Strategic Marketing

McGraw-Hill/Irwin Series in Marketing

Alreck & Settle
The Survey Research Handbook
Third Edition

Alsem & Wittink
Strategic Marketing: A Practical Approach
First Edition

Anderson, Beveridge, Lawton & Scott
Merlin: A Marketing Simulation
First Edition

Arens
Contemporary Advertising
Tenth Edition

Arnould, Price & Zinkhan
Consumers
Second Edition

Bearden, Ingram & LaForge
Marketing: Principles & Perspectives
Fourth Edition

Belch & Belch
Advertising & Promotion: An Integrated Marketing Communications Approach
Sixth Edition

Bingham & Gomes
Business Marketing
Third Edition

Cateora & Graham
International Marketing
Twelfth Edition

Cole & Mishler
Consumer and Business Credit Management
Eleventh Edition

Cooper & Schindler
Marketing Research
First Edition

Cravens & Piercy
Strategic Marketing
Eighth Edition

Cravens, Lamb & Crittenden
Strategic Marketing Management Cases
Seventh Edition

Crawford & Di Benedetto
New Products Management
Eighth Edition

Duncan
Principles of Advertising and IMC
Second Edition

Dwyer & Tanner
Business Marketing
Third Edition

Eisenmann
Internet Business Models: Text and Cases
First Edition

Etzel, Walker & Stanton
Marketing
Thirteenth Edition

Forrest
Internet Marketing Intelligence
First Edition

Futrell
ABC's of Relationship Selling
Eighth Edition

Futrell
Fundamentals of Selling
Ninth Edition

Gourville, Quelch & Rangan
Cases in Health Care Marketing
First Edition

Hair, Bush & Ortinau
Marketing Research
Third Edition

Hawkins, Best & Coney
Consumer Behavior
Ninth Edition

Johansson
Global Marketing
Fourth Edition

Johnston & Marshall
Churchill/Ford/Walker's Sales Force Management
Eighth Edition

Johnston & Marshall
Relationship Selling and Sales Management
First Edition

Kerin, Hartley & Rudelius
Marketing: The Core
First Edition

Kerin, Berkowitz, Hartley & Rudelius
Marketing
Eighth Edition

Lehmann & Winer
Analysis for Marketing Planning
Sixth Edition

Lehmann & Winer
Product Management
Fourth Edition

Levy & Weitz
Retailing Management
Fifth Edition

Mason & Perreault
The Marketing Game!
Third Edition

McDonald
Direct Marketing: An Integrated Approach
First Edition

Mohammed, Fisher, Jaworski & Paddison
Internet Marketing: Building Advantage in a Networked Economy
Second Edition

Molinari
Marketing Research Project Manual
First Edition

Monroe
Pricing
Third Edition

Mullins, Walker & Boyd
Marketing Management: A Strategic Decision-Making Approach
Fifth Edition

Nentl & Miller
SimSeries Simulations: SimSell SimSales Management SimMarketing SimMarketing Research SimCRM
First Edition

Perreault & McCarthy
Basic Marketing: A Global Managerial Approach
Fifteenth Edition

Perreault & McCarthy
Essentials of Marketing: A Global Managerial Approach
Tenth Edition

Peter & Donnelly
A Preface to Marketing Management
Tenth Edition

Peter & Donnelly
Marketing Management: Knowledge and Skills
Seventh Edition

Peter & Olson
Consumer Behavior
Seventh Edition

Purvis & Burton
Which Ad Pulled Best?
Ninth Edition

Quelch, Rangan & Lal
Marketing Management Text and Cases
First Edition

Rayport & Jaworski
Introduction to e-Commerce
Second Edition

Rayport & Jaworski
e-Commerce
First Edition

Rayport & Jaworski
Cases in e-Commerce
First Edition

Richardson
Internet Marketing
First Edition

Roberts
Internet Marketing: Integrating Online and Offline Strategies
First Edition

Spiro, Stanton & Rich
Management of a Sales Force
Eleventh Edition

Stock & Lambert
Strategic Logistics Management
Fourth Edition

Ulrich & Eppinger
Product Design and Development
Third Edition

Walker, Boyd, Mullins & Larreche
Marketing Strategy: A Decision-Focused Approach
Fifth Edition

Weitz, Castleberry & Tanner
Selling: Building Partnerships
Fifth Edition

Zeithamel & Bitner
Services Marketing
Fourth Edition

Strategic Marketing

Eighth Edition

David W. Cravens
M.J. Neeley School of Business
Texas Christian University

Nigel F. Piercy
Warwick Business School
The University of Warwick

Boston Burr Ridge, IL Dubuque, IA Madison, WI New York San Francisco St. Louis Bangkok
Bogotá Caracas Kuala Lumpur Lisbon London Madrid Mexico City Milan Montreal
New Delhi Santiago Seoul Singapore Sydney Taipei Toronto

STRATEGIC MARKETING
Published by McGraw-Hill/Irwin, a business unit of The McGraw-Hill Companies, Inc., 1221 Avenue of the Americas, New York, NY, 10020.

Some ancillaries, including electronic and print components, may not be available to customers outside the United States.

This book is printed on acid-free paper.

1 2 3 4 5 6 7 8 9 0 CCW/CCW 0 9 8 7 6 5

ISBN 0-07-296634-3

Editorial director: *John E. Biernat*
Publisher: *Andy Winston*
Editorial assistant: *Jill M. O'Malley*
Executive marketing manager: *Dan Silverburg*
Producer, Media technology: *Damian Moshak*
Project manager: *Trina Hauger*
Production supervisor: *Debra R. Sylvester*
Design coordinator: *Cara David*
Photo research coordinator: *Lori Kramer*
Photo researcher: *Keri Johnson*
Media project manager: *Joyce J. Chappetto*
Supplement producer: *Gina F. DiMartino*
Developer, Media technology: *Brian Nacik*
Cover image: © Corbis Images
Typeface: *10/12 Times Roman*
Compositor: *SR Nova Pvt Ltd., Bangalore, India*
Printer: *Courier Westford*

Page 12: © Reuters/CORBIS; page 32: Courtesy of Google, Inc.; page 71: Courtesy of Samsung Telecommunications America; page 107: Courtesy of ACCOR; page 169: Courtesy of Intel; page 200: Courtesy of AFLAC Incorporated; page 264: Courtesy of BMW of North America, LLC; page 327: © 2004 Dell Inc. All Rights Reserved; page 342: Courtesy of Singapore Airlines; page 414: Justin Sullivan/Getty Images; page 422: Michael Newman/PhotoEdit

Library of Congress Cataloging-in-Publication Data

Cravens, David W.
Strategic marketing/David W. Cravens, Nigel F. Piercy.–8th ed.
p. cm. – (McGraw-Hill/Irwin series in marketing)
Various multi-media instructional materials are available to supplement the text.
Includes bibliographical references and index.
ISBN 0-07-296634-3 (alk. paper)
1. Marketing–Decision making. 2. Marketing–Management.
3. Marketing–Management–Case studies. I. Piercy, Nigel. II. Title. III. Series.
HF5415.135.C72 2006
658.8′02–dc22

2004061068

www.mhhe.com

To Sue and Karen

DWC

To the memory of Helena G. Piercy
(1911–2001)

NFP

Preface

The challenges of providing superior value to customers have become critical to many companies around the world in their efforts to achieve high levels of performance. Delivering value requires understanding markets, buyers, and competition, and deciding how to match the organization's distinctive capabilities with promising value opportunities. Understanding markets and how they will change in the future is essential in guiding business and marketing strategies.

Strategic marketing's demanding role in business performance is demonstrated in the market-driven strategies of successful organizations competing in a wide array of market and competitive situations. Superior customer value, leveraging distinctive capabilities, responding rapidly to diversity and change in the marketplace, developing innovation cultures, and recognizing global business challenges are demanding initiatives that require effective marketing strategies for gaining and sustaining a competitive edge. *Strategic Marketing* examines the concepts and processes in designing and implementing market-driven strategies.

Market-Driven Strategy

Gaining a competitive advantage requires providing superior value to customers. Several initiatives are necessary in achieving customer objectives.

- Marketing strategy provides the concepts and processes that are essential in delivering superior customer value.
- Marketing is a major stakeholder in essential organizational core processes—new product development, customer relationship management, value/supply-chain management, and business strategy implementation.
- The use of cross-functional teams to manage core business processes is rapidly changing the role and structure of the traditional hierarchical organization.
- Collaborative relationship initiatives place new priorities on forging effective relationships with customers, suppliers, value-chain members, and competitors.
- Understanding customers, competitors, and the market environment requires the active involvement of the entire organization to manage market knowledge decisively.
- Developing processes that enable the organization to continually learn from customers, competitors, and other sources is vital to sustaining a competitive edge.
- The powerful technologies provided by the Internet and the World Wide Web, corporate intranets, and advanced communication and collaboration systems for customer and supplier relationship management underpin effective processes.
- The environmental and ethical aspects of business practice are critical concerns for individual executives as well as their companies, requiring management direction and active involvement by the entire organization.

Customer diversity and new forms of competition create impressive growth and performance opportunities for those firms that successfully apply strategic marketing concepts and analyses in business strategy development and implementation. The challenge to become market-driven is apparent in a variety of industries around the world. Analyzing market behavior and matching strategies to changing conditions require a hands-on approach to marketing strategy development and implementation. Penetrating financial analysis is an important skill of the marketing professional.

Strategic Marketing examines marketing strategy using a combination of text concepts, application processes, and cases to develop decision-making processes and apply them to business situations. The book is designed for use in undergraduate capstone management marketing courses and in the MBA marketing core and advanced strategy courses.

New and Expanded Scope

Regardless of business size and scope, competing in any market today requires a global perspective. The eighth edition accentuates this global perspective. The author team provides an extensive range of global involvement. The shrinking time-and-access boundaries of global markets establish new competitive requirements. The rapid emergence of powerful new competitive forces throughout the world, often facilitated by new business models, mandates an international viewpoint for executives in most organizations. The global dimensions of marketing strategy are integrated throughout the chapters of the book and also considered in several cases.

Customer relationship management (CRM) has been given special attention in this edition. There is a new CRM Appendix to Chapter 7. The topic is also covered in several chapters.

Internet initiatives comprise a vital part of the marketing strategies of many companies. Internet strategies are rapidly expanding in most companies. Because of the nature and scope of the various uses of the Internet, we have integrated this important topic into several chapters rather than developing a separate chapter. Internet Features are included in all chapters.

Brand leveraging coverage is examined along with related topics on brand identity, brand strategy, and brand portfolio management. Sustaining and disruptive innovation strategies are examined.

Special attention has been given to marketing metrics throughout the book. Similar emphasis is placed on segmentation, positioning, and value creation.

The Text

Strategic Marketing uses a decision process perspective to examine the key concepts and issues involved in selecting strategies. It is apparent that many instructors want to consider a marketing strategy perspective that extends beyond the traditional emphasis on the marketing program (4Ps). Coverage on services as well as goods is continued in the eighth edition. The length and design of the book offer flexibility in the use of the text material and cases. Internet and Feature applications are also included in each chapter. They can be used for class discussion and assignments.

The book is designed around the marketing strategy process with a clear emphasis on analysis, planning, and implementation. Part I provides an overview of market-driven strategy and business marketing strategies. Part II considers markets, segments, and customer value. Part III discusses designing market-driven strategies. Part IV considers market-driven program development. Finally, Part V examines implementing and managing market-driven strategies. Various decision process guides are provided throughout the book to assist the reader in applying the analysis and strategy development approaches discussed in the text.

The Cases

There are 28 new cases out of a total of 44. Many are well-known companies that students should find both interesting and challenging. Shorter application-focused cases are placed at the end of each part of the book. These cases are useful in applying the concepts and methods discussed in the chapters, and they can be used for class discussion, hand-in assignments, and/or class presentations. The cases consider a wide variety of business environments, both domestic and international. They include goods and services; organizations at different value-chain levels; and small, medium, and large enterprises. The features in every chapter provide additional case illustrations and information for consideration and discussion.

Many of the cases examine the marketing strategies of well-known companies. The cases are very timely, offering an interesting perspective on contemporary business practice. These companies have available extensive financial and product information on the Internet, which expands analysis opportunities.

Part VI includes comprehensive cases that offer students a variety of opportunities to apply marketing strategy concepts. Each case considers several important strategy issues. The cases represent different competitive situations for consumer and business goods and services as well as domestic and international markets.

Changes in the Eighth Edition

The eighth edition of *Strategic Marketing* follows the basic design of previous editions. Nevertheless, the revision incorporates many significant changes, additions, and updated examples. Every chapter includes new material and expanded treatment of important topics.

Features are included in each chapter. They follow a theme, emphasizing topics such as strategy, ethics, Internet, cross-functional relationships, innovation, and global applications.

Each chapter has been revised to incorporate new concepts and examples, improve readability and flow, and encourage reader interest and involvement. Topical coverage has been expanded (or reduced), where appropriate, to better position the book for teaching and learning in today's rapidly changing business environment. An expanded set of Internet and Feature applications is included at the end of each chapter. Financial analysis guidelines are in the Chapter 2 Appendix, and sales forecasting materials are included in the Chapter 3 Appendix. A discussion of customer relationship management (CRM) is provided in the Chapter 7 Appendix.

Teaching/Learning Resources

A complete and expanded teaching-learning portfolio is available on the Instructor's Resource CD-ROM. It includes an Instructor's Manual with course-planning suggestions, answers to end-of-chapter questions, Internet application guidelines, Feature application guidelines, instructor's notes for cases, and a multiple-choice question bank. A PowerPoint® presentation for each chapter is also included on the CD-ROM. The PowerPoint presentations provide an organized coverage of the chapter topics.

This edition of the manual has been substantially revised and expanded to improve its effectiveness in supporting course planning, case discussion, and examination preparation. Detailed instructor's notes concerning the use of the cases are provided, including epilogues when available. Additional information such as chapter summaries and case studies can be found on the book's Web site *www.mhhe.com/cravens06.*

The text, cases, Web site and Instructor's Manual offer considerable flexibility in course design, depending on the instructor's objectives and the course for which the book is used.

Acknowledgments

The eighth edition has benefited from the contributions and experiences of many people and organizations. Business executives and colleagues at universities in many countries have influenced the development of *Strategic Marketing*. While space does not permit thanking each person, a sincere note of appreciation is extended to all. We shall identify several individuals whose assistance was particularly important.

A special thank you is extended to the reviewers of this and prior editions and to many colleagues that have offered numerous suggestions and ideas. Throughout the development of the eighth edition, several individuals made important suggestions for improving the book.

We are also indebted to the case authors who gave us permission to use their cases. We appreciate the opportunity to include them in the book. Each author or authors are specifically identified with each case.

Special thanks to the management and professional team of McGraw-Hill/Irwin for their support and encouragement on this and prior editions of *Strategic Marketing*: Andy Winston, as publisher, has provided an important editorial leadership role; Editorial Assistant Jill O'Malley, has been a constant source of valuable assistance and encouragement; Dan Silverburg provided important marketing direction for the project; Trina Hauger guided the book through the various stages of production while Cara David polished the design.

Many students provided various kinds of support that were essential to completing the revision. In particular, we appreciate the excellent contributions to this edition made by Jose Guerra and Andrew Soule, TCU graduate assistants. We also appreciate the helpful comments and suggestions of many students in our classes.

We appreciate the support and encouragement provided by Shannon Shipp, Chair of the TCU Marketing Department and Howard Thomas, Dean of Warwick Business School. Special thanks are due to Connie Clark at TCU and Sheila Frost and Janet Biddle at Warwick University for typing the manuscript and for their assistance in other aspects of the project.

David W. Cravens

Nigel F. Piercy

About the Authors

David W. Cravens

David W. Cravens holds the Eunice and James L. West Chair of American Enterprise Studies and is Professor of Marketing in the M.J. Neeley School of Business at Texas Christian University. Previously, he was the Alcoa Foundation Professor at the University of Tennessee, where he chaired the Department of Marketing and Transportation and the Management Science Program. He has a Doctorate in Business Administration and MBA from Indiana University. He holds a Bachelor of Science in Civil Engineering from Massachusetts Institute of Technology. Before becoming an educator, Dave held various industry and government management positions. He is internationally recognized for his research on marketing strategy and sales management and has contributed over 100 articles and 25 books. Dave is a former editor of the *Journal of Academy of Marketing Science*. He has held various positions in the American Marketing Association and the Academy of Marketing Science. He received the Lifetime Achievement Award from the American Marketing Association in 2002 and was selected as the 1996 Outstanding Marketing Educator by the Academy of Marketing Science. He serves on the editorial boards of several academic journals. He has been a visiting scholar at universities in Austria, Australia, Chile, Czech Republic, England, Ireland, Italy, Germany, Mexico, The Netherlands, New Zealand, Singapore, Switzerland, and Wales. He has conducted management seminars and executive briefings in many countries in Asia, Europe, and South America. He is a frequent speaker at management development seminars and industry conferences.

Nigel F. Piercy

Nigel F. Piercy is Professor of Marketing at Warwick Business School, in the University of Warwick, United Kingdom, where he also leads the Sales and Account Management Strategy research unit. He was previously Professor of Strategic Marketing and Head of the Marketing Group at Cranfield School of Management, and for a number of years was the Sir Julian Hodge Chair in Marketing and Strategy at Cardiff University. He has been a visiting scholar at Texas Christian University; University of California, Berkeley; Fuqua School of Business, Duke University; Columbia Business School; Athens Laboratory of Business Administration; and Vienna University of Business and Economics. He has extensive experience in executive education and as a management workshop speaker. He has worked with managers and business students in the United States, Europe, the Far East, South Africa, and Zimbabwe. He holds a PhD from the University of Wales, and MA from Durham University Business School, and a BA from Heriot-Watt University, Edinburgh, Scotland. He has been awarded the distinction of a higher doctorate (Doctor of Letters) from Heriot-Watt University, for his published research work. Prior to academic life, Nigel was in retail management and latterly in strategic market planning with Nycomed Amersham plc. His research is in the areas of marketing strategy and implementation, and sales management. He has published some 200 articles and chapters and 16 books. He is editor of the *Journal of Strategic Marketing* and serves on the editorial boards of several scholarly journals.

Brief Contents

Table of Contents

Chapter 7
Strategic Relationships 189

Appendix 7A
Customer Relationship Management (CRM) 215

Chapter 8
Planning for New Products 221

Cases for Part Three 250

PART FOUR
MARKET-DRIVEN PROGRAM DEVELOPMENT 264

Chapter 9
Strategic Brand Management 264

Chapter 10
Value-Chain Strategy 292

Chapter 11
Pricing Strategy and Management 316

Chapter 12
Promotion, Advertising, and Sales Promotion Strategies 338

Chapter 1

Market-Driven Strategy

The challenges from radical market change and ever fiercer competition confronting executives around the world are complex and rapidly escalating. Market and industry boundaries are often difficult to define because of the entry of new and disruptive forms of competition. Customers' demands for superior value from the goods and services (products) they purchase are unprecedented, as they become yet more knowledgeable about products and more perceptive in the judgments they make. External influences from diverse pressure groups and lobbyists have increased dramatically in country after country. Major change initiatives are under way in many industries ranging from aerospace to telecommunications. Innovative business models that alter the traditional roles of an industry are defining a new agenda for business and marketing strategy development. Companies are adopting market-driven strategies guided by the logic that all business strategy decisions should start with a clear understanding of markets, customers, and competitors.[1] Increasingly, it is clear that enhancements in customer value provide a primary route to delivering superior shareholder value.[2]

Procter & Gamble (P&G), the household products giant, is an interesting example of a company that was slow to adapt to major market changes and competitive initiatives in the 1990s. P&G lost its lead market position in product categories such as diapers and toothpaste. By 2000 it was apparent that P&G needed to strengthen its market-driven strategy. P&G's stock experienced a 43 percent decline, growth had leveled, and profit margins had declined. A. G. Lafley was appointed chief executive officer (CEO) in the summer of 2000. Lafley's market-driven strategy initiatives have resulted in impressive market position gains and financial performance.

The new CEO placed major emphasis on making the customer the focal point of P&G's total operations.[3] Gaining an understanding of the benefits customers are seeking from products is a high priority throughout the company. Management is encouraging innovation synergies through collaboration between P&G business units to develop new products. Leveraging of these distinctive capabilities has resulted in several new products such as Crest Whitestrips, Dawn Power Dissolver, and Tide Stain Brush. P&G has been unusually successful in matching customers' value requirements with the distinctive capabilities of its business units.

P&G's performance since 2000 highlights the positive impact of market-driven strategy. The stock price is up from a low in 2000 of $53 to $105 in mid-2004. Sales increased from $40 billion to nearly $50 billion in 2004. The Crest toothpaste brand regained its lead position from Colgate, and P&G moved from fifth position to the lead position with the Iams pet food brand. P&G's earnings displayed consistent increases during this period.

We begin with a discussion of market-driven strategy, and its pivotal role in designing and implementing business and marketing strategies. Then, we look closely at the importance and process of becoming market-oriented. Next, we examine the capabilities of market-driven organizations, followed by discussion of creating value for customers. Finally, we look at the initiatives that are necessary to become market-driven, and the challenges that marketing executives face in making effective decisions in an era of unprecedented complexity and change.

Market-Driven Strategy

The underlying logic of market-driven strategy is that the market and the customers that form the market should be the starting point in business strategy formulation. "Considerable progress has been made in identifying market-driven businesses, understanding what they do, and measuring the bottom-line consequences of their orientation to their markets."[4] Importantly, as illustrated by P&G, market-driven strategy provides a companywide perspective, which mandates more effective integration of activities and processes that impact customer value. We examine the characteristics of market-driven strategy and discuss several issues associated with adopting the strategy.

Characteristics of Market-Driven Strategies

A key advantage of becoming market-oriented is gaining an understanding of the market and how it is likely to change in the future. This knowledge provides the foundation for designing market-driven strategies. Developing this vision about the market requires obtaining information about customers, competitors, and markets; viewing the information from a total business perspective; deciding across business functions how to deliver superior customer value; and taking these actions to provide value to customers.[5] There is compelling support from research findings and business practice indicating that market-driven strategies enhance business performance.

The major characteristics of market-driven strategies are shown in Exhibit 1.1. The organization's market orientation helps management to identify customers whose value requirements provide the best match with the organization's distinctive capabilities. Successful market-driven strategy design and implementation should lead to superior performance for an organization. Dell Inc.'s successful market-driven strategy is illustrative. Dell's value-chain strategy combines technologies from Intel, IBM, and Microsoft to serve customers efficiently and with state-of-the-art computer technology. Dell is able to introduce next generation products faster than its competitors can because its market-driven strategy is developed around a direct sales, built-to-order business design. This distinctive process capability is supported by effective supplier, distribution, and service partnerships with other companies. Dell's management understands its customers since company personnel are in close contact with buyers who make inquiries and place orders. Not only does Dell process some 500,000 calls each week, 65,000 corporate customers are linked to Dell through their own Dell Premier Pages on the Internet. Dell's 2004 sales should exceed $47 billion.

EXHIBIT 1.1 Characteristics of Market-Driven Strategies

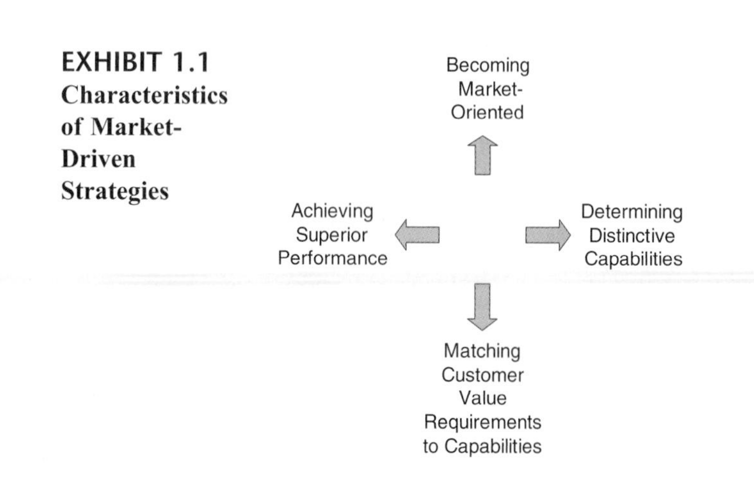

We examine each market-driven characteristic in the remainder of the chapter. A discussion of relevant strategy concepts, methods, and applications is provided throughout the book, beginning with the marketing strategy overview developed in Chapter 2.

Why Pursue a Market-Driven Strategy?

While our understanding of market-driven strategy is far from complete, the available evidence indicates a strong supporting logic for pursuing this type of strategy.[6] Importantly, the characteristics shown in Exhibit 1.1 offer guidelines for strategy development rather than advocating a particular strategy. Market-driven strategy needs to be linked to the organization's unique competitive strategy.

The achievements of companies that display market-driven characteristics are impressive. Examples include Dell Inc., Louis Vuitton, Southwest Airlines, Tesco PLC, Tiffany & Co., Wal-Mart, and Zara. Many other companies are in the process of developing market-driven strategies. We examine successful and unsuccessful strategies of several companies throughout the book, to illustrate the underlying strategy concepts.

The development of a market-driven strategy is not a short-term endeavor. A considerable amount of effort is necessary to build a market-driven organizational culture and processes. Also, the methods of measuring progress extend beyond short-term financial performance measures. While financial performance is important, it may not indicate whether progress is being made in pursuing a successful market-driven strategy. Responding to this need, "balanced scorecard" measures are being adopted by an increasing number of companies.[7] The scorecard approach includes the use of customer, learning and growth, and internal business process measures as well as financial performance measures. This approach recognizes that short-term cost savings and profit enhancements may undermine the achievement of strategic goals and the building of superior customer value.

Becoming Market-Oriented

A market orientation is a business perspective that makes the customer the focal point of a company's total operations. "A business is market-oriented when its culture is systematically and entirely committed to the continuous creation of superior customer value."[8] Importantly, achieving a market orientation involves the use of superior organizational skills in understanding and satisfying customers.[9]

Becoming market-oriented demands ethical behavior within the organization and with customers, suppliers, and other stakeholders. The Ethics Feature describes the consequences of questionable ethical behavior concerning Boeing Co. executives' relationships with an Air Force procurement officer.

Becoming market-oriented requires the involvement and support of the entire workforce. The organization must monitor rapidly changing customer needs and wants, determine the impact of these changes on customer satisfaction, increase the rate of product innovation, and implement strategies that build the organization's competitive advantage. We now describe the characteristics and features of market orientation and discuss several issues in becoming market-oriented.

Characteristics of Market Orientation

A market-oriented organization continuously gathers information about customers, competitors, and markets; views the information from a total business perspective; decides how to deliver superior customer value; and takes actions to provide value to customers.[10] Importantly, these initiatives involve cross-functional participation. Market orientation requires participation by everyone in the organization. An organization that is market-oriented has both a culture committed to providing superior customer value and processes for creating value for buyers. Market orientation requires a customer focus, competitor intelligence, and cross-functional cooperation and involvement. This initiative extends beyond the marketing function in an organization.

Ethics Feature

Customer Relationship Management

Boeing Co. terminated its chief financial officer (CFO) in November 2003 because of concerns about questionable ethical behavior regarding initiatives involved in obtaining lucrative defense contracts.

An employment negotiation with an Air Force procurement officer was apparently initiated by the CFO when the officer was in a position to influence the Defense Department contract to purchase Boeing 767 tankers. The officer was subsequently employed by Boeing, and was terminated by Boeing with the CFO.

There was mounting concern in Washington over the methods used by Boeing to obtain lucrative defense contracts. The allegations of misconduct regarding the $18 billion 767 tanker contract were the latest in a series of ethical lapses by Boeing.

Responding to pressure from the Boeing board, the CEO resigned on December 1, 2003. In addition to ethical concerns, there were questions about Boeing's strategic direction.

Sources: "Boeing: Caught in Its Own Turbulence," *BusinessWeek*, December 8, 2003, 37; Stanley Holmes, "Boeing: What Really Happened," *BusinessWeek*, December 15, 2003, 33–38.

Customer Focus. The marketing concept has proposed a customer focus for half a century, yet until the 1990s this emphasis had limited impact on managers as a basis for managing a business.[11] There are similarities between the marketing concept and market orientation, although the former implies a functional (marketing) emphasis. The important difference is that market orientation is more than a philosophy since it consists of a process for delivering customer value. The marketing concept advocates starting with customer needs/wants, deciding which needs to meet, and involving the entire organization in the process of satisfying customers. The market-oriented organization understands customers' preferences and requirements and effectively deploys the skills and resources of the entire organization to satisfy customers. Becoming customer-oriented requires finding out what values buyers want to help them satisfy their purchasing objectives. Buyers' decisions are based on the attributes and features of the product that offers the best value for the buyers' use situations. A buyer's experience in using the product is compared to his/her expectations to determine customer satisfaction.[12]

Dell Inc.'s direct contact with its buyers is an important information source for guiding actions to provide superior customer value. The direct, built-to-order process used by Dell avoids stocking computers that may not contain state-of-the-art technology. Also, each computer contains the specific features requested by the buyer. Dell's competitors that market their computers through distributors and retailers have higher costs because price reductions for purchased components (e.g., chips) cannot be utilized on computers in inventory. Dell's built-to-order business model enables taking advantage of lower prices and technology improvements of components.

Competitor Intelligence. A market-oriented organization recognizes the importance of understanding its competition as well as the customer:

> The key questions are which competitors, and what technologies, and whether target customers perceive them as alternate satisfiers. Superior value requires that the seller identify and understand the principal competitors' short-term strengths and weaknesses and long-term capabilities and strategies.[13]

Failure to identify and respond to competitive threats can create serious consequences for a company. For example, Polaroid's management did not define its competitive area as all forms of photography, concentrating instead on its instant photo monopoly position, and eventually the company was outflanked by digital photography. Had Polaroid been market-oriented its management might have better understood the changes taking place, recognized the competitive threat, and developed strategies to counter the threat. Instead, the company filed for bankruptcy.

Cross-Functional Coordination. Market-oriented companies are effective in getting all business functions working together to provide superior customer value. These organizations are successful in removing the walls between business functions—marketing talks with research and development and finance. Cross-functional teamwork guides the entire organization toward providing superior customer value.

Performance Implications. Companies that are market-oriented begin strategic analysis with a penetrating view of the market and competition. Moreover, an expanding body of research findings points to a positive relationship between market orientation and superior performance.[14] Companies that are market-oriented display favorable organizational performance compared to companies that are not market-oriented. The positive market orientation/performance relationship has been found in several studies.

Becoming a Market-Oriented Organization

Becoming a market-oriented company involves several interrelated requirements. The major activities include information acquisition, interfunctional assessment, shared diagnosis, and coordinated action. The objective is to deliver superior customer value.

Superior Customer Value. Customer value is the trade-off of benefits less the costs involved in acquiring a product. The bundle of benefits includes the product, the supporting services, the personnel involved in the purchase and use experience, and the perceived image of the product (brand). The costs include the price of purchase, the time and energy involved, and the psychic costs (e.g., perceived risk).

Information Acquisition. "A company can be market-oriented only if it completely understands its markets and the people who decide whether to buy its products or services."[15] Gaining these insights requires proactive information gathering and analysis. In many instances a wealth of information is available from company records, information systems, and employees. The challenge is to develop an effective approach to gathering relevant information that involves participation of all business functions, not just sales and marketing personnel.

P&G's CEO encourages employees to think of brands as consumers rather than as scientists seeking technical perfection.[16] For example, in 2004 the P&G baby care division launched a new product line, Pampers Feel'n Learn Advanced Trainers, based on findings from the diaper-testing center indicating that parents are frustrated by lengthy toilet training experiences.

A key part of information acquisition is learning from experience. Learning organizations encourage open-minded inquiry, widespread information dissemination, and the use of mutually informed managers' visions about the current market and how it is likely to change in the future.[17] For example, Intuit's obsession with customer service gave its Quicken design team revealing insights into the problems users encounter with the Quicken personal finance software and the preferences users have concerning software features. Making the Quicken software simple to use requires understanding market needs, extensive use testing, customer feedback, and continuous product improvement.

Cross-Functional Assessment. Zara, the Spanish apparel retailer, is very effective in overcoming the hurdles of getting people from different functions to share information about the market and to work together to develop innovative products. Delivering superior customer value at Zara involves all business functions. Zara designs and produces some 12,000 apparel styles each year, and each is available in stores in only four weeks. Zara stores renew nearly half their stock every two weeks. The short time span between new ideas and their transformation into store offerings is impressive. Zara's shared vision about customers and competition guides the design process, and information technology plays a vital role in Zara's success. Zara's business design and operations are described in the Cross-Functional Feature. Inditex sales were $5.6 billion in 2003, growing at a 25 percent rate.[18] Inditex opened 364 stores and launched Zara Home in 2003. Zara's U.S. coverage includes stores in New York, Washington, Miami, Orlando, and Las Vegas.

Cross-Functional Feature

Zara Moves New Clothing Designs from Concept to Store Rack in Two Weeks

The Zara boutique is buzzing on Calle Real in the rainy northern Spanish city of La Coruña. Customers are buying out the newly designed red tank tops and black blazers, but they're pining for beige and bright purple ones, too. Most fashion companies would need months to retool and restock. Not Zara. Every Saturday the store manager pulls out a Casio handheld computer and types in orders for new clothes. They arrive on Monday.

Zara is the Dell Computer Inc. of the fashion industry. The Spanish star is using the Web to churn out sophisticated fashion at budget prices, turning the industry's traditional fashion cycle completely on its well-coiffed head. Now, a new design can go from pattern to store in two weeks, rather than six months. Founded two decades ago in a remote, impoverished area of the Iberian peninsula, Zara's privately held parent, Inditex, has become a flourishing $2 billion company with 924 stores in 31 countries.

Traditionally, fashion collections are designed only four times a year. And major retailers outsource most of their production to low-cost subcontractors in far-off developing countries such as China. Zara ignores the old logic. For quick turnaround, it makes some two-thirds of its clothes in a company-owned facility in Spain, restocks stores around the globe twice a week, and continually redesigns its clothes—an astounding 12,000 different designs a year.

Here's how Zara does it: A store manager sends in a new idea to La Coruña headquarters. The 200-plus designers decide if it's appealing, then come up with specs. The design is scanned into a computer and zapped to production computers in manufacturing, which cut the material needed to be assembled into clothes by outside workshops. The manufacturing plant is futuristic, too, stuffed with huge clothes-cutting machines that are run by a handful of technicians in a laboratory-style computer-control center.

Eventually, Zara will begin using the Web to sell clothes since finding new store sites is becoming more difficult. In America, e-tailing could boost its low profile. "Americans have less reluctance to buy online than here in Southern Europe," says Inditex CEO José María Castellano. Thanks to Zara, Americans could begin to associate Spain with Internet innovation as well as stylish tank tops.

—*William Echikson*

Source: "The Fashion Cycle Hits High Gear," *BusinessWeek E.Biz*, September 18, 2000, EB66.

Shared Diagnosis and Action. Becoming market-oriented requires moving beyond information gathering and analysis to deciding what actions to take to provide superior customer value. This involves shared discussions among company personnel and analysis of alternatives in meeting customer needs.[19] Cross-functional collaboration facilitates diagnosis and coordinated decision making and implementation. The speed of Zara's new-product introduction and inventory turnover highlights the importance of all business functions working together toward a common purpose.

Becoming market-oriented often requires making major changes in the culture, processes, and structure of the traditional pyramid-type organization typically structured into functional units. Nonetheless, the mounting evidence suggests that the market-oriented organization has an important competitive advantage in providing superior customer value and achieving superior performance.

Distinctive Capabilities

Identifying an organization's distinctive capabilities (competencies) is a vital part of market-driven strategy (Exhibit 1.1). "Capabilities are complex bundles of skills and accumulated knowledge, exercised through organizational processes, that enable firms to coordinate activities and make use of their assets."[20] The major components of distinctive capabilities are shown in Exhibit 1.2, using Southwest Airlines' business model to illustrate each component.

The airline's growth and financial performance are impressive. Although Southwest is the fourth largest U.S. airline, its market capitalization is greater than the total capitalization of AMR (American Airlines), Delta Airlines, and UAL Corp. Southwest's revenues will approach

EXHIBIT 1.2
Southwest Airline's Distinctive Capabilities

Organizational Processes

Southwest has a point-to-point route system rather than the hub-and-spoke design used by many airlines. The airline offers services to 57 cities in 29 states, with an average trip about 500 miles. The carrier's value proposition consists of low fares and limited services (no meals). Nonetheless, major emphasis throughout the organization is placed on building a loyal customer base. Operating costs are kept low by using only Boeing 737 aircraft, minimizing the time span from landing to departure, and developing strong customer loyalty. The company continues to grow by expanding its point-to-point route network.

Skills and Accumulated Knowledge

The airline has developed impressive skills in operating its business model at very low cost levels. Accumulated knowledge has guided management in improving the business design over time.

Coordination of Activities

Coordination of activities across business functions is facilitated by the point-to-point business model. The high aircraft utilization, simplification of functions, and limited passenger services enable the airline to manage the activities very efficiently and to provide on-time point-to-point services offered on a frequent basis.

Assets

Southwest's key assets are very low operating costs, loyal customer base, and high employee esprit de corps.

$7 billion in 2005, compared to $5.6 billion in 2000. In contrast to the major airlines, favorable net profits were recorded during the same period.

Zara's new-product development process illustrates the retailer's distinctive capabilities. The new-product development process applies the *skills* of the design team and benefits from the team's *accumulated knowledge. Coordination of activities* across business functions during new-product development is facilitated by information technology. For example, Zara's product designs take into account manufacturing requirements as well as offering high fashion products. *Assets* such as Zara's strong brand image help to launch new products.

It is apparent from the Southwest Airlines and Zara examples that an organization's capabilities are not a particular business function, asset, or individual, but instead consist of core processes of the organization. Michael Porter indicates that "the essence of strategy is in the activities—choosing to perform activities differently or to perform different activities than rivals."[21] His concept of activity networks is consistent with viewing distinctive capabilities as groupings of skills and accumulated knowledge, applied through organizational processes. Dell Inc.'s direct-to-the-customer, built-to-order process is a distinctive capability that operates using Dell's skills and accumulated knowledge in coordinating the activities that comprise the process, and benefiting from Dell's strong brand image in the personal computer market. The outcome of the process is the delivery of superior customer value to the organizations that purchase Dell's computers (over 90 percent of Dell's buyers are businesses rather than consumers).

Organizational capabilities and organizational processes are closely related:

> It is the capability that enables the activities in a business process to be carried out. The business will have as many processes as are necessary to carry out the natural business activities defined by the stage in the value chain and the key success factors in the market.[22]

We know that processes are not the same across industries or for businesses in the same industry. For example, Dell Inc. and Hewlett-Packard have different processes, and the activity networks for Dell will differ from those of Wal-Mart. Compared to the retailer, Dell is at an earlier stage in the value chain that links suppliers, manufacturers, distributors/retailers, and end users of goods and services.

We now look more closely at the distinctive capabilities of an organization, followed by a discussion of different types of capabilities. Then, we examine the relationship between capabilities and customer value.

Identifying Distinctive Capabilities

Understanding the organization's distinctive capabilities and how they relate to customers' value requirements are important considerations in marketing strategy design. Management should place a company's strategic focus on its distinctive capabilities.[23] These capabilities may enable the organization to compete in new markets, provide significant value to customers, and create market-entry barriers to potential competitors. For example Hewlett-Packard (H-P) has a strong capability in ink-jet printer technology, which enabled the company to become the world leader in computer printers. H-P leveraged this capability to develop the ink-jet fax through a strategic alliance with a Japanese partner, which contributed a distinctive capability in fax technology.

Capabilities are important factors in shaping corporate and business strategies. Many companies are deciding what they do best, concentrating their strategies around their distinctive capabilities. For example, in the late 1990s Tandy Corporation, after unsuccessful ventures into computer manufacturing, computer retailing, megastore electronics, and appliance retailing, exited from these businesses and focused its growth initiatives on the core capabilities of the Radio Shack retail chain. The corporation's name was changed to Radio Shack to provide brand focus.

A distinctive capability: (1) offers a disproportionate (higher) contribution to superior customer value, or (2) enables an organization to deliver value to customers in a substantially more cost-effective manner.[24] Southwest Airlines' distinctive capability is its business design, enabling the carrier to offer travelers low fares in combination with satisfactory services.

An important issue is deciding which capability to emphasize.[25] How, for example, did Wal-Mart's management decide to invest heavily to build its information and logistics system? Why did Dell choose the direct sales, built-to-order business design? What supporting logic led Hewlett-Packard to invest heavily in ink-jet technology and to position its printers against dot matrix printers rather than laser printers? These choices are not always apparent, and may involve developing new capabilities that offer the potential of being distinctive.

The starting point in deciding which capability to pursue is identifying and evaluating the organization's existing capabilities. The three characteristics shown in Exhibit 1.3 are useful criteria for identifying distinctive capabilities. The capability must be superior to the competition and difficult to duplicate. GORE-TEX fabric technology satisfies these criteria. Moreover, various applications of GORE-TEX materials have been developed (e.g., fabric for raincoats,

EXHIBIT 1.3
Desirable Capabilities

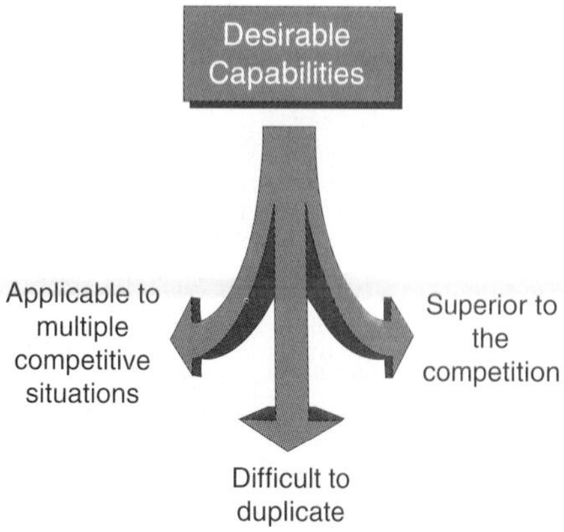

medical supplies, and dental floss. A capability may not always be applicable to multiple competitive situations, but in order to be sustainable it needs to be superior to competition and difficult to duplicate. Multiple competitive situation applications add additional strength to the capability.

Types of Capabilities

Classifying the organization's capabilities is useful in identifying distinctive capabilities. As shown in Exhibit 1.4, one way of classification is to determine whether processes operate from outside the business to inside, inside out, or spanning processes. The processes shown are illustrative rather than a complete enumeration of processes. Moreover, since a company may have unique capabilities, the intent is not to identify a generic inventory of processes.

The process capabilities shown in Exhibit 1.4 differ in purpose and focus.[26] The outside-in processes connect the organization to the external environment, providing market feedback and forging external relationships. The inside-out processes are the activities necessary to satisfy customer value requirements (e.g., manufacturing/operations). The outside-in processes play a key role in offering direction for the spanning and inside-out capabilities, which respond to the customer needs and requirements identified by the outside-in processes. Market sensing, customer linking, channel bonding (e.g., manufacturer/retailer relationships), and technology monitoring supply vital information for new-product opportunities, service requirements, and competitive threats.

This process view of capabilities highlights the interrelated nature of organizational processes and points to several important issues:[27]

- The market-driven organization has a clear external focus.
- Capabilities typically span several business functions, involving teams of people.
- Processes need to be clearly defined and have identifiable owners.
- Information should be shared with all process participants.
- Processes are interconnected to other processes and management needs to coordinate the linkages.

While many companies are structured according to business functions, an increasing number are placing emphasis on cross-functional processes. As companies alter their traditional organizational hierarchies, they may retain functional groupings (e.g., engineering, finance, marketing, etc.), while placing emphasis on processes like those shown in Exhibit 1.4.

EXHIBIT 1.4
Classifying Capabilities

Source: Chart from George S. Day, "The Capabilities of Market-Driven Organizations," *Journal of Marketing*, October 1994, 41. Reprinted with permission of the American Marketing Association.

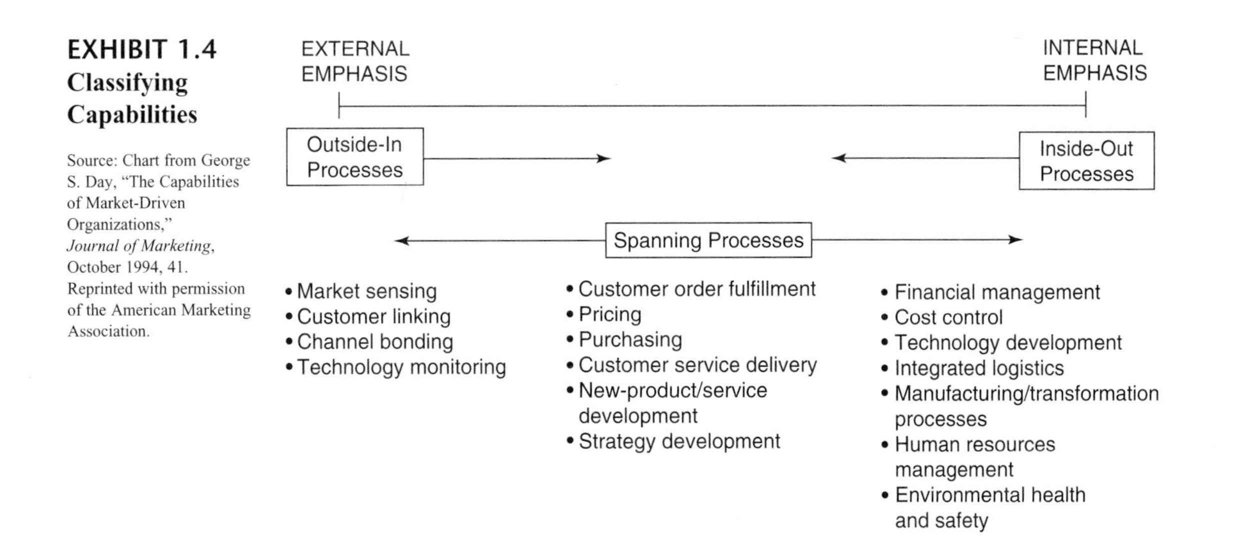

The organizational process view of distinctive capabilities requires shifting away from the traditional specialization of business functions (e.g., operations, marketing, research and development) toward a cross-functional process perspective. Implications of these changes include:[28]

- Managing and participating in process-driven organizations create new skill requirements and challenges.
- Functional organizations require individual skills in information gathering, data analysis, and external collaboration.
- Process-driven organizations emphasize skills in relationship management, internal communication and persuasion, team building, information interpretation, and strategic reasoning.

Value and Capabilities

Value for buyers consists of the benefits and costs resulting from the purchase and use of products. Value is perceived by the buyer. Superior value occurs when there are positive net benefits. A company needs to pursue value opportunities that match its distinctive capabilities. A market-oriented company uses its market sensing processes, shared diagnosis, and cross-functional decision making to identify and take advantage of superior value opportunities. Management must determine where and how it can offer superior value, directing these capabilities to customer groups (market segments) that result in a favorable capability/value match.

Creating Value for Customers

"Customer value is the outcome of a process that begins with a business strategy anchored in a deep understanding of customer needs."[29] The creation of customer value is an important challenge for managers. The priority placed on customer value is the result of companies' experience with Total Quality Management, intense competition, and the increasing demands of customers. Several benefits of value initiatives reported by executives in a study conducted by The Conference Board are shown in Exhibit 1.5. The purpose of the study was to determine if companies are taking actions to improve customer value, and obtain an assessment of the results (benefits) of the value initiatives. Exhibit 1.5 offers positive evidence of companies' proactive efforts to increase customer value. About half of the study respondents were from the quality function, nearly one-third from marketing, and the rest from other business functions. About 80 percent of the participating companies were from the United States, and the remaining from Europe.

We take a closer look at the concept of customer value, and consider how value is generated. Then we look at the progress being made in the value initiatives of companies.

EXHIBIT 1.5
A Self-Assessment: Results of Customer Value Initiative

Source: Graph from Kathryn Troy, *Change Management: Striving for Customer Value* (New York: The Conference Board, 1996), 6. Reprinted with permission from The Conference Board.

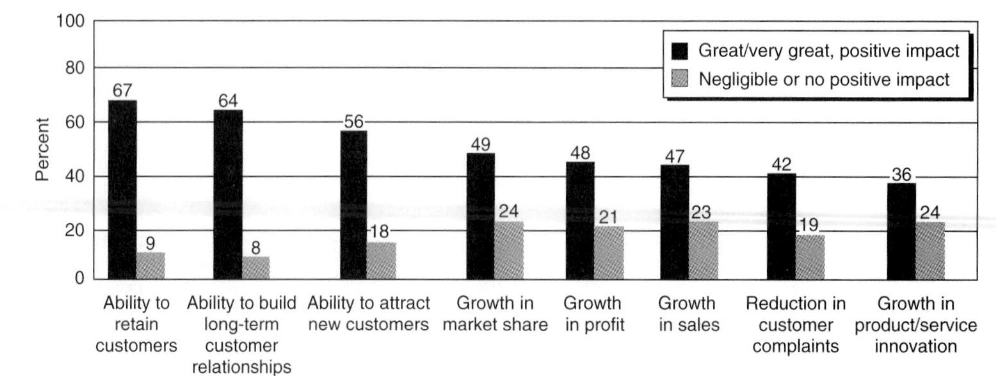

Those choosing a "moderate" impact are not shown on the chart but account for the difference between the percentages shown and 100 percent.

Internet Feature The World of eBay

eBay is the world's largest personal online trading community, where individuals buy and sell items across thousands of categories.

The idea for eBay grew out of a conversation between computer systems developer Pierre Omidyar and his wife, who was trying to locate Pez sweet containers for her collection. An Internet advertisement led to a massive response and the establishment of eBay as an online auction site.

eBay was launched in 1995, and now has a community of more than 105 million registered users. eBay users buy and sell items in more than 9,000 categories worldwide. Each day eBay hosts over 10 million auctions, with one million new items joining the "for sale" list every 24 hours. The site receives more than 120,000 hits a second and 175 million searches a day.

Every item auctioned has a strict time limit for bids to be made, creating high levels of user excitement and involvement. The eBay "community" chats at the eBay Café and uses online bulletin boards to communicate. eBay has become part of its users' lifestyle, with many creating second businesses and giving up regular jobs to buy and sell through eBay. In 2001, 10,000 people in the United States gave up their jobs to become full-time eBay traders, and by 2004 the number of people in the United States making their living part-time or full-time on eBay had reached 430,000.

In the first quarter of 2004, gross sales had reached $8 billion. In 2003, the company's market value had reached $40 billion. Estimates suggest that $100 invested in eBay on the first day of trading stock in 1999 would have been worth $2,272 only five years later.

Sources: David Thomas, "Weird World of eBay," *Daily Mail*, June 10, 2004, 32–33; eBay.com Web site.

Customer Value

Offering superior customer value is at the core of the eBay business design. Consider how conventional companies would have reacted to a proposal for this business only a few years ago. eBay's impressive customer value delivery is described in the Internet Feature.

Buyers form value expectations and decide to purchase goods and services based on their perceptions of products' benefits less the total costs incurred.[30] Customer satisfaction indicates how well the product use experience compares to the buyer's value expectations. Superior customer value results from a very favorable use experience compared to buyers' expectations and the value offerings of competitors.

Providing Value to Customers

As discussed earlier, the organization's distinctive capabilities are used to deliver value by differentiating the product offer, offering lower prices relative to competing brands, or a combination of lower cost and differentiation.[31] Deciding which avenue to follow requires matching capabilities to the best value opportunities.

Consider, for example, Hewlett-Packard's (H-P) very successful ink-jet printer strategy which positioned the printer as an alternative to dot matrix technology. H-P's management decided not to target laser printers by offering the ink-jet as a lower-cost option to laser printers. The dot matrix strategy offered H-P a much larger market opportunity. The H-P product management team's vision about the market was correct in that dot matrix users would soon become dissatisfied with the quality and capabilities of the printers.

Value Initiatives

The Conference Board customer value survey indicates that a majority of companies consider value initiatives to be producing positive results. Strong progress was reported in the following areas:

- Analyzing customer needs and instilling customer-focused behavior in frontline employees (70 percent or more);
- Analyzing target markets and boosting service quality (60 to 70 percent);

- Using cross-functional teams to develop products and services (about half);
- Achieving operational excellence (about half); and
- Innovating (about half).[32]

Twenty-five of the companies that have completed the implementation of a value initiative report major progress in instilling customer-focused behavior for employees not in frontline contact with customers.[33] These same companies indicate stronger performance in expanding market share, innovation, and retaining customers, when compared to companies that are beginning value initiatives. The companies that have value initiatives under way are becoming market-oriented and leveraging their distinctive capabilities. The results offer substantial support for the benefits of market-driven strategy.

Nonetheless, there is an important distinction between value and innovation. An *Economist Intelligence Unit Report* in 1999 contained interviews with executives from many leading companies throughout the world: "What counts, conclude the participants, is value innovation. This is defined as creating new value propositions . . . that lead to increased customer satisfaction, loyalty and—ultimately—sustainable, profitable growth. Market leaders are just that—pioneers."[34]

Innovation in customer value coming from outside the traditional industry boundaries and disrupting conventional ways of doing business is underlined by Apple's iPod and iTunes innovations in recorded music described in the Strategy Feature. While competitors prepare to develop yet better ways of delivering value to the consumer of music, the success of iPod illustrates the payoff of effective value innovation (see accompanying iPod photo).

Becoming Market-Driven

The discussion so far points to the importance of becoming market-oriented, leveraging the distinctive capabilities, and finding a good match between customers' value requirements and the organization's capabilities. The supporting logic for these actions is that they are expected to lead to superior customer value and organizational performance. Moreover, research evidence indicates that these characteristics are present in market-driven organizations, which display higher performance than their counterparts that are not market-driven.

Strategy Feature

Revolution in the Music Industry

Major music producers entered the 21st century facing a strategic dilemma: The availability of high-quality digital music downloads from the Internet was undermining the market for their recorded CDs across the world. While fighting legal battles to close music Web sites like Napster, where users could share each other's music collections at no cost, the music industry searched in vain for a business model that would allow traditional firms to profit from digital music downloading from the Internet.

The breakthrough came from Steve Jobs at Apple Computer, Inc. The iPod is a small, elegantly designed, easy-to-use handheld device that can store 10,000 songs in a unit that is smaller than a deck of cards, and sells for around $300. The consumer can store collections of downloaded music on the iPod (or "burn" the music onto a blank CD disk). Strategic leverage came from Jobs' unprecedented success in persuading all the major record labels to make their music available—legally—on a single Web site. This site is Apple's online music store—iTunes, with approximately 700,000 songs available for download. A million songs were sold in iTunes' first week, and in the first seven months of iTunes' existence more than 30 million songs were downloaded from Apple's store. After a free 30-second preview, costs are roughly $1 for each song downloaded. In the third quarter of 2004, Apple sold over 800,000 iPods. By 2004, Apple was coming through with the $249 iPod mini, in a partnership with Hewlett-Packard to sell iPods and to load iTunes onto millions of personal computers. Forecasts for 2004 were iPod sales of $931 million and iTunes revenues of $220 million.

However, radical change in delivering customer value does not stand still. By late 2003, Apple's e-music dominance based on the iPod was threatened by emerging competitive innovations—interestingly still not from the traditional music companies:

- Dell's Digital Jukebox—a player that beats the iPod on price and works with more music services.
- Samsung YP109GS—a product similar to the iPod designed to work with a new service provided by the former free music site operator Napster.
- Rio Nitrus—a new breed of player that is cheaper and smaller than the iPod, but holds fewer songs.

Microsoft began testing an online music service in late 2004, designed to compete with Apple's iTunes. Additionally, Microsoft is providing software for more than 60 digital music players, and there are concerns that consumers will reject the iTunes business model (the iPod works only with iTunes and iTunes works only with the iPod) in favor of greater flexibility. Music buyers may prefer to be able to use sites like MusicMatch, Napster 2.0, or BuyMusic.com. Further strategic concerns for the traditional record producers are that there may be little market left for their conventional CD albums, as consumers prefer to "cherrypick" the tracks they actually want from the Web site. There are signs that some artists may choose to release music only through Web-based outlets, and that consumers may prefer to temporarily "rent" music rather than buy it outright.

Sources: Nick Wingfield, "Online Music's Latest Tune," *The Wall Street Journal*, August 27, 2004, B1-B2. Peter Burrows, "Everybody Wants a Piece of the iPod," *BusinessWeek*, October 27, 2003, 40. Peter Burrows, "Showtime!" *BusinessWeek*, February 2, 2004, 35–41.

A market-driven organization must identify which capabilities to develop and which investment commitments to make. These decisions can benefit from:

> a shared understanding of the industry structure, the needs of the target customer segments, the positional advantages being sought, and the trends in the environment.[35]

A major objective of this book is examining the concepts and processes that are relevant in gaining a shared understanding of customers and deciding how to satisfy their needs and preferences by favorably positioning the organization's value offer.

Market Sensing and Customer Linking Capabilities

Market orientation research, evolving business strategy paradigms, and the Conference Board study all point to the importance of market sensing and customer linking capabilities in achieving successful market-driven strategies.[36]

Market Sensing Capabilities. Market-driven companies have effective processes for learning about their markets. Sensing involves more than collecting information. It must be shared across functions and interpreted to determine what actions need to be initiated. Zara's close contact with store managers by telephone and computer generates valuable information for diagnosis and action.

Developing an effective market sensing capability requires finding and processing information from various sources. Sources must be identified and processes developed to collect and analyze the information. Information technology plays a vital role in market sensing activities. Different business functions have access to useful information and need to be involved in market sensing activities.

Customer Linking Capabilities. There is substantial evidence that creating and maintaining close relationships with customers are important in market-driven strategies.[37] These relationships offer advantages to both buyer and seller through information sharing and collaboration. Customer linking also reduces the possibility of a customer shifting to another supplier. Customers are valuable assets.

Quintiles Transnational (services for drug companies) has very effective customer linking capabilities.[38] Its drug testing and sales services are available in 27 countries. The company has extensive experience in clinical trials and marketing. Quintiles' customers are located in many countries around the world. Ongoing collaborative relationships are essential to Quintiles' success. It offers specialized expertise, assisting drug producers to reduce the time necessary in developing and testing new drugs.

Aligning Structure and Processes

Becoming market driven may require changing the design of the organization, placing more emphasis on cross-functional processes. Market orientation and process capabilities require cross-functional coordination and involvement. Many of the companies in the Conference Board study discussed earlier made changes in organization structures and processes as a part of their customer value initiatives. The initiatives included improving existing processes as well as redesigning processes. The processes that were primary targets for reengineering included sales and marketing, customer relations, order fulfillment, and distribution.[39] This emphasis was no doubt the result of the extensive work during the last decade on quality improvement that was concentrated in operations (manufacturing and services).

The objectives of the business process changes made by the companies in the Conference Board survey were to improve the overall level of product quality, reduce costs, and improve service delivery.[40] Nine out of the ten participating companies made changes in their business processes as part of their customer value effort. Interestingly, 42 percent of the companies' change initiatives came from the top of the organizations, while nearly as many initiatives (40 percent) were grass roots (bottom-up) approaches. This indicates the benefits of both top-down and bottom-up initiatives.

Underpinning such changes and initiatives is the importance of what has been called "implementation capabilities," or the ability of an organization to execute and sustain market-driven strategy, and do so on a global basis.[41] In addition to formulating the strategies essential to delivering superior customer value, it is vital to adopt a thorough and detailed approach to strategy implementation.

Challenges of a New Era for Strategic Marketing

At the midpoint of the first decade of the 21st century it is apparent that executives face unprecedented challenges in strategic marketing to cope with turbulent markets, competitive revolution, and escalating customer demands for value superiority. In this chapter we describe the rationale for market-driven strategy and its components as a business approach relevant to the new challenges of the present and future.

Importantly, the personal demands for incisiveness and ingenuity in creating and implementing innovative and robust marketing strategies should not be ignored. In addition to the technical skills of analysis and planning required to implement market-driven strategy, capabilities for understanding new market and competitor phenomena will be at a premium. Societal and global change also mandates high levels of personal integrity in managers and leaders, and the reflection of these qualities in the social responsiveness of organizations.

Escalating Globalization

The internationalization of business is well recognized in terms of the importance of export/import trade and the growth of international corporations, particularly in the Triad, comprising North America, Europe, and Japan. However, for strategic marketing in the 21st century, such a view of the international marketing issue may be shortsighted. The most intriguing and surprising challenges are likely to come from outside the mature Triad economies. It is important to understand the degree and extent of difference between the developed economies and the new world beyond.

For example, considerable attention is being given to the growing roles of China and India in the global economy. Consider that while the United States has a gross national income per capita of $35,400 and the United Kingdom has a comparable figure of $25,510, the same indicator of individual income in India is $470 and in China is $960. Then compare the population figures that show the United States has 293 million people, while India has 1.1 billion and China has 1.3 billion. The implications of these massive differences are beginning to impact dramatically.

For example, it is clear that major customers may source from countries with a massive cost advantage in labor costs. In 2004, Wal-Mart was the world's largest purchaser of Chinese goods, spending $15 billion in China in 2003, making the company China's fifth largest trading partner, ahead of countries like Russia and Britain. Indeed, U.S. consumers are reacting to price differences for medical treatments by traveling abroad. While a heart bypass may cost $25–35,000 in the United States, the operation is available in Thailand and India for $8–15,000.[42]

However, what is less predictable are the other ways in which economic differences may have dramatic effects. For example, there has been some concern about the trend for Western-based companies to outsource functions like back-office operations, call centers, and software development to India and China to take advantage of the low labor costs available.[43] Surprisingly, by mid-2004 Indian companies had quickly purchased a dozen or more U.S. call centers and business processing outsourcers in a form of reverse migration.[44]

Consider, further, that if one important source of profitable growth is serving the world's poor profitably—on the grounds that four billion people in the world have purchasing power of less than $2,000 per year[45]—then the expertise to achieve this goal may be located within the developing world not in the advanced economies. The most important exports from countries like India and China may well be new business models, which will impact established ways of doing business in the developed world.

It is apparent that a new kind of transnational business organization is emerging, which is effectively "stateless."[46] For example, Trend Micro operates a computer virus center in low-cost Manila with six smaller virus-response laboratories around the world, allowing this Taiwanese/American/Japanese company to guarantee delivery of inoculation against major viruses in less than two hours. Similarly, the R&D expertise being deployed by Korean multinationals like LG Electronics, Daewoo Electronics, Samsung Electronics, and Salus Biotech is being acquired in Russia where Russian engineers have considerable expertise and work for very low wages.[47]

It is illustrative of changing global priorities that in an unprecedented break with industry norms, GlaxoSmithKlein Biologicals, the world's largest vaccine company, plans a "south-first strategy" with its vaccine products—they will be introduced first in Latin America and Asia, and only subsequently in Europe. The effect is to take the vaccine first to where it is needed most and to achieve the company's goal of being the vaccine maker for the world. [48]

The global marketplace is dynamic and changing in complex ways with fundamental effects on the competitiveness and viability of companies in many sectors. Those who underestimate the rate of change and important shifts in international relationships run the risk of being outmaneuvered.

Technology Diversity and Uncertainty

The impact of technology on business may also be underestimated. There is nothing surprising in recognizing that technological advances will continue to produce new-product opportunities. What is more surprising is the radical nature of an increasing number of those opportunities. Consider, for example, the innovations described in Exhibit 1.6.

The skills and vision required to decide which radical innovation opportunities can be successfully commercialized will be extremely demanding, and the risks of failure will be high. These examples identify innovations that have the potential to revolutionize a range of different industries. They demand a strategic perspective that accepts the potential for revolution but balances this with commercial imperatives. The danger is that conventional approaches and shortsighted management may miss out on the most important opportunities.

EXHIBIT 1.6
Radical Product Opportunities from New Technologies

A Self-Cleaning Fabric from Nanotechnology. Research in Hong Kong offers the potential for fabrics that are self-cleaning. The innovation uses an ultrathin layer of titanium dioxide, a natural chemical compound used in toothpaste, foodstuffs, and sunscreen as a coating for cotton. When the treated cotton is exposed to sunlight a reaction is triggered in the titanium dioxide nanoparticles, which are 20,000 times thinner than a human hair, causing them to react with oxygen in the air and create an oxidizing agent which breaks down dirt, micro-organisms, and pollution into water and carbon dioxide. The prospect is a fabric for apparel and household products that cleans itself.[1]

Private Space Travel. In 2004, private space travel became a potentially commercial product. The world's first private space plane—SpaceShipOne—is currently being tested with the prospect of inexpensive access to space. The plane took only three years and $25 million to develop, and was funded by Paul G. Allen, cofounder of Microsoft. The pioneer of SpaceShipOne predicts that within 15 years space tourism will become a multibillion dollar business.[2]

The Digital Home. Consumers have growing opportunities to set up home electronics room-by-room to share high-speed Internet access and to exchange music, video, and other content. Home PC-networks offer the potential for networked appliances and features. Philips Electronics believes the goal is to achieve "ambient intelligence," where household devices get smarter and adapt to individual users in the household, all the way from the refrigerator that automatically reorders the milk when the carton is empty, to the mirror that turns into a flat-screen terminal and television, to the cooker that lets the cook know by phone that the food is nearly ready, to automated control of the temperature in the building.[3]

Self-Cleaning Windows. Pilkington in the United Kingdom has spent a decade developing its Activ product—glass with a microscopic coating that reacts with sunlight to dissolve dirt and grime, leaving a residue that is washed away by the rain. Activ is 20 times more expensive than normal glass, but avoids the need for chemical cleaners and labor in conventional window cleaning. The company is researching ways to adapt the product for automobile applications. Other potential uses of the technology are self-cleaning surfaces, using the coating to break down bacterial infections.[4]

[1]Robin Yapp, "The Hi-Tech Shirt That You'll Never Have to Wash," *Daily Mail*, June 15, 2004, 7.
[2]Otis Port, "Private Space Travel: We May Have Lift Off," *BusinessWeek*, June 21, 2004, 48.
[3]"Digital Homes," *BusinessWeek*, Special Report, July 21, 2003, 56–59.
[4]Andy Dolan, "Self-Cleaning Window," *Daily Mail*, June 9, 2004, 17.

Ethical Behavior and Social Responsiveness

The demands on individuals with high levels of personal integrity will likely increase in the future. Increasing levels of transparency mandate that manager behavior should meet the highest standards. The penalties for failing to meet the highest standards are likely to be severe. Growing emphasis is placed on corporate citizenship and the establishment and protection of secure corporate reputation as an asset with a financial return associated.[49] Throughout our examination of the elements of strategic marketing we emphasize the ethical and corporate responsibility issues of which a manager should be aware.

While these forces of change describe a challenging yet exciting environment for strategic marketing, across the world marketing professionals are finding new and better ways to respond to the new realities, to deliver superior customer value to their markets, and enhance shareholder value. Underpinning processes of reinvention and radical innovation are principles of robust marketing strategy. The goal of this book is to identify and illustrate these principles, and provide processes for responding to the challenges.

Summary

Market-driven strategies begin with an understanding of the market and the customers that form the market. The characteristics of market-driven strategies include becoming market-oriented, determining distinctive capabilities, finding a match between customer value and organizational capabilities, and obtaining superior performance by providing superior customer value. The available evidence indicates a strong supporting logic for adopting market-driven strategies, recognizing that a long-term commitment is necessary to develop these strategies.

Achieving a market orientation requires a customer focus, competitor intelligence, and coordination among the business functions. Becoming market-oriented involves making major changes in the culture, processes, and structure of the traditional pyramid organization organized into functional units. Several interrelated actions are required, including information acquisition, sharing information within the organization, interfunctional assessment, shared diagnosis, and decision making. The objective of market orientation is to provide superior customer value.

Leveraging distinctive capabilities is a key part of developing a market-driven strategy. Capabilities are organizational processes that enable firms to coordinate related activities and employ assets using skills and accumulated knowledge. Distinctive capabilities are superior to the competition, difficult to duplicate, and applicable to multiple competitive situations. Capabilities can be classified as outside-in, inside-out, and spanning processes. The outside-in processes provide direction to the inside-out and spanning processes by identifying customer needs and superior value opportunities.

The creation of superior customer value is a continuing competitive challenge in sustaining successful market-driven strategies. Value is the trade-off of product benefits minus the total costs of acquiring the product. Superior customer value occurs when the buyer has a very favorable use experience compared to his/her expectations and the value offerings of competitors. The avenues to value may be product differentiation, lower prices than competing brands, or a combination of lower cost and differentiation.

Becoming market-driven is a continuing process beginning with deciding which capabilities to develop. Capabilities need to be identified and analyzed, market sensing and customer linking capabilities developed, and necessary organizational changes implemented.

The new era of strategic marketing creates several important challenges for executives. Escalating globalization presents an array of complex opportunities. Radical innovations will produce many new product opportunities, requiring skill and vision in deciding which options to pursue. Moreover, the new era promises to increase the demands for ethical behavior and social responsibility.

Our discussion of the major components of market-driven strategy (Exhibit 1.1) provides an essential perspective concerning the development of business and marketing strategies. In Chapter 2, we examine the major decisions necessary in developing and implementing marketing strategy.

Internet Applications

A. Discuss how Dell Inc.'s Web site (*www.Dell.com*) supports its mission, value proposition, and brand image. What advantages (and limitations) does the Web site provide to business buyers?

B. Go to *www.travelocity.com* and investigate the site. How does travelocity.com collect information about its customers and how might this prove valuable to the company and ultimately the customer? What privacy issues could arise?

C. Review the McKinsey & Co. Web site. Are there indications that the consulting company is market-oriented?

Feature Applications

A. Read the Cross-Functional Feature—Zara Moves New Clothing Designs from Concept to Store Rack in Two Weeks and identify the strengths of Zara's business model. Consider how other fashion retailers might respond to protect their market share.

B. Review the Strategy Feature—Revolution in the Music Business and consider what is likely to happen next in the music business. In particular, where do these innovations and new types of competition leave the music production companies?

Questions for Review and Discussion

1. Discuss some of the reasons why managing in an environment of continuing change will be necessary in the future.
2. Explain the logic of pursuing a market-driven strategy.
3. Examine the relevance of market orientation as a guiding philosophy for a social service organization, giving particular attention to user needs and wants.
4. How do the organization's distinctive capabilities contribute to developing market-driven strategy?
5. Discuss the relationship between customer value and a company's distinctive capabilities.
6. What role does product/service innovation play in providing superior customer value?
7. How would you explain the concept of superior customer value to a new finance manager?
8. Suppose you have been appointed to the top marketing post of a corporation and the president has asked you to explain market-driven strategy to the board of directors. What will you include in your presentation?
9. Discuss the importance of developing a strategic vision about the future for competing in today's business environment.
10. Discuss the issues that are important in transforming a company into a market-driven organization.
11. How is the Internet likely to contribute to an organization's market-driven strategy in the future?
12. Develop a list of the personal challenges confronting the marketing executive, and consider the qualities and capabilities that may be most relevant to meeting these challenges.

Notes

1. George S. Day, "The Capabilities of Market-Driven Organizations," *Journal of Marketing*, October 1994, 37–52.
2. Peter Doyle, *Value-Based Marketing-Marketing Strategies for Corporate Growth and Shareholder Value* (Chichester: John Wiley, 2000).
3. Patricia Sellers, "P&G: Teaching an Old Dog New Tricks," *Fortune*, May 31, 2004, 167–180.
4 Day, "The Capabilities of Market-Driven Organizations," 37.
5. Stanley F. Slater and John C. Narver, "Market Orientation, Customer Value, and Superior Performance," *Business Horizons*, March/April 1994, 22–27.
6. Day, "The Capabilities of Market-Driven Organizations."
7. See, for example, Robert S. Kaplan and David P. Norton, *The Balanced Scorecard* (Boston: Harvard Business School Press, 1996).
8. Slater and Narver, "Market Orientation", 22.
9. George S. Day, *Market-Driven Strategy: Processes for Creating Value* (New York: Free Press, 1990).
10. Slater and Narver, "Market Orientation," 23.
11. Day, "The Capabilities of Market-Driven Organizations," 37.
12. Philip Kotler, *Marketing Management*, 8th ed. (Englewood Cliffs, NY: Prentice-Hall, 1994), Chapter 2.
13. Slater and Narver, "Market Orientation," 23.
14. Rohit Deshpandé and John V. Farley, "Organizational Culture, Market Orientation, Innovativeness, and Firm Performance: An International Research Odyssey," *International Journal of Research in Marketing* 21, 2004, 3–22.
15. Benson P. Shapiro, "What the Hell Is Market Oriented?" *Harvard Business Review*, November/December 1988, 120.
16. Sellers, "P&G," 172.
17. George Day, "Continuous Learning about Markets," *California Management Review*, Summer 1994, 9–31.

18. "Inditex! Spain's World Beating Business Model," *BusinessWeek*, June 7, 2004, 78–79.
19. Shapiro, "What the Hell Is Market Oriented?" 122.
20. Day, "The Capabilities of Market-Driven Organizations," 38.
21. Michael Porter, "What Is Strategy?" *Harvard Business Review*, November/December 1996, 64.
22. Day, "The Capabilities of Market-Driven Organizations," 38.
23. C. K. Prahalad and Gary Hamel, "The Core Competence of the Corporation," *Harvard Business Review*, May/June 1990, 79–91.
24. Day, "The Capabilities of Market-Driven Organizations," 38.
25. Ibid., 39–40.
26. Ibid., 40–43.
27. Ibid.
28. Frederick E. Webster Jr., "The Future Role of Marketing in the Organization," in *Reflections on the Futures of Marketing*," Donald R. Lehmann and Katherine E. Jocz (eds.) (Cambridge, MA: Marketing Science Institute, 1997), 39–66.
29. Kathryn Troy, *Change Management: Striving for Customer Value* (New York: The Conference Board Inc., 1996), 5.
30. Philip Kotler, *Marketing Management*, 9th ed., (Upper Saddle River, NJ: Prentice-Hall, 1997), Chapter 2.
31. George S. Day and Robin Wensley, "Assessing Advantage: A Framework for Diagnosing Competitive Superiority," *Journal of Marketing*, April 1988, 1–20.
32. Troy, "Change Management," 6.
33. Ibid., 6.
34. Laura Mazur, "Wrong Sort of Innovation," *Marketing Business*, June 1999, 49.
35. Day, "The Capabilities of Market-Driven Organizations," 49.
36. Ibid., 43–45.
37. Ibid.
38. David W. Cravens, Gordon Greenley, Nigel F. Piercy, and Stanley Slater, "Mapping the Path to Market Leadership: The Market-Driven Strategy Imperative," *Marketing Management*, Fall 1998.
39. Troy, "Change Management," 7.
40. Ibid.
41. Nigel F. Piercy, "Marketing Implementation: The Implications of Marketing Paradigm Weakness for the Strategy Execution Process," *Journal of the Academy of Marketing Science* 13(213), 1999, 113–131.
42. "Over the Sea, Then Under the Knife," *BusinessWeek*, February 16, 2004, 20–22.
43. "Job Exports: Europe's Turn," *BusinessWeek*, April 19, 2004, 20–21.
44. Manjeet Kripalani, "Now It's Bombay Calling the U.S.," *BusinessWeek*, June 21, 2004, 30.
45. C. K. Prahalad and Allen Hammond, "Serving the World's Poor Profitability," *Harvard Business Review*, September 2002, 48–57.
46. Steve Hamm, "Borders Are So 20th Century," *BusinessWeek*, September 22, 2003, 70–71.
47. Moon Ihlwan, "Want Innovation, Hire a Russian," *BusinessWeek*, March 8, 2004, 22.
48. Bruno Stevens, "Big Pharma Booster Shot," *BusinessWeek*, June 7, 2004, 66.
49. Roger L. Martin, "The Virtue Matrix: Calculating the Return on Corporate Responsibility," *Harvard Business Review*, March, 2002, 69–75.

Chapter 2

Corporate, Business, and Marketing Strategy

Business and marketing strategies are being altered and renewed in a wide range of companies by executives in their efforts to survive and prosper in an increasingly complex and demanding business environment. Choosing high performance strategies in this environment of constant change requires vision, sound strategic logic, and commitment. Market-driven organizations develop closely coordinated business and marketing strategies. Executives in many companies are reinventing their business models with the objective of improving their competitive advantage. These changes include altering market focus, expanding product scope, partnering with other organizations, outsourcing manufacturing, and modifying internal structure.

Strategic imperatives have shifted to a priority emphasis on developing a superior capacity for reinventing the business model. Key issues underpinning strategic choices are:

- **Revolution**—In many industries, the drivers of radical, revolutionary change have created most of the new wealth over the last decade. Examples include JetBlue, Costco, and eBay.
- **Renewal**—To survive, existing companies must innovate with respect to their traditional business models. P&G's renewal initiatives are impressive as discussed in Chapter 1.
- **Resilience**—The capacity for continuous reconstruction requires innovation with respect to the organizational values, processes, and behaviors that systematically favor perpetuating the past rather than innovation for renewal.[1]

The strategic initiative pursued by Airbus, the European airplane giant, to achieve a dominant position in the global aviation industry with its 555-seater super-jumbo airplane is an example of innovation-driven strategy. With its multinational production design, new technology to reduce the weight of the massive plane, and potential cost advantages for international airlines, many industry analysts are positive concerning Airbus' strategy, but some question the underlying forecast of demand for the super-jumbo, upon which profit depends. The company's strategy is described in the Global Feature.

Corporate strategy consists of deciding the scope and purpose of the business, its objectives, and the initiatives and resources necessary to achieve the objectives. Marketing strategy is guided by the decisions top management makes about how, when, and where to compete. This should be a two-way relationship—while corporate strategy defines strategic direction, allocates resources, and defines constraints on what cannot be done, executives responsible for marketing strategy have a responsibility to inform corporate strategists about external change in the market that identifies opportunities and threats, as shown in Exhibit 2.1.

Global Feature

The A380: A Pan-European Plane

Airbus is building the biggest airliner ever, and more than 100 A380s have been ordered by the airlines. The question is whether this is a brilliant strategy or a huge mistake for the company.

- The A380 is a massive plane, with capacity for more than 555 passengers. It uses a wing that is so long it would top a nine-story building if stood on end. List price is $250 million per plane.
- Development and production costs will exceed $13 billion before the plane flies. Contractors and suppliers have contributed more than $2 billion.
- Airbus is building major components in four countries—France, Germany, Britain, and Spain—and bringing them together for assembly in Toulouse. The logistics problems are severe. Airbus has had to build its own oceangoing ferry, buy large customer-built canal barges, and contribute to road-widening costs to accommodate the oversize loads it is moving from plant to plant.
- There is a substantial problem with the weight of the aircraft—at 560 tons, nearly 100 tons heavier than planned, to accommodate customer requests for quieter (and therefore heavier) engines.
- Key competitor Boeing has rejected the super-jumbo option. The Boeing strategy is based on the assumption that, as in the United States, passengers will want to fly on direct routes on midsize planes, and airlines will want smaller and more versatile aircraft to reduce financial and operational risks.
- Some U.S. airlines like Continental predict passenger resistance to the super-jumbo—who wants to check in with 500 other passengers, wait for service with 500 other passengers, and wait for bags with 500 other passengers.
- Airbus predicts that on long-haul flights, the A380 will cost airlines 15 percent less per seat mile by spreading costs over a much larger passenger base.
- Shortages of take-off slots at major international airports like London's Heathrow also favor larger aircraft.
- The biggest question remains whether Airbus has correctly gauged the long-term demand for the super-jumbo.
- If successful, the A380 will change the balance of power in global aviation, while failure will bring massive financial losses and could threaten Airbus's survival.

Source: Carol Matlock and Stanley Holmes, "Megaplane," *BusinessWeek*, November 10, 2003, 50–56.

EXHIBIT 2.1
Corporate, Business, and Marketing Strategy

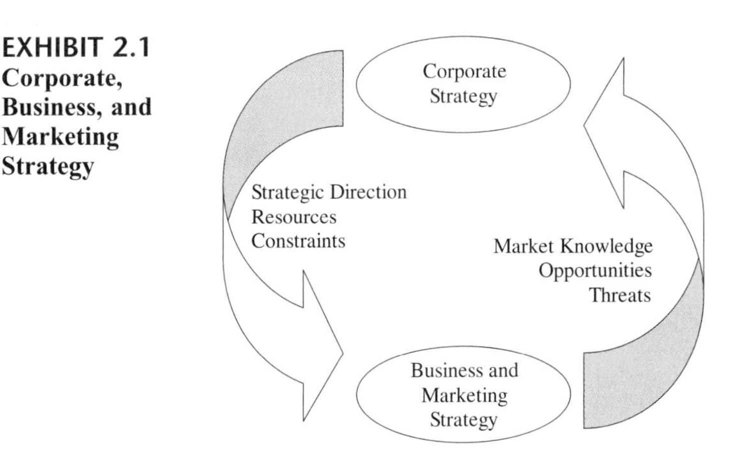

For example, planning at IBM is complex because of the sheer size and diversity of the company—revenues in excess of $80 billion and 315,000 staff. Marketing is closely involved with the strategy of evolving the company toward becoming a service business. Marketing planning is carried out by marketing managers in brand/business units and customer-based organizations.

As they develop strategies around brands and customers, marketing managers have to bid for and "buy" the resources they need for execution from the corporate level of the organization.[2] Because of this close relationship between different levels of strategy, it is important to examine the major aspects of designing and implementing business strategy.

We begin the chapter with a look at the nature and scope of corporate strategy. A discussion of business and marketing strategy relationships follows. Next, the marketing strategy process is described and illustrated. Finally, we examine the steps in preparing the strategic marketing plan.

Corporate Strategy

We describe the characteristics of corporate strategy and consider how organizations are changing. The section is concluded with a discussion of the major dimensions of corporate strategy.

What Is Corporate Strategy?

It is important to reach a reasonable consensus concerning the nature and scope of corporate strategy. One authority, Michael Porter, indicates that an effective strategy should display these characteristics:

- Unique competitive position for the company.
- Activities tailored to strategy.
- Clear trade-offs and choices vis-à-vis competitors.
- Competitive advantage arising from fit across activities.
- Sustainability coming from the activity system, not the parts.
- Operational effectiveness as a given.[3]

This concept of strategy views distinctive capabilities as comprised of business activities which are aligned to form processes. An example is Wal-Mart's distribution system comprised of various activities such as tracking each item in inventory. Other examples are Dell Inc.'s direct personal computer sales and built-to-order process, and Southwest Airline's city-to-city business design coupled with very efficient performance of the activities needed to transport passengers from point to point.

Corporate strategy consists of the decisions made by top management and the resulting actions taken to achieve the objectives set for the business. The major strategy components and several key issues related to each component are shown in Exhibit 2.2. The issues highlight important questions that management must answer in charting the course of the enterprise. Management's skills and vision in addressing these issues are critical to the performance of the corporation. Essential to corporate success is matching the capabilities of the organization with opportunities to provide long-term superior customer value.

It is apparent that in the 21st century marketing environments, companies are drastically altering their business and marketing strategies to get closer to their customers, counter competitive threats, and strengthen competitive advantages. The challenges to management include escalating international competition, new types and sources of competition, political and economic upheaval, dominance of the customer, and increasing marketing complexity.

Organizational Change

In recent decades massive changes were made in the size and structure of many business firms. These changes are described as rightsizing, reengineering, and reinventing the organization. The renewal (reforming) of the traditional organization typically moves through three phases: vertical disaggregation, internal redesign, and network formation.[4]

Vertical Disaggregation. Disaggregation reduces the *size* of the organization by eliminating jobs and layers of middle managers and leveling the hierarchy. The Conference Board, Inc. reports that 90 percent of its members downsized during the 1990s and about two-thirds of the executives representing a broad cross section of business say downsizing will continue.[5]

EXHIBIT 2.2
Corporate Strategy Components and Issues

Source: Orville C. Walker, Jr., Harper W. Boyd, Jr., and Jean-Claude Larréché, *Marketing Strategy* (Homewood, IL: Richard D. Irwin, 1992), 38. Copyright © The McGraw-Hill Companies. Used with permission.

Strategy Component	Key Issues
Scope, mission, and intent	• What business(es) should the firm be in? • What customer needs, market segments, and/or technologies should be focused on? • What is the firm's enduring strategic purpose or intent?
Objectives	• What performance dimensions should the firm's business units and employees focus on? • What is the target level of performance to be achieved on each dimension? • What is the time frame in which each target should be attained?
Development strategy	• How can the firm achieve a desired level of growth over time? • Can the desired growth be attained by expanding the firm's current businesses? • Will the company have to diversify into new businesses or product-markets to achieve its future growth objectives?
Resource allocation	• How should the firm's limited financial resources be allocated across its businesses to produce the highest returns? • Of the alternative strategies that each business might pursue, which will produce the greatest returns for the dollars invested?
Sources of synergy	• What competencies, knowledge, and customer-based intangibles (e.g., brand recognition, reputation) might be developed and shared across the firm's businesses? • What operational resources, facilities, or functions (e.g., plants, R&D, sales force) might the firm's businesses share to increase their efficiency?

The resulting flat corporation may organize its activities into a small number of key processes (e.g., new-product planning, sales generation, and customer service).[6] Alternatively, organizations may retain functional departments, overlaying them with processes. Cross-functional teams manage the processes, and providing superior customer value is a key objective and measure of performance. Employees are encouraged to make regular contact with suppliers and customers.

Internal Redesign. Organizational renewal is more than just reducing staff, eliminating layers of management, and adopting worker empowerment processes. The second phase alters the internal design of the organization. The new organization forms are lean, flexible, adaptive, and responsive to customer needs and market requirements.[7] The altered business designs involve innovation in designing products to meet customer needs, arranging supply and distribution networks, and constantly staying in touch with the marketplace. A priority of these organizations is understanding customer needs, offering value to customers, and retaining customers.

New Organization Forms. The third phase of organizational change involves the formation of relationships with other organizations and the use of processes as the basic organizing concept. Although interorganizational relationships are often present in the traditional organization, companies are expanding these relationships with suppliers, customers, and even competitors. These new organization forms are called networks since they involve several collaborative arrangements. Networks are more likely to be launched by entrepreneurs, since the traditional vertically integrated, hierarchically organized company finds difficulty in shifting to the network

Innovation Feature

Tightly Integrated Software versus Software Alliances—Oracle versus IBM

- Oracle's strategy is to develop and offer corporate customers a complete and integrated package of software for managing financial operations, manufacturing, sales force, logistics, e-commerce, and suppliers.
- IBM's strategy is to assemble and apply the best package of software from more than 50 software partners, leveraging the distinctive capabilities of each partner.
- The corporate software market for databases applications (e.g., sales force automation, supply-chain management) is an estimated $50 billion.
- Oracle's management indicates that IBM's objective is to market its consulting services for applying corporate software packages.
- IBM's software is about one-fifth the price of Oracle's software, but IBM also charges consulting fees to install and integrate software packages from partners such as SAP, Siebel Systems, Ariba, and PeopleSoft.
- The customer value issue is a combination of software price and software performance. Some corporate buyers are finding that IBM's total price is below Oracle's. Performance of the two firms' software packages appears to be comparable.
- Industry authorities are split concerning which software system will win the competitive battle. IBM and Oracle are expected to remain the strongest firms in the market.

Source: "IBM vs. Oracle: It Could Get Bloody," *BusinessWeek*, May 28, 2001, 65–66.

paradigm. Transformation means fewer people on the corporate payroll, different management challenges, drastic cultural changes, and complex collaborative relationships with other organizations. Nevertheless, traditional companies like IBM are successfully transforming themselves to more flexible and adaptive network forms. The Innovation Feature describes how IBM is using software alliances to compete with Oracle Corp.

Components of Strategy

Recognizing that there are several definitions of corporate strategy, we utilize this definition:

> Corporate strategy is the way a company creates value through the configuration and coordination of its multimarket activities.[8]

This definition emphasizes value creation, considers the multimarket scope of the corporation (product, geographic, and vertical value-chain boundaries), and points to how the organization manages its activities and businesses that fall under the corporate umbrella. A key premise of this view of strategy is that the multibusiness corporation must contribute to the competitive advantage of its units.[9] Thus, there needs to be a close relationship between the corporation and the businesses that are part of the firm.

A useful basis for examining corporate strategy that is consistent with the earlier definition consists of (1) management's long-term vision for the corporation; (2) objectives that serve as milestones toward the vision; (3) assets, skills, and capabilities; (4) businesses in which the corporation competes; (5) structure, systems, and processes; and (6) creation of value through multimarket activity.[10] We examine each strategy component.

Deciding Corporate Vision. Management's vision defines what the corporation is and what it does and provides important guidelines for managing and improving the corporation. The founder initially has a vision about the firm's mission, and management may alter the mission over time. Strategic choices about where the firm is going in the future—choices that take into account company capabilities, resources, opportunities, and problems—establish the vision of the enterprise. Developing strategies for sustainable competitive advantage, implementing them, and adjusting the strategies to respond to new environmental requirements is a continuing process. Managers monitor the market and competitive environment. The corporate vision may, over time, be changed because of problems or opportunities identified by monitoring. For example, IBM's management is placing major emphasis on consulting services as a direction of future growth.

Early in the strategy-development process management needs to define the vision of the corporation. It is reviewed and updated as shifts in the strategic direction of the enterprise occur over time. The vision statement sets several important guidelines for business operations:[11]

1. The reason for the company's existence and its responsibilities to stockholders, employees, society, and other stakeholders.
2. The firm's customers and the needs (benefits) that are to be met by the firm's goods or services (areas of product and market involvement).
3. The extent of specialization within each product-market area and the geographical scope of operations.
4. The amount and types of product-market diversification desired by management.
5. The stage(s) in the value-added chain where the business competes from raw materials to the end user.
6. Management's performance expectations for the company.
7. Other general guidelines for overall business strategy, such as technologies to be used and the role of research and development in the corporation.

Objectives. Objectives need to be set so that the performance of the enterprise can be gauged. Corporate objectives may be established in the following areas: *marketing, innovation, resources, productivity, social responsibility,* and *finance*.[12] Examples include growth and market-share expectations, improving product quality, employee training and development, new-product targets, return on invested capital, earnings growth rates, debt limits, energy reduction objectives, and pollution standards. Objectives are set at several levels in an organization beginning with those indicating the enterprise's overall objectives.

The time frame necessary for strategic change often goes beyond short-term financial reporting requirements. Companies are using more than financial measures to evaluate longer-term strategic objectives, and nonfinancial measures for short-term budgets. The "balanced scorecard" approach provides an expanded basis for tracking organizational performance.[13] It considers both long-term and short-term performance metrics. This method of keeping score includes objectives, measures, targets, and initiatives regarding financial, customer, internal business processes, and learning and growth perspectives. The balanced scorecard method is being used by many companies as a basis for managing and evaluating market-driven strategies.

Capabilities. As we discussed in Chapter 1, it is important to place a company's strategic focus on its distinctive capabilities.[14] These capabilities may offer the organization the potential to compete in different markets, provide significant value to end user customers, and create barriers to competitor duplication. For example, Hewlett-Packard developed a distinctive capability in ink-jet printer technology, enabling the company to become the world leader in printers.

We know that distinctive capabilities are important in shaping the organization's strategy. In contrast to the diversification wave of the 1970s, many companies are deciding what they do best and concentrating their efforts on these distinctive capabilities. A key strategy issue is matching capabilities to market opportunities. Capabilities that can be leveraged into different markets and applications are particularly valuable. For example, the GoreTex high performance fabric is used in many applications from apparel to dental floss.

Acknowledging the constraining nature of capabilities, resources, opportunities, and problems, management has a lot of flexibility in selecting the mission as well as changing it in the future. Sometimes the priorities and preferences of the CEO or the board of directors may override factual evidence in selecting the business mission. For example, many of the diversifications pursued by companies in the 1980s did not work well, and resulted in the restructuring and downsizing of many companies during the last decade.

Business Composition. Defining the composition of the business provides direction for both corporate and marketing strategy design. In single-product firms that serve one market, it is easy to determine the composition of the business. In many other firms it is necessary to separate the business into parts to facilitate strategic analyses and planning. When firms are serving multiple markets with different products, grouping similar business areas together aids decision making.

Business segment, group, or division designations are used to identify the major areas of business of a diversified corporation. Each segment, group, or division often contains a mix of related products, though a single product can be assigned such a designation. The term *segment* does not correspond to a market segment (subgroup of end users in a product-market), which we discuss throughout the book. Most large corporations break out their financial reports into business or industry segments according to the guidelines of the Financial Accounting Standards Board. Some firms may establish subgroups of related products within a business segment that are targeted to different customer groups.

A business segment, group, or division is often too large in terms of product and market composition to use in strategic analysis and planning, so it is divided into more specific strategic units. A popular name for these units is the *strategic business unit* (SBU). Typically SBUs display product and customer group similarities. A strategic business unit is a single product or brand, a line of products, or a mix of related products that meets a common market need or a group of related needs, and the unit's management is responsible for all (or most) of the basic business functions. The characteristics of the ideal SBU are described in Exhibit 2.3. Typically, the SBU has a specific strategy rather than a shared strategy with another business area. It is a cohesive organizational unit that is separately managed and produces sales and profit results.

Virgin Group is an interesting example of the formation of a large and diverse portfolio of business enterprises. The founder, Richard Branson, was knighted in England in 2000 for his entrepreneurship initiatives in launching an array of businesses under the Virgin Group corporate umbrella. With 200 separate companies, the Virgin brand identifies hundreds of products from travel to financial services to entertainment.[15] Core businesses are Virgin Atlantic, Virgin Express (a Brussels-based discount airline), Virgin Blue (an Australian no-frills airline), Virgin Rail (running two of Britain's main train services), and Virgin Mobile (Britain's fastest-growing mobile telephone company). New projects include Virgin USA, a discount airline business to fill the gaps left by Southwest and JetBlue, and Virgin Mobile USA, a joint venture with Sprint. Branson describes his business as a "branded venture-capital firm," and for most new ventures he supplies the brand, a small initial investment and takes majority control while partner organizations provide the main funding. Not all of the Virgin Group initiatives have been successful, but the successes have made him a very wealthy entrepreneur.

In a business that has two or more strategic business units, decisions must be made at two levels. Corporate management must first decide what business areas to pursue, and set priorities for allocating resources to each SBU. The decision makers for each SBU must select the strategies for implementing the corporate strategy and producing the results that corporate management expects. Corporate-level management is often involved in assisting SBUs to achieve their objectives.

Corporate strategy and resources should help the SBU to compete more effectively than if the unit operates on a completely independent basis. "To remain competitive, corporations must provide their business units with low-cost capital, outstanding executives, corporate R&D, centralized marketing where appropriate and other resources in the corporate arsenal."[16] Corporate resources and synergies help the SBU establish its competitive advantage. The strategic focus and priorities of corporate strategy guide SBU strategies. Finally, top management's expectations for the corporation indicate the results expected from an SBU, including both financial and nonfinancial objectives. When viewed in this context, the SBUs become the action centers of the corporation. One criticism of the SBU concept is that distinctive competencies are

EXHIBIT 2.3
Characteristics of the Ideal Strategic Business Unit

Source: Orville C. Walker Jr., Harper W. Boyd, Jr., and Jean-claud Larréché, *Marketing Strategy* (Homewood, IL: Richard D. Irwin, 1992), 76.

Characteristic	Rationale
• Serves a homogeneous set of markets with a limited number of related technologies	Minimizing the diversity of business unit's product-market entries enables the unit's manager to do a better job of formulating and implementing a coherent and internally consistent business strategy.
• Serves a unique set of product-markets	No other SBU within the firm should compete for the same set of customers with similar products. This enables the firm to avoid duplication of effort and helps maximize economies of scale within its SBUs.
• Has control over the factors necessary for successful performance, such as R&D, production, marketing, and distribution	This is not to say than an SBU should never share resources, such as a manufacturing plant or a sales force, with one or more business units, but the SBU should have authority to determine how its share of the joint resource will be used to effectively carry out its strategy.
• Has responsibility for its own profitability	Because top management cannot keep an eye on every decision and action taken by all its SBUs, the success of an SBU and its managers must be judged by monitoring its performance over time. Thus, the SBU's managers should have control over the factors that affect performance and then be held accountable for the outcomes.

not leveraged across a corporation's businesses. However, the successful vertical movement of the retailer Gap into the higher-quality/price apparel segment with Banana Republic and Old Navy into the lower-quality/price segment suggests just the opposite. Both initiatives leveraged Gap's competencies in design, outsourcing, and retail operations and merchandising.

Structure, Systems, and Processes. This aspect of strategy considers how the organization controls and coordinates the activities of its various business units and staff functions.[17] Structure determines the composition of the corporation. Systems are the formal policies and procedures that enable the organization to operate. Processes consider the informal aspects of the organization's activities:

> In establishing a firm's infrastructure, corporate managers have a wide array of organizational mechanisms at their disposal, from the formal boxes in an organization chart to the more subtle elements of corporate culture and style. Because every corporate strategy is different, there is not one optimal set of structures, systems, and processes.[18]

The logic of how the business is designed is receiving considerable attention because of the threats of customers being attracted by designs that better satisfy their needs and requirements. "A business design is the totality of how a company selects its customers, defines and differentiates its offerings, defines the tasks it will perform itself and those it will outsource, configures its resources, goes to market, creates utility for customers, and captures profit."[19] The business design (or business model) provides a focus on more than the product and/or technology, instead looking at the processes and relationships that comprise the design. For example, Dell's direct built-to-order business design is viewed by many business buyers as offering superior value.

Corporate Competitive Advantage. This part of corporate strategy looks at whether the strategy components create value through multimarket activity.[20] The strategic issues include evaluating the extent to which a business contributes positive benefits minus costs somewhere in the corporation and whether the corporation creates more value for the business than might be created by another owner. JC Penney's management decided in 2004 that its Eckerd retail drug chain was not a good strategic fit with the core business and the unit was sold to the CVC drug chain.

Business and Marketing Strategy

During the 1990s many strategy guidelines were offered by consultants, executives, and academics to guide business strategy formulation. These strategy paradigms propose a range of actions including reengineering the corporation, total quality management, building distinctive competencies, reinventing the organization, and strategic partnering. It is not feasible to review the various strategy concepts and methods that are available in many books, seminars, and consulting services. The corporate strategy framework presented in this chapter offers a basis for incorporating relevant strategy perspectives and guidelines.

An important issue is whether selecting a successful strategy has a favorable impact on results. Does the uncontrollable environment largely determine business performance or, instead, will the organization's strategy have a major impact on its performance? Successful businesses can be found operating in very demanding market and competitive environments. Examples include JetBlue Airlines (air travel), Samsung (electronics), and Wal-Mart (discount retailing). Of course, favorable environments would further enhance the performance of these companies.

The evidence suggests that strategic choices matter.[21] While environmental factors such as market demand, intensity of competition, government, and social change influence corporate performance, the strategic choices made by specific companies also have a significant impact on their performance. Importantly, the impact may be positive or negative. For example, Kmart held the leading market position over Wal-Mart in 1980, yet Wal-Mart overtook Kmart by investing heavily in information systems and distribution to develop a powerful customer-driven, low-cost retail network. Kmart declared bankruptcy in early 2002.

Developing the Strategic Plan for Each Business

Strategic analysis is conducted to: (1) diagnose business units' strengths and limitations, and (2) select strategies for maintaining or improving performance. Management decides what priority to place on each business regarding resource allocation and implements a strategy to meet the objectives for the SBU. The strategic plan indicates the action agenda for the business. An example of a business plan outline is shown in Exhibit 2.4. The "major strategies" shown in Part VI of the plan include the strategic actions planned for business development, marketing, quality, product and technology, human resources, manufacturing/facilities, and finance.

The strategic analysis guides establishing the SBU's mission, setting objectives, and determining the strategy to use to meet these objectives. The SBU's strategy indicates market target priorities, available resources, financial constraints, and other strategic guidelines needed to develop marketing plans. Depending on the size and diversity of the SBU, marketing plans may either be included in the SBU plan or developed separately. If combined, the marketing portion of the business plan will represent half or more of the business plan. In a small business (e.g., retail store, restaurant, etc.), the marketing portion of the plan may account for most of the plan. Plans may be developed to obtain financial support for a new venture, or to spell out internal business and marketing strategies.

Business and Marketing Strategy Relationships

An understanding of business purpose, scope, objectives, capabilities, and strategy is essential in designing and implementing marketing strategies that are consistent with the corporate and business unit plan of action.

EXHIBIT 2.4
Plan Outline—A High-Technology Products Manufacturer

Source: Excerpt from Rochelle O'Connor, *Facing Strategic Issues: New Planning Guides and Practices,* Report No. 87 (New York: The Conference Board, 1985), 32. Reprinted with permission from The Conference Board.

I. Management Summary
II. Business Definition
  Mission
  Purpose
  Role
III. Progress Report
  Comparison of key financial and market indicators
  Progress made on major strategies
IV. Market and Customer Analysis
  Potential versus served market
  Market segmentation
V. Competitive Analysis
  Description of three major competitors
  Analysis of competitor's strategies
VI. Objectives, Strategies, and Programs
  Key objectives
  Major strategies to accomplish the objectives
  Action programs to implement strategies
  Major assumptions and contingency programs
  Market share matrix
VII. Financial Projections
  Financial projections statement
  Personnel projections

The chief marketing executive's business strategy responsibilities include (1) participating in strategy formulation, and (2) developing marketing strategies that are consistent with business strategy priorities and integrated with other functional strategies. Since these two responsibilities are closely interrelated, it is important to examine marketing's role and functions in both areas to gain more insight into marketing's responsibilities and contributions. Peter F. Drucker describes this role:

> Marketing is so basic that it cannot be considered a separate function (i.e., a separate skill or work) within the business, on a par with others such as manufacturing or personnel. Marketing requires separate work and a distinct group of activities. But it is, first, a central dimension of the entire business. It is the whole business seen from the point of view of its final result, that is, from the customer's point of view.[22]

Frederick E. Webster describes the role of the marketing manager: "At the corporate level, marketing managers have a critical role to play as advocates for the customer and for a set of values and beliefs that put the customer first in the firm's decision making, and to communicate the value proposition as part of that culture throughout the organization, both internally and in its multiple relationships and alliances."[23] This role includes assessing market attractiveness in the markets available to the firm, providing a customer orientation, and communicating the firm's specific value advantages.

Strategic Marketing

Marketing strategy consists of the analysis, strategy development, and implementation activities in:

> Developing a vision about the market(s) of interest to the organization, selecting market target strategies, setting objectives, and developing, implementing, and managing the marketing program positioning strategies designed to meet the value requirements of the customers in each market target.

Strategic marketing is a market-driven process of strategy development, taking into account a constantly changing business environment and the need to deliver superior customer value. The focus of strategic marketing is on organizational performance rather than a primary concern about increasing sales. Marketing strategy seeks to deliver superior customer value by combining the customer-influencing strategies of the business into a coordinated set of market-driven actions. Strategic marketing links the organization with the environment and views marketing as a responsibility of the entire business rather than a specialized function.

Because of marketing's boundary orientation between the organization and its customers, channel members, and competition, marketing processes are central to the business strategy planning process.[24] Strategic marketing provides the expertise for environmental monitoring, for deciding what customer groups to serve, for guiding product specifications, and for choosing which competitors to position against. Successfully integrating cross-functional strategies is critical to providing superior customer value. Customer value requirements must be transformed into product design and production guidelines. Success in achieving high-quality goods and services requires finding out which attributes of goods and service quality drive customer value.

Marketing Strategy Process

The marketing strategy analysis, planning, implementation, and management process that we follow is described in Exhibit 2.5. The strategy stages shown are examined and applied in Parts II through V of the book. The strategic situation analysis considers market and competitor analysis, market segmentation, and continuous learning about markets. Designing marketing strategy examines customer targeting and positioning strategies, marketing relationship strategies, and planning for new products. Marketing program development consists of product, distribution, price, and promotion strategies designed and implemented to meet the value requirements of targeted buyers. Strategy implementation and management consider organizational design and marketing strategy implementation and control. We overview each part of the strategy process in the rest of this chapter.

Strategic Situation Analysis

Marketing management uses the information provided by the situation analysis to guide the design of a new strategy or change an existing strategy. The situation analysis is conducted on a regular basis after the strategy is under way to evaluate strategy performance and identify needed strategy changes.

EXHIBIT 2.5
Marketing Strategy Process

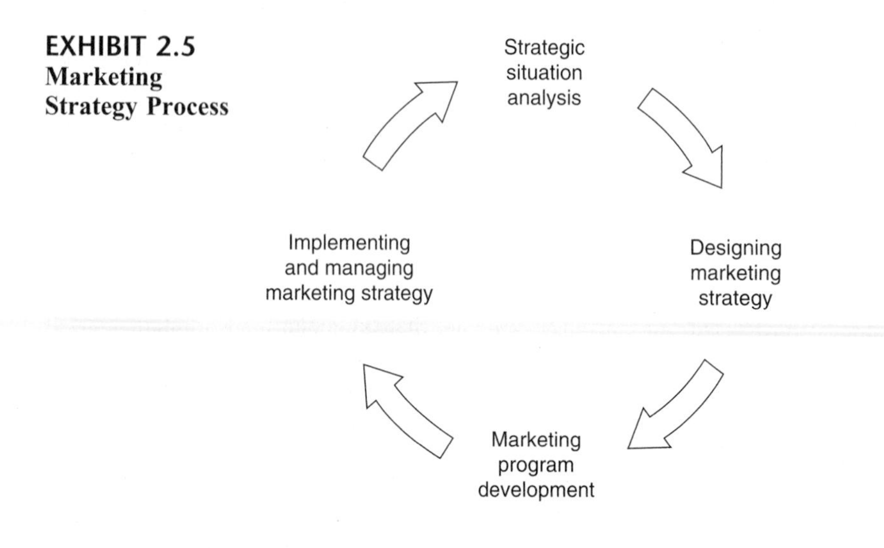

Market Vision, Structure, and Analysis. Markets need to be defined so that buyers and competition can be analyzed. For a market to exist, there must be (1) people with particular needs and wants and one or more products that can satisfy buyers' needs, and, (2) buyers willing and able to purchase a product that satisfies their needs and wants. A product-market consists of a specific product (or line of related products) that can satisfy a set of needs and wants for the people (or organizations) willing and able to purchase it. We use the term *product* to indicate either a physical good or an intangible service.

Analyzing product-markets and forecasting how they will change in the future are vital to business and marketing planning. Decisions to enter new product-markets, how to serve existing product-markets, and when to exit unattractive product-markets are critical strategic choices. The objective is to identify and describe the buyers, understand their preferences for products, estimate the size and rate of growth of the market, and find out what companies and products are competing in the market.

Evaluation of competitors' strategies, strengths, limitations, and plans is also a key aspect of the situation analysis. It is important to identify both existing and potential competitors. Competitor analysis includes evaluating each key competitor. The analyses highlight the competition's important strengths and weaknesses. A key issue is trying to figure out what each competitor is likely to do in the future.

Google Inc. provides an interesting example of a company that has reinvented the Internet search process to build a business now estimated to be worth $20 billion. Google's massive bank of servers process more than 3,000 searches every second of the day. Launched in 1998, Google powers over 50 percent of all Web searches. The start-up was based on a breakthrough search algorithm and a super-fast search process. The Google founders kept their home page free of advertising and links to other Web pages; scorned advertising in favor of word-of-mouth to build the brand, and built a business out of selling advertising alongside search results. Nonetheless, Google faces major competitive initiatives.[25] The competitive situation facing Google is outlined in Exhibit 2.6.

Segmenting Markets. Market segmentation looks at the nature and extent of diversity of buyers' needs and wants in a market. It offers an opportunity for an organization to focus its business capabilities on the requirements of one or more groups of buyers. The objective of segmentation is to examine differences in needs and wants and to identify the segments (subgroups) within the product-market of interest. Each segment contains buyers with similar needs and wants for the product category of interest to management. The segments are described using the various characteristics of people, the reasons that they buy or use certain products, and their preferences for certain brands of products. Likewise, segments of industrial product-markets may be formed according to the type of industry, the uses for the product, frequency of product purchase, and various other factors.

Each segment may vary quite a bit from the average characteristics of the entire product-market. The similarities of buyers' needs within a segment enable better targeting of the organization's capabilities to buyers with corresponding value requirements. For example, active individuals comprise an important market segment for Gatorade, the popular thirst-quenching sports drink. Teenagers are an important market segment for carbonated beverages since they have not yet developed strong brand preferences.

Continuous Learning about Markets. One of the major realities of achieving business success today is the necessity of understanding markets and competition. Sensing what is happening and is likely to occur in the future is complicated by competitive threats that may exist beyond traditional industry boundaries. For example, microwave dinners compete with McDonald's fast foods, CD-ROMs compete with books, and fax transmission competes with overnight letter delivery.

Managers and professionals in market-driven firms are able to sense what is happening in their markets, develop business and marketing strategies to seize opportunities and counter

EXHIBIT 2.6
The Outlook for Google in the Internet Search Business

Source: Ben Elgin, "Google," *BusinessWeek*, May 3, 2004, 50–56.

Google's days as unchallenged king of Internet searches are over. Microsoft and Yahoo are going to make this a highly contested market.

Brand: The Google name has been turned into a verb; Google powers 50% of all Web searches. Its brand has the edge.

Technology: Google's lead has been narrowed. Yahoo's search engine is almost as good, and Yahoo has 141 million registered users to personalize search results.

Reach: The future is universal search—a single search engine letting you search archived e-mail, Word documents, and Web pages with a single click. By 2006 Microsoft plans to integrate Web search into Windows for a clear advantage over Google and Yahoo.

Bankroll: All three contenders have financing, but Microsoft has made its intentions to compete in search crystal-clear, and Bill Gates' $4.7 billion R&D budget is nearly double the combined revenues of Yahoo and Google.

Advertisers: With 150,000 small business advertisers, Google has 50% more than Yahoo. Yahoo's revenue will suffer even more if Microsoft decides to create its own ad product and stop carrying Yahoo's search ads.

Execution: Google's unconventional management structure may impede decisive action. Microsoft has to build a search engine from scratch. Yahoo looks strongest here.

threats, and anticipate what the market will be like in the future.[26] Several market sensing methods are available to guide the collection and analysis of information. For example, company databases on customers created through Customer Relationship Management systems offer valuable data mining opportunities.

Designing Market-Driven Strategies

The strategic situation analysis phase of the marketing strategy process identifies market opportunities, defines market segments, evaluates competition, and assesses the organization's strengths and weaknesses. Market sensing information plays a key role in designing marketing strategy, which includes market targeting and positioning strategies, building marketing relationships, and developing and introducing new products. The Strategy Feature describes how BMW is rebuilding its positioning in the global premium automobile market.

Strategy Feature

BMW—Positioning Premium Automobiles

- Rebuilding the strategy for Bayernishe Motoren Werke (BMW) was an imperative as the global auto market fragmented into new niches, and demand for luxury sedans—BMW's core business—started to shrink as a percentage of all auto sales.
- The goal is to expand annual sales by 40 percent over five years, and to beat Mercedes-Benz as the number one maker of premium cars in the world.
- The company launched a new model nearly every three months during 2004 with more planned for 2005—ranging from the Rolls Royce Phantom, to the cult-car the MINI, to a new 5 Series sedan, to the X3, a downsized sports-utility vehicle.
- "BMW is the brand people aspire to own. When people get to the point they can afford a luxury car, they buy a BMW 3 Series," says one industry expert.
- BMW shows an obsession with performance and brand image. The brand image is closely tied to technical and design innovation.
- "BMW captured the performance space in the market for themselves. They own it," says one commentator.
- In the United States, BMW sales have overtaken those of Toyota's Lexus, and are substantially ahead of Mercedes-Benz, as the premium car market leader.

Source: Gail Edmondson, Chris Palmeri, Brian Grow, and Christine Tierney, "BMW," *BusinessWeek*, June 9, 2003, 19–24.

Market Targeting and Strategic Positioning. Marketing advantage is influenced by several situational factors including industry characteristics, type of firm (e.g., size), extent of differentiation in buyers' needs, and the specific competitive advantage(s) of the company designing the marketing strategy. The core issue is deciding how, when, and where to compete, given a firm's market and competitive environment.

The purpose of the **market targeting strategy** is to select the people (or organizations) that management wishes to serve in the product-market. When buyers' needs and wants vary, the market target is usually one or more segments of the product-market. Once the segments are identified and their relative importance to the firm determined, the targeting strategy is selected. The objective is to find the best match between the value requirements of each segment and the organization's distinctive capabilities. The targeting decision is the focal point of marketing strategy since targeting guides the setting of objectives and developing a positioning strategy. The options range from targeting most of the segments to targeting one or a few segments in a product-market. The targeting strategy may be influenced by the market's maturity, the diversity of buyers' needs and preferences, the firm's size compared to competition, corporate resources and priorities, and the volume of sales required to achieve favorable financial results. Deciding the objectives for each market target spells out the results expected by management. Examples of market target objectives are desired levels of sales, market share, customer retention, profit contribution, and customer satisfaction. Marketing objectives may also be set for the entire business unit and for specific marketing activities such as advertising.

The targeting and positioning strategies used by ConAgra Inc. for the Healthy Choice frozen food line helped the new brand successfully enter the market in the early 1990s. The low-calorie, low-cholesterol, low-sodium frozen food line quickly gained a strong market position.[27] Frozen food is a very competitive supermarket category because freezer space in stores is limited. Healthy Choice was introduced into the stagnant male-oriented frozen dinner segment of the market. It was positioned as a "health product." This positioning was successful even though it conflicts with conventional marketing guidelines: The female-oriented frozen food is the rapid growth segment and "health" positioning had been used to describe poor-tasting, low-calorie brands. Health is an issue of great concern to men and the taste of Healthy Choice is appealing to consumers who try the brand. The new line of frozen foods gained an impressive 25 percent market share in the

$700 million frozen dinner market. Healthy Choice extended its brand in the early 1990s to include breakfast items, deli meats, and soups. By 1992 intense price competition, new products, and promotion actions of the competition eroded Healthy Choice's share of the frozen dinner market, demonstrating the realities of competing against experienced food marketers. Nonetheless, during the 1990s Healthy Choice built a strong brand position across several food categories.

The marketing program **positioning strategy** is the combination of product, value-chain, price, and promotion strategies a firm uses to position itself against its key competitors in meeting the needs and wants of the market target. The strategies and tactics used to gain a favorable position are called the marketing mix or the marketing program.

The positioning strategy seeks to position the brand in the eyes and mind of the buyer and distinguish the product from the competition. The product, distribution, price, and promotion strategy components make up a bundle of actions that are used to influence buyers' positioning of a brand. General Motors Corp.'s (GMC) positioning problems with its automobile brands illustrate the strategic importance of positioning. In 1995, GMC launched a major marketing effort to reposition its brands. The objective was to identify the market segment targeted by each brand and to develop a unique positioning strategy appropriate for the target. The problem is that GM's car brands are perceived by many buyers to be very similar. The objective of GM's new strategy is to give each brand a distinct identity geared to the preferences of the brand's market target. GM's management decided to drop the Oldsmobile brand in 2000, apparently because GM was unable to sustain a competitive position for the brand.

Marketing Relationship Strategies. Marketing relationship partners may include end user customers, marketing channel members, suppliers, competitor alliances, and internal teams. The driving force underlying these relationships is that a company may enhance its ability to satisfy customers and cope with a rapidly changing business environment through collaboration of the parties involved. Relationship strategies gained new importance in the last decade as customers became more demanding and competition became more intense. Building long-term relationships with customers and value-chain partners offers companies a way to provide superior customer value. Although building collaborative relationships may not always be the best course of action, this avenue for gaining a competitive edge is increasing in popularity.

Strategic partnering has become an important strategic initiative for many well-known companies and brands. Many firms outsource the manufacturing of their products. Examples include Motorola cell phones, Baskin-Robbins ice cream, Calvin Klein jeans, Pepsi beverages, and Nike footwear. Strong relationships with outsourcing partners are vital to the success of these powerful brands. The trend of the 21st century is partnering rather than vertical integration.

Planning for New Products. New products are needed to replace old products because of declining sales and profits. Strategies for developing and positioning new market entries involve all functions of the business. Closely coordinated new-product planning is essential to satisfy customer requirements and produce products with high quality at competitive prices. New-product decisions include finding and evaluating ideas, selecting the most promising for development, designing the products, developing marketing programs, use and market testing the products, and introducing them to the market.

The new-product planning process starts by identifying gaps in customer satisfaction. The differences between existing product attributes and those desired by customers offer opportunities for new and improved products. Over the decades 3M Co. was recognized as one of corporate America's most inventive and innovative companies.[28] Surprisingly, this core strength began to drift in the last decade. 3M has not had a real winner since it launched Post-it Notes nearly 25 years ago. The new CEO is aggressively working to renew 3M's innovative culture and processes through redirection of R&D efforts, implementing Total Quality Management (Six Sigma), and acquiring innovative companies. 3M's innovation priorities highlight the pivotal role of new-product planning in business strategy.

Global Feature

How Nestlé Builds Its Brands throughout the World

- Global brand strategy.

  Largest branded food company in Mexico, Brazil, Chile, and Thailand—building rapidly in Vietnam and China.

  Builds both a manufacturing and a political presence.

  Negotiated over a decade to get into China.
- Owns nearly 8,000 brands worldwide—but only 750 are registered in more than one country—only 80 in 10 countries.

  The ingredients or processing technology are adapted for local conditions—often using the local brand name.
- Moves into a new market with a handful of labels—from its 11 strategic brand groups.

  Nestlé is the market leader in instant coffee in Australia (71%), France (67%), Japan (74%), and Mexico (85%).
- Nestlé's Thailand manager has worked there for 30 years.

  The 100 managers worldwide stay in only one region of the world (a key competitive advantage because they know local markets, competition, and governmental requirements).

  Coffee sales in Thailand were $25 million (1987) compared to $100 million (1994).
- Developed an entire milk distribution system in China from the farmer to the factory—produced 10,000 tons of powdered milk in 1994 ($700 million in sales by 2000).
- Nestlé is importing sales team and brand management techniques to supermarket chains in Thailand and other countries in the region.

Source: Carla Rapoport, "Nestlé's Brand Building Machine," *Fortune,* September 19, 1994, 147–48, 150, 154, 156.

EXHIBIT 2.7
Positioning Strategy Development

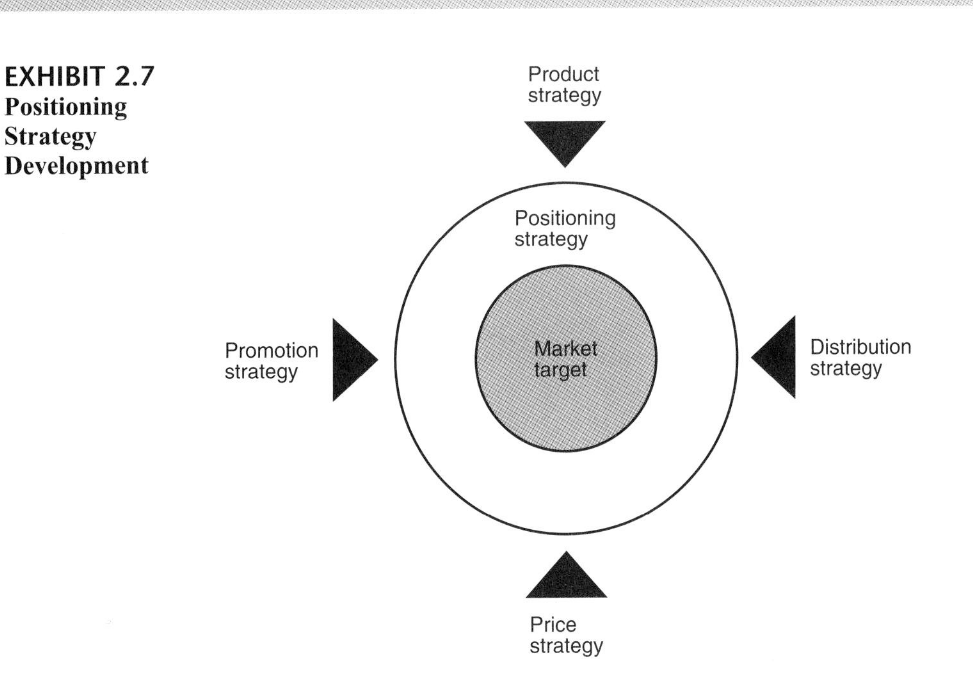

Market-Driven Program Development

Market targeting and positioning strategies for new and existing products guide the choice of strategies for the marketing program components. Product, distribution, price, and promotion strategies are combined to form the positioning strategy selected for each market target. The relationship of the positioning components to the market target is shown in Exhibit 2.7.

The marketing program (mix) strategies implement the positioning strategy.[29] The objective is to achieve favorable positioning while allocating financial, human, and production resources to markets, customers, and products as effectively and efficiently as possible.

Strategic Brand Management. Products (goods and services) often are the focal point of positioning strategy, particularly when companies or business units adopt organizational approaches emphasizing product or brand management. Product strategy includes: (1) developing plans for new products, (2) managing programs for successful products, and (3) deciding what to do about problem products (e.g., reduce costs or improve the product). Strategic brand management consists of building brand value (equity) and managing the organization's portfolio of brands for overall performance.

Nestlé, the Swiss food company, has a successful product and brand management strategy for competing in world markets. As described in the Global Feature, the company's brand strategy includes responding to local preferences, providing career tracks to keep managers in the same regional areas, and applying global food processing technology to gain cost and quality advantages.

Value-Chain, Price, and Promotion Strategies. One of the major issues in managing the marketing program is deciding how to integrate the components of the mix. Product, distribution, price, and promotion strategies are shaped into a coordinated plan of action. Each component helps to influence buyers in their positioning of products. If the activities of these mix components are not coordinated, the actions may conflict and resources may be wasted. For example, if the advertising messages for a company's brand stress quality and performance, but salespeople emphasize low price, buyers will be confused and brand damage may occur.

Market target buyers may be contacted on a direct basis using the firm's sales force or by direct marketing contact (e.g., Internet), or, instead, through a value-added chain (distribution channel) of marketing intermediaries (e.g., wholesalers, retailers, or dealers). Distribution channels are often used in linking producers with end user household and business markets. Decisions that need to be made include the type of channel organizations to use, the extent of channel management performed by the firm, and the intensity of distribution appropriate for the product or service. The choice of distribution channels influences buyers' positioning of the brand. For example, expensive watches like the Rolex brand are available from a limited number of retailers with prestigious images. These retailers help to reinforce the brand's image.

Price also plays an important role in positioning a product or service. Customer reaction to alternative prices, the cost of the product, the prices of the competition, and various legal and ethical factors establish the extent of flexibility management has in setting prices. Price strategy involves choosing the role of price in the positioning strategy, including the desired positioning of the product or brand as well as the margins necessary to satisfy and motivate distribution channel participants. Price may be used as an active (visible) component of marketing strategy, or, instead, marketing emphasis may be on other marketing mix components (e.g., product quality).

Advertising, sales promotion, the sales force, direct marketing, and public relations help the organization to communicate with its customers, value-chain partners, the public, and other target audiences. These activities make up the promotion strategy, which performs an essential role in communicating the positioning strategy to buyers and other relevant influences. Promotion informs, reminds, and persuades buyers and others who influence the purchasing process. Hundreds of billions of dollars are spent annually on promotion activities. This mandates planning and executing promotion decisions as effectively and efficiently as possible.

Implementing and Managing Market-Driven Strategy

Selecting the customers to target and the positioning strategy for each target moves marketing strategy development to the action stage (Exhibit 2.5). This stage considers designing the marketing organization and implementing and managing the strategy.

Designing Effective Market-Driven Organizations. An effective organization design matches people and work responsibilities in a way that is best for accomplishing the firm's marketing strategy. Deciding how to assemble people into organizational units and assign responsibility to the various mix components that make up the marketing strategy are important influences on performance. Organizational structures and processes must be matched to the business and marketing strategies that are developed and implemented. Organizational design needs to be evaluated on a regular basis to assess its adequacy and to identify necessary changes. Restructuring and reengineering of many organizations in the 1990s led to many changes in the structures of marketing units. Organizational change continues to be an important initiative in the 21st century.

Strategy Implementation and Control. Marketing strategy implementation and control consist of: (1) preparing the marketing plan and budget; (2) implementing the plan; and (3) using the plan in managing and controlling the strategy on an ongoing basis. The marketing plan includes details concerning targeting, positioning, and marketing mix activities. The plan spells out what is going to happen over the planning period, who is responsible, how much it will cost, and the expected results (e.g., sales forecasts). We discuss the preparation of the marketing plan in the last section of the chapter.

The marketing plan includes action guidelines for the activities to be implemented, who does what, the dates and location of implementation, and how implementation will be accomplished. Several factors contribute to implementation effectiveness including the skills and commitment of the people involved, organizational design, incentives, and the effectiveness of communication within the organization and externally.

Marketing strategy is an ongoing process of making decisions, implementing them, and tracking their effectiveness over time. In terms of its time requirements, strategic evaluation is far more demanding than planning. Evaluation and control are concerned with tracking performance and, when necessary, altering plans to keep performance on track. Evaluation also includes looking for new opportunities and potential threats in the future. It is the connecting link in the strategic marketing planning process shown in Exhibit 2.5. By serving as both the last stage and the first stage (evaluation before taking action) in the planning process, strategic evaluation assures that strategy is an ongoing activity.

Rubbermaid Inc. offers an interesting insight into evaluation and control. After more than a decade of superior performance, the company began to experience problems in 1995.[30] Sales slowed down and profits declined. Increases in the costs of resin used in plastic products triggered price increases to retailers. This irritated retailers, who reduced Rubbermaid's shelf space. The already slow consumer demand for housewares was further impacted by higher retail prices. Rubbermaid's management implemented cost reductions, sped up new-product introductions, and increased promotions to consumers to move results closer to expectations.

Internet Strategy

The explosive growth of Internet initiatives has resulted in a variety of Web strategies which may impact the business and marketing strategies of existing firms, and lead to the formation of new business designs. We consider the reasons why the Internet is a major force for change, and discuss alternative Internet strategies for existing companies and new business ventures.

Major Force for Change

The Internet era provides a new way of developing relationships between end user customers, value-chain members, and alliance partners.[31] The Web offers a compelling opportunity to enhance one-on-one relationships. These impressive knowledge systems enable organizations to link pricing, product, design, and promotion information with suppliers and customers.

Various strategic initiatives are altering the basic processes underlying business transactions. The reverse auction is illustrative. The reverse designation is because prices are being bid downward rather than upward. Suppliers of business-to-business companies have the opportunity via the Internet to offer competing bids to the customer. At the end of the process the low bid obtains the sale. Other Web-based initiatives are impacting buying processes. The effects can be dramatic. Major corporate buyers like Boeing and Motorola have warned that suppliers not making the transition to Web-based commerce may find themselves locked out of their businesses. The Covisint online exchange, formed by General Motors, Daimler-Chrysler, and Ford and now including other auto manufacturers, already links tens of thousands of suppliers to these major customers, and is seen as a prototype for other "industry-led" online exchanges.

It is apparent that the Internet has a pervasive potential for change that is likely to impact a wide range of products and businesses. The challenge for existing businesses is how to capture the advantages of the Internet without damaging important existing relationships. Avon Products Corp.'s challenges in sustaining its direct sales model while pursuing an Internet strategy are illustrative. In 2000, after 115 years of selling to the consumer at home, Avon changed its strategy and took its products into department stores and shopping malls for the first time.

Strategy and the Internet

While some authorities argue that the Internet will make conventional strategies obsolete, a more compelling logic is that the Internet is a powerful complement to traditional business and marketing strategies.[32] Nonetheless, competitive boundaries are likely to be altered and competition will become more intense. Tesco, the leading British supermarket retailer, illustrates both points. Tesco has adopted a "bricks and clicks" strategy for its Tesco Direct online business, combining the strength of its chain of stores with Internet-based ordering. Groceries are selected on a Web page reflecting the customer's local store, and are picked manually from the shelves of that same store for delivery to a customer. No additional warehousing or picking facilities are required. Tesco is now leveraging its online customer base to sell a growing range of high-margin nonfood products, from fresh flowers to apparel, as well as financial services. They may even sell automobiles by this route.

While there are various strategy initiatives regarding the Internet, they correspond to one of the following:

- Formation of a separate business model as an independent venture or an initiative by an existing company.

  Amazon.com Inc. is an example of the former whereas Sabre's Travelocity.Com venture was initiated by an existing company.

- Creation of a separate value-chain channel direct from the producer to the end user.

  Dell Inc. uses this Internet strategy.

- Using the Internet as an information resource.

  This initiative is used by various organizations such as *BusinessWeek.*

- Using the Web for advertising and sales promotion activities.

  These activities may be provided for one or more sponsors by a Web-based enterprise that offers users information at no charge. Ad revenues support the enterprise.

An organization may pursue more than one of the above initiatives, and the strategies may be interrelated. Also, alliances may be formed between traditional companies and Internet ventures.

Independent Internet business models have experienced several failures. In more than a few cases, the failures have been due to management's optimistic estimation of patronage and the failure to consider basic business and marketing strategy guidelines. The analysis of Webvan's lack of success in the Internet groceries market is described in the Internet Feature. It is notable that the most successful Internet grocery business in the world is operated by Tesco in the United Kingdom. The Internet channel is seen as only one way to reach the consumer, alongside regular stores, not a separate business.

Internet strategy is further considered in Chapters 10 and 13. Internet Features are included in many chapters.

Internet Feature

Webvan Left the Basics on the Shelf

Despite some clear advantages—backing from such savvy financiers as Goldman Sachs and Sequoia Capital, a well-respected management team led until April by former Andersen Consulting Chief George Shaheen, and more than $1 billion cash—Webvan's business model was fundamentally untenable. It simply made little sense to pour huge amounts of capital into the grocery business—which ekes out net margins averaging barely over 1%—without evidence that enough shoppers would change their habits.

But Webvan built a huge infrastructure that could only work if droves of consumers quickly embraced buying their peaches and plenty more online. That never happened. What's more, Webvan depended too much on technology as the driver of its business while overlooking the basics of the grocery industry. "We made the assumption that capital was endless, and demand was endless," new CEO Robert Swan said in a June interview.

Bad assumptions both. In its short life, Webvan burned through more than $1 billion building automated warehouses and pricey tech gear. Never was the overspending clearer than when Webvan merged with rival HomeGrocer.com last year. Its go-for-broke approach stood in stark contrast to HomeGrocer's slower-moving, more conservative strategy.

Webvan shelled out more than $25 million for each of its massive facilities vs. HomeGrocer's $5 million or so for smaller, lower-tech operations. Webvan's warehouses needed some 1,000 servers and 16 employees, to run the back end, but HomeGrocer's got by with just 100 servers and two employees, insiders say. And while Webvan needed about 4,000 orders a day to break even per facility, HomeGrocer required just 1,500. . . .

So does Webvan's failure mean that online grocer's prospects are no better than that of a carton of milk past the sell-by date? Not necessarily. Some believe it can still be a solid business, though one that will likely mature more slowly than anything Webvan anticipated. A soon-to-be-released study from IBM's consulting arm predicts that by 2004, enough demand will exist in some metropolitan areas to support at least three profitable grocers in those markets. "There is demand, and there are profitable ways of servicing these markets," says IBM's Ming Tsai.

Source: Linda Himelstein, "Commentary," *BusinessWeek*, July 23, 2001, 43.

Preparing the Marketing Plan

Marketing plans vary widely in scope and detail. Nevertheless, all plans need to be based on analyses of the product-market and segments, industry and competitive structure, and the organization's value proposition. We look at several important planning issues that provide a checklist for plan preparation.

Planning Relationships and Frequency

Marketing plans are developed, implemented, evaluated, and adjusted to keep the strategy on target. Since the marketing strategy normally extends beyond one year, it is useful to develop a three-year strategic plan and an annual plan to manage marketing activities during the year. Budgets for marketing activities (e.g., advertising) are set annually. Planning is really a series of annual plans guided by the marketing strategic plan.

The frequency of planning activities varies by company and marketing activity. Market targeting and positioning strategies are not changed significantly during the year. Tactical changes in product, distribution, price, and promotion strategies may be included in the annual plan. For example, the aggressive response of competitors to Healthy Choice's successful market entry required changes in Con Agra's pricing and promotion tactics for the frozen food line.

Planning Considerations

Suppose that you need to develop a plan for a new product to be introduced into the national market next year. The plan for the introduction should include the expected results (objectives), market targets, actions, responsibilities, schedules, and dates. The plan indicates details and deadlines, product plans, a market introduction program, advertising and sales promotion actions, employee training, and other information necessary to launching the product. The plan needs to answer a series of questions—what, when, where, who, how, and why—for each action targeted for completion during the planning period.

Responsibility for Preparing Plans. A marketing executive or team is responsible for preparing the marketing plan. Some companies combine the business plan and the marketing plan into a single planning activity. Regardless of the format used, the marketing plan is developed in close coordination with the strategic plan for the business. There is also much greater emphasis today to involve all business functions in the marketing planning process. A product or marketing manager may draft the formal plan for his/her area of responsibility, coordinating and receiving inputs from advertising, marketing research, sales, and other marketing specialists. Coordination and involvement with other business functions (R&D, finance, operations) are also essential.

Planning Unit. The choice of the planning unit may vary due to the product-market portfolio of the organization. Some firms plan and manage by individual products or brands. Others work with product lines, markets, or specific customers. The planning unit may reflect how marketing activities and responsibilities are organized. The market target is a useful focus for planning regardless of how the plan is aggregated. Using the target as the basis for planning helps to place the customer in the center of the planning process and keeps the positioning strategy linked to the market target.

Preparing the Marketing Plan

The Conference Board offers several examples of plan formats in its excellent reports on marketing planning.[33] Format and content depend on the size of the organization, managerial responsibility for planning, product and market scope, and other situational factors. An outline for a typical marketing plan is shown in Exhibit 2.8. We take a brief look at the major parts of the planning outline to illustrate the nature and scope of the planning process. In this discussion the market target serves as the planning unit.

The Situation Summary. This part of the plan describes the market and its important characteristics, size estimates, and growth projections. Market segment analysis indicates the segments to be targeted and their relative importance. The competitor analysis indicates the key competitors (actual and potential), their strengths and weaknesses, probable future actions, and the organization's competitive advantage(s) in each segment of interest. The summary should be very brief. Supporting detailed information for the summary can be placed in an appendix or in a separate analysis.

Describe the Market Target. A description of each market target, size and growth rate, end users' characteristics, positioning strategy guidelines, and other available information useful in planning and implementation are essential parts of the plan. When two or more targets are involved, it is helpful to indicate priorities for guiding resource allocation.

Objectives for the Market Target(s). Here we spell out what the marketing strategy is expected to accomplish during the planning period. Objectives are needed for each market target, indicating financial performance, sales, market position, customer satisfaction, and other desired results. Objectives are also usually included for each marketing program component.

Marketing Program Positioning Strategy. The positioning statement indicates how management wants the targeted customers and prospects to perceive the brand. Specific strategies and tactics for product, distribution, price, and promotion are explained in this part of the plan. Actions to be taken, responsibilities, time schedules, and other implementation information are included at this point in the plan.

Planning and implementation responsibilities often involve more than one person or department. One approach is to assign a planning team the responsibility for each market target and marketing mix component. Product and geographical responsibilities are sometimes allocated to individuals or teams. The responsibilities and coordination requirements need to be indicated for marketing units and other business functions. Importantly, the planning process should

EXHIBIT 2.8
Outline for Preparing an Annual Marketing Plan

Strategic Situation Summary

A summary of the strategic situation for the planning unit (business unit, market segment, product line, etc.).

Market Target(s) Description

Define and describe each market target, including customer profiles, customer preferences and buying habits, size and growth estimates, distribution channels, analysis of key competitors, and guidelines for positioning strategy.

Objectives for the Market Target(S)

Set objectives for the market target (such as market position, sales, and profits). Also state objectives for each component of the marketing program. Indicate how each objective will be measured.

Marketing Program Positioning Strategy

State how management wants the firm to be positioned relative to the competition in the eyes and mind of the buyer.

A. *Product Strategy*
   Set strategy for new products, product improvements, and product deletions.
B. *Distribution Strategy*
   Indicate the strategy to be used for each distribution channel, including role of middlemen, assistance and support provided, and specific activities planned.
C. *Price Strategy*
   Specify the role of price in the marketing strategy and the planned actions regarding price.
D. *Promotion Strategy*
   Indicate the planned strategy and actions for advertising, publicity, Internet, personal selling, and sales promotion.
E. *Marketing Research*
   Identify information needs and planned projects, objectives, estimated costs, and timetable.
F. *Coordination with Other Business Functions*
   Specify the responsibilities and activities of other departments that have an important influence on the planned marketing strategy.

Forecasts and Budgets

Forecast sales and profit for the marketing plan and prepare the budget for accomplishing the forecast.

encourage participation from all of the areas responsible for implementing the plan. Contingency plans may be included in the plan. The contingencies consider possible actions if the anticipated planning environment is different from what actually occurs.

Forecasting and Budgeting. Financial planning includes forecasting revenues and profits and estimating the costs necessary to carry out the marketing plan (see the Appendix to Chapter 2 for financial analysis details). The people responsible for market target, product, geographical area, or other units should prepare the forecasts and budgets. Comparative data on sales, profits, and expenses for prior years is useful to link the plan to previous results.

International Planning Process. Planning for global operations is more complex than domestic planning. The major phases of planning for a multinational firm operating in several countries are shown in Exhibit 2.9. The first step in the planning process is the market opportunity analysis. This may represent a major activity for a company that is entering a foreign market for the first time. Several applications are discussed in subsequent chapters. Because of the risks and uncertainties in international markets, the market assessment is very important for both new market entrants and experienced firms.

EXHIBIT 2.9
International Planning Process

Source: Philip R. Catteora and John L. Graham, *International Marketing*, 12th ed. (Burr Ridge, IL: McGraw-Hill/Irwin, 2005), 322. Copyright © The McGraw-Hill Companies. Used with permission.

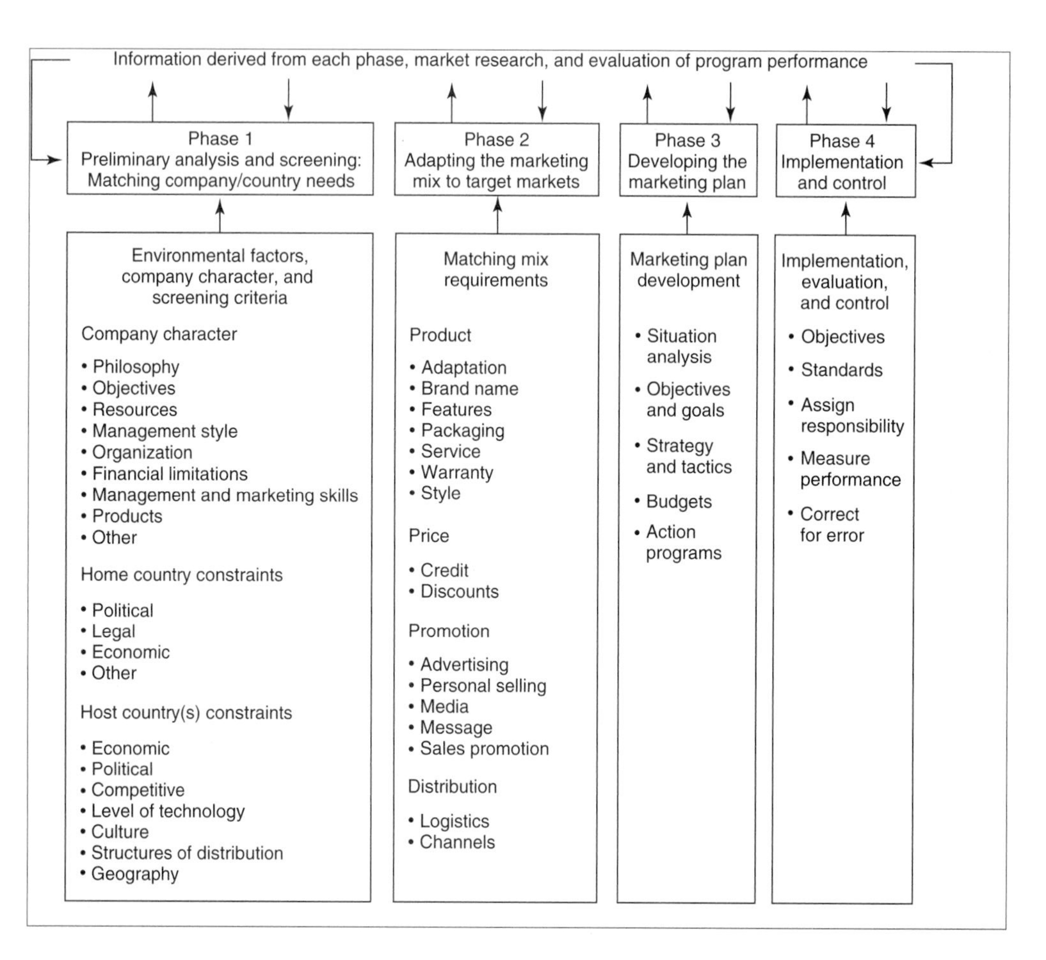

Phase 1 determines which targets to pursue and establishes relative priorities for resource allocation. Phase 2 fits the positioning strategy to each target market. The objective is to match the mix requirements to the needs identified and the positioning concept management selects. Phase 3 consists of the preparation of the marketing plan. Included are the situation assessment, objectives, strategy and tactics, budgets and forecasts, and action programs. Finally, in Phase 4, the plan is implemented and managed. Results are evaluated and strategies adjusted when necessary to improve results. Although the international market planning process is similar to planning domestic marketing strategies, the environment is far more complex and uncertain in international markets.

Summary

Strategy formulation for the corporation includes: (1) defining the corporate mission and setting objectives, (2) determining strategic business units, and (3) establishing strategy guidelines for long-term strategic planning of the corporation and its business units. Top management must select the corporate strategy to move the firm toward its objectives. After implementing the strategy, management considers how the strategy is progressing and what adjustments are needed. Successfully executing these steps requires penetrating and insightful analyses.

The corporate vision or mission statement spells out the nature and scope of the business and provides strategic direction for the corporation. The firm's objectives indicate the performance desired by management. If management decides to move away from the core business, several paths of corporate development are possible, including expansion into new products and/or markets as well as diversification.

The available evidence indicates that well-formulated and executed business strategies lead to superior performance. While there are several approaches to strategy development, they share common features including the objective of superior customer value, achieving a market orientation, and competing with distinctive capabilities.

Business unit strategies are guided by corporate strategy guidelines. The process begins by considering each business unit's market opportunity, position against competition, financial situation and projections, and strengths and weaknesses. The situation analysis spells out the strategy alternatives for the business unit. Management selects a strategy and develops a strategic plan, which is then implemented and managed.

Marketing strategy is an analysis, planning, implementation, and control process designed to satisfy customer needs and wants by providing superior customer value. The first part of the process includes product-market analysis, market segmentation, competition analysis, and continuous learning about markets. These analyses guide the choice of marketing strategy. Market definition establishes the overall competitive arena. Market segmentation describes possible customer groups for targeting by businesses. Competitor analysis looks at the strengths, weaknesses, and strategies of key competitors. Continuous learning about markets supplies information for analysis and decision making.

Designing the marketing strategy is the second stage in strategy development. The selection of the people (or organizations) to be targeted is guided by the situation analysis. The market target decision indicates the buyer groups whose needs are to be satisfied by the marketing program positioning strategy. The positioning strategy indicates how the firm will position itself against its key competitors in meeting the needs of the buyers in the market target. The relationship strategy spells out the extent of collaboration with consumers, other organizations, and company personnel. New-product strategies are essential to generate a continuing stream of new entries to replace mature products that are eliminated.

The third phase of the strategy process consists of market-driven program development. Specific marketing mix strategies for products, distribution, price, and promotion must be developed to implement the positioning strategy management has selected. The objective is to combine the marketing mix components to accomplish market target objectives in a cost-effective manner.

The last phase of the process consists of marketing strategy implementation and management. These activities focus on the marketing organizational design and marketing strategy implementation and control. This is the action phase of marketing strategy.

The marketing plan spells out the actions to be taken, who is responsible, deadlines to be met, and the sales forecast and budget. The plan describes the marketing decisions and guides the implementation of the decisions, and the evaluation and management of the marketing strategy.

Internet Applications

A. Examine the Web sites of Borders (*www.borders.com*) and Amazon (*www.amazon.com*). Compare and contrast the two approaches to using a Web site as part of each company's competitive strategy.

B. Examine the Web sites of both ebay.com (*www.ebay.com*) and uBid.com (*www.uBid.com*). Compare and contrast the two approaches to using a Web site as part of each company's competitive strategy. Analyze the differences and similarities and suggest improvements as well as a marketing strategy for the two companies (i.e., solely Internet-based).

Feature Applications

A. Review the material in the Global Feature—The A380: A Pan-European Plane. How can the risks being taken by Airbus with this venture be justified? What are the major concerns that should be monitored as the project proceeds?

B. Consider the points in the Strategy Feature—BMW: Positioning Premium Automobiles. How would you describe BMW's market targeting and positioning strategy? How does it compare to other premium car producers?

Questions for Review and Discussion

1. Top management of companies probably devoted more time to reviewing (and sometimes changing) their corporate vision (mission) in the last decade than in any other period. Discuss the major reasons for this increased concern with the vision for the corporation.
2. Discuss the role of organizational capabilities in corporate strategy.
3. What is the relationship between the corporate strategy and the strategies for the businesses that comprise the corporate portfolio?
4. Discuss the major issues that top management should consider when deciding whether or not to expand business operations into new business areas.
5. Discuss the environmental factors that should be assessed on a regular basis by a large retail corporation like Target Corp.
6. Discuss what you consider to be the major issues in trying to divide a corporation into strategic business units, indicating for each problem suggestions for overcoming it.

7. Develop an outline of how you would explain the marketing strategy process to an inventor who is forming a new business to develop, produce, and market a new product.
8. Discuss the role of market targeting and positioning in an organization's marketing strategy.
9. What is the relationship between the strategic plan for a business in the corporate portfolio and the marketing plan for the business?
10. You have been asked to develop a marketing plan for a metro-bank that has six branch offices. How would you approach this assignment?

Notes

1. Gary Hamel and Liisa Välikangas, "The Quest for Resilience," *Harvard Business Review*, September 2003, 52–63.
2. Anthony Marsella, Gerry Bell, Ian Ruddleston, and Merlin Stone, "Meeting Demand," *Marketing Business*, January 2004, 22–24.
3. Michael E. Porter, "What Is Strategy?" *Harvard Business Review*, November–December 1996, 74.
4. Raymond Miles and Charles Snow, "Fit, Failure, and the Hall of Fame," *California Management Review*, Spring 1984, 10–28; and James Brian Quinn, *Intelligent Enterprise* (New York: Free Press, 1992), Chapter 5.
5. Preston Townley, Comments made by the Conference Board CEO during an address at Texas Christian University in Fort Worth, Texas, February 15, 1994.
6. George S. Day, "Aligning the Organization to the Market," in *Reflections on the Future of Marketing*, Donald R. Lehmann and Katherine E. Joez (eds.) (Cambridge, MA: Marketing Science Institute, 1997), 67–93.
7. "The Virtual Corporation," *BusinessWeek*, February 8, 1993, 98–102.
8. David J. Collis and Cynthia A. Montgomery, *Corporate Strategy* (Chicago: Irwin, 1997), 5.
9. Ibid., 7 and 8.
10. Ibid., 7–12.
11. Based in part on George S. Day, *Strategic Market Planning* (St. Paul, MN: West Publishing, 1984), 18–22.
12. Peter F. Drucker, *Management* (New York: Harper & Row, 1974), 100.
13. Robert S. Kaplan and David P. Norton, *The Balanced Scorecard* (Boston: Harvard Business School Press, 1996).
14. C. K. Prahalad and Gary Hamel, "The Core Competence of the Corporation," *Harvard Business Review*, May–June 1990, 79–91; George S. Day, "The Capabilities of Market-Driven Organizations," *Journal of Marketing*, October 1994, 37–52.
15. Melanie Wells, "Red Baron," *Forbes*, July 3, 2000, 151–160; Kerry Capell and Wendy Zellner, "Richard Branson's Next Big Adventure," *BusinessWeek*, March 8, 2004, 16–17.
16. This discussion is based on Boris Yavitz and William H. Newman, "What the Corporation Should Provide Its Business Units," *Journal of Business Strategy* 3, no. 1 (Summer 1982), 14.
17. Collis and Montgomery, *Corporate Strategy*, 10–11.
18. Ibid., 11.
19. Adrian J. Slywotzky, *Value Migration* (Boston: Harvard Business School Press, 1996), 4.
20. Collis and Montgomery, *Corporate Strategy*, 11–12.
21. Shelby D. Hunt and Robert M. Morgan, "The Comparative Advantage Theory of Competition," *Journal of Marketing*, April 1995, 1–15.
22. Drucker, *Management*, 63.
23. Frederick E. Webster, "The Changing Role of Marketing in the Organization," *Journal of Marketing*, October 1992, 11.
24. George S. Day, *Strategic Market Planning* (St. Paul: West Publishing, 1984), 3.
25. Ben Elgin, "Google," *BusinessWeek*, May 3, 2004, 50–56.
26. George S. Day, "Continuous Learning about Markets," *California Management Review*, Summer 1994, 9–31.
27. This example is based on D. John Loden, *Megabrands* (Homewood, IL: Business One Irwin, 1992, 184–85.
28. Michael Arndt, "3M's Rising Star," *BusinessWeek*, April 12, 2004, 63–70.
29. Webster, "The Changing Role of Marketing," 13.
30. Paulette Thomas, "Rubbermaid Stock Plunges over 12% on Projected Weak 2nd Quarter Profit," *The Wall Street Journal*, June 12, 1995, B6.
31. The following discussion is based on material developed by Dr. John R. Nevin, Granger Wisconsin Distinguished Professor, University of Wisconsin.
32. Michael E. Porter, "Strategy and the Internet," *Harvard Business Review*, March 2001, 63–78.
33. David S. Hopkins, *The Marketing Plan* (New York: The Conference Board Inc., 1981). See also Howard Sutton, *The Marketing Plan in the 1990s* (New York: The Conference Board Inc., 1990).

Appendix 2A

Financial Analysis for Marketing Planning and Control

Several kinds of financial analyses are needed for marketing analysis, planning, and control activities. Such analyses represent an important part of case preparation activities. In some instances it will be necessary to review and interpret the financial information provided in the cases. In other instances, analyses may be prepared to support specific recommendations. The methods covered in this appendix represent a group of tools and techniques for use in marketing financial analysis. Throughout the discussion, it is assumed that accounting and finance fundamentals are understood.

Unit of Financial Analysis

Various units of analysis that can be used in marketing financial analysis are shown in Exhibit 2A.1. Two factors often influence the choice of a unit of analysis: (1) the purpose of the analysis and (2) the costs and availability of the information needed to perform the analysis.

Financial Situation Analysis

Financial measures can be used to help assess the present situation. One of the most common and best ways to quantify the financial situation of a firm is through ratio analysis. These ratios should be analyzed over a period of at least three years to discern trends.

Key Financial Ratios

Financial information will be more useful to management if it is prepared so that comparisons can be made. James Van Horne comments upon this need.

> To evaluate a firm's financial condition and performance, the financial analyst needs certain yardsticks. The yardstick frequently used is a ratio or index, relating two pieces of financial data to each other. Analysis and interpretation of various ratios should give an experienced and skilled analyst a better understanding of the financial condition and performance of the firm than he would obtain from analysis of the financial data alone.[1]

As we examine the financial analysis model in the next section, note how the ratio or index provides a useful frame of reference. Typically, ratios are used to compare historical and/or future trends within the firm or to compare a firm or business unit with an industry or other firms.

Several financial ratios often used to measure business performance are shown in Exhibit 2A.2. Note that these ratios are primarily useful as a means of comparing:

1. Ratio values for several time periods for a particular business.
2. A firm to its key competitors.
3. A firm to an industry or business standard.

There are several sources of ratio data.[2] These include data services such as Dun & Bradstreet, Robert Morris Associates' *Annual Statement Studies*, industry and trade associations, government agencies, and investment advisory services.

Other ways to gauge the productivity of marketing activities include sales per square feet of retail floor space, occupancy rates of hotels and office buildings, and sales per salesperson.

[1]James C. Van Horne, *Fundamentals of Financial Management*, 4th ed. (Englewood Cliffs, NJ: Prentice-Hall, 1980), 103–4.

[2]A useful guide to ratio analysis is provided in Richard Sanzo, *Ratio Analysis for Small Business* (Washington, DC: Small Business Administration, 1977).

EXHIBIT 2A.1 Alternative Units for Financial Analysis

Market	Product/Service	Organization
Market	Industry	Company
Market niche(s)	Product mix	Segment/division/unit
Geographic area(s)	product line	Marketing department
Customer groups	Specific product	Sales unit:
Individual customers	Brand	Region
	Model	District branch
		Office/store

EXHIBIT 2A.2 Summary of Key Financial Ratios

Source: Adapted from Arthur A. Thompson, Jr., and A. J. Strickland III, *Strategy and Policy*, 4th ed. (Homewood, IL: Richard D. Irwin, 1987), 270–1.

Ratio	How Calculated	What It Shows
Profitability ratios:		
1. Gross profit margin	$\frac{\text{Sales} - \text{Cost of goods sold}}{\text{Sales}}$	An indication of the total margin available to cover operating expenses and yield a profit.
2. Operating profit margin	$\frac{\text{Profits before taxes and before interest}}{\text{Sales}}$	An indication of the firm's profitability from current operations without regard to the interest charges accruing from the capital structure.
3. Net profit margin (or return on sales)	$\frac{\text{Profits after taxes}}{\text{Sales}}$	Shows after-tax profits per dollar of sales. Subpar profit margins indicate that the firm's sales prices are relatively low, its costs are relatively high, or both.
4. Return on total assets	$\frac{\text{Profits after taxes}}{\text{Total assets}}$ or $\frac{\text{Profits after taxes} + \text{Interest}}{\text{Total assets}}$	A measure of the return on total investment in the enterprise. It is sometimes desirable to add interest to after-tax profits to form the numerator of the ratio, since total assets are financed by creditors as well as by stockholders; hence, it is accurate to measure the productivity of assets by the returns provided to both classes of investors.
5. Return on stockholders' equity (or return on net worth)	$\frac{\text{Profits after taxes}}{\text{Total stockholders' equity}}$	A measure of the rate on stockholders' investment in the enterprise.
6. Return on common equity	$\frac{\text{Profits after taxes} - \text{Preferred stock dividends}}{\text{Total stockholders' equity} - \text{Par value of preferred stock}}$	A measure of the rate of return on the investment which the owners of common stock have made in the enterprise.
7. Earnings per share	$\frac{\text{Profits after taxes} - \text{Preferred stock dividends}}{\text{Number of shares of common stock outstanding}}$	Shows the earnings available to the owners of common stock.
Liquidity ratios:		
1. Current ratio	$\frac{\text{Current assets}}{\text{Current liabilities}}$	Indicates the extent to which the claims of short-term creditors are covered by assets that are expected to be converted to cash in a period roughly corresponding to the maturity of the liabilities.
2. Quick ratio (or acid-test ratio)	$\frac{\text{Current assets} - \text{Inventory}}{\text{Current liabilities}}$	A measure of the firm's ability to pay off short-term obligations without relying on the sale of its inventories.

Ratio	Calculation	What it measures
3. Cash ratio	$\frac{\text{Cash \& Marketable securities}}{\text{Current liabilities}}$	An indicator of how long the company can go without further inflow of funds.
4. Inventory to net working capital	$\frac{\text{Inventory}}{\text{Current assets} - \text{Current liabilities}}$	A measure of the extent to which the firm's working capital is tied up in inventory.
Leverage ratios:		
1. Debt to assets ratio	$\frac{\text{Total debt}}{\text{Total assets}}$	Measures the extent to which borrowed funds have been used to finance the firm's operations.
2. Debt to equity ratio	$\frac{\text{Total debt}}{\text{Total stockholders' equity}}$	Provides another measure of the funds provided the creditors versus the funds provided by owners.
3. Long-term debt to equity ratio	$\frac{\text{Long-term debt}}{\text{Total stockholders' equity}}$	A widely used measure of the balance between debt and equity in the firm's overall capital structure.
4. Times-interest-earned (or coverage ratios)	$\frac{\text{Profits before interest and taxes}}{\text{Total interest charges}}$	Measures the extent to which earnings can decline without the firm's becoming unable to meet its annual interest costs.
5. Fixed-charge coverage	$\frac{\text{Profits before taxes and interest} + \text{Lease obligations}}{\text{Total interest charges} + \text{Lease obligations}}$	A more inclusive indication of the firm's ability to meet all of its fixed-charge obligations.
Activity ratios:		
1. Inventory turnover	$\frac{\text{Cost of goods sold}}{\text{Inventory}}$	When compared to industry averages, it provides an indication of whether a company has excessive inventory or perhaps inadequate inventory.
2. Fixed-assets turnover*	$\frac{\text{Sales}}{\text{Fixed assets}}$	A measure of the sales productivity and utilization of plant and equipment.
3. Total-assets turnover	$\frac{\text{Sales}}{\text{Total assets}}$	A measure of the utilization of all the firm's assets; a ratio below the industry average indicates the company is not generating a sufficient volume of business given the size of its asset investment.
4. Accounts receivable turnover	$\frac{\text{Annual credit sales}}{\text{Accounts receivable}}$	A measure of the average length of time it takes the firm to collect on the sales made on credit.
5. Average collection period	$\frac{\text{Accounts receivable}}{\text{Total sales} \div 365}$ or $\frac{\text{Accounts receivable}}{\text{Average daily sales}}$	Indicates the average length of time the firm must wait after making a sale before it receives payment.

*The manager should also keep in mind the fixed charges associated with noncapitalized lease obligations.

Contribution Analysis

When the performance of products, market segments, and other marketing units is being analyzed, management should examine the unit's profit contribution. Contribution margin is equal to sales (revenue) less variable costs. Thus, contribution margin represents the amount of money available to cover fixed costs, and contribution margin less fixed costs is net income. An illustration of contribution margin analysis is given in Exhibit 2A.3. In this example, product X is generating a positive contribution margin. If product X were eliminated, $50,000 of product net income would be lost, and the remaining products would have to cover fixed costs not directly traceable to them. If the product is retained, the $50,000 can be used to contribute to other fixed costs and/or net income.

Financial Analysis Model

The model shown in Exhibit 2A.4 provides a useful guide for examining financial performance and identifying possible problem areas. The model combines several important financial ratios into one equation. Let's examine the model, moving from left to right. Profit margin multiplied by asset turnover yields return on assets. Moreover, assuming that the performance target is return on net worth (or return on equity), the product of return on assets and financial leverage determines performance. Increasing either ratio will increase net worth. The values of these ratios will vary considerably from one industry to another. For example, in grocery wholesaling, profit margins are typically very low, whereas asset turnover is very high. Through efficient management and high turnover, a wholesaler can stack up impressive returns on net worth. Furthermore, space productivity measures are obtained for individual departments in retail stores that offer more than one line, such as department stores. The measures selected depend on the particular characteristics of the business.

Evaluating Alternatives

As we move through the discussion of financial analysis, it is important to recognize the type of costs being used in the analysis. Using accounting terminology, costs can be designated as fixed or variable. A cost is *fixed* if it remains constant over the observation period, even though the volume of activity varies. In contrast, a *variable* cost is an expense that varies with sales over the observation period. Costs are designated as mixed or semivariable in instances when they contain both fixed and variable components.

Break-Even Analysis

This technique is used to examine the relationship between sales and costs. An illustration is given in Exhibit 2A.5. Using sales and costs information, it is easy to determine from a break-even analysis how many units of a product must be sold in order to break even, or cover total costs. In this example 65,000 units at sales

EXHIBIT 2A.3 Illustrative Contribution Margin Analysis for Product X ($000)

	Sales	$300
Less:	Variable manufacturing costs	100
	Other variable costs traceable to product X	50
Equals:	Contribution margin	150
Less:	Fixed costs directly traceable to product X	100
Equals:	Product net income	$50

EXHIBIT 2A.4 Financial Analysis Model

Profit margin		Asset turnover		Return on assets		Financial leverage		Return on net worth
↓		↓		↓		↓		↓
Net Profits (after taxes) / Net sales	×	Net sales / Total assets	→	Net Profits (after taxes) / Total assets	×	Total assets / Net worth	=	Net Profits (after taxes) / Net worth

EXHIBIT 2A.5 Illustrative Break-Even Analysis

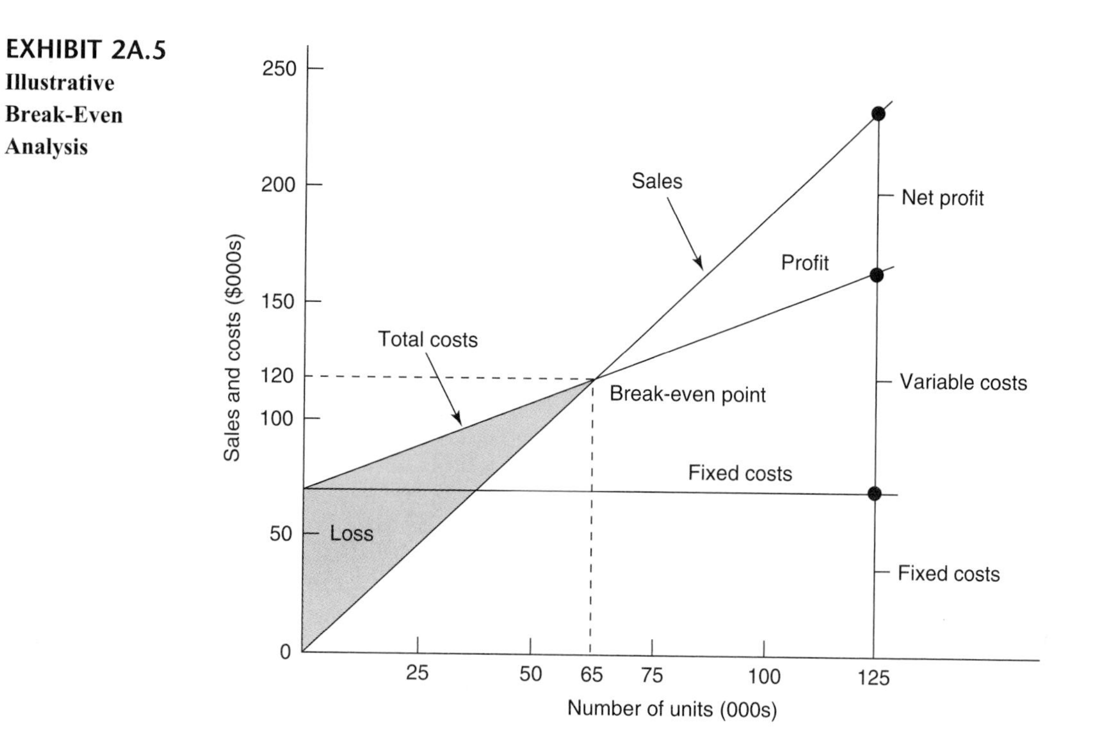

of $120,000 are equal to total costs of $120,000. Any additional units sold will produce a profit. The break-even point can be calculated in this manner:

$$\text{Break-even units} = \frac{\text{Fixed costs}}{\text{Price per unit} - \text{Variable cost per unit}}$$

Price in the illustration shown in Exhibit 2A.5 is $1.846 per unit, and variable cost is $0.769 per unit. With fixed costs of $70,000, this results in the break-even calculation:

$$\text{BE units} = \frac{\$70{,}000}{\$1.846 - \$0.769} = 65{,}000 \text{ units}$$

To determine how many units must be sold to achieve a target profit (expressed in before-tax dollars), the formula is amended as follows:

$$\text{Target profit units} = \frac{\text{Fixed costs} + \text{Target profit (before tax)}}{\text{Price per unit} - \text{Variable cost per unit}}$$

Using the same illustration as above and including a target before-tax profit of $37,700, the target profit calculation becomes:

$$\text{Target profit units} = \frac{\$70{,}000 + \$37{,}700}{\$1.846 - \$0.769} = 100{,}000 \text{ units}$$

EXHIBIT 2A.6 Cash Flow Comparison ($000s)

	Project X	Project Y
Start-Up Costs	<1,000>	<1,000>
Year 1	500	300
Year 2	500	400
Year 3	300	600

Break-even analysis is not a forecast. It indicates how many units of a product at a given price and cost must be sold in order to break even or achieve a target profit. Some important assumptions that underlie the above break-even analysis include the use of constant fixed and variable costs, a constant price, and a single product.

In addition to break-even analysis, several other financial tools are used to evaluate alternatives. Net present value of cash flow analysis and return on investment are among the most useful. For example, assume there are two projects with the cash flows shown in Exhibit 2A.6.

Though return on investment is widely used, it is limited by its inability to consider the time value of money. This is shown in Exhibit 2A.7. Return on investment for *both* projects X and Y is 10 percent. However, a dollar today is worth more than a dollar given in three years. Therefore, in assessing cash flows of a project or investment, future cash flows must be discounted back

EXHIBIT 2A.7 Present Value of Cash Flows

	Time	Cash Flow	PV Factor	NPV of Cash Flow
Project X				
	0	<1,000>	$1/(1+.12)^0 = 1$	<1,000>
	1	500	$1/(1+.12)^1 = 0.8929$	= 446.45
	2	500	$1/(1+.12)^2 = 0.7972$	= 398.60
	3	300	$1/(1+.12)^3 = 0.7118$	= 213.54
			Present value	+ 58.59
Project Y				
	0	<1,000>	$1/(1+.12)^0 = 1$	<1,000>
	1	300	$1/(1+.12)^1 = 0.8929$	= 267.87
	2	400	$1/(1+.12)^2 = 0.7972$	= 318.88
	3	600	$1/(1+.12)^3 = 0.7118$	= 427.08
			Net present value	+ 13.83

to the present at a rate comparable to the risk of the project.

Discounting cash flows is a simple process. Assume that the firm is considering projects X and Y and that its cost of capital is 12 percent. Additionally, assume that both projects carry risk comparable to the normal business risk. Under these circumstances, the analyst should discount the cash flows back to the present at the cost of capital, 12 percent. Present value factors can be looked up or computed using the formula $1/(1+i)^n$, where i equals our discounting rate per time period and n equals the number of compounding periods. In this example, the present value of cash flows would be as shown in Exhibit 2A.7.

Because both projects have a positive net present value, both are good. However, if they are mutually exclusive, the project with the highest net present value should be selected.

Financial Planning

Financial planning involves two major activities: (1) forecasting revenues and (2) budgeting (estimating future expenses). The actual financial analyses and forecasts included in the strategic marketing plan vary considerably from firm to firm. In addition, internal financial reporting and budgeting procedures vary widely among companies. Therefore, consider this approach as one example rather than the norm.

The choice of the financial information to be used for marketing planning and control will depend on its relationship with the corporate or business unit strategic plan. Another important consideration is the selection of performance measures to be used in gauging marketing performance. The objective is to indicate the range of possibilities and suggest some of the more frequently used financial analysis.

Pro forma income statements can be very useful when one is projecting performance and budgeting. Usually, this is done on a spreadsheet so that assumptions can be altered rapidly. Usually, only a few assumptions need be made. For example, sales growth rates can be projected from past trends and adjusted for new information. From this starting point, cost of goods can be determined as a percentage of sales. Operating expenses can also be determined as a percentage of sales based on past relationships, and the effective tax rate as a percentage of earnings before taxes. However, past relationships may not hold in the future. It may be necessary to analyze possible divergence from past relationships.

In addition, pro forma income statements can be used to generate pro forma cash flow statements. It is then possible to compare alternative courses of action by employing a uniformly comparable standard cash flow.

Supplemental Financial Analyses

The preceding sections of this appendix detailed the various forms of traditional financial analysis useful in marketing decision making. There are supplemental forms of analysis that can also be helpful in different types of marketing decisions. These supplemental techniques draw mainly from the management accounting discipline and rely on data that are available only to internal decision makers. Many of the financial analyses in the earlier sections employed data from published financial statements.

Only recently have marketing decision makers been able to look to management accounting to provide an additional set of quantitative tools to aid in the decision process.[3] These tools may be referred to collectively as strategic management accounting practices. Simmonds is generally credited with originating the term *strategic management accounting*, which he defines as "the provision and analysis of management accounting data about a business and its competitors for use in developing and monitoring the business strategy."[4] Although academic researchers may disagree about the specific techniques which constitute strategic management accounting, there are a wide selection of management accounting practices available for use in marketing decision making. These practices are described in Exhibit 2A.8 and include activity-based costing, attribute costing, benchmarking, brand valuation budgeting and monitoring, competitor cost assessment, competitive position monitoring, competitor performance appraisal, integrated performance measurement, life cycle costing, quality costing, strategic costing, strategic pricing, target costing, and value-chain costing.[5]

Exhibit 2A.8 also provides a description of the various marketing applications of strategic management accounting practices in terms of specific decision-making situations. Most of these practices require the marketing decision maker to gather information additional to that normally used for the preparation of external financial statements. In most cases, this information is already available in the accounting information system of the firm. However, it may be necessary to compile data from outside the firm in a more formalized manner to perform analysis using some of these strategic management accounting practices.

[3]George Foster and Mahendra Gupta, "Marketing, Cost Management and Management Accounting," *Journal of Management Accounting Research* 6 (1994), 43–77.

[4]K. Simmonds, "Strategic Management Accounting," *Management Accounting* (UK) 59, no. 4 (1981), 26–29.

[5]For a comprehensive description of strategic management accounting techniques and differences in attitudes toward the use of these techniques between accounting and marketing managers, see Karen S. Cravens and Chris Guilding, "An Empirical Study of the Application of Strategic Management Accounting Techniques," *Advances in Management Accounting* 10 (2001), 95–124.

EXHIBIT 2A.8 Supplemental Financial Analyses Using Management Accounting Practices

Strategic Management Accounting Practice	Description of the Practice	Description of Marketing Application
Activity-based costing	Indirect costs are assigned to a product or service in relation to the activities used to produce the product or provide the service. Decision making focuses on the collection of activities necessary to produce the product or service rather than the costs in a specific category.	This technique is particularly useful in determining the costs of customization or the provision of additional services to customers. Since the activities are the central focus for costing, decision makers can evaluate customers and markets in terms of the activities required to serve their needs.
Attribute costing	Products or services are costed in terms of attributes that appeal to customers. Thus, the cost object is not the entire product but a collection of features that respond to customer needs.	The nature of the cost object can be modified to support different strategic decision-making situations. As customers modify their preferences, decision makers can consider how particular product attributes satisfy their needs relative to marketing positioning strategies.
Benchmarking	Benchmarking is improving existing processes by looking to an ideal standard. The standard may be established from an external source such as a competitor, a partner, or an unrelated industry or company or by another area of the same firm.	Benchmarking provides an opportunity to assess processes for improvement and strategic advantage in terms of operational effectiveness. Critical lapses in customer service or customer contact situations can be remedied.
Brand valuation—budgeting and monitoring	Brand valuation assesses the current and future potential of a brand in quantitative terms. A "capitalized" value for internally developed brands can be created even though in the United States this value may not be included on a balance sheet.	Current spending on brand promotion activities can be evaluated in terms of future benefits. This can assist with budgeting decisions relative to a portfolio of brands or products and in monitoring the mix and potential of existing products.
Competitive position monitoring	This type of analysis is used in evaluating the market strategy of a competitor. Overall competitor positions in the market and industry are assessed, including sales and trend information, along with market share and cost estimates.	Since this technique requires an external focus, it allows decision makers to assess the position of a product in terms of existing and future strategy relative to competitors. Situations allowing a firm to improve competitive position can be identified and acted upon.
Competitor performance appraisal	This form of analysis is a detailed part of competitive position monitoring and focuses on preparing a quantitative analysis of the competitor's external financial statements.	Decision makers can identify the key areas of a competitor's market advantage and relate areas of advantage to strategic decisions.

Integrated performance measurement	This form of analysis uses performance appraisal based on measures that are developed in terms of a customer focus. Integrated measures may be linked to customer satisfaction and may include nonfinancial measures monitored at the individual and departmental levels.	Measures focusing on the customer can be linked to overall strategic objectives throughout the organization. Decision makers can get a clear picture of how their decisions (and performance) affect overall corporate performance.
Life cycle costing	A product or service is costed based on stages in the life of a product rather than financial reporting periods.	Decision makers can adopt a longer-term perspective to evaluate the performance of a product without the constraints of annual reporting periods.
Quality costing	Accounting measures support determining the cost of quality and the cost of a quality failure.	Decision makers can evaluate the impact on customers and market position when choices are made regarding quality issues.
Strategic costing	Strategic costing involves recognizing that the ultimate objective of expenditures related to a product or service may be more long-term in perspective. Thus, cost minimization is not the prime objective. Choices involving costs are evaluated in terms of long-term issues and the future potential of strategies.	Long-term strategy and strategic objectives considering product positioning and market penetration can be evaluated more completely. The long-term implications of a decision receive precedence over the short-term effect.
Strategic pricing	Strategic pricing adopts a more long-term and demand-focused approach to pricing rather than considering a cost-based and historical foundation.	Pricing decisions can be evaluated more in terms of competitive and market choices.
Target costing	A market-based approach is used to determine the target cost for a future product. The target cost is the remainder after a desired profit margin is subtracted from the estimated market price of a new product.	Since the product is designed to meet the target cost, decision makers know that the product will be able to enter the market at a price that allows an adequate level of profits. External rather than internal factors determine the price.
Value-chain costing	The cost of a product is evaluated over the entire value chain of production from research and development to customer service. This value chain may include multiple functional areas within the organization and cover different financial accounting reporting periods.	Operational efficiencies and competitive positioning can be evaluated at all stages of the value chain, not merely from the costs incurred during production. Links to suppliers, customers, and competitors can be considered at all points of the value chain.

Cases for Part 1

Case 1-1

Nokia Corp.

It's fast becoming the Helsinki conundrum. When cell-phone king Nokia is thrashing Ericsson and Motorola, and those two announce dreadful earnings, what's to stop jittery tech investors from punishing the whole sector, including Nokia? In markets like today's, where fear rules supreme, absolutely nothing. So Nokia Chairman Jorma Ollila is taking preemptive steps. A day or two before his rivals release their numbers, Ollila often puts out some good news of his own. It's nod and a wink to investors.

And sometimes it backfires. On Jan. 9, Nokia Corp. proudly previewed 2000 numbers. They showed Nokia extending its lead in handsets, rising to one-third of the 405 million unit global market—and double its closest competitor, Motorola Inc. In total, the Finns sold 128 million handsets, up an impressive 64% from 1999.

Yet as soon as the Nokia release hit the wires, all hell broke loose. Investors brushed past Nokia's competitive gains and zeroed in on the size of the market: 405 million seemed puny, some 20 million smaller than earlier analysts' projections! Suddenly fearful that the world's love affair with cell phones could be topping out, investors ditched Nokia stock, dropping the share price 9% and axing $17 billion from its market value. The current worry is that Nokia could announce disappointing results when it unveils its fourth quarter, on Jan. 30. "In this environment, any negative surprise will take the stock down," says Edward F. Snyder, analyst at J.P. Morgan H&Q in San Francisco. And a long-term bear market in telecom could dry up the pool of desperately needed capital for next-generation wireless systems.

Killer Brand

Setting aside jumpy markets, the story in cell phones is one of growing dominance. The Finnish giant, neck-and-neck with its top two rivals barely two years ago, is now lapping the field. The $27 billion company boosts its share simply by nudging down margins to a still-hefty 19%, this while the rest of the industry is struggling to make money (Exhibit 1). Nokia sits, debt-free, with $2.5 billion in cash, the biggest research-and-development budget in the industry, a killer brand, and unrivaled leverage not only over suppliers but also over customers. Those are the world's biggest phone companies, from AT&T to Deutsche Telekom, who supply millions of cell phones to the public. They pay top dollar to have the snazziest Nokias on hand. Few can afford to pass. "Nokia's the gorilla," says Joris de Beul, equity strategist at Fortis Investment Management in Brussels.

Sure, cell-phone growth will slow down from this year's 45%, especially in near-saturated Western Europe. But even pessimists project an additional 140 million units next year, many of them in developing markets such as China, India, and the United States. Within three years, the cell-phone market should reach 1 billion units per year, says International Data Corp. No one's better positioned to cash in on this monster market than Nokia. The Finns predict 25% to 35% sales growth through the next three years.

EXHIBIT 1 **Nokia Isn't the Biggest ...**

Data: J.P. Morgan H&Q

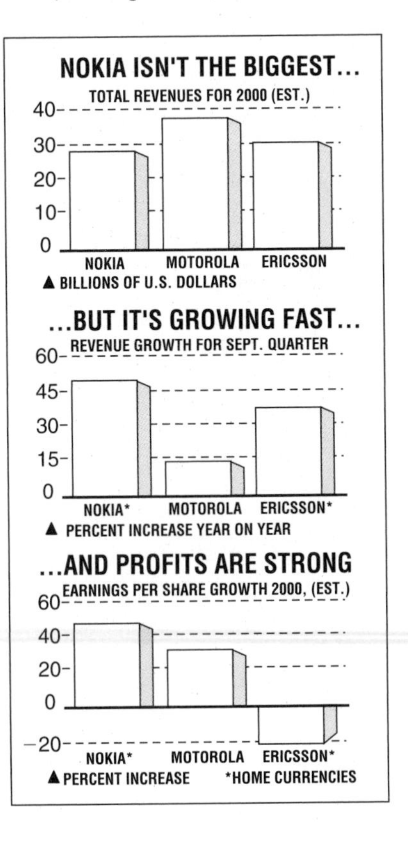

Yet in this sluttish climate, even a slight stumble on Nokia's part could jeopardize more than the Finnish giant's stock price. At risk is the company's whole ambitious gamble on the mobile Internet, which barely exists today. More than any other outfit, Nokia is spurring the global phone industry ahead on this trillion-dollar push. If the strategy pans out, the Finns could well sit atop the next stage of the Web, kings not just of Web-surfing machines, but also a power in software and networks.

Deep Debt

This is a dicey situation, however, because Nokia can never go back to just selling phones. It also needs huge commitments from its partners, the phone companies, to forge the wireless Web. But all the telcos have plunged deeply into debt. And in this new ball game Nokia faces fierce competition from the world's leading tech companies, from Silicon Valley to Tokyo.

Only a year ago, the wireless Web seemed to be falling nearly into place. The phone companies dutifully accepted Nokia's thesis that this high-speed mobile Net, known as Third Generation (3G), was the next big thing: To miss it meant death, no matter how much it cost. With that, the telcos went on one of the biggest spending binges in history, throwing billions of dollars at spectrum licenses like so much cab fare. When Britain's Vodafone Group PLC launched a $183 billion takeover of Germany's Mannesmann, the markets barely quivered. They were too busy applauding.

It was back in those cheery times, one evening at Nokia headquarters, that Chairman Ollila mentioned his company's market value and broke into laughter. "$250 billion," he said, shaking his head. Suddenly, it didn't seem like much money.

Today, it does. In a manic market, the noise surrounding 3G is every bit as grisly as the soundtrack of *Scream 3*. Phone companies are spending a spine-tingling $125 billion just for spectrum licenses in Europe, plus another $100 billion for the networks—this before any of them have figured out how to make a business from data on mobile phones. In a switch from cockeyed optimism to paranoia, investors have punished phone stocks, driving down giants like Deutsche Telekom and British Telecommunications PLC by 60% since last summer (Exhibit 2).

Such stampedes throw plenty of dust on Nokia. For now, though, the Finns' drive to build and dominate the mobile Web is not even off schedule. And the telcos, battered as they are, remain committed to 3G. Most of them are locked in, by the terms of their spectrum licenses, and ready to plow ahead.

Hazards lurk up ahead, though. The drive to 3G is pushing Nokia from the simple radio-based handsets it knows so well into the dizzying world of computers and consumer goodies, from digital cameras to tiny video machines—all of which will soon communicate with one another over the wireless Net. This process is known as digital convergence. And it's leading Nokia away from its home-telephone counter at Best Buy into different sections of the electronics store. It's here the Finns run smack into Microsoft Corp. and Sony Corp., which are busy making similar machines.

For Niklas Savander, Nokia's mission is like that of a surfer looking for the next wave. Savander, Nokia's vice-president for software applications, says that with mobile voice, Nokia caught a tsunami in the '90s. The

EXHIBIT 2 Nokia's New Firmament

The Bright Side . . .	. . . And the Dark
• Nokia is the world's fifth most valuable brand, ahead of Sony, Nike, and Mercedes-Benz.	• The European market for the current generation of handset is nearly saturated.
• It makes nearly one-third of all cell phones sold, enjoying huge economies of scale.	• The cellular market is struggling with the failure of early global-Internet software, called WAP.
• Its handset operating margins are 20%, compared with 5% for Motorola and –30% for Ericsson.	• Nokia's key customers, Europe's telcos, are $125 billion in debt, incurred to pay for 3G licenses.
• Nokia's strong management team has come through many crises unscathed.	• Investors are running from 3G and telcos are seeing credit ratings fall.
• It has global relationships with all the major phone companies.	• Nokia will likely be late in 3G phones and in an earlier Net-enabled format called GPRS.
• It has world-class research, design, and engineering teams.	• In handsets, Nokia faces well-capitalized Japanese rivals.

first company to design colorful phones and build a consumer brand, Nokia left competitors such as Motorola and Ericsson floundering in its wake. Those engineering companies viewed mobile phones for far too long as boring and expensive business tools. And Motorola made a disastrous bet on analog phones, just as Nokia was pushing digital (Exhibit 3). But those triumphs are in the past. "The next wave," says Savander, looking out the window at the lapping Baltic, "is the mobile Net. The question is whether we can catch two in a row."

"Close-Knit"

Five floors up from Savander at the Nokia House, Jorma Ollila scowls at the wave analogy. "It's a bit too simple," the 50-year-old Nokia chairman says in his clipped British accent, a product of a stint in London at Citibank. Ollila insists that his close-knit team of managers, the same five Finns who mapped out Nokia's course in current cell phones, have been preparing the company for the mobile Web for years. He notes that Nokia produced the first Web-surfing mobile phone—a brick known as the Communicator—way back in 1996, the Jurassic era of the wireless Web. From his glass-walled office. Ollila has been reassigning radio engineers into software and Internet technologies for the past three years. And he's been preparing his managers. More than smart software, Nokia's debt-free balance sheet, or its heavyweight brand, it's Ollila's inner circle of managers that promises to power Nokia in the coming wireless Web wars.

All Finns, these top execs took over Nokia as thirty-something managers when the national icon was wavering on the brink of bankruptcy. They jettisoned much of the company to focus on wireless. There they pushed

EXHIBIT 3 Motorola Can't Seem to Get out of Its Own Way

On the frozen plains of Schaumburg, Ill., executives at Motorola Inc. might happily trade their snow boots for Nokia's shoes. Sure, Nokia's hiccup in handset sales sent its shares tumbling. But that pain pales next to Motorola's chronic performance woes.

Since last March, the one-time high-tech bellwether has lost two-thirds of its value as its shares have collapsed to $20 from $60 a share. And on Jan. 10, Motorola reported fourth-quarter earnings of $335 million–down from last summer's expectations of $615 million–on sales of $10.1 billion. Motorola, says Jane A. Snorek, vice-president at Firmco, a Milwaukee investment house that owns shares in the company, "is in a lot of trouble."

What's bugging Motorola? Certainly the $37.6 billion company–which depends on semiconductor sales for about 20% of revenues–suffers from the cyclical swings of the chip industry. But its biggest problems stem from its $13.3 billion wireless business. In the past two years, Motorola's market share in cell-phone handsets has fallen to 13% from 17%, says researcher Dataquest Inc., while Nokia today controls a third of the market, up from 27% in 1999.

Simply put, Motorola can't quickly and profitably produce the phones consumers want. The company missed the transition to digital in the mid-'90s and today grapples with a product line that's too complex and hard to manage.

Compare Motorola's product line to Nokia's. The Finnish company uses just a handful of basic designs that share components such as screens, batteries, and some chips. Motorola, by contrast, juggles many different model platforms with little overlap among parts–making it nearly impossible to get the economies of scale Nokia enjoys.

And Motorola phones haven't clicked with consumers. U.S. cellular operator Cingular Wireless, for example, says Nokia phones dominate. At Sprint PCS Group outlets, Samsung Co. usually wins. The reason: customers say Motorola designs are clunky, and too many top $200–higher than most people will pay.

The greatest challenge for CEO Christopher B. Galvin is to develop a production process matching Nokia's. To that end, Motorola is whittling its model platforms to fewer than a half-dozen, sharing many basic components such as keypads. By mid-year, Motorola should churn out handsets far more quickly–and at far lower prices, says Leif G. Soderberg, head of strategy for Motorola's phone unit. "We're going to have fewer products and make the ones we've got killers," Soderberg says.

Better hurry. Even if sleek new phones are ready as soon as promised, Motorola can't afford more lost ground. It "could fall so far behind it'll never catch up," says Edward F. Snyder, analyst at J.P. Morgan H&Q. With so much at stake, Motorola execs must be shaking in their snow boots.

By Roger O. Crockett in Chicago

design and branding, and set up a low-cost industrial scheme that gave Nokia a head start when the cell phone became a mass-consumer good.

But while winning the cellular wars, Ollila was busy training his team for the challenges ahead. He shifted their jobs every two or three years. He dispatched his chief financial officer, Olli-Pekka Kallasvuo, to run the U.S. division in Dallas. There, the money man learned not just about manufacturing, but the all-important U.S. capital markets. Ollila sent his networks chief, Sari Baldauf, to run Asia—giving her a good look at the jumping-off markets for 3G.

Perhaps most important, Ollila pulled his No. 2 and heir apparent, Pekka Ala-Pietila, away from handsets in 1998 and sent him to Silicon Valley. Ollila says he has always counted on the 44-year-old Ala-Pietila as a visionary, and he makes a point of talking to him every day. Ala-Pietila's mandate is nothing less than to define the future of the wireless Web—and put Nokia on track to get rich there.

From Nokia's leafy campus in Mountain View, Calif., Ala-Pietila is piecing together an entire Internet division. The idea is a bold one for a hardware company: Nokia can make all the fancy phones it wants, from almond-size units that nestle in the ear to combo phone-organizers with color touch screens and the zippiest games. But all of these phones are going to flounder—and Nokia will, too—if the network they depend on falls flat. This is driving Nokia to funnel much of its $2.5 billion R&D budget into 3G projects extending far beyond the mere handset.

Some 20,000 engineers from California to Nokia's labs in Oulu, just south of the Polar Circle, are venturing far from their radio roots, reaching into nearly every technology that touches the Web. They're developing tiny Web-browsers and firewalls, e-commerce security systems, and vast programs known as "middleware" that will allow phone companies to manage the expected blizzard of 3G traffic. Nokia's risk? In an industry where companies zero in on specialties—Ericsson on transmission towers, Qualcomm Inc. on chip design—Nokia's covering the wireless waterfront. "Nokia is clinging to a vertical industrial model," says Hjalmar Widbladh, general manager of Microsoft's stockholm-based mobility division. "That goes against the times."

And the complexity of 3G systems is daunting. Consider a phone-toting German businesswoman in Malaysia. The network must locate her, offer a full load of German-language-services, from a list of vegetarian restaurants in Kuala-Lumpur to travel sites that permit her to postpone her Lufthansa flight by a day—and pay the $50 penalty, by phone of course. For the system to work, phone companies the world over must trace the steps of hundreds of millions of customers, adjust services to billions of different Web-surfing machines, and figure out the right billing for each customer's subscription. Building these systems "may be the most complex job humanity has ever faced," says Greg Papadopoulos, chief technology officer at Sun Microsystems Inc.

Redmond Rival

One of the few companies with resources to tackle it is Microsoft. The software giant is pulling out all the stops to extend its dominance from the desktop to the wireless Web. Three years ago, Nokia and Ericsson headed up an effort to block Microsoft from mobile-Net operating systems. Joined later by Motorola, they created a London-based joint venture called Symbian to produce a competing system.

But in the past year, Microsoft has flexed its mobile muscles. Last winter, it forged a joint venture with Ericsson to develop mini-Web browsers for handsets. "We can't do everything on our own," says Ericsson President Kurt Hellstrom. Months later, Microsoft hired away a key Symbian executive. In November, the Redmond giant unveiled prototypes of its first Internet phone, a joint venture with French phonemaker Sagem. The product is a slick palmtop device with a color screen, games, and a speaker phone—similar to Symbian-based products still in the lab. It's designed for generation 2.5, the next step in Europe's mobile Net, which should roll out this year. The worst part? Microsoft's product, due out within months, could beat Nokia to the marketplace.

The Japanese promise to arrive early, as well. While Europeans thrash about to finance their next-generation systems and the U.S. debates which part of the airwaves to devote to it, the Japanese are forging ahead. Generation Three should debut by May in Tokyo. Already, Japanese powerhouses Sony and Matsushita Communication Industrial Co. are unveiling zippy new phones, some connected to MP3 players, others to cameras and mini-game consoles. What's more, when the first 3G systems open in Europe, early next year, the Japanese will likely be ready first with handsets. "Panasonic is going to be a good six months ahead of Nokia," says Lloyd Carney, president of wireless Internet solutions at Nortel Networks.

One question is what the machines will look like. Nokia developers predict a broad and wacky wireless world. They see wireless Barbie Dolls and Yankee caps, phones equipped with global positioning hitched to dog collars and planted in school lunch boxes. They see people eventually accumulating gobs of wireless machines, just the way we pile up clocks and radios today. "The market will be big enough for everyone," predicts Ollila. But amid the tumult, Nokia's betting that users will continue to buy phone-like devices—albeit with a camera or game console or electronic organizer attached. Those multifeatured phones will remain Nokia's core market.

WAP Woes

But don't expect the market to take off like a rocket. When 3G rolls out, the service is likely to be spotty and pricey for months, perhaps longer. Nokia is betting, with the confidence of a powerhouse, that the market won't truly develop until the Finnish giant thunders onto the stage, complete with its phones, software, and a host of service providers in tow—and a massive P.R. campaign.

Chances are the market will continue to be iffy long after Nokia arrives. That was certainly the case with Europe's first generation of the mobile Internet, a disaster known as WAP, or wireless access protocol. Launched amid great fanfare 16 months ago, WAP has limped from the beginning, hobbled by slow connections, high prices, lackluster services and, most embarrassingly, undependable phones. "Nokia's first [WAP] phones were buggy as hell," says Nigel Deighton, Gartner Group analyst.

The next phase promises to be rocky too. The market is likely to swoon every time Ericsson beats Nokia to a 3G contract, every time a Net phone appears with bugs. But from the very start, Nokia's managers have thrived precisely when they're working through crises. Every tumble Nokia takes hardens it for the wild ride ahead. It's bound to be bruising. But these Nordics are proving they have the patience, the riches, and the smarts to withstand the heat.

By Stephen Baker in Helsinki, with John Shinal in Mountain View, Calif., and Irene M. Kunii in Tokyo

Source: "Is Nokia's Star Dimming?" *BusinessWeek*, January 22, 2001, 66–72.

Epilogue

Funny it took them so long. Years after the auto and computer industries shipped out much of their factory work, mobile-phone makers stuck to piecing together handsets in company-owned plants from Stockholm to Harvard, Ill. Now their old-fashioned ways are rapidly ending.

Battered by Finland's Nokia, Sweden's Ericsson threw in the towel, announcing on Jan. 26 that it was abandoning manufacturing. It turned the works—including six factories and 4,200 workers—over to contract manufacturer Flextronics International Ltd. Ericsson's retreat came only a month after Motorola Inc. said it would outsource much of its production. Nokia says it, too, will boost its use of low-cost outsiders to 15% of its handset production. In fact, 80% of this work will be done by contract labor in a few years, predicts Flextronics CEO Michael E. Marks.

The cost-cutting couldn't come a moment too soon. An abrupt slowdown is on the way. Nokia Chairman Jorma Ollila predicted on Jan. 30 that phone sales, projected earlier to grow 30% in 2001, to 560 million units, may come in closer to 500 million.

Leverage

But is shipping out manufacturing the best way to gird for rough times? Nokia insists it will keep most of its factory work in-house. Ollila maintains that producing its own phones constitutes one of Nokia's key advantages over its rivals. In fact, he's counting on Nokia's manufacturing edge to produce at the lowest costs in the industry, enabling the company to drive down prices. "We'll add to our share," he says, which now tops 30% of the global market.

So who's right, the outsourcing Swedes and Americans, or the do-it-yourself Finns? The answer may be both. To date, size has been Nokia's strength. With its explosive growth in the past two years, the company now towers over its rivals, producing more phones than No. 2 Motorola and No. 3 Ericsson combined. This gives Nokia a crucial edge in scale, along with leverage over suppliers, especially makers of computer chips that power these handsets (Exhibit 4).

Indeed, to take on this behemoth Ericsson is in effect creating another manufacturing giant by allying with

EXHIBIT 4 Nokia Pulls Ahead

Source: Company reports, Bank of America Securities

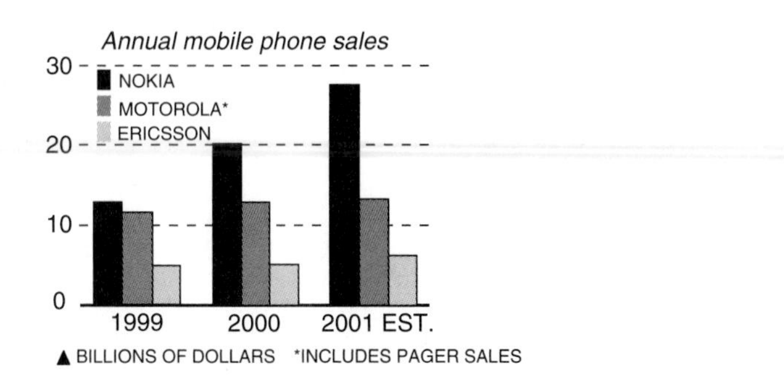

Flextronics. The $13 billion company, run from San Jose, Calif., may well become the other caller that chipmakers can't put on hold. "When it comes to scale, our partner is very, very big," points out Jan Ahrenbring, Ericsson's vice-president for marketing. Outsourcing should also go a long way in helping the laggards cut costs. Motorola's margins on phones have shrunk to a measly 3%. Ericsson's are even worse, posting a punishing yearend loss of $1.7 billion in its cell-phone unit. With the outsourcing deal, the Swedes "are looking for hundreds of millions of savings per year," says Marks.

Ugly Phones

But outsourcing alone won't save the day. What's required in this market is snazzy design, powerful marketing and, above all, teams that can anticipate consumer tastes—skills that are glaringly absent at Motorola and Ericsson. And ominously, while they're handing off more assembly work, they're both continuing to do design, engineering, and marketing internally. "If they make ugly phones that no one wants, lower costs won't help much," asserts Tim Sheedy, a wireless analyst at International Data Corp.

Still, nimble manufacturing has been a key to Nokia's success. The company, which was nearly bankrupt nine years ago, restructured for the global economy in the early '90s. "We didn't have factories in every country, like our competitors," says Ollila. Benefiting from streamlined design and manufacturing, Nokia produces two dozen new phones each year, a regimen rivals can't match.

But Nokia can't rest. Boutique manufacturers in Europe and America now envision disposable mobile phones with an hour of talk time to be sold for $10 in vending machines. When the cell phone, once a symbol of wealth and privilege, descends into the throwaway bin, even giants can't cut costs fast enough.

Source: Stephen Baker, "Commentary," ***BusinessWeek*****, February 12, 2001, 38.**

CASE 1-2

Charles Schwab Corp.

Charles R. "Chuck" Schwab is never happier than when he's waging war against Wall Street. In fact, it has been his business model ever since 1973, when he founded the discount brokerage that bears his name. His aim back then: to exploit the end of fixed-rate commissions in 1975—a traumatic event that slashed brokers' revenues and drove dozens of old-line firms out of business. His successful OneSource no-fee mutual-fund supermarket, launched in 1992, brought about a profound change in that business. And Schwab's stellar performance after its 1996 leap into online trading eventually forced the mighty Merrill Lynch & Co., one of the last holdouts, to follow suit in 1999.

Now the 64-year-old chairman and co-chief executive of Charles Schwab Corp. is again trying to rewrite the rules on Wall Street. On May 16, he announced moves aimed at capturing the most profitable customers of the likes of Merrill, Morgan Stanley Dean Witter, Salomon Smith Barney, and UBS PaineWebber—affluent clients with $500,000 to $5 million to invest. They constitute a huge market: By some estimates, they control nearly $11 trillion of investments in stocks, bonds, mutual funds, and cash, or about half the total of all such investments owned by Americans.

Schwab's attack plays directly off the crisis of confidence that's currently rocking the Street. Corporations blame bankers' bad advice for their troubled mergers and lackluster equity offerings. Betrayed individual investors fault their brokers for losing trillions of dollars of stock wealth since the dot-com bust in the spring of 2000. And they and others condemn the stock market's oracles—research analysts—for overly rosy stock recommendations.

Now, Schwab is trying to turn the Street's woes to his own advantage. Along with President and co-CEO David S. Pottruck, 53, he's launching an aggressive marketing campaign that fingers rivals' shortcomings and holds his firm up as the model of the squeaky-clean financial adviser. Hard-hitting print and TV ads emphasize that Schwab brokers, unlike their peers on the Street, aren't paid based on how much they encourage customers to trade, and that the company isn't beholden to big corporate clients because it doesn't have an investment-banking arm. "At Schwab, we're not focused on investment banking... To us, it's a potential conflict of interest," says one ad. "Is your broker's idea of an investment plan a never-ending series of hot stock tips?" asks another. "We're promoting a model different from all those other firms, and we will not be shy about promoting how different we are," says Schwab.

The centerpiece of Schwab's offering is a new stock-rating system coupled with a private-client service and, soon, insured banking products. For a flat fee, customers can talk one-on-one with a personal adviser who provides investment ideas on matters ranging from asset allocation to stock selection. Next year, it hopes to add FDIC-insured banking products. Both services are commonplace on Wall Street. What's unique, though, is how Schwab comes up with stock picks. Using a new in-house computer model, it grades more than 3,000 stocks on an A to F scale based on 24 measures, such as a company's free cash flow and sales growth (Exhibit 1). "It's a systematic approach with nothing but objectivity, not influenced by corporate relationships, investment banking, or any of the above," says Pottruck. Last year, he claims, investors who bought the top 30 A selections would have beaten the Standard & Poor's 500-stock index by 4.6 percentage points.

Schwab could do with a big lift. Ever since the tech stock bust in the spring of 2000, its mainstay online trading has fallen sharply, slashing its revenues and operating margins. The resulting squeeze was so hard that Schwab had to fire nearly one in four of its 26,000 workers last year—the first layoffs since the 1987 stock market crash. In the scramble to shore up profits, it is slapping on extra charges, such as a $3 transaction fee on online trades. And it has a minor rebellion on its hands among the independent financial advisers whose clients pony up about one-third of the $858 billion of Schwab's total client assets. Some claim Schwab is hanging onto clients it should be referring to them. A few are so angry that they have stopped placing new money with the firm.

The new strategy will cause plenty of strains at Schwab. Signing up thousands of upmarket clients and making money for them—and from them—is sure to be tough. By launching a private-client service, Schwab is straying further than ever from its discount-brokerage roots. It is hoping to extend its well-established brand without sacrificing the core brokerage business, which still accounts for 38% of its operating earnings. Schwab's top execs are well aware of the magnitude of the challenges they face. "The changes we're making are profound," says Pottruck, a former champion wrestler and football player at the University of Pennsylvania who is charged with making the strategy work. "This is retesting what the company stands for." The 18-year company veteran, long seen as Schwab's heir apparent, has been co-CEO since 1998. He serves as the firm's hands-on, day-to-day manager while Schwab serves as the big-picture strategist and public face of the company. Says Schwab: "I'm the inspirational leader, and Dave makes it happen."

If the duo can succeed, they'll do far more than revive their own business. They'll demonstrate that Wall Street can turn an honest penny without fleecing investors—and that it's possible to earn big bucks from a standalone brokerage and research operation.

As the firm strives to do that, it's finding some unexpected allies among the regulators. On May 21, Merrill reached a $100 million settlement with New York Attorney General Eliot Spitzer, who charged that its analysts issued misleading research to win banking business from Internet companies. Merrill also agreed to change its research standards and even the way that its analysts are paid. Other firms will likely follow suit. Spitzer is also investigating Salomon Smith Barney, Morgan Stanley, and at least three other firms. Meantime, the Securities & Exchange Commission hinted that Spitzer may not have the final word. "While this settlement is an important milestone for investor protection, it is not the finish line, and will not preclude our own efforts on behalf of the investing public," says SEC Director of Enforcement Stephen M. Cutler. The SEC has also launched a probe into the practices at 10 firms. And plaintiffs' lawyers are filing a flurry of class actions against Wall Street firms.

All the same, Schwab may find that it isn't alone in bragging about having no conflicts for very long. Merrill immediately tried to turn the May 21 settlement to its advantage, saying that it was setting a "new industry standard" for research—a boast that will be backed by an ad campaign. "Merrill Lynch can consider this a victory because they won a significant competitive advantage over their rivals," says John Coffee, professor of securities law at Columbia University. "They not only escaped crucifixion but they are blessed with holier analysts than the rest of their competitors." The same day, Goldman, Sachs & Co. appointed an investment research ombudsman and expanded its audit committee's responsibilities to include monitoring the integrity of its research. And on May 22, Salomon said it would adopt the same changes as Merrill.

While most of Wall Street quietly dismissed Schwab's offensive as a marketing ploy, Merrill pointed out a potential Achilles' heel. On May 16, it said in a rare statement that Schwab's attempt to recast itself as a source of advice simply reflected the woes of its discount-brokerage business. "They will be hard-pressed to deliver on that promise for the majority of their clients," it said.

Merrill may well be right. Schwab's culture is being severely tested. Employees hired mainly as order-takers are finding that they're underqualified as Schwab strives to upgrade its branch staff with more experienced—and more expensive—financial advisers. Meanwhile, there

EXHIBIT 1 Schwab's Soft Sell of Hard Stock Data: Commentary By Gary Weiss

Brokerage firms have a serious problem: No matter how much they might finesse it, a large and vital portion of their business is tied to the level of public enthusiasm (or, nowadays, lack thereof) for buying stocks. So it's easy to dismiss Charles Schwab Corp.'s new Equity Ratings as a marketing ploy that capitalizes on the analyst woes plaguing its competitors. Every week, Schwab will issue grades to more than 3,000 stocks, with the top 60 heralded for customers on the Schwab Web site. The stockpicking will be done by computer, without the fouling human touch. Or as Schwab puts it, "free from investment-banking and commissioned-based sales conflicts."

Translation: Wall Street research has lost whatever credibility it may have once possessed, and here comes Schwab to the rescue—of its own flagging revenue stream. Well, such cynicism is justified, but only up to a point.

Sure, there's a heavy, if not dominant, marketing component to the Schwab Equity Ratings, which were announced on May 16 and have a starring role in Schwab's new advertising campaign. Grading stocks is not new—Value Line Inc. has done it for years—and brokerages have their own overenthusiastic, buy-hold-never-sell stock-rating systems. Schwab is cleverly playing off public dissatisfaction with Wall Street research. And by doing so, the firm is engaging in a classic soft sell—gently prodding its customers off their duffs to buy stocks. "The lists are intended to provoke thinking—just to get our clients thinking," says Jerry Chafkin, a Schwab executive vice-president in charge of the new ratings.

At a time when investors have ample reason to think about anything but buying stocks, that's a smart strategy. It's also a reasonable enough investment tool. The general idea—objective, computer-driven research—certainly makes sense. If Wall Street research is not to be trusted, how else does an investor pick stocks? Advocates of efficient market theory believe a throw of a dart is as good a method as any. They may be right. But other market mavens, notably author and former Fidelity Magellan fund manager Peter Lynch, believe that investors should focus on stocks they know, and do their own research.

The Schwab rating system is a kind of middle ground. It offers customers an old-fashioned stock-screening mechanism, as do many other firms and Web sites. But such screens are a perilous method of stockpicking if the criteria are not properly selected. So Schwab is taking the idea a step further by doing a weekly screen for its customers, using 24 criteria involving mainly fundamental factors such as earnings and cash flow, plus analyses of analyst upgrades and downgrades. Chafkin says the aim of the ratings is to give investors a tool to use if they decide to alter their portfolios, not to encourage them to buy stocks. And, he says, the list is not expected to change dramatically from week to week. He also warns against using the screens to cherry-pick stocks.

Schwab's rating system is refreshing counterpoint to the hype that is routinely generated by Wall Street houses. The list criteria were designed by quantitative analysts who came on board from Chicago Investment Analytics, which Schwab acquired in November, 2000. Under the supervision of Chicago Investment co-founder Greg Forsythe, now Schwab's director of equity research, the computer will cull weekly through a list of nearly every stock with over $75 million in market value that isn't a real estate investment trust or a limited partnership.

The top 10% will be rated A and the bottom 10% will be rated F. The biggest category of stocks—40% of the lot—will always be rated C. Forsythe won't discuss the results of backtesting the new system because of regulatory constraints. But he says a model portfolio of 100 stocks, using the same basic approach as the ratings system, beat the market by 4.6 percentage points in 2001 and 6 points in the first quarter of 2002.

The top stocks on the list are diverse. The latest A-listers include such widely held companies as Anheuser-Busch, Kellogg, and Mattel, as well as less well-known names such as Commercial Metals, Sanderson, Farms, and Walter Industries.

But the system sneers at some widely held stocks, including a few that have lately generated a lot of Street interest. General Motors Corp., up 34% this year in a bad market, gets a C rating (great momentum, mediocre fundamentals and valuation). Is bedraggled IBM a buy? So say three-quarters of analysts covering the stock. But its momentum is cruddy, says the Schwab ratings, so it gets a C. Ditto for AOL Time Warner, while Citigroup draws a B, and Merrill Lynch, Schwab's beleaguered rival, gets a C.

And Schwab? Well, the firm, of course, does not rate its own stock. But its stockpicking system will only get an A from Schwab's shareholders if clients are roused from their stupor—and start generating commissions.

has been turmoil at the top. Steven L. Scheid, who headed the retail business, abruptly left in February because he wanted more "autonomy," according to the company. Scheid declined to comment. Pottruck is filling in for him while the company looks inside for a replacement.

The company's relationship with 5,000 independent advisers has been fraying ever since 2000, when Schwab bought U.S. Trust Corp., a 149-year-old advisory firm catering to multimillionaires. As Schwab pushes deeper into the advice business, many are feeling much more threatened and blame the firm for eating in to their business. "We feel Schwab's competing with us," says Christiane Delessert, an adviser in Newton, Mass., who keeps about $150 million in client assets at Schwab. "They are angering a lot of people." Schwab has tried to mollify the elite group of 330 outside advisers who form Schwab's Advisor Network. It has set up an incentive for branches to refer clients to them as they're supposed to—but the advisers have to turn over a small cut of the fees they earn from clients.

However risky the strategy might be, Schwab and Pottruck have little alternative but to bet big. (Exhibit 2). The firm is still reeling from the financial aftershocks of Nasdaq's nosedive in 2000. Pummeled by a 34% drop in daily average trades, revenue dropped 25% last year, to $4.35 billion, while net income plunged 72%, to $199 million. With little prospect of quick improvement, Pottruck moved to slash costs: Apart from the layoffs, he also dumped millions of dollars' worth of computer equipment to save the costs of running and maintaining it. "Obviously, we weren't going to succeed based on online trades," says Pottruck. Trading levels are "not going to go back to where they were in 2000, ever."

That realization also put the advice strategy on the front burner. Schwab had been quietly putting it in place well before the tech bust. By then, Schwab had already announced plans to acquire U.S. Trust. That move was designed to help Schwab retain customers who were leaving because it didn't provide trust and estate services. But Schwab still needed a service to offer to the legions of people with $500,000 or more in assets who want to keep control of their own accounts but need an adviser to give them ideas.

Launched on May 16, Schwab Private Client is Schwab's play for this market. For a fee of 0.6% of assets—or a minimum of $1,500—per year, customers meet face-to-face with an adviser to work out an investment plan and return to the same consultant for further advice. The adviser might call the client to discuss market or industry developments and their impact on the portfolio. What clients don't get: legal, tax, and estate-planning advice. Nor do Schwab's private-client advisers actually manage the client's money or decide what to buy and sell. That's still the client's job.

The service, which is by appointment only, will be available in most Schwab branches. But Schwab has also opened nine separate, plusher offices in upmarket neighborhoods for customers wanting to avoid the hoi polloi at regular branches. The discreet fourth-floor office in Santa Clara, Calif., in the heart of Silicon Valley, is furnished with dark wood furniture, flowers, and a conference room where customers can bring their tax advisers, estate planners, and attorneys for powwows with the Schwab adviser. "It feels like a private-client atmosphere," says John Molskness, who heads the office. "It's not designed for the walk-in client."

EXHIBIT 2 **Why Schwab Needs New Business–Fast**

Continued →

SCHWAB STILL DOMINATES ONLINE TRADING...

Market share of 2001 online trading volume	
SCHWAB	20.5%
E*TRADE	13.9
AMERITRADE	12.1
TD WATERHOUSE	11.6
DATEK	11.2
FIDELITY	8.4

Market share of $920 billion online account assets	
SCHWAB	37.2%
FIDELITY	33.7
TD WATERHOUSE	10.1
E*TRADE	4.9
AMERITRADE	3.4
QUICK & REILLY	2.7

...AND IS CLOSING THE ASSET GAP WITH MERRILL LYNCH...

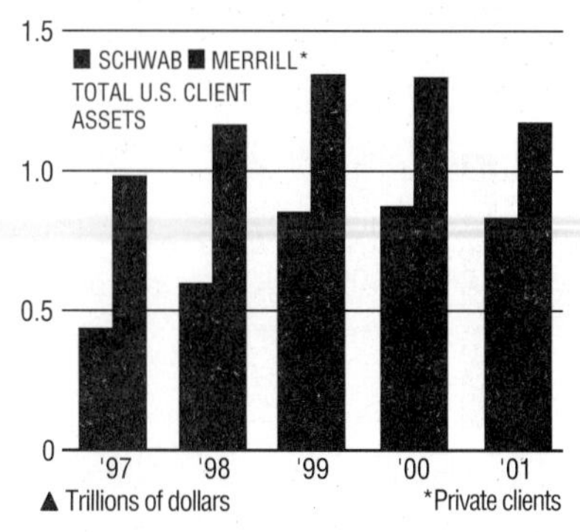

Pottruck credits U.S. Trust staffers for helping Schwab figure out how to structure its new service. They warned, for instance, that unlike Schwab's do-it-yourself customers, private clients don't appreciate being told to phone a call center if their adviser isn't available. But in other areas, the relationship hasn't been too fruitful. It quickly became clear that Schwab wouldn't be able to scale down U.S. Trust's high-maintenance hand-holding of clients to accounts as small as $500,000. And U.S. Trust stock analysts balked at putting their own research reports on Schwab's Web site. Pottruck says that was "a little bit of a disappointment," but Schwab realized that the analysts covered too few stocks to make the effort worthwhile. Instead, Schwab is offering Goldman Sachs' research to top-drawer clients.

Now, Schwab faces a reality check as it starts selling advice to a wider public. During a year of testing, the service attracted about 1,000 clients—mostly existing Schwab account holders—and $1.5 billion of assets, of which just $225 million was new money. Chuck Schwab is projecting the private-client business to reach between $3 billion and $4 billion in assets by yearend. Can he succeed? Some observers believe he has a decent shot at making the service work because many customers, burned by the tech meltdown, want advice. "Customers will want it because customers need it," says Morty Schaja, president of New York-based Baron Funds, which owns 22.3 million Schwab shares. "With the new service, they'll successfully fill in the gap between U.S. Trust and the discount-brokerage online trader. Now they can compete favorably with Merrill Lynch and Morgan Stanley." (Exhibit 3).

Others are far less sanguine because so many other banks and brokers are chasing the same affluent clients. "They're going into a very crowded marketplace," says David Thompson, consultant at NFO WorldGroup Inc. Adds Ward Harris of financial-services consulting firm McHenry Consulting Group: "I don't know if Schwab has the history or experience needed to succeed at this." While Schwab's advisers may be able to handle basics such as asset allocation, he says, they may cope less well with more complex issues such as managing options.

In pushing itself as a financial adviser to the affluent, Schwab's biggest hurdle may be finding the right staff. It now faces an urgent need to develop a cadre of qualified advisers for its private-client service. It has only 150 in place, but plans to double that number by yearend. If it can't find them within its existing ranks, it must look outside. That's already happening. Before he came to the then-new Santa Clara office about a year ago, the 34-year-old Molskness worked at the financial-advice operations of Prudential Financial and American Express. All four advisers in Santa Clara have years of experience in giving financial advice. But three of them lack a certified financial planner qualification, although they are currently completing the coursework to receive it.

Even with a qualified staff, Schwab may still be battling what Pottruck calls a "credibility gap" that keeps many potential customers from seeing Schwab as a legitimate source of advice. "We're not yet trusted for our market wisdom or the nature and depth of our client relationships," he says.

As its adviser staff boosts its qualifications, they're sure to demand higher salaries, something Schwab traditionally isn't known for. A former manager who voluntarily left the company in early 2001 notes an inside joke: Schwab is a discount broker that offers a "discount paycheck." Says Erick F. Maronak, head of research at Newbridge Partners LLC, which in early May sold about 6 million Schwab shares: "Where it cuts back on order-takers, it's got to replace with advice givers, and they cost more. If they want to compete with Merrill Lynch, it will require a lot of capital." Daniel O. Leemon,

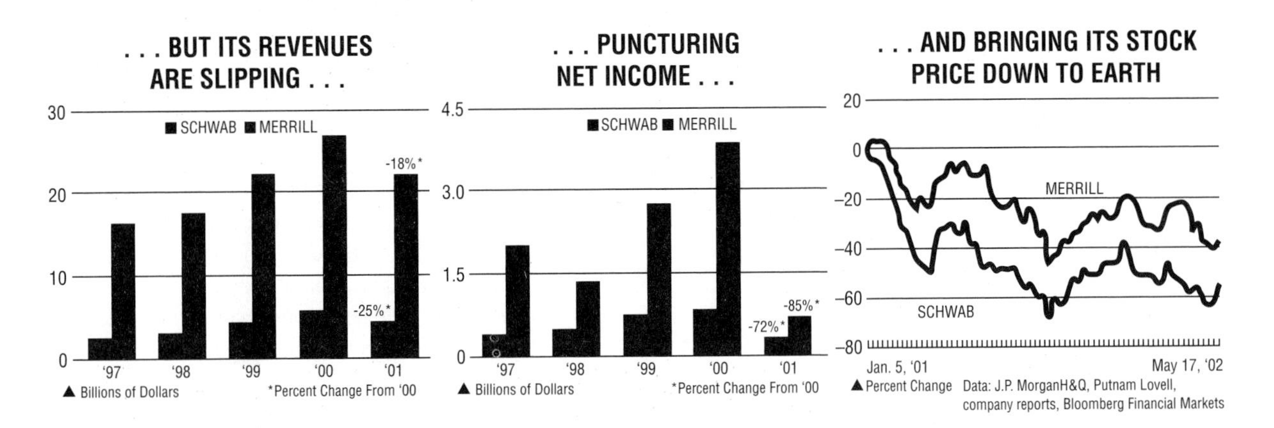

EXHIBIT 3 Schwab: Tackling the Bull: How different is the Schwab model from the fee-based offering of its biggest competitor, Merrill Lynch?

Data: Schwab, Merrill Lynch

SCHWAB	MERRILL
• **RETAIL BUSINESS** Sells equity offerings underwritten by Goldman Sachs, but does not have investment-banking business. Retail clients account for 60% of revenues and 37% of operating profits.	• Retail services contribute 44% of revenues and 31% of pretax earnings. But investment banking, which accounts for 65% of pretax earnings, is the bigger moneymaker.
• **RESEARCH** Employs no in-house research analysts. Distributes proprietary research based on quantitative models that it considers more objective. Also distributes Goldman Sachs research reports to investors with $500,000 of assets.	• Employs 800 research analysts and distributes proprietary research to financial consultants. Provides technical research based on quantitative calculations, but maintains that fundamental research by analysts beats computer models.
• **CHARGES** Charges annual fees of 0.6% for $2 million or less in assets. No fee on cash or money-market funds. Minimum charge $1,500.	• Charges annual fees of 1.5% on client's first $1 million in equities, 1% on mutual funds, 0.5% on bonds and cash. Minimum charge $1,500.
• **TRADING FEES** Fifty free trades a year for clients with $1 million or less in assets.	• Unlimited free trades for $1 million accounts, 300 for those over $500,000.
• **ADVISERS** Network of 150 advisers in nine private-client offices, and dozens of Schwab branches. Plus network of 330 independent advisers.	• Network of 14,000 in-house advisers in 700 branches across the U.S.

Schwab's chief strategy officer, counters that expected increased revenue and efficiency will offset rising payroll costs in the future.

Schwab also faces a real danger that customers will view its private-client advice as a one-size-fits-all product. Private-client advisers make heavy use of in-house computerized systems to develop investment plans for clients. Without them, serving each client would take so much time that Schwab's costs would spin out of control. "You run the risk of [getting into] a slippery slope where before you know it, you've reinvented the cost structure of your most expensive competitors," says Pottruck. "The key for Schwab is our ability to use technology and automation to keep the cost structure down."

Using a consistent computerized system to analyze client needs also protects clients from the whims or offbeat personal preferences of the adviser, Schwab executives say. But it's a small step from consistent to cookie-cutter. That's a perception Schwab has been aware of and wants to avoid. "None of us is so naive to think there's a model that works for everyone all the time," says Jeremiah H. Chafkin, an executive vice-president who is overseeing the advice service. "No one wants a relationship with a computer." The new ads try to counter any such perception, insisting that advisers "take the time to study your financial needs" and "listen to you and your goals."

That may produce hollow laughter from Schwab's traditional clients. Schwab no longer pays postage on envelopes customers can use to mail in checks. Since last fall, households with less than $50,000 in their accounts have to pay $30 a quarter, unless they trade eight times a year. And starting on June 1, the company will raise its minimum fee for broker-assisted trades by 41% and automated-phone trades by 65%. It also plans to start charging a $60 fee for all customers when they want to close an account. "It obviously wants to chase smaller customers out of there," sniffs Muriel Siebert, chairwoman of Muriel Siebert & Co., a rival discount broker that hasn't changed its fees. "Schwab could lose a lot of goodwill." Adds Baron Capital's Schaja: "The risk is that the customer that isn't profitable today might be a profitable customer in five years."

Pottruck clearly has to execute a delicate balancing act. The company's ambitious financial targets for this year don't leave him much room to maneuver—requiring him both to cut costs and bag significant new revenues. Schwab is targeting operating profit margins of 12% to 14% by yearend and aiming to boost revenue per employee to $300,000 in 2003, up from $190,000 in

EXHIBIT 4 Leading the Charge—Schwab's relentless innovation has redefined the brokerage business several times already

1973 Former equity analyst and portfolio manager Charles R. "Chuck" Schwab founds the brokerage to exploit the end of fixed-price stock trading commissions in May, 1975.

1975 Opens first branch in Sacramento. Now has 400 branches nationwide.

1983 Schwab sells his firm to Bank of America for $57 million, but quickly becomes dissatisfied and buys it back within four years.

1989 Launches Telebroker, a touch-tone trading and quote system.

1992 Introduces One-Source, a mutual-fund supermarket allowing customers to buy fund shares without paying loads or fees.

1996 Begins online trading, a business it now dominates with over 37% of $920 billion in online account assets.

2000 Announces merger with U.S. Trust, a 149-year-old adviser to multimillionaires.

2002 Takes on Wall Street directly with launch of Schwab Private Client and Schwab Equity Rating stock-picking system.

2001. In addition, it hopes to garner $125 billion in net new assets, a considerable jump from the $74 billion added in 2001—all the while nurturing the new private-client service.

In the past, Schwab has had its snafus. In 1999, it set up Epoch Partners Inc. along with TD Waterhouse, Ameritrade, and three venture-capital firms, to underwrite initial public offerings of technology companies to sell to clients, a market that froze after the tech bust. In June of last year, it sold its stake to Goldman Sachs, which acquired all of Epoch. Other ill-timed initiatives have included PocketBroker, a wireless trading service for handheld gadgets that Schwab acknowledges hasn't taken off, and CyberTrader, a service for active online traders that it is still trying to expand.

But it would be dangerous for Wall Street to assume that Schwab's private-client service will fall flat. Time and again, Chuck Schwab's rivals have pooh-poohed his ideas as impractical or unnecessary; time and again, his ideas have wrought major changes in the way Wall Street operates. If Schwab can show that a large-scale advice business can work profitably without being inextricably wed to an investment bank, he'll blow the Street's current business model out of the water—probably to the cheers of millions of disgruntled investors (Exhibit 4).

By Louise Lee in San Francisco, with Emily Thornton in New York

Source: "Schwab vs. Wall Street," *BusinessWeek*, June 3, 2002, 65–68, 70, and 71.

CASE 1-3

McKinsey & Co.

Shortly after Enron Corp. tumbled into bankruptcy last December, McKinsey & Co. Managing Partner Rajat Gupta was worried. It wasn't only because former Enron CEO Jeffrey K. Skilling was once a McKinsey & Co. partner and loyal alum. Or that his firm had advised the giant energy trader for nearly 18 years on basic strategy, even sitting in on boardroom presentations to Enron's directors. Or even that many of the underlying principles of Enron's transformation, including its "asset-light" strategy, its "loose-tight" culture, and the securitization of debt, were eagerly promoted by McKinsey consultants.

Gupta was worried about something much more immediate: Had McKinsey crossed a legal line that would drag it into the unfolding morass? In a stunning exercise for the world's whitest of white-shoe management consultants, Gupta dispatched his chief legal counsel to McKinsey's offices in Houston to review the firm's work at Enron. The mission was to find any evidence linking McKinsey to the massive fraud behind Enron's business model.

The lawyer came back with good news: There were no shredded documents, à la Arthur Andersen LLP, and, more important, says Gupta, there was nothing in the files to show that McKinsey ever helped Enron engineer its controversial off-balance-sheet financing or its financial reporting strategy. "In all the work we did with Enron," maintains Gupta, "we did not do anything that is related to financial structuring or disclosure or any of the issues that got them into trouble. We stand by all the work we did. Beyond that, we can only empathize with the trouble they are going through. It's a sad thing to see."

Still, outsiders marvel that the secretive partnership has not been drawn into the debacle, given its extensive involvement at Enron. "I'm surprised that they haven't been subpoenaed as a witness, at least," says Wayne E. Cooper, CEO of Kennedy Information, a research and publishing firm that keeps tabs on consultants. "There was so much smoke coming out of the Andersen smoking gun that all the firefighters went after that one. McKinsey was lucky. They dodged a bullet."

The bad news, however, is that Enron, which was paying McKinsey as much as $10 million in annual fees, is just one of an unusual number of embarrassing client failures for the elite consulting firm. Besides Enron, there's Swiss-air, Kmart, and Global Crossing—all McKinsey clients that have filed for bankruptcy in relatively short order. And those are just the biggest. McKinsey also finds itself improbably lining up with other creditors to collect unpaid fees from recently bankrupt companies that soared during the late '90s only to crash later. Battery maker Exide Technologies and NorthPoint Communications Group Inc., an upstart telecom provider, are two such examples.

All of which raises uncomfortable questions about the world's most prestigious—and enigmatic—consulting firm. Did McKinsey's partners get caught up in the euphoria of the late '90s and suffer lapses of judgment? And if so, what does that say about the quality of its expensive advice? Did it stray from its core values? What accountability does it—or any consulting firm—have for the ideas and concepts it launches into a company?

After all, McKinsey was a key architect of the strategic thinking that made Enron a Wall Street darling. In books, articles, and essays, its partners regularly stamped their imprimatur on many of Enron's strategies and practices, helping to position the energy giant as a corporate innovator worthy of emulation. The firm may not be the subject of any investigations, but its close involvement with Enron raises the question of whether McKinsey, like some other professional firms, ignored warning flags in order to keep an important account.

The breakdowns of such visible clients could not have come at a more trying time. Instead of celebrating the end of his third and final three-year term as managing director, Gupta, 53, finds his firm roiled by a rare and potentially disruptive downturn in its business. Like most other consulting firms, McKinsey rode the e-business wave to record revenues—and record partner payouts—in 2000. When the boom turned to bust, the firm was stuck with far too many consultants and not nearly enough assignments. The utilization rate, or billable time, of its consultants has fallen to its lowest level in more than 32 years: just 52%, vs. the heady 64% level during the dot-com boom. (Exhibit 1).

That's not to say that McKinsey has lost its standing. The firm remains the high priest of high-level consulting, with the most formidable intellectual firepower, the classiest client portfolio, and the greatest global reach of any adviser to management in the world. (Exhibit 2). Most of the firm's top clients pay $10 million a year and up in fees, while McKinsey's largest client—which it declines to name—doled out $60 million for its

EXHIBIT 1 McKinsey By The Numbers

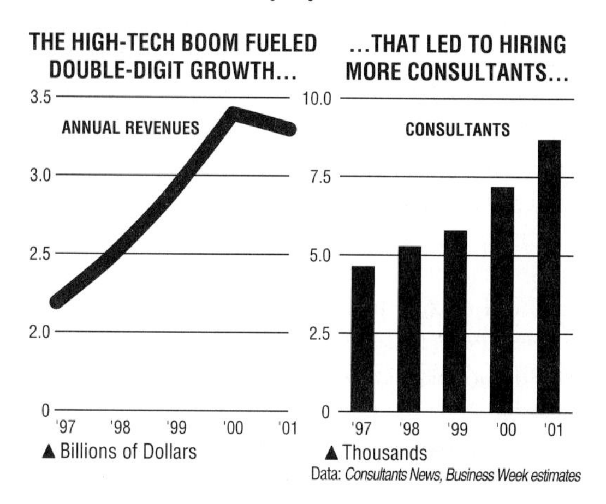

EXHIBIT 2 McKinsey and Its Rivals

Firm	Fiscal 2001 Revenues (Billions)	Change from 2000	Market Share Among Major Firms
McKINSEY	$3.4	−2%	40.6%
BOOZ, ALLEN & HAMILTON	1.6	4	19.1
A.T. KEARNEY*	1.2	−7	14.4
BOSTON CONSULTING GROUP	1.1	−5	12.5
BAIN	0.8	1	9.7
MONITOR	0.3	9	3.6

*A unit of EDSData: *Consultants News, BusinessWeek* estimates

EXHIBIT 3 McKinsey's Blue-Chip Client Roster

Data: *BusinessWeek*

Hewlett-Packard	A key adviser to CEO Carly Fiorina on H-P's recent acquisition of Compaq
Johnson & Johnson	A longtime, highly successful client that has used McKinsey on dozens of engagements over 30 years
General Motors	Continues to assist the big auto maker, which has shown gains over the competition in the past year
Siemens	Longtime counselor to vast German conglomerate on everything from sourcing parts from low-cost nations to factory consolidation
Home Depot	Advised the big-box retailer on its expansion into Latin America
Aeroflot	Assisted in the turnaround of Russia's biggest airline

advice last year. McKinsey serves 147 of the world's 200 largest corporations, including 80 of the top 120 financial-services firms, 9 of the 11 largest chemical companies, and 15 of the 22 biggest health-care and pharmaceutical concerns. (Exhibit 3).

McKinsey partners learn early on to protect and cultivate their client relationships. The firm says that it has served more than 400 active clients for 15 years or longer. It may be the priciest of the management consultants, but longtime clients say it gives top service. "McKinsey will bring its most senior people in to discuss the things they would do if they were in our shoes," says Klaus Kleinfeld, CEO of Siemens Corp., a longstanding client. "You have lunch. You have dinner. And then projects evolve. Very often, competitive bidding doesn't happen."

Gupta shows little concern over the meltdown of high-profile clients. "In these turbulent times, with our serving more than half the Fortune 500 companies, there are bound to be some clients that get into trouble," he says matter-of-factly. "We wouldn't have as many ongoing client situations if we didn't do good-quality work." And to be fair, McKinsey was hardly the only consultant to tie up with some high-flying upstarts in the '90s that later crashed.

When he became McKinsey's managing partner in 1994, Gupta's challenge was clear: He had to keep up McKinsey's growth while ensuring that size would not destroy the ethos of the close-knit partnership or undermine the firm's guiding principles. McKinseyites refer to these precepts, laid down by the firm's early leader, Marvin Bower, with near-religious conviction. Among the high-minded goals: Hire the best people and urge them to always put the client first—ahead of the interests of the firm.

In Gupta's early days as managing partner, some colleagues argued for keeping McKinsey small, to safeguard its culture and quality. Gupta was of another mind: He aggressively expanded abroad, opening up far-flung branches throughout Asia and Eastern Europe. In all, he expanded McKinsey's network to 84 worldwide locations from 58, boosted the consulting staff to 7,700 from 2,900, and lifted revenues to $3.4 billion from $1.2 billion in 1993. Meanwhile, the number of partners grew from 427 to 891. "It's a less personal place than it used to be," says Nancy Killefer, a senior partner in Washington, D.C. "In the old days, you knew everybody. That's not possible anymore."

Some observers believe the changes in McKinsey's culture went even deeper. Quietly, some current and former McKinsey consultants say the firm strayed from some of the ingrained values that have long guided the firm. Through the dot-com boom, for example, McKinsey allowed its focus on building agenda-shaping relationships with top management at leading companies to slip, as the firm took on some distinctly downmarket clients and projects. Increasingly, McKinsey began advising upstarts and divisional managers at less prestigious companies.

Worse, some argue, there was a noticeable tilt toward bringing in revenue at the expense of developing knowledge—a claim McKinsey vehemently disputes. "In [an earlier] era, the whole place had this tremendous focus on ideas," recalls a former McKinsey consultant. "I think knowledge has taken a backseat to revenue generation. The more revenues you create, the more your compensation and standing in the firm increases."

Gupta downplays any shift in priorities. "The pendulum does swing a little bit. I'd say that client development in the last year or two is more in the forefront, simply because that is the biggest need right now," he says, using McKinsey-speak for bringing in new business.

Perhaps the most visible example of this shift, say observers, was the rise of Ron Hulme, an affable, low-key senior partner and a leader of its energy practice, who managed the Enron account from McKinsey's

Houston offices. Like many of the firm's consultants, Hulme penned essays extolling the virtues of Enron. As McKinsey's annual billings climbed higher and higher at Enron—at one recent point exceeding $10 million—Hulme commanded greater influence in the firm, helping to lead partner conferences and key initiatives. Some insiders even considered him a potential successor to Gupta, though that's now an unlikely prospect, given Enron's collapse. "Despite his young age, he had tremendously high standing and power that derived from the Enron relationship," says a former McKinseyite. Hulme declined to comment.

Hulme did not initiate McKinsey's Enron business. Like many of the deepest and most lucrative corporate relationships, it began with one consultant who instantly impressed a client with his brilliance and insights. Jeffrey Skilling, then McKinsey's partner in charge of the worldwide energy practice, began advising Enron in the late '80s, but the relationship was cemented when he joined Enron in 1990 with the mandate to create a new way of doing business. Skilling, who once said he felt as if he were "doing God's work" at McKinsey, had proposed that Enron create a portfolio of fixed-price purchase and supply contracts that would supposedly eliminate supply risks and minimize the price fluctuations of the spot market for trading natural gas.

After joining Enron, Skilling repeatedly turned to McKinsey teams for analytical help and advice. "They infiltrated Enron with Jeff, and he was just the tip of the iceberg," says a former McKinsey consultant who worked at Enron. "There were all sorts of McKinsey people who went in over the years. They were so happy they had Enron locked up."

Indeed, several other prominent McKinsey consultants migrated to Enron as employees, including partner Doug Woodham, who left the firm in 1994 for a four-year stint as vice-president at Enron Capital & Trade Resources, where he led a team that developed an electric power and natural gas hedge fund. As Enron work became more financially driven, McKinsey teams there increasingly drew on partners with expertise in trading, risk management, and investment banking. At any given time, McKinsey had as many as 20 consultants at the energy company, several stationed in Enron's offices.

By and large, most of McKinsey's assignments at Enron were tactical or technical in nature: doing the prep work for entering new markets, formulating strategy for new products and services, and deciding whether Enron should acquire or partner with another company to gain access to a pipeline. But McKinsey also helped Enron formulate its now-discredited broadband strategy, in which it built a high-speed fiber network to support the trading of communications capacity. Among other things, McKinsey, over about six months, helped to gauge the size and growth of the market. And, like Enron and many others, it didn't see the telecom meltdown coming. McKinsey also helped to set up the finance subsidiary that Enron later portrayed as its growth engine, and also assisted the firm with its commodity risk management operations.

A former Enron senior executive says McKinsey consultants wielded influence throughout the organization. "They were all over the place," he says. "They were sitting with us every step of the way. They thought, 'This thing could be big, and we want credit for it.'" The extent of its work there and its access to senior management exposed the firm to much of Enron's inner workings. Over the years, McKinsey partners Hulme and Suzanne Nimocks had numerous one-on-one discussions with Skilling, according to former Enron executives.

Richard N. Foster, a senior partner, even became an adviser to Enron's board, attending a half-dozen board meetings in the 12 months up until October, 2001. Foster was frequently asked to step out of those meetings while the partners conferred with company lawyers over confidential matters. Competitors privately gloat that the title of Foster's most recent book, *Creative Destruction*, aptly captures what went wrong at Enron. Embarrassingly, the book, published in April, 2001, is filled with glowing references to Enron. "Dick Foster was very happy to see practice that enforced his theories of creative destruction at Enron," says a partner at another consulting firm. "McKinsey seems to have partners who develop academic theories and then run clinical trials on their clients." Foster declined to comment.

Some insiders offer a less benign interpretation of what went wrong at Enron. They don't claim McKinsey did anything illegal but do suggest it might have turned a blind eye to signs of trouble to preserve a lucrative relationship. "The problem for McKinsey with Enron isn't Andersen-type issues," says the former McKinsey consultant who worked at Enron. "Rather, it's 'Could they have seen the organization malfunctioning and spoken up?' The answer is yes. When you have a mega-client, 'This is what the client should hear' is twisted into, 'This is what is going to let us stay at the boardroom level.'"

Gupta won't be drawn into a detailed conversation on Enron. "Our view is not so much to have a public point of view here," he says. "I won't specifically talk about our work at Enron. We're constantly assessing whether we served everybody in the right way. I think we have."

Perhaps so. But many of the intellectual underpinnings of Enron's transformation from pipeline company to trading colossus can be traced directly to McKinsey thinking. Senior partner Lowell Bryan, one of the most influential of the firm's big thinkers today, has written extensively on securitized credit—the process of converting loans or receivables into securities. As far back as 1987, just after McKinsey began consulting for Enron, Bryan was writing that "securitization's potential . . . is great because it removes capital and balance sheets as constraints on growth." It was Bryan, too, who has written and spoken extensively on how capital-intensive companies such as Enron can generate greater value by finding ways to run low-asset businesses—what Skilling referred to as his "asset-light" strategy. Bryan was brought into Enron to convey these ideas to the company's top 100 executives. But he insists his ideas are not to blame. "I never said anything about fraud, accounting, or any of those issues."

If McKinsey has been humbled by the Enron experience, it certainly doesn't show it. When New York headquarters asked all consultants who favorably mentioned Enron in articles whether they wanted their citations taken off McKinsey's Web site, not a single consultant said yes. So all of the nearly 30 separate references to Enron in McKinsey-authored articles remain on the site.

As things began to unravel at Enron, some other important clients were also going off the rails. At Kmart, McKinsey produced work supporting the retailer's decision to sell more groceries in a bid to get shoppers to visit stores. It also was instrumental in creating BlueLight.com, which was intended to be spun off in an initial public offering but never made it to market.

McKinsey began consulting for the retailer in 1994. In the ensuing years, Kmart's competitive position steadily eroded. "That is a long enough time for a firm to know if its advice has impact," says an ex-McKinsey consultant. "But senior partners need to show revenue growth, so they are willing to continue to work with clients even if they feel there is no light at the end of the tunnel." McKinsey ended its relationship in 2000 after disagreeing with new CEO Charles Conaway, who pursued a disastrous price war against Wal-Mart. Still, McKinsey's involvement through the mid- to late 1990s, when Kmart swiftly and steadily lost ground to Wal-Mart, did not serve either client or consultant well.

At Swissair Group, McKinsey advised a major shift in strategy that led the once highly regarded airline to spend nearly $2 billion buying stakes in many small and troubled European airlines. The idea was for Swissair to expand into aviation services, providing everything from maintenance to food for other airlines as a way to increase revenues and profits. The strategy backfired, causing massive losses and a bankruptcy filing last October. McKinsey maintains it can't be held responsible for the outcome because it wasn't involved in the implementation of the strategy. At Global Crossing Ltd., McKinsey says its work was limited to only three projects, two of which involved information-technology outsourcing, so it cannot be blamed for the telecom provider's implosion.

The Internet boom posed an especially difficult challenge for McKinsey. The blanket assumption was that the rules of the game were changing, and many McKinseyites saw their former MBA classmates emerge overnight as multimillion-dollar entrepreneurial celebrities. Inside the firm, Gupta was faced with all kinds of new pressures: whether McKinsey should start a venture-capital fund, or go public itself, or start its own dot-com ventures as offshoots of the firm's consulting business; whether to accept equity instead of cash for an assignment with a startup. The partnership declined to sell shares, as Goldman Sachs had done, but in other important ways it veered from the course it had long followed.

One of the most noticeable changes was a drift away from its longstanding policy of not linking its fees to client performance. Bower believed alternative fee arrangements could tempt consultants to focus on the wrong things. During the past 18 months, McKinsey has been structuring dozens of deals with blue-chip companies that call for the payment of an assignment-ending bonus if a client is satisfied with the results. In the past three years, it also began accepting payment in stock from approximately 150 upstart companies, though McKinsey points out that this is a small percentage of its 12,000 engagements in that time. Gupta says the change allowed the firm to serve smaller, innovative companies that didn't have the cash to pay McKinsey's standard fees of $275,000 to $350,000 a month. The equity was then sunk into a blind trust and liquidated as soon as possible into a profit pool for its partners. In another case, that of Spain's Telefónica, it added a clause in its contract giving it a cash kicker based on the rising stock price of an Internet offshoot McKinsey was advising. The firm collected a $6.8 million bonus.

Yet even these concessions to the bonanza mentality during the boom's height didn't prevent defections. Many McKinsey consultants left for dot-com startups with names like Pet Quarters, Cyber Dialogue, Virtual Communities, and CarsDirect.com, many of which are now relegated to the junk heap of irrational exuberance. Across the firm, attrition rose only slightly during the boom, to over 22% a year in 1999 and 2000 from more typical levels of 18%. But some of the best people left, and some offices were hit hard by the exodus. In San Francisco, where McKinsey employs 150 professionals, a full third of the staff departed for other opportunities in 1999. "There was a whole group of people in the bubble who lost their way," says Larry Mendonca, the McKinsey partner who manages the San Francisco office. "They were trying to get their share of the bubble."

McKinsey got its share, of course. In its quest for revenue growth, it pursued a whole new class of clientele. Demand for consulting soared from both startups and large corporate clients, many of which had grown fearful that they were falling behind the Internet curve. During the peak two years of the dot-com boom, McKinsey alone did more than 1,000 e-commerce assignments, even as partners internally debated the true impact of the Net on clients. "I was in the room saying, 'You're smoking dope here on this dot-com stuff,'" recalls Roger Kline, a longtime McKinsey partner who oversees the financial-services practice.

But the firm even set up "accelerators," or facilities, to help entrepreneurs launch new dot-coms with direct McKinsey help. "Maybe we should have been a little more circumspect than we were," concedes Gupta. "But I don't think we made any big errors or excesses."

Not surprisingly, some of McKinsey's dot-com clients fared little better than Pets.com Inc. EB2B Commerce Inc., which engaged McKinsey in early 2000 to help it develop a strategy after a merger, was recently warned by Nasdaq that its stock could be delisted. The company's shares have plummeted to 15¢ from $190 when McKinsey started working with it. Another high-tech client, Applied Digital Solutions Inc., which McKinsey helped in exchange for equity, is in the midst of a meltdown, with first-quarter losses of $17 million. Applied Digital's auditors resigned the account in May after an accounting dispute with the company, which describes itself as a developer of "life-enhancing personal safeguard technologies." Shares of Applied Digital now trade for 57¢.

To be sure, McKinsey's core blue-chip clients, which range from General Motors Corp. to Johnson & Johnson, remain the firm's true bread and butter—partly because only those big companies can afford its fees. "McKinsey is expensive," says Ralph Larsen, former CEO of J&J. "But what they provide is a fresh look at our thinking and a certain detachment. We use them carefully for selected projects, things of great significance, and they have been valuable to us."

In managing the firm through the boom and the bust, Gupta now finds himself caught in a classic supply-demand squeeze, the sort of management dilemma for which a client would turn to McKinsey for advice: He hired too many people just as demand began to plummet. In an average year, McKinsey will offer consulting jobs to 3,100 MBAs and professionals in the expectation of getting roughly 2,000 acceptances. In 2000, however, more than 2,700 people accepted offers to join the firm. They apparently knew what McKinsey didn't yet get: The boom was over. By the following year, with the bubble clearly burst, the firm's attrition rate fell to only 5%. Suddenly, just as demand for business started falling off, McKinsey had too many consultants on the payroll, with fewer leaving for other opportunities. "We honored every offer and didn't push people out," says Gupta, "and we had no professional layoffs other than our traditional up-or-out stuff."

As McKinsey begins its months-long process early next year to elect a new managing partner, the firm will likely toast Gupta as the man who led the firm to new growth records in new markets around the world. "In every generation, there are issues that come up that define the firm," he says. "We've had our share in the last decade. But I feel very proud of where we've come out." The question for his successor is whether he expanded the firm at the cost of the culture and values that made McKinsey tower above its peers.

Source: John A. Byrne, "Inside McKinsey" *BusinessWeek*, July 8, 2002, 66–76.

Chapter 3

Markets and Competitive Space

Markets are increasingly complex, turbulent, and interrelated, creating challenges for managers in understanding market structure and identifying opportunities for growth. Consider, for example, the pervasive impact of digital technology on computer, telecommunications, photography, and office equipment markets and competitive space. Rapid technological change, Internet access, global competition, and the diversity of buyers' preferences in many markets require continuous monitoring to identify promising business opportunities, determine if new technologies are disruptive, assess the shifting requirements of buyers, evaluate changes in competitive positioning, and guide managers' decisions about which buyers to target and how to position brands to appeal to targeted buyers. A broad view of the market is important, even when management's interest centers on one or a few market segments within a particular market. Understanding the scope and structure of the entire market is necessary to develop strategy and anticipate market changes and competitive threats. Understanding markets and how they are likely to change in the future are vital inputs to market-driven strategies.

There is perhaps no better example of the importance of understanding markets and developing a vision of how they are likely to change in the future than the market for cell phones. (See accompanying Samsung Electronics phone advertisement). This market is only 20 years old, yet is expected to dominate U.S. communications by 2005. In 2003 in the United States there were 147 million wireless phones compared to 187 million traditional phone lines.[1] The rapid changes in the market are cannibalizing the core businesses of local telecommunications providers, negatively impacting their revenues and profits. Companies that are not offering wireless services are confronted with even more severe challenges. Also on the horizon is the expanding threat of Internet phone services. The value migration from traditional to cell phones is also a significant threat to telecom-equipment producers such as Lucent Technologies and Nortel Networks. Consolidation of suppliers is likely in their efforts to cope with the changes in the market and competitive space. Not surprisingly, wireless suppliers' revenues and profits are growing rapidly. An analysis of expected market changes is described in the Strategy Feature.

Strategy Feature

A Wireless World

Phone Companies

As traffic shifts to wireless, traditional carriers such as Verizon and SBC will see profit margins fall from 39% in 2001 to an average of 35% this year.

Equipment Makers

Prices for wireless gear are falling fast because penny-pinching phone companies are putting the squeeze on gear makers. Consolidation looms.

Regulators

The move from regulated phones to unregulated wireless means sweeping changes. Governments everywhere will have less influence in telecom.

Consumers

Lower prices, better gadgets, and a wave of innovative new services such as gambling and multimedia messaging will make consumers the clear winners in the wireless world.

Businesses

Mobile Net access is transforming industries. Productivity, for example, gets a boost since salespeople are able to spend more time with customers.

Source: "A Wireless World," *BusinessWeek*, October 27, 2003, 111.

The mobile phone illustration highlights several important issues concerning markets. The changes described show how competitive threats may develop from new business designs (wireless providers). Importantly, the rapid growth of cell phones points to the importance of market vision in assessing the nature and scope of new competitive threats and guiding strategic initiatives to counter the threats.

The chapter begins with a discussion of how markets and strategies are interrelated, followed by an approach for determining product-market scope and structure. Next, we look at how buyers are described and analyzed, and then we discuss competitor analysis. Guidelines follow for developing a strategic vision about the scope and composition of markets in the future. Finally, we consider how to estimate market size. Additional market forecasting guidelines are provided in Appendix 3A.

Markets and Strategies

Market knowledge is essential in guiding business and marketing strategies. First, we look at how markets impact strategy. Next, we examine the concept of value migration, and how it affects market opportunities. The section is concluded with a discussion of developing a shared vision about how the market is expected to change in the future.

Markets and Strategies Are Interlinked

Market changes often require altering business and marketing strategies. Managers that do not understand their markets, and how they will change in the future, may find their strategies inadequate as buyers' value requirements change and new products become available that better satisfy buyers' requirements. Many forces are causing the transformation of industries and are changing the structure of markets and nature of competition. The drivers of change include deregulation, global excess capacity, global competition, mergers and acquisitions, new technologies, changing customer expectations, disintermediation, demographic shifts, and changing life and work styles.[2] These influences create both market opportunities and threats by altering the nature and scope of markets and competitive space. Market-driven companies proactively alter their strategies to provide superior value to existing and new customers. For example, PepsiCo shows impressive performance in understanding and catering to changing tastes in the beverage and snacks market, rather than trying to change them. The company faces the facts about market change and adapts products to them. To capitalize on the growing market for New Age herbally enhanced beverages, PepsiCo acquired SoBe Beverages in 2001, and extended the brand into an energy drink for the school-age market—SoBe No Fear—and SoBe Fuerte aimed at the Hispanic market. Sabritas chips were brought in from PepsiCo's Mexican subsidiary targeting the foreign-born segment of the 46 million strong U.S. Hispanic market. Sabritas U.S. sales will exceed $100 million in 2004. The company defines its mission as serving the consumer, not protecting its existing brands.[3]

Digital photography has had a major impact on the market for cameras and film. Digital technology pushed Polaroid Corp. into bankruptcy. Kodak is making major shifts in business and marketing strategies to cope with unexpected large declines in film sales by trying to reinvent itself for the Digital Age.[4] Kodak's management announced new investments of $3 billion for expanded digital initiatives in 2003. Drops of 10 to 12 percent in film sales were expected annually through 2006. Some industry observers expected even more rapid sales declines. Profit margins are much lower for digital products. Kodak's managers recognized the digital threat, but their vision about the future did not anticipate the speed and magnitude of digital market entry. Digital technology requires major changes in the business and marketing strategies of Fuji, Kodak, and other camera and film companies. The rapid growth of camera phone sales has further compounded the scope and complexity of the market.

Value Migration

Value migration describes the process of customers shifting their purchases away from the products generated by outmoded business designs to new ones that offer superior value.[5] Examples include value migration from conventional typewriters to word processing and computers, reference books to CD-ROM format, and full-service airlines to discount airlines. Anticipating value migration threats is an essential aspect of market-driven strategy. Importantly, these threats may emerge from disruptive technologies that managers of existing products do not consider to be relevant competitive threats.

Value migration may affect a product category, a company, or an entire industry. Forecasting the exact nature, scope, and timing of migration may be difficult but is, nonetheless, essential. For example, Kodak's management did not forecast the rapid impact of digital photography on the imaging market. Market knowledge is a key input to assessing migration and disruptive technology trends. Value migration points to the close relationship between strategies and markets, and the need to define and understand the market and competitive arena. The value migration concept also highlights the importance of constant organizational learning and implementing strategy changes to proactively respond to value migration situations.

For-profit colleges are an interesting example of value migration from traditional universities to publicly traded businesses that have displayed explosive growth during the last decade.[6] These organizations comprise a new dimension in higher education. The top ten for-profit colleges have more than half a million students. The typical for-profit tuition charges are about $11,000 a year, midway between the average private and public university. The for-profits target age 20–30 working adults, and nearly one-half are minorities. Some 10 percent of Master of Business Administration students are enrolled in for-profit programs. For-profit students comprise over 40 percent of the online-degree market. Apollo Group/University of Phoenix has an enrollment of 200,000 in regular programs and another 80,000 pursuing online degrees.

Product-Market Scope and Structure

The activities involved in gaining an understanding of markets are shown in Exhibit 3.1. The first step is to define the market's boundaries and describe its structure. Markets can be defined in many different ways, and they are constantly changing as illustrated by the telecommunications, photography, and higher education examples. We look at how buyers' needs coupled with product benefits help to define product-markets, and we discuss several considerations in forming product-markets. Steps 2–4 of Exhibit 3.1 are discussed in following sections.

EXHIBIT 3.1
Gaining an Understanding of Markets

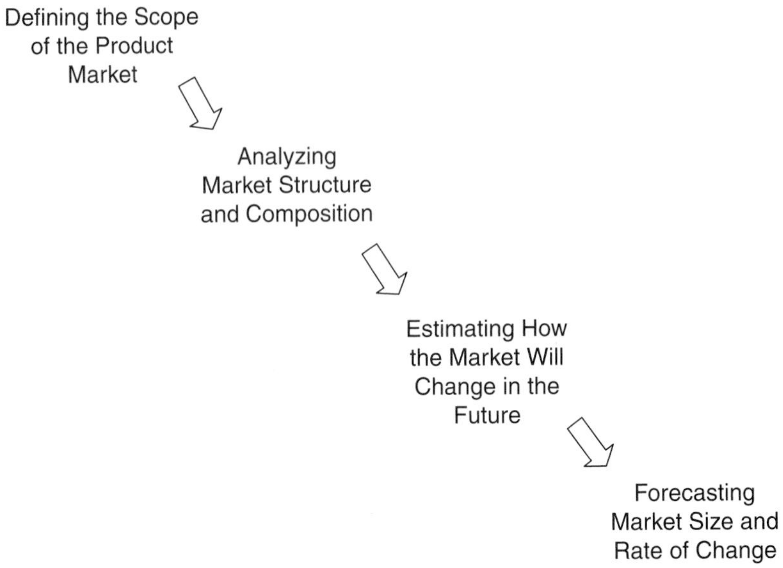

Defining the Scope of the Product Market
↓
Analyzing Market Structure and Composition
↓
Estimating How the Market Will Change in the Future
↓
Forecasting Market Size and Rate of Change

Matching Needs with Product Benefits

The term *product-market* recognizes that markets exist only when there are buyers with needs who have the ability to purchase goods and services (products) and products are available to satisfy the needs. There is a compelling argument that competitive strength comes from putting customer needs at the center of a company's operations, and that this perspective should guide management thinking about markets. For example, Progressive Insurance shows remarkable sales growth and shareholder value creation by its focus on the most important needs of its customers. The Innovation Feature describes how the company has changed its operations and how it meets customer needs.

Intuitively, it is easy to grasp the concept of a product-market, although there are differences in how managers define the term. Markets are comprised of groups of people who have the *ability* and *willingness* to buy something because they have a need for it.[7] The ability to buy and willingness to buy indicate that there is a demand for a particular product or service. People with needs and wants buy the benefits provided by a good or service to satisfy either a household or an organizational use situation. A product-market matches people with needs—needs that lead to a demand for a good or service—to the product benefits that satisfy those needs. Unless the product benefits are available, there is no market—only people with needs. Likewise, there must be people who have a use situation that can be satisfied by the product. Thus, a product-market combines the benefits of a product with the needs that lead people to express a demand for that product. Therefore, markets are defined in terms of needs substitutability among different products and brands and by the different ways in which people choose to satisfy their needs. "A product-market is the set of products judged to be substitutes within those usage situations in which similar patterns of benefits are sought by groups of customers."[8] The influence of competing brands becomes stronger, the closer the substitutability and the more direct the competition. The Ford Taurus competes directly with the Toyota Camry, whereas in a less direct yet relevant way, other major purchases (e.g., vacation travel) compete with automobile expenditures due to the consumer's budget constraints.

As an example, a financial services product-market for short-term investments may include money market accounts, mutual funds, U.S. Treasury bills, bank certificates of deposit, and other

Innovation Feature

Progressive Insurance: Customer Needs at the Center of Strategy

- In the period 1994 to 2004, Progressive Insurance increased sales from $1.3 billion to $9.5 billion, and ranks high in the *BusinessWeek* Top 50 U.S. companies for shareholder value creation.
- The company invents new ways of providing services to save customers time, money, and irritation, while often lowering costs at the same time.
- Loss adjusters are sent to the road accidents rather than working at the head office, and they have the power to write checks on the spot.
- Progressive reduced the time needed to see a damaged automobile from seven days to nine hours.
- Policyholders' cars are repaired quicker, and the focus on this central customer need has won much automobile insurance business for Progressive.
- These initiatives also enable Progressive to reduce its own costs—the cost of storing a damaged automobile for a day is $28, about the same as the profit from a six-month policy.

Source: Adapted from Adrian Mitchell, "Heart of the Matter," *The Marketer*, June 12, 2004, 14.

short-term investment alternatives. If one type of product is a substitute for another, then both should be included in the product-market.

By determining how a firm's specific product or brand is positioned within the product-market, management can monitor and evaluate changes in the product-market to decide whether alternate targeting and positioning strategies and product offerings are needed. In mapping the product-market, it is essential to establish boundaries that are broad enough to contain all of the relevant product categories that are competing for the same buyer needs.

Determining Product-Market Boundaries and Structure

Product-market boundaries and structure provide managers with important information for developing business and marketing strategies, and alert management to new competition. Considering only a company's brands and their direct competitors may mask potential competitive threats or opportunities.

Product-Market Structure. A company's brands compete with other companies' brands in generic, product-type, and product-variant product-markets. The **generic product-market** includes a broad group of products that satisfy a general, yet similar, need. For example, several classes or types of products can be combined to form the generic product-market for kitchen appliances. The starting point in product-market definition is to determine the particular need or want that a group of products satisfies, such as performing kitchen functions. Since people with a similar need may not satisfy it in the same manner, generic product-markets are often heterogeneous, containing different end user groups and several types of related products (e.g., kitchen appliances).

The **product-type product-market** includes all brands of a particular product type or class, such as ovens. The product-type is a product category or product classification that offers a specific set of benefits intended to satisfy a customer's need or want in a specific way. Differences in the products within a product-type (class) product-market may exist, creating **product-variants.**[9] For example, electric, gas, and microwave ovens all provide heating functions but employ different technologies.

Guidelines for Definition. In determining the scope of the product-market, it is helpful to identify (1) the basis for identifying buyers in the product-market of interest (geographical area and buyer characteristics such as age group), (2) the market size and characteristics, and (3) the brand and/or product categories competing for the needs and wants of the buyers included in the product-market.

EXHIBIT 3.2
Determining the Structure of a Product-Market

Start with the generic need satisfied by the product category of interest to management.

Identify the product categories (types) that can satisfy the generic need.

Identify the specific product-markets within the generic product-market.

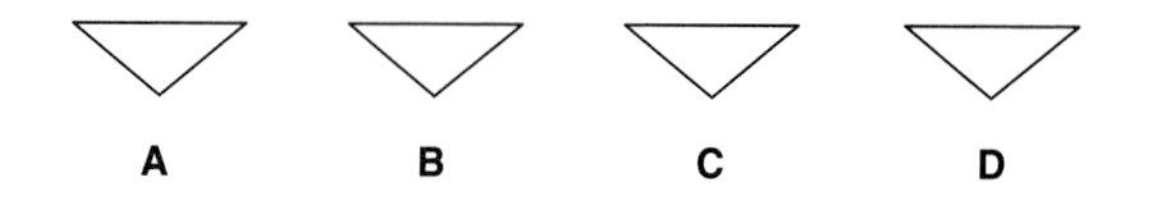

The scope and structure (composition) of a product-market can be determined by following the steps shown in Exhibit 3.2. We consider how this process can be used to define the structure in the kitchen appliance product-market. Suppose top management of a kitchen appliance firm wants to expand its mix of products. The company's present line of laundry and dishwashing products meets a generic need for the kitchen functions of cleaning. Other kitchen use situations include heating and cooling of foods. In this example the generic need is performing various kitchen functions. The products that provide kitchen functions are ways of satisfying the generic need. The breakout of products into specific product-markets (e.g., A, B, C, and D) would include equipment for washing and drying clothing, appliances for cooling food, cooking appliances, and dishwashers. The buyers in various specific product-markets and the different brands competing in these product-markets can be analyzed. The process of mapping the product-market structure begins by identifying the generic need (function) satisfied by the product of interest to management. Need identification is the basis for selecting the products that fit into the product market.

A simplified example of the product-market structure that includes the fast-food market is shown in Exhibit 3.3. A fast-food restaurant chain such as McDonald's should consider more than its regular customers and direct competitors in its market opportunity analysis. The consumption need being satisfied is fast and convenient preparation of food. The buyer has several ways of meeting the need, such as purchasing fast foods, microwave preparation in the home, patronizing supermarket delis, buying prepared foods in convenience stores, and ordering takeouts from traditional restaurants. The relevant competitive space includes all of these fast-food sources. It is essential to analyze market behavior and trends in the product-markets shown in Exhibit 3.3. Competition may come from any of the alternative services.

Forming Product-Markets

The factors that influence how product-market boundaries are determined include the purpose for analyzing the product-market, the rate of changes in market composition over time, and the extent of market complexity.

Purpose of Analysis. If management is deciding whether or not to exit from a business, primary emphasis may be on financial performance and competitive position. Detailed analysis of the product-market may not be necessary. In contrast, if the objective is finding one or more attractive market segments to target in the product-market, a much more penetrating analysis is necessary. When different products satisfy the same need, the product-market boundaries should contain all relevant products and brands. For example, the photography product-market should include digital cameras,

EXHIBIT 3.3
Illustrative Fast-Food Product-Market Structure

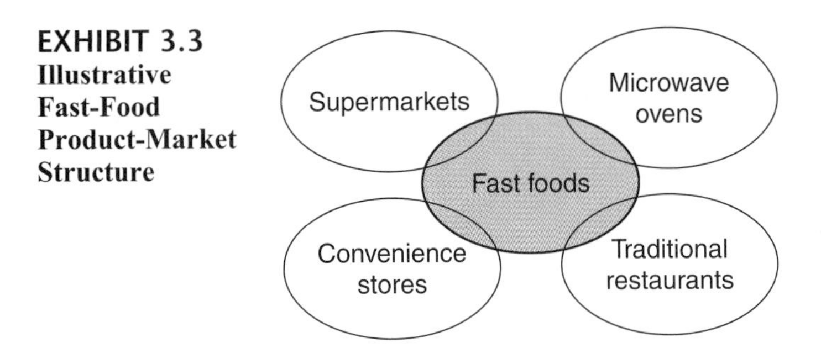

other equipment, and services, and conventional cameras, film, and services. Product-market boundaries should be determined in a manner that will be of strategic value, allowing management to capitalize on existing and potential opportunities and to avoid possible threats.

Changing Composition of Markets. Product-market composition may change as new technologies become available and new competition emerges. New technologies offer buyers different ways of meeting their needs. For example, fax technology gave people in need of overnight letter delivery an alternative way to transmit the information. The entry into the market by new competitors also alters market composition. Importantly, a focus by management on existing markets may provide an incomplete strategic perspective.[10]

Industry classifications often do not clearly define product-market boundaries. For example, people may meet their needs for food with products from several industries as shown in Exhibit 3.3. Industry-based definitions do not include alternative ways of meeting needs. Industry classifications typically have a product supply rather than a customer demand orientation. Of course, since industry associations, trade publications, and government agencies generate a lot of information about products and markets, information from these sources should be included in market analysis. However, market analysis activities should not be constrained by industry boundaries.

Extent of Market Complexity. Three characteristics of markets capture a large portion of the variation in their complexity: (1) the *functions* or uses of the product required by the customer, (2) the *technology* contained in the product to provide the desired function, and (3) the different *customer segments* using the product to perform a particular function.[11]

Customer function considers what the good or service does. It is the benefit provided to the customer. Thus, the function provides the capability that satisfies the value requirements of the customer. Functions consider the types of use situations each user encounters.[12] In the case of the personal computer, the function performed may be entertainment for the household, e-mail transmission, Internet purchasing, or various business functions.

Different *technologies* may satisfy the use situation of the customer. Steel and aluminum materials meet a similar need in various use situations. The technology consists of the materials and designs incorporated into products. In the case of a service, technology relates to how the service is rendered. Voice calls can be sent via the Internet, traditional phone lines, and wireless phones.

Customer segment recognizes the diversity of the needs of customers in a particular product-market such as automobiles. A specific brand and model won't satisfy all buyers' needs and wants. Two broad market segments for automobile use are households and organizations. These classifications can be further divided into more specific customer segments, such as preferences for European-style luxury sedans, sport-utility vehicles, and sports cars.

It is helpful to focus on the consumer (or organizational) end user of the product when defining the market, since the end user drives demand for the product. When the end users' needs and wants change, the market changes. Even though a manufacturer considers the distributor to which its products are sold to be the customer, the market is really defined by the consumer and organizational end users who purchase the product for consumption.

EXHIBIT 3.4
Illustrative Product-Market Structure

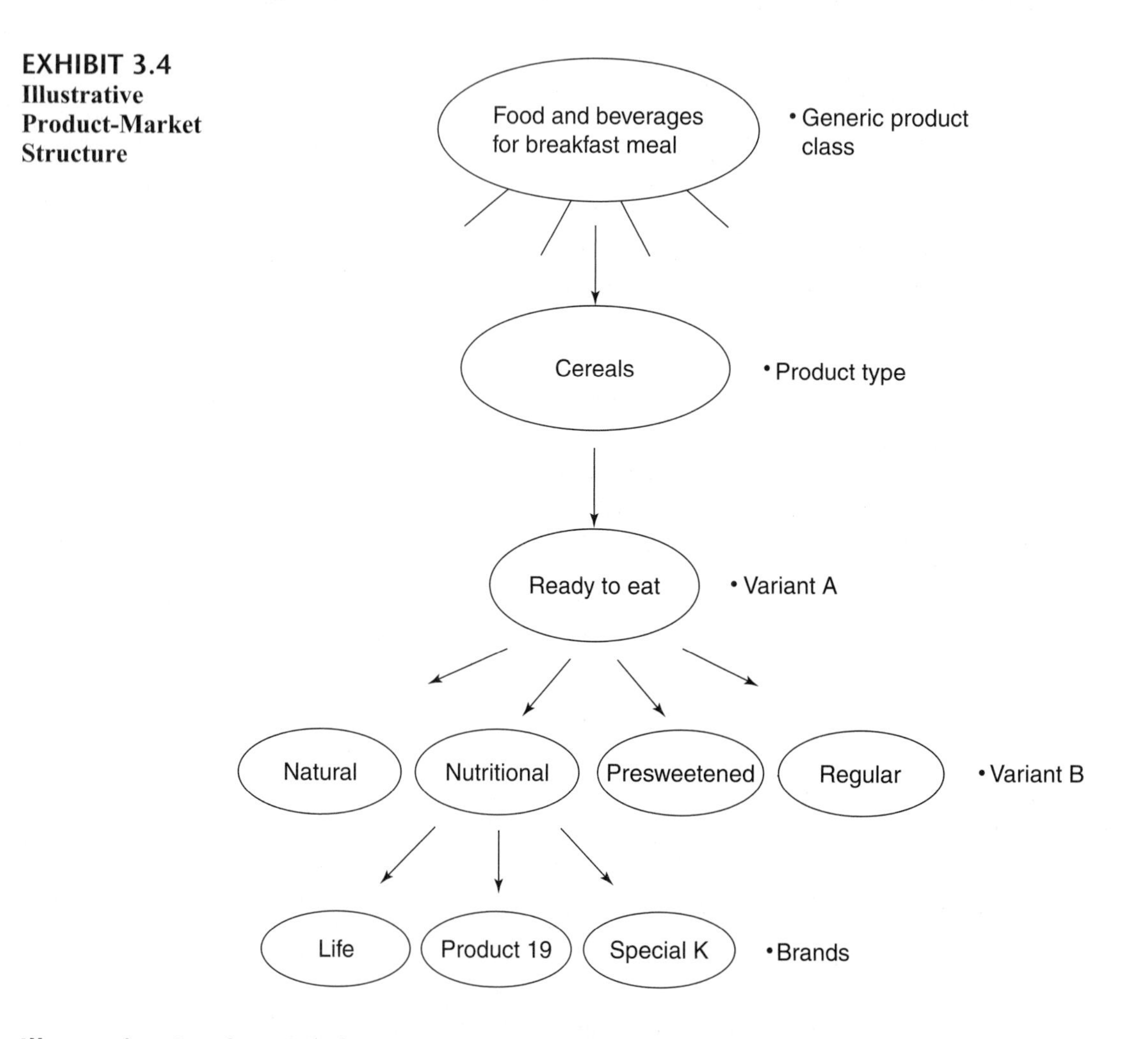

Illustrative Product-Market Structure

Suppose you are a brand manager for a cereal producer. You know that brands like Life, Product 19, and Special K compete for sales to people who want nutritional benefits from cereal. Nonetheless, our earlier discussion highlights the value of looking at a more complete picture of how competing brands like Life, Product 19, and Special K also may experience competition from other ways of meeting the needs satisfied by these brands. For example, a person may decide to eat a Kellogg's Nutri-Grain cereal bar instead of a bowl of cereal, and the consumer may want to vary the type of cereal, such as eating a natural or regular type of cereal. Because of the different product types and variants competing for the same needs and wants, the cereal brand manager needs to develop a picture of the product-market structure within which her/his brand is positioned. Exhibit 3.4 describes an illustrative product-market structure for cereals. The diagram can be expanded to portray other relevant product types (e.g., breakfast bars) in the generic product-market for food and beverages.

Describing and Analyzing End Users

After determining the product-market structure it is useful to develop profiles of end user buyers for the generic, product-type, and product-variant levels of the product-market. Buyers are identified, described, their value requirements indicated, and external environmental influences (e.g., interest

Global Feature

Profile of the Russian Middle Class

Class		Lower Middle	Middle Middle	Upper Middle
Monthly Income	Moscow	$800 to $1,500	$1,500 to $3,500	$3,500 to $7,000
	Provinces	$300 to $550	$550 to $1,500	$1,500 to $3,500
Job		Receptionist, driver, security guard	Computer programmer, junior manager, accountant	Senior manager, small-business owner, investment banker
Car		Late-model Russian-made Lada	New Toyota Corolla	New Opel Cadet or used BMW
Dacha		Homemade wooden cottage, outdoor sauna	Contractor-constructed, indoor plumbing and heating	Stone and brick walls, terrace, indoor garage
Summer Vacation		Resort towns on Black Sea, in Soviet-style hotel	Turkish seashore resort of Antalia	Majorca on Spanish Riviera

Source: "Russia's Middle Class," *BusinessWeek*, October 16, 2000, 79.

rate trends) determined. Analysis of the buyers in the market segments within a product-market is considered in Chapter 4.

Identifying and Describing Buyers

Characteristics such as family size, age, income, geographical location, sex, and occupation are often useful in identifying buyers in consumer markets. Illustrative factors used to identify end users in organizational markets include type of industry, company size, location, and types of products. Many published sources of information are available for use in identifying and describing customers. Examples include U.S. Census data, trade association publications, and studies by advertising media (TV, radio, magazines). When experience and existing information are not adequate in determining buyers, research studies may be necessary to identify and describe customers and prospects.

An interesting profile of the Russian middle class and illustrative product preferences are provided in the Global Feature, divided into three income categories:[13] The estimates assume a family of two parents and one child. The size of the Russian middle class is estimated to range from 8 to 20 percent of that country's 145 million people. This population group emerged from the economic crisis Russia experienced in 1998, making size estimation difficult. The Russian population information is useful in identifying and describing buyers where income is a relevant predictor of purchases of goods and services such as automobiles and vacation services.

How Buyers Make Choices

Often, simply describing buyers does not provide enough information to guide targeting and positioning decisions. We also need to try to find out *why* people buy products and specific product brands. In considering how customers decide what to buy, it is useful to analyze how they move through the sequence of steps leading to a decision to purchase a particular brand. Buyers normally follow a decision process. They begin by recognizing a need (problem recognition); next, they seek information; then, they identify and evaluate alternative products; and finally, they purchase a brand. Of course, the length and complexity of this process vary by product and purchasing situation. Decisions for frequently purchased products and for which a buyer has past experience tend to be routine. One part of studying buyer decision processes is finding out

EXHIBIT 3.5
Comparing the Stages in Consumer and Organizational Purchases

Source: Eric N. Berkowitz, Roger A. Kerin, Steven W. Hartley, and William Rudelius, *Marketing*, 5th ed. (Chicago: Richard D. Irwin, 1997), 192. Copyright © The McGraw-Hill Companies. Used with permission.

Stage in the Buying Decision Process	Consumer Purchase: CD Player for a Student	Organizational Purchase: Headphones for a CD Player
Problem recognition	Student doesn't like the sound of the stereo system now owned and desires a CD player.	Marketing research and sales departments observe that competitors are including headphones on their models. The firm decides to include headphones on its own new models, which will be purchased from an outside supplier.
Information search	Student uses past experience, that of friends, ads, and *Consumer Reports* to collect information and uncover alternatives.	Design and production engineers draft specifications for headphones. The purchasing department identifies suppliers of CD player headphones.
Alternative evaluation	Alternative CD players are evaluated on the basis of important attributes desired in a CD player.	Purchasing and engineering personnel visit suppliers and assess (1) facilities, (2) capacity, (3) quality control, and (4) financial status. They drop any suppliers not satisfactory on these factors.
Purchase decision	A specific brand of CD player is selected, the price is paid, and it is installed in the student's room.	They use (1) quality, (2) price, (3) delivery, and (4) technical capability as key buying criteria to select a supplier. Then they negotiate terms and award a contract.
Postpurchase behavior	Student reevaluates the purchase decision, may return the CD player to the store if it is unsatisfactory, and looks for supportive information to justify the purchase.	They evaluate suppliers by using a formal vendor rating system and notify supplier if phones do not meet its quality standard. If problem is not corrected, they drop the firm as a future supplier.

what criteria people use in making decisions. For example, how important is the brand name of a product in the purchase decision?

Illustrations of the buying decision process stages for a consumer purchase and an organizational purchase are shown in Exhibit 3.5. The consumer purchase involves a CD player, whereas the organizational purchase is for a CD player component from an outside supplier. Both processes move through the major process stages, but the issues and activities are quite different.

Environmental Influences

The final step in building customer profiles is to identify the external factors that influence buyers and thus impact the size and composition of the market over time. These influences include government actions (e.g., tax cut), social change, economic shifts, technology, and other factors that may alter buyers' needs and wants. Typically, these factors are not controlled by the buyer or the

EXHIBIT 3.6
Population Trends for the 50 States in the United States: 1995–2025

Source: U.S. Bureau of the Census, Population Division, PPL-47.

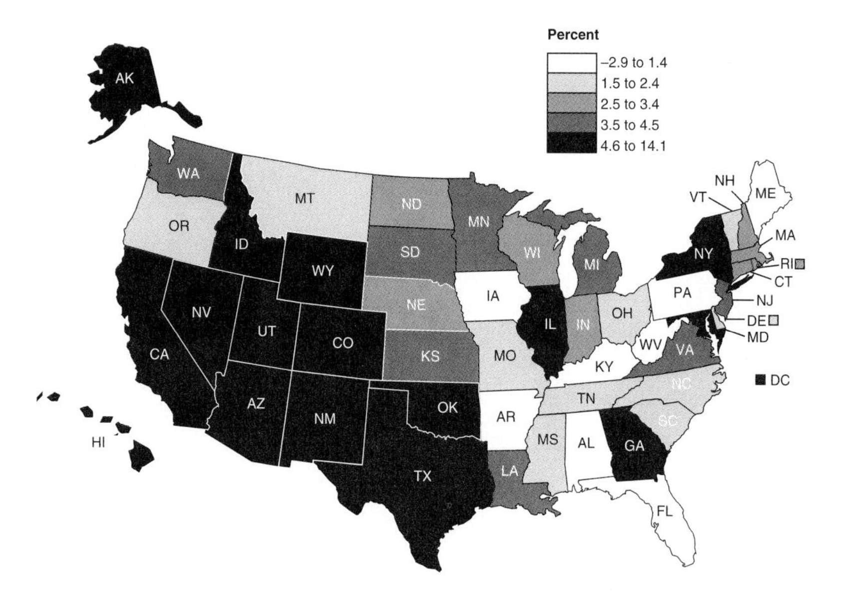

firms that market the product, and substantial changes in environmental influences can have a major impact on customers' purchasing activities. Therefore, it is important to identify the relevant external influences on a product-market and to estimate their future impact. During the past decade various changes in market opportunities occurred as a result of uncontrollable environmental factors. Illustrations include the shifts in population age-group composition, changes in tax laws affecting investments, and variations in interest rates. Consider, for example, the population trends for the 50 states in the United States from 1995 to 2025. Note that some states (Exhibit 3.6) display high growth rates while others are declining in size.

Building Customer Profiles

Describing customers starts with the generic product-market. At this level customer profiles describe the size and general composition of the customer base. For example, the commercial air travel customer profile for a specified geographical area (e.g., South America) would include market size, growth rates, mix of business and pleasure travelers, and other general characteristics. The product-type and variant profiles are more specific about customer characteristics (needs and wants, use situations, activities and interests, opinions, purchase processes and choice criteria, and environmental influences on buying decisions). Normally, product-type analysis considers the organization's product and closely related product types.

In developing marketing strategy, management is concerned with deciding which buyers to target within the product-market of interest, and how to position to each target. The customer profiles help to guide these decisions. The profiles are also useful in deciding how to segment the market. More comprehensive customer analyses are undertaken in market segmentation analysis, which we discuss in Chapter 4.

Analyzing Competition

Competitor analysis considers the companies and brands that compete in the product-market of interest. Analyzing the competition follows the five steps shown in Exhibit 3.7. We begin by determining the competitive arena in which an organization competes and describing the characteristics of the competitive space. Steps 2 and 3 identify, describe, and evaluate the organization's key competitors. Steps 4 and 5 anticipate competitors' future actions and identify potential new competitors that may enter the market.

EXHIBIT 3.7
Analyzing Competition

1. Define the competitive arena for the generic, specific, and variant product-markets.
2. Identify and describe key competitors.
3. Evaluate key competitors.
4. Anticipate actions by competitors.
5. Identify potential competitors.

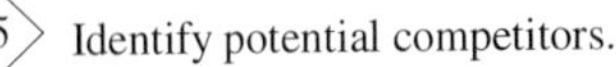

EXHIBIT 3.8
Example of Levels of Competition

Source: Donald R. Lehmann and Russell S. Winer, *Analysis for Marketing Planning,* 4th ed. (Burr Ridge, IL: Richard D. Irwin, 1997), 22. Copyright © The McGraw-Hill Companies. Used with permission.

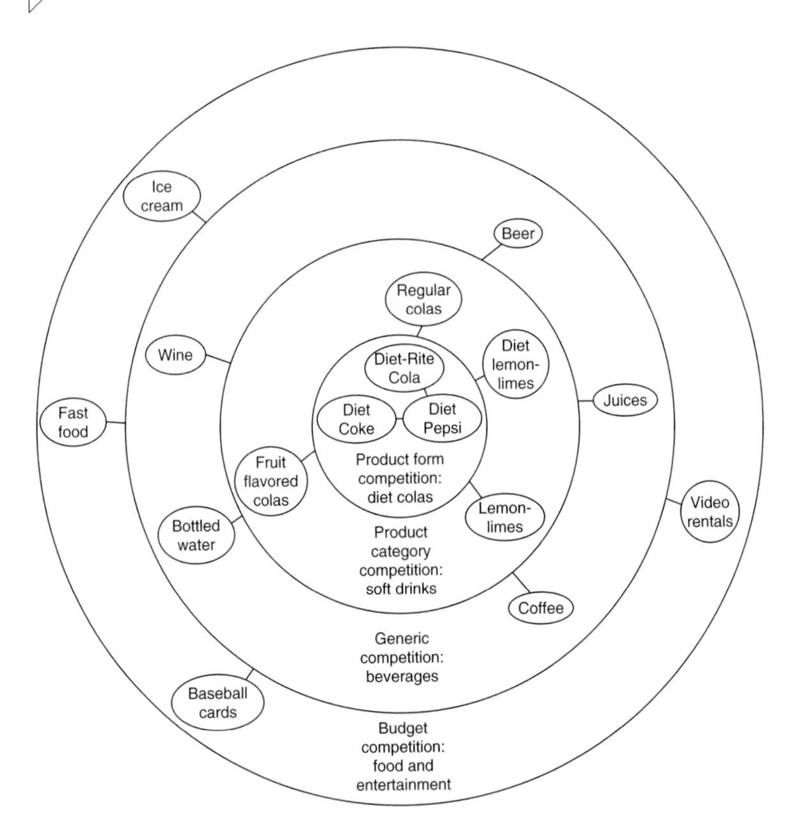

Defining the Competitive Arena

Competition often includes more than the firms that are considered to be direct competitors, like Coke and Pepsi. For example, the different levels of competition for diet colas are shown in Exhibit 3.8. The product-variant is the most direct type of competition. Nevertheless, other product categories of soft drinks also compete for buyers, as do other beverages. A complete understanding of the competitive arena helps to guide strategy design and implementation. Since competition often occurs within specific industries, an examination of industry structure is useful in defining the competitive arena, recognizing that more than one industry may be competing in the same product-market, depending on the complexity of the product-market structure. For example, digital camera competitors include traditional camera and film producers and electronics firms like Hewlett-Packard, Samsung, and Sony.

Industry Analysis. Competitor analysis is conducted from the point of view of a particular firm. For example, a soft drink firm such as Coca-Cola should include other beverage brands in its industry analysis. This analysis looks at two kinds of information: (1) a descriptive profile of the industry, and (2) an analysis of the value-chain (distribution) channels that link together the various organizations in the value-added system from suppliers to end users. Thus, the industry analysis is horizontal and covers similar types of firms (e.g., soft drink producers), whereas the value-chain analysis considers the vertical network of firms that supply materials and/or parts, produce products (and services), and distribute the products to end users.

The industry analysis includes: (1) industry characteristics and trends, such as sales, number of firms, and growth rates; and (2) operating practices of the firms in the industry, including product mix, service provided, barriers to entry, and geographical scope. An interesting example of analysis of business magazine competitors in France is included in the Capital case (6-7) in Exhibits 6 through 11. The Capital case considers the possible launch of a new business magazine.

First, we need to identify the companies that comprise the industry and develop descriptive information on the industry and its members. It is important to examine industry structure beyond domestic market boundaries, since international industry developments often affect regional, national, and international markets. For example, comparison of U.S. market shares from 1984 to 1999 for personal computer (PC) manufacturers is shown in Exhibit 3.9. Included are the Home, Business, and Education markets.[14] U.S. and global PC producers are shown and global producers are included in the "others" category. In 2001, global industry sales growth of PCs began to slow down, whereas handheld devices were experiencing rapid growth.

The industry identification is based on product similarity, location at the same level in the value chain (e.g., manufacturer, distributor, retailer), and geographical scope. The industry analysis considers:

- Industry size, growth, and composition.
- Typical marketing practices.
- Industry changes that are anticipated (e.g., consolidation trends).
- Industry strengths and weaknesses.
- Strategic alliances among competitors.

Analysis of the Value-Added Chain. The study of supplier and distribution channels is important in understanding and serving product-markets. While producers may go directly to their end users, many work with other organizations through distribution channels. The extent of vertical integration by competitor backward (supply) and forward toward end users is also useful information. The types of relationships (collaborative or transactional) in the distribution channel should be identified and evaluated. The extent of outsourcing activities in the value chain is also of interest. Different channels that access end user customers should be included in the channel analysis. For example, the electronic distribution channel initiatives taken by Charles Schwab & Co. to achieve the No. 1 online broker position are described in the Internet Feature. Case 1-2 describes Schwab's strategic challenges in 2002. By looking at the distribution approaches of industry members, we can identify important patterns and trends in serving end users. Value-chain analysis may also uncover new market opportunities that are not served by present channels of distribution. Finally, information from various value-chain levels can help in forecasting end user sales.

The use of outsourcing of manufacturing and other business functions expanded rapidly in the United States and Europe during the last decade. By outsourcing, an organization may gain strategic advantage by focusing on its core competencies, while outsourcing other necessary business functions to independent partners. Thus, analysis of outsourcing activities may be an important aspect of competitor analysis.

EXHIBIT 3.9
Personal Computer Market Shares in the United States for 1984, 1987, and 1999 (based on unit sales)

Source: Peter Burrows, "Apple," *BusinessWeek*, July 31, 2000, 108.

Home Market					
Maker	**1984**	**Maker**	**1987**	**Maker**	**1999**
Packard Bell	32.4%	Packard Bell NEC	23.3%	Compaq	19.0%
Apple	14.7	Compaq	18.8	H-P	16.1
Compaq	11.5	Gateway	11.1	Gateway	15.3
IBM	6.1	IBM	7.0	Emachines	11.0
Gateway	5.5	Acer	5.9	Packard Bell NEC	7.3
		Apple	5.0	Apple	7.1
Others	29.8	Others	28.9	Others	24.2
Business Market					
Maker	**1984**	**Maker**	**1987**	**Maker**	**1999**
Compaq	14.2%	Compaq	15.7%	Dell	22.4%
IBM	10.1	Dell	12.8	Compaq	15.0
Apple	6.4	IBM	9.5	IBM	9.2
Dell	5.9	H-P	8.0	H-P	6.0
Gateway	5.3	Toshiba	5.6	Toshiba	4.7
		Apple	1.4	Apple	1.3
Others	58.1	Others	47.0	Others	41.4
Education Market					
Maker	**1984**	**Maker**	**1987**	**Maker**	**1999**
Apple	47.0%	Apple	27.2%	Dell	21.4%
IBM	8.5	Compaq	13.2	Apple	16.5
Dell	4.3	Dell	10.7	Gateway	13.6
Gateway	3.3	Gateway	7.8	Compaq	9.2
Compaq	3.2	IBM	6.9	IBM	3.8
Others	33.0	Others	34.2	Others	35.5

Competitive Forces. Different competitive forces are present in the value-added chain. The traditional view of competition is expanded by recognizing Michael Porter's five competitive forces that impact industry performance:

1. Rivalry among existing firms.
2. Threat of new entrants.
3. Threat of substitute products.
4. Bargaining power of suppliers.
5. Bargaining power of buyers.[15]

The first force recognizes that active competition among industry members helps determine industry performance, and it is the most direct and intense form of competition. The aggressive competition between Coke and Pepsi is illustrative. Rivalry may occur within a market segment or across an entire product-market. The nature and scope of competition may vary according to the type of industry structure. For example, competition in an emerging industry consists of the market pioneer and a few other early entrants. A mature industry like personal computers includes many firms (Exhibit 3.9).

The second force highlights the possibility of new competitors entering the market. Existing firms may try to discourage new competition by aggressive expansion and other types of market

Internet Feature

How Charles Schwab & Co. Leverages Value-Chain Initiatives

It's a no brainer. We all know that Charles Schwab & Co. gets the Web. It's the No. 1 online broker and a leader in developing products and services for wired investors. With 4.1 million online accounts and a 21 percent share of all Web trades, the game is Schwab's to lose.

So how does it intend to stay ahead? By ensuring that customers get what they want, when they want, and how they want it. In recent months, Schwab has launched a wireless trading service and new online research tools that let customers take investment courses and hear live audio feeds of lectures. It's also building more branch offices and phone centers to complement its online services. By integrating the online and offline worlds, says e-commerce expert David K. Pecaut, president of the business development firm iFormation Group, "Schwab has become the benchmark for others going online."

And how. Some 81 percent of its trades are now done online, *vs.* 36 percent three years ago. That's great for Schwab, since processing online trades costs 80 percent less than offline ones. But the savings go further than that. With customers doing their own trades and research, branch employees are freer to promote higher-margin services. In June, Schwab introduced Portfolio Consultation, which lets customers meet with a Schwab adviser for $400. And a new wireless trading service went live in July.

Schwab has given offline investors more choices, too. It has added 23 branches this year, bringing the total to 363. And it's opening a fifth phone center to add 3,500 operators. That will help Schwab boost service even more, letting it process more phone trades when the still-too-frequent Web site crashes occur. All these offerings are aimed at folks like James Getzoff, a retiree in Marina del Rey, Calif., who frequently visits Schwab's site but just as often phones up the company. When a stock moves, says Getzoff, "I get right onto the site and research that company. If there's not enough there, I call one of the brokers to read me reports."

One hitch: Getzoff could do that now with rivals E*Trade Group or Merrill Lynch & Co., which are mirroring Schwab's multichannel strategy. Imitation may be the sincerest form of flattery, but it also means that Schwab will have to keep mining the Web to hang on to the top spot. *—Louise Lee*

Source: Louise Lee, "When You're No. 1, You Try Harder," *BusinessWeek E.Biz*, September 18, 2000, EB88.

entry barriers. The entry of Wal-Mart into the supermarket business has substantially expanded and intensified the competitive arena in this market.

The third force considers the potential impact of substitutes. New technologies that satisfy the same customer need are important sources of competition. Including alternative technologies in the definition of product-market structure identifies substitute forms of competition. This type of analysis is very important in assessing the impact of disruptive technologies like digital photography.

The fourth force is the power that suppliers may be able to exert on the producers in an industry. For example, the high costs of labor exert major pressures on the commercial airline industry. Companies may pursue vertical integration strategies to reduce the bargaining power of suppliers. Alternatively, collaborative relationships are useful to respond to the needs of both partners.

Finally, buyers may use their purchasing power to influence their suppliers. Wal-Mart, for example, has a strong influence on the suppliers of its many products. Understanding which organizations have power and influence in the value chain provides important insights into the structure of competition. Power may be centered at any level in the channel, though producers and retailers often display strong buying power. However, major component suppliers like Intel may exert substantial influence on value-chain members.

A major consequence of Michael Porter's view of competition is that the competitive arena may be altered as a result of the impact of the five forces on the industry. The five competitive forces also highlight the existence of vertical and horizontal forms of competition. The intensity of vertical competition is related, in part, to the bargaining power of suppliers and buyers. The location (level) of an organization in its value chain and the extent of its control over the channel may have a major influence on the organization's marketing strategy. Indeed, a strategic imperative may be to take action to change the impact of competitive forces on a company, for example through collaboration and alliance, rather than accepting the existing situation.

Key Competitor Analysis

Competitor analysis is conducted for the firms directly competing with each other (e.g., Nike and Reebok) and other companies that management may consider important in strategy analysis (e.g., potential market entrants). The rapid expansion of competitor intelligence activities by many companies in the last decade highlights the high priority executives place on monitoring competitors' activities.[16] Many companies around the world have developed very effective intelligence units. The Futures Group (business intelligence consultants) rates Microsoft as having the most effective corporate intelligence capabilities. Motorola, IBM, P&G, and General Electric also receive high ratings.

We now look at two major aspects of competitor analysis: (1) preparing a descriptive profile for each competitor, and (2) evaluating the competitor's strengths and weaknesses (Steps 2 and 3 of Exhibit 3.7).

Describing and Evaluating the Competitor. A *key competitor* is any organization going after the same market target as the firm conducting the analysis. American, Delta, and United Airlines are key competitors on many U.S. routes and certain international routes. Key competitors are often brands that compete in the same product-market or segment(s) within the market (Coke and Pepsi). Different product types that satisfy the same need or want may also actively compete against each other. Thus, microwave foods may compete with fast-food operators.

Information which is typically included in the competitor profile is shown in Exhibit 3.10. Sources of information include annual reports, industry studies by government and private organizations, business magazines and newspapers, trade publications, reports by financial analysts (e.g., *Value Line Investment Survey*), government reports, standardized data services (e.g., Information Resources, Inc., and Nielsen), databases, suppliers, customers, company personnel, and salespeople. Industry trade publications (e.g., *Aviation Week & Space Technology*) are useful in tracking industry trends, examining current issues, and obtaining special research studies. Direct contact with the research directors of trade publications is an important source of information about the industry and key competitors.

It is important to gain as much knowledge as possible about the background, experience, qualifications, and tenure of key executives for each major competitor. This information includes the executives' performance records, their particular areas of expertise, and the firms where they were previously employed. These analyses may suggest the future strategic initiatives of a key competitor.

Market coverage analysis centers on the market segments targeted by the competitor and the competitor's actual and relative market-share position. Relative market position is measured by comparing the share of the firm against the competitor with the highest market share in the segment. All segments in the product-market that could be targeted by the firm should be included in the competitor evaluation.

The competitor's past performance offers a useful basis for comparing competitors. The customer value proposition offered by the competitor for each segment is important information. This may indicate competitive opportunities as well as a possible threat. The competitor's distinctive capabilities need to be identified and evaluated.

Perceptual maps are useful in analyzing the competitive positioning of competing brands. A perceptual map for the brands competing in the analgesics product-market is shown in Exhibit 3.11. Note the area of vulnerability in the upper-right quadrant. Tylenol dominates the market, but there may be opportunities for new competitor brands. The map indicates how competitors are positioned relative to each other and alerts management to potential competitive threats.

An analysis of each competitor's past sales and financial performance indicates how well the competitor has performed on a historical basis. Competitor ratings are also useful in the comparisons (e.g., *Consumer Reports*). A typical period of analysis is three to five years or longer depending

EXHIBIT 3.10
Describing and Evaluating Key Competitors

- Business scope and objectives
- Management experience, capabilities, and weaknesses
- Market position and trends
- Scope of market coverage
- Market target(s) and customer base
- Positioning strategy for each target
- Distinctive capabilities
- Financial performance (current and historical)

EXHIBIT 3.11
Perceptual Map of Analgesics Brands

Source: William R. Dillon, Thomas J. Madden, and Neil H. Firtle, *Marketing Research in a Marketing Environment*, 3rd ed. (Burr Ridge, IL: Richard D. Irwin, 1994), 36. Copyright © The McGraw-Hill Companies. Used with permission.

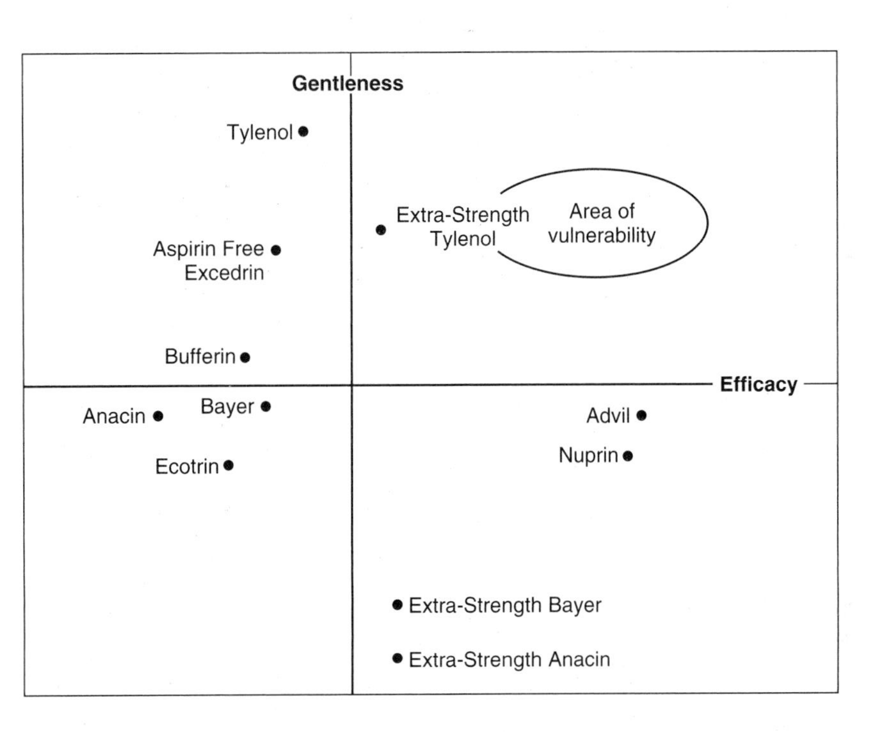

on the rate of change in the market. Performance information may include sales, market share, net profit, net profit margin, cash flow, and debt. Additionally, for specific types of businesses other performance information may be useful. For example, sales-per-square-foot is often used to compare the performance of retail stores. Operating cost per passenger mile is a popular measure for airline performance comparisons.

Assessing how well competitors meet customer value requirements requires finding out what criteria buyers use to rate each supplier. Customer-focused assessments are more useful than relying only on management judgments of value delivery. Measurement methods include customer comparisons of value attributes of the firm versus its competitors, customer surveys, loyalty measures, and the relative market share of end use segments.[17] Preference maps like the one shown in Exhibit 3.11 are useful in comparing the competing brands for attributes that are important determinants of customer satisfaction.

Using the competitor information, we can develop an overall evaluation of the key competitor's current strengths and weaknesses. Additionally, the summary assessment of distinctive capabilities includes information on the competitor's management capabilities and limitations, technical and operating advantages and weaknesses, marketing strategy, and other key strengths and limitations. Since competitors often display different capabilities, it is important to highlight these differences.

Anticipating Competitors' Actions

Steps 4 and 5 in competitor analysis (Exhibit 3.7) consider what each key competitor may do in the future, and identify potential competitors. The information obtained in the previous steps of the analysis should be helpful in estimating future trends, although possible strategy shifts by competitors may occur.

Estimating Competitors' Future Strategies. Competitors' future strategies may continue the directions that they have established in the past, particularly if no major external influences require changing their strategies. Nevertheless, assuming an existing strategy will continue is not wise. Competitors' current actions may signal probable future threats.

An interesting development in the telecommunication market is the rapid growth in the use of Internet calling. The technology is called voice over Internet protocol (VOIP).[18] First introduced in 1995, VOIP experienced start-up problems but by 2003, the technology was a rapidly growing share of home and business markets. Accounting for nearly 3 percent of global phone calls, VOIP has so far had a small impact on the phone market. Nonetheless, industry authorities expect the technology to become a significant competitive threat. VOIP subscribers in the U.S. are estimated to increase to eight times the 2003 level by 2004. Global Internet phone subscribers are expected to exceed 17 million by 2008.

Identifying New Competitors. New competitors may come from four major sources: (1) companies competing in a related product-market; (2) companies with related technologies; (3) companies already targeting similar customer groups with other products; and/or (4) companies competing in other geographical regions with similar products. Market entry by a new competitor is more likely under these conditions:

- High profit margins are being achieved by market incumbents.
- Future growth opportunities in the market are attractive.
- No major market-entry barriers are present.
- Competition is limited to one or a few competitors.
- Gaining an equivalent (or better) competitive advantage over the existing firm(s) serving the market is feasible.

If one or more of these conditions are present in a competitive situation, new competition will probably appear.

Developing a Strategic Vision about the Future

Market development and competitive space may not follow clearly defined and predictable paths. Nonetheless, signals can be identified that are useful in pointing to possible market changes. Answers to the following questions may indicate the possibility of a market changing significantly in the future:

1. Are industry boundaries clear and static? Are customers and competitors identifiable? Or are industry boundaries blurring and evolving?
2. Do firms compete as "distinct entities" or as families of suppliers and end product firms?
3. Is there competition for managing migration paths?
4. Is competition taking place at product line, business, and corporate levels? Do these levels of competition influence each other?
5. Can there be competition between clusters of firms to influence standards and industry evolution?[19]

Phases of Competition

It is useful to distinguish between different phases in the development of competition. In the initial stage, companies compete in identifying product concepts, technology choices, and building competencies.[20] This phase involves experimentation with ideas, and the path to market leadership is not clearly defined. The digital photography market moved through this stage in the early 2000s. Phase 2 may involve partnering of companies with the objective of controlling industry standards, though these firms eventually become competitors. Finally, as the market becomes clearly defined and the competitive space established, the competition concentrates on market share for end products and profits. The personal computer market is currently in this stage.

Anticipating the Future

Increasingly, we find that change and turbulence, rather than stability, characterize many product-markets. Moreover, as discussed above, it is often possible to identify the forces under way that will alter industry structure. Though, these influences are not easily identified and analyzed, the organizations that choose to invest substantial time and effort in anticipating the future create an opportunity for competitive advantage. Fuji appears to have done a better job of anticipating the future of digital photography than has Kodak. Executives in market-driven companies recognize the importance of developing these capabilities.

Hamel and Prahalad offer a compelling blueprint for analyzing the forces of change. While the details of their process cannot be captured in a few pages of discussion; the following questions are illustrative of the information needed to anticipate the future:[21]

- What are the influences (discontinuities) present in the product-market that have the potential to profoundly transform market/competitor structure?
- Investigate each discontinuity in substantial depth.
  - How will the trend impact customers?
  - What is the likely economic impact?
  - How fast is the trend developing?
  - Who is exploiting this trend?
  - Who has the most to gain/lose?
  - What new product opportunities will be created by this discontinuity?
  - How can we learn more about this trend?

Following the blueprint requires looking in depth at the relevant forces of change in a product-market and other markets that are interrelated. Anticipating the future requires searching beyond the existing competitive arena, for influences that promise to impact product-market boundaries. The process requires the involvement of the entire organization, and it demands a substantial amount of time. A company with a market orientation and cross-functional processes should be able to utilize these processes for anticipating the future. Also, it is apparent that developing a vision about the future needs to be an ongoing process.

The forces of change span across many markets, industries, and products. Illustrative situations that call for developing a process for anticipating the future include understanding the interlinkages of traditional telecommunications with wireless phones, cable television, and the Internet. The following observation is illustrative of these challenges:

> It is well accepted that the traditional television and PC will, in the not too distant future, be one product, capable of multiple functions—entertainment, education, or work. Sony, Philips, and Matsushita would like to influence this migration from the consumer electronics perspective. Silicon Graphics, Compaq, and Apple would like this migration to be influenced by the PC industry. Microsoft would like the software producers to be in the driver's seat. Groups of firms starting from different vantage points have different preferred routes toward the same goal, thus, there is competition to influence the migration paths.[22]

Market Size Estimation

An important part of market opportunity analysis is estimating the present and potential size of the market. Market size is usually measured by dollar sales and/or unit sales for a defined product-market and specified time period. Other size measures include the number of buyers, average purchase quantity, and frequency of purchase. Three key measures of market size are: *market potential, sales forecast,* and *market share.*

Market Potential

Market potential is the maximum amount of product sales that can be obtained from a defined product-market during a specified time period. It includes the total opportunity for sales by all firms serving the product-market. Market potential is the upper limit of sales that can be achieved by all firms for a specified product-market. Often, actual industry sales fall somewhat below market potential because the production and distribution systems are unable to completely meet the needs of all buyers who are both *willing* and *able* to purchase the product during the period of interest.

Sales Forecast

The sales forecast indicates the expected sales for a defined product-market during a specified time period. The industry sales forecast is the total volume of sales expected by all firms serving the product market. The sales forecast can be no greater than market potential and typically falls short of potential as discussed above. A forecast can be made for total sales at any product-market level (generic, product type, variant) and for specific subsets of the product-market (e.g., market segments). A company sales forecast can also be made for sales expected by a particular firm.

An interesting forecasting application is estimating the market for commercial aircraft. The lead-time in developing and producing these expensive products requires forecasts several years into the future. Moreover, passenger travel forecasts are needed to guide the aircraft forecasts. The Boeing Commercial Airplanes Group prepares an annual world forecast that includes 20-year air travel and aircraft sales projections. Boeing's 20-year aircraft forecast is shown in Exhibit 3.12. The Boeing *Current Market Outlook* is a very complete analysis of demand for commercial airplanes and aviation support services. It is a useful basic forecasting guide for the various companies serving the commercial aviation market.

Market Share

Company sales divided by the total sales of all firms for a specified product-market determines the market share of a particular firm. Market share may be calculated on the basis of actual sales or forecasted sales. Market share can be used to forecast future company sales and to compare actual market position among competing brands of a product. Market share may vary depending on the use of dollar sales or unit sales due to price differences across competitors.

It is essential in preparing forecasts to specify exactly what is being forecasted (defined product-market), the time period involved, and the geographical area. Otherwise, comparisons of sales and market share with those of competing firms will not be meaningful. Additional forecasting guidelines are provided in the Appendix to Chapter 3.

Evaluating Market Opportunity

Since a company's sales depend, in part, on its marketing plans, forecasts and marketing strategy are closely interrelated. Alternative positioning strategies (product, distribution, price, and promotion) should be evaluated for their estimated effects on sales. Because of the marketing effort/sales relationship, it is important to consider both market potential (opportunity) and planned marketing expenditures in determining the forecast. The impact of different sales forecasts must be evaluated from a total business perspective, since these forecasts affect production planning, human resource needs, and financial requirements.

EXHIBIT 3.12
Commercial Aircraft 20-Year Forecast

Source: Excerpt from *Current Market Outlook 2004* (Seattle: Boeing Commercial Airplanes Group, June 2004), 3, 5.

The market for airplanes is $2.0 trillion over 20 years. World air travel is projected to grow annually at 5.2% and air cargo at approximately 6.2% during the long-run forecast period. The world fleet is expected to more than double, with total fleet size growing to 35,000 by 2023. About 60% of the fleet operating today is projected to still be in operation 20 years from now. In the two decades, 18,600 new airplanes will be needed to fill capacity demand and 6,400 to replace active commercial airplanes.

Type of Aircraft	2003–2022*
Smaller Regional Jets	17%
Single-Aisle	58
Twin-Aisle	21
747 and Larger	4
Total Deliveries 2004–2023	**25,000 Airplanes**

*Percent of total

Forecasting Internet purchasing usage is an interesting forecasting challenge. It was estimated that by 2004 the 200 million Americans who had Web access would spend more than $120 billion.[23] Estimates for business-to-business Web purchases were in excess of $1 trillion a year. The Internet has also become an essential information source for consumers before purchasing from retail stores.

Sales forecasts of target markets are needed so that management can estimate the financial attractiveness of both new and existing market opportunities. The market potential and growth estimates gauge the overall attractiveness of the market. The sales forecast for the company's brand in combination with cost estimates provides a basis for profit projections. The decision to enter a new market or to exit from an existing market depends heavily on financial analyses and projections. Alternate market targets under consideration can be compared using sales and profit projections. Similar projections of key competitors are also useful in evaluating market opportunities.

Summary

Analyzing markets and competition is essential to making sound business and marketing decisions. The uses of product-market analyses are many and varied. An important aspect of market definition and analysis is moving beyond a product focus by incorporating market needs into the analysts' viewpoint.

Business strategies and markets are interrelated, and companies that do not understand their markets and how they are likely to change in the future are at a competitive disadvantage. Effective market sensing is essential in guiding business and marketing strategies. Value migration, the process of customers shifting their purchases to new products that better meet their needs, should be anticipated and counter strategies developed. An essential part of becoming market-oriented is identifying future directions of market change.

This chapter examines the nature and scope of defining product-market structure. By the use of different levels of aggregation (generic, product-type, and product-variant), products and brands are positioned within more aggregate categories, thus helping to better understand customers, product interrelationships, industry structure, distribution approaches, and key competitors. This approach to product-market analysis offers a consistent guide to needed information, regardless of the type of product-market being analyzed. Analyzing market opportunity includes (1) defining product-market boundaries and structure, (2) describing and analyzing end users, (3) conducting industry and value-chain analyses (4) evaluating key competitors, and (5) estimating market size and growth rates.

After the product-market boundaries and structure are determined information on various aspects of the market is collected and examined. First, it is useful to study the people or organizations who are the end users in the product-market at each level (generic, product type, and variant). These market profiles of customers help to evaluate opportunities and guide market targeting and positioning strategies. Next, we identify and analyze the firms that market products and services at each product-market level to aid strategy development. Industry and key competitor analysis considers the firms that compete with the company performing the market opportunity analysis. Thus, industry analysis for a personal computer producer would include the producers that make up the industry. The analysis should also include firms operating at all stages (levels) in the value-added system, such as suppliers, manufacturers, distributors, and retailers.

The next step in analyzing market opportunity is a comprehensive assessment of the major competitors. The key competitor analysis should include both actual and potential competitors that management considers important. Competitor analysis includes: (1) describing the company, (2) evaluating the competitor, and (3) anticipating the future actions of competitors. It is also important to identify possible new competitors. Competitor analysis is an ongoing activity and requires coordinated information collection and analysis.

Developing a strategic vision about the future and how markets are expected to change is an important part of market opportunity analysis. The mounting evidence about markets points to the critical importance of understanding and anticipating changes in markets. In gaining these insights, it is useful to view competition as a three-stage process of experimentation, partnering to set industry standards, and then pursuing market share and profits. Analyzing the forces of change provides a basis for anticipating the future.

The final step in product-market analysis is estimating market potential and forecasting sales. The forecasts often used in product-market analysis include estimates of market potential, sales forecasts of total sales by firms competing in the product-market, and the sales forecast for the firm of interest. This information is needed for various purposes and is prepared for different units of analysis, such as product category, brands, and geographical areas. The forecasting approach and techniques should be matched to the organization's needs. Forecasting methods are discussed in the Appendix.

Internet Applications

A. Airbus and Boeing are the primary competitors in the large commercial aircraft market. Discuss how the information available at Web sites (*www.boeing.com* and *www.airbus.com*) may be useful in competitive analysis. Market size information is available at: *www.boeing.com/commercial/cmo*.

B. Visit Hoover's Web site (*www.hoovers.com*). Investigate the different options for competitive and market analysis provided. How can these online tools best be utilized? What limitations apply?

C. Johnson & Johnson is currently competitive in the surgical stent market (a device inserted surgically as an artery to enable blood flow). The device is described in Case 2.4. Perform an Internet analysis of the stent market indicating past and current unit sales levels and forecasts for 2004–2006.

D. Samsung Electronics is one of the top producers of cell phones. Draw from Internet sources to prepare an analysis of the global cell phone market.

Feature Applications

A. Review the Strategy Feature, "A Wireless World," and describe this industry in terms of the competitive forces we have discussed. Consider the issues to be examined by telecom providers in building a strategic vision for the future.

B. Examine the material in the Internet Feature, "How Charles Schwab & Co. Leverages Value-Chain Initiatives." How does the growth of online trading services change the ways in which a company like Schwab should define its market boundaries and competitive arena?

Questions for Review and Discussion

1. Discuss the important issues that should be considered in defining the product-market for a totally new product.
2. Under what product and market conditions is the end user customer more likely to make an important contribution to product-market definition?
3. What recommendations can you make to the management of a company competing in a rapid growth market to help it identify new competitive threats early enough so that counterstrategies can be developed?
4. There are some dangers in concentrating product-market analysis only on a firm's specific brand and those brands that compete directly with a firm's brand. Discuss.
5. Using the approach to product-market definition and analysis discussed in the chapter, select a brand and describe the generic, product type, and brand product-markets of which the brand is a part.
6. For the brand you selected in Question 5, indicate the kinds of information needed to conduct a complete product-market analysis. Also suggest sources for obtaining each type of information.
7. Select an industry and describe its characteristics, participants, and structure.
8. A competitor analysis of the 7 UP soft drink brand is being conducted. Management plans to position the brand

against its key competitors. Should the competitors consist of only other noncola drinks?

9. Outline an approach to competitor evaluation, assuming you are preparing the analysis for a regional bank holding company.
10. Discuss how a small company (less than $1 million in sales) should analyze its competition.
11. Many popular forecasting techniques draw from past experience and historical data. Discuss some of the more important problems that may occur in using these methods.
12. What are the relevant issues a cross-functional team should consider in developing a strategic vision about the future for the organization's product-market(s)?

Notes

1. This illustration is based on "A Wireless World," *BusinessWeek*, October 27, 2003, 110–111, 114, and 116.
2. C. K. Prahalad and Gary Hamel, "Strategy as a Field of Study and Why Search for a New Paradigm?" *Strategic Management Journal*, Summer 1994, 5–16.
3. Diane Brady, "A Thousand and One Noshes," *BusinessWeek*, June 14, 2004, 44.
4. "No Excuse Not to Succeed," *BusinessWeek*, May 10, 2004, 96 and 98; William C. Symonds, "The Kodak Revolt Is Short-Sighted," *BusinessWeek*, November 3, 2003, 38.
5. Adrian J. Slywotzky, *Value Migration* (Boston: Harvard Business School Press, 1996).
6. "Cash-Low Universities," *BusinessWeek*, November 17, 2003, 71, 72, and 74.
7. This discussion is based upon suggestions provided by Professor Robert B. Woodruff of the University of Tennessee, Knoxville.
8. Rajendra K. Srivastava, Mark I. Alpert, and Allan D. Shocker, "A Customer-Oriented Approach for Determining Market Structures," *Journal of Marketing*, Spring 1984, 32.
9. George S. Day, *Strategic Marketing Planning: The Pursuit of Competitive Advantage* (St. Paul, MN: West Publishing, 1984), 72.
10. C. K. Prahalad, "Weak Signals versus Strong Paradigms," *Journal of Marketing Research*, August 1995, iii–vi.
11. Derek F. Abell, *Defining the Business: The Starting Point of Strategic Planning* (Englewood Cliffs, NV: Prentice Hall, 1980).
12. George S. Day, "Strategic Market Analysis: A Contingency Perspective," Working Paper, University of Toronto, July 1979.
13. "Russia's Middle Class," *BusinessWeek*, October 16, 2000, 79.
14. Peter Burrows, "Apple," *BusinessWeek*, July 31, 2000, 108.
15. Michael E. Porter, *Competitive Advantage* (New York: Free Press, 1985), 5.
16. William Green, "I Spy," *Forbes*, April 20, 1998, 91, 94, 96, 100.
17. George S. Day and Robin Wensley, "Assessing Advantage: A Framework for Diagnosing Competitive Superiority," *Journal of Marketing*, April 1998, 12–16.
18. Peter Grant and Almar Latour, "Circuit Breaker," *The Wall Street Journal*, October 9, 2003, A1 and A9; "Net Phones Start Ringing Up Customers," *BusinessWeek*, December 29, 2003, 45–46; Ken Brown and Almar Latour, "Phone Industry Faces Upheaval As Ways of Calling Change Fast," *The Wall Street Journal*, August 25, 2004, A1 and A8.
19. The following discussion is based on Prahalad, "Weak Signals," vi.
20. Ibid., 101–102.
21. Gary Hamel and C. K. Prahalad, *Competing for the Future* (Boston: Harvard Business School Press, 1994), 101.
22. Prahalad, "Weak Signals," v.
23. "E-Commerce Takes Off," *The Economist*, May 15, 2004, 9.

Appendix **3A**

Forecasting Guidelines

The steps in developing sales forecasts consist of (1) defining the forecasting problem, (2) identifying appropriate forecasting techniques, (3) evaluating and choosing a technique, and (4) implementing the forecasting system. A brief review of each step indicates important issues and considerations.[1]

Defining the Forecasting Problem

The requirements the forecasting method should satisfy, and the output required must be decided. Illustrative requirements include the time horizon, the level of accuracy desired, the uses to be made of the forecast results, and the degree of disaggregation (nation, state, local), including product/market detail, units of measurement, and time increments to be covered.

Identify, Evaluate, and Select Forecasting Technique(s)

Since several forecasting methods are available, each with certain features and limitations, the user's needs, resources, and available data should be matched with the appropriate techniques. Companies may incorporate two or more techniques into the forecasting process. Typically, one technique is used as the primary basis of forecasting, whereas the other technique is used to check the validity of the primary forecasting method. Also, techniques offer different outputs. Some are effective in obtaining aggregate forecasts, and others are used to estimate sales for disaggregated units of analysis (e.g., products). An overview of the major forecasting techniques is provided here in "Forecasting Techniques."

Implementation

Many firms begin with very informal forecasting approaches based on projections of past experience coupled with a subjective assessment of the future market environment. As the forecasting needs increase, more formalized methods are developed. Factors that often affect the choice of a forecasting system include the type of corporate planning process used, the volatility and complexity of markets, the number of products and markets, and the organizational units that have forecasting needs.

[1] The following discussion is based on Lawrence R. Small, *Sales Forecasting in Canada* (Ottawa: The Conference Board of Canada, 1980), 3–7.

Forecasting Techniques

The major approaches used to prepare forecasts are described briefly. Forecasting techniques generally follow two basic avenues. The first involves making direct estimates of brand sales. The second forecasts brand sales as a product of several components (e.g., industry sales and market share).[2] Several methods used for forecasting sales are described below:

Judgmental Forecasting. A common approach relies on a jury of executive opinion to obtain sounder forecasts than might be made by a single estimator. To put the results in better perspective, the jury members are usually given background information on past sales, and their estimates are sometimes weighted in proportion to their convictions about the likelihood of specific sales levels being realized.

Sales Force Estimates. The sales personnel of some firms—field representatives, managers, or distributors—are considered better positioned than anyone else to estimate the short-term outlook for sales in their assigned areas.

User's Expectations. Although the dispersion of product users in many markets (or the cost of reaching them) would make such an approach impractical, some manufacturers serving industrial markets find it possible to poll product users about their future plans and then use that information in developing their own forecasts.

Traditional Time-Series Analysis. In a familiar approach, the historical sales series may be broken down into its components—trends and cyclical and seasonal variations, including irregular variations—which are then projected. Time-series analysis has the advantage of being easy to understand and apply. However, there is a danger in relying on strictly mechanized projections of previously identified patterns.

Advanced Time-Series Analysis. For short-term forecasting purposes, several advanced time-series

[2] Vithala R. Rao and James E. Cox, Jr., *Sales Forecasting Methods: A Survey of Recent Developments* (Cambridge, MA: Marketing Science Institute, 1987), 17.

methods have been generating new interest and acceptance. Most rely on a moving average of the data series as their starting point, and requisite computer software facilitates their use. The methods include variants of exponential smoothing, adaptive filtering, Box Jenkins models, and the state-space technique. All assume that future movements of a sales series can be determined solely from the study of its past movements. However, certain of these methods have the alternative advantage of being able to take into account external variables as well.

Econometric Methods. The econometric approach provides a mathematical simplification, or "model," of measurable relationships between changes in the series being forecast and changes in other related factors. Such models are employed most often in the prediction of overall market demand, thus requiring a separate estimate of a company's own share. Increased interest in this approach reflects a growing concern with macroeconomic events as well as a preference for spelling out assumptions that underlie forecasts.

Input-Output Analysis. When developing forecasts for intermediate or commodity products, some firms are finding it advantageous to employ input-output measures within comprehensive forecasting systems that begin with macroeconomic considerations and end with estimates of industry sales. Still other methodologies must be employed in such systems, and specialists are required for the correct application and interpretation of input-output analysis.

New-Product Forecasting. New products pose special problems that are hard for the forecaster to circumvent. A sales forecast for a new product may rest upon any of several bases, including results of marketing research investigations, assumptions about analogous situations in the past, or assumptions about the rate at which users of such products or services will substitute the new item for ones they are currently buying.[3]

Several advantages and limitations of the various forecasting techniques are highlighted in Exhibit 3A.1. A more comprehensive discussion of forecasting techniques is provided by David M. Georgoff and Robert Murdick, "Managers' Guide to Forecasting," *Harvard Business Review*, January–February 1986, 110–20.

[3] David L. Hurwood, Elliott S. Grossman, and Earl L. Bailey, *Sales Forecasting* (New York: The Conference Board, 1978), i–ii.

EXHIBIT 3A.1 Summary of Advantages and Disadvantages of Various Forecasting Techniques

Source: Mark W. Johnston and Greg W. Marshall, *Sales Force Management*, 7th ed. (New York: McGraw-Hill/Irwin, 2003), 131.

Sales Forecasting Method	Advantages	Disadvantages
User expectations	1. Forecast estimates obtained directly from buyers 2. Projected product usage information can be highly detailed 3. Insightful method aids planning marketing strategy 4. Useful for new product forecasting	1. Potential customers must be few and well defined 2. Does not work well for consumer goods 3. Depends on the accuracy of user's estimates 4. Expensive, time-consuming, labor-intensive
Sales force composite	1. Involves the people (sales personnel) who will be held responsible for the results 2. Is fairly accurate 3. Aids in controlling and directing sales effort 4. Forecast is available for individual sales territories	1. Estimators (sales personnel) have a vested interest and therefore may be biased 2. Elaborate schemes sometimes are necessary to counteract bias 3. If estimates are biased, process to correct the data can be expensive
Jury of executive opinion	1. Easily done, very quick 2. Does not require elaborate statistics 3. Utilizes "collected wisdom" of the top people 4. Useful for new or innovative products	1. Produces aggregate forecasts 2. Expensive 3. Disperses responsibility for the forecast 4. Group dynamics operate
Delphi technique	1. Minimizes effects of group dynamics	1. Can be expensive and time-consuming
Market test	1. Provides ultimate test of consumers' reactions to the product 2. Allows assessment of the effectiveness of the total marketing program 3. Useful for new and innovative products	1. Lets competitors know what firm is doing 2. Invites competitive reaction 3. Expensive and time-consuming to set up 4. Often takes a long time to accurately assess level of initial and repeat demand
Time-series analysis	1. Utilizes historical data 2. Objective, inexpensive	1. Not useful for new or innovative products 2. Factors for trend, cyclical, seasonal, or product life-cycle phase must be accurately assessed and included 3. Technical skill and good judgment required
Statistical demand analysis	1. Great intuitive appeal 2. Requires quantification of assumptions underlying the estimates 3. Allows management to check results 4. Uncovers hidden factors affecting sales 5. Method is objective	1. Factors affecting sales must remain constant and be identified accurately to produce an accurate estimate 2. Requires technical skill and expertise 3. Some managers reluctant to use method due to the sophistication

Chapter 4

Strategic Market Segmentation

Segmenting markets is a foundation for superior performance. Understanding how buyers' needs and wants vary is essential in designing effective marketing strategies. Segmenting markets may be critical to developing and implementing market-driven strategy.

For example, in the early 1990s, traditional mainframe computer manufacturer IBM faced sluggish sales and profits. IBM was organized around product groups and powerful geographically organized sales divisions. In 1991 the company restructured, driven by a new segmentation approach to its markets. The company abandoned geographic sales regions as market segments, because they did not provide a way to group customers with similar needs and were a poor basis for target marketing. The focus for marketing strategy and efforts to stimulate market demand became Industry Solution Units (ISUs), focusing on major industrial sectors: banking, insurance, retail, government, utilities. The ISU organization at IBM helped to improve revenue performance by sharpening its market focus and providing clearer sales targets and positioning messages. By 1994 IBM had moved back into profitability. Much of the market-driven culture change at IBM has been linked to its move from a sales-led structure to one based on customer segments.[1]

Moreover, the need to improve an organization's understanding of buyers is escalating because of buyers' demands for uniqueness and an array of technology available to generate products to satisfy these demands. Companies are responding to the opportunities to provide unique customer value with products ranging from customized phone pagers for business users to self-designed greeting cards for consumers, and even postage stamps with customers' own photographs incorporated.

Buyers vary according to how they use products, the needs and preferences that the products satisfy, and their consumption patterns. These differences create market segments. Market segmentation is the process of identifying and analyzing subgroups of buyers in a product-market with similar response characteristics (e.g., frequency of purchase). Recognizing differences between market segments, and how they change, better and faster than competitors is an increasingly important source of competitive advantage.

Indeed, for companies producing consumer goods and services, the concept of a "one-size-fits-all mass market" is no longer relevant. Many consumer markets show signs of fragmentation into "microsegments" driven by diverse product preferences and media usage and demanding "right for me" in products purchased.[2] This is why Nike offers more than 300 varieties of sport shoe, not just one. Exhibit 4.1 illustrates some of the pressures on consumer goods companies to focus on buyer differences in developing market-led strategy.

The most specific form of market segmentation is to consider each buyer as a market segment. This is the basis for "one-to-one marketing."[3] Such fine-tuned segmentation is possible for an expanding array of goods and services due to mass customization techniques. It offers an exciting new approach to serving the unique needs and wants of individual buyers. Custom-designed

EXHIBIT 4.1 From Mass Markets to Micro Markets

Source: Adapted from Anthony Bianco, "The Vanishing Mass Market," *BusinessWeek*, July 12, 2004, 68.

	Old	New
Consumers	Passively receive whatever the TV networks broadcast.	Empowered media users control and shape content thanks to TiVo, iPod, and the Internet.
Aspirations	To keep up with the crowd.	To stand out from the crowd.
TV Choice	Three networks plus maybe a PBS station.	Hundreds of channels plus video on demand.
Magazines	Age of the big glossies: *Time*, *Life*, *Look*, and *Newsweek*.	Age of the special interest: a magazine for every age and affinity group.
Ads	Everyone hums the Alka-Seltzer jingle	Talking to a group of one, ads go ever narrower.
Brands	Rise of the big, ubiquitous brands, from Coca-Cola to Tide.	Niche brands, product extensions, and mass customization mean many product variations.

products satisfy individual buyer's needs and wants at prices comparable to mass-produced products. The growing adoption of Customer Relationship Management systems that integrate all information about each individual customer into a single location provides unprecedented opportunities to learn about customer needs from their actual behavior.

For example, BMW collects and integrates customer data from a variety of sources: new and used car buying records, warranty and service records, BMW financial services records, direct mail and Internet sources, and external information such as competitive sales data. The database is used for several purposes. Often it is used to predict when individual customers are likely to change their cars. Response rates to BMW advertising have tripled because the marketing database allows the company to segment and target customers accurately and to focus on those most likely to respond.[4]

Indeed, by coupling information technology and production efficiencies, products are designed to meet a customer's needs at prices that are competitive with mass-produced products. For example, a woman can walk into an Original Levi Store in New York, be measured by a salesperson, and try on a few pairs of jeans selected by computer from over 400 pairs to match her specific measurements. If one does not provide a perfect fit, the information is put into the computer to refine the specifications. The final match is a perfect fit at a price only $10 more than the mass-produced jeans. Since stocking a supply of each of the 400 jeans in every store would be very costly, the buyer's pair of jeans is shipped to the store or the buyer from the distribution center. Similarly, Japanese bicycle manufacturer Panasonic pioneered "made to measure" bicycles, where the retail customer is measured as if for a suit of clothes and the custom-made bicycle delivered to the store within a few days.

Decision makers face renewed dilemmas in making segmentation choices, driven by escalating market complexity and turbulence. Many traditional assumptions about markets are becoming obsolete. Consider the contrast in Exhibit 4.2 between the possible characteristics of complex and simple, and turbulent and stable markets. Clinging to erroneous assumptions that markets are simple and stable is likely to critically undermine the ability of an organization to develop and implement effective market-driven strategy.

We begin the chapter with a discussion of the role of market segmentation in marketing strategy, followed by a discussion of the variables used to identify segments. Next, we look at the methods for forming segments, followed by a review of high-variety strategies. Finally, we consider the issues and guidelines involved in selecting the segmentation strategy and in its implementation.

EXHIBIT 4.2
Market Characteristics and Market Segments

Source: Adapted from Brian Smith, "Made to Measure," *The Marketer*, June 2004, 8.

Market Complexity	
Complex Markets	**Simple Markets**
Have many segments. Have many sources of competition. Have multiple distribution channels. Have complex value propositions around a mix of product, service, and brand attributes. Customer decision-making process may be complicated and involve many people.	Have only one or two segments. Have relatively few sources of competition. Have one main distribution channel. Have simple value propositions around the core product or service. Customer decision-making process is simple and involves only a few people.
Market Turbulence	
Turbulent Markets	**Stable Markets**
Market segmentation changes rapidly and frequently. The nature of the competition changes rapidly and frequently. The number and type of distribution channels change rapidly. Value propositions change often and rapidly. The customer decision-making process may change frequently.	Market segmentation changes rarely and slowly. The nature of the competition changes rarely and slowly. The number and type of distribution channels are not changing significantly. Value propositions do not change significantly over time. The customer decision-making process is generally stable.

Segmentation and Market-Driven Strategy

Market segmentation needs to be considered early in the development of market-driven strategy. Segments are determined, customer value opportunities explored in each segment, organizational capabilities matched to promising segment opportunities, market target(s) selected from the segment(s) of interest, and a positioning strategy developed and implemented for each market target (Exhibit 4.3). We examine each of these activities to indicate the role of segmentation in the marketing strategy process.

Market Segmentation and Value Opportunities

Market segmentation is the process of placing the buyers in a product-market into subgroups so that the members of each segment display similar responsiveness to a particular positioning strategy. Buyer similarities are indicated by the amount and frequency of purchase, loyalty to a particular brand, how the product is used, and other measures of responsiveness. So segmentation is an identification process aimed at finding subgroups of buyers within a total market. The opportunity for segmentation occurs when differences in buyers' demand (response) functions allow market demand to be divided into segments, each with a distinct demand function.[5] The term "market niche" is sometimes used to refer to a market segment that represents a relatively small portion of the buyers in the total market. We consider a niche and a segment to be the same.

Segmentation identifies customer groups within a product-market, each containing buyers with similar value requirements concerning specific product/brand attributes. A segment is a possible market target for an organization competing in the market. Segmentation offers a company an opportunity to better match its products and capabilities to buyers' value requirements. Customer satisfaction can be improved by providing a value offering that matches the value proposition considered important by the buyer in a segment.

EXHIBIT 4.3 Segmentation and the Market-Driven Strategy Process

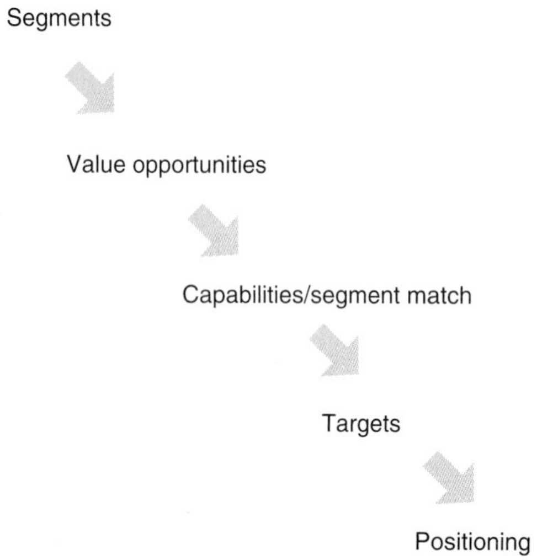

Segments

↘

Value opportunities

↘

Capabilities/segment match

↘

Targets

↘

Positioning

Creating New Market Space

Importantly, market analysis may identify segments not recognized or served effectively by competitors. There may be opportunities to tap into new areas of value and create a unique space in the market. For example, in France Accor has established the highly successful Formula 1 hotel chain by building a new market segment in between the traditional strategic groups in the hotel market. Traditional one-star hotels offer low prices, while two-star hotels offer more amenities and charge higher prices. Accor's analysis of customer needs found that customers choose the one-star hotel because it is cheap, but trade up from the one-star hotel to the two-star hotel for the "sleeping environment"—clean, quiet rooms with more comfortable beds—not all the other amenities that are offered. Formula 1 provides the superior "sleeping environment" of the two-star hotel, but not the other facilities, which allows it to offer this at the price of the one-star hotel. By 1999, Formula 1 had built a market share larger than the sum of those of the next five largest competitors.[6]

Matching Value Opportunities and Capabilities

While broad competitive comparisons can be made for an entire product-market, more penetrating insights about competitive advantage and market opportunity result from market segment analyses. Examining specific market segments helps to identify how to (1) attain a closer match between buyers' value preferences and the organization's capabilities, and (2) compare the organization's strengths (and weaknesses) to the key competitors in each segment.

Customer value requirements can often be better satisfied within a segment, compared to the total market. Consider, for example, Atlas Air Inc., a transportation company that offers outsourcing freight services for global air carriers. Launched in 1992, the founder identified an emerging customer need because carriers were replacing older aircraft with fuel efficient planes having half the cargo space of those being replaced.[7] Atlas customers include British Airways, China Airlines, KLM, Lufthansa, Swissair, and SAS, all attracted by low cost and reliable services. Atlas carries flowers and shoes from Amsterdam to Singapore for KLM and fish, cattle, and horses from Taipei to Europe for China Air.

Market Targeting and Strategic Positioning

Market targeting consists of evaluating and selecting one or more segments whose value requirements provide a good match with the organization's capabilities. Companies typically appeal to only a portion of the people or organizations in a product-market, regardless of how many segments are targeted. Management may decide to target one, a few, or several segments to gain the

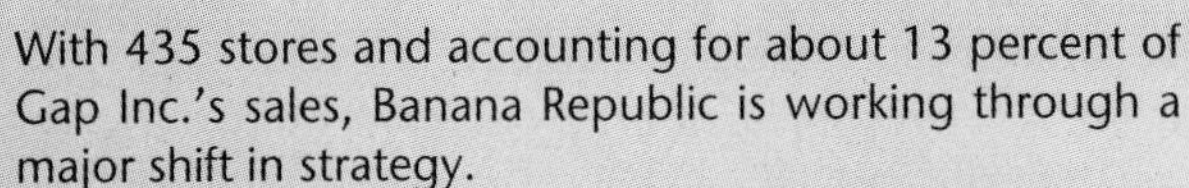

Segmentation and Positioning Challenges for Banana Republic

With 435 stores and accounting for about 13 percent of Gap Inc.'s sales, Banana Republic is working through a major shift in strategy.

Banana Republic is established as a seller of chic basics—casual office wear in blacks and beige—clothes for the dressed-down workplace. It is now positioning in the high fashion market, competing with brands like Polo Ralph Lauren, Calvin Klein, Ann Taylor, and Ellen Tracy. The move from fashion basics to $128 strapless dresses and Italian silk shirts reflects several strategic imperatives:

- Banana has to distinguish itself from the khakis and basics market segment where The Gap competes.
- Gap Inc. went into a three-year downturn in late 1999, partly because the overlap between The Gap and Old Navy stores led Gap shoppers to head for the lower prices at Old Navy.
- The Gap recovered by returning to basics like cropped pants, jeans, and khakis.
- Gap no longer looked like Old Navy—now it looked like Banana Republic.
- The solution is to shift Banana away from staple apparel towards fashion trends.
- The problem with the strategy is that consumers do not think of Banana for fashion, color, and new styles.

The transformation of Banana Republic by shifting strategic position is underpinned by four innovative approaches to build strength in the high fashion segment:

- Merchandise: emphasizing trendiness and color over basics and neutrals.
- Décor: making stores feel more upscale by adding touches such as potted plants and flowers.
- Promotion: persuading fashion editors to use the store's clothes in their editorial pages.
- Image: depicting ordinary, real-world settings in ads so the clothes appear accessible and wearable.

Source: Louise Lee, "Yes, We Have a New Banana," *BusinessWeek*, May 31, 2004, 74–75.

strength and advantage of specialization. Alternatively, while a specific segment strategy is not used, the marketing program selected by management is likely to appeal to a particular subgroup of buyers within the market. Segment identification and targeting are obviously preferred. Finding a segment by chance does not give management the opportunity of evaluating different segments in terms of the financial and competitive advantage implications of each segment. When segmentation is employed, it should be by design, and the underlying analyses should lead to the selection of one or more promising segments to target.

Recall the Chapter 2 description of positioning strategy as the combination of organizational actions management takes to meet the needs and wants of each market target. The strategy consists of product(s) and supporting services, distribution, pricing, and promotion components. Management's choices about how to influence target buyers to favorably position the product in their eyes and minds help in designing the positioning strategy.

The Strategy Feature describes the segmentation and positioning challenges at Banana Republic in the retail fashion marketplace. A special problem at Banana Republic, owned by Gap Inc., is to successfully position in a target market that does not lead to cannibalizing the sales of The Gap or Old Navy—both owned by Gap Inc.

Market segmentation lays the groundwork for market targeting and positioning strategies. The skills and insights used in segmenting a product-market may give a company important competitive advantages by identifying buyer groups that will respond favorably to the firm's marketing efforts. The previous Atlas Air example is illustrative.

Of course, faulty segmentation reduces the effectiveness of targeting and positioning decisions. For example, in 2000 General Motors made the decision to axe the Oldsmobile brand—the oldest auto brand in the United States. Although sometimes a symbol of innovation and style, Oldsmobile failed to establish a strong position in a long-term market niche or segment—it did not deliver the "class" of Cadillac and Buick nor the wider market appeal of Chevrolet.[8]

Selecting the Market to Be Segmented

Market segmentation may occur at any of the product-market levels shown in Exhibit 4.4. Generic-level segmentation is illustrated by segmenting supermarket buyers based on shopper types (e.g., limited shopping time). Product-type segmentation is shown by the differences in price, quality, and features of shaving equipment. Product-variant segmentation considers the segments within a category such as electric razors.

An important consideration in defining the market to be segmented is estimating the variation in buyers' needs and requirements at the different product-market levels and identifying the types of buyers included in the market. In the Atlas Air example, management defined the product-market to be segmented as air freight services for business organizations between major global airports. Segmenting the generic product-market for air freight services was too broad in scope. The market definition selected by Atlas Air excluded buyers (e.g., consumers) that were not of primary interest to management while including companies with different freight service needs.

In contemporary markets, boundaries and definitions can change rapidly, underlining the strategic importance of market definition and selection, and the need for frequent reevaluation.

Market Segmentation Activities and Decisions

The process of segmenting a market involves several interrelated activities and decisions beginning with defining the market to be segmented (Exhibit 4.5). It is necessary to decide how to segment the market, which involves selecting the variable(s) to use as the basis for identifying segments. For example, frequency of use of a product (e.g., frequent, moderate, and occasional) may be a possible basis for segmentation. Next, the method of forming segments is decided. This may consist of managers using judgment and experience to divide the market into segments as illustrated by the Atlas Air example. Alternatively, segments may be formed using statistical analysis. The availability of customer purchase behavior information in CRM systems, for example, provides a growing base for this analysis. Part of forming segments is deciding whether finer (smaller) segments should be used. Finally, strategic analysis is conducted on each segment to assist management in deciding which segment(s) to target.

Identifying Market Segments

After the market to be segmented is defined, one or more variables are selected to identify segments. For example, the United States Automobile Association (USAA) segments by type of employment. Although unknown to many people, USAA has built a successful business serving the automobile insurance needs of U.S. military personnel located throughout the world. USAA has close relationships with its 2.6 million members using powerful information technology. The USAA service representative has immediate access to the client's consolidated file, and the one-to-one service encounter is highly personalized. USAA achieves a 98 percent retention rate in its market chosen segment.[9]

First, we discuss the purpose of segmentation variables, followed by a review of the variables that are used in segmentation analyses.

EXHIBIT 4.4
Identifying the Health and Beauty Supplies Market Segments

Level of Competition	Product Definition	Illustrative Competitors	Need/Want Satisfied
Generic	Health and beauty aids	Consumer products companies	Enhancement of health and beauty
Product type	Shaving equipment	Gillette, Remington, Bic	Shaving
Product variant	Electric razors	Braun, Norelco, Remington, Panasonic	Electric shaving

EXHIBIT 4.5
Market Segmentation Activities and Decisions

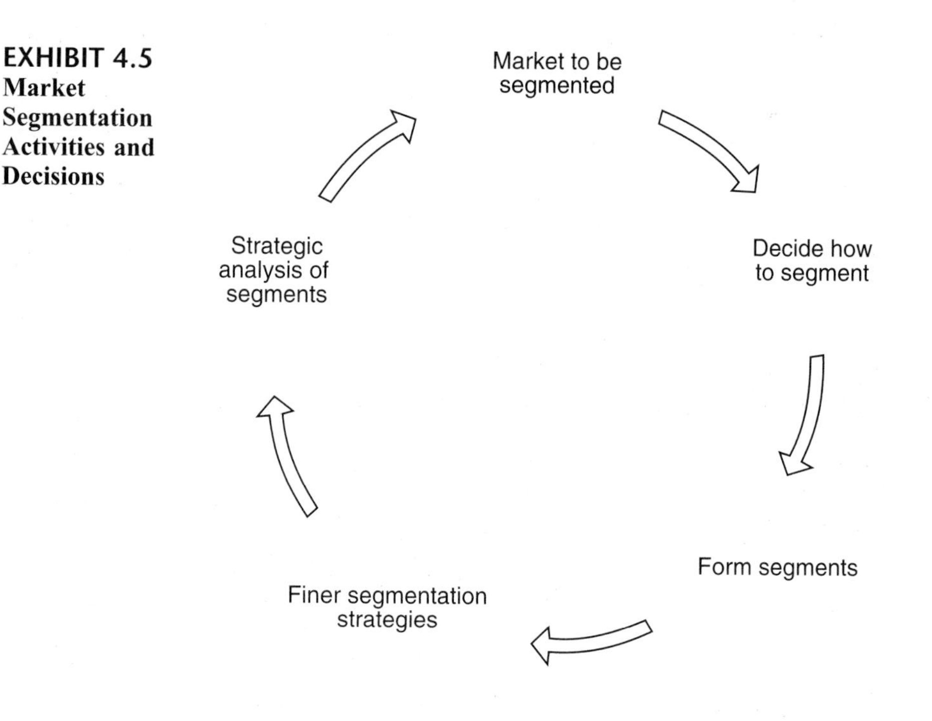

Purpose of Segmentation Variables

One or more variables (e.g., frequency of use) may be used to divide the product-market into segments. *Demographic* and *psychographic* (lifestyle and personality) characteristics of buyers are of interest, since this information is available from the U.S. Census reports and many other sources including electronic databases. The *use situation* variables consider how the buyer uses the product, such as purchasing a meal away from home for the purpose of entertainment. Variables measuring buyers' *needs* and *preferences* include attitudes, brand awareness, and brand preference. *Purchase-behavior* variables describe brand use and consumption (e.g., size and frequency of purchase). We examine these variables to highlight their uses, features, and other considerations important in segmenting markets.

Characteristics of People and Organizations

Consumer Markets. The characteristics of people fall into two major categories: (1) geographic and demographic, and (2) psychographic (lifestyle and personality). Demographics are often more useful to describe consumer segments after they have been formed rather than to identify them. Nonetheless, these variables are popular because available data often relate demographics to the other segmentation variables. Geographic location may be useful for segmenting product-markets. For example, there are regional differences in the popularity of transportation vehicles. In several U.S. states the most popular vehicle is a pickup truck. The "truck belt" runs from the upper Midwest south through Texas and the Gulf coast states. The Ford brand is dominant in the northern half of the truck belt while Chevrolet leads in the southern half.

Demographic variables describe buyers according to their age, income, education, occupation, and many other characteristics. Demographic information helps to describe groups of buyers such as heavy users of a product or brand. Demographics used in combination with buyer behavior information are useful in segmenting markets, selecting distribution channels, designing promotion strategies, and other decisions on marketing strategy.

Lifestyle variables indicate what people do (activities), their interests, their opinions, and their buying behavior. Lifestyle characteristics extend beyond demographics and offer a more penetrating description of the consumer.[10] Profiles can be developed using lifestyle characteristics.

Global Feature — The BMW MINI

- Notwithstanding depressed car markets in the United States and Europe, BMW's remake of the 1959 classic is becoming one of the most successful model overhauls ever. Sales of 176,000 cars in 2003 were up 22.4 percent from 2002, and the Oxford, England, factory is running at capacity. Estimates are that 2003 sales were $3.4 billion, producing pretax profit of $61.5 million.
- The new MINI look is a cute snout and bulldog-like stance offering an appealing contrast to boxy sports utility vehicles. While based on the original MINI, this is a premium priced vehicle, packed with technology.
- The car is positioned to be "quintessentially cool"—its biggest selling point is its individualistic appeal.
- Budget for the U.S. launch was only $13 million, so BMW used event-focused "guerrilla tactics," unconventional stunts, and irreverent humor to spark an infectious buzz.
- One of the first MINI sightings in the United States was a MINI strapped to the roof of a sports-utility vehicle with the sign "What are you doing for fun this weekend?"
- The MINI also appeared seated in football stadiums like a fan watching the game.
- The cool status of the MINI was cemented in place when it was used in the 2003 remake of the movie *The Italian Job*.
- When the MINI convertible comes to the United States and European market in 2004, the cars will be delivered with the top down and a seal that is to be broken when the roof is raised for the first time. Buyers will be asked to sign a mock contract committing them to keep the roof down as long as they can—to stay true to the MINI convertible's open-minded spirit. The company expects contests to see how long owners can go before breaking the seal.
- BMW has nurtured MINI mania by keeping supply just short of demand. More than half of buyers custom-order the MINI and wait three months for delivery.

Source: Gail Edmondson and Michael Eidam, "The MINI Just Keeps Getting Mightier," *BusinessWeek*, April 5, 2004, 26.

This information is used to segment markets, help position products, and guide the design of advertising messages.

An array of specialty magazines enables companies to identify and access very specific lifestyle segments. For example, Peterson Publishing Co. publishes 23 monthlies, 9 bimonthlies, and 45 annuals.[11] The company's magazine portfolio includes *Motor Trend*, *MTB* (mountain bikes), *Circle Track*, and *Teen* magazine. Specialty magazines match buyers' lifestyle interests with articles that correspond to the interests. Subscriber profiles help companies match their market target profiles with the right magazine(s). Many of the specialty magazines conduct subscriber research studies that are useful to companies targeting lifestyle segments. The availability of new technologies also enables more general publications to create themed sections or demographically targeted editions. For example, *Time* magazine can produce customized versions of its national edition—at the extreme as many as 20,000 different versions of a single issue.[12]

The Global Feature describes the success of BMW in positioning its MINI as a lifestyle vehicle, promoted through unconventional routes that fit with buyer characteristics in this niche of the automobile market.

Organizational Markets. Several characteristics help in segmenting business markets. The type of industry (sometimes called a vertical market) is related to purchase behavior for certain types of products. For example, automobile producers purchase steel, paint, and other raw materials. Since automobile firms' needs may vary from companies in other industries, this form of segmentation enables suppliers to specialize their efforts and satisfy customer needs. Other variables for segmenting organizational markets include size of the company, the stage of industry development, and the stage of the value-added system (e.g., producer, distribution, retailer). Dell, for example, targets the following organizational segments: global enterprises, large companies, midsize companies, government agencies, education, and small companies. Organizational segmentation is aided by first examining (1) the extent of market concentration, and (2) the degree of product customization.[13] Concentration considers the number of customers and their relative buying power. Product customization determines the extent to which the supplier must tailor the product to each organizational buyer. If one or both of these factors indicate quite a bit of diversity, segmentation opportunities may exist.

Boeing caters to the specific needs of each air carrier purchasing commercial aircraft. For example, an airline ordering a 747 has a choice of four configurations for the interior wall at the front of the rear cargo compartment.[14] This decision impacts how 2,550 parts are installed. While Boeing's efforts to provide customized designs are preferred by its customers, the costs are high and Boeing has had to evaluate the value/cost relationships of its attempts to satisfy the needs of single airline segments.

Product Use Situation Segmentation

Markets can be segmented based on how the product is used. As an illustration, Nikon, the Japanese camera company, offers a line of high performance sunglasses designed for activities and light conditions when skiing, driving, hiking, flying, shooting, and participating in water sports. Nikon competes in the premium portion of the market with prices somewhat higher than Ray-Ban, the market leader. Timex uses a similar basis of segmentation for its watches.

Needs and preferences vary according to different use situations. Consider, for example, segmenting the market for prescription drugs. Astra/Merck identifies the following segments based on the type of physician/patient drug use situation:

- **Health care as a business**—customers such as managed care administrators who consider economic factors of drug use foremost.
- **Traditional**—physicians with standard patient needs centered around the treatment of disease.
- **Cost sensitive**—physicians for whom cost is paramount, such as those with a sizable number of indigent patients.
- **Medical thought leaders**—people on the leading edge, often at teaching hospitals, who champion the newest therapies.[15]

A sales representative provides the medical thought leader with cutting-edge clinical studies, whereas the cost-sensitive doctor is provided information related to costs of treatments.

Mass customization offers a promising means of responding to different use situations at competitive prices. For example, Lutron Electronics gives its buyers customized light dimmer switches by programming desired features using computer chips built into the switches—the company holds 80 percent of all dimmer patents, and has achieved a 75 percent market share, with a product catalog including several thousand product variations in dozens of colors.[16]

Buyers' Needs and Preferences

Needs and preferences that are specific to products and brands can be used as segmentation bases and segment descriptors. Examples include brand loyalty status, benefits sought, and proneness to make a deal. Buyers may be attracted to different brands because of the benefits they offer. For example, seeking to generate additional revenues in the mid-1990s, Credit Lyonnaise, France's largest commercial bank, segmented and began targeting customers with annual incomes in excess of 500,000 francs ($100,000 at the time) that wanted quality service, financial advice, and upscale facilities.[17] Several new branch offices were designed to appeal to Credit Lyonnaise's wealthy clients. One office in Bordeaux, called Club Tourney, had an elegant townhouse with salons where clients met with advisors to discuss financial needs. The branch served 100 wealthy clients.

Consumer Needs. Needs motivate people to act. Understanding how buyers satisfy their needs provides guidelines for marketing actions. Consumers attempt to match their needs with the products that satisfy their needs. People have a variety of needs, including basic physiological needs (food, rest, and sex); the need for safety; the need for relationships with other people (friendship);

and personal satisfaction needs.[18] Understanding the nature and intensity of these needs is important in (1) determining how well a particular brand may satisfy the need, and/or (2) indicating what change(s) in the brand may be necessary to provide a better solution to the buyer's needs.

Attitudes. Buyer's attitudes toward brands are important because experience and research findings indicate that attitudes influence behavior. Attitudes are enduring systems of favorable or unfavorable evaluations about brands.[19] They reflect the buyer's overall liking or preference for a brand. Attitudes may develop from personal experience, interactions with other buyers, or by marketing efforts, such as advertising and personal selling.

Attitude information is useful in marketing strategy development. A strategy may be designed either to respond to established attitudes or, instead, to attempt to change an attitude. In a given situation, relevant attitudes should be identified and measured to indicate how brands compare. If important attitude influences on buyer behavior are identified and a firm's brand is measured against these attitudes, management may be able to improve the brand's position by using this information. Attitudes are often difficult to change, but firms may be able to do so if buyers' perceptions about the brand are incorrect. For example, if the trade-in value of an automobile is important to buyers in a targeted segment and a company learns through market research that its brand (which actually has a high trade-in value) is perceived as having a low trade-in value, advertising can communicate this information to buyers.

Perceptions. Perception is defined as "the process by which an individual selects, organizes, and interprets information inputs to create a meaningful picture of the world."[20] Perceptions are how buyers select, organize, and interpret marketing stimuli, such as advertising, personal selling, price, and the product. Perceptions form attitudes. Buyers are selective in the information they process. As an illustration of selective perception, some advertising messages may not be received by viewers because of the large number of messages vying for their attention. For example, Exhibit 4.6 lists products where substantial proportions of TV advertisements are actively ignored or skipped using a personal video recorder. Negative attitudes and perception may be a major barrier to communicating with consumers. Or, more simply, for example, a salesperson's conversation may be misunderstood or not understood because the buyer is trying to decide if the purchase is necessary while the salesperson is talking.

People often perceive things differently. Business executives are interested in how their products, salespeople, stores, and companies are perceived. Perception is important strategically in helping management to evaluate the current positioning strategy and in making changes in this

EXHIBIT 4.6
Television Viewers Watch Fewer Ads

Source: Survey of the 15 largest U.S. television markets in 2003 by CNW Marketing Research Inc. reported in Anthony Bianco, "The Vanishing Mass Market," *BusinessWeek*, July 12, 2004, 65.

	Ads Actively Ignored on Television	Ads Skipped Using Personal Video Recorder
Beer	4.8%	31.9%
Movie trailers	11.6	44.1
Soft drinks	21.6	82.7
Drug	32.3	45.6
Specialty clothing	33.4	62.4
Home products	41.6	90.3
Fast food	45.1	95.7
Cars (national)	52.8	68.8
Pet-related	55.5	81.5
Credit cards	62.7	94.2
Mortgage financing	74.1	94.7
Upcoming program	75.3	94.4
Unweighted average	43.1	71.6

positioning strategy. Perception mapping is a useful research technique for showing how brands are perceived by buyers according to various criteria. We discuss how preference mapping is used to form segments later in the chapter.

Purchase Behavior

Consumption variables such as the size and frequency of a purchase are useful in segmenting consumer and business markets. Marketers of industrial products often classify customers and prospects into categories on the basis of the volume of the purchase. For example, a specialty chemical producer concentrates its marketing efforts on chemical users that purchase at least $100,000 of chemicals each year. The firm further segments the market on the basis of how the customer uses the chemical.

The development of CRM systems offers fast access to records of actual customer purchase behavior and characteristics. CRM and loyalty programs are generating insights into customer behavior and segment differences, and providing the ability to respond more precisely to the needs of customers in different segments. For example, Consodata is a CRM company working for the Jigsaw consortium of some of the largest fast-moving consumer goods companies in the world. Unilever, Kimberley-Clark, and Cadbury Schweppes are sharing the costs of a giant database that can divide countries into any size segment and determine exactly who lives there, where they shop, what they buy, their lifestyles, and attitude data. Initial applications are in the precise merchandising of supermarket shelves to reflect local segment characteristics.

Similarly, Accor, the French-based hotel group, has adopted sophisticated business intelligence systems for its Sofitel and Novotel hotels in the United States. (See accompanying Sofitel advertisement). The potential benefit is to identify different customers' preferences, to differentiate and to customize. Using survey data, records of guests' visits and preferences or problems, the data are mined to draw up "golden nugget maps" to identify which customer segments have major potential, which already have been heavily exploited, and which have limited potential.[21] More details about CRM as a source of market understanding are given in the Appendix to Chapter 7.

Since buying decisions vary in importance and complexity, it is useful to classify them to better understand their characteristics, the products to which they apply, and the marketing strategy implications of each type of purchase behavior. Buyer decisions can be classified according to the extent to which the buyer is involved in the decision.[22] A high-involvement decision may be an expensive purchase, have important personal consequences, and impact the consumer's ego and social needs. The decision situation may consist of extended problem solving (high involvement), limited problem solving, or routine problem solving (low involvement). The characteristics of these situations are illustrated in Exhibit 4.7.

These categories are very broad since the range of involvement covers various buying situations. Even so, the classifications provide a useful way to compare and contrast buying situations. Also, involvement may vary from individual to individual. For example, a high-involvement purchase for one person may not be such for another person, since perceptions of expense, personal consequences, and social impact may vary across individuals.

EXHIBIT 4.7
Consumer Involvement in Purchase Decisions

Source: Eric N. Berkowitz, Roger A. Kerin, Steven W. Hartley, and William Rudelius, *Marketing*, 5th ed. (Chicago: Richard D. Irwin, 1997), 156. Copyright © The McGraw-Hill Companies. Used with permission.

	Consumer Involvement		
	High		Low
Characteristics of Purchase Decision Process	**Extended Problem Solving**	**Limited Problem Solving**	**Routine Problem Solving**
Number of brands examined	Many	Several	One
Number of sellers considered	Many	Several	Few
Number of product attributes evaluated	Many	Moderate	One
Number of external information sources used	Many	Few	None
Time spent searching	Considerable	Little	Minimal

EXHIBIT 4.8
Illustrative Segmentation Variables

	Consumer Markets	Industrial/Organizational Markets
Characteristics of people/organizations	Age, gender, race Income Family size Lifecycle stage Geographic location Lifestyle	Type of industry Size Geographic location Corporate culture Stage of development Producer/intermediary
Use situation	Occasion Importance of purchase Prior experience with product User status	Application Purchasing procedure New task, modified rebuy, straight rebuy
Buyers' needs/preferences	Brand loyalty status Brand preference Benefits sought Quality Proneness to make a deal	Performance requirements Brand preferences Desired features Service requirements
Purchase behavior	Size of purchase Frequency of purchase	Volume Frequency of purchase

Exhibit 4.8 summarizes the various segmentation variables and shows examples of segmentation bases and descriptors for consumer and organizational markets. As we examine the methods used to form segments, the role of these variables in segment determination and analysis is illustrated.

Forming Segments

The credit card division of American Express (AMEX) identifies market segments based on purchase behavior. One group of cardholders pays the annual fee for the card but rarely (or never) uses it.[23] This group of zero spenders is made up of (1) those who cannot afford much discretionary spending, and (2) those who use cash or competitors' cards. AMEX's objective is to identify the second group of potential buyers because they offer card usage opportunities and may potentially give up their card. AMEX uses self-selecting incentive offers (e.g., two free airline tickets for heavy card use over six months) to identify the valuable nonuser cardholders. While this segmentation approach is expensive, it costs less than obtaining a new customer to

Internet Feature

Monster.com

- Monster.com was founded in 1994 by Jeff Taylor, known as Chief Monster at Monster.com, and by 2004 claimed a 50 percent share of the online recruitment agency or job-search business, ahead of HotJobs (owned by Yahoo) and CareerBuilder (owned by three big newspaper groups).
- Jobseekers supply the Web site with eye-catching résumés and pay nothing while employers pay to scan the résumés or to post help-wanted ads. Nearly 50,000 people a day post résumés at the Monster.com site.
- Monster was the first to develop a database of résumés with user names and passwords; the first to develop the job-search agent that is now common in the industry; the first to develop a talent auction for free agents; and the first to develop a specific area on the Web devoted to finding jobs for top-level executives.
- A new service will allow jobseekers to contact each other for advice, mentoring, and career management, but this will not be free.
- The power of the Monster.com Internet business model is that it speeds up hiring and vastly increases the accuracy of the job-search process.
- An employer who knows exactly what he wants can use Monster's search filters to search vast numbers of résumés with pinpoint accuracy.
- With its low costs and wide reach Monster takes business away from traditional bricks-and-mortar recruitment agencies, headhunters, and conventional newspaper advertising. Monster demonstrates how an electronic marketplace can offer a reach and efficiency that physical markets cannot rival.
- The Monster brand is supported by the Chief Monster's sense of youthful fun and antiestablishment zest, as well as a big advertising budget including prime time slots around the Super Bowl and infectious slogans like "Never settle" and "Today's the day."

Sources: Adapted from "Business: A Monster Success; Face Value," *The Economist*, March 27, 2004, 86; Robert Barker, "Monster's Monstrous Appetite for Cash," *BusinessWeek*, May 17, 2004, 138; Caitlin Mollinson, "The Interview," *InternetWorld*, May 1, 2001.

replace one who leaves AMEX. It also does not require using expensive marketing research to identify cardholders with the ability (financial) to use their cards.

The requirements for segmentation are discussed first, and then the methods of segment formation are described and illustrated.

Requirements for Segmentation

An important question is deciding if it is worthwhile to segment a product-market. For example, Gillette has successfully adopted a "one product for all" strategy in the razor market. While in many instances segmentation is a sound strategy, its feasibility and value need to be evaluated. Nonetheless, the growing fragmentation of mature mass markets into segments with different needs and responsiveness to marketing actions may mandate segmentation strategy. Correspondingly, the growth of narrowcast media—cable television and radio; specialized magazines; cell-phone and personal digital assistant screens; and the Internet—makes major changes in the costs of reaching market segments. Segment targets that could not traditionally be reached with communications and product variants to match their needs at reasonable costs to the seller may now be accessible targets.[24]

For example, the Internet Feature describes how Monster.com has reinvented the recruitment agency business by its use of the Internet to match jobseekers with relevant employment opportunities in a way which no traditional business model can rival. Jobseekers can be categorized by type of job sought (e.g., sales, accountancy) and level, and these groups can be matched with employers in 20 different countries at great speed and with absolute precision.

It is important to decide if it is worthwhile to segment a product-market. Five criteria are useful for evaluating a potential segmentation strategy.

Response Differences. Determining differences in the responsiveness of the buyers in the product-market to positioning strategies is a key segment identification requirement. Suppose the customers in a product-market are placed into four groups, each a potential segment, using a variable such as income (affluent, high, medium, and low). If each group responds (e.g., amount of purchase) in the same way as all other groups to a marketing mix strategy, then the four groups are not market segments. If segments actually exist in this illustration, there must be differences in the responsiveness of the groups to marketing actions, such as pricing, product features, and promotion. The presence of real segments requires actual response differences. Simply finding differences in buyers' characteristics such as income is not enough.

For example, income is useful in finding response differences in India. A study conducted by a New Delhi think tank identifies a premium segment in the Indian consumer market.[25] Families with an annual income in excess of 1 million rupees ($29,200 at the time of the study) have as much buying power as a U.S. family with three times the same income. Living costs for the Indian family are very low (e.g., two-bedroom apartment for $130 a month). The premium segment is a promising target for luxury goods brands like Mercedes-Benz, Cartier, and Christian Dior. There are 600,000 Indian households in the premium segment, including 200,000 in Bombay (now Mumbai). Several Japanese, U.S. and European auto manufacturers plan to produce luxury cars in India.

Identifiable Segments. It must be possible to identify the customer groups that exhibit response differences, and sometimes finding the correct groups may be difficult. For example, even though variations in the amount of purchase by customers occur in a market, it may not be possible to identify which people correspond to the different response groups in the market. While it is usually feasible to find descriptive differences among the buyers in a product-market, these variations must be matched to response differences. Recall AMEX's approach to identifying cardholders with buying power who use the card infrequently. Incentives are used to attract nonuser cardholders with buying power.

Actionable Segments. A business must be able to aim a marketing program strategy at each segment selected as a market target. As discussed earlier, specialty magazines offer one means of selective targeting. Ideally, the marketing effort should focus on the segment of interest and not be wasted on nonsegment buyers. Cable television, magazine, and radio media are able to provide coverage of narrowly defined market segments. The Internet offers great potential for direct marketing channels to reach specialized segments. Similarly, databases offer very focused access to buyers.

Cost/Benefits of Segmentation. Segmentation must be financially attractive in terms of revenues generated and costs incurred. It is important to evaluate the benefits of segmentation. While segmentation may cost more in terms of research and added marketing expenses, it should also generate more sales and higher margins. The objective is to use a segmentation approach that offers a favorable revenue and cost combination.

For example, British-based ICI Fertilisers experienced substantial losses in the late 1980s, but rebuilt its business around an innovative market segmentation strategy. Research showed that farmers' priorities in fertilizer purchasing were dominated by price only in 10 percent of cases; instead, farmers were more influenced by advanced technology, loyalty to traditional merchants, and loyalty to brands. ICI created new product ranges around these needs, restructured the business around these ranges, and built impressive profitability.[26]

Stability over Time. Finally, the segments must show adequate stability over time so that the firm's marketing efforts will have enough time to produce favorable results. If buyers' needs change too fast, a group with similar response patterns at one point may display quite different patterns several months later. The time period may be too short to justify using a segmentation strategy. However, this question is also one where the impact of narrowcast media and advanced production technology may drastically reduce the time over which a segment target needs to be stable for it to be an attractive target.

Product Differentiation and Market Segmentation. The distinction between product differentiation and market segmentation is not always clear. *Product differentiation* occurs when a product offering is perceived by the buyer as different from the competition on any physical or nonphysical product characteristic, including price.[27] Using a product differentiation strategy, a

EXHIBIT 4.9
Approaches to Segment Identification

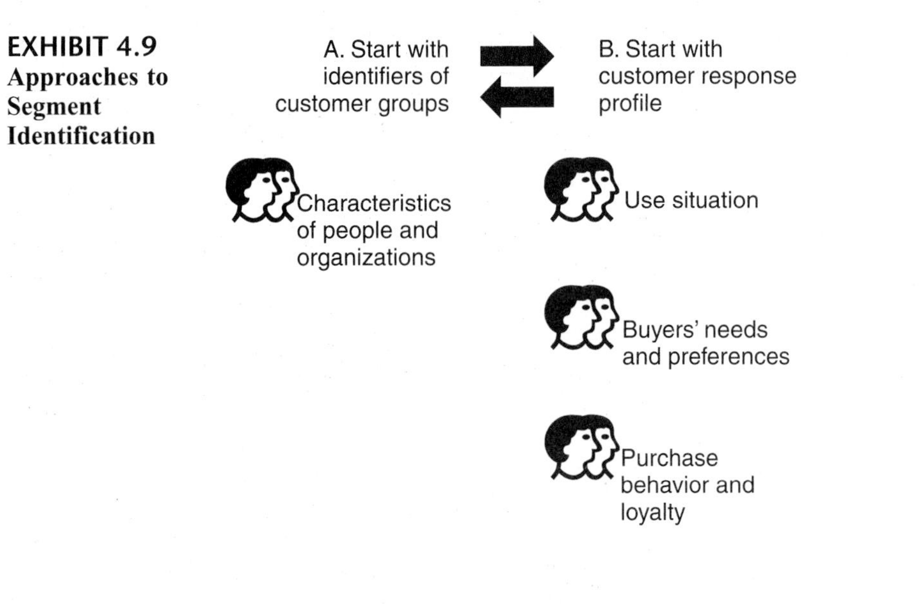

firm may target an entire market or one (or more) segments. Competing firms may differentiate their product offerings in trying to gain competitive advantage with the same group of targeted buyers. Market targeting using a differentiation strategy is considered further in Chapter 6.

Approaches to Segment Identification

Segments are formed by: (A) grouping customers using descriptive characteristics and then comparing response differences across the groups, or (B) forming groups based on response differences (e.g., frequency of purchase) and determining if the groups can be identified based on differences in their characteristics.[28] Exhibit 4.9 illustrates the two approaches. Approach A uses a characteristic such as income or family size believed to be related to buyer response. After forming the groups, they are examined to see if response varies across groups. Approach B places buyers with similar response patterns into groups and then develops buyer profiles using buyer characteristics. We describe each approach to show how it is used to identify segments.

Customer Group Identification

After the product-market of interest is defined, promising segments may be identified, using management judgment in combination with analysis of available information and/or marketing research studies. Consider, for example, hotel lodging services. Exhibit 4.10 illustrates ways to segment the hotel lodging product-market. An additional breakdown can be made according to business and household travelers. These categories may be further distinguished by individual customer and group customer segments. Groups may include conventions, corporate meetings, and tour groups. Several possible segments can be distinguished. Consider, for example, Marriott's Courtyard hotel chain. These hotels fall into the midpriced category and are targeted primarily to frequent business travelers who fly to destinations, are in the 40-plus age range, and have relatively high incomes.

When using the customer group identification approach, it is necessary to select one or more of the characteristics of people or organizations as the basis of segmentation. Using these variables, segments are formed by (1) management judgment and experience, or (2) supporting statistical analyses. The objective is to find differences in responsiveness among the customer groups. We look at some of the customer grouping methods to show how segments are formed.

Experience and Available Information. Management's knowledge of customer needs is often a useful guide to segmentation. For example, both experience and analysis of published information are often helpful in segmenting business markets. Business segment variables include

EXHIBIT 4.10 Product-Market Segment Dimensions for Hotel Lodging Services

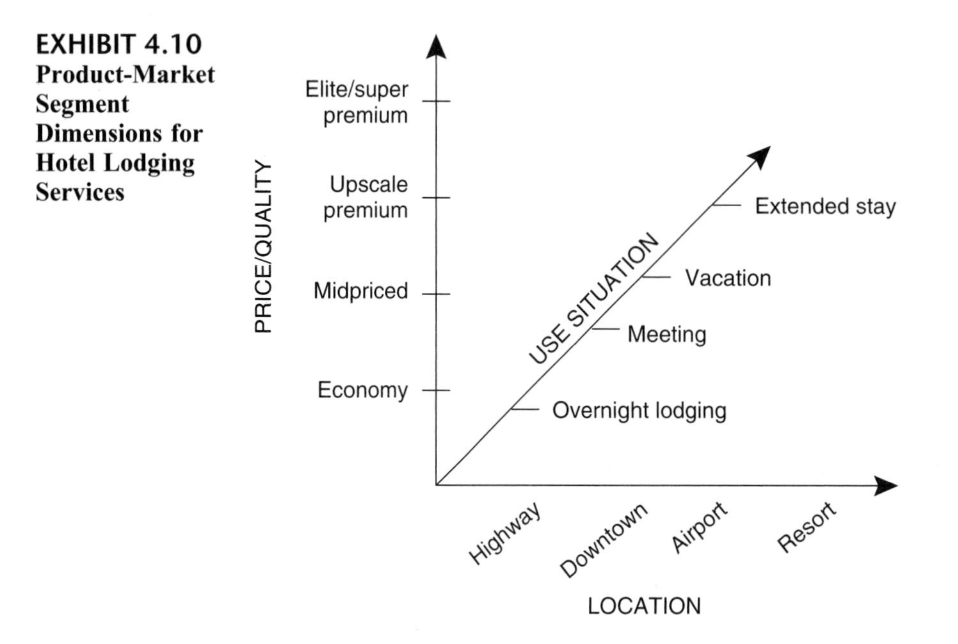

type of industry, size of purchase, and product application. Company records often contain information for analyzing the existing customer base. Published data such as industry mailing lists can be used to identify potential market segments. These groups are then analyzed to determine if they display different levels of response.

Segmenting using management judgment and experience, the Italian fashion producer and retailer Prada markets an expensive array of dresses, handbags, hats, shoes, and other women's apparel.[29] The best-selling $450 backpacks are designed to appeal to affluent women that do not want to flaunt their status. Each knapsack has a small triangular logo. Prada's products offer an antistatus (lifestyle) appeal to a segment of affluent women. The luxury retailer has 47 stores including 20 in Japan and two in the United States. Prada's goods are also sold in department stores.

Cross Classification Analyses. Another method of forming segments is to identify customer groups using descriptive characteristics and compare response rates (e.g., sales) by placing the information in a table. Customer groups form the rows and response categories form the columns. Review of industry publications and other published information may identify ways to break up a product-market into segments. Standardized information services such as Information Resources Inc. collect and publish consumer panel data on a regular basis. These data provide a wide range of consumer characteristics, advertising media usage, and other information that are analyzed by product and brand sales and market share. The data are obtained from a large sample of households through the United States. Similar statistical data are available in many overseas countries.

Information is available for use in forming population subgroups within product-markets. The analyst can use many sources, as well as management's insights and hunches regarding the market. The essential concern is whether a segmentation scheme identifies customer groups that display different product and brand responsiveness. The more evidence of meaningful differences, the better chance that useful segments exist. Cross-classification has some real advantages in terms of cost and ease of use. There may be a strong basis for choosing a segmenting scheme that uses this approach. This occurs more often in business and organizational markets, where management has a good knowledge of user needs, because there are fewer users than there are in consumer product-markets. Alternatively, this approach may be a first step leading to a more comprehensive type of analysis.

Database Segmentation. The availability of computerized databases offers a wide range of segmentation analysis capabilities. This type of analysis is particularly useful in consumer market segmentation. Databases are organized by geography and buyers' descriptive characteristics. They may also contain customer response information as shown in the AMEX cardholder illustration. Databases can be used to identify customer groups, design effective marketing programs, and improve the effectiveness of existing programs. The number of available databases is rapidly expanding, the costs are declining, and the information systems are becoming user friendly. Several marketing research and direct mail firms offer database services.

Segmentation Illustrations. Mobil Corporation studies buyers in the gasoline market to identify segments. The findings, including information obtained from over 2,000 motorists, are summarized in Exhibit 4.11. The research identified five primary purchasing groups.[30] Interestingly, Mobil found that the Price Shopper spends an average of $700 annually, compared to $1,200 for the Road Warriors and True Blues. Mobil's marketing strategy is to offer gasoline buyers a quality buying experience, including upgraded facilities, more lighting for safety, responsive attendants, and quality convenience products. The target segments are Road Warriors and Generation F3, involving a major effort in convenience stores and reduced time at the gas pump based on the Mobil *Speed Pass*. The test results from the new strategy raised revenues by 25 percent over previous sales for the same retail sites.

As shown by the profiles described in Exhibit 4.11, needs and preferences vary quite a bit within a market. Trying to satisfy all of the buyers in the market with the same marketing approach is difficult. Analyzing both the customer and the competition is important. Specific competitors may be better (or worse) at meeting the needs of specific customer groups (e.g., Mobil's Road Warriors). Finding gaps between buyers' needs and competitors' offerings provides opportunities for improving customer satisfaction. Also, companies study competitors' products to identify ways to improve their own.

By identifying customer groups using descriptive characteristics and comparing them to a measure of customer responsiveness to a marketing mix such as product usage rate (e.g., number of fax ink cartridges per year), potential segments can be identified. If the response rates are

EXHIBIT 4.11
Diversity of Gasoline Buyers

Source: Alanna Sullivan, "Mobil Bets Drivers Pick Cappuccino over Low Prices," *The Wall Street Journal*, January 30, 1995, B1. Wall Street Journal. Central Edition [Staff Produced Copy Only] by Alanna Sullivan. Copyright 1995 by Dow Jones & Co Inc. Reproduced with permission of Dow Jones & Co Inc. in the format Textbook via Copyright Clearance Center.

Road Warriors:	True Blues:	Generation F3:	Homebodies:	Price Shoppers:
Generally higher-income, middle-aged men, who drive 25,000 to 50,000 miles a year . . . buy premium with a credit card . . . purchase sandwiches and drinks from the convenience store . . . will sometimes wash their cars at the carwash.	Usually men and women with moderate to high incomes who are loyal to a brand and sometimes to a particular station . . . frequently buy premium gasoline and pay in cash	(for fuel, food, and fast): Upwardly mobile men and women—half under 25 years of age—who are constantly on the go . . . drive a lot and snack heavily from the convenience store.	Usually housewives who shuttle their children around during the day and use whatever gasoline station is based in town or along their route of travel.	Generally aren't loyal to either brand or a particular station; and rarely buy the premium line . . . frequently on tight budgets . . . efforts to woo them have been the basis of marketing strategies for years.
16% of buyers	**16% of buyers**	**27% of buyers**	**21% of buyers**	**20% of buyers**

similar within a segment, and differences in response exist between segments, then promising segments are identified. Segments do not always emerge from these analyses, because in some product-markets distinct segments may not exist, or the segment interrelationships may be so complex that an analysis of these predetermined groupings will not identify useful segments. Product differentiation strategies may be used in these situations.

In an era of increased globalization, it is also important to recognize that segmentation has an international dimension in many markets. This is not simply country differences, for example, differences in sizes of products like apparel and household furniture based on ethnic identity in overseas countries. Roper Starch Worldwide, based on interviews about core values with 1,000 people in each of 35 countries, identify six global consumer segments, existing to varying degrees in each country:

- *Strivers*: Place more emphasis on material and professional goals than do the other groups.
- *Devouts*: Tradition and duty are very important.
- *Altruists*: Interested in social issues and social welfare.
- *Intimates*: Value close personal and family relationships.
- *Fun seekers*: High consumption of restaurants, bars, movies.
- *Creatives*: Strong interest in education, knowledge, and technology.

The global study found that people in different segments generally pursued different activities, purchased different products, and used different media.[31]

Forming Groups Based on Response Differences

The alternative to selecting customer groups based on descriptive characteristics is to identify groups of buyers by using response differences to form the segments. A look at a segmentation analysis for the packaging division of Signode Corporation illustrates how this method is used.[32] The products consist of steel strappings for various packaging applications. An analysis of the customer base identified the following segments: programmed buyers (limited service needs), relationship buyers, transaction buyers, and bargain hunters (low price, high service). Statistical (cluster) analysis formed the segments using 12 variables concerning price and service trade-offs and buying power. The study included 161 of Signode's national accounts. Measures of the variables were obtained from sales records, sales managers, and sales representatives. The segments vary in responsiveness based on relative price and relative service.

The widespread adoption of CRM systems offers greater opportunity for timely and detailed analysis of response differences between customers. The "data warehouse," by integrating transactional data around customer types, makes possible complex analyses to understand differences in the behavior of different customers groups, observe customer life cycles, and predict behavior.[33] We discuss CRM in the Appendix to Chapter 7.

Response difference approaches draw more extensively from buyer behavior information than the customer group identification methods discussed earlier. Note, for example, the information on Signode's customer responsiveness to price and service. We now look at additional applications to more fully explore the potential of the customer response approaches.

Cluster Analysis. Cluster analysis (a statistical technique) groups people according to the similarity of their answers to questions such as brand preferences or product attributes. This method was useful to form segments for Signode Corporation. The objective of cluster analysis is to identify groupings in which the similarity within a group is high and the variation between groups is as great as possible. Each cluster is a potential segment.

Perceptual Maps. Another promising segmentation method uses consumer research data to construct maps of buyers' perceptions of products and brands. The information helps select market-target strategies, and decide how to position a product for a market target.

While the end result of perceptual mapping is simple to understand, its execution is demanding in terms of research skills. Although there are variations in approach, the following steps are illustrative:

1. Select the product-market area to be segmented.
2. Decide which brands compete in the product-market.
3. Collect buyers' perceptions about attributes for the available brands (and an ideal brand) obtained from a sample of people.
4. Analyze the data to form one, two, or more composite attribute dimensions, each independent of the other.
5. Prepare a map (two-dimensional X and Y grid) of attributes on which are positioned consumer perceptions of competing brands.
6. Plot consumers with similar ideal preferences to see if subgroups (potential segments) will form.
7. Evaluate how well the solution corresponds to the data that are analyzed.
8. Interpret the results as to market-target and product-positioning strategies.

An example of a perception map is shown in Exhibit 4.12. Each Group (I–V) contains people from a survey sample with similar preferences concerning expensiveness and quality for the product category. The Brands (A–E) are positioned using the preference data obtained from the survey participants. Assuming you are product manager for Brand C, what does the information indicate concerning possible targeting? Group V is a logical market target and III may represent a secondary market target. To appeal most effectively to Group V, we will probably need to change somewhat Group V consumers' price perceptions of Brand C. Offering a second brand less expensive than C to appeal to Group IV is another possible action. Of course, it is necessary to study the research results in much greater depth than this brief examination of Exhibit 4.12. Our intent is to illustrate the method of segmenting and show how the results might be used.

EXHIBIT 4.12
An Illustrative Consumer Perception Map

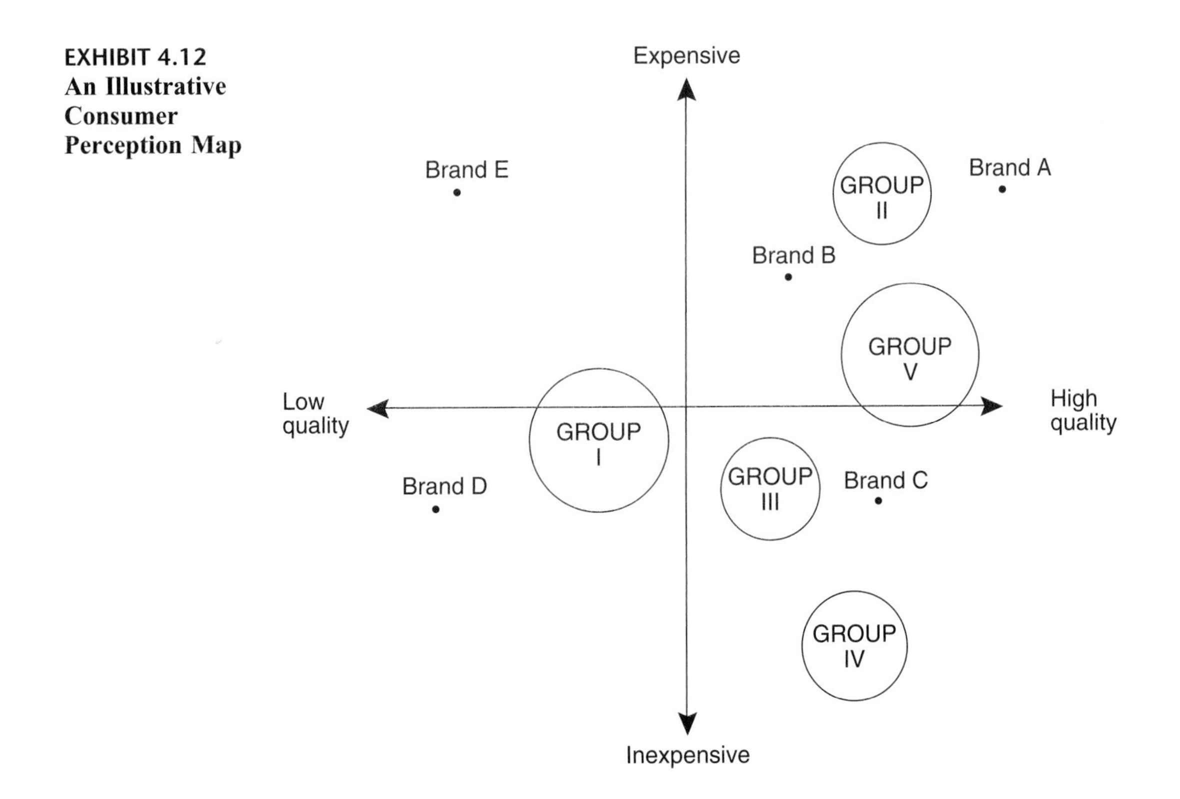

Perceptual mapping, like many of the research methods used for segment identification, is expensive and represents a technical challenge. When used and interpreted properly, these methods are useful tools for analyzing product-market structure to identify possible market targets and positioning concepts. Of course, there are many issues to be considered in specific applications such as choosing the attributes, identifying relevant products and brands, selecting the sample, and evaluating the strength of results.

Finer Segmentation Strategies

A combination of factors may help a company utilize finer segmentation strategies. Technology may be available to produce customized product offerings. Furthermore, highly sophisticated databases for accessing buyers can be used, and buyers' escalating preferences for unique products encourage consideration of increasingly smaller segments. In some situations, an individual buyer may comprise a market segment. Thus, an important segmentation issue is deciding how small segments should be.

We consider the logic of finer segments followed by a discussion of the available finer segmentation strategies.

Logic of Finer Segments

Several factors working together point to the benefits of considering very small segments—in some cases, segments of one. These include (1) the capabilities of companies to offer cost-effective, customized offerings; (2) the desires of buyers for highly customized products; and (3) the organizational advantages of close customer relationships.

Customized Offerings. Offering customized products may be feasible because of extensive information flow and comprehensive databases, computerized manufacturing systems, and integrated value chains.[34] At the center of these capabilities to provide buyers with customized offerings is information technology. Database knowledge, computer-aided product design and manufacturing, and distribution technology (e.g., just-in-time inventory) offer promising opportunities for serving the needs and preferences of very small market segments. This technology combined with the Internet has led to the emergence of "sliver" companies or "micromultinationals"—small, flexible organizations selling highly specialized products across the world.

Diverse Customer Base. The requirements of an increasingly diverse customer base for many products are apparent. Buyers seek uniqueness and companies such as Lutron Electronics try to respond to unique preferences. Global competitors seek to offer more attractive value in their goods and services.

Close Customer Relationships. Companies recognize the benefits of close relationships with their customers. By identifying customer value opportunities and developing cost-effective customized offerings, relationships can be profitable and effective in creating competitive barriers.

Finer Segmentation Strategies

We examine three approaches for finer segmentation opportunities: microsegmentation, mass customization, and variety seeking.[35]

Microsegmentation. This form of segmentation seeks to identify narrowly defined segments using one or more of the previously discussed segmentation variables (Exhibit 4.8). It differs from more aggregate segment formation in that microsegmentation results in a large number of very small segments. Each segment of interest to the organization receives a marketing mix designed to meet the value requirements of the segment.

Mass Customization. Providing customized products at prices not much higher than mass-produced items is feasible using mass customization concepts and methods. Achieving mass customization objectives is possible through computer-aided design and manufacturing software, flexible manufacturing techniques, and flexible supply systems.

There are two forms of mass customization. One employs standardized components but configuring the components to achieve customized product offerings.[36] For example, using standardized paint components, retail stores are able to create customized color shades by mixing the components. The other mass customization approach employs a flexible process. Through effective system design, variety can be created at very low costs. For example, Casio's customization approach enables the company to offer 5,000 different watches.

Variety-Seeking Strategy. This product strategy is intended to offer buyers opportunities to vary their choices in contrast to making unique choices.[37] The logic is that buyers who are offered alternatives may increase their total purchases of a brand. Mass customization methods also enable companies to offer an extensive variety at relatively low prices, thus gaining the advantages of customized and variety offerings.

Finer Segmentation Issues. While the benefits of customization are apparent, there are several issues that need to be examined when considering finer segmentation strategies:[38]

1. How much variety should be offered to buyers? What attributes are important in buyers choices and to what extent do they need to be varied? Boeing is considering this issue for its customized aircraft designs.
2. Will too much variety have negative effects on buyers? Is it possible that buyers will become confused and frustrated when offered too many choices?
3. Is it possible to increase buyers' desire for variety, creating a competitive advantage?
4. What processes should be used to learn about customer preferences? This may entail indirect methods (e.g., database analysis) or involving buyers in the process.

High variety strategies, properly conceived and executed, offer powerful opportunities for competitive advantage by providing superior value to customers. As highlighted by the above issues, pursuing these finer segmentation strategies involves major decisions including which strategy to pursue and how to implement the strategy. Important in deciding how fine the segmentation should be is estimating the value and cost trade-offs of the relevant alternatives.

Selecting the Segmentation Strategy

We have considered several approaches to market segmentation, ranging from forming segments via experience and judgment to finer segmentation strategies. We now discuss deciding how to segment the market, and strategic analysis of the segments that have been identified.

Deciding How to Segment

The choice of a segmentation method depends on such factors as the maturity of market, the competitive structure, and the organization's experience in the market. The more comprehensive the segmentation process, the higher the costs of segment identification will be, reaching the highest level when field research studies are involved and finer segmentation strategies are considered. It is important to maximize the available knowledge about the product-market. An essential first step in segmentation is analyzing the existing customer base to identify groups of buyers with different response behavior (e.g., frequent purchase versus occasional purchase). Developing a view of how to segment the market by managers may be helpful. In some instances this information will provide a sufficient basis for segment formation. If not, experience and existing information are often helpful in guiding the design of customer research studies.

The five segmentation criteria discussed earlier help to evaluate potential segments. Deciding if the criteria are satisfied rests with management after examining response differences among the segments. The segmentation plan should satisfy the responsiveness criterion plus the other criteria (end users are identifiable, they are accessible via marketing program, the segment[s] is economically viable, and the segment is stable over time). The latter criterion may be less of an issue with mass customization since changes can be accommodated.

It is useful to consider the trade-off between the costs of developing a better segmentation scheme and the benefits gained. For example, instead of one variable being used to segment, a combination of two or three variables might be used. The costs of a more insightful segmentation scheme include the analysis time and the complexity of strategy development. The potential benefits include better determination of response differences, which enable the design of more effective marketing mix strategies. Importantly, segmentation should not be viewed as static, but as dynamic—as Dell learned more about the PC market, the segmentation approach evolved and developed.

The competitive advantage gained by finding (or developing) a new market segment can be very important. Segment strategies are used by a wide range of small companies with excellent performance records. Consider, for example, segmenting the market for paper. One way to segment is according to the use situation. The uses of paper include newspapers, magazines, books, announcements, letters, and other applications. Crane & Company, a firm competing in this market, is the primary supplier of paper for printing money.[39] This segment of the high-quality paper market consists of a single customer—the U.S. Treasury. The company's commitment to making quality products has sustained its competitive advantage in this segment since 1879. In the early 1990s Crane introduced a new currency paper, designed to identify counterfeit bills by placing a polyester thread in the paper. The other three-quarters of Crane's sales includes fine writing papers and high-quality paper products.

Strategic Analysis of Market Segments

Each market segment of interest needs to be studied to determine its potential attractiveness as a market target. The major areas of analysis include customers, competitors, positioning strategy, and financial and market attractiveness.

Customer Analysis. When forming segments, it is useful to find out as much as possible about the customers in each segment. Variables such as those used in dividing product-markets into segments are also helpful in describing the people in the same segments. The discussion of customer profiles in Chapter 3 includes information needed to profile a product-market. Similar information is needed for the segment profile, although the segment-level analysis is more comprehensive than the product-market profile.

The objective is to find descriptive characteristics that are highly correlated to the variables used to form the segments. Standardized information services are available for some product-markets including foods, health and beauty aids, and pharmaceuticals. Large markets involving many competitors make it profitable for research firms to collect and analyze data that are useful to the firms serving the market.

Information Resources Inc., a Chicago-based research supplier, has combined computerized information processing with customer research methods to generate information for market segmentation. Its Behavior Scan system electronically tracks total grocery store sales and individual household purchase behavior through complete universal product code (UPC) scanner coverage. People in the 2,500 household samples in each of several metropolitan markets covered by the service carry special identification cards and are individually tracked via scanner in grocery stores and drugstores. IRI publishes *The Marketing Fact Book*, which has consumer purchase data on all product categories. An example is shown in Exhibit 4.13. The database can be used for follow-up, in-depth analyses to meet the needs of specific companies.

An essential part of customer analysis is determining how well the buyers in the segment are satisfied. We know that customer satisfaction is measured by comparing customer *expectations* about the product and supporting services with the *performance* of the product and supporting services.[40] Some researchers indicate the *prior experience* may be a better basis of comparison than *expectations*.[41]

EXHIBIT 4.13
Analysis of Age of Soap Purchasers

Source: From *The Marketing Fact Book®* (Chicago: Information Resources, 1986), 10. Reprinted with permission.

Demographics

Q. Within which demographic segments is Ivory Liquid share strongest? Weakest? How do I go about building the weaker segments?

A. With respect to age of female household head, Ivory Liquid performance differs dramatically.

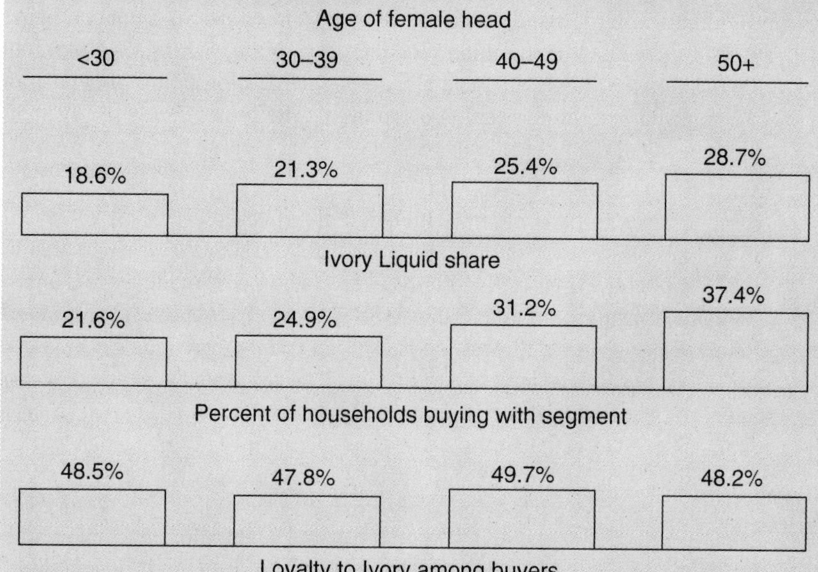

The relatively weaker performance among younger households traces to fewer buyers. Among those who *did* buy, loyalty was similar in all segments.

To build a share, promotions (perhaps high-value coupons) and/or advertising aimed at trial generation among younger female household heads should be considered.

This analysis can, of course, include a full range of additional demographic variables.

Note: *The above data are entirely fictional. Brand names are used only to add an element of reality. Any similarity to actual brand data is entirely coincidental.*

Customer satisfaction depends on the perceived performance of a product and supporting services and the standards that customers use to evaluate that performance.[42] The customer's standards complicate the relationship between organizational product specifications (e.g., product attribute tolerances) and satisfaction. Standards may involve something other than prepurchase expectations such as the perceived performance of competing products. Importantly, the standards are likely to vary across market segments.

Competitor Analysis. Market segment analysis considers the set of key competitors currently active in the market in which the segment is located plus any potential segment entrants. In complex market structures, mapping the competitive arena requires detailed analysis. The competing firms are described and evaluated to highlight their strengths and weaknesses. Information useful in the competitor analysis includes business scope and objectives; market position; market target(s) and customer base; positioning strategy; financial, technical, and operating strengths; management experience and capabilities; and special competitive advantages (e.g., patents). It is also important to anticipate the future strategies of key competitors.

Value-chain analysis can be used to examine competitive advantage at the segment level. A complete assessment of the nature and intensity of competition in the segment is important in determining whether to enter (or exit from) the segment and how to compete in the segment. Examining the five forces suggested by Porter (Chapter 3) is useful to determine segment attractiveness.

Positioning Analysis. We consider positioning strategy in Chapter 6. Segment analysis involves some preliminary choices about positioning strategy. One objective of segment analysis is to obtain guidelines for developing a positioning strategy. Flexibility exists in selecting how to position the firm (or brand) with its customers and against its competition in a segment. Positioning analysis shows how to combine product, distribution, pricing, and promotion strategies to favorably position the brand with buyers in the segment. Information from positioning maps like Exhibit 4.12 is useful in guiding positioning strategy. The positioning strategy should meet the needs and requirements of the targeted buyers at a cost that yields a profitable margin for the organization.

Estimating Segment Attractiveness. The financial and market attractiveness of each segment needs to be evaluated. Included are specific estimates of revenue, cost, and segment profit contribution over the planning horizon. Market attractiveness can be measured by market growth rate projections and attractiveness assessments made by management.

Financial analysis obtains sales, cost, and profit contribution estimates for each segment of interest. Since accurate forecasting is difficult if the projections are too far into the future, detailed projections typically extend two to five years ahead. Both the segment's competitive position evaluation and the financial forecasts are used in comparing segments. In all instances the risks and returns associated with serving a particular segment need to be considered. Flows of revenues and costs can be weighted to take into account risks and the time value of revenues and expenditures.

It should be recognized that as information availability grows, for example, through the data warehouses associated with CRM systems, the evaluation of segment attractiveness also has the potential for identifying unattractive market segments and even individual customers, which may be candidates for deletion.

Segmentation "Fit" and Implementation. One important aspect of evaluating segment attractiveness is how well the segments match company capabilities and the ability to implement marketing strategies around those segments.[43] There are many organizational barriers to the effective use of segmentation strategies. New segment targets that do not fit into conventional information reporting, planning processes, and budget systems in the company may be ignored or not adequately resourced. Innovative models of customer segments and market opportunities may be rejected by managers or the culture of the organization.

There are dangers that managers may prefer to retain traditional views of the market and structure information in that way, or that segmentation strategy will be driven by existing organizational structures and competitive norms.[44] It is important to be realistic in balancing the attractiveness of segments against the ability of the organization to implement appropriate marketing strategies to take advantage of the opportunities identified. Building effective marketing strategy around market segmentation mandates an emphasis on actionability as well as technique and analysis.[45]

Many of the issues we consider in later chapters impact on the operational capabilities of a company to implement segmentation strategies: for example, strength in cross-functional relationships may be a prerequisite to deliver value to new segments; the ability to work with partners may be needed to develop new products and services to build a strong position in a key market segment. The existence of these capabilities, or the ability to develop them, should be considered in making segmentation decisions.

Segment Analysis Illustration. An illustrative market segment analysis is shown in Exhibit 4.14. A two-year period is used for estimating sales, costs, contribution margin, and market share. Depending on the forecasting difficulty, estimates for a longer time period can be used. When appropriate, estimates can be expressed as present values of future revenues and costs. Business strength in Exhibit 4.13 refers to the present position of the firm relative to the competition in the segment. Alternatively, it can be expressed as the present position and an

EXHIBIT 4.14
Segment Financial and Market Attractiveness Analysis

	Segment		
Estimated ($ millions)	**X**	**Y**	**Z**
Sales*	10	16	5
Variable costs*	4	9	3
Contribution margin*	6	7	2
Market share†	60%	30%	10%
Total segment sales	17	53	50
Segment position:			
Business strength	High	Medium	Low
Attractiveness‡	Medium	Low	High

*For a two-year period.
‡Percent of total sales in the segment.
‡Based on a five-year projection.

estimated future position, based upon plans for increasing business strength. Attractiveness is typically evaluated for some future time period. In the illustration a five-year projection is used.

The example shows how segment opportunities are ranked according to their overall attractiveness. The analysis can be expanded to include additional information such as profiles of key competitors. The rankings are admittedly subjective since decision makers will vary in their weighing of estimated financial position, business strength, and segment attractiveness. Place yourself in the role of a manager evaluating the segments. Using the information in Exhibit 4.14, rank segments X, Y, and Z as to their overall importance as market targets. Unless management is ready to allocate a major portion of resources to segment Z to build business strength, it is a candidate for the last-place position. Yet Z has some attractive characteristics. The segment has the most favorable market attractiveness of the three, and its estimated total sales are nearly equal to Y's for the next two years. The big problem with Z is its business strength. The key question is whether Z's market share can be increased. If not, X looks like a good prospect for top rating, followed by Y, and by Z. Of course, management may decide to go after all three segments.

Summary

Market segmentation is often a requirement for competing in many product-markets because buyers differ in their preferences for products and services. Finding out what these preferences are and grouping buyers with similar needs is an essential part of business and marketing strategy development. Market segmentation is an opportunity for a small firm to focus on buyers where its competitive advantages are most favorable. Large firms seeking to establish or protect a dominant market position can often do so by targeting multiple segments.

Segmentation of a product-market requires that response differences exist between segments, and that the segments are identifiable and stable over time. Also, the benefits of segmentation should exceed the costs. Segmenting a market involves identifying the basis of segmentation, forming segments, describing each segment, and analyzing and evaluating the segment(s) of interest. The variables useful as bases for forming and describing segments include the characteristics of people and organizations, use situation, buyers' needs and preferences, and purchase behavior.

Segments can be formed by identifying customer groups using the characteristics of people or organizations. The groups are analyzed to determine if the response profiles are different across the candidate segments. Alternatively, customer response information can be used to form customer groupings and then the descriptive characteristics of the groups analyzed to find out if segments can be identified. Several examples of segment formation are discussed to illustrate the methods that are available for this purpose.

Finer segmenting strategies present attractive options for moving toward small segments and responding to buyers' unique value requirements. Technology, buyer diversity, and relationship opportunities are the drivers of finer segmentation strategies. These strategies include microsegmentation, mass customization, and variety seeking. While potentially attractive, finer segmentation strategies are more complex than other forms of segmentation and require comprehensive benefit and cost evaluations.

Segment analysis and evaluation consider the strengths and limitations of each segment as a potential market target for the organization. Segment analysis includes customer descriptions and satisfaction analysis, evaluating existing and potential competitors and competitive advantage, marketing program positioning analysis, and financial and market attractiveness. Segment analysis is important in evaluating customer satisfaction, finding new-product opportunities, selecting market targets, and designing positioning strategies. Nonetheless, it is also important to understand the organizational barriers to implementing segmentation strategy which may exist in a company, and to evaluate the "fit" of segmentation with company capabilities. Effectively implemented, a good segmentation strategy creates an important competitive edge for an organization.

Internet Applications

A. Explore several of the following Web sites:

www.adquest.com *www.americanet.com*
www.autosite.com *www.mlm2000.com*
www.sidewalk.com *www.monster.com*
www.realtor.com

How does the information from these sites affect our traditional concept of market segmentation? How is the segmentation process altered by such Internet providers?

B. Evaluate the following site for additional ideas and material concerned with market segmentation and the types of support that can be provided for companies: *www.marketsegmentation.co.uk*

Feature Applications

A. Review the material in the Strategy Feature, "Segmentation and Positioning Challenges for Banana Republic." Examine the product ranges at Gap's three branded store chains (The Gap, Banana Republic, and Old Navy) by visiting the Gap Inc. Web page (*www.gapinc.com*) and the pages for each type of store. Consider whether the company has succeeded in positioning its three brands in different segments and the challenges in maintaining this separation.

B. Review the BMW MINI case in the Global Feature, "The BMW MINI." Do you believe that BMW has built a robust niche or segment strategy, or is the car a fashion item with limited lasting appeal to car buyers, like other "retro" attempts?

Questions for Review and Discussion

1. Competing in the unified European market raises some interesting market segment questions. Discuss the segmentation issues regarding this multiple-country market.
2. Why are there marketing strategy advantages in using demographic characteristics to break out product-markets into segments?
3. The real test of a segment formation scheme occurs after it has been tried and the results evaluated. Are there ways to evaluate alternative segmenting schemes without actually trying them?
4. Suggest ways of obtaining the information needed to conduct a market segment analysis.
5. Why may it become necessary for companies to change their market segmentation identification over time?
6. Is considering segments of one buyer a reality or a myth? Discuss.
7. Is it necessary to use a unique positioning strategy for each market segment targeted by an organization?
8. Under what circumstances may it not be possible to break up a product-market into segments? What are the dangers of using an incorrect segment formation scheme?
9. What are some of the advantages in using mass customization technology to satisfy the needs of buyers?
10. Does the use of mass customization eliminate the need to segment a market?

Notes

1. Adapted from case material compiled by Neil A. Morgan and Garry Veale, originally published in Nigel F. Piercy, *Market-Led Strategic Change: Transforming the Process of Going to Market* (Oxford: Butterworth-Heinemann, 1997), 303–311.
2. Anthony Bianco, "The Vanishing Mass Market," *BusinessWeek*, July 12, 2004, 62–68.
3. Don Peppers and Martha Rogers, *Enterprise One-to-One* (New York: Doubleday, 1997).
4. Don Shultz and Heidi Schultz, "Individual Matters," *Marketing Business*, March 2004, 12–15.
5. Peter R. Dickson and James L. Ginter, "Market Segmentation, Product Differentiation, and Marketing Strategy," *Journal of Marketing*, April 1987, 1–10.

6. W. Chan Kim and Renee Mauborgne, "Finding Rooms for Manoeuvre," *Financial Times*, May 27, 1999.
7. James Samuelson, "Flying High," *Forbes*, August 2, 1996, 84–85.
8. Nikki Tait, "Mixed Emotions as Olds Guard Bows Out," *Financial Times*, December 20, 2000, 27.
9. Leonard L. Berry, "Relationship Marketing of Services—Growing Interest, Emerging Perspectives," *Journal of the Academy of Marketing Science*, Fall 1995, 238–240.
10. Henry Assael, *Consumer Behavior and Marketing Action*, 2nd ed. (Boston: PWS-Kent Publishing, 1984), 225.
11. Jerry Flint, "The Magazine Factory," *Forbes*, May 22, 1995, 160–162.
12. Anthony Bianco, "The Vanishing Mass Market."
13. Jay L. Laughlin and Charles R. Taylor, "An Approach to Industrial Market Segmentation," *Industrial Marketing Management* 20 (1991), 127–136.
14. Ronald Henkoff, "Boeing's Big Problem," *Fortune*, January 12, 1998, 96–99, 102–103.
15. Daniel S. Levine, "Justice Served," *Sales & Marketing Management*, May 1995, 53–61.
16. Michael Malone, "Pennsylvania Guys Mass Customize," *Forbes ASAP*, April 10, 1995, 82–85.
17. Nicholas Bray, "Credit Lyonnaise Targets Wealthy Clients," *The Wall Street Journal*, July 24, 1994.
18. A. H. Maslow, "Theory of Human Motivation," *Psychology Review*, July 1943, 43–45.
19. Assael, *Consumer Behavior and Marketing Action*, 650.
20. Bernard Berelson and Gary A. Steiner, *Human Behavior: An Inventory of Scientific Findings* (New York: Harcourt Brace Jovanovich, 1964), 88.
21. Christopher Field, "Loyalty Cards Are Unlikely to Carry All the Answers," *Financial Times*, May 3, 2000, IV; Marian Edwards, "Your Wish Is on My Database," *Financial Times*, February 28, 2000, 20.
22. Eric N. Berkowitz, Roger A. Kerin, Steven W. Hartley, and William Rudelius, *Marketing*, 5th ed. (Chicago: Richard D. Irwin, 1997), 155–156.
23. Louise O'Brien and Charles Jones, "Do Rewards Really Create Loyalty?" *Harvard Business Review*, May–June 1995, 78.
24. Anthony Bianco, "The Vanishing Mass Market."
25. Miriam Jordan, "In India, Luxury Is within Reach of Many," *The Wall Street Journal*, October 17, 1995, A15.
26. Malcolm McDonald, "A Slice of the Action," *Marketing Business*, July/August 1998, 47.
27. Dickson and Ginter, "Market Segmentation," 4.
28. George S. Day, *Market Driven Strategy* (New York: The Free Press), 1990, 101–104.
29. Nancy Rotenier, "Antistatus Backpacks, $450 a Copy," *Forbes*, June 19, 1995, 118–120.
30. Allanna Sullivan, "Mobil Bets Drivers Pick Cappuccino over Low Prices," *The Wall Street Journal*, January 30, 1995, B1 and B4.
31. *Marketing News*, July 20, 1998.
32. V. Kasturi Ranga, Rowland T. Moriarity, and Gordon S. Swartz, "Segmenting Customers in Mature Industrial Markets," *Journal of Marketing*, October 1992, 72–82.
33. *Financial Times, Understanding Customer Relationship Management, London: Financial Times*, Spring 2000.
34. Ali Kara and Erdener Kaynak, "Markets of a Single Customer: Exploiting Conceptual Developments in Market Segmentation," *European Journal of Marketing*, no. 11/12, 1997, 873–895.
35. Barbara E. Kahn, "Dynamic Relationships with Customers: High-Variety Strategies," *Journal of the Academy of Marketing Science*, Winter 1998, 45–53.
36. Kahn, "Dynamic Relationships"; Joseph B. Pine II, *Mass Customization: The New Frontier in Business Competition* (Boston: Harvard Business School Press, 1993).
37. Kahn, "Dynamic Relationships."
38. Kahn, "Dynamic Relationships."
39. Linda Killian, "Crane's Progress," *Forbes*, August 19, 1991, 44.
40. A. Parasuraman, Valarie A. Zeithaml, and Leonard L. Berry, "A Conceptual Model of Service Quality and Its Implications for Future Research," *Journal of Marketing*, Fall 1985, 41–50.
41. Robert B. Woodruff, Ernest R. Cadotte, and Roger L. Jenkins, "Modeling Consumer Satisfaction Processes Using Experienced-Based Norms," *Journal of Marketing Research*, August 1983, 296–304.
42. The following discussion of customer satisfaction is based on discussions with Robert B. Woodruff, The University of Tennessee, Knoxville.
43. Nigel F. Piercy and Neil A. Morgan, "Strategic and Operational Segmentation," *Journal of Strategic Marketing* 1, no. 2, 1993, 123–140.
44. Noel Capon and James M. Hulbert, *Marketing Management in the 21st Century* (Upper Saddle River, NJ: Prentice-Hall, 2001), 185–186.
45. D. Young, "The Politics behind Market Segmentation," *Marketing News*, October 21, 1996, 17.

Capabilities for Continuous Learning about Markets

Understanding markets and competition is critical to achieving market orientation. "Every discussion of market orientation emphasizes the ability of the firm to learn about customers, competitors, and channel members in order to continually sense and act on events and trends in present and prospective markets."[1] Market-driven companies display superior skills in gathering, interpreting, and using information to guide their business and marketing strategies.

Increasingly, learning about markets is more about interpreting information rather than finding it. With resources like online Internet searches, in-company information and intelligence systems, marketing research agency reports and surveys, and burgeoning technical literature in most fields, executives may be in danger of being overwhelmed by information. Research suggests that how accurate executives are about the competitive environment may be less important for strategy and the organizational changes that follow strategy than the way they interpret information about their environments. This suggests that investments in enhancing and shaping those interpretations may create a more durable competitive advantage than investments in obtaining more information.[2] The imperative in market-led strategy is the quest for superior interpretation and market understanding.

Consider the case of the personal computer market leader Dell Inc. From the outset, Dell's business model exploited the advantages of selling direct to customers and building products to order instead of estimating demand and building to stock. The direct business model was ideally placed to use the Internet to full advantage. However, underpinning the success of Dell's direct business model are processes of learning and responsiveness to customers, utilizing the company's technology and the Internet, but also the human processes of listening to customers and learning from them. Dell and suppliers share information and plans freely—external suppliers are treated as if they were internal to Dell's organization. Internet and direct selling relationships with customers also provide Dell with unique insights into their needs, preferences, and changing requirements. Sales account managers work with customers to develop plans to meet future IT needs. Dell works with customers to save them money by standardizing their global PC purchasing (providing the company with information about its own global PC purchasing patterns). Major customers have their own Dell Premier Pages on the Internet, providing an interactive product catalog, but also access to Dell support tools and technical resources. Dell's market sensing and learning capabilities have created a new competitive advantage, which is uniquely difficult for competitors to equal.[3]

A theme linking companies in many sectors is their capabilities in superior market sensing and their abilities to develop competitive advantage from their learning processes. The Cayenne sports utility vehicle from Porsche in Germany has been highly successful with U.S. consumers, lifting Porsche's sales by 15 percent and profits by 22 percent in 2004. The Cayenne product concept was based on painstaking intelligence gathering to establish that the consumer would pay a premium for the speed, for which Porsche is famous, in the shape of a sports-utility vehicle. Similarly, the British retailer Tesco is highly skilled in mining data from its loyalty card scheme, supplemented by customer feedback from telephone and written surveys, to identify and exploit new market opportunities. For example, in 2003 Tesco detected early signs that food consumers wanted more nutritional information, allowing a swift marketing response with a new labeling system providing shoppers with more detailed information on the fat, salt, and sugar content of hundreds of products ahead of the competition.[4]

The challenge is increasingly one of knowledge management to build companywide understanding of the marketplace and responsiveness, rather than simply collecting information.

In this chapter we examine how continuous learning about markets improves competitive advantage. First, we look at the relationship between market orientation and organizational learning. Next, we discuss several sources of information. Then we overview information methods and capabilities, including marketing research, standardized information services, management information systems, database systems, and decision support systems. Finally, several important issues are highlighted concerning the collection and use of information in the organization and the growing importance of knowledge management to effective market-driven strategy.

Market Orientation and Organizational Learning

The ability to learn from customers underpins the management decision making at companies like Autodesk—which holds roughly 80 percent of the world market for PC computer-aided design (CAD) software. Autodesk's successful spin-off Buzzsaw.com originated with discussions with customers about how they used the company's software in designing buildings and what they wanted in new software. The surprise was that customer priorities were not CAD sophistication but managing complex collaborative construction projects. The challenge was to create a better way for dozens of participants in a construction project to share drawings electronically and manage projects from beginning to end. After extensive research into how the various participants in a construction project worked, the solution was a well-designed Internet work space, with online tools for customers to manage their own work space. Within a year of the launch of Buzzsaw.com there were around 150,000 users of the Internet work space, communicating and sharing drawings across the world.[5]

Companies like Dell, Tesco, Porsche, and Autodesk illustrate the close relationship between a market-oriented culture and organizational learning. We review the characteristics of market orientation and look at the role of organizational learning in creating superior customer value. Next, the process of learning about markets is described, followed by a discussion of how learning helps to create superior customer value. Finally, we examine and illustrate the available methods of obtaining information.

Market Orientation

Market orientation is both a culture and also a process committed to achieving superior customer value (Chapter 1). The process consists of information acquisition, broad information dissemination, and shared diagnosis and coordinated action.[6] Market orientation provides the foundation for organizational learning, although some cautions need to be considered in achieving the potential of learning:[7]

1. Market intelligence may be so focused that opportunities or threats outside the current product-market are ignored.

2. Prevailing views of market orientation consider current customers and competitors, whereas other learning sources including suppliers, noncompeting businesses, consultants, and government may provide important information.

The market orientation perspective needs to extend beyond traditional market boundaries to include all of the relevant sources of knowledge and ideas. A key issue is deciding how broad this orientation should be. The section on learning about markets offers several guidelines concerning this issue.

Characteristics of the Learning Organization. Our understanding of the learning organization continues to unfold as the processes used by successful organizations are studied and interpreted. These organizations share several common characteristics:

> Learning organizations are guided by a shared vision that focuses the energies of organizational members on creating superior value for customers. These organizations continuously acquire, process, and disseminate throughout the organization knowledge about markets, products, technologies, and business processes. They do not hesitate to question long held assumptions and beliefs regarding their business. Their knowledge is based on experience, experimentation, and information from customers, suppliers, competitors, and other sources. Through complex communication, coordination, and conflict resolution processes, these organizations reach a shared interpretation of the information, which enables them to act swiftly and decisively to exploit opportunities and defuse problems. Learning organizations are exceptional in their ability to anticipate and act on opportunities in turbulent and fragmenting markets.[8]

Additional research promises to further expand our knowledge about these complex organizational processes.

Learning and Competitive Advantage. The advantage gained from learning is that the organization is able to quickly and effectively respond to opportunities and threats, and to satisfy customers' needs with new products and improved services.[9] Learning reduces the time necessary to accomplish projects such as new product development. For example, Manco is a distributor of duct tape, mailer envelopes, shelf liners, and related products. After listening to a customer, Manco developed its nonadhesive shelf liner, which is similar to rubber mesh and can be easily cut and fitted in and out of shelves. In 1997 the product had sales of $30 million, accounting for nearly one-fifth of Manco's annual sales.[10] Superior learning capabilities and speed of learning create a new competitive advantage, which may be extremely difficult for competitors to imitate or equal.

Learning about Markets

Learning about markets requires developing processes throughout the organization for obtaining, interpreting, and acting on information from sensing activities. The learning processes of market-oriented companies include a sequence of activities beginning with open-minded inquiry.[11]

In some cases, learning from the market may be a critical element of rebuilding performance by aligning company capabilities better with market characteristics. Consider the recovery program under way at The Bombay Company which is described in the Strategy Feature. Specialty retailer Bombay saw a steady decline in its performance through the late 1990s. A change of management team and enhanced market focus has driven a recovery in the early 2000s. The basis of this recovery has been extensive customer research and systematic management response to the lessons learned.

Objective Inquiry. One danger to be avoided is not exploring new views about markets and competition, because they are not taken seriously. Searching for information is of little value if management already has a fixed view on which new information will have no influence whatever it indicates.

Strategy Feature

Recovery at The Bombay Company Inc.

- The Bombay Company is a specialty retailer selling a range of traditional furniture, prints, and accessories through retail outlets, catalogs, and online. The early part of the 2000s has seen a substantial turnaround in the company's declining performance.
- A new management team undertook a major rebranding program based on customer research undertaken by Publicis USA in 2002, examining shopping experiences and what consumers really wanted from a home furnishings retailer.
- The research showed Bombay's products were liked, but the company had lost the ability to give the customers ideas about how to use the products and to decorate the home.
- This drove major changes in how goods were displayed and presented, with related goods kept together and furniture accessorized to provide the consumer with home decorating ideas. Confused merchandizing and pricing were rationalized.
- The research suggested Bombay was stuffy and took itself too seriously. Merchandizing was reoriented with a "points of view" program to style parts of each store around a theme and create a mood–such as "Bohemian" to mirror the gypsy trend prevalent in womens' fashion.
- The research showed catalogs were used for decorating ideas, not product listings, so they have been restyled around lifestyle choices.
- Further expansion ideas are the Bombay Kids outlets and the sale of Bombay furniture through Amazon.com's Home and Garden channel.
- The recovery strategy at Bombay involves reinventing the brand and redefining its store and catalog interiors. These changes are driven by extensive and continuing marketing research and response to customer feedback.

Source: Adapted from Arundhati Parmar, "Redecoration: Bombay Style," *Marketing News,* March 15, 2004, 9–10; and information available on the company Web site (*www.bombaycompany.com*).

As discussed in Chapter 1, the members of market-oriented organizations recognize the importance of market sensing and coordinated interpretation of market intelligence to guide strategies. Nonetheless, not all companies see the value in continuous learning about markets. Managers who are not part of market-driven cultures may be unwilling to invest in information to improve their decision-making results. The same companies often encounter problems because of faulty or incomplete market sensing.

A framework of the type shown in Exhibit 5.1 can be used as a participative, cross-functional structure for market sensing. This challenges managers to identify the most significant events impacting their business and its markets over a three- to five-year horizon, and to position the events in the matrix according to estimated probability and the effect of the event on the business. Importantly, by including external views, such as suppliers, technology experts, distributors, and customers, it is possible to build a view of the world that breaks free of traditional company beliefs, challenges management assumptions, and identifies the highest priorities for information collection and use in making strategic decisions.[12]

Developing processes for continuous learning allows firms to capture more information about customers, suppliers, and competitors. This capability provides the potential for growth based on informed decisions and a more complete mapping and analysis of the competitive environment. Also, firms can respond much more quickly to competitors' actions and take advantage of situations in the marketplace. Open-minded inquiry also helps to anticipate value migration threats, which are frequently initiated by competitors from outside the traditional market or industry.[13] For example, monitoring potential competitors such as electronic imaging companies by conventional film producers is essential in designing strategies for coping with the competitive threats from electronic technology.

Information Distribution for Synergy. This step encourages the widespread distribution of information in the organization. The objective is to leverage the value of the information

EXHIBIT 5.1
A Framework for Market Sensing

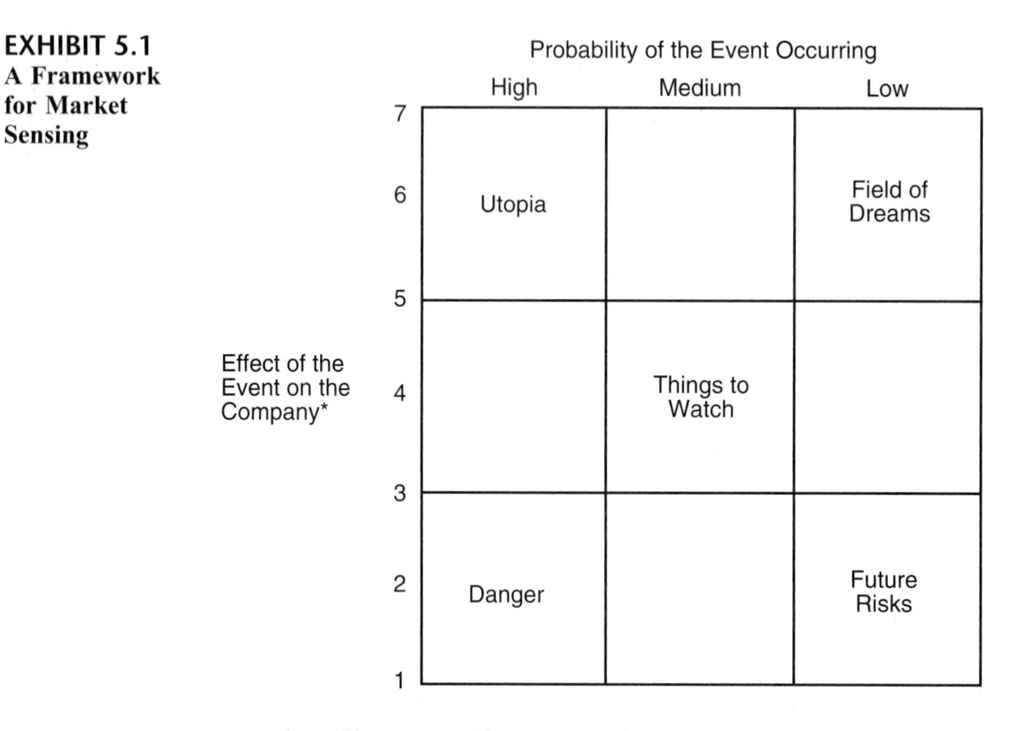

by cutting across business functions to share information on customers, value-chain channels, suppliers, and competitors. Traditional information processing in organizations allocates relevant information to each business function, and information possession becomes a source of internal power. Synergistic distribution works to remove functional hurdles and practices. Cross-functional teams are useful to encourage transfer of information across functions.

The explosion in information connectivity (access) resulting from electronic communication facilitates widespread information distribution.[14] Unbundling information from its physical carrier such as salespeople will provide access as well as speed in organizations. This will help cross-functional teams and alter hierarchical structures and proprietary information systems. Expanded information connectivity promises to encourage cooperation among functions, reduce the power of information possession, and enhance organizational learning.

Mutually Informed Interpretations. The mental model of the market guides managers' interpretation of information. The intent is to reach a shared vision about the market and about the impact that new information has on this vision. The market-oriented culture encourages market sensing. But the process requires more than gathering and studying information. "This interpretation is facilitated by the mental models of managers, which contain decision rules for deciding how to act on the information in light of anticipated outcomes."[15] The model reflects the executives' vision about the forces influencing the market and likely future directions of change. Learning occurs as members of the organization evaluate the results of their decisions based on their vision at the time the decisions were made. The market sensing framework in Exhibit 5.1 may support addressing these issues.

Deciding to take the high risk of cutting-edge ventures requires managers to reach a shared vision about uncertain future market opportunities. For example, the British supermarket company Tesco operates an outstanding and successful Internet grocery channel alongside its store network. The planning for this venture started in the mid-1990s, long before the much-publicized "dot-com revolution" was under way, leading to a national rollout in 2000, at a time when other Internet ventures were crashing in ruins. The five-year gestation period involved close study of what consumers wanted from Internet grocery shopping and a developing understanding that shoppers wanted the Internet channel to provide a complement store-based shopping, not a substitute. The management team has sustained its vision that an Internet channel would become a profitable part of the core business over a seven-year period before reaching operating profitability.

Accessible Memory. This part in the learning process emphasizes the importance of keeping and gaining access to prior learning. The objective is not to lose valuable information that can continue to be used. Doing this involves integrating the information into the organizational memory, and not losing information when people leave the organization. Hewlett-Packard's (H-P) vision about computer printer technology was that inkjet technology would replace dot matrix printers, providing an excellent growth opportunity. H-P beat Japanese companies to the market even though Canon had the technology. Hewlett-Packard's inkjet product design team continued to learn how to improve the product and develop strategies based on monitoring competitors' actions. For example, prices were lowered when the team sensed that Japanese competitors were about to enter the market.

Urban Outfitters Inc. is a successful specialty retailer that is guided by management's shared and constantly renewed vision about the market based on an effective learning process. The company targets style-conscious young adults. Sales in 2000 ran at $210 million, but this has grown at an average annual rate of 21 percent, reaching $548 million in 2004. The retailer's products include fashion apparel, accessories, household items, and gifts. Urban Outfitters' unique value proposition is the shopping environment it provides to the 18–30 targeted age group. To stay ahead of its unpredictable buyers with whimsical tastes, management employs over 75 fashion spies who sense what is happening in fashion in neighborhoods in New York, California, London, and Paris.[16] Salaries and expenses of this market sensing team total several million dollars annually. Market feedback guides new-product decisions and signals when buyer interest is slowing down. Stores are located near colleges and places where youths gather. Catalogs and the Web site reflect this identity. Management's close understanding of the fashion market has led to new retail concepts in its 50 Anthropologie stores, designed to appeal to its buyers when they move to an older age group in the life cycle. The target is women aged 30 to 45, focused on fashion, career, and home. The Free People operation is the company's more general branded wholesaler of casual clothes, sold through department and specialty stores.

Information, Analysis, and Action

Deciding what information is needed is the starting point in planning for and acquiring information. Because of the costs of acquiring, processing, and analyzing information, the potential benefits of needed information need to be compared to costs. Normally, information falls into two categories: (1) information regularly supplied from internal and external sources, and (2) information obtained as needed for a particular problem or situation. Examples of the former are sales costs analyses, information from 800 number calls, market share measurements, and customer satisfaction surveys. Information from the latter category includes new-product concept tests, brand preference studies, and studies of advertising effectiveness.

Several types of marketing information are available. A description of each type of information follows:

Marketing Research Studies. These studies consist of customized information collected and analyzed for a particular research problem. A study of customers' reactions to a new-product concept is an example. The information may be obtained through field surveys, online responses, and/or published sources.

Standardized Information Services. This information is available from outside vendors on a subscription or single-purchase basis. The services collect and analyze information that is sold to several customers such as prescription sales for drugs marketed to pharmaceutical firms.

Management Information Systems (MIS). Computerized systems supply information for a variety of purposes such as order processing, invoicing, customer analysis, and product performance. The information in these systems may include both internal and external data.

Database Systems. This special form of MIS includes information from internal and external sources that is computerized and used for customer and product analyses, mailing lists, identifying sales prospects, and other marketing applications.

Decision Support Systems. These computerized systems provide decision-making assistance to managers and staff. Their capabilities are more advanced than a MIS. American Airlines' revenue (pricing and yield) management system for aircraft seat utilization includes effective decision support techniques to assist analysts in obtaining maximum revenue for each flight.

Customer Relationship Management (CRM) Systems. Designed to manage the relationship with a customer more effectively, by integrating all needed information sources and systems to provide seamlessness at the point of contact with the customer, CRM systems also provide rich information sources relating to customers' actual purchase behavior. Frequently associated are "data warehouses," which are capable of being "mined" for customer information, CRM systems are providing a formidable new type of marketing information. (See the Appendix to Chapter 7.)

Competitor Intelligence Systems. Companies are using competitor intelligence systems to help monitor existing and potential competitors. Intelligence activities include searching databases, conducting customer surveys, interviewing suppliers and other channel members, forming strategic alliances with competitors, hiring competitors' employees, and evaluating competitors' products.

The firm's complete information needs should be considered before deciding what types of information to use. Most firms benefit from a routine and complete evaluation of their information situation. Cooperation among departments can save the firm countless employee-hours and dollars. Far too often a department launches an expensive information-gathering project only to discover later that another department already had the type of information sought. Synergistic information distribution encourages sharing.

In the remainder of the chapter, we examine the various methods of acquiring and processing information for use in marketing decision making. The objective is to show how the various information capabilities assist decision makers in strategic and operating decisions. A good marketing information management strategy takes into account the interrelationship of these capabilities.

Marketing Research Information

The starting point in obtaining marketing research information is defining the problem to be studied, indicating specific objectives, and determining what information is needed to help solve the problem. Problem definition examples for a new candy product and the quality of fast-food services are shown in Parts A and B of Exhibit 5.2.

Marketing research information is obtained from internal records, trade contacts, published information, surveys, and many other sources. An example of a research study is shown in Exhibit 5.3. It is a proposed test of the effectiveness of an advertising commercial. Marketing research studies range in cost from less than $10,000 to over $100,000.

Marketing research is "the systematic gathering, recording, processing, and analyzing of marketing data, which—when interpreted—will help the marketing executive to uncover opportunities and to reduce risks in decision making."[17] Strategies for obtaining marketing research information include collecting existing information, using standardized research services, and conducting special research studies.

EXHIBIT 5.2
Illustrative Marketing Research Problem Definitions

Source: William R. Dillon, Thomas J. Madden, and Nell H. Firtle, *Marketing Research in a Marketing Environment,* 3rd ed. (Burr Ridge, IL: Richard D. Irwin, 1994), 34.

Problem Setting A: A Consumer Package Goods Firm	
Project:	A major package goods firm is deciding on whether to continue development of a new "hard candy" product. The new product is a line extension offering a distinctive new ingredient that should be attractive to at least some category users. Brand managers want to collect information on the likely success of the new product.
Research Objective:	To determine the likely market success of a new "hard candy" product containing ingredient X and its relation to existing products.
Possible Research Questions:	1. What volume and market share will the new product achieve when it is rolled out nationally? 2. What trial rate can be expected? 3. Will the new product cannibalize existing products in our line? 4. Which existing products does the new product draw its share from? 5. Are there segments of consumers who have a greater likelihood of trying the new product? 6. Are there segments of consumers who are particularly attracted to the new ingredient?
Problem Setting B: A Fast-Food Chain	
Project:	The corporate management of a national fast-food chain wants to determine whether customer perceptions of service are uniform across their franchises. The parent corporation has followed a policy of minimizing variation in services provided. The intent of management is to assess whether customer perceptions of services are consistent with corporate standards.
Research Objective:	To evaluate customers' perceptions of the services provided by franchise operators and to identify areas that need attention.
Possible Research Questions:	1. What is the relevant set of service features on which franchises should be evaluated? 2. What is the perceived value of each service feature? 3. Do perceptions of services vary by meal? 4. Does the value of a service feature vary by meal? 5. Are there regional differences across franchises in terms of services provided? 6. What factors contribute to any differences that are observed?

Collecting Existing Information

The internal information system of the firm affects the extent and ease of the collection of existing information. The nature and scope of the information and the information system network will vary greatly from firm to firm and among industries. Many firms have extensive internal information systems, or at least the capability to implement such systems. Recall the new customer information resources being created by CRM systems.

EXHIBIT 5.3
Off-Air Test Marketing Research Project Proposal

Source: William R. Dillon, Thomas J. Madden, and Neil H. Firtle, *Marketing Research in a Marketing Environment,* 3rd ed. (Burr Ridge, IL; Richard D. Irwin, 1994), 611. Copyright © The McGraw-Hill Companies. Used with permission.

Brand: Colgate.

Project: Copy Test: "Midnight Delight."

Background and purpose: A new commercial has been developed—"Midnight Delight." Brand Group is interested in determining its effectiveness. The objectives of this study will be to determine
- Brand recall.
- Copy recall.
- Purchase intent shifts.
- Comparison with previous copy testing results.

Research method: This research will be conducted using central location mall facilities in Boston, Atlanta, Milwaukee, and San Francisco. Each commercial will be viewed by 200 past-30-week toothpaste users as follows:

		Age Group	Number of Respondents
Males	50%	8–11	30
Females	50%	12–17	50
		18–24	25
		25–34	25
		35–49	10
		50+	10
			150

Information to be obtained:
- Brand recall.
- Copy recall.
- Pre- and postpurchase intentions.

Action standard: This study, which is being done for information purposes, will be used in conjunction with previous copy testing results.

Cost and timing: The cost for one commercial will be $6,500 ± 10%. The following schedule will be established:

Field work	3 weeks
Top-line reports	1 week
Final report	3 weeks
Total	7 weeks

Supplier: Legget Lustig Firtle, Inc.

There is considerable value and potential in using the information in the organization's current system. This is essential for the strategic mission of the firm, as well as for efficient utilization of assets. Information is a resource that needs to be consciously managed.[18] Management should structure the information system to capture this resource and control its use. Information is not a by-product of activities of the firm. It is a scarce, valuable resource that affects the future success or failure of the firm. Management may not have control over the actions of competitors or consumers, but an effective information system provides a way to anticipate and react.

The product mix and the nature of business operations influence what type of internal marketing information system is appropriate in a particular firm. Nonetheless, electronic information systems are necessary in all kinds of companies. The system needs to be designed to meet the information needs of the organization. Manufacturers have different information requirements from retailers or wholesalers. The size and complexity of the firm also influence the composition of the information system.

The costs and benefits of the information must be evaluated for both short-term and long-term planning. Incremental efforts and expenditures in the early stages of creating an internal information system may avoid future costly modifications. Achieving long-term performance may require temporary losses to finance a system. It is critical to consider a long-term perspective in evaluating information system decisions.

Harrah's Entertainment is an example of a company developing market-led strategy on the basis of existing information. Harrah's operates 26 casinos in 13 states and in 2002 had more than $4 billion in revenue. In a sector known for fickle customers, Harrah's has built a strategy based on customer loyalty. Harrah's has used the data in its customer loyalty program—the Total Gold card—to uncover consumer preferences based on tracking the millions of individual transactions conducted. Harrah's found that 26 percent of its customers generated 82 percent of their revenues. These were not the high-rollers targeted by competitors, they were former teachers, doctors, bankers, and machinists—middle-aged and senior adults with discretionary time and income. They typically do not stay in casino hotels, but visit a casino on the way home from work or on a weekend night out. They respond differently to marketing and promotions because they enjoy the anticipation and excitement of gambling itself. Harrah's strategy is one of providing visibly higher levels of service to the customers with greatest value to the company. The transactional data can even be used to see which particular customers are playing which slot machines and to identify what it was about the particular machine that appealed to them. Harrah's successful strategy is driven by leveraging an existing information source to build competitive differentiation.[19]

Standardized Information Services

A wide variety of marketing information is available for purchase in special publications and on a subscription basis. In some instances, the information may be free, for example, in online statistical databases. Sources include government agencies, universities, private research firms, industry and trade organizations, and consultants. A key advantage to standardized information is that the costs of collection and analysis are shared by many users. The major limitation is that the information may not correspond well with the user's individual needs. These services offer substantial cost advantages, and many are quite inexpensive (for example, data distributed from the U.S. Census of Population and most governmental statistical services in developed countries). Many services allow online access to data, enabling subscribers to automatically input external information into their own information systems.

Many standardized information services are available to meet a wide range of decision-making needs. Some examples follow:[20]

Nielsen Media Research (*www.nielsenmedia.com*) collects information on television audience measurement, with measurement meters in 5,100 homes assessing the viewing habits of 14,000 individuals. Decisions to continue or drop shows often depend on these ratings.

The Petroleum Information Corporation unit (now part of IHS Energy) supplies information on drilling and production for firms interested in oil and gas exploration activities around the world (*www.ihsenergy.com*).

VNU in 2004 launched Homescan Online, a new service to measure how Internet use affects offline purchase behavior among 14,000 Homescan panel households (*www.vnu.com*).

Information Resources Inc.'s InfoScan retail tracking service and ConsumerNetwork panel services provide weekly sales, price, and store condition information for a sample of food, drug, and mass merchandise stores (*www.infores.com*).

ACNielsen Corp. (*www.acnielsen.com*) offers product movement data for food, drug, and other retail stores in more than 80 countries. Its ScanTrack service captures data through checkout scanners or in-store audits and provides weekly data on packaged goods in the United States.

IMS International (*imshealth.com*) provides information such as pharmaceutical audits of sales to the pharmaceutical and health care industries worldwide. Audits are available in over 100 countries.

Using the large data banks collected and organized by these services, many different analyses can be made, depending on a company's information needs. The cost of the information for use by one company would be prohibitive. By sharing the database, a wide range of company information needs can be met.

Information Resources Inc. (IRI) uses electronic retail store scanning systems to record purchases by people participating on consumer panels. Scanning systems in stores automatically record consumers' purchases, eliminating the need for diaries and providing accurate data. The InfoScan panel data are obtained from a sample of 60,000 households. IRI installs a complete electronic monitoring system in each city where it has a consumer panel. IRI can also monitor the television programs watched by participants and insert test commercials into programming. Advertisements can be targeted to households with specific demographic characteristics since these data are recorded for all participants. Subsequent purchases measure the effect of the commercial. The use of coupons can be monitored to test products and the strength of competitors. With this network, IRI can respond to various queries from clients such as Campbell Soup Company, P&G, Johnson & Johnson, and General Foods Corporation. IRI monitors consumer reactions and preferences without alerting them to which products are being tested. Firms can introduce advertising campaigns and determine optimal marketing strategies.

Special Research Studies

Research studies are initiated in response to problems or special information needs. Examples include market segmentation, new-product concept tests, product use tests, brand-name research, and advertising recall tests. Studies may range in scope from exploratory research based primarily on analysis of published information to field surveys involving personal, phone, or mail interviews with respondents who represent target populations. Considerable recent attention has been given to qualitative research using focus groups, rather than broader more representative surveys.

Recent developments include online market research services, offering less expensive and more rapidly available market research surveys. For example, launched in 1999, InsightExpress provides clients with a survey template to build an online questionnaire, allowing them to sample from a panel of 700,000 respondents, pay by credit card, and download results within a few days. A research project costing perhaps $25,000 using traditional services is estimated to cost only $1,000 online.[21] Reservations exist regarding the quality of the data produced by online services, but they provide a cheap route to sensing the market quickly.

Research studies follow a step-by-step process beginning with defining the problem to be investigated and the objectives of the research. An example of a project proposal for a study of customers' usage of low-salt/unsalted crackers is shown in Exhibit 5.4. The proposal indicated the objectives, research method, sampling plan, method of analysis, and cost. The project illustrates the steps involved in the research process (problem definition, information required, research method, sampling plan, questionnaire design, data collection, analysis, and research report).

In deciding whether to employ marketing research and when interpreting the results, several considerations are important.

Defining the Problem. Care must be exercised in formulating the research problem. It is essential to spell out exactly what information is needed to solve the problem. If this cannot be done, exploratory research should be conducted to help define the research problem and determine the objectives of the project. Caution should be exercised to avoid defining a symptom rather than the underlying problem—do falling sales reflect declining market size, new competitive activity, or ineffective promotion?

It is useful to prepare a written statement of the research problem, specific objectives, the information that is needed, information sources, and when the information is needed. Many companies contract with research firms to do the research. It is important that the supplier be as familiar as possible with the problem to be studied. Management needs to clearly define the intended project and may choose to involve the research supplier in defining the problem.

EXHIBIT 5.4 Illustrative Marketing Research Proposal

Source: William R. Dillon Thomas J. Madden, and Neil H. Firtle. *Marketing Research in a Marketing Environment,* 3rd ed. (Burr Ridge, IL: Richard D. Irwin, 1994). 49. Copyright © The McGraw-Hill Companies. Used with permission.

Category:	Low-salt crackers
Project:	Market study
Objectives:	To continue to build low-salt/unsalted cracker business and to effectively defend these brands against new competitive entries, a better understanding of consumers' use of low-salt/unsalted crackers and their attitudes toward low-salt/unsalted crackers is needed.
Research method:	A two-phase research study (screening and follow-up) will be conducted among households who are members of the supplier's mail panel.
Screening phase:	To address the marketing questions outlined above, it will be necessary to obtain a basic sample of low-salt/unsalted cracker users and readable samples (N = 150 in follow-up phase) for each of the brands of interest.
Sampling frame:	Screening questionnaires will be mailed to a nationally balanced sample of 36,000 panel member households. Within each household, men and women, age 18 or older, will complete the questionnaire. Returns are expected from 25,200 individuals, a response rate of 70 percent. A random sample of 2,000 of these respondents will be fully processed in the second phase of the study.
Follow-up phase:	In the follow-up phase, an extensive self-administered survey will be mailed to individuals having certain characteristics (i.e., category/specific brand usage) as identified in the screening phase.
Analysis:	Analysis will include standard cross-tabular analyses plus a number of multivariate statistical techniques (specifically a segmentation analysis) to help answer key research questions. For example: 1. What is the underlying need structure within the low-salt cracker market? 2. How is the market segmented in terms of usage dynamics? 3. What are the (particular brand's) strengths and weaknesses among its franchise?
Action standard:	Not applicable.
Cost:	The cost for conducting the study as specified within this proposal will be $121,500 ± 10% ($28,500 for screener and $93,000 for follow-up). This cost includes sample selection, questionnaire production, first-class postage (out and back), reminder postcards (follow-up study only), respondent incentives (follow-up study only), and data processing up to 12 cards and 6 open ends), four banners of tabulations at the follow-up phase, all necessary multivariate statistical analyses, and one presentation or report.
Timing:	Scheduling for the study will be as follows:

	Weeks Elapsed (from start of field, August 3)
Screeners returned	4
Phase I data available	7
Phase II commences	8
Phase II data collection ends	12
Phase II data available	16
Draft presentation available	20

Understanding the Limitations of the Research. Most studies are unable to do everything that the user wishes to accomplish and also stay within the available budget. Priorities for the information that is needed should be indicated. Also, obtaining certain information may not be feasible. For example, measuring the impact of advertising on profits may not be possible due to the influence of many other factors on profits.

Research suppliers should be able to indicate the limitations that may exist for a particular project. Discussions with a potential supplier are advisable before making a final commitment to the project. This will be useful in finalizing information need priorities.

Quality of the Research. There are many challenges to obtaining sound research results. The available evidence indicates that some studies are not well designed and implemented and may contain misleading results. Factors that affect the quality of study results include the experience of the research personnel, skills in carefully managing and controlling the data collection process, the size of the sample, the wording of questions, and how the data are analyzed. This classic example highlights the difficulties in achieving reliable results:[22]

> A Gallup poll sponsored by the disposable diaper industry asked: "It is estimated that disposable diapers account for less than 2 percent of the trash in today's landfills. In contrast, beverage containers, third-class mail and yard waste are estimated to account for about 21 percent of trash in landfills. Given this, in your opinion, would it be fair to ban disposable diapers?"

Not surprisingly, because of the wording of the question, 84 percent of the respondents answered "no" to the question.

Evaluating and Selecting Suppliers. Typically, research studies are not conducted by the user. When selecting a supplier, it is important to talk with two or three prior clients to determine their satisfaction with the research firm. It is also important to identify consultants who are experienced in conducting the particular type of research needed by the user. Familiarity with the industry may also be important.

Spending some time in evaluating a potential research supplier is very worthwhile. Experience and qualifications are important in selecting the supplier. Several useful screening questions are shown in Exhibit 5.5. These could be used to evaluate possible suppliers before asking for a detailed research proposal from the supplier.

Costs. Customized research studies are expensive. The factors that affect study costs include sample size, the length of the questionnaire, and how the information will be obtained. The complexity of the study objectives and the analysis methods also increases the professional capabilities of research personnel. Study costs may range from less than $10,000 (Exhibit 5.3) to over $100,000 (Exhibit 5.4).

Standardized subscription services (e.g., IRI's InfoScan) are also expensive, but for companies with various product types the annual cost is reasonable compared to the benefits and considerably below the cost of a company collecting and analyzing its own data in traditional ways.

Qualitative Research. It is important to recognize that research problems to be addressed may indicate the appropriateness of qualitative research methods, rather than surveys and other quantitative approaches. The use of focus groups is a typical way of collecting rich qualitative data, as compared to the more representative information from a survey or market test. For example, companies like Nokia use customer focus groups for several purposes. Testing a new messaging product for the U.S. market involved small groups giving individual feedback on product features that were changed before the product launch. The global positioning statement for the Nokia 3390 phone—"You Make It You"—was created from unfavorable focus group reactions to company attempts to describe positioning.[23]

The Marketing Research Industry. Suppliers of quantitative and qualitative research are likely to be marketing research firms. In 2003, the top 50 U.S. marketing research firms had revenues of $11.6 billion.[24] Nearly half these revenues were from outside the United States. Exhibit 5.6 shows the top 10 companies in 2003. Interestingly, six of the ten largest research

EXHIBIT 5.5
Ten Questions for Screening a New Supplier

Source: Seymour Sudman and Edward Blair, *Marketing Research: A Problem-Solving Approach* (Burr Ridge, IL: Irwin/McGraw-Hill, 1998), 67. Copyright © The McGraw-Hill Companies. Used with permission.

1. Ask the supplier's recent clients: *Would you recommend this supplier?* The biggest mistake research buyers make is not checking references. Do not let the supplier give you just any three references; ask for references from the five most recent jobs, and check dates as well as evaluations.
2. Ask the supplier: *Do you have sufficient funds for this job?* Get a bank reference, and check it. Underfinanced suppliers are tempted to cut corners. If the supplier is well qualified but not well financed, make arrangements such as a fieldwork drawing fund to ensure that the supplier has enough cash to do all work properly.
3. Ask the supplier: *What parts of the project will be subcontracted, and how do you control subcontractors?* Many suppliers subcontract parts of the research, and you should know how they manage their subcontractors. A ready answer indicates that the supplier understands the issue and has procedures in place.
4. If the research involves survey interviews, ask the supplier: *May I see your interviewer's manual and data entry manual?* You don't have to read these manuals but they should be readily available and should appear well used. The use of manuals suggests that formal management procedures are in place.
5. Also ask: *How do you train and supervise interviewers?* Supervision and training cost money and are not visible to clients, so some suppliers cut corners in these areas. The best suppliers do a good job of supervision and training as a matter of professional standards and welcome the chance to show off these standards.
6. Also ask: *What percentage of interviews are validated? How many invalid questionnaires are needed for you to do a 100 percent check on an interviewer's work?* If the answer is "What numbers do you want?" ask "What are your usual standards?" Interviewer cheating is most likely to occur in operations that do not have standards for finding and correcting it. You are looking for those standards, and you want them to be as high or higher than your own.
7. If the research involves survey interviews, ask the supplier: *May I see a typical questionnaire?* If the supplier shows you a questionnaire written for one of your competitors, leave immediately, because this is a violation of confidentiality and is unacceptable. Check whether the questionnaire will be easy for the respondent, the interviewer, and data entry people to use.
8. If the research involves any type of sampling, ask the supplier: *Who draws your samples?* Sampling is a technical aspect of research in which novices can easily make mistakes.
9. If the research involves any data being entered into the computer, ask the supplier: *What percentage of your data is verified?* Again, you are looking for standards, and the standard for data entry is 100 percent verification.
10. Ask your managers: *What do you think about this supplier?* Don't limit the value of research by using a supplier that your managers have doubts about. Also, the most useful research is research that produces new, even counterintuitive information, and managers often resist new information by raising the possibility that the supplier "did it wrong" or "didn't understand the issues." Make them raise any doubts at the start of the project, and save credibility questions for other problems.

organizations are owned by organizations based outside the United States. Agency research is predominantly market measurement studies, media audience research, and customer satisfaction measurement. Research into the impact of the Internet on markets is growing rapidly.

With the increasing globalization of brands and international competition, growing emphasis is being placed on a global perspective on marketing research. Particular interest is being shown in research in China and India, but also Latin America and parts of Africa, as well as eastern Europe and Russia. Particular problems in global research are cross-cultural differences that impact on information quality and characteristics. For example, an industry rule of thumb is that

EXHIBIT 5.6
Top Ten U.S. Marketing Research Firms in 2003

Source: Table from "Honomichi Top 50" Special Section of the *Marketing News,* June 15, 2004, p. H4. Reprinted with permission of the American Marketing Association.

U.S. Rank 2003	Organization	Headquarters	Web site	Worldwide research revenues ($ millions)	Percent non-U.S. revenues
1	VNU Inc.	New York	*www.vnu.com*	3,045.0	47.2
2	IMS Health Inc.	Fairfield, Conn.	*imsheath.com*	1,381.8	61.1
3	Information Resources Inc.	Chicago	*www.infores.com*	554.3	30.0
4	Westat Inc.	Rockville, Md.	*www.westat.com*	381.6	—
5	TNS USA	London	*www.tns-global.com*	1,290.1	71.6
—	TNS	London	*www.tns-i.com*	217.4	8.1
—	TNS NFO	Greenwich, Conn.	*www.nfow.com*	171.6	2.9
6	The Kantar Group	Fairfield, Conn.	*www.kantargroup.com*	1,002.1	66.1
7	Arbitron Inc.	New York	*arbitron.com*	273.6	2.9
8	NOP World US	New York	*www.nopword.com*	336.3	38.9
9	Ipsos	New York	*www.ipsos-na.com*	644.2	72.7
10	Synovate	Chicago	*www.synovate.com*	357.7	55.0

in the Americas the further north you go, the more reserved consumers are in what they express. The same consumer perception of the quality of a product might receive high scores in Latin America, average marks in the United States, and less favorable reviews in Canada, because of cultural differences. For companies in international markets, making allowances for such cultural differences in examining global marketing research is an important challenge.[25]

The Impact of the Internet on Marketing Information Costs and Availability

It is important to consider the impact of the Internet on both the way in which information can be collected and the type of information available. Many traditional guidelines to the availability and use of existing information, standardized services, and special studies are challenged by the major impact of the Internet. The Web offers greatly enhanced access to online information resources as diverse as the World Bank statistics on overseas countries, and individual company Web sites. The costs of using these resources are limited to the time it takes to access them. In addition, new and speedy ways of conducting survey studies using electronic questionnaires and panels are expanding rapidly. The Internet Feature summarizes some of the fundamental impacts of the Internet on marketing information collection.

Information Systems

There are many types of information systems within the organization. Manual systems are also used and may provide crucial information. Yet, for purposes of this chapter, attention is focused on computer-based information systems. "Strategic systems are those that change the goals, products, services, or environmental relationships of organizations."[26] These information systems alter how a firm does business with competitors, suppliers, and customers. Since the scope of strategic planning is so broad, information generated by the system is invaluable in strategic marketing planning. The system may provide information to assist decision makers with strategic planning, or may actually prepare a plan and formulate decisions. We briefly describe management information systems, database systems, and decision-support systems as possible ways to enhance the quality of information available to marketing decision makers.

Internet Feature The Web and Marketing Information

Online Surveys

- Surveys based on the Internet are a fast and inexpensive way to generate feedback on products and marketing communications. Limitations are that only online customers can participate and there is growing resistance to unsolicited marketing messages and spam among Web users.
- They may use tools companies already have at hand—the Web site, targeted e-mails, e-mail blasts, or other formats like Personal Digital Assistants.
- The only cost for the research may be employee time in writing the survey and posting it. Cheaply available self-service Web tools like Zoomerang or SurveyMonkey allow users to type in questions and click on the survey report.
- Companies unable to fund traditional marketing research can now afford to survey customers and uncover new business opportunities at low cost.

Customer Feedback and Peer-to-Peer Web Communication

- Some companies have designed online systems to allow consumers to voice opinions and describe experiences and evaluations of products and services.
- Online customer feedback is a form of digitized word-of-mouth communication.
- Channels for online feedback include message boards, discussion forums, opinion forums, newsgroups, and chat rooms.
- There are a growing number of independent online goods and service review forums, such as Epinions.com and Rateitall.com, where buyers pool product assessments on a peer-to-peer basis.

Monitoring Customer Web Behavior

- Controversially, there has been a major increase in the use of spyware and adware among Internet companies. Many have ethical reservations about this technology and some user reactions are hostile.
- Spyware and adware are cookies that users download from the Internet—some say often unwittingly and without intention—that hide themselves on the user's hard drive.
- Spyware collects personal data and tracks the user's Web site use, while adware observes Web visits and provides relevant pop-up ads based on the user's Internet use.

Sources: Ben Elgin, "Guess What—You Asked for Those Pop-Up Ads," *BusinessWeek,* June 28, 2004, 88–90; Catherine Arnold, "Cast Your Net," *Marketing News,* Nov. 24, 2003, 15–19; Robin T. Peterson and Zhilin Yang, "Web Product Reviews Help Strategy," *Marketing News,* April 1, 2004, 18–20.

Management Information Systems

Management information systems (MIS) provide raw data to decision makers within a firm. The system collects data on the transactions of the firm and may include competitor and environmental information. The decision makers (and systems analysts) are responsible for extracting the data relevant for a decision and in the appropriate format to facilitate the process. The system can provide information for decisions at all levels of the organization. Lower and middle-level managers are likely to use the system most often for operating decisions. The system may generate routine reports for frequent operating decisions, such as weekly sales by product, or may be queried for special analyses on an as-needed basis. Nonroutine decisions may consist of tracking the sales performance of a sales district over several months, determining the number of customer returns for a particular good, or listing all customers or suppliers within a given geographic area. The basic MIS collects data and allows for retrieval and manipulation of format in an organized manner. Typically, the MIS does not interact in the decision-making process. More advanced MIS capabilities provide important decision analysis capabilities.

Consider this MIS application. A sophisticated marketing information system enables a major airline to focus on the needs of specific market segments.[27] The system determines mileage awards for frequent flyers and provides a reservation support database, organized by market segments. The company's top 3 percent of customers accounts for 50 percent of sales. These key accounts are highlighted on all service screens and reports. Reservations agents are alerted that a person is an important customer. The frequent flyers receive a variety of special services including boarding priority and first-class upgrades.

Database Systems

Database systems comprise an important information resource in many companies. For example, the Target Corporation uses an effective database system to respond to customer diversity in its stores. Management's model of the market takes into account differences in product needs and preferences by store location, to tailor store offerings to customer differences.[28] Similarly, in its European retail operation, supermarket Tesco uses its loyalty club data to indicate demographic, income, and housing characteristics of consumers in the catchment area of a store to design appropriate product assortments—stores near large universities may concentrate on high-value ready-meal replacements from pizzas to take-away, precooked curries, while stores in family residential areas emphasize extensive food choices, cooking ingredients, and products for babies and children.

Databases are a form of MIS. Some database systems offer capabilities similar to decision-support systems. Computerized databases are indispensable for companies pursuing direct marketing strategies. Discussion of database marketing as a form of promotional strategy is included in Chapter 13.

The components of database systems include relational databases, personal computers, electronic publishing media, and voice systems.[29] The intent of database marketing is effectively using a computerized customer database to facilitate a significant and profitable communication with customers.

One of the challenges in the use of databases is identifying what patterns are present in the huge accumulations of information. Data mining software technology is being developed to assist in diagnosing patterns in databases.[30] Computer power enables analysis of as many as 10,000 customer attributes to help identify key patterns such as how to keep the best customers. For example, MCI Communications Corp. through data mining software has developed a highly secret set of 22 statistical profiles to monitor on a regular basis. While companies are only beginning to consider data mining technology, it promises to become an increasingly important database capability.

Recall earlier comments regarding the growing role of Customer Relationship Management (CRM) technology in building new databases—or data warehouses—from the company's own customer contacts. These new data sources are likely to be the focus of many data mining exercises and create new insights into customer behavior. For example, Wal-Mart's discovery of a correlation between Friday evening purchases of disposable diapers and beer is associated with the identification of a new product category comprising leisure and family products for families with small children.

Decision-Support Systems

A decision-support system (DSS) assists in the decision-making process using the information captured by the MIS. A marketing decision-support system (MDSS) integrates data that are not easily found, assimilated, formatted, or readily manipulated with software and hardware into a decision-making process that provides the marketing decision maker with assistance when needed.[31] The MDSS allows the user flexibility in applications and in format. A MDSS can be used for various levels of decision making ranging from determining reorder points for inventory to launching a new product.

The components of the MDSS consist of the database, the display, the models, and the analysis capabilities.[32]

Database. Various kinds of information are included in the database such as standardized marketing information produced by Nielsen and other research suppliers, sales and cost data, and internal information such as product sales, advertising data, and price information. The design and updating of the database are vital to the effectiveness of MDSS. The information should be relevant and organized to correspond to the units of analysis used in the system.

Display. This component of the MDSS enables the user to communicate with the database. Managers and staff professionals need to interact with the database:

> They must be able to extract, manipulate, and display data easily and quickly. Required capabilities range from simple ad hoc retrieval to more formal reports that track market status and product performance. Also needed are exception reports that flag problem areas. Many presentations should have graphics integrated with other materials.[33]

Models. This component of the MDSS provides mathematical and computational representations of variables and their interrelationships. For example, a sales force deployment model would include an effort-to-sales response function model and a deployment algorithm for use in analyzing selling effort allocation alternatives. The decision-support models are useful in analysis, planning, and control.

Analysis. This capability consists of various analysis methods such as regression analysis, factor analysis, time series, and preference mapping. Software capabilities may be included in the system. Analysis may be performed on a data set to study relationships, identify trends, prepare forecasts, and examine the impact of alternative decision rules.

MDSSs may operate autonomously or instead may require interaction with the decision maker during the process. There may be several stages before a recommendation is formed where the decision maker responds to queries to refine the scenario. Thus, an interactive MDSS requires more assistance from the decision maker and has more room for variation than an autonomous MDSS. The system is dependent on the quality and accuracy of the information and assumptions that are used in designing the system. The process should be viewed as a tool to assist in decision making, and is not a final product in itself.

Ideally, the experience and shared vision of management are built into the model. But often information is missing, and the decision maker has the best grasp of the entire situation. The most complete decisions incorporate the recommendation of the MDSS, but do not solely rely upon them. However, a DSS often serves to create or support a consensus, and evidence exists that a DSS does yield favorable decision-making performance when it is properly designed and applied to appropriate decision situations. Evaluations of DSS effectiveness show some positive results.[34] Using controlled laboratory tests of senior undergraduate students enrolled in a business policy course, researchers found that groups using the DSS made significantly better decisions than their non-DSS counterparts. Nevertheless, further evaluation is needed to better define the conditions and applications where success is likely to occur.

The concept of the MDSS as a tool is most apparent when considering strategic decisions rather than operating decisions. Clear, concise answers may not always be possible, yet the system is a very valuable tool in the process. Consider the following:

> A DSS developed by William Luther analyzes key success factors in the marketplace and makes comparisons with competitors. This system is called a Strategic Planning Model, and is most useful for smaller companies. Managers input their definition of key success factors by means of a standardized questionnaire format. Comparisons are made between the firm and competitors for these factors. The factors can be weighted for importance, and multiple situations can be considered. The model makes projections and recommendations of strategies.[35]

In using this system it is important that managers identify key success factors; otherwise the model will lose a great deal of credibility. When properly applied it offers a useful framework for decision makers, recognizing that it is not a complete replica of the decision-making situation.

Marketing Intelligence Systems and Knowledge Management

Importantly, the emphasis on market sensing in market-driven companies does not rely on hard data alone. Many companies are now investing in in-company intelligence units to coordinate and disseminate "soft" or qualitative data and improve shared corporate knowledge.[36] Intelligence may come from published materials in trade and scientific journals, salesperson visit reports, programs of customer visits by executives, social contacts, feedback from trade exhibitions and personal contacts, or even rumor in the marketplace.

For example, when Southwestern Bell Telephone Co. heard rumors about new competitors entering the market with special packages for home renters, they were able to counter this rapidly by appointing apartment complex managers as Southwestern Bell sales agents. Similarly, market feedback suggesting that new "micro" phone companies appealed particularly to younger telephone renters led Southwestern to move resources into product offers and promotions based on colleges.[37] This shows a market sensing capability based on market intelligence.

Conversely, there is widespread evidence that while it may take a substantial time for information about a company's shortcomings to reach senior executives, they are well known to customers and employees much earlier.[38] For example, the performance of British retailer Marks & Spencer collapsed during the late 1990s, its share value falling from 650p to 150p between 1997 and 2000. Customer surveys in 1997 and 1998 showed rapidly declining customer satisfaction and increasing defection. Retiring CEO Sir Richard Greenbury said in 2000 that he simply did not know that there were customer problems and that the decline in sales was a "surprise."[39] Market information that is ignored by management, interpreted incorrectly, or poorly communicated to them cannot impact effectively on decision making.

Knowledge Management

There is increasing recognition that knowledge about customers should be managed as a strategic asset, because competitive advantage can be created not merely by possessing current market information but by knowing how to use it. Market knowledge is inextricably linked to organizational learning and market orientation in the market-driven company.[40]

Peter Drucker argues, for example, that often 90 percent of the information that companies collect is internal—market research and management reports that only tell executives about their own company—while the real challenge is to build knowledge about new markets they do not yet serve and new technologies they do not yet possess.[41] Knowledge that builds competitive advantage involves major emphasis on rigorous customer perspectives and competitor comparisons.[42]

Role of the Chief Knowledge Officer

To meet this challenge, some companies have established positions with titles such as chief knowledge officer. While the titles and the job responsibilities vary, all appear linked to improving an organization's knowledge management and learning processes. This may be a staff position with only a few people involved, or, instead, responsibility for databases, a technical infrastructure, and related knowledge functions.[43] The position may report to chief executive officer, information officer, or other high-level executive. Companies that have these positions include Ernst & Young, IBM, and the World Bank.

While there appear to be differences between the role and functions of knowledge and learning officers, both positions do not occur in the same company.[44] Knowledge management is concerned with knowledge (information) collection and linking information within the organization. While the future of the position is not clear, as it develops there is likely to be a relationship between knowledge management and the discussion in this chapter of continuous learning about markets.

Innovation Feature Knowledge Sharing at Buckman Labs

- President of Manistique Papers Inc., Leif Christensen, was concerned with the effectiveness of the peroxide used in his new recycling plant to remove ink from old magazines—the paper produced was just not white enough.
- Christensen told Buckman Labs sales representatives about his whiteness problem.
- The salespeople immediately posted a message on Buckman's Internet discussion group. Buckman has 54 Internet discussion groups focused on its main products. Typically, employees post 50 to 100 messages a day.
- The company has amassed an easily searchable database of in-house expertise and past lessons learned—all accessible to employees and customers via a Web browser.
- Within hours of Christensen's white paper problem being posted, other Buckman personnel in Finland and Belgium helped explain the problem—a rare bacteria that breaks down the peroxide.
- Christensen was notified immediately with the information and the antidote. The total time elapsed between Buckman's learning about the problem and delivering the solution to the customer was around 48 hours. In the past this kind of problem solving would have taken weeks, if it had happened at all.
- Harnessing the brainpower of an entire global specialty chemicals company to assess and solve one customer's problem fast, underlines the power of knowledge sharing and the Internet.
- The customer's comment: "I don't think Buckman's competitors can pool the whole brainpower of the organization like Buckman can . . ."

Source: Marcia Stepanek, "Spread the Knowhow," *BusinessWeek E.Biz*, October 23, 2000, EB 52.

For example, Xerox claims a saving of $200 million from a single project that uncovered and shared expertise across the group. Internal benchmarking found its Austrian subsidiary was unusually successful at persuading customers to renew contracts. Sharing the Austrian approach with other groups brought 70 percent up to the Austrian standard in three months.[45] The Innovation Feature illustrates the potential power of innovative uses of Internet-based technology at Buckman Labs to enhance this form of knowledge sharing to solve customer problems in market-driven companies.

Leveraging Customer Knowledge

Several methods are being employed by companies to improve the availability and use of customer knowledge in impacting strategic decisions.[46] A discussion follows:

Creating "Customer Knowledge Development Dialogues." For example, DaimlerChrysler's Jeep division runs customer events called "Jeep Jamborees," attracting enthusiasts for the vehicle. Jeep employees connect with customers through informal conversations and semiformal round tables. Engineers and ethnographic researchers focus on the Jeep owner's relationship with the vehicle, driving changes to existing models and plans for new models.

Operating Enterprisewide "Customer Knowledge Communities." IBM, for example, uses collaborative Internet workspace called the *CustomerRoom* with major accounts, where individuals throughout its divisions and functions can exchange knowledge with each other and with the customer.

Capturing Customer Knowledge at the Point of Customer Contact. Customer Relationship Management systems capture customer behavior and response information which offers rich potential for better insights into issues like customer defection and competitors' strengths, as well as emerging customer needs and perceptions.

Management Commitment to Customer Knowledge. Management responsibility includes investing resources, time, and attention in maintaining customer dialogues and communities as a commitment to enhanced organizational understanding of the customer. For example, the vice president of marketing at Ford's LincolnMercury division actively participates in customer-related chat rooms on the Internet, and encourages other employees to follow his lead. Other approaches include planned programs of customer visits by cross-functional teams of executives as a systematic way of acquiring customer information, but also building superior understanding of and responsiveness to customer perspectives.[47]

Ethical Issues in Collecting and Using Information

Lastly, important privacy and ethical issues concerning the role of information in the organization need to be assessed by managers and professionals. Questions regarding ethical and socially responsible behavior are escalating in importance for individual executives and organizations. These questions may particularly impact approaches to collecting customer information, and the uses made of that information.

Invasion of Customer Privacy

The dramatic increase in use of databases has generated concerns about the invasion of privacy of individuals. Companies have responded to the issue by asking customers to indicate their preferences concerning mailing lists and other uses of the information. Nonetheless, concerns about this issue will undoubtedly continue as the sophistication of communications technology and software continues to develop.

Consider, for example, the use of patient information in the drug industry. Database marketing by pharmaceutical companies is guided by information obtained from toll-free number calls, subscriptions to magazines, and pharmacy questionnaires.[48] This information can be used to guide database marketing programs, targeting people with specific health concerns such as depression, arthritis, and other problems. Some patients are objecting about the use of their prescription data to guide direct mail and other promotional efforts. Yet further objections relate to the possible sharing of medical information databases of this kind with other parties, such as insurance companies who may want to determine premiums on the basis of health data for existing patients and their children.

Information and Ethics

Related to the issue of invasion of privacy is the issue of how companies and research suppliers should respond to ethical issues. For example, should a prospective client share a supplier's detailed project proposal with a competing supplier? A central issue concerns which organization pays for the cost of preparing the proposal. If the proposal is prepared at the expense of the supplier, then the proposal is the property of the supplier.[49] Sharing the proposal with its competition would be an issue of questionable ethics.

Other issues relate to the ways in which information is collected and from whom it is collected. There are major professional restrictions, for example, on collecting marketing information from children. In terms of the dilemmas that may emerge in how information is collected, consider the use of medical brain scanning technology to capture clues as to consumer product preferences and reactions to marketing messages described in the Ethics Feature. Executives face difficult issues in deciding if "neuromarketing" is an acceptable use of medical technology or whether it breaches the individual's right to privacy.

Information sharing with research suppliers, other external contractors, strategic alliance partners, and acquisition/merger prospects often involves highly confidential information. There are many possible situations that present ethical questions and concerns. Companies normally sign confidentiality agreements. Nonetheless, revealing trade secrets is a risk that relies primarily on the ethical behavior of the participants. Moreover, these situations offer excellent opportunities for learning.

Ethics Feature

Neuromarketing

- Medical research has created the magnetic resonance imaging (MRI) scanner to detect injury and disease associated with the brain.
- More recent MRI technology and software allows the machine to picture the flow of blood in the brain in response to visual stimuli—almost a picture of thoughts pinpointing what part of the brain recognizes things, enabling researchers to understand better the very essence of the mind and how it thinks, decides, and feels. This is "functional" MRI technology (fMRI).
- A controversial use of fMRI is probing customer preferences—sometimes called "neuromarketing." Researchers at Harvard, Emory, Caltech and Baylor are studying how consumer preferences for different kinds of products track with activity in different parts of the brain, as well as reactions to marketing messages.
- A new company in California offers a service to Hollywood studios to test audiences as they watch movie trailers to see which generate the most "brain buzz."
- Consumer watchdog Gary Ruskin complains, "It's wrong to use a medical technology for marketing, not healing."
- Other ethical concerns include the issue of privacy.
- Prominent neurobiologist Donald Kennedy, former head of the U.S. Food and Drug Administration, urges caution in collecting brain data: "Our brains are us, marking out the special character of our personal capacities, emotions, and convictions . . . As to my brainome, I don't want anyone to know it for any purpose whatsoever."
- A further issue is whether brain scan data should be made available to insurers, employers, and even law enforcement agencies.

Source: Joan O'C. Hamilton, "Journey to the Center of the Mind," *BusinessWeek*, April 19, 2004, 66–67.

Summary

Information performs a vital strategic role in an organization. Information capability creates a sustainable competitive advantage by improving the speed of decision making, reducing the costs of repetitive operations, and improving decision-making results. Market sensing is vital to the effectiveness of the market-oriented company. Managers' models of their markets guide the interpretation of information and resulting strategies designed to keep the firm ahead of its competition. Learning about markets necessitates open-minded inquiry, widespread distribution of information within the organization, mutually informed interpretation, and developing a memory to provide access to prior learning.

Marketing information capabilities include marketing research, marketing information systems, database systems, decision-support systems, and expert systems. Research information supports marketing analysis and decision making. This information may be obtained from internal sources, standardized information services, and special research studies. The information may be used to solve existing problems, evaluate potential actions such as new-product introductions, and as inputs to computerized data banks.

Computerized information systems include management information systems, database systems, CRM technology, and decision-support systems. These systems include capabilities for information processing, analysis of routine decision making, and decision recommendations for complex decision situations. The vast array of information processing and telecommunications technology that is available offers many opportunities to enhance the competitive advantage of companies.

The development of useful information systems is a key success requirement for competing in the rapidly changing and shrinking global business environment. Marketing decision-making results are improved by the use of effective information systems. Importantly, gaining information advantage requires more than technology. The systems demand creative (and cost-effective) design that focuses on decision-making information needs.

In addition, we recognize the growing importance of knowledge management in strategic marketing as a vital source of competitive advantage, the role of the chief knowledge officer, and several approaches to enhancing the development of customer knowledge.

Finally we consider some important issues in collecting and using information. These include invasion of customer privacy, and information and ethics.

Internet Applications

A. Revisit the list of major marketing research agencies in Exhibit 5.6. Visit several of the Web sites listed. Examine the major types of information provided both as standardized services and special study capabilities. List these and identify the ways in which such resources can impact on marketing decisions.

B. Select a well-known company or brand and use a search engine to find Web pages that include its name. Review the content of Web pages from different sources. Discuss the impact of Internet-based information on traditional ideas about confidentiality and privacy.

Feature Applications

A. Revisit the Internet Feature "The Web and Marketing Information." What are the major advantages of the Web in developing marketing information resources, but what are the potential disadvantages? How do these two lists balance against each other?

B. Examine the marketing information example described in the Ethics Feature "Neuromarketing." Should limits be placed on the ability of commercial organizations to capture and exploit information about individuals for reasons of privacy? Why should such issues concern marketing executives?

Questions for Review and Discussion

1. Discuss how an organization's marketing information skills and resources contribute to its distinctive capabilities.
2. How would you explain to a group of top-level executives the relationship between market orientation and continuous learning about markets?
3. Outline an approach to developing an effective market sensing capability for a regional full-service bank.
4. Compare and contrast the use of standardized information services as an alternative to special research studies for tracking the performance of a new packaged food product.
5. Discuss the probable impact of cable television on marketing research methods during the next decade as this medium penetrates an increasing number of U.S. households and closer relationships are developed with telecommunications companies.
6. Comment on the usefulness and limitations of test-market data as a source of marketing information.
7. Suppose the management of a retail floor covering (carpet, tile, wood) chain is considering a research study to measure household awareness of the retail chain, reactions to various aspects of wallpaper purchase and use, and identification of competing firms. How could management estimate the benefits of such a study in order to determine if the study should be conducted?
8. Are there similarities between marketing strategic intelligence and the operations of the U.S. Central Intelligence Agency? Do companies ever employ business spies?
9. Discuss how manufacturers of U.S. and Swiss watches could have used market sensing to help avoid the problems that several firms in the industry encountered as Seiko and other Japanese companies entered the watch market.
10. Examine the strategic implications for small independent retailers and regional chains concerning the expanding strategic use of information technology by large retailers like Wal-Mart.
11. Data mining from databases is receiving increased attention in many companies. Discuss the underlying logic of data mining.
12. What are the relevant issues that need to be considered when obtaining the services of an outside supplier for a marketing research project?

Notes

1. George S. Day, "The Capabilities of Market-Driven Organizations," *Journal of Marketing,* October 1994, 43.
2. Kathleen M. Sutcliffe and Klaus Weber, "The High Cost of Accurate Knowledge," *Harvard Business Review,* May 2003, 74–82.
3. Adapted from Nigel F. Piercy, *Market-Led Strategic Change: A Guide to Transforming the Process of Going to Market* (Oxford: Butterworth-Heinemann, 2002), 202–204.
4. David Fairlamb, Gail Edmondson, Laura Cohn, Kerry Capell, and Stanley Reed, "The Best European Performers," *BusinessWeek,* June 28, 2004, 48–53.
5. Patricia B. Seybould, "Get inside the Lives of Your Customers," *Harvard Business Review,* May 2001, 81–89.
6. Stanley F. Slater and John C. Narver, "Market Orientation, Customer Value, and Superior Performance," *Business Horizons,* March/April 1994, 22–27.
7. Stanley F. Slater and John C. Narver, "Market Orientation and the Learning Organization," *Journal of Marketing,* July 1995, 63–74 at 71. Reprinted with permission of the American Marketing Association.
8. Ibid., 71.
9. Ibid.
10. Roger D. Blackwell, *From Mind to Market* (New York: HarperBusiness, 1997), 9.
11. The following discussion is based on Day, "The Capabilities of Market-Driven Organizations." See also Stanley F. Slater

and John C. Narver, "Market-Oriented Isn't Enough: Build a Learning Organization," Report No. 94-103 (Cambridge, MA: Marketing Science Institute, 1994).

12. Nigel F. Piercy and Nikala Lane, "Marketing Implementation: Building and Sustaining a Real Market Understanding," *Journal of Marketing Practice: Applied Marketing Science* 2, no. 3, 1996, 15–28.
13. Adrian J. Slywotzky, *Value Migration* (Boston: Harvard Business School Press, 1996).
14. Philip B. Evans and Thomas S. Wuster, "Strategy and the New Economics of Information," *Harvard Business Review,* September–October 1997, 70–82. See also Philip Evans and Thomas S. Wurster, *Blown to Bits: How the New Economics of Information Transforms Strategy* (Boston, MA.: Harvard Business School Press, 2000).
15. Day, "The Capabilities of Market-Driven Organizations," 43.
16. Robert La Franco, "It's All about Visuals," *Forbes,* May 22, 1995, 108, 110, and 112.
17. William R. Dillon, Thomas J. Madden, and Neil H. Firtle, *Marketing Research in a Marketing Environment,* 3rd ed. (Burr Ridge, IL: Richard D. Irwin, 1994), 737.
18. Kenneth C. Laudon and Jane Price Laudon, *Management Information Systems* (New York: Macmillan, 1988), 235.
19. Gary Loveman, "Diamonds in the Data Mine," *Harvard Business Review,* May 2003, 109–113.
20. A description of the top 50 companies in the marketing research industry can be found in the "Honomichl 50" Special Section of the *Marketing News,* June 15, 2004. Reprinted with permission of the American Marketing Association.
21. Valerie Marchant, "First E-Marketing, Now E-Research," *Time.com,* January 24, 2000.
22. Cynthia Crossen, "Margin of Error," *The Wall Street Journal,* November 11, 1991, A1. Wall Street Journal. Central Edition (staff produced copy only) by Cynthia Crossen. Copyright 1991 by Dow Jones & Co Inc. Reproduced with permission of Dow Jones & Co Inc. in the format Textbook via Copyright Clearance Center.
23. Deborah L. Vence, "Turned on a Dime," *Marketing News,* March 15, 2004.
24. Jack Honomichl, "Gradual Gains," *Marketing News,* June 15, 2004, H1–H53.
25. Catherine Arnold, "Global Perspective," *Marketing News,* May 15, 2004, 43.
26. Laudon and Laudon, *Management Information Systems,* 62.
27. Michael Miron, John Cecil, Kevin Bradicich, and Gene Hall, "The Myths and Realities of Competitive Advantage," *DATAMATION,* October 1, 1988, 76.
28. Gregory A. Patterson, "Different Strokes: Target 'Micromarkets' Its Way to Success; No Two Stores Are Alike," *The Wall Street Journal,* May 31, 1995, A1 and A9.
29. Bob Shaw and Merlin Stone, "Competitive Superiority through Database Marketing," *Long Range Planning,* October 1988, 24–40.
30. "Coaxing the Meaning out of Raw Data," *BusinessWeek,* February 3, 1997, 134, 136–138.
31. John D. C. Little and Michael Cassettari, *Decision Support Systems for Marketing Managers,* New York: AMA, 1984, 7.
32. Ibid., 12–15.
33. Ibid., 14.
34. A discussion of DSS effectiveness is provided in Ramesh Sharda, Steve H. Barr, and James C. McDonnell, "Decision Support System Effectiveness: A Review and an Empirical Test," *Management Science* 34, no. 2 (February 1988), 139–159.
35. Reprinted from *Business Horizons*, May-June 1987, Robert J. Mockler, "Computer Information Systems and Strategic Corporate Planning," Copyright 1987, with permission from Elsevier.
36. Thomas A. Stewart, "Getting Real about Brainpower," *Fortune,* November 27, 1995.
37. Pat Long, "Turning Intelligence into Smart Marketing," *Marketing News,* March 27, 1995.
38. Michael Skapinker, "How to Bow Out without Egg on Your Face," *Financial Times,* March 8, 2000, 21.
39. Kate Rankine, "Marks Ignored Shoppers Fall in Faith," *Daily Telegraph,* October 30, 2000, 21.
40. Rohit Deshpande, "From Market Research Use to Market Knowledge Management," in Rohit Deshpande (ed.), *Using Market Knowledge,* Thousand Oaks, CA.: Sage, 2001, 1–8.
41. Peter Drucker, *Peter Drucker on the Profession of Management* (Boston, MA.: Harvard Business School Press, 1998).
42. George S. Day, "Learning about Markets," in Rohit Deshpande (ed.), *Using Market Knowledge* (Thousand Oaks, CA: Sage, 2001), 9–30.
43. Thomas A. Stewart, "Is This Job Really Necessary?" *Fortune,* January 12, 1998, 154–155.
44. Ibid.
45. Vanessa Houlder, "Xerox Makes Copies," *Financial Times,* July 14, 1997, 10.
46. Eric Lesser, David Mundel and Charles Wiecha, "Managing Customer Knowledge," *Journal of Business Strategy,* November/December 2000, 35–37.
47. Edward F. McQuarrie and Shelby H. McIntyre, "Implementing the Marketing Concept through a Program of Customer Visits," in Rohit Deshpande (ed.), *Using Market Knowledge,* Thousand Oaks, CA: Sage, 2001, 163–190.
48. William M. Bulkeley, "Prescriptions, Toll-Free Numbers Yield a Gold Mine for Marketers," *The Wall Street Journal,* April 17, 1998, B1 and B3.
49. Dillon, Madden, and Firtle, *Marketing Research in a Marketing Environment,* 48. Elizabeth MacDonald and Joanne S. Lublin, "In the Debris of a Failed Merger: Trade Secrets," *The Wall Street Journal,* March 10, 1998, B1 and B10.

Cases for Part 2

Case 2-1

Wi-Fi

Engineers on runways in Seattle and Frankfurt are tinkering with antennas and satellite links. This isn't the usual avionics, though. Instead, Boeing Co. is preparing a brand new business: flying cybercafés. By early next year, more than 100 Boeing jets are scheduled to be equipped with speedy wireless technology known as Wi-Fi. For $25 or so per flight, laptop-luggers will be able to log on to the Net while soaring above the clouds—shopping on eBay Inc., restocking their companies' inventories, perhaps even making voice calls over the Web. Boeing is so gung-ho on the new technology that over the next decade it hopes to outfit nearly 4,000 planes with Wi-Fi service. Says Scott E. Carson, president of the company's Connexion by Boeing unit: "Wi-Fi is on an explosive growth path."

After four years as a plaything for techno-geeks and home hobbyists, Wi-Fi is beginning to beam its way into Corporate America. Its superfast connections to the Web cost only a quarter as much as the gaggle of wires companies use today. And they're proving irresistible to businesses willing to venture onto the wireless edge. From General Motors to United Parcel Service to CareGroup, companies are using Wi-Fi for mission-critical jobs in factories, trucks, stores, and even hospitals. "We firmly believe that this is the tipping point," says Intel Corp. CEO Craig R. Barrett.

What is Wi-Fi? It's a radio signal that beams Internet connections out 300 feet. Attach it to a broadband modem and any nearby computers equipped with Wi-Fi receptors can log on to the Net, whether they're in the cubicle across the hall, the apartment next door, or the hammock out back. To date, Wi-Fi has grown on the scruffy fringes of the networked world. It shares an unregulated radio spectrum with a motley crew of contraptions, including cordless phones and baby monitors.

Yet Wi-Fi networks, known as hot spots, have popped up faster than fleas on a circus dog. Thousands of do-it-yourselfers worldwide have rigged antennas to create their own hot spots. They've joined together to form networks so that the public can zap e-mails and surf blogs for free, no matter where they are. From street corners in Sydney to mountaintops outside Seattle, some 5,000 free hot spots have emerged. This is Wi-Fi Nation. More than 18 million people worldwide have logged on, and the numbers are growing daily (Exhibit 1).

The challenge facing the tech industry is to transform this unruly phenomenon into a global business. This means turning Wi-Fi Nation into Wi-Fi Inc. That involves transforming a riot of hit-or-miss hot spots into coherent, dependable networks. It means coming up with billing systems, roaming agreements, and technical standards—jobs the phone companies are busy tackling. The goal, says Anand Chandrasekher, vice-president and general manager of the mobile-platforms group at Intel, is to "take Wi-Fi from a wireless rogue activity to an industrial-strength solution that corporations can bet on."

If successful, Wi-Fi has the power to fit the Internet with wings. A constellation of dependable Wi-Fi hot spots could extend dramatically the range and expanse of the Web, changing its very nature. The path ahead, analysts say, is sure to have its share of bumps. But it could lead to cascades of up-to-the-minute information zipping around offices, homes, even remote disaster sites. MeshNetworks Inc. in Maitland, Fla., is working on Wi-Fi systems that would allow emergency-response teams to create networks among themselves by simply turning on their laptops or handhelds—even if cellular or wired networks have been knocked out.

Corporations aren't waiting for fine-tuned industrial versions of Wi-Fi to hit the market. The potential productivity gains are so compelling that many are investing in custom-built systems. United Parcel Service Inc. is equipping its worldwide distribution centers with wireless networks at a cost of $120 million. The company says that as loaders and packers scan packages, the information zips instantly to the the UPS network, leading to a 35% productivity gain. IBM is devising Wi-Fi-powered systems to monitor the minute-by-minute operations of distant machines, from potato fryers at restaurants to air conditioners in computer labs.

Other tech titans are rushing in, too. Intel is spending $300 million to market its Centrino computer chips, which come equipped for Wi-Fi. In March, Cisco Systems Inc. agreed to spend $500 million for Linksys, a Wi-Fi equipment maker. For the first time, that will put Cisco into head-to-head competition with Microsoft Corp., which plowed into Wi-Fi network gear last year. And Cometa Networks, the new joint venture made up of Intel, IBM, and AT&T, is building a nationwide network of 20,000

EXHIBIT 1 Why It's Taking Off

Wireless networking, or Wi-Fi, is a runaway success. The grassroots movement has soared to 18 million users, up from 2.5 million in 2000. Now, the technology is quickly moving into the mainstream. Here's why it has caught on:

Wi-Fi–Ready Devices
Dell, Toshiba, and TiVo are building Wi-Fi into computers and digital recording devices. Over 90% of new laptops will be Wi-Fi–ready by 2005, up from 35% by yearend 2003.

Nationwide Network Bets
At least four commercial Wi-Fi networks are in operation or under development in the U.S. They include VoiceStream, Toshiba, Boingo, and Cometa Networks, which is backed by IBM, Intel, and AT&T. That will raise awareness and push prices lower.

Broadband Lift-Off
Wi-Fi is getting a boost from the popularity of broadband, which is growing 30% this year. That's because Wi-Fi is an inexpensive way to connect several household computers to a single high-speed Internet connection.

Tech Titans Jump In
Intel, Microsoft, Cisco, and IBM are pushing Wi-Fi just as hard as pioneers like Boingo are. In March, Cisco bought Wi-Fi gearmaker Linksys Group for $500 million. And Intel is spending $300 million to promote its Centrino Wi-Fi chips.

Rampant Innovation
Wi-Fi technology is advancing fast. Intel and MeshNetworks are developing antennas that can reach for miles instead of today's 300 feet. Next: Wi-Fi–ready cell phones, PDAs, and hot spots on trains and buses.

Falling Prices
The price of Wi-Fi equipment is dropping. An antenna for a laptop now costs $46, down from $189 in 1999. Lower prices are opening the market to a broader group of buyers.

Grassroots Phenom
Pioneers in Portland, Ore., New York, Barcelona, and Sydney continue to expand community networks in parks, bars, and coffee shops. There are now 5,000 of these free networks worldwide.

Data: In-Stat/MDR, IDC, Yankee Group, Wireless Node Database Project

hot spots over the next three years. Phone companies, including Verizon Communications Inc. and T-Mobile USA Inc., are following suit. "You'd have to have your head in the sand to not see the news about hot-spot deployments," says Edward M. Cholerton, SBC Communications Inc.'s vice-president for Internet product management.

The giants are joined by legions of small fry. Last year alone, in the depths of the tech downturn, U.S. venture-capital firms pumped $2.8 billion into 296 wireless startups, says researcher Thomson Venture Economics. And as more companies pile in, prices for Wi-Fi equipment are plummeting. Installing an industrial-strength hot spot costs only $2,000 now, one-fifth what it cost two years ago. Home-gear prices are also in free fall. More than 50 companies are in the chip market alone, estimates Gartner Inc. As the tech powerhouses storm into the market, a painful wave of consolidation is all but assured.

Even for the mighty, this gold rush crosses hazardous terrain. Off-the-shelf versions of Wi-Fi are often unreliable and rough to install. This undermines confidence in the technology. And key initiatives are untested. Will corporate and consumer users dish out $30 to $50 a month for access to a nationwide grid of Wi-Fi hot spots? Will the number of subscriptions justify big network investments? "Can anyone make money in the home-networking or wireless world?" asks David Schmertz, a vice-president at Efficient Networks Inc., a broadband subsidiary of Siemens. "We're looking at that question hourly."

The riches won't flow until Wi-Fi security reaches industrial grade. Corporations are hankering for the power and flexibility of Wi-Fi networks, but many are postponing rollouts in strategic areas until they're convinced that hackers, spies, and competitors can't intercept wireless data. General Motors Corp. has deployed Wi-Fi in 90 manufacturing plants but is holding off on Wi-Fi at headquarters until next year. Why? Execs worry that until new encryption is in place, guests at a Marriott Hotel across the street could log on to GM's network and make off with vital memos and budgets. Industry analysts say a slew of airtight Wi-Fi security systems will be out next year. But delays or news of security breaches could pummel confidence in the technology.

A wild card is the possible overlap between Wi-Fi and the multibillion-dollar project for a high-speed cellular system known as Third Generation (3G). Like Wi-Fi, 3G promises a wireless Internet. It's coming onstream in Europe and Asia and will be spreading in North America in the next two years. As a phone system, 3G provides far broader coverage than Wi-Fi's constellation of hot spots. But Wi-Fi's hot spots are targeted precisely in the hotels, airports, and commercial centers where mobile Net surfers are most likely to be swarming. This upsets revenue projections for phone companies. Still, they're plowing ahead with Wi-Fi deployments on three continents, hoping they can bill customers for a menu of wireless services, including both Wi-Fi and 3G.

Wi-Fi represents a disruptive force. Yet if history is an indicator, it will ultimately pay rich dividends. The upstart technology appears to follow a pattern that has become common in the Internet age. New technologies surge from the grass roots, pushing companies to race madly, trying first to cope with the new sensations and later to transform them into businesses. This happened with the Net itself, and with Linux, the free software operating system. Now, the Internet has not only defined an age, it has spawned a host of successful companies. Some 40% of publicly traded Net companies are profitable today. Linux, developed within a populist movement similar in spirit to Wi-Fi, holds 13.7% of the $50.9 billion market for server software and is breathing down Microsoft's neck.

Wi-Fi promises similar fireworks. And the beleaguered tech industry is counting on it for a welcome shot of growth. In the short term, the direct payoff is likely to be moderate. Wi-Fi spending on hardware and subscriptions is expected to reach $3.4 billion this year and is growing at a 30% clip. Network buildouts over the next two years will chip in $8.2 billion more. That's welcome in a downturn but not enough to sway a $1 trillion global tech economy. And Wi-Fi subscriptions aren't likely to catch on until national networks are up and running, perhaps two years from now.

Instead, it's as an amplifier of other technologies that Wi-Fi packs its punch. It turns nearly every machine, from laptops to cash registers, into network devices. And it fuels demand for always-on broadband connections. This, in turn, paves the way for the next generation of Internet services. Analyst Christopher Fine of Goldman, Sachs & Co. compares the power of Wi-Fi to the networking of computers in the early 1990s or the telephone exchanges that spread in the 1920s.

Intel and computer makers are betting on it to spur laptop sales, which even without Wi-Fi carry profit margins 50% higher than those on desktops. Microsoft is pushing its Windows XP operating system, which is specially adapted to handle Wi-Fi. "You could say that Wi-Fi is the killer app that gets people to upgrade to Windows XP," says Pieter Knook, the company's vice-president for network service providers. On April 15, Intel announced that strong laptop sales, powered by Wi-Fi–ready Centrino chips, helped boost first-quarter profits.

The consumer-electronics industry is counting on Wi-Fi, too, to link a host of appliances in the home. Already, gadget-meisters are sending MP3 songs and videos from their computers to TVs and stereos via Wi-Fi. This could become a breeze over the next two years as the new generation of Wi-Fi rolls out, lifting connection speeds to 54 megabits—or nearly an hour of MP3 music—per second. Motorola, Nokia, and Ericsson are working on Wi-Fi phones that would let people move from Wi-Fi to cellular networks without even noticing. These should be ready in 18 months. In time, Wi-Fi could even feed data into smart networks in the home or factory to automatically monitor climate controls or industrial supply chains. "There's no upper limit to how you can use this technology," says Dean Douglas, vice-president for telecommunications at IBM Global Services. "In that, it's like the Web."

In its infancy, long before Wi-Fi took shape, the radio technology belonged to businesses. The year was 1985. The Federal Communications Commission had opened up slivers of the radio spectrum for experimentation. Researchers at a vanguard of companies, including NCR, Symbol Technologies, and Apple Computer, started building wireless networks. Their goal was to link everything from cash registers to auto assembly lines. But momentum slowed in the late '80s as the companies developed systems that didn't work together.

An NCR Corp. scientist named Vic Hayes stepped into the mess in 1990. Hayes led the movement toward a standard. It was a long and combative process, but in 1997, it led to the release of 802.11b, now known as Wi-Fi, or Wireless Fidelity. Two years later, Apple kick-started the market by adding Wi-Fi to its iBook portables for the then-stunningly low price of $99.

The race was on. In cities worldwide, tech geeks began setting up wireless networks. Led by pioneers such as Rob Flickenger in San Francisco and Anthony Townsend in New York, these techies jerry-built Linux-based hot spots and cheap alternatives to expensive gear. Famously, they improvised antennas using empty Pringles cans. And in the 21st century equivalent of barn-raisings, they united to link neighbors to the growing community networks. Says Townsend, who co-founded NYCwireless in 2000 with Terry Schmidt: "Our model of Wi-Fi is if you charge people to use it, it's not useful." Now the pair runs a business that builds community networks.

While Wi-Fi Nation was taking shape in the streets, a smattering of businesses were adapting the new networks to their own needs. At CareGroup Inc. hospitals in Massachusetts, engineers installed wireless systems to connect more than 2,000 doctors and nurses to the corporate system. This way, whether they were in emergency rooms or intensive-care units, they could access patient records, add observations to the database, and check on medicines. "It's cost-effective, and the doctors love it," says Chief Information Officer John D. Halamka, who estimates that the system helps reduce costly medical errors by 50%.

Early on, entrepreneurs saw opportunity in the burgeoning Wi-Fi community. Sky Dayton, founder of Internet service Earthlink Inc., believed that if anyone could unite the ragtag collection of hot spots and network communities into a secure nationwide network, there was a fortune to be made. In 2001, he founded Boingo Wireless Inc. The idea was to certify networks everywhere as Boingo providers. Then, when subscribers paying up to $50 a month turned on their laptops and saw a Boingo connection, they'd log in. Boingo, based in Santa Monica, Calif., and local providers would split the take.

It was a good idea. So good that lots of others came up with it, too. In the past two years, scores of networks have been launched, causing the number of commercial hot spots to mushroom to 16,000. Starbucks Corp. piled in, teaming with T-Mobile to offer consumers Wi-Fi surfing at more than 2,100 coffee shops for $40 a month. Fast-food giant McDonald's Corp. has deployed Wi-Fi at 10 restaurants in New York and plans to add hundreds more hot spots by yearend. The idea there is less to make money on Wi-Fi services, which go for $3 per hour, than to attract new customers and boost sales. McDonald's is offering a free hour of Wi-Fi with each Extra Value Meal.

To date, though, few commercial hot spots have thrived—and analysts have plenty of doubts about the new ventures at Boeing and McDonald's (Exhibit 2). Why? No carrier can offer seamless nationwide coverage, security is still touch-and-go, and many potential users feel it costs

EXHIBIT 2 The Many Challenges Wi-Fi Faces

Wireless networking must overcome a slew of technological and economic hurdles to win its battle to join the mainstream.

Challenge	Solution
Standards Are Unclear Wi-Fi developers harness different chunks of unlicensed radio spectrum. Some companies are holding back because there's no single standard.	Equipment makers are replacing transmitters with gear that covers the whole Wi-Fi spectrum.
Security Is Spotty In the past, Wi-Fi systems have allowed unauthorized users to sneak onto networks and steal bandwidth and even data from private computers.	New systems have encryption software but are still playing catch-up with traditional corporate networks.
Prices Are Too High Wi-Fi is cheaper than most other wireless Internet access, such as cell phones. But at up to $50 a month, a subscription to a commercial Wi-Fi network is still too pricey for mass adoption.	Eventually, rival networks will drive the price to $10 a month or less, or bundle it into a phone bill. That may be years away.
Range Is Limited Wi-Fi hot spots provide Web access at 300 feet or less. And that range can be reduced by walls or even foliage.	Signal boosters are available now. New antennas with a range in miles are being developed.
Hidden Costs A corporate hot spot can be had for $1,000. But installation and maintenance can add $3,000.	New gear drives down cost for big installations.
Inter-Operability No carrier is national, let alone global. For coverage on the road, a user would have to subscribe to several networks.	Networks must create roaming agreements similar to those in the cell-phone industry.

too much. "We don't subscribe to any of these services," says Tripp McCune, senior vice-president and director of information technology at ad agency Deutsch Inc. "The coverage isn't widespread enough for our people to use."

The job now is to build Wi-Fi into a solid pillar of the networked world. And Intel is out to lead the charge. Last year, CEO Barrett put $150 million into a Wi-Fi-oriented venture fund. He assigned 800 engineers to work on Wi-Fi, and in December he joined IBM and AT&T to launch Cometa. Unlike Boingo, Cometa will build its own hot spots. By next March, it plans to have 5,000 up and running.

The next job is to establish Wi-Fi as a global mainstay, and Intel is responding, naturally, with a chip. The Centrino family of chips, released in March with a $300 million media campaign, embeds a Wi-Fi receptor into the innards of a laptop computer. The effect should be dramatic. By this summer, every Dell Computer Corp. laptop and 70% of Hewlett-Packard Co.'s consumer offerings will be Wi-Fi-ready. For most users, this should ease the transition into the new technology. The current process is so complicated that it often irks novices. Intel and Microsoft are hoping that with the new systems (Exhibit 3), Wi-Fi installation will eventually become as easy as activating a modem: click "yes" six or seven times and then "finish."

Wi-Fi isn't likely to become a rock-solid standard until hot spots are dependable. That's pushing more than 100 Intel engineers on a worldwide mission. They're labeling hot spots the world over as "Centrino-certified." The idea is to unify the Wi-Fi world around Intel's brand, giving Centrino the Wi-Fi equivalent of the *Good Housekeeping* Seal of Approval.

Across the industry, engineers are coming up with security systems to satisfy the most demanding customers. Cranite Systems Inc. in San Jose, Calif., sold security for the $960,000 Wi-Fi installation at the U.S. Army's West Point Academy. Colonel Donald J. Welch, an associate dean for information and educational technology, says the military put the system through rigorous antihacking tests. "We don't want to be a launching pad [for hackers] to the Defense Dept.'s network," he says.

He has reason to be hypervigilant. Every step of the way, the technology manages to remind the Wi-Fi industry of the tough road ahead. At Intel's glitzy launch of its Centrino chips in March at the Hammerstein Ballroom in New York, CEO Barrett was on hand. The room shook to the sounds of *Goin' Mobile* by the Who. The crowd watched a live video hookup as an executive demonstrated how to use a Wi-Fi-equipped laptop to make a phone call. All he got, though, was dead air.

EXHIBIT 3 Making Wi-Fi Work

Millions of people are setting up wireless networks. Here's how it's done, using a network with a PC and one or more laptops:

1. Get a High-Speed Net Connection. You can subscribe to a cable-modem or DSL phone service for about $40 a month. The modem is usually free, and you can do the installation yourself in a few minutes.

2. Buy a Wi-Fi Access Point. The size of a clock radio, this box includes an Internet router and a two-way Wi-Fi radio. It costs $100 to $250.

3. Connect Access Point to Modem and Desktop. Plug cables into the back of the modem and PC. Install the software on the PC and follow the directions.

4. Buy a Wireless Antenna for Each Laptop. These credit-card size devices run $30 to $50.

5. Install Antenna and Antenna Software on Laptop. Install the antenna before you install the software, or it won't work properly.

6. Congratulations! Your network is up and running. Test the signal strength by wandering around with the laptop.

7. Whoops! The signal is weak. Most people find reception in their homes is hampered by walls and other obstructions. Signal strength will remain stronger if you move upstairs or downstairs just above or below the access point.

8. Don't Panic! You have options. You can buy a signal booster, which attaches to the router and costs about $100. You can sometimes boost the strength of the router's signal online, with help from the manufacturer's service department.

9. Telecommuting? O.K., Panic! If you work at home with a laptop that has been configured for the office, you may need to reconfigure it with help of your employer.

10. Expand! Now that you have connected the desktop and the laptop to your network, you can buy another antenna to include your TiVo, digital home theater, or gaming console in the network.

As technology companies scramble to transform Wi-Fi into a business, they'll come up against a lot more dead air. But it will all be worth it if Wi-Fi lives up to its promise to unleash the Internet.

By Heather Green, with Steve Rosenbush in New York, Roger O. Crockett in Chicago, and Stanley Holmes in Seattle.

Source: "Wi-Fi Means Business," *BusinessWeek*, April 28, 2003, 86–92.

Case 2-2

Nike Inc.

It's hard to say exactly when Nike Inc., one-time corporate brat, began to transform itself into a pillar of the community. But it may have been during a meeting in 1998, at a time when the company was under attack for allegedly exploiting overseas factory workers. Nike, in its usual maverick style, had initially tried to slough off the issue. But now, as managers argued over whether to raise the minimum age of workers in those factories from 14 to 18, Nike Chairman and co-founder Philip H. Knight ended the debate with a surprising call: Just do it.

The issue became a galvanizing force for both him and Nike. One of Corporate America's true free spirits, the brash Knight had long cultivated an aloof, even arrogant, style. When the outcry over working conditions in Nike's overseas factories started in the late '90s, he glossed over the complaints, claiming he had little control over suppliers. But as protests mounted on college campuses, Knight seemed to snap to attention. Suddenly, he was scouring the negative press coverage for errors; writing college presidents about the issue; and bringing in Maria S. Eitel from Microsoft Corp. as vice-president for corporate responsibility. "Phil made clear from the day I started that this is a huge priority," says Eitel.

These days, Knight is plugged into Nike's operations like never before. He has little choice. The backlash against Nike's labor practices isn't the only crisis the company faces. Two years ago, jolted by shifting teen fashions and the Asian economic downturn, sales of its sneakers and sports apparel hit a brick wall, and the hard times aren't over. On February 8, Nike told analysts that earnings this year and next would fall short of estimates because important retail chains are closing stores and the strong dollar is resulting in unfavorable currency translations (Exhibit 1). Immediately, the stock swooned 18%, to 37, lopping a stunning $2.4 billion off Nike's stock market valuation. "Investors feel that the turnaround they've been waiting for is being pushed off again," says Dana Eisman Cohen, an analyst with Donaldson, Lufkin & Jenrette. "People are losing patience."

With that kind of pressure, Knight, the ultracompetitive former college miler who co-founded Nike 28 years ago by selling running shoes out of his car trunk, is struggling to rebuild the company from top to bottom. That's required a huge attitude adjustment at Nike's headquarters in Beaverton, Ore. Knight quadrupled sales in the '90s with a buccaneer style that had Nike thumbing its nose at the sports Establishment. This, for example, was the company that in 1994 paid $25,000 to help defend skating outcast Tonya Harding. But two years ago, Knight, 61, woke up to discover that Nike was so big that it had become the Establishment. And like a middle-aged rock-and-roller who finds himself raising a family in the 'burbs, he has had to learn to accept the responsibility that comes with age. "There are some things you can do as a $100 million company that you can't get away with as a $9 billion company," Knight explains to *BusinessWeek* in his first major interview about Nike's new strategy. "We're not as rebellious as we were five years ago."

No wonder—many of the rebels are gone. Over the past two years, Knight and his No. 2, President Thomas E. Clarke, have trimmed Nike's payroll by 1,600, or 8%. At the same time, several executives identified with Nike's go-go years left, replaced by outsiders schooled at some of the nation's biggest corporations. Nine of Nike's 41 vice-presidents have worked at the company for fewer than two years, compared with just one of 27 four years ago. Three months ago, Nike hired a chief financial officer from PepsiCo Inc. Other newly minted vice-presidents have

EXHIBIT 1

Data: Footwear Market Insights, Nike, Inc., Black & Co., Bloomberg Financial Markets.

come from Disney, General Motors, and SBC Communications. Competitors say Nike needed to upgrade and deepen its management ranks. "I'm sure Nike's looking for fresh perspective, and newcomers bring a fresh perspective," says Paul Heffernan, vice-president for global marketing at Boston-based New Balance Athletic Shoe Inc.

The new team is immersed in the effort to reinvent Nike. Newcomers are heading initiatives that include a unit charged with reaching nontraditional markets, particularly extreme-sports enthusiasts such as skateboarders and snowboarders. Others are revamping Nike's manufacturing and logistics systems. Even the swoosh is no longer sacred. The logo is shrinking on some items and may disappear entirely from others.

The biggest change around the Beaverton campus, though, is that for the first time in years, Nike executives are taking a hard look at costs. Years of breakneck growth encouraged free spending. In the past, managers had plenty of big-picture goals but no hard budget numbers to rein them in. "Cost controls were a far second to boosting sales," recalls former marketing executive Elizabeth G. Dolan, who worked at Nike for a decade before leaving in 1997 to start her own consulting firm. Now, managers have to hold expense increases to about 3% below revenue increases. Nike also recently launched an effort to streamline manufacturing and logistics. "We grew really fast from 1994 to 1997, but I don't think anybody would suggest we were efficient," says Knight. "We couldn't be. We were just chasing the growth."

That chase was breathtaking while it lasted. In the mid-'90s, Nike blew away competitors such as Reebok and Adidas, its sales exploding from $3.8 billion in 1994 to $9.2 billion in 1997. Investors reaped a 320% increase in the stock price from Jan. 1, 1995, to a high of 75 in early 1997. But in 1998, the sprinter pulled up lame. Sales plummeted in Asia and stalled in the U.S. For the fiscal year ended May 31, sales slipped 8%. Even after overseas markets recovered late last year, Nike's domestic sales rose a paltry 2%. Now, the company has lowered sales projections for this year to an increase of just 3% to 4% from last year's $8.8 billion.

Nike's new lean focus helped it eke out a 13% increase in net income last year. But hopes for a 31% gain in 2000 were dashed when Clarke told analysts that earnings would come in slightly below estimates for this year and next. He said earnings-per-share growth would be held to "at least 20%" in fiscal year 2000 and to the mid-teens in 2001. Jennifer Black, an analyst at Black & Co. in Portland, Ore., believes Nike can generate a net earnings increase of 28% this year, still far below the glory days in 1996 and 1997 when Nike racked up gains of 38% and 44%, respectively.

Nike's news was especially troubling because, like other mature consumer-products companies, it was counting on overseas markets to speed growth. But with a weak euro, big gains in Europe are unlikely. Meanwhile, Knight expects only single-digit sales gains in the U.S. for the next few years. "Back in the mid-1990s, it was nirvana in the U.S. That's over," says Susan Zeeb, an analyst at Northern Trust Corp., which manages about 1 million Nike shares for wealthy individuals.

The result is a more measured, but hardly humbled, Phil Knight. He still tools around Beaverton in a black '92 Acura with NIKEMN (Nike Man) license plates and may be the only major American CEO to have his corporate logo tattooed on his ankle. And he's just as visible back at headquarters, where he still runs five miles a day. When top Nike-sponsored athletes drop by—golfer Tiger Woods, for instance, whom the company will pay an estimated $60 million to $80 million over five years—Knight is right by their side.

Knight may not have lost his ebullience, but his company is still in recovery from a downturn that hit it like a body blow. Starting in 1997, thousands of fickle teens suddenly switched from Nike Air Jordans to hiking boots and casual leather shoes. In 1994, athletic shoes accounted for 38% of all shoes sold in the U.S.; four years later, that had slipped to 31%, according to industry researcher Footwear Market Insights. Of course, that's still a healthy slice of the overall market, and Nike dominates the category with a 40% share. Nike's own sales slide was accelerated by its lingering association with arrogant millionaire athletes and overseas sweatshops.

Knight was blindsided by the ferocity of the anti-Nike sentiment about its overseas workers. The damage to the brand was real—and not just on college campuses. "They exploit people with what they pay as minimum wage in Third World countries," said Peter George, a runner from Melbourne, Australia, just after he finished competing in last November's New York City Marathon. He was wearing Asics shoes.

Once Knight figured out that the critics weren't going away, he abruptly changed tactics. "As part of our evolution, we've chosen to engage our critics rather than saying that they're wrong, which is my natural instinct," he says. Since Eitel came on board in 1998, her staff has doubled, to 95, one of the company's few areas of expansion. Nike maintains that it has made real progress on the issue, citing for example a literacy program it started for workers in Indonesia. Even activists acknowledge some basic improvements in working conditions. For instance, Nike has replaced the solvent toluene, which can produce harmful fumes, with a water-based cement on most production lines. Still, critics say they haven't done enough. "You get the sense they're flailing around, trying to make enough changes to satisfy critics without making changes that cost lots of money," says Medea Benjamin, executive director of Global Exchange, a San Francisco-based activist group.

Getting Nike back on the fast track will require a broad effort. Knight must wean it away from the Old Nike, sometimes literally. Last year, he carved off the part of the business that makes products for extreme sports into a separate unit called ACG—short for "all-conditions gear." The ACG group moved into its own floor in a building away from the main footwear business and built its own staff, budget, and marketing plan.

Why the separation? Nike has failed to build credibility among fans of nontraditional sports, a small but important demographic that tends to originate fashion trends among teens. "To certain kids who are still excited about the NFL, Nike might still be cool. But to the portion of Generation Y that's individual-oriented and identifies with these newer sports it isn't relevant," says Gary H. Schoenfeld, CEO of Vans Inc., maker of shoes and clothing for skateboarders, snowboarders, and surfers.

Even at the Magdalena Ecke Family YMCA Skate Park in Encinitas, Calif., which Nike helped to rebuild a few years ago with a $100,000 donation, many kids don't know that Nike makes a skateboard shoe. Some of those who do aren't impressed. "Nikes aren't good at all," says 10-year-old Jesse Satterfield, who wears Osiris shoes. "They wear down easily, and they're not comfortable."

ACG is supposed to change that. Knight put the business under the charge of Gordon O. McFadden, a 17-year veteran of Norwegian outdoor-apparel maker Helly Hansen. Four of the five top ACG executives are outsiders, hired from places like Dr Pepper/Seven Up Inc. and Fila Holding. A skier, snowboarder, and mountain biker himself, McFadden, 49, is developing new products, such as a $175 snowboarding jacket with a dozen pockets designed to hold such essentials as gloves, goggles, and headphones. To learn these markets, he's putting 15 or 20 designers in a studio close to the action in Southern California, the epicenter of the skateboarding and surfing worlds. And ACG will soon take the wraps off a clog-like shoe, the Rufus, that it hopes will slow the onslaught of "brown shoes," the hiking boots and other casual footwear that many young customers prefer over athletic shoes.

But ACG knows that cool new products alone won't solve Nike's problems: The company needs a new image to go with them. ACG plans to start its first big marketing push in June, with new print ads and in-store promotions. And starting this September, McFadden intends to open dozens of ACG stores at ski lodges and outdoor resorts. The new stores and products will bear ACG's logo: an inverted triangle with the letters ACG underscored by a swoosh. McFadden expects ACG's sales of action-sports products to grow by about 20% annually, compared with an 8% rate before the unit was given its independence. "We've got a startup mentality," says McFadden. "They want us to break rules, be the kind of renegade Nike was when Phil started."

But this isn't the '70s. To project that kind of attitude in the new millennium, a strong Internet presence is a must. Until recently, however, Nike was clueless when it came to cyberspace. But last summer, Knight invited a star-studded cast of Net-industry executives to educate Nike employees about the Web. One speaker, Novell Inc. CEO Eric E. Schmidt, recalls: "Phil got up at the beginning and said: 'I don't understand all this stuff, but it's incredibly important, and we're going to get ahead of it.'"

Now, Knight meets with his Internet team daily. Topics include ways to drive traffic to Nike.com and partnerships, such as the one with Ask Jeeves Inc., which recently added an automated customer-service feature to the site. Nike's electronic commerce site, which has been selling shoes for almost a year, was jazzed up recently to let customers choose colors and personalize them with a name or jersey number.

Nike is pushing the envelope in other key areas, too. It now takes Nike, and much of the industry, about 18 months to design and produce a shoe. Roland Wolfram, hired from SBC's Pacific Telesis unit in 1998, is trying to cut that to 12 months, and even shorter on some products. "Traditionally, Nike has relied on its product excellence and brand moxie, but we also want to have this other leg of the stool to stand on," says Wolfram.

Shortening the design and manufacturing cycle has implications up and down the sales chain. Right now, Nike has to place its bets far in advance of actual demand, leaving it vulnerable to swift changes in fashion. Last year, for instance, it ordered 400,000 pairs of one of its sports sandals from its contract factories. But when the actual retail orders came in months later, they totaled more than a million pairs, leaving Nike scrambling to fill the demand.

Nike is also putting in place an automatic replenishment system that ships out basic, high-volume merchandise without waiting for retailers to place orders. In the past, retailers often ran out of simple polo-style tops or shorts. That hurt sales of higher-priced items like halter tops, since consumers frequently purchase basic and fashion items together. Nike is now selling $100 million of merchandise a year through auto-replenishment. Retailers say the improvements have smoothed out many of the supply problems that dogged the company in 1998. "They're delivering on time, something that was a real challenge," says John Douglas Morton, CEO of Denver-based Gart Sports Co., which operates 130 apparel and equipment stores.

If this sounds like a more disciplined and calculated approach to doing business, it is. A good part of the enforcement has fallen to Clarke, a 20-year Nike veteran who became president in 1994. He has spent much of the past two years increasing financial accountability around the company to make employees more conscious of sales performance and expenses. In 1998, Nike gave managers in each region—the U.S., Europe, Asia, and Latin America—their own profit-and-loss statements and now ties compensation more closely to performance.

As part of the new emphasis on financial responsibility, Knight and Clarke are pounding home the need to cut costs. Layoffs and cutbacks have hit every area of the company. Nike last year held its annual executive retreat in Beaverton—a far cheaper alternative to the seaside resort in the Netherlands where managers gathered a few years back. Little things count, too, these days: In the past, Nike paid its advertising agency to assemble videos highlighting new products for the retreat. Last year, it did that work itself.

Knight admits that his unconventional style—he was known to disappear from day-to-day operations for weeks at a time—contributed to his company's current predicament. In April, 1998, Knight summoned the headquarters staff to "the Bo," Nike's gymnasium named for former football/baseball star Bo Jackson. There, Knight apologized for taking his eye off the ball during Nike's boom years and failing to prepare it for the rough times that followed (Exhibit 2).

Despite that mea culpa, Knight shrugs off any suggestions that the struggles of the past two years have transformed him personally. But he acknowledges that he has had to swallow some pride. "There's a fine line between being a certain size and being a bully. And we don't want to be a bully," he says. He acknowledges that creating a big-company culture "is not as much fun, but I think it's part of the evolution you've got to go through."

Knight hasn't given up hope that his company can regain its old stride. "I don't think we're middle-aged, I think we're in our twenties. I think there is great opportunity for growth," he says gamely. But putting Nike back on track will require a delicate balancing act—taming the company's brash, in-your-face style while injecting a new sense of vigor. Nike's CEO likes to point out that he has weathered other rough patches. "This is the fourth downturn in 18 years as a public company. I said going into the 1990s that if we can get through it with only two downturns, we'll have a great decade. And I'll look forward to 2000 through 2010 coming up with the same statement." That may be the only good thing about slowing down as you get older—it gives you a chance to put things in perspective.

Source: Louise Lee, "Can Nike Still Do It?" *BusinessWeek*, February 21, 2000, 120–22, 124, 126, 128.

Epilogue

Nike marketing execs couldn't have written a better script themselves. On June 30, Brazilian superstar Ronaldo, sporting a pair of special lightweight, silver-coated Nike soccer shoes, knocked in two goals in the final game to win the World Cup for his soccer-mad country. The 2-0 victory over Germany was sweet redemption for Ronaldo, who bad battled back from career-threatening injuries. And it marked a coup for Nike Inc., which sponsored the Brazilian national team and its star in a bid to crack the $2.5 billion global soccer-gear business dominated by German rival Adidas-Salomon.

That's just the sort of deft footwork that Nike will need if it's going to break free from a moribund U.S. sneaker market. The Beaverton (Ore.) giant still gets more than half of its nearly $10 billion in annual sales from shoes. And much of the news lately has been grim: U.S. shoe sales were flat in the three months ended Aug. 31, and orders for future quarters dropped 3%. Factoring in a $266 million charge to reflect goodwill on past acquisitions, Nike reported a $48.9 million net loss. The biggest shock of all; Nike's top customer, Foot Locker Inc., canceled orders for as much as $250 million worth of business. Now Nike has to scramble to find retailers to take all those $160 Vince Carter Shox and $200 Air Jordans.

But the gloom is deceiving. Behind the scenes, Nike is finally making headway in its year-long quest to get back on the growth track. A few short years after some pronounced the brand finished on the basis of tepid product launches, shifting customer tastes, and its ties to Third World sweatshops, Nike appears to be displaying financial discipline for the first time and proving that it can squeeze growth out of something other than shoes.

Even Nike apparel, a chronic under-achiever, finally is making significant contributions. Shirts, shorts, and other clothing generated $2.9 billion in sales for the fiscal year ended May 31, or 30% of Nike's total, and kicked in its first meaningful profit. Global soccer revenues rose 24%,

EXHIBIT 2 Take Our Swoosh. Please

In the old days, Nike Inc. didn't have to do a lot of research to figure out what kids thought was cool. The answer was "Nike." For years, the brand was a mainstay of Young & Rubicam's annual survey of preferred labels among teens. But three years ago, it fell off the list and has yet to climb back on. Even sales of its once hot Air Jordan sneakers are down. Business at its glitzy NikeTown stores has dropped off, too. Says Marian Salzman, who heads the Brand Futures Group at Young & Rubicam Inc.: "Nike just ain't cool."

What went wrong? Nike was hurt by accusations that it fosters sweatshop factory conditions overseas. But there were basic marketing mishaps, too. Lackluster ads, a series of fashion miscues, and overexposure of the swoosh all damaged Nike's image. To fight back, the company is listening hard these days to what kids say they're interested in—instead of assuming it already knows.

Gen Bending

Take its latest TV ads, launched in January. They're a complex blend of celebrity athletes, teenspeak, and the Internet. In one, champion sprinter Marion Jones challenges viewers to a race. The camera weaves through a maze of streets and houses and winds up crashing into a man juggling chainsaws. It ends with a shot of airborne, whirring saws, a scream—and a Web address, whatever.nike.com. There, visitors can choose from among several possible conclusions, including one in which Jones punches the viewer in the nose. In another, the viewer is decapitated by a chainsaw. It's more than just an attention-getting ad: The company says the campaign has boosted online orders for sneakers. Another recent campaign features famous athletes displaying the physical costs of competition: scars, missing fingers, and knocked-out teeth.

But Nike has also figured out that national ad campaigns only go so far with younger consumers. "Generation Y wants a sense of having discovered it themselves," says Wendy Liebmann, president of New York-based marketing consultant WSL Strategic Retail. That means getting the message out through narrowly targeted sponsorships or events, like the stickball game that Nike staged last year between the Yankees and the Mets.

Nike is still doing plenty of big-ticket endorsements and sponsorships. But it is targeting some of those dollars differently, Nike's push into women's and girl's athletic gear got a huge boost from the company's support of the Women's World Cup soccer tournament last summer. The company followed up the famous image of a victorious Brandi Chastain ripping off her jersey by rolling out products such as its line of $47 "Inner Actives" sports bras. "Athletic bras that work without smashing you down," says one ad.

To combat a sense among kids that Nike is simply ubiquitous, the company is starting to use its powerful swoosh symbol more selectively. One former Nike executive recalls a meeting in early '98 where product designers and marketers scrutinized a running shoe and discovered it had at least nine swooshes. "No one had ever really counted," he says. Now, Nike CEO Philip H. Knight is looking for less obvious ways to use the logo. "If you blast it on every T shirt, every sign in the soccer match, you dilute it," says Knight. "There's more thought given to how we use it."

The biggest blow to Brand Nike has been the controversy surrounding its overseas labor practices. Top execs now take the issue seriously and have made efforts, from contests to ads in college papers, to keep kids informed of the changes they've made. Knight thinks Nike is making headway. "You're seeing a bit of resurgence with the younger consumer," he says hopefully. Now, if he can just translate that momentum into store traffic, he just might score a come-from-behind victory with kids.

By Louise Lee in Beaverton, Ore.

to $450 million, last year, a dramatic jump considering Nike had virtually no soccer credibility—or sales—at the time of the 1994 World Cup. Even in golf, Nike seems to be on the way to becoming a power, on the strength of its sponsorship of Tiger Woods and the refinement of a lineup that includes balls, clubs, and shoes.

The result: Nike returned to double-digit profit growth in fiscal 2002, with net income rising 12%, to $663.3 million. Profits should grow another 13% in the year ending May 31—albeit on only 5% sales growth, according to Wells Fargo Securities (Exhibit 3). "I think now we're a pretty well-run $10 billion company, and we're ready to grow again," says Nike Chairman and CEO Philip H. Knight.

Even Nike's vaunted image-making machinery—so crucial to the rise of the brand in the 1990s—appears to be back on track. Whimsical television advertisements that show an entire city engaged in a giant game of tag have helped soften a brand that was too often associated with hard work rather than play. For the World Cup,

EXHIBIT 3

Data: Company reports, Wells Fargo Securities.

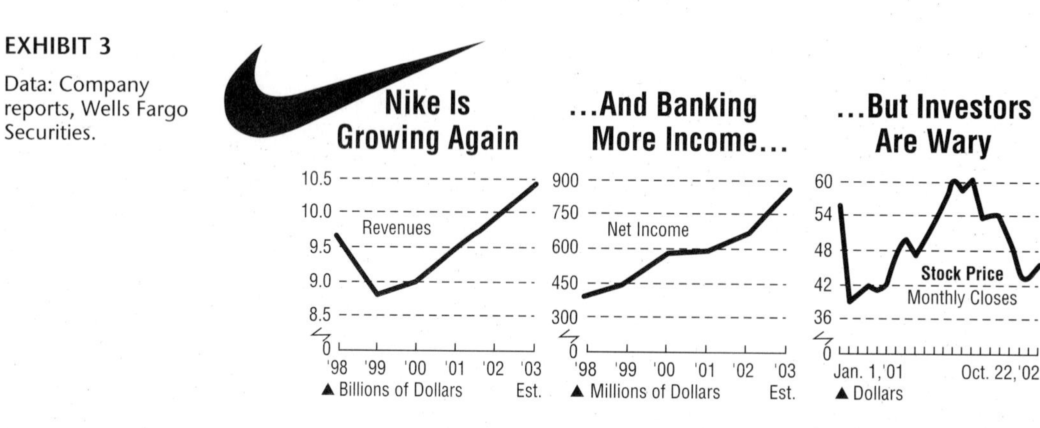

Nike created global buzz with an ad that pitted its stable of soccer stars in street-style matches inside a steel cage aboard a tanker.

Knight, the enigmatic company co-founder, finally acknowledged early last year that he needed to shake things up. After a torrid run in the mid-1990s—capped by a 50% burst in sales during 1997—the company simply outgrew its inventory and other systems. By 1999, sales had dropped, and profits, which peaked at $795 million in '97, fell to $451 million. Having accumulated the titles of chairman, CEO, and president, Knight admits he was part of the problem: "We got to be a $9 billion company with a $5 billion management."

The turnaround began when Knight handed over day-to-day control to a pair of Nike veterans, co-Presidents Mark G. Parker, 47, and Charlie Denson, 46. While yoking two ambitious execs can be a recipe for indecision, or worse, Parker and Denson so far have forged a smooth relationship, insiders say. Parker, originally a shoe designer, brought to market such innovations as Nike's flexible Presto and spring-soled Shox. Now he is leading an assault on sub-$100 footwear. Denson, meanwhile, used his sales background to pare down a near billion-dollar inventory bulge, which threatened to implode the supply chain. Among other things, he installed new computer systems to better track goods.

Although Knight has stuck with insiders for the top posts, he has reached outside for some key hires. They have blended surprisingly well with Nike's notoriously insular, athlete-dominated culture. Chief Financial Officer Donald W. Blair, hired from PepsiCo Inc. in 1999, has fostered fiscal discipline at a company that loves to spend money on product development and marketing. For the first time in a decade, Nike's gross margin last quarter exceeded 40% of revenues. Meanwhile, Mindy Grossman, a fast-talking New Yorker hired two years ago from the Polo Ralph Lauren Corp., is pumping life into Nike apparel. She has slashed lead times to put new outfits on the shelf from 18 months to 11 and is launching a line of active lifestyle fashions. "I think they are bridging lifestyle and sport a lot better and creating more fashionable looks and fabrics," says Shawn Neville, CEO of retailer Footaction.

Nike will need to draw on all of its new discipline and brand strength to stay one step ahead of fierce shoe competitors such as Adidas and New Balance Athletic Shoe Inc., which have been gaining U.S. market share. The tense standoff with Foot Locker, which accounts for 11% of Nike's sales, didn't help. The mess, sparked by slow sales of Nike's premium shoes, will take months to clear up. A bigger challenge, though, is to prove Nike can be a force in lower-priced shoes. Whereas some teens once bought eight pairs of pricey shoes a year, cell phones and other gizmos now compete for their money.

That erosion of Nike's core business is a big reason its shares are down 30% since hitting a two-year high of $63.99 in late March. To respond, Nike is offering a relaunch of the classic Air Jordan 9 at $125. Admitting that the initial design and high price of the Vince Carter Shox doomed sales, it will launch the redesigned second edition at the NBA All-Star Game in February. Says a sobered Eric Sprunk, Nike's footwear vice-president: "We're not going to $200. We probably pushed that too aggressively."

Fortunately, Nike is now much less dependent on the U.S. market. Its overall international revenues have gradually grown to $4.4 billion, now nearly matching U.S. revenues of $4.7 billion. In the most recent quarter, Nike's sales grew 15% in Europe and 24% in Asia. A key driver of overseas growth will be soccer footwear and equipment. Last spring, to coincide with the World Cup, Nike introduced a line of radically designed shoes, jerseys, and equipment, including the Mercurial Vapor, worn by Ronaldo. It spent $155 million on endorsements and $100 million on ads, an interactive Web site, and 13 mini theme parks scattered across the globe.

The payoff? Nike believes global soccer revenues should hit $1 billion within five years. Even more promising, Nike seems to be recapturing excitement among younger consumers. "When you're walking down the street, people notice—ooh, Nikes. They don't remark on Adidas," says Fahri Gurlir, a 14-year-old German soccer fan from Frankfurt. Nike isn't over the hump yet. But far from the basketball court, it seems to be getting its head back into the game.

By Stanley Holmes in Beaverton, Ore., with Christine Tierney in Frankfurt.

Source: "How Nike Got Its Game Back," *BusinessWeek*, November 4, 2002, 129–131.

Case 2-3

Campbell Soup Co.

CAMDEN, N.J.—When R. David C. Macnair, Campbell Soup Co.'s chief technical officer, summoned doctors and nutritionists for a preview of the company's promising new product, he wasn't prepared for the gasps as he unveiled a helping of mashed potatoes.

Unexpectedly, they were glowing bright green.

The fluorescent spuds might have been a harbinger for Campbell back in 1992, as the soup company pursued its most ambitious and secretive product in a century: a regimen of nutrient-fortified meals promising therapeutic benefits and called Intelligent Quisine.

IQ would go beyond the increasingly popular low-fat products of the time, and Campbell backed its therapeutic claims with clinical trials at eight universities. Several medical experts and groups heralded the IQ line as a breakthrough: the first foods scientifically proven to lower high levels of cholesterol, blood sugar and blood pressure.

The testimonials were one reward for the seven years and $55 million Campbell would eventually invest in developing IQ, but a bigger payoff was expected in the marketplace. As the company began selling 41 breakfasts, lunches, dinners and snacks in a market test in Ohio in January 1997, then-Chief Executive David W. Johnson told analysts that Campbell foresaw $200 million in annual sales when the brand went nationwide.

But after 15 months in Ohio, Campbell yanked the line last March, surrendering to problems outside and within the company. While many test subjects enjoyed the meals and added their testimonials to those of the experts, others found the IQ line too expensive or lacking in variety. In the end, sales fell far short of expectations. Inside Campbell, Mr. Johnson's enthusiasm collided with the skepticism of his eventual successor, Dale Morrison. And in hindsight, some observers suggest that Campbell may have pulled out too soon, noting that IQ's therapeutic side made it analogous to a new drug, which can take more than two years to garner the support it needs from the medical establishment.

Campbell's own postmortem suggests the company may have bitten off more than it could chew. Spokesman Michael Kilpatric says, "Business results in Ohio didn't meet expectations and would have required more health-care resources, and that is not a core competency of Campbell." After its bold plunge into innovation, the big conservative company, built on one main product, went back to its breadwinner. Mr. Kilpatric says Campbell made a decision to exit the frozen-food business and "put our resources behind soup."

Did Campbell quit too soon? Other companies continue to regard so-called functional foods—snacks and meals with medical benefits—as the next blockbuster to snap stagnant sales in the $650 billion food industry, which has been suffering from a shortage of innovative hits. Kellogg Co., which spent $75 million to open a functional-food lab, is expected to launch new products early next year. ConAgra Inc. and Nestle SA are also developing what the industry has dubbed "nutraceuticals." By some estimates, sales of functional foods could reach $24 billion a year by 2001, as the huge baby-boomer population enters old age.

Campbell began casting about for a cutting-edge health food in 1990. At the time, the company was still king of soup, with more than three-quarters of the American market. But soup consumption had stalled, leaving the company worried about where future growth would come from just as rivals were digging into a hot new market. ConAgra's Healthy Choice and H. J. Heinz & Co.'s Weight Watchers frozen meals were taking off as Americans became more aware of the link between diet and disease.

So Campbell researchers began working to push the envelope, with foods that could help people manage or prevent ailments such as diabetes and cardiovascular disease. Campbell saw a demographic gold mine. About 58 million Americans have high-blood pressure and other forms of cardiovascular disease, America's No. 1 killer.

An additional 16 million Americans have diabetes, the seventh leading cause of death.

In 1991, Dr. Macnair. who has a Ph.D. in biochemistry, assembled a medical advisory board comprising specialists in nutrition, heart disease and diabetes to help Campbell run its foods through the scientific gauntlet. It would be an expensive undertaking, but it had a lot of support at the top from Mr. Johnson, IQ's biggest champion.

Plucked from the chief executive's job at Novartis AG's Gerber Products, Mr. Johnson arrived at Campbell in 1990 with orders to boost sagging earnings and soup sales. He soon resurrected an early version of the healthful food product, which had been referred to internally as Project Apple. He was drawn to the "explosive potential," as he now puts it, of "something that tastes great, is good for you, and is therapeutically as effective as a drug."

Soon he was dropping in on the medical advisory board, sitting through technical discussions on systolic and diastolic blood pressures. "Wouldn't you be dumbfounded by the opportunity to take a quantum leap and develop a product that could help improve the health and nutrition of the world?" asks Mr. Johnson, now 66 years old and Campbell's chairman.

Few inside Campbell knew anything about the development work, which was initially code-named Project Nightingale (as in Florence). Campbell kept IQ researchers away from the rest of the company, and organized some of them into small, segregated groups that focused on snacks or desserts. Mr. Johnson and Dr. Macnair were so fearful of a leak that many top Campbell executives were kept in the dark. Marketing tasks were farmed out with demands for total confidentiality.

Developing a menu of meals packed with vitamins and minerals pushed Campbell's food-technology skills to the limit, and not just on mashed potatoes. (Dr. Macnair says he never figured what caused the green glow; he suspects it had something do with oxidation or heating of the nutrients added.) Of the early entrees, Mary Winston, a retired science consultant at the American Heart Association, says, "The best analogy would be airline meals." An early fiber-enriched dinner roll "could have been marketed as a hockey puck," Dr. Macnair recalls.

By late 1994, Campbell had developed what it considered 24 palatable meals, or about a week's worth, and the medical advisory board began conducting clinical trials at the eight universities where the board members worked. Of the 560 subjects who ate the meals for a 10-week period, 73% lowered their blood cholesterol from what were considered high levels, 75% reduced their blood pressure and 62% reduced their blood sugar. None of the testers experienced any side effects that can accompany medications, Campbell says, though some reported having a little gas.

"I've never had so much blood drawn before in my life," says Mary Ann Haisch, 57, a trial participant from Vancouver, Wash. She was provided with free chow for 10 weeks. In return, she had to check into a clinic regularly, have four samples of blood taken and answer questions about her well-being, including her sex life. Her cholesterol dropped to 200 milligrams a deciliter from 240, and she lost 13 pounds. And the food? "Best raisin bran I ate in my life," she says. But the dinner roll, speckled with nutrients, she says, tasted like a grainy "energy bar."

With the clinical trials going well, Campbell turned to marketing issues, preparing for a yearlong market test. Up to this point, trial subjects had gotten their meals in plain, white boxes. But Campbell's marketing department and consultants began conjuring up a name for the food and flashy packaging. It chose "Intelligent Quisine" and designed medicinal-looking blue boxes and cans for dishes such as French toast with sausage, New England clam chowder and sirloin beef tips. Each week, 21 meals, most of them frozen, would be delivered to a buyer's door by United Parcel Service.

By early 1995, at Dr. Macnair's suggestion, Mr. Johnson created a new division called the Center for Nutrition and Wellness, with the nutritionists' "food pyramid" as its logo. It employed more than 30 nutrition scientists, dietitians and others, and was based at the Camden, N.J., headquarters in Building 81, known for its wide open offices and occasional squirrel infestations.

Two years later, in January 1997, IQ was ready to stride into Ohio with fanfare. "Introducing the first and only meal program clinically proven to help people reduce high cholesterol, blood pressure and blood sugar," blared a print ad in Ladies' Home Journal. A 10-minute infomercial showed men and women in lab coats, inspecting tomatoes, cauliflower and spices.

All the ads featured trial participants. "When I was first diagnosed with high cholesterol, I got scared. . . . Now I get the food I love and my cholesterol went down 36 points," one testified. Another proclaimed: "I ate cheesecake on the meal program and my cholesterol went down 15 points."

At Campbell's phone bank in Salt Lake City, the toll-free switchboard lit up, but when the callers were told that IQ's one-week "sample pack" cost $80 and that the recommended 10-week plans went for $700, many hung up. The price was just too high for many older people who live on Social Security and other sources of fixed income. Etta Saltos, a nutritionist at the U.S. Department of Agriculture, ordered a week's worth of meals for her father, a diabetic who lived alone in Ohio. "When he found out what they cost," she says, he "put them in the freezer for a rainy day."

Campbell also tapped the medical community for marketing help. The company sought what it called the "implied endorsement" of hospitals, health-maintenance organizations and insurers, which could then target their thousands of members in direct mailings. The IQ team quickly persuaded the Cleveland Clinic, for one, to distribute meals and promotional material to its heart patients.

In addition, Campbell hired 24 part-time pharmaceuticals salespeople to storm doctors offices around Ohio. May Ann DiStasi of Cincinnati met with 25 physicians a week, zapping IQ meals in their office microwaves, and serving them for lunch or a snack. After her pitch, she left behind IQ "scratch pads" resembling prescription pads.

IQ wasn't always warmly received. In January 1997, at a lunch at the American Heart Association's Columbus, Ohio, office, about 40 dietitians and other professionals noshed on salad with IQ dressing, and chicken divan with rice, as Campbell touted IQ's clinical-trial results. But in the back of the room, some dietitians groused that IQ offered nothing more than a motivated person could whip up on his own, recalls Yvonne Sebastian, a program manager with the American Diabetes Association who attended the meeting.

Meanwhile, Mr. Johnson was working the Wall Street crowd, bragging to analysts at a food-industry convention in Florida of the healing power of IQ. Most had paid little attention to the embryonic product. The headline for one analyst's report in late 1996 reflected the skepticism: "UPS T.V. Dinners Drive Top Line?"

By March 1997, the doubts had surfaced in-house: Several division presidents at Campbell had begun questioning the costly project they knew so little about. To appease them, Mr. Johnson called for a review, and a team of consultants from the Boston Consulting Group swept into Building 81 to size up the business prospects for IQ. Mr. Morrison, Campbell's new head of international and specialty foods and a leading contender to succeed Mr. Johnson, thought IQ's $20 million budget was excessive, slashed it to $13 million, and poured the savings into Campbell's overseas expansion.

Two months later, with the consultants still hovering, sales results in Ohio were looking bad. Fewer than 2,500 people had ordered slightly more than six weeks' worth of food on average—far short of the yearlong target of 40,000 orders. Desperate to rev up sales, Campbell had its salespeople cold-call those who had previously ordered IQ meals, offering discounts.

Some IQ diners did notice dramatic changes in their health and lifestyle. Yvonne Holsinger, 72, saw her blood sugar dip to between 110 and 135 milligrams a deciliter from more than 300 after 10 weeks. So dedicated was she that she was able to quit taking the medication Glyburide for her adult-onset diabetes.

Others, however, found the IQ meal program tedious. Patricia Bowers, a 68-year-old diabetic, got tired of the same eight or nine dinners over about 40 weeks. She called the IQ 800 number to complain and was happy to hear there was a pizza on the drawing board.

In June, the consultants recommended to Mr. Morrison that Campbell quit trying to drum up grassroots support from consumers and individual doctors and instead set up storefronts near medical clinics where the infirm could pick up their meals and receive dietary counseling.

But by July 1997, the tide was turning against IQ within Campbell. Mr. Johnson relinquished his position as chief executive officer, and Mr. Morrison, as expected, became president and CEO. The former executive of PepsiCo Inc.'s Frito-Lay unit had a specific game plan: to focus on key brands and expand overseas. He spun off Campbell's huge Swanson and Vlasic businesses and smaller lines, representing $1.4 billion of Campbell's $7.9 billion in sales for the fiscal year ended July 1997.

And he began the death watch for IQ by putting it on the corporate back burner. With no marketing budget for the project, Campbell stopped promoting IQ, although it continued funding new clinical trials and working with the Cleveland Clinic. Researchers at the Center for Nutrition and Wellness were reassigned to other Campbell divisions. Finally, last fall, Campbell made plans to sell IQ, at a price tag that has varied from as much as $15 million to as little as $3 million.

Campbell certainly had gathered some important market intelligence on functional foods. IQ showed that many Americans resist a long-term eating plan; they want a quick fix, a magic bullet. The project's fate also may reflect the impatience of food companies.

Dr. Macnair and some marketing people began making IQ presentations at companies including Bristol-Myers Squibb Co. and Monsanto Co. And the team prepared for IQ's sale by creating a "due-diligence room" at Building 81, with all of the marketing material, clinical-trial results and packaging on display. No prospects showed, and today that room in Building 81 is empty and dark.

Source: Vanessa O'Connell, "Food for Thought: How Campbell Saw a Breakthrough Menu Turn into Leftovers," *The Wall Street Journal*, October 6, 1998, A1, A12.

Case 2-4

Johnson & Johnson

Lots of executives at Johnson & Johnson have stories about William C. Weldon's powers of persuasion. The onetime drug salesman who now leads the health-care giant is famed for his ability to convince, cajole, or sometimes just sweet-talk colleagues into seeing things his way. A couple of years ago, Dr. Per A. Peterson, the chief of pharmaceutical research and development, was fed up with personnel headaches and told Weldon he was thinking of leaving the company. The next morning, Peterson, who lives minutes from Weldon in central New Jersey, got a call from the boss at 5:30, inviting him over for breakfast. As Weldon tended to the skillet, the two men discussed Peterson's concerns. And then they talked some more: Their conversation lasted well into the afternoon. Eventually, Peterson agreed to stay, and within a week Weldon had made the changes Peterson sought. "What else can you say to a guy who cooks you an omelette at six in the morning?" says Peterson with a laugh. "You say yes."

Weldon, 54, and one year into the job, will need those skills in spades as he guides J&J in the new century. The 117-year-old company is an astonishingly complex enterprise, made up of 204 different businesses organized into three divisions: drugs, medical devices and diagnostics, and consumer products. Much of the company's growth in recent years has come from pharmaceuticals; they accounted for almost half of J&J's sales and 61% of its operating profits last year. With revenue of $36 billion, J&J is one of the largest health-care companies in the U.S. That allows it to take bigger risks: When a surgical device business lost some $500 million between 1992 and 1995, J&J hardly felt it.

Consumers know Johnson & Johnson for its Band-Aids and baby powder. But competitors know the company as a fierce rival that boasts a rare combination of scientific expertise and marketing savvy. It regularly develops or acquires innovative products and then sells them more aggressively than almost anyone around. Even if a hospital might prefer to purchase its surgical tools from one company and its sutures from another, it could likely end up buying both from J&J because J&J offers favorable prices to hospitals that buy the whole package. J&J can also trade on its "heritage," as Weldon calls it, when it comes to persuading doctors to try its new drugs and devices. Or when it comes to persuading consumers: When J&J launched anemia drug Procrit in 1991, few expected it to make much of a difference to the company's performance. Not only did J&J spend millions to educate physicians about the condition, it also ran a series of ads on television—an unusual move considering that the drug is marketed specifically to treat anemia in chemotherapy patients. But it worked: Procrit is now J&J's best-selling drug.

The company Weldon inherited from his predecessor, Ralph S. Larsen, has been one of the most consistent, most successful health-care companies for years. Others around it are suffering as patents for important drugs expire with little of real consequence to replace them. That's expected in an industry so dependent on the unpredictable pace of scientific innovation. But not at J&J. The company is famed for delivering at least 10% earnings growth year in and year out going back nearly two decades. In the first quarter, it reported a 13% rise. Its stock price, meanwhile, has increased from less than $3, split-adjusted, in the mid-1980s to almost 20 times that now. Over the past two years, as the Standard & Poor's 500-stock index has fallen 28.1%, J&J stock has increased 19.4%. And in 2002, J&J earned $6.8 billion (excluding special charges), compared with $5.9 billion the previous year.

Maintaining that record could be Weldon's biggest challenge: Just to keep up, he must in essence create a new $4 billion business every year. But J&J's crucial drug business is finally succumbing to the pressures slowing down the rest of the industry. Procrit sales were nearly flat in the first quarter because of a new rival, news that sent the stock down 3% in one day. And like its peers, J&J doesn't have much coming out of its labs now. Meanwhile, its new drug-coated stent has been held up at the Food & Drug Administration. Approval still seems highly likely. But if the device does not get the O.K., it would be a huge blow to J&J.

What makes matters worse for Weldon is that the other component of J&J's growth—acquisitions—could become more problematic, too. Over the past decade, J&J has bought 52 businesses for $30 billion; 10% to 15% of its top-line growth each year comes from such investments. But to buy something that really affects overall performance is a different proposition for a $36 billion company than it is for a $10 billion company. "You get to a point where finding acquisitions that fit the mold and make a contribution becomes increasingly difficult," warns UBS Warburg analyst David Lothson. "This puts pressure on the sustainability of this strategy, and ultimately it could break down."

J&J's success has hinged on its unique culture and structure. But for the company to thrive in the future, that system has to change. Each of its far-flung units operates pretty much as an independent enterprise. Businesses set their own strategies; they have their own finance and human resources departments, for example. While this degree of decentralization makes for relatively high overhead costs, no chief executive, Weldon included, has thought that too high a price to pay. Johnson & Johnson has been able to turn itself into a powerhouse precisely because the businesses it buys, and the ones it starts, are given near-total autonomy. That independence fosters an entrepreneurial attitude that has kept J&J intensely competitive as others around it have faltered.

Now, though, the various enterprises at J&J can no longer operate in near isolation. Weldon believes, as do most others in the industry, that some of the most important breakthroughs in 21st century medicine will come from the ability to apply scientific advances in one discipline to another. The treatment of many diseases is becoming vastly more sophisticated: Sutures are coated with drugs to prevent infections; tests based on genomic research could determine who will respond to a certain cancer drug; defibrillators may be linked to computers that alert doctors when patients have abnormal heart rhythms.

The company should be perfectly positioned to profit from this shift toward combining drugs, devices, and diagnostics, claims Weldon, since few companies will be able to match its reach and strength in those three basic areas (Exhibit 1). "There is a convergence that will allow us to do things we haven't done before," he says. Indeed, J&J has top-notch products in each of those categories. It has been boosting its research and development budget by more than 10% annually for the past few years, which puts it among the top spenders, and now employs 9,300 scientists in 40 labs around the world.

But J&J can cash in only if its fiercely independent businesses can work together. In effect, Weldon wants J&J to be one of the few companies to make good on that often-promised, rarely delivered idea of synergy. To do so, he has to decide if he's willing to put J&J's famed autonomy at risk. For now, Weldon is creating new systems to foster better communication and more frequent collaboration among J&J's disparate operations.

Already J&J has been inching toward this more cohesive approach: Its new drug-coated stent, which could revolutionize the field of cardiology, grew out of a discussion in the mid-1990s between a drug researcher and one in J&J's stent business. Now Weldon has to promote this kind of cooperation throughout the company without quashing the entrepreneurial spirit that has made J&J what it is today. Cultivating those alliances "would be challenging in any organization, but particularly in an organization that has been so successful because of its decentralized culture," says Jerry Cacciotti, managing director at consulting firm Strategic Decisions Group. Weldon, like every other leader in the company's history, worked his way up through the ranks. Among other things, it made him a true believer in the J&J system. Whatever he hopes to achieve, he doesn't expect to undermine that.

In many ways, Weldon personifies the Johnson & Johnson ethos. Though he was one of the first J&J executives to go casual in the 1990s and sometimes schedules business lunches at his favorite burger joint in Manhattan, Weldon is compulsively competitive. As he says, "it's no fun to be second." One of his first bosses recalls how Weldon badgered him to release sales figures early because Weldon was desperate to know if he had

EXHIBIT 1 It's Not Really about Baby Powder

Pharmaceuticals
The most profitable and fastest-growing of J&J's businesses, but expected to slow considerably as competition for its key drugs increases. The company wants to use drug-delivery technology to come up with new formulations of existing products.

SHARE OF SALES	47.2%
SHARE OF OPERATING PROFITS	60.9%

Devices & Diagnostics
Its drug-coated stent could be a multibillion-dollar blockbuster. But with the FDA approval process dragging on, J&J could also face a competing product before yearend. The diagnostic group hopes to develop gene-based tests linked to promising new treatments.

SHARE OF SALES	34.7%
SHARE OF OPERATING PROFITS	26.2%

Consumer
It's the least profitable and slowest-growing of J&J's businesses, but with widely known products such as Johnson's Baby Shampoo and Band-Aids, the operation cloaks the company in an image of decency that indirectly benefits every J&J sales rep. A key opportunity: over-the-counter versions of drugs that lose their patents.

SHARE OF SALES	18.1%
SHARE OF OPERATING PROFITS	12.9%

won a company competition. Weldon is such an intense athlete that he was just a sprint away from ruining his knee altogether when he finally gave up playing basketball. It's not easy for him to keep a respectable distance from his managers now. "It's like a barroom brawl [where] you are outside looking in when you want to be in the middle of it," he says.

Weldon became famous for setting near-impossible goals for his people and holding them to it. "There was rarely an empty suit around Bill," says one former J&Jer. "If you weren't pulling your weight, you were gone." In the 1990s, when Weldon ran a business that sold surgical tools, executives back at headquarters in New Brunswick, N.J., used to systematically upgrade the reviews he gave his employees.

With that in mind, consider what Weldon is willing to do so that his changes don't threaten J&J's ecosystem: restrain himself. Although he talks incessantly about synergy and convergence, the steps he's actually taking to make sure his units cross-fertilize are measured ones. He isn't pushing specific deals on his managers. For example, industry sources say J&J has held on-and-off talks with Guidant Corp., which makes implantable defibrillators. That field of cardiovascular medicine is a growing market that's perfectly suited for some of these emerging combination therapies. But Weldon isn't leading the way in those talks. And he's delegating crucial decisions about how to spend R&D dollars.

Weldon is subtly turning up the heat on cooperation between his different units, however. J&J experts in various diseases have been meeting quarterly for the past five years to share information. Weldon and James T. Lenehan, vice-chairman and president of J&J, are now setting up two groups, focused on two diseases (they won't say which), that will work together more formally. After six months, each group will report on potential strategies and projects.

To understand Weldon's vision for the new J&J, it's useful to look at how he reshaped the pharmaceutical operation when he took it over in 1998. At the time, J&J's drug business was posting solid growth thanks to popular products such as the anemia drug Procrit and the anti-psychotic medication Risperdal. But the drug R&D operation was sputtering after several potential treatments had failed in late-stage testing. Weldon's solution was to create a new committee comprised of R&D executives and senior managers from the sales and marketing operations to decide which projects to green-light. Previously, those decisions were made largely by scientists in the company's two major R&D operations; there was no such thing as setting common priorities. Weldon also created a new post to oversee R&D and gave the job to Peterson. "Some people may have thought Bill curtailed their freedom," says Peterson. "But we've improved the decision-making to eliminate compounds that just won't make it."

Although most of the changes Weldon instituted in the pharmaceutical business won't yield real results for years, there is some evidence that this new collaboration is working (Exhibit 2). Shortly after taking charge of the drug unit, Weldon visited J&J's research facility in La Jolla, Calif., to learn about the company's genomic studies. Researchers were focused on building a massive database using gene patterns that correlate to a certain disease or to someone's likely response to a particular drug. When they told Weldon how useful the database could be for J&J's diagnostic business, he in turn urged Lenehan, who oversees the unit, to send his people out. Now, Peterson says, the diagnostics team is developing a test that the drug R&D folks could use to predict which patients will benefit from an experimental cancer therapy. If the test works, it could significantly cut J&J's drug-development costs.

Even the company's fabled consumer brands are starting to take on a scientific edge. Its new liquid Band-Aid is based on a material used in a wound-closing product sold by one of J&J's hospital-supply businesses. And a few years ago, J&J turned its prescription antifungal treatment, Nizoral, into a dandruff shampoo. Indeed, these kinds

EXHIBIT 2 What Synergy Could Look Like at J&J

Improved Drugs
J&J's pharmaceutical operation is working with the company's drug-delivery operation, Alza, to come up with a new formulation of the epilepsy drug Topamax. The drug has been shown to also promote weight loss, and this would make it a more tolerable obesity treatment.

New Medical Tests
A new diagnostic unit is working with data generated by drug researchers; they could, for example, develop a gene-based test to identify patients most likely to respond to experimental cancer treatments.

Cutting-Edge Consumer Products
In 2002, J&J rolled out the new Band-Aid Brand Liquid Bandage, a liquid coating that is applied to cuts on hard-to-cover areas like fingers and knuckles. The product is based on a material used in a wound-closing product sold by J&J's hospital-products company, Ethicon.

of products are one reason operating margins for the consumer business have increased from 13.8% in 2000 to 18.7% in 2002.

But perhaps the most promising result of this approach is J&J's drug-coated stent, called Cypher (Exhibit 3). A few years after that first meeting between researchers, J&J created teams from the drug business and the device operation to collaborate on manufacturing the stent, which props open arteries after angioplasty. "If we didn't have all this [expertise]," Weldon says, "we'd probably still be negotiating with [outside] companies to put this together." And to show that he is letting managers mind their own businesses, Weldon says that he only gets briefed about the stent's progress every month (though he does invite Robert W. Croce, the division head, to dinner for more casual updates). "They are the experts who know the marketplace, know the hospitals, and know the cardiologists," Weldon says of the Cypher team. "I have the utmost confidence in them."

With that empowerment, though, comes the clear expectation that J&J's experts will go after their markets with the same tenacity Weldon displayed in his climb to the top. Before heading up the drug division, Weldon made his reputation at J&J in the early '90s as head of a new unit, Ethicon Endo-Surgery Inc. Ethicon Endo was supposed to establish itself in the emerging field of endoscopic surgery. J&J did what only a company of its resources can: It poured hundreds of millions

EXHIBIT 3 The Race to Keep Arteries Clear—and Rivals at Bay

There are a lot of "ifs" when it comes to Johnson & Johnson's new drug-coated stent, called Cypher. The biggest question is timing: The stent could be a billion-dollar product this year if the Food & Drug Administration approves it in time to give J&J a head start against rivals. A stent is used to prop open arteries after angioplasty; the new device is coated with a drug that prevents those arteries from re-clogging. The agency has held off giving its O.K. over a number of issues, including the shelf life of the stent. A short shelf life could hinder J&J's ability to meet initial market demand, since it wouldn't be able to sell all the stents it has manufactured already. The company says it has addressed all FDA concerns.

Even if the stent hits the market soon, as J&J has said, rivals won't be far behind. Boston Scientific Corp. is developing a stent coated with a different drug that it could launch by year's end. And if the two devices are equally effective, doctors may not favor J&J's version. That's because analysts say Boston Scientific's metal stent itself, as well as the system for inserting it into the body, is more flexible and easier to use.

Then there's the risk of a backlash against the cost of J&J's new stent. In 1994, when J&J introduced the first widely used one, the company irked cardiologists with the stent's steep price: $1,600. Nor had J&J gotten additional Medicare reimbursement for hospitals. To make matters worse, it took the company three years to develop a meaningful improvement on the original. The result is that J&J lost its dominance in a crucial market it helped to create. Robert W. Croce, company group chairman for Cordis, the unit developing the stent, says J&J has successfully lobbied for increased Medicare reimbursement in advance this time (good thing, since the stent might go for as much as $3,000) and plans to roll out a new and better version every 15 months

But Brue Chandler, executive vice-president at St. Joseph's Health System in Atlanta, says he has already heard Cordis sales representatives mention the possibility of discounts on other company products to help offset the price of the stent. "I find that objectionable, because it doesn't go to the core issue of introducing a product at a [reasonable] price," says Chandler. He adds: "They've already begun alienating the purchasing market." J&J's Croce says the company will work with hospitals to deal with their concerns about the stent's cost. And it won't do so by offering selective discounts on other products. Still, if J&J isn't careful, history could repeat itself.

By Amy Barrett in New Brunswick, N.J.

How Cypher Works

1. A catheter, with a balloon at the tip, is threaded into the patient through the femoral artery in the groin until it reaches the clogged artery. The balloon is expanded, opens the artery, and is removed.
2. A catheter, now with a stent at the end with a balloon inside, is inserted. When it reaches the artery, the balloon is inflated, propping open the stent. The catheter and balloon are removed, leaving the stent in place.
3. Over time, the drug sirolimus, which is coated onto the stent, is released into the blood vessel wall. It acts to block the creation of excessive amounts of scar tissue that could reclog the artery.

into building a full line of tools for surgeons. And Weldon did what he does best: He went after the leading company, United States Surgical Corp., as if it were a mortal threat.

Weldon spent much of his time on the road, traveling the country from his base in Cincinnati to meet with surgeons and hospital executives. Once he canceled a flight home from San Diego after hearing that a potential customer was wavering. He went back the following morning to nail down the deal. Weldon often set more ambitious goals than headquarters did. Nick Valeriani, who was then vice-president of sales and marketing, recalls: "We'd have a great year and Bill would say, 'Nice job. Why couldn't it have been 25% higher?'" By 1996, J&J surpassed U.S. Surgical, which was later bought by Tyco International Ltd.

That's not to say that Weldon doesn't understand the power of positive reinforcement. Twice he wheedled higher bonuses for his managers out of New Brunswick. Another time at Ethicon Endo, he closed up shop for a day of rest after a particularly harried couple of months. He never told anyone at headquarters. And no one in New Brunswick ever said a word about it. "Hell, you are the goddamn boss," he says. "Sometimes it is better to beg forgiveness than to ask permission."

And for those executives who fell short, Weldon made it clear he didn't like to be disappointed. When a new J&J drug business, Centocor Inc., failed to meet the aggressive sales goals it set for 2000, Weldon was at the offices in Malvern, Pa., before the week was out. David P. Holveck, former company group chairman of Centocor who now runs J&J's venture-capital arm, says of Weldon: "He is a man of few words. But his body language was very clear: In this game there are two strikes. In 2001, we were expected to get it right." They did.

Not everybody appreciated Weldon's demands. None would speak for attribution, but several former executives at Ethicon Endo say Weldon alienated those he felt weren't part of the team. "He is an intimidator and a dominator," says one former executive who claims Weldon turned on him after he opposed an acquisition.

Weldon hasn't really ever taken much for granted. His father was a stagehand on Broadway for several years. While his mother, a seamstress, worked on costumes for the ballet and theater, Weldon would watch the shows from backstage. She handled Marilyn Monroe's wardrobe the night the actress sang *Happy Birthday* to President John F. Kennedy in 1962, and she retired last year at the age of 80. "My parents were very hardworking, union people," Weldon says. "It's a tough life."

When Weldon was in elementary school, the family moved to Ridgewood, N.J., which former classmates describe as a wealthy and somewhat socially competitive town. There, Weldon grew up in one of the less prosperous neighborhoods. He was an indifferent student but a determined athlete who played on both the basketball and football teams.

Weldon put himself through Quinnipiac University in Hamden, Conn., by working as a mover in Newark, N.J., on weekends and holidays. He says he got serious about his studies after he married his high school sweetheart, Barbara Dearborn, midway through college. Shortly after graduating with a major in biology, Weldon had his one and only interview at J&J. Howard Klick, who hired him as a sales rep at the McNeil Pharmaceutical unit, recalls asking him for a sales pitch on a pen. Weldon took the pen apart, then gave Klick the hard sell. "He was hungry," Klick says. "He had fire in the belly."

He'll need that drive if he's to maintain J&J's growth trajectory. At this point, most of J&J's important drugs are under assault from competitors. Growth of the company's biggest-selling product, the $4.3 billion Procrit franchise, has stalled in the face of Aranesp, a drug from archrival Amgen Inc. And side-effect problems have plagued the European version, called Eprex. As a result, Procrit, which grew at a 20%-plus rate over the past few years, may actually post a 2% decline in worldwide sales in 2003, according to J.P. Morgan Securities analyst Michael Weinstein. Meanwhile, J&J's $1.3 billion rheumatoid arthritis drug Remicade faces competing products from Amgen and Abbott Laboratories.

Weldon downplays the threat. He argues that Remicade has tremendous potential because it can be used to treat other conditions, including Crohn's disease, and that Procrit will continue to dominate the anemia market. And J&J does have 56 drugs in late-stage testing (though only eight are truly new).

With J&J's blockbusters slowing, Weldon may expect his successor at the drug unit to do something dramatic. That's what he did two years ago when he completed the company's biggest acquisition ever: buying drug-delivery player Alza Corp. for $13.2 billion to shore up the business. There are supposed synergies here too, he says. Alza's technology could help J&J devise safer and more effective formulations of existing drugs. Among them: a new sustained-release version of the epilepsy drug Topamax that could be used to treat obesity.

But buying growth is likely to be more of a challenge for J&J these days. For one thing, nearly every pharmaceutical operation around is looking to make deals. And there are relatively few companies with products that are far enough along and important enough to make a real difference to J&J.

Of course, the drug business' problems now fall to its new boss, Christine A. Poon, whom Weldon helped recruit from Bristol-Myers Squibb Co. But Weldon still jumps in every now and then. One weekend earlier this year, several senior executives were hammering out details on the $2.4 billion acquisition of Scios Inc., a biotech company that has a drug for congestive heart failure. They called Weldon at home to ask for his input on one point. Weldon decided to go to the office to give his answer. And he stayed until well after midnight. Weldon says he wanted to make an appearance because it was Poon's first major acquisition. "I wanted to be there, if nothing else, to give her some moral support," he says.

But you know he got a thrill from being back in the thick of things. As Weldon leads the company into a new era, he'll have to be careful not to cross the line between supporting his executives and encroaching on their territory. Their autonomy has been central to Johnson & Johnson's success. To refine the J&J way, Weldon will have to be among the most disciplined and restrained of executives. Keeping a company on top can be just as hard as getting it there.

Source: Amy Barrett, "Staying on Top," *BusinessWeek*, May 5, 2003, 60–68.

Chapter 6

Market Targeting and Strategic Positioning

Deciding which buyers to target and how to position the firm's products for each market target are the core components of market-driven strategy, guiding the entire organization in its efforts to provide superior customer value. Effective targeting and positioning strategies are essential in gaining and sustaining superior organizational performance. Faulty decisions negatively affect performance.

Through effective targeting and positioning Costco Wholesale has gained a strong position against Wal-Mart's Sam's Club in the U.S. warehouse club market. Costco targets more affluent and sophisticated urban dwellers whereas Sam's concentrates on the mass middle-market located in smaller cities.[1] Costco's value offering enables buyers to trade up for branded luxury items and trade down for private label products such as paper towels, detergent, and vitamins. Markups are set at 14 percent, resulting in very attractive prices. Costco's sales for 2005 should exceed $52 billion. Costco's annual sales have been greater than Sam's sales with fewer warehouses but nearly double the average sales per Costco outlet. Costco has a strong ethics-driven corporate culture. Sam's has been reducing prices to gain market share, and has also adjusted its merchandise mix to offer more upscale items. Industry experts indicate that the growth of the warehouse club market segments (households and businesses) is likely to slow down in the future.

In the analysis of the successful marketing strategies of companies like Costco, one feature stands out. Each has a market target and positioning strategy that is a positive contributor to gaining a strong market and financial position for the firm. Examples of effective targeting and positioning strategies are found in all kinds and sizes of businesses, including companies marketing industrial and consumer goods and services.

We begin the chapter by examining market targeting strategy and discussing how targets are selected. Next, we consider strategic positioning and look at what is involved in developing a positioning strategy for each market target. We conclude with a discussion of how positioning effectiveness is evaluated.

Market Targeting Strategy

The market targeting decision identifies the people or organizations in a product-market toward which an organization directs its positioning strategy. Selecting good market targets is one of management's most demanding challenges. For example, should the organization attempt to serve all buyers who are willing and able to buy a particular good or service, or instead selectively focus on one or more subgroups? Study of the product-market, its buyers, the organization's capabilities

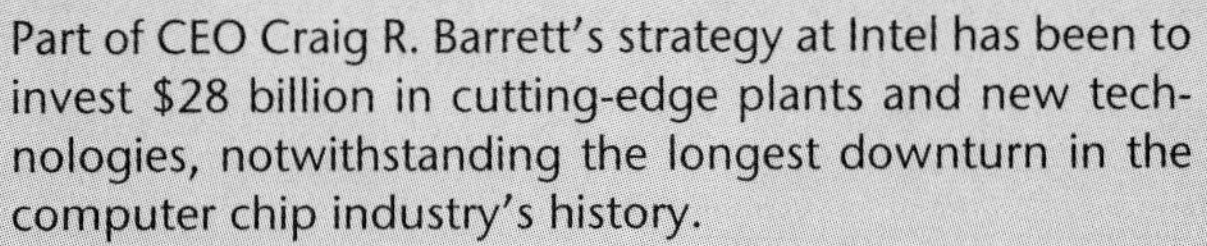

Strategy Feature

Intel's Market Initiatives

Part of CEO Craig R. Barrett's strategy at Intel has been to invest $28 billion in cutting-edge plants and new technologies, notwithstanding the longest downturn in the computer chip industry's history.

His goal is to have Intel chips at the heart of products in several new markets in addition to personal computers and servers. Intel is branching out from computer chips to semiconductors for a range of new products, which will in turn boost Intel's core personal computer and server business.

Intel's primary product-markets are:

- **PCs and Servers.** The core business, where Intel has an 83 percent market share of a $27 billion market.
- **Flat-Panel Televisions.** A $10 billion market where Intel's processors for decoding TV signals could halve the cost of flat-panel screens.
- **Handhelds.** Intel's chips power half of all handheld computers in a market worth $2 billion.
- **Personal Media Players.** Intel is positioned to become a leading producer of processors and memory chips in the emerging market for portable video players.
- **WiMax.** Intel's new technology should deliver high-speed Net access to a PC within 30 miles of a transmission point.
- **Cellular Phones.** Intel currently holds 20 percent of a $9 billion market for memory chips and digital signal processors.

Source: Cliff Edwards, "Intel," *BusinessWeek*, March 8, 2004, 42–50.

and resources, and the competition is necessary in order to make this decision. The chapters in Part II provide important information for the targeting decision.

Consider, for example, the development of Intel's marketing strategy of progressively adding new product-markets to the existing core business. (See Intel advertisement.) Intel's product strategy is described in the Strategy Feature.

Targeting and positioning strategies consist of: (1) identifying and analyzing the segments in a product-market, (2) deciding which segment(s) to target, and (3) designing and implementing a positioning strategy for each target.

Many companies use some form of market segmentation, since buyers have become increasingly differentiated as to their value requirements. Microsegmentation (finer segmentation) is becoming popular, aided by effective segmentation and targeting methods such as database marketing and mass customization. Moreover, the Internet offers an opportunity for direct access to individual customers. In the following discussion we assume that the product-market is segmented on some basis. Emerging markets may require rather broad macrosegmentation, resulting in a few segments, whereas more mature markets can be divided into several micro segments. A new market may need to advance to the growth stage before meaningful segmentation is feasible.

Targeting Alternatives

The targeting decision determines which customer group(s) the organization will serve. Management may select one or a few segments or go after more complete coverage of the product-market by targeting most of the segments. A specific marketing effort (positioning strategy) is directed toward each target that management decides to serve. For example, Pfizer's targeting strategy for the 2003 launch of its new drug Relpax is as follows:

> Pfizer for the first time launched a new product—Relpax—without any TV advertising at all. Relpax is a prescription medicine for migraine headache relief. Pfizer identified **active young mothers as**

the prime target group for Relpax and adjusted its media mix accordingly. "They are listening to the radio in the car, [going] on the Internet late at night, or reading a magazine in a quiet moment," says Dorothy L. Weitzer, a Pfizer marketing vice-president. "They are not watching TV."[2]

Pfizer's market target strategy is guided by market segmentation based on buyers' characteristics (active mothers).

Market targeting approaches fall into two major categories: segment targeting and targeting through product differentiation. As shown by Exhibit 6.1, segment targeting ranges from a single segment to targeting all or most of the segments in the market. American Airlines uses extensive targeting in air travel services, as does General Motors with its different brands and styles of automobiles. An example of selective targeting is Autodesk's targeting of architects with its line of computer-aided design software.

When segments are difficult to identify, even though diversity in preferences may exist, companies may appeal to buyers through product specialization or product variety. While differences may exist in needs and wants, buyers' preferences are diffused, making it difficult to define segments.[3] Specialization involves offering buyers a product differentiated from competitor's products and designed to appeal to customer needs and wants not satisfied by competitors. The Vanguard Group offers a wide variety of mutual funds to investors, which are not targeted to particular investor segments. Vanguard's variety-based positioning is intended to appeal to a wide array of customers, but in most cases meeting a subset of their investment needs.[4]

Factors Influencing Targeting Decisions

Market segment analysis discussed in Chapter 4 helps to evaluate and rank the overall attractiveness of the segments under consideration by management as market targets. These evaluations include customer information, competitor positioning, and the financial and market attractiveness of the segments. An important factor in targeting is determining the value requirements of the buyers in each segment. Market segment analysis is used to evaluate both existing and potential market targets.

Management needs to decide if it will target a single segment, selectively target a few segments, or target all or most of the segments in the product-market. Several factors influence the choice of the targeting strategy:

- Stage of product-market maturity
- Extent of diversity in buyer preferences
- Industry structure
- Organizational capabilities and resources
- Opportunities for gaining competitive advantage

EXHIBIT 6.1
Market Targeting Approaches

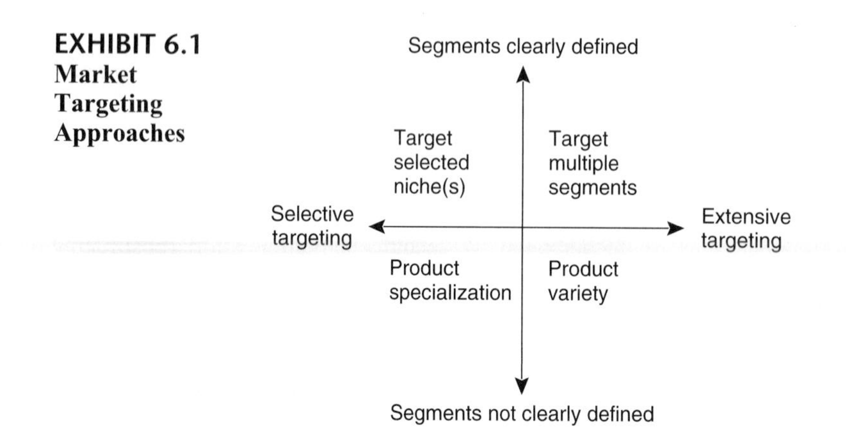

Since these influences may vary according to stage of product-market maturity, we use maturity as the basis for considering different targeting situations. The objective is to look at how each factor affects the market target strategy.

Targeting in Different Market Environments

The industry environment is influenced by the extent of concentration of its firms, the stage of its maturity, and its exposure to international competition. Five generic environments portray the range of industry structures:[5]

Emerging. Industries newly formed or reformed are categorized as emerging, created by factors such as a new technology, the changing needs of buyers, and the identification of unmet needs by suppliers. The satellite radio service industry is illustrative.

Fragmented. Typically, a large number of relatively small firms make up the fragmented industry. No company has a strong position regarding market share or influence in this industry structure. Industrial chemical distribution and home security services are examples of fragmented industries.

Transitional. These industries are shifting from rapid growth to maturity, as indicated by the maturing product life cycles of the products in the industry. Growing rapidly until reaching high levels of household penetration, microwave ovens are now in the maturity stage.

Declining. A declining industry is actually fading away instead of experiencing a temporary decline or cyclical changes. Camera and film products are moving into the declining stage as digital photography gains momentum.

Global. Firms in this category compete on a global basis. Examples include automobiles, consumer electronics, and telecommunications. This classification may include transitional or declining industry market situations.

The five industry categories are neither exhaustive nor mutually exclusive. Moreover, changing environmental and industry conditions may alter an industry classification. Also, rapid growth may occur in some countries while industry growth is mature or declining in other countries or regions.

The stages of the life cycles of the products in the industry offer useful insights about the industry environment. The market environments discussed above are closely related to the product life cycle (PLC) stages. Looking at competition during the stages of the product life cycle and at different product-market levels (generic, product type, and variant) provides insights into different types and intensities of competition. We know that products, like people, move through life cycles, and products' life cycles are increasingly shorter due to the rapid pace of technological change in the 21st century.

The life cycle of a typical product is shown in Exhibit 6.2. Sales begin at the time of introduction and increase over the pattern shown. Profits initially lag sales, since expenses often exceed sales during the initial stage of the product life cycle as a result of heavy introductory expenses. Industry sales and profits decline after the product reaches the maturity stage. Often profits fall off before sales.

Since an industry may contain more than one product-market and different industries may compete in a given market, it is useful to consider the market environment as the basis of discussion. Emerging, growth, mature, declining, and global market environments are discussed to illustrate different targeting situations.

Emerging Markets

"The most pervasive feature of emerging markets is uncertainty about customer acceptance and the eventual size of the market, which process and product technology will be dominant, whether cost declines will be realized, and the identity, structure, and actions of competitors."[6] Internet

EXHIBIT 6.2
Life Cycle of a Typical Product

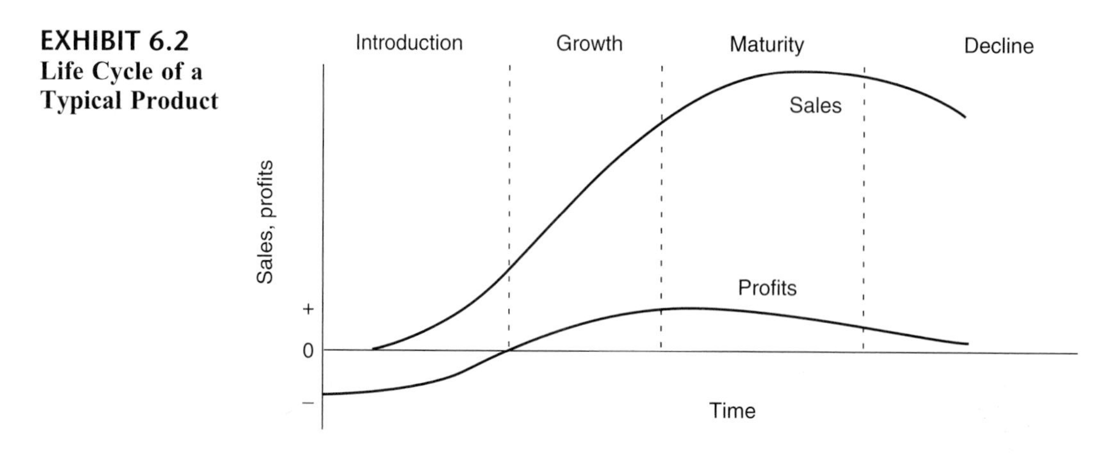

telecommunications is an example of an emerging market. Market definition and analysis are rather general in the early stages of product-market development. Buyers' needs and wants are not highly differentiated because they do not have experience with the product. Determining the future scope and direction of growth of product-market development may be difficult, as will forecasting the size of market growth.

There are two types of emerging markets: (1) the development of a totally new product-market, and (2) a new product entry into an existing market. In the first situation, the emerging market is formed by people/organizations whose needs and wants have not been satisfied by available products. A cure for the AIDS virus is an example. In the second situation, the market entry is a new product that provides an alternative value proposition to buyers in an existing market. The entry of digital photography into the traditional camera and film market is an example of entry into an existing market.

Buyer Diversity. The similarity of buyers' preferences in a new product-market often limits segmentation efforts. It may be possible to identify a few broad segments. For example, heavy, medium, and low product usage can be used to segment a new product-market where usage varies across buyers. If segmentation is not feasible, an alternative is to define and describe an average or typical user, directing marketing efforts toward these potential users.

Industry Structure. Study of the characteristics of market pioneers indicates that new enterprises are more likely to enter a new product-market than are the large, well-established companies. The exception is a breakthrough innovation in a large company coupled with strong entry barriers. The pioneers that develop a new product-market "are typically small new organizations set up specifically to exploit first-mover advantages in the new resource space."[7] These entrepreneurs often have limited access to resources and must pursue product-market opportunities that require low levels of investment.

Industry development is influenced by various factors, including the rate of acceptance of the product by buyers, entry barriers, performance of firms serving the market, and future expectations. The pioneer's proprietary technology may delay entry by others until the potential entrants can gain access to the technology. Major change in market composition and competition during the initial years is a common feature of emerging industries.

Capabilities and Resources. A firm entering an existing product-market with a new product is more likely to achieve a competitive edge by offering buyers unique benefits rather than lower prices for equivalent benefits, though cost may be the basis of superior value when the new product is a lower-cost alternate technology to an existing product. For example, fax transmission of letters and brief reports is both faster and less expensive than overnight delivery services. Similarly, the development of e-mail capabilities gave e-mail transmission an advantage over fax transmissions.

Innovation Feature An Emerging Market for Satellite Radio Services

Satellite Radio Powers Up

Satellite radio is catching on, with some 700,000 subscribers today and forecasts for 1.5 million by yearend.

What Is Satellite Radio? These systems beam CD-quality signals from space to special radios, most of which are installed in cars. Customers can also listen at home or on the go.

Where Is It Available? Two carriers offer nationwide coverage. XM, based in Washington, DC, is $9.99 a month; Sirius, based in New York, is $12.95.

What Do You Get? The services offer about 100 channels. Sirius is commercial-free, while XM broadcasts a limited number of ads. Programs range from music to news and comedy.

Who Is Backing Satellite Radio? Carmakers, who are eager for a stake in a new, fast-growing business. GM funded XM, and DaimlerChrysler is backing Sirius. Others are picking one of the two technologies, which are not currently compatible.

Do Most Cars Have Satellite Radio? The systems are available on many new models for about $300. Within two years, satellite radio is expected to be available on many new cars.

What about Home and Portable Systems? You can buy a palm-size receiver from Sirius or XM. They are available from retailers like Circuit City and Wal-Mart for about $200, including adapters. You can carry these, using them at home or in the car. For an additional $99, XM's can be used with a special portable boom box.

XM has the lead position in the market but faces major financial challenges, and is spending $20 million in cash each month. With less than 1 million subscribers, XM needs 7.5 million and $1 billion in revenues to cover capital and interest costs.

Source: "This Is the Dawning of the Age—XM?" *BusinessWeek*, July 7, 2003, 90–92.

Entry of disruptive technologies into existing product-markets may present competitive threats to incumbents.[8] The threat is that the value proposition of the new technology (e.g., digital photography) may eventually attract buyers away from incumbent firms. Disruptive technology is discussed in Chapter 8.

Targeting Strategy. Despite the uncertainties in an emerging industry, there is evidence which indicates "that more successful or longer-living firms engage in less change than firms which fail."[9] Instead these experienced firms select and follow a consistent strategy on a continuing basis. If this behavior is characteristic of a broad range of successful new ventures, then choosing the entry strategy is very important.

Satellite radio service is an interesting example of an emerging market. This market situation displays many of the characteristics we have been discussing. The Innovation Feature describes the opportunities, challenges, and risks confronting XM Satellite Radio in early 2004.

Growth Market

Segments are likely to be found in the growth stage of the market. Identifying customer groups with similar value requirements improves targeting, and "experience with the product, process, and materials technologies leads to greater efficiency and increased standardization."[10] During the growth stage the market environment moves from highly uncertain to moderately uncertain. Further change in the market is likely, but at this stage there is a level of awareness about the forces that influence the size and composition of the product-market.

Patterns of use can be identified and the characteristics of buyers and their use patterns can be determined. Segmentation by type of industry may be feasible in industrial markets. Demographic characteristics such as age, income, and family size may identify broad macrosegments for consumer products such as food and drugs. Analysis of the characteristics and preferences of existing buyers yields useful guidelines for estimating market potential.

Industry Structure. We often assume that high-growth markets are very attractive, and that early entry offers important competitive advantages. Nevertheless, there are some warnings for industry participants:

> First, a visible growth market can attract too many competitors—the market and its distribution channel cannot support them. The intensity of competition is accentuated when growth fails to match expectations or eventually slows. Second, the early entrant is unable to cope when key success factors or technologies change, in part because it lacks the financial skills or organizational skills.[11]

For example, the fiber-optic cable network market in the United States attracted far too many competitors (some 1,500). Most of the networks were not being used in the early 2000s due to significant overbuilding.

Generalizations about industry structure in growth markets are difficult. There is some evidence that large, established firms are more likely to enter growth markets rather than entering emerging markets. This is because the companies may not be able to move as quickly as small specialist firms in exploiting the opportunities in the emerging product-market.[12] The established companies have skills and resource advantages for achieving market leadership. These powerful firms can overcome the timing advantage of the market pioneers. Later entrants also have the advantage of evaluating the attractiveness of the product-market during its initial development.

Capabilities and Resources. Survival analysis of firms in the minicomputer industry highlights two performance characteristics in the rapid growth stage of the product-market: (1) survival rates are much higher for aggressive firms competing on a broad market scope compared to conservative firms competing on the same basis, and (2) survival rates are high (about three-quarters) for both aggressive and conservative specialists.[13] This research suggests that survival requires aggressive action by firms that seek large market positions in the total market. These firms must possess the capabilities and resources necessary to achieve market position. Other competitors are likely to be more successful by selectively targeting one or a few market segments.

Targeting Strategy. There are at least three possible targeting strategies in growth market situations: (1) extensive market coverage by firms with established businesses in related markets, (2) selective targeting by firms with diversified product portfolios, and (3) very focused targeting strategies by small organizations serving one or a few market segments.[14]

A selective targeting strategy is feasible when buyers' needs are differentiated or when products are differentiated. The segments that are not served by large competitors provide an opportunity for the small firm to gain competitive advantage. The market leader(s) may not find small segments attractive enough to seek a position in the segment. If the buyers in the market have similar needs, a small organization may gain advantage through product specialization. This strategy would concentrate on a specific product or component.

The objective of the targeting strategy is to match the organization's distinctive capabilities to value opportunities in the product-market. The number of specific targets to pursue depends on management's objectives and the available segments in the market.

Strategies for Mature Markets

Not all firms that enter the emerging and growth stages of the market survive in the maturity stage. The needs and characteristics of buyers also change over time. Market entry at the maturity stage is less likely than in previous life cycle stages.

Buyer Diversity. Segmentation is often essential at the maturity stage of the life cycle. At this stage, the product-market is clearly defined, indicating buyers' preferences and the competitive structure. The factors that drive market growth are often apparent. The market is not likely to expand or decline rapidly. Nonetheless, eventual decline may occur unless actions are taken to extend the product life cycle through product innovation and new applications of existing products.

Identification and evaluation of market segments are necessary to select targets that offer each firm a competitive advantage. Since the mature market has a history, experience should be available concerning how buyers respond to the marketing efforts of the firms competing in the product-market. Knowledge of the competitive and environmental influences on the segments in the market helps to obtain accurate forecasts, and select positioning strategies.

The maturity of the product-market may reduce its attractiveness to the companies serving the market, so the market-driven organization may benefit from (1) scanning the external environment for new opportunities that are consistent with the organization's skills and resources (core competencies); (2) identifying potential disruptive technology threats/opportunities to the current technologies in meeting customer needs, and selecting strategies for responding to the opportunities; and/or (3) identifying opportunities within specific segments for new and improved products.

Buyers in mature markets are experienced and increasingly demanding. They are familiar with competing brands and display preferences for particular brands. The key marketing issue is developing and sustaining brand preference, since buyers are aware of the product type and its features. Many top brands like Coca-Cola, Gillette, and Wrigley's have held their leading positions for more than half a century. This highlights the importance of obtaining and protecting a lead position at an early stage in the development of a market.

Industry Structure. The characteristics of mature industries include intense competition for market share, emphasis on cost and service, slowdown in new-product flows, international competition, pressures on profits, and increases in the power of channel of distribution organizations that link suppliers and producers with end users.[15] Deciding how to compete successfully in a mature product-market is influenced by the composition of competitive space and the extent of differentiation in buyers' value requirements.

The typical mature industry structure consists of a few companies that dominate the industry and several other firms that pursue market selectivity strategies. The larger firms may include a market leader and two or three competitors with relatively large market positions compared to the remaining competitors. Entry into the mature product-market is often difficult because of major barriers and intense competition for sales and profits. Those that enter normally follow market or product selectivity strategies. Acquisition may be the best way of market entry rather than trying to develop products and marketing capabilities. Mature industries are increasingly experiencing pressures for global consolidation. Examples include automobiles, banking, foods, household appliances, prescription drugs, telecommunications, and consumer electronics.

Capabilities and Resources. Depending on the firm's position in the mature market, management's objective may be cost reduction, selective targeting, or product differentiation. Poor performance may lead to restructuring the corporation to try to improve financial performance. If improvement is not feasible, the decision may be to exit from the business.

Audi AG implemented a major turnaround strategy in the mid-1990s designed to appeal to more automobile buyers with an exciting image. The midrange Audi A4 introduced in 1995 attracted new buyers and was part of a major new product strategy to increase sales and profits. Leveraging Audi's capabilities and resources, the A4's initial entry was very successful. Supported by a major advertising campaign, the new model attracted younger buyers. Appealing to this target was a major objective of the new marketing strategy. Audi's A6 and A8 models were targeted to additional market segments.

Targeting. Both targeting and positioning strategies may change in moving from the growth to maturity stages of the product-market. Targeting may be altered to reflect changes in priorities among market targets. Positioning within a targeted market may be adjusted to improve customer satisfaction and operating performance. Nonetheless, consistency in positioning over time is important. During the maturity stage management is likely to place heavy emphasis on efficiency.

Strategy Feature

Levi Strauss Expands Its Levi Jeans Brands Up and Down

Levi Strauss has experienced major sales and profit declines since the mid-1990s. Revenues fell from $7.1 billion in 1996 to $4 billion in fiscal 2003.

For years the Levi brand targeted the middle price and quality market, avoiding discounters like Wal-Mart, Target, and Kohl's. Management also failed to recognize the significance of the boom in high-fashion denim. In a surprising turnaround initiative Levi has expanded its jeans market coverage to target both price- and fashion-conscious buyers.

The new Levi Signature brand is available from Target, Wal-Mart and other discounters. The more expensive Premium Red Tab is targeted to upscale customers of retailers like Nordstrom and Neiman-Marcus.

Attempting to appeal to a wide range of market targets with a variety of poorly differentiated Levi jeans brands is risky. A potential consequence is damage to the Levi brand, and the brand strategy may not have a major impact on Levi's sales and profits.

Levi Strauss' failure to respond to changes in its core jeans market is illustrative of the challenges of competing in highly competitive mature markets. Recognizing the seriousness of the problem, management retained a turnaround consulting firm in late 2003.

Source: Wendy Zellner, "Lessons from a Faded Levi Strauss," *BusinessWeek*, December 15, 2003, 44.

Targeting segments is appropriate for all firms competing in a mature product-market. The strategic issue is deciding which segments to serve. Market maturity may create new opportunities and threats in a company's market target(s). The Strategy Feature describes Levi Strauss' challenges in the mature jeans market.

Firms pursuing extensive targeting strategies may decide to exit from certain segments. The targets that are retained in the portfolio can be prioritized to help guide product research and development, channel management, pricing strategy, advertising expenditures, and selling effort allocations.

Global Markets

Understanding global markets is important regardless of where an organization decides to compete, since domestic markets often attract international competitors. The increasingly smaller world linked by instant communications, global supply networks, and international finance markets mandates evaluating global opportunities and threats. In selecting strategies for global markets, there are two primary options for consideration: (1) the advantages of global reach and standardization; and (2) the advantages of local adaptation.[16]

Global Reach and Standardization. This strategy considers the extent to which standardization of products and other strategy elements can be used to compete on a global basis. The world is the market arena and buyers are targeted without regard to national boundaries and regional preferences. Global standardized products are not commodities. They are differentiated, but standardized across national boundaries. The objective is to identify market segments that span global markets and to serve these opportunities with global positioning strategies. For example, Gap, McDonald's and Rolex employ standardization strategies.

Local Adaption. In some international markets, domestic customers are targeted and positioning strategies are designed to consider the value requirements of domestic buyers. A wide variety of social, political, cultural, economic, and language differences among countries affects buyers' needs and preferences. These variations need to be accounted for in targeting and positioning strategies. For example, food and beverage preferences vary across national and regional boundaries. Instant coffee is popular in Britain but not in France. Responding to national differences, Nestlé employs domestic and regional strategies for several of its food products.

Industry Structure. Industry structure and competition are changing throughout the world as companies seek to improve their competitive advantage in the rapidly shrinking global marketplace. Corporate actions include restructuring, acquisitions, mergers, and strategic alliances.

Global Feature

Bollywood

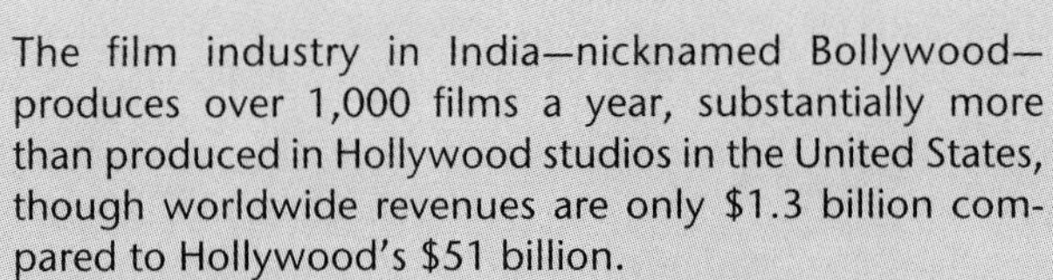

The film industry in India—nicknamed Bollywood—produces over 1,000 films a year, substantially more than produced in Hollywood studios in the United States, though worldwide revenues are only $1.3 billion compared to Hollywood's $51 billion.

With low budgets, chaotic organization, unsophisticated scripting, suspicions of mob money associations, and low marketing expenditure, Bollywood films traditionally succeeded primarily in the local Indian marketplace and in emerging Asian markets. For example, the first film shown in Kabul after the Taliban fled Afghanistan's capital was a Bollywood epic. However, the flamboyant and colorful productions have also proved popular with Indian expatriates working overseas, and with Indian immigrant communities across the world.

Indeed, more recent Bollywood films have attracted growing developed world attention. In 2002, *Lagaan*, a Bollywood blockbuster, was nominated for Best Foreign Film at the Academy Awards. Mira Nair's *Monsoon Wedding*, about a New Delhi wedding, earned over $30 million worldwide on an investment of just $1.5 million, and is set to become a Broadway play.

The surge of popularity of Bollywood firms in the West has resulted in several forms of collaboration with Hollywood distributors and studios:

- A musical comedy, *Marigold*, including characteristically flamboyant song-and-dance sequences in Hindi and English, is the first fully fledged production joint venture between Hollywood and Bollywood.
- In the United States, Sony's Columbia TriStar Motion Picture Group distributed *Laagan* and *Mission Kashmir* and has a dozen more Bollywood movies lined up.
- Twentieth Century Fox has signed a deal with popular Bollywood producer Ram Gopal Verma to market and distribute his next three films in India, and potentially internationally.

Source: Manjeet Kripalani and Ron Grover, "Bollywood," *BusinessWeek*, December 2, 2002, 42–46.

For example, General Mills has a strategic alliance with Nestlé to market General Mills' products in Europe, offering a major opportunity for General Mills to increase sales of cereal products. Nestlé has the experience and distribution network needed to tap the global cereal market.

Targeting. Strategies for competing in international markets range from targeting a single country, regional (multinational) targeting, or targeting on a global basis. The strategic issue is deciding whether to compete internationally, and, if so, how to compete. Also, the choice of a domestic focus requires an understanding of relevant global influences on the domestic strategy.

Cateora and Graham discuss three strategies for competing in international markets:[17]

1. Selling domestic products in foreign markets with little or no adaption of the domestic marketing program.
2. Multidomestic market strategy utilizing distinct marketing programs for each country.
3. Global strategy targeting an entire set of country markets using a standardized marketing program.

The domestic market extension strategy targets markets where there is a good match with the domestic market. The multidomestic strategy is decentralized, with strategy operating relatively independently. The global strategy seeks to pursue a similar strategy in all international markets. Airbus and Boeing use this strategy for commercial aircraft.

One market entry option is establishing a strategic alliance with one or more companies that provide market access and other global distinctive capabilities (see Chapter 7). The Global Feature demonstrates how local filmmaking in India—Bollywood—has become more successful internationally.[18] U.S. distributors and studios are responding with collaborative efforts.

Positioning Strategy

Positioning strategy is discussed in the rest of the chapter. First, we provide an overview of what is involved in strategic positioning and consider the selection of the positioning concept. Next, we examine the composition of the positioning strategy and how the positioning components are combined into an integrated strategy. Finally, we look at how positioning effectiveness is evaluated.

Positioning may focus on an entire company, a mix of products, a specific line of products, or a particular brand, although positioning is often centered on the brand. Importantly, positioning is closely linked to business strategy. The major initiatives necessary in strategic positioning are described in Exhibit 6.3. The buyers in the market target are the focus of the positioning strategy. The *positioning concept* indicates management's desired positioning of the product (brand) in the eyes and minds of the targeted buyers. It is a statement of what the product (brand) means guided by the value requirements of the buyers in the market target.[19] Positioning is intended to deliver the value proposition appropriate for each market target pursued by the organization. For example, Gatorade is targeted to active people experiencing hot and thirsty use situations. The drink is positioned as the best thirst quencher and replenisher, backed by scientific tests. Selecting the desired positioning requires an understanding of buyers' value requirements and their perceptions of competing brands.

The *positioning strategy* is the combination of marketing program (mix) strategies used to portray the desired positioning of management to targeted buyers. This strategy includes the product, supporting services, distribution channels, price, and promotion actions taken by the organization. *Positioning effectiveness* considers how well management's positioning objectives are being achieved in the market target.

As shown in Exhibit 6.4 the positioning objective is to have each targeted customer perceive the brand distinctly from other competing brands and favorably compared to the other brands. Of course, the actual positioning of the brand is determined by the buyer's perceptions of the firm's positioning strategy (and perceptions of competitors' strategies). The intent is to gain a relevant, distinct, and enduring position that is considered important by the buyers that are targeted. Management must design and implement the positioning strategy to achieve this result. A company's positioning strategy (marketing program) works to persuade buyers to favorably position the brand.

Achieving a distinct and valued position with targeted buyers is a pivotal initiative in Hyundai's plan to gain market position in the U.S. automobile market. The Korean carmaker is using new models, attractive prices, and a generous warranty to attract buyers of U.S. automobiles as described in Exhibit 6.5. A key component of the plan was the new 2001 XG 300, which offers full-size luxury at prices substantially below Japanese brands. Hyundai's market position has shown major growth since 1998. Hyundai's competitive threat is likely to impact U.S. car brands rather than European or Japanese companies.

EXHIBIT 6.3
Strategic Positioning Initiatives

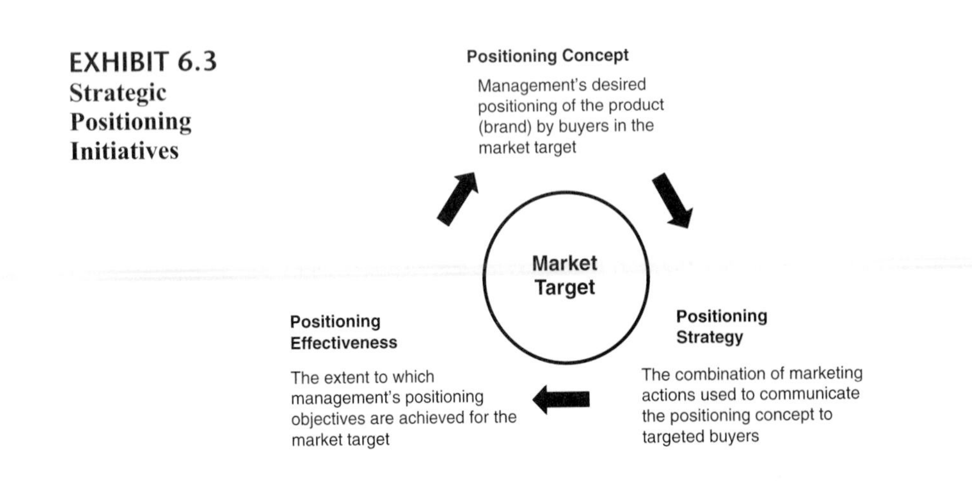

EXHIBIT 6.4
Positioning in Perspective

Objective:	Match the organization's distinctive capabilities with the customer value requirements in each market target. (How do we want to be perceived by targeted buyers?)
Desired Result	Gain a relevant, distinct, and enduring position that is considered important by the buyers in the target market.
Action by the Organizations	Design and implement the positioning strategy (marketing program) for the market target.

EXHIBIT 6.5
Hyundai, the Korean Carmaker, Positions Its New Luxury Model

Source: "And Now, A Luxury Hyundai," *BusinessWeek*, February 26, 2001, 33.

- The 2001 XG 300 full-size sedan is priced $10,000 above the previous high-end entry, the Sonata.
- The new entry is attracting a lot of buyers, even though Hyundai experienced quality problems during the 1990s.
- The XG is priced $10,000 below the Toyota Avalon and Infiniti I-30.
- Hyundai sold 90,000 cars in 1998 in the United States but received very low quality rankings.
- Hyundai offers a generous 10-year warranty on engines and transmissions.
- Management's 2001 sales estimates exceed 300,000 cars.
- Central to Hyundai's plan is its customer value-driven positioning strategy.
- Current buyers of U.S. automobile brands are the primary targets for Hyundai's cars.

Selecting the Positioning Concept

The positioning concept indicates the perception or association that management wants buyers to have concerning the company's brand. Aaker and Shansby comment on the importance of this decision:

> The position can be central to customers' perception and choice decisions. Further, since all elements of the marketing program can potentially affect the position, it is usually necessary to use a positioning strategy as a focus for the development of the marketing program. A clear positioning strategy can insure that the elements of the marketing program are consistent and supportive.[20]

Choosing the positioning concept is an important first step in designing the positioning strategy. The positioning concept of the product (brand) is "the general meaning that is understood by customers in terms of its relevance to their needs and preferences."[21] The positioning strategy is the combination of marketing mix actions that are intended to implement the product (brand) concept to achieve a specific position with targeted buyers.

Positioning Concepts.[22] The positioning concept should be linked to buyers' value preferences (value proposition). The concept may be *functional*, *symbolic*, or *experiential*. The *functional* concept applies to products that solve consumption-related problems for externally generated consumption needs. Examples of brands using this basis of positioning include Crest toothpaste (cavity prevention), Clorox liquid cleaner (effective cleaning), and a checking account with ABC Bank (convenient services). *Symbolic positioning* relates to the buyer's internally generated need for self-enhancement, role position, group membership, or ego-identification. Examples of symbolic positioning are Rolex watches and Louis Vuitton luxury goods. Finally, the *experiential* concept is used to position products that provide sensory pleasure, variety, and/or cognitive stimulation. BMW's automobile brands are positioned using an experiential concept that emphasizes the driving experience.

Three aspects of positioning concept selection are important.[23] First, the positioning concept applies to a specific brand rather than all of the competing brands in a product classification such as toothpaste. Second, the concept is used to guide positioning decisions over the life of the brand, recognizing that the brand's specific position may change over time. However, consistency is important. Third, if two or more positioning concepts, for example, functional and experiential, are used to guide positioning strategy, the multiple concepts are likely to confuse buyers and perhaps weaken the effectiveness of positioning actions. Of course, the specific concept selected may not fall clearly into one of the three classifications.

The Positioning Decision. In deciding how to position, it is useful to study the positioning of competing brands using attributes that are important to existing and potential buyers of the competing brands. The objective is to try to determine the preferred (ideal) position of the buyers in each market segment of interest and to compare this preferred position with the actual positions of competing brands. Marketing research may be necessary in identifying customers' ideal positioning. Management then seeks a distinct position that corresponds with the buyers' preferred position for the target of interest.

Determining the existing positioning of a brand by targeted buyers and deciding whether the position satisfies management's objectives are considered later in the chapter. We discuss developing the positioning strategy, and examine resource allocation guidelines for integrating the positioning components.

Developing the Positioning Strategy

The positioning strategy places the marketing program (mix) components into a coordinated set of actions designed to achieve the positioning objective(s). Developing the positioning strategy includes determining the activities and results for which each marketing program component (product, distribution, price, promotion) will be responsible, choosing the amount to spend on each program component, and deciding how much to spend on the entire program.

Selecting the positioning strategy may be guided by a combination of management judgment and experience, analysis of prior activities and results, experimentation (e.g., test marketing), and field research. We look at several considerations regarding targeting and supporting activities, followed by deciding how to develop the positioning strategy.

Scope of Positioning Strategy

The positioning strategy is usually centered on a single brand (Total toothpaste) or a line of related products (kitchen appliances) for a specific market target. Whether the strategy is brand-specific or greater in scope depends on such factors as the size of the product-market, characteristics of the good or service, the number of products involved, and product interrelationships in the consumer's use situation. For example, the marketing programs of Johnson & Johnson, P&G, and Sara Lee focus on positioning each of their various brands, whereas firms such as General Electric Company, Caterpillar, IBM, and Nike use the corporate name to position the product-line or product-portfolio. When serving several market targets, an umbrella strategy covering multiple targets may be used for some of the marketing program components. For example, advertising may be designed to appeal to more than a single target, or the same product (coach airline seats) may be targeted to different buyers through different distribution channels, pricing, and promotion activities.

Marketing Program Decisions

A look at Pier 1 Imports' positioning strategy illustrates how the specialty retailer combines marketing mix components into a coordinated strategy.[24] The company competes in the United States, Canada, England, and Mexico. Pier 1's 2004 sales should exceed $2 billion, double 1996 sales. Profits have grown at an even faster rate. Pier 1's positioning strategy includes unique merchandise, national and local advertising, strategically located stores, attractive store environments, outstanding customer service, and modern retail systems. Most of the retailer's goods are imported from China and India.

Product Strategy. Pier 1's array of merchandise includes decorative home furnishings, furniture, housewares, and bed and bath products. The merchandise is unique and ever-changing, imported from 1,500 suppliers. Management's objective is to create a casual, sensory store environment. The merchandise offers customers an opportunity to satisfy their desire for diversity.

Value-Chain Strategy. The retailer manages the value chain from supplier to end user, integrating its global supply network with its retail stores. Pier 1 has over 1,000 stores in 48 states. It uses freestanding and strip retail sites that can be quickly and conveniently accessed by customers. Store layouts and exteriors are attractively designed. Information systems are installed throughout company operations to provide real-time information to manage the business. Regional distribution centers supply merchandise to the retail store networks.

Pricing Strategy. Pier 1's global supply network and purchasing know-how result in merchandise costs that enable the company to offer quality merchandise at attractive prices. Information systems target slow-moving merchandise for possible pricing actions. The pricing strategy emphasizes the value and uniqueness of the merchandise.

Promotion Strategy. The retailer uses an effective combination of advertising, sales promotion, personal selling, and public relations to communicate with customers. Its aggressive national television advertising strategy positions Pier 1 as "The Place to Discover." Television advertising and store enhancements have helped to generate impressive sales growth. Attractive color catalogs encourage people to visit the stores. Experienced store managers and sales associates convey the corporate culture of a customer-driven company. The customer service policy states, "The customer is always right."

Competitive Advantage. Pier 1 Imports' distinctive capability is a combination of value and uniqueness of merchandise that is competitively priced and deployed in a strong retail network. The specialty retailer has been very effective in building brand image and customer loyalty. The slowdown in household relocation during the 1990s encouraged spending on accent pieces and decorative home furnishings. These pressures forced many small retailers to close, strengthening Pier 1's market position. Management's continual investment in market research studies keeps the retailer's strategy focused on customers' needs and wants.

An overview of the various decisions that are made in developing a positioning strategy is shown in Exhibit 6.6. Several of these actions are described in the Pier 1 illustration. We examine each positioning strategy component in detail in Chapters 9–13. The present objective is to show how the components fit into the positioning strategy. The positioning concept is the core focus for designing the integrated strategy. The positioning strategy indicates how (and why) the product mix, line, or brand is to be positioned for each market target. This strategy includes:

- The product strategy, including how the product(s) will be positioned against the competition in the product-market.
- The value-chain (distribution) strategy to be used.
- The pricing strategy, including the role and positioning of price relative to competition.
- The advertising and sales promotion strategy and the objectives these promotion components are expected to achieve.
- The sales force strategy, direct marketing strategy, and Internet strategy, indicating how they are used in the positioning strategy.

Designing the Positioning Strategy. First, it is necessary to set the major strategy guidelines for each marketing program component. For example, will more than one channel of distribution be utilized? Second, management strategies for each of the program components are

EXHIBIT 6.6 Positioning Strategy Overview

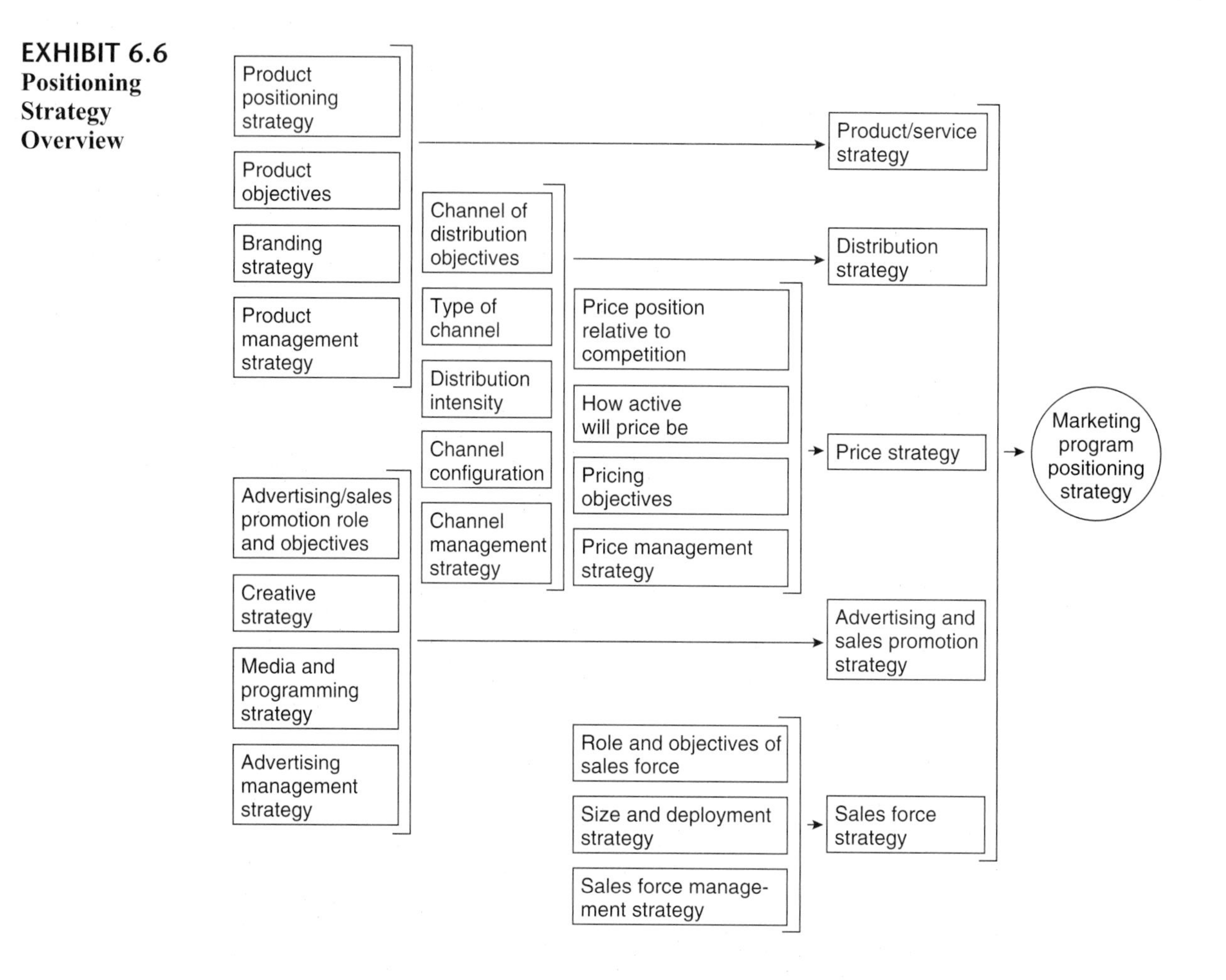

implemented. For example, Pier 1's retail management strategy involves informing store managers about new merchandise, providing logistical support to the stores, and making necessary changes in the strategy over time.

Cross-Functional Relationships. Responsibilities for the positioning strategy components (product, distribution, price, and promotion) are often assigned to various functional units within a company or business unit. This separation of responsibilities (and budgets) highlights the importance of coordinating the positioning strategy. Responsibility should be assigned for coordinating and managing all aspects of the positioning strategy. Some companies use strategy teams for this purpose. Product and brand managers may be given responsibility for coordinating the positioning strategy across functional units.

Determining Positioning Effectiveness

Estimating how the market target will respond to a proposed marketing program, and, after implementation, determining how the target is responding to the program that has been implemented are essential in selecting and managing positioning strategies. Positioning evaluation should include customer analysis, competitor analysis, and internal analysis.[25] Importantly, these analyses need to be conducted on a continuing basis to determine how well the positioning strategy is performing. "Positioning helps customers know the real differences among competing products so that they can choose the one that is of most value to them."[26] Positioning shows how a company or brand is differentiated from its competitors. Buyers position companies or brands using

EXHIBIT 6.7
Determining Positioning Effectiveness

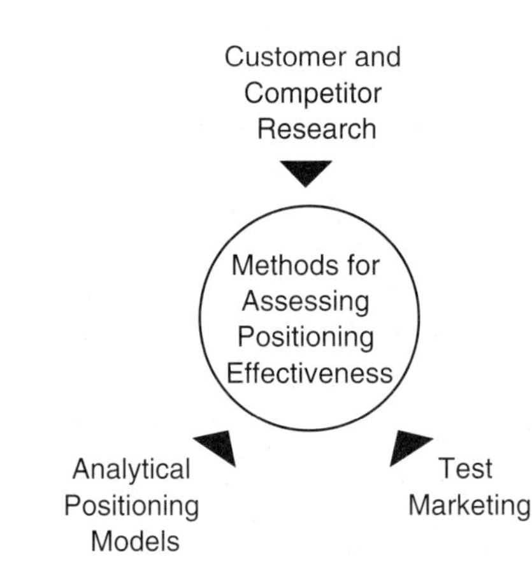

specific attributes or dimensions about products or corporate values. Management's objective is to gain (or sustain) a distinct position that corresponds to target customers' value preferences for the brand or company being positioned.

Several methods are available for analyzing positioning alternatives and determining positioning effectiveness. These include customer and competitor research, market testing of proposed strategies, and the use of analytical models (Exhibit 6.7).

Customer and Competitor Research

Research studies provide customer and competitor information which may be useful in designing positioning strategy and evaluating strategy results. Several of the research methods discussed in Part II help to determine the position of a brand. For example, preference maps are useful in determining a marketing program strategy by mapping customer preferences for various competing brands.

Methods are available for considering the effects on sales of several marketing program components. For example, using multivariate testing (MVT), a screening experiment can be conducted to identify important causal factors affecting market response.[27] The advantage of MVT is testing the effects of several factors at the same time. For example, a medical equipment producer identified seven factors as possible influences on the sales of a new product for use by surgeons in the operating room. The factors include: (1) special product training for salespeople; (2) monetary incentives for salespeople; (3) vacation incentives for salespeople; (4) distributing product information to physicians; (5) mailing product information to operating room supervisors; (6) a letter from the president of the firm describing the product; and (7) offering a customized surgical product (in contrast to a standardized product). The effect of each factor can be measured using field tests to vary the amount of the factor exposed to targeted buyers. For example, the high level of factor 1 consisted of training whereas the low-level treatment was no training. A fractional factorial experimental design was used to evaluate the effects of the seven factors. Different factor combinations were tested. One factor combination included no training, a monetary incentive, no vacation incentive, no mailing to physicians, mailing to operating room supervisors, letter from the president, and the standard product. A sample of 64 salespeople was randomly selected, and groups of eight were randomly assigned to each of the eight treatment combinations. The eight treatment combinations were designed to enable testing the effects of each factor plus the influence of various combinations of factors.

One useful finding of the screening experiment was that several of the factors had no impact on sales. For example, the customized product did not sell as well as the standard product. This information saved the firm an estimated $1 million in expenses by eliminating the need to offer customized product designs. Before conducting the experiment, management had planned to customize the product for surgeons' use. The other results of the screening experiment were useful in designing the positioning strategy for the product. Interestingly, the vacation incentive had the largest effect on sales of all of the factors, surpassing even the money incentive.

Test Marketing

Test marketing generates information about the commercial feasibility of a promising new product or about new positioning strategies for new products. The research method can also be used to test possible changes in the marketing program components (e.g., different amounts of advertising expenditures). The decision to test market is influenced by the following factors:

1. How much risk and investment are associated with the venture? When both are low, launching the product without a test market may be appropriate.
2. How much of a difference is there between the manufacturing investment required for the test versus the national launch? A large difference would favor a test market.
3. What are the likelihood and speed of the competitive response to the product offering?
4. How do the marketing costs and risks vary with the scale of the launch?[28]

While usually costing less than a national introduction, test marketing is nevertheless expensive. Market tests of packaged consumer products often cost $2 million or more depending on the scope of the tests and locations involved.[29] The competitive risks of revealing one's plans must also be weighed against the value of test market information. The major benefits of testing are risk reduction through better demand forecasts and the opportunity to fine-tune a marketing program strategy.

Test marketing provides market (sales) forecasts and information on the effectiveness of alternative marketing program strategies. Forecasts and other information are highly dependent on how well results from one or a few test markets provide accurate projections of how the national market or regional market will respond to the marketing program being tested. Model-based analysis helps overcome problems associated with idiosyncrasies of test cities.[30] A detailed behavioral model of the consumer is used to analyze test market information and develop forecasts that can be made for the effect of modified marketing strategies. We continue the discussion of test marketing of new products in Chapter 8.

Virtual shopping is a potentially powerful computer-simulated environment for testing buyers' reactions to new products and developing positioning strategies.[31] A virtual retail store can be created as a marketing laboratory for testing new-product concepts before commercial introduction. In addition to evaluating new-product concepts, the virtual shopping laboratory can test alternative retail display formats and other marketing program components such as product styles and sizes.

Positioning Models

Obtaining information about customers and prospects, analyzing it, and then developing strategies based on the information coupled with management judgment is the crux of positioning analysis. Some promising results have been achieved by incorporating research data into formal models for decision analysis. These models are developed using historical sales and marketing program data. A wide range of software is available for marketing model applications (e.g., advertising media allocation models).[32] Comprehensive discussion of marketing model applications is available from various sources.[33]

Determining Positioning Effectiveness

How do we know if we have a good positioning strategy? Does the strategy yield the results that are expected concerning sales, market share, profit contribution, growth rates, customer satisfaction, and other competitive advantage outcomes? Gauging the effectiveness of a marketing program strategy using specific criteria such as market share and profitability is more straightforward than evaluating competitive advantage. Yet developing a positioning strategy that cannot be easily copied is an essential consideration. For example, a competitor would need considerable resources—not to

Strategy Feature

- Motorcycle icon Harley-Davidson is world renowned for its sale of distinctive "dream machines"—high price, high performance motorcycles. It sells more than 300,000 machines a year, and in many locations demand outstrips supply so dealers can charge a price premium.
- The core market for the hogs is middle-aged male baby-boomers. The CEO once stated: "What we sell is the ability for a 43-year-old accountant to dress up in black leather, ride a motorcycle through town, and make people instantly afraid of him." However, this is an aging customer base.
- The challenge for the company is to broaden its market and attract female customers and younger users of the bikes, without undermining its positioning in its core market.
- The gamble is that new product features and services aimed to attract new types of customer will not alienate existing customers.
- Product features on new Harleys to appeal to the broader market targets include: smaller handlebar grips, an easier-pulling clutch, and lower seats; new materials and engine technology will make the bikes more powerful but easier to handle; Harley dealers are providing riders' education classes to help novices learn to ride and get licensed.

Source: Michael L. Abramson, "Hurdles on the Road to Hog Heaven," *BusinessWeek*, November 10, 2003, 60–62.

mention a long time period—to duplicate the powerful Revenue Management decision support system developed by American Airlines. In contrast, an airline can respond immediately with a price cut to meet the price offered by a competitor.

Companies do not alter their positioning strategies on a frequent basis, although adjustments are made at different stages of product-market maturity and in response to environmental, market, and competitive forces. For example, Pier 1 began national television advertising in 1995, and the expenditures generated very favorable sales response. Even though frequent changes are not made, a successful positioning strategy should be evaluated on a regular basis to identify shifting buyer preferences and changes in competitors' strategies.

The importance of clear, strong positioning is undermined by faulty positioning, which can subvert a company's marketing strategy. Positioning errors include:

- *Underpositioning*—when customers have only vague ideas about the company and its products and do not perceive anything distinctive about them.
- *Overpositioning*—when customers have too narrow an understanding of the company, product, or brand. For example, Mont Blanc sells pens for several thousand dollars, but it is important to the company that the consumer is aware that Mont Blanc pens are available in much cheaper models.
- *Confused positioning*—when frequent changes and contradictory messages confuse customers regarding the positioning of the brand.
- *Doubtful positioning*—when the claims made for the product or brand are not regarded as credible by the customer.[34]

Positioning and Targeting Strategies

Positioning strategies become particularly challenging when management decides to target several segments. The objective is to develop an effective positioning strategy for each segment. The use of a different brand for each targeted segment is one way of focusing a positioning strategy. The Gap employs this strategy with its Gap, Banana Republic, and Old Navy brands.

It is a challenge for a company with a clear positioning and segment choice in place to target additional segments which may undermine the strength of positioning in the existing segment. This may be particularly important to maintaining growth in mature markets. The Strategy Feature describing the positioning and targeting dilemma for Harley-Davidson is illustrative.

Summary

Choosing the right market target strategy can affect the performance of the enterprise. The targeting decision is critical to guiding the positioning of a brand or company in the marketplace. Sometimes a single target cannot be selected because the business competes in several market segments. Moreover, locating the firm's best match between its distinctive capabilities and a market segment's value requirements may first require a detailed analysis of several segments. Targeting decisions establish key guidelines for business and marketing strategies.

The market targeting options include a single segment, selective segments, or extensive segments. Choosing among these options involves consideration of the stage of product-market maturity, buyer diversity, industry structure, and the organization's distinctive capabilities. When segments cannot be clearly defined, product specialization or product variety strategies may be used.

Market targeting decisions need to take into account the product-market life cycle stage. Risk and uncertainty are high in the emerging market stage because of the lack of experience in the new market. Targeting in the growth stage benefits from prior experience, although competition is likely to be more intense than in the emerging market stage. Targeting approaches may be narrow or broad in scope based on the firm's resources and competitive advantage. Targeting in mature markets often involves multiple targeting (or product variety) strategies by a few major competitors and single/selective (or product specialization) strategies by firms with small market shares. Global targeting ranges from local adaptation to global reach.

The positioning concept describes how management wants buyers to position the brand. The concept used to position the brand may be based on the functions provided by the product, the experience it offers, or the symbol it conveys. Importantly, buyers position brands whereas companies seek to influence how buyers position brands. Success depends on how well the organization's distinctive capabilities correspond to the value requirements of each targeted segment.

Developing the positioning strategy requires integrating the product, value-chain, price, and promotion strategies to focus them on the market target. The result is an integrated strategy designed to achieve management's positioning objectives while gaining the largest possible competitive advantage. Shaping this bundle of strategies is a major challenge to marketing decision makers. Since the strategies span different functional areas and responsibilities, close cross-functional coordination is essential.

Building on an understanding of the market target and the objectives to be accomplished by the marketing program, the positioning strategy matches the firm's capabilities to buyers' value preferences. These programming decisions include selecting the amount of expenditure, deciding how to allocate these resources to the marketing program components, and making the most effective use of resources within each mix component. The factors that affect marketing program strategy include the market target, competition, resource constraints, management's priorities, and the product life cycle. The positioning strategy describes the desired positioning relative to the competition.

Central to the positioning decision is examining the relationship between the marketing effort and the market response. Positioning analysis is useful in estimating the market response as well as in evaluating competition and buyer preferences. The analysis methods include customer/competitor research, market testing, and positioning models. Analysis information, combined with management judgment and experience, are the basis for selecting a positioning strategy.

Internet Applications

A. Procter & Gamble (P&G) competes in the United States and many other countries. Consider how P&G may utilize maps in analyzing and selecting market targets (see *tiger.census.gov* and *www.nationalgeographic.com*).

B. Go to *www.jnj.com* and click on "Background" and then on "Fast Facts." Describe the different business segments and units of Johnson & Johnson.

C. Go to *www.mcdonalds.com* and analyze McDonald's revitalization plan and discuss possible marketing strategies for McDonald's.

D. Based on information available at *www.cisco.com* describe Cisco Systems' positioning strategy.

Feature Applications

A. Review the Global Feature "Bollywood," and consider what market targeting and strategic positioning choices are faced by a Bollywood studio targeting the U.S. marketplace.

B. Examine the issues described in the Strategy Feature "Harley-Davidson," and identify the problem Harley faces concerning positioning in its core market segment while trying to gain business from new segments with different needs. How can the company resolve this dilemma?

Questions for Review and Discussion

1. Discuss why it may be necessary for an organization to alter its targeting strategy over time.
2. What factors are important in selecting a market target?
3. Discuss the considerations that should be evaluated in targeting a macromarket segment whose buyers' needs vary versus targeting three microsegments within the macrosegment.
4. How might a medium-sized bank determine the major market targets served by the bank?
5. Select a product and discuss how the size and composition of the marketing program might require adjustment as the product moves through its life cycle.
6. Suggest an approach that can be used by a regional family restaurant chain to determine the firm's strengths over its competitors.
7. Describe a positioning concept for three different brands/products that corresponds to functional, experiential, and symbolic positioning.
8. Discuss some of the more important reasons why test market results may *not* be a good gauge of how well a new product will perform when it is launched in the national market.
9. "Evaluating marketing performance by using return-on-investment (ROI) measures is not appropriate because marketing is only one of several influences upon ROI." Develop an argument against this statement.
10. Two factors complicate the problem of making future projections as to the financial performance of marketing programs. First, the flow of revenues and costs is likely to be uneven over the planning horizon. Second, sales may not develop as forecasted. How should we handle these factors in financial projections?
11. Discuss the relationship between the positioning concept and positioning strategy.
12. Select a product type product-market (e.g., ice cream). Discuss the use of functional, symbolic, and experiential positioning concepts in this product category.
13. Discuss the conditions that might enable a new competitor to enter a mature product-market.
14. Competing in the mature market for air travel promises to be a demanding challenge in the 21st century. Discuss the marketing strategy issues facing Delta Airlines during the next decade.
15. Assume you are assisting Motorola in determining information needs for monitoring its cell phone targeting and positioning strategies. What are your recommendations?

Notes

1. Based in part on John Helyar, "The Only Company Wal-Mart Fears," *Fortune*, November 2, 2003, 158–166: *Ratings and Reports*, *The Value Line Investment Survey*, November 12, 2004, 1677.
2. Anthony Bianco, "The Vanishing Mass Market," *BusinessWeek*, July 12, 2004, 63.
3. Ravi S. Achrol, "Evolution of the Marketing Organization: New Forms for Turbulent Environments," *Journal of Marketing*, October 1991, 82–83.
4. Michael E. Porter, "What Is Strategy?" *Harvard Business Review*, November–December 1996, 66.
5. Michael E. Porter, *Competitive Strategy* (New York: Free Press, 1980), Chapter 9.
6. Mary Lambkin and George S. Day, "Evolutionary Processes in Competitive Markets: Beyond the Product Life Cycle," *Journal of Marketing*, July 1989, 4.
7. Ibid., 13.
8. Clayton M. Christensen and Michael E. Raynor, *The Innovator's Solution* (Boston: Harvard Business School Press, 2003), Chapter 1.
9. Elaine Romanelli, "New Venture Strategies in the Minicomputer Industry," *California Management Review*, Fall 1987, 161.
10. Lambkin and Day, "Evolutionary Processes in Competitive Markets," 14.
11. Romanelli, "New Venture Strategies in the Minicomputer Industry," 161.
12. Lambkin and Day, "Evolutionary Processes in Competitive Markets," 11.
13. Romanelli, "New Venture Strategies in the Minicomputer Industry," 170–172.
14. Lambkin and Day, "Evolutionary Processes in Competitive Markets," 12.
15. Porter, Competitive Strategy, 238–240.
16. George S. Day, *Market-Driven Strategy* (New York: The Free Press, 1990), 266–270.
17. Philip R. Cateora and John L. Graham, *International Marketing*, 12th ed. (New York: McGraw-Hill/Irwin, 2005), 22–23.
18. Manjeet Kripalani and Ron Grover, "Bollywood," *BusinessWeek*, December 2, 2002, 42–46.
19. C. Whan Park, Bernard J. Jaworski, and Deborah J. Macinnis, "Strategic Brand Concept-Image Management," *Journal of Marketing*, October 1986, 135–145.
20. Reprinted from *Business Horizons*, May-June 1982, David A. Aaker and J. Gary Shansby, "Positioning Your Product," Copyright 1982, with permission from Elsevier.
21. C. W. Park and Gerald Zaltman, *Marketing Management* (Chicago: The Dryden Press, 1987), 248.

22. This discussion is based on Park, Jaworski, and Macinnis, "Strategic Brand Concept-Image Management," 136–137, and David A. Aaker, *Building Strong Brands* (New York: The Free Press, 1996), 95–101.
23. Ibid.
24. This illustration is drawn from discussions with Pier 1 executives, *Annual Reports*, and published information.
25. Aaker, *Building Strong Brands*, Chapter 6.
26. Edward D. Mingo, "The Fine Art of Positioning," *The Journal of Business Strategy*, March/April 1988, 34.
27. Rita Koselka, "The New Mantra: MVT," *Forbes*, March 11, 1996, 114–116; David W. Cravens, Charles H. Holland, Charles W. Lamb Jr., and William C. Moncrief III, "Marketing's Role in Product and Service Quality," *Industrial Marketing Management*, November 1988, 301.
28. N. D. Cadbury, "When, Where, and How to Test Market," *Harvard Business Review*, May–June 1975, 97–98.
29. Glen L. Urban and John R. Hauser, *Design and Marketing of New Products*, 2nd ed. (Englewood Cliffs, NJ: Prentice-Hall, 1993), 495.
30. Ibid.; See Chapter 17 for a discussion of alternative methods for analyzing test markets.
31. Raymond R. Burke, "Virtual Shopping: Breakthrough in Marketing Research," *Harvard Business Review*, March–April 1996, 120–131.
32. Gary L. Lilien and Arvind Rangaswamy, *Marketing Engineering: Computer Assisted Marketing Analysis and Planning* (Reading, MA: Addison-Wesley, 1998).
33. See, for example, Gary L. Lillien, Phillip Kotler, and K. Sridhar Moorthy, *Marketing Models* (Englewood Cliffs, NJ: Prentice-Hall, 1992).
34. Graham J. Hooley, John A. Saunders, and Nigel F. Piercy, *Marketing Strategy and Competitive Positioning*, 3rd ed. (London: Prentice-Hall Europe, 2003), 269.

Chapter 7

Strategic Relationships

Strategic relationships among suppliers, producers, distribution channel organizations, and customers (end users of goods and services) occur for several reasons. The objective may be to gain access to markets, enhance value offerings, reduce the risks generated by rapid environmental change, share complementary skills to acquire new knowledge, or obtain resources beyond those available to a single enterprise. These relationships are not recent innovations, but they are escalating in importance because of the environmental complexity and risks of a global economy, and the skill and resource limitations of a single organization.[1] Strategic alliances, joint ventures, and supplier-producer collaborations are examples of cooperative relationships between independent firms.

An interesting example of an evolving relationship strategy is the Business Development Initiative launched by RadioShack in 2004. As part of its mission to demystify new technology for the consumer—"You've Got Questions. We've Got Answers."—RadioShack relies on strategic alliances to bring technology to its 7,000 stores and the one million consumers who visit one of them every day. Through the late 1990s RadioShack pioneered cobranding alliances with leading brands in the electronics and computer industry to pursue "stores within a store"—for example, "The Sprint Store at RadioShack" brought wireless phone and other telephone services to RadioShack stores, while "The RadioShack Cool Things" gave Radioshack a bridge from consumer electronics into the home entertainment industry.

The alliance approach continues to underpin RadioShack's strategy. In 2003 RadioShack announced a strategic alliance with GlobeSecNine in Washington, DC, to identify declassified military and security technology that could provide consumer products (such as "smart" cameras and tracking systems). A major move in 2004 also saw a RadioShack alliance with Motorola to leverage joint development, sourcing, and licensing power (e.g., in Bluetooth wireless technology accessories and broadband networking products). The same year saw another alliance for RadioShack with EchoStar Communications Corp. and SIRIUS satellite radio to position EchoStar's DISH network and SIRIUS as the only satellite entertainment brands offered in RadioShack.[2]

Marketing relationships are important avenues to building strong bonds with customers. The RadioShack illustration indicates how essential it is to consider all of the participating organizations involved in linking buyers with sellers in the relationship strategy. The objective is to offer end user customers superior value through collaboration of the organizations involved in the process. However, it is also important to recognize that collaborative relationship strategies may radically transform traditional buyer-seller and competitor structures in unexpected ways.

Increasingly, business and marketing strategies involve more than a single organization. In this chapter we examine the nature and scope of the strategic relationships among various

EXHIBIT 7.1
Strategic Relationships

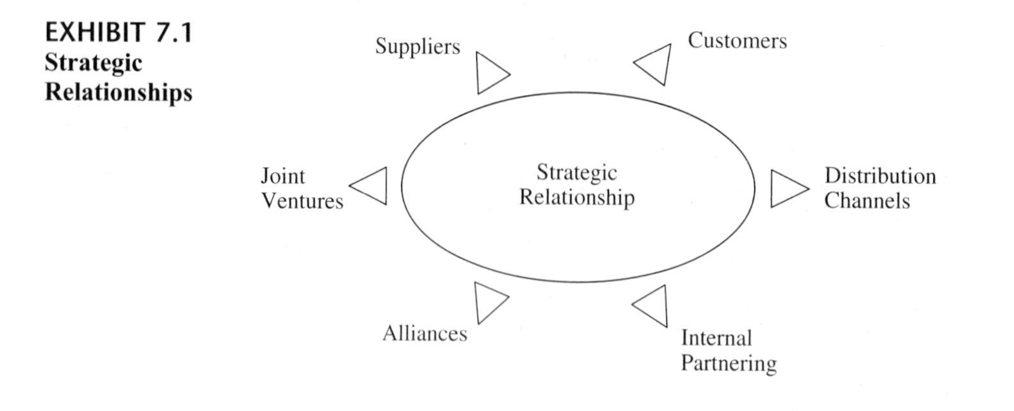

partners. We consider the full range of strategic relationships shown in Exhibit 7.1. First, we consider the rationale for interorganizational relationships and discuss the logic underlying collaborative relationships. Next, we look at different kinds of relationships among organizations, followed by a discussion of several considerations that are important in developing effective interorganizational relationships. We emphasize the risks and strategic vulnerabilities that new types of business relationship strategies may create. Finally, we discuss several issues that are important concerning global relationships.

The Rationale for Interorganizational Relationships

In the past, companies frequently established relationships to achieve tactical objectives such as selling in smaller overseas markets.[3] Today strategic relationships among organizations consider the elements of overall competitive strength—technology, costs, and marketing. Unlike tactical relationships, the effectiveness of these strategic agreements among companies can affect their long-term performance and even survival.

Several factors create a need to establish cooperative strategic relationships with other organizations. These influences include the opportunities to enhance value offerings to customers; the diversity, turbulence, and riskiness of the global business environment; the escalating complexity of technology; the existence of large resource requirements; the need to gain access to global markets; and the availability of an impressive array of information technology for coordinating intercompany operations. As shown in Exhibit 7.2, the various drivers of relationships fall into three broad categories: (1) value-enhancing opportunities by combining the competencies of two or more organizations, (2) environmental turbulence and diversity, and (3) skill and resource gaps.

Value-Enhancing Opportunities

The opportunity present in many markets today is that organizations can couple their competencies to offer superior customer value. Even when partnering is not required, a relationship strategy may result in a much more attractive value offering.

RadioShack's "Store-within-a-Store" concepts give customers the combined advantages of strong producer/service supplier and retail brands. Customers work with experienced electronics retailers and also gain access to strong product brands. Similar logic underpins the deal between Amazon and The Bombay Company. Amazon will sell furniture by Bombay Company and Bombay Kids online—Amazon leverages its database expertise to promote Bombay through

EXHIBIT 7.2
Drivers of Interorganizational Relationships

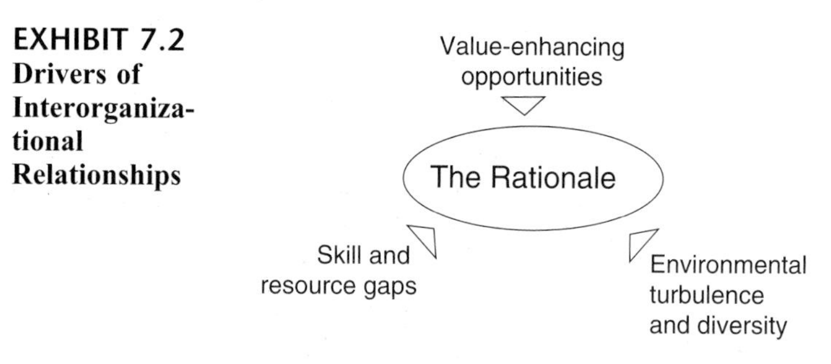

targeted e-mails and other forms of personalized marketing, using technology not otherwise available to Bombay.[4]

Modularity in product and process design offers a promising basis for leveraging interorganizational capabilities to create superior customer value. It consists of "building a complex product or process from smaller subsystems that can be designed independently yet function together as a whole."[5] A key feature of modularity is the flexibility gained by designers, producers, and product users. Companies are able to partner with others in design and production of modules or subsystems. The computer industry has performed a leadership role in advancing the use of modularity. Chip designers, computer manufacturers, component specialists, and software firms are able to make unique contributions to product design, manufacture, and use by working within the framework of an integrated architecture, which indicates how the modules fit together and the functions each will perform.[6]

A similar logic underpins the strategy developed at TiVo Inc., the pioneering producer of digital video recorders that allow TV viewers to pause live television, zip through commercials, and automatically record their favorite programs. Faced with lower price competition from cable TV companies offering similar services, and new competitors entering the market, TiVo is striking alliances to have its software incorporated into fast-selling consumer electronics like DVD players and laptop computers, aiming to build business from the premium services it can then offer consumers. The challenge is to make "TiVo Inside" successful across several sectors.[7]

Environmental Turbulence and Diversity

Since the changing and turbulent global business environment is examined in several chapters, the present discussion is brief. Diversity refers to differences between the elements in the environment, including people, organizations, and social forces affecting resources.[8] Interlinked global markets create important challenges for companies.

Coping with diversity involves both the internal organization and its relationships with other organizations. Environmental diversity reduces the capacity of an organization to respond quickly to customer needs and new product development.[9] Organizations meet this challenge by (1) altering their internal organization structures, and (2) establishing strategic relationships with other organizations.

Environmental diversity makes it difficult to link buyers and the goods and services that meet buyers' needs and wants in the marketplace. Because of this, companies are teaming up to meet the requirements of fragmented markets and complex technologies. These strategies may involve supplier and producer collaboration, strategic alliances between competitors, joint ventures between industry members, and network organizations that coordinate partnerships and alliances with many other organizations.[10] Examples of these organization forms are discussed later in the chapter.

Exhibit 7.3 illustrates growth trends in strategic relationships. Major organizations throughout the world display escalating dependence on alliances to build business, and this trend appears set to continue.

EXHIBIT 7.3
Growth in Strategic Relationships

Sources: Loren Gary, "A Growing Reliance on Alliance," *Harvard Management Update*, April 2004, 3–4. Matthew Schifrin, "Partner or Perish," *Forbes*, May 21, 2001, 26–28. Maria Gonzalez, "Strategic Alliances," *Ivey Business Journal*, September/October 2001, 47–51. J. R. Harbison and P. Pekar, *Smart Alliances: A Practical Guide to Repeatable Success* (San Francisco: Jossey-Bass, 1998).

- It was estimated in 2001 that the top 500 global businesses have an average of 60 major strategic alliances each.
- At the end of the 1990s, it was reported that the number of U.S. alliances had grown by more than 25 percent annually for the previous five years.
- Consulting firm Accenture estimates that U.S. companies with at least $2 billion in sales each formed an average of 138 alliances from 1996 to 1999.
- In 1993, when Lou Gerstner took over as CEO, only 5% of IBM's sales outside personal computers were derived from alliances. By 2001, IBM was managing almost 100,000 alliances, which contribute over one-third of its income.
- A 2003 survey by Accenture of major companies found that nearly one-third expect alliances to account for more than one-third of their market value by 2005.
- A survey of global alliances by Accenture Consulting in 1999 found that:
  - Eighty-two percent of executives surveyed believed that alliances will be the prime vehicle for growth.
  - Alliances account for an average of 26 percent of *Fortune* 500 companies' revenues—up from 11 percent fiver years earlier.
  - Alliances account for 6 to 15 percent of the market value of companies surveyed, and this is expected to increase to 16 to 25 percent of the average company's market value within five years.
  - Senior management at 25 percent of companies surveyed expects alliances to contribute more than 40 percent of their company's value within five years.
- A Vantage Partners survey of the top 1,000 U.S. companies found in 2003 nearly 20 percent of their revenue resulted from alliances, with forecasts this would reach 30 percent in 2004. Reliance on alliances was even higher in European companies.

Skill and Resource Gaps

The skill and resource requirements of technologies in many industries often surpass the capabilities of a single organization. Even those companies that can develop the capabilities may do so faster via partnering. Thus, the sharing of complementary technologies and risks are important drivers for strategic partnerships. In addition to technology, financial constraints, access to markets, and availability of information systems encourage establishing relationships among independent organizations. For example, airframe manufacturer Boeing, seeking to provide airline passengers with live television and Internet access, joined forces with units of Loral Space and Communications Ltd., Italy's Finmeccanica SpA, and Japan's Mitsubishi group to create an inflight-communications venture, which also includes CNN and CNBC to provide news content.[11]

An interesting and unusual illustration is provided by the Anglo-German alliance between Warren Kade, a small British clothing company, and Siemens, the German engineering and electronics conglomerate. The alliance helps position Siemens' mobile phones as fashion accessories associated with designer clothing on the Paris catwalk, but with the potentials for new design concepts to be incorporated in the phones, and advanced electronics to be designed into fashion clothing. The alliance unusually brings fashion and technology closer together.[12]

Increasing Complexity of Technology. Technology constraints impact industry giants as well as smaller firms. Small companies with specialized competitive strengths are able to achieve impressive bargaining power with larger firms because of their high levels of competence in specialized technology areas, and their ability to substantially compress development time. The partnerships between large and small pharmaceutical companies are illustrative. The small firm gains financial support, while the large firm gets access to specialized technology.

Strategy Feature

Aerospace Industry Leadership

European, British, and American aerospace companies are fighting over alliances and partnerships, amid accusations of unfair subsidies and reports of technology blockages that threaten to derail transatlantic programs like the Joint Strike Fighter.

- Industry leaders are Boeing, in Washington, and Airbus Industrie in Europe. Airbus is 80 percent owned by EADS (European Aeronautic Defence & Space Co.), a Franco-German-Spanish combine formed by folding together the best of Europe's aerospace companies in July 2000. The remaining 20 percent of EADS is owned by BAE Systems in the United Kingdom.
- Airbus is accused of receiving hidden government subsidy, while Boeing tries to recover from the alleged unethical behavior of its executives in bidding for a new tanker order from the U.S. airforce.
- While in 2003 Boeing had revenues of $50.5 billion compared to Airbus' $37 billion, by 2004 EADS was the dominant player in the commercial airlines business and Europe's most important defense contractor.
- The United States leads the world in military spending, in 2003 accounting for 47 percent of the global defense budget of $956 billion. EADS has set up a U.S. subsidiary providing Boeing with competition on its own turf.
- Planned transatlantic collaborations in technology-sharing to avoid duplication in research have been largely unsuccessful—export licensing regulations are a problem, and the U.S. military are protective of their technology.
- The MEADS missile system being developed by EADS and a European consortium with Lockheed Martin is stalled over problems with access to sensitive U.S. radar technology.
- Commentators fear these roadblocks to collaboration are forcing European industry to develop its own capabilities independently from the United States, and to become a competitor rather than a partner.
- It is apparent that the European market is not large enough to support EADS and their collaborators.
- EADS' U.S. operation has gained U.S. Coast Guard orders for turboprop transport planes, and EADS is targeting a symbolically much larger coup—its Eurocopter unit is bidding for a contract to furnish the White House with a new fleet of Presidential helicopters.

Source: Rachel Tiplady, "EADS: Europe's Giant Keeps Climbing," and "Aerospace & Aviation," *BusinessWeek*, July 26, 2004.

Similarly, in 2001 IBM formed 59 strategic software alliances to bring "the hot, the cool, the fast, where IBM needs it."[13]

Access to technology and other skills, specialization advantages, and the opportunity to enhance product value are important motivations for establishing relationships among organizations. These relationships may be vertical between suppliers and producers or horizontal across industry members.

The global aerospace and defense industry provides a compelling illustration of the risks driven by technology complexity and the importance of managing alliances effectively. The Strategy Feature describes the problematic relationships between U.S. and European producers, and the danger that failure to collaborate effectively and share risks may increase risk by turning potential partners into powerful competitors.

Financial Constraints. The financial needs for competing in global markets are often greater than the capacity of a single organization. As a result, many companies must seek partners in order to obtain the resources essential for competing in many industries, or to spread the risks of financial loss with another firm.

The development of large commercial aircraft described in the Strategy Feature illustrates the limitations of one company trying to compete in this global market. Boeing and Airbus Industrie, the industry leaders, are confronting the challenge of developing strategies for competing effectively in the 21st century. The two companies display intensive rivalry and are fiercely competitive for market share in the depressed airliner market. However, the two companies are launching new aircraft in different markets instead of going head-to-head for the same customers.

The Airbus vision is that airport congestion will be relieved by reducing the number of aircraft flying from them, and has invested $10.7 billion in the development of the A380 super-jumbo carrying 555 passengers. Airbus can spread its risk over its consortium members (four companies from England, France, Germany, and Spain form Airbus). Boeing will invest $6 billion in developing its new 200–300-seat 7E7 Dreamliner, because it believes that major airport congestion will be countered by more point-to-point flying between smaller cities. Importantly, both companies have risk-sharing partners. Collaborators are investing $3.1 billion in new technologies for the double-decker A380, including 18 Japanese technology partners. Airbus claims the A380 is the first of its models with more than 50 percent U.S. content (excluding engines). Boeing's 7E7 will be the least American of any Boeing model with foreign companies supplying up to 70 percent of some versions. Thirty-five percent of the 7E7—the wings and forward fuselage section—will come from Mitsubishi, Kawasaki, and Fuji in Japan in a $2.26 billion deal to develop these parts from carbon fiber reinforced plastic supplied by Toray Corp. in Japan. This is the first time in its history that Boeing has outsourced the design and development of its critical wing and center fuselage.[14]

Access to Markets. Organizational relationships are also important in gaining access to markets. Products have traditionally been distributed through marketing intermediaries such as wholesalers and retailers in order to access end user markets. These vertical channels of distribution are important in linking supply and demand. Horizontal relationships have often been established between competing firms to access global markets and domestic market segments not served by the cooperating firms. These cooperative marketing agreements expand the traditional channel of distribution coverage and gain the advantage of market knowledge in international markets.

International strategic alliances are used by many companies competing throughout the world. Commercial air travel is one of the more active industries involving overseas partners and competing through strategic alliances. The Global Feature demonstrates how essential these strategic relationships have become to competing in this industry. In effect competition is between alliances rather than between individual organizations.

Information Technology. Information technology makes establishing organizational relationships feasible in terms of time, cost, and effectiveness. Advances in information technology provide an important resource for improving the effectiveness of both internal and interorganizational communications:

> Advances in information technology and telecommunications have removed many of the communications barriers that prevented companies from drawing on overseas technical resources. Indeed, the ability to transmit documents and even complex design drawings instantaneously from one part of the globe to another by electronic mail means that it is often more efficient to collaborate globally in product development.[15]

Information systems enable organizations to effectively communicate even though the collaborating firms are widely dispersed geographically. In particular, the Internet provides a powerful means, for example, to reduce product development times by sharing designs for components and subassemblies with suppliers, customers, and collaborators throughout the world.[16] Electronic mail, file-sharing, and Web-based conferencing and collaboration tools do much to support working across traditional corporate boundaries.

An interesting example of a new business model based on the Internet that reshapes relationships between buyers and sellers is described in the Internet Feature. Swedish-based ABB Group is a leader in power and automation technologies. ABB uses the Internet to provide an integration platform—IT Industrial—that allows industrial customers to manage installations better and to have real-time access to their own customers and suppliers.

Global Feature

Global Airline Alliances

The accompanying table shows the major global airline alliances. In their short history alliances have seen numerous airlines switching alliances and the Qualiflyer alliance has been disbanded while the Wings arrangement between KLM and Northwest stopped operating after KLM was bought by Air France in 2004.

Major International Airline Alliances

Alliance	Slogan	Founded	Market Share*	Members	Comments
Star Alliance	"A more civilised way to fly the world"	May 1997	23%	Air Canada	
				Air New Zealand (1999)	
				Ansett Australia (1999)	Ansett collapsed 2001.
				All Nippon Airways (1999)	
				Asiana Airlines (2003)	
				Austrian Airlines (2000)**	
				BMI British Midland (2000)	
				LOT Polish Air (2003)	
				Lufthansa	
				Mexicana (2000)	Membership ends 2004.
				SAS Scandinavian	
				Singapore (2000)	
				Spanair (2003)	
				Thai Air International	
				United Airlines	
				US Airways (2004)	
				Varig Brazilian Airways (October 1997)	
					Industry experts predict the Star members will merge if in the future the U.S. government allows transnational airlines.
Oneworld	"The alliance that revolves around you"	February 1999	17%	Aer Lingus (2000)	
				American Airlines	
				British Airways	
				Canadian Airlines	Left after sold to Air Canada in 2004.
				Cathay Pacific	
				Finnair (September 1999)	
				Iberia (September 1999)	
				LanChile (2000)	
				Swissair	Released from commitment to join in 2003.
				Qantas	
				17 affiliate members provide regional services in association with full alliance members	
SkyTeam	"Caring more about you"	June 2000	13%	Air France	Air France merged with KLM in 2004 to form Air France-KLM.

Major International Airline Alliances (continued)

Alliance	Slogan	Founded	Market Share*	Members	Comments
				Aeromexico Alitalia (2001) CSA Czech (2001) Delta Korean Air KLM (2004) Continental (2004) Northwest (2004)	
Wings	"Worldwide reliability"	KLM/NW cooperation since 1993	11	KLM Continental Northwest	The merger of KLM with Air France in 2004 effectively merges Wings into SkyTeam. KLM had previously sought code-sharing with BA and AA cutting across the alliances.
Qualiflyer	"Flying European style"	March 1998	–	Formed from 12 European airlines, defections to Star and Oneworld weakened the alliance	Disbanded in 2002 by the seven remaining members, who are expected to join other alliances.

Source: Tourism Futures International, *www.tourismfuturesintl.com*, July 2004. Reprinted with permission.
* IATA estimates for 2002.
** Includes Lauda Air and Tyrolean.

Examining the Potential for Collaborative Relationships

Collaborative relations include shared activities such as product and process design, cooperative marketing programs, applications assistance, long-term supply contracts, and just-in-time inventory programs.[17] The amount of collaboration may vary substantially across industries and individual companies. Moreover, in a given competitive situation a firm may pursue different degrees of collaboration across its customer base. For example, some supplier-customer relationships are transactional, but the same supplier may seek collaborative relationships with other customers.

There are several factors that need to be evaluated when considering possible collaborative relationships with other organizations. We examine each factor, indicating important issues concerning how the factor may impact a strategic relationship.

What Is the Strategic Logic? Partnering is the result of two organizations working together toward a common objective such as sharing technologies, market access, or compressing new product development time. For example, a supplier may benefit from a customer's leading-edge application of the supplier's product.[18]

When Wal-Mart wanted to expand in Mexico in anticipation of NAFTA, it established a joint venture with Mexico's Cifra, providing Wal-Mart with a firm base and greatly reducing its learning time in a new market. Cifra/Wal-Mart is now Mexico's leading retailer under the name Wal-Mart de Mexico. Interestingly, Wal-Mart has taken that experience and applied it to Brazil and other parts of Latin America.[19]

Internet Feature ABB's Internet Model

The Swiss-Swedish owned ABB group, with sales of $20 billion is one of the three largest electrical engineering companies in the world. Several events underline the link between the Internet and relationship strategy:

- In 2000, CEO Gran Lindahl resigned because he was convinced that ABB's leadership required an information technology background, not traditional engineering skills.
- Instead of using the Web just to support buying and selling of goods and services, ABB's e-business model tries to use the Web as a communications pathway to feed its technology expertise and knowledge of industry trends to customers.
- Moreover, the Internet relationship provides the means for customers to share ideas and problems with each other as well as with ABB.
- By linking customers to ABB's "brainpower"—the knowledge of its employees—the Internet provides the basis for knowledge sharing within the company and with customers.
- Information sharing is between customers as well—Lindt, the Swiss chocolate company can use its ABB Web page to see how other customers use "preventative maintenance" to operate factories efficiently.
- The model brings ABB's R&D closer to customers and to business decisions, speeding up the commercialization of technology and reducing overlap between research projects, with savings estimated as tens of millions of dollars.

Source: Excerpt from Peter Marsh, "Welding Metal to the Internet," *Financial Times*, October 30, 2000. Reprinted with permission.

Research by Accenture on alliance issues and trends in 2003 finds that for nearly half the companies involved in strategic alliances, learning was seen as the critical goal. Achieving learning goals through alliances is highly associated with successful alliances.[20]

The key issue is that there should be a strong underlying logic for collaboration. The alignment between alliance strategy and business strategy is crucial to success in partnering.[21]

Is Partnering a Promising Strategy? This factor considers the costs as well as the benefits of partnering with customers, suppliers, and competitors. Strategic relationships are demanding in terms of both time and resources. The relationship may require substantial investments by the partners, and often cannot be transferred to other business relationships.[22] Because of this, the benefits need to be candidly assessed and compared to the costs. This requires careful planning of the relationship to spell out activities, participants, and costs.

How Essential Is the Relationship Strategy? Normally, relationships are formed because the partners believe that combining their efforts is essential, and that pursuing the project alone is not feasible. However, experience indicates that strategic relationships are more likely to succeed when dependence is important and equivalent between the collaborating organizations.

Are Good Candidates Available? Promising partners may be unwilling to collaborate or already involved with other organizations. For example, many of the desirable global airline alliance partners have established relationships (see the Global Feature on Airline Strategic Alliances), and partnering with weaker companies is increasingly undesirable in this sector.

Do Relationships Fit Our Culture? The corporate cultures of the partners should be adaptable to the partnership.[23] This issue is particularly important for partners from countries with substantial national cultural differences. The partners' approach to business activities and priorities should be compatible.

For example, the global alliance between British Telecom (BT) and AT&T aimed to combine resources around "Concert"—a product to provide multinational corporations with a single, global telecoms source based on "virtual private networks," with target sales of $10 billion. BT had a history of failed partnerships in its globalization initiatives. AT&T lacked experience in collaborative situations, and its earlier global alliance—Unisource—had broken down over AT&T's reluctance to cooperate with foreign partners or commit to common investment with them. After a relationship of persistent squabbling between BT and AT&T, the Concert alliance collapsed after only two years. Costs to BT of unwinding from the alliance are estimated at $2.1 billion, with charges of $5.5 billion to AT&T from Concert's demise.[24]

We will discuss shortly the related question of partnering capabilities. It is becoming clear that the ability to operate effective relationship strategies between organizations relies on skills and capabilities which vary considerably between organizations.

Types of Organizational Relationships

The types of relationships that may be formed by a firm are shown in Exhibit 7.4. Included are supplier and buyer (vertical), lateral (horizontal), and internal relationships. A useful way to examine organizational relationships is to consider whether the tie between firms is vertical or horizontal. The focal firm may participate in both vertical and horizontal relationships. We first look at vertical relationships among organizations, and, then, strategic alliances and joint ventures, followed by internal relationships. Evolving global, relationships among organizations are examined in a subsequent section.

Customer-Supplier Relationships

Moving products through various stages in the value-added process often involves linking suppliers, manufacturers, distributors, and consumer and business end users of goods and services into vertical channels. Functional specialization and efficiency create the need for different types of organizations. For example, wholesalers stock products in inventory and deploy them when needed to retailers, thus reducing the delays of ordering direct from manufacturers.

Over recent years the use of supplier/manufacturer collaborative relationships has expanded in many industries. While problems such as industrial secrets, labor objections, and loss of control occurred, the benefits of leveraging of distinctive capabilities of partners are substantial in developing new products and manufacturing processes. These relationships are extensively used in the automotive and computer industries.

A related development is the outsourcing of activities such as transportation, repair and maintenance services, information systems, and human resources. It has been suggested that outsourcing parts of the value-chain process to partners is a form of leveraged growth—it allows a company to expand sales without capital investment in all stages of the value chain.[25]

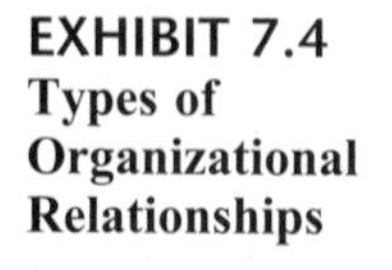

EXHIBIT 7.4
Types of Organizational Relationships

Source: Figure from Robert M. Morgan and Shelby D. Hunt, "The Commitment–Trust Theory of Relationship Marketing" *Journal of Marketing*, July 1994, 21. Reprinted with permission of the American Marketing Association.

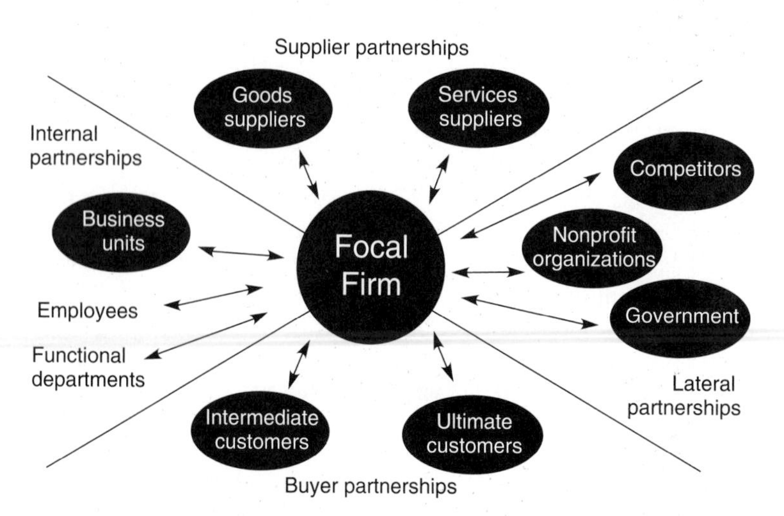

Innovation Feature BMW Outsourcing Strategy

In 2000 BMW struck a deal with Magna Steyr in Austria to outsource the engineering and production of its new X3 compact sport utility vehicle. The 5,000-page agreement pioneered a huge handover of in-house engineering and production technology by the premium brand manufacturer.

Magna had already produced cars for Mercedes-Benz, Audi, Volswagen, Jeep and Chrysler, but nothing as large-scale as the X3. The agreement was to get from concept to production in a record breaking 28 months—several months faster than BMW's normal in-house performance.

The benefits are:

- Using the contractor's engineers lets the carmaker keep down head counts.
- The car company avoids building a billion dollar factory.
- A contract deal often means that the carmaker can produce more models quickly.
- Working with various clients, contractors acquire new skills and expertise.

The risks are:

- If the builder botches the quality, the car company's reputation suffers.
- Depending on how the deal is structured, a contractor can get stuck with unused capacity when sales fall below a certain threshold.
- In a fast-moving market, the niches these partnerships typically target can vanish before rewards are reaped.

It is as yet unclear if outsourcing will reshape the global auto industry but a growing number of manufacturers throughout the world are using the new manufacturing model for niche market vehicles.

Source: Gail Edmondson, "Look Who's Building Bimmers," *BusinessWeek*, December 8, 2003, 18–19.

The suppliers and buyers of a vast array of raw materials, parts and components, equipment, and services (e.g., consulting, maintenance) are linked together in vertical channels of distribution. The relationships between the supplier and customer range from transactional to collaborative. A provocative example is provided in the Innovation Feature. For the first time in its history, luxury automobile manufacturer BMW is outsourcing production of its vehicles. The new manufacturing model offers major benefits, but also carries substantial risks.

Distribution Channel Relationships

Vertical relationships also occur between producers and marketing intermediaries (e.g., wholesalers and retailers). These value-chain relationships provide the producer access to consumer and organizational end users. Interorganizational relationships vary from highly collaborative to transactional ties. A strong collaborative relationship exists in a vertical marketing system (VMS).[26] These systems are managed by one of the channel members such as a retailer, distributor, or producer. The VMS may be owned by a channel firm, linked together contractually (e.g., a franchise system), or the relationship held together by the power and influence of the firm administering the channel relationships.

For example, the American Family Life Assurance Company (AFLAC) is increasingly well known in the United States from its advertising featuring the "AFLAC duck", (see photo on the following page). In fact, three-quarters of AFLAC's $12 billion revenues come from Japan, where it is the largest foreign life insurance company. AFLAC operates in Japan in the niche category of supplemental insurance (cancer, medical, and other life insurance products that supplement the national health-care system). While traditional Japanese life insurers employ sales employees who call on customers at their home to sell policies and collect premiums, AFLAC established a broad-based distribution network of corporate partners. The corporate partners are affiliated with companies and reach those companies' employees, suppliers, and customers. By 2004, some 95 percent of companies listed on the Tokyo Stock Exchange offer AFLAC products to their employees, and AFLAC has insurance products in 25 percent of Japanese households. Marketing through collaboration with employers enables AFLAC to reach large numbers of consumers economically to minimize the costs of premium collection (they are collected through payroll deductions), and avoid paying high commissions.

There is considerable evidence that the organizations in distribution channels are becoming involved to a greater extent in collaborative relationships compared to traditional power and dependence ties. Examples include the Radio Shack store-within-a-store relationships with other companies, and AFLAC's ties with Japanese companies. We discuss value-chain relationships in Chapter 10.

End User Customer Relationships

The driving force underlying strategic relationships is that a company may enhance its ability to satisfy customers and cope with a rapidly changing business environment through partnering. Several examples are shown in Exhibit 7.5. Some believe that the future of competition lies in co-creation initiatives with customers—only by letting individual corporate customers and consumers shape products and service can real fit with customer needs be achieved.[27]

For example, Sumerset Houseboats Inc. in Kentucky custom-builds boats, engaging each individual customer in a dialogue through design and construction. Through the Internet, it also connects to a community of Sumerset houseboat owners so they can compare notes, which boosts customer satisfaction but also provides Sumerset with unique design insights for future products.[28]

Although building collaborative relationships may not always be the best course of action, this avenue for gaining a competitive edge is increasing in popularity. We examine developing a customer focus and assessing customer value.

Customer Focus. Relationship marketing starts with the customer—understanding needs and wants and how to satisfy requirements and preferences:

> Customers think about products and companies in relation to other products and companies. What really matters is how existing and potential customers think about a company in relation to its competitors. Customers set up a hierarchy of values, wants, and needs based on empirical data, opinions, word-of-mouth references, and previous experiences with products and services. They use that information to make purchasing decisions.[29]

The importance of understanding customers' needs and wants encourages developing long-term collaborative relationships. Driving the necessity of staying in close contact with buyers is the reality that customers often have several suppliers of the products they wish to purchase. Customer diversity complicates the competitive challenge. Consistent with being market-oriented, developing a customer-oriented organization includes:

- Instilling customer-oriented values and beliefs supported by top management.
- Integrating market and customer focus into the strategic planning process.
- Developing strong marketing managers and programs.
- Creating market-based measures of performance.
- Developing customer commitment throughout the organization.[30]

EXHIBIT 7.5
Illustrative Partnering with Customers

Company/Brand	Customer Partner
• Boeing (commercial aircraft)	Involving airlines in the design of the Boeing 777
• Harley-Davidson (motorcycles)	Harley Owners Group with over 100,000 members
• Marriott (hotels)	Partnering with corporate customers
• Dell Computer	Partnering with large corporate customers

The development of Customer Relationship Management (CRM) systems provides an extension of relationship marketing to customers. CRM provides structure for managing the point of customer contact by integrating information technology and data around the customer. CRM is an important development and is discussed in more detail in the Appendix to this chapter.

Similarly, in the management of relationships with large corporate customers, many organizations have moved to the adoption of Key Account Management structures and Global Account Management approaches as ways of building teams dedicated to managing the relationship with the most valuable customers.[31]

Assessing Customer Value. An important issue is selecting the customers with which to develop relationships since some may not want to partner and others may not offer enough potential to justify partnering with them. A look at Marriott's partnering strategy is illustrative.

> Building customer relationships is the core sales strategy of Marriott International Inc.'s Business Travel Sales Organization. The travel manager is the target for the selling activities of the 2,500-person sales organization. The key features of the major account sales strategy are: (1) choose customers wisely (Marriott follows a comprehensive customer evaluation process); (2) build customer research into the value proposition (understanding what drives customer value and satisfaction); (3) lead with learning by following a step-by-step sales process; (4) invest in the customer's goal-setting process, rather than Marriott's; and (5) develop a relationship strategy with a sense of purpose, trust, open access, shared leadership, and continuous learning. Marriott's management recognizes that customers who regularly purchase the company's services are valuable assets who demand continuous attention by high-performance teams. Rapidly changing markets and customer diversity add to the importance of developing strong ties with valuable customers to stay in touch with their changing requirements.[32]

Relationship strategies need to recognize differences in the value of customers to the seller as well as the specific requirements of customers.[33] Marriott's emphasis on carefully selecting business customers with whom to partner illustrates the importance of prioritizing sales strategies by segmenting accounts for corporate influence and profit. Relationship building is appropriate when large differences exist in the value of customers. Valuable customers may want close collaboration from their suppliers concerning product design, inventory planning, and order processing, and they may proactively pursue collaboration. The objective is to develop buyer and seller relationships so that both partners benefit from the relationship.

Frequent flyer programs have been very successful in building long-term relationships with customers. The Advantage program pioneered by American Airlines attracted other airlines as well as hotel chains, credit card companies, and rental car companies. In many different business situations, a small percent of customers account for a very large percentage of purchases. The 80/20 rule is illustrative, which states that 20 percent of customers are the source of 80 percent of sales.

Strategic Alliances

A strategic alliance between two organizations is an agreement to cooperate to achieve one or more common strategic objectives. The relationship is horizontal in scope, between companies at the same level in the value chain. While the term *alliance* is sometimes used to designate supplier-producer partnerships, it is used here to identify collaborative relationships between companies that are competitors or in related industries. The alliance relationship is intended to be long-term and strategically important to both parties. Several reasons for forming strategic alliances are shown in Exhibit 7.6. The following discussion assumes an alliance between two parties, recognizing that there may be more than two alliance partners.

Each organization's contribution to the alliance is intended to complement the partner's contribution. The alliance requires each participant to yield some of its independence: "Alliances mean sharing control."[34] The rationale for the relationship may be to gain access to markets, utilize existing distribution channels, share technology development costs, or obtain specific skills or resources.

The alliance is not a merger between two independent organizations, although the termination of an alliance may eventually lead to an acquisition of one partner by the other partner. It is different from a joint venture launched by two firms or a formal contractual relationship between organizations. Moreover, the alliance involves more than purchasing stock in another company. Instead, it is a commitment to actively participate on a common project or program that is strategic in scope.

Weaknesses in alliances may come from several causes. For example, in 2000 as part of its drive to build the world's number one car and truck company, DaimlerChrysler formed a partnership with Korean automaker Hyundai—taking a 10.5 percent ownership stake in Hyundai and promising to build small cars and 100,000 trucks a year in a 50-50 joint venture. The relationship was dogged by acrimonious disputes, cultural clashes, and power struggles, with an increasingly self-confident Hyundai determined to be treated as an equal partner. By 2004, the plan to develop small cars had gone nowhere, and the $700 million truck project was stalled. The timeline of the partnership is illustrative:

- September 2000—Daimler takes an initial 10 percent stake in Hyundai for $381 million, aiming to set up a 50-50 joint venture to build 100,000 trucks a year.
- November 2001—Daimler and Hyundai break ground for a $260 million truck engine plant due to start up in 2004.
- October 2003—Hyundai halts the project, angry over Daimler's new alliance with Beijing Automotive to produce Mercedes-Benz autos in the fast-growing Chinese market—Hyundai already had an exclusive pact with Beijing to make autos in China.
- April 2004—Insiders say the alliance is near collapse.[35]

Poorly structured partnerships may be extremely damaging to all concerned. First, we discuss the success record of alliances. Next, different uses of alliances are described. Finally, several alliance success requirements are examined.

Success of Alliances. The competitive realities of surviving and prospering in the complex and rapidly changing business environment encourage companies to form strategic alliances in many different industries. Some strategic partnerships have endured for substantial periods—a Fuji-Xerox partnership entered its 42nd year in 2004, and Samsung and Corning have been working together since the 1970s.[36]

Nonetheless, the record of success of alliances is not favorable, and success rates of less than 50 percent have often been found by researchers.[37] While the alliance is a promising strategy for enhancing the competitive advantage of the partners, several failures have occurred due to the complexity of managing these relationships.

EXHIBIT 7.6
Motives Underlying Entry of Firms into Strategic Alliances

Source: From P. Rajan Varadarajan and Margaret H. Cunningham, "Strategic Alliances: A Synthesis of Conceptual Foundations," *Journal of the Academy of Marketing Science*, Fall 1995, 285. Copyright © 1995 by the Academy of Marketing Science. Reprinted by permission of Sage Publications, Inc.

Market entry- and market position-related motives
Gain access to new international markets.
Circumvent barriers to entering international markets posed by legal, regulatory, and/or political factors.
Defend market position in present markets.
Enhance market position in present markets.

Product-related motives
Fill gaps in present product line.
Broaden present product line.
Differentiate or add value to the product.

Product/market-related motives
Enter new product-market domains.
Enter or maintain the option to enter evolving industries whose product offerings may emerge as either substitutes for, or complements to, the firm's product offerings.

Market structure modification-related motives
Reduce potential threat of future competition.
Raise entry barriers/erect entry barriers.
Alter the technological base of competition.

Market entry timing-related motives
Accelerate pace of entry into new product-market domains by accelerating pace of R&D, product development, and/or market entry.

Resource use efficiency-related motives
Lower manufacturing costs.
Lower marketing costs.

Resource extension- and risk reduction-related motives
Pool resources in light of large outlays required.
Lower risk in the face of large resource outlays required, technological uncertainties, market uncertainties, and/or other uncertainties.

Skill enhancement-related motives
Learning new skills from alliance partners.
Enhancement of present skills by working with alliance partners.

The Conference Board Inc. surveyed the chief executive officers (CEOs) of 350 companies in the United States, Europe, Canada, and Mexico concerning their experiences with strategic alliances. The CEOs considered about half of their recent alliances to be successful. Several reasons are cited for those that were not successful, which are summarized in Exhibit 7.7. The alliance failures are divided into logic and process failures.

Kinds of Alliances. An alliance typically involves a marketing, research and development, operations (manufacturing), and/or financial relationship between the partners (Exhibit 7.6). Capabilities may be exchanged or shared. In addition to functions performed by the partners, other aspects of alliances may include market coverage and effectively matching the specific characteristics of the partners.

The alliance helps each partner to obtain business and technical skills and experience that are not available internally. One partner contributes unique capabilities to the other organization in return for needed skills and experience. The intent of the alliance is that both parties benefit from sharing complementary functional responsibilities rather than independently performing them.

EXHIBIT 7.7
Why Strategic Alliances Fail

Source: Chart from Margaret Hart and Stephen J. Garone, *Making International Strategic Alliances Work*, R-1086 (New York: The Conference Board, 1994), 19. Reprinted with permission from The Conference Board.

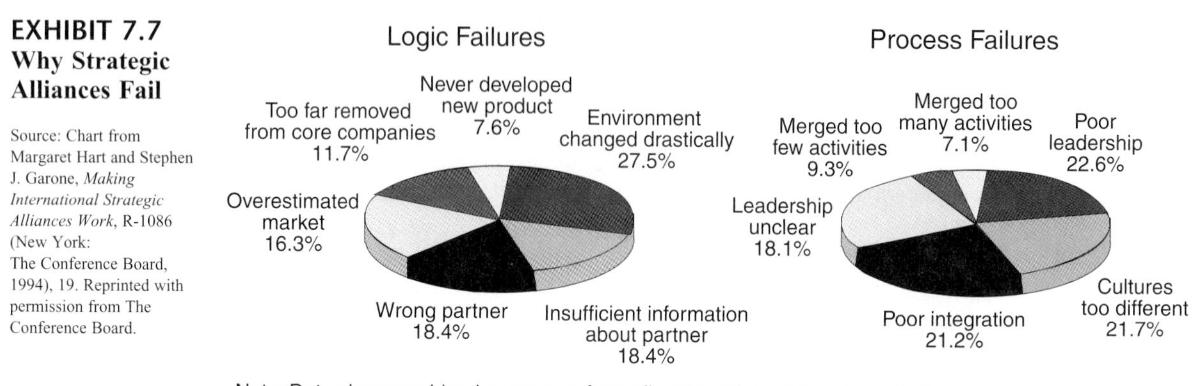

Alliance Success Requirements. The success of the alliance may depend heavily on effectively matching the capabilities of the participating organizations and on achieving the full commitment of each partner to the alliance. The benefits and the trade-offs in the alliance must be favorable for each of the partners. The contribution of one partner should fill a gap in the other partner's capabilities.

One important concern in the alliance relationship is that the partner may gain access to confidential technology and other proprietary information. While this issue is important, the essential consideration is assessing the relationship's risks and rewards and the integrity of the alliance partner. A strong bond of trust between the partners exists in most successful relationships. The purpose of the alliance is for each partner to contribute something distinctive rather than to transfer core skills to the other partner.[38] It is important for the managers in each organization to evaluate the advisability and risks concerning the transfer of skills and technologies to the partner.

Alliance Vulnerabilities. Relatedly, it is important to recognize that alliance relationships may be fragile and difficult to sustain effectively, particularly if there is a lack of trust or mutuality of interest between partners.[39] Moreover, careful analysis is required of the impact of a failed alliance on a company's remaining ability to compete and survive. For example, in 2001, when Motorola withdrew from a joint project with Psion to develop a product to rival the Palm Pilot, Psion's shares fell 20 percent on the day, and the company was left without sufficient resources to complete the project alone.[40]

The higher the level of dependence on a partner organization, the greater the strategic vulnerability created if the alliance fails. Some estimates suggest that as many as 70 percent of alliances fail. It is important that every alliance agreement should include an exit strategy. Recognizing that alliances are impermanent may maximize their useful life.[41]

Joint Ventures

Joint ventures are agreements between two or more firms to establish a separate entity. These relationships may be used in several ways: to develop a new market opportunity; to access an international market; to share costs and financial risks; to gain a share of local manufacturing profits; or to acquire knowledge or technology for the core business.[42] For example, Coca-Cola has a long-standing 50-50 joint venture with Nestlé—Beverage Partners Worldwide (formerly Coca-Cola and Nestlé Refreshments)—to take its tea and coffee brands into global markets alongside Nestlé products. In some cases, joint ventures can grow valuable assets—in 2001 Xerox was able to sell half its stake in Fuji Xerox Co. to Fuji for $1.3 billion, to counter liquidity problems.[43]

While joint ventures are similar to strategic alliances, a venture results in the creation of a new organization. Environmental turbulence and risk set the rationale for the venture more so than a major skill/resource gap, although both pressures may be present.

Honeywell Inc. has several joint ventures worldwide. The manufacturer and marketer of control systems and components for homes and businesses has been operating outside the United States for nearly 60 years. The company's chief executive officer, Michael R. Bonsignore, describes one venture:

> *Sinopec-Honeywell* involves one of Honeywell's customers, the Chinese National Petroleum Company—Sinopec. In January 1993, Honeywell entered into a joint equity company with Sinopec for a number of reasons: geographic expansion, market share, and risk diversification. Orders from Sinopec doubled in the first year and Honeywell has since attained the central government's acceptance. However, says Bonsignore, "we do have a number of concerns that we monitor constantly, such as MFN, the potential for Sinopec to become a competitor, and ongoing decentralization of the decision authority in the Chinese government."[44]

Internal Partnering

Internal partnerships may occur between business units, functional departments, and individual employees (Exhibit 7.4). The intent is to encourage and facilitate cross-functional cooperation rather than specialization. Key internal processes such as new-product development benefit from cross-functional cooperation in areas such as research and development, marketing, purchasing, finance, and operations working together to identify, evaluate, develop, and commercialize new-product concepts.

For example, P&G uses a corporate collaboration network—*My Idea*—to allow employees throughout the company to send ideas to an innovation panel. Projects selected can tap into P&G's entire global resource base. P&G's Corporate New Ventures Group was established in 1997, and by the end of 1998, 58 new products had been launched—compared to no new products launched in some years. The *Swiffer* cleaning product reached market in 10 months, half the normal P&G time.[45]

The success of internal relationship strategies requires developing strong internal collaboration that cuts across functional boundaries. As noted in earlier chapters, many companies are using teams of people from various functions to manage processes such as new-product development, customer relationships, order processing, and delivery of products.

As we discussed in Chapter 1, a market-oriented organization is committed to delivering superior customer value through market sensing, interfunctional cooperation, and shared decision making. Several guidelines for developing effective internal relationships follow:[46]

1. Demonstrate management support.
2. Start with a pilot team.
3. Keep the teams small—and together.
4. Link the teams to the strategy.
5. Seek complementary skills for the team—and look for potential.
6. Educate and train.
7. Address the issue of team leadership.
8. Motivate and reward team performance, not just individual performance.

The relationship strategy requires attention to the internal structure. The starting point is building a collaborative customer-driven internal culture.

The importance of effective internal partnering to support market-driven strategy is underlined by the remarkable performance of warehouse club Costco compared to archrival Sam's Club, owned by Wal-Mart. Costco combines higher compensation and more generous employment terms for its employees with higher productivity than Sam's Club can achieve. The Cross-Functional Feature describes Costco's clever marketing strategy supported by strong employee relationships driving competitive advantage.

Cross-Functional Feature

Costco versus Sam's Club People Costs

Costco has achieved a major position in the U.S. warehouse club business, against major competitors Sam's Club, owned by Wal-Mart, and BJ's Wholesale Club.

- Costco's success is underpinned by selling a mix of higher margin products to more affluent customers—catering better than competitors for small shop owners and high-income consumers.
- Costco searches constantly for innovation and higher productivity—new ways to repackage goods into bulk items, saving labor and increasing supply chain efficiency; the first wholesale club to offer fresh meat, pharmacies, and photo labs.
- Remarkably, Costco compensates its employees more generously to motivate and retain good workers—one fifth of whom are unionized—and gets lower staff turnover and higher productivity. *BusinessWeek* comparisons show how Costco pays its people more but gets higher productivity in return:
- The 102,000 Sam's Club employees in the United States generated $35 billion in sales in 2003, while Costco did $34 billion with one-third fewer employees.
- Costco has one of retailing's most productive and loyal workforces.

It Pays a Lot More Than Wal-Mart . . .

	Costco	Wal-Mart's Sam's Club
Average hourly wage	$15.97	$11.52
Annual health costs per worker	$5,735	$3,500
Covered by health plan	82%	47%
Annual retirement costs per worker	$1,330	$747
Covered by retirement plans	91%	64%

But Gets More Out of Its Workers . . .

	Costco	Walmart's Sam's Club
Employee turnover	6% a year	21% a year
Labor and overhead costs	9.8% of sales	17% of sales
Sales per square foot	$795	$516
Profits per employee	$13,647	$11,037
Yearly operating income growth	10.1%	9.8%

Source: Stanley Holmes and Wendy Zellner, "The Costco Way," *BusinessWeek*, April 12, 2004, 56–57.

Developing Effective Relationships between Organizations

We know that forming and managing effective collaborative partnerships between independent organizations is complex, so we need to look further into the process of developing effective relationships. The objective of the relationship is first considered, followed by a discussion of several relationship management guidelines.

Objective of the Relationship

We look at possible strategic objectives of relationships.[47] In some situations collaborative action may be an option rather than a requirement.

Identifying and Obtaining New Technologies and Competencies. This objective is a continuing challenge for many companies because of the increasing complexity of technology and the short time span between identifying and commercializing new technologies.

There are several ways to locate and exploit external sources of research and development:

- Collaboration with university departments and other research institutions.
- Precompetitive collaborative R&D to spread research resources more widely.
- Corporate venturing—making systematic investments in emerging companies to gain a window on the technologies and market applications of the future.
- Joint ventures and other forms of strategic partnership that enable a company to acquire new competencies by "borrowing" from a company with a leadership position.[48]

Japanese companies aggressively pursue all of these strategies, whereas U.S. companies rely more heavily on internal R&D. However, the future trend is toward expanded use of external research and development collaboration by United States and other companies throughout the world. For example, collaboration is extensive among component manufacturers, personal computer producers, and software firms.

The role of the Internet in encouraging and facilitating technology sharing is becoming significant. Italian company Olivetti has pioneered multinational collaboration between companies and research institutions in its multimedia product development project.[49]

Developing New Markets and Building Market Position. Alliances and other collaborative relationships may be promising alternatives for a single company interested in developing a market or entering a global market. This strategy requires finding potential partners that have strong marketing capabilities, and/or market position. Collaboration may be used to enter a new product market or to geographically expand a position in a market already served.

Increasingly, major corporations are pursuing collaborative strategies in research and development and in gaining market access. General Electric has a corporate objective of globalization, which requires participation in each major market in the world:

> This requires several different forms of participation: trading technology for market access; trading market access for technology; and trading market access for market access. This "share to gain" becomes a way of life.[50]

GE's globalization objective has led to forming over 100 collaborative relationships.[51]

Market Selectivity Strategies. Competing in mature markets often involves either market domination or market selectivity strategies. Competition in these markets is characterized by a small core of major firms and several smaller competitors that concentrate their efforts in market segments. Firms with small market position need to adopt strategies that enable them to compete in market segments where they have unique strengths and/or the segments are not of interest to large competitors. Cooperative relationships may be appropriate for these firms. The possible avenues for relationships include purchasing components to be processed and marketed to one or a few market segments, subcontracting to industry leaders, and providing distribution services to industry leaders.

The high entry barriers in producing semiconductors encourage the formation of strategic alliances.[52] Partnerships are essential in developing niche markets in this industry. Alliances exist between small U.S. firms that have specialized design expertise and Japanese, Korean, Taiwanese, and European companies with large-scale electronics manufacturing capabilities. The alliances make possible market entry for the design specialists. The cost of moving a complex new chip design to commercialization is in excess of $1 billion.

Restructuring and Cost-Reduction Strategies. Competing in international markets often requires companies to restructure and/or reduce product costs. Restructuring may result in forming cooperative relationships with other organizations. Cost reduction requirements may encourage the firm to locate low-cost sources of supply. Many producers in Europe, Japan, and the United States establish relationships with companies in newly industrialized countries such as Korea, Taiwan, and Singapore. These collaborative relationships enable companies to reduce plant investment and product costs.

Relationship Management Guidelines

While collaborative relationships are increasingly necessary, the available concepts and methods for managing these partnerships are limited. Contemporary business management skills and experience apply primarily to a single organization rather than offering guidelines for managing interorganizational relationships. However, the experience that companies have gained in managing distribution-channel relationships provides a useful, although incomplete, set of guidelines. To expand the existing base of management knowledge, Collins and Doorley conducted a major global study of strategic partnerships.[53] Companies in North America, Europe, Japan, and Korea participated in the study. The research identified the eight key guidelines for strategic-partnership management shown in Exhibit 7.8. A brief discussion of each guideline follows.

Planning. Comprehensive planning is critical when combining the skills and resources of two independent organizations to achieve one or more strategic objectives. The objectives must be specified, alternative strategies for achieving the objectives evaluated, and decisions made concerning how the relationship will be structured and managed. To determine the feasibility and attractiveness of the proposed relationship, the initiating partner may want to evaluate several potential partners before selecting one.

Trust and Self-Interest. Successful partnerships involve trust and respect between the partners and a willingness to share with each other on various self-interest issues. Confrontational relationships are not likely to be successful. Prior informal experience may be useful in showing whether participants can cooperate on a more formalized strategic project.

Trust is enhanced by meaningful communication between the partners.[54] The process of building trust leads to better communication. Thus, building and sustaining partnership relationships require both communication and the accumulation of trust between the organizations. Trust, in turn, leads to better cooperation among the partners.

Conflicts. Realizing that conflicts will occur is an important aspect of the relationship. The partners must respond when conflicts occur and work proactively to resolve the issues:

> Even firms in successful partnerships would readily acknowledge that disagreements are inevitable. Rather than allowing these conflicts to run their course capriciously, however, adroit partner firms develop mediating mechanisms to diffuse and settle their differences rapidly.[55]

Mechanisms for conflict resolution include training the personnel who are involved in relationships, establishing a council or interorganizational committee, and appointing a mutually acceptable ombudsman to resolve problems.

Leadership Structure. "Failure to create an effective leadership structure can be fatal; it makes coordination difficult and expensive, slows down development, and can seriously erode the decision-making process."[56] Strategic leadership of the partnership can be achieved by

EXHIBIT 7.8
Relationship Management Guidelines

- Planning
- Trust/Self-interest
- Conflicts
- Leadership
- Flexibility
- Technology transfer
- Learning

(1) developing an independent leadership structure, or (2) assigning the responsibility to one of the partners. The former may involve recruiting a project director from outside. The latter option is probably the more feasible of the two in many instances.

Flexibility. Recognizing the interdependence of the partners is essential in building successful relationships. Each organization has different objectives and priorities. "Management must be predominantly by persuasion and influence, with a willingness to adapt as circumstances change."[57] Relationships change over time. The partnership must be flexible in order to adjust to changing conditions and partnership requirements.

Cultural Differences. Strategic relationships among companies from different nations are influenced by cultural differences. Both partners must accept these realities. If partners fail to respond to the cultural variations, the relationship may be adversely affected. These differences may be related to stage of industrial development, political system, religion, economic issues, and corporate culture.

Technology Transfer. When the partnership involves both developing technology and transferring the technology into commercial applications, special attention must be given to implementation. Important issues include organizational problems, identifying a commercial sponsor, appointing a team to achieve the transfer, and building transfer mechanisms into the plan. Planners, marketers, and production people are important participants in the transfer process.

Learning from Partner's Strengths. Finally, the opportunity for an organization to expand its skills and experience should be exploited. Japanese companies are particularly effective in taking advantage of this opportunity. One objective of the partnership should be to learn the skills of the cooperating firm, as well as completing a specific project or program.[58] Surprisingly, U.S. companies often fail to capitalize on this opportunity in their interorganizational relationships. Japanese companies view cooperative ventures as another form of competition where they can transfer acquired skills to other parts of the business.

Partnership Capabilities

In addition to establishing a sound process for designing and managing alliances, it is important to consider what is necessary to build an organizational competence in strategic relationships. The capability to manage effectively through partnerships does not exist in all organizations. Recall the collapse of the BT and AT&T strategic alliance for global telecommunications described earlier. Partnering effectively with other organizations is a key core competence, which may need to be developed. Eli Lilly is recognized as a company that generates value from its alliances, and this company addresses the skills gap by running partnership training classes for its managers and for its partners. Other successful alliance strategies are operated by companies like Hewlett-Packard and Oracle by establishing a dedicated strategic alliance function in the company.[59]

Control and Evaluation[60]

Many conventional approaches to control and evaluation are inappropriate and ineffective in managing interorganizational collaborations. Alliance performance evaluation is a critical success factor, which requires the development and implementation of a formal evaluation process that reflects the unique differences between alliances and more traditional organizational forms. A "balanced scorecard" approach allows evaluation criteria to be specified in financial, customer focus, internal business process, and learning and growth dimensions. The goal is to have measurement metrics with both short- and long-term importance, and to incorporate not only quantitative measures (e.g., sales, growth, costs) but also important qualitative measures that speak to the strength and sustainability of the alliance (e.g., trust, communications flows, conflicts, culture gaps). Importantly, particularly in the early stages of an alliance relationship, qualitative metrics may be the most important predictors of success.

The challenge of developing appropriate ways to assess alliance performance and strength is considerable. It is useful to consider measures and metrics against the following principles:

- Metrics should be comparable across alliances.
- Metrics should be defined and discussed with alliance partners.
- There should be clarity about the implications of alliance performance.
- A process for auditing alliance performance should be implemented.
- Alliance performance should be linked to individual performance review.
- A forum should be created for reviewing and acting on alliance performance data.[61]

Global Relationships among Organizations

Several kinds of organizations compete in global markets. One form is the multinational corporation that may operate in several countries, using a separate organization in each country. The present discussion considers organizational forms that involve relationships with other organizations.

Examples of joint ventures and strategic alliances competing in international markets are discussed throughout the chapter. The use of cooperative agreements by companies in the United States, Japan, and the European Union expanded during the 1990s and 2000s. Global relationships offer significant advantages in gaining market access and leveraging the capabilities of individual firms.

The need to develop more flexible organizational forms for competing in rapidly changing global markets is illustrated by two types of organizations: (1) the network corporation, and (2) the Japanese form of trading company.[62] We also discuss the strategic role of government in global relationships among organizations.

The Network Corporation. This kind of organization consists of a core corporation that coordinates activities and functions between sources of supply and end users of the product. The network, or hollow corporation, has a relatively small work force, relying instead on independent organizations for manufacturing and distribution, often located at several places throughout the world. The organizations are linked by a sophisticated information system. The core company may be vertically integrated at the retail level or, instead, may utilize an independent distribution system.

One organization of the network manages the various partnerships and alliances. This network organization coordinates R&D, finance, global strategy, manufacturing, information systems, marketing, and the management of relationships.[63] The primary organizing concept is a small network control center that uses independent specialists to perform various functions. Thus, the priority is placed on "buying" rather than "producing" and on "partnership" rather than "ownership." The network organization must define the skills and resources that it will use to develop new knowledge and skills. For example, a core competency of the network organization may be designing, managing, and controlling partnerships with customers, suppliers, distributors, and other specialists.

Trading Companies. The use of trading companies dates far back into history in Asia. Since they share certain of the characteristics of network organizations, a look at this organization form provides additional insights into interorganizational relationships. Japanese companies have been very successful in developing and coordinating extensive global operations and information management.[64] These *sogo shosha* concentrated primarily on commodity products, worked most directly with suppliers, and maintained a strong national (rather than global) perspective.

The skills and experience developed by Japanese companies through the *sogo shosha* provide these companies an important competitive advantage in developing other forms of flexible organizations, like the network company discussed above. Japan's needs for natural resources were important influences on the development of trading companies. Today, these giant organizations are active in helping emerging countries develop their markets such as China and Vietnam.

The Strategic Role of Government

While the role of the government in the United States is largely one of facilitating and regulating free enterprise, governments in several other countries play a proactive role with business organizations. For example, the Japanese government encouraged the development of the *sogo shosha*. In considering the role of government, we look at three types of relationships between government and private industry: (1) the single-nation partnership; (2) the multiple-nation partnership; and (3) the government corporation.

Single-Nation Partnership. A country's government may form a partnership with one or a group of companies to develop an industry or achieve some other national objective. Japan has successfully used this method of creating a national competitive advantage in a targeted industry in several instances.[65] For example, the Japanese Ministry of International Trade and Industry (MITI) performs a coordinating role in industry development. MITI resources and personnel establish alliances among companies, provide planning and technical assistance, and sponsor research. Government policy helped Japan build its competitive advantage by encouraging demand in new industries, fostering intraindustry competition, and identifying and encouraging the development of emerging technologies.

Multiple-Nation Partnerships. Regional cooperation among nations may encourage companies to form consortium relationships in selected industries. Recall the Strategy Feature describing the Airbus Industrie consortium. Airbus Industrie members have received massive loans from the governments of the participating companies.[66] Boeing and McDonnell Douglas dominated the industry until government subsidies and multinational sharing of skills and resources enabled Airbus to gain second place in the worldwide market for large commercial aircraft in the early 1990s. Government subsidies for Airbus continue in the 21st century.

International partnerships may create significant market change and shifts in international trading patterns. Consider the relationship between Korea and China. In the 1990s Korea's focus was on the U.S. market and its foreign relations were centered on Washington, DC. Increasingly in the 21st century, Korea looks at China as the regional leader in diplomacy and statecraft. In 2003, South Korean businesses invested more in China—$4.4 billion—than U.S. companies who put $4.2 billion into China. Some 25,000 Korean companies manufacture in China. Companies like Samsung and LG are using China as a major manufacturing base to produce goods more cheaply and increase global market share for their electronics products and appliances. While some fear the effects of the export of Korean jobs and technology to China, the relationship between the two countries has major global implications for the future.[67]

Government Corporations. Nations may operate government-owned corporations, though in recent years a trend toward privatization of these corporations occurred in the United Kingdom, Australia, Mexico, and other countries. Nevertheless, government-supported corporations continue to compete in various global industries, including air transportation, chemicals, computers, and consumer electronics. Not surprisingly, competitors often are critical of government organizations because of their unfair advantage resulting from government financial support. Interestingly, in the European airline industry, the privatized carriers show substantially stronger profit performance compared to state-owned carriers.[68]

Government Legislation. Antitrust laws in the United States prohibit certain kinds of cooperation among direct competitors in an industry. The intense global competition and loss of competitiveness in many industries seem to be changing the traditional view of lone-wolf competition among companies. While the antitrust laws continue to be in place, there may be more flexibility by government agencies in interpreting whether collaboration among firms in an industry is an antitrust issue. For example, the granting of antitrust immunity is essential in certain aspects of the airline alliances described in the Global Feature.

Summary

The competitive realities of surviving and prospering in the complex and rapidly changing business environment encourage teaming up with other companies, so cooperative strategic relationships among independent companies are escalating in importance. The major drivers of interorganizational relationships are value opportunities, environmental turbulence and diversity, and skill and resource gaps. The increasing complexity of technology, financial constraints, the need to access markets, and the availability of information technology all contribute to skill and resource gaps.

In examining the potential for collaborative relationships several criteria need to be evaluated. Important criteria include determining the underlying logic of the proposed relationship, deciding whether partnering is the best way to achieve the strategic objective, assessing how essential is the relationship, determining if good candidates are available, and considering whether collaborative relationships are compatible with the corporate culture.

Relationships between organizations range from transactional exchange to collaborative partnerships. These relationships may be vertical in the value-added chain or horizontal within or across industries. Vertical relationships involve collaboration between suppliers and producers and distribution channel linkages among firms. Horizontal partnerships may include competitors and other industry members. The horizontal or lateral relationships include strategic alliances and joint ventures.

Collaborative relationships are complex, and, not surprisingly, generate conflicts. Many horizontal relationships have not been particularly successful, even though the number of these partnerships is escalating throughout the world. Trust and commitment between the partners are critical to building a successful relationship. Planning helps to improve the chances of success. The capability to manage effectively through partnerships requires distinct skills and new approaches, not available in all organizations.

Several objectives may be achieved through strategic relationships, including gaining access to new technologies, developing new markets, building market position, implementing market segmentation strategies, and pursuing restructuring and cost-reduction strategies. The requirements for successfully managing interorganizational relationships include planning, balancing trust and self-interest, recognizing conflicts, defining leadership structure, achieving flexibility, adjusting to cultural differences, facilitating technology transfers, and learning from partners' strengths. The development of appropriate control and evaluation approaches for these new business forms has become a priority.

Global relationships among organizations may include conventional organizational forms, alliances, joint ventures, network corporations, and trading companies. Governments in several countries play a proactive role in organizational relationships through coordination, financial support, and government corporations.

Internet Applications

A. Visit the Web site *www.alliancestrategy.com* and review the presentations and material available at the site. Summarize what factors should be considered in making alliances between organizations effective.

B. Go to the investor information and company history information on *www.amazon.com*. Identify the evolving network of strategic relationships with customers, suppliers, and collaborators both on the Web and with conventional organizations. Which of these relationships are the most important to Amazon?

Feature Applications

A. Review the airline alliance lists, statistics, and news in the Global Feature in this chapter. Examine the changes happening and predicted in airline alliances by searching "airline alliances" on the Internet. What conclusions can be drawn about the strategic vulnerabilities of alliances?

B. Examine the material presented in the Cross-Functional Feature. How can it be possible for Costco to perform well against competitors when it carries a burden of higher labor costs? Are there issues in this case, which may be worth considering in other situations where a company faces strong low-cost, low-price competition?

Questions for Review and Discussion

1. Discuss the major factors that encourage the formation of strategic partnerships between companies.
2. Compare and contrast vertical and horizontal strategic relationships between independent companies.
3. Discuss the similarities and differences between strategic alliances and joint ventures.
4. A German electronics company and a Japanese electronics company are discussing the formation of a strategic alliance to market the other firm's products in their respective countries. What are the important issues in making this relationship successful for both partners?
5. Establishing successful interorganizational relationships is difficult, according to authorities. Will the success record improve in the future as more companies pursue this strategy?
6. Are vertical relationships more likely to be successful than horizontal relationships? Discuss.
7. Suppose you are seeking a Japanese strategic alliance partner to market your French pharmaceutical products in Asia. What characteristics are important in selecting a good partner?
8. Discuss how alliances may enable foreign companies to reduce the negative reaction that is anticipated if they tried to purchase companies in other countries.
9. Discuss how government may participate in helping domestic companies develop their competitive advantages in an industry such as aerospace products.
10. Identify and discuss important issues in deciding whether to create internal cross-functional relationships.

Notes

1. David W. Cravens, Shannon H. Shipp, and Karen S. Cravens, "Analysis of Cooperative Interorganizational Relationships, Strategic Alliance Formation, and Strategic Alliance Effectiveness," *Journal of Strategic Marketing*, March 1993, 55–70.
2. Information collated from company Web site: *www.radioshack.com*, July 2004.
3. Timothy M. Collins and Thomas L. Doorley, *Teaming Up for the 90s* (Homewood, IL: Business One Irwin, 1991), 5.
4. Arundhati Parmar, "Redecoration: Bombay Style," *Marketing News*, March 15, 2004, 9–10.
5. Carliss Y. Baldwin and Kim B. Clark, "Managing in an Age of Modularity," *Harvard Business Review*, September–October 1997, 84–93 at 84.
6. Ibid.
7. Cliff Edwards, "Will Souping Up TiVo Save It?" *BusinessWeek*, May 17, 2004, 82–83.
8. Ravi S. Achrol, "Evolution of the Marketing Organization: New Forms for the Turbulent Environments," *Journal of Marketing*, October 1991, 78–79.
9. Ibid.
10. Frederick E. Webster Jr., "The Changing Role of Marketing in the Organization," *Journal of Marketing*, October 1992, 1–17.
11. Andy Pasztor and Jeff Cole, "Boeing Plans TV, Web Alliance for Inflight Access," *Wall Street Journal*, April 28, 2000, 5.
12. Gill South, "Upwardly Mobile," *The Business*, September 2, 2000, 26–29.
13. Matthew Schifrin, "Partner or Perish," Forbes, May 21, 2001, 26–28.
14. "Aerospace & Aviation," *BusinessWeek*, July 26, 2004, 46–48.
15. Collins and Doorley, *Teaming Up for the 90s,* 8.
16. Andrew Baxter, "Internet Heralds New Era of Collaboration," *Financial Times*, November 1, 2000, V.
17. The following discussion is based on James C. Anderson and James A. Narus, "Partnering as a Focused Market Strategy," *California Management Review*, Spring 1991, 96–97.
18. Ibid., 100–103.
19. Matthew Schifrin, "Partner or Perish," *Forbes*, May 21, 2001, 26–28.
20. Nick Palmer, "Alliances: Learning to Change," *www.accenture.com*, January 2003.
21. Salvatore Parise and John C. Henderson, "Knowledge Resource Exchange in Strategic Alliances," *IBM Systems Journal* 40, no. 4, 2001, 908–924.
22. Lars Hallen, Jan Johanson, and Nazeem Seyed-Mohamed, "Interfirm Adaptation in Business Relationships," *Journal of Marketing*, April 1991, 30.
23. Anderson and Narus, "Partnering as a Focused Market Strategy."
24. "Concertina'd," *Financial Times*, October 17, 2001, 28.
25. John Hagel, "Leveraged Growth: Expanding Sales without Sacrificing Profits," *Harvard Business Review*, October 2002, 69–77.
26. Bert C. McCammon Jr., "Perspectives for Distribution Programming," in *Vertical Marketing Systems*, ed. Louis P. Bucklin (Glenview, IL: Scott, Foresman, 1970), 43.
27. C. K. Prahalad and Venkat Ramaswamy, *The Future of Competition: Co-Creating Unique Value with Customers* (Cambridge, MA: Harvard Business School Press, 2004).
28. Ibid.
29. Regis McKenna, *Relationship Marketing* (Reading, MA: Addison-Wesley Publishing Company, 1991), 43.
30. Frederick E. Webster Jr., "The Rediscovery of the Marketing Concept," *Business Horizons*, May–June 1988, 37.

31. Noel Capon, *Key Account Management and Planning* (New York: Free Press, 2001).
32. David W. Cravens, "The Changing Role of the Salesforce in the Corporation," *Marketing Management*, Fall 1995, 50.
33. Ibid.
34. Kenichi Ohmae, *The Borderless World* (New York: Harper Business, 1990), 114.
35. Gail Edmondson and Moon Ihlwan, "Driving in Different Directions," *BusinessWeek*, May 3, 2004, 24.
36. Loren Gary, "A Growing Reliance on Alliance," *Harvard Management Update*, April 2004, 3–4.
37. Salvatore Parise and John C. Henderson, "Knowledge Resource Exchange in Strategic Alliances," *IBM Systems Journal* 40 (4), 2001, 908–924.
38. Gary Hamel, Yves L. Doz, and C. K. Prahalad, "Collaborate with Your Competitor—and Win," *Harvard Business Review*, January–February 1989, 135–136.
39. Douglas M. Lambert, Margaret A. Emmelhainz, and John T. Gardner, "So You Think You Want a Partner?" *Marketing Management*, Summer 1996, 25–41.
40. Caroline Daniel, "Psion Falls 19% After Motorola Pulls Out of Project," *Financial Times*, January 30, 2001, 38.
41. Maria Gonzalez, "Strategic Alliances," *Ivey Business Journal*, September/October 2001, 47–51.
42. Collins and Doorley, *Teaming Up for the 90s*, 205–209.
43. Matthew Schifrin, "Partner or Perish," *Forbes*, May 21, 2001, 26–28.
44. Margaret Hart and Stephen J. Garone, *Making International Strategic Alliances Work*, R-1086 (New York: The Conference Board Inc.,1994), 19.
45. *BusinessWeek E.Biz*, December 18, 1999.
46. Leonard L. Berry, *On Great Service* (New York: Free Press, 1995), 139–142.
47. The following discussion is based on Collins and Doorley, *Teaming Up for the 90s*, Chapter 3.
48. Ibid., 30.
49. P. Zagnoli and C. Cardini, "Patterns of International R&R Cooperation for New Product Development: The Olivetti Multimedia Product," *R&D Management*, 24, no. 1, 1994, 3–15.
50. General Electric Company, *Operating Objectives to Meet the Challenges of the 90s* (Fairfield, CT: General Electric Company), March 14, 1988.
51. George S. Day, *Market Driven Strategy* (New York: The Free Press, 1990), 275–276.
52. William B. Scott, "Global Alliances Spur Development of Niche Market Semiconductors," *Aviation Week and Space Technology*, September 9, 1991, 70–71.
53. The following discussion is drawn from Collins and Doorley, *Teaming Up for the 90s*, Chapter 5.
54. James C. Anderson and James A. Narus, "A Model of Distributor Firm and Manufacturer Firm Working Partnerships," *Journal of Marketing*, January 1990, 45.
55. Ibid., 56.
56. Collins and Doorley, *Teaming Up for the 90s*, 108.
57. Ibid., 110.
58. Bernard Wysocki, Jr., "Global Reach," *The Wall Street Journal*, March 26, 1990, A1 and A5.
59. Jeffrey H. Dyer, Prashant Kale, and Harbir Singh, "How to Make Strategic Alliances Work," *Sloan Management Review*, Summer 2001, 37–43.
60. This discussion is based on: Karen Cravens, Nigel Piercy, and David Cravens, "Assessing the Performance of Strategic Alliances," *European Management Journal* 18, no. 5, 2000, 529–541.
61. Jonathan Hughes, *Implementing Alliance Metrics: Six Basic Principles*, Vantage Partners' White Paper, *www.vantagepartners.com/publications*, 2002.
62. Achrol, "Evolution of the Marketing Organization," 84–85; and Webster, "The Changing Role of Marketing," 8–9.
63. Webster, "The Changing Role of Marketing," 8–9.
64. Achrol, "Evolution of the Marketing Organization," 84.
65. Michael E. Porter, *The Competitive Advantage of Nations* (New York: The Free Press, 1990), 414–416.
66. David W. Cravens, H. Kirk Downey, and Paul Lauritano, "Global Competition in the Commercial Aircraft Industry: Positioning for Advantage by the Triad Nations," *Columbia Journal of World Business*, Winter 1992, 46–58.
67. Moon Ihlwan and Dexter Roberts, "Korea's China Play," *BusinessWeek*, March 29, 2004, 48–52.
68. Brian Coleman, "Among European Airlines, the Privatized Soar to the Top," *The Wall Street Journal*, July 19, 1995, B4.

Appendix **7A**

Customer Relationship Management (CRM)

Customer Relationship Management (CRM) systems have attracted wide attention in companies because of several benefits they offer. There are a number of major benefits attainable in improving the service received by customers but most particularly in building and leveraging powerful and insightful databases of customer information. However, fully realizing those benefits has proved difficult for many companies. CRM developments have paralleled the growth in e-business and the two areas have several connections, leading to the emergence of e-CRM to describe Internet-based initiatives. It is important that CRM strategy should be developed by marketing executives with the other business functions involved in CRM.

CRM offers sellers the opportunity to gather customer information rapidly, to identify the most valuable customers over a time period, and to increase customer loyalty by providing customized products and services. It may also facilitate cross-selling by attracting loyal customers to additional products and services, and make it easier to capture similar customers in the future.

This has been described as "tying in an asset," when the asset is the customer, and CRM supports a customer-responsive strategy, which gains competitive advantage when it:

- Delivers superior customer value by personalizing the interaction between the customer and the company.
- Demonstrates the company's trustworthiness and reliability to the customer.
- Tightens connections with the customer.
- Achieves the coordination of complex organizational capabilities around the customer.[1]

CRM underpins a focus on customer loyalty and retention, with a goal of winning a large share of the total lifetime value of each profitable customer.

The Meaning of Customer Relationship Management

The term CRM is somewhat open-ended because it means very different things in different circumstances. This reflects the rapid evolution and development of this approach to managing customer relationships. We identify several levels of CRM below. The term is often used to embrace anything from automated customer contact systems to increase salesforce productivity, to customer service centers and automated call centers, to enterprisewide systems to break down departmental barriers and integrate information about customers into a single access point.

To some, CRM refers to little more than building relationships with customers to match the product and service offer better with customer needs. Others see CRM as concerned with developing a unified and cohesive view of the customer, however the customer chooses to communicate with the organization (in person, by mail, Internet, or telephone), and emphasizing enhanced customer service and the use of call centers to provide consistency in how the company interacts with customers. To yet others, CRM focuses on the creation and use of a customer database to support decision makers.

Importantly, Peppers and Rogers turn our attention from the technology and hardware of CRM to its strategic importance when they define CRM as "making managerial decisions with the end goal of increasing the value of the customer base through better relationships with customers, usually on an individual basis."[2] The emphasis on strategy built around profitable customers as the primary concern of CRM is emphasized also by Bain & Co. In their view "CRM aligns business processes with customer strategies to build customer loyalty and increase profits over time."[3] Another useful viewpoint suggests that CRM consists of three main elements:

- Identifying, satisfying, retaining, and maximizing the value of a firm's best customers.
- Wrapping the firm around the customer to ensure that each contact with the customer is appropriate and based upon extensive knowledge of both the customer's needs and profitability.
- Creating a full picture of the customer.[4]

[1] George Day, "Tying in an Asset," in *Understanding CRM* (London: Financial Times, 2000).

[2] Don Peppers and Martha Rogers, *Managing Customer Relationships* (Hobroken, NJ: Wiley, 2004).

[3] Darrell K. Rigby, Frederick F. Reichheld, and Phil Schefter, "Avoid the Four Perils of CRM," *Harvard Business Review*, February 2002, 101–109.

[4] Lynette Ryals, Simon D. Knox, and Stan Maklan, *Customer Relationship Management: The Business Case for CRM. Financial Times Report* (London: Prentice Hall, 2000).

Levels of CRM

One way of categorizing CRM initiatives is to distinguish between operational, analytical, and strategic CRM levels, as shown in Exhibit 7A.1. All levels of CRM have important but different implications for strategic marketing.

EXHIBIT 7A.1
Levels of CRM

Source: Adapted from Charlotte Mason, "Perspectives on Teaching Analytically Oriented CRM," presentation at AMA CRM Faculty Consortium, 2004.

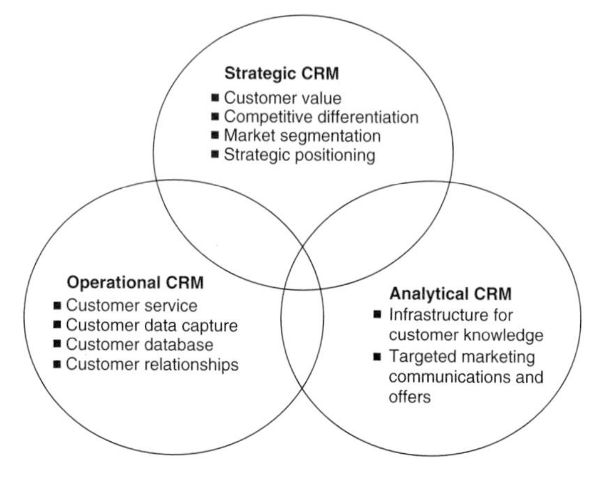

Operational CRM

A key element of CRM is to improve and make consistent the customer's service experience. The goal of CRM is to use every available source of information to build a detailed picture of each individual customer. It aims to capture information from every contact the customer has with any part of the organization, and to ensure it is available whenever the customer next interacts with the company.

One aim is to avoid inefficiencies for the customer—receiving mailshots from a bank offering a mortgage to an existing mortgage customer; waiting on the telephone to the utility company while files are retrieved; providing name and address details every time a book is purchased by mail order or on an Internet site. The integration of customer information through the CRM system should allow more accurate mailshots; a call center operative or help desk engineer with instant access to up-to-date and complete customer information; and Web sites that recognize a returning customer and remember dispatch and payment requirements.

The benefits to the customer from CRM initiatives may also include: improved response times when they request information; products and services that are better adapted to their requirements; immediate access to order status and history information; and more responsive technical support.

For example, the France-based hotel group Accor links CRM data to guest survey information in its U.S. Sofitel and Novatel hotels, to anticipate the preferences of frequent users. The VP for sales and marketing for Accor North America notes "It takes us back to the time when there were small inns and the owner knew every customer and treated them as an individual. It should help streamline check-in and accommodate preferences for guests who, for example, request the same room every time. The group will be able to market with a microscope instead of a telescope."[5]

[5] Marian Edmunds, "Your Wish Is on My Database," *Financial Times*, February 28, 2000, 16.

Analytical CRM

In addition to enhancing customer service efficiency and impacting on the quality of customer relationships, the integration and pooling of individual customer information by CRM systems also creates a powerful resource for analysis. Knowledge about which products and services a specific customer buys, through which channels, and at what times, offers unprecedented opportunities for more precise direct marketing offers and for focusing on the best prospects in a market, in terms of their profitability and growth potential for the seller. For example, bookseller Borders uses its customer database to send e-mails tailored to the customer's reading interests to alert them to upcoming releases.

The database created through CRM technology should contain information about the following:

- *Transactions*—this should include a complete purchase history for each customer with accompanying details (date, price paid, products purchased).
- *Customer Contacts*—with multiple channels of distribution and communication the database should record all customer contacts with the company and its distributors, including sales calls, service requests, complaints, inquiries, and loyalty program participation.
- *Descriptive Information*—for each individual customer, relevant descriptive data that provide the basis for market segmentation and targeted marketing communications.

- *Response to Marketing Stimuli*—whether the customer responded to specific advertising, a price offer, a direct marketing initiative, or a sales call, or any other direct contact.[6]

Increasingly sophisticated software is available to undertake data mining and to model data from the CRM database.

For example, while traditional approaches to market segmentation have identified groups of customers by their purchase behavior or descriptive data, CRM offers the opportunity to examine individual customers or narrowly defined groups, and to calculate what each offers the company in profits. The concept of *customer lifetime value* (CLV) is illustrative. CLV calculates past profit produced by the customer for the firm—the sum of all the margins of all the products purchased over time, less the cost of reaching that customer. To this is added forecasts of margins on future purchases (under different assumptions for different customers), discounted back to their present value (because profit we expect in five years' time is worth less to us than profit we make this year). The CLV calculation is a powerful tool for focusing marketing and promotional efforts where they will be most productive. Other novel data analyses facilitated by CRM include market basket analysis—that is, examining what products are purchased together by different customers, and "click analysis" based on Web site visits and purchases to better understand online customer behavior.[7]

Strategic CRM

Importantly, the creation of CRM information resources and the adoption of appropriate software tools[8] to make sense of the information is building an important source of competitive advantage for many companies that goes beyond the confines of call centers and targeted communications.

The strategic use of CRM resources reflects the shift in focus by marketing executives to the customer who delivers long-term profits, that is, an emphasis on customer retention rather than acquisition. Well-known metrics suggest that as little as a 5 percent increase in customer retention can have an impact as high as 95 percent on the net present value delivered by the customer.[9] Other studies by McKinsey find that repeat customers generate over twice as much gross income as new customers.[10] CRM makes it much easier for executives to focus strategy on customer profitability and the gains from reducing customer "churn."

Interestingly, as CRM evolves and offers executives deeper insights into their customer base, the new information may challenge strategic assumptions in important ways. For example, the points made above suggest a powerful linkage between enhanced customer loyalty and higher customer profitability. However, companies are discovering through CRM database analysis that this is not always true. Some groups of customers may not justify the costs required to retain them, because the real fit between their needs and the company's products is weak. Just because a group of customers was profitable in the past, it may be dangerous to assume this will always be true. For example, many nonloyal customers are initially profitable, causing the company to chase them for further profits—but once these customers have ceased buying, they become increasingly unprofitable if the company continues to invest in them. CRM data provide executives with a unique basis to address such issues as loyalty and profitability on the basis of fact instead of assumption, and to focus on individual customers, not groups containing many dissimilar buyers.[11] We say more about the strategic benefits of CRM below.

In short, while the "front-end" of CRM systems is about customer service and building stronger customer relationships, the analytical level provides a "back-end" or infrastructure for decision support, which links to the strategic level of CRM.

Requirements for Effective CRM Implementation

Corporate expenditures on CRM technology are running at very high levels across the world. Estimated expenditures rose from $20 billion in 2000 to $46 billion in 2003, with signs of continued growth. Nonetheless, the evidence of the performance of CRM systems has been disappointing for many companies. The Gartner Group concluded in 2002 that 55 percent of all CRM projects

[6] Russell S. Winer, "A Framework for Customer Relationship Management," *California Management Review* 43, no. 4, Summer 2001, 89–105.

[7] Ibid.

[8] For more information on the rapid development of software tools for data mining and interpretation, see the Useful Web sites for Additional CRM Material, listed at the end of the Appendix.

[9] Frederick F. Reichheld, *The Loyalty Effect* (Cambridge, MA: Harvard Business School Press, 1996).

[10] Russell S. Winer, op. cit.

[11] Werner Reinartz and V. Kumar, "The Mismanagement of Customer Loyalty," *Harvard Business Review*, July 2002, 86–94.

do not produce results, and the Bain & Co. 2001 survey of management tools ranked CRM in the bottom three for satisfaction—indeed, one in five users in the Bain survey reported their CRM initiatives had not only failed to deliver profitable growth, but had also damaged long-term customer relationships.[12]

One report suggests that the major components of the successful implementation of CRM are:

- A front office that integrates sales, marketing, and service functions across all media (call centers, people, retail outlets, Internet).
- A data warehouse that stores customer information and the appropriate analytical tools with which to analyze that data and learn about customer behavior.
- Business rules developed from the data analysis to ensure the front office benefits from the firm's learning about its customers.
- Measures of performance that enable customer relationships to continually improve.
- Integration into the firm's operational and support (or "back office") systems, ensuring the front office's promises are delivered.[13]

Indeed, there have been several suggestions that high failure rates associated with CRM are caused by managers underestimating the real organizational changes required for effective implementation that unlocks the benefits of CRM. While the front-end of CRM systems is concerned with building databases integrating customer data, providing better customer service, and establishing systems like automated call centers for enhanced responsiveness, achieving the full potential of CRM requires change in companywide processes, organization structure, and corporate culture.

Bain & Co. research suggests that there are four significant pitfalls to avoid in CRM initiatives:

1. Implementing CRM before creating a customer strategy—success relies on making strategic customer and positioning choices, and this outweighs the importance of the computer systems, software, call centers, and other technologies.
2. Putting CRM in place before changing the organization to match—CRM affects more than customer-facing processes, it impacts on internal structures and systems that may have to change.
3. Assuming that more CRM technology is necessarily better, rather than matching the technology to the customer strategy.
4. Investing in building relationships with disinterested customers, instead of those who value them.[14]

CRM and Strategic Marketing

From the perspective of strategic marketing, there are several reasons why CRM is important and why there should be marketing involvement in decisions about CRM.

Implementation

It is important that the adoption and implementation of CRM should be seen as more than technology focused on efficiency. There are significant implications for the strategic positioning of a company and its customer relationships, where the voice of marketing should be heard.

Customer Value

Operationally it is important not to assume that the drivers of value for all customers are the same, or that CRM is the key to all important customer relationships. For example, there are signs that many consumers are weary with call centers and automated responses.

Performance Metrics

The availability of CRM data provide the opportunity to update the measures used by managers to assess the success of products and services in the marketplace. Traditional financial and market-based indicators like sales, profitability, and market share will continue to be important. However, CRM allows the development of measures that are customer-centric and more insightful into marketing strategy effectiveness. CRM-based measures of performance (both online and offline) may include: customer acquisition costs; conversion rates (from lookers to buyers); retention/churn rates; same customer sales rates; loyalty measures; and customer "share of wallet."[15]

Short-Term versus Long-Term Value

It is important that when decisions are made about a company's customer priorities, for example, on the basis of historical customer profitability, that long-term issues should be considered. Customers who are currently unprofitable may be attractive long-term prospects for

[12] Rigby et al., op. cit.

[13] Simon Knox, Stan Maklan, Adrian Payne, Joe Peppard, and Lynette Ryals, *Customer Relationship Management: Perspectives from the Marketplace*, Oxford: Butterworth-Heinemann, 2003.

[14] Rigby et al., op. cit.

[15] Russell S. Winer, op. cit.

suppliers who maintain loyalty through the hard times until the customers become profitable, and customers who are currently profitable may not be the best prospects for the future. The simple availability of CRM information should not be allowed to override strategic choices of customers to be retained where a long-term relationship may be highly attractive. This is why the active participation of marketing executives in CRM initiatives remains a priority. Customer lifetime value is an attractive measure to focus on long-term customer attractiveness. For example, in many countries retail banks aggressively recruit young people as customers when they are undergraduate and graduate students (and likely to be unprofitable to the bank) with the goal of retaining the customer with a better than average chance of becoming a high-net-worth individual (and offering profitable opportunities to the bank).

Competitive Differentiation

If some customers are unprofitable, then rather than "firing" the customer, the competitive issue may be how to change the route to market to make then profitable to the company. For example, when British Airways made the decision to focus only on its profitable business-class passengers at the expense of economy travelers, Virgin Airways gained the economy-class passengers at BA's cost. CRM data may provide one of the most powerful tools for identifying different customers on the basis of their behavior and other characteristics, to locate those whose needs have good fit with a company's capabilities. As one-to-one marketing expert Don Peppers has noted: "For every credit card company that wants to concentrate on higher income customers, there's another credit card company that wants to concentrate on lower income customers, and they do it by streamlining their service and making it more cost-efficient."[16] It is important that decisions about customer choices should reflect strategic priorities.

Lack of Competitive Advantage

Investment in CRM to build competitive advantage may be an illusion if a company focuses only on automated call centers and customer complaint systems. The level of expenditure on CRM suggests that most competitors in most markets will have similar resources, and may be quicker to get to the real competitive strengths in aligning resources and capabilities around customers. Competitive advantage is likely to require more than just investment in CRM technology, particularly if it is poorly implemented. Similar CRM technology is available to most companies in most markets, and the issue for competitive advantage enhancement is not having the technology but how it is used.

Information-Based Competitive Advantage

One of the most important aspects of CRM from a strategic marketing perspective is the creation of a major new source of customer knowledge. Used appropriately the databases and information stores created through CRM technology may be one of the most valuable resources in the company for uncovering new value-creating opportunities for customers and for developing market understanding and insights ahead of the competition. As a further resource for developing and exploiting market sensing capabilities, CRM systems have enormous potential, which some organizations are now beginning to exploit to build competitive advantage.

Useful Web Sites for Additional CRM Material

www.dbmarketing.com
The Web site of the Database Marketing Institute, with a number of articles and speeches concerning recent developments in database marketing, available to be downloaded.

www.thearling.com
A site with extensive information about developments in data mining, and articles and papers on this topic for download.

www.1to1.com
The Web site of the Peppers & Rogers Group features the work and consultancy of Don Peppers and Martha Rogers. White Papers are available for download. A free subscription to the inside 1to1 newsletter is also available.

www.teradata.com
The Web site of the Teradata Division of NCR. It contains an interesting technical library on data warehousing and data mining as well as customer case studies.

[16] Richard Tomkins, "Goodbye to Small Spenders," *Financial Times*, February 4, 2000, 13.

Chapter 8

Planning for New Products

Innovation is essential to all organizations' continuing growth and performance in the global marketplace. Innovation takes many forms, including new goods and services, organizational processes, and business designs. Importantly, even when the critical role of innovation is recognized by managers, deciding which innovation opportunities to pursue is a demanding challenge. Organizations must develop a culture of innovation and build effective processes to identify innovation opportunities and transform ideas into new-product successes.

The economic pressures and market turbulence that impacted companies in a wide range of industries during the early years of the 21st century shifted many executives' strategic priorities away from the development of cutting-edge new products.[1] The innovation processes of companies like Boeing, Kodak, Motorola, and 3M were not meeting the challenges of aggressive development of cutting-edge new products. Instead, short-term, bottom-line performance was the center of attention. These short-term cost initiatives may sometimes be necessary, but it is essential to sustain long-term innovation strategies. Innovation creates competitive advantage and value for customers and the organization.

Breakthrough innovations provide vital avenues for company growth. Consider, for example, light-emitting diodes (LEDs). "LEDs promise to replace today's glass encased incandescent and fluorescent light bulbs: LED lights use far less electricity than an average bulb, and they shine for a far longer time before burning out."[2] The market potential is exciting but there are many challenges in developing LEDs for broad-based lighting applications. Several companies are pursuing initiatives to move LED technology into the $40 billion lighting market.[3] The players include General Electric, Philips, and other electronic firms. Two major hurdles are cost of the diode and the quality of the light. The breakthrough is at least a few years away and probably longer.

In this chapter we consider the planning of new products, beginning with a discussion of customer needs analysis. Next, we discuss the steps in new-product planning, including generating ideas, screening and evaluating the ideas, business analysis, product development and testing, designing the market entry strategy, market testing, and new-product introduction. The chapter concludes with a discussion of variations in the generic new-product planning process.

New-Product Planning as a Customer-Driven Process

New-product opportunities that offer superior value to customers range from totally new products to improvements in existing products. First, we consider the different types of new products. Next, the importance of finding customer value opportunities is discussed. Finally, important drivers of successful innovations are examined.

Innovation Feature Microsoft and Intel Moving In on PC Makers Turf

For years, personal computer makers have cheered whenever their biggest suppliers, Intel Corp. and Microsoft Corp., have hawked new processors or software at industry trade shows. But they aren't likely to coo about what those companies will introduce at this year's Consumer Electronics Show on January 5 and 6.

Rather than unveil new goodies for PCs, the two will preview computerlike appliances that could siphon consumer dollars spent on PCs. The moves could also cut off promising new markets for PC makers. Intel will reveal a digital music player, while Microsoft will show off its much anticipated Xbox game console.

The introductions could kick off a more troubled era between PC makers and the chip and software kingpins. Although the Wintel duo has dabbled in selling hardware such as mice and home-networking gear to consumers, this is the first time it will go head-to-head with PC makers in markets with sizable potential. "You're going to step on a lot of toes when you start competing for the same consumer dollars as your customers," observes IDC analyst Bob O'Donnell. The assault couldn't come at a worse time for PC makers. Partly because of market saturation, computer sales are expected to slow dramatically in 2001. Furthermore, electronic appliance makers such as Palm Inc. and Nintendo have been busy picking off niche PC functions like personal organizers, photography, music players, and games. Analysts now expect sales of non-PC devices to grow at least 40 percent through 2004, versus mid-teen growth for PCs.

Of course, it's far from certain whether Microsoft and Intel will be successful. Neither has much experience competing against long-established electronics suppliers such as Sony and Panasonic, much less Compaq and Gateway. But both have spent billions on brand recognition, and analysts say their new offerings are technologically superior.

Source: *BusinessWeek*, January 15, 2001, 41.

Types of New Products

New goods and services introductions can be classified according to (1) newness to the market and (2) the extent of customer value created, resulting in the following types of new products:[4]

- *Transformational Innovation:* Products that are radically new and the value created is substantial. Examples include CNN News Channel, Automatic Teller Machines (ATMs), and digital cameras.
- *Substantial Innovation:* Products that are significantly new and create important value for customers. Examples include Kimberly-Clark Huggies/Nappies and Diet Coke.
- *Incremental Innovations:* New products that provide improved performance or greater perceived value (or lower cost). An example is a new Coca-Cola flavor.

A company's new-product initiatives may include innovation in one or more of the three categories. The reality is that many new products are extensions of existing product lines and incremental improvements of existing products rather than totally new products. These extensions and improvements account for as much as 70 to 80 percent of all innovations. The planning process we discuss in this chapter applies to any of the three categories and is used in planning new services as well as tangible products. The Innovation Feature describes some interesting innovation initiatives by Intel and Microsoft that extend outside their core business focus but leverage their brand recognition and proprietary technologies. We discuss brand leveraging in Chapter 9.

New-product initiatives are guided by customer needs analysis. Even transformational product ideas should have some relationship to needs that are not being met by existing products. However, as we discuss shortly, potential customers may not always be good sounding boards for radically new innovations. Importantly, these innovations sometimes have a disruptive impact on existing products.

EXHIBIT 8.1
Finding New-Product Opportunities

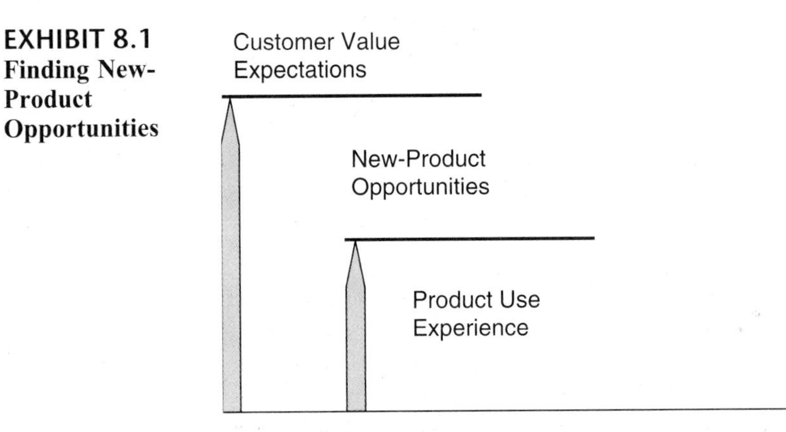

Finding Customer Value Opportunities

Customer needs yield important information for determining where value opportunities exist in developing new products. Market segment identification and analysis help identify which segments offer new-product opportunities to the organization. Extensive study of existing and potential customers and the competition are vital in guiding effective new-product planning.

We know that customer value is the combination of benefits provided by a product minus all of the costs incurred by the buyer (Chapter 1). Customer satisfaction indicates how well the product use experience compares to the value expected by the buyer. The closer the match between expectations and the use experience, the better the resulting value.

Customer Value. The objective of customer value analysis is to identify needs for (1) new products, (2) improvements in existing products, (3) improvements in the processes that produce the products, and (4) improvements in supporting services. The intent is to find gaps (opportunities) between buyers' expectations and the extent to which they are being met (Exhibit 8.1). Everyone in the organization needs to be involved in this process. This market-driven approach to product planning helps to avoid a mismatch between technologies and customer needs.

A difference between expectations and use experience may offer a new-product opportunity. For example, an alert U.S. Surgical Corporation (USS) salesperson saw an opportunity to satisfy a surgical need that was not being met with existing products. USS's products include staplers for skin closure and other surgical applications. The close working relationship of USS sales representatives with surgeons in operating rooms gives USS a critical competitive advantage.[5] The salesperson identified the new-product opportunity by observing surgeons' early use of self-developed instruments to perform experiments in laparoscopy. Using this procedure, the surgeon inserts a tiny TV camera into the body with very thin surgical instruments. USS responded quickly to this need by designing and introducing a laparoscopic stapler. The product is used in gall bladder removal and other internal surgical applications.

Buyers' satisfaction with existing products and brands is evaluated by considering various product/service attributes that identify buyers' preferences and comparisons of competing brands. The comparisons may include preference mapping and other analyses that we discussed in earlier chapters. The USS surgical product idea is an example of "lead" customer analysis. Lead customers are those that are the first to anticipate new product trends. The objective of the various preference analysis techniques is to identify the important preferences for the buyers in specific market segments.

Matching Capabilities to Value Opportunities. Each value opportunity should be considered in terms of whether the organization has the capabilities to deliver superior customer value. Organizations will normally have the capabilities needed for product line extensions and incremental improvements. Developing products for a new product category requires realistic assessment of the organization's capabilities concerning the new category. Partnering with a company that has the needed capabilities is an option concerning the addition of a new product category. For example, Healthy Choice (ConAgra) Foods Inc. partnered with Kellogg to offer a new line of breakfast cereals.

Transformational Innovations. Customers may not be good guides to totally new product ideas that may be called radical or breakthrough innovations since they create new families of products and businesses.[6] When such ideas are under consideration, potential customers may not understand how the new product will replace an existing product. The problem is that customers may not anticipate a preference for a revolutionary new product.[7] For example, initial response from potential users of optical fibers, VCRs, Federal Express, and CNN was not encouraging. In these situations, management must form a vision about the innovation and be willing to make the commitment to develop the technology as Corning Inc. did with optical fiber technology. The risk, of course, is that management's vision may be faulty.

A study of successful U.S. firms competing against Japanese companies in electronics-related markets points to the critical role of both radical innovations and incremental product improvements:

> These businesses built and renewed, and continue to build and renew, their competitive advantage through radical and generational innovations. They sustained that advantage over time through incremental product line improvements and extensions—but it is on the basis of the riskier, failure-laden, expensive and time-consuming efforts to pioneer new businesses and new generations of technology that their competitive advantage was and still is established.[8]

Incremental product improvements are guided by analyzing customer value opportunities (Exhibit 8.1), whereas conventional approaches to finding new-product opportunities are not very useful in evaluating potential transformational innovations:

> The familiar admonition to be customer-driven is of little value when it is not at all clear who the customer is—when the market has never experienced the features created by the new technology. Likewise, analytic methods for evaluating new product opportunities (e.g., discounted cash flow and market diffusion analyses) appear to be much more appropriate for incremental than for discontinuous innovation.[9]

Radical innovations have the potential of disrupting existing (sustaining) technologies, and creating negative impacts on the leading firms that pursue innovation strategies using existing technologies.[10] Examples of disruptive innovations include Amazon.com, JetBlue (airline), salesforce.com, and steel minimills. LED lighting is a potential disruptive threat to incandescent and fluorescent light bulbs. These disruptive technologies are often not considered to be threats by firms pursuing sustaining technologies. Identifying threats and developing viable strategies for disruptive technologies is a major management challenge. Clayton Christensen and Michael E. Raynor in *The Innovators Solution* offer a compelling analysis of these threats and provide important guidelines for managing disruptive innovations.[11] The challenge for companies confronted with potential disruptive opportunities and threats is recognizing that product planning processes differ for sustaining and disruptive innovations. Executives must manage both processes. It may be necessary to position the disruptive technology in a separate organization independent from the core organization.

To avoid missing out on new technologies, IBM has changed the way it identifies and pursues promising new ideas. Because new ideas fall between organizational boundaries and may conflict with existing business units, the ideas are managed separately and differently:

- *Horizon One Businesses* are traditional, mature businesses such as mainframe computers.
- *Horizon Two Businesses* are the current growth businesses.

EXHIBIT 8.2
Characteristics of Successful Innovators

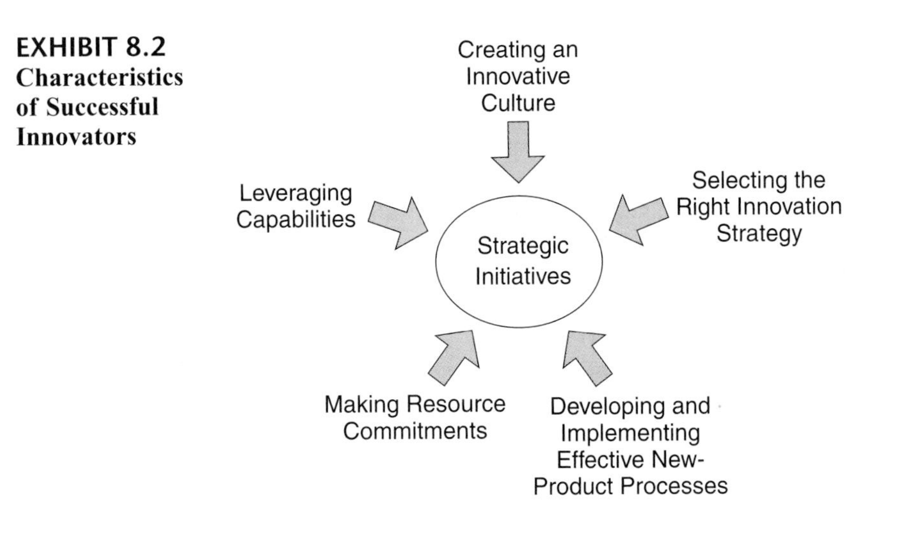

- *Horizon Three Businesses* are new, young businesses that are put in separate organizational units, are insulated from traditional management methods and performance yardsticks, and receive personal sponsorship from senior managers to protect them from other interests in the company.[12]

Unless these initiatives are taken, the sustaining technology is likely to dominate innovation activities. A good market/technology match is important in being successful with radical technologies. Priority should be given to market niches that the traditional technology does not serve well. Christensen and Raynor also propose that products from disruptive technologies that are not currently valued by customers may match future value requirements very well. The eventual strong preference for digital photography displayed by buyers is illustrative.

The new-product planning process we discuss in this chapter is appropriate for planning incremental product improvements, and it can also be used in radical innovation, as a separate organizational initiative. We discuss variations to the generic new-product planning process at the end of the chapter.

Characteristics of Successful Innovators

Certain companies seem to consistently excel over others in developing successful new products. Successful innovators often display similar characteristics. Importantly, the strategic initiatives shown in Exhibit 8.2 have consistently been good predictors of successful innovation based on research studies, management judgment and experience, and analysis of specific companies' innovation experience. These initiatives refer to the organization as an innovator rather than specific new-product projects, which may be impacted by situation specific factors.

Creating an innovative culture is essential to generating successful new products. Research findings constantly point to the importance of an innovative organizational climate and culture.[13] This requires positioning innovation as a distinct organizational priority, and communicating the importance of innovation to all employees. Moreover, deciding the right innovation strategy involves defining the product, market, and technology scope of the organization. Corporate purpose and scope set important guidelines and boundaries for new-product planning. High-quality new-product planning processes are essential to implement the organization's innovation strategy. Importantly, achieving successful new-product outcomes requires allocating adequate resources to new-product initiatives. Finally, the extent to which the organization can leverage its capabilities into promising new-product and market opportunities enhances innovation performance (if the leveraging efforts are successful). Our earlier Innovation Feature discussion of the Intel and Microsoft consumer products is an example of leveraging.

Steps in New-Product Planning

A new product does not have to be a high-technology breakthrough to be successful, but it must deliver superior customer value. Post-it Notes have been a big winner for 3M Company.[14] We know that the notepaper pads come in various sizes and each page has a thin strip of adhesive on the back which can be attached to reports, telephones, walls, and other places. The idea came from a 3M researcher. He had used slips of paper to mark songs in his hymnbook, but the paper kept falling out. To eliminate the problem, the employee applied an adhesive that had been developed in 3M's research laboratory that failed to provide the adhesive strength needed in the original use situation. The adhesive worked fine for marking songs in the book. Interestingly, office-supply vendors initially saw no market for the sticky-back notepaper. The 3M Company employed extensive sampling to show the value of the product. Over the signature of the CEO's administrative assistant, samples were sent to executive assistants at all *Fortune* 500 companies. After using the supply of samples, the executive assistants wanted more. Today, Post-it-Notes are indispensable in both offices and homes.

Creating an innovative culture is an important foundation for innovation (Exhibit 8.2). It is also necessary to set some boundaries concerning the types of new products to be considered for possible development. We examine these issues followed by a discussion of the steps in the new-product planning process.

Developing a Culture and Strategy for Innovation

Open communications throughout the organization and high levels of employee involvement and interest are characteristic of innovative cultures. Recognizing the importance of developing a culture and innovation strategy, Intel's CEO has pursued several actions intended to encourage innovation initiatives beyond the core chip business. Management also changed the structure of the organization to make it more flexible to allow new ideas to thrive (see earlier Innovation Feature). Evidence of innovative cultures may be found in corporate mission statements, advertising messages, presentations by top executives, and case studies in business publications.

Creating (or strengthening) an innovation culture can be encouraged by several interrelated management initiatives:[15]

- Plan and implement a two-day innovation workshop of top executives to develop an innovation plan. This would involve use of cross-functional teams, resource allocations, rewards, and innovation performance metrics.
- Develop an innovation declaration highlighting the company's objectives and senior management's roles and responsibilities.
- Conduct innovation training programs for employees and managers to encourage commitment and involvement.
- Communicate the priority of innovation via articles, newsletters, and presentations to employees, shareholders, and customers.
- Schedule innovation speakers on a regular basis to expose employees to innovation authorities.

The organization's innovation strategy spells out management's choice of the organization's most promising opportunities for new products. This strategy needs to be formulated by taking into account the organization's distinctive capabilities, relevant technologies, and the market opportunities that provide a good customer value match with the organization's capabilities. A major benchmarking study of 161 business units from a broad range of industries in the United States, Germany, Denmark, and Canada indicates that a carefully formulated and communicated new-product innovation strategy is one of three cornerstones of superior new-product performance.[16] A successful new-product strategy includes:

1. Setting specific, written new-product objectives (sales, profit contribution, market, share, etc.).
2. Communicating across the organization the role of new products in contributing to the goals of the business.
3. Defining the areas of strategic focus for the corporation in terms of product scope, markets, and technologies.
4. Including longer-term, transformational projects in the portfolio along with incremental projects.

Implementing each of these new-product strategy guidelines should assist management in selecting the right innovation strategy.

In 2004 Philips, Europe's consumer-electronics giant, launched new innovation strategy guidelines:[17]

- All products should conform to the philosophy "designed around you"—the consumer.
- Products should be easy to use but not through low technology.
- Products should be advanced.

The strategy is intended to guide a transformation process for Philips, which is clearly focused on the customer (Exhibit 8.1). Interaction across business units is encouraged.

Developing Effective New-Product Planning Processes

Creating the right culture and selecting the right innovation strategy are essential but not sufficient initiatives in successful innovation (Exhibit 8.2). Innovation must be achieved through the processes put in place by the organization. The previously discussed benchmarking study found that having a high-quality new-product process in place is the most important cornerstone of new-product planning performance, ahead of both selecting the right innovation strategy and committing necessary resources to new-product development.

Developing successful new products requires systematic planning to coordinate the many decisions, activities, and functions necessary to move the new-product idea to commercial success. A generic planning process can be used in planning a wide range of new products. There may be necessary modifications in the process in certain situations and these issues are discussed in the last section of the chapter. The major stages in the planning process are shown in Exhibit 8.3. We examine each process stage to see what is involved, how the stages depend on each other, and why cross-functional coordination of new-product planning is very important.

EXHIBIT 8.3
New-Product Planning Process

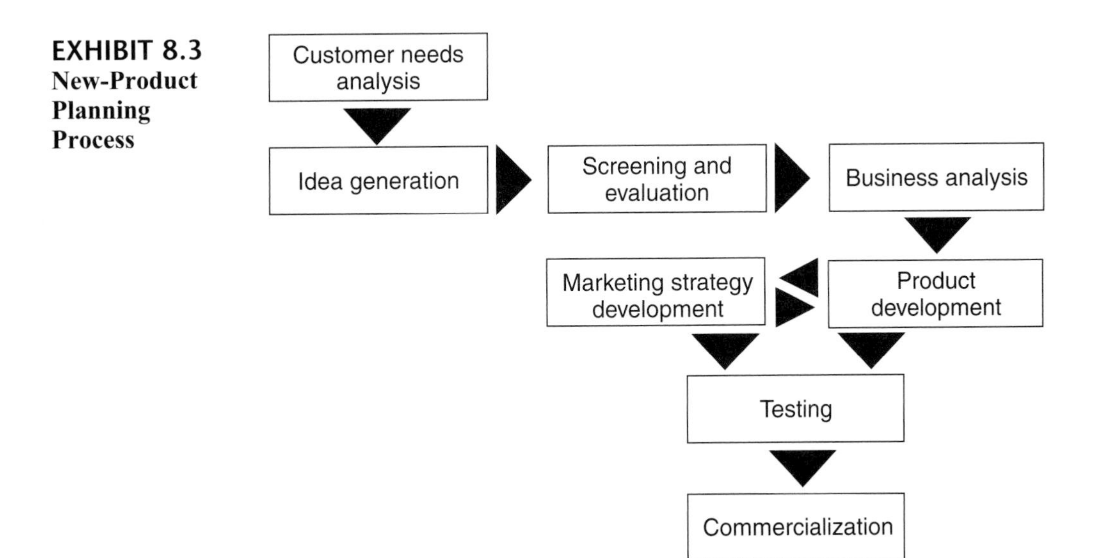

Successful new-product planning requires: (1) generating a continuing stream of new-product ideas that will satisfy the organization's requirements for new products and (2) putting in place processes and methods for evaluating new-product ideas as they move through each of the planning stages.

The following initiatives are important in effectively applying the planning process to develop and introduce new products. First, the process involves different business functions, so it is necessary to develop ways of coordinating and integrating cross-functional activities in the planning process. Second, compressing the time span for product development creates an important competitive advantage. For example, U.S. Surgical's quick response to laparoscopy equipment development enabled the company to establish first position in the market. Third, the product planning activities consume resources and must be managed so that the results deliver high levels of customer satisfaction at acceptable costs. Finally, the planning process is used for new-service development as well as physical products. Certain differences in new-service planning are highlighted as we discuss the planning stages.

Responsibility for New-Product Planning

Since new product development involves different business functions such as marketing, finance, operations, human resources, and research and development (R&D), ways of encouraging cross functional interaction and coordination are essential. Various organizational designs may be employed to coordinate interfunctional interactions that are necessary in developing successful new products, including:[18]

- Coordination of new-product activities by a high-level business manager.
- Interfunctional coordination by a team of new-product planning representatives.
- Creation of a cross-functional project task force responsible for new-product planning.
- Designation of a new-products manager to coordinate planning among departments.
- Formation of a matrix organizational structure for integrating new-product planning with business functions.
- Creation of a design center which is similar in concept to a new-product team, except the center is a permanent part of the organization.

The design team and design center are more recent new-product coordination mechanisms. Though cross-functional teams are widely cited as promising new-product planning mechanisms, research findings suggest that they may be most appropriate for planning truly new and innovative products.[19] The more traditional bureaucratic structures (e.g., new-products manager) may be better in planning line extensions and product improvements. The danger of the traditional structure is failing to identify new-product opportunities outside the scope of existing new-product planning.

The nature and scope of new-product projects may influence how the responsibilities are allocated. Several characteristics of various new-product development efforts are described in Exhibit 8.4. Consider, for example, the enormous team of people involved in developing the Boeing 777 commercial aircraft. The organizational design for such a large-scale project is likely to be more formal than a small-scale project like the Stanley screwdriver. Interestingly, the complete design and production for the 777 aircraft was accomplished by computer that linked together the various people and functions involved as well as partnering companies. We discuss organizational designs further in Chapter 14.

Idea Generation

Guided by the new-product innovation strategy, finding promising new ideas is the starting point in the new-product development process. Idea generation ranges from incremental improvements of existing products to breakthrough products. An example of an incremental

EXHIBIT 8.4 Attributes of Five Products and Their Associated Development Efforts (all figures are approximate, based on publicly available information and company sources)

Source: Karl T. Ulrich and Stephen D. Eppinger, *Product Design and Development*, 2nd ed. (Burr Ridge, IL: Irwin/McGraw-Hill, 2000), 6. Copyright © The McGraw-Hill Companies. Used with permission.

	Stanley Tools Jobmaster Screwdriver	Rollerblade In-Line Skate	Hewlett-Packard DeskJet Printer	Volkswagen New Beetle Automobile	Boeing 777 Airplane
Annual production volume	100,000 units/year	100,000 units/year	4 million units/year	100,000 units/year	50 units/year
Sales lifetime	40 years	3 years	2 years	6 years	30 years
Sales price	$3	$200	$300	$17,000	$130 million
Number of unique parts (part numbers)	3 parts	35 parts	200 parts	10,000 parts	130,000 parts
Development time	1 year	2 years	1.5 years	3.5 years	4.5 years
Internal development team (peak size)	3 people	5 people	100 people	800 people	6,800 people
External development team (peak size)	3 people	10 people	75 people	800 people	10,000 people
Development cost	$150,000	$750,000	$50 million	$400 million	$3 billion
Production investment	$150,000	$1 million	$25 million	$500 million	$3 billion

improvement is Pepsi's vanilla flavor carbonated drink introduced in 2003. An example of a totally new product is a drug that will cure AIDS.

Sources of Ideas

New-product ideas come from many sources. Limiting the search for ideas to those generated by internal research and development activities is far too narrow an approach for most firms. Sources of new-product ideas include R&D laboratories, employees, customers, competitors, outside inventors, acquisition, and value-chain members. Both solicited and spontaneous ideas may emerge from these sources. Some companies are developing "open-market innovation" approaches using licensing, joint ventures, and strategic alliances. By opening their boundaries to suppliers, customers, outside researchers, even competitors, businesses are increasing the import and export of new ideas to improve the speed, cost, and quality of innovation. For example, when Pitney-Bowes was challenged with protecting consumers and postal workers from envelopes tainted with anthrax spores by terrorists, they had no in-house response—their expertise is in secure metering systems to protect postal revenues. They collected ideas from fields as diverse as food handling to military security, before working with outside inventors to introduce new products and services to secure mail against bioterrorism—specialized scanners and imaging systems to identify suspicious letters and packages.[20]

For many major companies, the slowdown in traditional R&D spending has mandated a broad global search for new ideas from any source. For example, giant chemical companies like Dow and BASF post research problems at a Web site run by Eli Lilly & Co.'s InnoCentive Inc., to match scientists anywhere in the world with research problems. InnoCentive has a community of 30,000 scientists worldwide and pays up to $100,000 for solutions posted to the site. Others like Intel are locating satellite research facilities close to leading research universities to tap into academic expertise. In some cases the breakthrough ideas come from research-based collaboration. For example, Xerox has broken with its tradition to look to outsiders to help develop optical-network

Strategy Feature

Benetton's Strategy to Revive Apparel Idea Generation

"We didn't take advantage of the [industry's] quick transformation," says Silvana Cassano, the ex-Fiat manager who assumed the post of chief executive of Benetton Group on May 5.

That transformation saw the best retailers turn into cutting-edge users of digital technology. Benetton's competitors—notably Spain's Zara and Sweden's Hennes & Mauritz (H&M)—have raised the bar for the entire industry. These retailers can beam new styles from the catwalk to the shop floor in less than a month—and at bargain prices. Both deploy sophisticated technology to track which items are selling and which aren't, so winners can be speedily restocked and slow movers yanked down from the racks. They've got the look down, too—cool and minimal for the working women who love Zara, and over-the-top trendy for H&M's teen fans. And Benetton's look? Bland. "The Benetton brand is out of fashion," says Sagra Maceira de Rosen, retail analyst at J.P. Morgan Chase & Co. in London.

Cassano is out to change that. The message he delivered in his first encounter with shareholders was short and powerful: Benetton is going to refocus on the apparel business, which encompasses the Sisley and Benetton brands.

It's no secret that Benetton's core casualwear business has suffered neglect. In 1994, founder Luciano Benetton launched an ill-fated diversification into sports equipment, snapping up trophy brands such as Prince (tennis rackets), Rollerblade (in-line skates), and Killer Loop (snowboards). But the strategy foundered and last year, Benetton sold the entire equipment division, booking $190 million in write-offs. The company posted its first annual loss—$10.5 million, on revenues of $2.3 billion.

Source: "Has Benetton Stopped Unraveling?" *BusinessWeek*, June 30, 2003, 76.

technology. One result is the inclusion of Xerox's imaging technology expertise in a joint project with Intel, to produce a new microprocessor tailored to document imaging.[21] In complex and rapidly changing markets, many companies are exploring new and faster ways to capture new ideas from diverse sources as the basis for developing new products and services.

It is essential to establish a proactive idea-generation and evaluation process that meets the needs of the enterprise. Answering these questions is helpful in developing the idea-generation program:

- Should idea search activities be targeted or open-ended? Should the search for new-product ideas be restricted to ideas that correspond to the firm's new-product strategy?
- How extensive and aggressive should new-product idea search activities be?
- What specific sources are best for generating a regular flow of new-product ideas?
- How can new ideas be obtained from customers?
- Where will responsibility for new-product idea search be placed? How will new-product idea generation activities be directed and coordinated?
- What are potential threats from alternative technologies that may satisfy customers better than our products (e.g., digital rather than camera and film photography)?

An important issue is deciding how far to expand beyond the organization's core new-product strategy in generating new-product ideas. These initiatives may be risky as discussed in the Strategy Feature, which describes Benetton's neglect of its core apparel business resulting from venturing into sports equipment.

For most companies, the idea search process should be targeted within a range of product and market involvement that is consistent with corporate mission and objectives and business-unit strategy. While some far-out new-product idea may occasionally change the future of a company, more often open-ended idea search dissipates resources and misdirects efforts. However, management should be proactive in monitoring potential disruptive technologies and opportunities beyond the core product focus.

EXHIBIT 8.5
Adding Customers to the Design Team

Source: Review of C. K. Prahalad and Venkat Ramaswamy, *The Future of Competition* (Boston: Harvard Business School Press, 2004), in *BusinessWeek*, March 1, 2004, 22.

This isn't about tweaking a few management techniques and business processes. Fundamental changes must be made not only to the CEO's role but also every corporate function, from product development to sales and marketing.

Models include British Petroleum, which, through an online system, pulls in market information from customers, distributes it to the managers and staff who need to know about it, and provides forums for discussing and acting on it. BP is formally organized on geographic lines, which meet only at the top. But the online system reorganizes it around knowledge rather than rank. There's also Deere & Co., which is developing a GPS-based technology that tracks how farmers use its equipment, diagnoses emerging problems, and warns of potential equipment failures.

Identifying the best idea sources depends on many factors including the size and type of firm, technologies involved, new-product needs, resources, management's preferences, and corporate capabilities. Management should consider these issues and develop a proactive strategy for idea generation that will satisfy the firm's requirements. Creating an innovative culture should encourage generating new-product ideas. The innovation strategy provides idea generation guidelines.

Many new-product ideas originate from the users of products and services. Lead user analyses offer promising potential for the development of new products.[22] The earlier U.S. Surgical example is illustrative of lead-user opportunities. These companies identify gaps between their satisfaction with available products and users' value expectations, and lead users pursue initiatives to meet their needs. Implementing this approach to idea generation requires major internal and external initiatives. The benefits can be significant as described in Exhibit 8.5. The objective is to identify the companies that pioneer new applications and to study their requirements to guide new-product development in product markets that change rapidly. The intent is to satisfy the lead users' needs, thus accelerating new-product adoption by other companies.

Involving customers in the innovation process goes much further than direct customer feedback for some companies in their search for new ideas that create customer value. These companies have gone to the extent of equipping customers with the tools to develop and design their own products—ranging from minor modifications to major innovations. For example, Bush Boake Allen (BBA) is a global supplier of specialty flavors to companies like Nestlé. BBA has developed a toolkit that enables customers to develop their own flavors, which BBA then manufactures. In the materials business, GE provides customers with Web tools to design better plastic products. The trend toward customers as innovators has transformed some industries. In the semiconductor business it has led to a custom-chip business that has grown to more than $15 billion.[23]

One view is that "co-creating" value with customers provides a model indicating the future of competitive strategy—only by allowing customers to design products and services will companies be able to provide the added value for which customers will pay.[24] For example, Dow Chemical Co. has developed what it calls "inventing to order," when it collects a "wish list" of products or technical characteristics from customers, which provide input to the R&D laboratory. This is similar to "open market innovation" we describe elsewhere, but aims to build in guaranteed demand to underwrite R&D expenditure.

Methods of Generating Ideas

There are several ways of obtaining ideas for new products. Typically, a company considers multiple options in generating product ideas. Various approaches to idea generation are shown in Exhibit 8.6. A discussion of idea-generation methods follows.

Search. Tapping several information sources may be helpful in identifying new-product ideas. New-product idea publications are available from companies that wish to sell or license

EXHIBIT 8.6 Problem-Based Concept Generation

Source: Chart from C. Merle Crawford and C. Anthony DiBenedetto, *New Products Management*, 7th ed. (Burr Ridge, IL: Irwin/McGraw-Hill, 2003), 96. Copyright © The McGraw-Hill Companies. Used with permission.

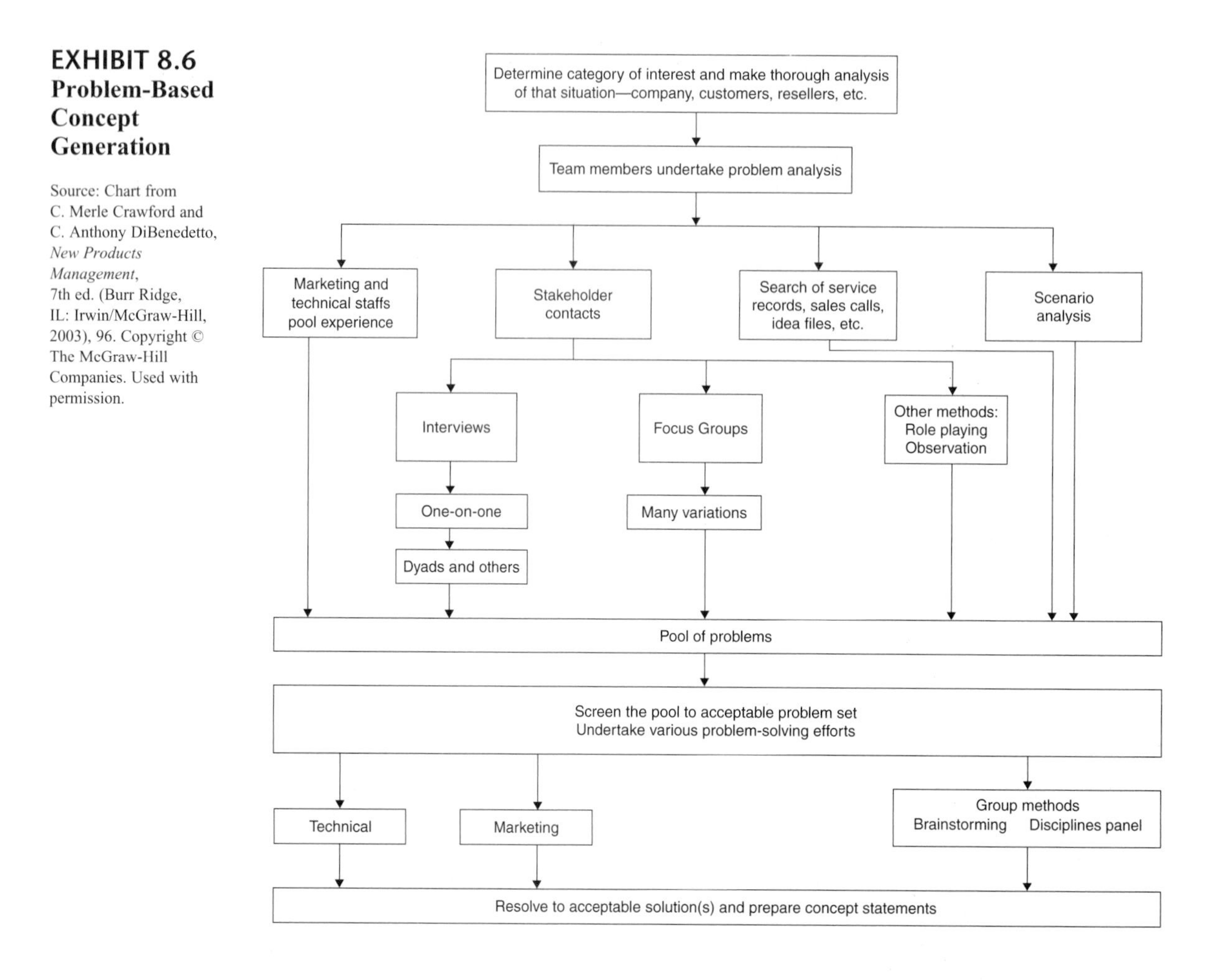

ideas they do not wish to commercialize. New technology information is available from commercial and government computerized search services. News sources may also yield information about the new-product activities of competitors. Many trade publications contain new-product announcements. Companies need to identify the relevant search areas and assign responsibility for idea search to an individual or team.

Marketing Research. Surveys of product users help to identify needs that can be satisfied by new products. The focus group is a useful technique to identify and evaluate new-product concepts, and the research method can be used for both consumer and industrial products. The focus group consists of 8 to 12 people invited to meet with an experienced moderator to discuss a product-use situation. Idea generation may occur in the focus group discussion of user requirements for a particular product-use situation. Group members are asked to suggest new-product ideas. Later, focus group sessions may be used to evaluate product concepts intended to satisfy the needs identified in the initial session. More than one focus group can be used at each stage in the process. Focus groups can be conducted using value-chain members and company personnel as well as end user customers.

Another research technique that is used to generate new-product ideas is the advisory panel. The panel members are selected to represent the firm's target market. For example, such a panel for a producer of mechanics' hand tools would include mechanics. Companies in various industries, including telecommunications, fast foods, and pharmaceuticals, use customer advisory groups. These experienced users provide ideas and evaluations for new and existing products.

Internal and External Development. Companies' research and development laboratories continue to generate many new-product ideas. The United States is the leading spender on industrial research and development in the world and after the surge in R&D expenditure in the late 1990s, with the exception of countries like Japan and Korea, very few countries allocated a higher percentage of gross domestic product to R&D. However, U.S. expenditures fell from $198.8 billion between 2001 and 2002, with a small recovery in 2003. Major cut backs in R&D expenditure by large corporations like Xerox and AT&T may even lead to a steady decline in overall national spending.[25] These factors are driving innovative companies to explore new ways of matching R&D resources to value opportunities—through "open source innovation," strategic alliances, joint ventures, and the global search for promising innovation prospects.

New-product ideas may originate from development efforts outside the firm. Sources include inventors, government and private laboratories, and small high-technology firms. Strategic alliances between companies may result in identifying new-product ideas, as well as sharing responsibility for other activities in new-product development.

Other Idea-Generation Methods. Incentives may be useful to get new-product ideas from employees, marketing middlemen, and customers. The amount of the incentive should be high enough to encourage submission. Management should also guard against employees leaving the company and developing a promising idea elsewhere. For this reason many firms require employees to sign secrecy agreements.

Finally, acquiring another firm offers a way to obtain new-product ideas. This strategy may be more cost-effective than internal development and can substantially reduce the lead time required for developing new products. P&G's purchase of the battery-powered Crest SpinBrush from the inventor is an example.

Idea generation identifies one or more new-product opportunities that are screened and evaluated. Before comprehensive evaluation, an idea for a new product must be transformed into a defined concept, which states what the product will do (anticipated attributes) and the benefits that are superior to available products.[26] The product concept expresses the idea in operational terms so that it can be evaluated as a potential candidate for development into a new product.

Screening, Evaluating, and Business Analysis

Management needs a screening and evaluation process that will eliminate unpromising ideas as soon as possible while keeping the risks of rejecting good ideas at acceptable levels. Moving too many ideas through too many stages in the new-product planning process is expensive. Expenditures build up from the idea stage to the commercialization stage, whereas the risks of developing a bad new product decline as information accumulates about product performance and market acceptance. The objective is to eliminate the least promising ideas before too much time and money are invested in them. However, the tighter the screening procedure, the higher the risk of rejecting a good idea. On the basis of the specific factors involved, it is necessary to establish a level of risk that is acceptable to management.

Evaluation occurs regularly as an idea moves through the new-product planning stages. While the objective is to eliminate the poor risks as early as possible in the planning process, evaluation is necessary at each stage in the planning process. We discuss several evaluation techniques as the stages in new-product planning are examined. Typically, evaluation begins by screening new-product ideas to identify those that are considered to be most promising. These ideas are subjected to more comprehensive concept evaluation. Business analysis is the final assessment before deciding whether to develop the concept into a new product.

Screening

A new-product idea receives an initial screening to determine its strategic fit in the company or business unit. Two questions need to be answered: (1) Is the idea compatible with the organization's mission and objectives? (2) Is the product initiative commercially feasible? The compatibility of the idea considers factors such as internal capabilities (e.g., development, production, and marketing), financial needs, and competitive factors. Commercial feasibility considers market attractiveness, technical feasibility, financial attractiveness, and social and environmental concerns. The number of ideas generated by an organization is likely to influence the approach utilized in screening the ideas. A large number of ideas call for a formal screening process.

Screening eliminates ideas that are not compatible or feasible for the business. Management must establish how narrow or wide the screening boundaries should be, For example, managers from two similar firms may have very different missions and objectives as well as different propensities toward risk. An idea could be strategically compatible in one firm and not in another. Also, new-product strategies and priorities may change when top management changes as previously discussed in the Strategic Feature concerning Benetton.

After identifying relevant screening criteria, some firms use scoring and importance weighting techniques to evaluate the factors considered in the screening process. Summing the weighted scores obtains a score for each idea being screened. Management can set ranges for passing and rejecting. The effectiveness of these methods is highly dependent on including relevant criteria and gaining agreement on the relative importance of the screening factors from the managers involved.

Concept Evaluation

The boundaries between idea screening, evaluation, and business analysis are often not clearly drawn. These evaluation stages may be combined, particularly when only a few ideas are involved. After completion of initial screening, each idea that survives becomes a new-product concept and receives a more comprehensive evaluation. Several of the same factors used in screening may be evaluated in greater depth, including buyers' reactions to the proposed concept. A team representing different business functions is often responsible for concept evaluation.

Importance of Concept Evaluation. Extensive research on companies' new-product planning activities highlights the critical role of extensive market and technical assessments *before* beginning the development of a new-product concept.[27] These "up-front" evaluations should result in a clearly defined new-product concept indicating its market target(s), customer value offering, and positioning strategy. Research concerning product failures strongly suggests that many companies do not devote enough attention to "up-front" evaluation of product concepts.

The failure of the handheld CueCat scanner offers compelling evidence of the value and importance of concept evaluation. CueCat reads a bar code and, when attached to a personal computer, provides a direct access Web page for the product. The founder of Digital Convergence Corp. raised $185 million from investors to commercially launch CueCat.[28] Large investors included Belo Corp. ($37.5 million), Radio Shack ($30 million), and Young & Rubicam ($28 million). The business plan was to give away 50 million CueCats ($6.50 cost) and obtain revenues from advertisers and licensing fees. Four million CueCats were distributed but few were used. People did not want to carry the scanner around and could quickly access Web sites by typing the address. CueCat did not fill a consumer need. Importantly, this weakness could have been identified at the concept stage before large expenditures were made to produce and distribute the product.

Concept Tests. Concept tests are useful in evaluation and refinement of proposed new products. The purpose of concept testing is to obtain a reaction to the new-product concept from a sample of potential buyers before the product is developed. More than one concept test may be used during the evaluation process. The technique supplies important information for reshaping, redefining, and coalescing new-product ideas.[29] Concept tests help to evaluate the relative appeal of ideas or alternative product positionings, supply information for developing the product and marketing strategy, and identify potential market segments. A proposal to conduct a concept test for evaluating alternative investment products is described in Exhibit 8.7.

EXHIBIT 8.7
Project Proposal: New-Product Concept Screening Test

Source: Adapted from William R. Dillon, Thomas J. Madden, and Neil H. Firtle, *Marketing Research in a Marketing Environment*, 3rd ed. (Burr Ridge, IL: Richard D. Irwin, 1994), 562. Copyright © The McGraw-Hill Companies. Used with permission.

Brand:	New products.
Project:	Concept screening.
Background and objectives:	The New York banking group has developed 12 new-product ideas for investment products (services). The objectives of this research are to assess consumer interest in the concepts and to establish priorities for further development.
Research method:	Concept testing will be conducted in four geographically dispersed, central location facilities within the New York metropolitan area. Each of the 12 concepts plus 1 retest control concept will be evaluated by a total of 100 men and 100 women with household incomes of $25,000. The following age quotas will be used for both male and female groups within the sample: 18–34 = 50 percent 35–49 = 25 percent 50 and over = 25 percent Each respondent will evaluate a maximum of eight concepts. Order of presentation will be rotated throughout to avoid position bias. Because some of the concepts are in low-incidence product categories, user groups will be defined both broadly and narrowly in an attempt to assess potential among target audiences.
Information to be obtained:	This study will provide the following information to assist in concept evaluation: Investment ownership. Purchase interest (likelihood of subscription). Uniqueness of new service. Believability. Importance of main point. Demographics.
Action standard:	To identify concepts warranting further development, top-box purchase intent scores will be compared to the top-box purchase intent scores achieved by the top 10 percent of the concepts tested in earlier concept screening studies. Rank order of purchase intent scores on the *uniqueness, believability*, and *importance* ratings will also be considered in the evaluation and prioritization of concepts for further development.
Material requirements:	Fifty copies of each concept.
Cost and timing:	The cost of this research will be $15,000 ± 10% This research will adhere to the following schedule: Field work 1 week Top-line 2 weeks Final report 3 weeks
Supplier:	Burke Marketing Research.

The concept test is a useful way to evaluate a product idea very early in the development process. The costs of these tests are reasonable, given the information that can be obtained. Nonetheless, there are some important cautions. The test is not a definitive gauge of commercial success. Since the actual product and a commercial setting are not present, the evaluation is somewhat artificial.

The concept test is probably most useful in identifying very favorable or unfavorable product concepts. The research method also offers a basis for comparing two or more concepts. An

EXHIBIT 8.8
Concept Evaluation Issues

- What is the objective (purpose) of concept evaluation?
- How much time/resources should be allocated to evaluation?
- What are the risks?
- Who will perform the evaluation?
- Who decides the outcomes?
- What evaluation techniques are most useful?

important requirement of concept testing is that the product (good or service) can be described in words and visually, and the participant must have the experience and capability to evaluate the concept. The respondent must be able to visualize the proposed product and its features based on a verbal or written description and/or picture.

Computer technology offers very promising capabilities for visual testing of new-product concepts. Potential customers can be provided with multimedia virtual buying environment. Virtual methodology was used to evaluate the potential of new electric cars:

> Respondents viewed multimedia presentations, read on-line articles about the new product, talked with users of the vehicle, visited a showroom, and were able to virtually get into the vehicle and talk with salespeople.[30]

Several concept evaluation issues are highlighted in Exhibit 8.8. Evaluation includes more than concept tests. For example, the new-product team may perform competitor analyses, market forecasts, and technical feasibility evaluations. The questions indicated in Exhibit 8.8 are helpful in deciding how to evaluate the new-product concept.

Business Analysis

Before making the decision to move the concept into the product development stage, an assessment needs to be made of the estimated revenues and costs for developing and commercializing the new product. Business analysis estimates the commercial performance of the new-product concept. Obtaining an accurate financial projection depends on the quality of the revenue and cost forecasts. Business analysis is normally accomplished at several stages in the new-product planning process, beginning before the product concept moves into the development stage. Financial projections are refined at later stages.

Revenue Forecasts. The newness of the product, the size of the market, and the competing products all influence the accuracy of revenue projections. In the case of an established market such as breakfast cereals, potato chips, or toothpaste, estimates of total market size are usually available from industry information. Industry associations often publish industry forecasts and government agencies such as the U.S. Commerce Department forecast sales for various industries. The more difficult task is estimating the market share that is feasible for a new-product entry. A range of feasible share positions can be forecast at the concept stage and used as a basis for preliminary financial projections. Established markets also may have success norms based on prior experience. When available the success norm provides a basis for estimating the possibility of reaching a successful level of sales.

Nonetheless, major difficulties may exist in forecasting the demand for innovations. Consider, for example, the dilemma facing telecom companies with third-generation (3G) mobile phone services. The European carriers have spent some $250 billion buying 3G rights and new networks. Notwithstanding efficient data connections at broadband speeds, cheaper voice calls, Internet access, photo messaging, games, streaming video clips, and videoconferencing on 3G phones, consumers have shown limited interest in buying mobile multimedia. There is a possible risk that levels of business achieved may never pay back the cost of the 3G licenses acquired in 2001 and 2002.[31] After a very slow start the 3Q forecasts in 2004 became cautiously optimistic, indicating an evolution rather than a revolution.

Preliminary Marketing Plan. An initial marketing strategy should be developed as a part of the business analysis. Included are market target(s), positioning strategy, and marketing program plans. While this plan is preliminary, it is an early guide to strategy development and coordination among marketing, design, operations, and other business functions. The choice of the marketing strategy is necessary in developing the revenue forecast. Different approaches to marketing and different levels of effort in the marketing strategy guide estimates of the sales, which may be achieved in different parts of the market.

Cost Estimation. Several different costs occur in the planning and commercialization of new products. One way to categorize the costs is to estimate them for each stage in the new-product planning process (Exhibit 8.3). The costs increase rapidly as the product concept moves through the development process. Expenditures for each planning stage can be further divided into functional categories (e.g., marketing, research and development, and manufacturing).

Profit Projections. Analyses appropriate for new-product evaluation include break-even, cash flow, return on investment, and profit contribution (see Appendix to Chapter 2). Break-even analysis is particularly useful to show how many units of the new-product must be sold before it begins to make a profit. Management can use the break-even level as a basis for assessing the feasibility of the project. The issue is whether management considers reaching and exceeding break-even to be feasible.

The appropriate time horizon for projecting sales, costs, and profits should be determined. For example, the product may be required to recoup all costs within a certain time period. Business analysis estimates should take into consideration the probable flow of revenues and costs over the time span used in the analysis. Typically, new products incur heavy costs before they start to generate revenues.

Other Considerations. Several other issues are considered in the business analysis of a new-product concept. First, management often has guidelines for the financial performance of new products. These can be used to accept, reject, or further analyze the product concept. Another issue is assessing the amount of risk associated with the venture. This factor should be included either in the financial projections or as an additional consideration beyond the financial estimates. Finally, possible cannibalization of sales by the new-product from the firm's existing products needs to be considered. Cannibalization is not necessarily a negative factor since management's intent may be to cannibalize its brand and competitor's brands with the new product.

Product and Process Development

After completing the business analysis stage, management must decide either to begin product development or abort the project. During the development stage the concept is transformed into one or more prototypes. The prototype is the actual product, but may be custom-produced rather than by an established manufacturing process. Use testing of the product may occur during the development stage.

Our earlier discussion of customer-guided new-product planning emphasizes the importance of transforming customer preferences into internal product design guidelines. Product design decisions need to be guided by customer preferences and analysis of competitor advantages and weaknesses. Product development should involve the entire new-product planning team. We examine the product development process followed by a discussion of collaborative development.

Product Development Process

The development of the new-product includes product design, industrial design (ease-of-use and style), process (manufacturing) design, packaging design, and decisions to make or outsource various product components. Development typically consists of various technical activities, but also requires continuing interaction among R&D, marketing, operations, finance, and legal functions. The relative importance of development activities differs according to the product

Cross-Functional Feature — IDEO Redefined Good Design by Creating Experiences, Not Just Products

A company goes to IDEO with a problem. It wants a better product, service, or space—no matter. IDEO puts together an eclectic team composed of members from the client company and its own experts who go out to observe and document the consumer experience. Often, IDEO will have top executives play the roles of their own customers. Execs from food and clothing companies show off their own stuff in different retail stores and on the Web. Health care managers get care in different hospitals. Wireless providers use their own—and competing—services.

The next stage is brainstorming. IDEO mixes designers, engineers, and social scientists with its clients in a room where they intensely scrutinize a given problem and suggest possible solutions. It is managed chaos: a dozen or so very smart people examining data, throwing out ideas, writing potential solutions on big Post-its that are ripped off and attached to the wall.

IDEO designers then mock up working models of the best concepts that emerge. Rapid prototyping has always been a hallmark of the company. Seeing ideas in working, tangible form is a far more powerful mode of explanation than simply reading about them off a page. IDEO uses inexpensive prototyping tools—Apple-based iMovies to portray consumer experiences and cheap cardboard to mock up examination rooms or fitting rooms. "IDEO's passion is about making stuff work, not about being artists," says design guru Tucker Viemeister, CEO of Dutch-based designer Springtime USA. "Their corporate customers really buy into it."

Source: Bruce Nussbaum, "The Power of Design," *BusinessWeek*, May 17, 2004, 91.

involved. For example, product and process design are extensive for complex products like large commercial aircraft. In contrast, line extensions (e.g., new flavors and package sizes) of food products do not require extensive design activities.

Product Specifications. The R&D technical team needs guidelines in order to develop the product. Product specifications describe what the product will do rather than how it should be designed. These guidelines indicate the product planners' expectations regarding the benefits provided by the product based on customer analysis, including essential physical and operating characteristics.[32] This information helps the technical team in determining the best design strategy for delivering the benefits. The more complete the specifications for the product, the better the designers can incorporate the requirements into the design. The specifications also provide a basis for assessing design feasibility. In some situations benefit/cost assessments may require changing the specifications.

Industrial Design. Companies are placing increasing emphasis on the ease-of-use and style of products. Design consultants assist companies on various design initiatives. The design process of IDEO, the industry leader, is described in the Cross Functional Feature.

Prototype. The technical team uses the product specifications to guide the design of one or more physical products. Similar information is needed to guide software design and design of new services. At this stage the product is called a prototype since it is not ready for commercial production and marketing. Many of the parts may be custom-built, and materials, packaging, and other details may differ from the commercial version. Nevertheless, the prototype needs to be capable of delivering the benefits spelled out in the specifications. Scale models are used in some kinds of products such as commercial aircraft. Models can be tested in wind tunnels to evaluate their performance characteristics. Computer technology is also used in testing and evaluation of new products such as automobiles and aircraft.

Use Tests. When use testing of the prototype is feasible, designers can obtain important feedback from users concerning how well the product meets the needs that are spelled out in the product specifications. A standard approach to use testing is to distribute the product to a sample of users, asking them to try the product. Follow-up occurs after the test participant has had sufficient time to evaluate the product. The design of new industrial products may include the active involvement of users in testing and evaluating the product at various stages in the development process. The relatively small number of users in industrial markets compared to consumer markets makes use testing very feasible. Use tests are also popular for gaining reactions to new consumer products such as foods, drinks, and health and beauty aids. Clinical trials may also be conducted to support performance claims of products such as foods offering therapeutic benefits.

An example of a proposed use test for a new soup flavor is described in Exhibit 8.9. Unlike a market test, the use test normally does not identify the brand name of the product or the company name. While the use test is less accurate in gauging market success compared to the market test, the use test yields important information such as preferences, ratings, likes/dislikes, advantages/limitations, unique features, usage and users, and comparisons with competing products.[33]

Process Development. The process for producing the product in commercial quantities must be developed. Manufacturing the product at the desired quality level and cost is a critical determinant of profitability. The new-product may be feasible to produce in the laboratory but not in a manufacturing plant, because of costs, production rates, and other considerations. Initial production delays can also jeopardize the success of a new product.

The concepts of *mass customization* and *modularity* may have a major impact on product and process design.[34] As we discussed in Chapter 4, mass customization enables customizing product offerings at relatively low costs. Modularity involves developing and producing a product using interrelated modules, thus facilitating mass customization. The system architecture links the modules together, but each part can be designed and produced independently within the organization or by suppliers. Modularity was pioneered by the computer industry, but is applicable to many other products.

Collaborative Development

Collaborative research and development partnerships are used to increase the distinctive capabilities of a single company and reduce the time required to develop and market new products. These relationships may be strategic alliances or supplier-producer collaborations (Chapter 7). Collaborative development occurs in several industries including computer hardware and software, commercial aircraft, and automobiles.

Outsourcing of the manufacturing of new products to other firms became very popular over the last decade. For example, Sara Lee Corp., the $20 billion (2004) producer of an array of consumer brands from foods to apparel, announced a strategy in the late 1990s of shifting production of its products to independent producers. Previously, Sara Lee had produced many of its brands in-house. Pursuing similar initiatives, Tommy Hilfiger has about 3,100 employees (and $1.7 billion in sales in 2004) because of outsourcing and licensing its clothing and accessories. Coke and Pepsi outsource the bottling and distribution of their beverage brands. Outsourcing reduces the investment required by the product designer but requires close coordination with the producer firm.

Marketing Strategy and Market Testing

Guidelines for marketing strategy depend on whether the new-product being developed is an incremental improvement or new to the company. The latter requires complete targeting and positioning strategies (Chapter 6). An incremental product improvement may only need a revised promotion strategy to convey to target buyers information about the benefits the improved product offers. It is also important to consider how the new-product will impact the sales of existing products. Regardless of the newness of the product, reviewing the proposed marketing strategy helps to avoid market introduction problems.

EXHIBIT 8.9 Project Proposal: Product Test

Source: William R. Dillon, Thomas J. Madden, and Neil H. Firtle, *Marketing Research in a Marketing Environment*, 3rd ed. (Burr Ridge, IL: Richard D. Irwin, 1994), 583. Copyright © The McGraw-Hill Companies. Used with permission.

Brand:	New product: Hardy Soup.
Project:	Campbell's versus new Hardy Soup blind product test.
Background and objectives:	R&D has developed a new Hardy Soup in two different flavors (chicken noodle and mushroom). Additionally, each flavor has been developed at two different flavor strengths. The brand groups have requested that research be conducted to determine (1) whether this product should be considered for introduction, (2) If so, if one or both flavors should be introduced, and (3) which flavor variation(s) would be preferred most by the consumer. The objective of this research will be to determine consumers' preferences for each flavor variation of the new product relative to Campbell's Chunky products.
Method:	There will be four cells. In each cell, a blind paired-product test will be conducted between a different flavor variation of the new product and the currently marketed Campbell's product, as follows: • Campbell's Chunky Chicken Noodle versus Hardy's Chicken Noodle 1. • Campbell's Chunky Chicken Noodle versus Hardy's Chicken Noodle 2. • Campbell's Chunky Mushroom versus Hardy's Mushroom 1. • Campbell's Chunky Mushroom versus Hardy's Mushroom 2. In each cell, there will be 200 past-30-day ready-to-serve soup user/purchasers. Respondents will be interviewed in a shopping mall and given both products to take home and try. Additionally, to be used in the test, respondents must be positively disposed toward chicken noodle or mushroom flavors. Order of product trial will be rotated to minimize position bias. Telephone callbacks will be made after a one-week period.
Action standard:	Each new soup flavor will be considered for introduction if one or more of its flavor variations achieves at least absolute parity with its Campbell's Chunky control. If for either flavor alternative more than one flavor level variation meets the action standard, the one that is preferred over Campbell's at the highest level of confidence will be recommended to be considered for introduction. A single-sample *t*-test for paired comparison data (two-tail) will be used to test for significance.
Cost and timing:	The cost of this study will be $32,000 ± 10%. The following schedule will be established: Field work 2 weeks Top-line 2 weeks Final report 4 weeks
Research firm:	Burke Marketing Research.

Marketing Strategy Decisions

Evaluation efforts (e.g., use tests) conducted during product development supply information that may be helpful in designing the marketing strategy. Examples of useful planning guidelines include user characteristics, product features, advantages over competing products, types of use situations, feasible price range, and potential buyer profiles. The design of the marketing strategy should begin early in the new-product planning process since several activities need to be completed and reducing the time to market introduction is an important competitive advantage. Marketing strategy planning begins at the concept evaluation stage and continues during product development. Activities such as packaging, name selection, environmental considerations, product information, colors, materials, and product safety must also be decided between engineering, operations, and marketing.

Market Targeting. Selection of the market target(s) for the new-product range from offering a new-product to an existing target, to identifying an entirely new group of potential users. Examining the prior marketing research (concept tests and use tests) for the new-product may yield useful insights as to targeting opportunities. It may also be necessary to conduct additional research before finalizing the market targeting strategy.

Positioning Strategy. Several positioning decisions are resolved during the marketing strategy development stage. Product strategy regarding packaging, name selection, sizes, and other aspects of the product must be decided. The distribution strategy determines the channels of distribution to be used. It is also necessary to formulate a price strategy and to develop an advertising and sales promotion strategy. Testing of advertisements may occur at this stage. Decisions must be made as to how to use the Internet. Finally, sales management must design a personal selling strategy including deciding about sales force training and allocation of selling effort to the new product.

Market Testing Options

Market testing can be considered after the product is fully developed, providing the product is suitable for market testing. Market tests gauge buyer response to the new-product and evaluate one or more positioning strategies. Test marketing is used for consumer products such as foods, beverages, and health and beauty aids. Market tests can also be conducted for business-to-business goods and services. In addition to conventional test marketing, less expensive alternatives are available such as simulated test marketing and scanner-based test marketing.

An interesting description of the different new-product evaluation methods is shown in Exhibit 8.10.[35] The testing tools for each of the stages are indicated. Note how market testing fits into the planning process. The exhibit also provides an overview of the entire new-product planning process.

Simulated Test Marketing. One way of implementing simulated testing is recruiting potential buyers while they are shopping. The simulation technique:

> Involves intercepting shoppers at a high-traffic location, sometimes prescreening them for category use, exposing the selected individuals to a commercial (or concept) for a proposed new-product, giving them an opportunity to buy the new-product in a real life or laboratory setting, and interviewing those who purchased the new-product at a later date to ascertain their reaction and repeat-purchase intentions.[36]

Simulated tests offer several advantages including speed (12 to 16 weeks), low cost (less than $100,000 compared to more than $2 million for full-scale market tests), and the simulated tests yield relatively accurate forecasts of market response.[37] The tests also eliminate the risk present in conventional testing that competitors will jam the test.

Scanner-Based Test Marketing. This method involves testing in an actual market environment. The test product must be made available in each test city. Information Resources Inc.'s BehaviorScan system pioneered the use of cable television and a computerized database to track new products. The system uses information and responses from recruited panel members in

EXHIBIT 8.10
How Market Testing Relates to the Other Testing Steps

Source: Chart from C. Merle Crawford and C. Anthony Di Benedetto, *New Products Management,* 7th ed. (Burr Ridge, IL: Irwin/McGraw-Hill, 2003), 435. Copyright © The McGraw-Hill Companies. Used with permission.

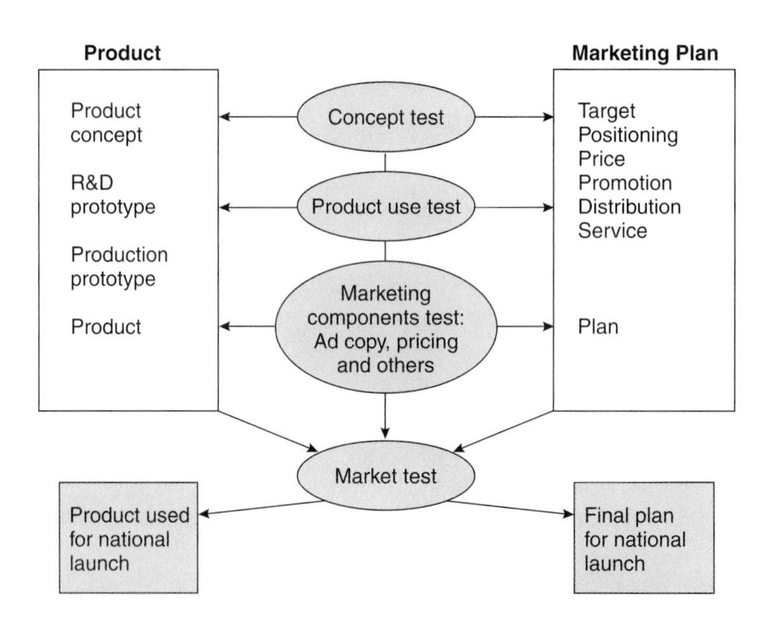

each test city. Each member has an identification card to show to participating store cashiers. Purchases are electronically recorded and transmitted to a central data bank. Cable television enables BehaviorScan to use controlled advertisement testing. Some viewers can be exposed to ads while the ads are being withheld from other viewers.

Conventional Test Marketing. This method of market testing introduces the product under actual market conditions in one or more test cities.[38] It is used for frequently purchased consumer products. Test marketing employs a complete marketing program including advertising and personal selling. Product sampling is often an important factor in launching the new-product in the test market. The product is marketed on a commercial basis in each city, and test results are then projected to the national or regional target market. Because of its high cost, conventional test marketing represents the final evaluation before full-scale market introduction. Management may decide not to test-market in order to avoid competitor awareness, high testing costs, and delayed introduction.

Testing Industrial Products. Market testing can be used for industrial products. Selection of test sites may need to extend beyond one or two cities to include sufficient market coverage. For example, a region of a country might be used for testing. The test firm has substantial control of an industrial products test since it can use direct mail, the Internet, and personal selling. The relatively small number of customers also aids targeting of marketing efforts. The product should have the characteristics necessary for testing: It should be producible in test quantities, relatively inexpensive, and not subject to extensive buying center influences throughout the customer's organization.

Selecting Test Sites. Test sites should exhibit the buyer and environmental characteristics of the intended market target. Since no site is perfect, the objective is to find a reasonable match between the test and market target for the new-product. These criteria are often used to evaluate potential test sites for consumer products.

1. Representation as to population size.
2. Typical per capita income.
3. Typical purchasing habits.
4. Stability of year-round sales.

5. Relative isolation from other cities.
6. Not easily jammed by competitors.
7. Typical of planned distribution outlets.
8. Availability of retailers that will cooperate.
9. Availability of media that will cooperate.
10. Availability of research and audit service companies.[39]

Some of the best metropolitan test markets in the United State are Detroit; St. Louis; Charlotte-Gastonia-Rock Hill, North Carolina–South Carolina; Fort Worth-Arlington, Texas; and Kansas City.[40]

Length of the Test. The length of the test affects the test results. Conventional market tests are usually conducted over several months. The longer the test period, the more accurate the results are in predicting future market performance. Market tests of more than a year are not unusual.

External Influences. Probably the most troublesome external factor that may affect test market results is competition that does not compete on a normal basis. Competitors may attempt to drive test market results awry by increasing or decreasing their marketing efforts and making other changes in their marketing actions. It is also important to monitor the test market environment to identify other unusual influences such as major shifts in economic conditions.

New-Product Models

New-product analytical models are useful in analyzing test market data and predicting commercial market success. They fall into two categories: (1) first-purchase models designed to predict the cumulative number of new-product tries over time, and (2) models designed to predict the repeat purchase rate of buyers who have tried the product.[41] The latter model combines a first-purchase model with a repeat-purchase model. The consumer adoption process for new products provides guidelines for using the models.

Extensive research concerning the adoption of innovations indicates that (1) new-product adopters follow a sequence of stages in their adoption process; (2) adopters' characteristics vary according to how soon they adopt the product after introduction; and (3) adoption findings may be of value in new-product planning. The adoption stages are awareness, interest, evaluation, trial, and adoption.[42] By finding and targeting the "early adopters," firms may be able to accelerate a new-product's adoption. Early adopters tend to be younger, of generally higher socioeconomic status, and more in contact with impersonal and cosmopolitan sources of information than later adopters.[43] The early adopter also uses a variety of information sources.

Commercialization

Introducing the new product into the market requires finalizing the marketing plan, coordinating market entry activities with business functions, implementing the marketing strategy, and monitoring and control of the product launch. P&G's entry into Japan's dish soap market in 1995 is an interesting new-product venture.[44] P&G's Joy brand gained a leading 20 percent share of the $400 million dish soap market by 1997. The successful strategy included offering new technology, packaging that retailers liked, attractive margins for retailers, and heavy spending on innovative commercials that got consumers' attention. At the time of market entry, Kao and Lion (Japanese companies) together had nearly 40 percent of the market. P&G developed a highly concentrated formula for Joy to eliminate consumers' concerns about Joy's strengths compared to other brands. Encouraged by commercials to try the new-product, Japanese homemakers were pleased with Joy's performance.

The Marketing Plan

Market introduction requires a complete marketing strategy that is spelled out in the marketing plan. The plan should be coordinated with the people and business functions responsible for the introduction, including salespeople, sales and marketing managers, and managers in other functional areas such as operations, distribution, finance, and human resources. Responsibility for the new-product launch is normally assigned to the marketing manager or product manager. Alternatively, companies may assign responsibility to product planning and market introduction teams.

The timing and geographical scope of the launch are important decisions. The options range from a national market introduction to an area-by-area rollout. In some instances the scope of the introduction may extend to international markets. The national introduction is a major endeavor, requiring a comprehensive implementation effort. A rollout reduces the scope of the introduction and enables management to adjust marketing strategy based on experience gained in the early stages of the launch. Of course, the rollout approach, like market testing, gives competition more time to react.

Monitoring and Control

Real-time tracking of new-product performance at the market entry stage is extremely important. Standardized information services are available for monitoring sales of products such as foods, health and beauty aids, and prescription drugs. Information for these services is collected through store audits, consumer diary panels, and scanner services. Special tracking studies may be necessary for products that are not included in standardized information services.

The Internet is rapidly becoming an essential new-product information gathering and monitoring capability. These activities include private online communities and research panels that provide companies with Shoppers' feedback. The Internet Feature describes how Coca-Cola, Kraft Foods, Hallmark Cards, and Stonyfield Farm use the Web to generate new-product ideas from consumers and spot problems with new products.

It is important to include product performance metrics with performance targets in the new-product plan to evaluate how well the product is performing. Often included are profit contribution, sales, market share, and return on investment objectives—including the time horizon for reaching objectives. It is also important to establish benchmarks for objectives that indicate minimum acceptable performance. For example, market share threshold levels are sometimes used to gauge new-product performance. Repeat purchase data are essential for tracking frequently purchased products. Regular measures of customer satisfaction are also relevant measures of market performance.

Variations in the Generic New-Product Planning Process

The new-product planning process (Exhibit 8.3) is based on the logic of being market driven and focused on customer needs. While a market-oriented focus is always important, some variations in the generic process we have been discussing may occur due to the new-product strategy of a particular company. The variants from the generic process fall into four categories: technology push, platform, process intensive, and customized products.[45] The major impact of the variants is on the types of ideas that are considered by the firm. Several characteristics of variations from the generic process are described in Exhibit 8.11. We examine each variant, highlighting situations where it may be applicable and the differences from the generic process. The chapter is concluded with a discussion of proactive cannibalization.

Internet Feature

Friendly Spies on the Net

HALLMARK CARDS

Research:

The company hosts an online bulletin board for 200 consumers who chat about everything from holiday decorating ideas to prayers for ill loved ones. Hallmark breaks in to steer the conversation or conduct surveys.

Payoff:

New ideas for cards such as less sentimental ones for mothers-in-law or sympathy cards for the anniversary of a death, and an entire new product line that Hallmark has yet to disclose.

STONYFIELD FARM

Research:

Stonyfield's higher-priced yogurt appeals to a niche audience that can't easily be found in phone surveys or mail interviews. So it went online to ask 105 yogurt eaters for feedback on new products.

Payoff:

The survey was done in two days, down from a month, for 20% less cost than a phone survey. The company ditched the name YoFemme after consumers panned it, in favor of YoSelf.

COCA-COLA

Research:

Coke created an online panel of 100 teenagers and asked how to remake its flagging Powerade sports drink. Coke wanted to move fast, and by going deep with the same panelists, it could count on quality results.

Payoff:

Powerade relaunched in June with B vitamins, thanks to input from the panel. Coke cut the time and cost of product-development research by 50%.

KRAFT FOODS

Research:

The company surveyed 160 panelists about frozen vegetables, then chose 24 to do a taste-test for a new product. Consumers sent responses via e-mail that were more detailed than traditional surveys.

Payoff:

Research was 30% faster and 25% cheaper than a typical focus group. And Kraft reached consumers nationwide rather than in just a few major cities.

Source: Faith Keenan, "Friendly Spies on the Net," *BusinessWeek E.Biz*, July 9, 2001, EB27.

Technology Push Processes

Technology-driven new-product planning starts with a new technology and the planning team looks for a market need that can be satisfied by the technology. The technology is the primary driver of the new-product planning process. Nonetheless, the various stages of generic process are applicable. The technology provides the focus for generating new-product ideas, which are based on the technology. The development of ink-jet technology by Hewlett-Packard (H-P) followed the technology push process. The printing capability was developed first, and then a product team pursued applications of the technology.

Platform Products

The platform product is the result of an organization developing a capability that can be used to generate other products. The planning process starts with an available platform. The platform is an existing design that can be adapted to other product extensions. The objective is to leverage the platform to develop other products. Platform strategies are used for automobile designs, computers, appliances, and many other products.

EXHIBIT 8.11
Summary of Variants of the Generic Development Process

Source: Karl T. Ulrich and Stephen D. Eppinger, *Product Design and Development*, 2nd ed. (Burr Ridge, IL: Irwin/McGraw-Hill, 2000), 21. Copyright © The McGraw-Hill Companies. Used with permission.

	Generic (Market Pull)	Technology Push	Platform Products	Process Intensive	Customized
Description	The firm begins with a market opportunity, then finds appropriate technologies to meet customer needs.	The firm begins with a new technology, then finds an appropriate market.	The firm assumes that the new product will be built around an established technological subsystem.	Characteristics of the product are highly constrained by the production process.	New products are slight variations of existing configurations.
Distinctions with respect to generic process		Planning phase involves matching technology and market. Concept development assumes a given technology.	Concept development assumes a technology platform.	Both process and product must be developed together from the very beginning, or an existing production process must be specified from the beginning.	Similarity of projects allows for a highly structured development process.
Examples	Most sporting goods, furniture, tools.	Gore-Tex rainwear, Tyvek envelopes.	Consumer electronics, computers, printers.	Snack foods, cereal, chemicals, semiconductors.	Switches, motors, batteries, containers.

Process-Intensive Products

Planning for process-intensive products centers on the production process that an organization has in place. The objective is to generate products that utilize the organization's process capabilities. New-product ideas are those that can be produced by the existing process. Examples of process-intensive products include foods, beverages, chemicals, and semiconductors. Pepsi's development of the Sierra Mist carbonated beverage is an example of a process-intensive product.

Customized Products

Customized products are incremental variations of existing products, and may be developed to meet specific needs of customers. The organization pursues a very structured and detailed development process. The intent is to customize the product to meet the customer's specific specifications. For example, large commercial aircraft orders are often customized to meet the specific preferences of airline carriers.

Proactive Cannibalization

Proactive cannibalization consists of the pursuit of a deliberate, ongoing strategy of developing and introducing new products that attract the buyers of a company's existing products. The strategic logic of this concept is offering buyers a better solution to a need currently being satisfied. Executive resistance to cannibalization is driven by the belief that it is unproductive for a company to compete with its own products and services, rather than targeting those of competitors. Nonetheless, the reality is that changes in market requirements and customer value opportunities will result in threats for existing products and technologies.

There are various examples of the negative consequences of avoiding cannibalization initiatives in the communications, financial services, retailing, and other sectors. Encyclopaedia Britannica's failure to recognize the threat of CD-ROM technology is illustrative. Proactive cannibalization may be essential to many firms to sustain a competitive advantage and achieve financial performance and growth objectives. In support of the logic of proactive cannibalization, research sponsored by the Marketing Science Institute indicates that managers of successful firms proactively resist the instinct to retain the value of past investments in product development.[46] They pursue proactive cannibalization initiatives.

Summary

New-product planning is a vital activity in every company, and it applies to services as well as physical products. Companies that are successful in new-product planning follow a step-by-step process of new-product planning combined with effective organization designs for managing new products. Experience and learning help these firms to improve product planning over time. The corporate cultures of companies, like Microsoft, encourage innovation.

Top management often defines the product, market, and technology scope of new-product ideas to be considered by an organization. The steps in new-product planning include customer needs analysis, idea generation and screening, concept evaluation, business analysis, product development and testing, marketing strategy development, market testing, and commercialization (Exhibit 8.3).

Idea generation starts the process of planning for a new-product. There are various internal and external sources of new-product ideas. Ideas are generated by information search, marketing research, research and development, incentives, and acquisition. Screening, evaluation, and business analysis help determine if the new-product concept is sufficiently attractive to justify proceeding with development.

Design of the product and use testing transform the product from a concept into a prototype. Product development creates one or more prototypes. Product testing obtains user reaction to the new-product. Manufacturing development determines how to produce the product in commercial quantities at costs that will enable the firm to price the product at a level attractive to buyers. Marketing strategy development begins early in the product planning process. A complete marketing strategy is needed for a totally new-product. Product line additions, modifications, and other changes require a less extensive development of marketing strategy.

Completion of the product design and marketing strategy moves the process to the market testing stage. At this point management may decide to obtain some form of market reaction to the new product before full-scale market entry. Testing options include simulated test marketing, scanner-based test marketing, and conventional test marketing. Industrial products are not market-tested as much as consumer products, although frequently purchased nondurables can be tested. Instead, use tests of product prototypes are more typical for industrial products. Commercialization completes the planning process, moving the product into the marketplace to pursue sales and profit performance objectives.

The market-driven, customer-focused generic planning process provides the basic guide to developing new products. Nonetheless, some variations are necessary in applying the process when technology plays a lead role, existing product platforms influence new-product development, manufacturing processes constrain product scope, or incremental variations are used to customize products. Finally, proactive cannibalization initiatives should be considered in the innovation strategies of all companies.

Internet Applications

A. Visit the Web site of the Gap (*www.gap.com*). Discuss how the Web can be used in new-product planning for a bricks-and-mortar retailer such as the Gap.

B. Virgin Group Ltd. is an interesting corporate conglomerate headed by British tycoon Richard C.N. Branson. Visit Virgin.com and develop a critical analysis of Virgin's new-product strategy of launching a portfolio of online businesses.

C. Dell Inc. is expanding its product portfolio. Go to *www.dell.com* and describe the product categories in which Dell competes.

D. Visit the H&M Web site and compare H&M's product offerings with those offered by Gap (*www.gap.com*).

Feature Applications

A. The Benetton Strategy Feature describes the potential risks of expanding too far beyond the core business. How should new-product planners avoid this problem without disregarding all potential opportunities beyond the core business?

B. The Cross-Functional Feature describes how the design consultant IDEO assists companies in new-product design. Discuss the advantages and limitations of having this activity performed by a consultant rather than internally.

C. Review the content of the Innovation Feature "Microsoft and Intel Moving In on PC Makers' Turf." Consider the risks for established companies in developing new products that put them in direct competition with their own customers. Is it appropriate for Microsoft and Intel to go in this direction?

Questions for Review and Discussion

1. Explain the relationship between customer satisfaction and customer value.
2. In many consumer products companies, marketing executives seem to play the lead role in new-product planning, whereas research and development executives occupy this position in firms with very complex products such as electronics. Why do these differences exist? Do you agree that such differences should occur?
3. Discuss the features and limitations of focus group interviews for use in new-product planning.
4. Identify and discuss the important issues in deciding how to organize for new-product planning.
5. Discuss the issues and trade-offs of using tight evaluation versus loose evaluation procedures as a product concept moves through the planning process to the commercialization stage.
6. What factors may affect the length of the new-product planning process?
7. Compare and contrast the use of scanner tests and conventional market tests.
8. Is the use of a single-city test market appropriate? Discuss.
9. Examine the new-product planning process (Exhibit 8.3), assuming a platform strategy is being used by the organization. How does the platform strategy alter the planning process?
10. Discuss the potential role of the Internet in the new-product planning process. Which stages of the process may benefit most from Internet initiatives?

Notes

1. Thomas D. Kuczmarski, Erica B. Seamon, Kathryn W. Spilotro, and Zachary T. Johnston, "The Breakthrough Mindset." *Marketing Management,* March/April 2003, 38–43.
2. David Talbot, "LEDS versus Lightbulb," *Technology Review*, May 2003, 32.
3. Daniel Lyons, "Bright Ideas," *Forbes*, October 14, 2002, 154–158.
4. Suzanne Treville, "Improving the Innovation Process," *OR/MS Today*, December 1994, 29.
5. "Getting Hot Ideas from Customers," *Fortune*, May 18, 1992, 86–87.
6. Gary S. Lynn, Joseph G. Morone, and Albert S. Paulson, "Marketing and Discontinuous Innovation: The Probe and Learn Process," *California Management Review*, Spring 1996, 8–37.
7. Ibid.
8. Joseph Morone, *Winning in High-Tech Markets* (Boston: Harvard Business School Press, 1993), 217.
9. Lynn et al., "Marketing and Discontinuous Innovation . . . ," 11.
10. Clayton M. Christensen, *The Innovator's Dilemma* (Boston: Harvard Business School Press, 1997).
11. Clayton M. Christensen and Michael E. Raynor, *The Innovator's Solution* (Boston: Harvard Business School Press, 2003).
12. Richard Walters, "Never Forget to Nurture the Next Big Idea," *Financial Times*, May 15, 2001, 21.
13. Robert Cooper, "Benchmarking new-product Performance: Results of the Best Practices Study, "*European Management Journal*, February 1998, 1–7; "Producer Power," *The Economist*, March 4, 1995, 70; Kuczmarski et al. "The Breakthrough Mindset."
14. Lawrence Ingrassia, "By Improving Scratch Paper, 3M Gets New-Product Winner," *The Wall Street Journal*, March 31, 1983, 27.
15. Kuczmarski et al. "The Breakthrough Mindset," 43.
16. Cooper, "Benchmarking New Product Performance."
17. "Simplifying Philips," *The Economist*, June 12, 2004, 66.
18. Eric M. Olsen, Orville C. Walker Jr., and Robert W. Ruekert, "Organizing for Effective New-Product Development: The Moderating Role of Product Innovativeness." *Journal of Marketing*, January 1995, 48–62.
19. Ibid.
20. Darrell Rigby and Chris Zook, "Open-Market Innovation," *Harvard Business Review*, October 2002, 80–89.

21. Jay Greene, John Carey, Michael Arndt, and Otis Port, "Reinventing Corporate R&D," *BusinessWeek*, September 22, 2003, 72–73.
22. Glen L. Urban and Eric von Hippel, "Lead User Analyses for the Development of New Industrial Products," *Management Science*, May 1988, 569–582.
23. Stefan Thomke and Eric von Hippel, "Customers as Innovators," *Harvard Business Review*, April 2002, 74–81.
24. Prahalad and Ramaswamy, *The Future of Competition*.
25. Jay Greene, John Carey, Michael Arndt, and Otis Port, "Reinventing Corporate R&D," *BusinessWeek*, September 22, 2003, 72–73.
26. C. Merle Crawford and C. Anthony Di Benedetto, *New Products Management,* 7th ed. (Burr Ridge, IL: Irwin/McGraw-Hill, 2003), Chapter 4.
27. Cooper, "Benchmarking New Product Performance."
28. Elliot Spagat, "A Web Gadget Fizzles Despite a Salesman's Dazzle," *The Wall Street Journal*, June 27, 2001, B1, B4.
29. William R. Dillon, Thomas J. Madden, and Neil H. Firtle, *Marketing Research in a Marketing Environment*, 3rd ed. (Burr Ridge, IL: Richard D. Irwin Inc., 1994).
30. Glen L. Urban, *Digital Marketing Strategy* (Upper Saddle River, NJ: Pearson Prentice Hall, 2004), 96.
31. Almar Latour, "Disconnected," *The Wall Street Journal*, June 5, 2001, A1, A8. "Vision, Meet Reality," *The Economist*, September 4, 2004, 63–65.
32. Crawford and Di Benedetto, *New Products Management*, Chapter 12.
33. Dillon, Madden, and Firtle, *Marketing Research*, 582–584.
34. See, for example, James H. Gilmore and B. Joseph Pine II, "The Four Faces of Mass Customization," *Harvard Business Review*, January–February 1997, 91–101; and Kathleen M. Eisenhardt and Shona L. Brown, "Time Pacing: Competing in Markets That Won't Stand Still," *Harvard Business Review*, March–April 1998, 67.
35. Crawford and DiBenedetto, *New Products Management*, 411.
36. Dillon, Madden, and Firtle, *Marketing Research*, 639.
37. Ibid.
38. Ibid.
39. Ibid.
40. Judith Waldrop, "All-American Markets." *American Demographics*, January 1992.
41. Gary L. Lillien, Phillip Kotler, and Sridhar Moorthy, *Marketing Models* (Upper Saddle River, NJ: Prentice Hall, 1992).
42. Everett M. Rogers, *Diffusion of Innovations* (New York: Free Press, 1962).
43. Ibid.
44. Norhiko Shirouzu, "P&G's Joy Makes an Unlikely Splash in Japan," *The Wall Street Journal*, December 19, 1997, B1 and B8.
45. The following discussion is based on Karl T. Ulrich and Steven D. Eppinger, *Product Design and Development*, 2nd ed. (Burr Ridge, IL: Irwin/McGraw-Hill Inc., 2000), 20–23.
46. Rajesh K. Chandy and Gerald J. Tellis, "Organizing for Radical Product Innovation," Innovation," *MSI Report No. 98–102*. (Cambridge, MA: Marketing Science Institute, 1998).

Cases for Part 3

Case 3-1

Samsung Electronics (A)

To managers of Samsung Electronics' sprawling television plant in Suwon, South Korea, it seemed like a no-brainer. During the depth of the country's economic crisis in early 1998, the Korean won was wallowing at 1,800 to the dollar—less than half its value of a year earlier. That provided a golden opportunity to throw production lines into overdrive and flood export markets with TVs while the currency was still cheap.

But rather than giving the green light, Samsung Electronics President Yun Jong Yong rebuked his eager managers. Just a few months earlier, he had shut down the Suwon plant for two months because so many unsold TVs and other appliances had piled up in Samsung warehouses. The costs of carrying that inventory had been devastating to the company's balance sheets. Samsung wouldn't repeat the mistake. Declaring war on unsold inventory, Yun said Samsung factories would only produce goods after orders were in hand and profitability assured.

Putting profitability before gross sales is basic business common sense in the West. But it was a radical concept at Samsung and other Korean conglomerates, which for decades had been obsessed with exports and record production runs. Now, Samsung Electronics managers hail Yun's profits-first decree as pivotal in a remarkable corporate comeback. "Shutting the TV plant sent a very strong signal to the staff," says Park Sung Chil, Samsung's director of supply-chain management. The just-in-time approach to production has enabled Samsung to shave $3 billion in inventory costs and accounts receivable (Exhibit 1).

High-End Focus

Yun is spearheading what may well be a revolution in Korean industry. Since he took the helm of the sprawling Samsung Group's electronics businesses in January, 1997, Yun, a 30-year company veteran, has been reversing many practices that have long characterized Korea's *chaebol.* Samsung Electronics has dramatically reduced its debts, sold or spun off dozens of assets unrelated to its core businesses, set up financial and managerial fire walls

EXHIBIT 1
Anatomy of a Turnaround
Source: *BusinessWeek*

ANATOMY OF A TURNAROUND

FINANCIAL RESTRUCTURING Some $10 billion in debt has been wiped out since 1997. Dozens of companies have been sold off or spun off. Stakes in money-losing Samsung Motor and computer maker AST have been written off.

PROFITS FIRST The old obsession with market share and setting production and export records is giving way to a focus on making money with high-end products based on innovative designs.

STREAMLINING Managers now strive to produce goods only after orders are placed and get them to customers within days, eliminating billions of dollars in inventory costs and accounts receivable.

DIVERSIFICATION Once dependent on commodity memory chips for half of sales and 90% of profits, Samsung Electronics has greatly broadened its base to become a global giant in telecom devices, flat-planel displays, and digital appliances. Is investing in nonmemory semiconductors.

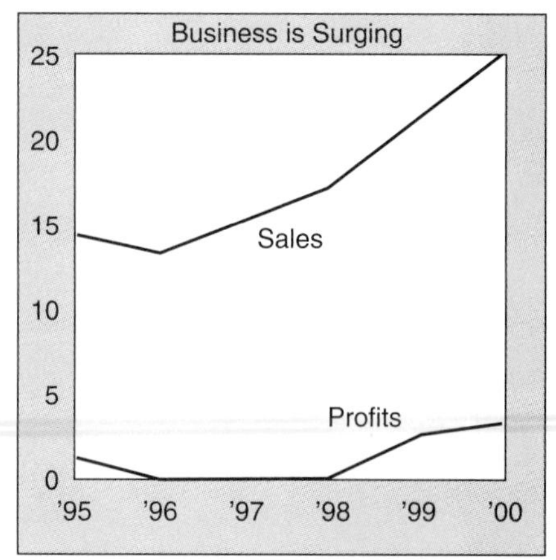

▲Billions of Dollars
Source: Samsung Electronics.
Projections by Salomon Smith Barney.

between itself and other Samsung companies, and cut a third of its workforce. And it is striving to abandon its dependence on cheap commodity products to focus instead on high-end goods employing innovative designs.

The ultimate aim is to guide the company into the global electronics elite. With core strengths in microelectronics, telecom equipment, PCs, and consumer appliances, Samsung is positioned in each major segment of the so-called "digital convergence" and aims to rank alongside the likes of Sony Corp. and Philips Electronics. In the coming years, Samsung plans to spin out a full range of Next Age products, from affordable digital televisions and "smart cards" loaded with movies and data to sleek wireless phones enabling users to access the Web, watch TV, and listen to music.

The management transformation is hardly complete. And many *chaebol* critics warn that the lack of accountability to outside shareholders means the founding families behind groups such as Samsung could resort to business as usual once they are safely out of crisis. "Sure, Samsung has built up competence in its core businesses," says Korea University finance professor Jang Ha Sung. "The problem is that changes in its financial and business structures could be temporary without a change in corporate governance."

"Exemplary Student"

But there's little doubt the improvement has been dramatic. After weathering a harrowing free fall in profits and sales that started with the 1996 slump in memory chips, Samsung Electronics is stronger than ever. This year, Salomon Smith Barney figures the company should post a net profit of at least $2.7 billion on a 24% increase in sales, to $22 billion. The results even reflect a $700 million write-off of Samsung Electronics' investments in cars and failed U.S. computer maker AST Research Inc. "Samsung has been an exemplary student," says Lee Hun Jai, chairman of the Financial Supervisory Commission, which is overseeing Korea's corporate and financial overhaul.

Of course, a strong rebound in demand for Samsung's bread-and-butter product, dynamic random access memory (DRAM) chips, accounts for a good chunk of this turnaround. Since June, prices for 64-megabit DRAMs have surged from around $4 to $10. Samsung, one of the few big memory chip producers that kept investing in capacity through the down cycle, benefited the most, blowing past Japanese rivals.

But memory chips are not the whole story. Although DRAMs probably will account for 45% of 1999 profits, other sectors also are coming on strong. Samsung Electronics has emerged as the world's leader in thin-film transistor flat-panel displays for computers, another sector where prices have leapt. Samsung's telecom division, bolstered by soaring demand at home for its $380 voice-activated SCH-A100 cell phone and a rising share of the U.S. cellular market, now ranks among the world's top six producers of wireless handsets. It also is the world's leading producer of computer monitors. All 15 of Samsung Electronics' main product groups, including the consumer-appliance unit that had lost money for five years, are now in the black. That's a claim Samsung couldn't make even in the fat mid-'90s.

Samsung Electronics' diversification means its business is much better balanced than before the crisis. In 1995, memory chips accounted for 90% of corporate profits and half of all sales. They now account for about 20% of sales, with the rest spread more evenly among computer and telecom products. Samsung also is making gains in nonmemory chips, where it badly lags U.S. and Japanese producers. The focus is now on chips used in Samsung's array of digital phones, TVs, cameras, and smart cards.

Samsung Electronics executives concede none of these vital changes would have occurred were it not for two disasters—the crash in memory-chip prices, followed in 1997 by Korea's financial collapse. A $3.2 billion profit in 1995, when 16-Mb DRAMs fetched $40 apiece, offset steady losses in many of the company's other businesses. When DRAM prices plunged, Samsung Electronics realized that its reliance on a volatile commodity product "was a very, very risky strategy," says Yun. The company long knew it had to improve efficiency, restructure, and pare back its workforce.

Public Pressure

Nor did Samsung Electronics seriously tackle its wasteful manufacturing practices. In TVs, the company was carrying up to three months of excess inventory by 1997. Not only was Samsung paying to finance the inventory, but also prices for its electronics products were often 30% lower by the time they were sold. "In the past, we were evaluated by unit manufacturing cost alone," explains supply-chain director Park. "So we produced and produced and produced, not caring whether or not it was sold." At the same time, Samsung Group Chairman Lee Kun Hee was under intense public pressure for allowing the group's debts to pile up so high and for forcing affiliates such as Samsung Electronics to subsidize such ill-considered investments as a $3.5 billion plunge into cars.

EXHIBIT 2
Growth Is Now Better Balanced

Source: Samsung Electronics. Projections by Salomon Smith Barney.

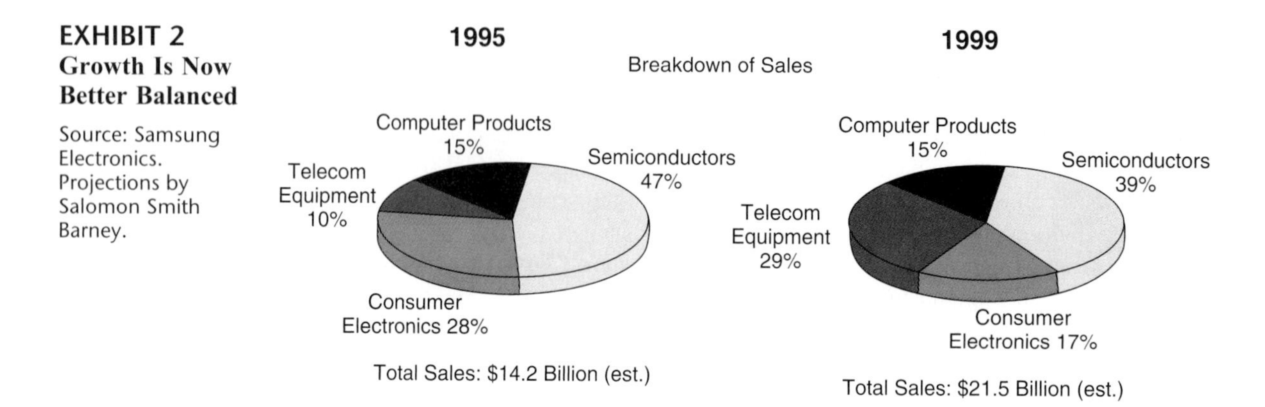

Since 1997, Yun has sold or spun off 57 businesses, from refrigerators and pagers to satellite receivers. Such asset sales have helped Samsung Electronics to slash debt by $10.8 billion. It also has cut the number of employees from 84,000 to 54,000.

The restructuring helped persuade bankers to keep Samsung's credit lines open at a critical time in the semiconductor cycle. Betting the DRAM market would rebound, Yun kept adding cutting-edge capacity while the Japanese held back. The move paid off when the cycle turned to boom again. Just as important was better supply-chain management, which has halved inventory from an average of $3.6 billion in 1997.

Samsung's next goal is to rank alongside the consumer-electronics giants of Japan and Europe. It has made the biggest strides in cellular phones (Exhibit 2). In Korea, the company expects to sell around 7 million wireless handsets this year. It already is marketing a new phone with a flip-up touch screen that allows users to send e-mails and access English/Korean dictionaries, the Bible, Buddhist songbooks, and games. Another phone has a built-in TV receiver; still another is small enough to wear as a wristwatch.

Samsung also is surging in the U.S. A team-up with Sprint PCS has helped it grab 19% of the CDMA phone market. One big hit is the SCH-3500, a $149 set that dials numbers on voice command. By test-marketing innovative products in Korea, "when they hit here, they have a product that's absolutely ready to go to market," says Andrew Sukawaty, president of Sprint's PCS unit. "We don't go through the teething problems we go through with some other vendors."

Samsung is making a similarly bold bet on digital TVs, hoping to grab 10% of the market when prices fall within reach of middle-class families. Because digital home appliances are evolving so rapidly, it's too early to tell whether Samsung Electronics will emerge a winner. Kimihide Takano, a Tokyo-based electronics analyst with Dresdner Kleinwort Benson Asia, warns that the consumer electronics sector is poised for a shakeout. To survive, he says, a company "won't be able to just churn out commodity products." That is a major reason why Samsung Electronics is now plowing much of its profits from DRAMs into nonmemory chips. By producing cutting-edge chips with telecom, graphics, and processing capability in-house, Samsung hopes to have an edge over rivals who depend on outsiders for key components.

While its manufacturing prowess is clear, Samsung Electronics has its work cut out showing it can also succeed as an innovator in specialty-chip design. But this year, the nonmemory unit hopes to earn up to $200 million on sales of $1 billion, with 50% sales growth expected in 2000. By next year, it hopes to supply half of Samsung's internal needs for telecom chips. Samsung also is making chip sets for digital TVs. And soon it will market Alpha microprocessors under license from Compaq Computer Corp. Rivals aren't counting Samsung out. "This is a company that is investing in technology and new equipment to stay ahead," says Kenji Tokuyama, who will head NEC's new DRAM venture with Hitachi. "We regard it as a formidable competitor."

A bigger question may be whether Samsung Electronics will maintain its financial discipline long enough to fulfill Yun's vision, especially if the government's *chaebol* watchdogs let down their guard. Insider practices and an obsession with expansion are deeply ingrained in Korea's industrial psyche. But the memories of Korea's economic catastrophe will be impossible to erase. If Samsung Electronics continues to win applause for profits and innovation—rather than size—it could have plenty of motivation to finish the job of reshaping a sprawling conglomerate into a focused, truly global enterprise.

By Moon Ihlwan and Pete Engardio in Seoul, with Irene Kunii in Tokyo and Roger Crockett in Chicago

Source: "Samsung: The Making of a Superstar," *BusinessWeek*, December 20, 1999, 137, 138, 140.

Case 3-2

McDonald's Corp.

Richard Steinig remembers beaming as if he had won the lottery. There he was, all of 27 when he became a junior partner with a McDonald's Corp. franchisee in 1973, just a year after starting as a $115-a-week manager trainee in Miami. "It was an incredible feeling," says Steinig. His two stores each generated $80,000 in annual sales, and he pocketed more than 15% of that as profit. Not bad at a time when the minimum wage was still under $2 an hour and a McDonald's hamburger and fries set you back less than a dollar, even with a regular Coke.

Fast-forward 30 years. Franchise owner Steinig's four restaurants average annual sales of $1.56 million, but his face is creased with worry. Instead of living the American Dream, Steinig says he's barely scraping by. Sales haven't budged since 1999, but costs keep rising. So when McDonald's began advertising its $1 menu featuring the Big N' Tasty burger, Steinig rebelled. The popular item cost him $1.07 to make—so he sells it for $2.25 unless a customer asks for the $1 promotion price. No wonder profit margins are no more than half of what they were when he started out. "We have become our worst enemy," Steinig says.

Welcome to Hamburger Hell. For decades, McDonald's was a juggernaut. It gave millions of Americans their first jobs while changing the way a nation ate. It rose from a single outlet in a nondescript Chicago suburb to become an American icon. But today, McDonald's is a reeling giant that teeters from one mess to another.

Consider the events of just the past three months: On Dec. 5, after watching McDonald's stock slide 60% in three years, the board ousted Chief Executive Jack M. Greenberg, 60. His tenure was marked by the introduction of 40 new menu items, none of which caught on big, and the purchase of a handful of non-burger chains, none of which were rolled out widely enough to make much difference. Indeed, his critics say that by trying so many different things—and executing them poorly—Greenberg let the burger business deteriorate. Consumer surveys show that service and quality now lag far behind those of rivals.

The company's solution was to bring back retired Vice-Chairman James R. Cantalupo, 59, who had overseen McDonald's successful international expansion in the '80s and '90s. Unfortunately, seven weeks later, the company reported the first quarterly loss in its 47-year history. Then it revealed that January sales at outlets open at least a year skidded 2.4%, after sliding 2.1% in 2002.

Can Cantalupo reverse the long slide at McDonald's? When he and his new team lay out their plan to analysts in early April, they are expected to concentrate on getting the basics of service and quality right, in part by reinstituting a tough "up or out" grading system that will kick out underperforming franchisees. "We have to rebuild the foundation. It's fruitless to add growth if the foundation is weak," says Cantalupo. He gives himself 18 months to do that with help from Australian-bred chief operating officer, Charles Bell, 42, whom Cantalupo has designated his successor, and Mats Lederhausen, a 39-year-old Swede in charge of global strategy (Exhibit 1).

But the problems at McDonald's go way beyond cleaning up restaurants and freshening the menu. The chain is being squeezed by long-term trends that threaten to leave it marginalized. It faces a rapidly fragmenting market, where America's recent immigrants have made once-exotic foods like sushi and burritos everyday options, and quick meals of all sorts can be found in supermarkets, convenience stores, even vending machines. One of the fastest-growing restaurant categories is the "fast-casual" segment—those places with slightly more expensive menus, such as Cosi, a sandwich shop, or Quizno's, a gourmet sub sandwich chain, where customers find the food healthier and better-tasting. As Lederhausen succinctly puts it: "We are clearly living through the death of the mass market."

If so, it may well mark the end of McDonald's long run as a growth company. Cantalupo seemed to

EXHIBIT 1

Out of the Frying Pan. . .

New CEO Cantalupo is giving himself 18 months to get McDonald's back on track. He faces a daunting to-do list:

Improve the Basics

McDonald's lags in consumer surveys. Using mystery shoppers and unannounced inspections, it will give special help to laggard franchisees. But if they flunk again, Cantalupo vows, they'll lose their shops.

Rekindle the Flame with Franchisees

Franchisees, who own 85% of all U.S. McDonald's, face stagnant sales. So any added costs from new equipment or programs cut into margins. Cantalupo has to get them to buy into his plan.

Whip up Something New

McDonald's last big hit was Chicken McNuggets in 1983. Rather than trying to do too much in his test kitchens, Cantalupo may encourage franchisees—who created the Big Mac and Egg McMuffin—to be more creative.

Stop Eating Your Own Lunch

Even with cutbacks, McDonald's plans to add 1,230 hamburger outlets worldwide in 2003. Some analysts say that to avoid cannibalization, Cantalupo needs to shutter more than the 500 sites he plans on closing this year.

acknowledge as much when he slashed sales growth estimates in the near term to only 2% annually, down from 15%. No one at Oak Brook (Ill.) headquarters blames the strong dollar or mad cow disease anymore for the company's problems—a big change from the Greenberg era. Perhaps most telling is that the chain plans to add only 250 new outlets in the U.S. this year, 40% fewer than in 2002. Sales in Europe rose only 1%, and the chain this year will add only 200 units to the 6,070 it has there—30% fewer new openings than last year. Meanwhile, it is closing 176 of its 2,800 stores in Japan because of the economic doldrums there.

Up until a few years ago, franchisees clamored to jump on board. But last year, in an exodus that was unheard of in Mickey D's heyday, 126 franchisees left the system, with 68, representing 169 restaurants, forced out for poor performance. The others left seeking greener pastures. The company buys back franchises if they cannot be sold, so forcing out a franchisee is not cheap. McDonald's took a pretax charge of $292 million last quarter to close 719 restaurants—200 in 2002 and the rest expected this year.

For their part, investors have already accepted that the growth days are over. Those who remain will happily settle for steady dividends. Last Oct. 22, when McDonald's announced a 1¢ hike in its annual dividend, to 23½¢, its stock rose 9%, to $18.95—even though the company said third-quarter profits would decline. It was the biggest one-day gain for McDonald's on the New York Stock Exchange in at least two years. Today, though, the stock is near an eight-year low of $13.50, off 48% in the past year (Exhibit 2). One of the few money managers willing to give McDonald's a chance, Wendell L. Perkins at Johnson Asset Management in Racine, Wis., says: "McDonald's needs to understand that it is a different company from 10 years ago and increase its dividend to return some of that cash flow to shareholders to reflect its mature market position."

The company has the cash to boost shareholder payouts. It recently canceled an expensive stock buyback program. Cantalupo won praise on Wall Street for killing an expensive revamp of the company's technology that would have cost $1 billion. But if increasing the dividend would make Wall Street happy, it would raise problems with its 2,461 franchisees. That would be essentially an admission that McDonald's is giving up on the kind of growth for which they signed up.

Already, franchisees who see the chain as stuck in a rut are jumping ship to faster-growing rivals. Paul

EXHIBIT 2 For Investors, Only Heartburn

Data: Bloomberg Financial Markets

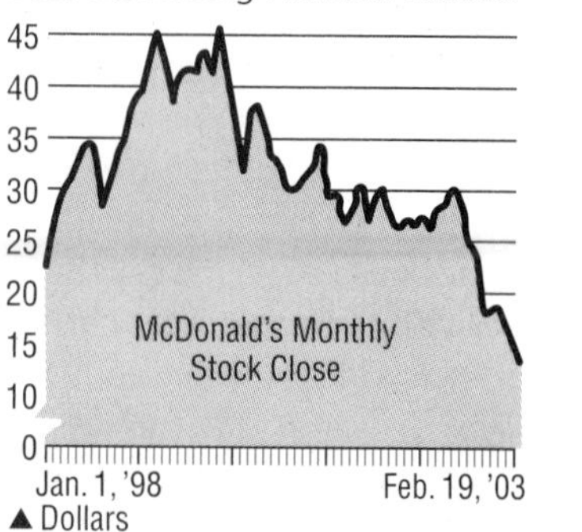

Saber, a McDonald's franchisee for 17 years, sold his 14 restaurants back to the company in 2000 when he realized that eating habits were shifting away from McDonald's burgers to fresher, better-tasting food. So he moved to rival Panera Bread Co., a fast-growing national bakery café chain. "The McDonald's-type fast food isn't relevant to today's consumer," says Saber, who will open 15 Paneras in San Diego.

In the past, owner-operators were McDonald's evangelists. Prospective franchisees were once so eager to get into the two-year training program that they would wait in line for hours when applications were handed out at the chain's offices around the country. But there aren't any lines today, and many existing franchisees feel alienated. They have seen their margins dip to a paltry 4%, from 15% at the peak. Richard Adams, a former franchisee and a food consultant, claims that as many as 20 franchisees are currently leaving McDonald's every month. Why? "Because it's so hard to survive these days," he says.

One of the biggest sore points for franchisees is the top-down manner in which Greenberg and other past CEOs attempted to fix pricing and menu problems. Many owner-operators still grumble over the $18,000 to $100,000 they had to spend in the late 1990s to install company-mandated "Made for You" kitchen upgrades in each restaurant. The new kitchens were supposed to speed up orders and accommodate new menu items. But in the end, they actually slowed service. Reggie Webb, who operates 11 McDonald's restaurants in Los Angeles, says his sales have dipped by an average of $50,000 at each of his outlets over the past 15 years. "From my perspective, I am working harder than ever and making less than I ever had on an average-store basis," says Webb. He'll have to open his wallet again if McDonald's includes his units in the next 200 restaurants it selects for refurbishing. Franchisees pay 70% of that $150,000 cost.

Franchisees also beef about McDonald's addiction to discounting. When McDonald's cut prices in a 1997 price war, sales fell over the next four months. The lesson should have been obvious. "Pulling hard on the price lever is dangerous. It risks cheapening the brand," says Sam Rovit, a partner at Chicago consultant Bain & Co. Yet Cantalupo is sticking with the $1 menu program introduced last year. "We like to wear out our competitors with our price," he says. Burger King and Wendy's International Inc. admit that the tactic is squeezing their sales. But in the five months since its debut, the $1 menu has done nothing to improve McDonald's results.

As a last resort, McDonald's is getting rid of the weakest franchises. Continuous growth can no longer bail out underperformers, so Cantalupo is enforcing a "tough love" program that Greenberg reinstated last year after the company gave it up in 1990. Owners that flunk the rating and inspection system will get a chance to clean up their act. But if they don't improve, they'll be booted.

The decline in McDonald's once-vaunted service and quality can be traced to its expansion of the 1990s, when headquarters stopped grading franchises for cleanliness, speed, and service. Training declined as restaurants fought for workers in a tight labor market. That led to a falloff in kitchen and counter skills—according to a 2002 survey by Columbus (Ohio) market researcher Global Growth Group, McDonald's came in third in average service time behind Wendy's and sandwich shop Chick-fil-A Inc. Wendy's took an average 127 seconds to place and fill an order, vs. 151 seconds at Chick-fil-A and 163 at McDonald's. That may not seem like much, but Greenberg has said that saving six seconds at a drive-through brings a 1% increase in sales.

Trouble is, it's tough to sell franchisees on a new quality gauge at the same time the company is asking them to do everything from offering cheap burgers to shouldering renovation costs. Franchising works best when a market is expanding and owners can be rewarded for meeting incentives. In the past, franchisees who beat McDonald's national sales average were typically rewarded with the chance to open or buy more stores. The largest franchisees now operate upwards of 50 stores. But with falling sales, those incentives don't cut it. "Any company today has to be very vigilant about their business model and willing to break it, even if it's successful, to make sure they stay on top of the changing trends," says Alan Feldman, CEO of Midas Inc., who was COO for domestic operations at McDonald's until January, 2002. "You can't just go on cloning your business into the future."

By the late 1990s, it was clear that the system was losing traction. New menu items like the low-fat McLean Deluxe and Arch Deluxe burgers, meant to appeal to adults, bombed. Non-burger offerings did no better, often because of poor planning. Consultant Michael Seid, who manages a franchise consulting firm in West Hartford, Conn., points out that McDonald's offered a pizza that didn't fit through the drive-through window and salad shakers that were packed so tightly that dressing couldn't flow through them. By 1998, McDonald's posted its first-ever decline in annual earnings and then-CEO Michael R. Quinlan was out, replaced by Greenberg, a 16-year McDonald's veteran.

Greenberg won points for braking the chain's runaway U.S. expansion. He also broadened its portfolio, acquiring Chipotle Mexican Grill and Boston Market Corp. But he was unable to focus on the new ventures while also improving quality, getting the new kitchens rolled out, and developing new menu items. Says Los Angeles franchisee Webb: "We would have been better off trying fewer things and making them work." Greenberg was unable to reverse skidding sales and profits, and after last year's disastrous fourth quarter, he offered his resignation at the Dec. 5 board meeting. There were no angry words from directors. But there were no objections, either.

Insiders say Cantalupo, who had retired only a year earlier, was the only candidate seriously considered to take over, despite shareholder sentiment for an outsider. The board felt that it needed someone who knew the company and could move quickly. Cantalupo has chosen to work with younger McDonald's executives, whom he feels will bring energy and fresh ideas to the table. Bell, formerly president of McDonald's Europe, became a store manager in his native Australia at 19 and rose through the ranks. There, he launched a coffeehouse concept called McCafe, which is now being introduced around the globe. He later achieved success in France, where he abandoned McDonald's cookie-cutter orange-and-yellow stores for individualized ones that offer local fare like the ham-and-cheese Croque McDo.

The second top executive Cantalupo has recruited is a bona fide outsider—at least by company standards. Lederhausen holds an MBA from the Stockholm School of Economics and worked with Boston Consulting Group Inc. for two years. However, he jokes that he grew up in a french-fry vat because his father introduced McDonald's to Sweden in 1973. Lederhausen is in charge of growth and menu development.

Getting the recipe right will be tougher now that consumers have tasted better burgers. While McDonald's says it may start toasting its buns longer to get the flavor right, rivals go even further. Industry experts point to 160-store In-N-Out, a profitable California burger chain. Its burgers are grilled when ordered—no heat lamps to warm up precooked food. Today, In-N-Out is rated No. 1 by fast-food consumers tracked by consultant Sandelman & Associates Inc. in San Diego. "The burger category has great strength," adds David C. Novak, chairman and CEO of Yum! Brands Inc., parent of KFC and Taco Bell. "That's America's food. People love hamburgers."

McDonald's best hope to recapture that love might be to turn to its most innovative franchisees. Take Irwin Kruger in New York, who recently opened a 17,000-square-foot showcase unit in Times Square with video monitors showing movie trailers, brick walls, theatrical lighting—and strong profits. "We're slated to have sales of over $5 million this year and profits exceeding 10%," says Kruger. Rejuvenated marketing would help, too: McDonald's called its top ad agencies together in February to draw up a plan that would go beyond the ubiquitous Disney movie tie-ins.

It will take nothing short of a marketing miracle, though, to return McDonald's to its youthful vigor. "They are at a critical juncture and what they do today will shape whether they just fade away or recapture some of the magic and greatness again," says Robert S. Goldin, executive vice-president at food consultant Technomic Inc. As McDonald's settles into middle age, Cantalupo and his team may have to settle for stable and reliable.

By Pallavi Gogoi and Michael Arndt in Oak Brook, Ill.

Source: "Hamburger Hell," *BusinessWeek*, March 3, 2003, 104–108.

Case 3-3

Apex Chemical Company

The Executive Committee of Apex Chemical Company—a medium-sized chemical manufacturer with annual sales of $60 million—is trying to determine which of two new compounds the company should market. The two products were expected to have the same gross margin percentage. The following conversation takes place between the vice president for research, Ralph Rogovin, the vice president for marketing, Miles Mumford, and the president, Paul Prendigast.

VP-Research: Compound A-115, a new electrolysis agent, is the one; there just isn't any doubt about it. Why, for precipitating a synergistic reaction in silver electrolysis, it has a distinct advantage over anything now on the market.

President: That makes sense, Ralph. Apex has always tried to avoid "me too" products, and if this one is that much better . . . what do you think, Miles?

VP-Marketing: Well, I favor the idea of Compound B-227, the plastic oxidizer. We have some reputation in that field; we're already known for our plastic oxidizers.

VP-Research: Yes, Miles, but this one isn't really better than the ones we already have. It belongs to the beta-prednigone group, and they just aren't as good as the stigones are. We *do* have the best stigone in the field.

President: Just the same, Ralph, the beta-prednigones are cutting into our stigone sales. The board of directors has been giving me a going-over on that one.

VP-Marketing: Yes, Ralph, maybe they're not as good scientists as we are—or think we are—but the buyers in the market seem to insist on buying beta-prednigones. How do you explain that? The betas have 60 percent of the market now.

VP-Research: That's your job, not mine, Miles. If we can't sell the best product—and I can prove it *is* the best, as you've seen from my data and computations—then there's something wrong with Apex's marketing effort.

President: What do you say to that, Miles? What *is* the explanation?

VP-Marketing: Well, it's a very tricky field—the process in which these compounds are used is always touch-and-go; everyone is always trying something new.

VP-Research: All the more reason to put our effort behind Compound A-115, in the electrolysis field. Here we know that we have a real technical breakthrough. I agree with Paul that that's our strength.

President: What about that, Miles? Why not stay out of the dogfight represented by Compound B-227, if the plastic oxidizer market is as tricky as you say?

VP-Marketing: I don't feel just right about it, Paul. I understand that the electrolysis market is pretty satisfied with the present products. We did a survey and 95 percent said they were satisfied with the Hamfield Company's product.

President: It's a big market, too, isn't it, Miles?

VP-Marketing: Yes, about $10 million a year total.

President: And only one strongly entrenched company—Hamfield?

VP-Marketing: Yes, I must admit it's not like the plastic oxidizer situation—where there are three strong competitors and about a half-dozen who are selling off-brands. On the other hand, oxidizers are a $40 million market—four times as big.

President: That's true, Miles. Furthermore our oxidizer sales represent 25 percent of our total sales.

VP-Research: But we've been losing ground the past year. Our oxidizer sales dropped 10 percent, didn't they, Miles? While the total oxidizer market was growing, didn't you say?

VP-Marketing: Well, the electrolysis field is certainly more stable. Total sales are holding level, and as I said before, Hamfield's share is pretty constant, too.

President: What about the technical requirements in the electrolysis field? With a really improved product we ought to be able . . .

VP-Marketing: Well, to tell you the truth, I don't know very much about the kind of people who use it and how they . . . you see, it's really a different industry.

President: What about it, Ralph?

VP-Research: It's almost a different branch of chemistry, too. But I have plenty of confidence in our laboratory men. I can't see any reason why we should run into trouble . . . It really does have a plus-three-point superiority on a scale of 100—here, the chart shows it crystal clear, Miles.

VP-Marketing: But aren't we spreading ourselves pretty thin—instead of concentrating where our greatest know-how . . . You've always said, Paul, that . . .

President: Yes, I know, but maybe we ought to diversify, too. You know, all our eggs in one basket.

VP-Marketing: But if it's a good basket . . .

VP-Research: Nonsense, Miles, it's the kind of eggs you've got in the basket that counts—and Compound A-115, the electrolysis agent, is scientifically the better one.

VP-Marketing: Yes, but what about taking eggs to the market? Maybe people don't want to buy that particular egg from us, but they would buy Compound B-227—the plastic oxidizer.

President: Eggs, eggs, eggs—I'm saying to both of you, let's just be sure we don't lay any!

Source: Edward C. Bursk and Stephen A. Greyser, *Cases in Marketing Management,* 2nd ed. (Englewood Cliffs, NJ: Prentice-Hall, 1975), 204–10. Reprinted by permission of Prentice-Hall, Englewood Cliffs, NJ.

Case 3-4

Cisco Systems Inc.

For the first few weeks of 2001, John T. Chambers, the irrepressibly optimistic CEO of Cisco Systems Inc., thought the networking giant might neatly sidestep the tech wreck. Twice he had canvassed his top lieutenants, only to rebuff their advice that he lay off workers for the first time in the company's history. But on the evening of Mar. 8, 2001, Chambers landed in Silicon Valley shaken by what he had learned during a two-week business trip around the world. Customer after customer had told him they were slashing spending. Finally, he succumbed: It was time for a massive overhaul. He stayed up all night, hitting the treadmill for hours in his Los Altos Hills home. "I just ran and ran and ran, and thought through the alternatives," he says. At 4 a.m., he decided to call a meeting of his top managers for 6:30 that morning.

It would be a gut-wrenching session. An unusually downbeat Chambers huddled with his top execs and then O.K.'d 8,500 layoffs—18% of the payroll. "This is the toughest decision I've ever had to make," he said, according to one person who was in the room. At 9:30, he left to break the news to employees at his monthly breakfast with workers celebrating birthdays that month. "He had serious feelings of remorse, of 'what could I have done differently?'" says Peter Solvik, the company's former chief information officer. "For a year after that, he was somber."

How times have changed. On Nov. 5, when Cisco announced its quarterly results, Chambers was back to his ebullient self—at one point jokingly asking a vice-president if he was sure he didn't want to raise his forecast in response to an analyst's question. His giddy mood spoke volumes, as did Cisco's results: The company's profits zoomed 76%, to $1.1 billion for the quarter, while sales hit $5.1 billion, the highest level since January, 2001. With orders on the upswing, Cisco said it expects to post 9% to 11% growth in the current quarter.

Cisco isn't just back in fighting trim—it's stronger than ever (Exhibit 1). The company's share of the total $92 billion communications-equipment business has jumped to 16% from 10% in 2001, according to Synergy Research Group Inc.—the biggest land grab in Cisco's history. While battered rivals Lucent Technologies and Nortel Networks are only now glimpsing black ink, Cisco is racking up record profits. It earned $3.6 billion in the most recent fiscal year, nearly a billion dollars more than its previous best in 2000. And with no long-term debt and $19.7 billion in cash and investments, Cisco's balance sheet is among the strongest in the tech industry. Says Chambers: "We've executed to the point that we have 100% of the industry's profits, 100% of the cash, and about 70% of the market cap."

EXHIBIT 1 Trouncing Rivals
The networking juggernaut took a tumble, along with the rest of the industry, in 2001. But it has recovered faster and increased its domination of competitors

Data: JMP Securities LLC

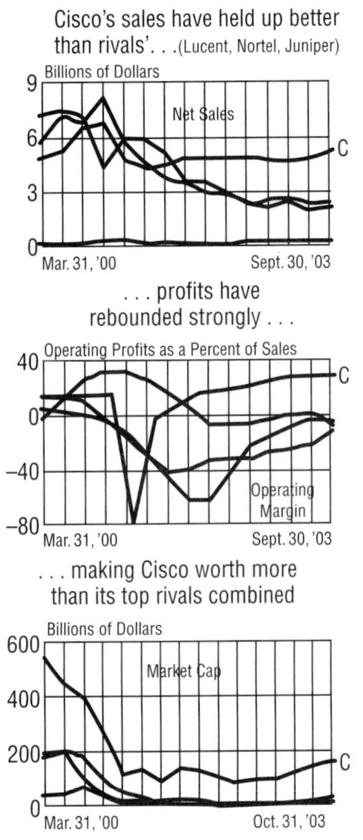

Rebuilt Foundation

Indeed, Cisco could be a case study of how a sullied high-flier can use a slump not only to clean house but also to build a better foundation. While Chambers was late to recognize the worst tech downturn in history, once he realized it was no mere dip, he seized the moment to rethink every aspect of the company—upending its operations, its priorities, even its culture (Exhibit 2).

Chambers replaced the chaos that went with growth at any cost with the order of a company managed for profits. Under a six-point plan, he imposed operating discipline on entrepreneurial staffers who had been too busy taking orders and cashing stock options to bother with efficiency, cost-cutting, or teamwork. Engineers who had been able to chase any idea willy-nilly suddenly had to work only on technologies approved by a newly appointed engineering czar. Midlevel managers with the authority to invest $10 million in a promising startup saw the open checkbook snapped shut. Execs encouraged to compete with one another found that teamwork would count for as much as 30% of their annual bonuses. And staffers who fueled Cisco's 73-company buying binge from 1993 to 2000 by scooping up any networking outfit with a shot at success were told they would be held personally accountable for a deal's financial results. "Process was a dirty word at Cisco, including for the CEO," admits Chambers.

In all, it's the rare tale of an Internet star that turned out to be more, rather than less, than it seemed to be. It would be hard to overstate the battering Chambers' reputation took in the first few months of 2001. He was relentlessly upbeat even as evidence of trouble mounted. Lucent, Gateway, and others announced layoffs, and still Chambers waxed optimistic. He didn't back off projections of 50% revenue growth until Feb. 6—and then only to 30%. He assured investors that Cisco's hyperefficient e-business systems enabled it to forecast demand with near-scientific precision. Then he was proven wildly wrong. After Cisco announced layoffs and a staggering $2.2 billion inventory write-down, Chambers looked like a corporate Goodtime Charlie, incapable of managing in turbulent times. But once his eyes were open, he threw himself into the reality of a new, harsher environment with the same near-religious zeal he had with the Internet boom.

Cisco's conversion has been agonizing for many involved. More than 3,000 resellers and 800 suppliers were squeezed out as Cisco reduced its partnerships to cut costs. Some employees felt the mass layoffs were a draconian overreaction. Even Chambers has paid a price. The 54-year-old West Virginian looks like he has aged 10 years in the past three, with the lines around his eyes and mouth visibly deeper. "It was obviously the most challenging time in my business career," he says.

With the trying times behind him, Chambers now wants to put more distance between Cisco and its rivals. While he won't commit publicly to a specific growth target after being burned so badly, two high-ranking executives say the internal goal is a scorching 20% a year. Is it possible? Cisco sees three engines of growth. For starters, the company already gets 14% of sales from six fast-growing markets it targeted during the downturn, including Wi-Fi and security software. It's also banking on an upgrade cycle in its primary business of selling routers and switches, the large computers that direct the flow of data on the Net and corporate networks. The third

EXHIBIT 2 Cisco's Savvy Overhaul

Here's how the networking giant has put itself back in the catbird seat:

Engineering
In the boom, engineers followed their geek muses wherever they led. In 2001, Cisco centralized engineering, and top execs started setting the tech road map.

Result: Since then, Cisco has cut its product line 27%, to 24,000 models, to focus on the most successful. That has helped win volume discounts worth hundreds of millions of dollars.

Operations
The company used to operate like a band of independent tech tribes. Each unit could choose its own suppliers and manufacturers. Now a committee oversees all such decisions.

Result: Since 2001, Cisco has cut its suppliers and manufacturers, and productivity is surging. Sales per worker has risen 24%, to $548,000, this year.

Acquisitions
Cisco had long been a binge buyer—of even unproven startups with no profits. Now it focuses on established companies that can contribute to earnings.

Result: Acquisitions tumbled from 23 deals in 2000 to two in 2001. And Cisco says home-networking leader Linksys, which Cisco bought in March, contributed to earnings from Day One.

Culture
The old Cisco was known for its *carpe diem* culture—with little coordinated planning. Now teamwork is emphasized.

Result: Some 92% of workers expect to be with Cisco in five years, according to an internal survey of 30,000 staffers, vs. 50% at most companies. And top execs are collaborating—partly because new compensation policies tie 30% of their annual bonuses to their ability to work with peers.

Information Systems
Cisco, an e-business pioneer, is upping the ante with thrice-yearly reviews where execs must map out new ways to use the Web. A goal: Improving Cisco's sales forecasts to prevent a repeat of the $2.2 billion inventory write-off in April, 2001.

Result: Cisco says it realized $2.1 billion in savings from using the Net in 2002. It's now spending $100 million on three big projects, including a database consolidation to improve forecasts.

Growth Strategy
In the past, Cisco focused almost exclusively on networking gear. Now it's pursuing six new markets, including security and Net phones. Over 50% of its $3.3 billion R&D budget in 2002 is for emerging markets, up from the past.

Result: Cisco is making headway in most new markets and gets 14% of its revenues from them. Now Cisco is introducing new products, including wireless gear, such as security cameras, for consumers.

leg of Chambers' growth plan: grabbing a large share of the telecom-gear market as the world's phone companies go from running separate networks for voice, data, and video to a single, more cost-effective network to handle all three. Chambers thinks Cisco can boost its share of the $64 billion telecom market from 3% now to at least 15%, though he won't specify a time frame. Investors are optimistic: Cisco's shares have surged 80% over the past year, to 23.

Still, Chambers will struggle to live up to such sky-high goals. Investors and top execs may think of Cisco as a turbocharged growth company, but it simply isn't anymore. Even in the much-celebrated first fiscal quarter, Cisco's revenues rose only 5%. And that's not going to improve much in the years ahead. Why? It's the law of large numbers: The networking-equipment biz that accounts for 80% of Cisco's revenues is expected to grow a piddling 6% in coming years, according to JMP Securities. Cisco will get a lift from expanding into new markets, particularly telecom, but it's unlikely that top-line growth will pass the low double digits for the foreseeable future. "I think they can get to 10%," says analyst Brantley Thompson of Goldman, Sachs & Co. "I don't think they can get to 15%. At some point, all the tech giants slow down."

Payback?

Ironically, the going may get tougher as the economy rebounds. At the downturn's nadir, most corporations grudgingly paid Cisco's premium prices rather than incur the cost of switching to weaker rivals that might not survive for long. Now customers are starting to shop around—and there are bargains to be had. Dell and China's Huawei Technologies, in particular, are aggressively undercutting Cisco's prices. "Cisco is in denial," says Dell Inc. President Kevin B. Rollins. "In every tech market we've seen, prices and margins come down. It's a law of gravity." Also worrisome are the resellers and suppliers Cisco squeezed during the slump. With the economy bouncing back, many bruised ex-partners, such as networking specialist Xtelesis Corp. in Burlingame, Calif., are eager to help rivals take Cisco down a notch. "They're not hurting now," says President Scott Strochak. "But once customers are investing again and Cisco has lost half of its smaller distributors, I'd like to think it will hurt them."

Cisco also must prove that its newfound discipline hasn't dampened its hard-charging zeal. Some recent departees say there have been frustrations with all the new procedures, and they worry that bureaucracy may slow Cisco down as it battles nimble rivals. One sign of potential trouble is Cisco's inability to hold off upstart Juniper Networks in the market for high-end routers that telephone companies use to handle massive data flows. While Juniper has been gaining share, insiders say Cisco's years-long effort to field a competing product has been stymied by engineering delays. "Cisco has been too conservative," says Tom Nolle, president of consulting firm CIMI Corp.

Still, there's no doubt that Cisco's rebound positions it as a powerhouse for years. The company is more disciplined and cohesive, and Chambers' plans for new markets may change the very nature of Cisco. Besides security software and wireless gear, it's moving into storage-networking products, optical gear, even consumer gadgets. Selling Wi-Fi gear is worth nearly $1 billion, and Cisco has begun rolling out consumer offerings, such as a $149 wireless security camera. All told, analysts expect the new businesses to count for 30% of Cisco's revenues in 2006.

The company's remarkable journey began as many difficult transitions do—reluctantly. In late 2000, contract manufacturers began warning that parts were piling up in their warehouses and asked for permission to cut back on orders. Cisco execs told them to keep ordering. Even after Cisco narrowly missed Wall Street's earnings expectations in the quarter that ended Jan. 30, 2001—its first miss in 11 years—Chambers couldn't break from his growth-oriented mind-set. "John had always boldly gone where no one else would go," says Gary Daichendt, his former No. 2, who retired in December, 2000.

All that changed during Chambers' around-the-world business trip in late February and early March. He realized the world had changed—and Cisco would have to adjust. "At times like those, you have to analyze what you did to yourself, vs. what the market did to you," says Chambers. "You almost always get surprised [by a downturn], but you determine how deep and long you think it will be, take appropriate actions, and start getting ready for the next upturn."

That process began at the meeting on the morning of the layoffs. From the start, the team agreed that the ultimate goal should be to maintain Cisco's net profit margin of 20%. They hammered out details of the six-point plan Chambers had begun sketching. Then they turned to the harsh task of determining how many jobs needed to go. Many were dismayed—even embarrassed—at having to issue so many pink slips just a month after they had hired 2,400 new workers. But Chambers wanted the layoffs to be large enough that he wouldn't have to issue wave after wave of cuts, as Hewlett-Packard, Sun Microsystems, and Siebel Systems have had to do. To ease the blow, Chambers insisted on rich severance packages and urged his team to be brutally frank about the deteriorating situation.

For weeks, Cisco's top 20 execs gathered daily in a conference room called Napa Valley, overlooking the green hills east of San Jose. One morning in April, then-CFO Larry R. Carter delivered more painful news: Because Cisco had been buying parts like mad until demand fell off a cliff, it had mountains of inventory that was obsolete. He recommended moving quickly to take a roughly $2 billion write-off—20% of Cisco's accumulated profits since it was formed in 1984. Senior Vice-President Randy Pond at one point offered to break the news to Cisco's board himself, since inventory was under his purview. Chambers cut him short. "Don't even go there," he said. "We got to this point based on decisions that were rational at the time." Still, even Chambers' reassuring tone couldn't soften the blow. "There were a lot of heads in hands," recalls Pond. When Cisco announced the $2.2 billion write-down on May 8, Cisco's battered stock slid 7% more, to 19.50.

It was over the summer of 2001 that Chambers and the rest of Cisco's management team began to control their own destiny. One of Chambers' first moves after the write-down was to visit Mario Mazzola, a well-respected engineer who had joined Cisco in 1993. The Italian native, now 57, had long planned to retire—an internal memo about his departure had already circulated. But over several meetings at Cisco's sprawling collection of squat, three-story office buildings, Chambers told Mazzola that Cisco needed him. The company's engineering efforts were a jumble of overlapping development projects. At one point, Cisco had five separate efforts aimed at data-storage switches, according to JMP analyst Sam Wilson. Chambers told Mazzola that only he could corral the company's 12,000 engineers and make Cisco a stronger innovator, less reliant on acquisitions. In August, Mazzola agreed.

Strict Diet

He quickly got to work. Many iffy projects were axed, including a broadband wireless technology when the two biggest potential customers decided not to pursue it. In all, Cisco cut the number of models it sells from 33,000 to 24,000. Still, insiders say there's far more fat to cut. Says a former exec: "If you're 50 pounds overweight, you can lose 20 pounds just by walking—but [it takes more] to lose that last 10 pounds."

There's no question Cisco has trimmed its once-freewheeling investment practices. In the past, acquisitions and investments in other companies were haphazard. That ended when Senior Vice-President Daniel A. Scheinman took over corporate development in August. An attorney who had been Cisco's general counsel, Scheinman set up an investment review board that analyzes investment proposals before they can move forward. Roughly 50% are O.K.'d, he says.

The acquisition free-for-all ended, too. Scheinman set up monthly meetings with the heads of operations, sales, and finance to vet potential deals. Besides making sure an acquisition makes sense for the company as a whole, the group works up detailed operational plans to make sure the business can be successfully integrated into Cisco—and a deal's sponsor must commit to sales and earnings targets. That put a screeching stop to the buying binge: Cisco bought two companies in fiscal 2001, down from 24 the year before. The company is doing deals again, but more carefully. When Cisco bought home-networking leader Linksys Corp. in March for $500 million, Scheinman and his group talked for six months before proceeding.

Some of the most painful progress began during the fall of 2001 on the operations front. With Cisco's sales plunging, Pond's staffers began playing hardball with suppliers to keep profits up. The CEO of one supplier said Cisco wanted to take 90 days to pay for his products instead of the normal 30. It also wanted the supplier to extend the warranty on its goods to three years from one. When he balked, the CEO got a call from a midlevel manager. "If you don't [agree to our terms], we'll instruct our people not to use your products," he recalls the manager saying. The supplier like many others in such tough times, couldn't afford to lose Cisco's business and buckled under.

Many others lost out entirely. Cisco's list of key suppliers has fallen from 1,300 to 420. That lowered administrative costs and led to volume discounts worth hundreds of millions of dollars each year. Pond also outsourced more production to lower costs, from 45% in 2000 to over 90% today. At the same time, he spent millions to shift production work from nine contract manufacturers to just four. And smaller resellers complain that Cisco began giving discounts to strategic distribution partners such as IBM and SBC Communications, leaving hundreds of smaller players unable to compete against these behemoths. "Cisco went from being our best partner in good times to our worst enemy in bad times," says the former CEO of one reseller. SBC says the closer relationship is helping it sell more to its business customers.

In early 2002, with Cisco making progress in adopting Chambers' new marching orders, the CEO considered an even more ambitious goal: He approached CIO Solvik and asked him if it was possible to double productivity, to $1 million per employee, by 2007. That way, Chambers figured, Cisco could capitalize on the next spending upturn without having to add many workers, sending profits through the roof. After a few months of studying industry leaders such as Wal-Mart Stores and Dell, Solvik said it was doable—but only if Cisco stopped behaving like a confederation of startups and more like a mature, cohesive corporation.

In Cisco's cowboy culture, this was explosive stuff. When Solvik explained his findings at Chambers' vacation home in Carmel, Calif., in April, 2002, the response was chilly. Execs listened uneasily while gazing at the 180-degree view of Monterey Bay. When Solvik asked for volunteers to investigate how Cisco could emulate the best company in a certain area—say, Dell in operating efficiency—not a single exec followed through. "It didn't resonate well with the group at all," recalls Pond. "But Pete wouldn't let go of it."

Chambers backed Solvik. Just after the Carmel gathering, he instituted an Internet Capabilities Review. Three times a year, top managers share how they use the Web to boost productivity. At the same time, they're measured on how well they implemented the best ideas from previous sessions. He also created a series of committees to get all parts of the company working together. Now, most decisions—what parts to buy, what products to design, what distributors to use—must be cleared by Business Councils that focus on Cisco's overall performance.

All the new procedures created some controversy. Product managers were stunned at the extra steps required to get anything done. Under the new structure, Ish Limkakeng, a product-development manager for switches, must get clearance from a committee of executives from various parts of the company rather than just chat up a few associates. He says the change was difficult, though he came to understand the benefits for the company.

Some salespeople still feel hamstrung. One of Chambers' initiatives is an e-customer project that will consolidate 19 different databases into a single repository. It's designed to boost efficiency and prevent mishaps such as the double ordering by customers that contributed to the inventory write-down. But a salesperson can no longer log in an order for a new customer without first clearing it with a support team that makes sure the customer isn't already in Cisco's records. One insider says salespeople in Europe have been "thumbing their noses" at the e-customer rules and not following the new guidelines. Sales chief Richard J. Justice acknowledges some griping and says Cisco may refine the process to address the complaints.

Calling Telecom

Chambers took other steps to rein in Cisco's Wild West culture during 2002. Most pointedly, he made teamwork a critical part of top execs' bonus plans. He told them 30% of their bonuses for the 2003 fiscal year would depend on how well they collaborated with others. "It tends to formalize the discussion around how can I help you and how can you help me," says Sue Bostrom, head of Cisco's Internet consulting group.

When it came time to divvy up those bonuses, it was clear that Chambers' overhaul had resulted in a leaner, more efficient Cisco. On Aug. 5, the company announced that it had earned $3.6 billion for the year—almost double net income for the year before, even though sales were flat, at $18.9 billion. And employees were getting more comfortable with the new Cisco. "There's been huge progress," says Justice. "There's a sense of redemption and vindication."

Today, revenue growth remains the biggest challenge (Exhibit 3). The company is off to a fast start in a number of promising markets. In security software, Cisco already has taken the lead from Check Point Software Technologies Ltd., with a 27.3% share in the second quarter, up from 20.1% in 2001, says Synergy Research. And Cisco is building quickly on its Linksys acquisition. Charles H. Giancarlo, a senior vice-president responsible for Linksys, says Cisco plans to introduce a dozen more home gizmos over the next year. "Who knows?" he says. "Linksys might become a household name, while Cisco may only be for portfolio planners."

Still, to get revenue growth back to double digits, Cisco will finally have to make headway with the big phone companies. And they're wary shoppers. Established carriers such as BellSouth Corp. had serious reliability problems with Cisco gear in the '90s. To make matters worse, Chambers served as the arms merchant for scores of their upstart rivals—only to see most of them disappear in the telecom bust.

EXHIBIT 3 The Challenges Ahead

Cisco still faces some knotty problems:

Seizing New Markets
Growth in its core business–supplying networking gear to corporations–is slowing. To boost revenues by 12% annually, as Wall Street expects, Cisco must dominate new, fast-growth markets, such as security and Internet-based phones.

Ring Up Sales to Phone Companies
Cisco aims to boost its share of the $64 billion telecom-equipment market to at least 15% from its current 3%. Trouble is, phone companies fear Cisco's gear isn't reliable enough.

Reverse Bad Karma with Partners
During the downturn, Cisco used all of its muscle to win discounts from sales-starved suppliers and resellers–then left many in a lurch by reducing the number of its business partners. The result: Widespread resentment of Cisco's 68% gross margins. If they see the chance, spurned partners may switch to Cisco's rivals.

Beware of Bureaucracy
The company has saved billions by imposing more controls and processes on its entrepreneurial troops. As the tech recovery gains steam, it must prove it can still move quickly and aggressively to hold off challengers.

Now, Cisco has been on a crusade to get into the telecom industry's good graces. Chambers himself called top telecom execs to apologize for his past arrogance. "He said maybe they'd forgotten one of their fundamental rules: Listen to your customer," recalls BellSouth Chief Technology Officer Bill Smith. Cisco also began pouring over 50% of its research and development budget into new gear that could be used more easily with the phone companies' existing switches. Cisco's most recent quarter suggests the plan is going well: Orders from carriers were up 20% over the previous year—far more than at rivals such as Lucent or Nortel. And phone company execs say Cisco has made progress. "I think they are capable of becoming a top one or two provider," says SBC Chief Technology Officer Ross Ireland. BellSouth plans to deploy a Cisco switch next year to handle voice and data traffic.

After a difficult three years, much has changed at Cisco. At one point during the annual sales powwow at a San Francisco convention center in August, a wizened Chambers came out from behind the podium to be closer to the 10,000 salespeople. Dressed in casual clothes, Chambers squatted on the steps of the stage and struck an intimate tone. Recalls sales manager Gregory H. Lynch: "Chambers said, 'I think we're ready to grow again. I'm asking you to help me.'" The words are toned down from the wild years, but Cisco looks poised to continue its dominance.

Source: Peter Burrows, "Cisco's Comeback," *BusinessWeek*, November 24, 2003, 118–124.

Chapter 9

Strategic Brand Management

Existing products as well as new products play an essential role in generating the sales and profits required to maintain the vitality of the business. Moreover, initiatives concerning new and existing products are closely interrelated. Management's challenge is to achieve the highest overall performance from the portfolio of products offered by the firm. This involves new-product initiatives, targeting and positioning existing products, tracking performance of the portfolio, and improving or eliminating poor-performing products. Companies may have one or more brands in the portfolio. Strategic brand management is an ongoing challenge, involving executives from all business functions

Bayerische Motoren Werke's BMW brand consists of an impressive portfolio of automobile lines and models (see accompanying BMW advertisement). Building strong brands is a high-priority management initiative at BMW:

Global Feature

BMW's Brand Portfolio

THE BIG THREE: BMW's CORE MODELS

3 SERIES

Sporty compact that is the leader in unit sales.
Starting price: $28,495

5 SERIES

BMW's linchpin model and profit-driver accounts for 30% of sales.
Starting price: $38,295

7 SERIES

Flagship luxury sedan offers wealthy buyers a more dynamic drive than rivals.
Starting price: $69,195

1 SERIES

A premium subcompact car arriving in 2005 aimed at younger buyers.
Starting price: NA

6 SERIES

Coupe to hit market in late 2003 and convertible in 2004. Both will revive a former 6 model last produced in 1989.
Starting price: NA

NEW MODELS ON THE MARKET OR IN THE WORKS

X3

Baby SUV with 6-cylinder engine set to launch in late 2003. Development and production entirely outsourced to Austria's Magna Steyr.
Starting price: NA

X5

Powerful sport-utility off-roader launched in 2001 ranked among the top-selling luxury SUVs in the U.S.
Starting Price: $40,195

Z4

Sleek new roadster hit showrooms in 2003 replacing the Z3 with improved suspension and bigger engine range.
Starting price: $33,795

MINI

BMW remade this British icon into a hot-selling premium small car that fetches $37,000 fully loaded.
Starting Price: $16,425

ROLLS ROYCE

Super luxury limousine revamped using BMW's 12-cylinder engine.
Starting Price: $320,000

Source: "BMW," *BusinessWeek*, June 19, 2003, 58–59.

> The Munich company is rolling out a new or updated model nearly every three months through 2005 in a ramp-up more ambitious than anything the company has tried before. "The [new-] product initiative is critical to our success," say BMW Chief Executive Helmut Panke. "We won't give up, and we don't rest on our laurels," says the 56-year old Panke. "We won't accept the position of No. 2."[1]

The expanding BMW family is described in the Global Feature. Management's fast-track brand initiatives present an array of strategic brand management challenges. The new model rollout is designed to move BMW to a new level of global brand position and profitability.[2] In the short run the resource demands of the new models are expected to reduce profit margins. Nonetheless, BMW has impressive distinctive capabilities including strong brand equity, strong technical skills, flexible production facilities, and a very talented and committed workforce.

EXHIBIT 9.1

Source: "BMW," *BusinessWeek*, June 9, 2003, 60.

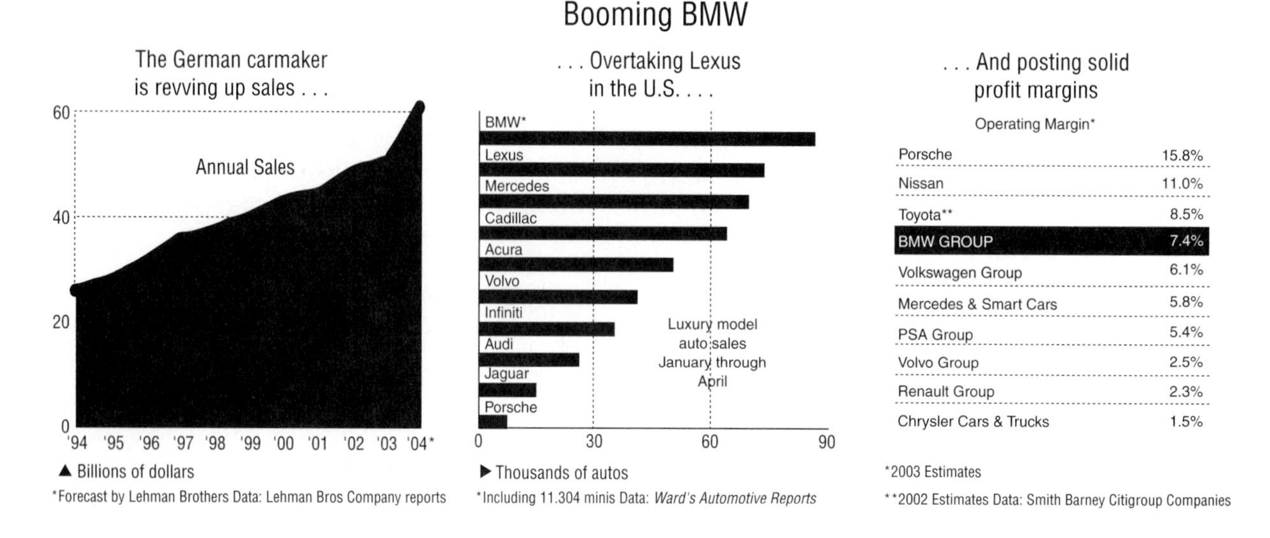

Moreover, as shown in Exhibit 9.1, BMW's performance continues to achieve new highs. The major risk is doing too much, too fast.

Strategic Brand Management requires several interrelated initiatives designed to build strong brands. First, we examine the challenges of brand building, and discuss the importance and scope of strategic brand analysis. Next, we look at brand identity strategies, and what is involved in managing the brand over time including brand leveraging initiatives. We follow this with a discussion of managing the brand system (portfolio).

Challenges in Building Strong Brands

It is important to distinguish between the terms product and brand. In practice they are often used interchangeably, although there are differences in meaning. "A product is anything that is potentially valued by a target market for the benefits or satisfactions it provides, including objects, services, organizations, places, people, and ideas."[3] This view of the product covers a wide range of situations, including tangible goods and intangible services. Thus, political candidates are products, as are travel services, medical services, refrigerators, gas turbines, and computers.

A brand is a company-specific identification of a company's products. The American Marketing Association defines a brand as follows:

> A **brand** is a name, term, sign, symbol, or design, or a combination of them, intended to identify the goods or services of one seller or group of sellers, and to differentiate them from those of competitors.

While the products of some companies are not identified as brands, most have some form of brand designation. Throughout the chapter when discussing a company's product, product line, or product mix (portfolio) we assume that the products have a brand identity.

We know that services differ from physical products in several ways. A service is intangible.[4] It cannot be placed in inventory; the service is consumed at the time it is produced. There is often variability in the consistency of services rendered. Services are often linked to the people who produce the service. Establishing a brand position for a service requires association with the tangible components such as people that produce the service or are somehow related to the service. The use of well-known personalities in the advertisements of the American Express

Card is an example. Internet-based brands are particularly illustrative of the problems faced in establishing effective brands for intangibles like services.

First, we look at the strategic role of brands. A discussion follows of brand management challenges. Next, we consider who is responsible for brand management. Finally, we examine the initiatives involved in strategic brand management.

Strategic Role of Brands

Strategic brand management is a key issue in many organizations and is not the domain only of packaged consumer goods companies. For example, in 2004 Sun Microsystems Inc. CEO, Scott McNealy, was struggling to turn the company around by creating a distinctive brand identity against Dell Inc., IBM, and other competitors. Sun's strategy is described below:

> While most rivals make plain-vanilla computers and slug it out on price, Sun's plan is to change the rules of the game. At the high end of the server market, Sun is developing "throughput computing" chips that can handle dozens of tasks at the same time. At the low end, Sun servers built around Advanced Micro Devices, Inc.'s inexpensive chips will handle not only processing tasks but also the basic networking that rivals' boxes can't. And its pricing approach is something no server company has dared try before: It's planning to give away low-end servers to customers that agree to buy its software for several years. "We have a maverick strategy," says McNealy. "I think there's a huge opportunity right now."[5]

Sun is attempting to pursue two very different brand strategies: developing low cost servers and inventing state-of-the-art technologies. These involve positioning the Sun brand as a premium brand and also offering bare-bones servers.[6]

A strategic brand perspective requires managers to be clear about what role brands play for the company in creating customer value and shareholder value. This understanding should be the basis for directing and sustaining brand investments into the most productive areas. One approach distinguishes between the functions of brands for buyers and sellers.[7]

For buyers, brands can:

- Reduce customer search costs, by identifying products quickly and accurately.
- Reduce the buyer's perceived risk, by providing an assurance of quality and consistency (which may then be transferred to new products).
- Reduce the social and psychological risks associated with owning and using the "wrong" product, by providing psychological rewards for purchasing brands that symbolize status and prestige.

For sellers, brands can play a function of facilitation, by making easier some of the tasks the seller has to perform. Brands can facilitate:

- Repeat purchases that enhance the company's financial performance, because the brand enables the customer to identify and re-identify the product compared to alternatives.
- The introduction of new products, because the customer is familiar with the brand from previous buying experience.
- Promotional effectiveness, by providing a point of focus.
- Premium pricing, by creating a basic level of differentiation compared to competitors.
- Market segmentation, by communicating a coherent message to the target audience, telling them for whom the brand is intended and for whom it is not.
- Brand loyalty, of particular importance in product categories where loyal buying is an important feature of buying behavior.

The potential contribution of brand strength to building customer value and competitive advantage has encouraged managers to focus attention on global estimates of the value of brands and the concept of brand equity.

The financial value of brands receives major attention from investors, particularly in changes in the estimated value of a company's brand.[8] Exhibit 9.2 shows the top-ranked 25 brands from the 2004 Interbrand valuations of global brands with a value greater than $1 billion. Interbrand calculates brand value as the net present value of the earnings the brand is expected to generate in the future. The Interbrand model bases brand earnings on forecasts of brand revenues allowing for risk and the role of the brand in stimulating customer demand. The Interbrand measure of brand strength includes: leadership (ability to influence the market); stability (survival ability based on customer loyalty); market (security from change of technology and fashion); geography (ability to cross geographic borders); support (consistency and effectiveness of brand support); and, protection (legal title).

Strong brands are major contributors to the distinctive capabilities of companies like General Electric, Johnson & Johnson, Nestlé, and Procter and Gamble. Sustaining and building brand strengths is a continuing challenge for managers. The earlier Global Feature describes several of BMW's brand-building initiatives. Customers' preferences change over time and competitors are continually seeking to improve their market positions.

Brand Management Challenges

Several internal and external forces create hurdles for product and brand managers in their efforts to build strong brands:[9]

- *Intense Price and Other Competitive Pressures.* Deciding how to respond to these pressures shifts managers' attention away from brand management responsibilities. For example, in 2003 Dell Inc. pursued aggressive tactics in lowering its personal computer prices. Hewlett-Packard and others were forced to alter their PC prices or face market share losses.
- *Fragmentation of Markets and Media.* Many markets have become highly differentiated in terms of customer needs. Similarly, the media (advertising and sales promotion) available to access market segments have become very fragmented and specialized. The Internet has compounded market targeting and access complexity.
- *Complex Brand Strategies and Relationships.* Multiple additions to core brands such as Pepsi have created complex brand management situations, compounded by the value-chain relationships essential in delivering superior value to end user customers. These complexities may encourage managers to alter strategies rather than building the existing strategies. Benetton's ill-fated entry into the sports equipment market is illustrative.
- *Bias against Innovation.* Brand complacency may result in a failure to innovate. Innovation may be avoided to prevent cannibalism of existing products. Polaroid's management waited too long to fully respond to the disruptive threat of digital photography.
- *Pressure to Invest Elsewhere.* A strong brand may generate complacency and cause management to shift resources to new initiatives. Motorola's allocation of resources to the Irridium Global Phone initiative is an example of neglecting the core brand, enabling Nokia to gain the lead position in cellular phones.
- *Short-Term Pressures.* Managers encounter many short-term pressures that shift their attention and resources away from important brand-building programs. Top management's need to achieve quarterly financial targets may cause these pressures.

The key to reducing these negative impacts on brand-building strategies is developing brand strategy guidelines, tracking initiatives on a regular basis, and critically assessing potential challenges that shift management attention away from core strategies.

Brand Management Responsibility

Responsibility for brand strategy extends to several organizational levels. Three management levels often are found in companies that have strategic business units, different product lines, and specific brands within lines.

EXHIBIT 9.2
The Global Brand Scoreboard

Source: "The 100 Top Brands," *BusinessWeek,* August 2, 2004, 68–69.

Rank 2004	Rank 2003	Brand	2004 Brand Value $Millions	2003 Brand Value $Millions	Percent Change	Country of Ownership	Description
1	1	Coca-Cola	67,394	70,453	–4%	U.S.	Little innovation beyond its flagship brand and poor management has caught up with Coke as consumers' thirst for cola has diminished.
2	2	Microsoft	61,372	65,174	–6	U.S.	Its logo pops up on 400 million computer screens worldwide. But virus plagues and rival Linux took some luster off Gates & Co.
3	3	IBM	53,791	51,767	4	U.S.	A leader in defining e-business, with services making up more than half of Big Blue's sales.
4	4	GE	44,111	42,340	4	U.S.	With acquisitions in areas from bioscience to bomb detection, it's easier to buy GE's new theme of "imagination at work."
5	5	Intel	33,499	31,112	8	U.S.	No longer just inside PCs, Intel is using its muscle to set the agenda for everything from wireless standards to the digital home.
6	7	Disney	27,113	28,036	–3	U.S.	Long the gold seal in family entertainment, but newcomers like Nickelodeon and Pixar are siphoning off some of its brand equity.
7	8	McDonald's	25,001	24,699	1	U.S.	Big Mac has pulled out of a two-year slump but still has to battle its reputation for supersizing the world's kids.
8	6	Nokia	24,041	29,440	–18	Finland	Tough times for the mobile-phone giant as its market share has slipped and younger buyers turn to rivals such as Samsung.
9	11	Toyota	22,673	20,784	9	Japan	With rock-solid quality and the edge in hybrid cars, the Japanese auto maker is on track to overtake Ford in worldwide sales.
10	9	Marlboro	22,128	22,183	0	U.S.	The No.1 name in cigarettes has cut prices and upped marketing to beat back the challenges of higher taxes and fewer smokers.
11	10	Mercedes	21,331	21,371	0	Germany	With wobbly profits and quality problems, the luxury car brand is struggling to retain premium status.
12	12	Hewlett-Packard	20,978	19,860	6	U.S.	Covering everything from digital cameras to service, the IT giant wants to dominate the middle ground between Dell and IBM.
13	13	Citibank	19,971	18,571	8	U.S.	New CEO Charles Prince has spurred on global expansion and boosted the consumer credit division.
14	15	American Express	17,683	16,833	5	U.S.	A recent federal court ruling that allows banks to issue Amex cards should give the brand another boost.
15	16	Gillette	16,723	15,978	5	U.S.	Despite the tougher competition from Schick, the King of Blades still reigns with new products like the battery-powered M3Power.

EXHIBIT 9.2
Continued

Rank 2004	2003		2004 Brand Value $Millions	2003 Brand Value $Millions	Percent Change	Country of Ownership	Description
16	17	Cisco	15,948	15,789	1%	U.S.	The networking behemoth used slick TV ads and key acquisitions like Linksys to extend its reach.
17	19	BMW	15,886	15,106	5	Germany	The Bavarian auto maker is powering higher sales with a raft of new models from the sleek 6 Series sports coupe to the X3 baby SUV.
18	18	Honda	14,874	15,625	–5	Japan	Overtaken by Nissan at home and falling further behind rival Toyota in the U.S. market.
19	14	Ford	14,475	17,066	–15	U.S.	Ford is trying to make quality "Job One" again after an embarrassing run of glitches, but leery consumers haven't yet regained trust.
20	20	Sony	12,759	13,153	–3	Japan	It was late to the LCD TV boom, and the PS2 video game console is slipping. Worse, rival Samsung is in Sony's face.
21	25	Samsung	12,553	10,846	16	S. Korea	No longer known just undercutting the prices of big Japanese brands, the Korean consumer-electronics dynamo is suddenly cool.
22	23	Pepsi	12,066	11,777	2	U.S.	Targeted marketing and ads abroad with stars like soccer icon David Beckham have enabled the No. 2 cola maker to steal some of Coke's fizz.
23	21	Nescafe	11,892	12,336	–4	Switzerland	It's still the world's favorite instant coffee but even products like Ice Java struggle against hip upscale brands like Starbucks.
24	22	Budweiser	11,846	11,894	0	U.S.	The growing global low-carb trend has left Bud flat. Plus, it's under attack from bulked-up and feisty rival Miller.
25	29	Dell	11,500	10,367	11	U.S.	With its reputation for low prices and fast delivery, Dell continues to leave competitors in the dust.

Product/Brand Management. Product or brand managers' responsibilities consist of planning, managing, and coordinating the strategy for a specific product or brand. Managers' activities include market analysis, targeting, positioning strategy, performance analysis and strategy adjustment, identification of new-product needs, and management and coordination of product/brand marketing activities. Marketing plans for specific brands are often prepared at this level. Product or brand managers typically do not have authority over all brand management activities. Nevertheless, they have responsibility for the performance of their brands. These managers are sponsors or advocates of specific products, negotiating and collaborating on behalf of their product/brand strategies with the salesforce, research and development, operations, marketing research, and advertising and sales promotion managers.

Product Group/Marketing Management. A business with several product categories and/or brands may assign responsibility for coordinating the initiatives of its product or brand managers to a product director, group manager, or marketing manager. This person coordinates and monitors the activities and approves the recommendations of a group of product or brand managers. The group responsibilities are to manage the brand systems (portfolio). Additionally, the product group manager coordinates product management activities and decisions with the business-unit management.

Product Portfolio Management. This responsibility is normally assigned to the chief executive at the SBU or corporate level of an organization or to a team of top executives. Illustrative decisions include product acquisitions, research and development priorities, new-product decisions, and resource allocation. Evaluation of brand/product portfolio performance may also be centered at this level. In a corporation with two or more SBUs, top management may coordinate and establish product management guidelines for the SBU management. We look further into the organization of marketing activities in Chapter 14.

By the mid-1990s many companies were reevaluating the traditional approaches to managing products. The changes were particularly apparent in fast-moving goods as described below:[10]

> Unilever's British soap unit and Elida Gibbs personal products division eliminated their marketing director positions.
>
> Marketing and sales groups were combined and focused on consumer research and product development.
>
> Customer development teams were formed to work with retailers across all of the companies' brands.

Similar changes are being made by other companies to integrate sales, marketing, and other business functions into cross-functional teams. A study by the Boston Consulting Group indicated that 90 percent of the responding companies have restructured their marketing departments. It is apparent that traditional product and brand-based organizations will increasingly evolve into customer and market-based approaches to implement more effectively the mandate for customer focus.[11]

Competitive pressures and the changing needs and wants of buyers help to explain why many companies devote a lot of attention to managing their products and brands. These strategies are often a key component in top management's plans for improving the performance of a business. Actions may include modifying products, introducing new products, and eliminating products.

Marketing's Role in Product Strategy. Marketing executives have three major responsibilities in the organization's product/brand strategy. First, market sensing is essential at all stages of new-product planning, providing information for matching new-product ideas with customer needs and wants. The knowledge, experience, and marketing research methods of marketing professionals are utilized in product strategy development. Customer and competitor information is needed in finding and describing unmet needs, in evaluating products as they are developed and introduced, and in monitoring the performance of specific brands and the brand portfolio.

Marketing's second responsibility in product/brand strategy concerns product specifications. Increasingly, top management is looking to marketing professionals for identifying the characteristics and performance features of products. Information about customers' needs and wants is translated into specifications for the product. Matching customer value requirements with the organization's distinctive capabilities is essential in designing and implementing successful strategic brand management.

The third responsibility of marketing in brand strategy is guiding target market and program-positioning strategies. These decisions are often critical to the success of both new and existing products. Since the choice of product specifications and positioning are very much interrelated, strategic positioning should be considered at an early stage in the product planning process. Positioning decisions may include a single product or brand, a line of products, or a mix of product lines within a business unit.

Strategic brand management decisions are relevant to all businesses, including suppliers, producers, wholesalers, distributors, and retailers. While many of these decisions involve the evaluation, selection, and dropping of products by producers, intermediaries may also develop new goods and services. Moreover, suppliers are faced with important brand management decisions.

Strategic Brand Management

Strategic brand management consists of several interrelated initiatives as shown in Exhibit 9.3.[12] We briefly describe each activity, examining them in greater depth in the following sections of the chapter.

Brand Identity. The intent of brand identity is to determine "a unique set of brand associations that the brand strategist aspires to create or maintain."[13] The identity may be associated with the product, the organization, a person, or a symbol.

Identity Implementation. This initiative determines what part of the identity is to be communicated to the target audience and how this will be achieved. The brand position statement describes the identity information to be used to position the brand in the eyes and minds of targeted buyers.

Managing the Brand over Time. The brand must be managed from its initial launch throughout its life cycle. While the brand strategy may be altered over time, the intent is to be consistent, build the strength of the brand, and avoid damaging the brand. Target's management has been very successful in managing the retailer's brand, whereas Kmart's faulty brand management eventually led to bankruptcy.

Managing the Brand Portfolio. This initiative consists of coordinating the organization's portfolio or system of brands with the objective of achieving optimal system performance. The focus is on the portfolio and its brand interrelations rather than an individual brand.

Leveraging the Brand. Leveraging involves extending the core identity to a new addition to the product line, or to a new product category. Nike's leveraging the core footwear brand to apparel and sports equipment is illustrative.

Brand Equity. Each of the strategic brand management initiatives shown in Exhibit 9.3 may have a positive or negative impact on the value of the brand. Brand equity recognizes the importance of brand value and identifies the key dimensions of equity. The objective is to build brand equity over time. Exhibit 9.2 illustrates one approach to brand valuation.

Strategic Brand Analysis. This initiative provides essential information for decision making for each of the brand management activities shown in Exhibit 9.3. Analysis includes market/customer, competitor, and brand information.

EXHIBIT 9.3
Strategic Brand Management

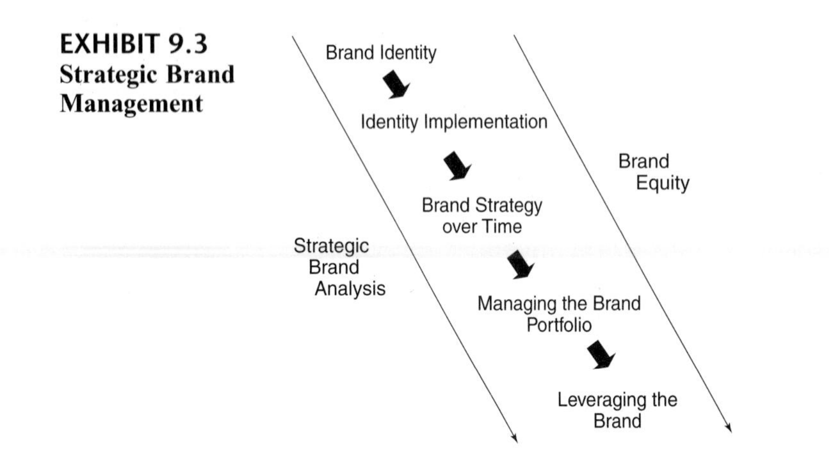

Strategic Brand Analysis

A company may have a single product, a product line, or a portfolio of product lines. In our discussion of managing existing products, we assume that product/brand strategy decisions are being made for a strategic business unit (SBU). The product composition of the SBU consists of one or more product lines and the specific product(s) that make up each line. The SBU may have a single product or single line or various lines and specific products within each line.

Strategic brand analysis includes market and customer, competitor, and brand analysis. Since Chapter 3 considers the two former activities, the present discussion centers on brand analysis. Various aspects of the brand may be examined including performance, portfolio interrelationships, leveraging strengths and weaknesses, and brand values.

Evaluating the performance of the brand portfolio helps guide decisions on new products, modified products, and eliminating products. Consider, for example, Apple's decision to drop the Newton handheld computer.[14] Apple invested an estimated $500 million in the brand extension from the beginning of the development in 1987. The core concept was a computer that could convert the user's handwriting into electronic format. Introduced in 1993 at around $1,000, Newton was too expensive for many users and there were problems with the handwriting recognition feature. Competition eventually emerged from the successful Palm Pilot introduced in 1996. Over one million units were sold in a two-year period. The designers created a handheld unit that could do a few things well. Apple's Message Pad was never profitable, although some industry observers suggest that Apple could have been the market leader by continuing product improvement. The Personal Digital Assistant units were a disruptive technology that required time to develop a position in the mainstream market (see Chapter 8).

Tracking Brand Performance

Evaluating existing products in the brand system (portfolio) requires tracking the performance of each product as shown in Exhibit 9.4. Management needs to establish the performance objectives and benchmarks for gauging product performance. Objectives may include both financial and nonfinancial factors. Because of the demand and cost interrelationships among products, it is necessary to sort out the sales and costs attributable to each product to show how well it is doing. The concepts and methods of activity-based cost analysis are useful for this purpose.[15]

The next step in tracking performance is selecting one or more methods to evaluate product performance. Several useful methods are shown in Exhibit 9.5. The results of the analyses should identify problem products and those performing at or above management's expectations. The information from the analyses also helps management consider whether to eliminate the problem product.

EXHIBIT 9.4
Tracking Brand Performance

Identify Problem Products

Decide How to Resolve the Problem

EXHIBIT 9.5 Methods for Analyzing Product Portfolio Performance

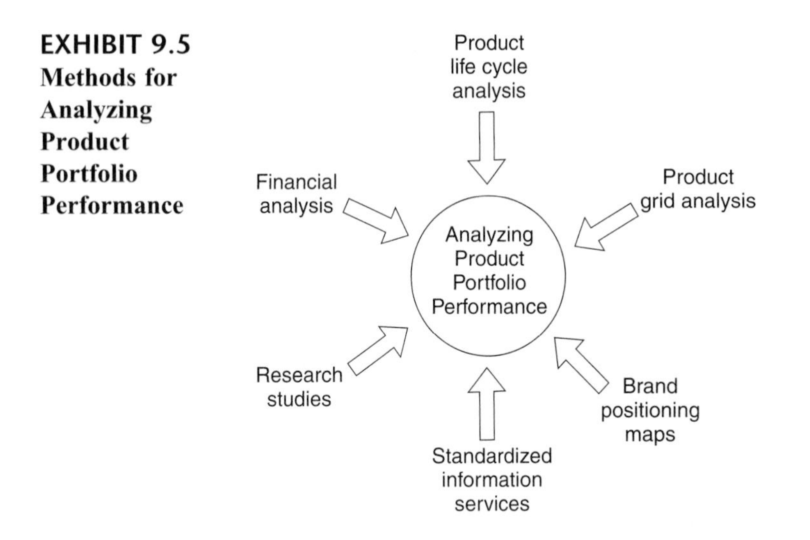

An interesting application of performance analysis for a service is the revenue management system used by American Airlines to evaluate route performance. Each route (e.g., Los Angeles—Dallas/Fort Worth) is a unit in the route system or network. Based on performance, forecasts of demand, competition, and other strategic and tactical considerations, the airline makes decisions to expand, reduce, or terminate service throughout the route network. Each analyst is responsible for a group of routes. Working with management guidelines, the analyst determines how many seats on each flight are to be allocated to AA advantage miles and those assigned to various fare classifications. American Airlines pioneered this system and is recognized throughout the industry for its distinctive revenue management capabilities. Assisting analysts are complex computer models developed using experience data and management science techniques.

We look at product life cycle analysis, product grid analysis, and positioning analysis to illustrate methods for diagnosing product performance and identifying alternatives for resolving problems. Standardized information services, research studies, and financial analysis are discussed in previous chapters.

Product Life Cycle Analysis

In Chapter 6 we describe the major stages of the product life cycle (PLC): introduction, growth, maturity, and decline. Relevant issues in PLC analysis include:

- Determining the length and rate of change of the product life cycle.
- Identifying the current PLC stage and selecting the product strategy that corresponds to that stage.
- Anticipating threats and finding opportunities for altering and extending the PLC.

Rate of Change. Product life cycles are becoming shorter for many products due to new technology, rapidly changing preferences of buyers, and intense competition. Cycles also vary for different products. A clothing style may last only one season, whereas a new commercial aircraft may be produced for many years after introduction. Determining the rate of change of the PLC is important because of the need to adjust the marketing strategy to correspond to the changing conditions.

New technologies may shorten and even terminate product life cycles. Failures may occur in the introductory stage. Recall our discussion of the CueCat scanner in the previous chapter. Moreover, DVD-audio and direct download from the Internet may make the CD obsolete.[16]

Product Life Cycle Strategies. The PLC stage of the product has important implications regarding all aspects of targeting and positioning (see Chapter 6). Different strategy phases are encountered in moving through the PLC. This calls for changing the focus of marketing strategy over the PLC. In the first stage the objective is to establish the brand in the market through brand development activities such as advertising. In the growth stage the brand is reinforced through marketing efforts. During the maturity stage, product repositioning efforts may occur by adjusting size, color, and packaging to appeal to different market segments. Finally, during the decline stage the features of the product may be modified.

Analysis of the growth rate, sales trends, time since introduction, intensity of competition, pricing practices, and competitor entry/exit information is useful in PLC position analysis. Identifying when the product has moved from growth to maturity is more difficult than determining other stage positions. Analysis of industry structure and competition helps in estimating when the product has reached maturity.

Product Grid Analysis

Product grid analysis considers whether each product is measuring up to management's minimum performance criteria, and assesses the strengths and weaknesses of the product relative to other products in the portfolio. The comparative analysis of products can be performed by incorporating market attractiveness and competitive strength assessments using two-way (horizontal and vertical) grids. These grids highlight differences among products. After the relative market attractiveness and competitive strength of the products in the portfolio are identified, more comprehensive analysis of specific performance factors may also be useful, including profit contribution; barriers to entry; sales fluctuations; extent of capacity utilization; responsiveness of sales to prices, promotional activities, and service levels; technology (maturity, volatility, and complexity); alternative production and process opportunities; and environmental considerations.[17]

Brand Positioning Analysis

Perceptual maps are useful in comparing brands.[18] Recall our discussion of these methods in earlier chapters. Preference mapping analysis offers useful guidelines for strategic targeting and product positioning. The analyses can relate buyer preferences to different brands and indicate possible brand repositioning options. New product opportunities may also be identified in the analysis of preference maps. Positioning studies over time can measure the impact of repositioning strategies.

Virtual shopping technology is another promising method for studying brand positioning. This research technique enabled Goodyear to assess its brand equity and pricing strategy for automobile tires and examine potential competitor actions. The Innovation Feature describes the research technique.

Other Analysis Methods

The financial analysis techniques in the Appendix to Chapter 2 are used to evaluate product financial performance. Other product analysis methods include research studies that show the relative importance of product attributes to buyers and rate brands against these attributes. This information indicates brand strengths and weaknesses. Many of the standardized information services provided by marketing research firms, such as Information Resources Inc. and A.C. Nielsen Company, are useful in monitoring the market performance of competing brands of food and drug products. Industry trade publications also publish market share and other brand performance data.

Product Cannibalization[19]

A major consideration when introducing new products that meet similar needs to a firm's existing brands is estimating how much sales volume the new product will attract from one or more existing brands. For example, Gillette's Sensor razor presented a possible cannibalization threat to the

Innovation Feature Virtual Shopping Research

Virtual shopping technology offers a powerful research approach for studying shoppers' reactions to new and existing products.

The approach employs a computer-simulated shopping environment in three dimensions. The imaging technology provides a way to study what attracts the customer's attention, and how to motivate buyers to select particular brands in retail stores.

Virtual store shoppers can move their carts down the aisle examining many products and brands. A particular brand can be imaged to the center of the computer screen, and rotated for inspection. It can be purchased by touching the shopping cart.

The computer records all of the details of the shopping process (e.g., quantity purchased, prices, sequence of purchase, and the time used in the purchase). While virtual shopping is a simulated experience, validation studies indicate that it offers a valuable research method for the kinds of products that can be displayed in this format.

Similar to other forms of simulated shopping, participants must be recruited. This may result in some differences compared to actual shopping behavior, but the technique offers very favorable cost/benefit trade-offs. The technology also can be used to study and develop strategies for Internet shopping.

Sources: Margaret Garrison, "Marketing Magic Is Created in IU's 3-D World of Virtual Shopping," *IU Business*, Spring 1997, 3; Raymond R. Burke, "Virtual Shopping," *OR/MS TODAY*, August 1995, 28–37.

company's Atra and Trac II sales.[20] Gillette's plan was to target disposable users, recognizing that some cannibalization of Atra and Trac II would occur. Also, the Sensor blades were priced about 25 percent higher than Atra. Since both Atra and Trac II were in the mature stages of their life cycles, the new brand was needed to strengthen Gillette's product portfolio performance. The Sensor performed even better than the sales and profit forecasts made by Gillette's management.

Decision makers with successful products may be reluctant to innovate because of the cannibalization threat. Nonetheless, as discussed in chapter 8, proactive cannibalization can yield positive benefits, and the willingness to risk cannibalization may be significant to innovation success.[21] Intel's continuous improvement of computer processors is illustrative of proactive cannibalization with positive effects.

Brand Equity

Brand equity measurement is an important part of strategic brand management. It is frequently a difficult concept for managers to accept, but effective strategic brand management requires that we understand brand equity and evaluate its impact when making brand management decisions:

> Brand equity is a set of brand assets and liabilities linked to a brand, its name, and symbol, that add to or subtract from the value provided by a product or service to a firm and/or to that firm's customers.[22]

The assets and liabilities that impact brand equity include brand loyalty, name awareness, perceived quality, brand associations (e.g., Nike's association with athletes), and proprietary brand assets (e.g., patents).

Measuring Brand Equity. Aaker proposes several measures to capture all relevant aspects of brand equity:[23]

- Loyalty (price premium, satisfaction/loyalty).
- Perceived quality/leadership measures (perceived quality, leadership/popularity).
- Associations/differentiation (perceived value, brand personality, organizational associations).
- Awareness (brand awareness).
- Market behavior (market share, price and distribution indices).

These components provide the basis for developing operational measures of brand equity.

Several methods for brand valuation have been proposed. Interbrand's approach was discussed earlier (Exhibit 9.2). One promising method is momentum accounting, which considers how the earning power of the brand changes over its life cycle because of the revenues and costs associated with the brand:

> Momentum accounting uses functions similar to depreciation curves in conventional accounting to monitor the sources of change in brand value over time. Momentum accounting tries to capture managers' intuition about the reasons for momentum change in terms of "impulses"—the marketing, competitive, and environmental events that affect a brand's value.[24]

Young & Rubicam (Y&R) has developed another brand evaluation tool, Brand Asset Valuator (BAV).[25] The technique uses the brand's vitality (relevance and differentiation) and brand stature (esteem and familiarity) to gauge the health of the brand. Since 1993 BAV has conducted studies with 300,000 consumers and 19,000 brands in 40 countries. Brands with high differentiation include Disney, Jaguar, and Victoria's Secret. AT&T and Kodak fall into the high relevance category. Brands with high esteem include Band-Aid and Rubbermaid, while Coca-Cola and Kellogg's fall into the high familiarity category.

Brand Health Reports. It is important to consider absolute brand values and investments, and the change in brand value over time that provides regular evaluation of brand health. Several major companies have adopted brand health report cards including indicators to assess the direction of change in brand equity and key issues to be addressed. Brand health reports can be compiled for individual brands or the entire brand portfolio.[26] The brand report card can assess the brand against the characteristics of the strongest brands by scoring against key criteria of brand strength:

- The brand excels at delivering the benefits customers truly desire.
- The brand stays relevant.
- The pricing strategy is based on consumers' perceptions of value.
- The brand is properly positioned.
- The brand is consistent.
- The brand portfolio and hierarchy make sense.
- The brand makes use of and coordinates a full repertoire of marketing activities to build brand equity.
- The brand's managers understand what the brand means to consumers.
- The brand is given proper support and that support is sustained over the long run.
- The company monitors sources of brand equity.[27]

Others suggest that brand health assessment measures should include market position (e.g., market share and repeat purchase behavior), perception (e.g., awareness, differentiation), marketing support (e.g., share of advertising spending in the sector compared to market share), and profitability.[28] Brand health reports need to be produced on a regular and systematic basis to alert managers to necessary changes in strategy and new market opportunities.

Brand Identity Strategies

Determining the brand identity strategy for an organization's products is a very important strategic initiative (Exhibit 9.3). Brand identification should span a long time horizon, providing a foundation for building brand equity:

> Brand identity is a unique set of brand associations that the brand strategist aspires to create or maintain. These associations represent what the brand stands for and imply a promise to customers from the organization members.[29]

We first discuss determining the brand identity and consider the role of brand position. Next, alternative levels of brand identity are described. Finally, we examine the process of brand identity implementation.

Extending the Brand Identification Concept

In addition to the brand as a product or the brand as an organization, David Aaker extends brand identification to the brand as a person and the brand as a symbol.[30] The brand as a person, or brand personality, perspective recognizes that strong brands may have an identity beyond the product or the company, which has positive impacts on the customer relationship and perception of value. The brand as a symbol underlines the role in brand building of visual imagery, metaphors, and brand heritage. For example, consider Nike's "swoosh" visual symbolism, the Energizer bunny metaphor for long battery life, and Starbucks' Seattle coffee house tradition. Relatedly, Don Schultz refers to this as "getting to the heart of the brand" to understand the promise that the brand makes to the customer and its value proposition.[31] A clear and effective brand identification strategy is a foundation for building brand strength.

While all four brand identity perspectives may not be employed by an organization, it is important to consider identity options beyond a product focus. Moreover, it is essential to recognize that brand identity articulates how management would like the brand to be perceived, whereas brand image indicates how buyers currently perceive the brand.

Value Proposition

The value proposition conveys the benefit(s) offered by the brand. These benefits may be functional, emotional, or self-expressive.[32] The intent is to consider the benefits that distinguish a brand from its competition. The value proposition expresses the underlying logic of the relationship between the brand and the customer.

Brand Identity Options

One of several brand identity options may be appropriate for a company. We look at the features of each. The major identification alternatives are shown in Exhibit 9.6. Branding applies to services as well as goods. We examine the features of each identity option.

Specific Product Branding. The strategy of assigning a brand name to a specific product is used by various producers of frequently purchased items, such as P&G's Crest toothpaste, Pampers diapers, and Ivory soap. The brand name on the product gives it a unique identification in the marketplace. Building a new brand name through advertising initially can cost over $50 million, plus the expense of maintaining the brand identity in the marketplace.

Product Line Branding. This strategy places a brand name on a line of related products. Palm Inc.'s popular line of personal digital assistants is an example of product line branding. It provides focus and offers cost advantages by promoting the entire line rather than each product. This strategy is effective when a firm has one or more lines, each of which contains an interrelated offering of product items. One advantage of product line branding is that additional items (line extensions) can be introduced utilizing the established brand name.

Corporate Branding. This strategy builds brand identity using the corporate name to identify the entire product offering. Examples include IBM in computers, BMW in automobiles, and Victoria's Secret in intimate apparel. Corporate branding has the advantage of using one advertising and sales promotion program to support all of the firm's products. It also facilitates the introduction and promotion of new products. The shortcomings of corporate branding include a lack of focus on specific products and possible adverse effects on the product portfolio if the company encounters negative publicity for one of its products.

Combination Branding. A company may use a combination of the branding strategies shown in Exhibit 9.6. Sears, for example, employs both product line and corporate branding (e.g., the Kenmore appliance and Craftsman tool lines). Combination branding benefits from the buyer's association of the corporate name with the product or line brand name. However,

EXHIBIT 9.6
Brand Identity Options

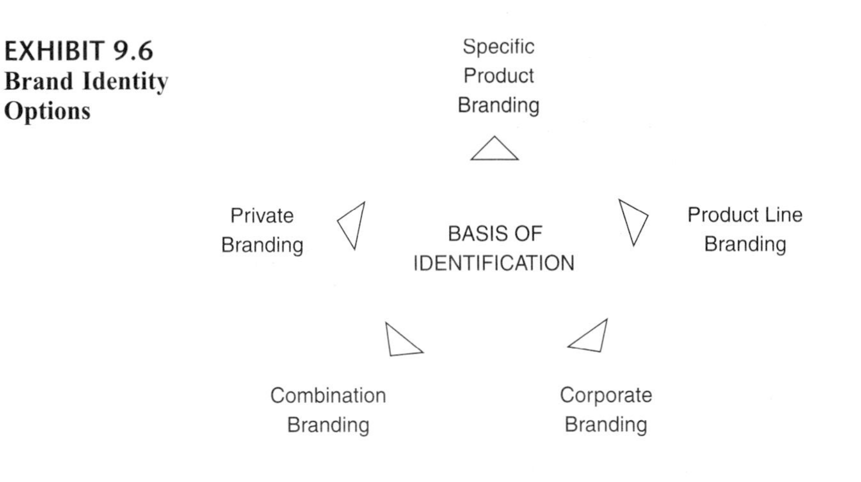

corporate advertising may not be cost-effective for inexpensive, frequently purchased consumer brands. For example, companies like P&G and Chesebrough-Ponds (Vaseline, Q-tips) do not actively promote the corporate identity.

Private Branding. In another form of corporate branding, retailers with established brand names, such as Costco, Krogers, Target, and Wal-Mart, contract with producers to manufacture and place the retailer's brand name on products sold by the retailer. Called private branding, the major advantage to the producer is eliminating the costs of marketing to end users, although a private-label arrangement may make the manufacturer dependent on the firm using the private brand. Nevertheless, the arrangement can yield benefits to both the producer and the value-chain member. The retailer uses its private brand to build store loyalty, since the private brand is associated with the retailer's stores.

Identity Implementation

Identity implementation involves deciding the components of the brand identity and value proposition to be included in the brand position statement. These questions should be answered in formulating the identity implementation strategy:[33]

1. Select a brand position that will be favorably recognized by customers and will differentiate the brand from its competitors.
2. Determine the primary and secondary target audiences.
3. Select the primary communication objectives.
4. Determine the points of advantage.

Determination of the brand position is the core of the implementation strategy. This decision involves selecting the part of the core identity to be communicated to the targets, including points of leverage and key benefits.[34]

Managing Products/Brands

Analyzing performance shows how well existing brand strategies are performing, helps management to identify new-product needs, and points to where existing strategies should be altered.

Brands that have been successful over a long time period offer useful insights about product strategies. Established brands like Budweiser, Hershey, IBM, and Intel continue to build strong market positions. The performance records of powerful brands are the result of (1) marketing skills, (2) product quality, and (3) strong brand preference developed through years of successful advertising.[35] The brand equity that has been built for a company's many famous brands is a valuable asset. A common characteristic of many enduring brands is that the targeting and positioning strategy initially selected has generally been followed during the life of each brand. Consistency in the marketing strategy over time is very important.[36]

The evidence suggests that selecting and implementing good brand strategies pays off. Research findings indicate that the leading brands in various product categories are as much as 50 percent more profitable than their nearest competitors.[37]

Strategies for Improving Product Performance

Product improvement strategies include decisions for each product, product line, and the product portfolio, as shown in Exhibit 9.7. Product line actions may consist of adding a new product, reducing costs, improving the existing product, altering the marketing strategy, or dropping the product. Product portfolio strategy may involve adding a product line, deleting a line, or changing the priority of a line (e.g., increasing the marketing budget for one line and cutting the budget for another line).

Once the need to change the strategy of an existing product is identified, there are several options for responding to the situation (Exhibit 9.7). We discuss each strategy to indicate the issues and scope of the action.

Additions to the Product Line. Management may decide to add a new product to the line to improve performance of a product or product line. Coca-Cola added new flavors to Coke in early 2003. Alternatively, a strong performing brand may provide an opportunity to leverage its strengths by adding a new related line or product category. For example, in 1998, the lingerie retailer Victoria's Secret launched a new line of cosmetics to be sold in its stores, and subsequently through its successful Web page direct marketing channel.[38] By the end of 2000, the growing line of prestige beauty products contributed 16 percent of Victoria's Secret sales, and the $150 million sales of the Dream Angels line made it the leading prestige fragrance in the United States. This success led Victoria's Secret into a joint venture with Shisheido for a 2002 launch of new cosmetics lines. We discuss line and brand extension options later in the chapter.

Cost Reduction. We know that low costs give a company a major advantage over the competition. As an illustration, Nabisco's Ritz Cracker was introduced in 1934 and is the

EXHIBIT 9.7
Strategies for Improving Product Performance

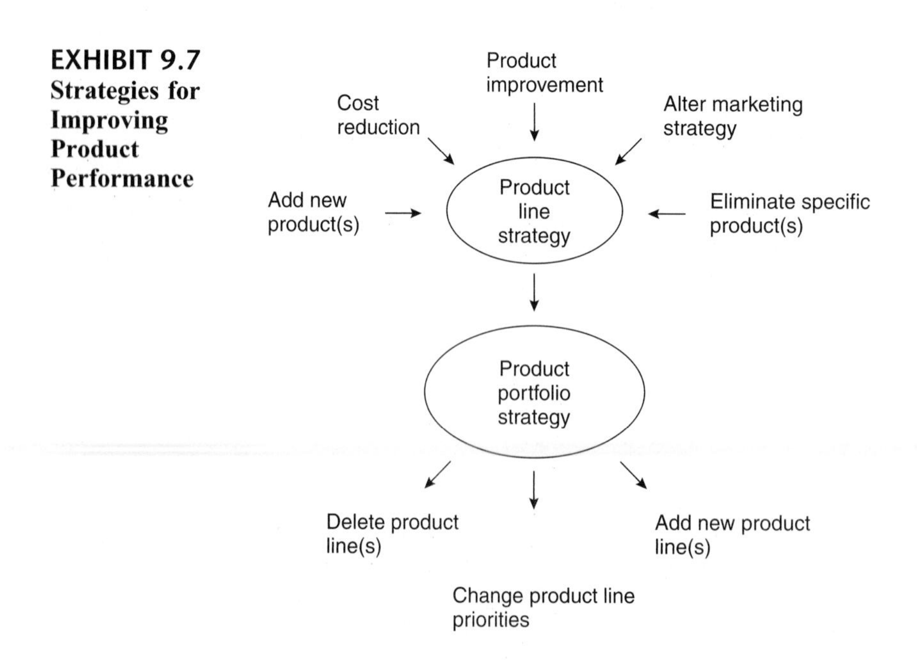

best-selling cracker in the world.[39] In 2000, Nabisco's Ritz had U.S. sales of $475 million, and a market share almost twice that of its nearest competitor.[40] In addition to a flavor that has wide appeal, Ritz's low price compared to other types of crackers gives it a major competitive advantage. Ritz's high-volume production helps to keep costs low. A product's cost may be reduced by changes in its design, manufacturing improvements, reduction of the cost of supplies, and improvements in marketing productivity.

Product Improvement. Products are often improved by changing their features, quality, and styling. Automobile features and styles are modified on a continuing basis. Many companies allocate substantial resources to the regular improvement of their products. Compared to a decade ago, today's products, such as disposable diapers, cameras, computers, and consumer electronics show vast improvements in performance and features. For example, the Skoda automobile brand was associated with low mechanical standards and reliability, until acquired by Volkswagen whose engineering and production expertise has transformed the Skoda product into one of the leading European brands.

One way to differentiate a brand against competition is with unique *features.* Another option is to let the buyer customize the features desired in a product. Recall, for example, the discussion of mass customization in earlier chapters. Optional features offer the buyer more flexibility in selecting a brand. The capability to produce products with varied features that appeal to market diversity is an important competitive advantage.

Style may offer an important competitive edge for certain product categories. Moreover, style may serve as a proxy for quality in some product categories. The impact of intangibles like style should not be underestimated. Trackers of trends have been surprised by the influence of Japanese design and culture in the early 2000s. Japanese designs are impacting on fields as diverse as toys (e.g., small dolls); cell phones (e.g., the Sony Ericsson camera phone); cars (e.g., Toyota's gas-electric Prius); and fashion (e.g., Louis Vuitton's Murakami bags). Japanese-style comics called *manga,* as thick as paperbacks, selling for $10 in Target and Borders, are at the center of pop culture, along with *anime,* the distinctive Japanese-style cartoons. Interestingly, Nike has experimented with releasing new sport shoes in Tokyo, and counting in days the time it takes for the shoes to appear on the feet of trendsetters in New York and London.[41]

Marketing Strategy Alteration. Changes in market targeting and positioning may be necessary as a product moves through its life cycle. However, the changes should be consistent with the core strategies. Problems or opportunities may point to adjusting the marketing strategy during a PLC stage. Tylenol's marketing strategy over its life cycle has been altered while maintaining a consistent positioning on its strong association with doctors and hospitals.

Product Elimination. Dropping a problem product may be necessary when cost reduction, product improvement, or marketing strategy initiatives are not feasible for improving the performance of the product. In deciding to drop a product, management may consider a variety of performance criteria in addition to the product's sales and profit contribution. Elimination may occur at any PLC stage, although it is more likely to occur in either the introduction or decline stages. Risks are involved in eliminating products that have loyal buyers; the elimination strategy should be carefully planned and implemented.

Environmental Effects of Products. Environmental issues concerning product labeling, packaging, use, and disposal need to be considered in the product strategies of companies whose products have potential environmental impact. Protection of the environment involves a complex set of trade-offs among social, economic, political, and technology factors. Companies like McDonald's, P&G, Rubbermaid, and many others incorporate environmental considerations into their product strategies. Moreover, these environmental issues are global in scope.

Environmental issues and concerns may be very complex, and require consumers to change their use and disposal behavior. Even technical authorities do not always agree on the extent to which environmental problems exist, or how to solve the problems. Nevertheless, many companies, governments, and special-interest groups are proactively working toward reducing environmental contamination.

In some cases, stringent legislative controls have been developed. The European Union's end-of-life vehicles directive comes into force in 2007 and mandates car manufacturers to cover the costs of recycling old vehicles, as well as ensuring that recyclable components make up 85 percent of the weight of new vehicles.

Manufacturers are already setting aside large funds to meet compliance costs. Some expect similar legislation to be developed in other countries and across other sectors such as white goods.[42]

Product Portfolio Modifications

Adding a new line of products to the product portfolio is a major product strategy change (Exhibit 9.7). The motivation for changing the product mix may be to:

- Increase the growth rate of the business.
- Offer a more complete range of products to wholesalers and retailers.
- Gain marketing strength and economies in distribution, advertising, and personal selling.
- Leverage an existing brand position.
- Avoid dependence on one product line or category.

The product portfolio may be expanded through internal development or by purchase of an entire company or a line of products. Purchase may be a favorable option compared to the costs of internal development. Acquisition is also a faster means of expanding the product mix. Strategic alliances among competitors are also used for expanding product lines.

Strategies for Brand Strength

The discussion so far centers on actions that may be taken for specific products in the portfolio. Managers in a company or business unit are also concerned with managing the portfolio for optimal performance. Companies may also decide to delete a product line from the portfolio. For example, Levi Strauss put its Dockers brand of apparel up for sale in 2004. Apparently, management decided to concentrate on managing the Levi brand. A cohesive, clearly defined brand portfolio is essential to achieving brand strength. The importance of a strategic brand management perspective is described:

> Brand portfolio strategy becomes especially critical as brand contexts are complicated by multiple segments, multiple products, varied competitor types, complex distribution channels, multiple brand extensions, and the wider use of endorsed brands and sub-brands.[43]

Nestlé, the world's largest food company, has over 8,000 brands.[44] Starting in 2001 management was pursuing initiatives to streamline operations to reduce cost, strengthening key product groups via acquisitions, outsourcing activities such as tomato canning and pasta production, and developing new products. By 2003, $1.5 billion in cost reductions had been achieved. Some critics observe that significantly expanded marketing expenditures may offset the cost reductions.

There are many powerful forces mandating critical strategic management focus on brands. These forces include overcapacity and intense price competition in many sectors; the proliferation of similar competing products; and, powerful retailers with their own category management and private branding interests.[45]

Strategies for building brand strength and sustaining that strength for the brand portfolio require attention to the implementation of brand identification in brand-building strategies, revitalizing brands in the later stages of their life cycles, and recognizing the strategic vulnerabilities of core brands, since brands may be vulnerable to competitive attack or changing market conditions.

Brand-Building Strategies. The essence of strategies for brand strength is that management should actively "build, maintain, and manage the four assets that underlie brand equity—awareness,

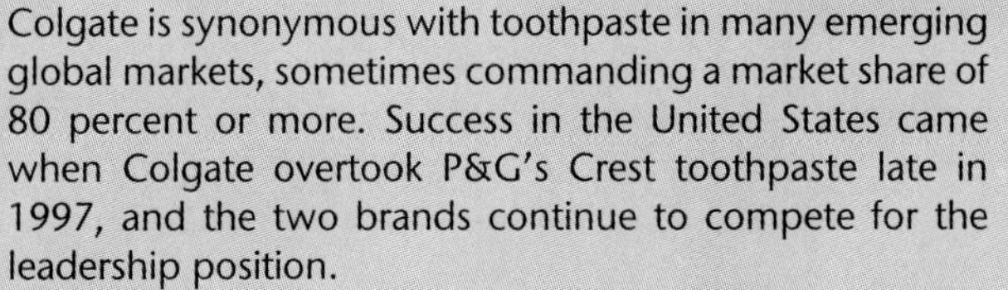

Colgate's Global Brand Strategy

Colgate is synonymous with toothpaste in many emerging global markets, sometimes commanding a market share of 80 percent or more. Success in the United States came when Colgate overtook P&G's Crest toothpaste late in 1997, and the two brands continue to compete for the leadership position.

Colgate's constant innovation and marketing power involves several initiatives:

- Every year Colgate sends its people around the world to reinforce the message of oral hygiene.
- The goal is to convert the world to Colgate—whether squeezing toothpaste onto neem sticks in India or pushing free toothbrushes into the hands of 50 million school children worldwide.
- Colgate has changed the product offer for different overseas markets—it is an inexpensive tooth powder in India, a chalky flavored paste in China, and elsewhere a trendy gel aimed at high-growth youth markets.
- Colgate is promoted at rock concerts, rural road shows, mobile dental clinics, schools—anywhere people bare their teeth.
- Colgate was first to market with a plaque-fighting product and the first to target gum disease with its products (important with an aging U.S. population), as well as products for sensitive teeth, and a "2 in 1" product for children.
- Colgate's brand strategy involves "touching consumers wherever they are"—from conventional advertising to sponsoring a contest with Blockbuster Video to pick which stars have the brightest smiles.

Source: "How Colgate Chomps on the Competition," *BusinessWeek Online*, August 6, 2001.

perceived quality, brand loyalty, and brand association."[46] Critical to this process is developing the brand identification strategy and implementing that identity throughout the company and the marketplace. Colgate Palmolive's successful initiatives in global brand building are described in the Global Feature.

In addition to creating brand identification, attention is frequently also needed in coordinating the brand identity across the organization, the different media it uses, and the different markets and segments it serves.[47] For example, IBM's corporate brand identifies a great number of products and company divisions in diverse end user markets. The challenge is to implement the brand identification consistently across these different situations. The risk of failing to do so is customer confusion and reduced brand equity.

Brand Revitalization. Mature brands that are important in the company's overall strategy may require rejuvenation. For example, P&G's Oil of Olay has a 53-year-old brand history and retains a strong position in the skin care market by adding products that link to the brand heritage.[48] Similarly, when P&G acquired the mature Old Spice men's fragrance brand, it was underperforming in its target market of older consumers. P&G successfully repositioned the brand to attract younger consumers and rebuilt market share. Apple Computers transformed the company's position with the launch of the iMac and its 1997 "Think Different" campaign directed at the loyal core of Macintosh users.[49]

Strategic Brand Vulnerabilities. A strategic perspective on brands also requires that decision makers be aware of the vulnerability of brands. When Skoda cars were first launched in the United Kingdom, with a heritage of low-quality vehicles assembled in part by convict labor in a then-Communist country, consumer tests revealed that perceived value was actually lower when the brand was known, than when the brand identification was removed from the cars.

In the early 1990s, Encyclopaedia Britannica rebuffed an approach from Microsoft to produce a digital version of their encyclopaedia. In less than two years Microsoft's Encarta dominated the market. When Encyclopaedia Britannica approached Microsoft to reopen negotiations, Microsoft's management indicated that research findings showed that Britannica had negative brand equity and would have to pay Microsoft to have its name on a joint product.[50]

Brand Leveraging Strategy

Established brand names may be useful to introduce other products by linking the new product to an existing brand name. The primary advantage is immediate name recognition for the new product. Methods of capitalizing on an existing brand name include line extension, stretching the brand vertically, brand extension, cobranding, and licensing.

Line Extension. This leveraging strategy consists of offering additional items in the same product class or category as the core brand. Extensions may include new flavors, forms, colors, and package sizes. Cherry Coke is an example. The primary danger is overextending the line and weakening the brand equity. Most new products are line extensions.

Stretching the Brand Vertically.[51] This form of line extension may include moving up or down in price/quality from the core brand. It may involve subbrands that vary in price and features. The same name may be used (e.g., BMW 300, 500, 700), or the brand name linked less directly (Courtyard by Marriott). The advantages of this strategy include expanded market opportunities, shared costs, and leveraging distinctive capabilities. The primary limitations are damage to the core brand when moving lower (e.g., lower price/quality versions of a premium brand) or difficulty in moving the brand to a higher price/quality level.

Brand Extension. This form of leveraging benefits from buyers' familiarity with an existing brand name in a product class to launch a new product line in another product class.[52] The new line may or may not be closely related to the brand from which it is being extended. Examples of related extensions include Ivory shampoo and conditioner, Nike apparel, and Swiss Army watches. Critics of brand extensions indicate that these initiatives often do not succeed and may damage the core brand. There are several potential risks associated with brand extensions: (1) diluting existing brand associations, (2) creating undesirable attribute associations, (3) failure of the new brand to deliver on its promise, (4) an unexpected incident (e.g., product recall), and (5) cannibalization of the brand franchise.[53] One of the more successful brand extensions of the 1990s was the various lines of Healthy Choice foods.

Regardless of the possible dangers of brand extension, it continues to be popular. Two considerations are important. There should be a logical tie between the core brand and the extension. It may be a different product type while having some relationship to the core brand. For example, in the United Kingdom, the successful fashion retailer French Connection is extending its branding from clothes to eyeglasses, cosmetics, underwear, and watches, as well as homewares such as towels and bed linen. The extension also needs to be carefully evaluated as to any negative impact on the brand equity of the core brand.

An interesting example of how the Virgin Group in the United Kingdom is extending the brand into new industries is described in Exhibit 9.8. Sir Richard Branson, CEO of Virgin Group, plans to launch Virgin USA, a discount airline, in 2005.

Cobranding. This strategy consists of two well-known brands working together in promoting their products. The brand names are used in various promotional efforts. Examples include airlines cobranding with credit card companies. Delta Airlines' cobranding alliance with American Express via the Sky Miles credit card is illustrative. The advantage is leveraging the customer bases of the two brands. Joint products may be involved or instead a composite product such as the Healthy Choice-Kellogg line of cereals may be cobranded.

Cobranding may involve business-to-business partners. Dell Inc. has an agreement with EMC to cobrand its Clarion line of data storage systems.[54] More commonly cobranding is used to link consumer brands. Disney, for examplè, is cobranding breakfast cereals, toaster pastries, and waffles with Kellogg, as well as Disney Xtreme! Coolers with Minute Maid.[55]

Cobranding occurs when brands from different organizations (or distinctly different businesses within the same organization) combine to create an offering in which brands from each play a driver role.[56] Promotional budgets can be shared and new-product introductions facilitated. The

EXHIBIT 9.8
Brand Extension in Action

Source: Excerpt from Stephen J. Garone, *Managing Reputation with Image and Brands* (New York: The Conference Board, 1998), 11. Reprinted with permission from The Conference Board.

An Experienced Virgin

Virgin Group is one of the greatest examples of extending a brand into new industries without diverging from its core values—irreverent, unconventional, creative, entertaining, active. "Each time Virgin entered a new business," explains John Mathers, director, Sampson Tyrrell Enterprise, "all the commercial pundits suggested it was stretching the brand too far. They reasoned that few people would want to buy financial services, for example, from a youth brand with a rock and roll image." But ever since its inception in the early 1970s, Virgin has been racking up an impressive number of notches on its corporate bedpost.

Virgin's businesses now include book publishing, radio and television broadcasting, hotel management, entertainment retail, trading and investments, and an airline—"a highly successful migration of core values that are very much the product of an ideology," says Interbrand's Tom Blackett.

Andrew Welch of Landor cites an example of how the Virgin megastore in Paris has been able to transcend its boundaries of being purely a retailer: "It has become a temple for young consumers and youth culture. Paris youth place their trust in Virgin for guidance on what is contemporary culture. As such, Virgin is considered the consummate specialist in all things for youth fashion and fashionability."

"Virgin has succeeded in many markets in creating a new reality that its competitors have been compelled to follow because it touches the consumer in a fundamental way," summarizes Blackett, "which may actually be the key to shaking up mature environments in the future."

important challenge is selecting the right brand combination and coordinating the implementation between two independent companies. An effective cobranding arrangement is a strong competitive strategy.

Licensing. Another popular method of using the core brand name is licensing. The sale of a firm's brand name to another company for use on a noncompeting product is a major business activity. Total U.S. retail sales of licensed products were estimated at more than $100 billion in 2000.[57] The firm granting the license obtains additional revenue with only limited costs. It also gains free publicity for the core brand name.

For example, Land Rover has taken its name into a range of product categories including outdoor clothing, and "adventure kit" for children, wristwatches, and an "all-terrain pushchair" for infants designed for off-road use like Land Rover vehicles. The company sees the advantages as additional revenue for the brand, but also reinforcing the rugged lifestyle identification of the brand. Similarly, PepsiCo Inc. employs licensing as a strategic tool to enhance and build the identification of the brand and generate additional revenue stream—the use of the Pepsi logo on young men's and women's apparel is intended to reflect the lifestyles of drinkers of Pepsi and Mountain Dew.[58]

The main limitation is that the licensee may create an unfavorable image for the brand. Licensing may be used for corporate, product line, or specific brands. Anheuser-Busch Companies Inc. (Budweiser beer) is one of the largest corporate licensors.

Overleveraging. Decision makers may be under great pressure to leverage their brands over a larger number of products to justify investments in brand building and to increase profitability. There may be significant risks in stretching brands too far. The brand extension may not succeed if it is not compatible with the established brand identification, and may even dilute or damage the brand equity for established products.[59] Regular brand health checks and a strategic brand system perspective are important to identifying and managing these risks.

Global Branding

Companies operating in international markets face various strategic branding challenges. For example, European multinational Unilever is reducing its brand portfolio from 1,600 to 400, to focus on its strong global brands like Lipton, while acquiring more global brands for its portfolio: SlimFast, Ben & Jerry's Homemade, and Bestfoods (Knorr, Hellmans). The company's global brand strategy is intended to position it favorably with international retailers.[60]

Increasingly cosmopolitan consumers in many countries with similar tastes drawn from exposure to similar media, as well as the economies of scale of global brand identification and communications, encourage the development of global brands. However, global brand identity may also create barriers to building strong identification with local markets, and for some companies the mantra has become "think global, act local."

Aaker and Joachimsthaler argue that global brand strategy is often misguided, and the priority should not be building global brands (although they may result); instead the priority should be working for global brand leadership—strong brands in all markets supported by effective, strategic global brand management.[61] Nonetheless, this may involve different approaches to those successful in the domestic market. For example, P&G has traditionally emphasized individual product brands instead of its corporate identity. However, in some overseas markets like Japan, Russia, and India, the company uses the corporate umbrella identification of P&G to create value. Japanese consumers want to know about the company behind the brands they buy.[62]

Multinational operations increasingly face the challenge of managing brand portfolios containing global, regional, and local brands. For example, Nestlé manages a four-level brand portfolio: 10 worldwide corporate brands (e.g., Nestlé, Carnation, Buitoni); 45 worldwide strategic brands (e.g., KitKat, Polo, Coffee-Mate), which are the responsibility of general management at the strategic business-unit level; 140 regional strategic brands (e.g., Stouffers, Contadina, Findus), which are the responsibility of strategic business units and regional management; and 7,500 local brands (e.g., Texicana, Brigadeiro, Rocky), which are the responsibility of local markets.[63] While some observers believe Nestlé's brand strategy may be overly complex, its performance is impressive.

Internet Brands

Some controversy surrounds the issue of branding on the Internet. That controversy relates mainly to the sustainability of brands that exist only on the Internet, but extends to how the Web can impact the brand equity of conventional brands. It is all but impossible for the decision maker to ignore the linkage between the brand and the Internet. The Internet Feature describes the struggle of Lastminute.com to establish its brand and value proposition as an Internet company.

Interestingly, successful online brands may be those adopting brand strategies that rely on traditional, offline forms of communications. For example, the career Web site Monster.com makes successful use of sponsoring the halftime report at the Super Bowl backed by advertising spots in the pregame and during the game. Monster's target is men and women aged 18 to 49, and the Super Bowl event gives excellent coverage, which coincides with the time of the year when many people are thinking of changing their jobs.[64]

The Internet can play a pivotal role in enhancing brand relationships and corporate reputation, by offering customers a new degree of interactivity with the brand, and speed and adaptability in the relationship-building process.[65] For established brands seeking to reinforce brand identification strategy and enhance brand equity through the Web, the Web site should:

- Create a positive experience, by being easy to use, delivering value, and being interactive, personalized and timely.
- Reflect and support the brand.
- Look for synergy with other communications programs.

Internet Feature Lastminute.com's Brand Development

Founded by Martha Lane Fox and Brent Hoberman in November 1998, Lastminute.com uses the reach of the Internet to offer reduced prices direct to consumers—theater tickets, airline tickets, hotel reservations, gifts, and "lifestyle services" for the cash-rich, time-poor urban consumer, who has not planned ahead. Started in the United Kingdom, Lastminute.com has Web sites in the United Kingdom, France, Italy, Spain, and Holland.

- The Lastminute.com business model could not operate without the Internet—it has created a "last minute marketplace," said to have been conceived by Hoberman because of his inability to plan anything in advance.
- The business is a "Web brand"—it provides only information and customer service, taking a commission from suppliers—it links buyers and sellers without involvement in fulfillment.
- Nonetheless, launch advertising was almost totally offline—London Underground posters, print and billboard advertising, promotional tie-ups with other companies, and a much-hyped "Blonde Ambition" PR tour by Martha Lane Fox.
- In 2000 Lastminute.com went public in a badly handled launch; it was grossly overvalued and between March 2000 and December 2000, share values fell from 560p to 120p.
- Late in 2000, Allan Leighton joined the company as nonexecutive chairman, bringing outstanding retailing skills—he is credited with the turnaround of Asda (the United Kingdom's number three supermarket chain), and headed Wal-Mart's European operations for a time.
- Christmas 2000, Lastminute.com ventured successfully into offline trading with a Christmas gifts catalog and telephone ordering of gifts.
- In 2001 Lastminute.com formed a Web-based alliance with travel company Thomas Cook.
- Under Allan Leighton's influence, Lastminute.com is increasing its focus on the core markets of the United Kingdom, France, and Germany, reducing staff levels, reducing advertising expenditures, and focusing on revenue growth instead of customer acquisition.
- With growing revenues and falling costs, predictions are for break-even by 2002 and full profitability after that.

Source: Reprinted from *Market-Led Strategic Change: A Guide to Transforming the Process of Going to Market*, Nigel F. Piercy, "LastMinute.com - Myth and Reality," Copyright 2001, with permission from Elsevier.

- Provide a home for the loyalist and extend the relationship with those customers.
- Differentiate, with strong subbranded content.[66]

While much remains to be learned about the requirements for effective brand building on the Internet, these initiatives should be included in strategic brand management responsibilities.

Managing the Brand Portfolio

Companies that have several different brands and product categories should manage them as a system rather than pursuing independent brand strategies:

> The brand portfolio strategy specifies the structure of the brand portfolio and the scope, roles, and interrelationships of the portfolio brands. The goals are to create synergy, leverage, clarity within the portfolio and relevant, differentiated, and energized brands.[67]

The importance of a brand portfolio perspective is illustrated by the DaimlerBenz response to a new-product test failure. In the late 1990s DaimlerBenz's management targeted the small car market with the new A-Class Baby Benz, alongside the prestigious Mercedez-Benz C- and E-Class lines. In 1997, wholly unexpectedly, in a test drive a Swedish journalist rolled the A-Class Benz when simulating a swerve around an imaginary elk (the "Elk Test"). The company responded with expensive changes to the vehicle—new tires, electronic stabilizing as standard—but after 3,000 cancelled orders they were forced to take the car off the market for three months to undertake chassis modifications. Rumors spread that the company had stretched itself too far too quickly to get into the mass car market, fuelled by the subsequent delay of the launch of the Smart car because of similar safety concerns. Nonetheless, the company survived the crisis and its measured and careful approach has protected the brands from long-term damage. The A-Class Benz is now a highly successful product line.[68]

A brand portfolio perspective encourages the use of brands to support the entire portfolio as well as its support of each brand:

> A key to managing brands in an environment of complexity is to consider them as not only individual performers, but members of a system of brands that must work to support one another. A brand system can serve as a launching platform for new products or brands and as a foundation for all brands in the system.[69]

A key concept that guides the management of the brand portfolio is that specific brands play different roles in the system. For example, one brand may play a lead or driver role whereas other brands in the system may play supportive roles.

An important issue in managing brand portfolios is deciding how many brands should comprise the system. Four questions are relevant in deciding whether to introduce a new brand name:

1. Is the brand sufficiently different to merit a new name?
2. Will a new name really add value?
3. Will the existing brand be placed at risk if it is used on a new product?
4. Will the business support a new brand name?[70]

Summary

Strategic brand management provides the foundation for selecting strategies for each of the remaining components of the positioning strategy. It forms the leading edge of efforts to influence buyers' positioning of the company's brands. Product strategy needs to be matched to the right distribution, pricing, and promotion strategies. Product decisions shape both corporate and marketing strategies, and are made within the guidelines of the corporate mission and objectives. The major product decisions for a strategic business unit include selecting the mix of products to be offered, deciding how to position an SBU's product offering, developing and implementing strategies for the products in the portfolio, selecting the branding strategy for each product, and managing the brand system.

Most successful corporations assign an individual or organizational unit responsibility for strategic brand management. Product managers for planning and coordinating product activities are used by many companies, although new customer- and market-based structures are emerging.

Evaluating a company's existing products and brands helps to establish priorities and guidelines for managing the product portfolio. The methods include the portfolio screening, analysis of the product life cycle, product grid analysis, positioning analysis, and financial analysis. Product cannibalization is an important issue in this analysis. It is necessary to decide for each product if (1) a new product should be developed to replace or complement the product; (2) the product should be improved (and, if so, how); or (3) the product should be eliminated. Product strategy alternatives for the existing products include cost reduction, product alteration, marketing strategy changes, and product elimination. Product mix modification may also occur.

Gap Inc. announced an interesting new brand initiative in late 2004.[71] The plan is to launch a new women's clothing brand, targeting women over 35. The initial rollout will consist of 10 stores to be opened in 2005. The new chain will have its own personality, differentiating it from the Gap, Old Navy, and Banana Republic brands.

The role of branding in positioning products is pivotal for many companies. Brand equity is a valuable asset that requires continuous attention to build and protect the brand's value. The equity of a brand includes both its assets and liabilities, including brand loyalty, name awareness, perceived quality, brand associations, and proprietary brand assets. Increasingly, companies are measuring brand equity to help guide product portfolio strategies, and adopting regular brand health checks. Mature brands may require specific revitalization approaches. Managers must be aware also of existing and emerging strategic brand vulnerabilities.

Brand identity may focus on the product, the organization, a person, or a symbol. Brand identification strategy involves deciding among private branding, corporate branding, product-line branding, specific product branding, and combination branding. Brand identification in the marketplace offers a firm an opportunity to gain a strategic advantage through brand equity and brand leveraging.

Opportunities for leveraging brands include line extensions in the existing product class, extending the line vertically, extending the brand to different product classes, cobranding with other brands, and licensing the brand name. Line extensions are widely used alongside the other forms of leveraging. For companies with international operations, additional concerns relate to global branding issues. Increasingly, attention is also required to the role of the Internet in implementing brand identification.

Finally, management is concerned with the system or network of brands in the portfolio. Each brand should contribute to the portfolio as well as benefiting from it. The objective should be to coordinate strategies across the system rather than managing each brand on an independent basis.

Internet Applications

A. Examine the Fortune Brands Web site (*www.fortunebrands.com*). Analyze and evaluate the strategic initiatives used by Fortune Brands in their strategic brand management.

B. Visit the Web site of Lastminute.com (*www.lastminute.com*). Map the business model used by this Web brand. Review the strengths and weaknesses of the model, and consider how the brand has been established and how it may be extended.

C. Go to (*www.e4m.biz*), operated by the United Kingdom's Marketing Council. Register at the site and choose the Business-to-Consumer area, and the Brand Consistency option under Strategy Area. Review several of the short cases describing how major companies are striving for consistency in their brand identification while using multiple channels including the Internet. What conclusions can you draw regarding the requirements for brand consistency across multiple channels?

D. Visit the Yahoo Inc. Web site. Describe Yahoo's brand portfolio.

Feature Applications

A. Review the BMW Global Feature. What are the important issues confronting BMW's management in managing the company's brand portfolio? How can a brand portfolio perspective assist in meeting these challenges?

B. Examine the case described in the Global Feature "Colgate's Global Brand Strategy." What are the major problems a company faces in taking branded consumer goods into overseas markets—can brand identity and image survive in globalization?

Questions for Review and Discussion

1. Eli Lilly & Company manufactures a broad line of pharmaceuticals with strong brand positions in the marketplace. Lilly is also a manufacturer of generic drug products. Is this combination branding strategy a logical one? If so, why?
2. Discuss the advantages and limitations of following a branding strategy of using brand names for specific products.
3. What is the role of strategic brand analysis in building strong brands?
4. To what extent are the SBU strategy and the product strategy interrelated?
5. Suppose that a top administrator of a university wants to establish a product-management function covering both new and existing services. Develop a plan for establishing a product planning program.
6. Many products like Jell-O reach maturity. Discuss several ways to give mature products new vigor. How can management determine whether it is worthwhile to attempt to salvage products that are performing poorly?
7. How does improving product quality lower the cost of producing a product?
8. Why do some products experience long successful lives while others have very short life cycles?
9. How can a company combine the strengths of global brands with the need to adapt to local market requirements in a multinational operation?
10. Discuss the underlying logic of managing brand systems.
11. What are the strengths and limitations in moving the Marriott brand vertically upward and downward in terms of price and quality?

Notes

1. "BMW," *BusinessWeek,* June 9, 2003, 57.
2. Ibid., 57–60.
3. David W. Cravens, Gerald E. Hills, and Robert B. Woodruff, *Marketing Management* (Homewood IL: Richard D. Irwin, 1987), 375.
4. Leonard Berry, "Services Marketing Is Different," *Business,* May–June 1980, 24–30.
5. Jim Kerstetter and Peter Burrows, "A CEO's Last Stand," *BusinessWeek,* July 26, 2004, 67.
6. Ibid.
7. The discussion in this section is based on Pierre Berthon, James M. Hulbert, and Leyland F. Pitt, *Brands, Brand Managers, and the Management of Brands: Where to Next?* Boston, MA: Marketing Science Institute, Report No. 97-122, 1997.
8. "The 100 Top Brands," *BusinessWeek,* August 2, 2004, 68.
9. David A. Aaker, *Building Strong Brands* (New York: The Free Press, 1996), 26–35.
10. "Death of the Brand Manager," *The Economist,* April 9, 1994, 67–68.
11. Pierre Berthon, James M. Hulbert, and Leyland F. Pitt, *Brands, Brand Managers, and the Management of Brands: Where to Next?* Boston, MA: Marketing Science Institute, Report No. 97-122, 1997.
12. David A. Aaker, *Building Strong Brands* (New York: The Free Press, 1996), 26–35.
13. Ibid., 68.
14. Jim Carlton, "Apple Drops Newton, An Idea Ahead of Its Time," *The Wall Street Journal,* March 2, 1998, B1 and B8.
15. Robert Cooper and Robert S. Kaplan, "Measure Costs Right: Make the Right Decisions," *Harvard Business Review,* September–October 1998, 96–103.
16. Michael J. Etzel, Bruce J. Walker, and William J. Stanton, *Marketing*, 13th ed. (McGraw-Hill/lrwin, 2004), 247.
17. George S. Day, "Diagnosing the Product Portfolio," *Journal of Marketing,* April 1977, 37.
18. The development of these maps is discussed in William R. Dillon, Thomas J. Madden, and Neil H. Firtle, *Marketing Research in a Marketing Environment*, 3rd ed. (Burr Ridge, IL: Richard D. Irwin, Inc. 1994), Appendix to Chapter 17.
19. This section is based on David W. Cravens, Nigel F. Piercy, and George S. Low, "The Innovation Challenges of Proactive Cannibalization and Discontinuous Technology," *European Business Review* 14, no. 4, 2002.
20. Lawrence Ingrassia, "Face-Off: A Recovering Gillette Hopes for Vindication in a High-Tech Razor," *The Wall Street Journal,* September 29, 1989, A1, A4.
21. Rajesh K. Chandry and Gerald J. Tellis, "Organizing for Radical Product Innovation: The Overlooked Role of the Willingness to Cannibalize," *Journal of Marketing Research,* November 1998, 474–487. Rajesh K. Chandry and Gerald J. Tellis, *Organizing for Radical Product Innovation* (Boston, MA): *Marketing Science Institute,* Report 98-102, 1998.
22. David A. Aaker, *Managing Brand Equity* (New York: The Free Press, 1991), 15.
23. Ibid., 102–120.
24. Peter H. Farquhar, Julie Y. Han, and Yuji Liri, "Brands on the Balance Sheet," *Marketing Management,* Winter 1992, 19.
25. Kevin Lane Keller, *Strategic Brand Management*, 2nd ed. Upper Saddle River: N.J. Pearson Education, Inc., 2003, 509–517.
26. Kevin Lane Keller, "The Brand Report Card," *Harvard Business Review,* January/February 2000, 147–157.
27. Ibid., 148–149.
28. Noel Capon and James M. Hulbert, *Marketing Management in the 21st Century,* Upper Saddle River, NJ: Prentice-Hall, 2001.
29. Aaker, *Building Strong Brands,* 68.
30. This discussion is based on Aaker, *Building Strong Brands,* Chapter 3.
31. Don E. Schultz, "Getting to the Heart of the Brand," *Marketing Management,* September/October 2000, 8–9.
32. Aaker, *Building Strong Brands,* 102.
33. Ibid., 183.
34. Ibid., Chapter 6.
35. Ronald Alsop, "Enduring Brands Hold Their Allure by Sticking Close to Their Roots," *The Wall Street Journal,* Centennial Edition.
36. Ibid.
37. Ibid.
38. Yumiko Ono, "Victoria's Secret to Launch Makeup with Sexy Names," *The Wall Street Journal,* September 14, 1998, B8.
39. "If It's Not Broken, Don't Fix It," *Forbes*, May 7, 1984, 132.
40. Kelly Beamon, "The Great Bake Off," *Supermarket Business,* August 15, 2000, 41.
41. Christopher Palmeri and Nanette Byrnes, "Is Japanese Style Taking Over the World?" *BusinessWeek*, July 26, 2004, 96–98.
42. Jonathan Guthrie, "Industry Left to Bear the Burden," *Financial Times,* March 19, 2001.
43. David A. Aaker, *Brand Portfolio Strategy* (New York: The Free Press, 2004), 13.
44. "Nestle Is Starting to Slim Down at Last," *BusinessWeek,* October 27, 2003, 56–57.
45. David A. Aaker and Erich Joachimesthaler, *Brand Leadership* (New York, The Free Press, 2000).
46. Aaker, *Building Strong Brands,* 35.

47. Ibid., 340.
48. Dana James, "Rejuvenating Mature Brands Can Be a Stimulating Exercise," *Marketing News,* August 16, 1999, 16–17.
49. James Heckman, "Don't Let the Fat Lady Sing: Smart Strategies Revive Dead Brands," *Marketing News,* January 4, 1999, 1.
50. L. Downes and C. Mui, *Unleashing the Killer App: Digital Strategies for Market Dominance* (Boston, MA: Harvard Business School Press, 1998).
51. Aaker, *Brand Portfolio Strategy*, Chapter 7.
52. Ibid.
53. Ibid., 210–213.
54. Joseph F. Kovar, "EMC-Dell Blockbuster," *Crn*, October 29, 2001, 3.
55. Stephanie Thompson, "The Mouse in the Food Aisle," *Advertising Age,* September 10, 2001, 73.
56. Aaker, *Brand Portfolio Strategy,* 20.
57. Robert Gray, "Brands Profit from Loaning Out Kudos," *Marketing,* October 4, 2000, 29.
58. Gary Khermouch, "'Whoa, Cool Shirt.' 'Yeah, It's a Pepsi,'" *BusinessWeek,* September 10, 2001, 84.
59. D. R. John, B. Loken, and C. Joiner, "The Negative Impact of Extensions: Can Flagship Products Be Diluted?" *Journal of Marketing* 62, January 1998, 19–32.
60. Richard Tomkins, "Manufacturers Strike Back," *Financial Times,* June 16, 2000, 14.
61. Aaker and Joachimsthaler, *Brand Leadership,* 309.
62. Alison Smith, "Moving Out of the Shadows," *Financial Times,* June 5, 1998, 22.
63. "A Dedicated Enemy of Fashion," *The Economist,* August 31, 2002, 47–48; A. J. Parsons, "Nestle: The Visions of Local Managers," *The McKinsey Quarterly,* No. 2, 1996, 5–29.
64. Michael Krauss, "Monster.com Exec Shares Vision for Brand," *Marketing News,* May 1, 2004, 6.
65. Larry Chiagouris and Brant Wansley, "Branding on the Internet," *Marketing Management,* Summer 2000, 34–38.
66. Aaker and Joachimsthaler, *Brand Leadership,* 2000, 242.
67. Aaker, *Brand Portfolio Strategy,* 13.
68. David Woodruff, "A-Class Damage Control at Daimler-Benz," *BusinessWeek,* November 24, 1997, 62. Rufus Olins and Matthew Lynn, "A-Class Disaster," *Sunday Times,* November 16, 1997, 54.
69. Aaker, *Building Strong Brands,* 241.
70. Ibid., 264–266.
71. Amy Merrick, "Gap's Greatest Generation," *The Wall Street Journal*, September 15, 2004, B1, B3.

Chapter 10

Value-Chain Strategy

A group of vertically aligned organizations that add value to a good or service in moving from basic supplies to finished products for consumer and organizational end users is a value chain. Strategic choices in value-chain options are an important part of market-led strategy.

We use the term value chain in preference to others that describe distribution activities from other perspectives (such as that of manufacturing or operations functions), to underline the central purpose of superior customer value. Terms such as physical distribution management, logistics, distribution, and supply chain management are all used to identify certain aspects of the value chain and its management, as well as new organizational units found in many companies. The term value chain focuses attention on the processes, activities, organizations, and structures that combine to create value for customers as products move from their point of origin to the end user.

The value chain (network) is the configuration of distribution channels linking value-chain members with end users. We examine the decisions faced by a company in developing a channel of distribution strategy. Channels of distribution are a central issue in managing the value chain. An effective and efficient distribution channel provides the member organizations with an important strategic edge over competing channels. Distribution strategy concerns how a firm reaches its market targets. We also emphasize the need for marketing decision makers to incorporate into their thinking the impact of innovations in supply chain strategy. The important goal is maintaining the ability of the market-driven company to realign its value chain when this is necessary to meet the changing needs of its customers and markets.

The strategic importance of value-chain decisions is illustrated by the recovery program in process at Benetton. On the basis of its distinctive casual wear and provocative advertising Benetton became one of the world's best-known brands in the 1980s. However, in the 1990s the company was left behind by new competitors which used digital technology to get new styles from the fashion house to stores in less than a month, and at bargain prices. Zara from Spain focused on the latest styles for working women, and Sweden's Hennes & Mauritz (H&M) aimed at very up-to-date clothes for teenagers. By comparison, Benetton's brand was seen as bland and poorly positioned.

Zara and H&M own their retail outlets and operate state-of-the-art unified supply chain systems to track global sales and respond to changes. Benetton was renowned for its outsourcing of production and also distribution—93 percent of sales came from franchise operations. By 2000, Benetton's retail locations were being suffocated by the aggressive international competition of its competitors—typically with larger, more attractive stores, which could respond at lightning speed to customer preferences.

In addition to rebuilding brand values to position better against Zara and H&M, Benetton's recovery strategy depends on several value-chain initiatives: installing up-to-date yield management technology to link all its several thousand retail outlets and improve its time-to-market with new fashions; enlarging existing outlets to carry the whole product range; where this is not possible, focusing smaller stores on a single market segment or product (e.g., only womens' clothes or only knitwear); and, opening large outlets on the main shopping streets of major cities. The aim is to develop a network of larger stores directly owned and managed by Benetton. By 2003, there were 166 Benetton "megastores." It is likely that Benetton's future performance will depend in large part on the success of its value-chain initiatives.[1]

We first look at the role of distribution channels in marketing strategy and discuss several channel strategy issues. Next, we examine the process of selecting the type of channel, determining the intensity of distribution, and choosing the channel configuration of organizations. A discussion of managing the distribution channel follows. We then look at distributing through international channels. Finally, we consider several important supply chain management issues.

Strategic Role of Distribution

A good distribution network creates a strong competitive advantage for an organization. The Benetton example above underlines how central distribution decisions can be to differentiating a company and building competitive strength.

In Chapter 7 we discussed partnering between international airlines to gain market access. However, the airlines example also underlines the impact of the Internet on distribution channels. For example, for a growing number of airlines, an e-mailed reservation number has replaced the multipart ticket that the traveler had to collect from a travel agent or receive through the mail. Significantly, European no-frills airlines like easyJet and Ryanair are working to achieve 100 percent direct Internet booking and ticketing, replacing the traditional functions of the travel agent. Channels are a major element of how airlines compete.

The huge impact of the Internet, creating new channels through which value can be delivered is illustrated in the Internet Feature. This describes the impact of computer kiosks and communication technology to remote villages and areas in India—one of the largest but also one of the poorest countries in the world.

We describe the distribution functions in the channel and then look at the distribution of services. We also examine several factors affecting the choice of whether to use distribution intermediaries or go direct to end users.

Distribution Functions

The *channel of distribution* is a network of value-chain organizations performing functions that connect goods and services with end users. The distribution channel consists of *interdependent* and *interrelated* institutions and agencies, functioning as a system or network, cooperating in their efforts to produce and distribute a product to end users. Thus, hospitals, ambulance services, physicians, test laboratories, insurance companies, and drugstores make up a channel of distribution for health care services.[2] Managed health care organizations are increasingly coordinating the activities of these channel members. Examples of channels of distribution for consumer and industrial products are shown in Exhibit 10.1. In addition to the intermediaries that are shown, many facilitating organizations perform services such as financial institutions, transportation firms, advertising agencies, and insurance firms.

Several value-added activities are necessary in moving products from producers to end users. *Buying and selling* activities by marketing intermediaries reduce the number of transactions

Impact of Technology in India

India is one of the largest countries in the world, but much of its population lives below the poverty line. Nonetheless, the creative use of innovative technology like computer kiosks—one or two personal computers linked to the Internet and available to the public are transforming many value chains in many sectors in India.

Source: Manjeet Kripalani, "The Digital Village," *BusinessWeek*, June 28, 2004, 28–30.

Technology for the Masses

Problem	Solution
E-Government	
Land titles were difficult and costly to get, so farmers faced major problems in getting credit or selling property.	Karnataka State has digitized 20 million deeds, so farmers, for just 30 cents, can get their property deeds from any of 200 computer kiosks.
Computer Kiosks	
Poor roads, power and phone networks hinder the delivery of services such as health care, banking, and education.	Solar-powered computer kiosks, where villagers can buy supplies and get market and health care information.
Agricultural E-Commerce	
Farmers must walk miles to market to buy seeds and fertilizer, and then sell their produce through middlemen at low prices.	Web site with market information that sells supplies and buys produce directly, eliminating middlemen.
Tele-Medicine	
Distances between villages and hospitals make it hard to diagnose and treat patients needing immediate care.	Urban doctors can now view tests from remote clinics and consult with rural caregivers via satellite video and data links.

for producers and end users. *Assembly* of products into inventory helps to meet buyers' time-of-purchase and variety preferences. *Transportation* eliminates the locational gap between buyers and sellers, thus accomplishing the physical distribution function. *Financing* facilitates the exchange function. *Processing and storage* of goods involve breaking large quantities into individual orders, maintaining inventory, and assembling orders for shipment. *Advertising and sales promotion* communicate product availability, location, and features. *Pricing* sets the basis of exchange between buyer and seller. *Reduction of risk* is accomplished through mechanisms such as insurance, return policies, and futures trading. *Personal selling* provides sales, information, and supporting services. *Communications* between buyers and sellers include personal selling contacts, written orders and confirmations, and other information flows. Finally, *servicing and repairs* are essential for many types of products. Increasingly, the Internet provides an enabling and information-sharing technology, changing the way in which these value-adding functions are carried out.

Developing the channel strategy includes determining the functions that are needed and which organizations will be responsible for each function. Middlemen offer important cost and time advantages in the distribution of a wide range of products. Steel service centers illustrate functional specialization.[3] The centers buy steel coil or bar in bulk from steel producers. They

EXHIBIT 10.1
Common Channels of Distribution

Source: Gilbert A. Churchill, Jr., and J. Paul Peter, *Marketing*, 2nd ed. (New York: Irwin/McGraw-Hill, 1998), 369, 371. Copyright © The McGraw-Hill Companies. Used with permission.

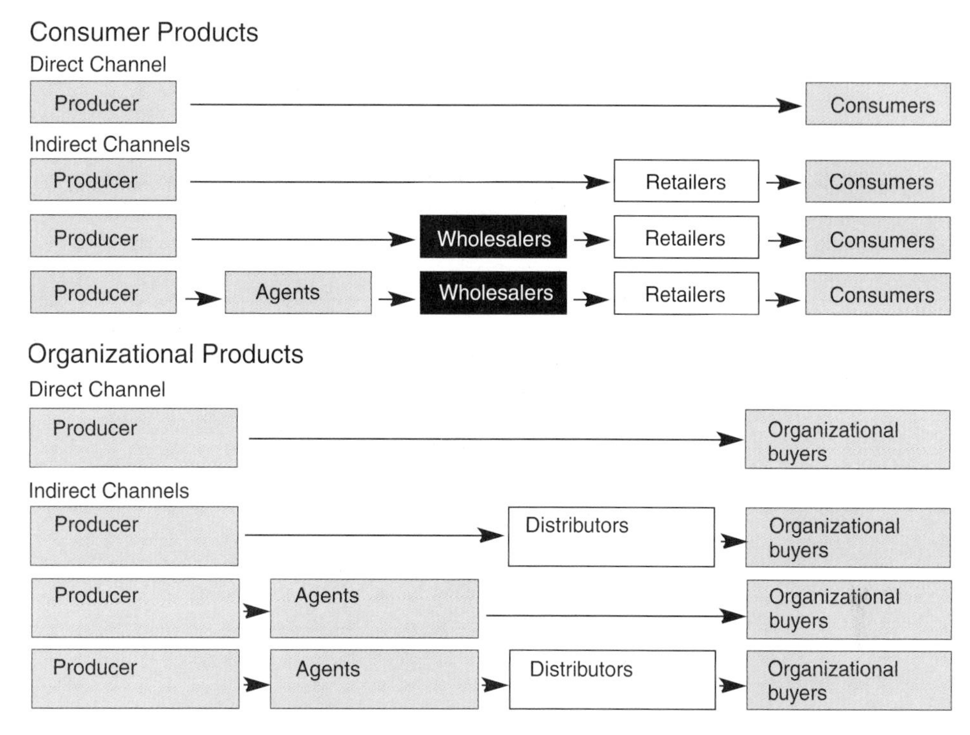

cut and shape the steel at lower costs than the producers, and value-added resellers can react more quickly than steel mills to customer needs. This responsiveness helps reduce the buyer's inventory.

When first selecting a channel of distribution for a new product, the pricing strategy and desired positioning of the product may influence the choice of the channel. For example, a decision to use a premium price and a symbolic positioning concept calls for retail stores that buyers will associate with this image. While the consumer can view and configure alternative models on the company's Web page, it is not possible to buy a new Rolex watch on the Internet.

The Strategy Feature describes the impressive turnaround strategy for Samsung, built on vertical integration (Samsung operates its own factories rather than favoring outsourcing), and a careful choice of markets and distribution partners. Much of the competitive differentiation built by Samsung is based on speed to market and rapid innovation.

Once the channel-of-distribution design is complete and responsibilities for performing the various marketing functions are assigned, these decisions establish guidelines for pricing, advertising, and personal selling strategies. For example, the manufacturers' prices must take into account the requirements and functions of middlemen as well as pricing practices in the channel. Likewise, promotional efforts must be matched to the various channel participants' requirements and capabilities. Consumer-products manufacturers often direct advertising to consumers to help *pull* products through distribution channels. Alternatively, promotion may be concentrated on middlemen to help *push* the product through the channel. Intermediaries may also need help in planning their marketing efforts and other supporting activities.

Channels for Services

Services such as air travel, banking, entertainment, health care, and insurance often involve distribution channels. The service provider renders the service to the end users rather than its being produced like a good and moved through marketing intermediaries to the end user. Because of this the distribution networks for services differ somewhat from those used for

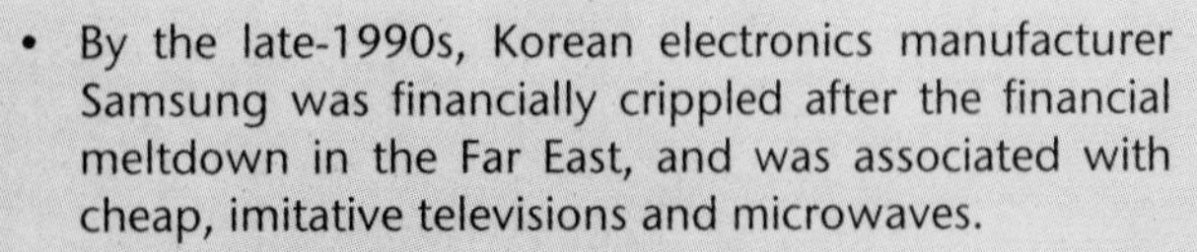

Transformation at Samsung

- By the late-1990s, Korean electronics manufacturer Samsung was financially crippled after the financial meltdown in the Far East, and was associated with cheap, imitative televisions and microwaves.
- By the mid-2000s, Samsung had become one of the world's coolest brands—stylish Samsung high-definition TVs, phones, plasma displays, and digital music and video players crowd the aisles at Best Buy, and the brand is tied into *The Matrix*: *Reloaded* through advertising featuring Trinity and Agent Smith and selling a wireless phone like the one used by Keanu Reeves in the movie.
- The company's feature-packed gadgets are winning design awards, the company is moving to the top of consumer brand awareness surveys, and aiming to oust Sony as number one in consumer electronics.
- In the United States, Samsung has taken its products off the shelves of Wal-Mart and Target, and positioned them with higher-end chains like Best Buy and Circuit City to reach the markets it wants.
- Samsung challenges many conventional strategic rules. The company refuses to enter the software market that offers higher margins, and aims to thrive in hardware—where rather than outsource manufacturing, Samsung builds new factories. The company is diversified and vertically integrated.
- To get to where it is now, Samsung went through aggressive restructuring and reduced headcount and bureaucracy to streamline operations.
- Samsung competes through hardware innovation, product customization, and speed—when T-Mobile in Germany agreed to market a new camera-phone, Samsung had a prototype in four months with an innovative lens that swivels 270 degrees and transmits photos wirelessly. Samsung gets new products to market in around half the time needed by Japanese rivals.
- Samsung sells only higher-end goods and resists pressures toward marketing low-price products.

Source: Cliff Edwards, N. J. Moon Ihlwan, and Pete Engardio, "The Samsung Way," *BusinessWeek*, June 16, 2003, 46–53.

goods. While channels for services may not require as many levels (e.g., producer, distributor, retailer), the network may actually be more complex.

A look at the distribution channels for commercial air travel services highlights several of the characteristics of channels for services. While the airline produces the services, it works with several distribution partners. Tickets may be obtained from independent travel agencies, from airline ticket offices, by telephone, direct from the airline's Internet site, from an Internet travel agent, and through special group arrangements. Airlines have cooperative arrangements with hotel chains, car rental companies, and tour groups. Airline sales forces may call on large corporate customers and other partners. Credit card companies offer charge services and may participate with the airlines' frequent flier programs. Strategic alliances with other airlines may extend a carrier's geographical coverage.

The objectives of channels for services are similar to those for goods, although the functions performed in channels differ somewhat from those for goods. Services are normally rendered when needed rather than placed into inventory. Similarly, services may not be transported although the service provider may go to the user's location to render the service. Processing and storage are normally not involved with services. Servicing and repair functions may not apply to many services. The other functions previously discussed apply to both goods and services (e.g., buying and selling, financing, advertising and sales promotion, pricing, reduction of risk (e.g., lost baggage insurance), and communications.

Direct Distribution by Manufacturers

We consider channel of distribution strategy from a manufacturer's point of view, although many of the strategic issues apply to firms at any level in the value chain—supplier, wholesale, or retail. Manufacturers are unique because they may have the option of going directly to end users through a company sales force or serving end users through marketing intermediaries. Manufacturers have three distribution alternatives: (1) direct distribution, (2) use of intermediaries, or (3) situations in which both (1) and (2) are feasible. The Internet direct channel makes alternative (1) open to many more companies. The factors that influence the distribution decision include buyer considerations, product characteristics, and financial and control factors.

Buyer Considerations. Manufacturers look at the amount and frequency of purchases by buyers, as well as the margins over manufacturing costs that are available to pay for direct selling costs. Customers' needs for product information and applications assistance may determine whether a company sales force or independent marketing intermediaries can best satisfy buyers' needs. Dell Inc's direct sales, built-to-order business design has proven to be a major competitive edge, reinforced by the Internet. However, Dell's targets are business buyers and relatively sophisticated consumers, which greatly influences the type and level of service required. The customer's "techno-readiness," or preparedness to deal over the Internet is an important consideration in evaluating the direct Internet channel possibility.[4]

Competitive Considerations. Distribution channels may be an important aspect of how a company differentiates itself and its products from others, and this may impel decision makers toward increased emphasis on direct channels. Dell is powerfully differentiated by its direct business model. The Internet can change the economics of distribution in favor of direct marketing.

For example, the last five years have shown substantial growth in custom online ordering, a form of mass customization. On its Web site Colorworks, Masterfoods USA (the division of Mars that makes M&M's, offers consumers a palette of 21 colors to coat M&M's—for example in their school colors. The cost is nearly three times that of regular M&M's, but it provides a growing niche business. Similarly, P&G allows consumers to design eye moisturizer and foundation makeup products at its reflect.com site; Yankee Candle Co. allows buyers to mix and match colors and scents to customize the candle; and Branches Hockey allows the enthusiast to specify the custom hockey stick. Advantages include higher prices and impressive customer loyalty. On the other hand, Nike's custom online ordering at Nikeid.com was constrained by the need for consumers to try on the sneaker—so they have moved to Web kiosks in Niketown stores to combine regular retail with the custom product.[5]

Product Characteristics. Companies often consider product characteristics in deciding whether to use a direct or distribution-channel strategy. Complex goods and services often require close contact between customers and the producer, who may have to provide application assistance, service, and other supporting activities. For example, chemical-processing equipment, mainframe computer systems, pollution-control equipment, and engineering-design services are often marketed directly to end users via company sales forces. Another factor is the range of products offered by the manufacturer. A complete line may make distribution by the manufacturer economically feasible, whereas the cost of direct sales for a single product may be prohibitive. High-volume purchases may make direct distribution feasible for a single product. Companies whose product designs change because of rapidly changing technology often adopt direct sales approaches. Also qualified marketing intermediaries may not be available, given the complexity of the product and the requirements of the customer. Direct contact with the end user provides feedback to the manufacturer about new product needs, problem areas, and other concerns. Many supporting services may be Web-based.

Financial and Control Considerations. It is necessary to decide if resources are available for direct distribution, and, if they are, whether selling direct to end users is the best use of the resources. Both the costs and benefits need to be evaluated. Direct distribution gives the manufacturer control over distribution, since independent organizations cannot be managed in the same manner as company employees. This may be an important factor to the manufacturer.

For example, in the early 2000s several high-technology manufacturers opened retail outlets. By 2004, Apple Computer had opened 75 stores in 3 years. The goal was to educate consumers about the company's computers and music players. It is a response to the threat of commodification in

EXHIBIT 10.2
Factors Favoring Distribution by the Manufacturer

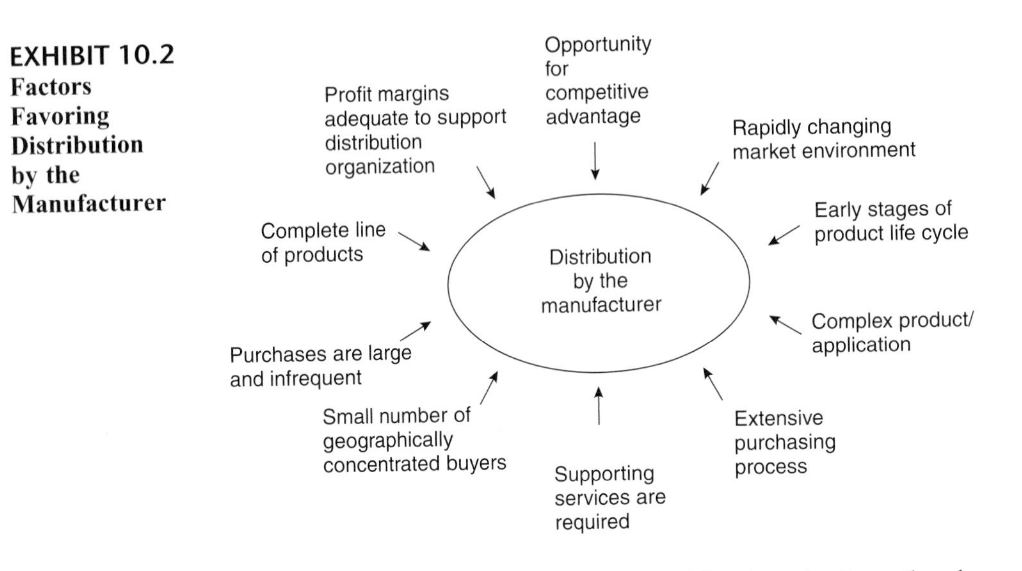

electronics—the consumer with little brand loyalty who buys the cheapest possible product. Similar motives underpin the opening of retail outlets by Sony Electronics and palmOne—the aim is to reinforce their brands with affluent consumers and gain better insight into fast-changing trends in consumer electronics. These moves underline the importance of market access and market learning in sustaining competitive differentiation.[6]

Exhibit 10.2 highlights several factors favoring distribution by the manufacturer. A firm's financial resources and capabilities are also important considerations. The producers of business and industrial products are more likely than producers of consumer products to utilize company distribution to end users. This is achieved by a direct to the end user network of company sales offices and a field sales force or by a vertically integrated distribution system (distribution centers and retail outlets) owned by the manufacturer. Companies with superior Internet capabilities may also favor the direct channel more than others.

A producer may decide to work through middlemen to avoid investing to provide direct contact, and to utilize the competencies of experienced value-added organizations. For example, most steel producers utilize independent service centers.[7]

Channel of Distribution Strategy

We now consider the decisions that are necessary in developing a channel of distribution strategy. They include (1) determining the type of channel arrangement, (2) deciding the intensity of distribution, (3) selecting the channel configuration (Exhibit 10.3).

Management may seek to achieve one or more objectives using the channel of distribution strategy. While the primary objective is gaining access to end user buyers, other related objectives may also be important, as shown in Exhibit 10.4. These include providing promotional and personal selling support, offering customer service, obtaining market information, and gaining favorable revenue/cost performance. Recall the moves into retail by Apple, Sony, and palmOne to build brand values with consumers.

Types of Distribution Channels

The major types of channels are conventional channels and vertical marketing systems (VMS). The conventional channel of distribution is a group of vertically linked independent organizations, each trying to look out for itself, with limited concern for the total performance of the channel. The relationships between the conventional channel participants are rather informal and the members are not closely coordinated. The focus of the channel organizations is on buyer-seller transactions rather than close collaboration throughout the distribution channel.

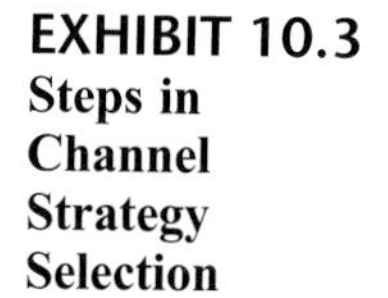

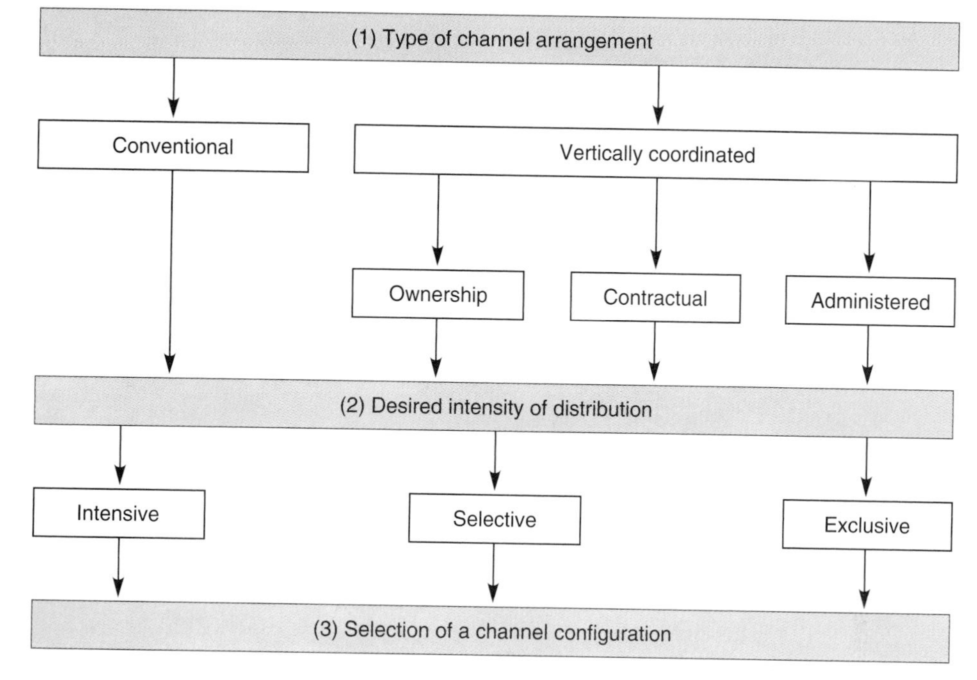

The second type of distribution channel is the vertical marketing system (VMS). Marketing executives in an increasing number of firms realize the advantages to be gained by managing the channel as a coordinated or programmed system of participating organizations. We consider later the influence of supply chain management approaches and the Internet on the operations of channels. These vertical marketing systems dominate the retailing sector and are significant factors in the business and industrial products and services sectors.

A primary feature of a VMS is the management (or coordination) of the distribution channel by one organization. Programming and coordination of channel activities and functions are directed by the firm that is the channel manager. Operating rules and guidelines indicate the functions and responsibilities of each participant. Management assistance and services are supplied to the participating organizations by the firm that is the channel leader.

Three types of vertical marketing systems may be used: *ownership, contractual,* and *administered*. During recent years, a fourth form of VMS has developed in which the channel organizations form collaborative relationships rather than control by one organization. We consider this as a *relationship* VMS.

Ownership VMS. Ownership of distribution channels from source of supply to end user involves a substantial capital investment by the channel coordinator. This kind of VMS is also less adaptable to change compared to the other VMS forms. For these reasons a more popular alternative may be to develop collaborative relationships with channel members (e.g., supplier/manufacture alliances). Such arrangements tend to reduce the coordinator's control over the channel but overcome the disadvantages of control through ownership. Nonetheless, in highly competitive markets, the need for control of distribution may make channel ownership more attractive. Globally, many auto manufacturers are establishing their own retail outlets and buying out independent franchisees and distributors to regain channel control to build an ownership VMS, replacing conventional channels.

Contractual VMS. The contractual form of the VMS may include various formal arrangements between channel participants including franchising and voluntary chains of independent retailers. Franchising is popular in fast foods, lodging, and many other retail lines. Traditional automobile dealerships are another example of a contractual VMS. Wholesaler-sponsored retail

EXHIBIT 10.4
Distribution Channel Objectives and Measurement Criteria

Source: Harper W. Boyd, Jr., Orville C. Walker, Jr., and Jean-Claude Larréché, *Marketing Management*, 3rd ed. (New York: Irwin/McGraw-Hill, 1998), 317. Copyright © The McGraw-Hill Companies. Used with permission.

Performance Objective	Possible Measures	Applicable Product and Channel Level
Product Availability		
• Coverage of relevant retailers	• Percent of effective distribution	• Consumer products (particularly convenience goods) at retail level
• In-store positioning	• Percent of shelf-facings or display space gained by product, weighted by importance of store	• Consumer products at retail level
• Coverage of geographic markets	• Frequency of sales calls by customer type; average delivery time	• Industrial products; consumer goods at wholesale level
Promotional Effort		
• Effective point-of-purchase (POP) promotion	• Percent of stores using special displays and POP materials, weighted by importance of store	• Consumer products at retail level
• Effective personal selling support	• Percent of salespeople's time devoted to product; number of salespeople receiving training on product's characteristics and applications	• Industrial products; consumer durables at all channel levels; consumer convenience goods at wholesale level
Customer Service		
• Installation, training, repair	• Number of service technicians receiving technical training; monitoring of customer complaints	• Industrial products, particularly those involving high technology; consumer durables at retail level
Market Information		
• Monitoring sales trends, inventory levels, competitors' actions	• Quality and timeliness of information obtained	• All levels of distribution
Cost-Effectiveness		
• Cost of channel functions relative to sales volume	• Middlemen margins and marketing costs as percent of sales	• All levels of distribution

chains are used by food and drug wholesalers to establish networks of independent retailers. Contractual programs may be initiated by manufacturers, wholesalers, and retailers. For example, the outstanding growth of Krispy Kreme doughnuts is based in part on franchised stores in the United States which provide a third of the company's income. Interestingly, Krispy Kreme's international expansion is based on the franchised part of its operation.[8]

Administered VMS. The administered VMS exists because one of the channel members has the capacity to influence channel members. This influence may be the result of financial strengths, brand image, specialized skills (e.g., marketing, product innovation), and assistance and support to channel members. For example, DeBeers managed the worldwide distribution of rough diamonds through its marketing cartel for over a century, acting as "buyer of last resort" to achieve market stability and steady price appreciation for diamonds—by 1998 DeBeers had a diamond stockpile of $5 billion. However, DeBeers shifted strategy in 2000 to leverage its "Diamonds Are Forever" positioning concept with consumers and to brand diamonds—the company has moved down the value chain to participate in the finished jewelry market.[9]

Relationship VMS. This type of channel shares certain characteristics of the administered VMS, but differs in that a single firm does not exert substantial control over other channel members. Instead, the relationship involves close collaboration and sharing of information. The relationship VMS may be more logical in channels with only two or three levels. An example is the relationship between Radio Shack and Sprint (telephone services).

The economic performance of vertical marketing systems is likely to be higher than that in conventional channels if the channel network is properly designed and managed. However, the participating firms in the channel must make certain concessions and be willing to work toward overall channel performance. There are rules to be followed, control is exercised in various ways, and generally there is less flexibility for the channel members. Also, some of the requirements of the total VMS may not be in the best interests of a particular participant. Nonetheless, competing in a conventional distribution channel against a VMS is a major competitive challenge, so a channel member may find membership in a VMS to be beneficial.

The remarkable story of Linux illustrates how informal relationship-building by parties at different stages in the value change can transform an industry. The Innovation Feature describes how IBM and Intel, producing computer hardware, and Dell, the leading reseller, have supported Linux's open-source software expansion. Commentators suggest that industry animosity toward the operating systems dominance of Microsoft has motivated much of the support given to Linux.

Distribution Intensity

Step 2 in channel strategy is selecting distribution intensity (Exhibit 10.3). Industrie Natuzzi SpA's management made an important distribution intensity decision in 1982 when it rejected the R.H. Macy & Company proposal to serve as the leather furniture producer's exclusive retailer in the New York area.[10] Instead, the Italian manufacturer decided to distribute its products in a wide range of retail outlets, though only to one in each price and quality category—the first product to reach the United States was "the peoples' sofa," priced at $999. By 2000, Natuzzi had 220 retail customers in New York alone, including Macy & Company. In the mid-2000s Natuzzi holds leading market shares in the United States and Europe, with 50 percent of its global sales made in the United States.

Distribution intensity is best examined in reference to how many retail stores (or industrial product dealers) carry a particular brand in a geographical area. If a company like Natuzzi decides to distribute its products in many of the retail outlets in a trading area that might normally carry such a product, it is using an *intensive* distribution approach. A trading area may be a portion of a city, the entire metropolitan area, or a larger geographical area. If one retailer or dealer in the trading area distributes the product, then management is following an *exclusive* distribution strategy. Examples include Lexus automobiles and Caterpillar industrial equipment. *Selective* distribution falls between the two extremes. Rolex watches and Coach leather goods are distributed on a selective basis.

Choosing the right distribution intensity depends on management's targeting and positioning strategies and product and market characteristics. The major issues in deciding distribution intensity are:

- Identifying which distribution intensities are feasible, taking into account the size and characteristics of the market target, the product, and the requirements likely to be imposed by prospective intermediaries (e.g., they may want exclusive sales territories).
- Selecting the alternatives that are compatible with the proposed market target and marketing program positioning strategy. For example, exclusive distribution was not consistent with Natuzzi's U.S. targeting strategy.

Innovation Feature The Linux Revolution

Linux is a penny-pinching open-source alternative to computer operating systems such as Microsoft's Windows and Sun Microsystem's Solaris. It is flexible enough to run everything from an IBM supercomputer to a Motorola cell phone.

"Open source" software means that Linux can be downloaded off the Web free (though typically it is bought by companies as part of a package that includes services). For example, Morgan Stanley is replacing 4,000 high-powered servers running traditional software, with much lower-priced machines running Linux—projected 5-year savings are $100 million.

Not only is the Linux software available free, it also improves—a rag-tag band of open-source programming volunteers around the world work on the software. Before using Linux, tech companies must sign a license in which they promise to give away innovations they build on top of it. Users like to be able to modify programs themselves to meet their needs and fix problems, and appear happy to share this with others.

Backed by technology companies like Intel, IBM, H-P and Dell, Linux is taking its cute penguin mascot mainstream. From almost a zero start in 2000, by 2006 Linux is expected to have 25 percent of the $50 billion market for server computers, and Linux is finding its way into countless consumer electronics products—Sony PlayStation, video game consoles, and TiVo TV program recorders.

Linux challenges the ability of producers to earn revenues and profits from the intellectual property right in software—in addition to Linux, basic open-source databases and e-mail are already available.

Source: Jim Kerstetter, Steve Hamm, and Spencer E. Ante, "The Linux Uprising," *BusinessWeek*, March 3, 2003, 48–56.

Linux Cuts Both Ways

The Winners	The Losers
IBM—selling twice as many Linux servers as any other company, and well-liked by Linux developers.	**Sun Microsystems**—customers are abandoning its Solaris software for Linux, which performs similar tasks.
Intel—the processor giant is taking Linux into the world of high-powered computing in corporate data centers.	**Microsoft**—Linux wins the price war and is attracting corporate customers who do not want to be locked into Microsoft.
Dell—can sell Linux servers cheaper than other major computer companies.	**Linux Start-ups**—other than Red Hat, there is not much room.
Red Hat—the leading seller of Linux has lined up distribution deals with just about every big computer company.	**Linux Purists**—Linux developers who don't like the idea of working with capitalists had better get used to the idea.

- Choosing the alternative that (1) offers the best strategic fit, (2) meets management's financial performance expectations, and (3) is attractive enough to intermediaries so that they will be motivated to perform their assigned functions.

The characteristics of the product and the market target to be served often suggest a particular distribution intensity. For example, an expensive product, such as a Toyota Lexus luxury automobile, does not require intensive distribution to make contact with potential buyers. Moreover, several dealers in a trading area could not generate enough sales and profits to be successful due to the luxury car's limited sales potential. Similarly, Samsung's move to the higher end of consumer electronics points to a selective rather than intensive distribution strategy. In contrast, Kodak film needs to be widely available in the marketplace.

The distribution intensity should correspond to the marketing strategy selected. For example, Estée Lauder distributes cosmetics through selected department stores that carry quality products. Management decided not to meet Revlon head-on in the marketplace, and instead concentrates its efforts on a small number of retail outlets. In doing this, Estée Lauder avoids huge national advertising expenditures and uses promotional tactics to help attract its customers to retail outlets. Buyers are offered free items when purchasing other specified items.

Strategic requirements, management's preferences, and other constraints help determine the distribution intensity that offers the best strategic fit and performance potential. The requirements of intermediaries need to be considered, along with management's desire to coordinate and motivate them. For example, exclusive distribution is a powerful incentive to intermediaries and also simplifies management activities for the channel leader. But if the company that is granted exclusive distribution rights is unable (or unwilling) to fully serve the needs of target customers, the manufacturer will not take advantage of the sales and profit opportunities that could be obtained by using more intermediaries.

Channel Configuration

The third step in selecting the distribution strategy is deciding: (1) how many levels of organizations to include in the vertical channel, and (2) the specific kinds of intermediaries to be selected at each level (Exhibit 10.3). The type (conventional or VMS) of channel and the distribution intensity selected help in deciding how many channel levels to use and what types of intermediaries to select. Different channel levels are shown in Exhibit 10.1. As an example, an industrial products producer might choose between distributors and sales agents (independent organizations that receive commissions on sales) to contact industrial buyers. Several factors may influence the choice of one of the channel configurations shown in Exhibit 10.1.

End User Considerations. It is important to know *where* the targeted end users might expect to purchase the products of interest. The intermediaries that are selected should provide an avenue to the market segments(s) targeted by the producer. Analysis of buyer characteristics and preferences provides important information for selecting firms patronized by end users. This, in turn, guides decisions concerning additional channel levels, such as the middlemen selling to the retailers that contact the market target customers.

Product Characteristics. The complexity of the product, special application requirements, and servicing needs are useful in guiding the choice of intermediaries. Looking at how competing products are distributed may suggest possible types of intermediaries, although adopting competitors' strategies may not be the most promising channel configuration. The breadth and depth of the products to be distributed are also important considerations since intermediaries may want full lines of products.

Manufacturer's Capabilities and Resources. Large producers with extensive capabilities and resources have a lot of flexibility in choosing intermediaries. These producers also have a great deal of bargaining power with the middlemen, and, the producer may be able (and willing) to perform certain distribution functions. Such options are more limited for small producers with limited capabilities and resource constraints.

Required Functions. The functions that need to be performed in moving products from producer to end user include various channel activities such as storage, servicing, and transportation. Studying these functions is useful in choosing the types of intermediaries that are appropriate for a particular product or service. For example, if the producer needs only the direct-selling function, independent manufacturers' agents may be the right middlemen to use. Alternatively, if inventory stocking and after-sales service are needed, then a full-service wholesaler may be essential.

Availability and Skills of Intermediaries. Evaluation of the experience, capabilities, and motivation of the intermediaries that are under consideration for channel membership is also important. Firms within the same industry often vary in skills and experience. Also, qualified channel members may not be available. For example, some types of middlemen will not distribute competing products.

A channel with only one level between the producer and end user simplifies the coordination and management of the channel. The more complex the channel network, the more challenging it is to complete various distribution functions. Nevertheless, using specialists at two (or more) levels (e.g., brokers, wholesalers, dealers) may offer substantial economies of scale through the specialization of functions. The channel configuration that is selected typically takes into account several important trade-offs. As an example, manufacturer's agents (independent sales representatives) may provide the producer greater channel control compared to full-service wholesalers. However, the agents make it necessary for the manufacturer to perform several functions, such as inventory stocking, invoicing, and service.

Selecting the Channel Strategy

The major channel-strategy decisions we have examined are summarized in Exhibit 10.3. Management (1) chooses the type(s) of channel to be used, (2) determines the desired intensity of distribution, and (3) selects the channel configuration. One of the first issues to be resolved is deciding whether to manage the channel, partner with other members, or be a participant. This choice often rests on the bargaining power a company can exert in negotiating with other organizations in the channel system and the value (and costs) of performing the channel management role. The options include deciding to manage or coordinate operations in the channel of distribution, becoming a member of a vertically coordinated channel, or becoming a member of a conventional channel system. The following factors need to be assessed in the choice of the channel strategy.

Market Access. As emphasized throughout the chapter the market target decision needs to be closely coordinated with channel strategy, since the channel connects products and end users. The market target decision is not finalized until the channel strategy is selected. Information about the customers in the market target can help eliminate unsuitable channel-strategy alternatives. Multiple market targets may require more than a single channel of distribution. One advantage of middlemen is that they have an established customer base. When this customer base matches the producer's choice of market target(s), market access is achieved very rapidly.

Value-Added Competencies. The channel selected should offer the most favorable combination of value-added competencies. Making this assessment requires looking at the competencies of each participant and the trade-offs concerning financial and flexibility and control considerations.

Financial Considerations. Two financial issues affect the channel strategy. First, are the resources available for launching the proposed strategy? For example, a small producer may not have the money to build a distribution network. Second, the revenue-cost impact of alternative channel strategies needs to be evaluated. These analyses include cash flow, income, return on investment, and operating capital requirements (see Appendix to Chapter 2).

Flexibility and Control Considerations. Management should decide how much flexibility it wants in the channel network and how much control it would like to have over other channel participants. An example of flexibility is how easily channel members can be added (or eliminated). A conventional channel offers little opportunity for control by a member firm, yet there is a lot of flexibility in entering and exiting from the channel. The VMS offers more control than the conventional channel. Legal and regulatory constraints also affect channel strategies in such areas as pricing, exclusive dealing, and allocation of market coverage.

Channel Strategy Illustration. Suppose a producer of industrial controls for fluid processing (e.g., valves, regulators) is considering two channel strategy alternatives: using independent manufacturer's representatives (agents) versus recruiting a company sales force to sell its products to industrial customers. The representatives receive a commission of 8 percent on their dollar sales volume. Salespeople will be paid an estimated $100,000 in annual salary and expenses. Salespeople must be recruited, trained, and supervised.

EXHIBIT 10.5
Illustrative Channel Strategy Evaluation

Evaluation Criteria	Manufacturer's Representatives	Company Sales Force
Market access	Rapid	One- to three-year development
Sales forecast (two years)	$10 million	$20 million
Forecast accuracy	High	Medium to low
Estimated costs	$1 million*	$2.4 million†
Selling expense (costs/sales)	10%	12%
Flexibility	Good	Fair
Control	Limited	Good

*Includes 8% commission plus management time for recruiting and training representatives.
†Includes $100,000 for 10 salespeople, plus management time.

An illustrative channel strategy evaluation is shown in Exhibit 10.5. The company sales force alternative is more expensive (using a two-year time frame) than the use of independent sales agents. Assuming both options generate contributions to profit, the trade-off of higher expenses needs to be evaluated against flexibility and control considerations. One possibility that is often used by manufacturers seeking access to a new market is to initially utilize manufacturer's representatives with a longer-term strategy of converting to a company sales force. This offers an opportunity to gain market knowledge while keeping selling expenses in line with actual sales.

Strategies at Different Channel Levels

We have looked at distribution largely from the producer's viewpoint. Wholesalers and retailers are also concerned with channel strategies, and some of them may exercise primary control over channel operations. For example, The Limited is a powerful force in its channels, as is Wal-Mart. Large food wholesalers and retailers are major factors in their channels of distribution. Moreover, decisions by wholesalers, distributors, brokers, and retailers about which manufacturers' products to carry often affect the performance of all channel participants.

Channel strategy can be examined from any level in the distribution network. The major distinction lies in the point of view (retailer, wholesaler, producer) used to develop the strategy. Intermediaries may have fewer alternatives to consider than producers and, thus, less flexibility in channel strategy. Nevertheless, their approach to channel strategy is often extremely active rather than passive.

Managing the Channel

After deciding on the channel design, the actual channel participants are identified, evaluated, and recruited. Finding competent and motivated intermediaries is critical to successfully implementing the channel strategy. Channel management activities include choosing how to assist and support intermediaries, developing operating policies, providing incentives, selecting promotional programs, and evaluating channel results. These activities consume much of management's time, since once established the channel design may be difficult to modify.

Importantly, changes in channel design may have serious consequences for the members. Consider, for example, the impact of adding a direct Internet channel to distribution strategy. Direct Internet sales compete with distributors and salespeople in the value chain. One of Dell's key advantages with its direct business model was that it was very difficult for existing market leaders like IBM and H-P to operate a direct business model—they were tied to traditional distribution channels and were reluctant to compete with their own distributors.

To gain a better insight into channel management, we discuss channel leadership, management structure and systems, physical distribution management, channel relationships, conflict resolution, channel performance, and legal and ethical considerations.

Channel Leadership

Some form of interorganization management is needed to assure that the channel has satisfactory performance as a competitive entity.[11] One firm may gain power over other channel organizations because of its specific characteristics (e.g., size), experience, and environmental factors, and its ability to capitalize on such factors. Gaining this advantage is more feasible in a VMS than in a conventional channel.

Performing the leadership role may also lead to conflicts arising from differences in the objectives and priorities of channel members. Conflicts with retailers created by the channel strategy changes are illustrative. The organization with the most power may make decisions that are not considered favorable by other channel members.

Management Structure and Systems

Channel coordination and management are often the responsibility of the sales organization (Chapter 13). For example, a manufacturer's salespeople develop buyer-seller relationships with wholesalers and/or retailers. The management structure and systems may vary from informal arrangements to highly structured operating systems. Conventional channel management is more informal, whereas the management of VMS is more structured and programmed. The VMS management systems may include operating policies and procedures, information system linkages, various supporting services to channel participants, and setting performance targets.

Physical Distribution Management

Physical distribution (logistics) management has received considerable attention from distribution, marketing, manufacturing, and transportation professionals. The objective is improving the distribution of supplies, goods in process, and finished products. The decision to integrate physical distribution with other channel functions or to manage it separately is a question that must be resolved by a particular organization. There are instances when either approach may be appropriate. Physical distribution is a key channel function and thus an important part of channel strategy and management. Management needs to first select the appropriate channel strategy, considering the physical distribution function and other essential channel activities. Once the strategy is selected, physical distribution management alternatives can be examined for the value-chain network. Recent moves to extend physical distribution management in the form of supply chain strategy are considered later in the chapter.

Channel Relationships

Chapter 7 considers various forms of relationships between organizations, examining the degree of collaboration between companies, the extent of commitment of the participating organizations, and the power and dependence ties between the organizations. We now look at how these issues relate to channel relationships.

Degree of Collaboration. Channel relationships are often transactional in conventional channels but may become more collaborative in VMSs. The extent of collaboration is influenced by the complexity of the product, the potential benefits of collaboration, and the willingness of channel members to work together as partners. Just-in-time inventory programs, total quality management activities, and supply chain models encourage collaboration and information sharing between suppliers and producers.

Commitment and Trust among Channel Members. The commitment and trust of channel organizations is likely to be higher in VMSs compared to conventional channels. For example, a contractual arrangement (e.g., franchise agreement) is a commitment to work together. Yet, the strength of the commitment may vary depending on the contract terms. For example, contracts between manufacturers and their independent representatives or agents typically allow either party to terminate the relationship with a 30-day notification.

Highly collaborative relationships among channel members call for a considerable degree of commitment and trust between the partners. The cooperating organizations provide access to confidential product plans, market data, and other trade secrets. Trust normally develops as the partners learn to work with each other and find the relationship to be favorable to each partner's objectives.

Power and Dependence. In VMSs, power is concentrated with one organization and the other channel members are dependent on the channel manager. This concentration of power does not exist with the relationship VMS. Power in conventional channels is less concentrated than it is in VMSs, and channel members are less dependent on each other. Conventional channel relationships may, nevertheless, result in some channel members possessing more bargaining power than others.

Hallmark Cards is the market leader in the greeting card industry. However, building and sustaining that position has required an evolving distribution strategy over time. These changes posed a difficult power and dependence challenge that had to be met. For decades Hallmark relied on independent specialty shops to sell its cards. Increasingly, through the 1990s mass merchandisers like Target stores accounted for a rapidly growing share of the market. Notwithstanding the impact on small specialty store owners, Hallmark had to expand into this distribution channel or continue to lose market share. By the late 1990s many mass merchandise retailers carried Hallmark cards. By the 2000s, Hallmark had partnered with Microsoft to offer personalized cards via the Internet, as well as selling software packages via Amazon.com to allow consumers to produce their own cards from templates, and providing e-cards and online greeting cards from its Web site.

In many sectors, suppliers face unprecedented pressure from powerful channel members. New merchandising strategies with this effect include house branding and category killers.[12] House branding includes retailers who have established the retail store network as the brand, such as Gap, Banana Republic, and Victoria's Secret. These retailers rely on contract manufacturers to produce their brands. Category killers are companies like Toys "R" Us, Home Depot, Staples, and Linens 'n Things that attempt to dominate one segment of the market, often with very low prices. Suppliers may have substantially less control over these channels than in the past. Responses may include suppliers reclaiming important value-added services from distributors to build stronger relationships with end users; eliminating layers in the conventional channel; or creating new channels.

Channel Globalization

Significantly for consumer goods suppliers, many major retail chains have expanded internationally. The globalization of distribution channels is underlined by the launch of Internet-based online exchanges. With the ability to source and merchandise globally, efficient supply chains, and powerful information technology, major retailers have more bargaining power than many of their suppliers.

Increasingly, industrywide forms include online exchanges on the Internet. For example, in retail, Sears Roebuck in the United States, Sainsbury in the United Kingdom, along with Germany's Metro and France's Carrefour have established GlobalNet Exchange (GNX). Other major organizations like Wal-Mart and Sun Microsystems are instead developing "private exchanges" on the Internet, linking them with their suppliers but not their competitors.[13]

Similarly, in 2000 another group of large retailers from around the world announced an Internet-based alliance to create the Worldwide Retail Exchange. Participants included Target, Albertsons, CVS, Kmart, and Safeway Inc. in the United States; Tesco, Marks & Spencer, Woolworth, and Kingfisher in the United Kingdom; Auchan and Casino in France; and Royal Holland in the Netherlands. The alliance had 64 members with combined revenues of $900 billion, and estimated it had taken $1 billion out of its members costs. In full operation the Exchange will link them with more than 100,000 suppliers in food, general merchandise, and health care products. The goal is to have suppliers located throughout the world compete with each other through a single Web site with complete price transparency. Though in their infancy, such schemes are likely to be a prototype for the globalization of channels of distribution.[14]

Although they are facing problems of technology integration as well as antitrust questions, it is estimated that Internet-based procurement systems may cut 30 percent off costs.[15] In business-to-business marketing, it is telling that beginning in 1999, major purchasers like Boeing and Motorola were warning that suppliers unable or unwilling to make the transition to Web-based commerce would be locked out of their businesses.[16]

The implication is that suppliers face competition at a global level even in what would previously have been seen as domestic business. Buyers able to access online exchanges or participate in online reverse auctions have in effect globalized the distribution channel.

Multichanneling

An important trend in distribution is the use of multiple channels to gain greater access to end user customers. For example, Dayton Hudson (renamed Target Corporation in 2000) after the sales of its Marshall Field's and Mervyns store groups in 2004, operates three retail formats: Target, Target Greatland and Super Target, as well as its online business Target.com.[17] Many suppliers are using the Internet channel to bypass traditional distributors. For example, Lego and Mattell offer their entire product ranges online, auto manufacturers sell direct to consumers over the Web, and business customers can buy electric motors from ABB.[18]

One implication is that increasingly suppliers face the challenge of managing multiple channels to the same market. The problem is to define innovative channel combinations that best meet customer needs. However, in many situations the way channels are used is defined by customer choice. Customers may "channel surf"—Forrester Research estimates that as many as half of all customers shop for information in one channel, then defect from that channel to make the purchase in another medium. Where customers have become more adversarial, buy more strategically, and have the information and technology to make more informed decisions, it may be risky to assume that discrete channels serving static market segments is a sustainable option. Channel decisions must be informed by understanding the various paths buyers follow as they move through the purchase process.[19]

For example, consider the case of the financial services supplier with three main channels all carrying the same products: a direct channel using the Internet, a network of retail branches, and financial services intermediaries. The challenge is to understand how different groups of customers use each channel—possibly the retail branch builds awareness, the intermediary provides information, and the Web site makes the sale. That understanding provides the basis for managing conflicts between the channels and investing selectively in each to match it to customer needs. Williams-Sonoma, for instance, has a cross-channel selling strategy with sales split 60/40 between retail outlets and online/catalog sales. The company continues to find ways of improving each channel so it drives results in the others—catalogs do not simply sell products, by acting as in-home advertising they bring the company to the attention of new customers who are encouraged to use the stores.[20]

Conflict Resolution

Conflicts are certain to occur between the channel members and in multichanneling between channels, because of differences in objectives, priorities, and corporate cultures. Looking at a proposed channel relationship by each participating organization may identify areas (e.g., incompatible objectives) that are likely to lead to major conflicts. In such situations, management may decide to seek another channel partner. Effective communications before and after establishing the channel relationships can also help to eliminate or reduce conflicts.

Several methods are used to resolve actual and potential conflicts.[21] One useful approach is to involve channel members in the decisions that will affect the organizations. Another helpful method of resolving or reducing conflict is developing effective communications channels between channel members. Pursuing objectives that are important to all channel members also helps to reduce conflict. Finally, it may be necessary to establish methods for mediation and arbitration.

Conflicts between channel members may require resolution in court if the stakes merit such extreme action. In 2001, Levi Strauss won a decision in the European Court of Justice against the powerful British retailer Tesco. In Europe Levi jeans are a premier brand sold at a premium price (the British manufacturer's recommended price for Levi 501s is around twice the U.S. price). Levi's refused to supply their jeans to the discounter supermarket Tesco. Tesco used their global sourcing to buy 501s outside Europe, imported them, and sold them in British supermarkets for around $40. Levi's view was that the supermarket distribution channel was undermining its brand, and that it had the right to determine where its products were sold. Levi's actions in upholding its rights to control the distribution channels for its brand have attracted considerable adverse consumer and media comment.[22]

Channel Performance

The performance of the channel is important from two points of view. First, each member is interested in how well the channel is meeting the member's objectives. Second, the organization that is managing or coordinating the channel is concerned with its performance and the overall performance of the channel. Tracking performance for the individual channel members includes various financial and market measures such as profit contribution, revenues, costs, market share, customer satisfaction, and rate of growth. Several criteria for evaluating the overall performance of the channel are shown in Exhibit 10.4.

Companies gain a strategic advantage by improving distribution productivity. Reducing distribution costs and the time in moving products to end users are high-priority action areas in many companies. Much of the impact of Toyota's successful strategy in the auto market is from huge cost savings in the value chain—from operations through supply chain to distribution.

Monitoring the changes that are taking place in distribution and incorporating distribution strategy considerations into the strategic planning process are essential strategic marketing activities. Market turbulence, global competition, and information technology create a rapidly changing distribution environment. Furthermore, multichanneling creates new challenges in measuring channel effectiveness.[23]

Legal and Ethical Considerations

Various legal and ethical considerations may impact channel relationships. Legal concerns by the federal government include arrangements between channel members that substantially lessen competition, restrictive contracts concerning products and/or geographical coverage, promotional allowances and incentives, and pricing practices.[24] State and local laws and regulations may also impact channel members.

The importance of ethics is shown by a research survey of *Fortune* 1000 companies indicating that 98 percent of the responding companies have formal ethics policy statements or documents, and more than one-half have an executive specifically assigned to deal with ethics and conduct issues.[25] Ethical issues are heavily influenced by corporate policies and practices. Corporate pressures on performance may create ethical situations. Deciding whether a practice is ethical is sometimes complex. Complexity increases in international channels crossing different cultures. Channel decisions that impact other channel members may create ethical situations. Many companies have established internal standards on how business should be conducted. Written statements of working relationships among channel members may also include such statements. For example, the Target Corporation publishes a statement of Standards of Vendor Engagement, specifying the ethical and environmental standards to be maintained by its suppliers, backed by a compliance inspection program.

International Channels

The distribution channels that are available in international markets are not totally different from the channels in a particular country such as the United States. Uniqueness is less a function of structural alternatives and more related to the vast range of operational and market variables

EXHIBIT 10.6 International Channel of Distribution Alternatives

Source: Phillip R. Cateora, and John L. Graham, *International Marketing*, 12th ed. (Burr Ridge, IL: McGraw-Hill/Irwin, 2005), 414. Copyright © The McGraw-Hill Companies. Used with permission.

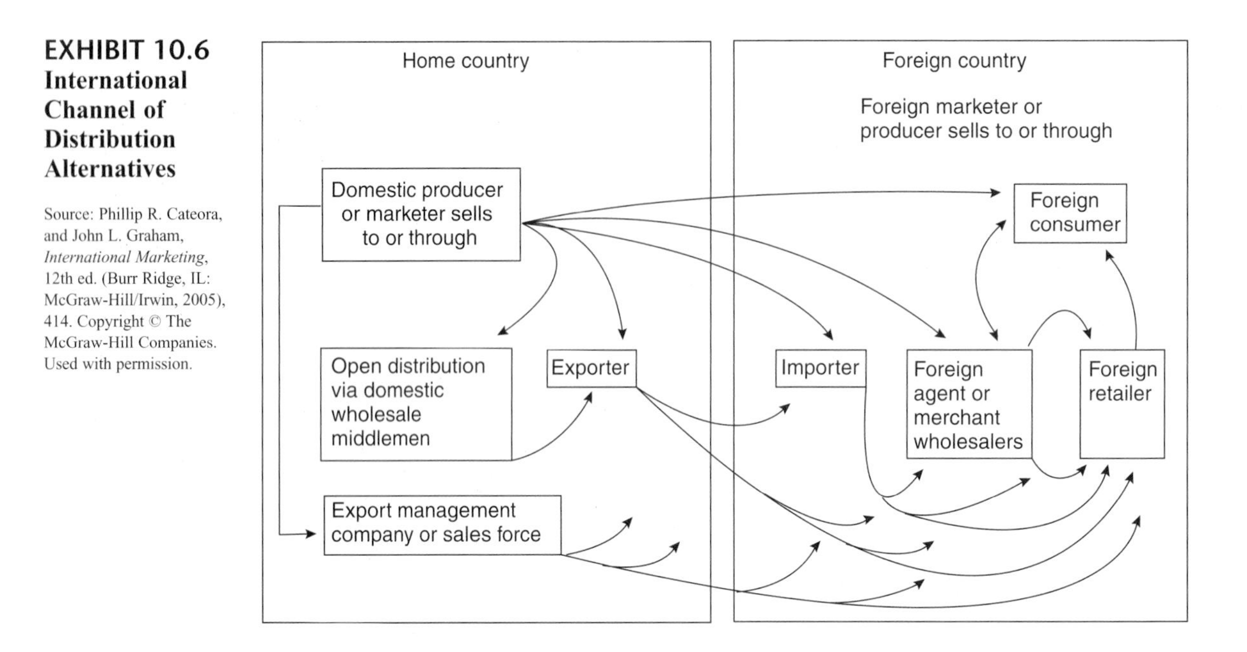

that influence channel strategy.[26] Several channel of distribution alternatives are shown in Exhibit 10.6. The arrows show many possible channel networks linking producers, middlemen, and end users.

Examining International Distribution Patterns

While the basic channel structure (e.g., agents, wholesalers, retailer) is similar across countries, there are many important differences in distribution patterns among countries. "Only when the varied intricacies of actual distribution patterns are understood can the complexity of the distribution task be appreciated."[27] Generalization about distribution practices throughout the world is obviously not possible.

Studying the distribution patterns in the nation(s) of interest is important in obtaining guidelines for distribution strategy. On one hand, various global trends such as satellite communications, the Internet, regional cooperative arrangements (e.g., European Union), and transportation networks (e.g., intermodal services) impact distribution systems in various ways reflecting globalization. Global market turbulence and corporate restructuring create additional influences on distribution strategies and practices.

However, even in the Internet era designing channels to reach overseas customers, particularly in the developing countries, may require some adaptability and the use of high technology may not always provide the solution. The Global Feature describes how Unilever has adapted its distribution strategy in Tanzania.

Factors Affecting Channel Selection

The channel strategy analysis and selection process presented in the chapter can be used for developing or evaluating international channel strategy, recognizing that many situational factors affect channel decisions in specific countries. The factors affecting the choice of international channels include cost, capital requirements, control, coverage, strategic product-market fit, and the likelihood that the middlemen will remain in business over a reasonable time horizon.[28] The political and economic stability of the country is, of course, very important. Stability needs to be evaluated early in the decision to enter the country.

Global Feature

Unilever's Distribution in Tanzania

The Dutch multinational's subsidiary, Unilever Tanzania, was established in 1998 to make inroads with a basic range of goods, in an economy where distribution had been dominated by traditional wholesalers.

Traditional distribution channels were unpromising. Local wholesaling: produced patchy product availability; brands lost their franchise; and pricing was difficult to manage.

Unilever chose to go direct to retail outlets, facing the immense challenge that Tanzania has 100,000 retail outlets spread across the country, in 9,000 villages—with half the population living below the poverty line, many consumers buy rice, maize, and flour in tiny quantities every day from minikiosks in lanes too narrow for vehicles.

- In the Tanzanian towns, Unilever delivers its goods by vans to larger shops.
- But to reach outlets in inaccessible rural areas, they have formed a "bicycle brigade."
- Wearing Unilever's "battle dress" of an "Omo" shirt (Omo is the leading detergent brand) and a yellow "Key" baseball cap (Key is a local soap brand), acting almost as mobile advertisements, salespeople on bicycles take Unilever products to the country's villages.
- Each salesperson has a company bicycle with large boxes welded on the back to transport small packages of detergent powder, margarine, soap and oil, and visits 20–30 shops a day on a fixed itinerary. When the goods are delivered the bicycle stocks are replenished at a central distribution point.
- A typical transaction sees salesman Sospeter Jackson cycling to a tiny outlet at the side of a dusty road near Kiwalani, to sell two bars of Key soap (conveniently marked on both sides so the shopkeeper can cut and sell chunks of soap for a few cents) and a dozen 50-gram sachets of Omo detergent.
- In the first five months of operations, the bicycle brigade grew Unilever's sales fivefold—making tiny packs of Omo detergent and Blue Band margarine into market leaders.

Source: Mark Turner, "Bicycle Brigade's Mission," *Financial Times*, August 16, 2000, 14. Reprinted with permission.

Supply Chain Management Issues

In addition to the design and management of channel systems, a strategic perspective for value-chain management requires consideration of several supply chain initiatives that have major impacts on channel strategy.

Supply Chain Management[29]

Many organizations have adopted supply chain management structures, which have developed out of physical distribution and operations management. However, the impact of supply chain strategies has extended beyond issues of transportation, storage, and stockholding to influence relationships between channel members and customer value. Consider for example, the Efficient Consumer Response (ECR) program. ECR is a cooperative partnership between retailers and manufacturers to reduce supply chain costs—lower stock levels, fewer damaged goods, simpler transaction management. The ECR approaches have achieved impressive cost savings:

> In a detergent project in Sweden, involving Lever Brothers, 20 percent of the category's stock-keeping units (SKUs) were delisted as surplus to consumer requirements, but the result of better focus resulted in a 9 percent sales increase.
> In the dental care market, a Colgate Palmolive project involved a 25 percent reduction in SKUs, but retailer market share increased 11 percent and profit margins by 9 percent.[30]
> As a result of ECR, retailer and supplier companies are collaborating in such areas as forecasting, category management, and electronic commerce.[31]

Collaboration and information sharing have become central to supply chain design. Integrating processes across organizational boundaries is essential to building the seamless supply chain, where "all players think and act as one."[32] The competitive impact of supply chain strength is emphasized: "It is supply chains that compete not companies."[33]

Lean Supply Chains.[34] A major development in supply chain management has emanated from Japanese management approaches, and the example of Toyota in the automotive field in particular (see Case 6.5). This development focuses on the application of lean thinking to supply chains.[35]

The foundation of the lean supply chain is defining value from the perspective of the end-customer, to identify the value stream of activities in the supply chain that are needed to place the correctly specified product with the customer. All non-value-creating activities are "muda," or waste, and should be eliminated. Attention is given to continuous flow of products in the supply chain, instead of traditional "batch and queue" approaches, to eliminate time wasting, storage, and scrap. Products are not produced upstream in the supply chain until ordered by the downstream customer, that is, pulled through the supply chain, removing the need for large inventories and customer waiting time.

The lean philosophy also advances the need for constant search for improvement and perfection. The goal is to remove demand instability through collaboration between suppliers and distributors, and ultimately to allow customers to order direct from the production system.[36] Examples of lean supply chains are provided by Dell Inc., and the industrywide ECR program in the U.S. grocery sector.

While the lean supply chain arguments are compelling, some critics suggest that the lean approach creates supply chains that are vulnerable to unexpected market change and do not have the capacity to be responsive to customers.

Agile Supply Chains. In response to the impact of turbulent volatile markets that are difficult to predict, new emphasis has been placed on creating supply chains that are not lengthy and slow-moving "pipelines," but agile and responsive to market change.[37] Supply chain agility means using market knowledge and a virtual corporation to respond to marketplace volatility, as opposed to the lean approach which seeks to remove waste and manage volatility out of the supply chain by leveling demand.[38] The agile supply chain reserves capacity to cope with unpredictable demand.[39] While lean supply chains require long-term partnership with suppliers, the agile model mandates fluid and market-based relationships to enhance responsiveness to the market and capacity for rapid change.[40] Agile supply chain models emphasize customer satisfaction rather than meeting a more limited set of value criteria based on reduced costs.

Internet-Based Supply Chains. It is important to note that in several approaches to designing modern supply chains, the Internet and customized intranets and extranets are essential enabling technologies that support interfirm collaboration, the integration of ordering and fulfillment processes, and the sharing of information. The role of the Internet in reshaping channels is expanded below.

Limitations and Risks in Supply Chain Strategies. In spite of the advances made in recent years, there remain substantial barriers to effective supply chain collaborations. Research suggests those barriers include complexity in technology integration and costs of integration; lack of trading partner technology sophistication; lack of clear benefits; cultural resistance to new trading partner paradigms; few Web-based applications available; and lack of shared technical standards.[41] Consideration should also be given to recovery from the collapse of supply chain collaborations and the impact on a company's competitive position.

The Impact of Supply Chain Management on Marketing. Already in many sectors, corporate purchasers are reducing their supplier numbers to improve their companies' supply chain efficiency, providing another competitive pressure on suppliers. However, in addition to this marketplace pressure, importantly supply chain strategies impact on several critical issues for marketing strategy and the value chain: product availability in the market, speed to market with innovations, the range of product choices offered to customers, product deletion decisions, prices, and competitive positioning.

In the market-driven company, a strategic value chain perspective requires collaboration and integration between marketing and supply chain management. Chapter 14 considers this critical interface between managers from different functions. Important issues to consider are that:

1. Supply chain decisions are made with an understanding of the real drivers of customer value in different market segments, and the forces for value migration, not simply on the basis of measurable quality and technical product specification.
2. Supply chain decisions do not create inflexibility and inability to respond to marketplace change.
3. Supply chain decisions should be made in the light of strategic marketing questions, such as brand identification, product choice for customers, product promotion, and building sustainable competitive advantage, not only short-term cost savings.
4. Supply chain strategy may not be a source of competitive advantage, if all players in the market have similar technology and designs.
5. Supply chain collaborations may be vulnerable to failure, and recovery strategies may be required.

Flexibility and Change

One important marketing task is the regular review and evaluation of the adequacy of existing distribution systems. Changes in distribution may improve both customer satisfaction and organizational effectiveness. While the supply chain manager's focus is on cost efficiency, the strategic value-chain issue is positioning in the market to build and sustain competitive advantage. Issues of cost efficiency in supply should not be allowed to obscure the importance of market strategy.

In addition, value-chain strategy and channel decisions should be regarded as variable not fixed. Importantly, a strategic value-chain perspective mandates that channel systems and surrounding issues should be realigned and restructured as an important source of competitive differentiation.

As market situations change, market-driven companies will respond in value-chain strategy adjustments. The speed and magnitude of change in many markets mandates that the value-chain and channel structures should be reviewed regularly as a source of competitive advantage in building superior value for customers. Recall the shift in Benetton's distribution strategy to address its competitive weaknesses and competitive position versus Zara and H&M.

Summary

The value chain consists of the organizations, systems, and processes that add to customer value in moving products to end users. A strategic value-chain perspective aims to align a company's value chain with changing customer and competitive requirements. The core of the value chain is the channel of distribution. A strong channel network is an important way to gain competitive advantage. Distribution channels provide access to market targets. The choice between company distribution to end users and the use of intermediaries is guided by end user needs and characteristics, product characteristics, and financial and control considerations.

Manufacturers select the type of channel to be used, determine distribution intensity, design the channel configuration, and manage various aspects of channel operations. These channels are either conventional or vertical marketing systems (VMS). The VMS, the dominant channel for consumer products, is increasing in importance for business and industrial products. In a VMS, one firm owns all organizations in the channel, a contractual arrangement exists between organizations, one channel member is in charge of channel administration, or members develop collaborative relationships. Channel decisions also include deciding on intensity of distribution and the channel configuration. Channel management includes implementing the channel strategy, coordinating channel operations, and tracking the performance of the channel.

The choice of a channel strategy begins when management decides whether to manage the channel or to assume a participant role. Strategic analysis identifies and evaluates the channel alternatives. Several factors are evaluated, including access to the market target, channel functions to be performed, financial considerations, and legal and control constraints. The channel strategy adopted establishes guidelines for price and promotion strategies.

International channels of distribution may be similar in structure to those found in the United States and other developed countries. Nevertheless, important variations exist in the channels of different countries because of the stage of economic development, government influence, and industry practices. Strategic alliances offer one means of gaining market access to the existing channels of a company operating in a country of interest to the firm. The Internet has a dramatic impact on the globalization of channels of distribution.

A strategic value-chain perspective requires that managers in the market-driven company regularly review the adequacy of their channels strategy, and consider the impact of major market and technology changes. This perspective emphasizes the entire value chain and the company's strategic positioning in its markets, rather than short-term cost savings. It also requires that managers incorporate new distribution and communications concepts into their channel design, where this provides competitive advantage.

Internet Applications

A. Examine the Web sites of Aveda (www.aveda.com) and The Body Shop (www.bodyshop.com). Compare and contrast the distribution networks of these two retailers.

B. Go to the site of the Worldwide Retail Exchange. (www.worldwideretailexchange.org) and review the public pages describing the history, membership, and operation of this international online exchange for retailers. Identify and list the ways in which the exchange alters distribution strategy for suppliers, and the impact on consumers.

Feature Applications

A. In the Innovation Feature, "The Linux Revolution," what has really happened in the value chain for software? Will the impact of open-source software change the way this sector delivers value to customers—if so, then how may this unfold and develop?

B. The Global Feature describes one company's adaptation of its distribution channel to local market conditions in Tanzania. What adaptations should international marketers review when planning channel strategy in developing countries and how can they find out what is required?

Questions for Review and Discussion

1. In the late 1990s several airlines started selling tickets using the Internet. Discuss the implications of this method of distribution for travel agencies.
2. Distribution analysts indicate that costs for supermarkets equal about 98 percent of sales. What influence does this high break-even level have on supermarkets' diversification into delis, cheese shops, seafood shops, and flowers?
3. Why do some large, financially strong manufacturers choose not to own their dealers but instead establish contractual relationships with them?
4. What are the advantages and limitations of the use of multiple channels of distribution by a manufacturer?
5. Discuss some likely trends in the distribution of automobiles in the 21st century, including the shift away from exclusive distribution arrangements.
6. In the late 1990s Radio Shack initiated cobranding strategies with Compaq Computer and Sprint. Discuss the logic of this strategy, pointing out its strengths and shortcomings.
7. Identify and discuss some of the factors that should increase the trend toward collaborative relationships in vertical marketing systems.
8. Why might a manufacturer choose to enter a conventional channel of distribution?
9. Suppose the management of a raw material supplier is interested in performing a financial analysis of a distribution channel comprised of manufacturers, distributors, and retailers. Outline an approach for doing the analysis.
10. Discuss some of the important strategic issues facing a drug manufacturer in deciding whether to distribute veterinary prescriptions and over-the-counter products through veterinarians or distributors.

Notes

1. Jack Ewing and Christina Passariello, "Has Benetton Stopped Unravelling?" *BusinessWeek,* June 23, 2003, 22–23; Arnaldo Camuffo, Pietro Romano, and Andrea Vinelli, "Back To the Future: Benetton Transforms Its Global Network," *Sloan Management Review,* Fall 2001, 46–52.
2. Louis W. Stern, Adel I. El-Ansary, and James R. Brown, *Management in Marketing Channels* (Englewood Cliffs, NJ: Prentice Hall, 1989), 4.
3. Chris Adams, "Steel Middlemen Are Finding Fatter Profits in the Metal," *The Wall Street Journal*, August 8, 1997, B4.
4. A. Parasuraman and Charles L. Colby, *Techno-Ready Marketing: How and Why Your Customers Adopt Technology* (New York: Free Press, 2001).
5. Faith Keenan, Stanley Holmes, Jay Greene, and Roger O. Crockett, "A Mass Market of One," *BusinessWeek,* December 2, 2002, 62–65.

6. Cliff Edwards, "Boutiques for the Flagging Brand," *BusinessWeek,* May 24, 2004, 68.
7. Chris Adams, "Steel Middlemen," B4.
8. Andy Serwer, "The Hole Story: How Krispy Kreme Became the Hottest Brand in America," *Fortune,* June 23, 2003.
9. "Cracks in the Diamond Trade," *BusinessWeek,* March 2, 1998, 106; Gillian O'Connor and Emma Muller, "De Beer's New Deal Loses a Little Sparkle," *Financial Times,* January 17, 2001, 34.
10. Lisa Bannon, "Natuzzi's Huge Selection of Leather Furniture Pays Off," *The Wall Street Journal,* November 17, 1994, B4.
11. For a complete discussion of channel management, see Louis W. Stern and Adel I. EI-Ansary, *Marketing Channels*. 4th ed. (Englewood Cliffs, NJ: Prentice Hall, Inc., 1992).
12. Robert Meehan, "Create, Revise Channels for Customers," *Marketing News,* October 23, 2000, 48.
13. Simon London, "Keeping It in the Family," *Financial Times,* Understanding SCM Supplement, Autumn 2001, 10.
14. Peter Cunliffe, "Worldwide Superstore for Retailers," *Daily Mail,* April 1, 2000; Dan Roberts, "Tesco Joins Online Consortium," *Daily Telegraph,* April 1, 2000.
15. Jonahan Fenby, "B2B, or Not to Be?," *Sunday Business,* March 26, 2000.
16. Weld Royal, "Death of a Salesman," *www.industryweek.com,* May 17, 1999, 59–60.
17. M. Howard Gelfand, "Dayton Hudson Keeps Its Vision," *Advertising Age,* July 9, 1984, 4, 46–47.
18. David Bowen, "How to Use the Web as a Recession-Busting Tool," *Financial Times,* January 18, 2001.
19. Paul F. Nunes and Frank V. Cespedes, "The Customer Has Escaped," *Harvard Business Review,* November 2003, 96–105.
20. Ibid.
21. James A. Narus and James C. Anderson, "Turn Your Industrial Distributors into Partners," *Harvard Business Review,* March–April 1986, 66–71.
22. Sally Pook, "Tesco Loses Fight to Sell Levi's at American Prices," *Daily Telegraph,* November 21, 2001, 7.
23. Matt Hobbs and Hugh Wilson, "The Multi-Channel Challenge," *Marketing Business,* February 2004, 12–15.
24. An expanded discussion of these issues is available in Lou E. Pelson, David Strutton, and James R. Lompkin, *Marketing Channels* (Chicago: Richard D. Irwin, 1997), Chapters 6 and 7.
25. Gary R. Weaver, Linda Klebe Trevino, and Philip L. Cochran, "Corporate Ethics Practices in the Mid-1990s: An Empirical Study of the *Fortune* 1000," *Journal of Business Ethics* 18, no. 3, 1999, 283–294.
26. Philip R. Cateora, *International Marketing*. 9th ed. (Burr Ridge, IL: Richard D. Irwin, 1996), Chapter 15.
27. Ibid., 449.
28. Cateora, *International Marketing,* Chapter 15.
29. This section of the chapter benefited from the advice and insightful contributions of Niall C. Piercy, School of Management, University of Bath, U.K.
30. Alan Mitchell, "ECR's Big Idea Requires Sharing of Information," *Marketing Week,* April 16, 1998, 22–23.
31. Mark Tosh, "ECR—A Concept with Legs, Heart and Soul," *Progressive Grocer,* December 1998, 4–5; Richard J. Sherman, "Collaborative Planning, Forecasting and Replenishment: Realizing the Promise of Efficient Consumer Response through Collaborative Technology," *Journal of Marketing Theory and Practice* 6, no. 4, 1998, 6–9.
32. Denis R. Towill, "The Seamless Supply Chain: The Predator's Strategic Advantage," *International Journal of Technology Management* 13, no. 1, 1997, 37–56.
33. Martin Christopher, *Marketing Logistics* (Oxford: Butterworth-Heinemann, 1997).
34. This section is based on Nigel F. Piercy, "Marketing Implementation: The Implications of Marketing Paradigm Weakness for the Strategy Execution Process," *Journal of the Academy of Marketing Science* 26, no. 3, 1998, 222–236.
35. James P. Womack and Daniel T. Jones, *Lean Thinking: Banish Waste and Create Wealth in Your Corporation* (New York: Simon and Schuster, 1996); James P. Womack and Daniel T. Jones, "Beyond Toyota: How to Root Out Waste and Pursue Perfection," *Harvard Business Review,* September/October 1996, 140–158; James P. Womack and Daniel T. Jones, "From Lean Thinking to the Lean Enterprise," *Harvard Business Review,* March/April 1994, 93–103.
36. Daniel T. Jones, "The Route to the Future," *Manufacturing Engineer,* February 2001, 33–37.
37. Martin Christopher, "The Agile Supply Chain," *Industrial Marketing Management* 29, no. 1, 2000, 37–44.
38. J. B. Naylor, M. M. Naim, and D. Berry, "Leagility: Interfacing the Lean and Agile Manufacturing Paradigm in the Total Supply Chain," *International Journal of Production Economics* 62, 1999, 107–118.
39. Martin Christopher and Denis R. Towill, "Supply Chain Migration from Lean to Functional to Agile and Customized," *Supply Chain Management* 5, no. 4, 2000, 206–221.
40. B. Evans and M. Powell, "Synergistic Thinking: A Pragmatic View of 'Lean' and 'Agile,'" *Logistics and Transport Focus* 2, no. 10, December 2000; Mark Whitehead, "Flexible: Friend or Foe," *Supply Management,* January 6, 2000, 24–27.
41. Steve Jarvis, "Up the Down Supply Chain," *Marketing News,* September 10, 2001, 3.

Chapter 11

Pricing Strategy and Management

The pricing strategies for goods and services are becoming increasingly challenging for many firms because of deregulation, informed buyers, intense global competition, slow growth in many markets, and the opportunity for firms to strengthen market position. Price impacts financial performance and is an important influence on buyers' value positioning of brands. Price may become a proxy measure for product quality when buyers have difficulty in evaluating complex products.

Low-cost airlines such as JetBlue, Southwest Airlines, and AirTran Airways created complex pricing situations for major airlines like American and Delta Airlines in the late 1990s and early 2000s. Initially, the majors avoided aggressive response to the low prices being offered by the discount airlines. However, the low-cost carriers doubled their share of U.S. domestic airline capacity from 10 percent in 1995 to an estimated 20 percent in 2004.[1] By 2004 it was apparent that the major airlines' pricing strategies for competing against the low-cost carriers were rapidly shifting from passive to aggressive pricing initiatives. The favorable economy and strengthened financial positions of the majors provided a better basis for meeting the discounters' low fares. Delta and United Airlines launched their own low-price carriers. Nonetheless, the low-cost airlines continue to create formidable competition for the majors by leveraging their substantial cost advantages while gaining strong customer loyalty. Selecting pricing strategies for competing with successful discounters like JetBlue and Southwest Airlines will be a continuing challenge for the major airlines. JetBlue and Southwest Airlines receive higher ratings for customer service than American and Delta Airlines.

Pricing decisions have substantial consequences for many companies as illustrated by the effects of price competition in the commercial airline industry. Once implemented, it may be difficult to alter price strategy—particularly if the change calls for a significant increase. Pricing actions that violate laws can land managers in jail. Price has many possible uses as a strategic instrument in business strategy.

The realities of the pricing environment are apparent.[2] Airline electronic revenue management pricing methods, which were pioneered by American Airlines in 1985, previewed the expanding role of technology in pricing today. The Internet is facilitating flexible pricing initiatives in other product categories. Aggressive price competition occurs frequently in a wide range of markets for both goods and services. The motivation for these actions includes attempts to operate at production capacity, pursue survival actions by companies in financial trouble, and respond to competitive pressures on market-share position. Goods and services providers have money invested in fixed assets that management is unable or unwilling to liquidate.

First, we examine the strategic role of price in marketing strategy and discuss several pricing situations. Following a step-by-step approach to developing or altering pricing strategy, we describe and illustrate the steps. We then present an approach to situation analysis for pricing decisions, using several application situations to highlight the nature and scope of pricing analysis. Next, deciding which pricing strategy to adopt is considered. Finally, we discuss pricing policies and look at several special pricing issues.

Strategic Role of Price

Several factors influence management's decisions about how price will be used in marketing strategy. An important concern is estimating how buyers will respond to alternative prices for a good or service. The cost of producing and distributing a product sets lower boundaries on the pricing decision. Costs affect an organization's ability to compete. The existing and potential competition in the market segments targeted by a company affects management's flexibility in selecting prices. Finally, legal and ethical constraints create pressures on decision makers.

The Internet promises to be an increasingly important influence on the role of prices in many organizations. The Internet Feature describes several aspects of the impact of the Internet on pricing.

A strategic perspective on pricing decisions may provide new opportunities and open new market space. For example, there may be advantages in pricing across the substitutes for a product rather than just against the immediate competition. Consider the advantage secured by Southwest Airlines by setting fares that were close to the road travel costs for short-haul journeys, not just against the established airlines' fares.

Another illustration of the competitive advantage that may be achieved in some situations by strategic pricing decisions that focus on the costs of alternatives and substitutes is provided by Berkshire Hathaway's Executive Jet Company. The company sells shares of small aircraft for corporate travel. While executives may prefer a private jet, these aircraft are extremely expensive. The bulk of executive travel involves first-class and business-class tickets for conventional airlines. Berkshire Hathaway's pricing strategy is to compete with conventional airlines for a greater share of the corporate travel budget by selling shares of time in a corporate jet. Companies obtain the cachet and convenience of private air travel at a cost comparable to the annual business-class travel budget for many companies. Berkshire took the business from premium-ticket airline customers, but also from companies preferring a time share to the full costs of owning a corporate jet that would spend much of its time sitting on the ground.[3]

A strategic pricing perspective also mandates understanding how price is viewed and understood by customers. For example, in the industrial lighting market, traditional strategies focus on corporate purchasing managers, who buy on the basis of how much light bulbs cost and how long they last. All competitors compete head-to-head on these aspects of value. Management of the Dutch company Philips reasoned that basic price and bulb life do not account for the full cost of lighting. The fluorescent bulb contains toxic materials that force business customers to pay high disposal costs. Typically, corporate purchasing officers are not accountable for disposal costs. Philips launched Alto, an expensive but environmentally friendly bulb, to appeal to chief financial officers (on lower total costs if disposal is included) and to appeal to marketing departments (on environmental image issues). The Alto bulb replaced more than 25 percent of the total market for traditional industrial fluorescent lamps in the United States.[4]

Price in the Positioning Strategy

Strategic choices about market targets, positioning strategies and product and distribution strategies set guidelines for both price and promotion strategies. Product quality and features, type of distribution channel, end users served, and the functions performed by value-chain members all help establish a feasible price range. When an organization forms a new distribution network,

Internet Feature

The Impact of the Internet on Pricing

- *Price Information.* The Web makes it simple for buyers to visit suppliers' sites or those of distributors to check and compare prices quickly and easily. In many product-markets, such as computers and software, books and CDs, and automobiles, price comparison services exist on the Web specifically to identify lower-priced outlets, such as pricewatch.com and bottomdollar.com. The impact of growing price transparency is likely to have a substantial impact on pricing. In some business-to-business markets companies are already finding that they no longer compete against the prices of conventional competitors but against the lowest price that the customer can find anywhere on the Web. Online exchanges are designed to achieve exactly this.
- *Auctions.* In many markets there are online auctions in which customers bid in a conventional way for products (e.g., eBay.com and uBid.com), but there are also reverse auctions like Priceline.com where customers declare the price they are willing to pay (for example, for an air ticket) and Priceline.com searches for a supplier at that price.
- *Group Buying.* Services have been established where the prices of products drop according to how many purchasers there are, encouraging customers to form groups and buy at the lower price, such as letsbuyit.com.
- *Price Differences.* The Web undermines the ability of a company to leverage differences in demand to charge different prices in different parts of the market. For example, The Gap sells blue jeans for around $30 in its U.S. stores and from its Web site. British customers can see those prices on the Web but then find they are paying £30 for the same blue jeans in British stores. The Gap's problem is that selling to British consumers from the U.S. Web site will undermine its store prices. Its current strategy is to refuse to supply British customers from the Web. Opportunities to charge price premiums in certain segments of the market will be increasingly rare.
- *Real-Time Pricing.* Puget Sound Energy has pioneered real-time pricing for customers for electricity. Smart meters and Internet-based technologies give customers nearly real-time information on the variable, time-sensitive cost of providing energy. Providing fast price signals in advance allows customers to reduce costs by choosing to consume power off-peak at lower prices. The effect is that consumers have the ability to react to and drive down wholesale market prices by reducing peak-hour energy use.

Source: Adapted from Gary B. Swofford, "The Imperative for Real-Time Pricing," *Utility Business,* September 2001, 36–38. Reprinted with permission of the author; Adapted from Robert J. Kauffman and Bin Wang, "New Buyers' Arrival under Dynamic Pricing Market Microstructure," *Journal of Management Information Systems* vol. 18, no. 2 (Fall 2001) 157–188. Used by permission of M.E. Sharpe, Inc.

selection of the channel and intermediaries may be driven by price strategy. The influence of price on other marketing mix components may vary in different strategy situations. In some cases, price plays a dominant role in the marketing strategy, whereas, in other situations, price may perform a more passive role. Nevertheless, the strategic role of price is too often not recognized. "Part of the reason that pricing is misused and poorly understood is the common practice of making it the last marketing decision. We think that we must design products, communication plans, and a method of distribution before we have something to price. We then use pricing tactically to capture whatever value we can."[5] This practice should be avoided. Pricing plays an important strategic role in marketing strategy.

Who Is Responsible for Pricing Decisions? Responsibility for pricing decisions varies across organizations. Marketing executives determine pricing strategy in many companies. Pricing decisions may be made by the chief executive officer in some firms such as aircraft producers and construction firms. Manufacturing and engineering executives may be assigned pricing responsibility in companies that produce customer-designed industrial equipment. The vital importance of pricing decisions argues strongly for cross-functional participation. Pricing impacts all business functions. Operations, engineering, finance, and marketing executives should participate in strategic pricing decisions, regardless of where responsibility is assigned. Coordination of strategic and tactical pricing decisions with other aspects of marketing strategy is also critical because of the interrelationships involved.

Product Strategy. When only one product is involved, the pricing decision is simplified. Yet, in many instances, a line or mix of products must be priced. Consider a situation involving a product and consumable supplies for the product. One popular strategy is to price the product at competitive levels and set higher margins for supplies. Examples include parts for automobiles and cartridge refills for computer printers. Also, the prices for products in a line do not necessarily correspond to the cost of each item. For example, prices in supermarkets are based on a total mix strategy rather than individual item pricing. Understanding the composition of the mix and the interrelationships among products is important in determining pricing strategy, particularly when the brand identity is built around a line or mix of products rather than on a brand-by-brand basis. Product quality and features affect price strategy. A high-quality product may benefit from a high price to help establish a prestige position in the marketplace and satisfy management's profit performance requirements. Alternatively, a manufacturer supplying private-branded products to a retailer like Wal-Mart or Target must price competitively in order to obtain sales. Pricing decisions require analysis of the product mix, branding strategy, and product quality and features to determine the effects of these factors on price strategy.

Distribution Strategy. Type of channel, distribution intensity, and channel configuration also influence price strategy. The functions performed and the motivation of intermediaries need to be considered in setting prices. Value-added resellers require price margins to pay for their activities and to give them incentives to obtain their cooperation. Pricing is equally important when distribution is performed by the manufacturer. Pricing in coordinated and managed channels reflects total channel considerations more so than in conventional channels. Intensive distribution is likely to call for more competitive pricing than selective or exclusive distribution. In multichannel situations, pricing may pose a particular challenge. For example, if the Web site offers a lower price than conventional channels, how will members of those channels react?

Pricing Situations

Pricing strategy requires continuous monitoring because of changing external conditions, the actions of competitors, and the opportunities to gain a competitive edge through pricing actions. Our earlier look at the competitive battle for commercial airline travelers is illustrative. There are various situations requiring pricing actions such as:

- Deciding how to price a new product or line of products.
- Evaluating the need to adjust price as the product moves through the product life cycle.
- Changing a positioning strategy that calls for modifying the current pricing strategy.
- Deciding how to respond to the pressures of competitive threats.

Decisions about pricing for existing products may include increasing, decreasing, or holding prices at current levels. Understanding the competitive situation and possible actions by competitors is important in deciding if and when to alter prices. Demand and cost information is a strong influence on new-product pricing. Deciding how to price a new product also should consider competing substitutes since few new products occupy a unique position in the market.

Gillette's Sensor razor was an outstanding success in the early 1990s, strengthening the company's market position and attracting shavers away from disposable razors. Gillette introduced a new razor, MACH3, in 1998. It was priced 35 percent higher than the SensorExcel, which was substantially higher priced than its predecessor, Atra.[6] Gillette's pricing strategy for MACH3 was value-driven, positioning the razor as offering a superior shaving experience. The triple-bladed shaving system cost $750 million to bring to the commercialization stage plus an estimated $300 million for marketing the new product in the first year. The key pricing issue was whether shavers would consider MACH3 to be worth a 35 percent premium over the cost of SensorExcel blades. The new razor was available in 100 countries by the end of 1999. Gillette's consumer use tests of MACH3 compared to SensorExcel, and competing brands gave the razor a 2:1 preference, strongly supporting the premium pricing strategy. Nevertheless, the venture involved substantial risk considering $1 billion plus investment. However, by 2000 it was apparent that MACH3 was performing even better than Sensor for the same time span after introduction.

Various Roles of Pricing

Prices perform various functions in the marketing program—as a signal to the buyer, an instrument of competition, a means to improve financial performance, and a substitute for other marketing program functions (e.g., promotional pricing).

Signal to the Buyer. Price offers a fast and direct way of communicating with the buyer. The price is visible to the buyer and provides a basis of comparison between brands. Price may be used to position the brand as a high-quality product or instead to pursue head-on competition with another brand.

Instrument of Competition. Price offers a way to quickly attack competitors or, alternatively, to position a firm away from direct competition. For example, off-price retailers use a low-price strategy against department stores and other retailers. Price strategy is always related to competition whether firms use a higher, lower, or equal price.

Improving Financial Performance. Since prices and costs determine financial performance, pricing strategies are assessed as to their estimated impact on the firm's financial statements, both in the short and the long run. Gillette's huge investment in the MACH3 razor is recovered and profits generated from the prices paid by buyers. Global competition has forced many firms to adopt pricing approaches that will generate revenues in line with forecasts. Both revenues and costs need to be taken into account in selecting pricing strategies.

Marketing Program Considerations. Prices may substitute for selling effort, advertising, and sales promotion. Alternatively, price may be used to reinforce these activities in the marketing program. The role of pricing often depends on how other components in the marketing program are used. For example, prices can be used as an incentive to channel members, as the focus of promotional strategy, and as a signal of value. In deciding the role of pricing in marketing strategy, management evaluates the importance of prices to competitive positioning, probable buyer's reactions, financial requirements, and interrelationships in the marketing program.

Pricing Strategy

The major steps in selecting a pricing strategy for a new product or altering an existing strategy are shown in Exhibit 11.1. Strategy formulation begins by determining pricing objectives, which guide strategy development. Next, it is necessary to analyze the pricing situation, taking into account demand, cost, competition, and legal and ethical factors. These analyses indicate how much flexibility there is in pricing a new product or changing the pricing strategy for an existing product. Interestingly, Gillette's consumer tests of MACH3 indicated that there was little buyer resistance to a price 45 percent above SensorExcel.[7] This information indicated that management had a lot of flexibility in deciding how to price MACH3. Next, based on the situation analysis and the pricing objectives, the pricing strategy is selected. Finally, specific prices and policies are determined to implement the strategy. Each step in the pricing strategy, overviewed in Exhibit 11.1, is examined in the rest of the chapter.

Pricing Objectives

Managers use their pricing strategies to achieve specific objectives. More than one pricing objective is usually involved, and sometimes the objectives may conflict with each other. If so, adjustments may be needed on one of the conflicting objectives. For example, if one objective is to increase market share by 30 percent and the second objective is to obtain a high profit margin, management should decide if both objectives are feasible. If not, one must be adjusted. Objectives set essential guidelines for pricing strategy.

Pricing objectives vary according to the situational factors present and management's preferences. A high price may be set to recover investment in a new product. This practice is typical in the pricing of new prescription drugs. A low price may be used to gain market position,

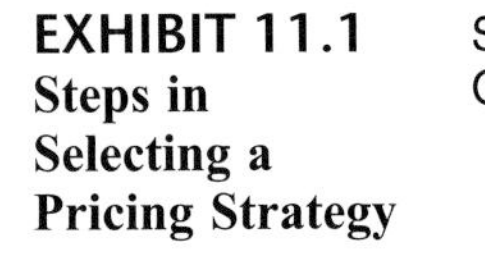

EXHIBIT 11.1 Steps in Selecting a Pricing Strategy

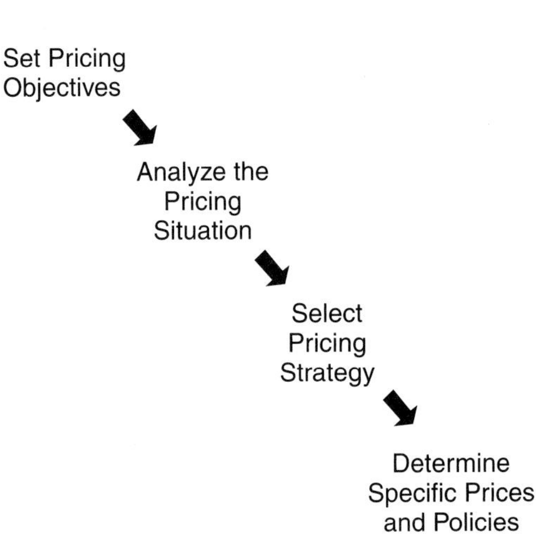

discourage new competition, or attract new buyers. Several examples of pricing objectives follow:

Gain Market Position. Low prices may be used to gain sales and market share. Limitations include encouraging price wars and reduction (or elimination) of profit contributions. Even though buyers may have been responsive to a price for MACH3 that was 45 percent above SensorExcel, Gillette's management used a 35 percent price increase that was more likely to gain market position.

Achieve Financial Performance. Prices are selected to contribute to financial objectives such as profit contribution and cash flow. Prices that are too high may not be acceptable to buyers. A key objective for Gillette's MACH3 pricing strategy was to achieve financial performance in combination with market position.

Product Positioning. Prices may be used to enhance product image, promote the use of the product, create awareness, and other positioning objectives. The visibility of price (high or low) may impact the effectiveness of other positioning components such as advertising.

Stimulate Demand. Price is used to encourage buyers to try a new product or to purchase existing brands during periods when sales slow down (e.g., recessions). A potential problem is that buyers may balk at purchasing when prices return to normal levels. Discount coupons for new products like Colgate's Total toothpaste help stimulate demand without actually lowering listed prices.

Influence Competition. The objective of pricing actions may be to influence existing or potential competitors. Management may want to discourage market entry or price cutting by current competitors. A price leader may want to encourage industry members to raise prices. One problem is that competitors may not respond as predicted.

Intel employed an interesting strategy for competing with inexpensive semiconductors that offered rapid graphics processing and posed a threat to Intel's flagship Pentium chip.[8] Rather than lowering the Pentium price to appeal to the price-sensitive market segment, Intel developed the Cirrus chip based on the Pentium platform, which eliminated additional design and tooling costs. Some of the Pentium capabilities were not activated in the new chip, which was priced to compete with competitors' products. Intel stimulated demand without lowering the price of its premium chip.

Analyzing the Pricing Situation

Pricing analysis is essential in evaluating new-product ideas, developing test marketing strategy, and selecting a new-product introduction strategy. Pricing analysis on a regular basis is also necessary for existing products because of changes in the market and competitive environment,

EXHIBIT 11.2
Factors Impacting the Pricing Situation

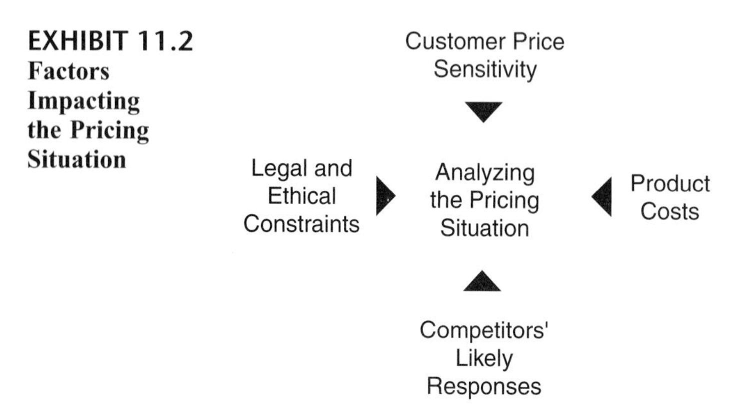

unsatisfactory market performance, and modifications in marketing strategy over the product's life cycle. Intel's analysis of pricing in the price-sensitive chip market segment is illustrative. The factors influencing the pricing situation include: (1) customer price sensitivity, (2) product costs, (3) current and potential competitive actions, and (4) legal and ethical constraints (Exhibit 11.2). We examine each factor and illustrate what is involved in the analyses.

Customer Price Sensitivity

One of the challenges in pricing analysis is estimating how buyers will respond to alternative prices. The pricing of P&G's analgesic brand, Aleve, illustrates this situation. The product was introduced in a highly competitive $2.38 billion market in 1994.[9] Aleve is the over-the-counter version of Naprosyn (developed by Syntex Corporation). P&G estimated first-year sales of $200 million. A $100 million marketing effort spearheaded Aleve's market entry. The pricing was the same as Advil's though Aleve lasts 8 to 12 hours compared to Advil's 8 hours. Aggressive promotional pricing (coupons) was anticipated from the leading competitors, Tylenol ($700 million sales) and Advil ($330 million). Some industry authorities expected Aleve to pose a greater threat to the weaker brands (Bayer, Bufferin, and Nuprin).

Analysis of buyers' responsiveness to price should answer the following questions:

1. Size of the product-market in terms of buying potential.
2. The market segments and market targeting strategy to be used.
3. Sensitivity of demand in each segment to changes in price.
4. Importance of nonprice factors, such as features and performance.
5. The estimated sales at different price levels.

Let's examine these questions for Aleve. The analgesic market was growing at about a 3 percent annual rate. Aleve offers extended relief benefits to arthritis sufferers and people with sore muscles. P&G apparently wanted to stress the brand's performance (value proposition) rather than encourage price competition. Management's $200 million sales estimate would position Aleve in third place behind Tylenol and Advil. Since forecasting product-market size, segmentation, and targeting is discussed in Chapters 3, 4, and 6, the last three questions are now considered.

The core issue in pricing is finding out what value (benefits-costs) the buyer places on the product or brand.[10] Pricing decision makers need this information in order to determine pricing strategy. Basing price only on cost may lead to pricing too high or too low compared to the value perceived by the buyer. Buyers see different values depending on their use situation, so market segment analysis is essential. For example, people who want an analgesic that lasts longer are likely to place a high value on Aleve.

Price Elasticity. Price elasticity is the percentage change in the quantity sold of a product when the price changes, divided by the percentage change in price. Elasticity is measured for changes in price from some specific price level so elasticity is not necessarily constant over the range of prices under consideration. Surprisingly, research indicates that in some situations people will buy more of certain products at *higher* prices, thus displaying a price-quantity relationship that slopes upward to the right, rather than the typical downward sloping volume and price relationship. In these instances, buyers seem to be using price as a measure of quality because they are unable to evaluate the product. Estimating the exact shape of the demand curve (price-quantity relationship) is probably impossible in most instances. Even so, there are ways to estimate the sensitivity of customers to alternative prices. Test marketing can be used for this purpose. Study of historical price and quantity data may be helpful. End user research studies, such as consumer evaluations of price, are also used. These approaches, coupled with management judgment, help indicate the sensitivity of sales to price in the range of prices that is under consideration.

An interesting discussion of the challenges in obtaining information from people about their willingness to purchase a product at different prices is provided in Exhibit 11.3. The differences in responses based on how price questions are presented highlight the importance of experience and research skills in guiding customer research surveys.

Nonprice Factors. Factors other than price may be important in analyzing buying situations. For example, buyers may be willing to pay a premium price to gain other advantages or, instead, be willing to forgo certain advantages for lower prices. Factors other than price that may be important are quality, uniqueness, availability, convenience, service, and warranty.

EXHIBIT 11.3
Effects of Price Presentation

Source: Kent B. Monroe, *Pricing*. 3rd ed. (Burr Ridge, IL: McGraw-Hill/Irwin, 2003), 223.

One problem in conducting price research is how to get information from respondents about their willingness to purchase a product at different prices. Ideally, we would like to know how the individual would respond to different prices. However, once they realize that we are trying to estimate their demand curve individuals may provide answers that reflect their understanding of the traditional demand curve—that they buy more at lower prices and less or none at higher prices. The problem is that price is presented as a cost or sacrifice to potential buyers, not as an attribute. To present price as an attribute means that other product or service information must be presented to the respondents.

One research study looked at a range of prices, but the researchers varied whether only one price was presented to respondents or whether multiple prices were presented. In the multiple price situation, prices were presented sequentially, either high to low or low to high. As the graph indicates, substantial differences occurred in the estimates. Presenting multiple prices produced downward sloping demand curves, but a single price presentation revealed increasing estimated usage between $3 and $9, declining thereafter.

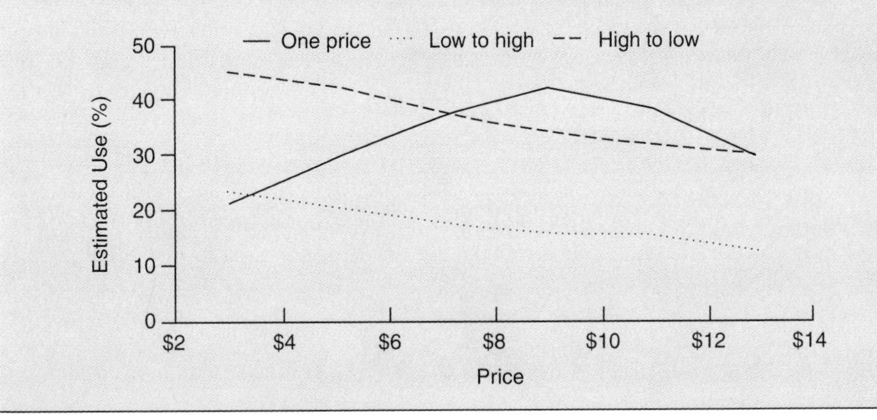

EXHIBIT 11.4
Buyers' Perceptions of Value Offerings of Brands A–E

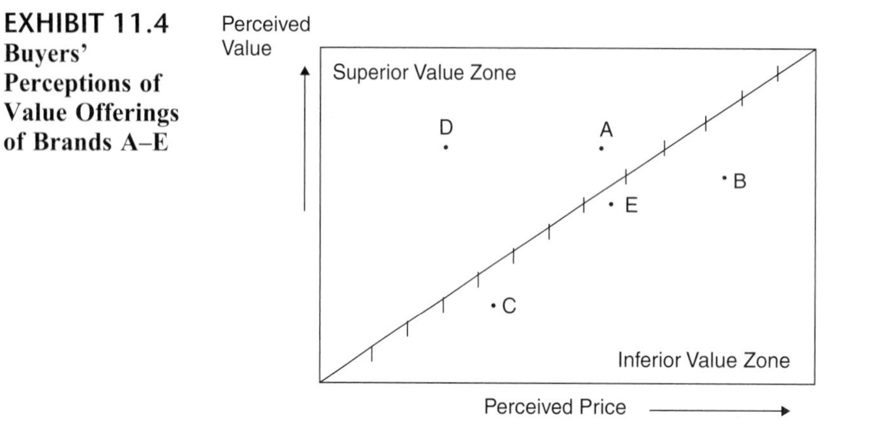

Value mapping is a useful technique for analyzing how buyers perceive the value offerings of different brands.[11] Value is the sum of benefits offered by the product less the costs of acquiring the product. One approach is to first develop the map based on managers' opinions, followed by obtaining value perceptions from a sample of consumers. The results of the two maps can then be compared and analyzed. An illustrative value map is shown in Exhibit 11.4 for brands A–E. Brands A and D offer better than fair value (the diagonal line).

In some instances the buying situation may reduce the importance of price in the buyer's choice process. The price of the product may be a minor factor when the cost is small compared to the importance of the use situation. Examples include infrequently purchased electric parts for home entertainment equipment, batteries for appliances, and health and beauty aids during a vacation. The need for important but relatively inexpensive parts for industrial equipment is another situation that reduces the role of price in the buyer's purchase decision. Quick Metal, an adhesive produced by Loctite Corporation, is used by maintenance personnel to repair production equipment such as a broken gear tooth. At less than $20 a tube, the price is not a major concern since one tube will keep an expensive production line operating until a new part is installed.

Other examples of nonprice factors that affect the buying situation include (1) purchases of products that are essential to physical health, such as pain relief; (2) choice between brands of complex products that are difficult to evaluate, such as DVD equipment (a high price may be used as a gauge of quality); and (3) image-enhancement situations such as serving prestige brands of drinks to socially important guests.

Forecasts. Forecasts of sales are needed for the price alternatives that management is considering. In planning the introduction of Aleve, P&G's management could look at alternative sales forecasts based on different prices and other marketing program variations. These forecasts, when combined with cost estimates, indicate the financial impact of different price strategies. The objective is to estimate sales in units for each product (or brand) at the prices under consideration.

Controlled tests can be used to forecast the effects of price changes. For example, a fast-food chain can evaluate the effects of different prices on demand through tests in a sample of stores. Experimental designs can be used to measure or control the effects of factors other than price. We discuss methods for analyzing the effects of positioning strategy components and positioning results in Chapter 6.

Cost Analysis

Cost information is also needed in making pricing decisions. A guide to cost analysis is shown in Exhibit 11.5.

EXHIBIT 11.5
Cost Analysis for Pricing Decisions

- Determine the components of the cost of the product.
- Estimate how cost varies with volume of sales.
- Analyze the cost competitive advantage of the product.
- Decide how experience in producing the product affects costs.
- Estimate how much control the organization has over costs.

Composition of Product Cost. First, it is necessary to determine the fixed and variable costs involved in producing and distributing the product. Also, it is important to estimate the amount of the product cost accounted for by purchases from suppliers. For example, a large portion of the costs of a personal computer are the components purchased from suppliers. It is useful to separate the costs into labor, materials, and capital categories when studying cost structure.

Activity-based costing (ABC) is a promising technique that provides information for pricing strategy. Many firms have adopted ABC as a costing mechanism to more appropriately assign indirect costs to goods and services. The key component of ABC is to assign costs based upon the activities that are performed to create the good or provide the service. With ABC, decision makers obtain a much more accurate representation of product costs. This information is useful in pricing decisions and comparisons across product lines and customer groups. Since ABC estimates the cost of the product in terms of a collection of activities, it is much easier to evaluate pricing for particular attributes or service levels. Similarly, it is possible to make comparisons to competitors by evaluating the costs of activities necessary to offer product enhancements.

Firms that successfully implement ABC do so initially as an accounting technique, yet the ultimate objective is to facilitate activity-based management (ABM). In this manner, the cost data become an integral part of the product strategy in terms of considering the entire value chain, encompassing suppliers, customers, and competitors. For example, products that may require packaging or delivery modifications incur additional costs. With ABM, decision makers have a better understanding of these additional costs, can price accordingly, and can consider these costs in conjunction with the offerings of competitors.

Volume Effect on Cost. The next part of cost analysis examines cost and volume relationships. How do costs vary at different levels of production or quantities purchased? Can economies of scale be gained over the volume range that is under consideration, given the target market and positioning strategy? At what volume levels are significant cost reductions possible? Volume effect analysis determines the extent to which the volume produced or distributed should be taken into account in selecting the pricing strategy.

Competitive Advantage. Comparing key competitors' costs is often valuable. Are their costs higher, lower, or about the same? Although such information is sometimes difficult to obtain, experienced managers can often make accurate estimates. In some industries such as commercial airlines cost information is available. It is useful to place key competitors into relative product cost categories (e.g., higher, lower, same). Analysts may be able to estimate competitive cost information from knowledge of types of costs, wage rates, material costs, production facilities, and related information.

Experience Effect. It is important to consider the effect of experience on costs. Experience or learning-curve analysis (using historical data) indicates whether costs and prices for various products decline by a given amount each time the number of units produced doubles. However, price declines may be uneven because of competitive influences. When unit costs (vertical axis) are plotted against total accumulated volume (horizontal axis), costs decline with volume. This effect occurs when experience over time increases the efficiency of production operations. The experience-curve effect may not be same across all product categories.[12]

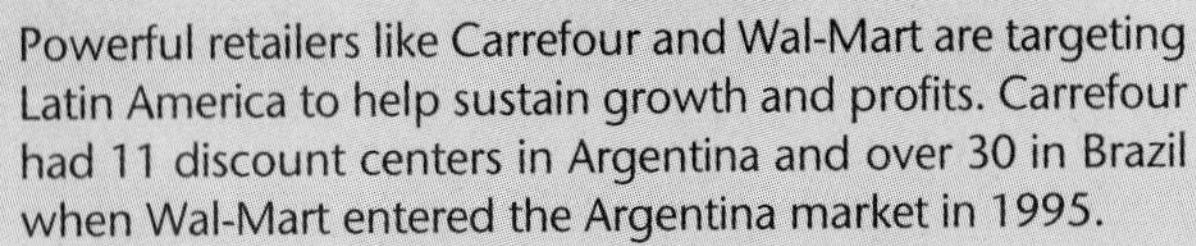

French Retailer Carrefour and Wal-Mart Compete in Argentina

Powerful retailers like Carrefour and Wal-Mart are targeting Latin America to help sustain growth and profits. Carrefour had 11 discount centers in Argentina and over 30 in Brazil when Wal-Mart entered the Argentina market in 1995.

Wal-Mart alleges that the French competitor is pressuring its local suppliers to stop supplying Wal-Mart with personal care, paper products, and other goods. Carrefour denies the charge. Wal-Mart's concern is that without strong support from local manufacturers, the retailer will be unable to purchase 85 percent of its goods in Argentina. Importing will substantially increase Wal-Mart's costs.

The battle for market position by the two giant discounters promises to be interesting. Carrefour has a head start with sales of $1.5 billion in Argentina. Both are matching prices. Wal-Mart is stressing customer service and trying to build collaborative relationships with suppliers. Carrefour does not have a strong reputation for service. The number of supermarkets, hypermarkets, and self-service outlets in Argentina nearly doubled from 1984 to 1994.

By 1997 Wal-Mart had strengthened its market position in Argentina. Store managers were responding to local preferences such as selling smokehouses because of the local taste for smoked meats. Worldwide, Carrefour competed in 13 international markets compared to 7 for Wal-Mart. Carrefour's sales were $12 billion compared to Wal-Mart's $56 billion.

Sources: Jonathan Friedland, "Big Discounters Duel Over Hot Market," *The Wall Street Journal*, August 23, 1995, A6. WALL STREET JOURNAL. CENTRAL EDITION [STAFF PRODUCED COPY ONLY] by JONATHAN FRIEDLAND. Copyright 1995 by DOW JONES & CO INC. Reproduced with permission of DOW JONES & CO INC in the format Textbook via Copyright Clearance Center; "Wal-Mart Spoken Here," *BusinessWeek*, June 23, 1997, 138–144.

Control over Costs. Finally, it is useful to consider how much influence an organization may have over its product costs in the future. To what extent can research and development, bargaining power with suppliers, process innovation, and other factors help to reduce costs over the planning horizon? These considerations are interrelated with experience-curve analysis, yet may operate over a shorter time range. The bargaining power of an organization in its channels of distribution, for example, can have a major effect on costs, and the effects can be immediate. An example of bargaining power with suppliers by the French retailer Carrefour in the fast-growing retail market in Argentina is described in the Global Feature.

Competitor Analysis

Each competitor's pricing strategy needs to be evaluated to determine (1) which firms represent the most direct competition (actual and potential) for buyers in the market targets that are under consideration; (2) how competing firms are positioned on a relative price basis and the extent to which price is used as an active part of their marketing strategies; (3) how successful each firm's price strategy has been; and (4) the key competitors' probable responses to alternative price strategies.

The discussion in Chapter 3 considers guidelines for competitor identification. It is important to determine both potential and current competitors. The fiber-optic cable network industry is an interesting competitor analysis situation. In 2001, an estimated 39 million miles of fiber networks covered the United States, while less than 3 percent of this capacity was actually in use.[13] The anticipated escalating demand for telecommunications bandwidth encouraged many firms like Quest Communications International Inc. and Level 3 Communications Inc., to rapidly build underground fiber-optic networks. Barriers to entry were low. Nearly 1,500 firms had developed cable networks by 2001. Global Crossing Ltd., losing money on over $1 billion in revenues, spent $20 billion to build a 100,000-mile global network. The excess capacity was expected to cause prices for network space to fall more than 60 percent in 2001. An industry shakeout is likely since there is not enough demand to support the large number of competitors. By 2004 Quest and Level 3 had experienced weak or negative profit performance for the previous five years.

The success of a competitor's price strategy is usually gauged by financial performance. One problem with using performance to gauge pricing success is accounting for influences other than price on profits.

Strategy Feature

The Prisoner's Dilemma

A popular exercise in seminars and executive briefings we hold is to ask executives to participate in a prisoner's dilemma pricing game. Each team must decide whether to price its products high or low compared to those of another team in 10 rounds of competition. The objective is to earn the most money; results are determined by the decision that two competitors make in comparison with each other.

The game fairly accurately simulates a typical profit/loss scenario for price competition in mature markets. The objective is to impart several lessons in pricing competition, the first being that pricing is more like playing poker than solitaire. Success depends not just on a combination of luck and how the hand is played but also on how well competitors play their hands. In real markets, outcomes depend not only on how customers respond but, perhaps more important, on how competitors respond to changes in price.

If a competitor matches a price decrease, neither the initiator nor the follower will achieve a significant increase in sales and both are likely to have a significant decrease in profits. In developing pricing strategy, managers need to anticipate the moves of their competitors and attempt to influence those moves by selectively communicating information to influence competitive behavior.

The second lesson is that managers must adopt a very long time horizon when considering changes in price. Once started, price wars are difficult to stop. A simple decision to drop price often becomes the first shot in a war that no competitor wins. Before initiating a price decrease, managers must consider how it will affect the competitive stability of markets.

Philip Morris discovered this when it initiated a price war in the cigarette business by cutting the prices of its top brands. Competitors followed, and the net result was a $2.3 billion drop in operating profits for Philip Morris, even as the Marlboro brand increased its market share seven points to 29%. The manufacturer of Camels experienced a $1.3 billion drop in profits.

The third lesson from the prisoner's dilemma is that careful use of a value-based marketing approach can reverse a trend toward price-based marketing. This is accomplished through signaling, a nonprice competitive tactic that involves selectively disclosing information to competitors to influence their behavior. The steel and airline industries provide prominent examples of the signaling strategy's use. They often rely on announcements that conveniently appear on the front pages of the *Wall Street Journal* to signal competitors of pending price moves and provide them with opportunities to follow. The strategy takes time to implement, but it provides a far better long-term competitive position for marketers who employ it.

Source: Excerpt from Reed Holden and Thomas T. Nagle, "Kamikaze Pricing," *Marketing Management*, Summer 1998, 34. Reprinted with permission of the American Marketing Association.

The most difficult of the four questions about competition is predicting what they will do in response to alternative price actions. No changes are likely unless one firm's price is viewed as threatening (low) or greedy (high). Competitive pressures, actual and potential, often narrow the range of feasible prices and rule out the use of extremely high or low prices relative to competition. In new-product markets, competitive factors may be insignificant, although very high prices may attract potential competitors.

The personal computer market offers an interesting look at the effects of intense competition. Dell Inc. reduced its PC prices in 2003 in major pricing actions designed to take market share from Hewlett-Packard Co.[14] Dell had launched similar initiatives against Compaq Computer in 2000, and Compaq was subsequently acquired by H-P. The aggressive price competition resulted in H-P's PC unit reporting a loss in third quarter 2003. A major competitive hurdle for H-P is Dell's low-cost direct-sales business model (see Dell Inc. photo).

Game theory is a promising method for analyzing competitors' pricing strategies. It can be used to analyze competitive pricing situations. The technique became very popular in the 1990s. An interesting application of game theory is discussed in the Strategy Feature. Note how game theory highlights the dilemmas involved in PC pricing.

Game theory was used to design the auction process for the simultaneous sale of several third generation (3G) wireless phone licenses in Britain.[15] The process was very successful for the government. After 150 rounds of bidding, final bidders for five licenses paid a total of $34 billion, more than seven times the amount anticipated by the government.

Legal and Ethical Considerations

The last step in analyzing the pricing situation is identifying possible legal and ethical factors that may affect the choice of a price strategy. A wide variety of laws and regulations affect pricing actions. Legal constraints are important influences on the pricing of goods and services in many different national and cooperative regional trade environments. Pricing practices in the United States that have received the most attention from government include:[16]

Horizontal Price Fixing. Price collusion between competitors. Products with narrow profit margins are more likely to lead to price fixing. The Sherman Antitrust Act prohibits price fixing between companies at the same level in the channel.

Price Discrimination. Charging different customers different prices without an underlying cost basis for discrimination. The Robinson-Patman Act prohibits price discrimination if it lessens or damages competition.

Deceptive Pricing. This pricing practice involves misleading the buyer by a high price that is subsequently reduced to the normal price. This practice is prohibited by the Federal Trade Commission Act.

Price Fixing in Channels of Distribution. The Consumer Goods Pricing Act places vertical price fixing under the jurisdiction of the antitrust laws.

Price Information. This practice involves violating requirements concerning the form and the availability of price information for consumers. Unit pricing and consumer credit requirements are examples. For example, the Consumer Credit Protection Act requires full disclosure of annual interest rates and other financial charges.

Ethical issues in pricing are more subjective and difficult to evaluate than legal factors. Companies may include ethical guidelines in their pricing policies. Deciding what is or is not ethical is often difficult. Possible ethical issues should be evaluated when developing a pricing strategy.

Ethical issues in the pricing of prescription drugs are a continuing challenge for the industry. The drug producers are under continuing pressure from consumers, elected officials, and special interest groups concerning high drug prices. Drug pricing raises possible ethical issues, although the companies indicate their prices are necessary due to large research and development expenses. Nonetheless, one study reported that the average price of 50 drugs most used by the elderly increased 3.9 percent in 1999 compared to the 2.2 percent inflation rate.[17] Price controls have been proposed by consumer groups. The pharmaceutical industry was criticized for spending $14 billion in 1999 on promotion, public relations, advertising, and drug samples to doctors. In the 2000s, international pharmaceutical companies are under intense pressure to provide drugs used in the treatment of AIDS at a very low price in countries where the disease is endemic.

Selecting the Pricing Strategy

Analysis of the pricing situation provides essential information for selecting the pricing strategy. Using this information management needs to (1) determine extent of pricing flexibility; and (2) decide how to position price relative to costs and how visible to make the price of the product. The pricing strategy needs to be coordinated with the development of the entire marketing program since in most, if not all, instances there are other important marketing program component influences on buyers' purchasing behavior.

Ethics Feature

The Price of Cigarettes in the Developing World

- The global tobacco industry supports about 100,000 jobs worldwide and duties on tobacco products provide huge tax revenues for governments throughout the developed world.
- Tobacco companies describe their product as "a legal and widely enjoyed consumer product," while also recognizing that cigarette smoking poses a severe health risk for both users and "passive smokers."
- Cigarette smoking is declining in many developed countries, but remains at high levels in the developing world.
- The industry is implementing several important initiatives in the developing world: campaigns against child labor in tobacco cultivation; is involved in programs to alleviate indigenous diseases in developing countries; encourages environmental protection.
- The dilemma is whether tobacco companies should be actively supporting cigarette smoking in developing countries, and the role of low-priced brands in developing these markets, compared to the effects of tobacco cultivation industry of declining demand.
- These dilemmas are shared with companies who transport and retail tobacco products.

EXHIBIT 11.6
Determinants of Pricing Flexibility

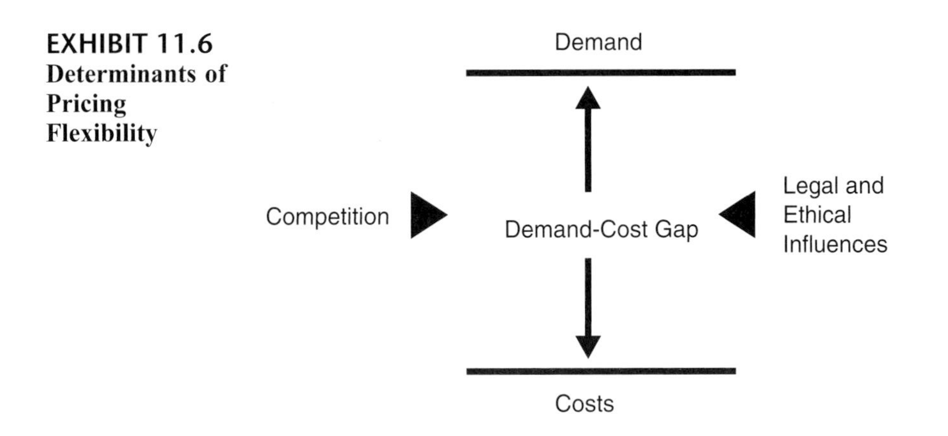

How Much Flexibility Exists?

Demand and cost factors determine the extent of pricing flexibility. Within these upper and lower boundaries, competition and legal and ethical considerations also influence the choice of a specific pricing strategy. Exhibit 11.6 illustrates how these factors influence flexibility. The price gap between demand and cost may be narrow or wide. A narrow gap simplifies the decision; a wide gap provides a greater range of feasible strategies. Choice of the pricing strategy is influenced by competitors' strategies, present and future, and by legal and ethical considerations. Management must determine where to price within the flexibility band shown in Exhibit 11.6. In competitive markets the feasibility range may be very narrow. Recall, for example, P&G's pricing of Aleve, which was priced the same as a key competitor's brand. New markets or emerging market segments in established markets may allow management more flexibility in strategy selection.

Consider the dilemma, for example, facing executives in the tobacco industry and those associated with it regarding the low pricing of cigarettes in the developing world described in the Ethics Feature.

A pricing strategy situation is described in the Cross-Functional Feature. Several important pricing issues are highlighted. Before reading the next paragraph, identify the issues that you believe need to be considered in deciding what action to take concerning the pricing of Novaton. Also decide whether you agree or disagree with the decision made by the pricing team.

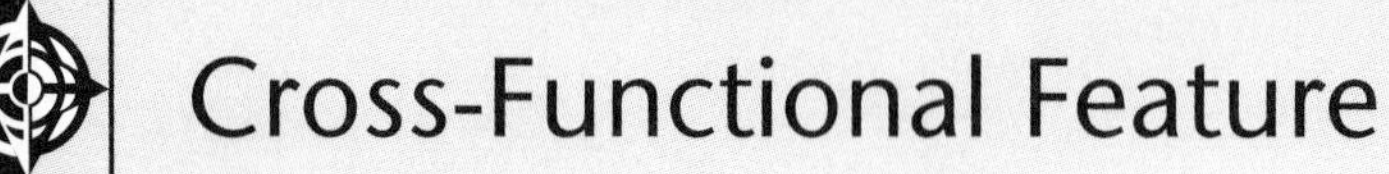

Cross-Functional Feature

Can You Identify the Pricing Issues in This Decision Situation?

The meeting was held on a snowy day in January. Novet's corporate offices, located in a large midwestern city, were quiet as people arrived late because of the new snowstorm. Mary Fritz, a marketing manager, started the discussion: "Let me review our progress on Novaton. We introduced it 18 months ago to a marketplace containing no competitive products, and we knew this product would be really valuable to our customers. We set our initial price at $250 per unit, expecting to sell 5,000 units in our first year, an additional 20,000 units this year, and 40,000 units next year. We just knew that as customers started to use the product, they would tell others. And word of mouth would be our best advertisement.

"We know this new product is really great," Fritz said, "and the customers who bought it like it a lot. But we've only sold 492 units so far. Now we're hearing Holycon Inc. is about to introduce a competing unit called the H-200. Some of our distributors have seen the H-200 and say it's just as good. Holycon has told the distributors they will price at 15 percent below us. In other markets where we've faced Holycon, we've had to be really aggressive in cutting prices in order to keep share. This time, we would like to get ahead of them, and use a preemptive strategy."

Fritz's group manager, Nina Pacofsky, responded: "OK, what do you suggest? And don't forget, we've committed to some very hefty profit goals this year. I'm not ready to tell Division we're not going to make it—especially this early in the year."

"Well, here's what we propose," said Fritz. "Since Holycon has always cut prices in the past, we're going to cut prices first this time and make it hard for them to compete. We propose to cut prices by 30 percent. In order to keep our profitability level, we're going to cut back on advertising. And, we figure that the lower price will not only discourage Holycon, but be so attractive when combined with our features that volume will go way up. We'll actually exceed our projected profit level for the year."

John Fine, the product manager, asked what the awareness level was for Novaton. Fritz didn't know, but Sally Olson found a note in a market research report indicating that awareness was about 25 percent.

Pacofsky hesitated. "Does anyone know if Holycon has actually built manufacturing facilities for their product?"

James Busky, the manufacturing manager, responded: "I heard from an extruder salesman that he had sold two extruders to Holycon. The salesman told me what the extruders were and said they were for a secret project. But, based on the type of extruders, they could only be used to compete with us. And, given the size of the extruders, Holycon's capacity will probably be about 40,000 units per year, almost 60 percent of our capacity."

Pacofsky wanted to know what Holycon's costs were likely to be and also wondered whether Holycon would be able to make any money if Novaton's prices were 30 percent lower.

"Based on our costs, and the fact that Holycon invested two years after us, we believe Holycon will have a margin of 3 percent on sales," said Tom Jeffries, the group competitive intelligence and market research specialist. "Because we were first to market, and customers know us better, we think Holycon will not get enough share to justify its entry. We think they'll drop out of the market if we cut our prices."

"OK," Pacofsky said. "Go ahead with the price cut. We know Holycon always cuts prices, and it's clear we're not getting customers to buy because our prices are too high. Keep me up-to-date on sales. And we've got to keep our profits up."

The meeting adjourned. Mary Fritz headed off to draft new price lists and announcements to the sales force. Heading to her office, she dropped into the advertising manager's office, and asked him to stop all advertising on Novaton.

Source: George E. Cressman Jr., "Snatching Defeat from the Jaws of Victory," *Marketing Management*, Summer 1997, 10. Reprinted with permission of the American Marketing Association.

The Novaton illustration highlights several factors to consider in analyzing the pricing situation (Exhibit 11.6). A central issue is determining why Novaton is not selling well in the market.[18] The problem may be price but it could also be very low customer awareness (25%). Surprisingly, the team's analyses did not consider customers' perceptions of Novaton. Depending on how customers position the brand, a price cut may not be effective. The information about Holycon's plans may be correct but the team is basing a very important pricing decision on very limited intelligence. Similarly, the competitor's manufacturing capacity information came from only one person. Finally, the competitor's costs were estimated by assuming Holycon had similar operations to Novaton's. This premise may be faulty.

These issues highlight serious questions about Fritz's pricing strategy.[19] It was later determined that the underlying problem was low awareness. Interestingly, customers actually considered Novaton to be better than Holycon. Novet's market sensing information was incomplete. Holycon's costs were 60 percent less than Novet's costs for Novaton. Holycon came into the market at prices 40 percent below Novaton's original price. After two years of tough price competition Novet dropped out of the market. This might have been avoided if the pricing team had recognized that a better pricing strategy would have been to position Novaton as offering superior value worth its original price, and aggressively communicated the value proposition to build awareness with potential buyers.

Price Positioning and Visibility

A key decision is how far above cost to price a new product within the flexibility band (Exhibit 11.6). A relatively low market entry price may be used with the objective of building volume and market position, or instead, a high price may be selected to generate large margins. The former is a "penetration" strategy whereas the latter is a "skimming" strategy. Analysis of the results of low-price strategies in highly competitive markets indicates that while the strategies are sometimes necessary, they should be used with considerable caution.[20]

Lack of knowledge about probable market response to the new product complicates the pricing decision. Several factors may affect the choice of a pricing approach for a new product, including the cost and life span of the product, the estimated responsiveness of buyers to alternative prices, and assessment of competitive reaction.

A decision should also be made about how visible price will be in the promotion of the new product. The use of a low entry price requires active promotion of the price to gain market position. When firms use a high price relative to cost, price often assumes a passive role in the marketing mix. Instead, performance and other attributes of the product are stressed in the marketing program.

Illustrative Pricing Strategies

The pricing strategy selected depends on how management decides to position the product relative to competition, and whether price performs an active or passive role in the marketing program. The use of price as an active (or passive) factor refers to whether price is highlighted in advertising, personal selling, and other promotional efforts. Many firms choose neutral pricing strategies (at or near the prices of key competitors), emphasizing nonpricing factors in their marketing strategies.[21] The neutral pricing strategy seeks to remove price as the basis of choosing among competing brands. We examine several strategies, describing their characteristics and features.

High-Active Strategy. The underlying logic of emphasizing the high price in promotional activities is to convey to the buyer that because the brand is expensive it offers superior value. While not widely used, this pricing strategy has been used to symbolically position products such as high-end alcoholic beverages. When the buyer cannot easily evaluate the quality of a product, price can serve as a signal of value. Making price visible and active can appeal to the buyer's perceptions of quality, image, and dependability of products and services. A firm using a high-price strategy is also less subject to retaliation by competitors, particularly if its product is differentiated from other brands.

High-Passive Strategy. High prices may be essential to gain the margins necessary to serve small target markets, produce high-quality products, or pay for the development of new products. Relatively high-priced brands are often marketed by featuring nonprice factors rather than using high-active strategies. Product features and performance can be stressed when the people in the target market are concerned with product quality and performance. BMW and Mercedes have successfully followed this strategy for many years. Nonetheless, the realities of competing against Japanese luxury automobiles required improving the value offerings of European brands in the late 1990s.

Low-Active Strategy. Several retailers use this pricing strategy, including Home Depot (home improvement), Dollar General Stores (apparel), Office Depot (office supplies), Wal-Mart (merchandise), and Pic 'N Pay Shoe Stores (family shoes). The low-active strategy is also popular with discount stock brokers. When price is an important factor for a large segment of buyers, a low-active price strategy is very effective, as indicated by the rapid growth of retailers like Wal-Mart. However, this strategy may encourage competitors to offer comparable prices. It is a more attractive option when the competition for the market target is not heavy or when a company has cost advantages and a strong position in the product-market. Southwest Airlines has performed very well using the low-active pricing strategy for its city-to-city route network.

Low-Passive Strategy. This strategy may be used by small manufacturers whose products have lower-cost features than other suppliers. By not emphasizing a low price, the firm runs less danger that potential buyers will assume the product quality is inferior to other brands. Some firms participating in conventional distribution channels may not spend much on marketing their products and, thus, can offer low prices because of lower costs. Other firms that have actual cost advantages for comparable competing products may decide to stress value rather than price even though they are offering prices lower than competing brands.

Determining Specific Prices and Policies

The last step in pricing strategy (Exhibit 11.1) is selecting specific prices and formulating policies to help manage the pricing strategy. Pricing methods are first examined, followed by a discussion of pricing policy. The chapter is concluded by discussing several special pricing issues.

Determining Specific Prices

It is necessary to either assign a specific price to each product item or provide a method for computing price for a particular buyer-seller transaction. Many methods and techniques are available for calculating price.

Price determination is normally based on cost, demand, competition, or a combination of these factors. Cost-oriented methods use the cost of producing and marketing the product as the basis for determining price. Demand-oriented pricing methods consider estimated market response to alternative prices. The most profitable combination of price and market response level is selected. Competition-oriented methods use competitors' prices as a reference point in setting prices. The price selected may be above, below, or equal to competitors' prices. Typically, one method (cost, demand, or competition) provides the primary basis for pricing, although the other factors have some influence.

Cost-Oriented Approaches. Break-even pricing is a cost-oriented approach that may be used to determine prices. The initial computation is as follows:

$$\text{Break-even (units)} = \frac{\text{Total fixed costs}}{\text{Unit price} - \text{Unit variable cost}}$$

When using this method, we select a price and calculate the number of units that must be sold at that price to cover all fixed and variable costs. Management must assess the feasibility of exceeding the break-even level of sales to generate a profit. One or more possible prices may be evaluated. Break-even analysis is not a complete basis for determining price, since both demand and competition are important considerations in the pricing decision. With break-even price as a frame of reference, demand and competition can be evaluated. The price selected is at some level higher than the break-even price.

Another popular cost-oriented pricing method is cost-plus pricing. This technique uses cost as the basis of calculating the selling price. Costco uses this method to determine its warehouse prices. A percentage amount of the cost is added to cost to determine price. A similar method, popular in retailing, markup pricing, calculates markups as a percentage of the selling price. When using markup pricing, this formula determines the selling price.

$$\text{Price} = \frac{\text{Average unit cost}}{1 - \text{Markup percent*}}$$

*Percent expressed in decimal form

Competition-Oriented Approaches. Pricing decisions are always affected by the actions of competitors. Pricing methods that use competitors' prices in calculating actual prices include setting prices equal to or at some specified percentage above or below the competition's. In industries such as air travel, one of the firms may be viewed by others as the price leader. When the leader changes its prices, other firms follow with similar prices. American Airlines has attempted to perform such a leadership role in the United States, although its pricing changes are not always adopted by competing airlines. Another form of competition-oriented pricing is competitive bidding where firms submit sealed bids to the purchaser. This method is used in the purchase of various industrial products and suppliers.

Reverse auction pricing is an interesting competitive form of Internet pricing. This method of determining price involves sellers bidding for organizational buyers' purchases:

> In many cases, suppliers (sellers) must be prequalified before their bids are considered. These sites generally will have links to prospective sellers. Many times, supplier performance is rated, and these ratings are presented by the site as a benefit to current and prospective buyers. Freemarkets.com conducts online auctions of industrial parts, raw materials, commodities, and services. Suppliers bid lower prices in real time until the auction is closed to fill the purchase orders of large buying organizations. In 1999 this site auctioned off more than $1 billion worth of purchases and saved buyers between 2 and 25 percent.[22]

Demand-Oriented Approaches. The buyer is the frame of reference for these methods. One popular method is estimating the value of the product to the buyer. The objective is to determine how much the buyer is willing to pay for the product based on its contribution to the buyer's needs or wants. This approach is used for both consumer and business products. Information on demand and price relationships is needed in guiding demand-oriented pricing decisions. Internet auction pricing is a demand-oriented method of pricing.

Many pricing methods are in use, so it is important to select specific prices within the guidelines provided by price strategy and to incorporate demand, cost, and competition considerations. Other sources provide extensive coverage of pricing decisions.[23]

Establishing Pricing Policy and Structure

Determining price flexibility, positioning price against competition, and deciding how active a component it will be in the marketing program do not spell out the operating guidelines necessary for implementing the pricing strategy. Policy guidelines must be determined for use in guiding pricing decisions and pricing structure.

Pricing Policy. An illustration shows how pricing decisions are guided by policies. Mervyn's, the 276-store retail chain, experienced poor performance in the early 1990s, due to faulty merchandise selection and pricing policy.[24] The retailer's pricing policy was to offer large price reductions on many items that were advertised one week each month. For example, a blanket was sale-priced at $17.99, compared to the regular $25 price. Since many buyers were aware of Mervyn's pricing policy, they waited until the week the item of interest was sale-priced. The faulty policy reduced sales and profits.

A pricing policy may include consideration of discounts, allowances, returns, and other operating guidelines. The policy serves as the basis for implementing and managing the pricing strategy. The policy may be in written form, although many companies operate without formal pricing policies.

Pricing Structure. Anytime more than one product item is involved, management must determine product mix and line-pricing interrelationships in order to establish price structure. Pricing structure concerns how individual items in the line are priced in relation to one another: The items may be aimed at the same market target or different end user groups. For example, department stores often offer store brands and premium national brands. In the case of a single product category, price differences among the product items typically reflect more than variations in costs. For example, large supermarket chains price for total profitability of their product offerings rather than for performance of individual items. These retailers have developed computer analysis and pricing procedures to achieve sales, market share, and profit objectives. Similarly, commercial airlines must work with an array of fares in the pricing structure.

The pricing of the Toyota Camry and the Lexus ES 330 is an interesting example of pricing products in relation to each other. The ES 330 is targeted to the semiluxury market. The ES 330 has essentially the same body as the Camry, but the Lexus sells for substantially more than the Camry. Of course, the Lexus offers certain unique features, but some of the price difference has to be image rather than substance. The performance of both brands is impressive.

Once product relationships are established, some basis for determining the price structure must be selected. Many firms base price structure on market and competitive factors as well as differences in the costs of producing each item. Some use multiple criteria for determining price structure and have sophisticated computer models to examine alternate pricing schemes. Others use rules of thumb developed from experience.

Most product-line pricing approaches include both cost considerations and demand and competitive concerns. For example, industrial-equipment manufacturers sometimes price new products at or close to cost and depend on sales of high-margin items such as supplies, parts, and replacement items to generate profits. The important consideration is to price the entire mix and line of products to achieve pricing objectives.

Special Pricing Situations

Special pricing situations may occur in particular industries, markets, and competitive environments. Some examples follow.

Price Segmentation. Price may be used to appeal to different market segments. For example, airline prices vary depending on the conditions of purchase. Different versions of the same basic product may be offered at different prices to reflect differences in materials and product features. Recall our earlier discussion of Intel's PC chip strategy. Industrial-products firms may use quantity discounts to respond to differences in the quantities purchased by customers. Price elasticity differences make it feasible to appeal to different segments.

Distribution Channel Pricing. The pricing strategies of producers using marketing middlemen should include consideration of the pricing needs (e.g., flexibility and incentives) of channel members. These decisions require analysis of cost and pricing at all channel levels. If producer prices to intermediaries are too high, inadequate margins may discourage intermediaries from actively promoting the producer's brand. Margins vary based on the nature and importance of the value-added activities that intermediaries in the channel are expected to perform. For example, margins between costs and selling prices must be large enough to compensate a wholesaler for carrying a complete stock of replacement parts. In the multichannel situation, the question of price differences across channels also has to be addressed.

Price Flexibility. Another special consideration is deciding how flexible prices will be. Will prices be firm, or will they be negotiated between buyer and seller? Perhaps most important, firms should make price flexibility a policy decision rather than a tactical response. Some companies' price lists are very rigid while others have list prices that give no indication of actual selling prices. It is also important to recognize the legal issues in pricing products when using flexible pricing policies.

EXHIBIT 11.7
Brand Counterfeiting in China

Source: Dexter Roberts, Frederick Balfour, Paul Magnusson, Pete Engardio, and Jennifer Lee, "China's Piracy Plague," *BusinessWeek*, June 5, 2000, 48.

Procter & Gamble The company estimates that 15% of the soaps and detergents bearing its Head & Shoulders, Vidal Sassoon, Safeguard, and Tide brands in China are fake, costing $150 million in lost sales.

Gillette As many as one-quarter of its Duracell batteries, Parker pens, and Gillette razors sold in China are believed to be pirated.

Bestfoods Bogus versions of Skippy Peanut Butter and Knorr boullion result in tens of millions of dollars in lost sales.

Yamaha The company estimates that five of every six JYM150-A motorcycles and ZY125 scooters bearing its name in China are fake. Some state-owned factories produce copies four months after a new model is launched.

Nike Replicas of its sport shoes and T-shirts are a growing problem in China.

Microsoft Counterfeiters are moving beyond crude knockoffs to high-quality versions of Windows and Windows NT—with packaging virtually indistinguishable from the real product—and sold in authorized outlets.

Anheuser-Busch Bogus Budweiser is sold in 640 ml bottles in China.

DaimlerChrysler Fake brake disks, windshields, oil filters, and shock absorbers for Mercedes cars are being made and sold in China.

Epson Copying machines as well as ink cartridges are counterfeited.

When considering reducing prices it is important to estimate how operating profits will be impacted. Estimates of how operating profits will be reduced for a 1 percent price cut provided by McKinsey & Co. consultants are 24 percent for food and drugstores, 13 percent for airlines, and 11 percent for computers and office equipment.[25] Smaller operating profit decreases are estimated for tobacco (5 percent) and diversified financials (2.4 percent). Thus, the impact of price cuts (and price wars) can be substantial.

Product Life Cycle Pricing. Some companies have policies to guide pricing decisions over the life cycle of the product. Depending on its stage in the product life cycle, the price of a particular product or an entire line may be based on market share, profitability, cash flow, or other objectives. In many product-markets, price declines (in constant dollars) as the product moves through its life cycle. Because of life cycle considerations, different objectives and policies may apply to particular products within a mix or line. Price becomes a more active element of strategy as products move through the life cycle and competitive pressures build, costs decline, and volume increases. Life cycle pricing strategy should be consistent with the overall marketing program positioning strategy used.

Counterfeit Products. The production and sales of counterfeit brands costs companies like Nike, Gillette, and Microsoft billions of dollars each year.[26] The competitive challenge for brand piracy is not to meet the prices for fakes, which are a small fraction of prices for the actual brands. Instead, companies whose brands are copied pursue initiatives to gain support from nations like China to prohibit and police the counterfeiting activities. Poor copies reduce the sales of the real brands and also cause brand damage. Exhibit 11.7 provides several examples of brand pirating in China.

Summary

Pricing strategy gains considerable direction from the decisions management makes about the product mix, branding strategy, and product quality. Distribution strategy also influences the choice of how price will work in combination with advertising and sales force strategies. Importantly, pricing strategy may also influence distribution strategy and other marketing program decisions. Price, like other marketing program components, is a means of generating market response, though price can be deployed much faster than other mix components.

Two important trends are apparent in the use of pricing as a strategic variable. First, companies are designing far more flexibility into their pricing strategies in order to cope with the rapid changes and uncertainties in the turbulent business environment. Second, price is more often used as an active rather than passive element of corporate and marketing strategies. This trend is particularly apparent in the retail sector where aggressive low-price strategies are used by firms such as Wal-Mart, Office Depot, and Home Depot.

Product, distribution, pricing, and promotion strategies must fit together into an integrated positioning strategy. Pricing strategy for new and existing products includes (1) setting pricing objectives, (2) analyzing the pricing situation, (3) selecting (or revising) the pricing strategy, and (4) determining specific prices and policies. Companies use their pricing strategies to achieve one or more of several possible objectives. These include gaining market position, achieving financial performance, positioning the product, stimulating demand, and influencing competition.

Analyzing the pricing situation is necessary to develop a pricing strategy for a mix or line of products, or to select a pricing strategy for a new product or brand. Underlying strategy formulation are several important activities, including analyses of customer price sensitivity, cost, competition, and legal and ethical considerations. These analyses indicate the extent of pricing flexibility, by determining the pricing zone between cost and probable demand for the good or service being analyzed.

Pricing may be relatively high (skimming), neutral, or relatively low (penetration) compared to competition. The choice of a pricing strategy includes consideration of price positioning and visibility. Alternative pricing strategies can be examined according to the firm's price relative to the competition and how active the promotion of price will be in the marketing program. Pricing approaches include high-active, high-passive, low-active, and low-passive strategies. Variations within the four categories occur. In many industries market leaders establish prices that are followed by other firms in the industry.

The determination of specific prices may be based on costs, competition, and/or demand influences. Implementing and managing the pricing strategy also includes establishing pricing policy and structure. Finally, several special pricing considerations include price segmentation, distribution channel pricing, price flexibility, product life cycle pricing, and counterfeit products.

Internet Applications

A. Explore the Web site of American Airlines (*www.aa.com*). Consider how the Web site can facilitate price discrimination.

B. Visit Amazon.com. Evaluate Amazon's pricing strategy. How do its prices compare to those of "brick and mortar" retailers? Critically evaluate the company's product offering and identify potential market segments.

C. Visit Oracle.com. Discuss how Oracle considers price in the information provided for its business process software suite.

D. Study the information available from Starbucks Web site (*www.starbucks.com*). Discuss how the Web site enhances the firm's ability to obtain premium prices.

Feature Applications

A. From the Cross-Functional Feature, develop a list of the pricing issues faced by the executives at Novet. What are the arguments that can be made for avoiding the price-cutting option?

B. Think about "The Prisoner's Dilemma" described in the Strategy Feature. What would be the ethical dilemmas for executives across different companies in a sector sharing information to coordinate prices? Why are such practices unlawful in most countries?

Questions for Review and Discussion

1. Discuss the role of price in the marketing strategy for Rolex watches. Contrast Timex's price strategy with Rolex's strategy.
2. The Toyota Camry and the Lexus ES 330 are very similar but the ES 330 is priced substantially higher than the Camry. Discuss the features and limitations of this pricing strategy.
3. Indicate how a fast-food chain can estimate the price elasticity of a proposed new product such as a chicken sandwich.
4. Real estate brokers typically charge a fixed percentage of a home's sales price. Advertising agencies follow a similar price strategy. Discuss why this may be sound price strategy. What are the arguments against it from the buyer's point of view?
5. Cite examples of businesses to which the experience-curve effect may not be applicable. What influence may this have on price determination?
6. In some industries prices are set low, subsidies are provided, and other price-reducing mechanisms are used to

establish a long-term relationship with the buyer. Utilities, for example, sometimes use incentives to encourage contractors to install electric- or gas-powered appliances. Manufacturers may price equipment low, then depend on service and parts for profit contribution. What are the advantages and limitations of this pricing strategy?

7. Discuss why it is important to consider pricing from a strategic rather than a tactical perspective.
8. Discuss some of the ways that estimates of the costs of competitors' products can be determined.
9. Discuss how a pricing strategy should be developed by a software firm to price its business-analysis software line.
10. Suppose a firm is considering changing from a low-active price strategy to a high-active strategy. Discuss the implications of this proposed change.
11. Describe and evaluate the price strategy used for the Lexus 430 European-style luxury sedan.

Notes

1. This illustration is based on "Look Who's Buzzing the Discounters," *BusinessWeek,* November 24, 2003, 48.
2. "CAPITAL: How Technology Tailors Price Tags," *The Wall Street Journal,* June 21, 2001, A1; Bill Saporito, "Why the Price Wars Never End," *Fortune,* March 23, 1992, 68–71, 74, 78.
3. W. Chan Kim and Renee Mauborgne, "Now Name a Price That's Hard to Refuse," *Financial Times,* January 24, 2001.
4. W. Chan Kim and Renee Mauborgne, "Creating New Market Space," *Harvard Business Review,* January–February 1999, 83–93.
5. Thomas Nagle, "Make Pricing a Key Driver of Your Marketing Strategy," *Marketing News,* November 9, 1998, 4.
6. See "Taking It on the Chin," *The Economist,* April 18, 1998, 60–61; Mark Maremont, "How Gillette Brought Its MACH3 to Market," *The Wall Street Journal,* April 15, 1998, B1, B8; Mark Maremont, "A Cut Above?" *The Wall Street Journal,* April 14, 1998, A1 and A10.
7. Maremont, "How Gillette Brought Its MACH3 to Market," B1.
8. This illustration is based on George E. Cressman Jr. and Thomas T. Nagle, "How to Manage an Aggressive Competitor," *Business Horizons,* March–April 2002, 26.
9. Laura Bird, "P&G's New Analgesic Promises Pain for Over-the-Counter Rivals," *The Wall Street Journal,* June 16, 1994, B9.
10. Robert J. Dolan, "How Do You Know When the Price Is Right," *Harvard Business Review,* September–October 1995, 174–183.
11. Guidelines for constructing value maps are discussed in George E. Cressman Jr., "Snatching Defeat from the Jaws of Victory," *Marketing Management,* Summer 1997, 14.
12. A guide to determining experience curves is provided in Kent B. Monroe, *Pricing: Making Profitable Decisions*. 3rd ed. (Burr Ridge, IL: McGraw-Hill/Irwin, 2003), Chapter 13.
13. Rebecca Blumenstein, "Overbuilt Web," *The Wall Street Journal,* June 16, 2001, A1 and A8; Deborah Solomon, "Global Crossing Finds That the Race Has Just Begun," *The Wall Street Journal,* June 22, 2001, B4.
14. "A Nasty Surprise from HP," *BusinessWeek,* September 1, 2003, 80; Gary McWilliams and Pui-Wing Tam, "Dell Price Cuts Put a Squeeze on Rival H-P," *The Wall Street Journal,* August 21, 2003, B1 and B7.
15. Almar Latour, "Disconnected," *The Wall Street Journal,* June 5, 2001, A1 and A8.
16. These and other aspects of marketing and the law are discussed in Gilbert A. Churchill Jr. and J. Paul Peter, *Marketing*. 2nd ed. (Chicago: Irwin/McGraw-Hill, 1998), 325–327.
17. Shailagh Murry and Lucette Lagnado, "Drug Companies Face Assault on Prices," *The Wall Street Journal,* May 11, 2000, B1 and B4.
18. The following issues are based on Cressman, "Snatching Defeat from the Jaws of Victory," *Marketing Management,* Summer 1997, 10–11.
19. Ibid.
20. Reed K. Holden and Thomas T. Nagle, "Kamikaze Pricing," *Marketing Management,* Summer 1998, 31–39.
21. Ibid.
22. Jeffrey F. Rayport and Bernard J. Jaworski, *e-Commerce* (New York: McGraw-Hill/Irwin, 2001), 157.
23. See, for example, Monroe, *Pricing,* Thomas T. Nagle and Reed K. Holden, *The Strategy and Tactics of Pricing*. 2nd ed. (Englewood Cliffs, NJ: Prentice Hall, 1995).
24. Gregory A. Patterson, "Mervyn's Efforts to Revamp Result in Disappointment," *The Wall Street Journal,* March 29, 1994, B4.
25. Janice Revall, "The Price Is Not Always Right," *Fortune,* May 14, 2001, 240.
26. "China's Piracy Plague," *BusinessWeek,* June 5, 2000, 44–48.

Chapter 12

Promotion, Advertising, and Sales Promotion Strategies

Promotion strategy integrates the organization's communications initiatives, combining advertising, personal selling, sales promotion, interactive/Internet marketing, direct marketing, and public relations to communicate with buyers and others who influence purchasing decisions. The Internet offers a fast-growing avenue for one-to-one marketing for business and consumer buyers. Billions are spent every week in the United States and around the world on the various promotion components. Effective management of these expensive resources is essential to gain the optimum return from the promotion expenditures. Combining the components into a consistent overall promotion strategy requires close coordination across the responsible units in the organization.

Promotion plays an essential role in achieving impressive growth and financial performance for Louis Vuitton, the largest and most profitable luxury brand in the world.[1] The French producer of handbags, briefcases, and wallets is continually developing new products, improving the quality and efficiency of production processes and aggressively promoting its brand against competitors. In 2003 Vuitton increased advertising expenditures by 20 percent while the competition (Prada, Gucci, Hermés, and Coach) cut back on spending. The 2003 advertising included a global campaign featuring Jennifer Lopez. Vuitton's 2004 ads feature supermodels. Even with its aggressive advertising strategy, the company spends only 5 percent of its revenues on advertising (half of the industry average). Vuitton's advantage is that its 2003 revenues ($3.80 billion) were nearly double those of the number two competitor, Prada ($1.95 billion). Vuitton's high volume and superior operating margin provides a strong foundation for advertising and sales promotion spending.

The communications activities that make up promotion strategy inform people about products and persuade the company's buyers, channel organizations, and the public at large to purchase brands. The objective is to combine the promotion components into an integrated strategy for communicating with buyers and others who influence purchasing decisions. Since each form of promotion has certain strengths and shortcomings, an integrated strategy incorporates the advantages of each component into a cost-effective promotion mix.

We begin the chapter with an overview of promotion strategy and examine the decisions that are involved in designing the strategy. The intent is to develop an integrated view of communications strategy to which each of the promotion components contributes. Next, we discuss each component beginning with the major decisions that comprise advertising strategy and the factors affecting advertising decisions. The final section considers the design and implementation of sales promotion strategies. Personal selling, direct marketing, and Internet strategies are discussed in Chapter 13.

Promotion Strategy

Promotion strategy consists of planning, implementing, and controlling an organization's communications to its customers and other target audiences. The purpose of promotion in the marketing program is to achieve management's desired communications objectives with each audience. An important marketing responsibility is planning and coordinating the integrated promotion strategy and selecting the specific strategies for each of the promotion components. It is important to recognize that word-of-mouth communications among buyers and the communications activities of other organizations may influence the firm's target audience(s).

The Composition of Promotion Strategy

Advertising. Advertising consists of any form of nonpersonal communication concerning an organization, product, or idea that is paid for by a specific sponsor. The sponsor makes payment for the communication via one or more forms of media (e.g., television, radio, magazine, newspaper). Advertising expenditures in the United States were expected to grow by 7 percent in 2004 to $266 billion.[2] Network and cable TV and Internet advertising would experience the highest growth rates (10–12 percent) compared to single-digit growth for radio, magazines, and newspapers. The United States accounts for about 53 percent of worldwide advertising. Large advertising expenditures are often necessary to introduce new consumer products and build the brand equity of existing products. For example, Energizer Holdings spent an estimated $120 million in the United States in 2003 to launch the new Schick three-bladed razor "Intuition" for women.[3] The intent was to take market share from Gillette's Venus three-bladed razor, the leading women's brand. Intuition, priced at $7.99, dispenses its own shaving gel. Schick's razors have an 18 percent global market share compared to 70 percent for Gillette.

Among the advantages of using advertising to communicate with buyers are the low cost per exposure, the variety of media (newspapers, magazines, television, radio, Internet, direct mail, and outdoor advertising), control of exposure, consistent message content, and the opportunity for creative message design. In addition, the appeal and message can be adjusted when communications objectives change. Cable television enables advertisers to target their communications to specific buyers with more focus than the large networks. Advertising also has some disadvantages. It cannot interact with the buyer and may not be able to hold viewers' attention. Moreover, the message is fixed for the duration of an exposure.

Personal Selling. Personal selling consists of verbal communication between a salesperson (or selling team) and one or more prospective purchasers with the objective of making or influencing a sale. Annual expenditures on personal selling are much larger than advertising, perhaps twice as much. Importantly, both promotion components share some common features, including creating awareness of the brand, transmitting information, and persuading people to buy. Personal selling is expensive. For example, in the U.S. pharmaceuticals sector, the industry spends more on salespeople than on scientists. Some 70,000 U.S. salespeople cost the industry an estimated $7 billion a year.[4] The cost of a sales call may reach $400 for industrial goods and services, and typically multiple calls are necessary to sell the product.[5] One reason for the high call cost is the increasing involvement of salespeople in nonselling activities. Personal selling has several unique strengths: Salespeople can interact with buyers to answer questions and overcome objections, they can target buyers, and they have the capacity to accumulate market knowledge and provide feedback. Top management may participate in selling by making calls on major customers.

Sales Promotion. Sales promotion consists of various promotional activities including trade shows, contests, samples, point-of-purchase displays, trade incentives, and coupons. Sales promotion expenditures are much greater than the amount spent on advertising, and as large as sales force expenditures. This array of special communications techniques and incentives offers several advantages: Sales promotion can be used to target buyers, respond to special occasions, and create an incentive for purchase. Sales promotion activities may be targeted to consumers, value-chain members, or employees (e.g., salespeople). One of the more successful sales promotion initiatives is the frequent flyer incentive program. American Airlines launched the innovative AAdvantage program in 1981. It was first developed with a core customer group of 250,000 frequent flyers.[6] The airline's reservation system enables the company to track mileage and efficiently manage the program. American's costs per member per year for communications and administration are very low.

Direct Marketing. Direct marketing includes the various communications channels that enable companies to make direct contact with individual buyers. Examples are catalogs, direct mail, telemarketing, television selling, radio/magazine/newspaper selling, and electronic shopping. The distinguishing feature of direct marketing is the opportunity for the marketer to gain direct access to the buyer. Direct marketing expenditures account for an increasingly large portion of promotion expenditures.

Interactive/Internet Marketing. Included in this promotion component are the Internet, CD-ROM, kiosks, and interactive television. Interactive media enable buyers and sellers to interact. The Internet performs an important and rapidly escalating role in promotion strategy. In addition to providing a direct sales channel, the Internet may be used to identify sales leads, conduct Web-based surveys, provide product information, and display advertisements. The Internet provides the platform for a complete business strategy in the case of Internet business models. Marketing strategies are increasingly linked to Internet initiatives. The Internet has become an important component of many communications programs.

In 2002 the largest portion of Internet users was in North America, accounting for one-third of the global online population.[7] Internet users in Europe and Asia are close behind and expanding much faster than North America. The United States has an estimated 150 million users and the next largest Internet users are in Japan (34 million). China has 26 million users, up from only 1 million in five years.

Public Relations. Public relations for a company and its products consist of communications placed in the commercial media at no charge to the company receiving the publicity. For example, a news release on a new product may be published in a trade magazine but the company does not pay for the communication. The media coverage is an article or news item. The objective of the public relations department is to encourage relevant media to include company-released information in media communications. Public relations activities can make an important contribution to promotion strategy when the activity is planned and implemented to achieve specific promotion objectives. (Public relations activities are also used for publicity purposes such as communicating with financial analysts.) Publicity in the media can be negative as well as positive, and cannot be controlled by the organization to the same extent as other promotion components. Since a company does not purchase the media coverage, public relations is a cost-effective method of communication. The media are usually willing to cover topics of public interest. Many companies retain public relations consultants who proactively pursue opportunities to feature their companies and brands. For many companies the active management of "corporate reputation" is a public relations priority because reputation impacts on many of the stakeholders in the company.

Technology plays an important role in many companies' promotion strategies. For example, the Internet provides buyers with access to important information in making purchase decisions. An interesting use of the Internet to promote new movies and gather viewer information is described in the Internet Feature.

Developing Promotion Strategy

Market target and positioning strategies guide promotion decisions as shown in Exhibit 12.1. Several activities are involved in designing the promotion strategy including (1) setting communication objectives, (2) deciding the role of each of the components that make up the promotion program, (3) determining the promotion budget, (4) selecting the strategy for each promotion component,

Internet Feature

Twentieth Century Fox's Internet Marketing Strategy That Promotes Its Movies

It's all part of the most elaborate Internet marketing blitz ever to hit Hollywood. In post-*Blair Witch* Internet marketing, Fox has few peers in mastering the interactive power of the Web to boost interest in its films. Besides egging on mutant snitchers, Fox used online games, chat-room talks with the stars, and even a series of fake news articles of mysterious events to whip up online chatter.

The results are promising. The Web campaign capped a $50 million marketing program that helped *X-Men* gross more than $150 million. Fox exit polls showed that 28 percent of those who saw the film had visited the *X-Men* Web site—nearly five times the number of moviegoers who usually surf movie sites, say Hollywood marketing experts.

The potential reward, say industry marketing experts: a whole new customer base to target during later promotions—and larger-than-ever focus groups on which to test future films and plotlines. Up to six months before the movie's opening, for instance, mutantwatch.com was full of phony news accounts of freak hurricanes started by mutants and Badger Scouts in Michigan patrolling the streets in search of mutants. That's what drew those 65,000 mutant spotters—and their valuable data.

To be sure, this "viral marketing," the online equivalent of word-of-mouth advertising, can't work miracles. The apocalyptic animated film *Titan A.E.*, for example, died at the box office despite a hefty Web campaign that included offline events, such as a well-publicized skateboard contest on the Fox Sports Channel designed to drive folks to the *Titan* site.

But it's that kind of wasted spending that spurred Fox to develop a $1 million Web-powered data analysis program, code-named Eight Ball, that allows execs to track sales for most Fox films even before the box office closes for the night. Using its own data—plus some from box-office tracker ACNielsen EDI Inc.—Fox can decide where to boost advertising and where to yank it before financial disaster strikes. If a movie bombs in Boise, for instance, Fox can pull it—or run more ads in areas where sales are starting to build.

Source: Ronald Grover, "Lights, Camera, Web Site," *BusinessWeek E.Biz*, September 18, 2000, EB55.

EXHIBIT 12.1
Developing Promotion Strategy

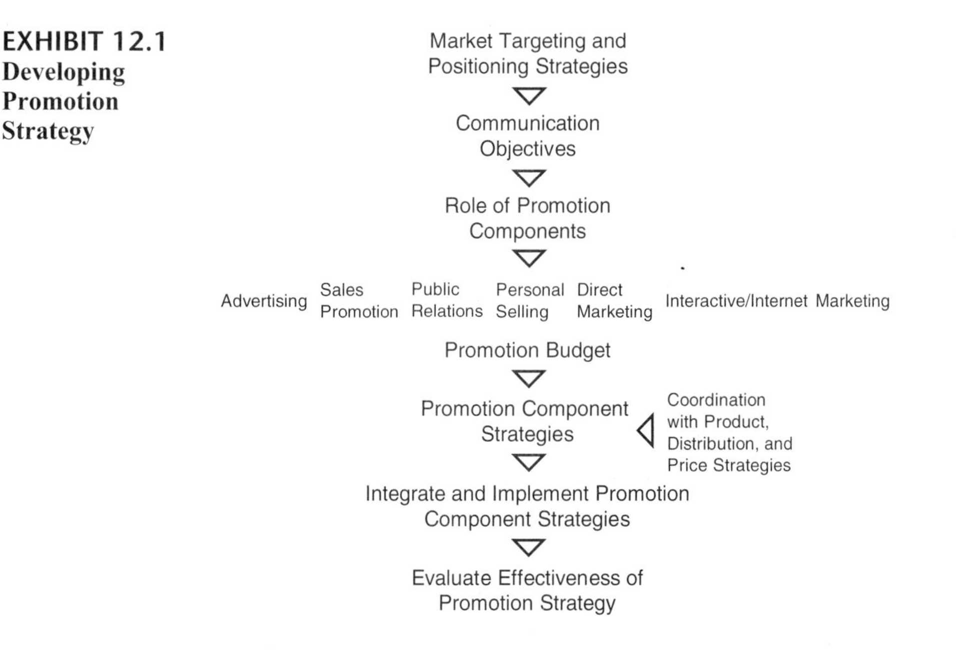

(5) integrating and implementing the promotion component strategies, and (6) evaluating the effectiveness of the integrated promotion strategies. Specific strategies must be determined for advertising, personal selling, sales promotion, direct marketing, Internet, and public relations, and these strategies need to be carefully integrated and coordinated to achieve communication objectives.

Market targets and product, distribution, and price decisions provide a frame of reference for (1) deciding the role of promotion strategy in the total marketing program, and (2) identifying the specific communications tasks of the promotion activities. One important question is deciding the role that the promotion strategy will play in marketing strategy. Advertising and personal selling

are often a major part of a firm's marketing strategy. In consumer package goods firms, sales promotion and advertising comprise a large portion of the promotion program. In business-to-business firms, personal selling often dominates the promotion strategy, with advertising and sales promotion playing a supporting role. The use of sales promotion and public relations varies considerably among companies. The role of direct marketing also differs across companies and industries. Internet initiatives are under way in a broad range of companies.

Interestingly, Singapore Airlines performs an important promotion role in marketing the nation (see accompanying Singapore Airlines advertisement). It is consistently one of the more profitable global airlines, although much smaller than the major carriers.[8] The airline's favorable image helps to position the country with executives, government officials, and tourists who experience Singapore Airlines' renowned services. The tiny city-state with a very small population has a strong brand image, enhanced by the airline's favorable reputation with customers and competitors throughout the world. The airline's advertising in business and travel magazines is designed to favorably position its distinctive bundle of values. Global air travel is expected to double in 2010 compared to 1990 and much of the growth is in Asia.

Communication Objectives

Communication objectives help determine how the promotion strategy components are used in the marketing program. Several illustrative communication objectives follow.

Need Recognition. A communication objective, which is important for new-product introductions, is to trigger a need. Need recognition may also be important for existing products and services, particularly when the buyer can postpone purchasing or choose not to purchase (such as life insurance). For example, P&G emphasized the need to control dandruff in its advertising of Head & Shoulders shampoo in China. The ads focused attention on how dandruff is very visible on people with black hair.

Finding Buyers. Promotion activities can be used to identify buyers. The message seeks to get the prospective buyer to respond. Recall, for example, the use of the Internet to attract potential movie viewers discussed in the earlier Internet Feature. Salespeople may be given responsibility for identifying and screening prospects. The use of toll-free numbers is often helpful in identifying customers as well as issues and problems of interest to the callers.

Brand Building. Promotion can aid a buyer's search for information. One of the objectives of new-product promotional activities is to help buyers learn about the product. Prescription drug companies advertise to the public to make people aware of diseases and the brand names of products used for treatment. In the past, they targeted only doctors through ads in medical journals and contacts by salespeople. Advertising is often a more cost-effective way to disseminate information than personal selling, particularly when the information can be exposed to targeted buyers by electronic or printed media.

Evaluation of Alternatives. Promotion helps buyers evaluate alternative products or brands. Both comparative advertising and personal selling are effective in demonstrating a brand's strengths over competing brands. An example of this form of advertising is to analyze competing brands of a product, showing a favorable comparison for the brand of the firm placing the ad. Specific product attributes may be used for the comparison. For example, PepsiCo's ads in 2001 for its leading bottled water brand, Aquafina, were positioned "to strip away the elite image to make it look accessible to everyone."[9] The objective was to differentiate Aquafina from competing brands as the most mouthwatering water available.

Decision to Purchase. Several of the promotion components may be used to stimulate the purchase decision. Personal selling is often effective in obtaining a purchase commitment from the buyers of consumer durable goods and industrial products. Door-to-door selling organizations such as Avon (cosmetics) and Cutco (knives) use highly programmed selling approaches to encourage buyers to purchase their products. Communication objectives in these firms include making a target number of contacts each day. Point-of-purchase sales promotions, such as displays in retail stores, are intended to influence the purchase decision, as are samples and discount coupons. One of the advantages of personal selling over advertising is its flexibility in responding to the buyer's objectives and questions at the time the decision to purchase is being made.

Customer Retention. Communicating with buyers after they purchase a product is an important promotional activity. Follow-up by salespeople, advertisements stressing a firm's service capabilities, and toll-free numbers placed on packages to encourage users to seek information or report problems are illustrations of post-purchase communications. Hotels leave questionnaires in rooms for occupants to use in evaluating hotel services.

As illustrated, various communication objectives may be assigned to promotion strategy. The uses of promotion vary according to the type of purchase, the stage of the buyer's decision process, the maturity of the product-market, and the role of promotion in the marketing program. Objectives need to be developed for the entire promotion program and for each promotion component. Certain objectives, such as sales and market share targets, are shared with other marketing program components. Examples of communication objectives include:

- Creating or increasing buyers' awareness of a product or brand.
- Influencing buyers' attitudes toward a company, product, or brand.
- Increasing the level of brand preference of the buyers in a targeted segment.
- Achieving sales and market share increases for specific customer or prospect targets.
- Generating repeat purchases of a brand.
- Encouraging trial of a new product.
- Attracting new customers.
- Encouraging long-term relationships.

In the following sections and the next chapter we discuss and provide examples of objectives for each promotion component.

Deciding the Role of the Promotion Components

Communication objectives are useful in deciding the specific role of each component in the promotion program. For example, the role of the sales force may be to obtain sales or, instead, to inform channel of distribution organizations about product features and applications. Advertising may be used to generate repeat purchases of a brand. Sales promotion (e.g., trade shows) may be used to achieve various objectives in the promotion mix. Direct marketing may play a major role in certain companies.

Early in the process of developing the promotion strategy, it is useful to set guidelines as to the expected contribution for each of the promotion program components. These guidelines help determine the strategy for each promotion component. It is necessary to decide which communication objective(s) will be the responsibility of each component. For example, advertising may be responsible for creating awareness of a new product. Sales promotion (e.g., coupons and samples) may encourage trial of the new product. Personal selling may be assigned responsibility for getting wholesalers and/or retailers to stock the new product. It is also important to decide how large the contribution of each promotion component will be, which will help to determine the promotion budget.

Determining the Promotion Budget

Selecting an optimal budget for promotion expenditures is complex because factors other than promotion also influence sales. Isolating the specific effects of promotion may be difficult due to lags in the impact of promotion on sales, effects of other marketing program components (e.g., retailers' cooperation), and the influences of uncontrollable factors (e.g., competition, economic conditions). Realistically, budgeting in practice is likely to emphasize improving promotion effectiveness compared to past results. Because of this, more practical budgeting techniques are normally used. These methods include (1) objective and task, (2) percent of sales, (3) competitive parity, and (4) all you can afford. These same approaches are used to determine advertising and sales promotion budgets. The personal-selling budget is largely determined by the number of people in the sales force and their qualifications. Direct marketing budgets are guided by the unit costs of customer contact such as cost per catalog mailed.

In many companies, the promotion budget may include only planned expenditures for advertising and sales promotion. Typically a separate budget is developed for the sales organization, which may contain sales promotion activities such as incentives for salespeople and value-chain members. Public relations budgets also are likely to be separate from promotion budgeting. Even so, it is important to consider the size and allocation of total promotion expenses when formulating the promotion strategy. Unless this is done, the integration of the components is likely to be fragmented. Internet budgets may be separate or included with the promotion component that utilizes Internet capabilities.

An example of a promotion budget (excluding sales force and public relations) for a pharmaceutical product is shown in Exhibit 12.2. Note the relative size of advertising and sample expenditures. The sampling of drugs to doctors by salespeople represents a substantial amount of the promotion budget. Sampling is an important promotion component in this industry.

Objective and Task. This logical and cost-effective method is probably the most widely used budgeting approach. Management sets the communication objectives, determines the tasks (activities) necessary to achieve the objectives, and adds up costs. This method also guides determining the role of the promotion components by selecting the component(s) appropriate for attaining each objective. Marketing management must carefully evaluate how the promotion objectives are to be achieved and choose the most cost-effective promotion components. The effectiveness of the objective and task method depends on the judgment and experience of the marketing team. The budget shown in Exhibit 12.2 was determined using the objective and task method. The pharmaceutical firm executives involved in the budgeting process included product managers, the division manager, sales management, and the chief marketing executive.

Percent of Sales. Using this method, the budget is calculated as a percent of sales and is, therefore, quite arbitrary. The percentage figure is often based on past expenditure patterns. The method fails to recognize that promotion efforts and results are related. For example, a 10 percent-of-sales budget may be too much or not enough promotion expenditures to achieve sales and other promotion objectives. Budgeting by percent of sales can lead to too much spending on promotion when sales are high and too little when sales are low. In a cyclical industry where sales follow up-and-down trends, a strategy of increasing promotion expenditures during low sales periods may be more appropriate.

EXHIBIT 12.2
Illustrative Promotion Budget for a Pharmaceutical Product

Promotional Activity	2006 Budget
Promotional material	$ 270,000
Samples	540,000
Direct mail	406,000
Journal advertising	472,000
Total budget	**$1,688,000**

Cross-Functional Feature

Promotion Budget Setting in Action

Researchers' in-depth interviews with managers in consumer products firms provide interesting insights into actual budget setting processes. The budget components included advertising, consumer promotion, and trade promotion.

Budgets are developed by cross-functional teams of managers from brand/category management, sales, trade marketing, manufacturing, accounting, and marketing research. The teams conduct situation analyses as the basis for marketing plan development. Out of this process, marketing objectives and the brand strategy are determined. The brand manager also forecasts sales and profits based on the strategy.

Using the strategy guidelines, the team makes a preliminary allocation of the promotion budget to advertising, consumer promotion, and trade promotion, guided by past expenditures. The budget is then modified to take into account estimated competitors' promotions and other market-driven factors. Next, the brand plan is presented to top management (e.g., president, vice presidents of marketing and sales, and group managers, including finance).

Based on top management's assessment and changes, the plan is finalized and implemented. The brand manager is responsible for managing the promotion budget during the year, making necessary tactical adjustments based on competitive and market factors.

Source: George S. Low and Jakki J. Mohr, "The Advertising Sales Promotion Trade-Off: Theory and Practice," Report No. 92-127 (Cambridge, MA: Marketing Science Institute, October 1992). Reprinted with permission.

Competitive Parity. Promotion expenditures for this budgeting method are guided by how much competitors spend. Yet competitors may be spending too much (or not enough) on promotion. Another key shortcoming of the competitive parity method is that differences in marketing strategy between competing firms may require different promotion strategies. For example, Revlon uses an intensive distribution strategy, while Estée Lauder targets buyers by distributing through selected department stores. A comparison of promotional strategies of these firms is not very meaningful, since their market targets, promotion objectives, and use of promotion components are different.

All You Can Afford. Since budget limits are a reality in most companies, this method is likely to influence all budget decisions. Top management may specify how much can be spent on promotion. For example, the guideline may be to increase the budget to 110 percent of last year's actual promotion expenditures. The objective and task method can be combined with the "all-you-can-afford" method by setting task priorities and allocating the budget to the higher priority tasks.

Budgeting in Practice. Research sponsored by the Marketing Science Institute indicates that in practice, promotion budgeting in consumer products firms involves a process that is a combination of rational, political, and expedient actions. The Cross-Functional Feature summarizes the study findings.

The Feature highlights the interactive nature of determining the promotion budget. Trade-offs must be evaluated concerning budget needs of promotion components, priorities among the components, and total budget limits. These discussions among the team members and top management play an important role in promotion strategy integration.

Promotion Component Strategies

Determining the strategy for each promotion component includes setting objectives and budget, selecting the strategy, and determining the activities (and timing) to be pursued. For example, advertising activities include choosing the creative strategy, formulating the message(s), and selecting the media to carry the ads.

In this chapter we discuss advertising and sales promotion strategy determination. Public relations strategy involves similar initiatives to advertising strategy determination. The following chapter examines sales force, Internet, and direct marketing strategies.

EXHIBIT 12.3 Illustrative Factors That Influence the Design of Promotion Strategy

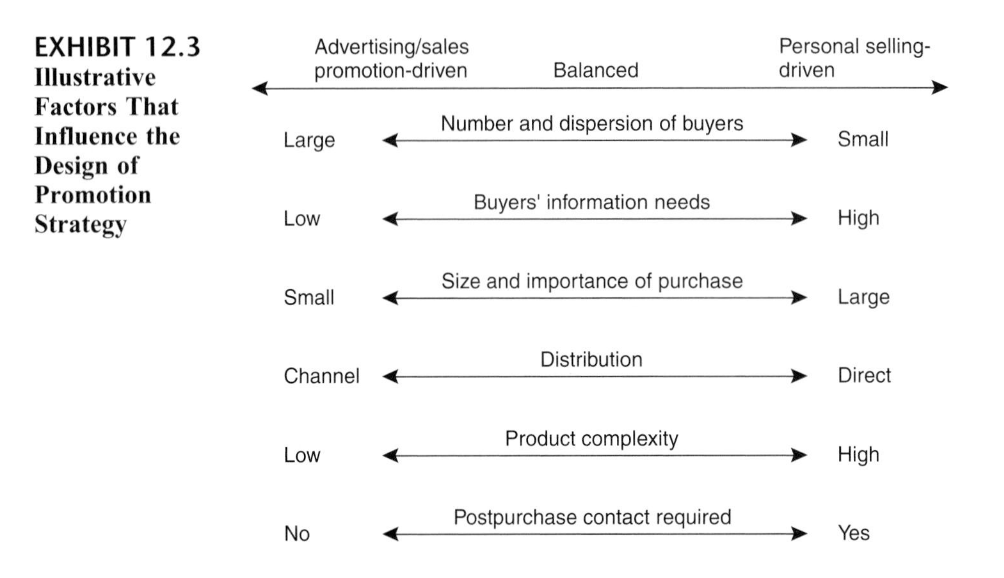

Integrating and Implementing the Promotion Strategy

Several factors may affect the composition of the promotion program as shown by Exhibit 12.3. Advertising, public relations, personal selling, direct marketing, Internet, and sales promotion strategies are likely to be fragmented when responsibility is assigned to more than one department. Moreover, there are differences in priorities, and evaluating the productivity of the promotion components is complex. For example, coordination between selling and advertising is difficult in firms marketing to industrial buyers, and these firms tend to follow personal-selling-driven promotion strategies. The separation of selling and advertising strategies also prevails in a variety of consumer products firms. An important marketing management issue is how to integrate the promotion strategy components.

Integrated marketing communications (IMC) strategies are replacing fragmented advertising, publicity, and sales programs. These approaches differ from traditional promotion strategies in several ways as described by the following characteristics of IMC strategies in retailing:

1. IMC programs are comprehensive. Advertising, personal selling, retail atmospherics, behavioral-modification programs, public relations, investor-relations programs, employee communications, and other forms are all considered in the planning of an IMC.
2. IMC programs are unified. The messages delivered by all media, including such diverse influences as employee recruiting and the atmospherics of retailers upon which the marketer primarily relies, are the same or supportive of a unified theme.
3. IMC programs are targeted. The public relations program, advertising programs, and dealer/distributor programs all have the same or related target markets.
4. IMC programs have coordinated execution of all the communications components of the organization.
5. IMC programs emphasize productivity in reaching the designated targets when selecting communication channels and allocating resources to marketing media.[10]

The Gap, the apparel retailer, has been unusually successful in implementing an integrated marketing-communications program.[11] Management positions advertising into the IMC strategy. Advertising plays a key role at the Gap but other marketing functions are equally important. The IMC strategy is effectively combined with the marketing strategy components.

Developing and implementing integrated communications strategies is essential for manufacturers as well as retailers, and for both consumer and business products. Effective management of these strategies has a positive impact on revenues and the productivity of promotion strategy:

> The move toward integrated marketing communications is one of the most significant marketing developments that occurred during the 1990s, and the shift toward this approach is continuing as we begin the new century. The IMC approach to marketing communications planning and strategy is being adopted by both large and small companies and has become popular among firms marketing consumer products and services as well as business-to-business marketers. There are a number of reasons why marketers are adopting the IMC approach. A fundamental reason is that they understand the value of strategically integrating the various communications functions rather than having them operate autonomously. By coordinating their marketing communications efforts, companies can avoid duplication, take advantage of synergy among promotional tools, and develop more efficient and effective marketing communications programs.[12]

Effectiveness of Promotion Strategy

Tracking the effectiveness of promotion strategy involves (1) evaluating the effectiveness of each promotion component, and (2) assessing the overall effectiveness of the integrated promotion strategy. In this and the next chapter we discuss measurement of effectiveness of the individual promotion components. Cross-functional teams can be used to assess overall promotion strategy effectiveness. Comparisons of actual results to objectives can be employed in the evaluation of each promotion component and the effectiveness of the integrated promotion strategy.

Advertising Strategy

Management's assessment of how advertising can contribute to the communication objectives has an important influence in deciding advertising's role. Estimating advertising's impact on buyers helps management to decide advertising's role and scope in the marketing program and choose specific objectives for advertising. As we discussed in the chapter introduction advertising plays a key role in Louis Vuitton's marketing strategy for its luxury products.

Identifying and describing the target audience are the first step in developing advertising strategy. Next, it is important to set specific objectives and decide on the advertising budget. There may be an adjustment (up or down) of this initial budget as the specific advertising activities and media choices are determined. The selection of the creative strategy follows. Specific messages need to be designed for each ad. Ads may be pretested. Choices of the advertising media and programming schedules implement the creative strategy. The final step is putting the advertising strategy under way and evaluating its effectiveness. We examine each of these activities, highlighting important features and strategy issues. In the discussion we assume that the target audience(s) has been selected.

Setting Advertising Objectives and Budgeting

Advertising Objectives. The earlier discussion of communication objectives identified various objectives that may be relevant for advertising. These include need recognition, identifying buyers, brand building, evaluation of alternatives, decision to purchase, and customer retention. More than one objective may be applicable for a particular advertising strategy.

Exhibit 12.4 shows alternative levels for setting advertising objectives. In moving from the most general level (exposure) to the most specific level (profit contribution) the objectives are increasingly more closely linked to the purchase decision. For example, knowing that advertising causes a measurable increase in sales is much more useful to the decision maker than knowing that a specific number of people are exposed to an advertising message. The key issue is whether objectives such as exposure and awareness are related to purchase behavior. For example, how much will exposure to the advertising increase the chances that people will purchase a product? Objectives such as exposure and awareness often can be measured, whereas determining the sales and profit impact of advertising may be more difficult to measure due to the impact of other factors on sales and profits. Because of the ease of measurement,

EXHIBIT 12.4
Alternative Levels for Setting Advertising Objectives

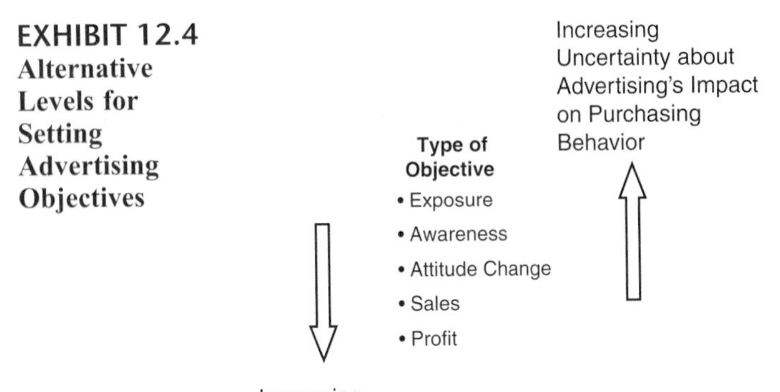

exposure and awareness objectives are used more often than attitude change, sales, and profit objectives.

Several questions are presented in Exhibit 12.5 that are useful in determining advertising objectives. The questions focus on alternative purposes of advertising ranging from generating immediate sales to brand image building. A checklist of specific objectives is shown for each of the nine questions. The intent is to suggest alternative objectives for each question.

Budget Determination. The budgeting methods for promotion discussed earlier in the chapter are also used in advertising budgeting. The objective and task method has a stronger supporting logic than the other methods. Consider, for example, the Italian government's advertising program intended to favorably position Italian fashion designers and craftsmen as the world's finest.[13] The objectives were to increase Italy's share of U.S. imports and enhance the prestige of its brands. The Italian Trade Commission budgeted $25 million on advertising and other promotion activities in the five-year period through 1997 to achieve these objectives. The aggressive campaign generated positive results with an increase in Italy's U.S. imported apparel share from 4.5 to 5.9 percent. Much larger increases were obtained by the more expensive imports like Versace and Giorgio Armani.

Analytical models of sales response have been developed to help guide advertising budgeting decisions for frequently purchased consumer products.[14] One model uses multiple regression analysis with ad expenditures and other predictors for estimating brand sales. Data from several previous time periods are used to build the models. A key assumption is that historical relationships will hold in the future.

Budget determination, creative strategy, and media/programming strategy are closely interrelated, so these decisions need to be closely coordinated. A preliminary budget may be set, subject to review after the creative and media/programming strategies are determined. Using objective and task budgeting, creative plans and media alternatives should be examined in the budgeting process.

Creative Strategy

The range of advertising objectives shown in Exhibit 12.5 indicates the possible focus of the creative strategy. For example, if the objective is to enhance the image of a brand, then the message conveyed by the ad would seek to strengthen the brand image. This theme is illustrated by one of BMW's 2004 magazine ads introducing the new X5 4.8: "No matter how we disguise it, its heritage keeps showing through."

The creative strategy is guided by the market target and the desired positioning for the product or brand. In Chapter 6, we discuss positioning according to the *functions* performed by the brand, the *symbol* to be conveyed by the brand, or the *experience* provided by the brand. The creative theme seeks to effectively communicate the intended positioning to buyers and others influencing the purchase of the brand.

EXHIBIT 12.5
Determining Advertising Objectives

1. Does the advertising aim at *immediate sales*? If so, objectives might be:
   - Perform the complete selling function.
   - Close sales to prospects already partly sold.
   - Announce a special reason for buying now (price, premium, and so forth).
   - Remind people to buy.
   - Tie in with special buying event.
   - Stimulate impulse sales.
2. Does the advertising aim at *near-term sales*? If so, objectives might be:
   - Create awareness.
   - Enhance brand image.
   - Implant information or attitude.
   - Combat or offset competitive claims.
   - Correct false impressions, misinformation.
   - Build familiarity and easy recognition.
3. Does the advertising aim at building a *long-range consumer franchise*? If so, objectives might be:
   - Build confidence in company and brand.
   - Build customer demand.
   - Select preferred distributors and dealers.
   - Secure universal distribution.
   - Establish a "reputation platform" for launching new brands or product lines.
4. Does the advertising aim at helping increase sales? If so, objectives would be:
   - Hold present customers.
   - Convert other users to advertiser's brand.
   - Cause people to specify advertiser's brand.
   - Convert nonusers to users.
   - Make steady customers out of occasional ones.
   - Advertise new uses.
   - Persuade customers to buy larger sizes or multiple units.
   - Remind users to buy.
   - Encourage greater frequency or quantity of use.
5. Does the advertising aim at some specific step that leads to a sale? If so, objectives might be:
   - Persuade prospect to write for descriptive literature, return a coupon, enter a contest.
   - Persuade prospect to visit a showroom, ask for a demonstration.
   - Induce prospect to sample the product (trial offer).
6. How important are supplementary benefits of advertising? Objectives would be:
   - Help salespeople open new accounts.
   - Help salespeople get larger orders from wholesalers and retailers.
   - Help salespeople get preferred display space.
   - Give salespeople an entrée.
   - Build morale of sales force.
   - Impress the trade.
7. Should the advertising impart information needed to consummate sales and build customer satisfaction? If so, objectives may be to use:
   - "Where to buy it" advertising.
   - "How to use it" advertising.
   - New models, features, package.
   - New prices.
   - Special terms, trade-in offers, and so forth.
   - New policies (such as guarantees).
8. Should advertising build confidence and goodwill for the corporation? Targets may include:
   - Customers and potential customers.
   - The trade (distributors, dealers, retail people).
   - Employees and potential employees.
   - The financial community.
   - The public at large.
9. What kind of images does the company wish to build?
   - Product quality, dependability.
   - Service.
   - Family resemblance of diversified products.
   - Corporate citizenship.
   - Growth, progressiveness, technical leadership.

Source: William Arens, *Contemporary Advertising*, 7th ed. (Burr Ridge, IL: Irwin/McGraw-Hill, 1999), R18.

There are several successful advertising campaign themes that have been used for many years. Examples include Nike's "Just Do It"; "You're in good hands with Allstate"; "Intel inside"; and Timex's "It takes a licking and keeps on ticking."[15] Interestingly, some of the highest-rated and lowest-rated ads have been created by the same advertising agency. (We discuss the agency's role later in the chapter.)

Creative advertising designs enhance the effectiveness of advertising by providing a unifying concept that binds together the various parts of an advertising campaign. Advertising agencies, which typically receive 15 percent of gross billings, are experts in designing creative strategies. The agency professionals may design unique themes to position a product or firm in some particular way or use comparisons with competition to enhance the firm's brands. Choosing the right creative theme for the marketing situation can make a major contribution to the success of a program. While tests are used to evaluate creative approaches, the task is more of an art than a science. Perhaps the best guide to creativity is an agency's track record.

Several challenges are impacting the creative process and changing the design of creative strategies:

> The new generation of advertising creatives will face a world of ever-growing complexity. They must handle many challenges of integrated marketing communications (IMC) as they help their clients build relationships with highly fragmented target markets. They will need to understand the wide range of new technologies affecting advertising (computer hardware and software, electronic networking, high-definition television, and more). And they have to learn how to advertise in emerging international markets.[16]

The creative strategy used for Murphy's Oil Soap shows the importance of a market segment focus and brand positioning through creative advertising. For nearly 100 years the soap was marketed in a single region of the United States.[17] Fourteen years after a national rollout program starting in 1976, the brand gained sixth position in its product category. Sales in 1990 increased to over $30 million, eight times more than in 1980. The brand was positioned as an effective wood cleaner. Its "Great Houses" advertising campaign displayed impressive old homes highlighting the beauty of wood and the special requirements of a wood-cleaning product. More recent advertising and sales promotion have positioned the soap as effective in "cleaning wood surfaces . . . and more."

Media/Scheduling Decisions

A company's advertising agency or media organization normally guides media selection and scheduling decisions. They have the experience and technical ability to match media and scheduling to the target audience(s) specified by the firm. The media, timing, and programming for television and radio decisions are influenced largely by two factors: (1) access to the target audience(s), and (2) the costs of reaching the target group(s). A comparison of advertising rates for several media is shown below:[18]

Medium	Vehicle	Cost	Reach	CPM*
TV	30 seconds on network prime time	$120,000	10 million households	$12
Consumer magazine	Page, 4-color in *Cosmopolitan*	$86,155	2.5 million paid readers	35
Online service	Banner on CompuServe's major-topic page	$10,000 per month	750,000 visitors	13
Web site	Banner on Infoseek	$10,000 per month	500,000 page views per month	20

*CPM=cost per thousand exposures.

Innovation Feature Reaching the Vanishing Mass Market

- The decline in prime-time television audience ratings and newspaper circulation since the 1970s has been accompanied by the development of a proliferation of digital and wireless communication channels: hundreds of narrowcast cable TV and radio channels; thousands of specialized magazines; millions of computer terminals, video game consoles, personal digital assistants and cell phone screens.
- In the 1960s an advertiser could reach 80 percent of U.S. women with a spot aired simultaneously on CBS, NBC, and ABC, while now an ad would have to run on 100 TV channels to get near this feat.
- Mass media's share of advertising is declining as marketers boost spending on more targetable, narrowcast media.
- The fastest form of online advertising is "paid search"—the search engine used displays paid advertisements or "sponsored links" with the search results. Internet users can be targeted by region and city.
- Online media are interactive, so advertisers can gather invaluable personal information from consumers, and get a more precise measurement of advertising impact.
- A recent study by Sanford C. Bernstein & Co. predicts by 2010 marketers will spend more for advertising on cable and the Internet, than on network TV or on magazines.

Source: Anthony Bianco, "The Vanishing Mass Market," *BusinessWeek*, July 12, 2004, 58–62.

The audience coverage varies considerably so the access to the target audience is also important. The various media provide extensive profile information on their viewers. *Standard Rates and Data Services* publishes advertising costs for various media. The costs are determined by circulation levels and the type of publication. In deciding which medium to use, it is important to evaluate the cost per exposure and the characteristics of the subscribers. The medium should provide coverage of the market target for the product or brand being advertised. High media costs help explain why companies may transfer resources to online advertising, such as banners and click-throughs, where production and media costs are much lower.

Media models are available to analyze allocations and decide which media mix best achieves one or more objectives.[19] These models typically use an exposure measure (Exhibit 12.4) as the basis for media allocation. For example, cost per thousand of exposure can be used to evaluate alternative media. The models also consider audience characteristics (e.g., age group composition) and other factors. The models are useful in selecting media when many advertising programs and a wide range of media are used.

The fragmentation of many consumer markets is driving significant amounts of advertising spending from traditional mass media to more focused narrowcast media. The Innovation Feature describes some of these changes.

Role of the Advertising Agency

Advertising agencies perform various functions for clients including developing creative designs and selecting media. Full-service agencies offer a range of services including marketing research, sales promotion, marketing planning. The typical basis of compensation is a 15 percent fee on media expenditures. For example, $1 million of advertising provides a commission of $150,000. The agency pays the $850,000 for the media space and bills the client $1,000,000. Cash discounts for payment may be involved.

Agency Relationship. The normal basis of operation between a corporate client and the agency is a cooperative effort. The client briefs the agency on the marketing strategy and the role of advertising in the marketing program. In some instances agency executives may be involved in the development of the marketing strategy. The better the agency understands the company's marketing program, the more effective the agency can be in providing advertising services. The agency may assign one or more personnel full-time to a client with a large advertising budget.

EXHIBIT 12.6
Checklist for Evaluating Advertising Agencies

Rate each agency on a scale from 1 (strongly negative) to 10 (strongly positive).

General Information
- ☐ Size compatible with our needs.
- ☐ Strength of management.
- ☐ Financial stability.
- ☐ Compatibility with other clients.
- ☐ Range of services.
- ☐ Cost of services; billing policies.

Marketing Information
- ☐ Ability to offer marketing counsel.
- ☐ Understanding of the markets we serve.
- ☐ Experience dealing in our market.
- ☐ Success record; case histories.

Creative Abilities
- ☐ Well-thought-out creativity; relevance to strategy.
- ☐ Art strength.
- ☐ Copy strength.
- ☐ Overall creative quality.
- ☐ Effectiveness compared to work of competitors.

Production
- ☐ Faithfulness to creative concept and execution.
- ☐ Diligence to schedules and budgets.
- ☐ Ability to control outside services.

Media
- ☐ Existence and soundness of media research.
- ☐ Effective and efficient media strategy.
- ☐ Ability to achieve objectives within budget.
- ☐ Strength at negotiating and executing schedules.

Personality
- ☐ Overall personality, philosophy, or position.
- ☐ Compatibility with client staff and management.
- ☐ Willingness to assign top people to account.

References
- ☐ Rating by current clients.
- ☐ Rating by past clients.
- ☐ Rating by media and financial sources.

Source: William F. Arens, *Contemporary Advertising*, 6th ed. (Burr Ridge, IL: Richard D. Irwin, 1996), 93. Copyright © The McGraw-Hill Companies. Used with permission.

Choosing an advertising agency is an important decision. It is also necessary to evaluate the relationship over time since a company's advertising requirements change. Good agency relationships are usually the result of teaming with an agency that has the capabilities and commitment needed by the client. Several factors that should be considered in evaluating an agency are shown in Exhibit 12.6.

Agency Compensation. The traditional method of compensation of the agency is a 15 percent commission on media expenditures. Most agencies operate on some type of commission arrangement, though the arrangement may involve a commission for media placement and a separate arrangement for other services. For example, media placement would receive a 5 percent commission, whereas other services associated with the advertising would yield an additional 10 percent. These changes in the original 15 percent commission are the consequence of advertising specialists (e.g., media buying) offering reduced fees.

Clients may work out flexible payment arrangements with their agency. The agency may keep a record of its costs and the client pays for the services it requires. The resulting compensation may be greater or less than the traditional 15 percent commission. In some arrangements agencies may share cost savings with the client.

Industry Composition. Large, full-service agencies like Dentsu in Tokyo and Young & Rubicam in New York account for the dominant portion of billings. Nonetheless, several local and regional agencies have created pressures for change throughout the industry. Concerns of clients about arbitrary commission rates and lack of flexibility in client services have led to placing business with small specialty agencies that provide media buying, creative design, and other services. There are many local and regional agencies that serve small and medium-size clients.

Problem Areas. Normally, an agency does not serve clients competing in the same industry. The agency requires access to sensitive information (e.g., sales by product line, by geographical area) in order to effectively serve the client. The advertiser is hesitant to share confidential information when the agency has clients who are viewed as competitors. Achieving the one-client objective is more difficult in working with companies that have smaller advertising budgets. It is important when selecting an agency to determine who its clients are and what sort of policies the agency follows concerning serving clients that are competitors.

Implementing the Advertising Strategy and Measuring Its Effectiveness

Before the advertising strategy is implemented, it is advisable to establish the criteria that will be used for measuring advertising effectiveness. Advertising expenditures are wasted if firms spend too much or allocate expenditures improperly. Measuring effectiveness provides necessary feedback for future advertising decisions. Importantly, the quality of advertising can be as critical to getting results as the amount of advertising.

Tracking Advertising Performance. As previously discussed, advertising's impact on sales may be difficult to measure because other factors also influence sales and profits. Most efforts to measure effectiveness consider objectives such as attitude change, awareness, or exposure (Exhibit 12.4). Comparing objectives and results helps managers decide when to alter or stop advertising campaigns. Services such as Nielsen's TV ratings are available for the major media. These ratings have a critical impact on the allocation of advertising dollars, although some recent research findings question the accuracy of the ratings. Various measurement concerns have resulted in several changes in the rating process.

Methods of Measuring Effectiveness. Several methods are used to evaluate advertising results. Analysis of historical data identifies relationships between advertising expenditures and sales using statistical techniques such as regression analysis. Recall tests measure consumers' awareness of specific ads and campaigns by asking questions to determine if a sample of people remembers an ad. Longitudinal studies track advertising expenditures and sales results before, during, and after an advertising campaign. Controlled tests are a form of longitudinal study in which extraneous effects are measured and/or controlled during the test. Test marketing can be used to evaluate advertising effectiveness. Effort/results models use empirical data to build a mathematical relationship between sales and advertising effort.

Consumer panels provide a useful method for measuring advertising effectiveness for frequently purchased consumer food and drug products in cities with cable TV. The panel is comprised of a group of consumers that agrees to supply information about their purchases on a continuing basis. Cash register scanning of the purchases of panel members provides data on brands purchased, prices, and other information. Samples of consumers can be split into groups that are exposed or not exposed to advertising on cable television. With the use of equivalent samples, the influence on sales of factors other than advertising can be controlled. The difference in sales between the control and the experimental (exposed) groups over the test period measures the effect of advertising.

Advertising research is used for more than just measuring the effectiveness of advertising. Research can be used for various activities in advertising strategy development, including generating and evaluating creative ideas and concepts, and pretesting concepts, ideas, and specific ads.

An example of a popular test used to evaluate TV commercials is shown in Exhibit 12.7. The test commercial is shown in selected test cities. After the commercial is shown, a sample of people who viewed the program is asked several questions to determine reactions to the commercial. The basis of the evaluation is the respondent's recall about the commercial. While such tests have been criticized because they do not evaluate ad quality or relevance, recall continues to be the primary way commercials are evaluated.

EXHIBIT 12.7
How TV Commercials Are Tested

Source: William R. Dillon, Thomas J. Madden, and Neil H. Firtle, *Marketing Research in a Marketing Environment.* 3rd ed. (Burr Ridge, IL: Richard D. Irwin, 1994), 612. Copyright © The McGraw-Hill Companies. Used with permission.

Brand:	Juicy Fruit.
Project:	"False Start" Burke on-air test.
Background and objectives:	The William Wrigley Company has requested a Burke on-air test for the new copy execution of "False Start." The objective of this research is to measure the communication effectiveness of the "False Start" execution.
Research method:	A sample of 150 past-30-day chewing gum users in the commercial audience will be interviewed. The air date is scheduled for the first Tuesday of the month in December, on "NYPD Blue." Interviewing will be conducted within five metro areas: Boston, Atlanta, Indianapolis, Dallas, and Phoenix.
Information to be obtained:	—Total commercial recall. —Copy recall. —Visual recall.
Action standard:	The commercial will be considered acceptable in the areas of memorability and sales message communication if: a. It generates 25 or better related recall score. b. At least 25 of the commercial audience remembers at least one sales message.
Timing and cost:	Fieldwork first Tuesday in December Top line 1 week Final report 4 weeks The cost for this research will be $15,000 ±10%.
Research supplier:	Burke Marketing Research.

Sales Promotion Strategy

Sales promotion expenditures are increasing more rapidly than advertising in many companies.[20] Manufacturers' expenditures for sales promotion are estimated to be as high as 75 percent of the total spent on the two promotion components. Both advertising and sales promotions are receiving major attention by companies in their attempts to boost productivity and reduce costs. When marketing expenditures account for one-third or more of total sales in many companies, the bottom-line impact of improving the effectiveness of promotion expenditures and/or lowering costs is substantial.

Sales promotion activities provide extra value or incentives to consumers and value-chain participants.[21] The intent is to encourage immediate sales. Managers often use the term *promotion* when referring to sales promotion activities. Sales promotion is some form of inducement (e.g., coupon, contest, rebate, etc.). It is intended to accelerate the selling process to build sales volume. Importantly, sales promotion activities can be targeted to various points of influence in the value chain.

We look at the nature and scope of sales promotion, the types of sales promotion activities, the advantages and limitations of sales promotion, and the decisions that make up sales promotion strategy.

Nature and Scope of Sales Promotion

Japanese companies employ an interesting form of promotion—showrooms that have hands-on new product displays.[22] The intent is to give people the opportunity to examine new products placed in attractive surroundings. The items displayed are not for sale in the showrooms. The sponsors want potential buyers to see the products, try them out, and become familiar with their features. For example, the Matsushita Electric Works showroom has a state-of-the-art home displaying the newest Japanese furnishings and appliances, as well as many gadgets.

The responsibility for sales promotion activities often spans several marketing functions, such as advertising, merchandising, product planning, and sales. For example, a sales contest for salespeople is typically designed and administered by sales managers and the costs of the contest are included in the sales department budget. Similarly, planning and coordinating a sampling or coupon refund program may be assigned to a product manager. Point-of-purchase promotion displays in retail stores may be the responsibility of the field sales organization.

Total expenditures for sales promotion by business and industry in the United States are much larger than the total spent on advertising, probably more than double advertising expenditures. The complete scope of sales promotion is often difficult to identify because the activities are included in various departments and budgets. Unlike advertising, sales promotion expenditures are not published.

A relevant issue is deciding how to manage the various sales promotion activities. While these programs are used to support advertising, pricing, channel of distribution, and personal selling strategies, the size and scope of sales promotion suggest that the responsibility for managing sales promotion should be assigned to one or a team of executives. Otherwise, sales promotion activities are fragmented, and may not be properly integrated with other promotion components. The chief marketing executive should assign responsibility for coordination and evaluation of sales promotion activities.

Sales Promotion Activities

Many activities may be part of the total promotion program, including trade shows, specialty advertising (e.g., imprinted calendars), contests, point-of-purchase displays, coupons, recognition programs (e.g., awards to top suppliers), and free samples. Expenditures for sales promotion may be very substantial. Companies may direct their sales promotion activities to consumer buyers, industrial buyers, channel members, and salespeople, as shown in Exhibit 12.8. Sales promotion programs fall into three major categories: incentives, promotional pricing, and informational activities.

EXHIBIT 12.8
Sales Promotion Activities Targeted to Various Groups

	Targeted to:			
Sales Promotion Activity	Consumer Buyers	Industrial Buyers	Channel Members	Salespeople
Incentives				
Contests	X	X	X	X
Trips	X	X	X	X
Bonuses			X	X
Prizes	X	X	X	X
Advertising support			X	
Free items	X	X		
Recognition			X	X
Promotional Pricing				
Coupons	X			
Allowances		X	X	
Rebates	X	X	X	
Cash	X			
Informational Activities				
Displays	X			
Demonstrations	X	X	X	
Selling aids			X	X
Specialty advertising (e.g., pens)	X	X	X	
Trade shows	X	X	X	

Strategy Feature

When the Factory Is a Theme Park

Ford's fancy $30 million visitor center, which reopens on May 3, doesn't present your typical factory tour. Rather, it's the latest example of what brand experts call "experiential" marketing. Frustrated by the growing difficulties of reaching consumers through traditional advertising, companies from Mattel Inc. to DaimlerChrysler are adding engrossing personal experiences to drive home the lessons behind their brand.

The beauty of a well-designed factory tour is that while it doesn't reach nearly as many people as a TV spot, it can attract the very consumers who are most likely to buy. Binney & Smith Inc.'s recently updated Crayola Factory in Easton, Pennsylvania, shows 375,000 kids and their families each year how crayons are made. But the real focus of the $9-a-head visit is finger painting, drawing, and other, well, hands-on projects using Crayola products in brightly colored play areas. Says marketing consultant Joe Pine, cofounder of Strategic Horizons: "You're getting potential customers to pay you to sell to them."

In a few cases, these "experiences" can be cash cows. Devotees of Mattel's American Girl historically themed dolls flock to its Chicago and New York emporiums, spending hundreds of dollars to take in musical shows, have their dolls' hair styled, or buy party packages. But for the most part, these setups are loss leaders geared at generating word of mouth. And if Ford's high-tech center succeeds in giving even some of its visitors a warm and fuzzy feeling about a manufacturing giant, it'll have pulled off a feat few ad campaigns could match.

Source: Kathleen Kerwin Dearborn, "When the Factory Is a Theme Park," *BusinessWeek*, May 3, 2004, 93.

Promotion to Consumer Targets. Sales promotion is used in the marketing of many consumer goods and services. It includes a wide variety of activities, as illustrated in Exhibit 12.8. A key management concern is evaluating the effectiveness of promotions such as coupons, rebates, contests, and other awards. The large expenditures necessary to support these programs require that the results and costs be objectively assessed.

The sponsoring of sports events and individuals is a major initiative by various companies and brands. Sales promotion results from the association of the brand with the event or person. An example is PepsiCo's sponsorship of the Pepsi 400 NASCAR race. Similarly, sports celebrities may be sponsored, such as cyclist Lance Armstrong in the Tour de France. The strategy issue is determining the benefits versus costs of these sales promotion activities.

The use of factory tours and visiting centers is an interesting form of sales promotion that is being aggressively pursued by various manufacturers of consumer products, in their efforts to overcome the difficulties of communicating to consumers via traditional advertising media. The Strategy Feature describes the "experiential marketing" initiatives of several companies.

Promotion to Industrial Targets. Many of the sales promotion methods that are used for consumer products also apply to industrial products, although the role and scope of the methods may vary. For example, trade shows perform a key role in small and medium-sized companies' marketing strategies. The advantage of the trade show is the heavy concentration of potential buyers at one location during a very short time. The cost per contact is much less than a salesperson calling on prospects at their offices. While people attending trade shows also spend their time viewing competitors' products, an effective display and buyer/seller interactions offer a unique opportunity to hold the prospects' attention.

The Internet has many of the features of trade shows while eliminating certain of their limitations. For example, the Web enables the French woolens manufacturer Carreman to provide its customers fabric samples in one day.[23] The company posted its top fabrics on the Etexx Web site for online sample ordering. Management is optimistic that its customers will respond favorably to the initiative. Etexx, a start-up based in Nice, created an e-marketplace for buyers and sellers of fabrics.

Sales promotion programs that target industrial buyers may consume a greater portion of the marketing budget than advertising. Many of these activities support personal selling strategies.

They include catalogs, brochures, product information reports, samples, trade shows, application guides, and promotional items such as calendars, pens, and calculators.

Promotion to Value-Chain Members. Sales promotion is an important part of manufacturers' marketing efforts to wholesalers and retailers for such products as foods, beverages, and appliances. Catalogs and other product information are essential promotional components for many lines. The Internet offers an alternative way to make catalog information available. Promotional pricing is often used to push new products through channels of distribution. Various incentives are popular in marketing to value-chain members. Specialty advertising items such as calendars and memo pads are used in maintaining buyer awareness of brands and company names.

Promotion to the Sales Force. Incentives and informational activities are the primary forms of promotion used to assist and motivate company sales forces. Sales contests and prizes are popular. Companies also make wide use of recognition programs like the "salesperson of the year." Promotional information is vital to salespeople. Presentation kits help salespeople describe new products and the features of existing products.

A high-tech promotion tool with strong potential is the automated sales presentation created with integrated use of sound, graphics, and video briefcase computers. These multimedia or interactive techniques give salespeople powerful presentation capabilities, allowing them access to a complete product information system available in the notebook computer.

Advantages and Limitations of Sales Promotion

Because of its wide array of incentive, pricing, and communication capabilities, sales promotion has the flexibility to contribute to various marketing objectives. A marketing manager can target buyers, channel members, and salespeople and the sales response of the sales promotion activities can be measured to determine their effectiveness. For example, a company can track its coupon redemption or rebate success. Many of the incentive and price promotion techniques trigger the purchase of other products.

Sales promotion is not without its disadvantages, however. In most instances, rather than a substitute for advertising and personal selling, sales promotion supports other promotional efforts. Control is essential to prevent some people from taking advantage of free offers, coupons, and other incentives. Value-added resellers may build inventories on products receiving manufacturers' trade discounts. Incentives and price-promotional activities need to be monitored. An effective advertisement can be run thousands of times, but promotional campaigns are usually not reusable. Thus, the costs of development must be evaluated in advance.

Sales Promotion Strategy

The steps in developing the sales promotion strategy are similar to the design of advertising strategy. It is necessary to first define the communications task(s) that the sales promotion program is expected to accomplish. Next, specific promotion objectives are set regarding awareness levels and purchase intentions. It is important to evaluate the relative cost-effectiveness of feasible sales promotion methods and to select those that offer the best results/cost combination. Both the content of the sales promotion and its timing should be coordinated with other promotion activities. Finally, the program is implemented and is evaluated on a continuing basis. Evaluation measures the extent to which objectives are achieved. For example, trade show results can be evaluated to determine how many show contacts are converted to purchases.

Summary

Promotion strategy is a vital part of the positioning strategy. The components—advertising, sales promotion, public relations, personal selling, direct marketing, and interactive/Internet marketing—offer an impressive array of capabilities for communicating with market targets and other relevant audiences. However, promotion activities are expensive. Management must decide the size of the promotion budget and allocate it to the promotion components. Each promotion activity offers certain unique advantages and also shares several characteristics with the other components.

Promotion strategy is guided by the market targeting and positioning strategies. Communication objectives must be determined and the role of each promotion component selected by marketing management. Budgeting indicates the amount and allocation of resources to the promotion strategy. The major budgeting methods are objective and task, percent of sales, competitive parity, and all you can afford. Several product and market factors affect whether the promotion strategy will emphasize advertising, sales promotion, personal selling, or seek a balance between the forms of promotion. The effective integration of the communications program is a major challenge for many firms. Finally, the effectiveness of the promotion strategy is evaluated.

The steps in developing advertising strategy include identifying the target audience, deciding the role of advertising in the promotional mix, indicating advertising objectives and budget size, selecting the creative strategy, determining the media and programming schedule, and implementing the program and measuring its effectiveness. Advertising objectives may range from audience exposure to profit contribution. Advertising agencies offer specialized services for developing creative strategies, designing messages, and selecting media and programming strategies. Measuring advertising effectiveness is essential in managing this expensive resource.

Our discussion of sales promotion highlights several methods that are available for use as incentives, advertising support, and informational activities. Typically, firms use sales promotion activities in conjunction with advertising and personal selling rather than as a primary component of promotion strategy. Promotion programs may target consumer buyers, industrial buyers, middlemen, and salespeople. Sales promotion strategy should be based on the selection of methods that provide the best results/cost combinations for achieving the communications objectives.

Internet Applications

A. Discuss how Godiva Chocolatier's Web site (*www.godiva.com*) corresponds to the brand image portrayed by its retail stores. What are the promotion objectives that Godiva's management seems to be pursuing on the Web site?

B. Go the Web sites of NBC and the BBC (*www.nbc.com* and *www.bbc.co.uk*). Contrast the ways NBC and the BBC promote their daily TV programs online. Which similarities and differences do you detect? Suggest ways of improvement considering the respective cultural frame of reference and target market for NBC and BBC.

C. Discuss how Apple's (*www.apple.com*) marketing strategy for iPod Mini is enhanced by a Web-based approach.

Feature Applications

A. Consider the promotion activities described in the Internet Feature. Discuss how these initiatives offer compelling advantages over traditional promotion strategies.

B. Review the Strategy Feature concerning the use of the factory as a theme park. Identify other products and markets where this sales promotion method may display favorable benefits and cost relationships.

Questions for Review and Discussion

1. Compare and contrast the role of promotion in an international public accounting firm with promotion by American Airlines.
2. Identify and discuss the factors that are important in determining the promotion program for the following products:
   a. Video tape recorder/player.
   b. Personal computer.
   c. Boeing 7E7 Dreamliner commercial aircraft.
   d. Residential homes.
3. What are the important considerations in determining a promotion budget?
4. Under what conditions is a firm's promotion strategy more likely to be advertising/sales promotion-driven rather than personal selling-driven?
5. Discuss the advantages and limitations of using awareness as an advertising objective. When might this objective be appropriate?
6. Identify and discuss the important differences between advertising and sales promotion strategies in the marketing promotion strategy.
7. Coordination of advertising and personal selling strategies is a major challenge in large companies. Outline a plan for integrating these strategies.
8. Discuss the role of sales promotion methods in the promotion strategy of a major airline.
9. How and to what extent is the Internet likely to be useful in companies' promotion strategies?

Notes

1. This illustration is based on "The Vuitton Machine," *BusinessWeek,* March 22, 2004, 98–100, 102.
2. "Mad Ave: The Sizzle Will Be a Harder Sell," *BusinessWeek,* January 12, 2004, 119.
3. Suzanne Vranica, "Schick Challenges Gillette with $120 Million Campaign," *The Wall Street Journal,* April 17, 2003, A18.
4. Gardiner Harris, "Drug Makers Go Hollywood, Finding Marketing Pays," *The Wall Street Journal,* July 6, 2000, 1.
5. Mark W. Johnston and Greg W. Marshall, *Sales Force Management.* 7th ed. (Burr Ridge, IL: McGraw-Hill/Irwin, 2003), 48.
6. "Exclusive Interview: Mike Gunn of American Airlines," *Colloquy* 3, no. 2 (1992), 8–10.
7. George E. Belch and Michael A. Belch, *Advertising and Promotion.* 6th ed. (Burr Ridge, IL: McGraw-Hill/Irwin, 2004), 695.
8. "SIA Presses for Higher Yields with New Aircraft, IFE Systems," *Aviation Week & Space Technology,* June 4, 2001, 69–70.
9. Betsy McKay, "PepsiCo Bases Water Ads on 'Nothing,'" *The Wall Street Journal,* June 25, 2001, B10.
10. Roger D. Blackwell, *From Mind to Market* (New York: Harper Business, 1997), 182–183.
11. Ibid.
12. Belch and Belch, *Advertising and Promotion,* 11.
13. Wendy Bounds and Deborah Ball, "Italy Knits Support for Fashion Industry," *The Wall Street Journal,* December 15, 1997, B8.
14. Advertising budgeting models are discussed in Gary L. Lilien, Phillip Kotler, and Sridhar Moerlhy, *Marketing Models* (Englewood Cliffs, NJ: Prentice-Hall, 1992), Chapter 6.
15. George E. Belch and Michael A. Belch, *Advertising and Promotion.* 5th ed. (New York: Irwin/McGraw-Hill, 2001), 262.
16. William F. Arens, *Advertising.* 9th ed. (Burr Ridge, IL: McGraw-Hill/Irwin, 2004), 384.
17. Dr. John Loden, *Megabrands* (Homewood, IL: Business One Irwin, 1992), 188–190.
18. Belch and Belch, *Advertising and Promotion.* 5th ed. 517.
19. Roland T. Rust, *Advertising Media Models* (Lexington, MA: D.C. Heath, 1986).
20. George S. Low and Jakki J. Mohr, "Advertising vs. Sales Promotion: A Brand Management Perspective," *Journal of Product & Brand Management* 9, no. 6 (2000), 389–414; Andrew J. Parsons, Focus and Squeeze: Consumer Marketing in the '90s," *Marketing Management,* Winter 1992, 51–55.
21. Belch and Belch, *Advertising and Promotion,* 6th ed., Chapter 16.
22. Mary Roach, "Attack of the Killer Showroom," *American Way,* November 15, 1995, 108, 110, and 112.
23. "Streamlining," *BusinessWeek,* E.Biz, September 18, 2000, EB70.

Chapter 13

Sales Force, Internet, and Direct Marketing Strategies

Sales organizations in many companies have experienced significant changes over the last decade. Transactional selling activities are being performed via the Internet, while salespeople are more focused on collaborative and consulting relationships. Contrary to some forecasts the role of selling has not deteriorated. However, major shifts have occurred in how the selling function is being performed. Personal selling, the Internet, and direct marketing responsibilities have been impacted by the changes. The Internet has become an important avenue of direct contact between customers and companies selling goods and services. Companies may use a combination of salespeople, direct marketing, and the Internet to perform selling and sales support functions. Coordinating an organization's activities across multiple customer contact initiatives is essential to avoid conflicts and enhance overall results.

Salesforce.com is an interesting example of a dot.com start-up, which has developed a successful business model supplying customer management software over the Net for use by salespeople. A key feature of the software is that it is sold as a service to customers at $65 per month for each individual user. Salesforce.com has nearly 10,000 customers like SunGuard Data Systems Inc., which purchase the customer management software service for 1,000 salespeople worldwide.[1] The company has customers in 65 countries. Salesforce.com illustrates how Internet information technology can enhance the capabilities and efforts of salespeople. By replacing large up-front software purchases with monthly service charges Salesforce.com offers customers a compelling value opportunity. Since this feature can be duplicated by software competitors such as Siebel Systems, Oracle, and PeopleSoft, Salesforce.com may have difficulty sustaining its competitive edge.

Office Depot Inc. is an interesting example of a company that has successfully implemented an Internet strategy while avoiding conflict with the large direct sales force of its Business Services Group that sells to medium-to-large size organizational customers. The company's Internet strategy is described in the Internet Feature.

In this chapter we first discuss developing and implementing sales force strategy. Next, we consider the issues and initiatives concerning Internet strategy. Finally, we describe and illustrate the various methods used in direct marketing.

Developing and Implementing Sales Force Strategy

Sales force strategy is concerned with deciding how to use personal selling to contact sales prospects and build the types of customer relationships that management considers necessary to accomplish the organization's marketing objectives. Personal selling activities vary considerably

Internet Feature

Office Depot's Successful Internet Strategy

- Using a seamless network, Web operations are integrated into Office Depot's existing businesses.
- An easy-to-use electronic link is provided between the online store and internal networks.
- Purchasing authorizations and limits are incorporated into the system.
- Ease of use rather than technology is the key priority for improving the online network.
- Bonuses are offered to salespeople to encourage corporate customers to use online ordering.
- Sales applicants are tested concerning Internet familiarity and informed of the importance of Office Depot's online initiatives during the hiring process.
- Office Depot's Internet-sourced sales have increased at double digit rates from $1 billion in 2000. The online business was profitable in its first year.

Source: Charles Haddad, "Office Depot's E-Diva," *BusinessWeek E.biz*, August 6, 2001, EB22–EB24.

EXHIBIT 13.1
Developing Sales Force Strategy

Determine the role of the sales force in the promotion strategy

⇩

Define the selling process (how selling will be accomplished)

⇩

Decide if and how alternative sales channels will be utilized

⇩

Design the sales organization

⇩

Recruit, train, and manage salespeople

⇩

Evaluate performance and make adjustments where necessary

across companies based on how personal selling contributes to marketing positioning strategy and promotion strategy. For example, a Pfizer pharmaceutical salesperson maintains regular contact with doctors and other professionals, but actual purchases are made at retail outlets where the prescriptions are filled. Nonetheless, Pfizer's salespeople play a vital role in the company's marketing strategy. The drug salesperson provides information on new products, distributes samples, and works toward building long-term relationships.

Developing sales force strategy includes six major steps as shown in Exhibit 13.1. First, the role of the sales force in the promotion strategy is determined. This requires deciding how personal selling is expected to contribute to the marketing program. Second, the selling process must be determined, indicating how selling will be accomplished with targeted customers. Third, in selecting sales channels, management decides how field selling, major account management, telemarketing, and the Internet will contribute to the selling process. Fourth, the design of the sales organization

Ethics Feature

Challenges in Selling and Sales Management

Two sets of ethical dilemmas are of particular concern to sales managers. The first set is embedded in the manager's dealings with the salespeople. Ethical issues involved in relationships between a sales manager and the sales force include such things as fairness and equal treatment of all social groups in hiring and promotion, respect for the individual in supervisory practices and training programs, and fairness and integrity in the design of sales territories, assignment of quotas, and determination of compensation and incentive rewards. Ethical issues pervade nearly all aspects of sales force management.

The second set of ethical issues arises from the interactions between salespeople and their customers. These issues only indirectly involve the sales manager because the manager cannot always directly observe or control the actions of every member of the sales force. But managers have a responsibility to establish standards of ethical behavior for their subordinates, communicate them clearly, and enforce them vigorously.

Source: Mark W. Johnston and Greg W. Marshall, *Sales Force Management*. 7th ed. (Burr Ridge, IL: McGraw-Hill/Irwin, 2003), 21.

must be examined to determine its effectiveness. A new design needs to be selected for a new organization. Fifth, salespeople are recruited, trained, and managed. Finally, the results of the selling strategy are evaluated and adjustments are made to narrow the gap between actual and desired results.

Salespeople's interactions with many customers and the geographical dispersion of salespeople are likely to create more ethical issues than are experienced in other types of jobs. Sales managers may encounter a wide range of ethical issues as discussed in the Ethics Feature.

The Role of Selling in Promotion Strategy

Salespeople's responsibilities may range from order takers to extensive collaboration as consultants to customers. While management has some flexibility in choosing the role and objectives of the sales force in the marketing program, several factors often guide the role of selling in a firm's marketing strategy, as shown in Exhibit 13.2. Considerable direction as to how personal selling will be used is provided by the target market, product characteristics, distribution policies, and pricing policies. The selling effort needs to be positioned into the integrated communications program. It is also useful to indicate how the other promotion-mix components, such as advertising, support and relate to the sales force. Sales management needs to be aware of the plans and activities of other promotion components.

The objectives assigned to salespeople frequently involve management's expected sales results. Sales quotas are used to state these expectations. Companies may give incentives to salespeople who achieve their quotas. Team selling incentives may also be used. Objectives other than sales are important in many organizations. These include increasing the number of new accounts, providing services to customers and channel organizations, retaining customers, selecting and evaluating middlemen, and obtaining market information. The objectives selected need to be consistent with marketing strategy and promotion objectives, and measurable so that salesperson performance can be evaluated.

Sales & Marketing Management uses four categories of responsibilities to define the range of personal selling roles. The categories are as follows:[2]

- **Transactional Selling.** Selling is largely based on price and the products involved are often commodities.
- **Feature/Benefit Selling.** In these selling situations, price and features are equally important.
- **Solution Selling.** The product is matched to clients' needs and price is secondary to obtaining a successful product application.

EXHIBIT 13.2 Factors Influencing the Role of Personal Selling in a Firm's IMC Strategy

Source: Mark W. Johnston and Greg W. Marshall, *Sales Force Management*. 7th ed. (Burr Ridge, IL: McGraw-Hill/Irwin, 2003), 87. Copyright © The McGraw-Hill Companies. Used with permission.

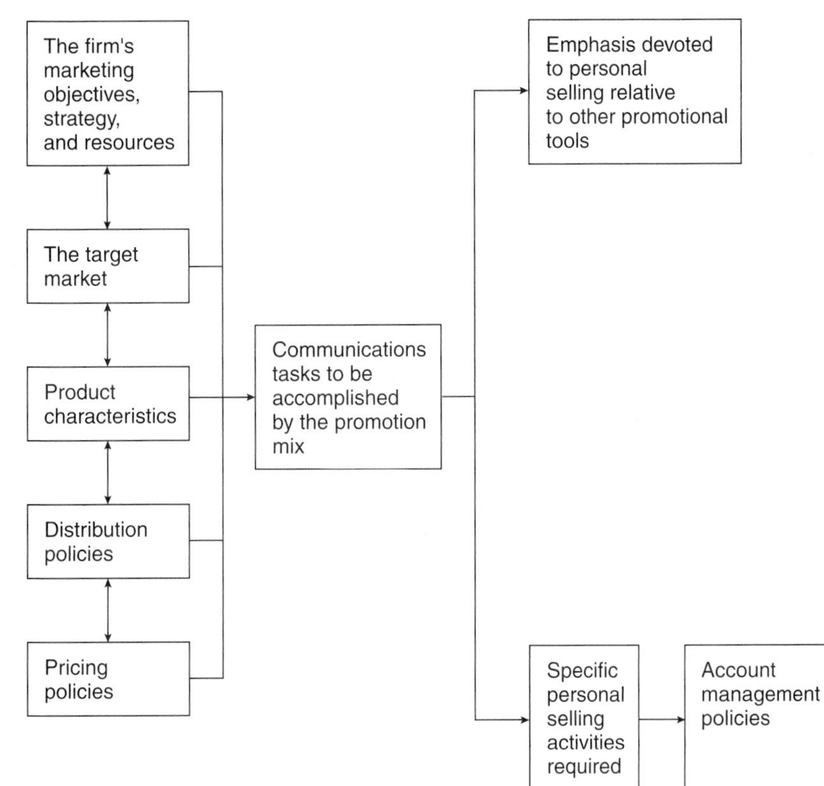

- **Value-Added Selling.** These situations involve consulting-type relationships using team approaches. Price is relevant but is not the driver.

The Internet is replacing salespeople in transactional selling, whereas it is more likely to provide support for the other three categories.

The *Sales & Marketing Management* compensation survey reported average total compensation for top-performance salespeople at $153,417 in 2003.[3] Incentive pay (bonus and commissions) was 43 percent of total compensation. Average compensation for midlevel performers was $92,337. Substantial 2004 pay increases for salespeople were forecast by most of the executives surveyed in the *S&MM* survey.

Types of Sales Jobs

The salespeople that sell to ultimate consumers (door-to-door sales, insurance sales, real estate brokers, retail store sales, etc.) comprise a major portion of the number of salespeople, but a much greater volume of sales is accounted for by organizational (business-to-business) salespeople.[4] Organizational sales may be to resellers (e.g., retail chains), business users, and institutions. Consumer and organizational sales are similar in several respects, but organizational sales may involve more complex products, larger and more extensive purchasing processes, different selling skills, and more extensive management processes (e.g., training, coaching, directing, and evaluating).

Illustrative sales positions for organizational salespeople include new business, trade selling, missionary selling, and consultative/technical selling.[5]

New Business Selling. This selling job involves obtaining sales from new buyers. The buyers may be one-time purchasers or repeat buyers. For example, recruiting a new online business customer by an Office Depot salesperson is an illustration of a one-time selling situation. Alternatively, the selling strategy may be concerned with obtaining new buyers on a continuing basis. Commercial insurance and real estate sales firms use this strategy.

Trade Selling. This form of selling provides assistance and support to value-chain members rather than obtaining sales. A manufacturer marketing through wholesalers, retailers, or other intermediaries may provide merchandising, logistical, promotional, and product information assistance. PepsiCo's field sales organization assists retailers in merchandising and support activities, works closely with bottlers, and builds relationships with fast-food and other retailers selling drinks on premises.

Missionary Selling. A strategy similar to trade selling is missionary selling. In these selling situations the producer's salespeople work with the customers of a channel member to encourage them to purchase the producer's product from the channel member. For example, commercial airline sales representatives contact travel agencies and corporate customers, providing them with schedule information on new routes and encouraging them to book flights on their airline.

Consultative/Technical Selling Strategy. Firms that use this strategy sell to an existing customer base, and provide technical and application assistance. These positions may involve the sales of complex equipment or services such as management consulting. Selling of commercial aircraft to airlines is another example of consultative selling.

An organization may use more than one of the above selling strategies. For example, a transportation services company might use a new business strategy for expanding its customer base and a missionary selling strategy for servicing existing customers. The skills needed by the salesperson vary according to the selling strategy used.

Several changes are under way in many sales organizations. The reforming process requires redesigning the traditional sales organization, leveraging information technology to lower costs and provide quick response, designing the sales strategy to meet different customer needs, building long-term relationships with customers and business partners, and responding proactively to global competitive opportunities and challenges. The sales force continues to be essential in many organizations, but salespeople are being asked to assume new responsibilities, and the methods for keeping score are changing. An interesting analysis of the changes occurring in both consumer and business marketing is shown in the Strategy Feature. It highlights the evolving emphasis on customer relationship management and the use of the Internet and direct marketing methods in combination with personal selling processes.

Defining the Selling Process

Several selling and sales support activities are involved in moving from identifying a buyer's needs to completing the sale and managing the postsale relationships between buyer and seller. The resulting selling process includes (1) prospecting for customers, (2) opening the relationship, (3) qualifying the prospect, (4) presenting the sales message, (5) closing the sale, and (6) servicing the account.[6] The process may be very simple, consisting of a routine set of actions designed to close the sale. Alternatively, the process may extend over a long time period, with many contacts and interactions between the buyers, other people influencing the purchase, the salesperson assigned to the account, and technical specialists in the seller's organization. Recall the different selling roles discussed earlier, which range from routine actions (transactional selling) to consulting relationships (value-added selling).

Sales management determines the selling process by indicating the customers and prospects the firm is targeting and the guidelines for developing customer relationships and obtaining sales results. This process is management's strategy for achieving the sales force objectives in the selling environment of interest. Salespeople implement the process following the guidelines set by management, such as the product strategy (relative emphasis on different products), customer targeting and priorities, and the desired selling activities and outcomes.

Strategy Feature — The Shifting Language of Marketing

Decaying: **The Old Consumer Marketing Paradigm**	*Emerging:* **New Common Paradigm**	*Decaying:* **The Old Business Marketing Paradigm**
Broadcast communication, hard to customize	Conversations managed from the center	Communication in the field, hard to standardize
Segments	Markets of one	Territories
Market share	Share of customer	Account potential
Survey research	Transaction databases	Call reports
Products	Processes	Products
Brand equity	Customer equity	Account profitability
Brand managers	Customer relationship managers	Account managers

Source: John Deighton, "Commentary on Exploring the Implications of the Internet for Consumer Marketing," *Journal of the Academy of Marketing Science,* Fall 1997, 350.

The selling process is normally managed by the salesperson who has responsibility for a customer account, although an increasing number of companies are assigning this responsibility to customer relationship management teams. Account management includes planning and execution of the selling activities between the salesperson and the customer or prospect. Some organizations analyze this process and set guidelines for use by salespeople to plan their selling activities. Process analysis may result in programmed selling steps or alternatively, may lead to highly customized selling approaches where the salesperson develops specific strategies for each account. A company may also use team selling (e.g., product specialists and salesperson), major account management, telemarketing, and Internet support systems.

Corporate restructuring in the 1990s created the need to reengineer sales processes in many companies.[7] Indications of a possible need for a change in the sales process include faulty forecasting, inconsistent sales performances, sales declines, lost customers, new customers from acquisitions, drops in profit margins, and price wars. The changes made by FedEx Corp. are illustrative.[8] Management combined its air and ground freight sales forces in 2000. Rather than having to deal with separate sales forces, customers are now contacted by salespeople representing both air and ground services. The changes provided more uniform coverage and eliminated costly duplicated coverage. FedEx has had strong sales and profit growth since 2000, moving from $18.3 to an estimated $27 billion in sales for 2005 and $2.32 to an estimated $3.85 earnings per share in 2005 These changes are illustrative of customer management strategies being implemented by several companies.

The selling process provides guidelines for sales force recruiting, training, allocation of effort, organizational design, and the use of selling support activities such as telemarketing and the Internet. Understanding the selling process is essential in coordinating all elements of the marketing program.

Sales Channels

An important part of deciding the personal selling strategy is consideration of the alternative channels to end user customers. Management must decide (1) which channel(s) to use in contacting value-chain members and end users; and (2) how telemarketing, Internet, and direct marketing will be used to support the field sales force. For example, management may decide to contact major accounts using national or global account managers, contact regular accounts using the field sales force and service, small accounts via telemarketing or the Internet. The reality is that direct contact by face-to-face salespeople is very expensive and this resource should be analyzed in terms of benefits and costs.

The choice of a particular sales channel is influenced by the buying power of customers, the selling channel threshold levels, and the complexity of buyer-seller relationships.[9] We discuss customer contact requirements to illustrate the strengths and limitations of alternative sales channels.

Customer Buying Power. The purchasing potential of customers and prospects often places them into different importance categories. The "major" or "global" account represents the most important customer category. This customer (1) purchases a significant volume on an absolute dollar basis and as a percent of a supplier's total sales, and (2) purchases (or influences the purchase) from a central or headquarters location for several geographically dispersed organizational units.[10] The buying power of a supplier's total customer base may range from several major accounts to a large number of very low volume purchasers. Customers and prospects can be classified into (1) major accounts, (2) other customers requiring face-to-face contact, and (3) accounts whose purchases (or potential) do not justify regular contact by field salespeople.

Threshold Levels. The number of customers in each buying power category influences the selection of selling channels. The need for a multiple selling channel strategy should be determined. For example, the amount of telemarketing effort that is needed determines whether a telemarketing or electronic support unit should be considered. Similarly, enough major accounts should exist in order to develop and implement a major account program. If the customer base does not display substantial differences in purchasing power and servicing requirements, then the use of a single sales force channel may be appropriate.

Complexity of the Customer Relationship. The account management relationship is also a key factor as to the type of sales channel that is appropriate. For example, a customer that (1) has several people involved in the buying process; (2) seeks a long-term, cooperative relationship with the supplier; and (3) requires specialized attention and service creates a relatively complex buyer-seller relationship.[11] Such a relationship coupled with sufficient buying power suggests the use of a major account management channel. In contrast, a simple, routinized buying situation suggests direct marketing or Internet buyer-seller linkages. The field selling channel corresponds best to customer relationships that fall between very complex and highly routinized.

There is a trend toward greater use of customer management strategies by many companies. For example, Newell Rubbermaid Inc., producer of a range of consumer household products, has a major sales force initiative under way to introduce new products and build relationships with retailers.[12] The nearly 900 salespeople work with stores in spotlighting Newell Rubbermaid products and conduct product comparisons in the stores for end users. Hundreds of college graduates have been recruited to strengthen relationships with retailers.

Designing the Sales Organization

Designing a sales organization includes selecting an organizational structure and deciding the size and deployment of salespeople to geographical areas and/or customers and prospects.

Organizational Design. The organizational approach adopted should support the firm's sales force strategy. As companies adjust their selling strategies, organizational structure may also require changes. FedEx's shift to a single sales force for its air and ground services is illustrative. There is a clear trend toward a greater focus on customers (market driven) rather than products or geography as the basis for the design of the sales organization.

The characteristics of the customer base, the product(s), and the geographic location of buyers are the more important influences on the design of the sales organization. The answers to several questions are helpful in narrowing the choice of an organizational design.

1. What is the selling job? What activities are to be performed by salespeople?
2. Is specialization of selling effort necessary according to type of customer, different products, or salesperson activities (e.g., sales and service)?
3. Are channel-of-distribution relationships important in the organizational design?
4. How many and what kinds of sales management levels are needed to provide the proper amount of supervision, assistance, and control?
5. Will sales teams be used, and if so, what will be their composition?
6. How and to what extent will sales channels other than the field sales force be used?

The sales force organizational design needs to be compatible with the selling strategy and other marketing program strategies. The major types of organization designs are shown in Exhibit 13.3. These designs take into account the scope of the product portfolio and differences in customer needs. Whenever the customer base is widely dispersed, geography is likely to be relevant in the organizational design. The market-driven design is heavily influenced by the customer base, although geographical location may also influence the design. The product/market design takes both factors into account in determining how the organization is structured. Similar customer needs and a complex range of products point to the product-driven design. If the product or the customer base does not dominate design considerations, a geographical organization is used. The assigned area and (or) accounts that are the responsibility of the salesperson comprise the sales territory or work unit.

Sales Force Deployment. Sales management must decide how many salespeople are needed and how to deploy them to customers and prospects. Several factors outside the salesperson's control often affect his or her sales results, such as market potential, number and location of customers, intensity of competition, and market (brand) position of the company. Sales force deployment analysis needs to consider both salesperson factors and the relevant uncontrollable factors.

EXHIBIT 13.3
Sales Organization Designs

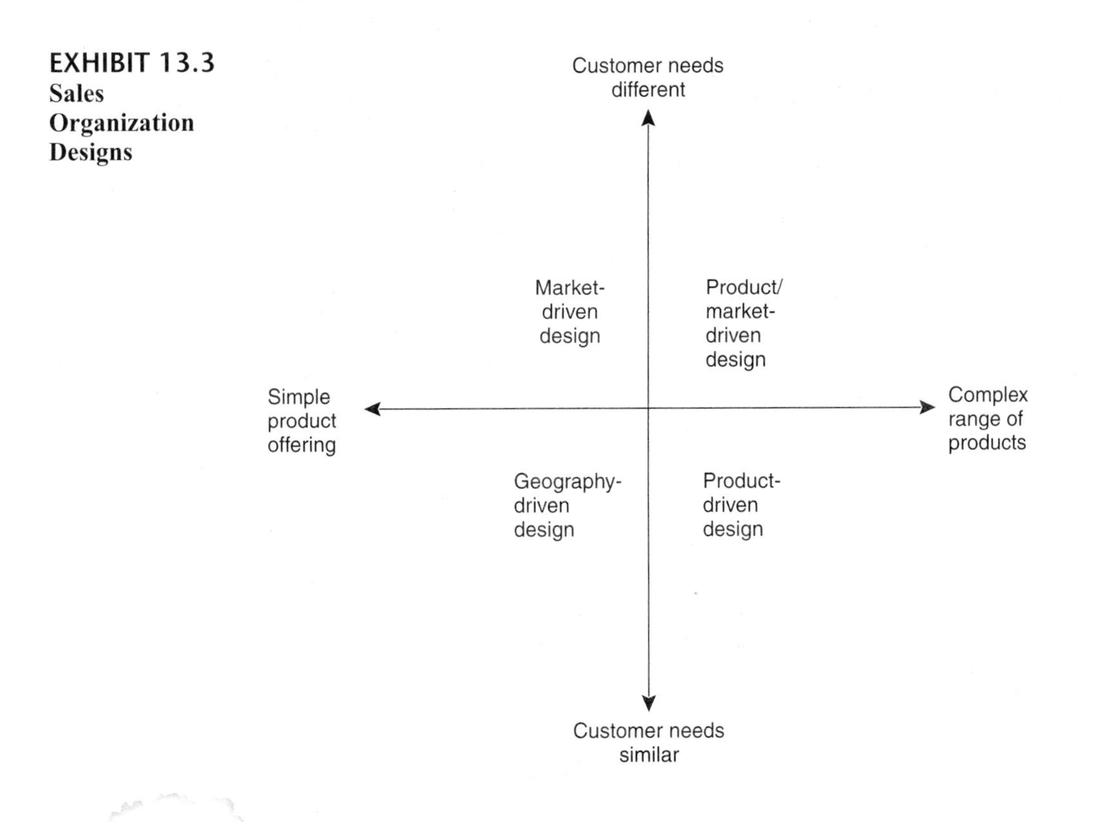

Several methods are available for analyzing sales force size and the deployment of selling effort including (1) revenue/cost analysis, (2) single-factor models, (3) sales and effort response models, and (4) portfolio deployment models. Normally, sales and/or costs are the basis for determining sales force size and allocation.

Revenue/cost analysis techniques require information on each salesperson's sales and/or costs. One approach compares each salesperson to an average breakeven sales level, thus helping management to spot unprofitable territories. Another approach analyzes the profit performance of accounts or trading areas, to estimate the profit impact of adding more salespeople, or to determine how many people a new sales organization needs. These techniques are very useful in locating high- and low-performance territories.

Single-factor models assume that size and/or effort deployment are determined by one factor, such as market potential or workload (e.g., number of calls required), whose values can be used to determine required selling effort. Suppose there are two territories, X and Y. Territory X has double the market potential (opportunity for business) of territory Y. If selling effort is deployed according to market potential, X should get double the selling effort of Y.

Consideration of multiple influences (e.g., market potential, intensity of competition, and workload) on market response can improve salesperson deployment decisions. Several promising *sales and effort response models* are available to assist management on sales force size and deployment decisions.[13] Exhibit 13.4 shows the information provided by one of these models. The analysis indicates that Jones's territory requires only about 36 percent of a person whereas Smith's territory needs about 2.36 people. The inadequate sales coverage in Smith's territory is risky in terms of dissatisfaction and loss of customers. The allocations are determined by incrementally increasing selling effort in high-response areas and reducing effort where sales response is low. Note that Exhibit 13.4 includes only two territories of a large sales organization. Sales response is determined from a computer analysis of the selling effort-to-sales response relationship.

EXHIBIT 13.4 Sales Force Deployment Analysis Illustration for Jones's and Smith's Territories

	Trading Area†	Present Effort (percent)	Recommended Effort (percent)	Estimated Sales* Present Effort	Estimated Sales* Recommended Effort
Jones:					
	1	10%	4%	$ 19	$ 13
	2	60	20	153	120
	3	15	7	57	50
	4	5	2	10	7
	5	10	3	21	16
	Total	100%	36%	$ 260	$ 206
Smith:					
	1	18%	81%	$ 370	$ 520
	2	7	21	100	130
	3	5	11	55	65
	4	35	35	225	225
	5	5	11	60	70
	6	30	77	400	500
	Total	100%	236%	$ 1,210	$ 1,510

*In $000.
†Each territory is made up of several trading areas.

The Swiss Drug Maker Novartis Strengthens Sales Force Capabilities

Novartis' 1999 sales growth was very low compared to rivals' double-digit sales increases. Top management launched a major turnaround strategy, spearheaded by new product initiatives and strengthening of the sales force.

- Salespeople were provided customer research information to focus their targeting efforts.
- The size of the sales force was increased from 2,815 to 6,200 in 2002.
- Collaboration and persistence were determined to be key traits of high-performance Novartis salespeople.
- Major efforts were initiated to upgrade the sales force and improve selling and product training.

Source: Excerpt from "New Prescription: Its Rivals in a Funk, Novartis Finds a Technique to Thrive," *The Wall Street Journal*, August 23, 2002, A1 and A5.

Managing the Sales Force

The Novartis pharmaceutical company headquartered in Basel, Switzerland, is an interesting example of a company that made changes to strengthen its sales force in the early 2000s. The Global Feature describes several of Novartis' actions.

We know that salespeople differ in ability, motivation, and performance. Managers are involved in selecting, training, monitoring, directing, evaluating, and rewarding salespeople. A brief look at each activity highlights the responsibilities and functions of a sales manager.

Finding and Selecting Salespeople. A major study of the chief sales executives in over 100 firms selling business-to-business products asked them to indicate on a 1 to 10 scale how important 29 salesperson characteristics are to the success of their salespeople.[14] The executives indicated that the three most significant success characteristics are (1) being customer-driven and highly committed to the job; (2) accepting direction and cooperating as a team player; and (3) being motivated by one's peers, financial incentives, and oneself.

Exhibit 13.5 shows several characteristics that are often important for different types of selling situations. The characteristics vary based on the type of selling strategy being employed, so we must first define the job that is to be performed. Managers use application forms, personal interviews, rating forms, reference checks, physical examinations, and various kinds of tests to assist them in making hiring decisions. The personal interview is widely cited as the most important part of the selection process for salespeople.

Training. Some firms use formal programs to train their salespeople; others use informal on-the-job training. Factors that affect the type and duration of training include size of firm, type of sales job, product complexity, experience of new salespeople, and management's commitment to training. Training topics may include selling concepts and techniques, product knowledge, territory management, and company policies and operating procedures.

In training salespeople, companies may seek to (1) increase productivity, (2) improve morale, (3) lower turnover, (4) improve customer relations, and (5) enable better management of time and territory.[15] These objectives are concerned with increasing results from the salesperson's effort and/or reducing selling costs. Sales training should be evaluated concerning its benefits and costs. Evaluations may include before-and-after training results, participant critiques, and comparison of salespeople receiving training to those that have not been trained. Product knowledge training is probably more widespread than any other type of training.

Supervising and Motivating Salespeople. The manager that supervises salespeople has a key role in implementing a firm's selling strategy. He or she faces several important management issues. Coordinating the activities of a field sales force is difficult due to lack of regular contact.

EXHIBIT 13.5 Characteristics Related to Sales Performance in Different Types of Sales Jobs

Source: Mark Johnston and Greg Marshall, *Sales Force Management*. 7th ed. (Burr Ridge, IL: McGraw-Hill/Irwin, 2003), 312. Copyright © The McGraw-Hill Companies. Used with permission.

Type of Sales Job	Characteristics That Are Relatively Important	Characteristics That Are Relatively Less Important
Trade selling	Age, maturity, empathy, knowledge of customer needs and business methods	Aggressiveness, technical ability, product knowledge, persuasiveness
Missionary selling	Youth, high energy and stamina, verbal skill, persuasiveness	Empathy, knowledge of customers, maturity, previous sales experience
Technical selling	Education, product and customer knowledge—usually gained through training, intelligence	Empathy, persuasiveness, aggressiveness, age
New business selling	Experience, age and maturity, aggressiveness, persuasiveness, persistence	Customer knowledge, product knowledge, education, empathy

Compensation incentives are often used to encourage salespeople to obtain sales. However, salespeople need to be internally motivated. As discussed earlier, sales executives want salespeople who are customer-driven and committed to the company and to team relationships.

The most widely used compensation plan is a combination of salary and incentive (80 percent salary and 20 percent incentive pay is a typical arrangement). The compensation plan should be fair to all participants and create an appropriate incentive. Salespeople also respond favorably to recognition programs and special promotions such as vacation travel awards.

Managers assist and encourage salespeople, and incentives highlight the importance of results, but the salesperson is the driving force in selling situations. Sales management must match promising selling opportunities with competent and self-motivated professional salespeople while providing the proper company environment, leadership, and collaborative support. Although most sales management professionals consider financial compensation the most important motivating force, recent research indicates that personal characteristics, environmental conditions, and company policies and procedures are also important motivating factors.[16]

A recent study involving a large (1,000+) sample of business-to-business salespeople found that salespeople who experienced higher levels of management monitoring and directing displayed higher performance, job satisfaction, and organizational commitment.[17] These findings suggest that higher levels of management control are associated with favorable salesperson attitudes and behavior.

Sales Force Evaluation and Control

Sales management is continually working to improve the productivity of selling efforts. During the last decade personal selling costs increased much faster than advertising costs, so achieving high sales force performance is important. The evaluation of sales force performance considers sales results, costs, salesperson activities, and customer satisfaction. Several issues are important in evaluation, including the unit(s) of analysis, measures of performance, performance standards, and factors that the sales organization and individual salespeople cannot control.

Unit of Analysis. Evaluation extends beyond the salesperson to include other organizational units, such as districts and branches. Selling teams are used in some types of selling. These companies focus evaluations on team results. Product performance evaluation by geographical area and across organization units is relevant in the firms that produce more than one product. Individual account sales and cost analyses are useful for customers such as national accounts and accounts assigned to salespeople.

Performance Measures. Management needs yardsticks for measuring salesperson performance. For example, the sales force of a regional food processor that distributes through grocery wholesalers and large retail chains devotes most of its selling effort to calling on retailers. Since the firm does not have information on sales of its products by individual retail outlet, evaluations are based on the activities of salespeople rather than sales outcomes. This type of control system focuses on "behavior" rather than "outcomes."

Sales managers may use both activity (behavior) and outcome measures of salesperson performance. Research indicates that multiple item measures of several activities and outcomes are useful in performance evaluation.[18] Illustrative areas include sales planning, expense control, sales presentation, technical knowledge, information feedback, and sales results. Achievement of the sales quota (actual sales/quota sales) is a widely used outcome measure of sales performance. Other outcome measures include new business generated, market share gains, new-product sales, and profit contributions.

Performance evaluation is influenced by the sales management control system used by the organization. Emphasis may be placed on salesperson activities, on outcomes, or a combination of activities and outcomes. The objective is to use the type of control that is most effective for the selling situation. Direct selling organizations like Avon and Mary Kay focus more on outcome control. Companies like American Airlines and Pfizer include both activity and outcome control. An important aspect of management control is the compensation plan. When salespeople are compensated primarily by commission earnings on sales results, pay becomes the primary management control mechanism.

Setting Performance Standards. Although internal comparisons of performance are frequently used, they are not very helpful if the performance of the entire sales force is unacceptable. A major problem in setting sales performance standards is determining how to adjust them for factors that are not under the salesperson's control (i.e., market potential, intensity of competition, differences in customer needs, and quality of supervision). A competent salesperson may not appear to be performing well if assigned to a poor sales territory (e.g., salesperson Jones in Exhibit 13.4). Such differences need to be included in the evaluation process since territories often are not equal in terms of opportunity and other uncontrollable factors.

We know that evaluating performance is one of sales management's more difficult tasks. Typically, performance tracking involves assessing a combination of outcome and behavioral factors. In compensation plans other than straight commission, performance evaluation may affect the salesperson's pay, so obtaining a fair evaluation is important.

By evaluating the organization's personal selling strategy, management may identify various problems requiring corrective action. Problems may be linked to individual salespeople or to decisions that impact the entire organization. A well-designed information system helps in the diagnosis of performance and guides corrective actions when necessary.

Internet Strategy

We now consider Internet strategy alternatives, examine integration of Internet initiatives with marketing and promotion strategies, discuss options for measuring effectiveness, and look at the Internet's future in business and marketing strategies. Also, recall our discussion of the topic in Chapters 2 and 11.

"The Internet is a worldwide means of exchanging information and communicating through a series of interconnected computers."[19] It offers a fast and versatile communications capability. Internet initiatives span a wide range of global industries and companies, and there have been successes but also many failures, stimulated by overly optimistic expectations and faulty implementation. Initiatives have been pursued by both traditional enterprises and new business designs. One of the more visible new Internet enterprises is Amazon.com Inc., the online retailer that reported its first profitable year in 2003 with sales of $5.3 billion. Business-to-business use

EXHIBIT 13.6
Hitting Pay Dirt in the Virtual World

Source: Michael J. Mandel and Robert D. Hof, "Rethinking the Internet: E-Biz: Down but Hardly Out," *BusinessWeek*, March 26, 2001, 128.

Electronic Commerce

Pegged to hit $6.8 trillion in 2004, with 90% of that coming from business-to-business sales, says Forrester Research. About 80% of Cisco Systems' orders are taken online, about $5 billion last quarter—saving the networking giant $760 million in annual operating costs.

E-Marketplaces

Transactions on e-marketplaces expected to reach $2.8 trillion in 2004, says AMR Research. Defense contractor United Technologies bought $450 million worth of metals, motors, and other products from an e-marketplace in 2000 and got prices about 15% less than what it usually pays.

Procurement

Businesses will buy $2.8 trillion in supplies over the Internet in 2004, excluding e-marketplace purchases, says AMR Research. Eastman Chemical is buying 19% of its supplies online now, up from almost nothing two years ago. That has helped boost productivity 9% per year.

Knowledge Management

Companies will spend $10.2 billion to store and share their employees' knowledge over the Net by 2004, says IDC. Electronics manufacturer Siemens has spent $7.8 million to create a Web site for employees to share expertise to help win contracts. The result: new sales of $122 million.

Customer Relationships

Corporations will invest $12.2 billion by 2004 on linking customers, sales, and marketing over the Web, says the META Group. Lands' End converts more than 10% of its Web visitors to buyers—compared with the average 4.9%—in part because it offers live chat and other customer-service extras. Even with the crash in Internet stocks, companies are investing heavily in online initiatives.

of the Internet is far more extensive than consumer adoption of the Internet. The impacts of the Internet on business organizations in the future are expected to be both transformational as well as incremental in scope.

Strategy Development

The first step in strategy development is to determine the role of the Internet in the organization's business and marketing strategies. As discussed in Chapter 2, this role may involve a separate business model, a value-chain channel, a marketing communications tool, or a promotional medium:

> Marketers lured by the Internet's promise of immediacy, interactivity, availability, customization, and global reach need to evaluate when it really pays to reach customers through the Internet and how the Internet best fits into overall marketing strategy. To do so, they need to pay even closer attention to customers and rethink how to evaluate market opportunities, set marketing strategy, and deploy marketing programs.[20]

Several examples of how companies are using the Internet are described in Exhibit 13.6. The various initiatives ranging from e-commerce to customer relationships show how the Internet is leveraging the operating processes of many companies.

Deciding Internet Objectives

The capabilities of the Internet fall into two broad categories: a communications medium, and a direct response medium enabling users to purchase and sell products. A summary of the communications features of the Internet follows:[21]

Creating Awareness and Interest. Advertising on the Internet offers important advantages to many companies. The opportunity for global exposure provides a useful brand building capability.

Disseminating Information. Providing product, application, and company information via the Internet is essential in the competitive marketplace. This capability offers an opportunity for direct one-on-one contact.

Obtaining Research Information. The Internet offers a very cost-effective means of obtaining information, such as user profiles. However, concerns have been voiced about invasion of consumer privacy.

Brand Building. Access to users provides an opportunity to build a brand that is unique compared to other media. This highlights the importance of developing effective designs for Web sites.

Improving Customer Service. The Internet offers an important avenue of after-the-sale customer contact. Dell Inc. offers a wide range of services to its corporate customers via the Internet.

We now consider what is involved in developing an e-commerce capability. This initiative may be pursued by an existing company such as Avon Products Corp. or a new Web-based business model.

E-Commerce Strategy

Designing and launching a new e-commerce business that enables buyers to purchase products is a major initiative. Moreover, faulty evaluation of market opportunities and inadequate planning have resulted in many Web-based business failures. Several interrelated decisions must be made:

1. Which customer groups should I serve?
2. How do I provide a compelling set of benefits to my targeted customer? How do I differentiate my "value proposition" versus online and offline competitors?
3. How do I communicate with customers?
4. What is the content, "look-and-feel," level of community, and degree of personalization of the Web site?
5. How should I structure my organization? What business services and applications software choices do I need to consider?
6. Who are my potential partners? Whose capabilities complement ours?
7. How will this business provide value to shareholders?
8. What metrics should I use to judge the progress of the business? How do I value the business?[22]

The intent of the present discussion is to describe what is involved in an e-business initiative; an extensive coverage of the topic is provided by several other sources.[23]

Value Opportunities and Risks

The earlier discussion highlights several unique features of the Internet as a communications medium. Properly designed and managed, Web-based initiatives provide important opportunities for offering superior customer value. These include:[24]

1. Very focused targeting is possible via the Web.
2. Messages can be designed to address the needs and preferences of the target audience.
3. The Web offers a compelling opportunity for interaction and feedback.
4. A core value offering of the Internet is access to a wide range of information.
5. The sales potential offered by the Internet is substantial (see Exhibit 13.6).
6. The Internet provides an exciting opportunity for communications innovation.
7. The exposure opportunities of the Internet are significant, enabling many small companies and professionals to attain cost-effective access to customers and prospects.
8. The speed of response via the Internet is impressive.

The extensive value opportunities offered by the Web explain the many initiatives pursued by companies. Nonetheless, there are some risks associated with the use of the Internet as a communications medium. These include difficulties in effectiveness measurement, changes in audience characteristics, access and response delays, multiple-ad exposure, potential for deception, and costs that may be higher than traditional media.[25]

Measuring Internet Effectiveness

Measurement problems associated with the Internet are particularly challenging. This is not surprising given the explosive growth of Web-based initiatives and the limited experience with the medium. Nonetheless, there are many sources of measurement data. Evaluating the quality and relevance of alternative measurement sources requires careful assessment by the organization pursuing Internet strategies.

In an attempt to provide guidelines for Internet effectiveness measurement an industry study was undertaken that resulted in a 2002 report.[26] The voluntary guidelines included five recommended measures for independent auditing and verification. The metrics proposed were ad impressions, clicks, unique visitors, total visits, and page impressions.

The Future of the Internet

Perhaps the Internet shakeout was inevitable because of the race to develop Internet capabilities and business designs. Acknowledging the setbacks, it is apparent that Internet initiatives will expand significantly in the future. Internet technology and applications will experience an exciting future:

> Although the specific details are unpredictable and unimportant, digital technology will inevitably accelerate, intensify, and reduce the cost of marketing activities. What is important is that marketing managers will help guide the company's customers toward better utilization of the company's products and services.[27]

The reality is that the Internet will not result in a massive transformation of business practices.[28] Its impact is expected to be much greater for companies and organizations that are very dependent on the flow of information. The impact of the Internet in the future promises to be revolutionary for certain industries and incremental for others. We have experienced the impact of the Internet on sales of books, music, and air travel. Internet evolutions forecast for the future include jewelry, payments, telecom, hotels, real estate, and software.[29] For example, while Internet jewelry sales account for only $2 billion of the $45 billion total industry sales, rapid growth is expected.

Direct Marketing Strategies

The purpose of direct marketing is to make direct contact with end user customers through alternative media (e.g., computer, telephone, mail, and kiosk). Many direct marketing methods are available, each offering certain advantages and limitations. The rapid growth of direct marketing during the last decade indicates that importance placed by many companies on these direct avenues to customers. For example, Williams-Sonoma, the kitchenware retailer, generates 40 percent of its annual revenues from catalog sales.[30] Using a two-stage strategy, the company first builds a catalog customer base in a metro area. At the second stage, Williams-Sonoma opens a retail store when sufficient catalog shoppers are identified, targeting catalog buyers with store promotion mailings.

First, we look at several considerations in the use of direct marketing. Next, the major direct marketing methods are discussed. Finally, we consider at how direct marketing strategies are developed and implemented.

Reasons for Using Direct Marketing

The expanding popularity of direct marketing methods is driven by a combination of factors such as socioeconomic trends, low costs, databases, and buyers' demands for value. We examine how these influences affect companies' use of mail, phone, media, and computers to contact individual buyers.

Socioeconomic Trends. Several trends make the availability of direct marketing purchases attractive to many buyers. Two working spouses impose major time constraints on households, so direct purchase via direct channels is a useful way of saving time as well as making contact at the convenience of the customer. Many single-person households also favor direct marketing purchases. Buyers can shop at home, save time, and avoid shopping congestion. Rapid response to order processing and shipping enables buyers to obtain their purchases in a few days. Liberal exchange policies reduce the risks of direct purchases.

Low Access Costs. While the cost per contact varies according to the method of direct contact, the marketer's costs are much lower than face-to-face sales contact. Telephone contact ranges from $10 to $20, compared to much lower costs per contact by computer, mail, and advertising media. The availability of databases that can target specific customer groups enables companies to selectively target buyers. Companies like American Express can market products to their credit card users. Similarly, airline frequent flyer mailing lists provide cost-effective access to buyers. The availability of credit cards simplifies the payment process.

Database Management. The use of computerized databases escalated during the last decade, driven by hardware and software technology advances. The availability of computerized databases is an important determinant of successful direct marketing.[31] The information in the systems includes internal data on customers and purchased data on customers and prospects. The customer and prospect information contained in databases can be used to generate mailing lists and prospect lists and to identify market segments. These segments offer a direct communications channel with customers and prospects.

Value. The shopping information provided via direct marketing, convenience, reduced shopping time, rapid response, and competitive prices give buyers an attractive bundle of value in many buying situations. Effective database management enables direct marketing to identify buyers who purchase on a continuing basis.

The differentiated needs and wants of buyers can be addressed through direct marketing, thus enhancing the value offered by the direct marketer. Offerings may be mass-customized when the direct marketer has the capability to modularize the product offering. For example, kiosks can be linked to information networks that transmit customized customer orders.

Direct Marketing Methods

Various direct marketing methods are shown in Exhibit 13.7. We briefly examine each method to highlight its features and limitations.

Catalogs and Direct Mail. Contact by mail with potential buyers may generate orders by phone or mail, or instead to encourage buyers to visit retail outlets to view goods and make purchases. Examples of companies using catalogs and other printed matter to encourage direct

EXHIBIT 13.7
Direct Marketing Methods

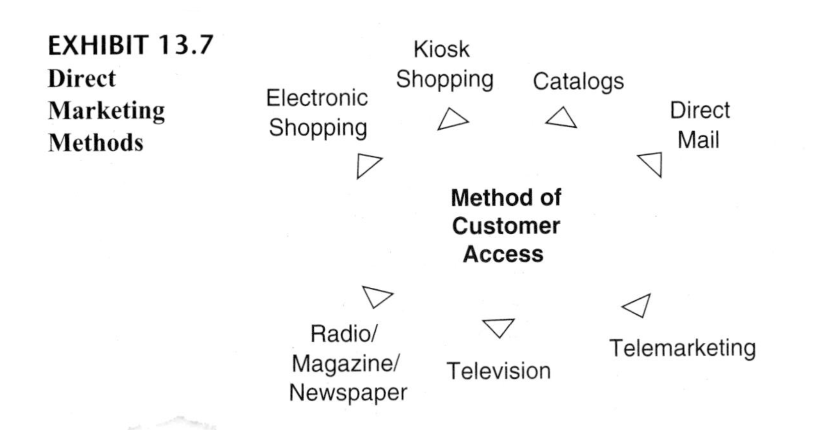

response include Lands' End (clothing), L.L. Bean (outdoor apparel and equipment), Calyx & Corolla (flowers), and the Conference Board Inc. (management conferences).

Telemarketing. This form of direct marketing consists of the use of telephone contact between the buyer and seller to perform all or some of the selling function. Telemarketing offers two key advantages—low contact cost and quick access by both buyer and seller. It may be used as the primary method of customer contact, or as a way to support the field sales force. Telemarketing escalated in importance during the last decade, and is a vital part of the selling activities of many companies. Telemarketing, like the Internet, is a potential avenue of conflict with an organization's face-to-face sales force, and may be an annoyance for consumers.

Direct Response Media. Many companies use television, radio, magazines, and newspapers to obtain sales from buyers. Direct response from the advertising is obtained by mail, telephone, and fax. People see the ads, decide to buy, and order the item from the organization promoting the product.

The TV Home Shopping Network markets a wide range of products for many companies. The products are displayed and their features described. Prices are discounted below list prices. The buyer places an order using a toll-free number. Individual companies may also market their products using commercials for specific products such as housewares, magazines, and music recordings.

Magazines, newspapers, and radio offer a wide range of direct marketing advertisements. The intent of the direct-response communications is to persuade the person reading or hearing the ad to order the product. The advantage of using these media is the very low cost of exposure. While the percent of response is also low, the returns can be substantial for products that buyers are willing to purchase through these media.

Electronic Shopping. The computer age has created two major methods of direct marketing: computer ordering by companies from their supplier, and consumer and business shopping via the Internet as discussed earlier in the chapter. Electronic shopping by business buyers is appropriate when the customer's requirements involve routine repurchase of standard items, and direct access to the buyer is not necessary. Electronic capabilities may be used to support a field sales force rather than as the sole method of customer contact. Computer ordering helps the seller establish a close link to customers, and reduces order cycles (time from order placement to receipt) and inventory stocks. Computer ordering enables the buyer to reduce inventory levels, cut costs, and monitor customer preferences. For example, Wal-Mart's computerized scanning equipment in its stores informs the retailer about what (and where) customers are buying and meeting their needs via the computerized ordering system. While some customers may resist becoming dependent on suppliers through electronic linkages, there is a strong trend toward closer ties between suppliers and organizational buyers.

As discussed earlier in the chapter virtual shopping on the Internet has received much publicity during the last few years. Many companies are considering the potential opportunities of direct marketing to computer users. The business-to-business sector accounts for the largest portion of total Internet sales. There are three types of networks: (1) The Internet is a global interlink of computer networks that have a common software standard; (2) The intranet is a company internal capability using Internet software standards; and (3) The extranet consists of providing external partners access to the intranet.[32] For example, a retail chain may serve customers via the Internet, coordinate store operations via the intranet, and utilize the extranet to interact with freelance product designers and other external partners.

Kiosk Shopping. Similar in concept to vending machines, kiosks offer buyers the opportunity to purchase from a facility (stand) located in a retail complex or other public area (e.g., airport). Kiosks may have Internet linkages. Airline tickets and flight insurance are examples of products sold using kiosks. In some instances the order may be placed at the kiosk but delivered to the customer's address. The advantage to the seller is exposure to many people, and the buyer benefits from the shopping convenience. Kiosks are best suited for selling products that buyers can easily evaluate due to prior experience.

Advantages of Direct Marketing

It is apparent that direct marketing offers several advantages for sellers.[33] This marketing approach enables selective reach and segmentation opportunities. Considerable flexibility in accessing potential buyers is provided via direct marketing. Timing contact can be managed and personalized. Importantly, the effectiveness of direct marketing can be measured from direct response.

Direct marketing also has certain limitations.[34] It may have negative image factors (e.g., junk mail). Accuracy of targeting is only as good as the lists used to access potential buyers. There may also be limited content support in direct-response advertising. Also, postal rates increase over time.

Direct Marketing Strategy

As highlighted in our discussion, direct marketing promotion has the primary objective of obtaining a purchase response from individual buyers. While the methods differ in nature and scope, all require the development of a strategy. Market target(s) must be identified, objectives set, positioning strategy developed, communication strategy formulated, program implemented and managed, and results evaluated against performance expectations.

The direct marketing strategy should be guided by the organization's marketing strategy. Direct marketing provides the way of reaching the customer on a one-to-one basis. Product strategy must be determined, prices set, and distribution arranged. Direct marketing may be the primary avenue to the customer as in the case of L.L. Bean Inc. in its targeting of the outdoor apparel niche using catalog marketing. Other companies may use direct marketing as one of several ways of communicating with their market targets. Dell Inc. employs direct sales contact with business customers, telephone sales, and Internet sales. The Internet may also be used by Dell's customers to obtain information before placing an order by phone.

Summary

Management analyzes the firm's marketing strategy, the target market, product characteristics, distribution strategy, and pricing strategy to identify the role of personal selling in the promotion mix. New business, trade selling, missionary selling, and consultative/technical selling strategies illustrate the possible roles that may be assigned to selling in various firms. The selling process indicates the selling activities necessary to move the buyer from need awareness to a purchase decision. Various sales channels are used in conjunction with the field sales force to accomplish the selling process activities.

Sales force organizational design decisions include the type of organizational structure to be used, the size of the sales force, and the allocation of selling effort. Deployment involves decisions regarding sales force size and effort allocation. Managing the sales force includes recruiting, training, supervising, and motivating salespeople. Evaluation and control determine the extent to which objectives are achieved and determine where adjustments are needed in selling strategy and tactics.

The Internet provides a unique and compelling means of electronic contact between buyers and sellers. The core capability of the Internet is communicating with buyers and prospects via an interactive process. The Internet is a new medium and companies are learning how to obtain its advantages and avoid its risks. The key organizational decision is deciding what role the Internet will play in the business and marketing strategies. The options range from a separate business model to a promotional medium.

The Internet offers several communications features including disseminating information, creating awareness, obtaining research information, brand building, encouraging trials, improving customer service, and expanding distribution. Developing an Internet business model is a major initiative involving the design of a new business. Faulty evaluation of market opportunities and inadequate planning have resulted in many Web-based failures.

The Internet's unique features offer important opportunities for providing superior customer value. It also has some potential risks in its use as a communications medium. A major challenge is measuring the effectiveness of Internet initiatives.

The purpose of direct marketing is to obtain a sales response from buyers by making direct contact using mail, telephone, advertising media, or computer. The rapidly expanding adoption of direct marketing methods that occurred in the last decade is the consequence of several influences including socioeconomic trends, low costs of exposure, computer technology, and buyers' demands for value. Direct marketing is used by many companies to contact organizational and consumer buyers.

Direct marketing offers several advantages including selective reach, segmentation opportunities, flexibility, timing control, and effectiveness measurement. However, certain direct methods may convey a negative image.

Companies have many options available for direct marketing to buyers. The methods include catalogs, direct mail, telemarketing, television, radio, magazines/newspapers, electronic shopping, and kiosk shopping. Developing a strategy for using each method includes selecting the market target(s), setting objectives, selecting positioning strategy, developing the communications strategy, implementing and managing the strategy, and evaluating results.

Internet Applications

A. Examine the Web site of Salesforce.com. Discuss how the Internet service provider can assist sales managers in their sales force management activities.

B. Visit Nokia's U.S. Web site (*www.nokiausa.com*). Evaluate Nokia's sales approach online. How does Nokia enhance its direct marketing strategy through Web-based offerings? How could the company increase traffic to its online sales platform without creating channel conflict?

C. Review the Web site of Merrill Lynch (*www.ml.com*). How does Merrill Lynch leverage its global position to adjust to local markets through the Internet? Why is the Internet particularly relevant for firms in the financial services industry?

Feature Applications

A. Review the Global Feature concerning Novartis' sales force initiatives. Discuss how these changes should be integrated with the drug company's promotion and marketing strategies.

B. The Strategy Feature highlights several changes in the "language of marketing." To what extent do these changes suggest marketing to consumer end users and business customers may involve several similar strategy characteristics?

Questions for Review and Discussion

1. What information does management require to analyze the selling situation?
2. Suppose an analysis of sales force size and selling effort deployment indicates that a company has a sales force of the right size but that the allocation of selling effort requires substantial adjustment in several territories. How should such deployment changes be implemented?
3. What questions would you want answered if you were trying to evaluate the effectiveness of a business unit's sales force strategy?
4. Discuss some of the advantages and limitations of recruiting salespeople by hiring the employees of companies with excellent training programs.
5. Is incentive compensation more important for salespeople than for product managers? Why?
6. Select a company and discuss how sales management should define the selling process.
7. What are the unique capabilities offered by the Internet to business users of the communications medium?
8. Discuss whether the Internet may replace conventional catalogs and direct mail methods of promotion.
9. Direct marketing is similar in many ways to advertising. Why is it important to view direct marketing as a specific group of promotion methods?
10. Discuss the reasons why many companies are interested in the marketing potential of the Internet.
11. Select one of the direct marketing methods and discuss the decisions that are necessary in developing a strategy for using the method.
12. Suppose you have been asked to evaluate whether a regional camera and consumer electronics retailer should obtain Internet space. What criteria should be used in the evaluation?

Notes

1. "Who Says CEOs Can't Find Inner Peace?" *BusinessWeek,* September 1, 2003, 77–78.
2. "What a Sales Call Costs," *Sales & Marketing Management,* September 2000, 79–81.
3. Christine Galea, "The 2004 Compensation Survey," *Sales & Marketing Management,* May 2004, 29–30.
4. The following discussion is based on Mark W. Johnston and Greg W. Marshall, *Sales Force Management.* 7th ed. (Burr Ridge, IL: McGraw-Hill/Irwin, 2003), 49–50.
5. Ibid.
6. Johnston and Marshall, *Sales Force Management,* 51–56.
7. Andy Cohen, "Starting Over," *Sales & Marketing Management,* September 1995.
8. Rick Brooks, "FedEx Fiscal Fourth-Quarter Profit Rose by 11%, Surpassing Expectations," *The Wall Street Journal,* June 29, 2000, B2.
9. The following discussion is drawn from Raymond W. LaForge, David W. Cravens, and Thomas N. Ingram, "Evaluating Multiple Sales Channel Strategies," *Journal*

of Business and Industrial Marketing, Summer/Fall 1991, 37–48.

10. Jerome A. Colletti and Gary S. Tubridy, "Effective Major Account Management," *Journal of Personal Selling and Sales Management,* August 1987, 1–10.
11. Ibid.
12. Erik Ahlberg, "Newell Rubbermaid Rebirth Is a Work in Progress," *The Wall Street Journal,* November 27, 2002, B3A.
13. Johnston and Marshall, *Sales Force Management,* Chapter 5.
14. David W. Cravens, Thomas M. Ingram, Raymond W. LaForge, and Clifford E. Young, "Hallmarks of Effective Sales Organizations," *Marketing Management,* Winter 1992, 56–67.
15. Johnston and Marshall, *Sales Force Management,* Chapter 10.
16. Ibid., Chapter 7.
17. David W. Cravens, Greg W. Marshall, Felicia G. Lassk, and George S. Low, "The Control Factor," *Marketing Management* 13, no. 1, January–February 2004, 39–44.
18. David W. Cravens, Thomas M. Ingram, Raymond W. LaForge, and Clifford E. Young, "Behavior-Based and Outcome-Based Sales Force Control Systems," *Journal of Marketing,* October 1993, 47–59.
19. George E. Belch and Michael A. Belch, *Advertising and Promotion*. 6th ed. (New York: McGraw-Hill Irwin, 2004), 486.
20. Bernard Jaworski and Katherine Jocz, "Rediscovering the Customer," *Marketing Management,* September/October 2002, 24.
21. The following is based on Belch and Belch, *Advertising and Promotion,* 492–493.
22. Jeffrey F. Rayport and Bernard J. Jaworski, *e-Commerce* (New York: McGraw-Hill/Irwin, 2001), 12.
23. See, for example, ibid.
24. Belch and Belch, *Advertising and Promotion,* 504–505.
25. Ibid., 505–506.
26 Ibid., 502–503.
27. Glen L. Urban, *Digital Marketing Strategy* (Upper Saddle River, NJ: Pearson Prentice Hall, 2004), 180.
28. Michael J. Mandel and Robert D. Hof, "Rethinking the Internet," *BusinessWeek,* March 26, 2001, 117–122.
29. Timothy J. Mullaney, "E-Biz Strikes Again," *BusinessWeek,* May 10, 2004, 80–90.
30. Sandra Baker, "Mail Bonding," *Fort Worth Star Telegram,* December 16, 1996, B1 and B3.
31. William J. McDonald, *Direct Marketing* (Burr Ridge, IL: Irwin/McGraw-Hill, 1998), 93.
32. "Log On, Link Up, Save Big," *BusinessWeek,* June 22, 1998, 136.
33. Belch and Belch, *Advertising and Promotion,* 480–481.
34. Ibid.

Cases for Part 4

Case 4-1

Planet Starbucks

The Starbucks coffee shop on Sixth Avenue and Pine Street in downtown Seattle sits serene and orderly, as unremarkable as any other in the chain bought 15 years ago by entrepreneur Howard Schultz. A little less than three years ago, however, the quiet storefront made front pages around the world. During the World Trade Organization talks in November, 1999, protesters flooded Seattle's streets, and among their targets was Starbucks, a symbol, to them, of free-market capitalism run amok, another multinational out to blanket the earth. Amid the crowds of protesters and riot police were black-masked anarchists who trashed the store, leaving its windows smashed and its tasteful green-and-white decor smelling of tear gas instead of espresso. Says an angry Schultz: "It's hurtful. I think people are ill-informed. It's very difficult to protest against a can of Coke, a bottle of Pepsi, or a can of Folgers. Starbucks is both this ubiquitous brand and a place where you can go and break a window. You can't break a can of Coke."

The store was quickly repaired, and the protesters have scattered to other cities. Yet cup by cup, Starbucks really is caffeinating the world, its green-and-white emblem beckoning to consumers on three continents. In 1999, Starbucks Corp. had 281 stores abroad. Today, it has about 1,200—and it's still in the early stages of a plan to colonize the globe. If the protesters were wrong in their tactics, they weren't wrong about Starbucks' ambitions. They were just early.

The story of how Schultz & Co. transformed a pedestrian commodity into an upscale consumer accessory has a fairy-tale quality. Starbucks has grown from 17 coffee shops in Seattle 15 years ago to 5,689 outlets in 28 countries. Sales have climbed an average of 20% annually since the company went public 10 years ago, to $2.6 billion in 2001, while profits bounded ahead an average of 30% per year, hitting $181.2 million last year. And the momentum continues. In the first three quarters of this fiscal year, sales climbed 24%, year to year, to $2.4 billion, while profits, excluding onetime charges and capital gains, rose 25%, to $159.5 million.

Moreover, the Starbucks name and image connect with millions of consumers around the globe. It was one of the fastest-growing brands in a *BusinessWeek* survey of the top 100 global brands published Aug. 5. At a time when one corporate star after another has crashed to earth, brought down by revelations of earnings misstatements, executive greed, or worse, Starbucks hasn't faltered. The company confidently predicts up to 25% annual sales and earnings growth this year. On Wall Street, Starbucks is the last great growth story. Its stock, including four splits, has soared more than 2,200% over the past decade, surpassing Wal-Mart, General Electric, PepsiCo, Coca-Cola, Microsoft, and IBM in total return. Now at $21, it is hovering near its all-time high of $23 in July, before the overall market drop.

And after a slowdown last fall and winter, when consumers seemed to draw inward after September 11, Starbucks is rocketing ahead once again. Sales in stores open at least 13 months grew by 6% in the 43 weeks through July 28, and the company predicts monthly same-store sales gains as high as 7% through the end of this fiscal year. That's below the 9% growth rate in 2000, but investors seem encouraged. "We're going to see a lot more growth," says Jerome A. Castellini, president of Chicago-based CastleArk Management, which controls about 300,000 Starbucks shares. "The stock is on a run."

But how long can that run last? Already, Schultz's team is hard-pressed to grind out new profits in a home market that is quickly becoming saturated. Amazingly, with 4,247 stores scattered across the U.S. and Canada, there are still eight states in the U.S. with no Starbucks stores. Frappuccino-free cities include Butte, Mont., and Fargo, N.D. But big cities, affluent suburbs, and shopping malls are full to the brim. In coffee-crazed Seattle, there is a Starbucks outlet for every 9,400 people, and the company considers that the upper limit of coffee-shop saturation. In Manhattan's 24 square miles, Starbucks has 124 cafés, with four more on the way this year. That's one for every 12,000 people—meaning that there could be room for even more stores. Given such concentration, it is likely to take annual same-store sales increases of 10% or more if the company is going to match its historic overall sales growth. That, as they might say at Starbucks, is a tall order to fill.

Indeed, the crowding of so many stores so close together has become a national joke, eliciting quips such as this headline in *The Onion*, a satirical publication: "A New Starbucks Opens in Rest-room of Existing Starbucks." And even the company admits that while its practice of blanketing an area with stores helps achieve market dominance, it can cut sales at existing outlets. "We probably self-cannibalize our stores at a rate of 30% a year," Schultz says. Adds Lehman Brothers Inc. analyst Mitchell Speiser: "Starbucks is at a defining point in its growth. It's reaching a level that makes it harder and harder to grow, just due to the law of large numbers."

To duplicate the staggering returns of its first decade, Starbucks has no choice but to export its concept aggressively. Indeed, some analysts give Starbucks only two years at most before it saturates the U.S. market. The chain now operates 1,200 international outlets, from Beijing to Bristol. That leaves plenty of room to grow. Indeed, about 400 of its planned 1,200 new stores this year will be built overseas, representing a 35% increase in its foreign base. Starbucks expects to double the number of its stores worldwide, to 10,000 in three years. During the past 12 months, the chain has opened stores in Vienna, Zurich, Madrid, Berlin, and even in far-off Jakarta. Athens comes next. And within the next year, Starbucks plans to move into Mexico and Puerto Rico. But global expansion poses huge risks for Starbucks. For one thing, it makes less money on each overseas store because most of them are operated with local partners. While that makes it easier to start up on foreign turf, it reduces the company's share of the profits to only 20% to 50%.

Moreover, Starbucks must cope with some predictable challenges of becoming a mature company in the U.S. After riding the wave of successful baby boomers through the '90s, the company faces an ominously hostile reception from its future consumers, the twenty- or thirty-somethings of Generation X. Not only are the activists among them turned off by the power and image of the well-known brand, but many others say that Starbucks' latte-sipping sophisticates and piped-in Kenny G music are a real turn-off. They don't feel wanted in a place that sells designer coffee at $3 a cup.

Even the thirst of loyalists for high-price coffee can't be taken for granted. Starbucks' growth over the past decade coincided with a remarkable surge in the economy. Consumer spending has continued strong in the downturn, but if that changes, those $3 lattes might be an easy place for people on a budget to cut back. Starbucks executives insist that won't happen, pointing out that even in the weeks following the terrorist attacks, same-store comparisons stayed positive while those of other retailers skidded.

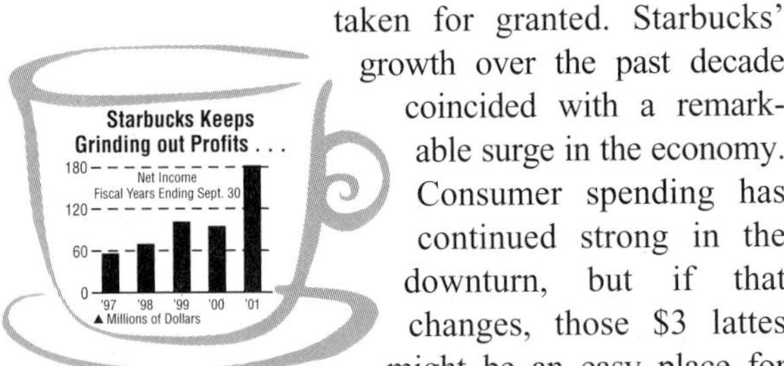

Starbucks also faces slumping morale and employee burnout among its store managers and its once-cheery army of *baristas*. Stock options for part-timers in the restaurant business was a Starbucks innovation that once commanded awe and respect from its employees. But now, though employees are still paid better than comparable workers elsewhere—about $7 per hour—many regard the job as just another fast-food gig. Dissatisfaction over odd hours and low pay is affecting the quality of the normally sterling service and even the coffee itself, say some customers and employees. Frustrated store managers among the company's roughly 470 California stores sued Starbucks in 2001 for allegedly refusing to pay legally mandated overtime. Starbucks settled the suit for $18 million this past April, shaving $0.03 per share off an otherwise strong second quarter. However, the heart of the complaint—feeling overworked and underappreciated—doesn't seem to be going away.

To be sure, Starbucks has a lot going for it as it confronts the challenge of maintaining its growth. Nearly free of debt, it fuels expansion with internal cash flow. And Starbucks can maintain a tight grip on its image because stores are company-owned: There are no franchisees to get sloppy about running things. By relying on mystique and word-of-mouth, whether here or overseas, the company saves a bundle on marketing costs. Starbucks spends just $30 million annually on advertising, or roughly 1% of revenues, usually just for new flavors of coffee drinks in the summer and product launches, such as its new in-store Web service. Most consumer companies its size shell out upwards of $300 million per year. Moreover, unlike a McDonald's or a Gap Inc., two other retailers that rapidly grew in the U.S., Starbucks has no nationwide competitor.

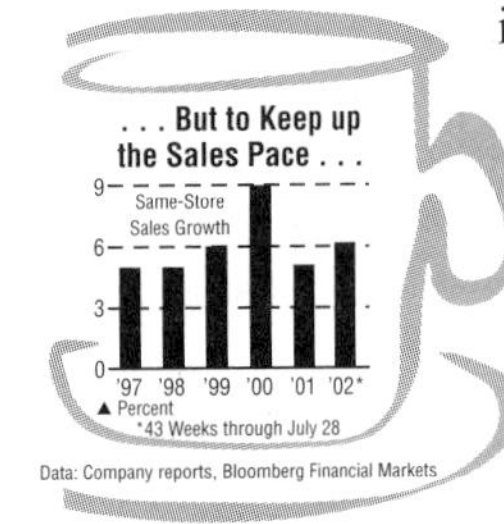

Starbucks also has a well-seasoned management team. Schultz, 49, stepped down as chief executive in 2000 to become chairman and chief global strategist. Orin Smith, 60, the company's numbers-cruncher, is now CEO and in charge of day-to-day operations. The head of North American operations is Howard Behar, 57, a retailing expert who returned last September, two years after retiring. The management trio is known as H_2O, for Howard, Howard, and Orin.

Schultz remains the heart and soul of the operation. Raised in a Brooklyn public-housing project, he found his way to Starbucks, a tiny chain of Seattle coffee shops, as a marketing executive in the early '80s. The name came about when the original owners looked to Seattle history for inspiration and chose the moniker of an old mining camp: Starbo. Further refinement led to Starbucks, after the first mate in *Moby-Dick*, which they felt evoked the seafaring romance of the early coffee traders (hence the mermaid logo). Schultz got the idea for the modern Starbucks format while visiting a Milan coffee bar. He bought out his bosses in 1987 and began expanding. Today, Schultz has a net worth of about $700 million, including $400 million of company stock.

Starbucks has come light years from those humble beginnings, but Schultz and his team still think there's room to grow in the U.S.—even in communities where the chain already has dozens of stores. Clustering stores increases total revenue and market share, Smith argues, even when individual stores poach on each other's sales. The strategy works, he says, because of Starbucks' size. It is large enough to absorb losses at existing stores as new ones open up, and soon overall sales grow beyond what they would have with just one store. Meanwhile, it's cheaper to deliver to and manage stores located close together. And by clustering, Starbucks can quickly dominate a local market.

The company is still capable of designing and opening a store in 16 weeks or less and recouping the initial investment in three years. The stores may be oases of tranquility, but management's expansion tactics are something else. Take what critics call its "predatory real estate" strategy—paying more than market-rate rents to keep competitors out of a location. David C. Schomer, owner of Espresso Vivace in Seattle's hip Capitol Hill neighborhood, says Starbucks approached his landlord and offered to pay nearly double the rate to put a coffee shop in the same building. The landlord stuck with Schomer, who says: "It's a little disconcerting to know that someone is willing to pay twice the going rate." Another time, Starbucks and Tully's Coffee Corp., a Seattle-based coffee chain, were competing for a space in the city. Starbucks got the lease but vacated the premises before the term was up. Still, rather than let Tully's get the space, Starbucks decided to pay the rent on the empty store so its competitor could not move in. Schultz makes no apologies for the hardball tactics. "The real estate business in America is a very, very tough game," he says. "It's not for the faint of heart."

Still, the company's strategy could backfire. Not only will neighborhood activists and local businesses increasingly resent the tactics, but customers could also grow annoyed over having fewer choices. Moreover, analysts contend that Starbucks can maintain about 15% square-footage growth in the U.S.—equivalent to 550 new stores—for only about two more years. After that, it will have to depend on overseas growth to maintain annual 20% revenue growth.

Starbucks was hoping to make up much of that growth with more sales of food and other noncoffee items, but has stumbled somewhat. In the late '90s, Schultz thought that offering $8 sandwiches, desserts, and CDs in his stores and selling packaged coffee in supermarkets would significantly boost sales. The specialty business now accounts for about 16% of sales, but growth has been less than expected. A healthy 19% this year, it's still far below the 38% growth rate of fiscal 2000. That suggests that while coffee can command high prices in a slump, food—at least at Starbucks—cannot. One of Behar's most important goals is to improve that record. For instance, the company now has a test program of serving hot breakfasts in 20 Seattle stores and may move to expand supermarket sales of whole beans.

What's more important for the bottom line, though, is that Starbucks has proven to be highly innovative in the way it sells its main course: coffee. In 800 locations it has installed automatic espresso machines to speed up service. And in November, it began offering prepaid Starbucks cards, priced from $5 to $500, which clerks swipe through a reader to deduct a sale. That, says the company, cuts transaction times in half. Starbucks has sold $70 million of the cards.

In early August, Starbucks launched Starbucks Express, its boldest experiment yet, which blends java, Web technology, and faster service. At about 60 stores in the Denver area, customers can pre-order and prepay for beverages and pastries via phone or on the Starbucks Express Web site. They just make the call or click the mouse before arriving at the store, and their beverage will be waiting—with their name printed on the cup. The company will decide in January on a national launch.

And Starbucks is bent on even more fundamental store changes. On Aug. 21, it announced expansion of a high-speed wireless Internet service to about 1,200 Starbucks locations in North America and Europe. Partners in the project—which Starbucks calls the world's largest Wi-Fi network—include Mobile International, a wireless subsidiary of Deutsche Telekom, and Hewlett-Packard. Customers sit in a store and check e-mail, surf the Web, or download multimedia presentations without looking for connections or tripping over cords. They start with 24 hours of free wireless broadband before choosing from a variety of monthly subscription plans.

Starbucks executives hope such innovations will help surmount their toughest challenge in the home market: attracting the next generation of customers. Younger coffee drinkers already feel uncomfortable in the stores. The company knows that because it once had a group of twentysomethings hypnotized for a market study. When their defenses were down, out came the bad news. "They either can't afford to buy coffee at Starbucks, or the only peers they see are those working behind the counter," says Mark Barden, who conducted the research for the Hal Riney & Partners ad agency (now part of Publicis Worldwide) in San Francisco. One of the recurring themes the hypnosis brought out was a sense that "people like me aren't welcome here except to serve the yuppies," he says. Then there are those who just find the whole Starbucks scene a bit pretentious. Katie Kelleher, 22, a Chicago paralegal, is put off by Starbucks' Italian terminology of *grande* and *venti* for coffee sizes. She goes to Dunkin' Donuts, saying: "Small, medium, and large is fine for me."

As it expands, Starbucks faces another big risk: that of becoming a far less special place for its employees. For a company modeled around enthusiastic service, that could have dire consequences for both image and sales. During its growth spurt of the mid- to late-1990s, Starbucks had the lowest employee turnover rate of any restaurant or fast-food company, largely thanks to its then unheard-of policy of giving health insurance and modest stock options to part-timers making barely more than minimum wage.

Such perks are no longer enough to keep all the workers happy. Starbucks' pay doesn't come close to matching the workload it requires, complain some staff. Says Carrie Shay, a former store manager in West Hollywood, Calif.: "If I were making a decent living, I'd still be there." Shay, one of the plaintiffs in the suit against the company, says she earned $32,000 a year to run a store with 10 to 15 part-time employees. She hired employees, managed their schedules, and monitored the store's weekly profit-and-loss statement. But she was also expected to put in significant time behind the counter and had to sign an affidavit pledging to work up to 20 hours of overtime a week without extra pay—a requirement the company has dropped since the settlement. Smith says that Starbucks offers better pay, benefits, and training than comparable companies, while it encourages promotions from within.

For sure, employee discontent is far from the image Starbucks wants to project of relaxed workers cheerfully making cappuccinos. But perhaps it is inevitable. The business model calls for lots of low-wage workers. And the more people who are hired as Starbucks expands, the less they are apt to feel connected to the original mission of high service—bantering with customers and treating them like family. Robert J. Thompson, a professor of popular culture at Syracuse University, says of Starbucks: "It's turning out to be one of the great 21st century American success stories—complete with all the ambiguities."

Overseas, though, the whole Starbucks package seems new and, to many young people, still very cool. In Vienna, where Starbucks had a gala opening for its first Austrian store last December, Helmut Spudich, a business editor for the paper *Der Standard*, predicted that Starbucks would attract a younger crowd than the established cafés. "The coffeehouses in Vienna are nice, but they are old. Starbucks is considered hip," he says.

But if Starbucks can count on its youth appeal to win a welcome in new markets, such enthusiasm cannot be counted on indefinitely. In Japan, the company beat even its own bullish expectations, growing to 368 stores after opening its first in Tokyo in 1996. Affluent young Japanese women like Anna Kato, a 22-year-old Toyota Motor Corp. worker, loved the place. "I don't care if it costs more, as long as it tastes sweet," she says, sitting in the world's busiest Starbucks, in Tokyo's Shibuya district. Yet same-store sales growth has fallen in the past 10 months in Japan, Starbucks' top foreign market, as rivals offer similar fare. Add to that the depressed economy, and Starbucks Japan seems to be losing steam. Although it forecasts a 30% gain in net profit, to $8 million, for the year started in April, on record sales of $516 million, same-store sales are down 14% for the year ended in June. Meanwhile in England, Starbucks' second-biggest overseas market, with 310 stores, imitators are popping up left and right to steal market share.

Entering other big markets may be tougher yet. The French seem to be ready for Starbucks' sweeter taste, says Philippe Bloch, cofounder of Columbus Café, a Starbucks-like chain. But he wonders if the company can profitably cope with France's arcane regulations and generous labor benefits. And in Italy, the epicenter of European coffee culture, the notion that the locals will abandon their own 200,000 coffee bars en masse for Starbucks strikes many as ludicrous. For one, Italian coffee bars prosper by serving food as well as coffee, an area where Starbucks still struggles. Also, Italian coffee is cheaper than U.S. java and, say Italian purists, much better. Americans pay about $1.50 for an espresso. In northern Italy, the price is 67¢; in the south, just 55¢. Schultz insists that Starbucks will eventually come to Italy. It'll have a lot to prove when it does. Carlo Petrini, founder of the antiglobalization movement Slow Food, sniffs that Starbucks' "substances served in styrofoam" won't cut it. The cups are paper, of course. But the skepticism is real.

As Starbucks spreads out, Schultz will have to be increasingly sensitive to those cultural challenges. In December, for instance, he flew to Israel to meet with Foreign Secretary Shimon Peres and other Israeli officials to discuss the Middle East crisis. He won't divulge the nature of his discussions. But subsequently, at a Seattle synagogue, Schultz let the Palestinians have it. With Starbucks outlets already in Kuwait, Lebanon, Oman, Qatar, and Saudi Arabia, he created a mild uproar among Palestinian supporters. Schultz quickly backpedaled, saying that his words were taken out of context and asserting that he is "pro-peace" for both sides.

There are plenty more minefields ahead. So far, the Seattle coffee company has compiled an envious record of growth. But the giddy buzz of that initial expansion is wearing off. Now, Starbucks is waking up to the grande challenges faced by any corporation bent on becoming a global powerhouse.

By Stanley Holmes in Seattle, with Drake Bennett in Paris, Kate Carlisle in Rome, and Chester Dawson in Tokyo, with bureau reports

For Coffee Growers, Not Even a Whiff of Profits

Is Starbucks Corp. profiting at the expense of the poor—that is, the poverty-stricken coffee farmers who supply the basic ingredient for the espressos and grande cappuccinos that affluent Americans buy?

Consider this: While company profits have tripled since 1997, to $181 million in fiscal 2000, many of the world's coffee farmers have been devastated by historically low prices. Coffee is now priced around 50¢ per pound, while production costs are around 80¢ per pound. "Small farmers are barely able to survive right now," says Guillermo Denaux, who monitors Central American Fair Trade cooperatives from El Salvador.

Starbucks' role as the world's fifth-largest buyer of coffee—behind the likes of Nestlé and Procter & Gamble—has placed it smack in the center of a controversy over how well-heeled corporations deal with poor farmers. The chain has a lot to lose if consumers, especially young ones, see it as a Third World profiteer. But the plight of the world's financially struggling coffee farmer is a complicated one—and not all the fault of corporate coffee buyers. Farmers are caught up in the harsh world of commodity markets, where prices are based on supply and demand in a highly fragmented industry. A chronic coffee surplus has resulted in years of low prices.

While undeniably benefiting from those cheap beans, Starbucks is striving to portray itself as a responsible global citizen. Chief Executive Orin C. Smith points to the company's involvement with various programs aimed at hiking the wages of farmers and improving the local environment. Starbucks recently unveiled guidelines that will pay farmers a premium price if they meet certain environmental, labor, and quality standards. Last year, the company joined TransFair, an organization that guarantees that farmers will receive most of the $1.26 per pound that coffee roasters pay for high-quality beans. "Our longtime suppliers couldn't make it if we weren't doing any of this," Smith says.

This year, Starbucks bought 150,000 pounds of fair-trade coffee from COOCAFE, the Consortium of Coffee Cooperatives of Guanacaste and Montes de Oro in Costa Rica. That's double what the cooperatives sold Starbucks last year but far below the 1.8 million pounds they had been hoping for. Groups such as Global Exchange and the Organic Consumers Assn. note that Starbucks is the only specialty coffee company that won't certify 5% of its coffee as "fair trade."

Critics contend that Starbucks spends more time polishing its image than it does tackling gaping inequities with suppliers. Starbucks makes sure everyone knows about the health clinic it built in Guatemala, says Deborah James, fair-trade director for Global Exchange, a San Francisco-based human-rights organization. "Building a clinic is a great thing," she says. "But it doesn't address the underlying poverty that is killing coffee farmers and their families."

Starbucks says it is working toward creating a sustainable business model in Guatemala, not trying to change its laws. Still, the company could do more for the people who have a big hand in its success, contends Stephen Coats, executive director for U.S./Labor Education in the Americas Project, another rights group. He would like to see Starbucks move faster to buy more fair-trade coffee. "Starbucks is moving very slowly, given the gravity of the situation, and tends to move only when pushed." It's time, activists suggest, for Starbucks to share the wealth.

By Stanley Homes in Seattle and Geri Smith in Mexico City

Source: "Planet Starbucks," *BusinessWeek*, September 9, 2002, 100–108.

Case 4-2
Hennes & Mauritz

Stefan Persson, chairman of Swedish retailer Hennes & Mauritz, vividly remembers his company's first attempt at international expansion. It was 1976, the year H&M opened its London store in Oxford Circus. "I stood outside trying to lure in customers by handing out ABBA albums," he recalls with a wry laugh. Persson, son of the founder and then age 29, waited for the crowds. And waited. "I still have most of those albums," he says.

Don't cry over that vinyl, Stefan. ABBA is still hot, but H&M is even hotter. Hotter than Shakira in July. Hotter even than harem pants—incidentally, an item flying out of H&M's stores this season. (Warning to female shoppers: If you don't want to be a fashion pioneer, those pants may not be for you. Try the peasant blouse instead.)

A slowing global economy, lackluster consumer spending: There's little sign of either at H&M. While rivals retreat from disastrous foreign forays and retailers across Europe and the U.S. struggle to post a profit, H&M's pretax income is set to hit $833 million in 2002, a 34% increase from the previous year, on sales of $5.8 billion, according to Keith Wills, Goldman, Sachs & Co.'s European retail analyst (Exhibit 1). The growth is being fueled not only by expansion: Wills also estimates same-store sales will be up between 4% and 5% this year. H&M has $1 billion in cash. Its market capitalization of $15 billion outstrips that of Gap Inc. and Zara International, its closest competitors (Exhibit 2). And at current sales levels, the chain is the largest apparel retailer in Europe. Although the stock has bounced around this year, it has nearly doubled since 1997 and has far outperformed the Stockholm index. This isn't a store chain. This is a money machine.

EXHIBIT 1

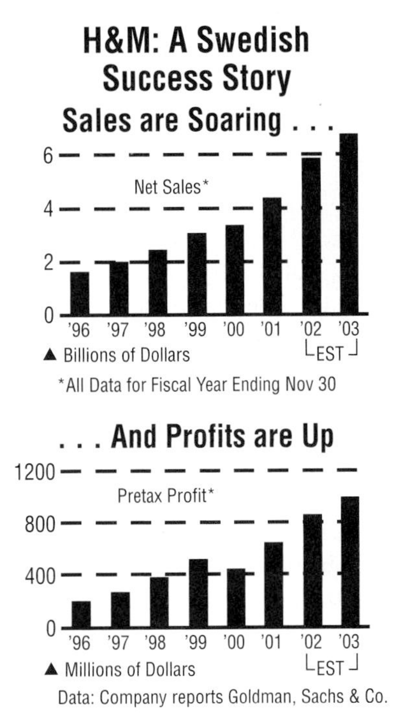

If you stop by its Fifth Avenue location in New York or check out the flagship at the corner of Regeringsgatan and Hamngatan in Stockholm, it's easy to see what's powering H&M's success. The prices are as low as the fashion is trendy, turning each location into a temple of "cheap chic." At the Manhattan emporium, mirrored disco balls hang from the ceiling, and banks of televisions broadcast videos of body-pierced, belly-baring pop princesses. On a cool afternoon in October, teenage girls in flared jeans and two-toned hair mill around the ground floor, hoisting piles of velour hoodies, Indian-print blouses, and patchwork denim skirts—each $30 or under. (The average price of an H&M item is just $18.) This is not Gap's brand of classic casuals or the more grown-up Euro-chic of Zara. It's exuberant, it's over the top, and it's working. "Everything is really nice—and cheap," says Sabrina Farhi, 22, as she clutches a suede trench coat she has been eyeing for weeks.

H&M is also shrewdly tailoring its strategy to fit the U.S. market. In Europe, H&M is more like a department store—selling a range of merchandise for men, women, teens, and children. Its U.S. stores are geared to younger, more fashion-conscious females. And while the pricing is cheap, the branding certainly isn't. H&M spends a hefty 4% of revenues on marketing. This year's photo ad campaign was shot by fashion-world legend Richard Avedon.

Behind this stylish image is a company so buttoned-down and frugal that you can't imagine its executives tuning into a soft-rock station, let alone getting inside a teenager's head. Stefan Persson, whose late father founded the company, looks and talks more like a financier than a merchant prince. A penny-pinching financier, at that. "H&M is run on a shoestring," says Nathan Cockrell, a retail analyst at Credit Suisse First Boston in London. "They buy as cheaply as possible and keep overheads

EXHIBIT 2 Clash of the Clothing Titans

	Style	Strategy	Global Reach	Financials
H&M	Motto is "fashion and quality at the best price." Translates into cutting-edge clothes.	Production outsourced to suppliers in Europe and Asia. Some lead time is just three weeks.	Has 809 stores in 14 countries. More than 88% of sales come from outside Sweden.	Estimated 2002 pretax profit of $833 million on sales of $5.8 billion.
GAP	Built its name on wardrobe basics such as denim, khakis, and T-shirts.	Outsources all production. An average of nine months for turnaround.	Operates 656 stores in Canada, Japan, and Europe, which produce 8% of sales.	Estimated 2002 pretax profit of $554 million on sales of $13.8 billion.
ZARA	Billed as Armani on a budget for its Euro-style clothing for women and men.	Bulk of production is handled by company's own manufacturing facilities in Spain.	Runs 507 outlets in 30 countries, but Spain still accounts for 50% of sales.	Parent Inditex does not break out sales.

Data: Company reports, Santander Central Hispano, BNP Paribas, Goldman, Sachs & Co.

low." Fly business class? Only in emergencies. Take cabs? Definitely frowned upon. To rein in costs, Persson even took away all employee mobile phones in the 1990s. Today, only a few key employees have cell-phone privileges.

But that gimlet eye is just what a retailer needs to stay on its game—especially the kind of high-risk game H&M is playing. Not since IKEA set out to conquer the world one modular wall unit at a time has a Swedish retailer displayed such bold international ambition. H&M is pressing full-steam ahead on a program that will bring its total number of stores to 844 by the end of 2002, a nearly 75% increase in the past six years. With the Nov. 1 opening of its latest Manhattan store, near Macy's, H&M will have 45 outlets in the U.S. It plans to open a further 20 American stores by yearend 2003. "No other European retailer has managed to expand so successfully beyond its own borders," says Wills.

Nevertheless, H&M is pursuing a strategy that has undone a number of rivals. Benetton tried to become the world's fashion retailer but retreated after a disastrous experience in the U.S. in the 1980s. Gap, once the hottest chain in the U.S., has lately been choking on its mismanaged inventory and has never taken off abroad.

Persson and his crew are undaunted. "When I joined in 1972, H&M was all about price," he says. "Then we added quality fashion to the equation, but everyone said you could never combine [them] successfully. But we were passionate that we could." Persson is just as passionate that he will be able to apply the H&M formula internationally.

What's that formula, exactly? Treat fashion as if it were perishable produce: Keep it fresh, and keep it moving. That means spotting the trends even before the trendoids do, turning the ideas into affordable clothes, and making the apparel fly off the racks. "We hate inventory," says H&M's head of buying, Karl Gunnar Fagerlin, whose job is to make sure the merchandise doesn't pile up at company warehouses. Not easy, considering that H&Ms sells 550 million items a year.

All major fashion retailers aim for fast turnaround these days, but H&M is one of the few in the winner's circle. All merchandise is designed in-house by a team of 95 in Stockholm. To keep costs down, the company out-sources manufacturing to a network of 900 garment shops located in 21 mostly low-wage countries, primarily Bangladesh, China, and Turkey. "They are constantly shifting production to get the best deal," says Johan Tisell, an analyst at Enskilda Securities in Stockholm.

Working hand-in-glove with suppliers, H&M's 21 local production offices have compressed lead times—meaning the time it takes for a garment to travel from design table to store floor—to as little as three weeks. Only Zara whose parent, Inditex, owns its own production facilities in Galicia, Spain, boasts a faster turnaround—a mere two weeks. Meanwhile, Gap Inc. operates on a nine-month cycle, a factor that analysts say is to blame for its chronic overstock problem.

H&M's speed maximizes its ability to churn out more hot items during any season, while minimizing its fashion *faux pas*. Stores are restocked daily—although sometimes, even that's not enough to meet demand. When the Manhattan flagship opened in the spring of 2002, crowds grew so large the store had to be restocked hourly.

Faster turnaround means higher sales, which helps H&M charge low prices and still earn gross margins of 53%, a key measure of a retailer's profitability. But cheap and fast don't cut it unless the fashion sense is there. H&M's young designers find their inspiration in everything from street trends and films to the bazaars of Marrakesh. Despite the similarity between *haute couture* and some of H&M's trendier pieces, copying from the catwalk is not permitted, swears Margareta van den Bosch, head of the design team. "Whether it's Donna Karan, Prada, or H&M, we all work on the same time frames," she says. "But we can add garments during the season."

Although H&M sells a range of clothing for women, men, and children, its cheap-chic formula goes down particularly well with the 15-to-30 set. Are you lusting after that Dolce & Gabbana corduroy trench coat but unwilling to cough up $1,000-plus? At $60, H&M's version is a steal. Sure, it's more Lycra than luxe and won't last forever. But if you're trying to keep *au courant*, one season is enough. "At least half my wardrobe comes from H&M," says Emma Mackie, a 19-year-old student in London. "It's really good value for money."

Acquiring this deft touch has taken decades. H&M founder Erling Persson, who died on Oct. 28 at 85, began his career working for his father delivering cheese to Stockholm restaurants. During a visit to New York in 1947, Persson marveled at the success of retailers such as Macy's. Upon his return, he launched small women's clothing chain Hennes—Swedish for "hers." The store's low prices proved a huge hit in Sweden, where retailing, as in the rest of Europe, was at that time still dominated by pricey department stores. By 1968, Hennes had morphed into H&M with the acquisition of Swedish men's retailer Mauritz, and its stores were dotted across Scandinavia. But it wasn't until after Stefan joined the company that H&M's international expansion really took off.

Persson's goal now is to enter a new country every second year. This year, the Swedish retailer is stepping into Portugal. Italy, Canada, and Eastern European nations may be next. The make-or-break market for H&M, though, will be the U.S., since 9 of the 13 European countries in which H&M operates are mature markets for the retailer. Breaking in hasn't been easy. Many of the U.S. outlets that H&M opened in 2000 were too big. The entire top floor of its massive 5,400-square-meter store in Carousel Center in Syracuse, N.Y., now sits empty. Poor location was another teething problem. H&M blundered when it set up shop in suburban Livingston Mall in Newark, N.J. The mall is dominated by numerous inexpensive chains such as Express, Old Navy, and Wet Seal, making it hard for H&M to stand out.

But H&M is learning from its mistakes. During the third quarter, it managed to halve the losses from U.S. outlets, to $6 million, and these are expected to break even by the end of 2002. "They've been quite sensible compared with other European retailers in the U.S.," says Wendy Liebmann, founder of WSL Strategic Retail in New York.

For H&M founder Erling Persson, however, the company's expansion at times seemed a bit too fast. "Sometimes, he asked me: 'Why are you in such a hurry?'" says Stefan. The answer is easy: When you're hot, you don't stop to cool off.

By Kerry Capell in Stockholm, with Gerry Khermouch in New York

Source: "HIP H&M," *BusinessWeek,* November 11, 2002, 106–110.

Case 4-3

Dell Inc.

When Dell CEO Michael S. Dell and President Kevin B. Rollins met privately in the fall of 2001, they felt confident that the company was recovering from the global crash in PC sales. Their own personal performance, however, was another matter. Internal interviews revealed that subordinates thought Dell, 38, was impersonal and emotionally detached, while Rollins, 50, was seen as autocratic and antagonistic. Few felt strong loyalty to the company's leaders. Worse, the discontent was spreading: A survey taken over the summer, following the company's first-ever mass layoffs, found that half of Dell Inc.'s employees would leave if they got the chance.

What happened next says much about why Dell is the best-managed company in technology. At other industry giants, the CEO and his chief sidekick might have shrugged off the criticism or let the issue slide. Not at Dell. Fearing an exodus of talent, the two execs focused on the gripes. Within a week, Dell faced his top 20 managers and offered a frank self-critique, acknowledging that he is hugely shy and that it sometimes made him seem aloof and unapproachable. He vowed to forge tighter bonds with his team. Some in the room were shocked. They knew personality tests given to key execs had repeatedly shown Dell to be an "off-the-charts introvert," and such an admission from him had to have been painful. "It was powerful stuff," says Brian Wood, the head of public-sector sales for the Americas. "You could tell it wasn't easy for him."

Michael Dell didn't stop there. Days later, they began showing a videotape of his talk to every manager in the company—several thousand people. Then Dell and Rollins adopted desktop props to help them do what didn't come naturally. A plastic bulldozer cautioned Dell not to ram through ideas without including others, and a Curious George doll encouraged Rollins to listen to his team before making up his mind.

Walking Databases

To some, the way Michael Dell handled sagging morale might seem like another tale of feel-good management. But to those inside the company, it epitomizes how this Round Rock (Tex.) computer maker has transformed itself from a no-name PC player into a powerhouse brand (Exhibit 1). Sure, Dell is the master at selling direct, bypassing middlemen to deliver PCs cheaper than any of its rivals. And few would quarrel that it's the model of efficiency, with a far-flung supply chain knitted together so tightly that it's like one electrical wire, humming 24/7. Yet all this has been true for more than a decade. And although the entire computer industry has tried to replicate Dell's tactics, none can hold a candle to the company's results. Today, Dell's stock is valued at a price-earnings multiple of 40, loftier than IBM, Microsoft, Wal-Mart Stores, or General Electric.

As it turns out, it's how Michael Dell manages the company that has elevated it far above its sell-direct business model. What's Dell's secret? At its heart is his belief that the status quo is never good enough, even if it means painful changes for the man with his name on the door. When success is achieved, it's greeted with five seconds of praise followed by five hours of postmortem on what could have been done better. Says Michael Dell: "Celebrate for a nanosecond. Then move on." After the outfit opened its first Asian factory, in Malaysia, the CEO sent the manager heading the job one of his old running shoes to congratulate him. The message: This is only the first step in a marathon.

Just as crucial is Michael Dell's belief that once a problem is uncovered, it should be dealt with quickly and directly, without excuses. "There's no 'The dog ate my homework' here," says Dell. No, indeedy. After Randall D. Groves, then head of the server business, delivered 16% higher sales last year, he was demoted. Never mind that none of its rivals came close to that. It could have been better, say two former Dell executives. Groves referred calls to a Dell spokesman, who says Groves's job change was part of a broader reorganization.

Above all, Michael Dell expects everyone to watch each dime—and turn it into at least a quarter. Unlike most tech bosses, Dell believes every product should be profitable from Day One. To ensure that, he expects his managers to be walking databases, able to cough up information on everything from top-line growth to the average number of times a part has to be replaced in the first 30 days after a computer is sold.

But there's one number he cares about most: operating margin. To Dell, it's not enough to rack up profits or grow fast. Execs must do both to maximize long-term profitability. That means products need to be priced low enough to induce shoppers to buy, but not so low that they cut unnecessarily into profits. When Dell's top managers in Europe lost out on profits in 1999 because they hadn't cut costs far enough, they were replaced. "There are some organizations where people think they're a hero if they

EXHIBIT 1 Managing the Dell Way

Michael Dell revolutionized the PC biz with a direct-sales model that keeps costs low and customer satisfaction high. That was 19 years ago, yet Dell is still outdistancing rivals. Credit his management principles:

Be Direct

It's an attitude, not just a business model. When the CEO talks, he doesn't mince words, and workers shouldn't either. They're supposed to question everything and **challenge their bosses.** And no one is exempt. In Dell's own annual 360-degree review, workers complained of his detached style, so he has pledged to be more emotionally engaged.

No Excuses

Dell believes in accountability above all else: "There's no 'The dog ate my homework' at Dell," he warns. A manager must quickly **admit a problem, confront it**, and never be defensive. Dell ruthlessly exposes weak spots during grueling quarterly reviews. And execs know they had better fix the problem before the next meeting.

No Victory Laps

To Dell, **celebration breeds complacency**. He once rejected an idea to display Dell artifacts in the company's lobby because "museums are looking at the past." When they succeed, managers must make due with a short e-mail or a quick pat on the back. The founder's mantra: "Celebrate for a nanosecond, then move on."

Leave the Ego at the Door

The company favors "two-in-a-box" management, in which two executives share responsibility for a product, a region, or a company function. That forces them to **work as a team**, playing off each other's strengths and watching out for each other's weaknesses.

No Easy Targets

It's not enough to rack up profits or turbocharge growth—execs must **do both.** Miss a profit goal, and you're not cutting costs fast enough, Overshoot it, and you're leaving sales on the table. In the past year, the server, storage, and networking chiefs were reassigned, despite solid results. "Pity the folks who didn't use all the bullets in their gun," says a former exec.

Worry about Saving Money, Not Saving Face

Unlike its rivals. Dell is quick to **pull the plug** on disappointing new ventures. The latest: Despite a year of work and extensive news coverage, Michael Dell spiked a plan to put e-commerce kiosks in Sears stores after just four were installed. Instead, kiosks are going into public areas in malls.

invent a new thing," says Rollins. "Being a hero at Dell means saving money."

It's this combination—reaching for the heights of perfection while burrowing down into every last data point—that no rival has been able to imitate. "It's like watching Michael Jordan stuff the basketball," says Merrill Lynch & Co. technology strategist Steven Milunovich. "I see it. I understand it. But I can't do it."

How did this Mike come by his management philosophy? It started 19 years ago, when he was ditching classes to sell homemade PCs out of his University of Texas dorm room. Dell was the scrappy underdog, fighting for his company's life against the likes of IBM and Compaq Computer Corp. with a direct-sales model that people thought was plain nuts. Now, Michael Dell is worth $17 billion, while his 40,000-employee company is about to top $40 billion in sales. Yet he continues to manage Dell with the urgency and determination of a college kid with his back to the wall. "I still think of us as a challenger," he says. "I still think of us attacking."

It's not that Michael Dell leads by force of personality. He's blessed with neither the tough-guy charisma of Jack Welch nor the folksy charm of the late Sam Walton. Once, after hearing about the exploits of flamboyant Oracle Corp. CEO Lawrence J. Ellison, he held up a piece of paper and deadpanned to an aide: "See this? It's vanilla and square, and so am I." This egoless demeanor permeates the company. Everyone is expected to sacrifice their own interests for the good of the business, and no one gets to be a star. If Michael Dell is willing to modify the personality traits he was born with, other top execs are expected to be just as self-sacrificing. Frequently, Dell pairs execs to run an important business, an approach called "two-in-a-box." That way, they work together, checking each others' weaknesses and sharing the blame when something goes wrong. One such executive calls Dell's senior leadership "the no-name management team."

All this has kept Dell on track as rivals have gone off the rails. Since 2000, the company has been adding market share at a faster pace than at any time in its history—nearly three percentage points in 2002. A renewed effort to control costs sliced overhead expenses to just 9.6% of revenue in the most recent quarter and boosted productivity to nearly $1 million in revenue per employee. That's three times the revenue per employee at IBM and almost twice Hewlett-Packard Co.'s rate.

Still, for the restless Michael Dell, that's not nearly enough. He wants to make sure the company he has spent half his life building can endure after he's gone. So he and Rollins have sketched out an ambitious financial target: $60 billion in revenues by 2006 (Exhibit 2). That's twice what the company did in 2001 and enough to put it in league with the largest, most powerful companies in the world. Getting there will require the same kind of success that the company achieved in PCs—but in altogether new markets. Already, Michael Dell is moving the company into printers, networking, handheld computers, and tech services. His latest foray: Dell is entering the cutthroat $95 billion consumer-electronics market with a portable digital-music player, an online music store, and a flat-panel television set slated to go on sale Oct. 28 (Exhibit 3).

Can Dell graduate from PC prodigy to corporate icon? Driving for nonstop growth will require grooming a new generation of leaders, which Rollins concedes is a major challenge given the company's pressure-cooker atmosphere. In the 1990s, after seasoned execs recruited from titans such as Intel and IBM quickly jumped ship, Dell learned that outsiders don't adapt easily to its demanding culture. And unlike in the past, Dell won't be able to count on stock options to make up for the discomfort. Some 32% of its outstanding options are priced above the current share price of $35, and the company has sliced grants to about 40 million shares this year, one-third the 2001 level. Little wonder that so far, Dell has achieved only a modest improvement in morale, according to its internal surveys. "They need to work a lot on appreciating people," says Kate Ludeman, an executive coach who has worked with Dell since 1995.

"One-Trick Pony"

Dell also faces an innovation dilemma. Its penny-pinching ways leave little room for investments in product development and future technologies, especially compared with rivals. Even in the midst of the recession, IBM spent $4.75 billion, or 5.9% of its revenues, on research and development in 2002, while HP ponied up $3.3 billion, or 5.8% of revenues. And Dell? Just a paltry $455 million, or 1.3%. Rivals say that handicaps Dell's ability to move much beyond PCs, particularly in such promising markets as digital imaging and utility computing. "Dell is a great company, but they are a one-trick pony," says HP CEO Carleton S. Fiorina. What's more, Dell has shown little patience for the costs of entering new markets, killing off products—like its high-end server—when they didn't produce quick profits, rather than staying committed to a long-term investment. "They're the best in the world at what they do," says IBM server chief William M. Zeitler. "The question is, will they be best at the Next Big Thing?"

For Michael Dell, inventing the Next Big Thing is not the goal. His mission is to build the Current Big Thing better than anyone else. He doesn't plan on becoming IBM or HP. Rather, he wants to focus on his strength as a superefficient manufacturer and distributor. That's why Dell continues to hone the efficiency of its operations. The company has won 550 business-process patents, for everything from a method of using wireless networks in factories to a configuration of manufacturing stations that's four times as productive as a standard assembly line. "They're inventing business processes. It's an asset that Dell has that its competitors don't," says Erik

EXHIBIT 2
Building a Behemoth

Data: Merrill Lynch & Co., Dell Inc.

Dell is gunning for $60 billion in revenue by 2006, an ambitious goal that requires it to grow 15% a year for the next four years. Here's how it plans to get there:

	2001	2002	2003*	2004*	2005*	2006*
PCs	$20	$23	$26	$27	$29	$30
Servers/Storage	5	5	7	8	9	10
Services	3	4	4	5	7	9
Software/Peripherals**	3	4	4	7	10	13
Total***	$31	$36	$41	$47	$54	$62

All figures are revenues in billions
*Estimated
**Including printers
***May not add up because of rounding

EXHIBIT 3 Beyond the PC

With 80% of its sales coming from the maturing PC market, Dell wants to apply its low-cost ways to new markets. If successful, it could maintain a brisk 15% annual growth rate.

	Consumer Electronics	PC Peripherals	Printers	Storage	Networking	Services
TOTAL 2003 MARKET	$95 Billion	$65 Billion	$50 Billion	$19.2 Billion	$11 Billion	$368 Billion
ESTIMATED DELL SALES FOR 2003	Negligible	$3.8 Billion	$500 Million	$1.5 Billion	$127 Million	$4.1 Billion
	Dell is dipping its toe into the cutthroat industry with flat-panel TVs, digital music players, and an online music service to appeal to its home PC customers. Dell spent $361 million on advertising last year, much of it to build its consumer brand.	Dell has sold its own monitors and digital projectors for years, and introduced its Axim personal digital assistant in late 2002. While it now sells wireless e-mail devices made by other companies, Dell is looking at going solo.	Rather than only resell other company's printers, this year Dell debuted six of its own models. Merrill Lynch thinks Dell's printer sales could rise to $1.4 billion in 2006—good, but not enough to undercut printer king Hewlett-Packard.	For the past two years, Dell has teamed with EMC to develop versions of the storage giant's low-cost models. That has helped Dell nab 5,400 new customers. Look for Dell to build the pricier models in the future.	Attracted by networking giant Cisco Systems' 70% gross margins, Dell sees a chance to take significant share with low-end switches that cost 50% less. The major challenge: Developing more sophisticated products.	Besides offering basic repair services, Dell now helps customers make better use of Dell gear–for instance, when a company needs guidance on setting up a corporate network. Dell hopes this will boost hardware sales—and margins.

Data: Dell, Merrill Lynch. Consumer Electronics Assn.

Brynjolfsson, director of the Center for eBusiness at the Massachusetts Institute of Technology's Sloan School of Management.

Dell's expansion strategy is carefully calibrated to capitalize on that asset. The game plan is to move into commodity markets—with standardized technology that's widely available—where Dell can apply its skills in discipline, speed, and efficiency. Then Dell can drop prices faster than any other company and prompt demand to soar. In markets that Dell thinks are becoming commoditized but still require R&D, the company is taking on partners to get in the door. In the printer market, for example, Dell is slapping its own brand on products from Lexmark International Inc. And in storage, Dell has paired up with EMC Corp. to sell co-branded storage machines. Dell plans to take over manufacturing in segments of those markets as they become commoditized. It recently took on low-end storage production from EMC, cutting its cost of goods 25%.

Dell's track record suggests the CEO will meet his $60 billion revenue goal by 2006. Already, Dell has grabbed large chunks of the markets for inexpensive servers and data-storage gear. After just two quarters, its first handheld computer has captured 37% of the U.S. market for such devices. And Rollins says initial sales of Dell printers are double its internal targets. With the potential growth in PCs and new markets, few analysts doubt that Dell can generate the 15% annual growth needed to reach the mark. The company has averaged better than 19% growth over the past four quarters, and on Oct. 8 Rollins assured investors that everything was on track. "It's almost machine-like," says Goldman, Sachs & Co. analyst Laura Conigliaro. For the year, analysts expect Dell to boost revenues 16%, to $41 billion, and profits 24%, to $2.6 billion, according to a survey of Wall Street estimates by First Call.

What should help Dell as it plunges into so many new markets is the founder's level-headed realism. A student of business history, he has paid close attention to how some of tech's legendary figures lost their way by refusing to admit mistakes. He cites Digital Equipment Corp.'s Ken Olsen as one who stuck with his strategy until the market passed him by and hints that Sun Microsystems Inc.'s Scott G. McNealy could be next.

Dell, on the other hand, has reversed course so fast he's lucky he didn't get whiplash. In 2001, he scrapped a plan to enter the mobile-phone market six months after hiring a top exec from Motorola Inc. to head it up. He decided the prospects weren't bright enough to offset the costs of entry. The next year, Dell wrote off its only major acquisition, a storage-technology company bought in 1999 for $340 million. Dell backed out of the high-end storage business because it decided its technology wasn't ready for market. "It's amazing how a guy who was so young when he founded the company could evolve as he has," says Edward J. Zander, former president of Sun Microsystems. "Guys that have been in the saddle for 15 and 20 years tend to get too religious. He's the exception to the rule."

Michael Dell, in fact, has one of the longest tenures of any founder who remains CEO. At 19 years and counting, he's second in the tech industry only to Oracle's Ellison. "This sounds strange coming from me," says William H. Gates III, who was CEO of Microsoft Corp. for 25 years before giving it up to be chairman and chief software architect, "but very few business leaders go from the early stage of extremely hands-on stuff to have a leadership style and management process that works for a company that's an absolutely huge and superimportant company."

One way Dell has done it is through his power-sharing arrangement with Rollins, à la his "two-in-a-box" philosophy. Brought on as a consultant in 1993 to help plot the company's first long-range plan, Rollins helped it recover from a series of miscues, including the bungled launch of its notebook business and a disastrous go at trading currencies. Three years later, Dell hired Rollins away from Bain & Co. to run North American sales.

Now, Rollins is the day-to-day general. He and Dell sit in adjoining offices separated by only a glass wall. During a pivotal meeting in the fall of 2001, Dell proposed they agree not to make a major move without the other's approval. Working in tandem helps avoid mistakes that the more entrepreneurial Dell or the more rigid Rollins might make alone. Says Dell: "This company is much stronger when the two of us are doing it together." And there's no question that Rollins is the successor. "If I get hit by a truck, he's the CEO. Everyone knows that."

The Gauntlet

Not that the current CEO is letting up. He maintains pinpoint control over the company's vast operations by constantly monitoring sales information, production data, and his competitors' activities. He keeps a BlackBerry strapped to his hip at all times. In the office, he reserves an hour in the morning and one each afternoon to do nothing but read and respond to e-mail, according to one former executive. "Michael can be a visionary, and he can tell you how many units were shipped from Singapore yesterday," says General Electric Co. CEO Jeffrey R. Immelt, a top Dell customer.

Dell's penchant for tracking every last detail can land him in hot water. On Oct. 10, during the trial of former Credit Suisse First Boston tech banker Frank P. Quattrone for allegedly obstructing an investigation into the bank's handling of hot initial public offerings, prosecutors revealed e-mails between Dell and Quattrone. In one July, 2000, exchange, Dell requested 250,000 shares in Corvis Corp., a promising networking company that was preparing to go public, for his corporate venture-capital fund. Dell suggested the allocation "would certainly help" the relationship between his company and CSFB. Dell declined to comment. But his spokesperson says he was merely trying to assist the fund and noted that the company did not do any investment-banking business with CSFB before or after the exchange. In a separate e-mail on which Michael Dell was copied, the manager of Dell's personal venture fund requested Corvis shares for the fund. A spokesperson for that fund says it had invested in Corvis in 1999 and there was nothing improper about the request.

Rollins has the same attention to detail as Michael Dell. He is overseeing a Six Sigma transformation of everything from manufacturing to marketing that is expected to help cut expenses $1.5 billion this year. The emphasis is on small surgical strikes on defects and waste, not massive restructurings. Consider a Six Sigma meeting one balmy July afternoon. Rollins listened to John Holland, a technician in Dell's server factory, describe how his team replaced the colored paper it used to print out parts lists with plain white paper, saving $23,000. "Where else do you get a supervisor making $40,000 a year presenting to the president of a $40 billion company?" says Americas Operations Vice-President Dick Hunter, Holland's boss.

The discipline in Michael Dell's management style is most apparent in how the company approaches new markets. Take Dell's plunge into the $50 billion printer business. Beginning in 2001, a team of Dell strategists spent more than a year researching the market. Dell only started serious planning after finding that nearly two-thirds of its customers said they would buy a Dell printer if they could get the same kind of service they got when they bought a PC or server. In the summer of 2002, Vice-President Tim Peters, a veteran of Dell's handheld launch, was tapped to lead the effort. But like any exec planning to put out a new product, he had to face the gauntlet of Dell and Rollins. After thinking up a strategy, he had to sit by while it was picked apart.

Nothing was left to chance. Dell prodded Peters to think about product features and the buying experience, while Rollins pushed him to keep costs low without sacrificing quality. Both bosses wanted to make sure the timing was right. That required intense discussions about how standardized printer technologies were and the state of the supply chain that Dell would use. One key challenge: ink. Customers typically buy replacement cartridges at a nearby retailer. It didn't seem likely that they would wait for days for an Internet order from Dell to arrive.

The toughest task in any product launch is the math. At Dell, a new line of PCs, which is good for $2 billion to $3 billion in annual revenue, costs roughly $10 million to launch. Any new idea must have a comparable return says G. Carl Everett, a Dell senior vice-president who retired in 2001, and turn a profit from the get-go. That's what Peters had to promise in printers. The rare exceptions occur only when Dell senses an opportunity that's critical to the company's future. Dell's server business, for instance, took 18 months to reach profitability, says former Vice-President Michael D. Lambert.

In the printer business, it took seven months for Peters to work everything out. The products debuted in March and were profitable immediately. Peters' proposed solution to the ink riddle: Every Dell printer comes loaded with software directing users to Dell.com, where they can order a new cartridge and have it delivered the next day. Still, Michael Dell never let up: The night before the launch, he sat up until 2 a.m. to watch the printers debut online and then zipped e-mails to Peters with suggestions for improvement. When initial sales came in at double the internal target, Peters' team got a very Dell-like reward: a quick trip to see *Terminator 3*.

That flick may turn out to have more than therapeutic value, considering that rival HP is determined to wipe out Dell's printer ambitions. HP's strategy is to leave Dell in the dust with a burst of innovation. It spends $1 billion a year on printer research—more than twice Dell's entire R&D budget. HP is using that money to develop products like high-end photo ink, which will last 73 years, nearly 10 times as long as what Dell offers. "Dell is going to hit a wall," says Jeff Clarke, HP's executive vice-president for global operations. "We view them as low-tech and low-cost. They're the Kmart of the industry." And some experts say Dell won't threaten HP's 60% market share anytime soon. Gartner Inc. estimates that Dell claimed less than 1% of the printer market in the second quarter, mostly at the low end of the business.

Attacking from Below

If past experience is any guide, Dell may struggle as it tries to move upmarket. With its bare-bones R&D budget, it had to kill off high-end servers that go head-to-head with fancy gear from Sun, saying the soft demand didn't merit its attention. And after two and a half years selling networking gear, Dell has failed to deliver products powerful enough to threaten Cisco Systems Inc.'s dominant market share. Yet Dell is betting that as technology improves, the low-end products it sells so deftly will become more than good enough for most customers, leaving rivals scrambling to find their next high-end innovation. "The history of the industry is [that] the attack from below works," says Merrill Lynch's Milunovich.

Indeed, Dell has had no trouble gobbling up sales as markets mature. In storage, its sales now account for 10% of EMC's revenue, some $600 million annually. In the low-margin home-PC market, which Dell long avoided, unit sales have grown an average of 46% in the past four quarters.

Michael Dell certainly would take exception to HP's jabs about his company being the Kmart of tech. But there are some striking similarities between Dell and another giant retailer: Wal-Mart. Like the behemoth from Bentonville, Ark., Dell has built a business as a super-efficient distributor, with the tightly run operations and thrifty management to enter any number of new markets quickly and easily. "We've always toyed with the idea that we could distribute anything," says Morton L. Topfer, a former Dell vice-chairman who now sits on the company's board. Maybe not anything. But Dell is striving to greatly expand his reach in the tech world. With his management philosophy of constant improvement, he seems well on his way.

By Andrew Park in Round Rock, Tex., with Peter Burrows in San Mateo, Calif., and bureau reports

Source: "What You Don't Know about Dell," *BusinessWeek*, November 3, 2003, 77–84.

Case 4-4

Sun Microsystems Inc. (A)

Late last June, Sun Microsystems Inc. President Edward Zander got the kind of call every tech executive dreads. After eBay Inc. suffered a 22-hour outage of its Web site and a spate of smaller crashes, CEO Margaret Whitman called to tell Zander that the problem was a bug in Sun's top-of-the-line server. Sun would learn something just as startling over the next few days of round-the-clock meetings with eBay: The Internet upstart didn't have a clue about running a $1 million-plus computer. The company hadn't provided sufficient air conditioning to keep the machine cool. And even though there had been a software problem with the machine for which Sun had issued a patch many months before, eBay had simply neglected to install it. The list went on—fueling the sentiment, as one Sun manager put it, that "selling computers to some of these dot-coms is like giving a gun to a 5-year-old."

That's when Zander realized things could get much worse. For most dot-coms, starting their business on a Sun server is almost a given. Already, more than 40% of the servers found in the computing centers that house most Web sites are Sun's, and that market is expected to boom as everyone from new Net companies to the click-and-mortar crowd set up shop online. "It suddenly hit me," says Zander. "How many future eBays are buying their first computer from us this very minute?" Adds Sun CEO Scott G. McNealy: "It was our Pentium moment," comparing the eBay incident to the lesson Intel Corp. learned in 1994 after the chip giant angered customers by initially trying to downplay a bug in its new Pentium chip. "That's when we realized it wasn't eBay's fault," says McNealy. "It was our fault."

McNealy and Zander didn't need another wake-up call. Since then, the two have been tearing apart Sun and rebuilding it in an effort to make the Net as reliable as the telephone system. Just as AT&T became Ma Bell, providing that always available dial tone, Sun is shooting for no less than Ma Web, the supplier of super-reliable Web tone. To do that, Sun is moving far beyond Web servers to providing many of the technologies required to make this possible: storage products, a vast array of e-business software, and consultants that not only supply all the gear but also hold customers' hands every step of the way (Exhibit 1).

Safe Bet

If the duo can pull it off, Sun could emerge as the King of the Net—every bit as dominant as Big Blue in its mainframe heyday or Microsoft Corp. in the PC era. Just as high-tech managers used to say, "No one gets fired for choosing IBM," Zander aims to have the same said of Sun. "I want to be the safe bet for companies that need the most innovative technology," he says.

Sun hopes to go down in the history books as that rare company with the vision to change an industry and the ability to cash in on that vision. Since it was founded in 1982, Sun has promoted the notion that "the network is the computer," a view of computing where the action isn't on desktop PCs but on big central servers where computing can be doled out in easy-to-use chunks, wherever and whenever desired. With the explosion of the Internet and rapid deployment of high-bandwidth networks, Sun's vision finally is becoming a reality. "McNealy held out for the pot of gold," says Bill Raduchel, a former Sun executive who is now chief technologist at America Online Inc. "It took a decade to play out, but now the pot of gold is here."

That's why Sun has been on a tear. In the most recent quarter, revenue climbed 35%—more than any other computer company, including PC darling Dell Computer Corp., which grew 30%. Sun is growing faster than at any time since 1991, when it was one-fifth the size it is today. And with gross profit margins of 52%, it is the most profitable computer maker in all of techdom.

McNealy vows this is just the beginning. Known for having the strategic vision, slickest sales reps, and hottest new products—but not the best service—Sun has made reliability the top priority. That means pumping up the services business and overhauling the way the company designs and sells its products. In the past year, Sun has reduced the number of configurations it sells from thousands by pushing customers to choose from under 200 models. And now, managers and sales reps are compensated largely on customer satisfaction. What's more, McNealy, a sometime golfing buddy of General Electric Co. Chairman John F. Welch, has become a convert of GE's Six Sigma quality program that builds in checks to make sure customers' operations stay up and running. By far, the boldest element of McNealy's plan is software. Sun is trying to define and dominate a new category of software that combines many of today's e-business software segments, including e-mail, e-commerce portals, and programs for serving up Web pages and wireless applications. The idea: Wrap a suite of applications into one fail-safe whole available on any Sun server. On July 17, iPlanet, Sun's Net software joint

EXHIBIT 1 The Net Effect

Almost from its founding in 1982, Sun has pursued a vision in which computing power resides on huge servers, whisking data and other services to PCs, handheld gadgets, and other devices. Thanks to the Web, Sun's vision is becoming reality. So Sun is honing its strategy, management techniques, and technology to become the dominant computer company in the Internet Age.

STRATEGY

Redefine Net Software: Today, hundreds of niche software outfits hawk a mind-numbing patchwork of applications. Sun wants to create a new category of software that combines many Net programs into one super-reliable whole that's included with its server.

As Reliable as the Phone Network: Sun is moving beyond just hardware to offer pretested configurations that include storage, Net software, and popular applications. That's how telco switchmakers like Lucent and Nortel managed to make the phone network fail-safe.

Lock Up the Service Providers: Having guessed right that software would be delivered over the Net rather than as CDs to be installed on PCs, Sun has the early lead with companies that will deliver the software—from Net newbies to huge telcos.

MANAGEMENT

Central Authority: On July 1, Sun created into one uber-sales operation, rather than fiercely independent server, software, chip, and services units. That way, customers can deal with one salesman. More important, engineers are working together to design resilient systems by making sure, for example, that Net software can detect chip or disk-drive failures.

No More Cowboys: Sun has been known as the freewheeling cowboy of the computer business. Now it's adding big-company processes—such as extensive audits of a customer's tech operations before taking the order.

TECHNOLOGY

The Grand Design: Sun is the architect of some of the sexier elements of the Web, such as its Java Net software. Now engineers are focusing on keeping the Net running all the time—like how to build backup systems to avoid failures in chips, servers, software, and networks.

Pay-as-You-Grow: Sun is working on hardware and software components that allow fast-growing customers to add what they need without ever having to scrap old equipment.

The Storage Is the Network: New VCR-sized storage devices that can be located anywhere on the Net—instead of just in central data centers—putting information closer to users.

LEADERSHIP

Forging Industry Standards: With Java a Net standard, Sun continues to push its Jini technology, which promises to let any digital device talk to any other. That way, your browser-equipped cell phone could print on any nearby Jini-ready printer.

Setting Ground Rules: Not all Net companies know how to operate around the clock. So Sun has a program to lay out best practices, from how to ensure backup to how to prevent data centers from becoming overheated. Some 300 companies have qualified for this stamp of approval of the Net Age.

venture formed with AOL last year, unveiled the new suite, along with an audacious goal: Within 18 months, the company expects to hit the $1 billion mark in e-commerce software sales, according to Margaret Breya, iPlanet's vice-president of marketing. By 2005, she says Sun could have a $5 billion to $10 billion software business. Other executives, however, say it may take a buying binge to get there.

Put it all together, and Sun is designing its own take on an old trend: vertical integration, in which it sells software, hardware, and services as one—just like telecom equipment makers Lucent Technologies or Nortel

Networks Corp. do with their phone switches. "The computing model of tomorrow is the telecom model of today," says Masood Jabbar, Sun's senior vice-president of sales. How does Sun fit in? It plans to make the "big frigging Webtone switches," as McNealy calls them—the powerful servers that can whisk billions of bits around the Net, along with the software that manages Web pages, dishes up data, and executes transactions. "The world's moving in our direction at 8 gazillion miles per hour. Our biggest problem is just trying to keep up," says McNealy.

That's why he has lit a bonfire under Sun. After the eBay incident, Zander called a meeting of all managers and read them the riot act. Late last summer, his staff identified 14 key initiatives, such as new processes for conducting customer audits, with one of Zander's top vice-presidents in charge of each. And on July 1, McNealy reorganized Sun, combining fiercely independent sales operations within product units into one single sales organization. Now, customers see one sales rep for their entire business, instead of being bombarded by reps from different divisions. And McNealy has created a Customer Advocacy Organization to make sure all divisions are putting reliability and customer satisfaction first. Division president Mel Friedman, for instance, has authority to request the redesign of any Sun product for suspected glitches. Says Breya: "It's about Sun growing up."

As we all know, though, growing up is hard to do. For Sun to shake off its upstart ways, it will have to make the shift from an engineering-driven company to a full-service company. That means mastering software sales, a historic weakness, and building up consulting to help companies design their e-business around Sun gear. And it must do all this while holding off heavyweights such as IBM and Hewlett-Packard. The stalwarts may have been slow to grok the Net, but they have a legacy of ultra-dependable products that could be a major advantage. "Sun rode the wave of dot-coms, but those companies have different needs now. And taking care of those needs is IBM's and HP's forte, not Sun's," says Bruce L. Chovnick, senior vice-president at Network Solutions, a Web registry company that recently ditched a Sun high-end server for a mainframe from IBM.

McNealy will have to stare down other challengers, as well. At a time when servers based on Sun's new UltraSparc3 chip are a few months late, longtime PC industry rivals are massing for yet another assault on the server market. Using Microsoft's four-month-old Windows 2000 program or the free Linux operating system, PC makers will continue to chip away at the market for less powerful servers—especially after Intel brings out its new IA-64 chips, due by year end. "Customers are willing to pay high prices and go with the safe bet [Sun] in these early days of the Net. But ultimately, we'll be able to redefine the economics of the Internet," says Compaq Computer Corp. CEO Michael D. Capellas. Adds International Data Corp. analyst Jean S. Bozman: "Everyone is shooting at Sun, there's no question about it."

The company with the most ammunition is Microsoft. On June 22, Microsoft announced its version of Sun's Webtone scheme—an initiative dubbed .net that is designed to make the Web much easier to use. In it, unrelated Web sites, Net services, and traditional Windows software programs can be linked together to do useful things—say, to get your bank's Web site to transfer money to your e-broker, who buys a stock and then records the trade to your Microsoft Money program on your PC. Such complexity requires software expertise, snorts Microsoft CEO Steve A. Ballmer, "and Sun's not really a software company." Counters Sun chief scientist Bill Joy: "I've been writing about network-based computing for 20 years. Microsoft embraced it last week."

Sniping aside, Sun faces even more software challenges. Throw into the mix programs such as Napster that make it easy to link files directly from PC to PC, altogether bypassing huge servers, and some analysts think McNealy & Co. could face a resurgence of powerful PCs that can store and move data around the Net. That could put a squeeze on server profits. Sanford C. Bernstein & Co. analyst Toni Sacconaghi thinks profit margins for Sun's servers could fall from the mid-50s to the low-30s within three years. So it's crucial that Sun crank up sales of hugely profitable software and storage products, with gross profit margins of 80% and 60%, respectively.

Only then can Sun continue to fund its $2 billion research-and-development effort and keep spending at an industry-leading rate of 10% of revenue. If it can't, Sun may find itself boxed into a high-end corner of the computer industry, adding to the list of once proud computer companies such as Digital Equipment Corp. that have been whittled away by PC makers.

Sun has managed to outfox the doomsayers before. In the early 1990s, when profits collapsed for the technical workstations that brought in 90% of the company's revenue, McNealy bet the next big opportunity would be servers. He poured billions into developing technologies such as the Solaris operating system. Now, servers and related gear bring roughly 80% of Sun's $11.7 billion in sales. Even more remarkable is Sun's assault on the high-end server market once dominated by IBM mainframes. While the market for $1 million-plus servers shrank 17.8%

EXHIBIT 2

Source: Data; Sanford C. Bernstein & Co.

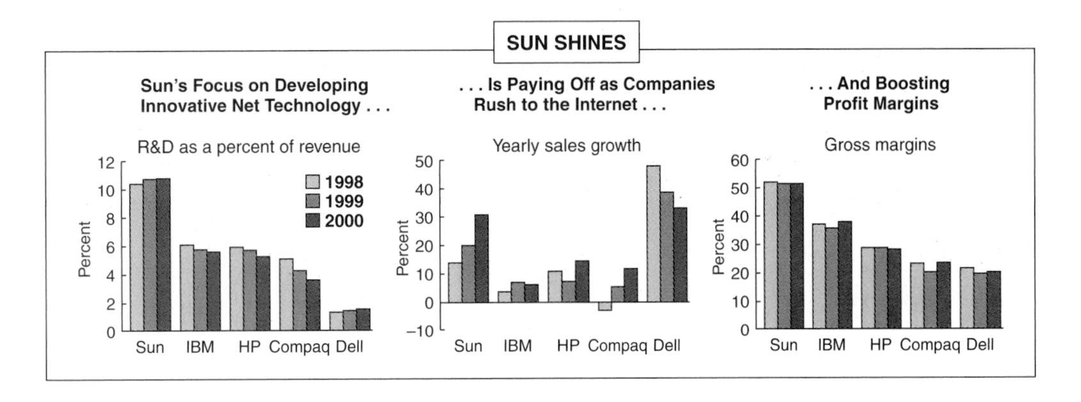

last year, to $11.4 billion, Sun's revenue has rocketed 28% because of runaway sales of its e10,000 Starfire machines, according to IDC (Exhibit 2).

Unlike high-tech dynasties such as IBM or Microsoft, Sun's grand plan is not based on locking customers into its own proprietary technology. IBM and Microsoft modulated the flow of new technology in the mainframe and PC eras largely by maintaining control of technical interfaces that others would need to create compatible programs and peripherals. But Sun wants to dominate Internet-style—that is, by doing as much innovation as possible, licensing leading-edge work as the standard for others, and then racing to stay ahead.

That puts the pressure on Sun's big thinkers, like Joy (Exhibit 3). For starters, Joy and Sun's other technologists have coined the term "Net Effects" to describe the challenge of keeping up with spiraling demand as a billion people use the Net more often, from more devices, and in different ways over the next few years. To keep pace, Sun's servers will have to accelerate in power at a rate at least 100 times faster than Moore's Law, which holds that chips double in speed every 18 months, says Sun chief technologist Greg Popadopolous. Sun is working on two tracks—massive single machines with millions of microprocessors, as well as distributed computing schemes so the computing load can be divvied up between smaller machines linked by high-speed networks.

Sun also is betting it can leapfrog the competition by giving customers the essential software they need to run their e-businesses in one neat, foolproof package. Today, companies face a blizzard of offerings—application servers to host and handle e-mail, Web servers to manage and send out Web pages, and portal programs on which to give the sites a unique look and feel. While these stand-alone software products may deliver the latest bells and whistles, it costs a fortune in consulting fees to make them work together.

Sun's approach is different. iPlanet packs snazzy programs into a suite known as the Internet Service Deployment Platform. Don't be fooled by the clunky name. Using this suite, customers can get up and running quickly because Sun has made sure the software works in sync. With the price starting at $500,000, Sun isn't looking to undercut the competition. Instead, customers will save on installation. "This could cut my development time by 30%," says Norbert Nowicki, a senior partner with Computer Sciences Corp., an El Segundo (Calif.) computer services consultancy.

Sun isn't the only company offering such a suite. Oracle, IBM, and Microsoft do, as well. But none of those companies is the dominant provider of the computers on which the software must run. "Sun isn't just dragging the software along anymore," says Goldman, Sachs &Co. analyst Laura Conigliaro. "It can be a serious driver of new business." Especially with partner AOL using the software suite internally and promoting it to its Net customers. "AOL is customer No. 1 for iPlanet," says David Gang, an AOL executive who recently became iPlanet's executive vice-president. "If we can build products that satisfy AOL, it should work for everyone else."

The irony of McNealy's software approach is that he's stealing a page from the Microsoft playbook—a twist on Microsoft's "embrace and extend" strategy of absorbing fresh technologies into its Windows software. Instead, Sun wants to either bundle or weave Net software into its Solaris operating system. The process already has begun. While competition used to be fierce in the market for arcane directory software, where companies store their databases of employees, customers, and suppliers, now

EXHIBIT 3 The Joy of Questioning

It was a bona fide mood killer. On May 15, the 100 or so chief technology officers at San Francisco's Palace Hotel were flying high. They spent the morning at a high-tech conference getting jazzed about how they could help their companies cash in on the limitless wealth-making potential of the Internet. Then Bill Joy took the stage. The Sun Microsystems Inc. chief scientist used his lunchtime keynote to lay out his view of technology: He fears that rapid high-tech advances could lead to man-made electronic and biological scourges—and the possible extinction of the human race by midcentury. For most of the speech, the audience sat in respectful silence. Then Joy gave a sense of what the future could hold by reading a long description of a horrific plague that wiped out much of medieval Greece. Nervous chuckles began to break the uncomfortable silence.

Joy is a surprising candidate to be making such dire warnings. After all, he has helped shape Sun's vision of superfast computers zipping all manner of digital transactions along the Net. And, he admits, it's computers from Sun and others that will make possible the scientific advances he fears. Still, no one at Sun is trying to talk Joy down from his high-tech bully pulpit. "The concept took me by surprise," admits Sun CEO Scott G. McNealy. "A lot of people think Bill is shooting the golden goose. But hey, I've got kids, too, and Bill's [discussing his views] in a very prudent, responsible way. He's not some lunatic. He's not a prophet of doom." Adds Melvin Schwartz, a Nobel prize winner for physics in 1988: "He's thinking about the things that should be thought about. What sounds wild today won't be in 20 to 30 years."

Indeed, Joy says he's out to shake the mindset that technology offers boundless good. Since publishing an article in *Wired* magazine last April entitled "Why the Future Doesn't Need Us," the 45-year-old Joy has been spending a third of his time on his latest concern. Discoveries in genetic engineering, robotics, and molecular-level engineering (nanotechnology) will soon make it possible for terrorists to unleash mayhem far more dangerous than the nuclear threat, he says. "These technologies are going to create a quadrillion dollars of wealth in the next century," says Joy. "But we do have to deal with the risks. The future is rushing at us at incredible speed, and people just haven't thought it through."

There have been plenty of doomsayers in the past, but few have Joy's credentials. In 1976, as a graduate student, Joy created a version of the Unix operating system that is the standard for most Web sites. In 1982, he co-founded Sun, and was a driving force behind its Java software. These days, Joy is working on new technology to make computers resistant to software bugs.

Joy is by no means turning his back on the Information Society that has made him rich. He says he's simply trying to start a debate. He suggests that companies exploring planet-threatening technologies pay high insurance premiums to discourage them from simply dabbling in such technology. Joy fears the only answer could be one that appalls scientists—including himself: put an end to the spirit of unfettered freedom of scientific inquiry. Lewis M. Branscomb, IBM's former chief scientist and a professor emeritus at Harvard University, credits Joy with raising important issues, but cautions that "once the politicians are allowed to start censoring 'dangerous knowledge,' we will lose both our democracy and our ability to understand how to manage our future." For Joy, the debate is just beginning.—*Peter Burrows*

Sun dominates because it has embedded directory software into the latest version of Solaris. "This could be every bit as big as Oracle's [$7.4 billion database] business," says Mark Tolliver, general manager of iPlanet.

In recent months, the company has made a push into hot new areas, such as a wireless server that will go head-to-head with IBM and others, and e-commerce and e-marketplace applications that will compete with offerings from Commerce One, Oracle, and others. And while iPlanet doesn't have a product to rival red-hot programs like Vignette's software for managing Web pages, Sun may develop offerings in this niche or buy the pieces necessary to offer it. "With our stock where it is, we'd be remiss if we didn't look at this," says Jonathan Schwartz, recently named Sun vice-president for corporate strategy.

Storage Breakthrough

One area where Sun hasn't been able to get off the ground is storage. The company has made two failed attempts to introduce new products in the last three years. "This business takes focus, but storage was an afterthought for Sun," says Raduchel. No more. Sun claims it has made a breakthrough and has created a specialized sales and support organization to push it. Never mind lining up big cabinet-size storage racks tethered to servers—the way most storage farms operate. Instead, customers put Sun's new T3 storage boxes wherever makes the most sense—without having to be within close proximity to a server. An Internet service provider, for example, could put one in a Boston office to speed Red Sox scores to the locals—regardless of whether that site uses servers from Sun or a rival. "The upside for Sun in storage is immense," says Goldman's Conigliaro, who thinks Sun's $2 billion business will grow 25% a year for the next three years. Still, in that time frame, rival EMC Corp. is expected to shoot past the $15 billion mark.

When did Sun get so serious about growing up? Rumblings began in 1998, when Sun's brain trust began to sense that customers' needs for keeping their Web sites up and running were far outstripping Sun's know-how. But for McNealy and Zander, the eBay incidents in mid-1999 underscored how fast those requirements were rising—and how far behind Sun really was.

Sun sprang into action to solve eBay's problem, and within weeks, it worked out a plan with software partners Oracle and Veritas Software Corp. to stabilize eBay's server—even devising back-up systems that have kept eBay out of the news despite six or so crashes in recent months. "We were pushing Sun's products to places they'd never had to go," says eBay Chief Technology Officer Maynard Webb, who last fall nearly switched to IBM. "For Sun to still have our business is a testament to their ability to solve those issues."

Zander was worried it was more like dumb luck. He knew last-minute heroics would not be possible should eBay-like debacles become commonplace. So in early July, Zander assigned Vice-President John C. Shoemaker to come up with a set of initiatives to meet customer demand for rock-solid gear. By the end of August, after key areas for improvement were identified, Zander decided it was time to turn up the pressure inside Sun, calling for daily 8 A.M. meetings with the management team to discuss any problems at customer sites. "Scott and I decided to ruin everyone's morning," he says.

Now, all high-end systems must be pretested with the customer's software before they ship. Another team is making sure that all new products can be monitored remotely from one of Sun's data centers, finally bringing it up to speed with rivals such as EMC and IBM. Sun has also done two-day, lengthy audits of 75 top customers, sometimes issuing 100-page reports that recommend making changes such as adding a humidity sensor to ensure that atmospheric conditions are optimal for Sun equipment.

And McNealy has become a crusader for the new quality program, dubbed Sun Sigma. Now, Sun's top execs will get four days of training and will then lead teams that will get four weeks of training in Six Sigma-style practices. Any manager who doesn't lead such a team over the next 18 months, says Zander, can forget getting promoted to vice-president.

Why the hardball tactic? With 35,000 employees, Sun will have to start behaving less like a mob of high-tech freedom fighters and more like an icon of big management control. If McNealy can pull that off, then Sun might one day truly be worthy of the nickname Ma Web.

Source: Peter Burrows, "Sun's Bid to Rule the Web," *BusinessWeek E.Biz*, July 24, 2000, EB 31–EB 42.

Chapter 14

Designing Market-Driven Organizations

An expanding base of evidence from a wide range of companies points to the critical importance of aligning the strategy and capabilities of the organization with the market in order to provide superior customer value.[1] Organizational change is essential in many companies to achieve this objective. The market-driven organization must alter its design, roles, and activities in line with customer value requirements.

Recent decades have seen a period of unprecedented organizational change, and this activity promises to continue. Companies have realigned their organizations to establish closer contact with customers, improve customer service, bring the Internet into operations and marketing, reduce unnecessary layers of management, decrease the time span between decisions and results, and improve organizational effectiveness in other ways. Organizational changes include the use of information systems to reduce organizational layers and response time, use of multifunctional teams to design and produce new products, development of new roles and structures, and creation of flexible networks of organizations to compete in turbulent business environments.

Procter & Gamble's (P&G) initiatives to become more market-driven are discussed in Chapter 1. Associated with those business and marketing strategy shifts were critically important organizational changes. P&G completed a massive global restructuring plan aimed to improve the company's innovation and competitiveness in June 2003. P&G's "Organization 2005" plan cost an estimated $2 billion. P&G is widely recognized for its powerful marketing capabilities, but at the end of the 1990s faced intense competition throughout the world and loss of position in several key product markets.

Previously organized into four business units covering the regions of the world, in 1998 seven new executives reporting to the CEO were given profit responsibility for global product units such as baby care, beauty, and fabric and home care (Global Business Units). Several of the Global Business Units are headquartered overseas. The new design concept also includes eight Market Development Units intended to tackle local market issues (e.g., supermarket retailing in South America), as well as Global Business Services and corporate functions. Key objectives were to increase the speed of decision making and move new products into commercialization faster, as well as managing the business on a global basis.

"Change agents" have been appointed to work across the Global Business Units to lead cultural and business change by helping teams to work together more effectively through using real-time collaboration tools. Virtual innovation teams are linked by intranets, which can be accessed by senior executives to keep up with developments. The program involves considerable downsizing in personnel, and substantial change—25 percent of P&G brand managers left the company in 18 months. The sales organization is being designed to focus salesperson attention more directly on individual brands.[2]

By the completion of the "Organization 2005" program, P&G had doubled its rate of sales growth, and left competitors complaining about P&G's renewed aggression in pricing and promotion. P&G is targeting profitable market segments throughout the world, where previously competitors were virtually unchallenged. The considerable savings from restructuring have been plowed back into market development.[3] The company is focused on big brands in big categories (laundry, hair care, diapers, and feminine protection); big developed markets; and partnerships with big retailers.[4]

P&G's changes in organizational design underline the nature of the fundamental changes facing many companies in realigning their structures and processes with the requirements of a turbulent and intensely competitive environment.

First, we examine several organization design issues, and then consider alternative designs and the features and limitations of each in different situational settings. Next, we discuss selecting an organization design. Finally, we look at several global aspects of organizations.

Considerations in Organization Design

Several factors influence the design of marketing organizations. They include (1) matching the design to the strategic goals and direction of the company; (2) determining the need to alter vertical structures of the organization; (3) deciding the extent of process-type organizational design; (4) integrating value-creating activities around customers; (5) partnering with independent organizations to perform marketing activities; and (6) understanding the impact of the Internet on the organization's processes.

Strategy and Organization Design

As strategies change and evolve in a company, it is increasingly necessary to examine organizational issues in the implementation of marketing strategy. Exhibit 14.1 describes several recent realignments of marketing structures in companies making major strategic changes. The examples show that across many sectors, companies are stimulated by many factors to rethink how they organize marketing—to counter performance shortfalls by better integration; to globalize products and brands effectively; to bring sales and marketing closer together; to focus on brands and products. Building new strategies in the market-driven company underlines the corresponding need to manage organizational change effectively.

Organizational Change

Organizational change is a continuing process in many companies. The trend is away from vertical structures toward flat horizontal structures with greater emphasis on processes (for example, new-product development) and less emphasis on functional specialization.

The vertical organization structure concerns the number of management levels and reporting relationships. Vertical design issues include determining reporting relationships, establishing departmental groupings, and creating vertical information linkages. Reporting relationships indicate who reports to whom in the organizational hierarchy. Departmental grouping considers how sets of employees are assigned responsibilities. Groupings may be according to function, geography, product, market, or combinations of these factors. Vertical information linkages are necessary to aid communications among organizational participants. Various techniques help to move information through the organization including approval of proposed actions, rules and procedures, plans and schedules, creation of additional levels or positions, and information systems.

Organizations today have fewer levels than traditional organizations and are beginning to organize around core business processes. These flat organizations have fewer managers and are information-based. Information storage, processing, and decision-support technology move information up and down and across the organization, and across organizational boundaries to partner

EXHIBIT 14.1 Strategic Change and Organizational Change

Sources: Jean Halliday, "GM Puts Final Nail in the Coffin of Brand Management," *Advertising Age,* April 5, 2004, 8; "K-C Creates Global Marketing Team," *Marketing Week,* January 22, 7; Steven Burke, "Ingram Reshapes U.S. Marketing Efforts," *CRN,* January 12, 2004, 66; Jean Halliday, "Chrysler Refits Brand Team," *Advertising Age,* May 14, 2001, 35; Theresa Howard, "Organization Next," *Brandweek,* July 31, 2000, 5; "Hershey Consolidates Marketing Group," *Candy Industry,* January 2000, 13–14.

- In 2004, faced with declining profits across the world, General Motors removed the last remnants of its failed brand management system, and replaced marketing teams around models with a single team per division, under a marketing director responsible for advertising, marketing and promotions for all models. This puts more control in the hands of marketing directors, who previously were less powerful than divisional advertising directors.
- Globalization at Kimberly-Clark led in January 2004 to a new global management structure, folding marketing and product development into one team. The European and North American personal care businesses were merged into a single North Atlantic division. Marketing and advertising have been brought together on a global basis.
- Computer industry distribution giant Ingram Micro appointed a new vice-president of marketing in 2004, to link sales and marketing more closely together. The goal is better execution of strategies with vendors.
- In 2001, the troubled Chrysler Group restructured its marketing organization, with Marketing communications directors and managers at Chrysler, Jeep and Dodge taking responsibility for total brand plans, including pricing and incentives. Previously their focus had been mainly on advertising strategy. The goal is greater product and brand focus and cultural change at Chrysler.
- PepsiCo's market strategy shows a greater emphasis on growing sales of noncarbonated beverages and focusing on ethnic markets. In 2000, the company split its marketing department into carbonated and noncarbonated beverages, and appointed a VP-level post dedicated to ethnic marketing. The company is also bringing the sales force closer to key retail customers with reorganization into five separate groups: field sales, national accounts sales, strategy and customer development, fountain beverage, and "Power of One" teams.
- Previously organized into business units focused on chocolate, nonchocolate, grocery, and special markets, Hershey Foods has replaced this structure with a consolidated U.S. marketing organization, to align marketing more closely with sales, and to emphasize brand equity and new products. The new VP U.S. Marketing manages six marketing units: seasons, new products, special channels, brand equity, pack-types, and event marketing.

organizations. Recall the use of virtual teams linked by intranet at P&G. Levels of management are usually eliminated, since people at those levels function primarily as information relays rather than as decision makers and leaders. In many organizations, management is under pressure to reduce operating costs, so eliminating organizational levels and increasing the number of people supervised to reduce staff size.

Exhibit 14.2 shows possible new structures as companies move away from traditional hierarchical structures.[5] A study of 73 companies by the Boston Consulting Group places 32 percent in the hierarchy, 38 percent in the process overlay, and 30 percent in the functional overlay form. No horizontal structures were reported. The prevailing organizational forms appear to be the hybrid overlay structures.

Hybrid, Process-Type Structures

As shown in Exhibit 14.2 the structures of large established companies are moving toward horizontal business processes while retaining integrating functions (marketing, human resources) and specialist functions (research and development, marketing).[6] The processes are major clusters of strategically important activities such as new-product development, order generation and fulfillment, and value/supply chain management. As companies adopt process structures, various organizational changes occur including fewer levels and fewer managers, greater emphasis on building distinctive capabilities using multifunctional teams, customer value-driven processes and capabilities, and continuously changing organizations that reflect market and competitive

EXHIBIT 14.2 Alternative Organizational Structures

Source: George S. Day, "Aligning the Organization to the Market," in *Reflections on the Future of Marketing,* Donald R. Lehmann and Katherine E. Jocz, eds. (Cambridge, MA: Marketing Science Institute, 1997), 69–73.

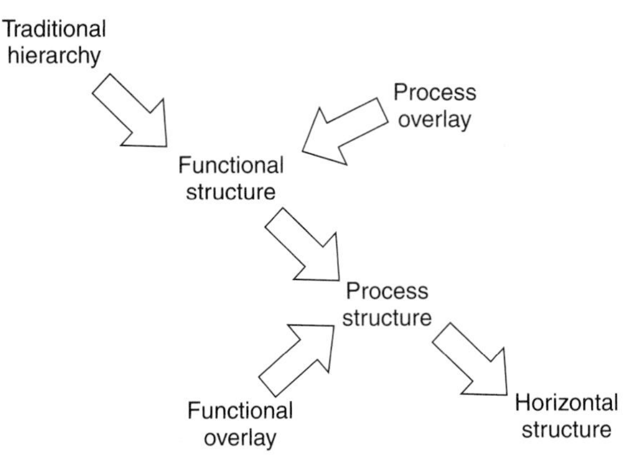

environment changes.[7] The Cross-Functional Feature highlights several characteristics of moving an organization from a functional toward a process orientation. These changes are likely to evolve rather than be immediately transformed.

Consumer packaged goods companies such as Kraft Foods have pioneered the move toward hybrid structures, and away from traditional product and brand management approaches in order to place emphasis on customer management:

> Teams are organized around three core processes: The consumer management team, replacing the brand management function, is responsible for customer segments; customer process teams, replacing the sales function, serve the retail accounts; and the supply management team, absorbing the logistics function, ensures on-time delivery to retailers. There is also a strategic integration team, to develop effective overall strategies and coordinate the teams. Although this team relies on deep understanding of the market, it might not be in the marketing function. While functions remain, their roles are to coordinate activities across teams to ensure that shared learning takes place, to acquire and nurture specialized skills, to deploy specialists to the cross-functional process teams, and to achieve scale economies.[8]

The design of an organization affects its ability (and willingness) to respond quickly. The advantage of doing things faster than the competition is clearly established in various kinds of business. Recall Zara's skill in moving women's apparel from design to the store in weeks instead of months, which enables the retailer to market new designs ahead of its competitors. At Toyota, teams of designers, engineers, product planners, workers, and suppliers are required to work face-to-face, in the process Toyota calls *obeya*—literally "big room." This dramatically cuts the time it takes to get from drawing board to showroom. It took only 19 months to develop the 2003 Solara—well below the industry average of about three years.[9] Organizations that set themselves up to do things faster have a competitive advantage.

The Challenge of Integration

The development of new organizational forms, with new specializations, internal relationships and processes, underlines the importance of effective integration around the drivers of customer value. There have been several problems related to integration between marketing and other activities in companies. Effectiveness depends on developing strong linkages between marketing and other functional units. This may involve a variety of approaches.

Integration Problems. Many traditional approaches to organization have hindered the ability of companies to coordinate and integrate activities around customer needs.[10] In some organizations there are major barriers to effective communication between marketing and other units, leading to misunderstanding and conflict, such as poor use of market information by R&D departments for reasons of rivalry and political behavior.[11] Additionally, the integration problem may be exacerbated by "ownership" of key activities by other functions

Cross-Functional Feature

Shifting from a Functional View of Marketing to a Process Orientation

- Managing and participating in process-driven organizations present new skill requirements and challenges.
- Functional organizations require individual skills in information gathering, data analysis, and (external) persuasion.
- The process-driven organization emphasizes skills in negotiation, conflict resolution, relationship management, internal communication and persuasion, managing interfaces, team building, teaching, information interpretation, and strategic reasoning.
- Central to the process orientation is defining the organization in terms of the capabilities and processes necessary to provide superior customer value.
- The market-driven enterprise will be customer focused rather than product or technology focused.
- This mandates positioning the organization in the value chain, market sensing, customer linking, and supply-chain management.

Source: Frederick E. Webster Jr., "The Future Role of Marketing in the Organization," in *Reflections on the Futures of Marketing,* Donald R. Lehmann and Katherine E. Jocz, eds. (Cambridge, MA: Marketing Science Institute, 1997), 39–66. Reprinted with permission.

1. Customer relationship management systems span departments and systems to integrate customer knowledge.
2. Critical new-product "pipelines" may place priority on leveraging R&D capabilities faster than the competitor.
3. The implementation of electronic commerce may leave traditional marketing behind.
4. Many of the people and processes that impact on customer value are outside the control of the marketing area.[12]

Accordingly, the imperative for integration becomes more urgent: "An organization can no longer consist of a group of unrelated activities and work groups because customers won't accept it."[13]

Marketing's Links to Other Functional Units. Increasingly, marketing and sales professionals must display superior skills in coordinating and integrating their activities with other functional areas of the business. Priorities will depend on the situation faced and the strategy in question, but illustrative examples of critical cross-functional relationships include:

- *Marketing and Finance/Accounting*—viewing customers as assets that impact on shareholder value provides a shared basis for avoiding traditional conflicts on marketing resource allocation, and lining internal systems up with customer value imperatives.
- *Marketing and Operations*—the challenge is matching internal capabilities in operations and supply chain management, for example, in speed, flexibility, quality management, operational systems—with market opportunities.
- *Marketing and Sales*—in many situations the sales force represents the ability of the company to implement marketing strategy, which is constrained by lack of "buy-in," and traditional sales management practices that do not support strategic change.
- *Marketing and R&D*—the challenge is building structures to link innovation and research capabilities with market opportunities.
- *Marketing and Customer Service*—customer service operations may represent the most important point of contact between a customer and the company and impact directly on customer perceptions of value, mandating alignment with strategic initiatives.
- *Marketing and Human Resource Management*—the key issue may be building competitive advantage through the quality of the people in the company, with major implications for

aligning processes of recruitment, selection, training, development, evaluation and reward with business strategy requirements.[14]

Effective cross-functional working is the key to many of the examples we have discussed. Many successful companies display characteristics of cross-functional effectiveness: Costco, Dell, Johnson Controls, and Toyota are illustrative. This capability may be a key attribute of the market-led company of the future. The move toward process-based organizations further underlines this requirement. Examples include new-product planning, distribution-channel coordination, pricing analysis, and strategic marketing alliances.

Mechanisms for enhancing the quality of marketing's links with other functional units include effective cross-functional teams, shared goals, superior internal communications, high levels of top management support, and attention to resolving internal disputes and conflicts.[15]

Approaches to Achieving Effective Integration. Several approaches to building effective integration may be considered as part of organization design. Formal mechanisms for integration include:

- Relocation and design of facilities to encourage communication and exchange of information.
- Personnel movement using joint training and job rotation to facilitate managers' understanding of other functions.
- Reward systems that prioritize higher-level goals (e.g., company profits from a cross-functional project) not just functional objectives.
- Formal procedures, for example, requiring coordinated input from marketing, finance, operations and IT to complete project documentation.
- Social orientation facilitating nonwork interaction between personnel from different functions.
- Project budgeting to centralize control over financial resources so they are channeled, for example, to a project or process team not to a functional department.[16]

Evidence relating to the effectiveness of these approaches is mixed. Nonetheless, the initiatives emphasize the need to examine more than simple structural choices in designing the effective market-driven organization. Interestingly, several routes to enhanced integration—increased personal communication, spatial proximity, social interaction—will become progressively more difficult in the intranet-based, hollow organization. In such cases, integration issues may become a high priority for management attention.

Interestingly, a number of companies adopt inclusion organization approaches to leveraging integration. JetBlue, the low-cost airline, has changed its chain of command so that technology reports to the marketing department. Similarly, chemicals giant DuPont has moved its technology department from its operations and services division to marketing and sales, and toymaker Mattel has long had IT reporting to marketing. The logic is that locating IT within marketing removes an integration barrier and ensures that technology will be used to solve customer problems.[17]

Building the "customer-engaged" organization may be one of the most formidable challenges facing marketing executives. Approaches to addressing the need to build customer focus throughout a company may include creating a Customer Value Guide that conveys the essence of what represents value to customers, for the benefit of decision makers in the organization; and conducting "customer engagement" workshops with all employees to focus thinking on customer value.[18]

The impact of effective integration between key functions is illustrated in the Strategy Feature describing the teamwork between marketing and sales and other functions at Johnson Controls Inc. Importantly, the Feature highlights the importance of considering information, process, and culture issues alongside structural choices in designing the market-driven organization for the future.

Strategy Feature

Marketing and Sales Teamwork at Johnson Controls

Johnson Controls is one of *Fortune's* list of "America's Most Admired Companies." The company is a market leader in automotive seating, interiors and batteries, with interests in automated control systems for buildings. In the mid-2000s, having survived the slump in high-technology markets, Johnson marked its 28th consecutive year of enhanced dividends. This year was the company's 57th year of uninterrupted sales gains and the 13th straight year of record earnings. The company's culture of teamwork underpins this remarkable performance:

- Executives from marketing and sales have frequent meetings, collaborate on marketing promotions, take training courses together, make sales calls together, and share information freely, with a shared focus on making sure customers get what they want.
- Making a sales call at Ford to win seat business in Ford's F Series truck, Johnson fields five employees—three from sales and two from marketing, with the goal of demonstrating such deep understanding of the consumer that Ford will not think of going to another supplier.
- Customer visits often involve sales, marketing, engineering and design personnel together.
- Salespeople are paid an end-of-year performance bonus, not commissions on sales, while marketing employees, engineers and product designers receive bonuses based on company performance.
- Auto manufacturers have shifted from buying parts from suppliers like Johnson to assemble into vehicles, toward buying systems (modules) of parts that basically just snap into the car.
- Johnson positioned itself to take advantage of this shift in customer needs by creating partnerships with its customers, undertaking exhaustive market research, and actively fostering an internal environment based on cooperation.
- Johnson's teamwork philosophy extends to its alliances, such as that with Philips for in-car DVD entertainment systems. Each alliance has an executive to oversee it, and a Web page for alliance partners to share critical information.

Sources: Andy Cohen, "In Control," *Sales and Marketing Management*, June 1999, 32–38; Harlan S. Byrne, "Johnson Controls: Back in Gear," *Barron's*, June 5, 2000, 21–22; Shirley A. Lazo, "Speaking of Dividends: Just Like Clockwork," *Barron's*, November 19, 2001, 37. Financial details from company Web site, July 2004.

Management philosophy at General Electric, the world's most valuable company and one of the most admired,[19] has long incorporated these themes:

> One clear message in our approach is the value of the borderless culture which breaks down the horizontal barriers between functions and the vertical barriers between organizational levels. This means that employees are encouraged to collaborate with others and given considerable freedom to turn their creativity into productivity.[20]

Partnering with Other Organizations

Selecting or modifying the marketing organization design should take into consideration the trade-offs between performing marketing functions within the organization and having external organizations perform the functions. The discussion of relationship strategies in Chapter 7 examines the use of partnering to perform various business functions. Contractual arrangements are often made for advertising and sales promotion services, marketing research, and telemarketing. Services are also available to perform marketing functions in international markets. Strategic alliances are popular market entry and product development strategies.

Outsourcing various business functions is an active initiative in many companies due to cost reduction pressures, availability of competent services, increased flexibility, and shared risk. There are various marketing functions that may be provided by independent suppliers. Examples include telemarketing, database marketing, field sales, logistics, Web site design and management, and information services. Dell Inc.'s outsourcing of computer services is illustrative.

Internal units provide more control of activities, easier access to other departments, and greater familiarity with company operations. The commitment of the people to the organization is often higher since they are part of the corporate culture. The limitations of internal units include difficulty in quickly expanding or contracting size, lack of experience in other business

Internet Feature

The Impact of the Internet on an Organization

Office supply company Staples Inc. shows the combination of the Internet's impact on customers and the organization itself.

- Staples Inc.'s Web sales reached $2.1 billion in 2004, growing 31 percent from the previous year, and contributing 16 percent of Staples' total sales.
- Internal business reports are distributed through an intranet—replacing the expensive process of printing hard copies in central data centers and mailing them to managers.
- Sales associates in stores use Web kiosks on the shop floor to access the intranet and customize reports to get the information most useful to their store, without leaving the floor to go to a back office. The company estimates saving $600,000 a year in paper and distribution costs.
- Staples also uses its intranet to distribute "Plan-O-Grams" providing schematics of how products and promotions should be displayed, customized to the store's location and size. This saves $250,000 annually in printing costs.
- Executives at headquarters buy material, furniture, and other supplies through a Web procurement application, which routes orders through the Internet to pre-approved vendors. The saving is $500,000, mostly in reduced administration costs and better control over the payment process.
- Previously, store managers completed employment forms for new hires and submitted them to corporate for approval through the mail. Now they do it through the intranet. What previously took four days now takes one. Savings from reduced labor are estimated at $1.2 million a year.

Source: Adapted from Ted Kemp, "Web Helps Merchants Save in Down Market," *InternetWeek*, October 15, 2001, 42–43. Copyright © 2004 by CMP Media LLC, 600 Community Drive, Manhasset, NY 11030, USA; Reprinted from *InternetWeek* with permission; "Staples' Web Sales Grow 31% and Account for 16% of All Sales", March 4, 2004, *www.InternetRetailer.com*.

environments, and limited skills in specialized areas such as advertising, marketing research, Web design, and database management.

External organizations offer specialized skills, experience, and flexibility in adapting to changing conditions. These firms may have lower costs than an organization that performs the function(s) internally. Obtaining services outside the firm also has limitations, including loss of control, longer execution time, greater coordination requirements, and lack of familiarity with the organization's products and markets. Identifying core competencies, coordinating relationships, defining operating responsibilities, establishing good communications, and monitoring and evaluating performance are essential to gaining effective use of external organizations.

The Impact of the Internet on Organizational Design Decisions

In addition to its impact on buyer-seller relationships by providing a direct marketing channel, the Internet impacts the internal processes and management of organizations. The Internet Feature illustrates the widespread impact not only of the Internet direct marketing channel, but also the company's intranet impact on internal processes.

The Internet requires attention to revision of the whole of the organization's structure, systems and processes, and new managerial roles and practices may be mandated by the Web.[21] However, Forrester Inc. research suggests that companies have made little progress in building the organizational structures needed to manage Internet-based business, and for many this remains an important challenge to be addressed.[22] It is likely that organizational issues reflecting the impact of the Internet on company processes will include:

- Fast access to information from any location in the organization and remote access from distributed locations for salespeople, distributors, customers, and partner organizations.
- Accelerated trends toward flatter organizations with whole levels of management removed to achieve faster response to market change.
- Virtual teams working on projects across geographical and traditional organizational boundaries.

- New integrated approaches to supplier relationship management (SRM) and customer relationship management (CRM) systems.
- Managing and controlling the outsourcing of more business processes and activities to specialist third-party suppliers.

Organizational Design Options

Functional specialization is often the first consideration in selecting an organizational design. Specialist functions are attractive because they develop expertise, resources, and skills in a particular activity. Emphasis on functions may be less appropriate when trying to direct activities toward market targets, products, and customers. Market targets and product scope also influence organizational design. When two or more targets and/or a mix of products are involved, companies often depart from functional organizational designs that place advertising, selling, research, and other supporting services into functional units (e.g., sales department). Similarly, distribution channels and sales force considerations may influence the organizational structure adopted by a firm. For example, the marketing of home entertainment products targeted to business buyers of employee incentives and promotional gifts might be placed in a unit separate from a unit marketing the same products to consumer end users. Geographical factors have a heavy influence on organization design because of the need to make the field supervisory structure correspond to how the sales force is assigned to customers.

In this discussion we assume that the marketing organization is part of a strategic business unit. Companies with two or more business units may have corporate marketing organizations as well as business-unit marketing organizations. Corporate involvement may range from a coordinating role to one in which the corporate staff has considerable influence on business-unit marketing operations. Also, the chief marketing executive and staff may participate in varying degrees in strategic planning for the enterprise and the business unit.

We first look at several traditional approaches to organizing marketing activities and assigning responsibilities, and then examine the role of corporate marketing. This is followed by a discussion of some new approaches in marketing organization design.

Traditional Designs

The major forms of marketing organizational designs are *functional, product, market,* and *matrix* designs.

Functional Organizational Design. This design assigns departments, groups, or individuals responsibility for specific activities, such as advertising and sales promotion, pricing, sales, marketing research, and marketing planning and services. Depending on the size and scope of its operations, the marketing organization may include some or all of these activities. The functional approach is often used when a single product or a closely related line is marketed to one market target.

Product-Focused Design. The product mix may require special consideration in the organizational design. New products often do not receive the attention they need unless specific responsibility is assigned to the planning and coordination of the new-product activities. This problem may also occur with existing products when a business unit has several products and there are technical and/or application differences. We examine several approaches to organizing using a product focus.

The **product/brand manager**, sometimes assisted by one or a few additional people, is responsible for planning and coordinating various business functions for the assigned products. Typically, the product manager does not have authority over all product-planning activities but may coordinate various product-related activities. The manager usually has background and experience in research and development, engineering, or marketing and is normally assigned to one of these departments. Product managers' titles and responsibilities vary widely across companies.

EXHIBIT 14.3
Product-Focused Structure

Source: Donald R. Lehmann and Russell S. Winer, *Product Management*. 2nd ed. (Chicago: Richard D. Irwin, 1997), 4. Copyright © The McGraw-Hill Companies. Used with permission.

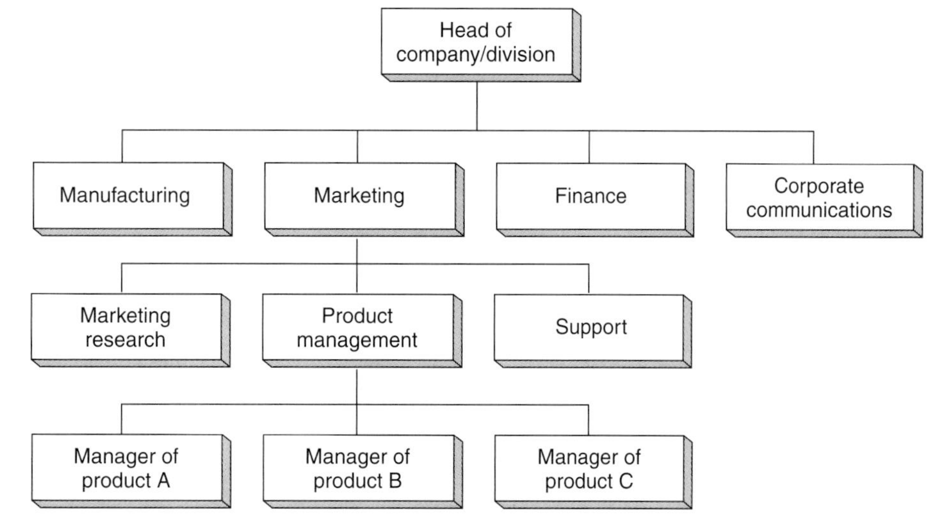

Product management structures continue to be used in many organizations even though there is a trend toward process designs.[23] The product management system assigns clear responsibility for product performance, and the system encourages coordination across business functions. These positions are also excellent training grounds for higher-level jobs. Nonetheless, the product focus may take emphasis away from the market. Also, there may be a short-term focus on financial performance. An example of a product-focused structure is shown in Exhibit 14.3.

One interesting observation is that traditional product management structure will evolve into customer-based structures, where several customer portfolios replace products as the "pillars" of the organization, and product managers will provide services to each customer portfolio group (as will functional specialists).[24]

Associated with the efficient consumer response approach to supply chain management (Chapter 10), one development in product-focused organization is the adoption of **category management** structures. Categories are groups of products defined by consumer purchase behavior patterns. For example, Nestlé and Interbrew are working with retailers to develop categories structures within which their brands can be developed, and restructuring their organizations around the categories.[25]

The **venture team** requires the creation of an organizational unit to perform some or all of the new-product planning functions. This unit may be a separate division or company created specifically for new-product or new-business ideas and initiatives.[26] Examples of successful products planned by venture units include the Boeing 757 aircraft, and the IBM personal computer line. Venture teams offer several advantages, including flexibility and quick response. They provide functional involvement and full-time commitment, and they can be disbanded when appropriate. Team members may be motivated to participate on a project that offers possible job advancement opportunities. The traditional venture team approach has been extended into a new organizational model—the Venture Marketing Organization—considered in the next section.

The **new-product team** is similar to a venture team in that it is comprised of functional specialists working on a specific new-product development project. The product team has a high degree of autonomy with the authority to select leaders, establish operating procedures, and resolve conflicts. The team is formed for a specific project although it may be assigned subsequent projects. Successful innovation at 3M is based on cross-functional new-product teams.[27]

Factors that often influence the choice of a product organization design are the kinds and scope of products offered, the amount of new-product development, the extent of coordination necessary among functional areas, and the management and technical problems previously encountered with new products and existing products. For example, a firm with an existing functional organizational structure may create a temporary team to manage and coordinate the development of a major new product. Before or soon after commercial introduction, the firm will shift responsibility for the product to the functional organization. The team's purpose is to allocate initial direction and effort to the new product so that it is properly launched.

Market-Focused Design. This approach is used when a business unit serves more than one market target (e.g., multiple market segments) and customer considerations are an important factor in the design of the marketing organization. For example, the customer base often affects the structuring of the field sales organization. A key advantage of this design is its customer focus.[28] Greater use of organization designs that focus on customer groups is predicted.[29] A potential conflict may exist if a company also has in place a product management system. Some firms appoint market managers and have a field sales force that is specialized by type of customer. The market manager operates much like a product manager, with responsibility for market planning, research, advertising, and sales force coordination. Market-oriented field organizations may be deployed according to industry, customer size, type of product application, or in other ways to achieve specialization by end user groups. Conditions that suggest a market-oriented design are (1) multiple market targets being served within a strategic business unit, (2) substantial differences in the customer requirements in a given target market, and/or (3) each customer or prospect purchasing the product in large volume or dollar amounts.

Matrix Design. This design utilizes a cross-classification approach to emphasize two different factors, such as products and marketing functions (Exhibit 14.4). Field sales coverage is determined by geography, whereas product emphasis is obtained using product managers. In addition to working with salespeople, product managers coordinate other marketing functions such as advertising and marketing research. Of course, other matrix schemes are possible. For example, within the sales regions shown in Exhibit 14.4, salespeople may be organized by product type or customer group. Also, marketing functions may be broken down by product category, such as appointing an advertising supervisor for Product II.

Combination approaches are effective in that they respond to important influences on the organization and offer more flexibility than the other traditional approaches. A major difficulty with these designs is establishing lines of responsibility and authority. Product and market managers frequently complain that they lack control over all marketing functions even though they are held accountable for results. Nevertheless, matrix approaches are popular, so their operational advantages must exceed their limitations.

Marketing's Corporate Role

An important organizational issue in firms with two or more operating units is deciding whether a corporate marketing function should be established, and if so, what its role and scope should be. Possible roles include:

1. Centralized provision of services like media purchases, marketing research, planning assistance, and other supporting activities, where there is economy of scale.
2. Monitoring the performance of operating level marketing and sales activities in such areas as pricing policies, new-product planning, sales force compensation, and other marketing expenditures and actions.
3. Providing specialized expertise to corporate management and operating units monitoring/control actions in areas like market segmentation analyses, new-product planning, and marketing strategy.

Nonetheless, influenced by the general trend in organizations toward decentralized management approaches, many corporations are moving marketing functions away from the corporate level to the business-unit level. Decentralization is a better way to cope with growing product and market complexity, and to enhance speed of response to market changes.[30]

EXHIBIT 14.4
A Marketing Organization Based on a Combination of Functions and Products

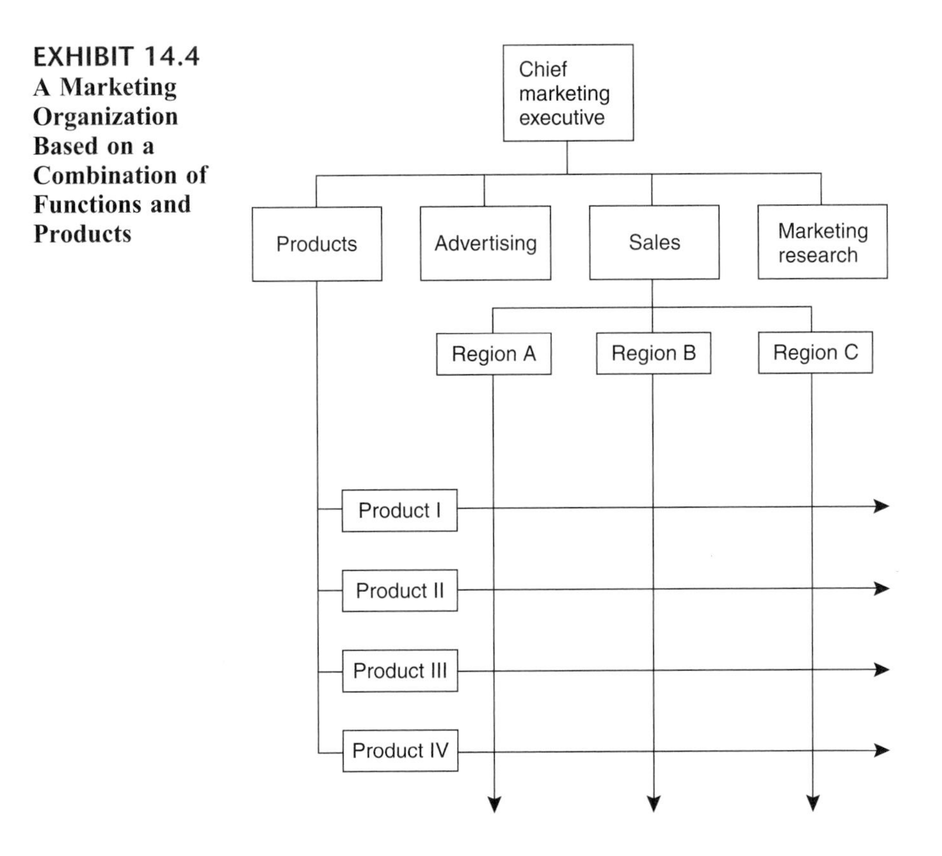

The corporate role of marketing is influenced by top management's approach to organizing the corporation, as well as the nature and complexity of business operations. Marketing strategy decisions are typically centered at the business-unit and product-market levels. Even so, it is very important for the top management team to include strategic marketing professionals. The market-driven nature of business strategy requires the active participation of marketing professionals.

New Forms of Marketing Organizations

As we discussed early in the chapter, the use of self-managing employee teams, emphasis on business processes rather than activities, and the application of information technology are creating major changes in organization design. However, the adoption of these organization designs is more likely to occur in newly formed companies or units rather than established companies. First, we explore how these influences are altering the traditional vertical organization. Then, we look at some new marketing organization designs.

New Marketing Roles. One issue facing managers is the emergence of new roles in marketing processes and how to locate them in the structure of the organization. Recall we described the potential for the chief knowledge or information officer in marketing (Chapter 5), and the possible role of the chief relationship officer (Chapter 7). The introduction of such roles requires attention to their organizational positioning.

One major issue faced by companies is where and how to position Internet-based channels in the marketing organization and the business unit. Early approaches isolated Internet channels from the rest of the business, while the real challenge for most companies is how to integrate the Internet into the core business.[31] Major "bricks and clicks" companies like Staples are rethinking the policy of separating their dot.com operations from the rest of the business, and bringing them back into the main operation.[32] The Web operations of successful retailers like Walgreens in the

United States and Tesco in the United Kingdom are closely integrated with their retail stores. Several important organizational issues are involved in achieving that integration.

Considerable attention is also being given to the impact of customer relationship management (CRM) systems on marketing organizations (Chapter 7). Some companies have, for example, appointed a chief customer officer, whose job focuses only on customer interactions and the customer experience. Large investment in CRM and its utilization in building relationship marketing strategy, may lead to the division of marketing into activities associated with customer acquisition processes and those focused on customer retention, since these are often very distinct and different processes.[33]

A number of major organizations have also developed key and global account management structures (KAM and GAM). We discuss major and global account management as a sales function in Chapter 13. There are signs that in some organizations KAM approaches are strategic marketing responses to the demands by major customers for specialized approaches. In the most advanced form, KAM is a new collaborative relationship with major accounts, focused on the customer's strategy and competitive advantage. The key account manager in these cases has a strategic responsibility for managing all contact between the seller and customer organization and planning jointly with the customer. Strategic key account management positions are senior positions that may not fit easily into the conventional sales organization, and carry major marketing and cross-functional responsibilities.[34]

Transforming Vertical Organizations. Corporate restructuring is changing how organizations are configured. This transformation involves defining the business as a group of interrelated processes rather than as functions of research and development, operations, marketing, and finance. Since most business processes involve several business functions, the basis of organization becomes the process rather than the function. Consider, for example, the process of "order generation and fulfillment."[35] The process owners are manufacturing and marketing. The process team responsible for defining, analyzing, and continually improving the process includes the workers that perform the various activities necessary to create the process outputs (completed orders delivered to customers).

The process concept of managing a business is a dramatic departure from traditional, functional organizational designs. The use of matrix and team-oriented designs provides experience in coordinating the activities of multifunctional teams. For example, a large industrial products company uses teams to develop and implement its marketing plans. Team members include product managers, research and development managers, manufacturing managers, sales management, finance executives, and top management. Nonetheless, making the transition to the true process-driven organization requires a major alteration in how the organization is designed and how it functions.

It is clear from the organizational changes which occurred during the last decade that structures are changing, and market-driven companies are seeking to more closely align the organization to the market. One strategy authority anticipates the following changes in structure:[36]

1. Companies will migrate toward hybrid organization forms by coupling the strengths of horizontal processes and vertical functional forms.
2. Organizational designs will differ significantly based on the organization's value strategy and core capabilities.
3. Data network advances will play a pivotal role in linking internal teams and obtaining information from the customer.
4. Greater dispersion of information and shared decision making throughout the organization will be essential to interactive strategies.

New Organization Forms. An example of one new organization form is the marketing coalition company shown in Exhibit 14.5.[37] This horizontally aligned organization is the control center for organizing a network of specialist firms. The core of this organization is a functionally specialized marketing capability that coordinates a network of independent functional units. They perform such functions as product technology, engineering, and manufacturing.

EXHIBIT 14.5
The Marketing Coalition Company

Source: Ravi S. Achrol, "Evolution of the Marketing Organization: New Forms for Turbulent Environments," *Journal of Marketing*, October 1991, 88. Reprinted with permission of the American Marketing Association.

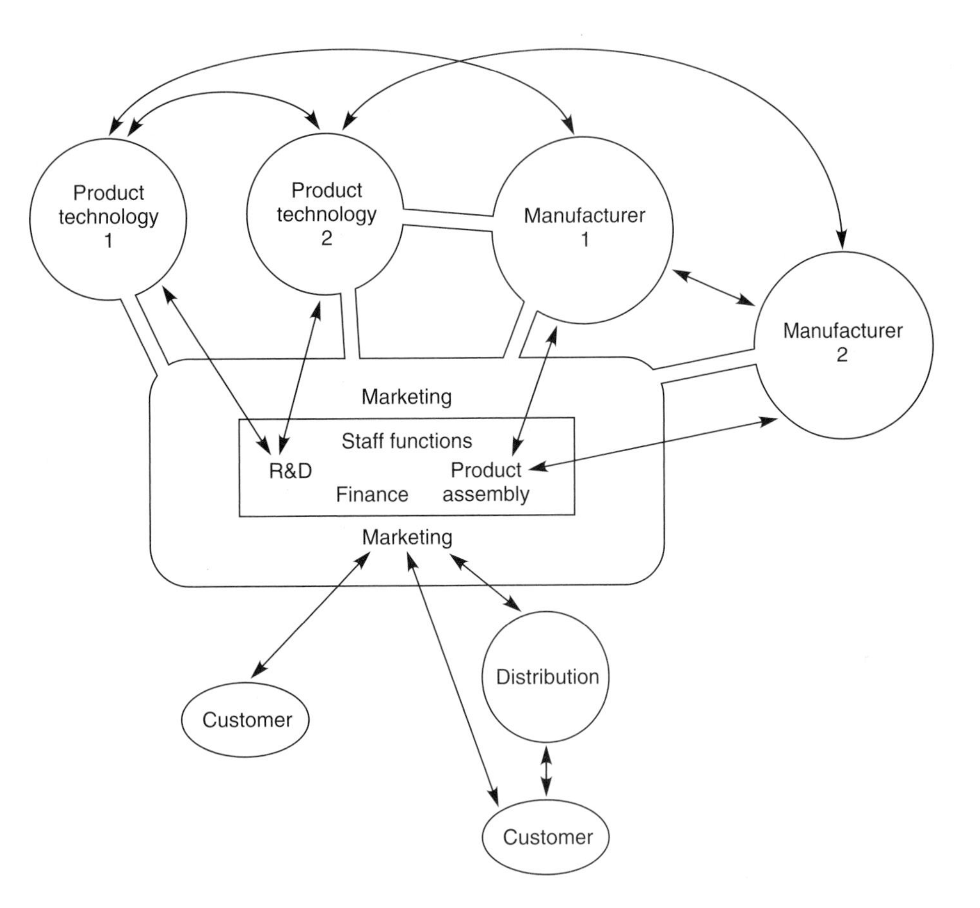

No pure forms of the marketing coalition company are known to exist. Several Japanese companies have certain characteristics of the coalition company. One U.S. furniture and houseware retail chain, the Bombay Company, is organized in a similar form to the coalition design in its supplier network. Bombay has a global network of specialized suppliers of its home furnishings. Specific components (e.g., legs, top) of a table are produced by different manufacturers, shipped to Bombay's product-assembly facility, and deployed through a national distribution system to Bombay's company-owned retail stores. While the Bombay design is not identical to Exhibit 14.5, there are several similarities.

The marketing coalition design is an example of a network organization. Networks are groups of independent organizations that are linked together to achieve a common objective.[38] They are comprised of a network coordinator and several network members who typically are specialists. Network organizations occur in new ventures and reformed traditional organizations. The underlying rationale for network formation is leveraging the skills and resources of the participating organizations. Many aspects of strategic alliances discussed in Chapter 7 are highly relevant to considering networked organizations.

Venture Marketing Organizations. An interesting new approach adopted by some companies extends the idea of venture teams as a way of responding to high-priority opportunities faster than conventional organizational approaches allow. The venture marketing organization (VMO) adopts the principles of venture capitalism: They aggressively seek new opportunities, allocate resources to the best, but cut their losses as they go. The VMO has a number of defining characteristics:

- Fluidity—to keep pace with the market, the VMO continually reconfigures, with little formal structure or fixed membership in opportunity teams.

Innovation Feature Venture Marketing Organization at Starbucks

The Venture Marketing Organization (VMO) is a fluid approach to identifying new opportunities and concentrating resources on the best. Starbucks has a VMO-style approach to innovation.

- Starbucks approaches new opportunities by assembling teams whose leaders often come from the functional marketing areas most critical to success. The originator of the idea may take the lead role only if qualified.
- If teams need skills that are not available internally they look outside. To lead the "Store of the Future" project, Starbucks hired a top executive with retail experience away from Universal Studios; and to develop its lunch service concept, it chose a manager from Marriott.

- After the new product is launched, some team members may stay to manage the venture, while others are redeployed to new-opportunity teams or return to line management. Success on a team is vital for promotion or a bigger role on another project.
- Teamwork extends to partner organizations. When pursuing a new ice cream project, Starbucks quickly realized they lacked the in-house packaging and channel management skills to move quickly. Teaming up with Dreyer's Grand Ice Cream got the product to market in half the normal time, and within four months it was the top-selling brand of coffee ice cream.
- Starbucks emphasizes the importance of identifying new opportunities throughout its organization. Anyone in the company with a new idea for an opportunity uses a one-page form to pass it to a senior executive team. If the company pursues the idea, the originator, regardless of tenure or title, is usually invited onto the launch team as a full-time member.
- In its first year, Starbucks' Frappuccino, a cold coffee drink, contributed 11 percent of company sales. The idea originated with a frontline manager in May 1994, gaining high-priority status from a five-person senior executive team in June. The new team developed marketing, packaging and channel approaches in July. A joint venture arrangement with PepsiCo was in place by August. The first wave of rollout was in October 1994, with national launch in May 1995.
- A high-level steering committee meets every two weeks to rate new opportunities against two simple criteria: impact on company revenue growth, and effects on the complexity of the retail store. The committee uses a one-page template to assess each idea, relying on a full-time process manager to ensure the information is presented consistently.

Sources: Nora A. Aufreiter, Teri L. Lawver, Candance D. Lun, "A New Way to Market," *The McKinsey Quarterly*, Issue 2, 2000, 52–61. Nora Aufreiter and Teri Lawver, "Winning the Race for New Market Opportunities," *Ivey Business Journal*, September/October 2000, 14–16.

- People are allocated roles, not jobs—the issue is managing talent within the organization and applying it to promising opportunities.
- Fast decision making is made from the top.
- Opportunity identification is everyone's job.
- Resources are focused on the highest payback opportunities and losers are quickly pruned.[39]

The impressive impact of a VMO-style approach to new market opportunities at Starbucks is described in the Innovation Feature.

Selecting an Organization Design

The design of the marketing organization is influenced by market and environmental factors, the characteristics and capabilities of the organization, and the marketing strategy followed by the firm. A good organizational scheme displays several characteristics:

> The organization should correspond to the strategic marketing plan. For example, if the plan is structured around markets or products, then the marketing organizational structure should reflect this same emphasis.
> Coordination of activities is essential to successful implementation of plans, both within the marketing function and with other company and business unit functions. The more highly specialized that marketing functions become, the more likely coordination and communications will be hampered.
> Specialization of marketing activities leads to greater efficiency in performing the functions. As an illustration, a central advertising department may be more cost-efficient than establishing an advertising unit for each product category. Specialization can also provide technical depth. For example, product or application specialization in a field sales force will enable salespeople to provide consultative-type assistance to customers.
> The organization should be structured so that responsibility for results will correspond to a manager's influence on results. While this objective is often difficult to fully achieve, it is an important consideration in designing the marketing organization.
> Finally, one of the real dangers in a highly structured and complex organization is the loss of flexibility. The organization should be adaptable to changing conditions. Recall the rationale for the venture marketing organization described earlier in the chapter.

Since some of these characteristics conflict with others, organizational design requires looking at priorities and balancing conflicting consequences.

First we look at several organizing concepts, followed by a discussion of organizing the sales force.

Organizing Concepts

How marketing activities are organized affects strategy implementation. For example, a classic view of four organizing concepts is shown in Exhibit 14.6. Note the usage context and performance characteristics of each structure. Since strategy implementation may involve a usage context that combines two of the structures, trade-offs are involved. The adopted organization structure may facilitate the implementation of certain activities and tasks. For example, the bureaucratic form should facilitate the implementation of repetitive activities such as telephone processing of air travel reservations and ticketing. Once management analyzes the task(s) to be performed and the environment in which they will be done, it must determine its priorities. An example is the objective performance and short-run efficiency or adaptability and longer-term effectiveness:

> Activities in different categories should be structured differently whenever feasible. Some firms appear to be moving in this direction, as shown by reports of cuts in corporate staff departments, the shifting of more planning and decision-making authority to individual business-unit and product-market managers, and the increased use of ad hoc task forces to deal with specific markets or problems—all of which indicate a shift toward more decentralized and flexible structures.[40]

Corporate culture may also have an important influence on implementation. For example, implementing new strategies may be more difficult in highly structured, bureaucratic organizations. General Motors' difficulty in responding to the global competitive pressures during the last decade is illustrative. Management should consider its own management style, accepted practices, specific performance of executives, and other unique characteristics in deciding how to design the organization.

The bureaucratic form in Exhibit 14.6 corresponds to the previously discussed traditional vertical organization forms. The relational form displays several characteristics of a network

EXHIBIT 14.6 Four Archetypical Organizational Forms

	Market versus Hierarchical Organization	
	Internal Organization of Activity	**External Organization of Activity**
Centralized Formalized Nonspecialized	Bureaucratic Form *Appropriate usage context* • Conditions of market failure • Low environmental uncertainty • Tasks that are repetitive, easily assessed, requiring specialized assets *Performance characteristics* • Highly effective and efficient • Less adaptive *Examples in marketing* • Functional organization • Company or division sales force • Corporate research staffs	Transactional Form *Appropriate usage context* • Under competitive market conditions • Low environmental uncertainty • Tasks that are repetitive, easily assessed, with no specialized investment *Performance characteristics* • Most efficient form • Highly effective for appropriate tasks • Less adaptive *Examples in marketing* • Contract purchase of advertising space • Contract purchase of transportation of product • Contract purchase of research field work
Structural Characteristics		
Decentralized Nonformalized Specialized	Organic Form *Appropriate usage context* • Conditions of market failure • High environmental uncertainty • Tasks that are infrequent, difficult to assess, requiring highly specialized investment *Performance characteristics* • Highly adaptive • Less efficient *Examples in marketing* • Product management organization • Specialized sales force organization • Research staffs organized by product groups	Relational Form *Appropriate usage context* • Under competitive market conditions • High environmental uncertainty • Tasks that are nonroutine, difficult to assess, requiring little specialized investment *Performance characteristics* • Highly adaptive • Highly effective for nonroutine, specialized tasks • Less efficient *Examples in marketing* • Long-term retainer contract with advertising agency • Ongoing relationship with consulting firm

Source: Robert W. Ruekert, Orville C. Walker Jr., and Kenneth J. Roering, "The Organization of Marketing Activities: A Contingency Theory of Structure and Performance," *Journal of Marketing,* Winter 1985, 20. Reprinted with permission of the American Marketing Assocation.

organization, though network design involves a more extensive group of independent partners. The transactional form may be used for certain repetitive, nonspecialized activities. The organic form has some similarities with the process-type organizations, but it also displays several characteristics of traditional structures.

Organizing the Sales Force

In many companies, the sales force comprises the largest part of the marketing organization. Therefore, organizing the sales force is often a central part of the marketing organization design. The design of the sales organization is discussed in Chapter 13, which also looks at designs that correspond to variations in product offering and customer needs. We now examine some additional aspects of organizing the sales force.

Organizing Multiple Sales Channels. Expanding the sales organization beyond the field sales force to include major-account programs, telemarketing, and/or Internet sales programs requires consideration as to how to organize the value-chain network. A key issue is whether to establish separate organizational units, or to combine two or more channels into one unit. For example, should the national account salespeople be placed in a separate organizational unit or instead be assigned to field sales units (e.g., regions or districts)? The use of multifunctional customer management processes discussed earlier in the chapter may affect these decisions.

When sales channel activities are relatively independent of the field sales force, a separate channel organization is appropriate. This occurs when major-account managers or telemarketing salespeople provide all contacts with assigned accounts. An example is the assignment of low sales volume accounts to telemarketing salespeople. A more likely situation is when contacts are made by both field personnel and other channels. These contacts require coordination between salespeople. The creation of independent sales-channel organizations complicates the coordination of selling activities.

Coordinating Major-Account Relationships. A look at the alternatives for coordinating key account relationships highlights several multiple-channel issues. A major-account program requires assignment of account responsibility to account managers. When the customer has several purchasing locations, coordination of selling and service activities is necessary. Several alternatives are available including (1) assigning key accounts to top sales executives (e.g., sales vice president); (2) creating a separate corporate division; and (3) establishing a separate major-accounts sales force.[41] Factors that influence the choice of an alternative include the number of major accounts served by the organization, the number of different geographical contacts with an account, the organizational level of contact (e.g., vice president versus maintenance supervisor), and the sales and service functions to be performed.

Global Dimensions of Organizations

Implementing the global strategies of companies creates several important organizational issues. A key issue is the degree to which products and marketing strategies and programs are standardized across domestic and international markets, as compared to being adapted to local market requirements.

Clearly, the Internet is playing a major role in the globalization of business. As more customers buy and make comparisons through the Web on an international basis, competition becomes global for many more companies. In addition the impact of the Internet on internal organizational processes and the development of intranets encourage teaming and projects that span geographical, cultural and time-zone barriers. Working in international project teams through an intranet mandates dealing with international issues as a necessity in the market-driven organization.[42]

Several issues in organizing global marketing strategies are examined followed by a discussion of organizational concepts that are used to manage global marketing activities. Much of the earlier material in the chapter applies to international operations. This discussion highlights several additional considerations.

Issues in Organizing Global Marketing Strategies

The important distinction in marketing throughout the world is that buyers differ in their needs, preferences, and priorities. Since such differences exist *within* a national market, the variations between countries are likely to be greater. Brands like Budweiser beer and Levi's jeans have significantly different market positions in international markets to those they occupy in the United States. Global market targeting and positioning strategies create several marketing organizational issues.

Variations in Business Functions. Global decisions concerning production, finance, and research and development are often more feasible than making the marketing decisions that span these markets. Marketing strategies often require sensitivity to cultural and linguistic differences. Foreign currencies, government regulations, and different product standards further complicate buyer-seller relationships. The important issue is recognizing when standardized marketing strategies can be used and when they must be modified.

Organizational Considerations. The marketing organization selected for competing in national markets is influenced by the market *scope* (e.g., single-country, multinational, or global strategy), and by the market *entry strategy* (export, licensing, joint venture, strategic alliance, or complete ownership). Recall the discussion of marketing strategies in global markets in Chapter 6. The adoption of a global strategy using joint ventures, alliances, and or complete ownership presents the most complex organizational challenge.

The marketing organization design in international operations may take one of three possible forms: (1) a global product division; (2) geographical divisions, each with product and functional responsibilities; or (3) matrix design incorporating (1) or (2) in combination with centralized functional support or instead a combination of area operations and global product management.[43] The global form corresponds to rapid growth situations for firms that have a broad product portfolio. The geographic form is used to obtain a close relationship with national and local governments. The matrix form is utilized by companies reorganizing for global competition. An example of a combination organization design is shown in Exhibit 14.7.

Coordination and Communication

Organizing marketing activities to serve international markets creates important coordination and communication requirements. Language and distance barriers complicate organizational relationships. Recall the major organizational shift at P&G in its "Organization 2005" change program. The company has moved to global management of its brand and businesses, coupled with new market development organizations for tailoring programs to local markets. By comparison, Unilever is struggling to compete with P&G, in part because of its greater degree of centralization and lesser ability to customize programs to local markets.[44]

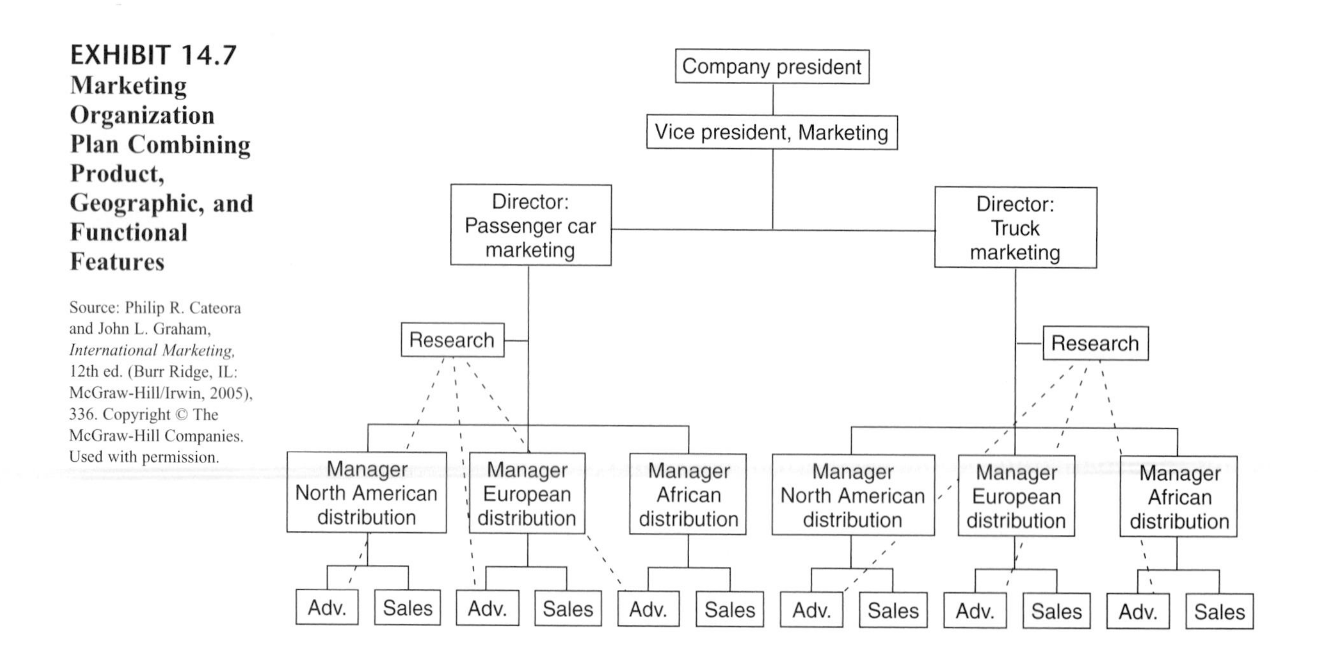

EXHIBIT 14.7
Marketing Organization Plan Combining Product, Geographic, and Functional Features

Source: Philip R. Cateora and John L. Graham, *International Marketing*, 12th ed. (Burr Ridge, IL: McGraw-Hill/Irwin, 2005), 336. Copyright © The McGraw-Hill Companies. Used with permission.

For many companies, growing emphasis on effective global teamwork is replacing traditional concepts of domestic versus international divisions. Many of the constraints to organizing globally have lessened, even for companies with a limited international involvement. Enabling technology provided by the Internet and collaboration software facilitates the operation and management of global teams.

Strategic Alliances. Recall the growth in alliance strategies among global firms described in Chapter 7. Expanded use of various types of alliances is expected to continue, particularly as a way of competing internationally. Importantly, the alliance relationship presents major interorganizational coordination and strategy implementation requirements. Recall, we discussed how the effectiveness of the alliance depends on how well operating relationships are established and managed on an ongoing basis and how well the partners can work together. These principles are highly relevant to the organizational change involved in globalizing.

Executive Qualifications. International experience and proven capabilities will increasingly be required for executive advancement in the 21st century.[45] Managing international marketing operations requires knowledge of finance, distribution, manufacturing and other business functions. The trend toward flat organizations with wide spans of control will make on-the-job executive development more difficult. Similarly, the qualifications for the chief executive's job will require experience in several areas. Market strategies will increasingly require management abilities to lead into new areas and to work in new ways that do not depend on formal authority, and the international context underlines the importance for the market-driven company of nurturing and retaining superior management talent.[46] International experience promises to become increasingly important to marketing executives in career development.

Summary

Differences in environmental situations create specific organization design requirements. The design and adaptation of organizations to their environments involves consideration of several important issues for marketing organization design including decisions regarding the use of internal and external organizations, designing the vertical structure, coordinating horizontal relationships, increasing speed of response, and analyzing environmental complexity and the forces of change. The Internet plays a major role as an enabling technology underpinning several aspects of organizational change.

Several traditional marketing organizations designs may be used to implement market strategy. The options include functional, product, market, and matrix designs. Increasingly, aligning the organization to the market is a central issue in organization designs. Building appropriate organization designs to integrate marketing with other functions, to position new marketing roles and responsibilities effectively, and to work with partner organizations are priorities for many companies.

The role and scope of corporate marketing is changing in many firms with multibusiness operations. The importance of corporate marketing appears to be declining in many firms, with marketing strategy emphasis instead being focused at the business level. The venture marketing organization is an interesting development being used by some companies.

New forms of marketing organizations are developing, driven by the use of cross-functional teams in organizations that manage business processes rather than functions, and the use of powerful information technology. These influences are transforming vertical organizations into horizontal ones. An example is the marketing coalition company.

The choice of an organization design involves finding a good structural environmental match. The match is influenced by the complexity of the environment and the unpredictability and interconnectedness of the environment. The design also involves selecting the best organizational form based on structural characteristics and the internal versus external orientation of marketing operations. The key role of the sales force in many organizations makes it a central part of marketing organization design.

Finally, the global strategies of companies highlight several marketing organizational issues. These include recognizing the differences in business functions in international operations and the increased coordination and communication requirements in international markets. Strategic alliances, an expanding area of global activity, present complex management and coordination situations. Executive qualifications in marketing and other business functions increasingly include international experience.

Internet Applications

A. Visit the Web site of the Strategic Account Management Association (*www.strategicaccounts.org*) and review some of the research library resources available at the site. What is the basis for suggesting that the strategic/key account manager is anything more than a senior salesperson working on major accounts? Why is it any different? Where can a strategic account manager be positioned in the marketing and sales organization?

B. Go to the Web site of Coca-Cola Inc. (*www.cocacola.com*). Use the corporate information pages (Our Company, Our Brands, and Around the World) to identify the growth in brands marketed by the company and its geographic emphasis. Identify the challenges for this company in organizing marketing for a growing brand portfolio in a diverse global marketplace.

Feature Applications

A. Compare the organizational approaches described in the Strategy Feature, "Marketing and Sales Teamwork at Johnson Controls" and the Innovation Feature, "Venture Marketing Organization at Starbucks." Develop a list of the common characteristics of the approaches taken by these companies, and consider what lessons can be learned.

B. Review the characteristics of process organization described in the Cross-Functional Feature, "Shifting from a Functional View of Marketing to a Process Orientation" (you may find that the framework in Exhibit 14.2 is also relevant). Attempt to produce organizational charts describing the structure and relationships in a hybrid, process-type structure, and a horizontal structure. Develop a list of what marketing organization may look like in major companies in 10 years' time.

Questions for Review and Discussion

1. The chief executive of a manufacturer of direct-order personal computers is interested in establishing a marketing organization in the firm. A small sales force handles sales to midsized businesses and advertising is planned and executed by an advertising agency. Other than the CEO, no one inside the firm is responsible for the marketing function. What factors should the CEO consider in designing a marketing organization?
2. Of the various approaches to marketing organization design, which one(s) offers the most flexibility in coping with rapidly changing market and competitive situations? Discuss.
3. Discuss the conditions where a matrix-type marketing organization would be appropriate, indicating important considerations and potential problems in using this organizational form.
4. Assume that you have been asked by the president of a major transportation services firm to recommend a marketing organizational design. What important factors should you consider in selecting the design?
5. Discuss some of the important issues related to integrating marketing into an organization such as a regional women's clothing chain compared to accomplishing the same task in The Limited Inc.
6. What are possible internal and external factors that may require changing the marketing organization design?
7. Is a trend toward more organic organizational forms likely in the future?
8. Summarize and chart the current and future impact of the Internet on marketing processes and organization.
9. Discuss the important organizational design issues in establishing an effective strategic alliance between organizations.
10. What are the major approaches to organizing the marketing function for international operations? Discuss the factors that may affect the choice of a particular organization design.
11. As companies begin to replace functions with processes, what are the possible effects on organizational designs?

Notes

1. George S. Day, "Aligning the Organization to the Market," in *Reflections on the Future of Marketing,* Donald R. Lehmann and Katherine E. Jocz, eds. (Cambridge, MA: Marketing Science Institute, 1997), 67–93.
2. Tara Parker-Pope and Joanne S. Lublin, "P&G Will Make Jager CEO Ahead of Schedule," *The Wall Street Journal,* September 10, 1998, B1 and B8. Steve Bell, "P&G Forced by Rivals to Change Old Habits," *Marketing,* June 17, 1999, 15. Patricia Van Arnum, "Procter & Gamble Moves Forward with Reorganization," *Chemical Market Reporter,* February 1, 1999, 12. John Bissell, "What Can We Learn from P&G's Troubles," *Brandweek,* July 10, 2000, 20–22. Christine Bittar, "Cosmetic Changes," *Brandweek,* June 18, 2001, 2.
3. Jack Neff, "P&G Outpacing Unilever in Five Year Battle," *Advertising Age,* November 3, 2003, 1–2.
4. Scott D. Horsburgh, "The Procter & Gamble Company," *Better Investing,* March 2003, 50.
5. Day, "Aligning the Organization to the Market," 69–72.
6. Ibid., 70–71.
7. Ibid.
8. Ibid., 72.
9. Kathleen Kerwin, Christopher Palmeri, and Paul Magnusson, "Can Anything Stop Toyota?" *BusinessWeek,* November 17, 2003, 62–70.
10. Don E. Schultz, "Structural Straitjackets Stifle Integrated Success," *Marketing News,* March 1, 1999, 8.

11. Elliot Maltz and Ajay Kohli quoted in Regina Fazio Maruca, "Getting Marketing's Voice Heard," *Harvard Business Review,* January/February 1999, 10–11. Elliot Maltz, William E. Souder, and Ajith Kumar, "Influencing R&D/Marketing Integration and the Use of Market Information by R&D Managers," *Journal of Business Research* 51, no. 2, 2001, 69–82.
12. Nigel F. Piercy, *Market-Led Strategic Change: A Guide to Transforming the Process of Going To Market* (Oxford: Butterworth-Heinemann, 2002), 242.
13. Don E. Schultz, "Integration Is Critical for Success in the 21st Century," *Marketing News,* September 15, 1997, 26.
14. James Mac Hulbert, Noel Capon, and Nigel F. Piercy, *Total Integrated Marketing: Breaking the Bounds of the Function* (New York: The Free Press, 2003).
15. Ibid.
16. Elliot Maltz and Ajay Kohli, "Reducing Marketing's Conflict with Other Functions: The Differential Effects of Integrating Mechanisms," *Journal of the Academy of Marketing Science,* Fall 2000, 479–492.
17. Nick Wreden, "Marketing Organization of the Future," *www.fusionbrand.blogs.com,* June 4, 2004.
18. William Band and John Guasperi, "Creating the Customer-Engaged Organization," *Marketing Management,* July/August 2003, 35–39.
19. "Special Report: The Global 1000," *BusinessWeek,* July 14, 2003, 40–55.
20. Robert Nardelli quoted in *Reinventing America: The 1993 BusinessWeek Symposium of Chief Executive Officers* (New York: BusinessWeek, 1994).
21. Jill Kickul and Lisa Gundry, "Breaking through Boundaries for Organizational Innovation: New Managerial Roles and Practices in E-Commerce Firms," *Journal of Management* 27, no. 3, 2001, 347–361.
22. Nicole Lewis, "E-Biz Goals Thwarted by Lack of Structure, Skills," *Ebn*, January 22, 2001, 64.
23. Donald R. Lehmann and Russell S. Winer, *Product Management.* 3rd ed. (Chicago: McGraw-Hill/Irwin, 2001).
24. Pierre Berthon, James M. Hulbert, and Leyland F. Pitt, *Brands, Brand Managers, and the Management of Brands* (Boston, MA: Marketing Science Institute), Report No. 97-122, 1997.
25. "FMCG Firms Need to Focus on Category before Brand," *Marketing,* September 27, 2001, 5.
26. Erick M. Olson, Orville C. Walker Jr., and Robert W. Ruekert, "Organizing for Effective New Product Development: The Moderating Role of Product Innovativeness,"*Journal of Marketing,* January 1995, 48–62.
27. Peter Doyle, *Marketing Management and Strategy.* 3rd ed. (London: Prentice Hall, 2002).
28. Lehmann and Winer, *Product Management.*
29. Christian Homburg, John P. Workman, and Ove Jensen, "Fundamental Changes in Marketing Organization: The Movement toward a Customer-Focused Organizational Structure," *Journal of the Academy of Marketing Science* 28, no. 4, 2000, 459–478.
30. Peter Doyle, 2002.
31. Michael Porter, "Strategy and the Internet," *Harvard Business Review,* March 2001, 63–78.
32. Andrew Edgecliffe-Johnson, "Staples Brings Dotcom Back into Fold, *Financial Times,* April 4, 2001.
33. Russell S. Winer, "A Framework for Customer Relationship Management," *California Management Review* 43, no. 4, 2001, 89–105.
34. Noel Capon, *Key Account Management and Planning* (New York: The Free Press, 2001). Christian Homburg, John P. Workman, and Ove Jensen, "A Configurational Perspective on Key Account Management," *Journal of Marketing,* April 2002, 38–60.
35. Thomas A. Stewart, "The Search for the Organization of Tomorrow," *Fortune,* May 18, 1997, 94.
36. Day, "Aligning the Organization to the Market," 93.
37. Ravi S. Achrol, "Evolution of the Marketing Organization: New Forms for Turbulent Environments," *Journal of Marketing,* October 1991, 77–93.
38. David W. Cravens, Nigel F. Piercy, and Shannon H. Shipp, "New Organization Forms for Competing in Highly Dynamic Environments, the Network Paradigm," *British Journal of Management* 7, 1996, 203–218.
39. Nora A. Aufreiter, Teri L. Lawver, and Candance D. Lun, "A New Way to Market," *The McKinsey Quarterly* 2, 2000, 52–61.
40. Quote from Robert W. Ruekert, Orville C. Walker Jr., and Kenneth J. Roering, "The Organization of Marketing Activities: A Contingency Theory of Structure and Performance," *Journal of Marketing,* Winter 1985, 23–24.
41. For an expanded discussion of this and other sales force organizational design issues, see Mark W. Johnston and Greg W. Marshall, *Sales Force Management.* 7th ed. (Burr Ridge, IL: Irwin McGraw-Hill, 2003), Chapter 4.
42. John A. Quelch and Lisa R. Klein, "The Internet and International Marketing," *Sloan Management Review,* Spring 1996, 60–68.
43. This discussion is based on Cateora and Graham, *International Marketing,* 335–338.
44. Jack Neff, "P&G Outpacing Unilever in Five-Year Battle," *Advertising Age,* November 3, 2003, 1–2.
45. Morgan W. McCall and George P. Hollenbeck, *Developing Global Executives: The Lessons of International Experience* (Boston, MA: Harvard Business School Press, 2001).
46. Stratford Sherman, "Leaders Are Learning Their Stuff," *Fortune,* November 27, 1995.

Chapter 15

Marketing Strategy Implementation and Control

The ultimate performance of market targeting and positioning decisions rests on how well the marketing strategy is implemented and managed on a continuing basis. Placing the strategy into action and adjusting it to eliminate performance gaps are essential success factors.

The importance of effective implementation and control approaches is illustrated by the strategic turnaround at Cisco Systems Inc.[1] In early 2001, customers across the world were drastically reducing orders, and Cisco was facing the need for a major strategy overhaul. In 2001, Cisco reduced the work force by 8,500 employees, took 18 percent off the payroll, and began to rebuild the business. By 2004 Cisco's revenue had grown to $22 billion with strong profit performance. Cisco's strategy for the future is to lead the next Internet revolution. This will include an array of new services, new applications, new products, and significant improvements in efficiencies. New

business ventures include net-phone service, storage, security, wireless, home networking gear, and optical networking.

Cisco still faces major strategic challenges, but its strategy overhaul illustrates the need for rigorous and systematic plan development allied with close attention to implementation and evaluation.

We begin with an overview of several issues in developing the marketing plan, followed by a discussion of implementing the plan. We examine internal marketing as an approach to effective implementation. Next, developing a strategic evaluation and control program is overviewed. Finally, the major evaluation activities are discussed and illustrated. These activities include conducting the strategic marketing audit, selecting performance criteria and measures, determining information needs and analysis, evaluating performance, and taking needed actions to keep performance on track.

The Marketing Plan

The marketing plan guides implementation and control, indicating marketing objectives and the strategy and tactics for accomplishing the objectives. Since Chapter 2 presents a step-by-step planning process, we briefly consider several planning issues and offer examples of marketing planning activities. Our perspective at this stage is more on implementation than analysis:

> A written plan is a key step in ensuring the effective execution of a strategic marketing program because it spells out what actions are to be taken, when and by whom.[2]

How the Marketing Plan Guides Implementation

The relationships between marketing strategy and the annual marketing plan are shown in Exhibit 15.1. The planning cycle is continuous. Plans are developed, implemented, evaluated, and revised to keep the marketing strategy on target. Since a strategy typically extends beyond one year, the annual plan is used to guide short-term marketing activities. The planning process is a series of annual plans guided by the marketing strategy. An annual planning period is necessary, since several of the activities shown require action within 12 months or less and budgets also require annual planning.

A look at the marketing planning process used by a large pharmaceutical company illustrates how planning is done. This process is described in Exhibit 15.2.

Contents of the Marketing Plan

An outline for developing the marketing plan is presented in Chapter 2. Many plans follow this general format. An executive summary provides top management and other executives not closely involved in implementation with an overview of the plan. The summary outlines the current situation, indicates marketing objectives, summarizes strategies, outlines action programs, and indicates financial expectations.[3]

EXHIBIT 15.1
Marketing Planning Relationships

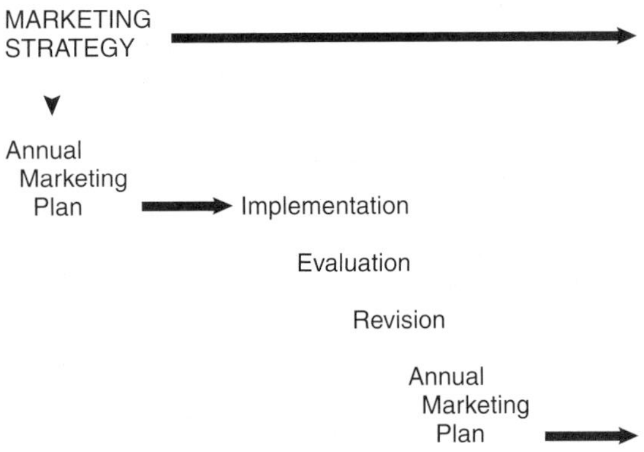

MARKETING STRATEGY →

↓

Annual Marketing Plan → Implementation

Evaluation

Revision

Annual Marketing Plan →

EXHIBIT 15.2 Marketing Planning Process at a Pharmaceutical Company

- Product managers are responsible for coordinating the preparation of marketing plans.
- A planning workshop is conducted midyear for the kickoff of the next year's plans. The workshop is attended by top management and product, research, sales, and finance managers. The firm's advertising agency account manager also participates in the workshop.
- The current year's plans are reviewed and each product manager presents the proposed marketing plan for next year. The workshop members critique each plan and suggest changes. Since the requested budgets may exceed available funds, priorities are placed on major budget components. Each product manager must provide strong support for requested funds.
- The same group meets again in 90 days and the revised plans are reviewed. At this meeting the plans are finalized and approved for implementation.
- Each product manager is responsible for coordinating and implementing the plan.
- Progress is reviewed throughout the plan year, and when necessary the plan is revised.

The marketing plan outline for Sonesta Hotels is shown in Exhibit 15.3. The activities include making the situation assessment, setting objectives, developing targeting and positioning strategies, deciding action programs for the marketing-mix components, and preparing supporting financial statements (budgets and profit-and-loss projections).

The typical planning process involves considerable coordination and interaction among functional areas. Team planning approaches like the pharmaceutical company's planning workshop are illustrative (Exhibit 15.2). Successful implementation of the marketing plan requires a broad consensus among various functional areas.[4] For example, a consensus is essential between product managers and sales management. Collaboration between product managers and sales managers is essential to provide sales coverage for the product portfolio. Multiple products require negotiation in reaching agreement on the amount of sales force time devoted to various products. Recall the Chapter 14 discussion of the importance of efforts to secure the integration of marketing with other functions and units in the organization, and approaches to achieving this.

Managing the Planning Process

Planning is an organizational process in which interactions and discussions between executives shape outcomes. Planning involves more than analytical techniques and computation. Research suggests that problems faced in making marketing planning effective may be addressed by considering the behavior of executives in conducting planning and the organizational context in which planning is done, as well as by formal training in planning techniques and procedures.[5] An effective planning process is closely linked to successful implementation of plans. Exhibit 15.4 shows the planning process as having three dimensions: analytical, behavioral and organizational, which should be managed consistently.

The analytical dimension of planning process consists of the tools for systematic planning—analytical techniques, formal procedures and systems—which are needed to develop robust and tested plans and strategies. The behavioral dimension of planning is concerned with how managers perceive planning activities and the strategic assumptions they make, as well as the degree and extent of participation in planning. Correspondingly, the organizational dimension of planning is concerned with the organizational structure in which planning is carried out, along with the associated information resources and corporate culture. One challenge to management is to manage all these aspects of the planning process in a consistent way.

The Innovation Feature describes how a manager addresses planning process issues at an SBU of the 3M Corporation in the United Kingdom. It illustrates the advantages of linking the planning process to implementation issues.

EXHIBIT 15.3 Sonesta Hotels: Marketing Plan Outline

Source: Adapted from Howard Sutton, *The Marketing Plan in the 1990s* (New York: The Conference Board, 1990), 34–35. Reprinted with permission from The Conference Board.

Note: Please keep the plan concise—maximum of 20 pages plus summary pages. Include title page and table of contents. Number all pages.

I. *Introduction.* Set the stage for the plan. Specifically identify marketing objectives such as "increase average rate," "more group business," "greater occupancy," or "penetrate new markets." Identify particular problems.

II. *Marketing Position.* Begin with a single statement that presents a consumer benefit in a way that distinguishes us from the competition.

III. *The Product.* Identify all facility and service changes that occurred this year and are planned for next year.

IV. *Marketplace Overview.* Briefly describe what is occurring in your marketplace that might have an impact on your business or marketing strategy, such as the economy, the competitive situation, etc.

V. *The Competition.* Briefly identify your primary competition (three or fewer), specifying number of rooms, what is new in their facilities, and marketing and pricing strategy.

VI. *Marketing Data*

- A. Identify top five geographic areas for transient business, with percentages of total room nights compared to the previous year.
- B. Briefly describe the guests at your hotel, considering age, sex, occupation, what they want, why they come, etc.
- C. Identify market segments with percentage of business achieved in each segment in current year (actual and projected) and projected for next year.

VII. *Strategy by Market Segment*

- A. Group
  1. *Objectives:* Identify what you specifically wish to achieve in this segment (for example, more high-rated business, more weekend business, larger groups).
  2. *Strategy:* Identify how sales, advertising, and public relations will work together to reach the objectives.
  3. *Sales Activities:* Divide by specific market segments.
     - *a.* Corporate
     - *b.* Association
     - *c.* Incentives
     - *d.* Travel agent
     - *e.* Tours
     - *f.* Other

     Under each category include a narrative description of specific sales activities geared toward each market segment, including geographically targeted areas, travel plans, group site inspections, correspondence, telephone solicitation, and trade shows. Be specific on action plans and designate responsibility and target months.
  4. *Sales Materials:* Identify all items so that they will be budgeted.
  5. *Direct Mail:* Briefly describe the direct mail program planned, including objectives, message, and content. Identify whether we will use existing material or create a new piece.
  6. *Research:* Indicate any research projects you plan to conduct in 1990, identifying what you wish to learn.
- B. Transient (the format here should be the same as group throughout)
  1. *Objective*
  2. *Strategy*

(continued)

EXHIBIT 15.3 *(concluded)*

3. *Sales Activities:* Divide by specific market segments.
   a. Consumer (rack rate)
   b. Corporate (prime and other)
   c. Travel agent: business, leisure, consortia
   d. Wholesale/airline/tour (foreign and domestic)
   e. Packages (specify names of packages)
   f. Government/military/education
   g. Special interest/other
4. *Sales Materials*
5. *Direct Mail*
6. *Research*

C. Other Sonesta Hotels

D. Local/Food and Beverage
1. *Objectives*
2. *Strategy*
3. *Sales Activities:* Divide by specific market segments.
   a. Restaurant and lounge, external promotion
   b. Restaurant and lounge, internal promotion
   c. Catering
   d. Community relation/other
4. *Sales Materials* (e.g., banquet menus, signage)
5. *Direct Mail*
6. *Research*

VIII. *Advertising*
- A. Subdivide advertising by market segment and campaign, paralleling the sales activities (group, transient, F&B).
- B. Describe objectives of each advertising campaign, identifying whether it should be promotional (immediate bookings) or image (longer-term awareness).
- C. Briefly describe contents of advertising, identifying key benefit to promote.
- D. Identify target media by location and type (newspaper, magazine, radio, etc.).
- E. Indicate percent of the advertising budget to be allocated to each market segment.

IX. *Public Relations*
- A. Describe objectives of public relations as it supports the sales and marketing priorities.
- B. Write a brief statement on overall goals by market segment paralleling the sales activities. Identify what proportion of your effort will be spent on each segment.

X. *Summary:* Close the plan with general statement concerning the major challenges you will face in the upcoming year and how you will overcome these challenges.

Implementing the Plan

Implementation effectiveness determines the outcome of marketing planning. The management of the planning process may enhance implementation effectiveness by building commitment and "ownership" of the plan and its execution. For example, actively managing the participation of different functions and executives from different specializations may improve the fit between the

Innovation Feature Planning for Commitment at 3M (UK)

3M is a global enterprise manufacturing more than 60,000 products from a base of 112 technology platforms, and 28 autonomous business units, of which Abrasive Systems Division (ASD) is one. ASD is 3M's original business and operates in a mature market, supplying abrasives mainly to manufacturing companies.

- At 3M (UK), the early 1990s saw ASD market share falling, accompanied by declining staff morale (compared to other company units and benchmark companies outside 3M).
- The appointment of Stuart Lane as ASD business unit manager in 1992 had three key goals: to restore sales growth to a minimum of 5 percent p.a., to return gross margin to the levels of the 1980s, and to bring the employee satisfaction level to at least the company average.
- Lane's first observations were that people felt they were not treated with respect or thanked for jobs well done; they lacked freedom to use initiative and make decisions; there was little information-sharing and too much bureaucracy.
- Lane's first decision was to double ASD's sales growth target from the 25 percent required by senior management (for 1992–1996) to 50 percent.
- In collaboration with 3M's Corporate Marketing business planners he designed what he describes as "a semi-formal, structured, iterative process" of planning for ASD.
- The new planning process started with a two-day planning workshop in spring 1992, followed by five further workshops over the following three months. Lane considers the workshops as critical to developing a robust plan for ASD, but also the team-building, ownership, enthusiasm and commitment to make the plan happen, and confidence among the team members that they were going to achieve the ambitious, "stretch" goals for ASD. Lane was prepared to sacrifice some sophistication in planning in favor of simplicity and involvement to win people's support.
- The planning was linked directly to an implementation process with three key elements:

1. A written plan, presented to management, but also reduced to an index card containing the essence of the plan in simple and memorable terms
2. The launch of the new plan to the ASD organization at the annual sales conference, and distribution of the index cards to be kept at the front of people's diaries
3. The introduction of Segment Action Teams (with a member of the management team as leader, but including people from sales, marketing, customer service and technical services from different levels in the organization), to take responsibility for segment-specific tactics and programmes. The Segment Action Teams have evolved into a key and permanent part of the ASD structure.

The results achieved by 1996 were a 53 percent growth in sales, a 100 percent growth in gross margin contribution, a 30 percent increase in market share, and employee satisfaction 12 percent above the company average. This was achieved, recall, in a mature market showing little growth.

Source: Adapted from Stuart Lane and Debbie Clewes, "The Implementation of Marketing Planning: A Case Study in Gaining Commitment at 3M (UK) Abrasives," *Journal of Strategic Marketing* 8, no. 3, 2000, 225–240. Reprinted with permission of Taylor & Francis Ltd., *www.tandf.co.uk/journals*.

plan and the company's real capabilities and resources, and avoid implementation barriers. Marketing managers may increasingly function as boundary-spanners both internally between functional areas and externally with suppliers, organizational partners, and customers.[6] Additional efforts to make the strategy implementation process more effective are a high priority in many companies. Many companies now recognize that implementation capabilities are an important corporate capability that requires detailed management attention.[7]

Implementation Process

Recent research underlines the influence of two sets of factors on marketing strategy implementation: *structural* issues, including the company's marketing functions, control systems, and policy guidelines, and *behavioral* issues, concerning marketing managers' skills in bargaining and negotiation, resource allocation, and developing informal organizational arrangements.[8] We consider several organizational and interpersonal aspects of effective implementation process.

A good implementation process spells out the activities to be implemented, who is responsible for implementation, the time and location of implementation, and how implementation will

EXHIBIT 15.4
Dimensions of Marketing Planning Process

Source: Adapted from Nigel F. Piercy, *Market-Lead Strategic Change: A Guide to Transforming the Process of Going to Market* (Oxford: Butterworth-Heinemann, 2002), 586.

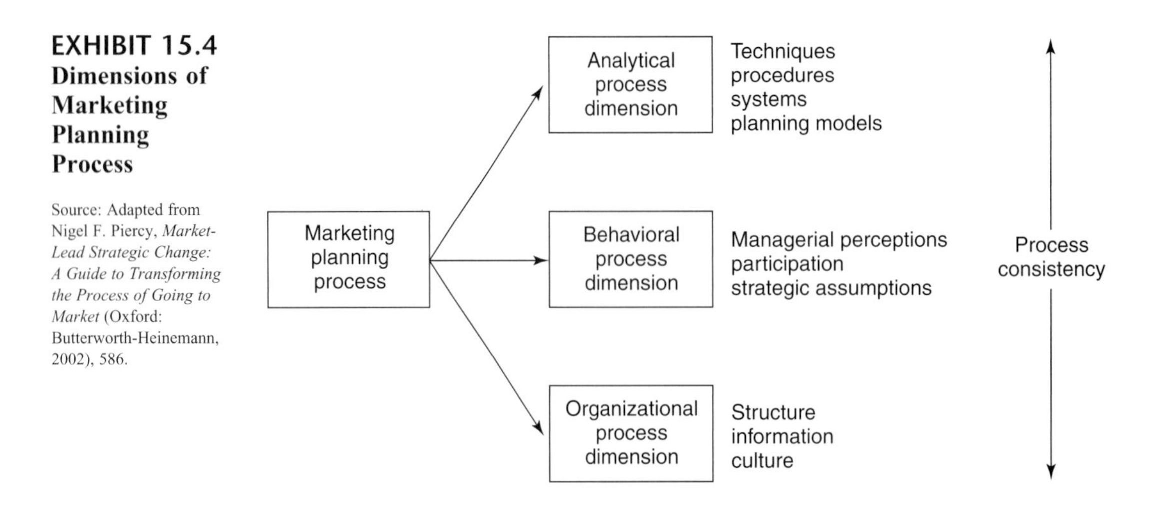

be achieved (Exhibit 15.5). Let's evaluate the following statement from a product manager's marketing plan:

> Sales representatives should target all accounts currently using a competitive product. A plan should be developed to convert 5 percent of these accounts to the company brand during the year. Account listings will be prepared and distributed by product management.

In this instance, the sales force is charged with implementation. An objective (5 percent conversion) is specified but very little information is provided as to *how* the accounts will be converted. A strategy is needed to penetrate the competitors' customer base. The sales force plan must translate the proposed actions and objective (5 percent conversion) into assigned salesperson responsibility (quotas), a timetable, and selling strategy guidelines. Training may be necessary to show the product advantages—and the competitors' product limitations—that will be useful in convincing the buyer to purchase the firm's brand.

The marketing plan can be used to identify the organizational units and managers that are responsible for implementing the various activities in the plan. Deadlines indicate the time available for implementation. In the case of the plan above, the sales manager is responsible for implementation through the sales force.

Improving Implementation

Managers are important facilitators in the implementation process, and some are better implementers than others. Planners and implementers often have different strengths and weaknesses. An effective planner may not be good at implementing plans. Desirable implementation skills include:

- The ability to understand how others feel, and good bargaining skills.
- The strength to be tough and fair in putting people and resources where they will be most effective.
- Effectiveness in focusing on the critical aspects of performance in managing marketing activities.
- The ability to create a necessary informal organization or network to match each problem with which they are confronted.[9]

Research underlines the importance of engendering a sense of role significance among those responsible for implementation.[10] In addition to skillful implementers, several factors facilitate the implementation process. These include *organizational design, incentives,* and *effective communications*. The features of each factor are highlighted.

Organizational Design. Certain types of organizational designs aid implementation. For example, product managers and multifunctional coordination teams are useful implementation methods.

EXHIBIT 15.5
The Implementation Process

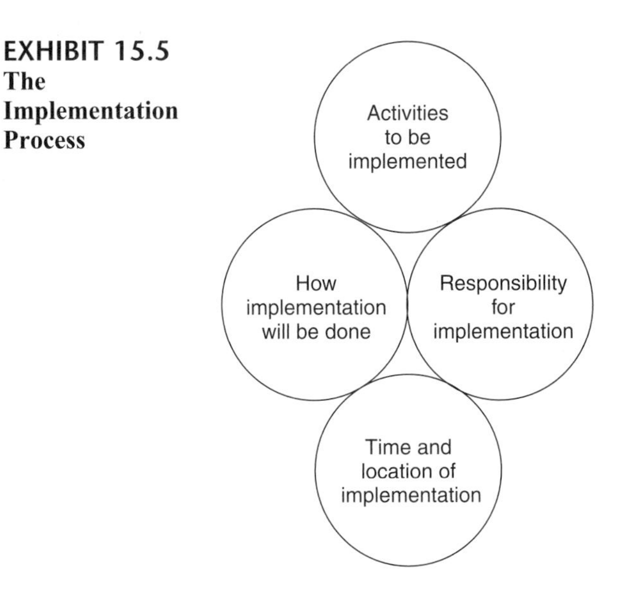

Management may create implementation teams consisting of representatives from the business functions and/or marketing activities involved. The flat, flexible organization designs discussed in Chapter 14 offer several advantages in implementation, since they encourage interfunctional cooperation and communication. Recall also the Chapter 14 discussion of venture marketing organizations as fluid groupings applying venture capitalism principles to develop and implement strategies around new opportunities. These designs are responsive to changing conditions.

As organizations shift from functional to process structures, the resulting changes promise to strengthen as well as complicate implementation strategies.[11] The use of cross-functional teams will aid implementation activities. The challenges of process definition, design, and management call for new skills and a multifunctional perspective, which will complicate implementation activities and require careful attention by management.

Incentives. Various rewards may help achieve successful implementation. For example, special incentives such as contests, recognition, and extra compensation are used to encourage salespeople to push a new product. Since implementation often involves teams of people, creation of team incentives may be necessary. Performance standards must be fair, and incentives should encourage something more than normal performance.

Communications. Rapid and accurate movement of information through the organization is essential in implementation. Both vertical and horizontal communications are needed in linking together the people and activities involved in implementation. Meetings, status reports, and informal discussions help to transmit information throughout the organization. Computerized information and decision-support systems like corporate intranets help to improve communications speed and effectiveness.

Problems often occur during implementation and may affect how fast and how well plans are put into action. Examples include competitors' actions, internal resistance between departments, loss of key personnel, supply chain delays affecting product availability (e.g., supply, production, and distribution problems), and changes in the business environment. Corrective actions may require appointing a person or team for troubleshooting the problem, increasing or shifting resources, or changing the original plan.

Internal Marketing

One interesting approach to enhancing strategy implementation effectiveness is the adoption of internal marketing methods. Internal marketing involves developing programs to win line management support for new strategies, to change the attitudes and behavior of employees working at key

EXHIBIT 15.6
Internal Marketing

Source: Reprinted from *Market-Led Strategic Change: A Guide to Transforming the Process of Going to Market*, Nigel F. Piercy, Copyright 2001, with permission from Elsevier.

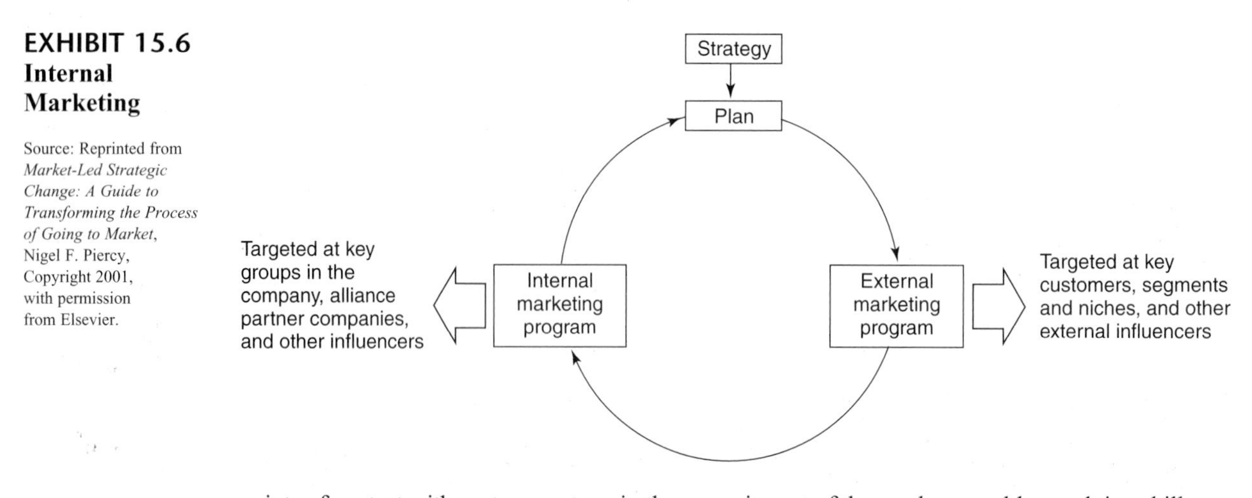

points of contact with customers, to gain the commitment of those whose problem-solving skills are important to superior execution of the strategy. Exhibit 15.6 shows internal marketing and external marketing programs as parallel outputs from the planning process. While external marketing positions the strategy in the customer marketplace, internal marketing is aimed at the internal customer within the company. Internal marketing goals may include promoting the external marketing strategy and how employees contribute, develop better understanding between customers and employees (regardless of whether they have direct contact), and provide superior internal customer service to support external strategy.[12]

An internal marketing approach involves examining each element of the external marketing program to identify what changes will be needed in the company's internal marketplace and how these changes can be achieved. If used as part of the planning process, analysis of the internal marketplace can isolate organizational change requirements (e.g., new skills, processes, organizational structures), implementation barriers (e.g., lack of support and commitment in key areas of the company), and new opportunities (by uncovering organizational capabilities otherwise overlooked).[13] Internal marketing is a promising way of identifying and resolving some of the implementation issues associated with the move from functional to process-based organizational designs.

One developing aspect of internal marketing is the opportunity to actively market plans and strategies not only inside the company, but also with partner organizations and their employees. Global advertising business, WPP, has targeted internal marketing as the fastest growth area for marketing services.[14] Effective implementation may rest also on company-wide efforts to put marketing plans and strategies into effect. The Cross-Functional Feature describes the operation of internal marketing at Southwest Airlines.

A Comprehensive Approach to Improving Implementation

One comprehensive way to deal with difficulty in the implementation of the marketing plan is to employ the balanced scorecard method.[15] This process is a formalized management control system that implements a given business-unit strategy by means of activities across four areas: financial, customer, internal business process, and learning and growth (or innovation).

The balanced scorecard was created by Kaplan and Norton in reaction to the difficulties that many managers experienced when trying to implement a particular strategy. A strategy is often not defined in a manner that describes how it might be achieved. Merely communicating the strategy to employees does not provide any instruction as to what actions they must take to help achieve the strategy. More importantly, managers might even take action to the detriment of other areas in an organization when attempting to implement the strategy. The balanced scorecard provides a framework to minimize such an occurrence by encouraging implementation of a common strategy, which is communicated and coordinated across all major areas of the organization. The "balanced"

Cross-Functional Feature

Implementing Excellence through Internal Marketing at Southwest Airlines

- The original "no-frills airline," Southwest is rated highly for offering customers below-market prices and above-average customer service. The company has won many industry awards for lowest customer complaints, most on-time arrivals, and highest quality baggage service.
- The company's internal marketing treats frontline employees as internal customers.
- Southwest uses high employee morale and service quality as a route to excellent and sustained profitability in a turbulent marketplace.
- At Southwest, internal marketing involves:

  1. Providing employees with a clear vision that is worth pursuing.
  2. Competing aggressively to attract the best people.
  3. Preparing people with the right skills and knowledge to perform.
  4. Emphasizing teamwork.
  5. Motivating employees through measurement and rewards.
  6. Providing people with the freedom to do well.
  7. Ensuring management understands the internal customer.

- Southwest's strong mission and vision shapes a unique corporate culture that puts employees first—they believe that the better they treat employees, the better they will perform in providing excellent service to customers.

Source: Adapted from Andrew J. Czaplewski, Jeffery M. Ferguson, and John F. Milliman, "Southwest Airlines: How Internal Marketing Pilots Success," *Marketing Management*, September/October 2001, 14–17. Reprinted with permission of the American Marketing Association.

component of the balanced scorecard reflects the need to consider how all areas of the organization function together to achieve a common goal of strategy implementation.

The major benefit of the balanced scorecard is that an often aggregate, broadly defined strategy is translated to very specific actions. Through execution and monitoring of these actions, management can assess the success of the strategy and also modify and adjust the strategy if necessary. Another major benefit of the balanced scorecard methodology is that it is feasible for any business-unit-level strategy and provides a means to link performance evaluation to strategy implementation.

For example, the marketing plan outline in Exhibit 15.3 for Sonesta Hotels can be adapted to the balanced scorecard format. The marketing plan for Sonesta Hotels is designed to achieve specific objectives through a set of strategies. In Part VII, A.3., the most difficult area is determining which activities will lead to achieving market segment objectives and ensuring that activities in the sales area do not interfere with activities in another area. The balanced scorecard approach allows consideration of specific sales activities, which will accomplish the objective but also formally includes an assessment of the strategy component (Part A.2.) across all aspects of the business unit at the same time. This assessment is more forward focused than concentrating only on sales, advertising, and public relations. It also helps to include performance measures and targets that are more long-term oriented and are not solely financially based. Therefore, a consideration of sales activities to execute a marketing strategy would also involve how these activities affect four major areas of the company: (1) the financial perspective; (2) the customer; (3) internal business processes; and (4) learning and growth. This integrated assessment would consider how the strategy would affect all major areas of the company and what performance indicators should be monitored in each of the four major areas. In this manner, it is much easier to integrate the marketing plan with the overall business strategy.

Internal Strategy-Structure Fit

It is important that the organization's competitive and marketing strategy be compatible with the internal structure of the business and its policies, procedures, and resources.[16] Several internal factors that may impact the implementation of marketing strategy are shown in Exhibit 15.7. These factors include higher-level corporate and business strategies, SBU and corporate relationships

EXHIBIT 15.7
Factors Affecting the Implementation of Business and Marketing Strategy

Source: Harper W. Boyd, Jr., and Orville C. Walker, Jr., *Marketing Management* (Burr Ridge, IL: Richard D. Irwin, 1990), 826. Copyright © The McGraw-Hill Companies. Used with permission.

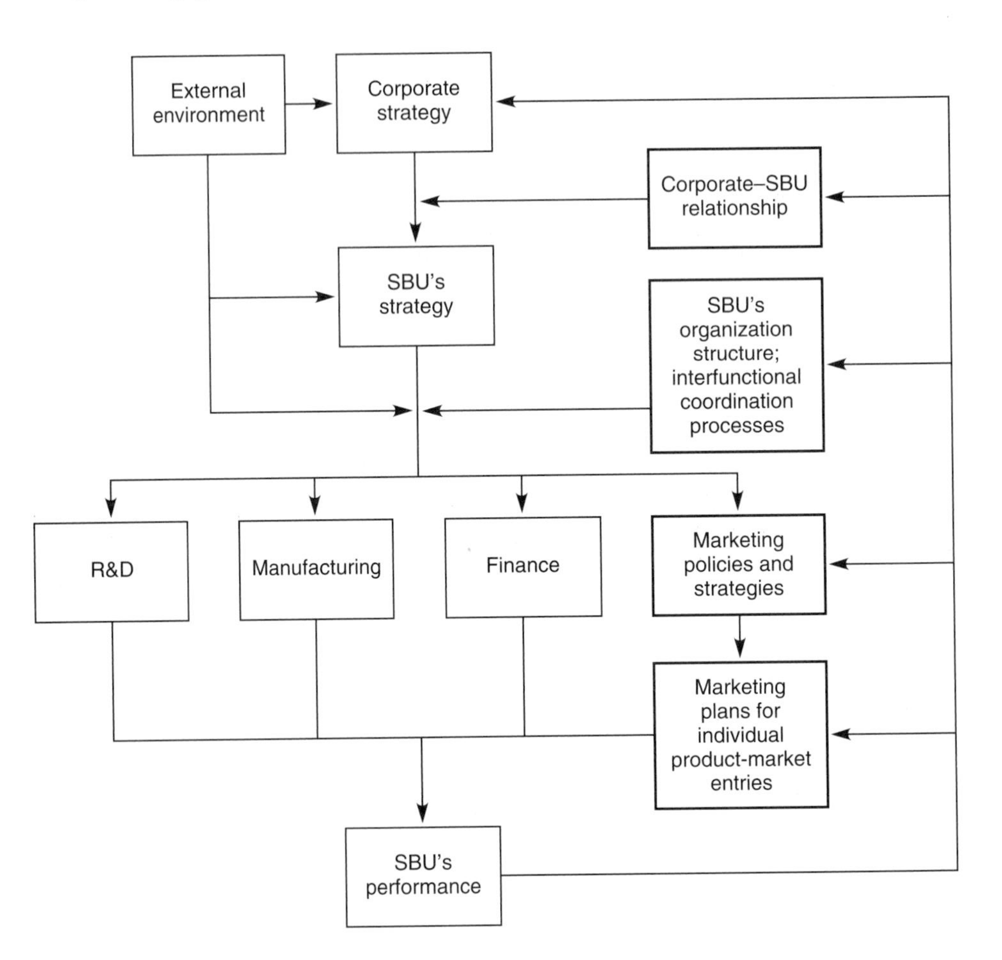

(e.g., extent of autonomy), the SBU's internal organization structure and coordination mechanisms, and the specific actions programmed in the marketing plan.

Coping with the influence of these factors during implementation requires close coordination of the strategies at the four levels shown in Exhibit 15.7. Marketing plans must be compatible with this internal structure. Otherwise implementation and performance are constrained. For example, a major objective of the marketing-planning process of the pharmaceutical company discussed earlier is to identify, communicate, and respond to issues and concerns at these four levels.

The importance of internal fit is shown by Hennes and Mauritz (H&M), the largest apparel retailer in Europe and a highly successful global fashion business. H&M sells "cheap chic"—very new, very extreme, very cheap fashion clothes to younger buyers. As well as outsourcing manufacturing to a huge network of garment shops in low-wage locations, H&M is run on principles of frugality internally as well. Overheads are minimized everywhere—executives rarely fly business class; taking cabs is frowned upon; all employee cell phones were taken away in the 1990s and even now only a few key employees have them. The fit between H&M's strategy and positioning, and its internal culture and management approach may help explain its success.[17]

Developing a Market Orientation

Encouraging and facilitating a market orientation throughout the business is an important responsibility of marketing management. The chief executive officer of a large transportation services company states that the marketing and operations functions are the customer-service components of the firm, and that the role of accounting, finance, human resources, and information systems is to support customer service activities. He emphasizes that the supporting functions are evaluated on the basis of how effectively they meet the needs of marketing and operations. Since the entire organization is concerned with delivering customer satisfaction, this CEO's operating philosophy encourages (and rewards) a customer-driven approach throughout the organization.

One of the major challenges for marketing executives is spreading the customer message throughout the company, its partners in alliances and networks, and its suppliers. The reality of integration may require nothing less.[18]

The Customer Is First. A key issue in developing a market orientation throughout the organization is convincing every employee that customer satisfaction is a shared responsibility. Training programs are used to achieve this objective. The starting point is getting the entire management team to recognize its role and responsibility for market-oriented leadership. Customer advisory groups are sometimes used in developing an internal awareness about the importance of the marketplace. Multifunctional (e.g., finance, marketing, operations) teams or task forces may also be helpful integrating methods.

Both the characteristics and culture of an organization affect the development of a market orientation. Small companies achieve this integration more easily than large, multilayered corporations. The corporate culture may aid or constrain integration. Managers of nonmarketing functions must be encouraged to recognize the importance of meeting customer needs through their activities. A strong commitment and active participation by the chief executive officer are essential to integrate marketing into the thinking and actions of everyone in the firm. The chief executive officer of Southwest Airlines has been very successful in achieving this objective (Cross-Functional Feature). The airline is a customer-driven organization.

The Role of External Organization

The implementation of marketing strategy is affected by external organizations such as strategic alliance partners, marketing consultants, advertising and public relations firms, channel members, and other organizations participating in the marketing effort. These outside organizations present a major coordination challenge when they actively participate in marketing activities. Their efforts should be identified in the marketing plan and their roles and responsibilities clearly established and communicated. There is a potential danger in not informing outside groups of planned actions, deadlines, and other implementation requirements. For example, the organization's advertising agency account executive and other agency staff members need to be familiar with all aspects of promotion strategy as well as the major aspects of marketing strategy (e.g., market targets, positioning strategies, and marketing-mix component strategies). Withholding information from participating firms hampers their efforts in strategy planning and implementation.

The development of collaborative relationships between suppliers and producers improves implementation. Supply chain management strategies encourage reducing the number of suppliers and building strong relationships (see Chapter 10). We noted earlier that internal marketing is playing a growing role in sustaining alliance and network-based organizations based on partnering. Companies that are effective in working with other organizations are likely to also do a good job with implementation inside the organization, since they have skills in developing effective working relationships. Total quality programs also encourage internal teamwork among functions.

Adaptation in the Balanced Scorecard. If the balanced scorecard approach is used in conjunction with a market orientation, some modification may be necessary.[19] The balanced scorecard advocates measures of performance across four main areas, which should remain in balance. However, many companies seeking a market orientation do so through emphasis on a particular core competency. These competencies may range from product or brand leadership to a strong customer focus. Consequently, companies with such a strong focus on an area of primary importance will continue to need a more extensive set of performance measures in those areas even with adoption of the balanced scorecard approach. Thus, a company competing on the basis of product leadership is dependent upon continual innovation to retain a strong market presence. Some advocate that in this case, the balanced scorecard should not be balanced and an emphasis should be placed on the innovation perspective. Similarly, other perspectives may be emphasized according to the organization's core competency.

Even with an "unbalanced" approach the balanced scorecard methodology assists in linking business strategy to actions. With a formalized consideration of all major areas in the business, it is more likely that appropriate performance measures can be created and that important areas will not be overlooked.

Strategic Evaluation and Control

Marketing strategy has to be responsive to changing conditions. Evaluation and control keep the strategy on target and show when adjustments are needed. The relentless pursuit of cost reduction and enhanced customer value through strategy adjustments is a reality for businesses/companies competing in the 21st century:

> For every line item in a marketing budget—product development costs, advertising and promotional expenses, costs for salespeople, and so on—specific and measurable standards of performance must be set so that each of these elements of marketing performance can be evaluated.[20]

Strategic evaluation requires analyzing information to gauge performance and taking the actions necessary to keep results on track. Managers need to continually monitor performance and, when necessary, revise their strategies due to changing conditions. Strategic evaluation, the last stage in the marketing strategy process, is really the starting point. Strategic marketing planning requires information from ongoing monitoring and evaluation of performance. Discussion of strategic evaluation has been delayed until now in order to first consider the strategic areas that require

EXHIBIT 15.8 Data Mining and CRM in Marketing Evaluation and Control

Sources: Roger D. Blackwell, *From Mind to Market* (New York: HarperBusiness, 1997), 188–189; Todd Wasserman, Gerry Khermouch, and Jeff Green, "Mining Everybody's Business," *Brandweek*, February 28, 2000, 32–36; Russell S. Winer, "A Framework for Customer Relationship Management." *California Management Review* 43, no. 4 (2001), 89–105.

Victoria's Secret	Data mining to improve merchandise managers' decisions concerning inventory levels.	The retailer stocked each bra style in 12 sizes, each with different colors. Restocking decisions were based on managers' judgment, and this resulted in an excess of certain items and a lack of others. A test was initiated to monitor sales and restock inventory according to decision rules applied to the database. Victoria's Secret's sales in the test stores increased by 30 percent using the new decision rules, with no increases in inventory.
Music marketing company	Data mining of purchase data revealed that a significant proportion of people over the age of 62 were buying rap music. They were not fans of Snoop Doggy Dogg but were buying presents for their grandchildren.	Senior citizen purchases had not been considered in the marketing strategy.The unexpected spending pattern produced a new profit center addressed through direct marketing emphasizing the company's low prices (for fixed-income senior citizens).
Wal-Mart	Uses data mining to allow each store to adapt its merchandise mix to local preferences.	Individual stores stock the range of colors, sizes, and price points that match spending patterns at the neighborhood level.
AT&T	Analyzes CRM data to identify the profitability of individual customers.	Service levels are adapted according to the profitability of the customer. Profitable customers receive personalized service, while less profitable customers are offered an automated, menu-driven service.

evaluation and to identify the kinds of information needed for assessing marketing performance. Thus, the first 14 chapters establish an essential foundation for building a strategic evaluation program. We now examine the impact of Customer Relationship Management systems, an overview of evaluation activities, and the role of the strategic marketing audit.

Customer Relationship Management

Recall that the widespread adoption of customer relationship management (CRM) systems to integrate all customer data from different sources, in combination with electronic point-of-sale customer data capture, offers several new and powerful resources for strategic evaluation and control (see Chapter 7 Appendix). For example, data mining is becoming an important tool for improving marketing strategies. Penetrating analysis of databases may reveal important purchasing patterns and the effect of marketing actions. Exhibit 15.8 illustrates this use of new data sources. Data mining applications indicate the important role of information technology in marketing strategy implementation and control.

The ability to identify profitability at the level of the individual customer by combining CRM and purchase data with other databases is becoming an especially important capability of strategic appraisal for marketing management. Together with growing emphasis on customer retention rather than just acquisition, a focus on customer lifetime value is important in guiding management decisions and evaluating the effectiveness of marketing strategy. CRM systems have the potential to greatly expand the measures of performance used, and to take a more fine-grained look at marketing effectiveness related to customer acquisition and defection rates, customer tenure, customer value and worth, proportion of inactive customers, and cross-selling.[21] The availability of CRM information is making new types of evaluation and control measurements available for management to assess the added-value achieved by marketing investments. We discuss marketing metrics further below.

An illustration of the powerful linkages between marketing information for evaluation and review and innovative strategies and organizational change is provided by the Whirlpool Corporation. This company's use of CRM data to drive a strategy of customer focus in a previously product-driven organization is described in the Strategy Feature.

Overview of Evaluation Activities

Evaluation consumes a high proportion of marketing executives' time and energy. Evaluation may seek to (1) find new opportunities or avoid threats, (2) keep performance in line with management's expectations, and/or (3) solve specific problems that exist.

An example of a threat identified via product-market analysis for an apparel company is the shift away from wearing suits and more formal business attire toward sports clothing. These changes in preferences are major threats for companies that produce men's suits. Similarly, Royal Doulton is a premier brand of formal chinaware, famed for its expensive dinnerplates, which saw its sales falling at 20 percent a year in the late-1990s, because of the move by consumers toward informal dining, and management's inability to reposition the brand. Closely tracking innovation in Web applications and earnings from acquisitions at Cisco Systems Inc. is an example of information to keep performance in line with management expectations. Finally, evaluating the effectiveness of alternative TV commercials is an example of solving specific problems.

Areas of evaluation include environmental scanning, product-market analysis, brand equity analysis, marketing program evaluation, and gauging the effectiveness of specific marketing mix components such as advertising. The major steps in establishing a strategic evaluation program are described in Exhibit 15.9. Strategic and annual marketing plans set the direction and guidelines for the evaluation and control process. A strategic marketing audit may be conducted when setting up an evaluation program, and periodically thereafter. Next, performance standards and measures need to be determined, followed by obtaining and analyzing information for the purpose of performance-gap identification. Actions are initiated to pursue opportunities or avoid threats, keep performance on track, or solve a particular decision-making problem.

Matching Metrics to Strategy at Whirlpool

Whirlpool Corporation is the world's largest manufacturer and retailer of home appliances with 2004 sales of more than $12 billion. Global Whirlpool brands include Whirlpool, KitchenAid, Brastemp, and Bauknecht.

Whirlpool's growth strategy—"Building unmatched customer loyalty"—focuses on winning the hearts and minds of customers.

Refocusing a traditionally product-driven engineering-oriented company toward a customer-driven strategy required new performance metrics and data. Traditionally, customer loyalty issues were delegated to the brand manager to achieve through marketing communications.

The corporate office of customer loyalty was established to design and implement a global customer loyalty measurement system and process.

The measurement system has two innovative elements: (1) a comprehensive view of all the customer touch points with the company, and (2) a clear distinction between the rational motivators and the emotional motivators of customer loyalty. These elements link directly to the marketing strategy.

The measurement system is backed by an IBM/Siebel CRM system to provide a single, enterprisewide source of customer information.

The new performance measurement system has revealed and allowed the organization to home in on previously untapped opportunities for building customer loyalty, and starts with an overall balanced scorecard measurement of the customer loyalty index for each brand.

New marketing initiative focus, for example, on the "Chief House Officer" (the homemaker who runs the house like a business). CHOs do not want the nuisance of taking some clothes to the dry cleaners or handwashing them—they even avoid buying clothes with delicate fabrics. Whirlpool has responded with the first washing machine that carries certification by The Woolmark Corporation that the machine is suitable for laundering machine washable wool garments.

Sources: Adapted from Lawrence A. Crosby and Sheree L. Johnson, "Do Metrics Reflect Your Market Strategy," *Marketing Management*, September/October 2003, 10–11. e-business solutions at *www.ibm.com*. Company information from www.whirlpool.com.

EXHIBIT 15.9 Strategic Marketing Evaluation and Control

Conduct strategic marketing audit
→ Select performance criteria and measures
→ Obtain and analyze information
→ Assess performance and take necessary action

The Strategic Marketing Audit

A marketing audit is useful when initiating a strategic evaluation program. Since evaluation compares results with expectations, it is necessary to lay some groundwork before setting up a tracking program. This complete review and assessment of marketing operations is similar in some respects to the situation analysis discussed in Part Two. However, the marketing audit goes beyond customer and competitive analysis to include all aspects of marketing operations. The audit is larger in scope than the situation analysis and is a more complete review of marketing strategy and performance. The audit can be used to initiate a formal strategic marketing planning

EXHIBIT 15.10 Guide to Conducting the Strategic Marketing Audit

I. CORPORATE MISSION AND OBJECTIVES
  A. Does the mission statement offer a clear guide to the product-markets of interest to the firm?
  B. Have objectives been established for the corporation?
  C. Is information available for the review of corporate progress toward objectives, and are the reviews conducted on a regular (e.g., quarterly, monthly) basis?
  D. Has corporate strategy been successful in meeting objectives?
  E. Are opportunities or problems pending that may require altering marketing strategy?
  F. What are the responsibilities of the chief marketing executive in corporate strategic planning?

II. BUSINESS COMPOSITION AND STRATEGIES
  A. What is the composition of the business (business segments, strategic planning units, and specific product-markets)?
  B. Have business strength and product-market attractiveness analyses been conducted for each planning unit? What are the results of the analyses?
  C. What is the corporate strategy for each planning unit (e.g., develop, stabilize, turn around, or harvest)?
  D. What objectives are assigned to each planning unit?
  E. Does each unit have a strategic plan?
  F. For each unit what objectives and responsibilities have been assigned to marketing?

III. MARKETING STRATEGY (FOR EACH PLANNING UNIT)
  A. Strategic planning and marketing:
    1. Is marketing's role and responsibility in corporate strategic planning clearly specified?
    2. Are responsibility and authority for marketing strategy assigned to one executive?
    3. How well is the firm's marketing strategy working?
    4. Are changes likely to occur in the corporate/marketing environment that may affect the firm's marketing strategy?
    5. Are there major contingencies that should be included in the strategic marketing plan?
  B. Marketing planning and organizational structure:
    1. Are annual and longer-range strategic marketing plans developed, and are they being used?
    2. Are the responsibilities of the various units in the marketing organization clearly specified?
    3. What are the strengths and limitations of the key members of the marketing organization? What is being done to develop people? What gaps in experience and capabilities exist on the marketing staff?
    4. Is the organizational structure for marketing effective for implementing marketing plans?
  C. Market target strategy:
    1. Has each market target been clearly defined and its importance to the firm established?
    2. Have demand, industry, and competition in each market target been analyzed and key trends, opportunities, and threats identified?
    3. Has the proper market target strategy been adopted?
    4. Should repositioning or exit from any product-market be considered?
  D. Objectives:
    1. Are objectives established for each market target, and are these consistent with planning-unit objectives and the available resources? Are the objectives realistic?
    2. Are sales, cost, and other performance information available for monitoring the progress of planned performance against actual results?
    3. Are regular appraisals made of marketing performance?
    4. Where do gaps exist between planned and actual results? What are the probable causes of the performance gaps?

(continued)

EXHIBIT 15.10 *(continued)*

E. Marketing program positioning strategy:
   1. Does the firm have an integrated positioning strategy made up of product, channel, price, advertising, and sales force strategies? Is the role selected for each mix element consistent with the overall program objectives, and does it properly complement other mix elements?
   2. Are adequate resources available to carry out the marketing program? Are resources committed to market targets according to the importance of each?
   3. Are allocations to the various marketing mix components too low, too high, or about right in terms of what each is expected to accomplish?
   4. Is the effectiveness of the marketing program appraised on a regular basis?

IV. MARKETING PROGRAM ACTIVITIES

A. Product strategy:
   1. Is the product mix geared to the needs and preferences that the firm wants to meet in each product-market?
   2. What branding strategy is being used?
   3. Are products properly positioned against competing brands?
   4. Does the firm have a sound approach to product planning and management, and is marketing involved in product decisions?
   5. Are additions to, modifications of, or deletions from the product mix needed to make the firm more competitive in the marketplace?
   6. Is the performance of each product evaluated on a regular basis?

B. Channel of distribution strategy:
   1. Has the firm selected the type (conventional or vertically coordinated) and intensity of distribution appropriate for each of its product-markets?
   2. How well does each channel access its market target? Is an effective channel configuration being used?
   3. Are channel organizations carrying out their assigned functions properly?
   4. How is the channel of distribution being managed? What improvements are needed?
   5. Are desired customer service levels being reached, and are the costs of doing this acceptable?

C. Price strategy:
   1. How responsive is each market target to price variations?
   2. What role and objectives does price have in the marketing mix?
   3. Should price play an active or passive role in program positioning strategy?
   4. How do the firm's price strategy and tactics compare to those of the competition?
   5. Is a logical approach used to establish prices?
   6. Are there indications that changes may be needed in price strategy or tactics?

D. Advertising and sales promotion strategies:
   1. Have a role and objectives been established for advertising and sales promotion in the marketing mix?
   2. Is the creative strategy consistent with the positioning strategy that is being used?
   3. Is the budget adequate to carry out the objectives assigned to advertising and sales promotion?
   4. Do the media and programming strategies represent the most cost-effective means of communicating with market targets?
   5. Do advertising copy and content effectively communicate the intended messages?
   6. How well does the advertising program measure up in meeting its objectives?

(continued)

EXHIBIT 15.10 *(concluded)*

E. Sales force strategy:
   1. Are the role and objectives of personal selling in the marketing program positioning strategy clearly specified and understood by the sales organization?
   2. Do the qualifications of salespeople correspond to their assigned roles?
   3. Is the sales force of the proper size to carry out its function, and is it efficiently deployed?
   4. Are sales force results in line with management's expectations?
   5. Is each salesperson assigned performance targets, and are incentives offered to reward performance?
   6. Are compensation levels and ranges competitive?

V. IMPLEMENTATION AND MANAGEMENT
   A. Have the causes of all performance gaps been identified?
   B. Is implementation of planned actions taking place as intended? Is implementation being hampered by marketing or other functional areas of the firm (e.g., operations, finance)?
   C. Has the strategic audit revealed areas requiring additional study before action is taken?

program, and it may be repeated on a periodic basis. Normally, the situation analysis is part of the annual development of marketing plans. Audits may be conducted every three to five years, or more frequently in special situations (e.g., acquisition/merger).

A guide to conducting the strategic marketing audit is shown in Exhibit 15.10. This format can be adapted to meet the needs of a particular firm. For example, if a company does not use indirect channels of distribution, this section of the audit guide will require adjustment. Likewise, if the sales force is the major part of a marketing program, then this section may be expanded to include other aspects of sales force strategy. The items included in the audit correspond to the strategic marketing plan because the main purpose of the audit is to appraise the effectiveness of strategy being followed. The audit guide includes several questions about marketing performance. The answers to these questions are incorporated into the design of the strategic tracking program.

There are other reasons besides starting an evaluation program for conducting a strategic marketing audit. Corporate restructuring may bring about a complete review of strategic marketing operations. Major shifts in business activities such as entry into new product and market areas or acquisitions may require strategic marketing audits. The growing impact of Internet-based business models may also encourage management to undertake an audit.

Performance Criteria and Information Needs

The next two stages in the evaluation and control process (Exhibit 15.9) are (1) selecting the performance criteria and the measures to be used for monitoring performance, and (2) identifying the information management needs to perform various marketing control activities.

Selecting Performance Criteria and Measures

As marketing plans are developed, performance criteria need to be selected to monitor performance. Specifying the information needed for marketing decision making is important and requires management's concentrated attention. In the past, marketing executives could develop and manage successful marketing strategies by relying on intuition, judgment, and experience. Successful executives in the 21st century need to combine judgment and experience with information and decision support systems. Similarly, the balanced scorecard approach is used by many companies to help select performance measures that are linked to strategy. Information systems are increasingly important in gaining a strategic edge in industries such as airline services, direct marketing, packaged foods, wholesaling, retailing, and financial services.

The purpose of objectives is to state the results that management is seeking and also provide a basis for evaluating the strategy's success. Objectives set standards of performance. Progress toward the objectives in the strategic and short-term plans is monitored on a continuing basis. In addition to information on objectives, management requires other kinds of feedback for use in performance evaluation. Some of this information is incorporated into regular tracking activities (e.g., the effectiveness of advertising expenditures). Other information is obtained as the need arises, such as a special study of consumer preferences for different brands.

Examples of performance criteria are discussed in several chapters. Criteria should be selected for the total plan and its important components. Illustrative criteria for total performance include sales, market share, profit, expense, and customer satisfaction targets. Brand-positioning map analyses may also be useful in tracking how a brand is positioned relative to key competitors. These assessments can be used to gauge overall performance and for specific market targets. Performance criteria are also needed for the marketing mix components. For example, new customer and lost customer tracking is often included in sales force performance monitoring. Pricing performance monitoring may include comparisons of actual to list prices, extent of discounting, and profit contribution. Since many possible performance criteria can be selected, management must identify the key measures that will show how the firm's marketing strategy is performing in its competitive environment and point to where changes are needed. Recall that the growing impact of CRM systems offers management access to a larger number of performance measures, particularly those relating to customer retention and defection.[22]

Marketing Metrics

The critical issue of selecting appropriate performance criteria is also illustrated by renewed attention given to the development of marketing metrics, or measures of the impact of marketing on the whole business, provided to senior management. The goal is to make better causal links between marketing activities and financial returns to the business.[23]

For example, Shell's large expenditure on sponsoring Ferrari in Formula One motor racing underlines the need for financial justification for this expenditure. Before signing a new five-year sponsorship contract, Shell management evaluated costs and benefits in five ways:

- Comparing attitudes toward the Shell brand of those who were aware of the Ferrari link, and those who were not.
- Examining change in purchasing behavior associated with shifts in attitudes toward the brand.
- Commissioning an independent evaluation of brand value, including branding, sales, price premium, and advertising effects.
- Making country-by-country comparisons—different Shell companies had merchandized the sponsorship locally to varying extents, so if the sponsorship was profitable, those who promoted it more should have obtained more benefit.
- Surveying manager opinion and their ratings of the impact of the sponsorship on return on investment.

After top management review, Shell approved the new five-year contract for the sponsorship as an important part of the company's marketing strategy.[24]

Tim Ambler, of London Business School, proposes the following questions to assess if a company's marketing tracking system, or performance measures, are adequate:

- Are the results reported to senior management regularly?
- Are the results compared with the forecast levels in business plans?
- Are they compared with key competitors using the same indicators?
- Is short-term performance adjusted to allow for changes in market-based assets?

EXHIBIT 15.11
Illustrative External and Internal Marketing Metrics

Sources: Adapted from Tim Ambler, "Marketing Metrics," *Business Strategy Review* 11, no. 2, 2000, 59–68. Tim Ambler, *Marketing and the Bottom Line*. 2nd ed. (Hemel Hempstead: Prentice Hall, 2003).

	External Market Metrics	
Financial measures	Sales value/volume Marketing investment Profits	
Brand equity	Relative satisfaction	Consumer preference or satisfaction relative to average for market/ competitors.
	Commitment	Index of "switchability," or measure of retention, loyalty, purchase intent or bonding.
	Relative perceived quality	Perceived quality satisfaction relative to average for market/competitors.
	Relative price	Market share by value/market share by volume.
	Availability	Distribution e.g., value-weighted percent of retail outlets carrying the brand.
	Internal Market Metrics	
Innovation health and employee alignment and commitment	Strategy	Awareness of goals Commitment to goals Active innovation support
	Culture	Appetite for learning Freedom to fail
	Outcomes	Number of initiatives in progress Number of innovations launched Percent of revenue due to launches in the last three years

- Is consumer behavior (purchase, frequency, retention, usage) researched and the drivers of behavior understood and monitored (e.g., satisfaction and brand awareness)?[25]

In Ambler's research into marketing metrics, the most important marketing metrics used by companies are: relative perceived quality; loyalty/retention; total number of customers; customer satisfaction; relative price (market share/volume); market share (volume or value); perceived quality/esteem; complaints (level of dissatisfaction); awareness; and distribution/ availability.[26] Conclusions about the types of metrics that may be useful are shown in Exhibit 15.11.

Importantly, metrics should be chosen to reflect strategic priorities and the issues most closely linking marketing investments with profits. For example, for monitoring external market performance, footwear retailer Payless ShoeSource uses two types of marketing metrics: (1) spending efficiency and effectiveness (e.g., ROI by advertising medium, advertising to sales spending ratios), and (2) business building (e.g., customer traffic, ratio of loyal to new customers). On the other hand, at food company Cadbury Schweppes, in the Managing for Value program, key measures include: performance against strategic milestones; market share, advertising spending, brand and advertising awareness, average purchases, and percent of total volume from new products.[27] Many major organizations are developing new sets of metrics to give top management better insight into performance against competitors and the value achieved from marketing investments.

Obtain and Analyze Information

The costs of acquiring, processing, and analyzing information are high, so the potential benefits of needed information must be compared to costs. Normally, information falls into two categories: (1) information regularly supplied to marketing management from internal and external sources, and (2) information obtained as needed for a particular problem or situation. Examples of the former are sales and cost analyses, market share measurements, and customer satisfaction surveys. Recall the growing impact of CRM systems in enhancing the availability of this type of information. Information from the latter category includes new-product concept tests, brand-preference studies, and studies of advertising effectiveness.

Several types of information may be needed by management. Information for strategic planning and evaluation can be obtained from these sources:

1. The *internal information system* is the backbone of any strategic evaluation program. These systems range from primarily sales and cost reports to highly sophisticated computerized marketing information systems and CRM/datamining technology.
2. *Standardized information services* are available by subscription or on a one-time basis, often at a fraction of the cost of preparing such information for a single firm. Nevertheless, these services are expensive. Standardized services are available in both printed form and in data files for computer analysis. Nielsen's TV rating data service is an example.
3. Marketing managers may require *special research studies.* A study of distributor opinions concerning a manufacturer's services is an example.
4. The firm's *strategic intelligence system* is concerned with monitoring and forecasting external, uncontrollable factors that influence the firm's product-markets. These efforts range from formal information activities to informal surveillance of the marketing environment.

Sources and types of marketing information are discussed in Chapter 5.

Performance Assessment and Action

The last stage in the marketing evaluation and control process is determining how the actual results compare with planned results. When performance gaps are too large, corrective actions are taken.

Opportunities and Performance Gaps

Strategic evaluation activities seek to (1) identify opportunities or performance gaps, and (2) initiate actions to take advantage of the opportunities or to correct existing and pending problems. Strategic intelligence, internal reporting and analysis activities, standardized information services, and research studies supply the information needed by marketing decision makers.

The real test of the value of the marketing information system is whether it helps marketing management to identify problems. In monitoring, there are two critical factors to take into account:

Problem/opportunity definition. Strategic analysis should lead to a clear explanation of an opportunity or problem since this will be needed to guide whatever strategic action may be taken. Often it is easy to confuse problem symptoms with problem causes.

Interpreting information. Management must also separate normal variations in performance from significant gaps in performance, since the latter are the ones that require strategic action. For example, how much of a drop in market share is necessary to signal a performance problem? Limits need to be set on the acceptable range of strategic performance.

No matter how extensive the information system may be, it cannot interpret the strategic importance of the information. This is the responsibility of management.[28]

An illustration of opportunity monitoring is provided by the emergence of concerns about environmental and "green" issues in many countries.

Environmental concerns are ongoing areas of strategic evaluation. Companies must identify important areas of concern and implement strategies that take into account consumer, public policy, and organizational priorities. Surprisingly, European consumers appear to be changing their priorities about eco-friendly products,[29] while in the United States, polls suggest in 2001 that only 50 percent of Americans considered themselves to be environmentalists, as compared to 76 percent in 1989.[30] Buyers may not be willing to pay a premium for green products.

Several explanations are offered for these changes including lower performance, higher prices, and environmentally responsible regular products. British supermarket chain Iceland decided in 2000 to move totally to organic produce in its own-label products, to make organic food part of mass market grocery shopping, in line with the growth of sales of this type of produce. In 2001, following a 6 percent fall in sales and loss of one-fifth of the company's market value, the decision was reversed. Iceland's largely blue-collar consumers did not find organic products appealing and objected to having the choice taken away. Philips, the European electronics multinational, claims that its success in marketing green products is based on understanding the need to link green product attributes like energy reduction, materials reduction and toxic substance reduction, with other consumer benefits (e.g., lower costs, convenience, higher quality of life).[31]

Company experiences with the paradoxes of consumer attitudes toward the purchase of green products underline the importance of extremely careful interpretation of the available evidence before decisions are made, and continuous monitoring of changes. Nonetheless, major changes in perceptions of environmental responsibility may also create important opportunities. The change in direction at Interfaces Inc. described in the Ethics Feature is an interesting example of a CEO combining his environmental and ethical judgment with responsiveness to customer concerns effectively.

In a quite different sector, John Browne running BP, the world's largest oil company, is happy to be cast as the "green" oilman. Browne's strategy of bold acquisitions and mergers, backed by insightful public relations efforts, has put BP at the forefront of the global energy industry. BP has branded itself the green energy company with its imaginative "Beyond Petroleum" advertising. Notwithstanding Browne being awarded an Earth Day Oscar by Greenpeace for "Best Impression of an Environmentalist," BP faces significantly fewer problems with the environmental lobby than rival Exxon.[32]

Determining Normal and Abnormal Variability

Operating results such as sales, market share, profits, order-processing time, and customer satisfaction display normal up and down fluctuations. The issue is determining whether these variations represent random variation or instead are due to special causes. For example, if a salesperson's sales over time remain within a normal band of variation, then the results are acceptable under the present operating conditions. Random high and low variations do not indicate unusually high or low performance. If this range of performance is *not* acceptable to management, then the system must be changed. This may require salesperson training, redesign of the territory, improvement in sales support, or other changes in the salesperson's operating system.

Statistical process-control concepts and methods are useful in determining when operating results are fluctuating normally or instead are out of control. Quality control charts can be used to analyze and improve results in marketing performance measures such as the number of orders processed, customer complaints, and territory sales.[33] Control-chart analysis indicates when the process is experiencing normal variation and when the process is out of control.

Ethics Feature

From Plunderer to Protector

- Ray C. Anderson is founder and now chairman of Atlanta-based Interface Inc., the world's largest manufacturer of commercial carpet tiles.
- In the mid-1990s, Interface was peppered by questions from interior designers about the dangers in the materials and processes it was using.
- Anderson convened a task force to answer his customers' questions. The members of the task force asked him for his environmental vision. Anderson comments, "But I had no vision, absolutely none . . ."
- He found his environmental vision in a book describing the need for sustainability to protect the earth's limited resources.
- Anderson pledged that by 2020 Interface would be a completely sustainable company, producing no dangerous waste, no harmful emissions, and using no oil.
- By 2004, Interface's eco-scorecard looked like this:

Interface's Eco-Scorecard

A decade ago, Interface founder, Ray Anderson, pledged that his $924 million company would stop using the earth's natural resources, eliminate waste, and emit no harmful emissions by 2020. Reductions made so far:

Waste	Down 80%
Water intake	Down 78%
Emission of greenhouse gases	Down 46%
Energy consumption	Down 31%
Use of petroleum-based materials	Down 28%
Total Savings	$231 million

Source: Michelle Conlin, "From Plunderer to Protector," *BusinessWeek*, July 19, 2004, 62–62.

The basic approach to control-chart analysis is to establish average and upper and lower control limits for the measure being evaluated. Examples of measures include order-processing time, district sales, customer complaints, and market share. Control boundaries are set using historical data. Future measures are plotted on the chart to determine whether the results are under control or instead fall outside the acceptable performance band determined by the upper and lower control limits. The objective is to continually improve the process that determines the results.

Deciding What Actions to Take

Many corrective actions are possible, depending on the situation. Management's actions may include exiting from a product-market, new-product planning, changing the target-market strategy, adjusting marketing strategy, or improving efficiency.

An illustration shows how strategic evaluation and control guide corrective action. Consider, for example, Nokia in Finland with unequaled brand recognition and distribution channels in the electronics sector, and huge purchasing power and manufacturing skills (see Case 1-1). In 2004, Nokia shocked investors by announcing a slow down in sales growth, and that market share had dropped below 30 percent for the first time.[34]

The warning indicators from the market were that while Nokia is still number 6 in the Interbrand survey of brands, there are some signs it is slipping in consumer surveys. Compared to rivals Samsung and Sony Ericsson, Nokia's phones are seen as dowdy, uninspired, and unfashionable—and the portfolio lacks a clamshell (flip-top) phone. The company was looking at a massive 21 percent drop in its average selling price. Furthermore, growth in the global mobile phone market is slowing. At the same time, basic wireless technology is becoming commoditized—average prices for phones are falling 4 percent annually. Commoditization opens the way for new low-cost competitors to enter the market.

In addition, Nokia's strengths in producing huge volumes of standardized phones is not set up to cope with increasing demands from operators for highly customized handsets. The company has been consistently late to market with new technologies, such as cameras, color screens, and fast data transfer rates.

Nokia management moved quickly to cut prices on selected handsets to hold market share, but then to address the larger issues emerging from their analysis of the market:

Problems	Strategies
Product choice: There are weaknesses in the handset portfolio, especially the lack of flip-phone	Will launch 40 phones in 2004, including flip-phones and high-end models with large color screens and top-of-the-line specifications.
Design problems: Nokia phones are seen as boring or bizarre	Still experimenting with novel approaches, but moving to a clean, modern look typified by the 6230.
Margins: Increasing commoditization and pressure on margins	To escape the low-end, expanding into mobile gaming, imaging, music, and even complex wireless systems for organizations.
Brand: Fading brand "buzz" among young people	Increasing marketing spending, sponsoring music festivals and snowboard championships, new wireless-video clips tie-in with National Basketball Association.

The challenge for Nokia is regaining market share and profit margins by finding a way out of the commoditized handsets business. The company has been through such turbulence before and emerged stronger.

Managing in a changing environment is what strategic marketing is all about. Responding to and anticipating change are the essence of evaluation and control. Executives develop innovative marketing strategies and monitor their effectiveness, altering the strategies as a result of changing conditions.

Summary

Marketing strategy implementation and control are vital links in a series of strategic marketing activities. These actions emphasize the continuing process of planning, implementing, evaluating, and adjusting marketing strategies. Strategic evaluation of marketing performance is the first step in strategic marketing planning and the last step after launching a strategy. The objective is to develop an approach to strategic evaluation, building on the concepts, processes, and methods developed in Chapters 1 through 14. Strategic evaluation is one of marketing management's most demanding and time-consuming responsibilities. While the activity lacks the glamour and excitement of new strategy development, perceptive evaluation often separates the winners from the losers. The management of successful companies anticipate and respond effectively to changing conditions and pressures. Regular strategic evaluation processes guide these responses.

Marketing strategy implementation and control are guided by the marketing plan and budget (Exhibit 15.1). The plan indicates the activities to be accomplished, how this is to be done, and the costs. The planning process moves into action through the annual marketing plan. It shows the activities to be implemented, responsibilities, deadlines, and expectations. Growing attention is being given to the management of planning process for effective strategy implementation, emphasizing not only analytical approaches, but also the commitment of managers to planning and the necessary organizational support.

Implementation (Exhibit 15.4) makes the plan happen. Many companies are concerned with enhancing implementation effectiveness. Organizational design, communications, and internal marketing may impact on implementation effectiveness. The balanced scorecard is a promising approach to coordinating a comprehensive approach to improving marketing implementation.

Much of the actual work of managing involves strategic and tactical evaluation of marketing options. Yet performing this function depends greatly on management's understanding of the planning process and the decisions that form plans. Strategic evaluation is a continuing cycle of making plans, launching them, tracking performance, identifying performance gaps, and initiating problem-solving actions. In accomplishing strategic evaluation, management must select performance criteria and measures and then set up a tracking program to obtain the information needed to guide evaluation activities. The choice and tracking of performance measures is increasingly impacted by the adoption of customer relationship management (CRM) systems. As an initial step in the strategic evaluation program (and periodically thereafter), a strategic marketing audit provides a useful basis for developing the program.

It is so easy for practicing managers to become preoccupied with day-to-day activities, neglecting to step back and review overall operations. The development of marketing metrics reporting the added-value of marketing to the whole company to senior management supports this need for strategic review. Regular audits and continuous monitoring of the market and competitive environment can prevent sudden shocks and can alert management to new opportunities. Building on findings from the strategic marketing audit, the chapter examines the major steps in acquiring and using information for strategic analysis. While the execution of the steps varies by situation, they offer a useful basis for guiding a strategic evaluation program in any type of firm. An important part of this process is setting standards for gauging marketing performance. These standards help determine what information is needed to monitor performance.

Internet Applications

A. Visit the Web site for 1-800-FLOWERS (*www.1800flowers.com*). How does this company employ its Web site to adapt to a constantly changing environment?

B. Enter the phrase "marketing implementation" into your search engine and review the first 20 sites indicated. View several of those representing consultants and agencies offering products and services to support marketing implementation. Which sound likely to be effective? What role, if any, can external agencies play in developing effective marketing strategy implementation initiatives?

Feature Applications

A. Review the Ethics Feature describing the environmental strategy implemented at Interfaces Inc. List the attractions from a marketing perspective of adopting an environmentally responsible position. Discuss whether companies can undertake environmental initiatives unless there is a commercial advantage.

B. Read the Cross-Functional Feature describing the internal marketing efforts at Southwest Airlines. Do "happy employees" always mean "happy customers"? Identify and list situations where you do not believe that this is true.

Questions for Review and Discussion

1. Discuss the similarities and differences between strategic marketing *planning* and *evaluation.*
2. What is involved in managing marketing planning as a process? What issues should be addressed in managing planning process in a company manufacturing high-technology components for the automotive sector?
3. Selecting the proper performance criteria for use in tracking results is a key part of a strategic evaluation program. Suggest performance criteria for use by a fast-food retail chain to monitor strategic marketing performance.
4. What justification is there for conducting a marketing audit in a business unit whose performance has been very good? Discuss.
5. Examination of the various areas of a strategic marketing audit shown in Exhibit 15.7 would be quite expensive and time consuming. Are there any ways to limit the scope of the audit?
6. Several kinds of information are collected for a strategic marketing evaluation. Develop a list of information that would be useful for a strategic evaluation in a life insurance company.
7. One of the more difficult management control issues is determining whether a process is experiencing normal variation or is actually out of control. Discuss how management can resolve this issue.
8. What role can internal marketing play in enhancing the effectiveness of both planning and implementation?
9. How can the "balanced scorecard" methods assist managers in their implementation efforts?
10. Discuss how management control differs for a strategic alliance compared to internal operations.
11. What are the important factors that managers should take into account to improve the implementation of strategies?
12. Discuss the role of customer relationship management (CRM) and data mining in improving marketing planning, implementation, and control activities.

Notes

1. This illustration is based on Quentin Hardy, "What Makes Cisco Run," *Forbes,* July 26, 2004, 66–74. Peter Burrows, "Cisco's Comeback," *BusinessWeek,* November 24, 2003, 42–48.
2. Orville C. Walker, Harper W. Boyd, John Mullins, and Jean-Claude Larréché, *Marketing Strategy: A Decision-Focused Approach.* 4th ed. (Burr Ridge IL: McGraw-Hill/Irwin, 2003), 319.

3. Donald R. Lehmann and Russell S. Winer, *Analysis for Marketing Planning*. 4th. ed. (Homewood, IL: Richard D. Irwin Inc., 1997), 10–13.
4. Ibid., 5–7.
5. Nigel F. Piercy and Neil A. Morgan, "The Marketing Planning Process: Behavioral Problems Compared to Analytical Techniques in Explaining Marketing Planning Credibility, *Journal of Business Research* 29, 1994, 167–178.
6. Frederick E. Webster, "The Future Role of Marketing in the Organization," in Donald R. Lehmann and Katherine E. Jocz (eds.), *Reflections on the Futures of Marketing* (Cambridge, MA: Marketing Science Institute, 1997, 39–66.
7. Nigel F. Piercy, "Marketing Implementation: The Implications of Marketing Paradigm Weakness for the Strategy Execution Process," *Journal of the Academy of Marketing Science* 26, no. 3, 1998, 222–236. Nigel F. Piercy and Frank V. Cespedes, "Implementing Marketing Strategy," *Journal of Marketing Management* 12, 1996, 135–160.
8. Charles H. Noble and Michael P. Mokwa, "Implementing Marketing Strategies: Developing and Testing a Managerial Theory," *Journal of Marketing,* October 1999, 57–73.
9. Thomas V. Bonoma, "Making Your Marketing Strategy Work," *Harvard Business Review,* March–April 1984, 75.
10. Noble and Mokwa, 71.
11. David W. Cravens, "Implementation Strategies in the Market-Driven Strategy Era," *Journal of the Academy of Marketing Science,* Summer 1998, 237–238.
12. Dana James, "Don't Forget Staff in Marketing Plan," *Marketing News,* March 13, 2000, 10–11.
13. Nigel F. Piercy and Neil A. Morgan, "Internal Marketing: The Missing Half of the Marketing Programme," *Long Range Planning* 24, no. 2, 1991, 82–93.
14. ". . . As Sorrell Starts Internal Marketing Drive," *Marketing Week,* July 12, 2001, 10.
15. Robert S. Kaplan and David P. Norton, *The Balanced Scorecard* (Boston: Harvard Business School Press, 1996).
16. This discussion is based on Harper W. Boyd Jr. and Orville C. Walker Jr. *Marketing Management* (Homewood, IL: Richard D. Irwin,1990), 824–825.
17. Kerry Capell and Gerry Khermouch, "Hip H&M," *BusinessWeek*, November 11, 2002, 39–42.
18. James Mac Hulbert, Noel Capon, and Nigel F. Piercy, *Total Integrated Marketing: Breaking the Bounds of the Function* (New York: The Free Press, 2003).
19. See Slater, Stanley F., Eric M. Olson, and Venkateshwar K. Reddy, "Strategy-Based Performance Measurement," *Business Horizons,* July–August 1997, 37–44, for a complete discussion on the modification of the balanced scorecard approach necessary to achieve a market orientation.
20. Orville C. Walker, Harper W. Boyd, John Mullins, and Jean-Claude Larréché, *Marketing Strategy: A Decision-Focused Approach*. 4th ed. (Burr Ridge, IL: McGraw-Hill/Irwin, 2003), 332.
21. Lawrence A. Crosby and Sheree L Johnson, "High Performance Marketing in the CRM Era," *Marketing Management,* September/October 2001, 10–11.
22. Larry Yu, "Successful Customer-Relationship Management," *Sloan Management Review,* Summer 2001, 18–29.
23. Wayne R. McCullough, "Marketing Metrics," *Marketing Management,* Spring 2000, 64.
24. "Marketers Still Lost in the Metrics," *Marketing,* August 10, 2000, 15–17.
25. Tim Ambler, *Marketing and the Bottom Line*. 2nd ed. (Hemel Hempstead: Prentice Hall, 2003).
26. Allyson L. Stewart-Allen, "Marketing Metrics for Corporate Boards," *Marketing News,* December 4, 2000, 14.
27. Tim Ambler, 2003.
28. An interesting evaluation of providing decision makers with support in the interpretation of evidence is found in D. V. L. Smith and J. H. Fletcher, *The Art and Science of Interpreting Market Research Evidence* (Chichester: Wiley, 2004).
29. Tara Parker-Pope, "Europeans' Environmental Concerns Don't Make It to the Shopping Basket," *The Wall Street Journal,* August 18, 1995, B3A.
30. Vadim Liberman, "The Green Conundrum," *Across the Board,* May/June 2001, 17–18.
31. Jacquelyn A. Ottman, "Green Marketing," *In Business,* September/October 2000, 31.
32. Nelson D. Schwartz, "Inside the Head of BP," *Fortune,* July 26, 2004, 56–61.
33. James Mac Hulbert, Noel Capon, and Nigel F. Piercy, *Total Integrated Marketing.*
34. This account is based on Andy Reinhardt, Adeline Bonnet, and Roger O. Crockett, "Can Nokia Get the Wow Back?" *BusinessWeek,* May 31, 2004, 18–21.

Cases for Part 5

CASE 5-1

Verizon Communications Inc.

Ivan G. Seidenberg hardly looks like Old Man Telecom. The chief executive of Verizon Communications Inc. is only 56 and has the build and intensity of someone much younger. But sitting in his sun-filled, 39th-floor office in Midtown Manhattan, Seidenberg points out that he joined the company as a cable splicer's assistant in the Bronx when he was 19. He even keeps his cable splicer's shears, knife, and sheaf tucked away in his desk. "It's hard to believe, but I've been here for 37 years, more than one-third of this company's history," he says. "I feel an obligation to make sure this company is well positioned for the next 100 years."

Now Seidenberg is launching a series of sweeping initiatives to make good on his vow. From hardball pricing tactics that have knocked rivals back on their heels to a capital-spending war chest that's the largest in telecom, he's determined to transform what was once just another sleepy phone company into the pacesetter for the industry. "When you're the market leader," says Seidenberg, "part of your responsibility is to reinvent the market."

At the heart of this reinvention is the most ambitious deployment of new telecom technology in years (Exhibit 1). Verizon plans to roll out fiber-optic connections to every home and business in its 29-state territory over the next 10 to 15 years, a project that might reasonably be compared with the construction of the Roman aqueducts. It will cost $20 billion to $40 billion, depending on how fast equipment prices fall, and allow the lightning-fast transmission of everything from regular old phone service to high-definition TV. No competitor yet dares follow suit, fearing it could be their financial Waterloo. "We'll watch them closely and go to school on them if they have found something economic," says Ross Ireland, chief technology officer at SBC Communications Inc., the second-largest phone company after Verizon.

Seidenberg is being no less aggressive when it comes to the wireless technology that has consumers and companies equally abuzz—Wi-Fi. In an unprecedented move, Verizon is blanketing Manhattan with more than 1,000 Wi-Fi hotspots that will let any broadband subscriber near a Verizon telephone booth use a laptop to wirelessly tap the Net for the latest news, sports scores, or weather report. If the rollout goes well, Verizon will duplicate this wireless grid in other major cities. Next up: third-generation wireless service, known as 3G, which lets customers make speedy Net connections from their mobile phones. Verizon will begin to deploy 3G in September, at least three months before any of its major competitors. "The other guys will say they want to be the best follower. The guy on the frontier takes a lot of arrows, so they say, 'Let someone else roll out 3G and fiber-to-the-home.' Well, that someone else is Verizon," says Alex Peters, lead manager of the $200 million Franklin Global Communications Fund, which bought an undisclosed number of the company's shares last year.

Verizon is leading the way with its pricing strategies, too. In March, the company became the first Bell to slice its broadband Internet service by 30%, to $35 a month. That's typically 10% to 20% cheaper than cable players such as AOL Time Warner Inc. and Comcast Corp., which have grabbed an early lead in broadband service. Even the musty long-distance business is getting a jolt of innovation: Earlier this year, Verizon became the first Bell to offer unlimited long-distance and local calls for one flat rate, typically $55 a month. Customers loved the idea, and Verizon quickly zoomed past Sprint Corp. to become the third-largest consumer long-distance player in the country. Now, every other Bell has introduced its own flat-rate service.

What's behind Seidenberg's sudden series of audacious moves? Two major reasons: competition from cable companies and the CEO's vision of his industry's future. The cable assault is most pressing because Comcast and its brethren are cutting into Verizon's cash-cow local-phone business and swiping most of the customers in broadband, the fastest-growing segment of telecom. To compete, Verizon plans to use its fiber-optic lines to offer Net access that's 20 times as fast as today's broadband—and bundle that with local phone service.

Just as important is Seidenberg's conviction that telecom as we know it is history. In its place will emerge what he calls a "broadband industry" that will use the new, superfast Net links and high-capacity networks to

EXHIBIT 1 Telecom's New Leader
Three years ago, Verizon looked like just another big phone company. But this year it has emerged as the industry pacesetter. Here's how:

Optics

Verizon is spending billions on blazingly fast optical lines to nearly every home and business in its territory over the next 10 to 15 years. This will challenge cable players in offering video, speedy Net access, and other services.

Impact Not only will the initiative result in new services for Verizon customers, but phone rivals will follow suit. That could spark a new round of capital investment.

Broadband

Cable-TV companies claim two-thirds of the 18 million U.S. broadband customers. In March, Verizon went on the attack, slashing the price of its rival DSL service by 30%, to $34.95. That's typically 10% to 20% cheaper than cable broadband.

Impact More customers will snap up broadband. That helps new band-width-gobbling Net services, like Apple's iTunes music service.

Wi-Fi

Verizon is blanketing Manhattan with 1,000 Wi-Fi hotspots, which let customers connect to the Net wirelessly within a range of several hundred feet. Verizon's DSL customers will get the service for free.

Impact Customers are the winners. They'll get a bargain on Wi-Fi in New York and maybe elsewhere. It will be tough for cable rivals to match the deal.

Wireless Data

In September, Verizon Wireless will roll out third-generation (3G) technology in Washington and San Diego. This will let users tap the Net directly from a cell phone or from a laptop at speeds faster than a DSL connection.

Impact Verizon will be first to market, pressing rivals like Cingular to keep pace. Customers will get more service for about the same price.

Research

As others cut back, Verizon's scientists are focusing more on novel products. One example: the Digital Companion, which next year will let you log on to a Web page from anywhere to see calls as they come in to your home, so you can route them elsewhere.

Impact By going beyond basic phone service, the company hopes to build consumer loyalty and add new revenue streams.

Long Distance

In January, Verizon became the first Bell to introduce unlimited local and long-distance calling for a flat fee. And it has displaced Sprint as the third-largest consumer long-distance company.

Impact All of the other major local-phone companies have followed Verizon's lead in offering flat-rate phone-service packages. Now Verizon can compete on an equal basis with rivals such as AT&T.

deliver video and voice communications services with all the extras, like software for security. If he's right, other companies will follow Verizon's lead and the communications industry will be remade. Seidenberg thinks ubiquitous broadband will transform broad swaths of the economy. High school students, for instance, could download the video of a biology lecture they missed. Doctors could use crystal-clear video-conferencing to examine patients in hard-to-reach rural areas. "The cable industry focuses on entertainment and games. The broadband industry will focus on education, health care, financial services, and essential government services," he says. "I think over the next five to 10 years, you will see five, six, seven [segments of the economy] reordering the way they think about providing services."

Over the long term, the strategy will put Verizon into completely new businesses. Though video may not be its primary focus, the company says that within five years it expects to distribute video services, which could include TV programming and movies on demand, so it can compete directly with cable companies. "I think it's terrific.... It could definitely work," says Sumner M. Redstone, chairman and CEO of Viacom Inc., whose holdings include MTV Networks and Paramount Pictures, and where Seidenberg is a director.

There are plenty of people, however, who think all that time spent up on the 39th floor has left Seidenberg a bit light-headed. Can any company afford to do what Verizon is attempting? The company says it will pump $12.5 billion to $13.5 billion into capital expenditures this year, the third-largest capital budget in the world after DaimlerChrysler and General Electric Co. (Exhibit 2). That's on top of the $3 billion a year it's paying in yearly interest because of its $54 billion debt load. How can Verizon pay for all this? Its business is one of the great cash machines of Corporate America. The largest local-phone operator and the largest wireless company, Verizon generates about $22 billion a year in cash from operations. That's 50% more than SBC, twice as much as BellSouth, and nearly three times as much as AT&T. More than any company in the industry, Verizon can make enormous bets and pay for them out of its own pocket. Seidenberg expects to cover the fiber-optic initiative without raising the capital budget above the current level, while he continues to reduce the company's debt. "Funding is not an issue," he says.

Still, plenty of critics question whether Seidenberg is leading the industry in the right direction. SBC and Qwest Communications International ventured onto a different path when they announced partnerships with satellite-TV service EchoStar Communications on July 21. The deal will allow them to combine voice, video, and data on a single bill—sooner than Verizon and at a fraction of the cost. And rather than a massive fiber rollout to offer broadband Net service, SBC is focused on DSL, where it has a big lead on Verizon. Other industry experts think Verizon's plan may not make financial sense. "Frankly, I'm skeptical," says former Federal Communications Commission Chairman William E. Kennard, managing director of investment company Carlyle Group.

The skepticism stems in part from history. Verizon was formed from the merger of Nynex and Bell Atlantic in 1997 and the melding of the combined companies and GTE in 2000. The predecessor companies tried, and failed, several times in the 1990s to capitalize on the convergence of television and communications. Bell

EXHIBIT 2 Verizon's Obstacle Course

Its ambitious agenda won't be easy to achieve. Here are the main hurdles, and prospects for overcoming them:

Phone Business

Revenue from Verizon's local-phone business declined 4.2% during the first quarter, as wireless rivals and resellers like AT&T ate into its business.

Outlook The trend can't be reversed, but Verizon can slow the losses by offering bundled services.

Losing Local-Phone Revenues

2, 0, −2, −4, −6

'02 I II III IV '03 II III IV —Est.—

▲ Percentage Decline, from Year-Earlier Quarter

Data: UBS Warburg

Debt

Verizon has managed to cut debt to $54 billion from $64 billion, but that's still high relative to rivals. Its ratio of net debt to earnings is 1.6, compared with 0.8 for SBC and 1.1 for BellSouth.

Outlook While Verizon has plenty of cash to cover debt payments and other obligations, it will need to keep reducing its debt to free up cash for new investments. That may require the sale of some assets, such as its international holdings.

Cable

Although cable companies have only 2% of the U.S. phone market, that will probably grow to 30% of the U.S. phone market over 10 years.

Outlook Verizon's investments in fiber should make it more competitive because the technology will allow it to offer TV service.

Cable on the Rise

Number of Phone Lines Provided by Cable Companies

4, 3, 2, 1, 0

'99 '00 '01 '02 '03 '04 '05 —Est.—

▲ Millions

Data: Kagan World Media

Costs

With a big union workforce and lots of older technology, Verizon's cost structure is higher than its younger rivals'. Its 228,000 workers each generate $294,000 in revenues, among the lowest in the industry.

Outlook Verizon is in contract talks with its unions and hopes to extract cost-saving concessions. Talks are tense, however, and a strike is becoming a real possibility.

Atlantic and Nynex helped launch Tele-TV in 1994 to develop interactive-TV programming, but the project folded after several years. Bell Atlantic also announced a merger with cable-TV powerhouse Tele-Communications Inc. in 1994, only to see the deal fall apart a few months later.

Now Verizon faces cable companies that are spoiling for a fight. The cable industry has spent more than $75 billion since 1995 to upgrade their networks for high-definition TV, fast Internet access, and telephone service. The phone companies "have to make sizable investments to catch up," says David N. Watson, executive vice-president for marketing at Comcast, the nation's largest cable operator. "And we won't be standing still." In fact, Comcast and the other cable companies are hell-bent on torpedoing Seidenberg's plans by destroying Verizon's profits before it can use them to get into the video business. Cable players are expected to nab 3.7 million phone lines nationwide by 2005, up from 2.2 million last year, according to market researcher Kagan World Media. That, along with competition from AT&T Corp. and wireless companies, caused Verizon to lose 3.7% of its local-phone lines in 2002.

The competitive threat is compounded by Verizon's labor situation. The company is locked in intense negotiations with its two main unions over a new contract for 75,000 of its 228,000 employees. Far apart over issues of health-care costs, work-rule flexibility, and organizing in the wireless unit, the two sides may very well be headed for a strike when the current contract expires on Aug. 2. Verizon has trained tens of thousands of managers to assume union duties should the talks fail. "There is no clear break. Sometimes you can see it in advance. This time, we can't," says George Kohl, director of research for the Communications Workers of America.

Verizon's labor issues won't disappear even if a strike is averted. More than half of its workers belong to a union, while rival cable companies are typically non-union shops. Verizon has what it says are the highest costs in telecom, with union workers in New York earning an average salary of $62,000, plus overtime and benefits. More important, Verizon has less flexibility than competitors when it comes to laying people off or reassigning them to high-growth units. On July 11, a labor mediator in New York ordered Verizon to rehire 2,300 workers the company had thought it had the right to lay off. It quickly announced it would rehire an additional 1,100 workers who were making similar claims in mediation.

Asked about all the skepticism, the understated Seidenberg responds with a wry smile. "People that watch our industry tend to be skeptical when there's hard work involved, but we've shown the resolve to get up every morning and do what it takes," he says.

Seidenberg and other execs insist much has changed at Verizon since the miscues of the '90s. In February, the FCC changed the regulations so that Verizon and other Bells won't have to share their new networks with rivals at government-controlled prices. Although final details have yet to be released, the decision strengthens the business case for building the networks. At the same time, the price of rolling out fiber to homes and offices has dropped by 50% over the past five years, and it will likely decline another 50% over the next few. "This is not a trial. It's a deployment," says Bruce S. Gordon, president of Verizon's consumer division. "The decision has been made, and it will happen. There's no going back."

If Seidenberg is right, he's positioning Verizon to thrive in the coming decades. Short-term, the deterioration in the core local-phone business probably will cancel out growth in new services. Analyst Simon Flannery of Morgan Stanley expects revenues to stay flat at $67 billion this year while net income declines 10%, to $7.5 billion, not including a $3 billion noncash charge for an accounting change and a write-down from international operations. Profits could even shrink again in 2004, to $7.2 billion. After that, Verizon's prospects look better. As broadband services are rolled out to more of its customers, Flannery estimates that the company's revenues will hit $70 billion in 2005 and net income will recover to $7.6 billion. "They are definitely the industry's future," says Brian Adamik, chief executive of market researcher Yankee Group.

Leave it to Seidenberg to do what others think impossible. The son of an air-conditioning repairman, he grew up in the working-class Gun Hill section of the Bronx. If he had potential for greatness, it was well hidden. Without the money for college, he started working for New York Telephone splicing cables in 1966. He was quickly drafted into the U.S. Army and wounded in Vietnam. After he returned to his old employer in 1968, his raw determination emerged. With his company helping to foot the bill, he earned a BA in mathematics from Lehman College, of the City University of New York, and an MBA at Pace University. He married his high school sweetheart, Phyllis, and they now have two children. During this time, he spent 12 straight years going to night school.

He worked hard on the job, too. As the youngest person on a work team laying cables at Co-op City in the Bronx, Ike, as he was called at the time, would remeasure the cable lines of other workers to see if they were the right length. Perhaps most surprising, he did it without getting throttled by more-senior workers. How? He never tried to take credit for the extra work from supervisors. He simply told the other workers so they could correct any errors as a team. Plus, he was a likable guy who played in the regular lunchtime football games. Seidenberg worked in operations and engineering before moving to Washington to handle regulatory affairs. In 1995, he became chairman and CEO of Nynex Corp.

It could have been a brief, shining moment of glory. When the local-telephone industry was deregulated in 1996, Nynex looked like takeover bait: too small to determine its own fate. Still, Seidenberg figured out a way to get the necessary scale by cutting savvy deals and sharing the spotlight. First, after the Bell Atlantic merger, he let Bell Atlantic Corp. CEO Raymond W. Smith run the combined companies for a couple of years before taking over. Then he waited his turn while GTE Corp. CEO Charles R. Lee ran the show, taking full control only after Lee stepped down as co-CEO last year, at the age of 62. "He's a master boardroom player," says Kennard.

Even now, Seidenberg is eager to let his lieutenants take the limelight. He often has Vice-Chairman Lawrence T. Babbio Jr., who runs the traditional phone business, and Verizon Wireless Services CEO Dennis F. Strigl represent the company in public forums. "All of these people could be CEOs in their own right. They are warriors, and they are on a mission," says Seidenberg. Yet they profess fierce loyalty to him and Verizon, which has been an island of stability in a churning sea.

The commander will need all the warriors he can get. Within two years, the cable-TV companies are expected to be in the phone business big time. They already have 15% of the market in a handful of Verizon neighborhoods where they offer phone service. Cable companies like Comcast, Cablevision Systems, and Cox Communications are planning to expand their phone operations in 2004 using Internet technology that's cheaper and packed with features like inexpensive second and third phone lines. At the current pace, the cable companies will probably have 30% of the phone market over the next decade, says telecom analyst John Hodulik of UBS.

The fiber strategy will help Verizon defend itself. By offering TV, superfast Web access, and feature-rich Internet-based phone services, Verizon could reduce potential customer churn by 50%, Hodulik estimates. Assuming fiber is deployed, he thinks the company will have 2007 net income of $7.9 billion on revenues of $79.7 billion. Those numbers are 2.5% and 5.7% higher than his forecasts before the fiber strategy was outlined.

Although these are the early days, high-speed fiber connections are proving popular with consumers. Verizon already is installing fiber in Brambleton, a planned community in Loudoun County, Va. Only 200 homes have been built so far, but that will grow to 6,000. Liz and Steve Levy are among the early adopters. The high-speed Net connection helps them stay in touch with neighbors over the community Web site, and Liz Levy uses it to maintain a Web site for her stationery business. They get pitched by satellite-TV companies all the time, but they won't switch. "It works really well, and I like getting all the services from a single company," she says.

Still, there's no guarantee that Seidenberg's broadband vision will become a reality. No company has attempted what he is doing on such a massive scale, and even smaller initiatives have shown mixed results. Construction of a fiber network in Eugene, Ore., was cut back because the economics of the effort didn't pan out. The city had originally planned to extend its optical links into homes and businesses, but it canceled the plan in March, 2002, as the economy soured. "We just couldn't make the numbers work," says Lance Robertson, communications coordinator for the Eugene Water & Electric Board.

Whether the numbers work for Verizon will depend on its costs for the new network. Installing a fiber-optic line in a home or business has dropped to about $2,000 today from more than $4,000 five years ago, according to market researcher Render, Vanderslice & Associates. The firm expects that will fall another 50%, to $1,000, in the next five years, although that will depend on how quickly Verizon and the Bells buy equipment. Doreen Toben, Verizon's chief financial officer, says costs have just now come down enough for the initiative to make financial sense. It should be profitable if the company's expense per line comes in between $1,200 and $1,800.

Verizon has a card up its sleeve. About 45% of its customers are wired via telephone poles and other above-ground connections, according to Verizon Chief Technology Officer Mark Wegleitner. That's compared to 32% for BellSouth, 28% for SBC, and 13% for Qwest. Why is that key? It's as much as 30% cheaper to upgrade a line on a phone pole than it is to upgrade one buried beneath a sidewalk or someone's lawn.

Despite the challenges, Seidenberg has a track record of patient investing that pays off in the end. Consider the wireless business, 45%-owned by Vodafone Group

PLC. In recent years, it invested more than its rivals and has reaped the reward. Today, with 33 million subscribers, it's far larger than No. 2 Cingular, a joint venture of BellSouth Corp. and SBC. And it's ahead on many financial metrics, from revenue and earnings growth to profitability. "We're trying to replicate wireless' successful model in other parts of the company, but it takes patience," says Babbio.

Verizon's wireless data plans should keep that growth engine humming. Beginning this September, it will introduce wireless systems in Washington and San Diego that let customers download data at peak speeds of 2.4 megabits a second. That's about five times faster than a DSL connection. While rivals are expected to deploy comparable technology, Verizon is ahead of the curve. Competitors won't roll out the technology until 2004 or 2005. By getting to market first, Verizon expects to maintain its above-average growth.

Rivals are skeptical. "The real question is, is the market ready for it," says William E. Clift, Cingular's chief technical officer. Seidenberg thinks all of these investments will create something of lasting importance and have a positive impact on the overall economy. "As broadband becomes more pervasive over the next three or four years, all the 'excess capacity' in long distance will get absorbed," Seidenberg says. "Microsoft or IBM would never say there's overcapacity. They envision a world in which you always need more capacity to handle all the things they can make. The problem is, we don't have that capacity where it needs to be ... in the home and office."

It will require near-perfect execution. But Seidenberg performs well under pressure. One afternoon in 1969, the young cable splicer and his buddies took a break for a game of touch football at Ferry Point Park in the Bronx. Pat LaScala, a cable splicer's assistant who had played high school football, told Seidenberg to go out for a pass as far as he could. "He ran right into a tree and got some big welt on his eye," LaScala recalled. "But he caught the ball." Today, he needs that poise more than ever. This time, it's no game.

With Tom Lowry in New York, Roger O. Crockett in Chicago, and Irene M. Kunii in Tokyo

Source: Steve Rosenbush, "Verizon's Gutsy Bet," *BusinessWeek*, August 4, 2003, 52–62.

CASE 5-2

General Motors Corp.

It's a chief executive's nightmare. The better you execute, the more improvements you make—the more your stock drops. That was the position G. Richard Wagoner Jr. found himself in last October. A day after General Motors Corp. announced that it had lifted operating earnings 30% in a stagnant car market, Standard & Poor's downgraded the auto maker's debt with no warning. Surprised investors rushed to sell, and the stock dropped 8%. Credit analysts pointed to GM's $76 billion pension fund, which they estimated at the time to be underfunded by as much as $23 billion. GM will have to plow in billions of dollars for years to keep the fund flush, they said.

The earnings gain was no accounting fluke, either. GM finished the year just as strong, with an operating profit of $3.9 billion, nearly double what it earned in 2001, on 5% higher sales of $186.2 billion. GM clearly leads the rest of the U.S. Big Three car companies, reflecting real operational improvements that Wagoner, 49, helped make in the past decade, starting when he was chief financial officer and later as chief operating officer. After GM lost a staggering $30 billion during a single three-year stretch in the early '90s, Wagoner and Chairman John F. "Jack" Smith Jr. forced GM back to basics. They slashed costs, cut payroll, and overhauled aging plants. Once he took over the corner office in May, 2000, CEO Wagoner pulled the efficiency collar even tighter. Now, GM ranks close to Honda Motor Co. and Toyota Motor Corp. in productivity and has made strides in quality. GM also recaptured leadership of the truck business from rival Ford Motor Co., a coup that made the company billions. Last year, GM even nudged up its share of the U.S. market, to 28.3% from 28.1% (Exhibit 1).

But as good as those moves are, they pale next to the problems of GM's weak car brands and gargantuan pension payments. In essence, Rick Wagoner is battling 30 years of management mistakes that have left him with immense burdens and very little room to maneuver. Chief executives from Frederic Donner to Roger Smith built up a bloated bureaucracy that cranked out boring, low-quality cars. Turf battles at headquarters sapped resources and diverted attention from a rising threat out of Asia and Europe. Those competitors drove away with the U.S. car market. Now they're aiming to do the same in sport-utility vehicles and trucks—the last bastion of

EXHIBIT 1

Data: General Motors Corp., Toyota Motor Corp., Harbour & Associates, Sanford C. Bernstein & Co.

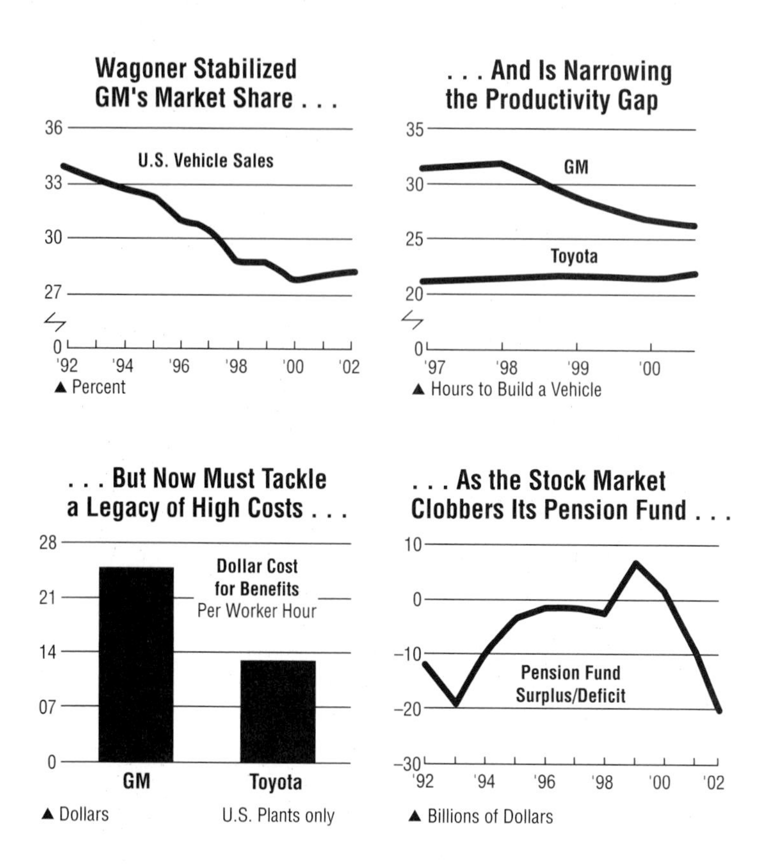

U.S. dominance. GM's most profitable segment is also under attack by environmentalists and safety regulators, and more and more buyers are flocking to smaller crossover SUVs.

Even worse for GM was the buildup of lavish health and retirement benefits for workers that it agreed to in fatter days as a way to buy peace with the United Auto Workers. The company says the gap between its pension funding and future liabilities is now $19.3 billion. That means GM will have to pump as much as $4 billion into the fund over this year and next. Providing health care to former and current workers will drain an additional $5 billion per year. The pension costs alone will cut projected 2003 net income from $4.2 billion to $2.8 billion. Providing for retirees saddles each car rolling off a GM assembly line with a $1,350 penalty vs. a Japanese car built in a new, nonunion U.S. plant, says analyst Scott Hill of Sanford C. Bernstein & Co. That's a daunting handicap in an industry that struggles to make an average operating profit of $800 per vehicle.

Those huge legacy costs explain why Wagoner has kept the heat on his competition with the 0% financing deals he unleashed after September 11, 2001. Closing plants and accepting a smaller chunk of the U.S. market—the route his rival, Ford, has taken—would give GM fewer vehicles over which to spread those big pension and health-care costs. And thanks to an onerous deal it struck in 1990 with the UAW, GM has to pay furloughed workers about 70% of their salary for years after they're laid off. Says Wagoner: "We have a huge fixed-cost base. It's 30 years of downsizing and 30 years of increased health-care costs. It puts a premium on us running this business to generate cash… . Our goal is to grow. We don't care who we take it from."

All that would make the outlook for GM pretty bleak, except for one thing: Eventually, those legacy costs start to diminish. Starting around 2008, the ranks of GM's elderly retirees will thin, relieving some of the burden. After that, more of the incremental gains Wagoner has been achieving will fall to the bottom line rather than to retirees. The results could be dramatic.

That makes Wagoner's imperative clear: He has to keep up cash flow to cover those costs until they start to shrink. At the same time, he must continue to rack up improvements in quality, efficiency, design, and brand appeal. If he can come anywhere close, he just might pull off an impressive turnaround. A stock market rebound would help immensely. GM's pension fund holds its own if it earns 9% a year on its investments. Each one-point rise above that is worth $700 million to the fund.

With much of the focus on GM's financial crunch, it's easy to lose sight of Wagoner's greatest achievement—and the best reason to believe that he might beat the legacy monster. Walk around GM's sprawling headquarters complex today and you soon realize that against all odds, Wagoner is making real progress in energizing GM's torpid culture. He broke with GM tradition by recruiting two respected outsiders for key positions—Robert A. Lutz as head of product development and John Devine as vice-chairman and chief financial officer. And he has given them extraordinary leeway to fix the company's problems.

To motivate his team, the self-effacing Wagoner leaves his ego at the door and lets his executives do their jobs. "Rick acts more like a coach than a boss," says David E. Cole, director of the Center for Automotive Research (CAR) in Ann Arbor, Mich. Thus it was Lutz who rolled out Cadillac's lavish Sixteen prototype luxury car at the Detroit auto show earlier this month as Wagoner sat in the background. Afterward, Wagoner chatted with a few reporters while Lutz held court beside the 16-cylinder vehicle, surrounded by a huge crowd, drinking a martini, and wearing someone's lipstick mark on his cheek.

That low-key style has helped Wagoner in tearing down GM's warring fiefdoms. Since giving the swaggering Lutz rule over product development, Wagoner has spiked the design-by-committee system and cut the time it takes to develop a new car to 20 months from nearly four years. GM used to have different studios for each division working on car designs that would get passed on to marketing, then engineering, then manufacturing. Lutz has one committee to cover the entire process. Every Thursday, he hashes out what vehicles should look like and which division will build them, along with a small group that includes Group Vice-President for Advanced Vehicle Development Mark T. Hogan, GM North America President Gary L. Cowger, Design Chief Wayne K. Cherry, and Chief Engineer James E. Queen.

But low-key doesn't mean hands-off. Lutz may make the day-to-day decisions on car design, but Wagoner reserves final say. He meets monthly with top execs, who see car designs much earlier in the process. The ones they think are promising move ahead fast. Says retired executive Richard C. Nerod, who ran GM's Latin America operations: "Rick cut out a lot of the infighting and the bull—."

Wagoner also exerts control by imposing tough performance standards. A legendary number-cruncher who rose up through GM's finance division, he holds top managers to strict measures. GM, like most big companies, always had performance goals. But they never went nearly as deep or into as much detail. Says Cowger: "Everything can be measured."

Everyone, too. Even Lutz, the larger-than-life product czar who flies his own fighter jet and sparked Chrysler's 1990s resurgence with cars such as the Dodge Viper and PT Cruiser, isn't exempt. Lutz was judged on 12 criteria last year, from how well he used existing parts to save money in new vehicles to how many engineering hours he cut from the development process.

Clearly, Wagoner's own ideas on how to fix GM have evolved. He seems to have learned from a brush with grand strategic vision back in the '90s, when, like now-deposed Ford CEO Jacques A. Nasser, he explored ways to grow outside of building cars. Wagoner was behind the decision to pump hundreds of millions into GM's OnStar Corp. telematics business and DirecTV satellite-TV service. Neither produced big revenues for GM. Now, with Devine applying a cold dose of realism to GM's finances, there's little illusion that such diversions can fix the cash crunch. "That was a dream a couple of years ago, but it's not reality," Devine says. "The math will tell you that the principal driver of revenue and profits is the car-and-truck business in North America and Europe."

If Wagoner has brought a new intensity to GM, he probably gets it from his mother, Martha, a onetime school teacher. Family members recall one Christmas several years ago when she doggedly kept baking cookies despite a broken arm. "My mom has a task orientation that you sometimes see in my brother," says Judy Pahren, a financial-services manager who is one of Wagoner's two sisters. Rick had a Norman Rockwell upbringing in Richmond, Va. He picked up a rabid devotion to Duke University basketball from his father, George, an accountant at Eskimo Pie Co. Wagoner got a chance to play for the Blue Devils as a walk-on. He demonstrated a deft shot but learned the limits of his athletic ability. "The knock on Rick was that you couldn't slide a phone book under his jump," says roommate Charles H. McCreary III. The devotion to alma mater remains, though: A few years ago, he ordered a custom "Duke blue" Suburban SUV.

After Duke, Wagoner got his MBA at Harvard Business School, surprising some upon graduation when he chose GM over potentially more lucrative jobs on Wall Street. Wagoner's knack for crunching numbers propelled him through stints at GM units in Canada, Europe, and Brazil. His big break came in 1992, when then-CEO Smith tapped him to be CFO after a boardroom coup. Even as CEO, Wagoner is known for a low-key lifestyle. He prides himself on juggling his work schedule to attend games and other activities of his three sons. And when entertaining, Wagoner is more likely to cook on his backyard grill than hire a caterer.

Wagoner's willingness to let others shine is a classic trait of leaders who have boosted their companies to exceptional performance, says Jim Collins, author of *Good to Great*. As a longtime GM insider, Wagoner has other advantages: He knows what brutal facts need to be confronted, and he can assess which veterans can handle key jobs. Says Collins: "Wagoner has the opportunity to take it back to great." But the odds are stiff—only 11 of 1,435 companies Collins studied made such a lasting transformation. And those that did required an average of seven years to get breakthrough results.

Still, competitors are impressed with the progress Wagoner has made. "I'm a big admirer of his management style," says crosstown rival William C. Ford Jr., chairman and CEO of Ford. He should be—GM's operating profit may not match the $4.6 billion No. 3 Toyota made in just the six months through September. And GM's stock, trading around 37, is down 26% from a year ago. But that performance sure beats Ford's $872 million operating profit and 36% lower stock price.

It's a testament to Wagoner's ability to cut costs that GM managed nearly to double margins in North America last year, to 2.6% of sales. Thanks to efficiency gains, GM is now one of the leanest car builders, with variable costs—labor, parts, outsourced production, etc.—amounting to 62% of revenues, according to UBS Warburg. That puts it ahead of Ford and Chrysler at 68%, and it isn't far behind leaders Toyota and Honda at 60%.

With lower costs than its domestic competition, GM is better able to withstand the price war it started with 0% financing. But Wagoner is betting that the cars he plans to launch in the next three years will be good enough to sell on merit, not price. A few "niche" vehicles, such as the hulking Hummer H2, are already out. But the assault begins in earnest later this year with the Chevy Malibu (Exhibit 2) family sedan and Equinox car/SUV crossover, Cadillac SRX small SUV, and Pontiac Grand Prix sedan. "This is one major last-ditch effort to save themselves in the car market," says Joseph Phillippi, a former Wall Street analyst who consults for the industry.

Wagoner, who's not a classic Detroit "car guy," seems content to rely on Lutz and his team to fix the lineup. During one trip through the design studio last year, he spotted a sexy two-door version of the Cadillac CTS sports sedan. "I hope you guys figure out a way to build that," Wagoner said, but offered no solutions, recalls one senior designer. "Rick trusts my judgment implicitly," Lutz says, "but if I came up with some wacky product proposals, he'd pull me back."

The most dramatic gains won't come on a sketch pad anyway but in the way GM selects new car designs and

EXHIBIT 2 Malibu on a Budget

One of Wagoner's biggest accomplishments has been reducing the time and money it takes to build vehicles. Here are some of the savings GM has wrung out of one mainstay car, the 2003 Chevy Malibu, compared with two other midsize sedans, the Oldsmobile Intrigue and Pontiac Grand Prix, that previously were built at the same Fairfax (Kan.) plant.

The Design GM designed the Malibu so that fewer workers can assemble more cars.
Payoff GM should be able to build the Malibu with 18 to 19 hours of labor instead of 24 hours.

The Platform GM engineers in the U.S., Germany, and Sweden worked together to share the same platform and other parts for the company's Chevrolet Malibu, Opel Vectra, and Saab 9-3 midsize sedans.
Payoff Engineering costs were cut by one-third.

The Interior GM gave French interior supplier Faurecia the contract for seats for the Malibu, Vectra, and Saab 9-3.
Payoff GM got seats made of more comfortable and durable materials for the price of cheaper seats.

The Gas Tank The Malibu and Saab 9-3 share the same gas tank, saving on engineering and safety tests.
Payoff The tank's cost is 30% lower.

then shepherds them through production. In the past, even if a bold design made it off a drawing board, it had little chance of surviving to the showroom. A concept would go from a designer to the marketing staff, which would try to tailor it to consumers. Then it would go to engineers, who would try to figure out how to build it, and so on. Separate teams worked with suppliers, factories, and parts suppliers on their individual slice of the process, with little interaction.

It was a recipe for mediocrity—and often disaster. The Aztek, which emerged in 2000 as a boxy, garish cross between an SUV and a minivan five years after designers first drew it up as a racy bid for younger drivers, is a prime example. Wagoner was determined to tear up that system by the roots. A few months after taking over, he ordered GM's product developers to ready the SSR concept vehicle for production. A combination of hot rod and pickup truck, it had been a big hit at the Detroit auto show. Wagoner thought its distinctive look, with chrome bars splitting the front grille and taillights, would be a great image builder. But the SSR still had to navigate the old GM system. Because it was announced before engineers had a precise blueprint to build it, the program quickly ran over budget. Today, its cost has ballooned way past the original $300 million projection, to almost $500 million. The $42,000 SSR will hit showrooms this summer, a quick turnaround for GM. But with only 5,000 sales projected per year, it makes for a very expensive showcase.

Since then, Wagoner and Lutz have smoothed things out a bit. Lutz, Cowger, Hogan, and the others decide what goes from the design studios into the funnel of cars that will be considered for funding by GM's Automotive Strategy Board, chaired monthly by Wagoner. Lutz says he and Wagoner have disagreed on some product decisions, but he hasn't been turned down yet. Now, 75% of the engineering work is finished when a program manager sits down to build a car.

That's how GM quickly green-lighted plans to resurrect the Pontiac GTO, its famous 1960s muscle car. For years, Pontiac and Chevrolet wanted a brawny car with rear-wheel drive, which is favored by driving enthusiasts. GM's Australian Holden Ltd. subsidiary had a promising candidate in its Monaro sports coupe, but the idea to bring it to the U.S. never made it out of committee. GM execs simply didn't want to spend what little money it would take to alter the Monaro to meet U.S. safety standards and American styling. Says Lutz: "I just asked, 'Why not?'" GM got the program together in less than 18 months. Later this year, Pontiac will roll out the GTO as a 340-horsepower Americanized Monaro.

Wagoner has also streamlined GM's factories. GM is now the most productive domestic auto maker, having cut the time it takes to assemble a vehicle from an average of 32 hours in 1998 to 26 hours in 2001, according to Harbour & Associates. That compares with 27 for Ford, almost 31 at DaimlerChrysler, 22.5 at Toyota, and 17.9 at Nissan. A big factor was expanding parts shared across vehicles. The new Chevy Malibu, for instance, uses the same platform and many of the same parts as the Saab 9-3 sedan (Exhibit 2). GM's plants are also more flexible—each of seven full-size pickup and SUV plants can make any of the vehicles designed on that platform.

The cars rolling off GM's assembly lines today are undeniably better built than they used to be. Once ranked below the industry average, GM trails only Honda and Toyota in J.D. Power & Associates Inc.'s initial quality survey, which measures problems in the first 90 days of ownership. Some cars, such as the Chevrolet Impala, even beat the likes of the Toyota Camry. Last year, *Consumer Reports* recommended 13 GM vehicles—representing 41% of its sales volume—up from 5 last year. But one of GM's most stubborn woes is that many buyers still perceive the Chevy, Pontiac, and Buick brands as musty and second-rate. GM needs incentives averaging $3,800 a vehicle—more than twice what Toyota spends.

The biggest risk to GM's lineup is at the top. Its popular SUVs and pickups accounted for about 90% of profits last year but are under increasing assault from foreign competitors and safety regulators. Like his competitors, Wagoner is banking on crossover vehicles, which combine SUV-like space and looks with a carlike ride and better fuel economy, as a hedge against a big-truck backlash. Cadillac's luxury SRX hits the market this year as a viable rival to the Lexus RX 330 and Mercedes M-class, and Chevy will launch its Equinox as an all-wheel drive crossover. Next year, GM will start offering pickups and SUVs with hybrid gas/electric engines. New designs are also in the works. Lutz has tentatively approved a highly stylized 2007 replacement for the Chevy Silverado and GMC Sierra pickups, which hold a commanding 40% of the pickup market. It will be based on the slick Cheyenne concept truck that GM unveiled in January, which has improved driver and passenger room and doors on each side of the pickup bed to provide easier cargo access. But in small SUVs and gas mileage, GM is playing catch-up to the Japanese.

Wagoner and his team have little choice but to wait out their biggest mess—those massive health and pension costs. Wagoner is brutally realistic: "We'd be accused of a pipe dream if we said in 10 years these issues will go away." GM pays its UAW workers only slightly more per hour than Toyota, Honda, and Nissan pay their American factory workers. But the cost of pension and health-care benefits for current workers is huge—about $24 per hour at GM, vs. $12 at the foreign factories. Pension obligations swelled after the 1990 contract, when then-Chairman Robert Stempel practically guaranteed almost no layoffs. Underestimating the speed of its decline, GM agreed to pay workers for years after a furlough. As losses mounted, GM resorted to early-retirement offers—avoiding billions in unemployment benefits but adding thousands of retirees. Since GM was shrinking faster than Ford, its pension rolls grew more quickly, to 2.5 retirees per worker today, vs. Ford's 1-to-1 ratio. Last year, GM plowed almost $5 billion into the pension fund to shore it up as stock prices fell. But Carol Levenson, an analyst for bond research firm Gimme Credit, points out that GM had to take on $4.6 billion in debt to do it. Until the stock and bond markets spring back, it's three steps forward and two steps back.

That pressure should ease somewhat over the next decade. GM's average worker is 48 years old—five years older than those at Ford or Chrysler. GM's total number of retirees will drop below existing levels by 2010, says CAR's labor and manufacturing analyst, Sean McAlinden. Wagoner believes that even without another bull market to boost the pension fund, GM can handle the drain and maintain its $7 billion capital-spending budget. Meanwhile, to pay down the pension shortfall, Devine is working to sell Hughes Electronics' DirecTV business, possibly to News Corp.

Closing the gap on health-care costs will be tougher. This summer, GM and the UAW will start working on a new four-year labor agreement. GM is almost certain to ask for higher co-payments from its 138,000 UAW employees. The union is almost certain to balk. "We don't have an interest in cost-shifting," says Richard Shoemaker, head of the UAW's GM department. GM also is one of many companies pushing to have Medicare pick up a greater share of retiree drug costs. But even Wagoner admits: "I don't see that happening soon."

Can Wagoner return GM to dominance? He has made heroic gains. But he's taking nothing for granted. At a speech in Detroit last year, he told the story of William C. Durant, who pulled together such companies as

GM's Big Three

Wagoner has handed over much of the responsibility for fixing the carmaker's long-term problems to two top lieutenants, Bob Lutz and John Devine. Hired out of retirement from Chrysler and Ford, they instantly raised GM's management profile.

G. Richard Wagoner Jr., 49
Current Title CEO and chairman-elect
Background Wagoner was hired as an analyst in GM's New York treasury office in 1977 and became a noted number-cruncher. Won the post of treasurer for GM's Brazil unit. Raced along the fast track through GM's finance operations until he was tapped by then-CEO Jack Smith to be CFO in 1992.
What He Has to Do Gets lots of credit for improving GM's efficiency and quality. Now, he has to keep the cash coming in and rebuild GM's market share while steadily working to reduce the carmaker's high costs for health-care and pension obligations.

Robert A. "Bob" Lutz, 70
Current Title Vice-chairman for product development
Background A classic "car guy," he worked at BMW and all of the Big Three carmakers, developing some of their hottest vehicles: Chrysler's Dodge Viper sports car, the Dodge Ram pickup, and the PT Cruiser. Retired after Chrysler's 1998 acquisition by Daimler, to run battery maker Exide.
What He Has to Do Lutz was hired to teach GM how to design cool cars again. He has already pushed through some hot roadsters and improved the craftsmanship of GM's interiors.

John M. Devine, 58
Current Title Vice-chairman and CFO
Background A numbers guy at Ford. Spent much of the '80s overseas, including running Ford Japan. Ditched Ford's ill-fated foray into banking. Retired in 1999 to work in venture capital because he didn't agree with now-deposed Ford CEO Jacques A. Nasser.
What He Has to Do Devine has brought new discipline to GM's dealmaking. Now he is working to sell GM's Hughes Electronics subsidiary, which will help make up some of the gap in pension funding.

Buick, Cadillac, and Olds to form GM in 1908. But Durant was more interested in cutting deals than managing, so he wound up running a bowling alley in Flint. "That fate has haunted GM chairmen for decades," Wagoner told his audience. He was joking, of course. But Wagoner will be the first to tell you that his own future is up in the air. It all depends on whether he can save GM from its past.

By David Welch, with Kathleen Kerwin, in Detroit

Source: "Rick Wagoner's Game Plan," *BusinessWeek*, February 10, 2003, 52–60.

CASE 5-3

Yahoo! Inc.

When Terry S. Semel walked into the Sunnyvale (Calif.) headquarters of Yahoo! Inc. for his first day as chief executive on May 1, 2001, he faced an unenviable task. Ad sales at the Internet icon were plummeting, and the new CEO was replacing the well-liked Timothy Koogle, who had been pushed aside by the company's board. Worse, leery employees quickly saw that Semel, a retired Hollywood exec, didn't know Internet technology and looked stiffly out of place at Yahoo's playful, egalitarian headquarters. Would this guy tour the Valley in the purple Yahoo car, as Koogle did, or play a Yahoo kazoo? Fat chance. And instead of bunking in nearby Atherton or Palo Alto, like other Silicon Valley execs, he rode off every evening in a chauffeured SUV to a luxury suite at San Francisco's Four Seasons Hotel.

Two years after taking control as chairman and CEO, Semel has silenced the doubters. By imposing his buttoned-down management approach on Yahoo, the 60-year-old has engineered one of the most remarkable revivals of a beleaguered dot-com. Once paralyzed by management gridlock and written off as another overhyped has-been, Yahoo is roaring back. The company earned $43 million on revenues of $953 million in 2002, compared with a $93 million loss in 2001 on $717 million in sales. And Yahoo's momentum is growing. Net income hit $47 million in this year's first quarter as revenues powered ahead 47%. Analysts predict that this year's profits will quadruple, to more than $200 million, while sales climb 33%, to $1.3 billion. "What he has done is just phenomenal," says Hollywood pal Barry Diller, CEO of USA Interactive Inc., a Yahoo competitor.

Semel has done nothing less than remake the culture of the quintessential Internet company. The new Yahoo is grounded by a host of Old Economy principles that Semel lugged up the coast from Los Angeles. The contrast with Yahoo's go-go days is stark. At Terry Semel's Yahoo, spontaneity is out. Order is in. New initiatives used to roll ahead following free-form brainstorming and a gut check. Now, they wind their way through a rugged gauntlet of tests and analysis. Only a few make the grade. It's a wrenching change. But Semel's self-effacing style, honed over years of navigating through the towering egos of Hollywood, helps soften the shock.

Yahoo's newfound success does, too. Semel has used the dealmaking skills that made him a legend in the movie business to land crucial acquisitions and partnerships that are producing rich new revenues for Yahoo (Exhibit 1). A deal with phone giant SBC Communications Inc. launched Yahoo into the business of selling broadband access to millions of American homes—which should add $70 million in revenue this year. The buyout of HotJobs.com last year put Yahoo into the online job-hunting business, adding $80 million in revenue. Most important, a partnership with Overture Services Inc. to carry ads on Yahoo's search-results pages is gushing some $230 million in revenue this year. The upshot? Semel's new businesses should make up half of Yahoo's top line in 2003. "We planted a lot of seeds a year and a half ago, and some are beginning to grow," he says (Exhibit 2).

Semel's strategy is gaining fans on Wall Street—and stoking new fears of a mini-Internet bubble. The company's shares have soared 200% in the past eight months, to $26. Sure, Yahoo's market capitalization is a mere 13% of its giddy all-time high of $127 billion in early 2000. But today's price-earnings ratio of 79 is triple that of heavyweight Microsoft Corp. and more than eBay Inc.'s 67, despite the online auctioneer's heftier revenues, profits, and growth projections. "Yahoo's valuation is a tough case to make," concedes Firsthand Funds Chief Investment Officer Kevin Landis, who nonetheless has bought 50,000 Yahoo shares in the past eight months based on the portal's turnaround and brighter industry trends.

EXHIBIT 1 Yahoo's Game Plan

Can CEO Semel lift Yahoo to greatness? The nine-year-old company is poised to notch its best-ever sales and profits in 2003. But Semel must accomplish even more to justify Yahoo's nosebleed market valuation, including a p-e of 79. Here are his biggest bets:

Paid Search

Revenues for selling links on its search-results pages rocketed from zilch to $130 million in 2002. With the overall paid-search market expected to grow 40% to 50% annually, paid search may be Yahoo!'s jet fuel in coming years.

2003 Projected Revenue
$230 million ▲ 77%

Outlook
Excellent This is the Internet's growth market, and few are positioned as well as Yahoo. Possible spoiler: Google.

Internet Advertising

Life is creeping back into Yahoo's longtime mainstay, traditional online advertising, which should top $600 million in 2003 sales. Yahoo expects to double the industry growth rate, with annual growth of at least 5% to 10% for the next several years.

2003 Projected Revenue
$615 million ▲ 18%

Outlook
Good The market is coming back, and Yahoo! has learned the hard way what works.

Paid Subscriptions

Only 1% of Yahoo's 232 million online users pay the company for services. Yahoo is working to bring in more cash outlays by offering a host of premium services, including online personals and supersize e-mail accounts.

2003 Projected Revenue
$251 million ▲ 25%

Outlook
Fair This is Yahoo's Achilles' heel. The potential is rich, but turning free Web surfers into paying subscribers is proving tough.

Broadband Access

A partnership with SBC Communications makes Yahoo a broadband player, generating fees and establishing Yahoo as a high-speed home page. But its failure to link up with other telecoms limits the offering, for now, to SBC's region.

2003 Projected Revenue
$70 million ▲ 900%

Outlook
Good Yahoo can grow with broadband, which is gaining 30% annually. The risk: It hinges on partnerships that could prove fragile.

Online Careers

Yahoo acquired Hotjobs.com in late 2001, which contributed $80 million to Yahoo's top line in 2002. But growth is slow in the stagnant U.S. employment market, and Yahoo trails job-search leader Monster.com

2003 Projected Revenue
$80 million ▲ 0%

Outlook
Good Online recruiting is expected to grow 18% a year for the next five years. Yahoo should grab a growing share.

Investors are betting on Semel to follow up his bold debut with a sizzling encore. Call it Act Two. For this next stage of growth, Semel envisions building Yahoo into a digital Disneyland, a souped-up theme park for the Internet Age. The idea is that Web surfers logging on to Yahoo's site, like customers squeezing through the turnstiles in Anaheim, will find themselves in a self-contained world full of irresistible offerings.

In the past, Yahoo attracted visitors with free services such as stock quotes and headlines and drew 90% of its revenue from online ads. Now, Semel is trying to charge for many services, coaxing Web surfers to spend hard cash on everything from digital music and online games to job listings and premium e-mail accounts with loads of extra storage. Already, he pulls in one-third of revenue from such offerings and hopes to drive it up to 50% by 2004. To do that, analysts say, he's likely to cut deals to add online travel and classified ads for cars.

But nothing is more key to Semel's strategy than his push into broadband. Lots of the services he's banking on, such as music and interactive games, are data hogs that appeal mostly to customers with high-speed links. Plus, broadband is always on, so many of Yahoo's customers will be lingering in Semel's theme park for hours on end, day after day. "The more time you spend on Yahoo, the more apt you are to sample both free and paid services," he says.

If Semel can pull it off, the new Yahoo could become one of the few enduring powerhouses on the Net. Customers who pay for its services could more

EXHIBIT 2 Yahoo's Turnaround

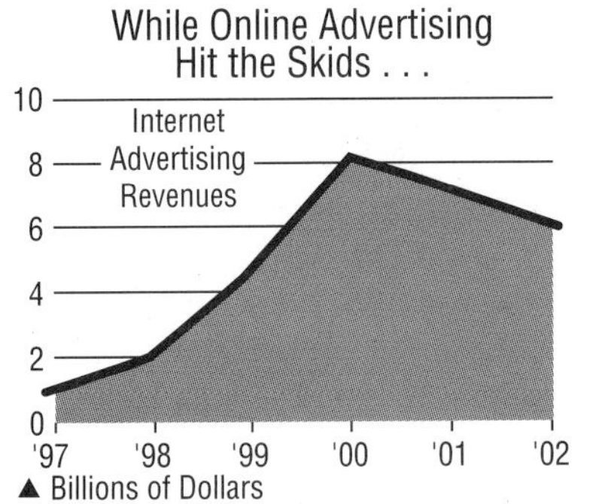

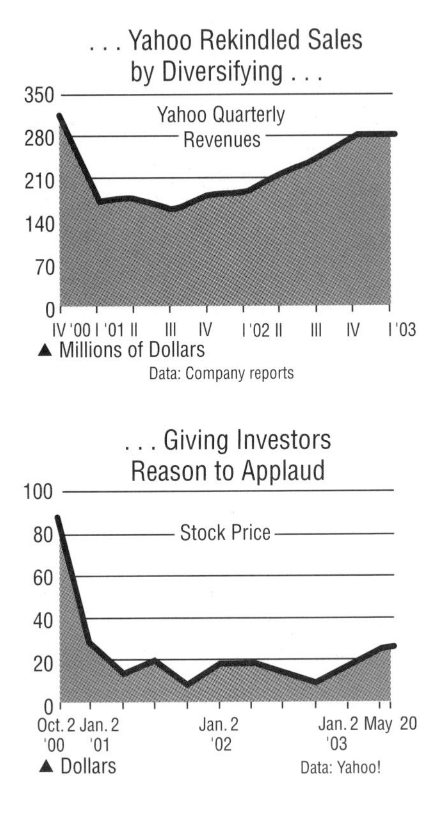

than triple, to 10 million in 2005 from 2.9 million now, analysts predict. Profits could soar 75% over the next two years, to $350 million, and sales could surge 30%, to $1.7 billion, analysts say. "Yahoo has emerged as a durable digital franchise," says Alberto W. Vilar, president of Amerindo Investment Advisors Inc., which has an undisclosed stake. "If you take the long view, this stock could still double or triple."

But Semel doesn't have a monopoly on digital theme parks. AOL Time Warner Inc. and Microsoft's MSN are pushing nearly identical agendas—and both boast advantages over Yahoo. AOL, despite its merger headaches, can tap into popular content from the world's largest media company, from CNN to Warner Music. MSN benefits from the software muscle and cash hoard of Microsoft, as well as broadband partnerships that cover 27% more lines into homes and businesses than Yahoo's SBC deal. It also may have an easier time getting Web surfers to pay for new offerings. "Yahoo's brand is built on free information services," says MSN Group Product Manager Lisa Gurry. She says coaxing Yahoo customers to pull out their wallets will be "very challenging."

An even greater challenge is coming from a newer competitor, Google Inc. In just four years, Google has turned into a global sensation and is now widely regarded as the preeminent search engine on earth. The risk to Yahoo is that the search king will give birth to a more potent business model. Instead of flocking to flashy theme parks such as Yahoo's, consumers are already starting to rely on Google's uncluttered search to find everything they need. Already, some online advertisers are moving their ad dollars to search engines. "We're shifting our emphasis away from portals [such as Yahoo, AOL, and MSN]," says Alan Rimm-Kaufman, vice-president for marketing at electronics retailer Crutchfield Corp. "The people stealing these ad dollars are [companies] like Google."

Hot competition in the search business could force Semel's next big move. His partnership with Overture, a company that delivers Internet advertising, is producing some 20% of Yahoo's revenues. Microsoft's MSN has a similar deal with Overture that also is paying off richly. Analysts say Semel could make an offer for Overture—if he thinks it's necessary to preempt a Microsoft acquisition. He is already sitting on $2.2 billion in cash, 50% more than the likely price tag for Overture. Still, Semel likely won't make a bid unless he's pushed into it because of the distractions of such a large merger. Yahoo and Overture declined comment on a possible deal.

Distraction is something Yahoo can ill afford as it adapts to the changes ahead. To date, Semel has honed the company's execution—cutting costs, filtering out iffy ideas, pursuing sure things, and making money. It's the perfect model for today's sickly market. But when the slump ends, new ideas will likely make a dramatic comeback. These could define the next generation of the Internet. The question is whether Yahoo, with its careful and laborious vetting process for new projects, risks losing out to Google or getting blindsided by a nimble newcomer.

Can Semel innovate, beat back the rising tide of competition, and live up to the latest round of great expectations for Yahoo? If he plays his cards right, yes. Despite the advantages of AOL and MSN, Yahoo has kept its position as the most popular site on the Web, according to Nielsen/Net Ratings. Yahoo claims 232 million monthly visitors. Semel is demonstrating the skills to turn this large chunk of humanity into paying customers, boosting the customer count eightfold, from 375,000 when he arrived two years ago. To combat Google, Semel is hurrying to beef up Yahoo's search capabilities. He closed a $290 million deal for search company Inktomi in March, and the marketing campaign to promote it blasted off in New York's Times Square on May 19. "Yahoo has reemerged as a potent force," says Derek Brown, an analyst at Pacific Growth Equities. "It's well-positioned to leverage its massive global user base and dominant brand."

The CEO's low-key approach has worked quiet magic through a 40-year career. When Brooklyn-born Semel arrived as a sales trainee at Warner Bros. in 1965, the 22-year-old accountant had little relevant experience but an understated confidence in himself. In an industry brimming with ego, Semel stayed offstage and worked to shine the light on others. It paid dividends. As he moved from Warner Bros. to Buena Vista and back again, Semel rose to the top on a vast network of friends and allies. He used these, along with his formidable negotiating skills, to create a giant. In a two-decade partnership as co-CEO with Bob Daly, Semel turned Warner Bros. from a $1 billion studio to an $11 billion behemoth, producing megahits such as *The Matrix*.

Through his retirement in 1999, Semel kept up the winning formula, making friends and minting millions. He says that in their two decades together, he and Daly never fought. If such a smooth track record is rare in high tech, it's even more uncommon in Hollywood. "When you're releasing 20 or 25 movies a year, you're navigating a minefield every weekend," says Barry M. Meyer, chairman and CEO of Warner Bros. Entertainment Inc. and a longtime Semel colleague. "His success at Yahoo does not surprise me at all."

It was Yahoo co-founder Jerry Yang who nudged Semel toward Yahoo in 2001. The two had met two years earlier at a media conference and had hit it off. By the spring of 2001, Yahoo was reeling from the falloff in Net advertising and needed a major overhaul. The question was whether the wealthy Semel, who was already dabbling in online entertainment companies, would dive into one of the biggest of them all at a time of crisis. Semel signed on with the proviso that Koogle step down as chairman.

When the new chief arrived, he ran into a few troubling surprises. Semel was shocked early on to learn that Yahoo did not have the technology in place to handle surging demand for services such as online personals, say two former executives. That spelled months of delay before Semel could push premium offerings.

Then there were the cultural challenges. Initially, Semel balked at the company's "cubicles only" policy, finally settling into a cube adjacent to a conference room so he could make phone calls in private. He stayed free of the Valley social scene, spending weeknights at the hotel in San Francisco and flying his private jet home to his swanky Los Angeles neighborhood of Bel Air on weekends.

Morale was also an issue. Compared with his predecessor, the relaxed and chatty Koogle, known by the troops as T.K., Semel came off at first as cold and rough. He chopped down the 44 business units he inherited to 5, stripping many execs of pet projects. Veteran Yahoo execs prodded Semel to mingle more with the rank and file and pushed him into grabbing lunch more often at the campus cafeteria. Still, such forays often fell flat. "T.K. was just one of the guys," says a former Yahoo manager. "When Semel talked to you, it felt like he was consciously making an effort to talk to employees."

Soon, Semel's strengths started to shine through. With his focus and dealmaking savvy, he appeared to have the tools to rescue Yahoo. Employees, with loads of underwater stock options, increasingly cheered him on. "People don't always agree with the direction they're getting, but they're happy the direction is there," says a current Yahoo manager who requested anonymity.

Walk through Yahoo's headquarters, past the purple cow in the lobby, the acres of cubicles, the workers in jeans, and you might think T.K. was still running the place. But sitting across from Semel, the change is evident. His voice quiet and steady, his language cordial yet deliberate, Semel seems incapable of the hype that once vaulted companies such as Yahoo into the stratosphere. This is the voice of the post-dot-com era. He steers attention to his colleagues. "I love [my managers] to do their homework," he says. "I love them to help make decisions, and they do. Somewhere in that process, I'll include myself—or they'll include me."

Semel's not kidding about the homework. In the old days, Yahoo execs would brainstorm for hours, often following hunches with new initiatives. Those days are long gone. Under Semel, managers must prepare exhaustively before bringing up a new idea if it's to have a chance to survive.

It's a Darwinian drama that takes place in near-weekly meetings of a group called the Product Council. Dreamed up by a couple of vice-presidents and championed by Semel and his chief operating officer, Daniel Rosensweig, a former president of CNET Networks Inc., the group typically includes nine managers from all corners of the company. It's chaired by Geoff Ralston and often includes key lieutenants such as Jeff Weiner and Jim Brock, all senior vice-presidents. The group sizes up business plans to make sure all new projects bring benefits to Yahoo's existing businesses. "We need to work within a framework," says Semel. "If it's a free-for-all ... we won't take advantage of the strengths of our company."

For years, managers built up their own niches around the main Yahoo site. No one, say former and current execs, appeared to be thinking about the portal as a whole, much less how the various bits and pieces could work together. "Managers would beg, borrow, and steal from the network to help their own properties," says Greg Coleman, Yahoo's executive vice-president for media and sales.

Semel wants to stitch it all together. He calls the concept "network optimization" and says it's a key goal for 2003. The idea is that every initiative should not only make money but also feed Yahoo's other businesses. It's the painstaking job of establishing these interconnections that eats up much of the time at council meetings. And the winnowing process is brutal. Of the 79 current ideas for premium services at some stage of planning inside Yahoo, only a few will launch in 2003, predicts Rosensweig.

Although some critics worry that innovative ideas may never see the light of day under Semel's tight control, he dismisses the prospect. Semel stresses instead the potential payoff: less clutter and a handful of high-performance services that feed each other. For a success story, he points to the company's recently relaunched search capabilities. Search for "pizza" and type in your area code, and Yahoo culls its Yellow Pages site to return addresses and driving maps to nearby pizza joints. Yahoo is the only heavyweight portal that integrates content this deeply with its search features.

Such smart execution was in dangerously short supply at Yahoo in the past. At the height of the Net bubble, Yahoo came off as arrogant. Its attitude, recalls Jeff Bell, a marketing vice-president at DaimlerChrysler Corp., was "Buy our stuff, and shut up." Semel has turned that around, hiring traditional media sales veterans and introducing more flexibility. The payoff: As the online ad market has recovered, advertisers are flocking back to Yahoo. Daimler's Bell says his Yahoo ad budget has doubled over the past two years.

Entertainment companies are joining the rush to buy key Yahoo ad space. Some 42 movies advertised on Yahoo in the first quarter, up from zilch in the first quarter of 2001. "Getting a presence on Yahoo's home page is huge," says Sarah Beatty, a senior marketing vice-president at USA Network, which is running seven ad campaigns on Yahoo in 2003.

Semel has supplemented Yahoo's ad revenues with dealmaking in other businesses. Consider the SBC pact to market broadband Net access. SBC pays Yahoo about $5 out of the $40 to $60 customers pay each month for service. Revenues from the deal should jump from $70 million this year to $125 million in 2004.

Still, Yahoo remains vulnerable in broadband. MSN has cut similar deals with Verizon Communications and Qwest Communications International Inc., which have 75 million lines to homes and businesses, vs. SBC's 59 million. Semel's efforts to land other broadband deals have come up short. More worrisome is the fragile nature of these partnerships. If SBC concludes that the Yahoo brand isn't a big draw, it could cut Yahoo out and save itself millions. An SBC spokesman says it is "happy" with Yahoo.

Of all Semel's deals, none shines brighter than the partnership with Overture Services. The companies team up to sell ads near Yahoo's search results, a business known as "paid search." If a user searches for "cookware," for instance, advertisers from Macy's to Sur La Table can bid to showcase their links near the results. Overture delivers the advertisers and forks over roughly two-thirds of the revenue. While Yahoo had debated such a partnership for years under Koogle, Semel drove it through in a hurry.

Just in time for paid search to blossom into the latest Web sensation. The partnership notched Yahoo more than $130 million in revenues last year—14% of its business. Analysts expect revenues from the partnership to increase 75% in 2003, accounting for nearly 20% of Yahoo's revenues.

That assumes that Goggle won't spoil Yahoo's fun. The wildly popular search engine has emerged as the fourth-most-trafficked site on the Internet, with an estimated $700 million in 2003 revenues. And the world may be heading Google's way. Industry analysts say that as Web surfers gain expertise, they visit general-interest sites such as Yahoo less and instead cut to the chase by typing in keywords on a search engine. According to analytics firm WebSideStory, the percentage of Web site visitors arriving via search engines doubled in the past year, to 13%.

Google's strength puts Semel in a bind. He licenses Google's search engine, which is popular among Yahoo's users. Trouble is, by keeping Google on Yahoo, he publicly endorses a rival. His likely goal, say analysts, is to replace Google soon with Inktomi, the search engine he acquired in March. That would save $13 million a year in licensing and pull the plug on Yahoo's apparent backing of Google. The danger? If Yahoo's Google-loving customers balk at switching to Inktomi, they could ditch Yahoo and surf straight to the Google site.

His answer is a national marketing campaign to boost Yahoo as a search brand. It kicked off on May 19 in New York's Times Square with the unveiling of a huge computer-screen ad featuring live searches on the Yahoo site. At street level in New York, teams of Yahoo's costumed "searchers" paraded among the crowds waving five-foot-long search bars.

It's all part of the growing buzz at Yahoo. Using his mix of discipline, sales, and dealmaking, Terry Semel has pulled off a stunning revival. But can he pull off Act Two and build Yahoo into the digital theme park of his dreams? If he does, Semel will be one of the biggest winners: When he took the helm, he bought 1 million shares of Yahoo at $17 apiece. Those shares are up 60%. The fact that Yahoo shares are banging on the ceiling and not the floor is a vivid sign that Semel's turnaround may be just getting started.

By Ben Elgin in Sunnyvale, Calif., with Ronald Grover in Los Angeles

Source: "Yahoo! Act Two," *BusinessWeek*, June 2, 2003, 70–76.

CASE 5-4

PSA Peugeot Citroën SA

Paris—Back in 1997, it looked as though French car maker PSA Peugeot Citroën SA was headed for a bleak, lonely future in an industry dominated by global mega-groups.

Heavily dependent on its home market and torn by a rivalry between its brands, the company was losing money and following a strategy that defied conventional wisdom. It had no plans to produce luxury cars or sport-utility vehicles, which generate much of the auto industry's profit, or to return to the U.S. market, which it fled in 1991 as sales dwindled.

Worst of all, rivals were merging to create titans such as DaimlerChrysler AG, based on the idea that massive scale would yield massive profits. But PSA, which had bad memories of messy acquisitions, including its 1974 purchase of Citroën, refused to consider combining with a rival. "A lot of people probably saw this as typical French egocentrism," Chief Executive Jean-Martin Folz recalled recently.

PSA's stubbornness paid off. Since the dark days of 1997, the company has become one of the most profitable car makers outside Japan. Between 1998 and 2002, sales climbed 62% to $61.8 billion, and the number of vehicles sold rose 55% to 3.27 million. That made PSA the world's sixth-largest car company, bigger than Honda Motor Corp. and Hyundai Motor Co. (Exhibit 1). Last year, on the strength of hot models such as the compact Peugeot 206, PSA's market share in Europe was 15.4%, up four points in five years. This year, PSA's market share has risen to 15.9%.

PSA's success adds fuel to the argument that the Big Three U.S. auto makers took a wrong turn when they poured billions into strategic alliances in the past half decade. Five years after its merger, Chrysler is again piling up losses. General Motors Corp. bought 20% of Fiat's crisis-ridden auto division and may get stuck with the rest, too. The European luxury brands Ford Motor Co. bought, such as Jaguar, lost about $500 million last year. In today's auto industry, Mr. Folz contends, expecting critical advantages from mergers is "simply hopeless."

Facing a severe industry downturn and a strong euro, PSA has seen profit fall this year, but its level of profitability is still higher than that of GM, Ford, Volkswagen AG and cross-town rival Renault SA.

Mr. Folz did it by making sure the company's brands, Peugeot and Citroën, stopped battling each other for the same customers—and stopped designing cars that looked alike. He saved money by combining production facilities and using the same basic parts for most of the company's vehicles. For international growth, he bet on China instead of the U.S. Mr. Folz acknowledges that PSA will have to return to the U.S. eventually, but he has no plans to do so in the near future.

The key to success these days, he argues, is not amassing economies of scale with a merger but producing

EXHIBIT 1
On a Fast Track

Sources: The company; Global Insight Automotive Group.

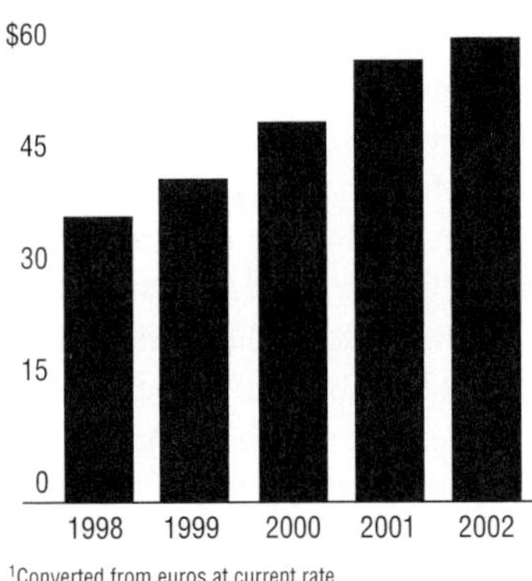

[1]Converted from euros at current rate

[2]Renault owns 44% of Nissan

innovative cars in rapid succession. That's because today's buyers want a far more diverse range of products than ever before—convertibles, SUVs, wagons, subcompacts and micro cars. Managers can't crank out that many products, Mr. Folz contends, if they're struggling to integrate two companies. Instead, he formed partnerships on particular projects to cut the cost of developing big-ticket components: diesel engines with Ford, a mini-car with Toyota Motor Corp. and small gasoline engines with Bayerische Motoren Werke AG.

Maintaining PSA's trajectory will be difficult. Its growth has been driven by smartly designed small cars, an area now targeted by luxury car makers, such as BMW with the Mini and Mercedes with its Smart and A-Class models. This fall, a redesigned Golf is due from Volkswagen, and a new Astra from GM's Opel. Both are expected to be big sellers in Europe, potentially at PSA's expense. Meanwhile, the models in PSA's pipeline are larger vehicles that typically sell at a lower volume.

An automotive outsider, Mr. Folz, 56, spent years in the sugar and aluminum industries, building a reputation as a top manager who ran companies efficiently. When the Peugeot family, which controls about a third of the auto maker's shareholder votes, recruited him to revive their operation, he spent two years as development chief before taking the top job in September 1997.

That year, PSA made two million vehicles and lost $457 million. Costs were out of whack, mostly because Peugeot and Citroën competed as much with each other as with anyone else. Run as independent companies, each spent millions on separate design teams, development programs and assembly plants. Similar vehicles used different sets of basic components, called "platforms" in industry jargon. Typical were two subcompacts, the Citroën Saxo and the Peugeot 106, which were nearly identical yet shared only 20% of their parts.

Four months after Mr. Folz became CEO, PSA presented a turnaround plan to analysts at its modest Paris headquarters. Peugeot and Citroën would become one, combining design, development and production. The company would replace the nine platforms then in use with three new ones, for small, midsize and large cars from both brands. Citroën now focuses on spacious, affordable vehicles, while Peugeot turns out sportier, stylish cars. "No more lookalikes," Mr. Folz says.

Mr. Folz also asserted his preference for partnerships over mergers. In the audience, eyes rolled. "Not many believed this was easily possible," says Smith Barney analyst John Lawson. His report on the presentation was headlined, "Folz Dawn?"

Three months later, underscoring the challenge Mr. Folz faced, Daimler-Benz AG and Chrysler Corp. announced their merger. The companies said brutal competition would soon leave fewer than a dozen car makers on the world stage.

Yet Mr. Folz had an ace in the hole: diesel. In the 1990s, PSA and other European firms developed cleaner diesel technology, and European governments began paying subsidies to encourage use of the fuel. At the time, Ford and GM were focused on global ambitions—but many decisions regarding Europe were being made in Detroit. Both companies missed the Continent's shift toward diesel.

So Mr. Folz invited Jacques Nasser, then Ford's CEO, to a chat in Paris. The PSA executive pointed out that a more powerful and fuel-efficient family of diesel engines would cost $1 billion to develop—a lot of money for one company but manageable for two. After more meetings, they had their agreement: PSA would lead the development of small diesels, Ford would work on larger ones, and they'd split the bill 50-50.

Then Mr. Folz approached Toyota President Fujio Cho with the minicar idea. Ultracompact cars that carry two people and some groceries were becoming a sizable niche in Europe. But these cars are tricky. They sell for under $9,700, so little that most manufacturers can't sell enough to recoup the development costs. As partners, Mr. Folz suggested, PSA and Toyota could make it work.

Other car makers, meanwhile, were bulking up. GM teamed with Fiat, in part to catch up on diesel. Looking for expertise on small cars, DaimlerChrysler took a big stake in Mitsubishi Motors Corp. Ford bought Volvo and Land Rover. Renault acquired part of Japan's then-ailing Nissan Motor Corp.

Nissan has since rebounded and generates income for Renault, but Renault is struggling to lift its own sales. Facing brutal competition in the U.S., Chrysler lost $2 billion in 2000, and $1 billion in the second quarter this year. Mitsubishi said it will lose $674 million this year.

GM and Fiat say they're saving millions by combining their purchasing operations, and merging their engine and transmission plants. Diesel engines developed by Fiat are now making GM cars more competitive in Europe. But Fiat's sales are plummeting and its losses widening, and GM is trying to wriggle out of an option that could compel it to buy the remaining 80% of Fiat's auto division.

Unhindered by integration headaches, PSA focused on using its new platforms to launch a succession of new vehicles—25 between 1999 and 2002. For Mr. Folz, keeping the models distinct became a personal mission. Once, he got word the front end of a Citroën sedan in development looked an awful lot like a car Peugeot was about to launch. So late one night, on Mr. Folz's orders, Citroën designers were quietly hustled across Paris to the Peugeot design center, given a peek at their colleagues' still-secret car and told to make theirs different.

PSA's biggest hit was the Peugeot 206, a compact with muscular contours. To keep sales rolling after the initial excitement, the company spun off a series of variants—a convertible, a five-door version, a sports model. Using many of the 206's underpinnings, Citroën created a rounded, bubble-shaped compact, the C3. "To customers, it's a totally different car," Mr. Peugeot says.

Then, instead of duplicating the 206's spinoffs, Citroën produced the C3 Pluriel, which transforms from a compact to a four-seat convertible to a pickup, and a smaller car, the C2.

Meanwhile, Mr. Folz brought together the two brands' production facilities. For example, about 200 miles west of Paris in Rennes, a plant that for decades produced nothing but Citroën cars now flies two flags out front: a red Citroën banner on one flagpole, a blue Peugeot standard on another. The facility will focus on producing large cars for both brands, while other PSA plants will concentrate on just small or midsize cars.

There are other new efficiencies. In the past, door panels for the Rennes plant were trucked a couple of hours from a supplier and stacked up for days until needed. Today, Visteon Inc. manufactures the panels in a new plant on what was farmland across the street from the Rennes facility. When PSA orders the panels, they arrive at the production line 138 minutes later, in the precise sequence required. Fuel tanks and air conditioners arrive the same way from other suppliers on the grounds.

These and similar improvements at other plants are supposed to save $682 million a year over the next three years, although analysts note PSA has a lot to save because it had been so inefficient.

To sustain its growth and protect margins, however, PSA has to expand into new segments and new countries. In the former case, it's not clear where PSA can go. Mr. Folz says PSA has no plans to develop SUVs, since they sell in limited volume in Europe. He's also not interested in adding a luxury brand, as so many other car makers are doing. Besides BMW and Mercedes, he says, "Who's making money with premium cars? Not Saab, not Jaguar."

Mr. Folz hopes two overseas partnerships will help PSA reach its goal of selling four million cars in 2006.

One was finalized in April 2002, when Mr. Folz joined Mr. Cho, the Toyota president, at a disused military airfield in the Czech Republic. There they broke ground for a plant where Toyota and PSA plan to build 300,000 mini-cars a year, 200,000 of them for PSA. The total cost: $1.7 billion, split equally.

The second culminated last October with a ceremony in the Great Hall of the People near China's Tienanmen Square. There, PSA and Dong Feng Motors, which already made Citroën cars in China, agreed to introduce Peugeot models to the Chinese market and double annual production capacity to 300,000 cars.

Source: Neal E. Boudette, "Road Less Traveled," *The Wall Street Journal*, August 4, 2003, A1 and A6.

Cases for Part 6

Case 6-1

Microsoft Corp.

Would you invest your hard-earned dollars in a company like this? Its revenues soared an average of 36% through the 1990s, but now it's heading into miserly single-digit growth. It has long been a powerful engine fueled by major updates of its products, yet the next major one, an unprecedented five years in the making, isn't expected until 2006. The company hasn't made much headway in newer, promising markets. And its share price is stuck exactly where it was in mid-1998. Not buying, huh? Well, tough luck: You probably already own a piece of this rock.

The company is Microsoft Corp., one of the most widely held stocks on the planet. And sure, for all its challenges, this icon of American capitalism still has a lot going for it. With a market cap of $279 billion, its valuation is the second highest in the world after General Electric Co. And it remains the most profitable company in the $1 trillion tech industry, pumping out $1 billion a month in cash.

But Microsoft just isn't the phenom it used to be. After 29 years, the software giant is starting to look like a star athlete who's past his prime. Growth is tepid. Expansion is stymied. Bureaucracy is a concern. And a company that used to be so intimidating it attracted antitrust suits on two continents seems, well, vulnerable (Exhibit 1).

The threats it faces are among the most serious in Microsoft's history (Exhibit 2) For starters, there's Linux, the software dubbed "open source" because the code is shared freely by developers around the world. With grass-roots and government support from Finland to China, Linux has become so popular that it's challenging Microsoft's core business as no rival ever has. Europe's trustbusters are coming down hard, too. On Mar. 24, they smacked the company with a ruling aimed at preventing Microsoft from leveraging Windows to gain ground in new markets, which could keep the giant tied up in court for years.

"Long Wait"

But most worrisome are delays of the new operating system, the very heart of Microsoft's business empire. Code-named Longhorn, the next version of Windows is an ambitious attempt to fundamentally change how people use computers. But critics have taken to calling it Long Wait. Already, execs concede that it won't debut until 2006, three years after researcher Gartner Inc. originally expected it to ship. That means Longhorn will come out five years after the last operating system, the longest gap ever between major Windows updates. And *BusinessWeek* has learned that to hit even that target, Microsoft is lowering its sights for the product, cutting back on key features such as an innovative way to store and search information on PCs. "Schedule is a priority for the release," wrote Microsoft Vice-President Joe Peterson in a Mar. 19 e-mail to employees on the project. "[We] expect teams to scale back features to meet target dates."

All this has Wall Street's best and brightest penciling in estimates for Microsoft that would have been an insult a few years back. Never mind 30%, or even 20% revenue growth. The optimistic forecast is for 11% growth over the next few years, shown here as the best-case scenario (charts). The Wall Street consensus is that the company will boost revenues 8% a year through 2006, according to Thomson First Call. That's right in line with the rate Gartner expects for the overall software industry. In other words, after nearly three decades of outracing the market, Microsoft is expected to be a middle-of-the-pack performer. "Microsoft is doing what large companies do—invest in new segments while maintaining the core," says David B. Yoffie, a professor at Harvard Business School. "So far, though, they're not doing it successfully."

The significance of this goes way beyond Microsoft's growth rate. For almost two decades, Gates & Co. have set the agenda for the tech industry, the most dynamic slice of the U.S. economy. Where Microsoft led, everyone from partners and rivals to Corporate America followed. The question now is whether Microsoft is losing the dynamism it needs to retain that leadership. Is mighty Microsoft becoming IBM in the 1980s—profitable but lumbering? Big but irrelevant? A giant but toothless? "They are already less relevant now than they were 10 years ago," says Michael A. Cusamano, professor at Massachusetts Institute of Technology's

EXHIBIT 1 Where's the Growth?

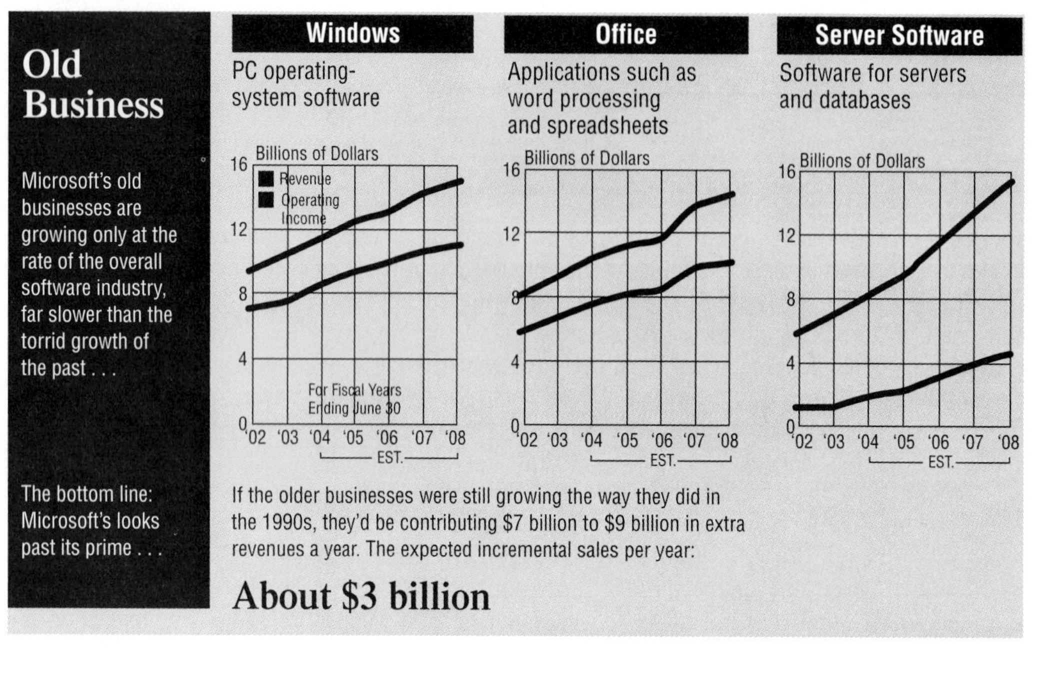

New Business

. . . And its younger businesses aren't growing fast enough to make up the difference

. . . While its forays into emerging sectors can't close the gap

Games

The Xbox video-game business and other home-entertainment products

Billions of Dollars

Revenue

Operating Income/Loss

8, 4, 0, –4, –8

'02 '03 '04 '05 '06 '07 '08

EST.

Internet

MSN and other Web operations

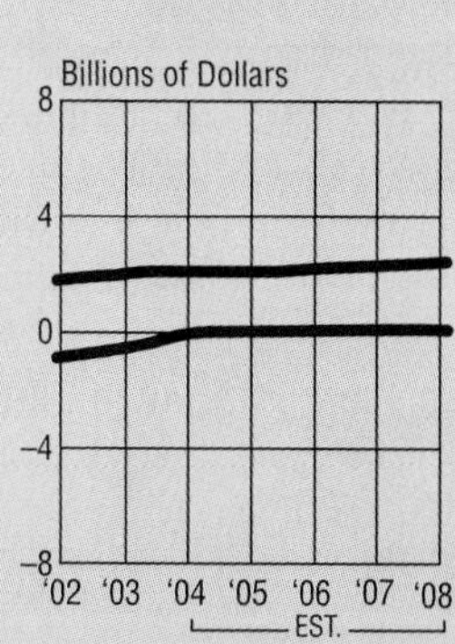

Business Software

Run-the-business applications for small and midsize companies

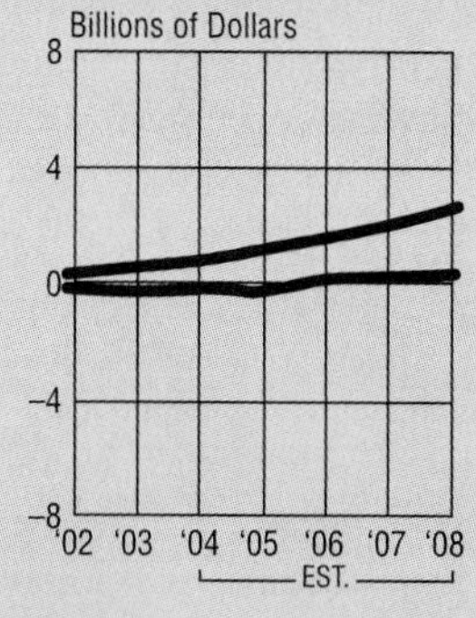

Phones/Handhelds

Software for mobile phones and handheld computers

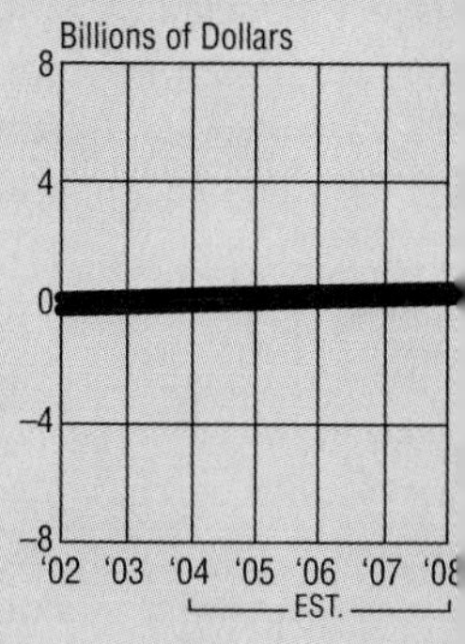

Microsoft has invested billions of dollars in these newer markets, and while their growth rates typically top those of Windows and Office, they're still too small to give a big boost to overall revenues. The expected incremental sales per year:

Less than $1 billion

Data: Sanford C. Bernstein

EXHIBIT 2
Trouble Ahead?
For more than two decades, Microsoft had rapid growth and fat profits. Now, serious challenges loom.

Slowing PC Sales Worldwide PC sales are expected to grow 11% this year but trail off to 8% in 2008, according to researcher IDC. Since Microsoft dominates desktop software, that puts a drag on its growth.

Security Problems Viruses and worms have forced cashstrapped corporate customers to buy security software, slowing Windows sales. Microsoft pulled workers off Longhorn, the next version of Windows, to focus on security improvements.

Linux The free operating-system software is all the rage for corporate server computers, retarding Microsoft's growth in this crucial market. Researcher Gartner says Linux' share will grow to 21% in 2007, while Windows' will slip to 68%. Overseas, Linux also is gaining momentum in desktop PCs.

The European Union Ruling If the EU decision prevents Microsoft from bundling new applications such as Web search and Net phone-calling with Windows, demand for upgrades could be depressed and Microsoft's attempts to enter new markets stymied.

Sloan School of Management and co-author of *Microsoft's Secrets*, a book on the company's success.

But ask CEO Steven A. Ballmer if Microsoft is past its prime, and he bristles. "No—in no sense do I feel like we're past our prime," he says during an interview in his windowless conference room. "The thing that I think is fair to say is we are past adolescence. Isn't adolescence when you grow really fast and you can sometimes be a little raucous? And then when you get into your prime, you're just hitting on every cylinder, you're having a great life, you're creating a family, you're rising to new responsibilities. We're in our prime, baby. We're post-adolescent. We are in our prime." He pulls out color-coded charts that show Microsoft outpacing a host of well-respected companies: Intel, GE, SAP. "Here's Dell, the great growth story of our industry," he says, pointing. "Growing more slowly than Microsoft."

Ballmer's right. Microsoft has boosted revenues 13% over the past three years, a stellar performance during tech's darkest days. But analysts are predicting a slow-mo future, and Ballmer declines to say whether they're wrong. "I'm not going to make some bold prediction of what a good growth rate is or a bad growth rate. I want to make sure that we're doing well relative to our industry."

Ballmer's boss of more than two decades, Chairman William H. Gates III, takes issue with the entire measurement of growth. He says it's naive to compare the $32 billion Microsoft with smaller players. "If growth is your metric, we're not your guy," Gates says, jumping out of his seat. Instead, the company's focus is on innovation, says Gates, who gave up the CEO title four years ago to become chief software architect. "We're doing more new things than any other company."

"The List"

While Ballmer drives day-to-day operations, the 48-year-old founder is taking personal control of the technology charge. He has put together what is now called "The List" around Microsoft's Redmond (Wash.) campus (Exhibit 3). It's a priority ranking of 50 or so initiatives that cut across product lines and are critical to making the next generation of products successful—everything from security software and the user interface to Web search and telephony. The List is so important that each item has been assigned to one top executive, who is responsible for driving it throughout the company. "We're using a lot of IQ to go after these things," says Gates.

A look down The List provides intriguing insight into Microsoft's concept of innovation. The company pours about $6 billion a year into research and development, and the vast majority of that goes to improve its monopoly businesses, Windows and Office. In the past, it developed ClearType technology for high-resolution text displays and grammar checking that identifies errors as people write with its word-processing software. Gates's work now on security and search also will be baked into Microsoft's most popular software. This approach, which he calls "integrated innovation," is the reason people continue to buy new versions of Windows. "I don't know if people really get what I'm saying or if they just think I'm being cute when I say our biggest competitor is our installed base," he says. "You can sit on the existing [products]—that's a perfectly legitimate choice. This is not a soft drink where you get thirsty and say, 'I drank my word processor. Let's have another.'"

EXHIBIT 3
Bill's To-Do List
Gates Keeps a tally of the top 50 tech initiatives he is responsible for pushing throughout the company. Here are six items on what is known at Microsoft as simply The List.

Search. Look out, Google. Microsoft plans to put search technology into the operating system. And it will let people search the Web and their PCs all at once.

Security. Spam and viruses and worms, oh my. Windows draws attacks like no other, and the company has drawn fire for not doing enough to plug security holes. Gates vows to do better.

Telephony. Forget old-fashioned phone calls. Gates wants to bring computer innovation to telecom. Think video voice mails. Or instant messaging with talk, not text.

Voice Recognition. Who wants to type? Microsoft is developing voice recognition so you won't have to. It's also developing software to read you your e-mail or Word documents.

FileSystem. Finding things on a PC is too cumbersome. New software will let you find not just digital photos but, for example, e-mails from the people in them.

Digital-Rights Management. Photos, music, and video are going digital. Microsoft is developing software to let people use that content without violating intellectual-property rights.

Microsoft's success in making people thirsty has been critical in the development of the entire personal-computer industry. From the biggest PC makers to the smallest software-application developers, almost all built their companies on top of Microsoft's creations. Critics may carp, but each time Microsoft gives users another reason to buy Windows or Office, it gives its partners another opportunity to sell their wares as well. That's why Ballmer bridles at criticism that Microsoft doesn't pioneer new markets. Important innovation, he says, is not simply dreaming up a new idea but also refining it enough to get people clamoring for it. "The thing that is most important is to be the guy who can come up with the innovation that gets the category to explode," he says. "The guy I really want to be is the category exploder." Perhaps more than any other company, Microsoft exploded the markets for PCs and for productivity software, such as Office's word processing and spreadsheets.

Now, however, the company seems to have misplaced its dynamite. The U.S. PC market is largely mature, so Microsoft has moved into new businesses. But these categories, such as online services and video-game consoles, already are dominated by large rivals—and they know Microsoft's tactics. So instead of opening new frontiers, Microsoft finds itself in pitched battles for existing territory. "Microsoft is the only company in the world that can afford to take fortified hills—and that's almost a disadvantage," says Richard E. Belluzzo, ex-Microsoft president and now CEO of data-storage player Quantum Corp. "They have too much money, too many good people, too much time—all of which can hurt [them] in some ways."

To bust out of this rut, Microsoft may need to put more focus on creating something altogether new. The company has spent a total of $32.6 billion on R&D since 1990, more than the next five largest software companies combined. Yet tech-industry observers marvel that it has produced so few breakthroughs. After all, it was Apple Computer Inc. that stole the show in digital music with its sleek iPod. And two Stanford University grad students came up with the search technology behind blockbuster Google Inc. "Plowing millions of dollars into me-too technology because you think there's indirect money you can make [through Windows and Office] is pure foolishness," says Cusamano.

Executive Squeeze

Some question whether Ballmer is doing enough to encourage innovation. In April, 2002, the chief divided the company into seven business units and gave each leader profit-and-loss responsibility (Exhibit 4). But he didn't give them complete independence. As part of integrated innovation, they're all supposed to coordinate their activities and align with the core Windows strategy. "They don't own 100% of their own destiny," says recently retired treasurer and deputy CFO Jean-Francois Heitz. Autonomy isn't the only issue. Ballmer's intense focus on financial details forced managers to spend untold hours boning up on the minutiae of their

EXHIBIT 4 Gates and Ballmer on 'Making the Transition'

In separate interviews, *Business Week's* Seattle bureau chief, Jay Greene, sat down with William H. Gates III, Microsoft's chairman, and CEO Steven A. Ballmer to discuss innovation, competition, and the company's future.

GATES

On Microsoft's growth prospects: If you want growth, don't go to the big guy. Go to the small guy. If growth is your story, you're looking in the wrong place. Now, if you're looking for innovation. . . we're more of a change agent for the way business is done, the way people work, the way people do things at home. We're 100 times more interested in [change] than we are [in] growth percentages or something like that.

On the company's innovation: With our $6 billion a year [in research and development], we're doing more new things than anyone else. Because of our high-volume approach, we can do a lot of new things that strengthen and maintain our profit pool and in some ways grow it. Percentage-wise it's not all that dramatic, and yet it's the most important work in the world.

On how its seven business units cooperate: We use this structure [profit and loss for each unit] to make sure that things are delegated and measured and fairly autonomous, and then we have various mechanisms that keep these P&Ls working together. The most interesting story for us is how we said: "O.K., give the P&Ls default autonomy, but then be very explicit about the things they need to work together on."

[These are] initiatives that I'm driving where many of the really big breakthrough things, like getting people to take advantage of [the new operating system] Longhorn, cut across the P&L structure. And that's just natural because it's integrated innovation.

We tried one approach, and it was just mediocre. Now we've got this new one that we put in place [last year], and it looks like this approach is really going to work well.

On the new approach: Gates's to-do list: So there's this list of [about 50] things. You see things on there like telephony. [These are technologies that cut across business units], where many P&Ls are involved, and it's so important to a scenario that we've got to get it right. They'd better be huge things, where if we get them right people go: "Wow, that's cool." They'd better be big-impact things. We're using a lot of IQ to go after these things. These are the things that, as they get into the products, define the excellence of the products.

This is the first time that we've really had a structure to formally deal with it. So it's not just "Hey, if you're confused, send mail to Bill"—something extremely ad hoc like that. This is very structured and very necessary for the breadth of things we're trying to do.

On Microsoft's real competition: I don't know if people really get what I'm saying or if they just think I'm being cute when I say our biggest competitor is our installed base. Yes, we have other competitors—Sony, Linux, Nokia, Oracle, and IBM. But the fact that you can sit on the existing [products]—that's a perfectly legitimate choice. This is not a soft drink where you get thirsty and say: "I drank my word processor, let's have another." No. Some people actually say to us: "There are no new things you can do." I know at least for the next decade that is just wrong. It's just wrong, and it will be fun to surprise them.

BALLMER

On Microsoft's growth prospects: we'll outperform the rest of our industry. The real issue isn't what's your growth rate. It's always got to be what's your growth rate relatively. Will there be startups that will be able to get a nice little boost early? Sure. Those same startups, if they were part of Microsoft, might not move our overall meter. We've grown a billion-dollar advertising business [in MSN] over the last several years. If that was a startup, it would look awfully darned good. So we sit here and look at the opportunities, and I couldn't be more excited.

On revenue growth vs. profit growth: We'll focus on both. In a sense, we have had the luxury of being able to have great profit growth without putting much of our IQ on the cost and efficiency side. We're putting more of our IQ on the cost and efficiency side. But, hey, the basic way all companies grow is with innovation. If we don't innovate, we don't grow. Yes, we'll apply more IQ on the efficiency and cost side. But still, the future to our growth will be innovation.

On innovation: Like all great companies, we have a mix of *de novo* innovation—that is, things that started here. And we have a mix of things where we provide a better innovation, better integration, better synthesis than somebody else may have done with a basic concept that they had come up with. But if you take a look at where we are today with TV software, we really pioneered the work. Smart phones, we really pioneered the work. Now the truth is, those categories are still nascent.

EXHIBIT 4 (continued)

The thing that is most important is to be the guy who can come up with the innovation that sets the category to explode, not the one that did the *de novo* innovation. Sometimes we're the category exploder. Sometimes we're the *de novo* guys. The guy I really want to be is the category exploder.

On his restructuring the company into seven business units: I know we did absolutely the right thing. I'm so excited about what we did two years ago. Everybody is kind of having to grow and get to the next level. It's really exciting to see, and I know it's absolutely the right thing for the long-term health of the company.

On giving more authority to execs: I think we are still really making the transition from the world in which we could think of ourselves, in a sense, as being in one or two businesses that could be run in a very centralized fashion to a business where we need to have strong business leadership really shepherding those businesses . . . I think really letting those talents grow, building the talents underneath them, that will be a critical part for us to realize our potential.

On comparisons of Longhorn to Cairo, an ill-fated Windows attempt in the 1990s: [Longhorn] will ship. It's got our best brainpower on it. The fact that we'll ship, of course, makes it dissimilar to the old Cairo project. But it's a firm project with a firm schedule with a team working on it. I think we pushed it back appropriately because of the need to focus in on security. But it is a very ambitious piece of work. It will be in the pantheon of most ambitious Windows releases of all times.

On whether the decision of European Commission trustbusters will force Microsoft to change Longhorn: I don't think so. We're now studying the 300-page document. At the last press conference, the commissioner went out of his way to say that he was acting consistently . . . with the precedent set in the U.S. courts and in the U.S. consent decree. In the U.S. consent decree, it's quite clear we can continue to innovate, to integrate new capabilities into Windows. So if in fact they are consistent, we should be able to continue down the path we've been on with Longhorn.

On whether Microsoft is having a midlife crisis: No, we're not having a midlife crisis. We're in a great mode. I don't know if you remember this old TV show, *The Mary Tyler Moore Show*. At the end she throws her hat up and says, "We're going to make it." That is kind of the spirit [we have]. We've got a lot to do, great opportunities, let's go, go, go, go, go, go, go.

businesses. He backed off after they complained, but some former execs think the planning process is still too much. "In the past, the system was optimized for people who could get [stuff] done," says a former exec. Now, "everybody is always preparing for a meeting."

Microsoft says these frustrations are just part of the growing pains of becoming a mature organization. Ballmer gives the new management system an A-. "I know it's absolutely the right thing for the long-term health of the company," he says.

Gates and Ballmer have led Microsoft through minefields before. In the 1990s, Gates engineered the company's powerful response to the Internet challenge, while Ballmer built a sales operation that penetrated corporations worldwide and ended the company's overdependence on desktop computing. Today, Microsoft is pushing hard on many fronts. Among them: applications for small and midsize businesses, the Xbox game console, Web-surfing cell phones, software for wristwatches that can get news updates, and most recently, speech-recognition systems. In each case, prospects for meaningful revenue growth are modest—at least for the next four years, for which analysts have done projections.

Cash Back?

With $53 billion in the bank, Microsoft could buy its way to faster growth. Indeed, it already has made a move in that direction, spending $2.5 billion over the past three years to move into the market for business applications for small to midsize companies. It could follow that up with acquisitions in a host of promising areas, such as security, collaboration, and game software.

But many analysts expect Microsoft to shy away from large deals and dole out more cash to shareholders—just like a mature company. It started paying a dividend last year and now spends $1.73 billion annually on it.

While shareholders have clamored for more, the company has said it needs the cash as an insurance policy against the European Commission antitrust probe and an antitrust suit brought by Sun Microsystems Inc. On Apr. 2, Microsoft settled the Sun case, paying its longtime nemesis nearly $2 billion. Now analysts expect Microsoft to start forking more cash over to shareholders, either in the form of a higher dividend or a big stock buyback. "Microsoft is growing up," says John Linehan, portfolio manager for the T. Rowe Price Value Fund, which recently became one of the company's top 10 shareholders. "It's a very attractive investment in the value camp."

Without acquisitions, however, Microsoft may struggle in new markets, given the shortcomings of its me-too approach. Consider Web access. Microsoft poured more than $10 billion into its MSN business in the past eight years, estimates Sanford C. Bernstein & Co. analyst Charles DiBona, much of it trying to catch America Online in attracting dial-up Net subscribers. While Microsoft succeeded in becoming AOL's most ferocious rival, the market has begun to evaporate as consumers migrate to broadband Net connections. Now, the money-losing business is dragging down the rest of MSN's numbers. "Some of that investment in MSN was not the best use of cash," says DiBona.

In some cases, Microsoft's track record of gobbling up profits has made potential partners leery. That's what's happening in the market for souped-up cell phones that can handle Web-surfing, e-mail, and photo-swapping. After four years of effort, Microsoft has persuaded a handful of mobile-phone makers to use its software, including Motorola Inc. But market leader Nokia Corp. and other major players are determined to thwart Microsoft's attempts to dominate their business the way it has the PC industry. Nokia and Sony Ericsson Mobile Communications use competing software from Symbian and have even taken equity stakes in the London company. "The name for this in the industry is ABM—anybody but Microsoft," says David Nagel, CEO of PalmSource, another maker of mobile-phone software.

Microsoft does better in markets adjacent to businesses it dominates. An example: Its foray into applications for small and midsize businesses. These companies typically own its Windows and Office products. Microsoft jumped in three years ago, buying two accounting-software companies, Great Plains Software and Navision. The business is growing at a healthy 20% a year, hitting $567 million in revenues in fiscal 2003.

That's little more than a rounding error at Microsoft today, but the plan is to keep offering ever-more-powerful software to these smaller businesses. Last year, Microsoft released its first homegrown application: customer-relationship management software for handling sales forces and customer-service staff. "It's all green fields," says Douglas J. Burgum, senior vice-president for Business Solutions Group. To stimulate demand, Microsoft is offering a promotion through June. It's selling its year-old CRM package for $99 per user for the first five users—a nearly $300 discount per user—if customers also buy Microsoft's $1,500 server product. It's classic Microsoft—and a tactic its rivals can't match, since they don't sell server software.

Logjam

Even here, though, Microsoft probably won't be able to add to overall revenue growth in a major way. Gartner expects the CRM market to rise an average of 5.5% a year through 2007, to $966 million. To add to Burgum's challenges, the next major version of his products, code-named Project Green, which meld the Great Plains and Navision products, won't be out until Longhorn debuts.

Indeed, Longhorn is becoming something of a logjam. Its delay is holding up the other products Microsoft usually debuts with a new operating system. A new version of Office often is released about the same time, with its applications fine-tuned to the new system's capabilities. Windows chief James E. Allchin pulled engineers off Longhorn to address security concerns in current products. That delayed what is already the most complex operating system Microsoft has ever built. The giant is debuting a new user interface, overhauling the way people store and retrieve files, and adding technology to let traditional applications interact with a new generation of programs called Web services. "Longhorn is an extremely ambitious project," says Gates.

The most important change is to the file system—the way information is stored on the PC. Microsoft is creating a new design not just for Windows but for all of its products that makes it easier to retrieve photos, documents, songs, and e-mail. That's important as users stash more and more files on their computers. If Microsoft gets it right, it will be simple, for example, for users to zip through thousands of pictures and sort them by date or by the people in them.

But Longhorn won't do everything Gates first envisioned. *BusinessWeek* has obtained copies of two internal e-mails showing that Microsoft is cutting some of the most ambitious technologies to get the product out the door. For example, Longhorn will now ship with a scaled-back version of the file system. The current plan, in practical terms, means people will be able to search their PCs for documents and information related to each other, but they won't be able to reach into corporate servers for similar files.

What's more, Microsoft is retreating from trying to link its two monopolies even more closely. *BusinessWeek* has learned that the company intended to develop the next version of Office so it would work only on Longhorn, not earlier versions of Windows. But in a videoconference with employees on Apr. 1, Microsoft's Peterson said such tight integration won't be possible given Longhorn's changes. "The great big version of Office that really takes advantage of the platform is something we're pushing out further in time," he said. "That's one big trade-off we've already made."

While Microsoft has been publicly vague on timing, Peterson wasn't. One e-mail said the company will ship the first beta version of the software next February and plans Longhorn's debut for the first six months of 2006. Microsoft confirmed the content of the e-mails and videoconference but declined to elaborate.

Getting Longhorn finished is critical because the delay is starting to take a toll. Customers who planned their software upgrades based on timing guidance from Microsoft must rejigger their plans. Those who can't wait for improved security and reliability will turn to alternatives, says Tony Yustein, a former Microsoft employee who now runs SoftCom Technology Consulting Inc., a Web-hosting company in Toronto. Yustein is adding Linux systems because of his growing frustration with his old company. "Microsoft has lost its perspective, concentration, and vision in operating systems," he says.

Viable Option

Linux poses the biggest threat to Microsoft since the Web burst on the scene in the mid-'90s. The 13-year-old operating system is attractive to tech companies and corporations alike because it gives them a viable alternative to Microsoft's products that they can modify at will. Also, since Linux computers run on the same processors as Windows and the software is available for free, for the first time Microsoft is confronted with competition that is cheaper to buy. Until now, Linux' momentum has come primarily at the expense of the Unix software in server computers.

But corporations increasingly are adopting Linux as a viable option to Windows. Robert W. Egan, vice-president for information technology at Boise Cascade Corp., is using Linux to run his company's internal Web site and network-maintenance programs—things he used to run on Windows. Other companies may follow suit: In a recent survey of corporate tech purchasers by Merrill Lynch & Co., 48% said they plan to boost their use of open-source software this year, and 34% of that subgroup are targeting applications that traditionally ran on Windows.

The place where Linux will likely have the most profound impact is in developing nations. Tech companies are staring hungrily at China and India as their next growth markets. Yet Microsoft likely won't dominate there, as it has in the U.S. Last November, China Standard Software Co., a consortium of government-funded companies, agreed to deploy a million computers in the next year using Linux on the desktop and Office rival StarOffice, made by Sun. "There are places, particularly in government, where people are making political decisions instead of right-minded decisions," says Ballmer.

The threat has Microsoft focused on Linux as Enemy No. 1. In the past two years, to win favor in China, Microsoft has pledged to spend more than $750 million on cooperative research, technology for schools, and other investments.

From Linux in China to Longhorn in waiting, Microsoft is increasingly stymied as it goes after new opportunities. But riding out the old businesses won't be enough. "The biggest challenge is to remain as tremendously successful as they have been in the past. That's a curse," says Hasso Plattner, chairman of the supervisory board at German software giant SAP. A lot of CEOs would probably accept Microsoft's curse and call it a blessing. But that's not good enough for Gates and Ballmer. "Some people actually say to us, 'There are no new things you can do,'" Gates says. "I know, at least for the next decade, that is just wrong. It's just wrong, and it will be fun to surprise them." There's no denying he has the will. Now he has to make it so.

With Jim Kerstetter and Peter Burrows in San Mateo, Calif., and Steve Hamm and Spencer E. Ante in New York

Source: Jay Greene, "Microsoft's Midlife Crisis," *BusinessWeek*, April 19, 2004, 88, 90–92, 94, 96–98.

Case 6-2

Samsung Electronics (B)

A black-suited Agent Smith sprints down a city street. As he is felled by an acrobatic kung fu kick from Trinity, the camera pulls back to show the action taking place inside a giant, floating Samsung TV. The screen rotates, revealing that the set is just three inches thick. "You cannot escape the Samsung 40-inch LCD flat-panel TV," intones the baritone voice of actor Laurence Fishburne. "Welcome to the new dimension."

The ad, now appearing in many U.S. theaters showing *The Matrix: Reloaded*, has an element of truth: Whether you're a consumer in America, Europe, or Asia, it's getting pretty darn hard to escape anything made by Samsung Electronics Co. Take the U.S. alone. Stroll the aisles of Best Buy Co. electronics stores, and stylish Samsung high-definition TVS, phones, plasma displays, and digital music and video players are everywhere. Log on to the home pages of USA Today, CNN, and other heavily trafficked sites, and Samsung's ads are first to pop out. You see its blue elliptical logo emblazoned on Olympic scoreboards. And expect more Matrix tie-ins: Samsung is selling a wireless phone just like the one Keanu Reeves uses to transport himself in the movie. Samsung will be even more visible in this fall's sequel, *The Matrix: Revolutions*.

Samsung's Matrix moment is the latest step in its reincarnation as one of the world's coolest brands. Its success in a blizzard of digital gadgets and in chips has wowed consumers and scared rivals around the world. The achievement is all the more remarkable considering that just six years ago, Samsung was financially crippled, its brand associated with cheap, me-too TVs and microwaves (Exhibit 1).

Now the company seems to be entering a new dimension. Its feature-jammed gadgets are racking up design awards, and the company is rapidly muscling its way to the top of consumer-brand awareness surveys. Samsung thinks the moment is fast arriving when it can unseat Sony Corp. as the most valuable electronics brand and the most important shaper of digital trends (Exhibit 2). "We believe we can be No. 1," says Samsung America Chief Executive Oh Dong Jin. Its rivals are taking the challenge seriously. "I ask for a report on what Samsung is doing every week," says Sony President Kunitake Ando.

A few measures of Samsung's progress: It has become the biggest maker of digital mobile phones using code division multiple access (CDMA) technology—and while it still lags No. 2 Motorola Inc. in handsets sold, it has just passed it in overall global revenues. A year ago, you'd have been hard pressed to find a Samsung high-definition TV in the U.S. Now, Samsung is the best-selling brand in TVs priced at $3,000 and above—a mantle long held by Sony and Mitsubishi Corp. In the new market for digital music players, Samsung's three-year-old Yepp is behind only the Rio of Japan's D&M Holdings Inc. and Apple Computer Inc.'s iPod. Samsung has blown past Micron Technology, Infineon Technologies, and Hynix Semiconductor in dynamic random-access memory (DRAM) chips—used in all PCs—and is gaining on Intel in the market for flash memory, used in digital cameras, music players, and handsets. In 2002, with most of techdom reeling, Samsung earned $5.9 billion on sales of $33.8 billion.

Can the good times last? That's a serious question, since Samsung is challenging basic New Economy dogma. In high tech, the assumption is that developing proprietary software and content gives you higher margins and a long lead time over rivals. Yet Samsung defiantly refuses to enter the software business. It's wedded to hardware and betting it can thrive in a period of relentless deflation for the industry. Rather than outsource manufacturing, the company sinks billions into huge new factories. Instead of bearing down on a few "core competencies," Samsung remains diversified and vertically integrated—Samsung chips and displays go into its own digital products. "If we get out of manufacturing," says CEO and Vice Chairman Yun Jong Yong, "we will lose."

Yet the industrial history of the past two decades suggests that this model does not work in the long run. The hazard—as many Japanese, U.S., and European companies learned in the 1980s and '90s—is that Samsung must keep investing heavily in R&D and new factories across numerous product lines. Samsung has sunk $19 billion over five years into new chip facilities. Rivals can buy similar technologies from other vendors without tying up capital or making long-term commitments. What's more, the life cycle of much hardware is brutally short and subject to relentless commoditization. The average price of a TV set has dropped 30% in five years; a DVD player goes for less than a quarter. The Chinese keep driving prices ever lower, leveraging supercheap wages and engineering talent. Meanwhile, the Japanese are building their own Chinese factories to

EXHIBIT 1
Climbing the Digital Ranks
From virtually nowhere a half-decade ago, Samsung is emerging as a market leader across the technology spectrum.

Cell Phones

Company	Global Market Share
1. Nokia	36%
2. Motorola	15
3. Samsung	10
4. Siemens	8

Data: Gartner

LCD Displays

Company	Global Market Share
1. Samsung	18%
2. LG Philips	17
3. AU Optronics	12
4. Sharp	9

Data: Display Search

Big-Screen TVs*

Company	Global Market Share
1. Samsung**	32%
2. Sony	25
3. Mitsubishi	25
4. Hitachi	11

*Priced $3,000 and above
**As of April 2003
Data: NPD Techworld

Flash Memory

Company	Global Market Share
1. Intel	27%
2. Samsung	14
3. Toshiba	11
4. Advanced Micro	10

Data: IC Insights

Dram Chips

Company	Global Market Share
1. Samsung	32%
2. Micron	19
3. Hynix	13
4. Infineon	12

Data: iSupply

Microwave Ovens

Company	Global Market Share
1. Samsung	25%
2. LG	22
3. Galanz	19
4. Sharp	15

Data: Samsung

MP3 Players

Company	Global Market Share
1. SonicBlue	18%
2. Apple	17
3. Samsung	13
4. Creative	12

Data: In-Stat/MDR

DVD Players

Company	Global Market Share
1. Toshiba	15%
2. Sony	14
3. Samsung	11
4. Panasonic	10

Data: NPDTechworld

lower costs. No wonder Samsung exited the low-margin market for TV sets 27 inches and under.

Faced with these perils, Samsung needs a constant stream of well-timed hits to stay on top. Even Sony has stumbled in this race: It now depends on PlayStation to support a consumer-electronics business whose glory days seem behind it. Other legendary hardware makers—Apple, Motorola, Ericsson—have learned the perils of the hardware way.

Investors got a sharp reminder of the risks Samsung is running when the company announced first-quarter results. In a tough environment, Samsung racked up the biggest market-share gain of any company in handsets, from 9.3% to 10.5%. Yet it had to lower prices to get there, and memory-chip prices also hit the bottom line. The result was a drop in first-quarter profits of 41%, to $942 million, on sales of $8 billion. Second-quarter profits could drop further, analysts say, hurt by lower sales in Korea's slumping economy—and in China and other Asian countries struck by the SARS epidemic. Controversy also flared in May when Samsung Electronics agreed to invest a further $93 million in a troubled credit-card affiliate. Many critics believe Samsung should divest the unit but that it is propping it up under orders of its parent, Samsung Group. Concern over corporate governance is the big reason Samsung continues to trade at a discount to its global peers. Even though it's regarded as one of the most transparent

EXHIBIT 2 Pink-Haired Designers, Red Cell Phones—Ka-Ching!

Take a close look at the latest products from Samsung Electronics Co., and you might be surprised. There's the ruby-red A220 cell phone—a $440 number that resembles a cosmetic compact and gives dieting tips, advises how to dress for the day's weather, and has a display that doubles as a mirror. You might like the $549 17-inch SyncMaster flat-panel computer display, which can be folded up and hung on a wall. Or check out the $1,200 Victoria LCD TV, which has a rounded back and half-inch-thick edges, making it look far thinner than rival models even though the total depth of 2.4 inches is about the same.

Could this be the same Samsung that a few years back was best known for selling me-too products whose main attraction was low price? Yep, and expect more cool stuff from the Korean dynamo. Samsung has come a long way in the past few years, and today it offers products that are the envy of tech companies—and their trend-conscious customers—from San Francisco to Stockholm. Last year, Samsung won five Industrial Design Excellence Awards for its digital appliances—a total matched only by Apple Computer Inc.

Samsung today employs 350 designers, twice as many as five years ago. Unlike their corporate brethren at what is still a very conservative Korean company, the designers clutter their desks with toys, often work in blue jeans and sneakers, and dye their hair pink, green, or blue. Despite an average age of just 33, they are the vanguard of Samsung's quest to come up with new, must-have products aimed at hip young consumers worldwide. "We used to work for engineers and product planners, but now we are key players in creating value," says An Yong Il, 34, Samsung's chief of user research.

Key to their value is the extent of their collaboration with the rest of the company. The design teams work closely with blue-sky market researchers, manufacturing experts, and engineers from across Samsung to create compelling gadgets that tap the company's breadth of expertise, look great, and work the way consumers want them to. One team dubbed the CNB Group, which stands for Creating New Business, constantly runs focus groups and user research to gauge consumer taste as far as five years in the future. "We aim to be remembered as the designers of iconic products," says Koo Ki Seol, who heads Samsung's Design Institute.

The focus on design is paying off in a constant stream of new models that let Samsung distinguish itself from competitors while accommodating both fickle consumer tastes and fast-changing technological improvements. A case in point is 29-year-old designer Kim Eui Seok's hanging LCD monitor. Besides redesigning the rectangular stand so the display can lie flat, Kim put hinges on the back of the screen and the stand so users can adjust the monitor's height and angle with a gentle push. The design enables the monitor to fit in a much smaller box, cutting air-shipment costs in half. "At my design school, I did not come across a single Samsung-designed product as an example to follow," says Kim. "But now we are creating buzz at markets and electronic shows." Given the resources Samsung is devoting to looking good, expect plenty more buzz in the future.

By Moon Ihlwan in Seoul

emerging-market companies anywhere, Korea's history of corporate scandals means many foreigners will always suspect its numbers.

If the earnings continue to soften, plenty of investors around the world will stand to lose. Samsung is the most widely held emerging-market stock, with $41 billion in market capitalization, and foreigners hold more than half its shares. Over the past five years, the shares have risen more than tenfold, to a recent $273. But concerns over 2003's earnings have driven the shares off their recent high this year.

The challenges are huge, but so are Samsung's strengths (Exhibit 3). It is used to big swings: Nearly half its profits come from memory chips, a notoriously cyclical business. Even in the weak first quarter, Samsung earned more than any U.S. tech company other than Microsoft, IBM, and Cisco. Meanwhile, Sony lost $940 million in this year's first three months and chip rivals Micron, Infineon, and Hynix lost a combined $1.88 billion. In cell phones, Samsung has kept its average selling price at $191, compared with $154 for Nokia and $147 for Motorola, according to Technology Business Research. What's more, since 1997 its debt has shrunk from an unsustainable $10.8 billion to $1.4 billion, leaving Samsung in a healthy net cash position. And its net margins have risen from 0.4% to 12%.

Driving this success is CEO Yun, a career company man who took over in the dark days of 1997. Yun and

EXHIBIT 3 Charging Through The Tech Best

Data: Samsung Electronics Co., Merrill Lynch & Co.

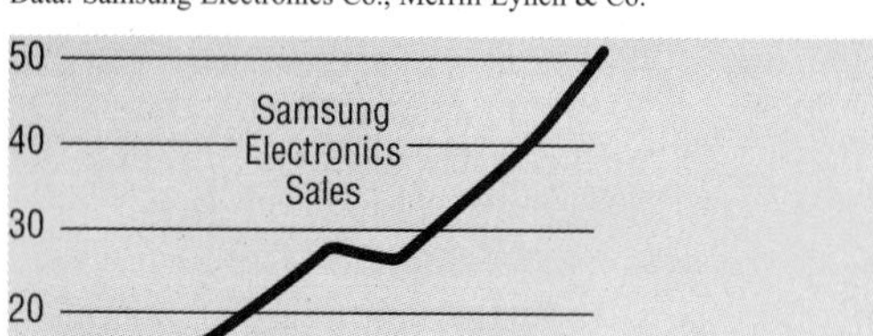

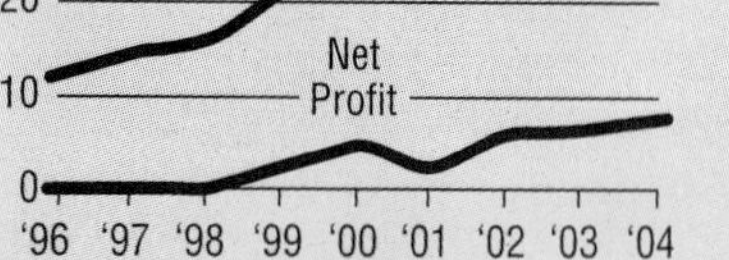

his boss, Samsung Group Chairman Lee Kun Hee, grasped that the electronics industry's shift from analog to digital, making many technologies accessible, would leave industry leadership up for grabs. "In the analog era, it was difficult for a latecomer to catch up," Yun says. But in the digital era, "if you are two months late, you're dead. So speed and intelligence are what matter, and the winners haven't yet been determined."

Samsung's strategy to win is pretty basic, but it's executing it with ferocious drive over a remarkably broad conglomerate. To streamline, Yun cut 24,000 workers and sold $2 billion in noncore businesses when he took over. Samsung managers who have worked for big competitors say they go through far fewer layers of bureaucracy to win approval for new products, budgets, and marketing plans, speeding up their ability to seize opportunities. In a recent speech, Sony Chairman Nobuyuki Idei noted Samsung's "aggressive restructuring" and said: "To survive as a global player, we too have to change."

Second, Samsung often forces its own units to compete with outsiders to get the best solution. In the liquid-crystal-display business, Samsung buys half of its color filters from Sumitomo Chemical Co. of Japan and sources the other half internally, pitting the two teams against each other. "They really press these departments to compete," says Sumitomo President Hiromasa Yonekura.

The next step is to customize as much as possible. Even in memory chips, the ultimate commodity, Samsung commands prices that are 17% above the industry average. A key reason is that 60% of its memory devices are custom-made for products like Dell servers, Microsoft Xbox game consoles, and even Nokia's cell phones. "Samsung is one of a handful of companies you can count on to bridge the technical and consumer experiences and bring them successfully to market," says Will Poole, Senior Vice President at Microsoft's Windows Client Business, which works with the Koreans.

The final ingredient is speed. Samsung says it takes an average of five months to go from new product concept to rollout, compared to 14 months six years ago. After Samsung persuaded T-Mobile, the German-U.S. cell-phone carrier, to market a new camera-phone last April, for example, it quickly assembled 80 designers and engineers from its chip, telecom, display, computing, and manufacturing operations. In four months, they had a prototype for the V205, which has an innovative lens that swivels 270 degrees and transmits photos wirelessly. Then Samsung flew 30 engineers to Seattle to field-test the phone on T-Mobile's servers and networks. By November, the phones were rolling out of the Korean plant. Since then, Samsung has sold 300,000 V205s a month at $350 each. Park Sang Jin, executive vice-president for mobile communications, estimates the turnaround time is half what Japanese rivals would require. "Samsung has managed to get all its best companies globally to pull in the same direction, something Toshiba, Motorola, and Sony have faced big challenges in doing," says Allen Delattre, director of Accenture Ltd. high-tech practice.

Samsung can also use South Korea as a test market. Some 70% of the country's homes are wired for broadband. Twenty percent of the population buys a new cell phone every seven months. Samsung already sells a phone in Korea that allows users to download and view up to 30 minutes of video and watch live TV for a fixed monthly fee. Samsung is selling 100,000 video-on-demand phones a month in Korea at $583 each. Verizon plans to introduce them in three U.S. cities this fall.

This year alone, Samsung will launch 95 new products in the U.S., including 42 new TVs. Motorola plans to introduce a dozen new cell-phone models, says Technology Business Research Inc. analyst Chris Foster. Samsung will launch 20. Nokia also is a whiz at snapping out new models. But most are based on two or three platforms, or basic designs. The 130 models Samsung will introduce globally this year are based on 78 platforms. Whereas Motorola completely changes its product line every 12 to 18 months, Foster says, Samsung refreshes its lineup every nine months. Samsung has already introduced the first voice-activated phones, handsets with MP3 players, and digital camera phones that send photos over global system for mobile (GSM) communications networks.

Samsung has been just as fast in digital TVs. It became the first to market projection TVs using new chips from Texas Instruments Inc. that employed digital-light processing (DLP). DLP chips contain 1.3 million micromirrors that flip at high speeds to create a sharper picture. TI had given Japanese companies the technology early in 1999, but they never figured out how to make the sets economically. Samsung entered the scene in late 2001, and already has seven DLP projection sets starting at $3,400 that have become the hottest-selling sets in their price range. "They'll get a product to market a lot faster than their counterparts," says George Danko, Best Buy's senior vice-president for consumer electronics.

Samsung hopes all this is just a warm-up for its bid to dominate the digital home (Exhibit 4). For years, Philips, Sony, and Apple have been developing home appliances, from handheld computers to intelligent refrigerators, that talk to each other and adapt to consumers' personal needs. Infrastructure bottlenecks and a lack of uniform standards got in the way.

Now, many analysts predict that digital appliances will take off within five years. By then, as many as 40% of U.S. households should be wired for high-speed Internet access, and digital TVs, home appliances, and networking devices will be much more affordable. Samsung is showing a version of its networked home in Seoul's Tower Palace apartment complex, where 2,400 families can operate appliances from washing machines to air conditioners by tapping on a wireless "Web pad" device, which doubles as a portable flat-screen TV.

It's a grandiose dream. But if the digital home becomes reality, Samsung has a chance. "They've got the products, a growing reputation as the innovator, and production lines to back that up," says In-Stat/MDR consumer-electronics analyst Cindy Wolf. With nearly $7 billion in cash, Samsung has plenty to spend on R&D, factories, and marketing.

Samsung Electronics' ascent is an unlikely tale. The company was left with huge debt following the 1997 Korean financial crisis, a crash in memory-chip prices, and a $700 million write-off after an ill-advised takeover of AST Technologies, a U.S. maker of PCs. Its subsidiaries paid little heed to profits and focused on breaking production and sales records—even if much of the output ended up unsold in warehouses.

A jovial toastmaster at company dinners but a tough-as-nails boss when he wants results, Yun shuttered Samsung's TV factories for two months until old inventory cleared. Yun also decreed Samsung would sell only high-end goods. Many cellular operators resisted. "Carriers didn't buy our story," says telecom exec Park. "They wanted lower prices all the time. At some point, we had to say no to them."

A top priority was straightening out the business in the U.S., where "we were in a desperate position,"

EXHIBIT 4 How Samsung's Pieces Fit Together
The company's latest cell phone shows the company's vertical integration at work, with all the divisions pulling together.

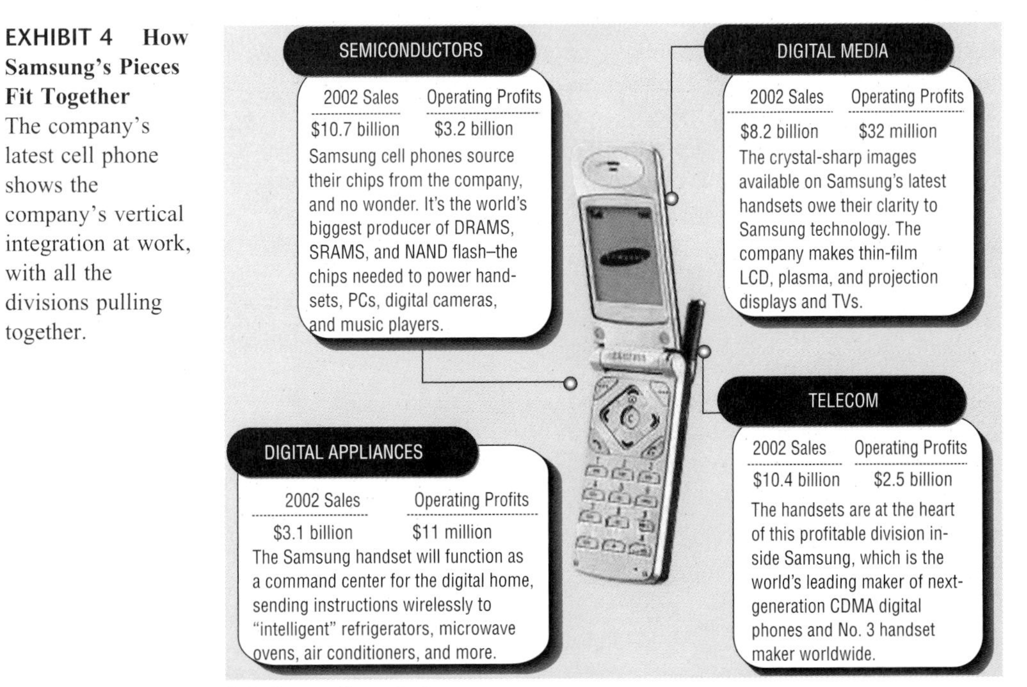

Data: Samsung Electronics Co.

recalls Samsung America chief Oh, appointed in early 2001. "We had a lot of gadgets. But they had nowhere to go." Samsung lured Peter Skaryznski from AT&T to run handset sales, and Peter Weedfald, who worked at ViewSonic Corp. and *ComputerWorld* magazine, to head marketing.

Yun brought new blood to Seoul, too. One recruit was Eric B. Kim, 48, who moved to the U.S. from Korea at age 13 and worked at various tech companies. Kim was named executive vice-president of global marketing in 1999. With his Korean rusty, Kim made his first big presentation to 400 managers in English. Sensing Kim would be resented, Yun declared: "Some of you may want to put Mr. Kim on top of a tree and then shake him down. If anybody tries that, I will kill you!"

The first coup in the U.S. came in 1997 when Sprint PCS Group began selling Samsung handsets. Sprint's service was based on CDMA, and Samsung had an early lead in the standard due to an alliance in Korea with Qualcomm Inc. Samsung's SCH-3500, a silver, clamshell-shaped model priced at $149, was an instant hit. Soon, Samsung was world leader in CDMA phones. Under Weedfald, Samsung also pulled its appliances off the shelves of Wal-Mart and Target and negotiated deals with higher-end chains like Best Buy and Circuit City.

Samsung's status in chips and displays, which can make up 90% of the cost of most digital devices, gives it an edge in handsets and other products. Besides dominating DRAM chips, Samsung leads in static random access memory and controls 55% of the $2 billion market for NAND flash memory, a technology mainly used in removable cards that store large music and color-image files. With portable digital appliances expected to skyrocket, analysts predict NAND flash sales will soar to $7 billion by 2005, overtaking the more established market for NOR flash, which is embedded onto PCs, dominated by Intel and Advanced Micro Devices.

The company's breadth in displays gives it a similar advantage. It leads in thin-film LCDs, which are becoming the favored format for PCs, normal-size TVs, and all mobile devices. Samsung predicts a factory being built in Tangjung, Korea, that will produce LCD sheets as big as a queen-size mattress will help to halve prices of large-screen LCD TVs by 2005. Samsung also aims to be No. 1 in plasma and projection displays.

If Samsung has a major flaw, it may be its lack of software and content. Samsung has no plans to branch out into music, movies, and games, as Sony and Apple have done. Sony figures that subscription-to-content will provide a more lucrative source of revenue. Samsung's execs remain convinced they're better off collaborating with content and software providers. They say this strategy offers customers more choices than Nokia, which uses its own software.

Yun has heard tech gurus, publications, and even Samsung execs warn him to forsake the vertical model. His response: Samsung needs it all. "Everyone can get the same technology now," he says. "But that doesn't mean they can make an advanced product." Stay at the forefront of core technologies and master the manufacturing, Yun believes, and you control your future. Many tech companies have tried that strategy and failed. Samsung is betting billions it can overcome the odds.

By Cliff Edwards in Ridgefield Park, N.J., Moon Ihlwan in Seoul, and Pete Engardio in Suwon

Source: "The Samsung Way," *BusinessWeek*, June 16, 2003, 56–64.

Case 6-3

General Electric Appliances*

Larry Barr had recently been promoted to the position of district sales manager (B.C.) for G.E. Appliances, a division of Canadian Appliance Manufacturing Co. Ltd. (CAMCO). One of his more important duties in that position was the allocation of his district's sales quota among his five salesmen. Barr received his quota for 2002 in October 2001. His immediate task was to determine an equitable allocation of that quota. This was important because the company's incentive pay plan was based on the salesmen's attainment of quota. A portion of Barr's remuneration was also based on the degree to which his sales force met their quotas.

Barr graduated from the University of British Columbia in 1993 with the degree of bachelor of commerce. He was immediately hired as a product manager for a mining equipment manufacturing firm because of his summer job experience with that firm. In 1996, he joined Canadian General Electric (C.G.E.) in Montreal as a product manager for refrigerators. There he was responsible for creating and merchandising a product line, as well as developing product and marketing plans. In January 1999, he was transferred to Coburg, Ontario, as a sales manager for industrial plastics. In September 2000, he became administrative manager (Western Region) and when the position of district sales manager became available, Barr was promoted to it. There his duties included development of sales strategies, supervision of salesmen, and budgeting.

Background

Canadian Appliance Manufacturing Co. Ltd (CAMCO) was created in 1998 under the joint ownership of Canadian General Electric Ltd. and General Steel Wares Ltd. (G.S.W.). CAMCO then purchased the production facilities of Westinghouse Canada Ltd. Under the purchase agreement, the Westinghouse brand name was transferred to White Consolidated Industries Ltd., where it became White-Westinghouse. Appliances manufactured by CAMCO in the former Westinghouse plant were branded Hotpoint. (See Exhibit 1.)

The G.E., G.S.W., and Hotpoint major appliance plants became divisions of CAMCO. These divisions operated independently and had their own separate management staff, although they were all ultimately accountable to CAMCO management. The divisions competed for sales, although not directly, because they each produced product lines for different price segments.

Competition

Competition in the appliance industry was vigorous. CAMCO was the largest firm in the industry, with approximately 45 percent market share, split between G.E., G.S.W. (Moffatt & McClary brands), and Hot-point. The following three firms each had 10 to 15 percent market share: Inglis (washers and dryers only), W.C.I. (makers of White-Westinghouse, Kelvinator, and Gibson), and Admiral. These firms also produced appliances under department store brand names such as Viking, Baycrest, and Kenmore, which accounted for an additional 15 percent of the market. The remainder of the market was divided among brands such as Maytag, Roper Dishwasher, Gurney, Tappan, and Danby.

G.E. marketed a full major appliance product line, including refrigerators, ranges, washers, dryers, dishwashers, and television sets. G.E. appliances generally had many features and were priced at the upper end of the price range. Their major competition came from Maytag and Westinghouse.

The Budgeting Process

G.E. Appliances was one of the most advanced firms in the consumer goods industry in terms of sales budgeting. Budgeting received careful analysis at all levels of management.

The budgetary process began in June of each year. The management of G.E. Appliances division assessed the economic outlook, growth trends in the industry, competitive activity, population growth, and so forth to determine a reasonable sales target for the next year. The president of CAMCO received this estimate, checked and revised it as necessary, and submitted it to the president of G.E. Canada. Final authorization rested with G.E. Ltd., which had a definite minimum growth target for the G.E. branch of CAMCO. G.E. Appliances was considered an "invest and grow" division, which meant it was expected to produce a healthy sales growth each year, regardless of the state of the economy. As

EXHIBIT 1 Organization Chart

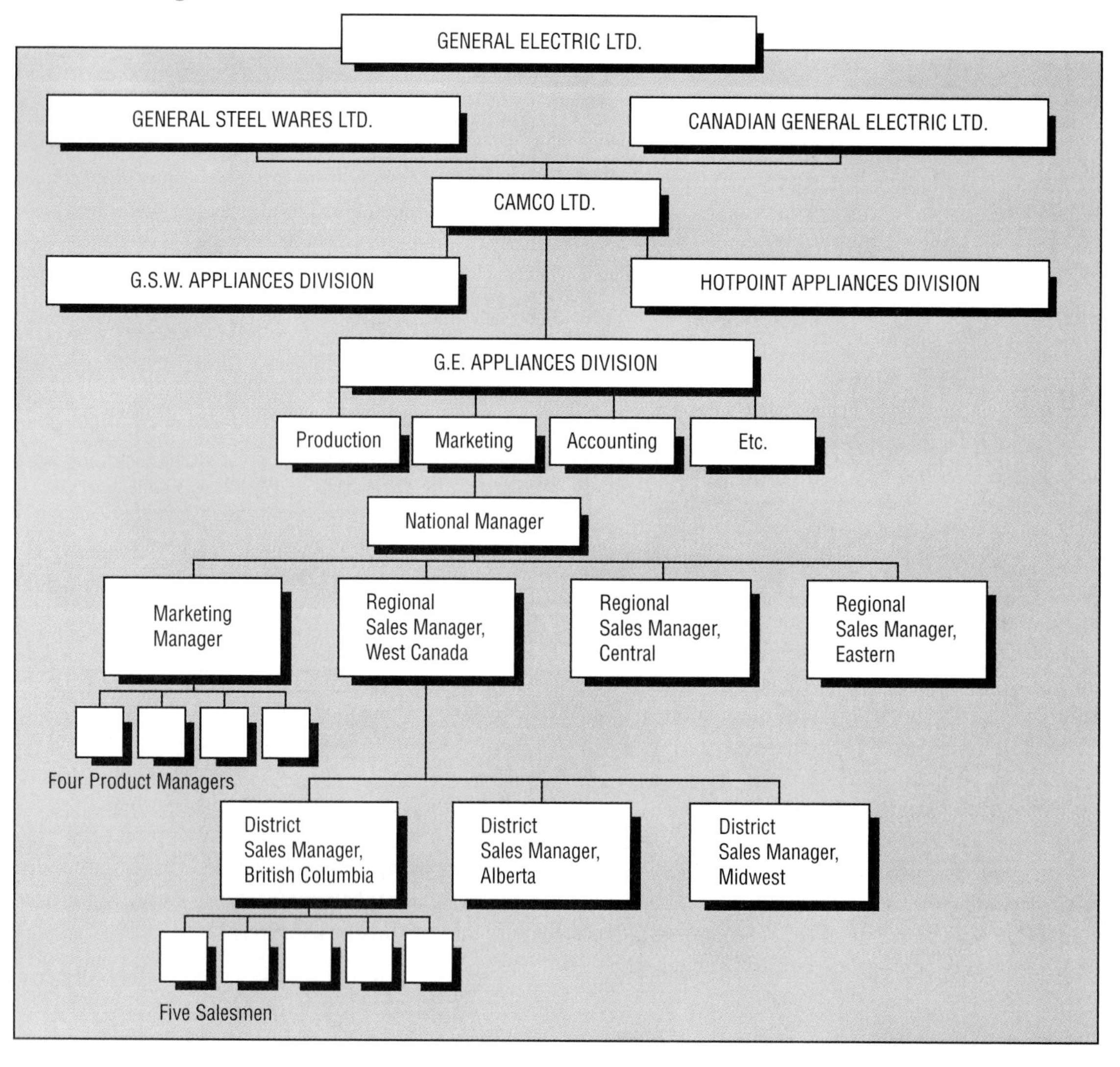

Barr observed, "This is difficult, but meeting challenges is the job of management."

The approved budget was expressed as a desired percentage increase in sales. Once the figure had been decided, it was not subject to change. The quota was communicated back through G.E. Canada Ltd., CAMCO, and G.E. Appliances, where it was available to the district sales managers in October. Each district was then required to meet an overall growth figure (quota), but each sales territory was not automatically expected to achieve that same growth. Barr was required to assess the situation in each territory, determine where growth potential was highest, and allocate his quota accordingly.

The Sales Incentive Plan

The sales incentive plan was a critical part of General Electric's sales force plan and an important consideration in the quota allocation of Barr. Each salesman had a portion of his earnings dependent on his performance with respect to quota. Also, Barr was awarded a bonus based on the sales performance of his district, making it advantageous to Barr and good for staff morale for all his salesmen to attain their quotas.

The sales force incentive plan was relatively simple. A bonus system is fairly typical for salesmen in any field. With G.E., each salesman agreed to a basic salary figure called "planned earnings." The planned salary varied according to experience, education, past performance, and competitive salaries. A salesman was paid 75 percent of his planned earnings on a guaranteed regular basis. The remaining 25 percent of salary was at risk, dependent on the person's sales record. There was also the possibility of earning substantially more money by selling more than quota (see Exhibit 2).

The bonus was awarded such that total salary (base plus bonus) equaled planned earnings when the quota was just met. The greatest increase in bonus came between 101 and 110 percent of quota. The bonus was paid quarterly on the cumulative total quota. A holdback system ensured that a salesman was never required to pay back previously earned bonus because of a poor quarter. Because of this system, it was critical that each salesman's quota be fair in relation to the other salesmen. Nothing was worse for morale than one person earning large bonuses while the others struggled.

Quota attainment was not the sole basis for evaluating the salesmen. They were required to fulfill a wide range of duties including service, franchising of new dealers, maintaining good relations with dealers, and

EXHIBIT 2
Sales Incentive Earnings Schedule: Major Appliances and Home Entertainment Products

Sales Quota Realization (percent)	Percent of Base Salary Total	Sales Quota Realization (Percent)	Incentive Percent of Base Salary Total
70%	0 %	105%	35.00%
71	0.75	106	37.00
72	1.50	107	39.00
73	2.25	108	41.00
74	3.00	109	43.00
75	3.75	110	45.00
76	4.50	111	46.00
77	5.25	112	47.00
78	6.00	113	48.00
79	6.75	114	49.00
80	7.50	115	50.00
81	8.25	116	51.00
82	9.00	117	52.00
83	9.75	118	53.00
84	10.50	119	54.00
85	11.25	120	55.00
86	12.00	121	56.00
87	12.75	122	57.00
88	13.50	123	58.00
89	14.25	124	59.00
90	15.00	125	60.00
91	16.00	126	61.00
92	17.00	127	62.00
93	18.00	128	63.00
94	19.00	129	64.00
95	20.00	130	65.00
96	21.00	131	66.00
97	22.00	132	67.00
98	23.00	133	68.00
99	24.00	134	69.00
100	25.00	135	70.00
101	27.00	136	71.00
102	29.00	137	72.00
103	31.00	138	73.00
104	33.00	139	74.00
		140	75.00

maintaining a balance of sales among the different product lines. Because the bonus system was based on sales only, Barr had to ensure the salesmen did not neglect their other duties.

A formal salary review was held each year for each salesman. However, Barr preferred to give his salesmen continuous feedback on their performances. Through human relations skills, he hoped to avoid problems that could lead to dismissal of a salesman and loss of sales for the company.

Barr's incentive bonus plan was more complex than the salesmen's. He was awarded a maximum of 75 annual bonus points broken down as follows: market share, 15; total sales performance, 30; sales representative balance, 30. Each point had a specific money value. The system ensured that Barr allocate his quota carefully. For instance, if one quota was so difficult that the salesmen sold only 80 percent of it, while the other salesmen exceeded quota, Barr's bonus would be reduced, even if the overall area sales exceeded the quota. (See Appendix, "Development of a Sales Commission Plan.")

Quota Allocation

The total 2002 sales budget for G.E. Appliances division was about $100 million, a 14 percent sales increase over 1999. Barr's share of the $33 million Western Region quota was $13.3 million, also a 14 percent increase over 1999. Barr had two weeks to allocate the quota among his five territories. He needed to consider factors such as historical allocation, economic outlook, dealer changes, personnel changes, untapped potential, new franchises or store openings, and buying group activity (volume purchases by associations of independent dealers).

Sales Force

There were five sales territories within B.C. (Exhibit 3). Territories were determined on the basis of number of customers, sales volume of customers, geographic size, and experience of the salesman. Territories were altered periodically to deal with changed circumstances.

One territory was comprised entirely of contract customers. Contract sales were sales in bulk lots to builders and developers who used the appliances in housing units. Because the appliances were not resold at retail, G.E. took a lower profit margin on such sales.

G.E. Appliances recruited M.B.A. graduates for their sales force. They sought bright, educated people who were willing to relocate anywhere in Canada. The company intended that these people would ultimately be promoted to managerial positions. The company also hired experienced career salesmen to get a blend of experience in the sales force. However, the typical salesman was under 30, aggressive, and upwardly mobile. G.E.'s sales training program covered only product knowledge. It was not felt necessary to train recruits in sales techniques.

Allocation Procedure

At the time Barr assumed the job of district sales manager, he had a meeting with the former sales manager, Ken Philips. Philips described to Barr the method he had used in the past to allocate the quota. As Barr understood it, the procedure was as follows.

EXHIBIT 3
G.E. Appliances—Sales Territories

Territory Designation	Description
9961 Greater Vancouver (Garth Rizzuto)	Hudson's Bay, Firestone, Kmart, McDonald Supply, plus seven independent dealers
9962 Interior (Dan Seguin)	All customers from Quesnel to Nelson, including contract sales (50 customers)
9963 Coastal (Ken Block)	Eatons, Woodwards, plus Vancouver Island north of Duncan and upper Fraser Valley (east of Clearbrook) (20 customers)
9964 Independent and Northern (Fred Speck)	All independents in lower mainland and South Vancouver Island, plus northern B. C. and Yukon (30 customers)
9967 Contract (Jim Wiste)	Contract sales Vancouver, Victoria All contract sales outside 9962 (50–60 customers)

The quota was received in October in the form of a desired percentage sales increase. The first step was to project current sales to the end of the year. This gave a base to which the increase was added for an estimation of the next year's quota.

From this quota, the value of contract sales was allocated. Contract sales were allocated first because the market was considered the easiest to forecast. The amount of contract sales in the sales mix was constrained by the lower profit margin on such sales.

The next step was to make a preliminary allocation by simply adding the budgeted percentage increase to the year-end estimates for each territory. Although this allocation seemed fair on the surface, it did not take into account the differing situations in the territories, or the difficulty of attaining such an increase.

The next step was examination of the sales data compiled by G.E. Weekly sales reports from all regions were fed into a central computer, which compiled them and printed out sales totals by product line for each customer, as well as other information. This information enabled the sales manager to check the reasonableness of his initial allocation through a careful analysis of the growth potential for each customer.

The analysis began with the largest accounts, such as Firestone, Hudson's Bay, and Eatons, which each bought over $1 million in appliances annually. Accounts that size were expected to achieve at least the budgeted growth. The main reason for this was that a shortfall of a few percentage points on such a large account would be difficult to make up elsewhere.

Next, the growth potential for medium-sized accounts was estimated. These accounts included McDonald Supply, Kmart, Federated Cooperative, and buying groups such as Volume Independent Purchasers (V.I.P.). Management expected the majority of sales growth to come from such accounts, which had annual sales of between $150,000 and $1 million.

At that point, about 70 percent of the accounts had been analyzed. The small accounts were estimated last. These had generally lower growth potential but were an important part of the company's distribution system.

Once all the accounts had been analyzed, the growth estimates were summed and the total compared to the budget. Usually, the growth estimates were well below the budget.

The next step was to gather more information. The salesmen were usually consulted to ensure that no potential trouble areas or good opportunities had been overlooked. The manager continued to revise and adjust the figures until the total estimated matched the budget. These projections were then summed by territory and compared to the preliminary territorial allocation.

Frequently, there were substantial differences between the two allocations. Historical allocations were then examined and the manager used his judgment in adjusting the figures until he was satisfied that the allocation was both equitable and attainable. Some factors that were considered at this stage included experience of the salesmen, competitive activities, potential store closures or openings, potential labor disputes in areas, and so forth.

The completed allocation was passed on to the regional sales manager for his approval. The process had usually taken one week or longer by this stage. Once the allocations had been approved, the district sales manager then divided them into sales quotas by product line. Often, the resulting average price did not match the expected mix between higher- and lower-priced units. Therefore, some additional adjusting of figures was necessary. The house account (used for sales to employees of the company) was used as the adjustment factor.

Once this breakdown had been completed, the numbers were printed on a budget sheet and given to the regional sales manager. He forwarded all the sheets for his region to the central computer, which printed out sales numbers for each product line by salesman, by month. These figures were used as the salesmen's quotas for the next year.

Current Situation

Barr recognized that he faced a difficult task. He thought he was too new to the job and the area to confidently undertake an account-by-account growth analysis. However, due to his previous experience with sales budgets, he did have some sound general ideas. He also had the records of past allocation and quota attainment (Exhibit 4), as well as the assistance of the regional sales manager, Anthony Foyt.

Barr's first step was to project the current sales figures to end-of-year totals. This task was facilitated because the former manager, Philips, had been making successive projections monthly since June. Barr then made a preliminary quota allocation by adding the budgeted sales increase of 14 percent to each territory's total (Exhibit 5).

Barr then began to assess circumstances that could cause him to alter that allocation. One major problem was the resignation, effective at the end of the year, of one of the company's top salesmen, Ken Block. His territory had traditionally been one of the most difficult,

EXHIBIT 4
Sales Results

Territory	1999 Budget (×1,000)	Percent of Total Budget	1999 Actual (×1,000)	1999 Variance from Quota (V%)
9967 (Contract)	$2,440	26.5%	$2,267	(7)%
9961 (Greater Vancouver)	1,790	19.4	1,824	2
9962 (Interior)	1,624	17.7	1,433	(11)
9963 (Coastal)	2,111	23.0	2,364	12
9964 (Ind. dealers)	1,131	12.3	1,176	4
House	84	1.1	235	—
Total	$9,180	100.0%	$9,299	1%

Territory	2000 Budget (×1,000)	Percent of Total Budget	2000 Actual (×1,000)	2000 Variance from Quota (V%)
9967 (Contract	$2,587	26.2%	$2,845	10%
9961 (Greater Vancouver)	2,005	20.3	2,165	8
9962 (Interior)	1,465	14.8	1,450	(1)
9963 (Coastal)	2,405	24.4	2,358	(2)
9964 (Ind. dealers)	1,334	13.5	1,494	12
House	.52	0.8	86	—
Total	$9,848	100.0%	$10,398	5%

EXHIBIT 5
Sales Projections and Quotas, 2001–2002

Projected Sales Results 2001

Territory	Oct. 2001 Year to Date	2001 Projected Total	2001 Budget	Percent of Total Budget	Projected Variance from Quota (V%)
9967	$2,447	$ 3,002	$ 2,859	25.0%	5%
9961	2,057	2,545	2,401	21.0	6
9962	1,318	1,623	1,727	15.1	(6)
9963	2,124	2,625	2,734	23.9	(4)
9964	1,394	1,720	1,578	13.8	
House	132	162	139	1.2	—
Total	$9,474	$11,677	$11,438	100.0%	2%

Preliminary Allocation 2002

Territory	2001 Projection	2002 Budget*	Percent of Total Budget
9967	$ 3,002	$ 3,422	25.7%
9961	2,545	2,901	21.8
9962	1,623	1,854	13.9
9963	2,625	2,992	22.5
9964	1,720	1,961	14.7
House	162	185	1.3
Total	$11,677	$13,315	100.0%

*2002 budget = 2001 territory projections + 14% = $13,315.

and Barr believed it would be unwise to replace Block with a novice salesman.

Barr considered shifting one of the more experienced salesmen into that area. However, that would have disrupted service in an additional territory, which was undesirable because it took several months for a salesman to build up a good rapport with customers. Barr's decision would affect his quota allocation because a salesman new to a territory could not be expected to immediately sell as well as the incumbent, and a novice salesman would require an even longer period of adaptation.

Barr was also concerned about territory 9961. The territory comprised two large national accounts and several major independent dealers. The buying decisions for the national accounts were made at their head offices, where G.E.'s regional salesmen had no control over the decisions. Recently, Barr had heard rumors that one of the national accounts was reviewing its purchase of G.E. Appliances. If it were to delist even some product lines, it would be a major blow to the salesman, Rizzuto, whose potential sales would be greatly reduced. Barr was unsure how to deal with that situation.

Another concern for Barr was the wide variance in buying of some accounts, Woodwards, Eatons, and McDonald Supply had large fluctuations from year to year. Also, Eatons, Hudson's Bay, and Woodwards had plans to open new stores in the Vancouver area sometime during the year. The sales increase to be generated by these events was hard to estimate.

The general economic outlook was poor. The Canadian dollar had fallen to 92 cents U.S. and unemployment was at about 8 percent. The government's anti-inflation program, which was scheduled to end in November 2002, had managed to keep inflation to the 8 percent level, but economists expected higher inflation and increased labor unrest during the postcontrol period.

The economic outlook was not the same in all areas. For instance, the Okanagan (9962) was a very depressed area. Tourism was down and fruit farmers were doing poorly despite good weather and record prices. Vancouver Island was still recovering from a 200 percent increase in ferry fares, while the lower mainland appeared to be in a relatively better position.

In the contract segment, construction had shown an increase over 2000. However, labor unrest was common. There had been a crippling eight-week strike in 2000, and there was a strong possibility of another strike in 2002.

With all of this in mind, Barr was very concerned that he allocate the quota properly because of the bonus system implications. How should he proceed? To help him in his decision, he reviewed a note on development of a sales commission plan that he had obtained while attending a seminar on sales management the previous year (see Appendix below).

Appendix: Development of a Sales Commission Plan

A series of steps are required to establish the foundation on which a sales commission plan can be built. These steps are as follows:

A. Determine Specific Sales Objectives of Positions to Be Included in Plan

For a sales commission plan to succeed, it must be designed to encourage the attainment of the business objectives of the component division. Before deciding on the specific measures of performance to be used in the plan, the component should review and define its major objectives. Typical objectives might be:

- Increase sales volume.
- Do an effective balanced selling job in a variety of product lines.
- Improve market share.
- Reduce selling expense to sales ratios.
- Develop new accounts or territories.
- Introduce new products.

Although it is probably neither desirable nor necessary to include all such objectives as specific measures of performance in the plan, they should be kept in mind, at least to the extent that the performance measures chosen for the plan are compatible with and do not work against the overall accomplishment of the component's business objectives.

Also, the relative current importance or ranking of these objectives will provide guidance in selecting the number and type of performance measures to be included in the plan.

B. Determine Quantitative Performance Measures to Be Used

Although it may be possible to include a number of measures in a particular plan, there is a drawback to using so many as to overly complicate it and fragment the impact of any one measure on the participants. A plan that is difficult to understand will lose a great deal of its motivation force, as well as be costly to administer properly.

For those who currently have a variable sales compensation plan(s) for their salespeople, a good starting point would be to consider the measures used in those plans. Although the measurements used for sales managers need not be identical, they should at least be compatible with those used to determine their salespeople's commissions.

However, keep in mind that a performance measure that may not be appropriate for individual salespeople may be a good one to apply to their manager. Measurements involving attainment of a share of a defined market, balanced selling for a variety of products, and control of district or region expenses might fall into this category.

Listed in Exhibit 6 are a variety of measurements that might be used to emphasize specific sales objectives.

For most components, all or most of these objectives will be desirable to some extent. The point is to select those of greatest importance where it will be possible to establish measures of standard or normal performance for individuals, or at least small groups of individuals working as a team.

If more than one performance measurement is to be used, the relative weighting of each measurement must be determined. If a measure is to be effective, it must carry enough weight to have at least some noticeable effect on the commission earnings of an individual.

As a general guide, it would be unusual for a plan to include more than two or three quantitative measures with a minimum weighting of 15 to 20 percent of planned commissions for any one measurement.

C. Establish Commission Payment Schedule for Each Performance Measure

1. Determine appropriate range of performance for each measurement. The performance range for a measurement defines the percent of standard performance (%R) at which commission earnings start to the point where they reach maximum.

The minimum point of the performance range for a given measurement should be set so that a majority of the participants can earn at least some incentive pay and the maximum set at a point that is possible of attainment by some participants. These points will vary with the type of measure used and the degree of predictability of individual budgets or other forms of measurement. In a period where overall performance is close to standard, 90 to 95 percent of the participants should fall within the performance range.

EXHIBIT 6
Tailoring Commission Plan Measurements to Fit Component Objectives

Objectives	Possible Plan Measurements
1. Increase sales/orders volume	Net sales billed or orders received against quota.
2. Increase sales of particular lines	Sales against product line quotas with weighted sales credits on individual lines.
3. Increase market share	Percent realization (%R) of shares bogey.
4. Do balanced selling job	%R of product line quotas with commissions increasing in proportion to number of lines up to quota.
5. Increase profitability	Margin realized from sales.
	Vary sales credits to emphasize profitable product lines.
	Vary sales credit in relation to amount of price discount.
6. Increase dealer sales	Pay distributor sales people or sales manager in relation to realization of sales quotas of assigned dealers.
7. Increase sales calls	%R of targeted calls per district or region.
8. Introduce new product	Additional sales credits on new line for limited period.
9. Control expense	%R of expense to sales or margin ratio. Adjust sales credit in proportion to variance from expense budget.
10. Sales teamwork	Share of incentive based upon group results.

For the commission plan to be effective, most of the participants should be operating within the performance range most of the time. If a participant is either far below the minimum of this range or has reached the maximum, further improvement will not affect his or her commission earnings, and the plan will be largely inoperative as far as he or she is concerned.

Actual past experience of %R attained by participants is obviously the best indicator of what this range should be for each measure used. Lacking this, it is better to err on the side of having a wider range than one that proves to be too narrow. If some form of group measure is used, the variation from standard performance is likely to be less for the group in total than for individuals within it. For example, the performance range for total district performance would probably be narrower than the range established for individual salespeople within a district.

2. Determine appropriate reward to risk ratio for commission earnings. This refers to the relationship of commission earned at standard performance to maximum commission earnings available under the plan. A plan that pays 10 percent of base salary for normal or standard performance and pays 30 percent as a maximum commission would have a 2 to 1 ratio. In other words, the participant can earn twice as much (20 percent) for above-standard performance as he or she stands to lose for below-standard performance (10 percent).

Reward under a sales commission plan should be related to the effort involved to produce a given result. To adequately encourage above-standard results, the reward to risk ratio should generally be at least 2 to 1. The proper control of incentive plan payments lies in the proper setting of performance standards, not in the setting of a low maximum payment for outstanding results that provides a minimum variation in individual earnings. Generally, a higher percentage of base salary should be paid for each 1%R above 100 percent than has been paid for each 1%R up to 100%R to reflect the relative difficulty involved in producing above-standard results.

Once the performance range and reward to risk ratios have been determined, the schedule of payments for each performance measure can then be calculated. This will show the percentage of the participant's base salary earned for various performance results (%R) from the point at which commissions start to maximum performance. For example, for measurement paying 20 percent of salary for standard performance:

Percent Base Salary Earned		Percent of Sales Quota
1% of base salary for each + 1%R	0%	80% or below
	20%	100% (standard performance)
1.33% of base salary for each + 1%R	60%	130% or above

D. Prepare Draft of Sales Commission Plan

After completing the above steps, a draft of a sales commission plan should be prepared using the outline below as a guide.

Keys to effective commission plans

1. Get the understanding and acceptance of the commission plan by the managers who will be involved in carrying it out. They must be convinced of its effectiveness to properly explain and "sell" the plan to the salespeople.
2. In turn, be sure the plan is presented clearly to the salespeople so that they have a good understanding of how the plan will work. We find that good acceptance of a sales commission plan on the part of salespeople correlates closely with how well they understood the plan and its effect on their commission. Salespeople must be convinced that the measurements used are factors they can control by their selling efforts.
3. Be sure the measurements used in the commission plan encourage the salespeople to achieve the marketing goals of your operation. For example, if sales volume is the only performance measure, salespeople will concentrate on producing as much dollar volume as possible by spending most of their time on products with high volume potential. It will be difficult to get them to spend much time on introducing new products with relatively low volume, handling customer complaints, and so on. Even though a good portion of their compensation may still be in salary, you can be sure they will wind up doing the things they feel will maximize their commission earnings.
4. One good solution to maintaining good sales direction is to put at least a portion of the commission earnings in an "incentive pool" to be distributed by the sales manager according to his or her judgment. This "pool" can vary in size according to some qualitative measure of the sales group's performance, but the manager can set individual measurements for each salesperson and reward each person according to how well he or she fulfills the goals.

5. If at all possible, you should test the plan for a period of time, perhaps in one or two sales areas or districts. To make it a real test, you should actually pay commission earnings to the participants, but the potential risk and rewards can be limited. No matter how well a plan has been conceived, not all the potential pitfalls will be apparent until you've actually operated the plan for a period of time. The test period is a relatively painless way to get some experience.
6. Finally, after the plan is in operation, take time to analyze the results. Is the plan accomplishing what you want it to do, both in terms of business results produced and in realistically compensating salespeople for their efforts?

Case 6-4

Slendertone

Local auctioneer Eamonn McBride still remembers clearly the day in 1990 when Kevin McDonnell arrived in the truck in Bunbeg: "Kevin had asked me to organize accommodations for some employees of a new business he was setting up. I went to look for him on the industrial estate. I found him outside the factory in a big truck. He pointed to the equipment in the back of the truck and said, 'That's it there,' referring to his new business. I was totally stunned." McDonnell wanted to buy the remaining assets of a company called BMR, which had gone into liquidation. The deal included ownership of the company's brand names, NeuroTech and Slendertone. McDonnell had decided, against the advice of many, to reestablish the business in an old factory on the industrial estate outside Bunbeg. Bunbeg is a remote, windswept coastal village in the Gaeltacht (Irish-speaking) region of northwest Donegal. Within a few weeks McDonnell and five employees had begun production.

McDonnell says that he knew little about the business he was getting into when he loaded the truck in Shannon and drove north to Donegal. An accountant by training, he thought that on paper it seemed like a viable business. He now employs over 150 people in Ireland and another 70 in international subsidiaries of his company, BioMedical Research Ltd. Company revenue in 1998 was £22 million, £17 million of which was from sales of Slendertone, up nearly 60 percent from the previous year.

This case was written by Michael J. Murphy, University College Cork. It is intended to be used as the basis for class discussion rather than to illustrate either effective or ineffective handling of a management situation. The case was made possible by the cooperation of BioMedical Research Ltd. Some of the figures, names, and other information in this case have been altered to protect company and customer confidentiality. However, all the data are representative of the actual position.

The company has received a number of design, export, and enterprise awards, and McDonnell was voted Donegal Businessman of the Year in 1995. But McDonnell has little time or desire to reflect on his substantial achievements to date—not while he has still to attain one of his greatest goals: to develop Slendertone into a world-class brand.

McDonnell believes that Slendertone can be a £100 million a year business by the year 2002. He likes to relate how Slendertone now outsells popular brands such as Impulse and Diet Pepsi in the United Kingdom; or how Slendertone is now available in Selfridges, the prestigious department store in London. McDonnell is under no illusions about the arduous challenge that lies ahead. However, he believes he has the strategy to achieve his goal. He is confident that the recent marketing strategy devised by Brian O'Donohoe will enable Slendertone to achieve sales of over £100 million in two years and become a world-class brand. O'Donohoe, now managing director of Slendertone, joined the company as marketing director for Slendertone in April 1997.

According to O'Donohoe, "BioMedical Research has gone from being a product-oriented company to a market-led one." In the process O'Donohoe has had to identify and deal with a number of critical issues. He believes that the foremost issue facing the Slendertone brand is credibility. He stresses the need to get away from the "gadget" image associated with Slendertone. O'Donohoe is confident that his strategy to reposition the brand will resolve this issue successfully. Product credibility is one of a number of important issues that have arisen since Slendertone's creation over 30 years ago. O'Donohoe knows that the future of Slendertone as a world-class brand depends on how well his strategy deals with these and other issues which have arisen more recently as a result of the company's dramatic growth.

Slendertone: The Early Years

Slendertone originally was developed by a company called BMR Ltd. in 1966. The company moved from England to the tax-free zone in Shannon in 1968. BMR manufactured a range of electronic muscle stimulation (EMS) devices under the Slendertone[1] and NeuroTech brands, serving the cosmetic and medical markets, respectively. By the end of the 1980s BMR's total annual sales were £1.5 million. Around 40 percent of revenue came from the sale of NeuroTech products, which were used by medical practitioners and physiotherapists to treat conditions such as muscle atrophy. The balance came from sales of Slendertone, which was used mostly for cosmetic purposes. Ninety-five percent of Slendertone sales were to the professional (beauty salon) market, with the remaining 5 percent coming from a limited range of home use products. The home use units were very basic and had few features. They retailed for between £250 and £400. Margins on all products were high. BMR claimed that Slendertone was available in over 40 countries by the late 1980s. All international sales were being handled by small local distributors or companies with diverse product interests (including an oil importer and a garden furniture dealer).

Kevin McDonnell was a creditor of BMR at the time of its liquidation; he had been supplying the company with printed circuit boards for four years. In that time he had learned something about the company's operations. When he heard BMR was going into liquidation, he immediately saw an opportunity. In an interview with *The Financial Times* in 1995 he stated: "I thought it was a bit odd that the company could go out of business, and yet, according to its business plan, it was capable of a 20 percent return on turnover." Few shared McDonnell's belief in the future of the Slendertone business. The managing director of BMR's German office felt that Slendertone was a fad which had little future.

McDonnell was not deterred. By the end of 1990 he had notched sales of £1.4 million, producing and selling much of the original BMR product range. With his focus initially on production, McDonnell continued to sell most of his products through distributors, many of which had previously worked with BMR. Over the next two years revenue grew gradually through increasing sales to distributors of the existing product range. McDonnell reinvested all his earnings in the business. Research into biomedical technology, with a view to developing new products, consumed much of his limited investment resources. The production facilities also were being upgraded: The company acquired a new and much larger factory in the Bunbeg industrial estate. McDonnell always believed that new product development was the key to future growth. By using distributors to develop export markets, he could focus his limited resources on developing better products.

[1] This case study focuses on the Slendertone division. Readers who are not familiar with EMS or Slendertone are advised to read the appendix before proceeding with the case.

The Gymbody 8

In late 1993 the Gymbody 8 was launched, the first "new" product produced by BioMedical Research Ltd. Designed primarily to meet the demands of a distributor in France, this "eight-pad stomach and bottom styler" was soon to outsell all the company's other products combined. Although it was much more stylish than anything else on the market at that time, initial sales of the Gymbody 8 were disappointing. Sales in general for home use products were very limited. Most sales of home use EMS-based consumer products were through mail order catalogs, small advertisements in the print media, and a very limited number of retail outlets, mainly pharmacies. After a few months of lackluster sales performance, the French distributor tried using an American-style direct response "infomercial" on the national home shopping channel, M6. This 30-minute "chat show," featuring interviews with a mixture of "ordinary" and celebrity users of the Gymbody 8, produced immediate results. Between interviews and demonstrations showing how the product worked, viewers were encouraged to order a Gymbody 8 by phone. By the end of 1994 Gymbody 8 sales (ex-factory) to the French distributor totaled £3.4 million. The French promotional strategy also involved the wide use of direct response (DR) advertisements in magazines and other print media. Over time retail distribution was extended to some pharmacies and a few sports stores. The soaring sales in France indicated a large untapped market for home use EMS products, a market larger than anyone in the company had anticipated.

Other Slendertone markets were slower to grow even after the introduction of the Gymbody 8. Those markets included mainland Europe, South America, Japan, and Australia. Sales in Ireland for the Gymbody 8 began to rise but were small relative to the sales in France. The Gymbody 8 was listed in a few English mail order catalogs, but sales were low. A distributor in Colombia was the only other customer of any significance for the Gymbody 8.

Distribution

With the exception of the home market, all sales of Slendertone were through distributors. By using distributors, the company believed it could develop new markets for Slendertone (or redevelop previous markets) more cost-effectively and quickly. The company's marketing resources were very limited because of the investments being made in research and production. Some of the distributors had handled Slendertone products previously for BMR, while others were newly recruited. Most of the distributors tended to be small operators, sometimes working from their homes. Most did not have the resources to invest in large-scale market development. Efforts to attract larger distributors already in the beauty market were proving unsuccessful in spite of the potential returns indicated by the ever-growing French market. Yet management was of the view that small distributors could also generate sales quickly by using direct marketing. Without the need to secure retail distribution and with an immediate return on all promotional spending, going direct would not require the levels of investment usually associated with introducing a new product to the market. The growing sales of Slendertone in Ireland from a range of direct marketing activities was proof of this.

Along with poorly resourced and inexperienced distributors, sluggish growth in most markets was blamed on legal restrictions on DR activity and cultural factors. In Germany, DR television was not allowed.[2] Combined with a very low use of credit cards, this did not augur well for a DR-oriented strategy in Germany. Other countries also had restrictions on DR activities. With regard to cultural factors, a number of BioMedical Research personnel felt that the Germans were less likely to be interested in a product like Slendertone than were the Spanish, the French, and the South Americans. It was believed that the latter countries had a stronger "body culture" and that their people were not as conservative as those in Germany and Switzerland. Yet, it was argued, this couldn't explain the rapidly growing sales of Slendertone in Ireland, a relatively conservative country.

Direct Response Television

In the summer of 1995 a small cable television company in Ireland agreed to broadcast a locally produced infomercial. The infomercial featured local celebrities and studio guests and adopted the French "chat show" format. Broadcast periodically throughout the summer to a potential audience of fewer than 200,000 viewers, the infomercial resulted in direct sales of almost 1,000 Gymbody 8's. Sales of Gymbody 8's also increased in a handful of retail outlets within the cable company's broadcast area. There appeared to be an increase in demand for Slendertone beauty salon treatments in this area. The success of the Irish infomercial campaign, along with the French campaign, convinced management that DR television was the best way to sell Slendertone. It was believed that if infomercials worked well in both France and Ireland, it was likely that they would work in most other countries. The focus of the sales strategy switched from developing local distributors to securing more DR television opportunities. Intensive research was undertaken to identify infomerical opportunities around the globe, from South America to the Far East. A number of opportunities were identified, but the initial costs of producing infomericals for separate far-flung markets were a constraint. It was then decided to target "home shopping" companies. These companies buy TV time in many countries and then broadcast a range of direct response programming.

By the end of 1995 a deal had been signed with Direct Shop Ltd., which was broadcasting home shopping programming in over 30 countries at that time. The advantages of using Direct Shop were that it had access to TV space across a number of markets, would handle all negotiations with the TV companies, would buy product up-front, and could handle large numbers of multilingual sales calls. BioMedical Research produced a new Slendertone infomercial exclusively for Direct Shop, using the successful chat show format. Direct Shop ran the infomercial on satellite channels such as Eurosport and Superchannel, usually late at night or early in the morning, when broadcasting time was available. The Slendertone infomericals often were broadcast alongside presentations for car care products, kitchen gadgets, fitness products and "exercisers," and various other products. Direct Shop, like all TV home shopping companies, operated on high margins. This meant that BioMedical Research would get less than 25 percent of the £120 retail price for the Gymbody 8. The company was selling this product to other distributors for around £40. Direct Shop also had a liberal customer returns policy. This resulted in return rates of product from customers as high as 35 percent. Very often the outer packaging hadn't even been opened by the purchasers. Direct Shop also returned much unsold product when TV sales were lower than expected for some countries.

[2] Restrictions on DR activity in Germany, including TV broadcasts, have since been relaxed.

Sales to Direct Shop were not as high initially as management had expected. After a few months sales began to increase, reaching monthly sales of around 3,000 Gymbody 8's. The majority of these sales were to television viewers in England.

The Direct Model

Total sales of Slendertone continued to grow rapidly. Sales (from the factory) to the French distributor totaled £5.6 million in 1995. By early 1996 it appeared that annual sales to France for that year would be considerably higher than the budgeted £7.2 million. Irish sales for 1995 were £0.4 million and were well ahead of budget in early 1996. Sales to Direct Shop were on the increase, though not by as much as management had budgeted. Sales on the order of £0.75 million were being made annually to the Colombian distributor. In early 1996 those four markets were accounting for over 90 percent of total Slendertone sales. Management continued to refine the direct model because of its success in those diverse markets.

One of the critical success factors of the direct approach was believed to be the way it allowed company representatives (either on the telephone directly to customers or through extended TV appearances) to explain clearly how the product worked. Management felt it would not be as easy to sell this product through regular retail channels. Retail sales, it was thought, required too much explanation by the sales staff, which might not be very knowledgeable about the products. Retail usually was limited to pharmacies and some sports stores. There was no definite strategy for developing retail channels. It was thought that there were some people who did not want to buy direct but who got their initial information from the infomercials, the company's telemarketing personnel, or other customers.

Going direct also allowed more targeted marketing efforts. While the target market for Slendertone was defined as "women between the ages of 25 and 55," a few niche segments also were targeted, including "prenuptials," "postnatals," and men. Postnatals were defined as women who had given birth recently and were now eager to regain their prepregnancy shape. Customer feedback had indicated that EMS was particularly effective in retoning the stomach muscles, which normally are "stretched" during pregnancy. This segment was reached by means of direct response advertisements in magazines aimed at new mothers and the "bounty bags" which are distributed in maternity wards. Bounty bags consist of free samples from manufacturers of baby-related products. The company would include a money-off voucher along with a specially designed brochure explaining how EMS can quickly and easily retone the stomach muscles. Prenuptials, those about to get married, were reached through wedding fairs and bridal magazines. EMS would allow the bride to be to quickly and easily tone up for the big day. It also was reported that increasing numbers of men were using the home use products. As an optional accessory the company supplied nonstick rubber pads which are attached to the body with a strap. These pads are suitable for men, for whom body hair can make adhesive pads uncomfortable.

Direct response enabled the company to gauge the effectiveness of all advertising and promotions directly. Advertisements were placed in a range of media, using different copy, graphics, and selling points to identify the most effective advertising methods. Direct response also meant that every advertisement produced immediate revenue or could be pulled quickly if it wasn't generating enough sales. This approach did not require the level of investment in brand development normally associated with introducing a new product to the market. In effect, all advertising became immediately self-financing.

Another important element of the direct strategy was to allow the company to develop an extensive customer database that could be used to market other products that the company would develop in the future. It had not yet been decided what those products would be other than that they would be sold under the Slendertone brand. The database also could be used to sell other products of interest to Slendertone customers and could be traded with other companies. The personal data from customers also proved useful for research purposes, helping the company identify its market.

Finally, for some customers, buying direct provided privacy when purchasing what some considered a personal product. One Irish pharmacist with a number of retail outlets reported that some customers would buy a Slendertone product at a pharmacy far from where they lived, presumably to avoid recognition by the staff or other customers. Some users of Slendertone products were reluctant to tell others they were using the company's products even when complimented on how well they were looking. The reasons given included, "No one says they are using these gimmicks" and "Because people would say to you, 'You don't need that.'" Some customers were reluctant to tell even a spouse that they had bought or were using Slendertone.

Customer Feedback

Attitudes regarding the sensitive nature of the purchase were revealed in a focus group of Irish customers conducted in 1995. A number of favorable comments about the Gymbody 8 were recorded, such as, "It's fabulous; I lost inches around the waist, and my sister got it and she looks fantastic." Some of the comments reflected an initial doubt about the efficacy of the product but subsequent satisfaction: "It's fabulous, I'm delighted, it's wonderful—it does actually work." One user was not so satisfied: "It's not very effective. I didn't see a visible difference; no one else did—no one commented."

The majority of the participants thought it was a very good value at £99. In determining "value" they tended to compare it to the cost of EMS treatment in a salon, joining a gym, taking fitness classes, or buying exercise equipment. The research also revealed generally low long-term use of the product. One issue raised related to uncertainty about using the unit, particularly how to place the pads on the body correctly. Another issue that arose was that using the products involved a certain amount of "hassle": attaching the pads to the unit, placing the pads on the body, and actually using the product for 40 minutes and then putting it all away again. All the focus group participants had bought their unit "off the TV," having seen the Irish infomercial. Most thought that the infomerical was very effective in explaining the product and that "it looked like a good product." Some found the TV presentation interesting and even entertaining (with some people watching it a number of times), while others thought it was "a bit over the top" or "false-looking."

The findings of this research supported anecdotal evidence and customer service feedback received by company personnel: initial doubt about the product's efficacy, a certain degree of surprise that it actually worked, mixed satisfaction (though mostly very high) with the results attained, and low long-term use. The low usage levels were confirmed by the low levels of replacement sales of the adhesive pads (which are used with the home use units to apply the current to the body and need to be replaced after 35 to 40 uses).

The Competition

Slendertone was the only product of its kind being marketed on television in 1995. A number of new EMS products entered the market during the mid-1990s, using a similar direct response approach in magazines, mail order catalogs, and other media. Other products had been available for many years, sold mostly through the mail order channel. With the exception of Ultratone, an English product, the competitor products in almost all markets tended to be of much poorer quality than Slendertone (though they were not necessarily much cheaper to buy). In this very fragmented market there were no international leaders. For instance, in Italy there were at least eight products on the market, none of which was sold outside the country. Other than the occasional mail order product, there did not appear to be any EMS units for sale in Germany. Ultratone was one of the biggest players in England but did not sell in France, which then was estimated to be the largest market for EMS products. In Spain a low-quality product called the Gymshape 8 was launched; it was priced lower than the Gymbody 8.

Management saw Slendertone as being at the "top end" of the market, based on its superior quality. Although the company had by then lost most of its mail order business to lower-priced (and lower-quality) competitors, management's attitude was that the biggest and most lucrative markets lay untapped. It was felt that the company had the products and the know-how to exploit those markets, as evidenced in France and Ireland. However, the increasing competition continued to put pressure on prices; most of the cost savings being achieved through more efficient production were being passed on to the distributors. From 1993 to the beginning of 1996 the retail price of the Gymbody 8 had fallen over £40 in France. To satisfy the French distributors' demand for cheaper products for certain channels, a "low-price" range under the Minibody and Intone brands was launched by BioMedical Research. Those products did not feature the Slendertone logo anywhere.

Given the fragmented nature of the market and a complete lack of secondary data for the EMS product class, it was hard to determine what market share different companies had. Lack of data also made it difficult to determine the size of the existing market for EMS products in each country. For planning purposes the company focused on the potential market for EMS, based on the belief that most countries had a large latent demand for EMS-based cosmetic products. Potential demand for each country was calculated on the basis of the size of the target market and the niche segments in that country. As revealed in the market research findings, the competition also had to be viewed in terms of the other means to improve body shape: the gym, fitness classes, exercise equipment, diets, diet foods, and the like.

The Professional Market

The salon business in Ireland experienced a big revival in the mid-1990s. The extensive marketing for the home use products helped create new or renewed awareness among salon users of EMS treatments and the Slendertone brand. Intensive media campaigns in Ireland were run to promote the salon products. In conjunction with salons, the company placed full-page "feature" advertisements in papers such as the *Sunday Independent.* A certain amount of tension arose between the company and the salon owners because the company was simultaneously marketing salon and home use units. For the price of 15 salon treatments one could buy a Gymbody 8.

The redevelopment of the salon market in the mid-1990s attracted a number of competitors to Ireland, including Ultratone, Eurowave, CACI, and Arysis. The increased competition led to greater promotional activity, which increased the demand for salon EMS treatments. Even though Slendertone had become a generic term for salon EMS treatment in Ireland, research in early 1996 indicated that some customers thought it represented "old" technology. Ultratone had positioned itself as the product with "newer" technology, one that was more effective and more comfortable and offered faster results in spite of using very similar, if not more basic, technology. In 1996 BioMedical Research promoted the fact that Slendertone had been in existence for 30 years. A special thirtieth-anniversary logo was featured on the promotional literature for the professional market. This was done to give buyers the assurance of long-term company marketing support and technical backup in the face of many new entrants into the market. Little effort was being made by the international distributors to develop the professional market in other countries in spite of very high margins on the larger professional units, which retailed at over £4,000. The French distributor was showing no interest in the professional market in France. It believed the size of the home use market offered much greater potential, and it did not require a sales team.

Product Development

After the success of the Gymbody 8, a number of other home use EMS products were developed by BioMedical Research before 1996, primarily to meet the requirements of the French distributor. Along with the low-cost Minibody and InTone brands, products developed under the Slendertone brand included the Bustyler (for lifting the breasts), the Face Up (a facial antiaging unit), and the Celluforme (to combat cellulite). Little market research was undertaken by the company while developing these products (the research that was done mostly consisted of prototype testing on a number of volunteers recruited locally in Galway, Ireland). The products would be developed, mostly in-house, according to criteria determined by the French distributor. The distributor also indicated the cost at which units would have to be supplied so that it could achieve certain retail price points in the targeted channels.

Rapid Growth

In March 1996 it appeared that annual Slendertone sales (from the factory) could break the £10 million barrier by year end. Sales for the Gymbody 8 represented over 70 percent of all Slendertone sales (including professional units). Over 75 percent of Gymbody 8 units being produced were for the French distributor. New employees were being recruited in a number of areas, including a large number of temporary workers in production. Many other workers chose to work overtime. There was a real sense of excitement throughout the company as orders continued to increase. The potential for Slendertone was enormous. If other countries achieved even a quarter of the per capita sales levels being attained in France or Ireland, the company would soon be a major Irish exporter. Plans were being drawn up to extend the factory and build a new headquarters in Galway. In spite of the impressive growth and the exciting potential, the board of the company was concerned about the growing dependence on one distributor.

The French distributor was becoming more demanding with regard to margins, product development, and pricing strategies. It continued to develop its own promotional material for the Slendertone range. The products were being sold as a form of "effortless exercise": "the equivalent of 240 sit-ups in just 40 minutes, while watching TV!" Some advertising featured topless models alongside sensational claims for the products' effectiveness: "the body you've always wanted in just three weeks." The distributor in France had arranged in 1996 for a well-known blond television celebrity to endorse the product. In the words of one of the Irish marketing staff, the distributor's approach was "very tacky." Still, few could argue with the ever-increasing sales. The distributor appeared to have found a large market that responded favorably to this type of promotion. Analysis of the French sales database, which was not computerized, indicated that sales were mostly to younger females; however, the distributor was very reluctant to share sales data with the company.

Developing the UK Market

A number of marketing meetings were held in April 1996 to develop a plan to reduce the company's growing dependence on this single customer. It was decided to develop the UK market directly, without any distributor involvement. This decision was made on the basis of a number of factors: the failure to attract good distributors in the past, the success of the company's direct campaign in Ireland, the reasonably successful sales to UK viewers by Direct Shop, and finally, geographic and cultural proximity to Ireland.

In May 1996 the board supported management's decision to develop the British market directly. This was going to require a substantial investment in terms of both money and management time. By the end of July an office had been established in London, with a general manager and two staff members. Direct response advertisements were soon being placed in a number of different print media, from *The Sunday Times Magazine* to the *News of the World*'s color supplement. Responses and sales were monitored closely to gauge the more likely market for the products. Sales were slow to grow; by the end of the first quarter the UK subsidiary was behind budget. The cost of maintaining an office in London also was affecting profitability. However, the Slendertone staff in both Ireland and England was optimistic about the longer-term prospects.

Slendertone in Turmoil

In late 1996 the size of the orders from the French distributor started to fall. Uncertainty about the reason for the sudden drop in French sales abounded, particularly as it was the buildup period to the normally busy Christmas season. The company quickly went from having a healthy cash surplus to being overdrawn. The banks were putting pressure on the company to address the situation. A decision was made to lay off all the temporary production workers. The situation continued to deteriorate. Over £1.5 million of raw material and stock, mostly for the French market, had accumulated in the factory. The staff was wondering whether the company could survive. McDonnell and his management team persevered with the plan to develop the UK market while addressing the serious situation developing in France.

After the slow start, sales in the United Kingdom were beginning to grow. Most sales were coming from direct response advertisements in magazines. Also, much public relations activity was being undertaken. Limited distribution had been secured in some nationwide retail chains, mostly on a trial basis in a few stores. Sales to Direct Shop (the television home-shopping company) were still disappointing, never rising above 4,000 Gymbody 8's a month. Sales in Ireland were up more than 30 percent over the previous year. Although sales to Ireland were now the highest per capita of any market, they still accounted for less than 10 percent of total sales. Sales to Colombia were about the same, while the sales of all the other distributors were down a little from the previous year.

The market in France deteriorated rapidly in early 1997. Subsequent analysis indicated that a number of factors were contributing to the dramatic loss of business there. The distributor had lost the television slot for the Gymbody 8 to a cheaper product. Other direct response channels seemed to have become "exhausted" or were being filled by cheaper products. To compound matters, a feature on EMS products in a consumer magazine gave poor ratings to many of the home-use products in the market. Although the Slendertone product range received the highest rating, this did not protect the company. A number of the low-quality competitors suddenly pulled out of the market, leaving a bad feeling in the "trade." The trade consisted of direct marketing companies that bought products from the distributors or manufacturers to sell to their existing customer base. It also included retailers: mostly pharmacies, sports shops, and a few department stores. The sudden fall in advertising for EMS products affected market demand and left many traders with unsold product. By the time BioMedical Research had received this information, it was too late to take any action. The company terminated its relationship with the French distributor later in the year, and all Slendertone sales in France soon came to an end.

At about the same time management ended its relationship with Direct Shop. The combination of lower than expected sales, low margins, and high return rates ensured that this was never going to be a profitable undertaking for the company. Furthermore, tension with existing distributors arose when Direct Shop began to broadcast across Europe, in many cases offering a price for the Gymbody 8 that was lower than what the distributors were charging for it locally. At least the company's own sales in the United Kingdom were growing. By selling direct to customers in the United Kingdom, BioMedical Research was earning a healthy margin (though the cost of the UK office and the increasing number of promotional campaigns had to be covered).

Restructuring

There had been a widespread belief throughout the company for many years that, in the words of one manager, "more marketing was needed." Efforts in 1995 and early 1996 to recruit a "marketing manager/marketing director designate," using advertisements in Irish and UK recruitment pages, were unsuccessful. It was suggested that the credibility issue concerning Slendertone might be having an effect on recruitment. With added urgency, the company succeeded in attracting O'Donohoe to the job of marketing director for Slendertone in April 1997. O'Donohoe had gained extensive marketing experience with Waterford Glass. He saw the opportunity to develop the Slendertone brand and welcomed the responsibility the job offered. But it was not easy at first: "When I joined in April, I had to go out to France, and everyone here in the office and factory would be waiting when I came back to see if I had gotten any new orders." Recognizing the opportunity presented by the trial placements for the Gymbody 8 in various UK stores, he immediately focused on developing the company's relationships in the retail channel.

While working on increasing retail sales, O'Donohoe initiated extensive research into the various markets for Slendertone. He started to build up a clearer picture of the markets for Slendertone and its brand positioning. His analysis of the French market identified the reasons for the drop in sales. It also revealed that Slendertone was not, nor ever had been, the market leader in France. Based on the distributor's reports, the company had been under the impression that Slendertone had had some 70 percent of the home-use EMS market. O'Donohoe's findings revealed that Slendertone's market share had been only a fraction of that figure. His analysis also revealed that sales of replacement pads had always been extremely low, indicating low customer product usage; it previously had been assumed that the French distributor was using a different supplier for the replacement pads. Focus group research in a number of countries showed that Slendertone had a very confused positioning: It was variously associated with dieting, weight loss, health, fitness, exercise, toning, and body shaping. The focus groups also reinforced the credibility issue. Many people's first thought on seeing the product being advertised was, Does it work? Secondary data showed the size of the different markets for areas such as health, fitness, and cosmetics in different countries. O'Donohoe also gathered data on consumer behaviour and motivations relating to those different markets.

The Business Defined

The next stage for O'Donohoe was to decide exactly what business the company was in. "I've read about this business being described as everything from the 'EMS business,' whatever that is, to 'passive gymnastics.' Our consumer research showed that Slendertone had a very confused message. We're in the self-confidence business," he states emphatically. "Self-confidence through improved appearance." He now defines the Slendertone brand as "the most effective and convenient appearance solutions." The new slogan for Slendertone will be "living life and loving it." In terms of people's deeper motivations with regard to health and fitness activities, O'Donohoe stresses a core need to look good. He states that most people work out to look good rather than to be healthy. Likewise, "people diet not for the sake of losing weight but to improve their appearance through their weight loss." It is this core need to look good which O'Donohoe is targeting with Slendertone. In spite of the company's involvement in the health market with its NeuroTech range of products, O'Donohoe is clear that Slendertone is about appearance, not health. He sees it as misleading to talk in terms of health and beauty, a trade category into which many products are placed. He puts a value of $170 billion on the self-confidence market in Europe; this figure includes the combined markets for cosmetics and fashion.

Also included in this market are men. Originally recognized as only a niche segment, male users now represent an important and fast-growing market for EMS cosmetic products. In late 1997 BioMedical Research modified the Gymbody 8 by adding rubber pads and redesigning the packaging and launched the Gymbody for Men. This was very successful and opened up a new market segment for Slendertone.

The company has begun extensive consumer trials at a clinic in Galway to gain a better understanding of the exact physiological benefits of Slendertone and to identify new ways to measure those benefits. According to O'Donohoe, "We want to get away from the earlier measurements of effectiveness, such as 'inch loss.'" He is conscious of the added psychological benefits that these products might offer users. BioMedical's researchers also are using these trials to identify ways to improve product convenience and comfort.

Repositioning Slendertone

By early 1999 Slendertone products were being stocked in over 2,300 retail outlets, primarily in the United Kingdom. O'Donohoe states that the increasing emphasis on retail has to be seen in terms of a complete repositioning of the Slendertone brand. "Using Direct Shop [television home shopping] was the worst thing ever for this company. And look at these [French] magazine advertisements: lots of exclamation marks, sensational product claims, very cluttered, and the models used!" he remarks, reviewing the earlier marketing of Slendertone. O'Donohoe says it is these promotional tactics which have resulted in a "gadget" positioning for Slendertone, one he is working on changing. Furthermore, he says, by making excessive product claims the company was unlikely to meet customer expectations. This was jeopardizing the opportunity for repeat purchases of Slendertone products by existing customers. Gone, says O'Donohoe, are the promises of "effortless exercise": "We are telling customers they need to work with the products to get results. This is resulting in a different type of customer for Slendertone; we want to get away from the 'gadget-freaks.'" It is this different type of customer O'Donohoe hopes will also purchase other Slendertone-branded products in the future. The target market for Slendertone now is women and men age 20 to 60 years. The earlier niche segments, such as the "postnatals," no longer are being targeted separately. O'Donohoe believes it is important to keep the Slendertone message focused rather than having different messages for different segments of the market.

Central to O'Donohoe's strategy is the development of Slendertone into a brand in its own right. From now on O'Donohoe wants people to associate Slendertone with "effective and convenient appearance solutions" rather than EMS devices: "Slendertone will be a brand that just happens to have EMS products." The Slendertone range could in the future include many types of products. The company has just created the position of brand extensions manager to plan the development of the Slendertone range. O'Donohoe believes the company is now in a position to create an international brand: "People will tell you it takes hundreds of millions to create an international brand. We don't agree."

A priority for O'Donohoe in his goal to develop the Slendertone brand is an increased emphasis on the Slendertone name. In addition to a redesign of all the product packaging to reflect more "real" users in "real" situations (see Exhibits 1 and 2), all the product names have been changed. The original Gymbody 8 will now be marketed as the Slendertone Body, the Face Up is now the Slendertone Face, and the Celluforme has become the Slendertone Body Plus. The male products will be the Slendertone Body Profile and the Slendertone Body Profile Sports, which has been adapted from the Total Body unit. Along with the Slendertone Total Body, these products constitute the full Slendertone home-use range, reduced from some 25 products three years earlier. A new professional unit, utilizing innovative touch-screen technology and "space-age" design, is about to be launched. O'Donohoe sees the professional market playing an important role in the development of Slendertone. He does not believe that the home-use and professional markets are competing; the company's experience has been that promotions for the home-use products raise awareness (and sales) for the professional market. The company currently has four staff members dedicated to developing the professional market in the United Kingdom.

Accessing the Market

O'Donohoe continues to put greater emphasis on developing retail channels, which, he says, "still represent over 95 percent of sales for all products sold worldwide in spite of the current hype about direct marketing." He believes he is able to secure retail space from important multiples because he is offering them unique access to the body-shape section of the appearance market. For these retailers Slendertone represents a new category of good, with higher than average revenues. On a shop-shelf "mock-up" in a small room at the back of the office, there is a display of the new Slendertone range, alongside massagers and shavers and other personal care products. O'Donohoe is conscious of the attention Slendertone has been attracting from the big players in the personal care market. In some cases they have been losing vital shelf space to this relatively unknown company from Ireland. He believes that BioMedical Research's expertise in the marketing of EMS products, a strong brand, and greater company flexibility (because of smaller size) will enable the company to defend itself against the multinational companies now looking at the EMS market.

The focus on retail does not mean an end to the use of direct marketing. Direct sales still account for around half of all UK sales. O'Donohoe sees direct marketing continuing to play an important role in developing the UK market and newer markets. The new direct response advertisements have been changed to reflect the move toward a stronger Slendertone brand identity and away from the "oversell" of earlier years.

The company will continue to use distributors for some markets. However O'Donohoe is determined to have greater company control over the brand than was the case in the past. By maintaining "control

EXHIBIT 1
The Cover of the Gymbody 8 Case (Used since 1994)

EXHIBIT 2
The Cover of the 'Slendertone Body' Case (Introduced in 1999)

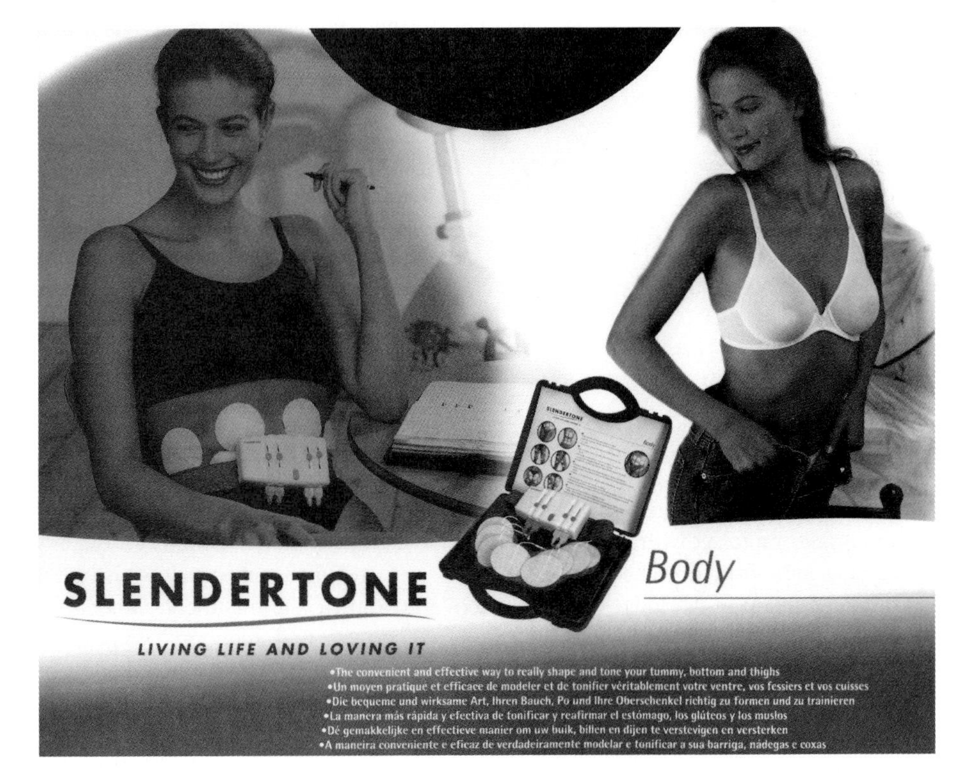

of the message" he believes the company can avoid a recurrence of what happened in the French market. Through a strong brand identity and a carefully controlled and differentiated image, he intends to protect the Slendertone name and market from the activities of other EMS companies. He does not plan to compete on price with the lower-quality producers; he believes that by investing in the Slendertone brand the company will be able to offer the customer greater total value at a higher price. The company will develop important markets such as Germany and France directly, as it has done successfully in the United Kingdom. Slendertone offices in Frankfurt and Paris have just been opened. O'Donohoe is conscious of the cost of establishing and maintaining international operations and the need to develop those markets successfully and promptly.

Slendertone: The Future

The company views the potential for Slendertone on two fronts: the existing potential for EMS-based products (including the existing Slendertone range and new, improved EMS products) and the potential for non-EMS Slendertone products. O'Donohoe believes he can restore Slendertone's fortunes in the French market: "The need is still there." He is conscious of bad feeling which may still exist within the trade, but other companies are operating again in this market (including BioMedical's former distributor, which now sells a lower-quality EMS product). There is still a lack of published secondary data for the EMS cosmetic market in any country. It is believed that the United Kingdom is now by far the largest EMS market. Company research indicates that the other markets with significant EMS sales are Spain and Italy. There is currently little EMS sales activity being observed by the company in Germany. In light of the level of sales being attained in Ireland (which has continued to grow every year since 1991) and the phenomenal recent growth in England, combined with a universal desire to look good, O'Donohoe envisages rapid growth for the existing Slendertone range in the short term. The potential for the extended Slendertone range in the longer term is much greater. Realizing this potential will depend on how effective the marketing strategy is in addressing all the issues and how well it is implemented.

For some the question might remain, Can Kevin McDonnell succeed in offering self-confidence to millions around the world from a factory in the wilds of Donegal? Certainly the locals in Bunbeg wouldn't doubt it.

Appendix
What Is Slendertone?

Beauty salons buy electronic muscle stimulation (EMS) units such as Slendertone so that they can provide their customers with a toning/body-shaping treatment. EMS devices work by delivering a series of electrical charges to the muscle through pads placed on the skin over the muscle area. Each tiny charge "fires" the motor points in the muscle. These charges are similar to the natural charges sent by the brain, through the nervous system, to activate particular muscles and thus cause movement. EMS therefore has the effect of exercising the muscle, but without the need to move the rest of the body. Customers use the EMS treatment over a period of weeks to help tone a particular area, primarily with the aim of improving body shape. This treatment also can improve circulation and the texture of the skin. EMS gives users improved body shape through improved muscle tone rather than through weight loss. Customers typically book a series of 10 or 15 one-hour treatments that are administered once or twice weekly. A qualified beautician who is trained in the use of EMS as part of the standard professional training for beauticians administers the treatment in the salon. A series of 10 salon treatments in Ireland costs in the range of £70. An alternative salon treatment to tone muscles is a manual "toning table," which works the muscles by moving different parts of the body attached to the table. Home use EMS units allow users to treat themselves in the comfort, privacy, and convenience of their own homes. A home use unit such as the Slendertone Body currently retails for £100 in Ireland. In terms of treatment, the home use unit should offer the user similar results to a salon treatment if used correctly and consistently.

Some customers prefer to go to a salon for EMS treatment, possibly enjoying the professional attention they get in a salon environment and the break it offers from everyday life. Booking and paying for a series of treatments in a salon also encourage customers to complete the treatment. Others prefer the convenience, privacy, and economy offered by the home use units. However, the home treatment requires a certain discipline to use the unit regularly. Home users sometimes report that they are uncertain if they are using the unit correctly; this mostly involves proper pad placement. EMS has been available in salons for over 30 years, but the home use market began to develop significantly only in the last 10 years.

Is EMS/Slendertone Safe?

EMS originally was developed for medical use. A common application of EMS is the rehabilitation of a muscle after an accident or a stroke. EMS frequently is used by physiotherapists for muscle rehabilitation after sports injuries and other injuries. Slendertone was developed to enable healthy users to "exercise" muscles without having to do any exercise. By remaining seated, lying down, or even doing minor chores, users could get the benefit of a vigorous workout. The effect of EMS is similar to that of regular exercise of a muscle. For many years the company compared the effect of using EMS (as applied to the abdominal muscles) to the effect gained from doing sit-ups. With the exception of well-stated contraindications (EMS should not be used by pregnant women, on or near open wounds, on or near ulcers, by diabetics, and on or near the throat area), EMS has proved to be perfectly safe for a variety of uses. Some people wonder what might happen when one stops using EMS. Again, the effect is like regular exercise: If one stops exercising, one may regain the shape one had before starting to exercise.

The U.S. Food and Drug Administration (FDA) has classified this type of EMS-based product as a Class II device. Class II devices must be prescribed by a "licensed practitioner" and only for very specified medical purposes. The FDA regulations governing the sale and use of EMS devices are based on proven efficacy and safety. According to the FDA, there is insufficient clinical evidence to support claims such as "body shaping," "weight loss," and "cellulite removal" for EMS treatments. The FDA's decision to impose stringent controls on the use of EMS was made after a number of home use EMS users suffered minor injuries. Users of a direct-current, home use EMS unit available in the United States in the 1970s suffered skin "burns" around the pad placement area. All Slendertone products, like the other cosmetic EMS products on the market today, only use alternating current, which will not cause burns.

Case 6-5

Toyota

YOI KANGAE, YOI SHINA! that's Toyota-speak for "Good thinking means good products." The slogan is emblazoned on a giant banner hanging across the company's Takaoka assembly plant, an hour outside the city of Nagoya. Plenty of good thinking has gone into the high-tech ballet that's performed here 17 hours a day. Six separate car models—from the Corolla compact to the new youth-oriented Scion xB—glide along on a single production line in any of a half-dozen colors. Overhead, car doors flow by on a conveyor belt that descends to floor level and drops off the right door in the correct color for each vehicle. This efficiency means Takaoka workers can build a car in just 20 hours.

The combination of speed and flexibility is world class (Exhibit 1). More important, a similar dance is happening at 30 Toyota plants worldwide, with some able to make as many as eight different models on the same line. That is leading to a monster increase in productivity and market responsiveness—all part of the company's obsession with what President Fujio Cho calls "the criticality of speed."

Remember when Japan was going to take over the world? Corporate America was apoplectic at the idea that every Japanese company might be as obsessive, productive, and well-managed as Toyota Motor Corp. We know what happened next: One of the longest crashes in business history revealed most of Japan Inc. to be debt-addicted, inefficient, and clueless. Today, 13 years after the Nikkei peaked, Japan is still struggling to avoid permanent decline. World domination? Hardly.

Except in one corner. In autos, the Japanese rule (Exhibit 2). And in Japan, one company—Toyota—combines the size, financial clout, and manufacturing excellence needed to dominate the global car industry in a way no company ever has. Sure, Toyota, with $146 billion in sales, may not be tops in every category. GM is bigger—for now. Nissan Motor Co. makes slightly more profit per vehicle in North America, and its U.S. plants are more efficient. Both Nissan and Honda have flexible assembly lines, too. But no car company is as strong as Toyota in so many areas.

Of course, the carmaker has always moved steadily forward: Its executives created the doctrine of *kaizen*, or continuous improvement (Exhibit 3). "They find a hole, and they plug it," says auto-industry consultant Maryann Keller. "They methodically study problems, and they solve them." But in the past few years, Toyota has

EXHIBIT 1 Global Push

Toyota's on the offensive around the globe. Here's a look at its worldwide operations:

Data: Toyota Motor, 2002 sales figures

North America	Europe	Southwest Asia	Southeast Asia
SALES: 1.94 million Toyota's products keep gaining on the Big Three's models, while Lexus is a luxury leader. Toyota employs 35,000 people and runs 10 factories in the region, and has 11.2% of the U.S. market.	SALES: 756,000 Has a 4.4% market share, led by the **Yaris** compact and a new **Avensis** with a cleaner diesel engine. Plans to boost production in Britain and France. Lexus though, is struggling.	SALES: 268,000 Builds cars in Bangladesh, India, Pakistan, and Turkey. The durable **Qualis** SUV is a big hit in India, and Toyota plans to start building transmissions there in mid-2004.	SALES: 455,000 Assembles cars in seven countries and is expanding its factories in Thailand and Indonesia. Plans to export trucks, engines, and components from the region to 80 countries.
South America	**Africa**	**China**	**Japan**
SALES: 97,000 Builds cars in Argentina, Brazil, Colombia, and Venezuela. Regionwide revenues fell 10% last year because of economic troubles in Argentina, but sales in Brazil grew after the launch of a new **Corolla.**	SALES: 140,000 Has manufacturing plants in Kenya and South Africa. Last year, it saw sales across the continent jump 10.5%, thanks to a new **Corolla** sedan and **Prado** SUV.	SALES: 58,000 Playing catch-up with rivals Volkswagen and GM. In April, it agreed with FAW to make the **Land Cruiser, Corolla,** and **Crown.** Share today is about 1.5%, but Toyota wants 10% by 2010.	SALES: 1.68 million Has maintained 40%-plus market share for five years running. New models this year include the **Sienta** compact minivan, the sportier **Wish** minivan, and a revamped **Harrier** SUV.

EXHIBIT 2 Way Ahead of the Pack

Data: Bloomberg Financial Markets, Harbour & Associates, J.D. Power & Associates, Toyo Keizai, Dresden Kleinwort, Burnham Securities. Research assistance by Susan Zegel.

	Market Cap*	Operating Profit*	Hours per Vehicle**	Defects***
Toyota	$110	$12.7	21.83	196
Nissan	54	7.5	16.83	258
Honda	40	6.1	22.27	215
DaimlerChrysler	38	5.7	28.04†	311
GM	24	3.8	24.44	264
Ford	22	3.6	26.14	287

*Billions **Average assembly time (North America) ***Problems per 100 vehicles on year 2000 models †Chryster only

accelerated these gains, raising the bar for the entire industry. Consider:

- Toyota is closing in on Chrysler to become the third-biggest carmaker in the U.S. Its U.S. share, rising steadily, is now above 11%.
- At its current rate of expansion, Toyota could pass Ford Motor Co. in mid-decade as the world's No. 2 auto maker. The No. 1 spot—still occupied by General Motors Corp., with 15% of the global market—would be the next target. President Cho's goal is 15% of global sales by 2010, up from 10% today. "They dominate wherever they go," says Nobuhiko Kawamoto, former president of Honda Motor Co. "They try to take over everything."
- Toyota has broken the Japanese curse of running companies simply for sales gains, not profit. Its operating margin of 8%-plus (vs. 2% in 1993) now dwarfs those of Detroit's Big Three. Even with the impact of the strong yen, estimated 2003 profits of $7.2 billion will be double 1999's level. On Nov. 5, the company reported profits of $4.8 billion on sales of $75 billion for the six months ended Sept. 30. Results like that have given Toyota a market

EXHIBIT 3 Kaizen in Action Toyota stresses constant improvement, or *kaizen*, in everything it does. Here's how the company revamped the 2004 Sienna minivan after the previous generation got disappointing reviews.

Data: Toyota Motor

Data: *BusinessWeek*, Edmunds.com Inc.

- The 3.3-liter, 230 hp engine is bigger and more powerful than before, but it gets slightly better gas mileage.
- Now has five-speed transmission instead of four.
- The 2004 is nimbler with a turning diameter of 36.8 feet–3.2 feet shorter than the previous model.
- At $23,495, it's $920 cheaper than the 2003.
- Third-row seats fold flat into the floor. On the older model they had to be removed to maximize cargo space.
- The new model is longer and wider than the 2003, with more headroom, leg room, and 12% more cargo space.

Camry
Bland? Sure, as bland as the bread and butter it is to Toyota. This reliable family sedan has been America's top-selling car in five of the past six years.
$19,560–$25,920

Prius
A funky-looking and earth-friendly gas-electric hybrid that gets 55 mpg–but offers the power and roominess of a midsize sedan.
$20,510

Scion xB
An attempt to be hip and edgy included underground marketing for this new car aimed at young people. Sales have been double Toyota's forecasts.
$14,165–$14,965

Yaris
The snub-nosed compact is Toyota's top-seller in Europe. Its Euro-styling has made it a hit in Japan too, where it's known as the Vitz. $11,787–$14,317

Tundra
This full-size pickup has built a loyal following as it has grown in bulk and power. A Double Cab model due in November will up the ante.
$16,495–$31,705*

Lexus RX330
The first Lexus built in North America, this luxury SUV boasts a smooth, car-like ride and nimble handling. It has been Lexus' U.S. sales leader.
$35,700–$37,500

*Doesn't include Double cab model, which isn't yet priced.

EXHIBIT 4 Toyota's Money Machine

Data: Toyota Motor Corp., Lehman Brothers Inc.

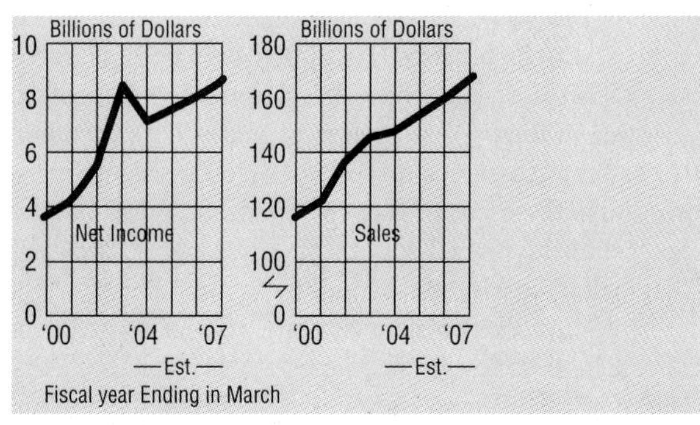

capitalization of $110 billion—more than that of GM, Ford, and DaimlerChrysler combined (Exhibit 4).

- The company has not only rounded out its product line in the U.S., with sport-utility vehicles, trucks, and a hit minivan, but it also has seized the psychological advantage in the market with the Prius, an eco-friendly gasoline-electric car. "This is going to be a real paradigm shift for the industry," says board member and top engineer Hiroyuki Watanabe. In October, when the second-generation Prius reached U.S. showrooms, dealers got 10,000 orders before the car was even available.
- Toyota has launched a joint program with its suppliers to radically cut the number of steps needed to make cars and car parts. In the past year alone, the company chopped $2.6 billion out of its $113 billion in manufacturing costs without any plant closures or layoffs. Toyota expects to cut an additional $2 billion out of its cost base this year.
- Toyota is putting the finishing touches on a plan to create an integrated, flexible, global manufacturing system. In this new network, plants from Indonesia to Argentina will be designed both to customize cars for local markets and to shift production to quickly satisfy any surges in demand from markets worldwide. By tapping, say, its South African plant to meet a need in Europe, Toyota can save itself the $1 billion normally needed to build a new factory.

If Cho gets this transformation right, he'll end up with an automotive machine that makes the Americans and Germans quake. Cost-cutting and process redesign will chop out billions in expenses. That will keep margins strong and free up cash to develop new models and technologies such as the Prius, to invest in global manufacturing, and to invade markets such as Europe and China. New models and new plants will build share, which will build more clout. And if there's a hiccup—well, there's a cash-and-securities hoard of $30 billion. "This is a company that does not fear failure," says Cho.

Roadblocks?

Can anything stop Toyota? There are some potential roadblocks. Toyota doesn't always get it right: Its early attempts at the youth market, minivans, and big pickup trucks all disappointed. It remains dependent on the U.S. business for some 70% of earnings. Its Lexus luxury sedans are losing ground to BMW, though Lexus' strong SUV sales are keeping the division in the game. The average Toyota owner is about 46, a number the company must lower or risk going the way of Buick. And most of Toyota's big sellers aren't exactly head-turners.

Meanwhile, Toyota's rivals are hardly sitting still. GM is finishing up a $4.3 billion revamp of Cadillac, and a revival is in the works: Overall GM quality is on an upswing too. "Toyota is a good competitor, but they're not unbeatable," says GM Chairman G. Richard Wagoner Jr. Over at Nissan, CEO Carlos Ghosn doubts Toyota's big bet on hybrids will pay off. "There will be no revolution," he predicts. And Detroit's Big Three are praying that a strong yen will batter Toyota. If the yen sticks at 110 to the dollar over the next 12 months, Toyota could see its pretax profits shrink by $900 million.

A strengthening yen might have hammered Toyota in the 1980s, and it will certainly have an impact next year. But today, three decades after starting its global push, Toyota can't be accused of needing a cheap yen to subsidize exports. Since starting U.S. production in 1986, Toyota has invested nearly $14 billion there. What's more, many of its costs are now set in dollars: Last year, Toyota's purchases of parts and materials from 500 North American suppliers came to $19 billion—more than the annual sales of Cisco Systems Inc. or Oracle Corp. The U.S. investment is an enormous natural hedge against the yen. "About 60% of what we sold here, we built here," Toyota Chairman Hiroshi Okuda said in a Sept. 10 speech in Washington.

Better for Toyota, those cars are also among the industry's biggest money-makers. Take SUVs: Ten years ago, Toyota had a puny 4% share. Today, it owns nearly 12% of that high-margin segment with eight models ranging from the $19,000 RAV4 to the $65,000 Lexus LX 470—and makes as much as $10,000 on each high-end model it sells. The company is steadily robbing Ford, Chrysler, and GM of their primacy in the cutthroat U.S. SUV market and has largely sat out the latest round of rebates: Toyota's average incentive per car this fall is just $647, compared with $3,812 at GM and $3,665 at Ford, according to market watcher Edmunds.com. This is one war of attrition where Detroit is clearly outgunned.

Toyota's charge into SUVs indicates a new willingness to play tough in the U.S., which it considers vital to its drive for a global 15% share. "The next era is full-size trucks and luxury, environmental, and youth cars," predicts James E. Press, chief operating officer at Toyota Motor Sales USA Inc. Toyota is already intent on boosting its 4.5% market share in pickups, the last profit refuge of the Big Three. Toyota is building an $800 million plant in San Antonio, Tex., that will allow it to more than double its Tundra output, to some 250,000 trucks a year by 2006, with rigs powerful and roomy enough to go head to head with Detroit's biggest models.

Toyota plans to extend its early lead in eco-cars by pushing the Prius and adding a hybrid Lexus RX 330 SUV next summer. The Lexus will get as much as 35 miles per gallon, compared with roughly 21 mpg for a conventional RX 330. And Toyota is vigorously attacking the youth market with the $14,500 Scion xB compact, which surprised Toyota-bashers with its angular, minimalist design. Since the Scion's U.S. launch in California in June, Toyota has sold nearly 7,700 of them, 30% better than forecast. Toyota Vice-President James Farley says three out of four buyers of the brand had no intention of buying a Toyota when they started looking. "That's exactly why we started the Scion," he says.

The Scion is evidence that Toyota's growing cash cushion gives it the means to revamp its lackluster designs. When Cho traveled through Germany in 1994, he recalls being asked: Why are Toyota cars so poorly styled? Part of the problem, says Cho, is that too many Toyotas were designed with Japanese consumers in mind and then exported. Some worked; some flopped.

These days, design teams on the West Coast of the U.S., in southern France, and back home compete for projects. That has paid off with models such as the

Yaris, Toyota's best-seller in Europe, where the company now has a 4.4% share, compared with less than 3% a decade ago. The Yaris was designed by a Greek, Sotiris Kovos, then imported successfully to Japan because of its "European" look. "Toyota has finally recognized that buyers want to feel like they have some level of style," says Wesley Brown, a consultant with auto researcher Iceology. The redesigned Solara sports coupe is getting high grades, too: A V-shape line flowing up from the grille gives it a more muscular silhouette, and its interior is 20% roomier than before.

Toyota Man

Leading Toyota to this new level of global vigor is Cho. He's Toyota Man personified: Self-effacing, ever smiling, but an executive whose radar seems to pick up every problem and opportunity. "Cho understands as much as anyone I've ever seen what's actually happening on the factory floor," says manufacturing consultant Ronald E. Harbour, whose firm's annual report on productivity is the industry bible.

That feel for the factory didn't come naturally. The 66-year-old company lifer studied law, not business, at the prestigious University of Tokyo and could have easily ended up as a faceless bureaucrat at the Ministry of Finance. But Cho learned the car business—and clearly learned it well—at the knee of Taichi Ohno, the creator of the legendary Toyota Production System, a series of in-house precepts on efficient manufacturing that changed the industry. Ohno, a brilliant but notoriously hot-headed engineer, lectured Cho about the need to be flexible and to look forward.

That advice is something Cho found invaluable when he was tapped to oversee the 1988 launch of Toyota's key U.S. plant in Georgetown, Ky., now the company's biggest U.S. factory and the maker of the Camry sedan. The good-natured and unpretentious Cho regularly worked the plant floor, making sure to shake hands with each line worker at Christmas to show his appreciation. He spoke at Rotary Club meetings and stopped to make small talk with the folks in Georgetown.

Given Toyota's booming U.S. sales in the late 1990s, few inside the company were surprised when Cho won the top job. Yet equally few had any clue that the new president was about to unleash so many powerful changes. Like his predecessor Okuda, Cho had long been frustrated by Toyota's glacial decision-making process and cultural insularity. Those had led to missed opportunities, such as when product planners at headquarters in Japan resisted calls from their U.S. colleagues to build an eight-cylinder pickup truck. Cho is rectifying that deficiency with a vengeance with the San Antonio plant.

Then three years ago, as Ghosn—"le cost killer"—was slashing billions at rival Nissan and cutting its supplier ranks in half, Cho had a revelation: If Nissan could do it, Toyota could do it better. The resulting program, called Construction of Cost Competitiveness for the 21st Century, or CCC21, taps into the company's strengths across the board to build cars more efficiently. It's also turning many operations inside out.

No Detail Too Small

Toyota has always valued frugality. It still turns down the heat at company-owned employee dormitories during working hours and labels its photocopy machines with the cost per copy to discourage overuse. But cost-cutting was often a piecemeal affair. With CCC21, Cho set a bold target of slashing prices on all key components for new models by 30%, which meant working with suppliers and Toyota's own staff to ferret out excess. "Previously, we tried to find waste here and there," says Cho. "But now there is a new dimension of proposals coming in."

In implementing CCC21, no detail is too small. For instance, Toyota designers took a close look at the grip handles mounted above the door inside most cars. By working with suppliers, they managed to cut the number of parts in these handles to five from 34, which helped cut procurement costs by 40%. As a plus, the change slashed the time needed for installation by 75%—to three seconds. "The pressure is on to cut costs at every stage," says Takashi Araki, a project manager at parts maker Aisin Seiki Co.

Just as Cho believes he can get far more out of suppliers, he thinks Toyota can make its workers vastly more productive. This is classic *kaizen*, but these days it has gone into overdrive (Exhibit 5). In the middle of the Kentucky plant, for instance, a *Kaizen* Team of particularly productive employees works in a barracks-like structure. The group's sole job is coming up with ways to save time and money. Georgetown employees, for instance, recommended removing the radiator support base—the lower jaw of the car—until the last stage of assembly. That way, workers can step into the engine compartment to install parts instead of having to lean over the front end and risk straining their backs. "We used to have to duck into the car to install something," explains Darryl Ashley, 41, a soft-spoken Kentucky native who joined Toyota nine years ago.

EXHIBIT 5
Deciphering Toyota-Speak
A handy glossary for understanding the company's vernacular.

Kaizen	PDCA	Obeya
Continuous improvement. Employees are given cash rewards for ferreting out glitches in production and devising solutions.	Plan, do, check, action. Steps in the development cycle aimed at quick decision-making in a task such as designing a car.	Literally, "big room," Regular face-to-face brainstorming sessions among engineers, designers, marketers, and suppliers
Pokayoke	**CCC21**	**GBL**
Mistake-proofing. Use of sensors to detect missing parts or improper assembly. Robots alert workers to errors by flashing lights.	Construction of Cost Competitiveness for the 21st century. A three-year push to slash costs of 170 components that account for 90% of parts expenses.	Global Body Line. A manufacturing process that holds auto frames together for welding with one brace instead of the 50 braces previously required.

In Cambridge, Ont., Cho is going even further: He's determined to show the world that Toyota can meet its own highest standards of excellence anywhere in its system. It was once company doctrine that Lexus could only be made in Japan. No longer. Production of the RX 330 SUV started in Cambridge on Sept. 26. If the Canadian hands can deliver the same quality as their Japanese counterparts, Toyota will be able to chop shipping costs by shifting Lexus production to the market where the bulk of those cars are sold (Exhibit 6).

The Japanese bosses put the Canadians through their paces. The 700 workers on the RX 330 line trained for 12 weeks, including stints in Japan for 200 of them. There, the Canadians managed to beat Japanese teams in quality assessment on a mock Lexus line. Cambridge has taken Toyota's focus on *poka-yoke*, or foolproofing measures, to another level. The plant has introduced "Circle L" stations where workers must double- and triple-check parts that customers have complained about—anything from glove boxes to suspension systems. "We know that if we can get this right, we may get to build other Lexus models," says Jason Birt, a 28-year-old Lexus line worker.

The Cambridge workers are aided by a radical piece of manufacturing technology being rolled out to Toyota plants worldwide. The system, called the Global Body Line, holds vehicle frames in place while they're being welded, using just one master brace instead of the dozens of separate braces required in a standard factory. No big deal? Perhaps, but the system is half as expensive to install. Analysts say it lets Toyota save 75% of the cost of refitting a production line to build a different car, and it's key to Toyota's ability to make multiple models on a single line. Better yet, the brace increases the rigidity of the car early in production, which boosts the accuracy of welds and makes for a more stable vehicle. "The end results are improved quality, shortened welding lines, reduced capital investment, and less time to launch new vehicles," says Atsushi Niimi, president of Toyota Motor Manufacturing North America.

Cho and his managers are not just reengineering how Toyota makes its cars—they want to revolutionize how it creates products. With the rise of e-mail and teleconferencing, teams of designers, engineers, product planners, workers, and suppliers rarely all convened in the same place. Under Cho, they're again required to work face to face, in a process Toyota calls obeya—literally, "big room." This cuts the time it takes to get a car from the drawing board to the showroom. It took only 19 months to develop the 2003 Solara. That's better than 22 months for the latest Sienna minivan, and 26 months for the latest Camry—well below the industry average of about three years.

If all this sounds like Toyota is riding a powerful growth wave, well, it is. While Cho is as mild-mannered and modest as they come, the revolution he has kicked off is anything but. Toyota is in the midst of a transformative makeover—and if Cho succeeds, the entire global auto industry is in for one, too.

With Kathleen Kerwin in Detroit, Christopher Palmeri in Los Angeles, and Paul Magnusson in Washington

EXHIBIT 6
Lexus: Still Looking for Traction in Europe

Source: Brian Bremner and Chester Dawson, "Can Anything Stop Toyota?" *BusinessWeek* November 17, 2003, 114–122.

When Dirk Lindermann was looking for a new luxury sedan last summer, he considered Mercedes and BMW before settling on a $40,000, black Audi A4. Lexus, though, didn't even enter into the game. "Lexus has no personality," says the 40-year-old Berlin advertising executive.

That's a problem for Toyota Motor Corp. The company's smooth-driving Lexus sedans sprinted from zero to luxury-market leader in the U.S. during the 1990s, overtaking German rivals Mercedes and BMW—as well as Cadillac and Lincoln—by offering better quality and service at a lower price. But Lexus is going nowhere fast in Europe: After 12 years in showrooms, last year it registered sales of just 21,156 cars—down 11% from 2001—compared with more than 234,000 in the U.S.

Toyota itself is fast shedding any *arriviste* stigma in the Old World. Since it began producing cars on the Continent in the '90s, European sales are up nearly 60%, to 734,000. Now it wants to crack the high-end with a renewed push for Lexus. The goal is to triple sales of the six Lexus models Toyota offers there by 2010, to at least 65,000 cars. "The potential in Europe for Lexus is every bit as great as in the U.S.," says Stuart McCullough, director of Lexus Europe.

To make Lexus a success, though, Toyota needs to establish it as a separate brand. Until now, the car has been sold in Europe mainly through Toyota's 250 dealerships, along with the far less lustrous Yaris, Corolla, and Avensis models. So Toyota is trying to set up dealerships that offer luxury-car buyers the kind of white-glove service they demand. "Lexus has to establish its own heritage, not just chase BMW and Mercedes," says Tadashi Arashima, president and chief executive of Toyota Motor Marketing Europe.

Will image-conscious Europeans warm up to Lexus if the cars are sold in tony showrooms? In Spain, where exclusive Lexus dealerships have been operating since 2000, sales are up 9% so far this year, though the brand sold just 969 vehicles in the country. "We've been able to show that these cars can compete with the big German brands in quality and also offer a lot more in terms of price," says Jorge Merino, head of sales at Axel, a three-year-old Lexus dealership in Madrid.

One big selling point is Lexus' six-year warranty. And the carmaker includes three years of free check-ups, maintenance, and roadside assistance. That compares with a standard guarantee of two years at most luxury brands. "I like BMW and Mercedes, but I have a feeling I may get more for my money with Lexus," says Ignacio Redondo, a legal consultant in Madrid who drives a Saab 900 but is mulling a new Lexus for the first time.

Harder, though, will be conforming to the European concept of luxury. Americans love comfort, size and dependability, while Europeans think luxury means attention to detail and brand heritage. "The biggest selling point for Lexus is that it doesn't break down," says Philipp Rosengarten, analyst at Global Insight Inc.'s automotive group. That's not enough to succeed in Europe. Instead, Lexus needs to create a desire to own the car—and even with plush dealerships and extended warranties, it has kilometers to go before reaching that goal.

By Gail Edmondson in Frankfurt, and Karen Nickel Anhalt in Berlin with Paulo Prada in Madrid

Case 6-6

Pfizer, Inc., Animal Health Products

Gail Oss, territory manager of the Pfizer, Inc., Animal Health Group in western Montana and southeastern Idaho, was driving back to her home office after a day of visiting cattle ranchers in her territory. The combination of the spring sunshine warming the air and the snow-capped peaks of the Bitterroot Mountains provided a stunningly beautiful backdrop for her drive, but the majestic beauty provided little relief for her troubled thoughts.

The North American Free Trade Agreement with Canada and Mexico had hit the local ranchers particularly hard. The influx of beef cattle into the U.S. market from those countries, as well as beef from other countries (e.g., Australia) that entered the United States as a result of more lenient import restrictions in Mexico, had wreaked havoc over the last year. Prices of beef had declined precipitously from the prior year. Ranchers in the past had retained sufficient reserves to come back from a bad year, but this year things were particularly bad. The prices being offered for the calves by the feedlot operators were in many cases lower than the costs of raising those calves. Ranchers' objectives had changed from making a modest income from their cattle operations to minimizing their losses.

In this environment, ranchers were actively seeking ways to cut costs. Gail sold high-quality animal health products, often at a premium price. One way in which ranchers could cut costs was to scrimp on animal health-care products such as vaccines and antibiotics or switch to a lower-cost alternative. The current environment posed a particularly severe threat not only to Gail's company but also to her livelihood. Gail had spent a substantial amount of time and effort cultivating long-term relationships with these ranchers, many of whom she had had to convince of her credibility, given her gender. Because of the time and effort she had spent cultivating these relationships, as well as the camaraderie she felt with her customers, she did not want to see the ranchers in her territory go under. Ranching was an important part of the history of Montana; many ranchers had ties to the land going back generations. They took pride in producing the food for many tables in the United States and other areas of the world. Gail felt that Pfizer could use its fairly significant resources to help these ranchers. Merely lowering the price of her products (if that was possible) would be merely a Band-Aid solution to the problem.

As part of Gail's weekly responsibilities, she communicated via an automated computer system to her sales manager, Tom Brooks (also in Montana), and to the marketing managers at headquarters (in Exton, Pennsylvania). She knew she needed to report the severity of the situation, but more important, she wanted to encourage headquarters to take the bull by the horns, so to speak. She was pondering the message she would write that evening from her kitchen table.

This case was prepared by Jakki Mohr and Sara Streeter, University of Montana. Some of the information in this case has been modified to protect the proprietary nature of firms' marketing strategies. The case is intended to be used as a basis for class discussion rather than to illustrate either effective or ineffective marketing strategies. Support from The Institute for the Study of Business Markets, Pennsylvania State University, is greatly appreciated.

Industry Background

The supply chain (Exhibit 1) for beef begins with the cow/calf producer (the commercial rancher). Commercial ranchers are in the business of breeding and raising cattle for the purpose of selling them to feedlots. Ranchers keep a herd of cows that are bred yearly. The calves generally are born in the early spring, weaned in October, and shipped to feedlots in late October and early November. The ranchers' objectives are to minimize death loss in the herd and breed cows that give birth to low-birth-weight calves (for calving ease), produce beef that will grade low choice by having a good amount of marbling, and produce calves that gain weight quickly. Success measures include the conception rate of cows exposed to bulls, live birth rates, birth weights, weaning weights, loss from death, and profitability. By the time a rancher sells the calves to the feedlot, the name of the game is pounds. The rancher generally wants the biggest calves possible by that time.

Within a commodity market, basic laws of supply and demand are influenced by those in a position to control access to the markets. Four meatpackers controlled roughly 80 percent of the industry. Meatpackers have acted as an intermediary between the meat consumer and the meat producer. This situation has not facilitated a free flow of information throughout the

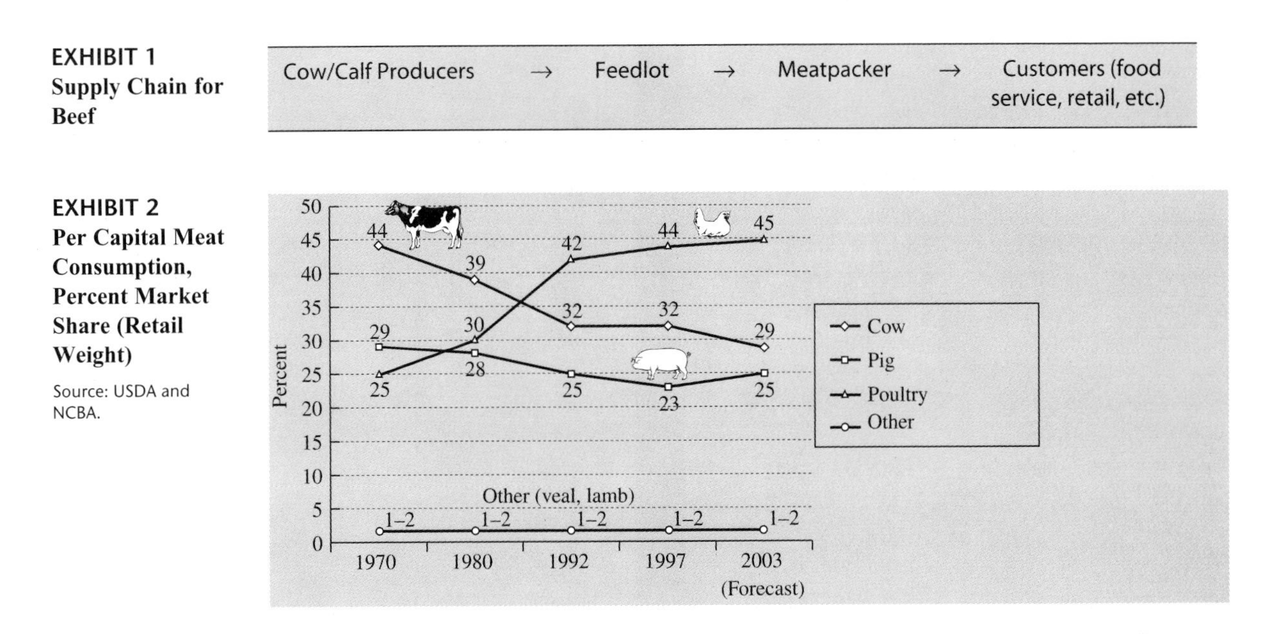

EXHIBIT 1
Supply Chain for Beef

EXHIBIT 2
Per Capital Meat Consumption, Percent Market Share (Retail Weight)

Source: USDA and NCBA.

supply chain, and therefore, the industry has not been strongly consumer-focused.

Exhibit 2 traces the market share for beef, pork, and poultry from 1970 through 1997 and projects changes in the market through 2003. The market share for beef has fallen from 44 percent in 1970 to 32 percent in 1997, a 27 percent drop.

Some of the reasons for the decline were

- Changes in consumer lifestyles (less time spent preparing home-cooked meals). An interesting statistic is that two-thirds of all dinner decisions are made on the same day; among those people, three-fourths don't know what they're going to make at 4:30 p.m.
- Health/nutritional issues (dietary considerations involving cholesterol, fat content, food-borne diseases, etc.).
- Switching to alternative meat products.

In addition, the pork and poultry industries had done a better job of marketing their products. During 1997, the number of new poultry products (for example, stuffed chicken entrees, and gourmet home meal replacements) introduced to the market increased 13 percent from the prior year, compared to an increase of only 3.5 percent for new beef products. And retail pricing for beef remained stubbornly high (although this high price did not translate into higher prices for the calves on a per weight basis to the ranchers, as discussed below).

Based on the historical data shown in Exhibit 3, the beef production cycle spans a 12-year period in which production levels expand and contract. As the exhibit shows, the amount of beef produced (bars in the chart, millions of pounds on the left-hand scale) increased through the mid-1990s despite the declining beef consumption in the United States shown in Exhibit 2. This relationship between production and consumption is consistent with other commodity markets, where there is an inverse relationship between supply and demand.

Some of the reasons for increased beef production in the mid-1990s were

- Herd liquidation: Low cattle prices coupled with the high cost of feed drove some producers out of business.
- Improved genetics and animal health/nutrition increased production yields; indeed, although cow numbers had decreased by 10 percent since 1985 (as noted in Exhibit 4, on next page), productivity per cow increased by 29 percent.
- Exports of beef increased sevenfold since 1985 (to 2 billion pounds); key markets include Japan (54 percent of export volume), Canada (16 percent), Korea (11 percent), and Mexico (9 percent).

Exhibit 3 also shows that the price the ranchers received for their beef cattle varied inversely with production (right-hand scale). Although calf prices were expected to rise slightly through the late 1990s and early 2000s, the prices paid were still far below the relatively high prices consumers paid at retail. One of the reasons given for the relatively low prices paid to ranchers on a per pound basis for their calves was the high degree of concentration at the meatpacker level of the supply chain. As was noted previously, four packing houses

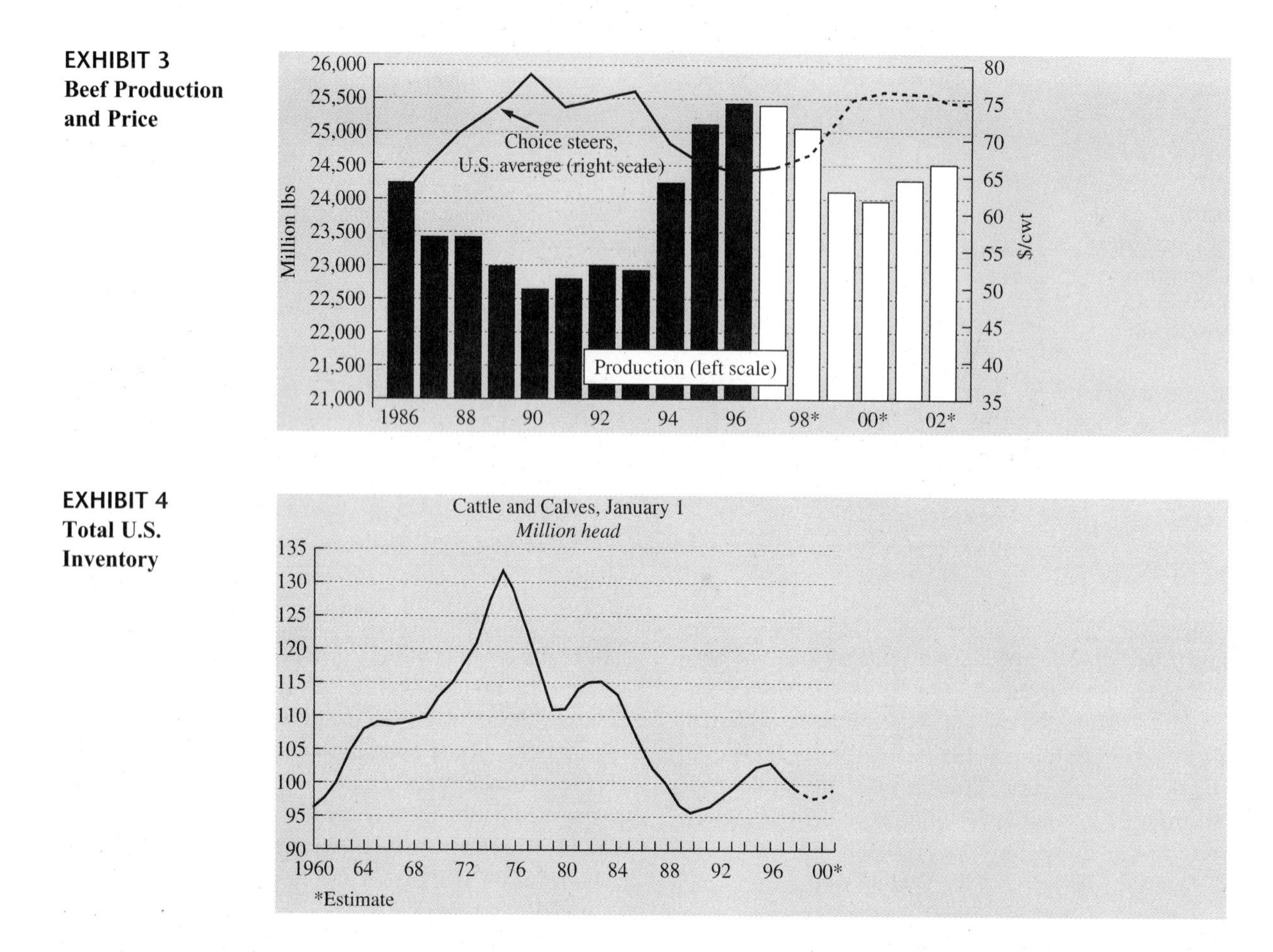

EXHIBIT 3
Beef Production and Price

EXHIBIT 4
Total U.S. Inventory

controlled access to the market. Some ranchers believed that this gave the packing houses near-monopoly power in setting prices both for what they would pay feedlot operators for the calves and for the prices charged to their downstream customers (the grocery store chains). Although the U.S. government had investigated the possibility of collusion among packers, the evidence was not sufficient to draw any firm conclusions.

To further complicate matters, NAFTA, passed in 1989, had given open access to the U.S. markets to Mexican and Canadian ranchers. The lowering of trade barriers, coupled with weakness in the Canadian dollar and the Mexican peso, made imported livestock cheap compared to U.S.-grown animals. As a result, thousands of head of cattle came streaming across the borders. The flow was heaviest from Canada.

During the summer of 1998, ranchers had been quite vocal in drawing attention to the influx of cattle from Canada. Local governments were somewhat responsive to their concerns. Indeed, trucks carrying Canadian cattle had been turned back at the border for minor infractions, such as licensing. In addition, the trucks often were pulled over for inspections. A private coalition of ranchers calling itself the Ranchers-Cattlemen Action Legal Foundation (R-CALF) filed three separate petitions with the U.S. International Trade Commission (ITC) on October 1, 1998, two against Canada and one against Mexico, asking for U.S. government trade investigations. The group requested that antidumping duties be levied on meat or livestock imports from those two countries. The Montana Stockgrowers Association had been an early and steadfast supporter of R-CALF.

The ITC determined that there was evidence to support the charge that the Canadian cattle imports were causing material injury to U.S. domestic cattle producers. The Department of Commerce began to collect information on Canadian subsidies and the prices at which Canadian cattle were sold in Canada and in the United States. In the case against Mexico, the ITC determined that there was no indication that imports of live cattle from Mexico were causing "material injury" to the domestic industry in the United States. Dissatisfied with the response, R-CALF decided to appeal the case to the Court of International Trade.

Ranchers were doing whatever they could to minimize the impact of NAFTA on their livelihoods; however, some could not sustain their operations in light of the lower cattle prices. The number of cattle operations was declining. In many cases, smaller ranchers were selling out to their larger neighbors. This reality was reflected in the cattle inventory statistics shown in Exhibit 4.

The number of cattle kept by U.S. ranchers had declined from a high of approximately 132 million head in 1975 to just under 100 million head in 1998. As was noted previously, improvements in genetics and animal health and nutrition allowed ranchers to increase production yields even with fewer head.

Additional Industry Changes

Some of the changes that had occurred in the poultry and pork industries, including more ready-to-eat products and branded products, were expected to import into the cattle industry. Industry analysts believed that the beef industry would need to develop products that could be more easily prepared and develop branded products that consumers could recognize and rely on for quality and convenience. In addition, industry analysts believed that the beef industry would have to improve the quality of its products (in terms of more consistent taste and tenderness), as currently only 25 percent of the beef produced met quality targets.

The development of branded beef would require a tracking system from "birth to beef" in the supply chain. Such tracking would allow standardized health, quality, and management protocols as well as improved feedback through the entire production model. This change would also necessitate that the producers be more closely linked to the feedlots to improve the quality of the beef. Branded beef production would move the industry from a cost-based (production) model to a value-added model. Better coordination along the supply chain would ensure an increased flow of information from the consumer to the producer. Alliances between the cow/calf producer and the feedlots would allow ranchers to better track the success of their calves (based on health and weight gain). Such data could allow the ranchers to further improve the genetics of their herds by tracking which cow/bull combinations had delivered the higher-yield calves. As part of these trends, some degree of integration or vertical coordination will occur in the beef industry. Ranchers will have to participate to ensure market access for their product. Ranchers will have to think beyond the boundaries of their own ranches.

Pfizer Animal Health Group

Pfizer, Inc., is a research-based, diversified health-care company with global operations. Pfizer Animal Health is one of the corporation's three major business groups (the other two being the Consumer Health Care Group and U.S. Pharmaceuticals). The Animal Health Products Group accounted for roughly 12 percent of the company's revenues in 1998.

Pfizer Animal Health products are sold to veterinarians and animal health distributors in more than 140 countries around the world for use by livestock producers and horse and pet owners; the products are used in more than 30 animal species. Pfizer Animal Health is committed to providing high-quality, research-based health products for livestock and companion animals. The company continues to invest significant funds for research and development. As a result, Pfizer has many new animal health products in its research pipeline, a number of which have already been introduced in some international markets and will become available in the United States in the next several years.

As Exhibit 5 shows, the Animal Health Group is divided into a North American Region with a U.S. Livestock Division, a U.S. Companion Animal Division (cats, dogs, etc.), and Canada. The Cow/Calf division falls under the Cattle Business Unit within the Livestock Division. That division is organized further by product type.

The marketing managers for each cattle market segment work closely with product managers and sales managers to ensure that timely, accurate information is received from the field. Territory managers responsible for all sales activities report to an area sales manager, who in turn reports to the national sales and marketing manager. Territory managers typically are compensated on a roughly 80 percent salary/20 percent commission basis. This percentage varies by salesperson by year: In a good year the commission might be a much higher percentage of overall earnings, while in a bad year the salary component might be a greater percentage of the salesperson's overall earnings.

Marketing Strategy

Pfizer's Cow/Calf Division offers a full range of products to cattle ranchers, including vaccines for both newborn calves and their mothers, medications (dewormers, antidiarrheals), and antibiotics (for pneumonia and other diseases). Pfizer's sophisticated research and development system has resulted in a number of new and useful products for the market. For

EXHIBIT 5
Pfizer Animal Health Organization

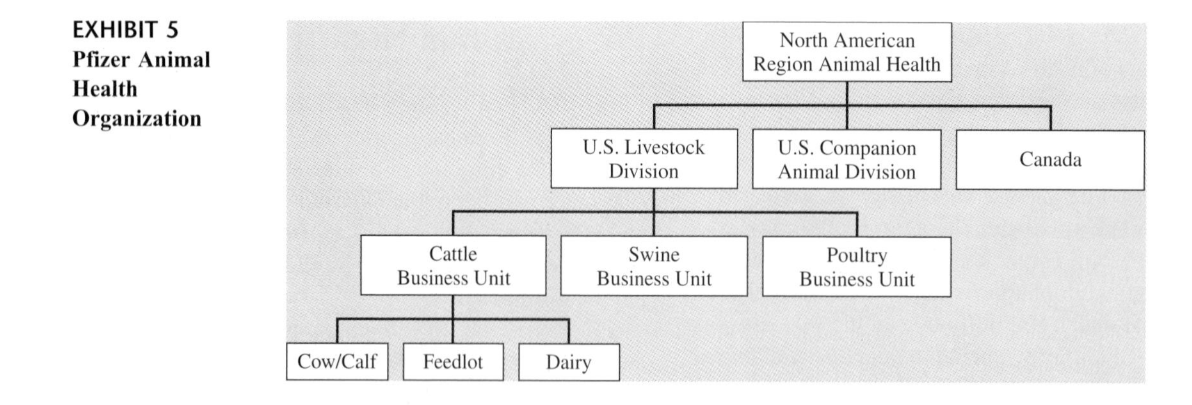

example, Pfizer developed a long-lasting dewormer that was poured along the cow's back. This technology was a significant time-saver for the rancher, eliminating the need to administer an oral medication or an injection. Moreover, Pfizer had been the first company to come up with a modified live and killed virus vaccine, a significant technological breakthrough which provided safety in pregnant animals and the efficacy of a modified live virus.

Pfizer offered a diverse product line to cow/calf ranchers. Some of Pfizer's key product lines are compared to those of competitors in Exhibit 6.

Pfizer segmented ranchers in the cow/calf business on the basis of herd size, as shown in Exhibit 7.

Hobbyists in many cases are ranchers who run their cattle businesses as a sideline to another job. Traditionalists' main livelihood comes from their cattle operations. Business segment operations are large ranches owned by either a family or a corporation.

Pfizer's extensive network of field sales representatives visits the ranchers to inform them about new and existing products. Time spent with accounts typically was allocated on the basis of volume of product purchased.

Pfizer positioned its products on the combination of superior science (resulting from its significant R&D efforts) and high-quality production/quality control techniques. For example, although other companies in the market (particularly producers of generics) used similar formulations in their products, on occasion they did not have good quality control in the production line, resulting in batches of ineffective vaccines and recalls. Pfizer backed its products completely, using its Technical Services Department. If ranchers had any kind of health or nutritional problem with their herds, they could call on a team of Pfizer technical specialists who would work with the local veterinarian, utilizing blood and other diagnostics to identify the problem and suggest a solution.

Pfizer also was very deeply involved in the cattle industry. Each territory manager was given an annual budget that included discretionary funds to be spent in his or her territory to sponsor industry activities such as seminars on herd health, stock shows, and 4-H. Gail Oss, for example, chose to spend a significant portion of her discretionary funds to sponsor meetings and conferences for the Montana Stockgrower's Association which might include a veterinarian or a professor from the extension office of a state university speaking on issues pertinent to ranchers.

The majority of Pfizer's trade advertising was focused on specific products and appeared in cattle industry publications such as *Beef Magazine* and *Bovine Veterinarian*. One ad read, "More veterinarians are satisfied with [Pfizer's] Dectomax Pour-On" and went on to describe veterinarians' greater satisfaction with and likelihood of recommending Dectomax compared to a key competitor, Ivomec:

> Eighty-four percent of veterinarians who recommended Dectomax Pour-On said they were satisfied or very satisfied with its performance—compared to only 51% who were satisfied or very satisfied with Ivomec Eprinex Pour-On . . . If choosing only between Dectomax and Ivomec, over three out of four veterinarians would choose to recommend Dectomax Pour-On.

Another ad read, "Calf Health Program Boosts Prices by Up to $21 More per Head." The data in the copy-intensive ad highlighted the fact that "cow-calf producers enrolled in value-added programs like Pfizer Select Vaccine programs are being rewarded for their efforts with top-of-the-market prices." Such programs are based on a consistent program of vaccinating animals with specific products and provide optimal disease protection. The programs result in cattle that perform more consistently and predictably in terms of weight

EXHIBIT 6 Comparison of Competitors' Product Lines

Source: Wood MacKenzie Animal Health Market Review and Veterinary Company Profiles, both done on a worldwide basis.

Company	Pfizer	American Home Products (Fort Dodge)	Bayer
Sales and, profitability	10-year average annual sales growth increase of 3.8%; average for global veterinary market is 6.9%. Profit rate in 1997 was 8.4%; market share in 1997 was 15.3%.	10-year average annual sales growth increase of 7.8%; average for global veterinary market is 6.9%. Profit rate in 1997 was 11.0%; market share was 9.0%.	10-year average annual sales growth increase of 10.2%; average for global veterinary market is 6.9%. Profit rate in 1997 was 16.8%; market share was 10.9%.
Bovine diseases covered by product range	IBR; P1-3; BVD; BRSV; leptospira; rotavirus; coronavirus; campylobacter; clostridia; *E. coli*; pasteurellosis; *Haemophilus*	Pasteurellosis; enterotoxaemia; chlamydia; salmonella; IBR; P1-3; brucellosis; rabies; *E. coli*; anaplasmosis; tetanus; BVD; BRSV; leptospirosis; trichomonas; campylobacter; papilloma; *Haemophilus*	IBR; FMD; IPV; P1-3; balanoposthitis; clostridia; *Haemophilus*; BRSV; BVD; leptospira; *E. coli*; rhinotracheitis; campylobacter
Significant products for cattle	Comprehensive product line; anti-infectives have formed basis of product line for many years; vaccine businesses also very important; also sells a performance enhancer, virginiamycin; parasiticides, led by Dectomax, starting to make significant impact on sales; Valbazen anthelmintic; broad range of general pharmaceuticals.	Predominantly a vaccine company; antibiotics centered on antimastitis products; anti-infectives based on penicillins, tetracyclines, sulphonamides, and quinolones; parasiticides led by Cydectin; main products in general pharmaceuticals are anabolic implants for muscle growth.	Product range biased toward parasiticides, particularly ectoparasiticides, and antibiotics; overall product range is diverse; some mastitis antimicrobials; wide range of pharmaceuticals, but sales value of each product is limited; focus is more on companion animal market.
Strengths	Strong manufacturing capabilities based on fermentation expertise and capacity; global marketing coverage supported by strategic local manufacture; strong range of new products in early commercialization; broad product range with strength in companion animals	Leading global vaccine business; good international exposure; comprehensive vaccine product range; potential for growth through Cydectin	Growing market in expanding companion animal sector; solid in-house manufacturing supported by global distribution capability; business focused on key market areas

EXHIBIT 6 (continued)

Company	Pfizer	American Home Products (Fort Dodge)	Bayer
Weaknesses	North America still dominates turnover; high proportion of sales due to off-patent products; heavily dependent on performance of livestock markets.	Business with disparate parts requiring strong central focus; except for vaccines, product range is dominated by commodity products; R&D likely to be reduced.	Underweight in United States; lack of critical mass in biologicals; no blockbuster product in North American market; narrow anti-infectives product portfolio; current R&D emphasis away from new product discovery.
Percent of R&D to sales*	5	3	3
Position on quality versus price†	5	3.5	3
Price support of distribution channel‡	2	4	3

*Specific ratios are considered proprietary. Hence, a general rating scale is used where 5 means a higher percentage of R&D/sales and 1 is a lower percentage.
†5 = focus on quality only; 1 = focus on low price only.
‡5 = strong emphasis on SPIFs (Special Promotional Incentive Funds) and price-related trade promotions; 1 = low emphasis.

EXHIBIT 7
Pfizer Market Segments, 1998

Segment	Number of Cattle	Number of Operations	Percent of National Cattle Inventory
Hobbyist	<100	808,000	50%
Traditionalist	100–499	69,000	36
Business	500+	5,900	14

gain and beef quality, resulting in higher prices at sale time.

Although the territory managers called on the ranchers (as well as the veterinarians, distributors, and dealers) in their territories, they sold no products directly to the ranchers. Ranchers could buy their animal health products from a local veterinarian or a distributor or dealer (such as a feed and seed store). The percentage of product flowing through vets or distributors and dealers varied significantly by region. In areas where feedlots (as opposed to cow/calf ranchers) were the predominant customers, 95 percent of the product might flow through distributors. In areas where ranchers were the predominant customers, vets might sell 50 percent of the product, depending on customer preferences.

Vets were particularly important in light of the fact that the overwhelming majority of ranchers said that the person they trusted the most when it came to managing the health of the herd was the veterinarian. Pfizer capitalizes on this trust in the vet in its marketing program. When the vet recommends a Pfizer product to a rancher, the vet gives the rancher a coded coupon which can be redeemed at either a vet clinic or a supply house. When the coupon is sent back to Pfizer for reimbursement, the vet is credited for servicing that product regardless of where the product is purchased.

Pfizer offers some trade promotions to vets and distributors, including volume rebate programs and price promotions on certain products during busy seasonal periods. However, Pfizer's competitors often gave much more significant discounts and SPIFs to distributors. As a result, when a rancher went to a distributor to buy a product the vet had recommended, the distributor might switch the rancher to a similar product on which the distributor was making more of a profit. If it was a Pfizer product the vet had recommended, the distributor might switch the rancher to a competitor's product. Pfizer historically had avoided competing on the basis of such promotional tactics, feeling instead that redirecting such funds back into R&D resulted in better long-term benefits for its customers.

As Gail pondered these various facets of the company's market position and strategies, she decided to take a strong stance in her weekly memo. It was time to cut the bull.

Case 6-7

Capital

It is the end of July 1991 and most Parisians are preparing to leave on holiday. But not Dr. Andreas Wiele. He, as project and executive manager, and the other members of the Prisma Presse team developing a new business magazine called *Capital* have other things on their minds. The zero issue of *Capital* went down well with the focus group they have just been watching over closed-circuit TV. The problem is the market itself. The economic situation is bad—advertising in business magazines has dropped by about 20 percent since the beginning of the year and circulation is still stagnant. Should they go ahead with the planned launch in September or postpone until the economic situation improves? If they do launch, key marketing decisions still remain to be taken: the magazine's price, its distribution, and communication policies.

Prisma Presse: Gruner+Jahr's French Subsidiary

Prisma Presse, with offices in the center of Paris close to the Champs-Elysèes, was founded in 1978 by the then 41-year-old Axel Ganz as the French subsidiary of Gruner+Jahr (Exhibit 1), the German publishing company headquartered in Hamburg, itself a subsidiary of the multimedia Bertelsmann Group. Trained as a journalist, Axel Ganz had already held various senior positions with leading magazine publishing companies.

During its 13 years, Prisma Presse has launched six magazines and acquired two more, increasing the circulation of the latter by a factor of three since taking them over in 1989. All Prisma Presse magazines are among the leaders in their segments (Exhibit 2). This compares favorably with the industry average. Of a total 173 new consumer magazines launched between 1987 and 1990 in France, only 119 (69 percent) were still going at the end of 1990. This enviable track record has earned Axel Ganz such sobriquets as "magazine alchemist" and "man with the Midas touch."

With a 1990–91 turnover of F2 billion (Exhibit 3), Prisma Presse has become the second biggest magazine publisher in France. It concentrates effort on text and layout in its magazines, and outsources such activities as documentation, photography, printing, and distribution. Prisma Presse is structured around the individual magazine (Exhibit 4). Each is headed by a duo consisting of an executive editor and an editor-in-chief, jointly responsible for editorial policies, staffing, circulation, and revenues of the magazine. The executive editor, often working on two magazines, is specifically responsible for financial results, while the editor-in-chief, usually assigned to one magazine only, is specifically responsible for execution of editorial policy. Each magazine has its own staff of journalists, art team, and advertising department. The advertising departments of the different magazines compete vigorously for business, sometimes against other Prisma Presse magazines. Coordination of advertising policy is one of the tasks of the corporate advertising business manager.

The staff of a successful magazine is regarded by management as a pool of talent from which inside members of future magazines are recruited. For example, *Prima* was the breeding ground for subsequent women's magazines. These insiders usually account for about half of the staff of a new magazine. They are used especially on the art team, because the visual concept across the range is basically the same. Outside recruitment brings in journalists with knowledge in content areas like economics, business, fashion, cooking, and travel.

Market research, production and distribution management, and some other functions are taken care of

This case was written by Reinhard Angelmar, professor of marketing, INSEAD, with the assistance of Wolfgang Munk (MBA 1992) and Thierry Azalbert (MBA 1992). It is intended to be used as a basis for class discussion rather than to illustrate either effective or ineffective handling of an administrative situation.

EXHIBIT 1
Gruner+Jahr Publications outside France

GERMANY
Magazines: *Art, Brigitte, Capital, Decoration, Elterns, Essen&Trinken, FF, Flora, Frau im Spiegel, Frau im Spiegel Rätsel, Geo, Geo Special, Geo Wissen, Häuser, Impulse, Marie-Claire,* Max,* Mein Kind und ich, Neues Wohnen, PM. Magazin, P.M. Logik Trainer, Schöner Wohnen, Prima, Saison, Sandra, Schöner Essen, Sonntagspost, Sports, Stern, Wochenpost, Yps.*
Newspapers: *Berliner Kurier, Berliner Zeitung, Dresdner Morgenpost, Chemnitzer Morgenpost, Hamburger Morgenpost, Mecklenburger Morgenpost, Leipziger Morgenpost, Sächsische Zeitung.*

SPAIN
Dunia, Geo, Mia, Mux Interessante, Natura, Ser Padres Hoy, Estar Viva, Cosmopolitan.*

UNITED KINGDOM
Best, Prima, Focus.

UNITED STATES
Parents, YM.

ITALY
Vera, Focus*.*

* Joint venture.

EXHIBIT 2 Prisma Presses: Product Portfolio, 1991

GEO
Travel/Discovery of the Beauty of Nature and Civilization
upper middle class
Monthly circulation: 580,000
Nr. 1 travel magazine
Launch: 1979

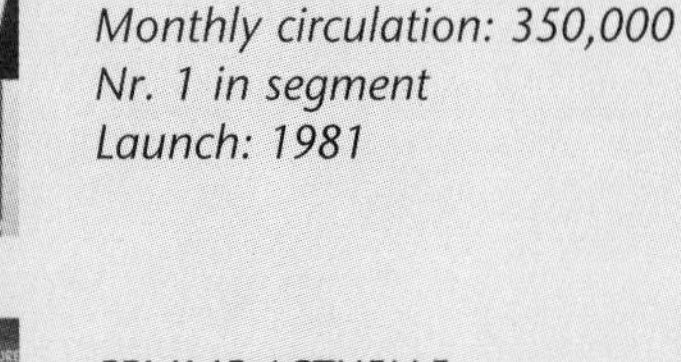

ÇA M'INTÉRESSE
Scientific Popularization
adolescents/young adults
Monthly circulation: 350,000
Nr. 1 in segment
Launch: 1981

PRIMA
Women's Magazine
good housekeepers and wives
Monthly circulation: 1,220,000
Nr. 1 women's monthly
Launch: 1982

FEMME ACTUELLE
Women's Magazine
Weekly circulation: 1,800,000
Nr. 1 women's weekly
Launch: 1984

TÉLÉ LOISIRS
TV Magazine
Weekly circulation: 1,220,000
Nr. 4 TV Magazine
Launch: 1986

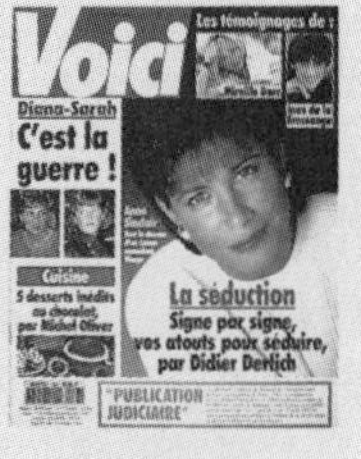

VOICI
The Celebrities' Private Lives
Weekly circulation: 600,000
Nr. 1 women's picture magazine
Launch: 1987

CUISINE ACTUELLE
Gourmet Magazine
Monthly circulation: 350,000
Nr. 1 food magazine
Acquired in 1989

GUIDE CUISINE
Family food magazine
Monthly circulation: 230,000
Nr. 2 food magazine
Acquired in 1989

CAPITAL
Monthly Business Magazine

Planned launch date:
September 1991

by specialized departments covering all Prisma Presse magazines. Tight cost controls create a sense of leanness throughout the organization.

Editorial Principles at Prisma Presse

Axel Ganz has strong convictions regarding the basic editorial principles that he imprints on all Prisma Presse magazines, regardless of their content area.

Reader/Circulation Focus

Magazines derive revenue both from readers (circulation) and advertising. In contrast to some publishers who are more advertiser- than reader-oriented, Axel Ganz's priority is clearly the reader: "Circulation is where the business is. You can act on it—and we must do everything we can to maximize it—whereas advertising also depends on factors beyond our control, like the overall economic situation." A Prisma Presse executive confirms: "Ganz is obsessed with circulation; when a

EXHIBIT 3
Key Data: Prisma Presse, Gruner+Jahr, Bertelsmann

	1987–88	1988–89	1989–90	1990–91
Prisma Presse (in Million FF)				
Total revenues	1,621	1,762	1,865	2,057
Growth		9%	6%	10%
Circulation revenues	1,253	1,335	1,433	1,606
Advertising revenues	347	401	405	424
Profits	83	104	119	159
% of revenues	5%	6%	6%	8%
Nr. of employees	414	448	481	527
Revenues/employee	4	4	4	4
Gruner+Jahr (in Million DM)				
Total revenues	2,773	2,987	3,099	3,284
Growth		8%	4%	6%
Profits	223	255	272	200
% of revenues	8%	9%	9%	6%
Nr. of employees	8,745	9,170	9,286	9,613
Bertelsmann Group (in Million DM)				
Total revenues	11,299	12,483	13,313	14,483
Growth		10%	7%	9%
Profits	362	402	510	540
% of revenues	3%	3%	4%	4%

Average 1991 exchange rates were: 3.3FF for 1DM, 5.6FF for 1$, 1.7DM for 1$. The financial year ends on June 30.

magazine's circulation starts declining, he sounds the alarm." Circulation determines the major part of bonus payments, which range from 60 percent of the annual salary for the managing duo to two months' additional salary for some of the regular staff. "When circulation objectives are not met, Axel Ganz puts on enormous pressure," comments one editor-in-chief. Managers who repeatedly fail to achieve objectives are asked to leave. "In this company, we get rid of teams that don't win," explains one executive.

Because the bulk of Prisma Presse circulation comes from volatile newsstand sales rather than from more stable subscriptions, reader appeal shows up quickly in circulation figures. Days when circulation figures come out have everyone in a state of feverish excitement. Outstanding results are celebrated, whereas disappointing circulation calls for quick remedial action, which may escalate from minor changes to a major overhaul. For example, *Voici*'s circulation increased from 240,000 at launch to 600,000 three years later, thanks to a series of changes resulting in the complete repositioning of *Voici* from a family magazine to one concentrating on the "celebrities' private lives."

A constant stream of market research data provides each magazine with information about its readers, and many team members are usually present to watch the focus groups which are organized regularly throughout France. This close attention to the reader is rather unusual in the French press. According to one Prisma Presse executive, "Competitors are managed by Parisian journalists who only think of their egos and their connections, and who impose the dictate of their good taste. This is intellectual terrorism. As for us, we can put ourselves in the shoes of the reader from the Creuse [a backward rural area in France]." One observer put it like this: "Prisma is to the French press what Disney is to the French cinema."

A Clear Concept and Consistent Implementation

Each magazine must have a clear concept (for example, "to discover and show the beautiful things on earth, which need to be preserved," *Geo*) and every aspect of the magazine (topics, style of presentation, visuals, layout, cover, etc.) must be consistent with this concept. To Axel Ganz, a successful magazine

EXHIBIT 4
Prisma Presse: Simplified Organization Chart, 1991

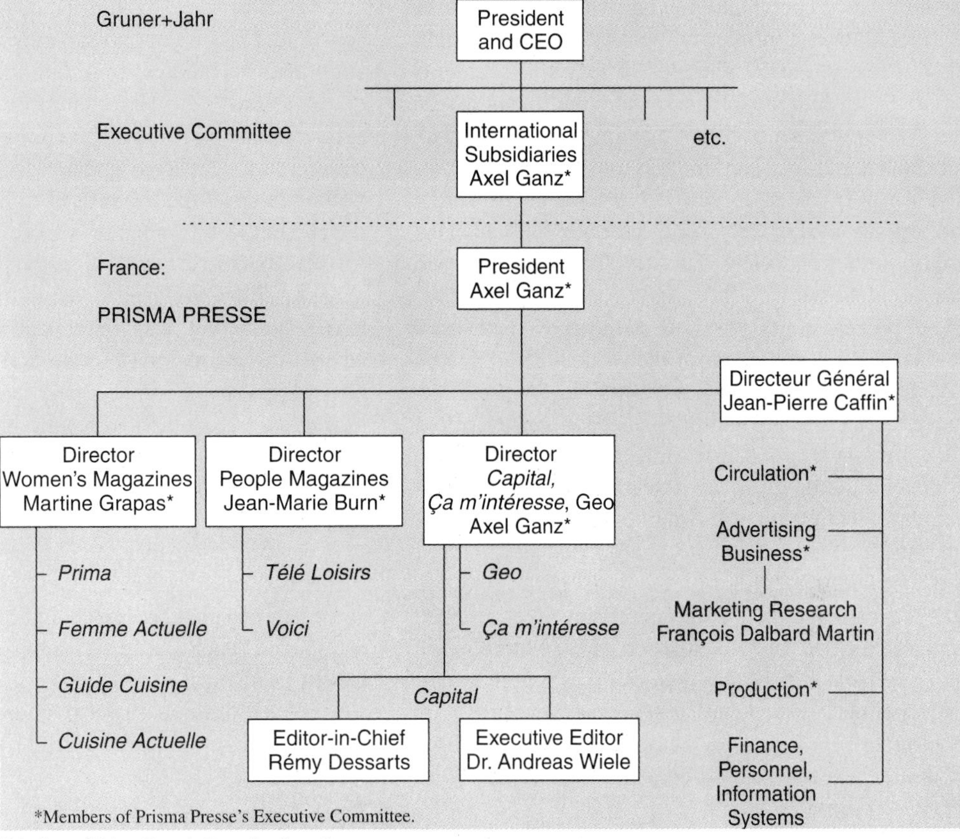

*Members of Prisma Presse's Executive Committee.

is like any other successful brand that acquires a distinctive identity: "Why does a reader prefer one magazine to another, although often both cover the same subjects? Because each title projects a specific image and creates a special kind of relationship with the reader." The managing team must ensure that every issue fits the concept: "There may be doubts and discussions, but the managing team must identify enough with the concept of their magazine to sense immediately, nine times out of 10, whether a topic is right or not," Axel Ganz comments.

Precise, Well-Researched Information

Prisma Presse has a strict policy of not allowing advertisers to interfere in editorial content, unlike some other publishers, where advertisers sometimes influence articles that they judge detrimental to their own interests, or where journalists use company press releases as main sources for their articles.

Attractive Presentation

Presentation in all Prisma Presse magazines is geared for maximum readability: short articles ("right length for a ride in the Metro"), short words ("no more than three syllables"), short sentences, and comprehensible titles. "You have to understand the conditions in which people read—poor lighting, ill-fitting glasses, etc.—it's these kinds of details that make the difference," explains one executive. The marrying of text and visuals is vital. The editorial policy of most Prisma Presse magazines stipulates that "topics are chosen only if it is possible to produce a matching visual representation."

The art directors are the guardians of the Prisma Presse formula for attractive presentation. They train the journalists in the magic formula, follow each issue through until the final check, and are always on the lookout for changes that would enhance appeal. Together with the editors-in-chief they comprise the main bottleneck and constraint for the launch of new magazines by Prisma Presse.

Searching for a New Idea

To sustain Prisma Presse's growth, Axel Ganz has set as an objective the launching of a new magazine every 18 months. The new products should have high circulation potential, be innovative rather than imitative, and use primarily newsstand distribution, Prisma Presse's main channel. The only segments specifically excluded are newspapers and news magazines. "There are sensibilities that should not be hurt," Axel Ganz explains. "Newspapers and news magazines deal with politics, and even if we took an objective stand on an issue, we would probably be accused of taking a German view. The time isn't right. In two generations, possibly. . ."

Axel Ganz, together with Martine Grapas and Jean-Marie Burn, directors for the women's and people magazines respectively, are responsible formally for coming up with ideas for magazines. Ideas may float around for many years, and only a few ever make it into development. In his own search for new product ideas, Axel Ganz monitors market trends in all segments and different countries, until "one day, out of this observation emerges a hunch that a particular area might be promising." Axel Ganz may see promise where others see only desolation. For example, he launched *Prima* and *Femme Actuelle* in a segment that, despite being crowded with 15 magazines, had been declining for 10 years. He reasoned that the decline was due not to a lack of demand, but because the offering was unsatisfactory.

Axel Ganz had a hunch that the business magazine market in France might be promising. Business magazines provide readers with business and economic news and analyses across all industries. The leading title in France was *L'Expansion* (a biweekly), which created the market in 1967, followed in 1975 by *Le Nouvel Economiste* (a weekly). In 1984, the Mitterrand presidency's sudden shift from anti- to probusiness gave rise to an increased interest in business information and triggered a rash of product launches, not all of which survived.

Fortune France, the most recent business magazine launched in February 1988, was an intriguing case. The intention was clear: Take advantage of *Fortune*'s awareness and image among international advertisers and top executives, while overcoming the language barrier which resulted, for the English-language edition, in a circulation of a mere 5,000 in France. *Fortune France* was published by a 50–50 joint venture between *Fortune*'s U.S. publisher Time–Warner and its French partner Hachette, the leading publisher in France. They shared the launch investment of F40 million and expected to reach payback within three years. The circulation goal was 50,000 initially, rising to 80,000 after three to four years.

Fortune France's editorial team consisted of eight full-time French journalists plus a network of correspondents. Changes in content, layout, and paper quality resulted in a glamorous, lifestyle-oriented magazine which had little in common with its American counterpart. "This magazine does not appear to be willing to upset the business establishment. One finds in it neither the bite nor the impertinence which account for the appeal of the U.S. magazine," commented one observer. *Fortune France* cost F30, sold mainly through newsstands, and was launched with a F2.5 million advertising campaign on radio and in the national press as well as by a direct mail campaign. Advertising business took off briskly despite high rates, but circulation remained low. Paid circulation reached 37,000 when *Fortune France* was eventually discontinued in June 1990.

Axel Ganz felt that the French business magazines suffered from two weaknesses. First, the older magazines had not changed much and looked somewhat old-fashioned. Second, all titles appeared light on editorial quality, and most seemed to believe more in attracting subscribers through expensive direct mail campaigns than through a high-quality product.

Recruitment of a Management Team to Fill a Blank Sheet of Paper

In Fall 1989 Axel Ganz transformed his hunch into a formal development project code-named *Hermès*, due for launch in 1991. Funds for development were budgeted in the three-year 1990–93 plan approved by Gruner+Jahr.

Gruner+Jahr was already familiar with the business magazine market as the publisher of Capital, the leading business magazine in Germany. But Axel Ganz decided to start from a blank sheet of paper, without any a priori ideas about the concept or name. "I don't believe in a Euro-magazine which would be completely identical in all countries. You can't simply export and translate magazines, which are cultural products. You can transpose to another country a concept which has proven its worth elsewhere, but you have to reshape and modify it to adapt it to the local context. Up-market magazines like Geo can be internationalized more easily, because these consumers become more similar, whereas mass market magazines like Prima address a more popular audience, for which local peculiarities—eating and leisure habits, for example—are very important."

In Spring 1990, Axel Ganz set out to recruit the management team for the new magazine. He found a project and executive manager in 28-year-old Dr. Andreas Wiele, an assistant to the president and CEO of Gruner+Jahr in Hamburg, who had previously worked for one year as a journalist for a Hamburg newspaper after studying law. Dr. Wiele joined Prisma Presse in Paris in July 1990.

Finding an appropriate editor-in-chief took much longer, despite the large number of candidates attracted by Prisma Presse's reputation. Ganz was looking for somebody with experience in the French business press, not a star journalist, but someone willing to apply Prisma Presse's editorial principles to business magazines. The choice finally went to 36-year-old Rèmy Dessarts, a graduate of a Paris business school who had spent eight years at *L'Expansion* before becoming associate editor of the business magazine *A pour Affaires.* Rèmy Dessarts joined in September.

Forty-eight-year-old Thierry Rouxel, assigned as art director for *Hermès*, was the third key member of the team. An old hand with Prisma Presse, Thierry Rouxel brought with him the all-important Prisma Presse presentation know-how to the project.

Through the recruitment process, word got out about Prisma Presse's intentions. But competitors did not take the project seriously, doubting that a company publishing mainly for women could successfully enter the business magazine market.

Analyzing the Market for Business Magazines

Dr. Wiele's major task during the initial months consisted of gathering and analyzing information on business magazines and other relevant publications (Exhibit 5). He found that circulation stagnation was hitting not only business magazines (Exhibit 6), but all segments of the economic press, with the exception of personal finance magazines like *Le Revenu Français* (170,000 circulation) and *Mieux Vivre* (139,000 circulation), which had enjoyed a compound annual growth of 8 percent over the last 10 years. The number of advertising pages in business magazines had been declining since 1988, with advertising revenues dipping slightly for the first time during 1990 (Exhibit 7).

Dr. Wiele noticed some striking differences between the French and German business magazine markets:

- Total circulation was higher in France, yet supply was much more fragmented. France had many more titles, each with a relatively small circulation; e.g., *L'Expansion*, with 150,000 was the leading title in France, compared to 250,000 for *Capital*, the leader in Germany.
- French magazines invested less in editorial content. They employed fewer journalists, everyone of whom had to produce more editorial pages than their counterparts in Germany.
- Subscription discounts and sales were both much higher in France than in Germany; e.g., 84 percent of *L'Expansion*'s circulation came from subscriptions (Exhibit 8) compared to 59 percent for *Capital.*
- German business magazines featured many more "personal service" topics (e.g., how to reduce taxes, manage one's career, invest money) than French business magazines, which left these subjects to specialized magazines such as *Le Revenu Français* and *Mieux Vivre*.

To obtain a broader perspective on the topics that could be covered by *Hermès*, Dr. Wiele analyzed the leading business magazines in Europe and the U.S. This survey provided the basis for a detailed content analysis of the French business magazines (Exhibit 9).

The total reader potential for business magazines in France was estimated at 4.8 million, comprising 1.5 million senior and middle managers in business firms (*chefs d'entreprise et cadres supèrieurs en entreprise*), 1.2 million top nonbusiness professionals such as lawyers, doctors, and senior civil servants, and 2.1 million entry-level managers (*cadres moyens*). Français Dalbard-Martin, Prisma Presse's market research specialist, pointed out that only 45 percent of the 4.8 million potential readers had actually read a business magazine during the preceding 12 months. The main reader target for *Hermès* would be the 1.5 million senior and middle managers in business firms. Only 59 percent of these were readers of business magazines.

Advertisers in French business magazines were also interested in reaching the top nonbusiness professionals, in addition to senior and middle managers in business. The combined 2.7 million person advertising target group was called the executives (*affaires et cadres supèrieurs*). The price which a business magazine could charge for advertising space depended mainly on (1) its absolute number (or, equivalently, its penetration) of "executive" readers, (2) the share of "executives" among its readers, and (3) the total number of buyers (paid circulation). Exhibit 10 shows the readership profile of the main competitors and the desired profile of *Hermès* readers.

Two focus groups were held with members from the *Hermès* target group in Fall 1990 to understand their

EXHIBIT 5 Main Economic Magazines in France, 1991

L'EXPANSION
general business magazine
twice a month
circulation: 149,000
Launch: 1967

LE NOUVEL ECONOMISTE
general business magazine
weekly
circulation: 89,000
Launch: 1975

SCIENCE & VIE ECONOMIE
general business magazine
monthly
circulation: 106,000
Launch: 1984

DYNASTEURS
general business magazine
monthly
circulation: 95,000
Launch: 1985

L'ENTREPRISE
business magazine for owners of
small businesses
monthly
circulation: 64,000
Launch: 1985

A POUR AFFAIRES
general business magazine
monthly
circulation: 42,000
Launch: 1985

CHALLENGES
general business magazine
monthly
circulation: 64,000
Launch: 1985

LE REVENU FRANÇAIS
personal finance magazine
monthly
circulation: 170,000
Launch: 1968

MIEUX VIVRE
personal finance magazine
monthly
circulation: 138,000
Launch: 1979

Note: All circulation figures refer to the average 1990 paid domestic circulation per issue.

perceptions and attitudes toward existing magazines, as well as their expectations. Exhibit 11 summarizes the results.

The Decisive Weekend: A New Concept Is Conceived

At the end of October 1990, Axel Ganz, Dr. Andreas Wiele, Rèmy Dessarts, Thierry Rouxel, and Françai̇s Dalbard-Martin met for a weekend to decide on the future course of the project. Most importantly, they decided to develop a prototype of *Hermès.* Prisma Presse develops products one at a time and, until now, every Prisma Presse project ever prototyped was subsequently launched.

The next major decision concerned the concept of the magazine. They decided that, compared to its competitors, the new magazine should be

- *Broader in scope.* In addition to the classic business coverage provided by French magazines, the new

EXHIBIT 6 Circulation of Main Business Magazines in France

	Launch Year	Frequency	Paid Domestic Circulation per Issue (in thousand copies)				Circulation Growth, 1987–90	Share of Monthly Paid Circulation, 1990	Gross Annual Circulation Revenue*** in million F (Estimate), 1990	Share of Annual Gross Circulation Revenue (Estimate), 1990
			1987	1988	1989	1990				
L'Expansion	1967	Biweekly	160	175	159	150	−6%	29%	74	31%
Le Nouvel Economiste	1975	Weekly	93	80	84	90	−3	34	56	24
Science & Vie Economie	1984	Monthly	111	116	117	107	−4	10	25	10
*Dynasteurs**	1985	Monthly	100	100	100	95	−5	9	31	13
L'Entreprise	1985	Monthly	61	62	65	65	7	6	20	8
*Tertiel/A pour Affaires***	1985	Monthly	33	34	35	47	42	4	11	5
Challenges	1986	Monthly	45	67	73	74	64	7	22	9
Total monthly paid domestic circulation (thousand copies)			1,042	1,049	1,044	1,048	1	100	239	100
Gross annual circulation revenue (millions of F)			217	233	240	239	10			

*Circulation as indicated by publisher. Circulation data of all other magazines are audited.

***Tertiel* relaunched as *A pour Affaires* in September 1989.

***Gross circulation revenue = Average price per copy (= Retail price − Subscription discount) × Total paid circulation (domestic and export).

EXHIBIT 7 Advertising in Main Business Magazines in France

	Number of Advertising Pages per Year				Growth in Net Rev., Adv. Pages 1987–90	Gross Share of Adv. Pages, 1990	Share of Advertising Revenue,** 1990 (million F)	Gross Adv. Revenue, 1990
	1987	1988	1989	1990				
L'Expansion	2,875	2,845	2,575	2,366	−18%	31%	274	42%
Le Nouvel Economiste	2,940	3,047	2,770	2,259	−23	30	184	28
Science & Vie Economie	242	231	225	224	−7	3	17	3
Dynasteurs	341	623	649	627	84	8	52	8
L'Entreprise	954	1,257	1,225	1,082	13	14	72	11
*Tertiel/A pour Affaires**	451	550	706	703	56	9	40	6
Challenges	222	223	352	343	55	5	19	3
Number of adv. pages per year	8,025	8,776	8,502	7,604	−5	100		
Gross advertising revenue per year (millions of F)	516	652	668	659	28		659	100

**Tertiel* relaunched as *A pour Affaires* in September 1989.
**Gross advertising revenue: List price per advertising page number of advertising pages.
The net revenue amounts to approximately 60 percent of the gross revenue, with the difference including the commission for media wholesalers and the advertising agency.

magazine should cover new trends, management techniques, and business philosophies (similar to the German *Manager Magazin*).

- *More entertaining.* The crucial role of individuals, with all their strengths and weaknesses, should be brought out more strongly; this required well-researched, thrilling success and failure stories, the description of interesting personalities, including those working outside Paris, an understanding of how they operated, and a coverage of lifestyle/leisure trends relevant to managers (similar to what the U.S. magazine *Forbes* offered).
- *More useful.* More coverage of personal interest topics like career management, continuing education, salaries, insurance, personal investments, etc. (similar to what the German magazines *Capital* and *DM* as well as *Le Revenu Français* and *Mieux Vivre* covered).
- *More informative.* All articles should be well researched and objective.
- *More international.* International aspects should be covered systematically and be based on facts rather than national stereotypes.
- *More visual.* The layout should be more attractive, reading should be facilitated, and the photographic material should be original, rather than relying on easily available photos of a small number of business celebrities.

This concept was immediately translated into a "flat plan." Such a plan allocates pages to the various content areas, defines specific articles in each content area, and, finally, describes the order of appearance of the articles. Development of the flat plan drew on everybody's industry knowledge, and many features were inspired by other magazines, both French and foreign. Two questions were asked throughout: (1) are the choices consistent with the product concept? and (2) do they lead to a clear competitive advantage?

The next immediate step was to produce a first prototype of the magazine by January 1991 and to test it with a group of potential readers. A second, revised prototype would be produced by April 1991 and a third by July 1991. The market launch was scheduled for September 1991.

Prototyping the New Concept

As Prisma Presse had no previous experience in the business market, five external journalists were recruited to work exclusively on the *Hermès* project. Some had extensive experience in the French business press, others were younger journalists. Just as for the editor-in-chief, it turned out to be difficult to find journalists having excellent business/economic knowledge, and willing to adapt to the editorial principles and culture of Prisma Presse. Recruitment remained a problem throughout, and several journalists were eventually asked to leave.

EXHIBIT 8 Marketing Mix and Revenue Structure of Business Magazines in France, 1990

	L'Expansion	Le Nouvel Economiste	Science & Vie Economie	Dynasteurs	L'Enterprise	A pour Affaires Economiques	Challenges
Marketing Mix: Circulation Market							
Product							
Avg. nr. pages/issue	189	112	107	140	190	162	109
Editorial/total nr. of pages	46%	60%	81%	59%	52%	57%	74%
Nr. issues/year	23	50	11	11	12	10	12
Total nr. of editorial pages/year	1,998	3,349	956	906	1,200	923	963
Avg. nr. of staff members	38	40	12	15	21	19	13
Nr. edit. pages/staff member/year	53	84	80	60	57	49	74
Price							
Newsstand price per copy	25F	15F	22F	30F	30F	27F	25F
Subscription discount*	48%	24%	18%	33%	41%	20%	23%
Distribution: newsstand unit sales							
% of total domestic paid circulation	16%	23%	34%	16%	32%	35%	22%
1990 media adv. (million F)	8.8	5.9	2.8	N.A	2.5	5.4	2.4
Per paid domestic copy (in F)	2.60F	1.30F	2.40F	N.A.	3.20F	11.40F	2.70F
% of gross newsstand revenue	68%	38%	31%	N.A.	33%	131%	55%
Marketing Mix: Advertising Market							
Price							
List price per 4-color page (in F)	117,600F	70,000F	65,000F	80,900F	61,900F	59,000F	59,500F
Cost per 1,000 paid domestic circul.	784F	778F	607F	825F	952F	1,255F	804F
Cost per 1,000 dom. exec. readers	162F	232F	230F	234F	141F	N.A.	342F
Advertising department (nr. persons)	7	8	4	4	7	4	5
Revenue Structure							
1990 gross revenue (estimate)							
Gross circulation revenue	74	56	25	31	20	11	22
Gross advertising revenue	274	184	17	52	72	40	19
Total gross revenue	348	240	42	83	92	51	41
Adv. rev. as a % of total gross rev.	79%	77%	40%	63%	79%	78%	47%
% of publisher's total gross rev.	35%	2%	N.A.	15%	9%	2.5%	10%
Name of publisher	L'Expansion	Hachette/ Filipacchi	Excelsior	Pearson France	L'Expansion	C.E.P.	Le Nouvel Observateur

*In calculating the subscription discount, the retail price of special issues (e.g., travel guides) made available free of charge to subscribers is included.

EXHIBIT 9 **Content Analysis of Business Magazines in France, 1990–91**

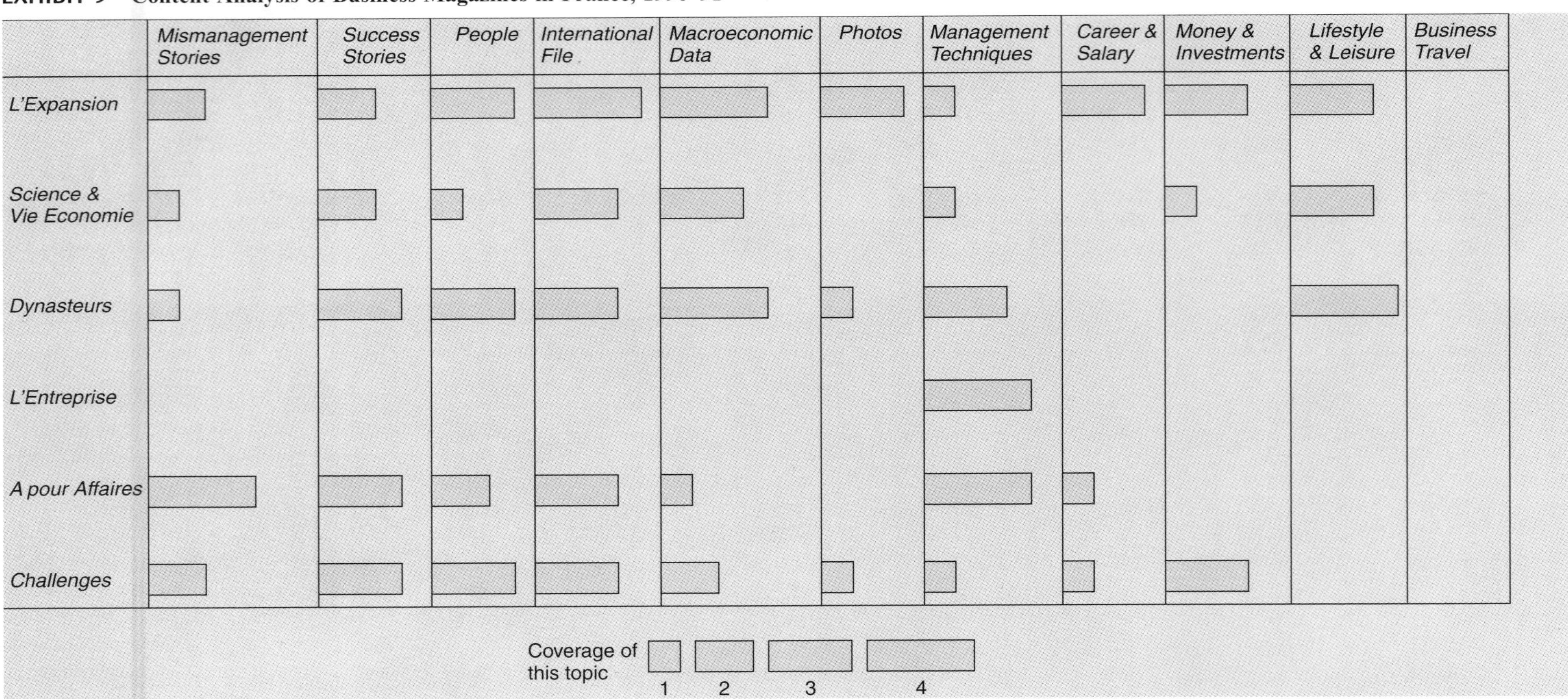

The team was given a separate, closed-off open-plan office in the Prisma Presse building. Access was highly restricted and, apart from the management duo, the art group, and Prisma Presse's senior management, the team had no contact with any other Prisma Presse staff, nor with other parts of the Gruner+Jahr organization, including the journalists working for Gruner+Jahr's *Capital* in Germany.

Organized around the main content areas of the magazine, the journalists immediately started to implement the flat plan. The important role of initiating them in the "Prisma Presse formula" fell to art director Thierry Rouxel, who discussed with each journalist at the outset the concept of the projected article, as well as the number and types of illustrations, and the layout on the page. Constant attention was paid to the integration of text, visuals, and layout as the articles progressed. At other magazines, the journalists' role was usually limited to writing articles, with editorial secretaries and visual staff adding their contributions afterwards. The tight schedule led to a very heavy workload, sometimes forcing journalists to work around the clock.

The first prototype was ready in January 1991. Kept under tight security control, the 50-page dummy had no cover page and no name. The articles chosen were deliberately sensational to find out how far one could go in the direction of entertainment and still be considered a serious business magazine. Many focused on power struggles (e.g., "1 seat for 3 pretenders," "The barons' conspiracy") or demolished well-known business figures (e.g., "Tapie doesn't have what it takes"). The dummy also included a psychological test ("Are you a real boss?"), an analysis of managers' difficulties with their children ("Daddy, I never see you!"), and a map of a fashionable Champs-Élysées restaurant indicating celebrities' preferred tables.

The dummy was immediately tested with two focus groups composed of target group members. After a first quick flick through they expressed pleasant surprise with the numerous photos, the big headlines, and the clear layout, which made for easy reading. But as they read the articles in greater depth, their mood turned negative and even angry. The magazine was too sensational, too negative ("vitriolic"), and too superficial for them—it was only good "to be read at the hairdresser's."

Undaunted, the team proceeded to produce a second prototype. They made small modifications in layout, headlines, and subheadings of articles already tested (Exhibit 12), and concentrated on producing other articles that would demonstrate the seriousness of the magazine. A 16-page article on the battle between European and Japanese automobile manufacturers was the longest and most intensively researched article.

The second, 100-page prototype, still without cover page or name, was tested with two focus groups in April 1991. The magazine's presentation was again very well received. But this time, the content was also praised for its diversity, factual grounding, and good summarizing of important information. The managers liked the editorial style, which was "the opposite of the bland, insipid style" of the habitual business journalism and reflected a desire to "see things the way they really are." Most of them felt like buying the magazine, reading it from cover to cover, and keeping it for future reference.

As always, Axel Ganz was watching the focus groups over closed-circuit TV. Before the second group drew to an end, he fetched some champagne, popped the corks, and declared "we will launch this magazine!"

Up to this point, the project had cost about F6 million. Funding for further development including a test launch was available through the development budget already approved by Gruner+Jahr. A test launch would require some more recruitment, but the team of journalists would receive no guarantee of continuing beyond the test phase. A full-blown launch like the one Axel Ganz had in mind, however, involved a more massive and longer-term commitment and required the formal approval of Gruner+Jahr and Bertelsmann. Dr. Wiele prepared a 10-page (plus exhibits) report, which summarized the market situation, explained the product and marketing concept for *Hermès,* and specified the main assumptions underlying the eight-year projected income. If circulation after six months failed to exceed 50,000, the magazine would be discontinued. It was estimated that cumulative investment would have reached F60 million at this point. As expected, the Gruner+Jahr and Bertelsmann boards gave the green light in May and June, respectively.

The Zero Issue: *Hermès* Becomes *Capital*

The third prototype was the magazine's "zero" issue. Identical to a real magazine in presentation and editorial content, its main purposes were to test readers' response to the real product, to scale up and test the production process, and, last but not least, to draw advertising.

To produce the zero issue, the magazine's staff was increased to 32, mostly by hiring from the outside. Almost all articles were new. The main editorial response to April's market research results was yet

EXHIBIT 10 1991 Readership Profile of Business Magazines in France

Source: IPSOS Cadres Actifs 1991.

	L'Expansion	Le Nouvel Economiste	Science & Vie Economie
All Target Groups: Magazine Penetration (in %)			
a. Senior and middle managers in business firms	21%*	10%	6%
b. Highly educated professionals	8	4	5
c. Entry-level managers	12	7	4
Total (a+b+c)	14	7	5
Advertising Target Group: "Executives" (a+b)			
Magazine penetration (in %)	15	7	5
Share of "executives" among readers (in %)	62	56	60
Hermes Reader Target Group			
Number of readers: senior & middle mgrs. in bus. firms	300,068	136,466	79,535
Reader profile: senior & middle mgrs. in bus. firms			
Sex (in %)			
Male	80	89	85
Female	20	12	15
Region (in %)			
Paris metropolitan region	42	47	39
Rest of France	58	53	61
Age (in %)			
<35	23	20	29
35–45	34	37	41
>45	42	44	30
Annual Income (1,000 F) (in %)			
<180	15	11	16
180–240	23	19	24
240–360	37	37	32
>360	19	27	21
Firm size (nr. employed) (in %)			
<10	22	17	18
10–50	20	17	20
50–200	14	16	22
200–500	13	14	11
>500	31	37	29
Type of business (in %)			
Manufacturing	32	41	31
Trade	17	17	12
Services	51	42	57

*Percentage of all French senior and middle managers in business firms who read the magazine during the week (*Nouvel Economiste*) or month (all other magazines) preceding the interview.

another increase in the number of pages devoted to "service" topics (management techniques, career and salary, personal finance) to 26 out of 110 editorial pages in total (Exhibit 13). A separate macroeconomic section printed on pink paper (the same color as the Financial Times and the economic supplement of a leading French newspaper) was added in the center of the magazine, and a tongue-in-cheek page appeared at the end.

What should the magazine be called? Because it was originally thought that the name *Capital* had negative connotations in France, other names had been considered, including the once more available *Fortune*, which

Dynasteurs	L'Enterprise	A pour Affaires Economiques	Challenges	Total (in million)	Hermes Target Profile
14%	16%	7%	5%	1,5	
2	3	0	2	1,2	
6	9	2	3	2,1	
7	10	3	4	4,8	
8	10	4	4	2,7	
63	57	66	58		
202,546	231,562	96,924	73,080	1,5	
				(in %)	(in %)
83	77	69	79	82	80
17	23	31	21	18	20
50	39	42	46	45	40
50	61	58	54	55	60
21	22	23	24	24	35
38	39	40	42	38	45
41	39	37	34	38	20
7	10	15	12	16	17
17	20	12	20	23	22
38	38	44	35	34	39
31	25	23	27	20	22
18	18	21	18	21	15
16	26	27	20	18	15
20	17	18	11	18	20
10	11	8	13	8	20
36	29	27	37	35	30
36	45	41	40	41	40
21	14	12	10	14	15
44	42	47	50	45	45

might open doors with advertisers and information sources. Negotiations failed, however, and in the end the name *Capital* was chosen, with the subtitle "The Essence of the Economy."

Capital was the first Prisma Presse magazine created with a completely integrated PC-based publishing system. This permitted several iterations before the final version was transmitted electronically to the Bertelsmann printing plant in Gtersloh, Germany.

Virtually everybody participated in the discussions of each version, including Axel Ganz. "He intervenes less in the content of articles than in the presentation, and occasionally shows a layouter how to solve a problem," commented Rèmy Dessarts. In the end, all remaining issues were solved by hierarchy and, as always, Axel Ganz gave the green light after having gone through the final version page by page, line by line.

EXHIBIT 11
Perceptions, Attitudes, and Expectations Concerning Business Magazines

Source: Report on two focus groups with senior and middle managers. Eliane Mikowski, Paris, Fall 1990.

1. The Existing Magazines

- Repetitive in content and style, from one issue to another, between one magazine and the others.
- No title with a clear profile; no originality.
- The journalists are not credible. They are either too ideologically dogmatic or mere spokesmen for the firms, or they provide inaccurate information.
- The readers feel trapped:
  They are obliged to read this press to be informed.
  The magazines make no effort to seduce them; reading is a real chore.
- Readers notice a timid change, but this more concerns the presentation (more color, more illustrations) than the content and basic philosophy of the magazines.

2. Readers' Expectations

- Useful information, instead of nebulous and pedantic discourse.
- Articles should be credible:
  The author's point of view should be clear.
  The article should be rigorous, well written, and well summarized.
  The issues should be put in perspective (comparisons over time, etc.).
- More controversy:
  Stop bootlicking well-known business figures and companies.
  Present conflicting theories and points of view.
  Show some detachment through humor and irony.
  Put issues in historical and geopolitical context.
- A wider angle:
  Greater international perspective, less French-oriented.
  Coverage of cultural topics.
  One or two humorous pages.
- A more attractive presentation:
  Clear table of contents.
  Facilitate reading through titles, subtitles, a clear visual code.
  Many illustrations and schemas.
  The articles should be more "airy."
  One or two very incisive and conclusive articles on specific topics (a double-page maximum).

To Launch or Not to Launch . . .

Hot off the press, the zero issue of *Capital* was tested with two focus groups on July 23 and 24, with positive results (Exhibit 14). Normally, this would be a good basis for drawing advertising, for which Constance Benquè, former head of *L'Expansion*'s advertising department, has just been recruited.

But is this the right time to launch a new business magazine? Since the beginning of the year, advertising volume in business magazines has declined by about 20 percent, and there are no signs of recovery, despite the end of the Gulf war. The entire economic press is suffering. The L'Expansion group, all of whose titles are in the economic press, is rumored to be in the red and reducing staff. *A pour Affaires* merged with *L'Entreprise* in June. *Science & Vie Economie* cut short its relaunch advertising campaign prematurely. The Reader's Digest group has just withdrawn its new personal finance magazine *Budgets famille* only six months after launch.

Dr. Wiele is wondering whether he should recommend that the planned September launch of *Capital* be postponed. If they go ahead with the launch, they have to decide on its price, distribution, and communication policies. Dr. Wiele sees two main alternatives: a "subscription" strategy and a "newsstand" strategy.

EXHIBIT 12
The Evolution of *Capital*

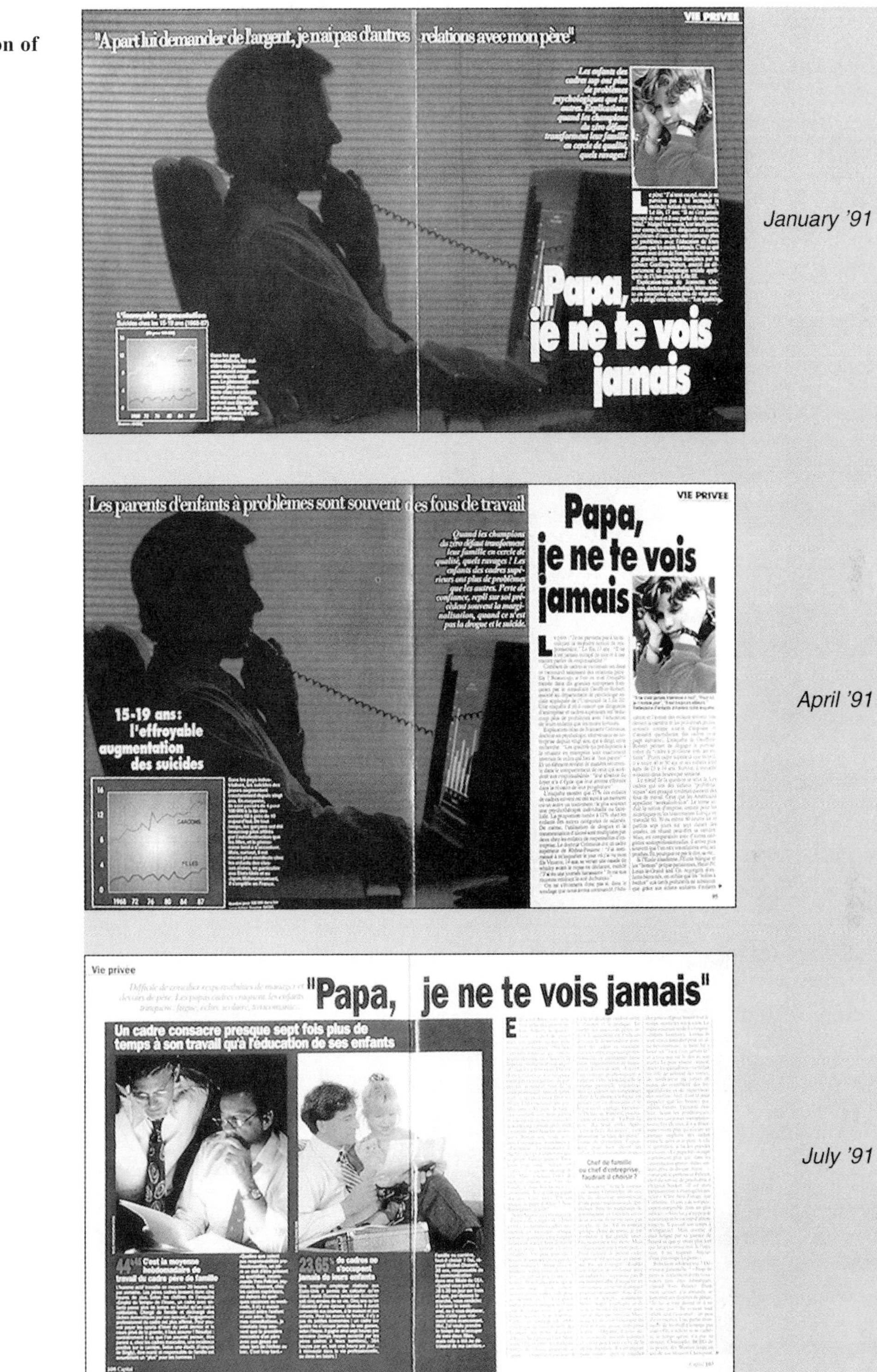

EXHIBIT 13
Number of Editorial Pages per Content Category

Content Categories	Capital		L'Expansion
	Flat Plan January 1991	Zero Issue July 1991	July 4–17 1991
People	14	12	3
Business	16	16	14
Success stories			
Mismanagement stories			
International file and macroeconomy	21	22	21
The economy in pictures and special topics	21	18	18
Service topics	15	26	1
Management techniques			
Career & salary			
Money & investments			
Lifestyle, leisure, business travel	21	16	5
Total number of editorial pages	108	110	62

EXHIBIT 14
Zero Number of *Capital:* Perceptions and Attitudes

Source: Report on two focus groups with senior and middle managers. Eliane Mikowski, Paris, July 23–24, 1991.

The main attitude is one of surprise in front of an object that is new in the context of the economic press. This is backed up by the following perceptions:

- Great richness and variety:
  "This is life, this is the world."
- Great density and true information.
- Great ease of reading:
  "Freedom of reading, depending on the circumstances, how much time I have, and how I feel."
  "One can read over lightly, for entertainment, or go for a detailed reading."
- A style:
  "Sharp." "The journalists take position," "interrogative"
- Professional:
  "Well researched," "The journalists have good access," "The magazine is pleasant. . .good pictures. . .attractive colors."

Overall, *Capital* will create an event in the market. It has great competitive potential both in the business magazine market and in the news magazine market. But readers hesitate regarding the magazine's identity and personality:

- A business or a news magazine?
- A "people" or a business information magazine?
- Superficial or dense?
- Structured or muddled?
- Judicious advice or consumerism?
- Specialization or popularization?

The subscription strategy would be in line with the other business magazines: a high newsstand price (e.g., F25) combined with a high subscription discount and a massive direct mail investments, resulting in subscription sales mainly.

The newsstand strategy would be a new approach for the business magazine market: a F15 newsstand price, identical to that of the weekly news magazines, combined with a low subscription discount and high mass media advertising. If *Capital* were published on the same day as these news magazines (Thursday or Friday) and displayed prominently, a significant share of the 600,000 buyers of weekly news magazines at the newsstands might pick up *Capital* once a month in addition to, or instead of, a news magazine. About 20 percent of news magazine readers fall into *Capital*'s reader target group.

Exhibits 15 and 16 summarize the key assumptions necessary to evaluate these alternative strategies. At Gruner+Jahr, magazines are expected to reach break-even within three to four years, pay back within five to eight years, and return 15 percent on investment in the long term.

EXHIBIT 15 Key Economic Assumptions for Capital

	1991–92	1998–99
Product		
Number of editorial pages/issue	110	120
Number of issues/year	10 (Oct.–July)	12 (August–July)
Editorial costs/editorial page	20,000 F	Increase: 3% p.a.
Mechanical costs/printed page	0.05 F	Increase: 3% p.a.
Department costs (management, advertising department)/year	6 F million	Increase: 5% p.a.
Newsstand Distribution		
Distribution margin (% of newsstand price)	55%	55%
% unsold rate (% of copies delivered to newsstands that are not sold)	50%	30%
Subscription Distribution		
Average cost of a new subscriber		
Via direct mail (mailing list purchase, direct mail)	300 F–1,000 F per subscription*	300 F–1,000 F per subscription*
Via self-promotion (subscription appeals included in *Capital*)	20 F per subscription	Increase: 3%
Self-promotion yield (share of newsstand copies for which subscription forms are sent)	1%	1%
Subscription renewal rate (%)	50–60%*	50–60%*
Average cost of renewing a subscription	20 F–80 F*	20 F–80 F*
Cost of serving a subscription (administration, postage, etc.)	4 F per copy	Increase: 3% p.a.
Advertising Market		
4-color ad page cost/1,000 circulation	755 F	Increase: 4% p.a.
Avg. net adv. revenue/adv. page	57%	57%
Advertising promotion/adv. page	3,200 F	Increase: 4% p.a.

*The greater the number of subscriptions, the higher the average cost of acquiring and renewing a subscription, and the lower the subscription renewal rate.

EXHIBIT 16 Circulation Market Mix

	"Subscription" Strategy			"Newsstand" Strategy		
Year	Newsstand Price (Subscr. Disc: 30%)	Media Adv. per Copy	Subscription Share (% of Total Circul.)	Newsstand Price (Subscr. Disc: 17.5%)	Media Adv. per Copy	Subscription Share (% of Total Circul.)
1991–92	25F	11F	70%	15F	21F	9%
1992–93	28F	5F	70	18F	10F	17
1993–94	30F	3F	70	20F	5F	24
1994–95	33F	3F	70	22F	5F	30
1995–96	35F	3F	70	22F	5F	34
1996–97	38F	3F	70	25F	5F	36
1997–98	40F	3F	70	25F	5F	37
1998–99	43F	3F	70	25F	5F	38

Case 6-8

Dura-plast, Inc.

Tom Parker, CEO of Dura-plast-Americas, Inc (DP-A), directs the U.S. subsidiary of a profitable international equipment manufacturer, Kovner DP International (DP International). He is responsible for directing DP-A's long-term growth and welfare, as well as meeting annual sales and profitability targets. As the head of the manufacturer's largest subsidiary, Parker also has been given the task of developing and implementing sales and marketing strategies that will support the entire Dura-plast group's profitability.

It is now January, 1995, and Mr. Parker is sitting in his office at DP-A's Flint, Michigan headquarters. He is thinking about the efforts his company made and the difficulties it encountered in presenting a successful sales contract to provide Techno Plastics, Inc. with Dura-plast granulator equipment. Techno Plastics, based in France, is a major international plastics producer which had decided to build a plant in the southeastern part of the United States. The sales process was complicated by the need for coordination across DP-A's different country-based subsidiaries and because Techno Plastics was a new customer for DP-A. Parker was pleased to receive reassurance from Techno Plastics that his bid would be successful, but, realizing that more and more plastics manufacturers are setting up global manufacturing operations, Parker wondered if changes were needed to better serve global accounts.

Source: *Written by Ryan Oliver under the supervision of Professor Joe Cannon as a basis for classroom discussion. As part of the case development, firm and individual specifics have been disguised.* Reproduced March 1996.

Granulation Equipment

DP-A and its parent company are in the business of designing, manufacturing, assembling, and selling plastics granulators. A plastics granulator is used to chop plastics waste (bad parts and production rejects) into small granules for closed-loop recycling. Granulators are most commonly used in industrial shops, where excess scrap is fed into the granulator hopper for conversion through rotating knives. The small uniform bits of processing scrap and bad parts which emerge from the granulator, called the "regrind," can then be recycled.

Granulators are specified by their infeed or throat size, throughput and weight, and by the composition and chemical makeup of the plastic waste they can process within an hour. Each is fitted with an infeed hopper designed to handle various plastics dimensions. Granulators positioned next to the plastic manufacturing machine to reclaim plastic scraps immediately are known as beside-the-press (B-T-P) granulators. Other types of granulators are placed in a central location (Central) in the plant and scraps are delivered to them manually or by conveyor or sold as smaller, stand alone (Automated) units.

The granulators sold range widely in price, feature, and quality/performance tradeoffs. Because granulators can be tailored to the specific production process of the customer, both the analysis and identification of customer requirements and customization costs are figured into the price of the product.

Thorton Group and Kovner DP International

DP-A is a wholly-owned subsidiary of the Norwegian Thorton Group member, DP International. The group consists of a number of medium-sized engineering companies in the producer-goods industry, each with the developing medium-sized industrial companies in a particular specialty area. The Thorton Group continues to grow through expanded sales and company acquisitions. Its operational structure and tactics support the growth of individual companies operating as important market makers in focused geographic areas. While most subsidiaries hold prominent positions near their customer bases, Thorton Company Headquarters have traditionally been placed close to their representative Norwegian manufacturing plants. Thorton and DP International specifics are provided in Exhibit 1 (Organizational Structure).

DP International follows a typical Thorton company organizational system: it develops and produces its granulation equipment in Norway and conducts sales through its international subsidiaries, thereby manufacturing globally with local market support. DP International invoiced sales totaling $233 and $326 million in 1992 and 1993 with respective earnings of $11 and $47 million. The parent company had a return on capital of over 35% during this period. In 1994, approximately 2700 units were sold in Europe, 2050 in America, and 500 in Asia. There has been substantial improvement in earnings as a result of the strong volume growth. However, DP International, with its high level of sales abroad, has also benefited from a weaker Norwegian krone rate.[1]

DP International's low-noise granulators have primarily been used for granulating plastic waste in connection with the automated manufacture of plastic products. A proprietary design offers technical superiority which has allowed the company to establish a strong global market presence. Its unique, patented reversible knife design is currently produced only in Norway.

In addition to supplying all the cutting chambers to its international subsidiaries, DP International sells a large number of complete machines because of the complexity of the electrical and drive systems. However, because products qualifying as locally made have lower costs due to lower import duties, DP International established an assembly and manufacturing plant in the US and an assembly plant in Germany. These run as autonomous P&L locations, typically assembling, customizing and adding local content to the larger granulators that are sourced from Norway for sale throughout the Americas and Europe. The small to medium-sized machines currently do not qualify as US products under NAFTA content requirements, and as such are not free from import duties.

DP International is planning further decentralization of its manufacturing operations with the establishment of a cutting chamber production facility in the US. This

[1] The unit of currency is the Norwegian krone, which is abbreviated NOK. NOK 1 = 100 ore. Note that all figures are in U.S. dollars unless otherwise noted. The assumed exchange rate is 7.00 NOK to $1 U.S.

EXHIBIT 1 Organizational Structure

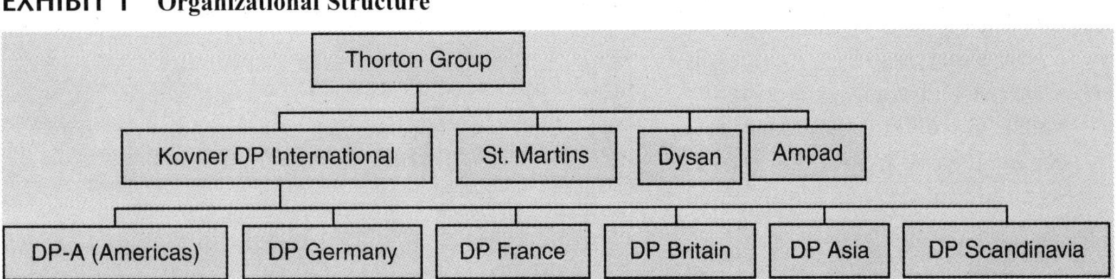

move will lower transportation costs, which currently add 6% or more to the final sale price of DP International units. In addition, it would enable the company to meet in-country product requirements, lessen the risk of international currency fluctuations, and lower tax and tariff duties.

DP International has responded to the cost of maintaining large product lines by developing flexibility in the manufacturing cycle. Increasingly, DP International has been able to customize its products to meet customer requirements, an important factor in DP International's low cost, high volume strategy. In fact, during 1992, DP International successfully launched a new product generation based on a modular product system, which brought about a strong volume increase in 1993. In 1994, the US subsidiary, DP-A, developed a US hopper welding cell which allowed for additional, in-house customization of the larger machines.

In order to handle market demand changes and increasing sales, DP International expanded its plant capacity in Norway this past year. When at full capacity, the new plant will allow the organization to expand sales from 5,000 to 7,000 with a substantial increase in its large-capacity machine production facilities.

Subsidiary Companies

Torger Erlandsen, the managing director of DP International, directs the integration of the international operations. Under his leadership, each of the subsidiary companies retains significant autonomy in both organizational structure and management. As a result, the operational manager in each of the countries functions in an atmosphere that offers a high degree of entrepreneurial freedom. Country managers make their own decisions with respect to sales strategy, pricing, and promotion. Erlandsen believes that granting this leadership independence is the most effective way to maximize the opportunities within the granulation equipment sales' niche marketplace.

While each of the subsidiary companies reports to the Norwegian headquarters, the subsidiary organizations do not have formal ties with each other. In a growing number of cases, however, an order may be generated from an area outside of a subsidiary's direct responsibility; the individual subsidiaries then have the responsibility to coordinate efforts which take into account specification development and business practice initiatives suitable to that business environment and culture. Final responsibility, however, and authority in decision making is given to the local subsidiary.

However, because of the interrelated nature between international marketing and manufacturing, there have been increasing problems regarding contract specification and pricing issues internationally. Some members of the DP International group, for instance, have begun to wonder if it might be a good idea to set a standard price internationally. With respect to sales strategy, some agree with the DP-A Vice President for Sales, Richard Foster, who argues that confusion in the sales cycle could be limited if the criteria for involvement in the sales relationship were more narrowly defined. His suggestion is for "involvement only when a person can enhance the sales relationship." Others suggest greater or lesser involvement across countries.

Traditionally, most countries have employed, Agents[2] to sell and distribute granulators. Agents buy the Duraplast granulators and then sell them to their own customer base, setting their own price levels. Prices in some cases are higher than DP International has wanted. In this set-up, the agent decides how he wants to sell in the market, and determines his own segmentation, targeting, and positioning, perhaps to the exclusion of some areas of the market. If the market is slumping, the agent argues that the price is too high. However, the manufacturer has limited knowledge of the specific competitors, contract terms, or agent mark-up. In fact, if the agent forgoes the contract, the manufacturer can lose an entire customer base.

One of DP International's new channel strategies is its transition to Manufacturer's Representative (MR)[3] relationships in each of the DP International offices worldwide—thus standardizing part of its selling strategy. This strategy focuses on generating sales through MRs contracts instead of through sales agents. One of the primary benefits of this strategy is to help DP International to protect its current and long-term market position by getting closer to the customer. It is important for DP International to understand where its machines

[2] Agents are generally businesses that contract with original equipment manufacturers to sell their products for a given period of time. Agents take ownership of the products and usually have protected territories.

[3] Manufacturing Representatives have been employed by many original equipment manufacturers because of their knowledge and ties within a particular industry. Manufacturer's Representatives represent multiple, noncompeting manufacturers, and are generally granted exclusive territories. They represent the supplier, but are not usually involved in distribution or installation. MRs do not take possession or ownership of equipment—they only operate as agents on behalf of (usually) multiple principals (i.e., manufacturers).

are being sold and to develop brand name loyalty in the market. The global program to take control of the customer has helped to clarify pricing and stabilize production. If the market is slumping, DP International's regional sales managers will be able to intensify the sales efforts or make strategic decisions, such as price reductions.

Each of DP International's subsidiaries handles the MR and other selling issues differently. The following sections provide more detail about DP International's subsidiaries in Germany, France, Britain and North America.

DP Germany (DPG)

Germany is a large market that is treated as an individual unit in DP International's international planning exercises. Germany's solo status and competitive advantage stems from its market size, homogeneity, and the location of a manufacturing plant which supplies the rest of Europe. The German market is almost as large as the US market with respect to the total number of customers.

German companies typically bid on a packaged basis. Each offer generally includes pricing and terms regarding auxiliary equipment, start-up and installation, plans, and long-term spare part commitments. Each part of the bid package is important to contract acquisition.

Germany recently changed its sales organization structure by shifting from an agent driven salesforce to one which includes both agents and MRs. Under the direction of a DPG sales manager who controls a group of sales reps and one agent, the country has been divided into territories where representatives are given regional exclusivity. In addition to managing the salesforce, the sales manager develops relationships and bids for larger granulation systems, calling on original equipment manufacturers (OEMs) and the largest potential purchasers.

DP France (DPF)

In France, as with the rest of Europe, sales cycles have traditionally been much longer than those in the US. The time from initial inquiry for granulation equipment to delivery averages 12–18 months. As a result, manufacturers and their customers have a longer time to plan and delineate product quote and specifications. Tom Parker suggests that "the introduction of MRs has allowed DP France to manage its customer base more closely." Consequently, DP France has developed sales relationships with several larger firms that have plants throughout France and worldwide. France is currently the smallest DP International European subsidiary. French customers typically expect bids to be presented in the same manner that German customers do—including all details on service, spare parts and support.

DP Britain (DP-UK)

The DP International office in Britain still uses an agent system to promote and sell its products. The agent system works because it is a generally accepted practice in the market and because of the limited interaction required in the sales process. Unlike the rest of Europe, distributors in Britain do not have to delineate each of the engineering and sales support requirements in the sales contract. DP-UK is a mid-sized DP International European subsidiary.

DP-Americas (DP-A)

DP-A, the biggest company in the DP International Group, faces the challenge of marketing within the quick cycle, volatile US, Canadian, and Mexican marketplaces. Strong in the US and Canada, DP-A has not made significant inroads into the Mexican, Latin American or South American markets as yet, principally because of practically non-existent safety standards, which allow competitors in these developing countries to build machines at a significantly lower cost.

DP-A's operations are led by a board of directors, consisting of Torger Erlandsen, a Norway-based manufacturing expert, and DP-A CEO Tom Parker. While Parker is responsible for day-to-day management of the DP-A activities, major decisions are approved by the board of directors. The board of directors currently meets on a quarterly basis with additional meetings as needed.

DP-A's domestic staff are split into three operational groups. The operations group manages the assembly and small-scale manufacturing operations in Flint, Michigan and a larger manufacturing plant just outside Knoxville, Tennessee, which will come on line in 1998. The Administration and Planning functions, as well as the Sales functions, are centralized in Flint.

The US bidding system is unlike Europe's. In addition to the faster selling cycle (the time from initial inquiry to final sale lasts between 2–8 months), US customers do not require the same amount of specificity and long-term price guarantees as those in Europe. DP-A, for instance, typically bids systems without the inclusion of auxiliary equipment and start-up costs. Start-up tends to be handled in-house and auxiliary equipment purchases are placed as needed. Most equipment installations are designed to be self-service—usually handled easily by in-plant engineers. DP-A does not bid for long-term spare part commitments or with detailed plant location specs either. Primarily because the market does not expect it, but also because the North American market is much more price-driven, bidding is more narrowly focused than in Europe.

DP-A's sales structure primarily relies on a network of Manufacturers Representatives. Each of DP-A's sales managers directs 4–5 MRs, spread out on a regional basis. Sales managers have responsibility for non-contiguous regions, such as a territory covering California, Canada, New England, and Texas. Richard Foster notes that noncontiguous sales areas give DP-A the ability to determine whether sales performance is a result of regional economic downturns or lackluster performance. Rising airline costs may cause DP-A to review this policy.

Currently, DP-A has exclusive, non-compete contracts with 25 MR groups, which in turn employ over 100 sales representatives. The DP-A MRs are located throughout the United States, Canada, and Mexico. MRs are the dominant distribution channel in the granulation industry because of their ability to cross-sell to the customer. A typical MR represents injection molding, blow molding, extrusion molding, vacuum systems for moving plastic, and drying systems equipment to the companies he or she visits. As such, representatives are a one-stop shop for a company's comprehensive plastic production equipment requirements.

The use of MRs allows DP-A to increase coverage while keeping full-time personnel to a minimum. MRs are not always the only contact with the end-user; however, their expertise and relationship with the buyers, built through the cross-sale of different types of plant equipment provides an effective and efficient sales strategy. MRs do not sell to all DP-A accounts. Larger sales are handled by DP-A's own marketing managers on the basis of leads generated from MRs and DP-A's direct advertising. If a lead generated by an MR generates a sale, the MR still receives the standard commission.

The best MRs generally carry the most effective and best known products because of their ability to close deals with a large group of well-established principals. MR groups have between 2–10 salespeople and close total sales in the range of 1 to 15 million dollars annually. Commissions on machines sales are generally 12% for mid-sized machines, 6% for the large-size machines, and 14% for machines under $ 10,000. If the MR and/or DP-A negotiated price discounts, these are generally split between the MR and DP-A.

MRs do not direct the installation or provide service for DP-A. Installation is not a critical sales factor for the smaller machines, because the machines arrive assembled and ready to run. For the larger central system machines, DP-A typically sends a service technician to the installation sight to check wiring and set-up specifications before the machine is first used. Service is directed from DP-A's central headquarters in Flint, Michigan.

Of DP-A sales, approximately 90% of all machines sold are used for new applications and 10% to replace outdated equipment. DP-A sales managers and MRs sell to a wide variety of individuals and companies on both a transactional and collaborative basis. DP-A classifies its current customers into the following categories.

- **Transactional accounts,** where customers purchase with both price and features in mind. In general, there are no long-term relationship or purchase commitments. Machines sold to these customers generally sell for under $10,000.
- **System accounts** are developed when MRs work with customers to define needs and establish fit. Granulators sold to customers in this category generally sell for between $10,000 and $50,000. While the service aspect of the sale provides ground for an ongoing relationship, there are no long-term purchase commitments.
- **Key accounts** represent the top 15% of DP-A sales and include large unit volume and annual dollar sales. The DP-A employee acts as a consultant in this relationship; more technologically proficient DP-A managers discuss the company's long-term plans and project goals. Currently, there are no formal long-term purchase commitments. Machines sold to these customers often cost more than $50,000.

Customers

The plastics industry uses two types of materials—thermoplastics and thermosets—in combination with stabilizers, colorants, flame retardants, and reinforcing agents in the plastic production process. These are then shaped or molded under heat and pressure to a solid state. Thermoplastics can be re-softened to their original condition by heat; however, thermosets cannot. Thermoplastics account for almost 90% of total plastic production and nearly 100% of granulation activity.

In general, thermoplastics output takes the form of pellets, flakes, granules, powders, liquid resins, sheeting, pipe, profile, parts, or film. It can be divided into four production categories:

Type	Examples	% Total Industry
Injection molding	Automobile parts, pudding cups	50
Blow molding	Soda and milk bottles	12
Extrusion	Trash bags, plastic pipes	30
Reclaim	Post consumer recycling	7

DP International sells the largest number of its granulators to injection molding companies. Nonetheless, it generates its highest level of profit from equipment utilizing extrusion processing, because the machines in this production category are significantly larger and more complex.

Large injection molding companies include Ford, Chrysler, and GM, as well as consumer product producers such as Black and Decker. Injection molding is a versatile and quick production process, and companies relying upon it have recently taken advantage of improvements in technology to expand productivity. In 1992 and 1993, this segment's plastic purchases grew by more than 11%.

Blow molding has shown high growth in the last few years because its resulting products are less expensive and easier to design. As new technology makes blow molding more profitable, blow molding firms, which include Coke, Pepsi, Tupperware, and Rubbermaid, have continued to expand their operations.

Extrusion is a popular method of producing large quantities of both uniform and dissimilar material that can be packaged into small units and distributed easily. The demand for plastics used in extrusion grew by over 12% for both 1992 and 1993. Future projections are not so rosy; growth in some segments of the extrusion industry which are expected to drop to less than 1% in 1995, and to contract by 4.4% in 1996, due to excess capacity.

Granulator Sales

DP-A offers approximately 30 different models in four primary product groups and one secondary product group through a strategic alliance with an original equipment manufacturer (OEM). The automation product group focuses on small, automated granulators for the injection molding market segment; the B-T-P product group is geared toward mid-size granulators for the injection molding/blow molding market; the central product group concentrates mostly in central reclamation in the extrusion market, while the parts/auxiliary/service product group is directed toward all customers.

The manufacturing process for DP-A equipment is a flexible multi-step process because of the unique design needs of individual clients. Compact machines generally require less customization. These machines come with DP-A's positive feed and rotating knife systems. Specifically, the design in the cutting chamber ensures positive feed of bulky materials and high throughputs. The reversible rotating knives allow the clearance between the cutting edges of the rotating and bed knives and the screen to remain constant. Both contribute to improved efficiency by reducing energy consumption and averting heat buildup.

The heavy-duty models include the positive feed and reversible rotating knife systems, as well as engineering systems capability and special hopper availability. Specialists in the engineering department are able to design a system to fit particular production requirements. As Tom Parker remarked, "the machines are generic but the applications are specific." Some applications require specially designed hoppers for maximum throughput and increased productivity. Energy efficiency remains a common concern in the design and purchase of both heavy-duty or compact machines.

In recent years, large global purchasers are increasingly seeking suppliers which can provide international turn-key solutions and services as opposed to sourcing from multiple suppliers for products and services. Using a single global supplier enhances negotiating power, standardizes spare parts, and allows the customer to build a closer relationship with one supplier. Global customers are asking granulator manufacturers to solve scrap recycling problems rather than simply sell them machines. This move is partly a result of the reduction in engineers at plastic manufacturer's production facilities. One customer commented that his firm wanted to focus its efforts on manufacturing, not on developing an expertise in recycling systems.

The trend is especially prevalent among European multinational firms, which traditionally have expected a high degree of supplier technical support. Additionally, rather than hiring technical expertise, purchasers are now contracting with companies which provide a centralized rather than local engineering focus.

A recent survey of DP-A customers and MRs found that they most value product performance, features, and the ability to customize the application. When asked to determine the most important attribute in the purchase decision, 41.7% of the customers chose quality/overall

EXHIBIT 2 Attribute Weighting

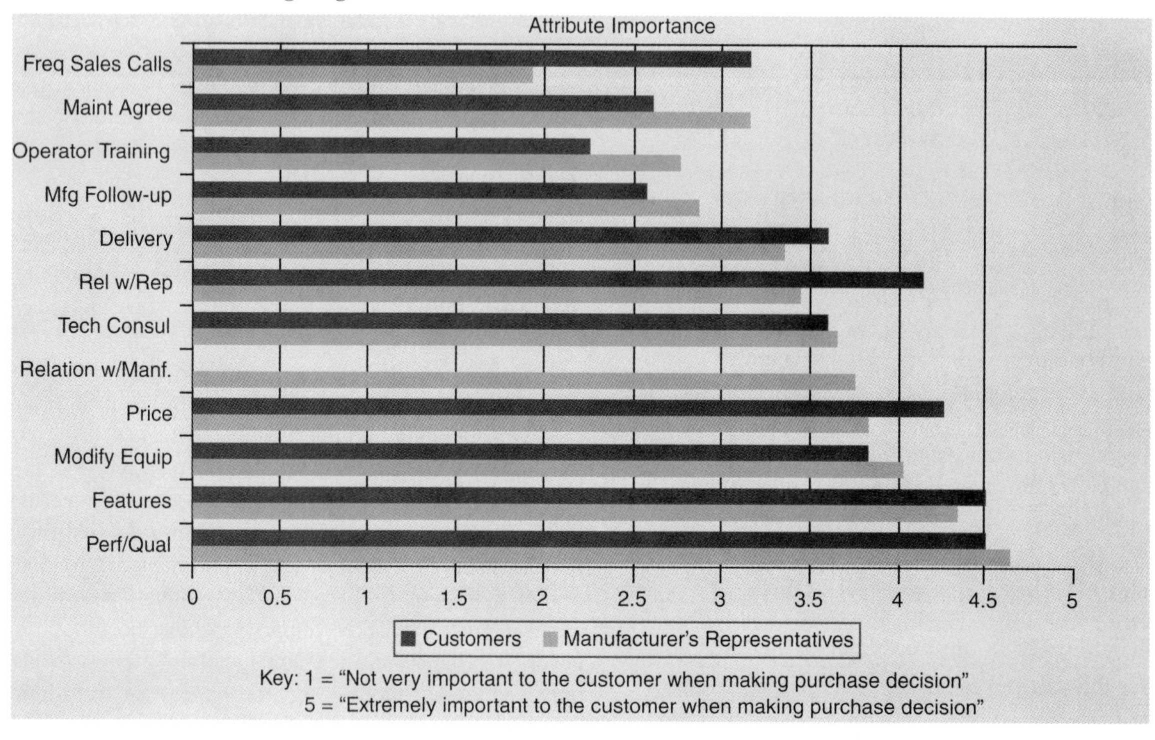

performance. In contrast, price was the most frequent response given by the MRs (31.4%). DP-A customers seem to view price as more of an order qualifier rather than an order winner. (Exhibit 2 provides a price/attribute comparison of DP-A customers and manufacturer representatives).

DP-A's most recent value-added solutions include its efforts within the injection molding, blow molding and film extrusion market segments of the plastic industry. Specialized niche development includes reclaim for scrap plastic, robot-fed injection molding, hot melt resin reclamation, edge trim film/sheet, post consumer waste bottle, vinyl siding and central thermoform scrap market segments. The niche markets are highly customized and provide high gross profits with limited competition. In support of these markets, DP-A engineers have worked with the market managers to further develop product engineered systems to meet their customer's application needs. Identification of these opportunities, however, continues to be a challenge.

DP-A's product portfolio overview provides information on each of the company's three major product groupings, the Automated, B-T-P, and Central. Individual components which are critical to application success and compliance include cutting chamber size, horsepower, rate screen, rotor configuration, RPM, and product features such as the tilt-back hopper and clam-shell screen cradle. Companies also have the choice of specialized features such as low infeed heights, oversized bearings, integral soundproofing, auger in feed, and conveyor infeed.

DP International is one of the largest producers of granulators worldwide and within the United States, DP-A has grown to be the largest supplier in unit volume of granulation equipment. Serving the entire range of companies in the plastic reclamation process, DP-A's installed customer account base includes over 6000 locations across the United States.

Part of this growth comes from the addition of a new OEM client to the DP-A portfolio. DP-A's strategic alliance with Fields (Powerflow) enables it to purchase and distribute up to 500 B-T-P units a year at a percentage discount. These units are sold under Powerflow's nameplate. DP-A is also considering the expansion of its OEM relationships to other major plastics manufacturers. Both partners benefit through these expanded relationships: DP International can increase market share and the OEMs can service their key accounts with a high quality product.

The key factors in DP-A's 1995 $21 million sales effort include the introduction of new machines, expanded service relationships, and enhanced marketing efforts, combined with further expansion of the OEM alliance with Powerflow.

For Tom Parker, DP-A volume leadership is "not a reason to be complacent." In addition to the company's drive for customer satisfaction and total quality management in the early 1990's, DP-A must now address issues related to account management and market change. Many of DP-A's larger machine segment clients now conduct business on both a domestic and international basis. Sales efforts have required significant synchronization of efforts between subsidiaries. In addition, under the goal of expanding profitability, management is working to raise the dollar volume on individual sales. Focusing on the mid- to large-size machine sales efforts has resulted in a mixed response from the salesforce. The numbers, however, continue to grow, with DP-A projecting dollar bookings of 45% of the US market in 1995.

In the last year, DP-A has posted record profits, with an average profit margin of 9% per sale. Gross profit, operating income, and net income information for 1993 and 1994 are presented in Exhibit 3.

Competition

DP-A was one of 15 competitors in the US Market which contributed to the 4500 granulators orders received overall in 1989 totaling $32.7 million and 7000 granulators in 1994 totaling $120 million.

Although DP-A is the newest competitor in the US granulator sales marketplace, it is currently the leader in volume sales, primarily through the OEM relationship with Powerflow. Before the linkage, it was number three in the market, driven by a strong sales push.

DP-A's price position in relation to that of its competitors may hamper unit sales in some market segments. Some of its competitors are large conglomerates which often use granulators as loss-leaders in negotiations to close higher dollar, turn-key system orders. DP-A has traditionally had a poor record in acquiring these orders, which are generally multi-unit contracts.

DP-A credits its success in the market to outperforming competitors by delivering the highest standard of customer service. While it has created the perception of technical design superiority through marketing proprietary concepts such as the "constant flow methodology," DP-A has traditionally viewed itself as the underdog. The company continues to resist complacency: one corporate motto states "we must provide better service than our competitors; as such, our customers are right 98% of the time."

EXHIBIT 3

Dura-plast, Inc.*	1993	1994
Gross Profit	$5,067,029	$6,995,259
Operating Income	$294,289	$1,697,332
Net Income	$167,055	$959,810

*Dura-plast, Inc. Income Statement as of December 31, 1994 and 1993.

The market leader in dollars sold is the Northway Corporation, which is owned by the Abrahams Group, a division of the German conglomerate Ludwig-Crow. It averages 35% gross margins on granulators, 60% on parts/knives, and 35% on pelletizers. Its profits last year averaged around 10%–14%.

Northway has a product management organizational structure with a vice president of Marketing and a product manager for its B-T-P/Automation, Central/Systems and Pelletizing product groups. Each product manager has an application engineer and clerical support. The company has a vice president of Sales who manages its regional sales managers, parts department and service department. The marketing group prepares their sales quotes and supports the sales group with marketing intelligence and new products. Northway recently acquired a manufacturer of screen changes and pelletizing which seems, at least in the short run, to have negatively affected the company's ability to support its granulator sales. Northway has, however, been able to use its multi-product sales to continue as a dominant force in the Central and System markets.

Northway distribution efforts have been shifted from a 20-man direct salesforce to 2 regional sales managers and 18 manufacturer representative agencies. Perhaps the two regional sales managers currently cannot provide the level of service necessary to meet customer retention requests; at any rate Northway now has the reputation of being hard to deal with and increasingly non-responsive.

Northway historically has had a wider range of products, as compared to DP-A, because of its ability to offer 20 machines in a market where DP-A has 3–4. Consequently DP-A has had to price aggressively to remain competitive, especially on granulator sales that fall into a DP-A market gap. There are times, for example, when customers want machines specified for power requirements and size that lie in between DP-A's offerings. In order to get the sale, DP-A has to bid its larger machine.

Northway currently is not advertising aggressively. In the past, however, it led the market in advertising dollars spent. The parent company, the Abrahams

EXHIBIT 4

	1989				1994			
Competitor	**Units**	**Unit %**	**Dollars**	**$ %**	**Units**	**Unit %**	**Dollars**	**$ %**
Northway	1200	26	$18 Million	28	1400	20	$33.5 Million	28
Grindall	150	33	16 Million	25	1650	23	27.5 Million	23
DP-A	650	14	8.5 Million	13	2050	28	30 Million	25
Fields (Powerflow)	450	10	6 Million	9	700	10	12 Million	10
Smith & Smith	400	8	5 Million	8	600	9	10 Million	8

Group, has a cooperative advertising strategy which promotes a comprehensive turn-key organization. This reputation supplements Northway's exceptional brand awareness and solid reputation. Northway also runs a direct mail program to targeted acquisition and retention customers on a quarterly basis.

DP-A, however, is the leading advertiser in the North American market. It runs full-page color and ¼-page black and white ads in five major publications. It also attends 5–7 trade shows per year in order to exhibit its new products. DP-A has invested heavily in high-tech contemporary literature to complement its quotations.

Techno Plastics Request for Proposals

Techno Plastics, located outside of Paris, is a multinational blow molding company that specializes in the production of hardened plastic fuel tank systems for automobiles. Part of its expansion plan includes the development plan, namely, to be the largest producer of fuel tanks globally. To meet its goals, the company decided to open a new fuel tank plant in the US.

DP International has developed a strong relationship with Techno Plastics over the past 12 years and is currently servicing Techno Plastics manufacturing plants in Germany, UK, and France. Despite this relationship, Techno Plastics submitted a request for proposals (RFP) to each of the major granulator producers as part of a plan to supply the plant it was building in Lawrenceville, Georgia. What follows is a summary and timeline of events related to the RFP, which originated in France. (Exhibit 5 provides an overview of organization teams within the DP International and Techno Plastics organizations.)

August 1994

DP International's US subsidiary submitted its first quote for Techno Plastics' Georgia granulator services in August of 1994. US executives visiting Europe on a planning trip were introduced to Techno Plastics personnel at a plastics convention. The local French contact for Techno Plastics, Jean Handel, a DP France sales manager, facilitated the introduction. In private, he explained Techno Plastics' strategic importance to DP International, in part due to its annual purchases of $1,000,000 in new equipment, parts and service.

At the plastics convention, the US team members demonstrated several of DP International's latest machines to Techno Plastics and began initial strategy discussions for the upcoming RFP response. Over the next few weeks, Jean Handel followed up with information regarding the US plant's specifications and also provided recommendations with respect to pricing.

With Handel's information, the DP-A bid was developed to mirror the specifications of Techno Plastics' German Plant, currently supplied by DP-G, with slightly higher pricing than the typical US bid. These specifications included a cooling device for regrind and a conveyer system, but did not include self-cleaning capabilities because these were not currently in place at the newest Techno Plastics plant in Germany.

DP-A proposed to provide a "system to meet Techno Plastics specifications," a standard practice for US bidding. Typical of DP-A's bids to its US customers, the bid not provide specifics regarding each piece of individual equipment, formalized engineering drawings, or spare part commitments.

In addition to the bid, the US sales executives traveled to the Lawrenceville plant to meet with Michel Duval, the plant manager. Scott Millar, DP-A Regional Manager, and Richard Foster presented a sales proposal to Duval and other Techno Plastics staff. Both the presentation and bid were well received.

September 1994

At another plastics convention in Paris in late September, US and European staff met in France for a second time with Stefan Sevan, the Techno Plastics engineer responsible for the Lawrenceville, Georgia

EXHIBIT 5 Organizational Structures

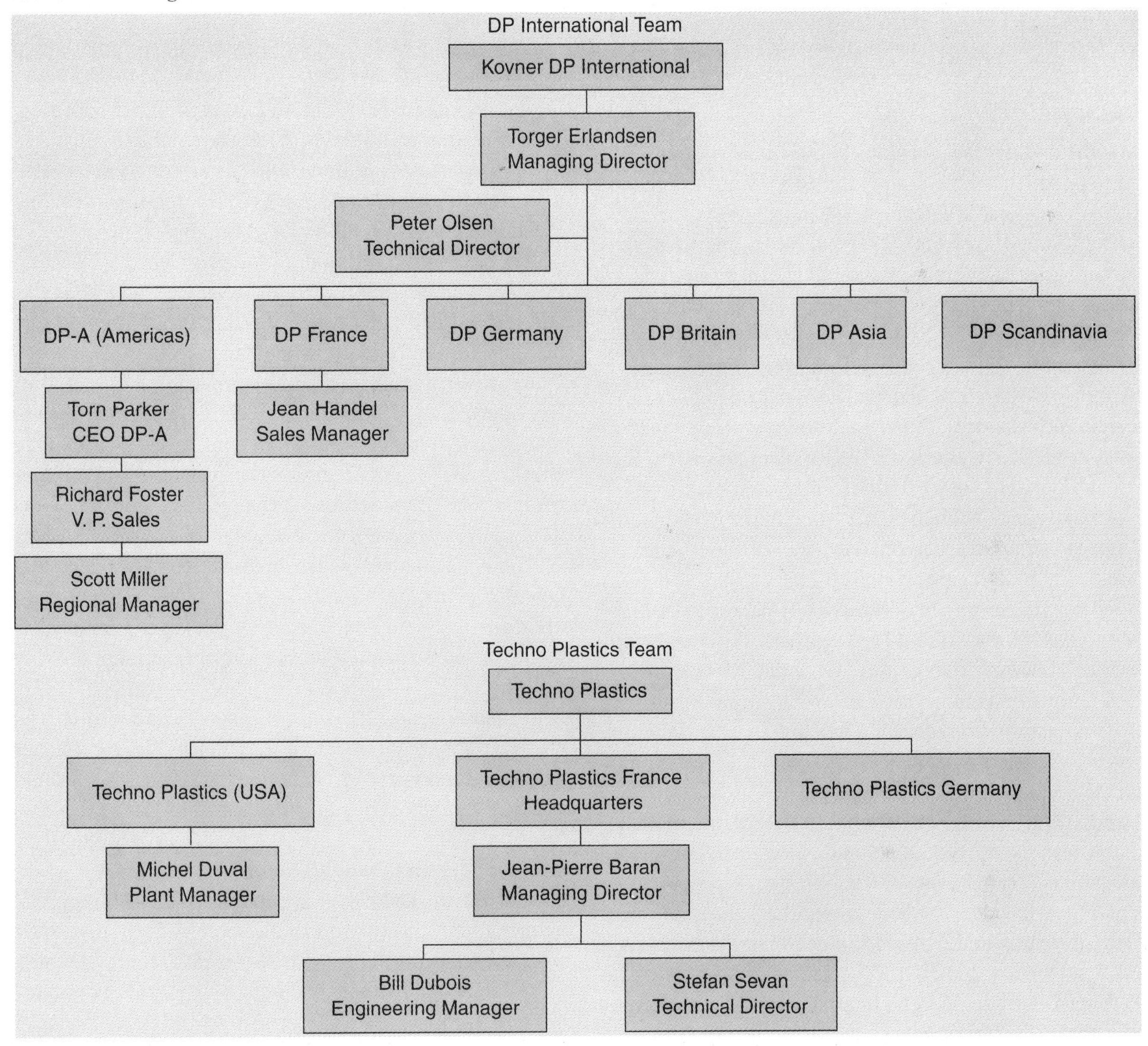

plant and Technical Director for Techno Plastics' Blow Molding Division. During this meeting, Sevan and his colleague Bill Dubois were led by Jean Handel in a discussion of the technical specification requirements for the new plant. On the basis of that discussion a new DP International product was offered to the Techno Plastics engineers. At the end of the meeting, Sevan requested that DP-A re-submit its quote for equipment and services, based on the new DP International machine and specification modifications.

The need for outside vendor support for the new offering and associated pricing of additional conveyor and blower equipment in the revised quote forced DP-A to delay its bid resubmittal for six weeks. At the end of this period, Sevan contacted DP International's US office regarding the quote. He requested that it be forwarded as soon as possible. Additional problems surfaced, however, when Sevan contacted DP-A again, telling them he had not received the offer. Evidently it had been misdirected by office staff. Neither side admitted to the error.

During this period, Sevan also contacted Peter Olsen, Technical Director for DP International's Norwegian Headquarters team, in an attempt to gain control over the sale. Following the quote's re-transmission and review, Sevan offered a temporary approval to the sale.

Richard Foster and Scott Miller traveled again to the Lawrenceville plant, following the third quote, to meet with Michel Duval. Duval was very pleased with DP-A following rigorous technical discussions.

January 1995

Notwithstanding the previous multi-quote issues, DP International seemed well positioned to acquire Techno Plastics' granulator business. Then reports from DP International European staff member visiting the Fukuma Plastics's trade show in Germany indicated another problem. The staff member had been informed by Stefan Sevan that the US subsidiary quotation was not adequate. The specifications had been quoted according to proposal requirements (the standard for project conformance), rather than to the current system in use at the Rothenburg, Germany plant. As such, the current bid would not meet all of Techno Plastics' needs.

The bid was re-submitted according to the Rothenburg set-up. However, Sevan contacted the DP International US Headquarters again, claiming that the bid still was not sufficient. Sevan encouraged Tom Parker to cut his price to ensure the order. DP-A responded by lowering its price, because Parker did not want to jeopardize DP-A's global position with Techno Plastics. To support the relationship, Parker and Richard Foster flew to France to find out more about the French specification expectations.

Caucusing with the French DP International subsidiary in Paris, a US, French, and Norwegian corporate management team reviewed the Techno Plastics case, preparing what they hoped would be the final bid. Although Jean Handel offered to negotiate on behalf of the US subsidiary, his offer was rejected, following what DP-A staff considered to be internal coordination errors and technical misinformation.

After lengthy intercompany caucusing, DP-A and Techno Plastics executives worked through plant specifications and at least half a dozen new issues developed in response to granulation requirements at the German plant. During this meeting, DP International offered its final quotation, following extensive technical discussions with Techno Plastics engineers and management. Both sides were elated with the outcome. Sevan reassured Parker at the meeting saying, "I told you, I've always been a Dura-plast man."

Epilogue

It is June, 1995, and Tom Parker, CEO of Dura-plast, Inc. (DP-A), is reconstructing DP-A's handling of the Techno Plastics granulation equipment order. He was surprised and extremely disappointed to learn that Techno Plastics had not selected DP-A to supply granulators for their new plant.

The considerable expenditure in human and capital resources, along with meetings in both the US and France to clarify issues related to equipment specification, time frame and bid pricing, were not to be justified by first-year earnings alone. DP-A's efforts were targeted at extending the ongoing DP International-Techno Plastics relationship in the US through a comprehensive order for both equipment and service for Techno Plastics' new plant in Lawrenceville, Georgia. The talks and the bid had been well received. It had seemed that the only formality left was the paperwork.

However, Torger Erlandsen, managing director of DP International Operations, recently informed Parker that the Lawrenceville plant bid was awarded to Northway, a US-based granulator producer and a major competitor. The news was delivered to Erlandsen by his DP France sales manager, Jean Handel.

To make matters worse, it now seems evident that DP-A sold to the wrong decision maker, and did not offer the right equipment and price package. Technically, there was no problem with the DP International product offering.

It also appears that the final purchase decision was made at the plant level in Lawrenceville by Michel Duval and in France by Stefan Sevan's boss, the Techno Plastics engineer responsible for the Lawrenceville, Georgia plant, Jean-Pierre Baran. DP-A had thought, that the decision would be made by DP-A's main contact, Sevan, and his direct reports. To DP-A's surprise, management in Lawrenceville commented that they were more comfortable with Northway, which "seemed more interested in their business and provided comprehensive information and service specifics in its bid." They also stated that, while price was not the order winner, the Northway offer was lower than the DP-A bid.

Re-examination of the bids, however, showed that Northway's slightly less expensive pricing did not include the same specifications as the DP-A offer. As a result, the Northway package, when complete, will actually be more expensive than the DP-A offer.

For Tom Parker, a significant problem with the Techno Plastics bid failure revolves around the issue of marketing coordination. As a group, Dura-plast did not understand who was the key player in charge and who was the key decision maker. While everyone intended to do the right thing, each member of the DP-A team made mistakes. Parker commented, "When Richard and I went to France and met with Stefan Sevan and his people, he assured us we had the order. We were convinced.

However, we never really had the order. Sevan may have thought he could give us the order, but he was not the decision maker. It was a nightmare. . . The only solution I see is structured coordination among the DP International groups."

Global accounts are raising new issues for DP International, particularly with respect to pricing, cross-subsidiary coordination, technology and marketing strategy. These issues were brought to a head in the Techno Plastics situation. Currently, Dura-plast is trying to price at the local market, in effect, to maximize the profit potential in each subsidiary. However, there are concerns regarding this practice as a long-term policy.

Up to this point, all of Techno Plastics' granulator purchases had been through a DPI subsidiary—it was very loyal to Dura-plast. Now, however, Northway is also threatening DPG and DP-UK because of disparities between European and US pricing. Northway's inroad is a major concern because it threatens other DP International key accounts.

Known for his critical evaluation and analysis, Mr. Parker is committed to supporting the current DP-A and DP International customer bases. He is currently working on a plan to regain the US Techno Plastics account and is outspoken regarding the importance of avoiding similar situations in the future. He is also committed to supporting business expansion through appropriate corporate change and new, viable projects. Mr. Parker wonders what is the best next step for DP-A.

Case 6-9

Wal-Mart

In business, there is big, and there is Wal-Mart. With $245 billion in revenues in 2002, Wal-Mart Stores Inc. is the world's largest company. It is three times the size of the No. 2 retailer, France's Carrefour. Every week, 138 million shoppers visit Wal-Mart's 4,750 stores; last year, 82% of American households made at least one purchase at Wal-Mart. "There's nothing like Wal-Mart," says Ira Kalish, global director of Deloitte Research. "They are so much bigger than any retailer has ever been that it's not possible to compare."

At Wal-Mart, "everyday low prices" is more than a slogan; it is the fundamental tenet of a cult masquerading as a company. Over the years, Wal-Mart has relentlessly wrung tens of billions of dollars in cost efficiencies out of the retail supply chain, passing the larger part of the savings along to shoppers as bargain prices. New England Consulting estimates that Wal-Mart saved its U.S. customers $20 billion last year alone. Factor in the price cuts other retailers must make to compete, and the total annual savings approach $100 billion. It's no wonder that economists refer to a broad "Wal-Mart effect" that has suppressed inflation and rippled productivity gains through the economy year after year.

However, Wal-Mart's seemingly simple and virtuous business model is fraught with complications and perverse consequences (Exhibit 1). To cite a particularly noteworthy one, this staunchly anti-union company, America's largest private employer, is widely blamed for the sorry state of retail wages in America. On average, Wal-Mart sales clerks—"associates" in company parlance—pulled in $8.23 an hour, or $13,861 a year, in 2001, according to documents filed in a lawsuit pending against the company. At the time, the federal poverty line for a family of three was $14,630. Wal-Mart insists that it pays competitively, citing a privately commissioned survey that found that it "meets or exceeds" the total remuneration paid by rival retailers in 50 U.S. markets. "This is a good place to work," says Coleman H. Peterson, executive vice-president for personnel, citing an employee turnover rate that has fallen below 45% from 70% in 1999.

Critics counter that this is evidence not of improving morale but of a lack of employment alternatives in a slow-growth economy. "It's a ticking time bomb," says an executive at one big Wal-Mart supplier. "At some point, do the people stand up and revolt?" Indeed, the company now faces a revolt of sorts in the form of nearly 40 lawsuits charging it with forcing employees to work overtime without pay and a sex-discrimination case that could rank as the largest civil rights class action ever. On Sept. 24, a federal judge in California began considering a plaintiff's petition to include all women who have worked at Wal-Mart since late 1998—1.6 million all told—in a suit alleging that Wal-Mart systematically denies women equal pay and opportunities for promotion. Wal-Mart is vigorously contesting all of these suits.

Wal-Mart might well be both America's most admired and most hated company. "The world has never known a company with such ambition, capability, and

EXHIBIT 1 The Long Arm of Bentonville, Ark. For better or worse, Wal-Mart is one of the most powerful companies in history. Here's how it flexes its muscles:

The Wal-Mart Economy

It's the largest company in the world, with $245 billion in sales last year. McKinsey estimates that an eighth of the productivity gains in the late '90s came from Wal-Mart's drive for efficiency, and the discounter has been at least partly responsible for the extraordinarily low inflation rate of recent years. Its $12 billion in imports from China last year accounted for a tenth of total U.S. imports from that nation.

Lowering Wages

With a global workforce of 1.4 million, Wal-Mart plays a huge role in wages and working conditions worldwide. Its hard line on costs has forced many factories to move overseas. Its labor costs are 20% less than those at unionized supermarkets. In 2001, its sales clerks made less, on average, than the federal poverty level.

Disrupting Communities

Wal-Mart's huge advantages in buying power and efficiency force many local rivals to close. For every Wal-Mart supercenter that opens in the next five years, two other supermarkets will close. And because the chain often extracts tax breaks, some economists believe that Wal-Mart's entry into a community doesn't result in any net increase in jobs and tax revenue.

Policing the Culture

In the name of protecting customers, Wal-Mart has forced magazines to hide covers it considers racy and has booted others off its racks entirely. It won't carry music or computer games with mature ratings. Record companies sell Wal-Mart sanitized versions of CDs. Elsewhere in the store, the chain declines to sell Preven, a morning-after pill. Most locations do offer inexpensive firearms.

Dominating Suppliers

In its relentless drive for lower prices, Wal-Mart homes in on every aspect of a supplier's operation—which products get developed, what they're made of, how to price them. It demands that every savings be passed on to consumers. No wonder one consultant says the second-worst thing a manufacturer can do is sign a contract with Wal-Mart. The worst? Not sign one.

momentum," marvels a Boston Consulting Group report. On Wall Street, Wal-Mart trades at a premium to most every other retailer. But the more size and power that "the Beast of Bentonville" amasses, the greater the backlash it is stirring among competing retailers, vendors, organized labor, community activists, and cultural and political progressives. America has a long history of controversial retailers, notes James E. Hoopes, a history professor at Babson College. "What's new about Wal-Mart is the flak it's drawn from outside the world of its competition," he says. "It's become a social phenomenon that people resent and fear".

Wal-Mart's marketplace clout is hard to overstate (Exhibit 2). In household staples such as toothpaste, shampoo, and paper towels, the company commands about 30% of the U.S. market, and analysts predict that its share of many such goods could hit 50% before decade's end. Wal-Mart also is Hollywood's biggest outlet, accounting for 15% to 20% of all sales of CDs, videos, and DVDs. The mega-retailer did not add magazines to its mix until the mid-1990s, but it now makes 15% of all single-copy sales in the U.S. In books, too, Wal-Mart has quickly become a force. "They pile up best-sellers like toothpaste," says Stephen Riggio, chief executive of Barnes & Noble Inc., the world's largest bookseller.

Wal-Mart controls a large and rapidly increasing share of the business done by most every major U.S. consumer-products company: 28% of Dial's total sales, 24% of Del Monte Foods', 23% of Clorox', 23% of

EXHIBIT 2 King Kong in Diapers Wal-Mart dominates sales in a number of categories:

Data: A.C. Nielsen, Retail Forward, *Home Textiles Today*

Category	Share
Disposable diapers	32%
Hair care	30
Toothpaste	26
Pet food	20
Home textiles	13

U.S. market share based on 2002 data; excludes Sam's Clubs

Revlon's, and on down the list. Suppliers' growing dependence on Wal-Mart is "a huge issue" not only for manufacturers but also for the U.S. economy, says Tom Rubel, CEO of consultant Retail Forward Inc. "If [Wal-Mart] ever stumbles, we've got a potential national security problem on our hands. They touch almost everything. . . . If they ever really went into a tailspin, the dislocation would be significant and traumatic."

Even so, Wal-Mart appears to be in no imminent danger of running afoul of federal antitrust statutes. The Robinson-Patman Act of 1936 was passed in large part to protect mom-and-pop grocers from the Great Atlantic & Pacific Tea Co., the Wal-Mart of its day. But contemporary antitrust interpretations eschew such David-and-Goliath populism. Giants like Wal-Mart have wide latitude to do as they wish to rivals and suppliers so long as they deliver lower prices to consumers. "When Wal-Mart comes in and people desert downtown because they like the selection and the low prices, it's hard for people in the antitrust community to say we should not let them do that," says New York University law professor Harry First.

CEO H. Lee Scott Jr. and other Wal-Mart executives are aware of the rising hostility the company faces and are trying to smooth its rough edges in dealing with the outside world. But they have no intention of tampering with its shopper-centric business model. "We don't turn a deaf ear to any criticism. We're most sensitive to what the customer has to say, though," says Vice-Chairman Thomas M. Coughlin. "Your customers will tell you when you're wrong."

Wal-Mart cites customer preferences as the reason it does not stock CDs or DVDs with parental warning stickers and why it occasionally yanks items from its shelves. In May, it removed the racy "lad" magazines *Maxim, Stuff*, and *FHM*. A month later, it began obscuring the covers of *Glamour, Redbook, Marie Claire*, and *Cosmopolitan* with binders. Why did Wal-Mart censor these publications and not *Rolling Stone*, which has featured a nearly naked Britney Spears and Christina Aguilera on two of its recent covers? "There's a lot of subjectivity," concedes Gary Severson, a Wal-Mart general merchandise manager. "There's a line between provocative and pornographic. I don't know exactly where it is."

Wal-Mart was the only one of the top 10 drug chains to refuse to stock Preven when Gynetics Inc. introduced the morning-after contraceptive in 1999. Roderick L. Mackenzie, Gynetics' founder and nonexecutive chairman, says senior Wal-Mart executives told his employees that they did not want their pharmacists grappling with the "moral dilemma" of abortion. Mackenzie was incensed but tried to hide it. "When you speak to God in Bentonville, you speak in hushed tones," says Mackenzie, who explained, to no avail, that Preven did not induce abortion but rather prevented pregnancy. Wal-Mart spokesman Jay Allen says "a number of factors were considered" in making the Preven decision, but he denies that opposition to abortion was one of them. "If anybody of any belief reads any moral decision [into] that, that's not right," he says.

Cultural Gatekeeper

There is no question that the company has the legal right to sell only what it chooses to sell, even in the case of First Amendment-protected material such as magazines. By most accounts, though, Wal-Mart's cultural gatekeeping has served to narrow the mainstream for entertainment offerings while imparting to it a rightward tilt. The big music companies have stopped grousing about Wal-Mart and are eagerly supplying the chain with the same sanitized versions of explicit CDs that they provide to radio stations. "You can't have 100% impact when you are taking an artist to a mainstream audience if you don't have the biggest player, Wal-Mart," says EMI Music North America Executive Vice-President Phil Quartararo.

This year alone, Wal-Mart hopes to open as many as 335 new stores in the U.S.: 55 discount stores, 210 supercenters, 45 Sam's Clubs, and 25 Neighborhood markets. An additional 130 new stores are on the boards for foreign markets. Wal-Mart currently operates 1,309 stores in 10 countries, ranking as the largest retailer in Mexico and Canada. If the company can maintain its current 15% growth rate, it will double its revenues over the next five years and top $600 billion in 2011 (Exhibit 3).

That's a very big if—even for Wal-Mart. Vice-Chairman Coughlin's biggest worry is finding enough warm bodies to staff all those new stores. By Wal-Mart's own estimate, about 44% of its 1.4 million employees will leave in 2003, meaning the company will need to hire 616,000 workers just to stay even. In addition, from 2004 to 2008, the company wants to add 800,000 new positions, including 47,000 management slots. "That's what causes me the most sleepless nights," Coughlin says.

At the same time, Wal-Mart will have to cope with intensifying grassroots opposition. The company's hugely ambitious expansion plans hinge on continuing its move out of its stronghold in the rural South and Midwest into urban America. This year, the company

EXHIBIT 3 41 Years of Nonstop Growth

Data: Wal-Mart Stores Inc.

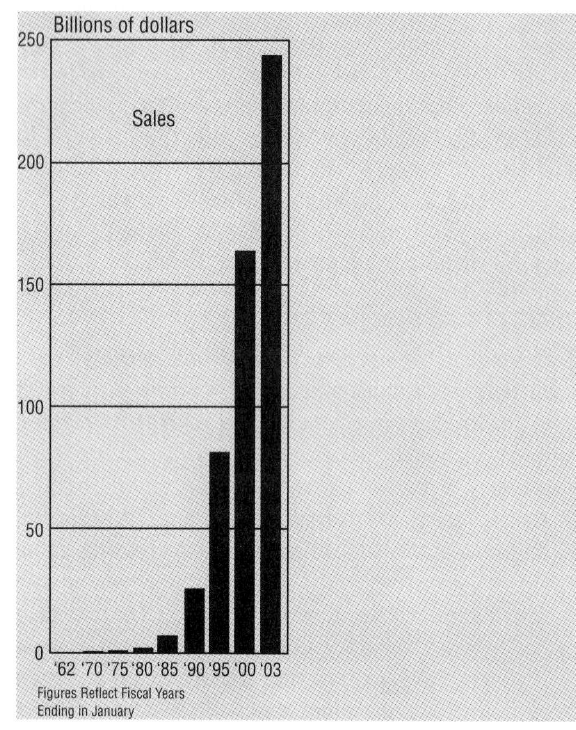

opened what it describes as "one of its first truly urban stores" in Los Angeles, not far from Watts. Everyday low prices no doubt appeal to city dwellers no less than to their country cousins. But Wal-Mart's sense of itself as definitively American ("Wal-Mart is America," boasts one top executive) is likely to be severely tested by the metropolis' high land costs, restrictive zoning codes, and combative labor unions—not to mention its greater economic and cultural diversity.

A Zero-Sum Game?

Certainly, Wal-Mart will be hard pressed to continue censoring its product lines using the justification of customer preference. The market for profanity-laced hip-hop may be tiny in Bentonville, Ark., but it is big in Los Angeles. Overseas, the company does not presume to impose a small-town, Bible Belt moral agenda on shoppers. "We adopt local standards," says John B. Menzer, CEO of Wal-Mart's international division. Why, then, should Los Angeles be any different?

The fact is, Wal-Mart doesn't know for certain how the majority of its customers feel about *Maxim*, or any other magazine, for that matter. It appears that the company makes no scientific attempt to survey shoppers about entertainment content but responds in ad hoc fashion to complaints lodged by a relative handful of customers and by outside groups, which are usually but not always of the conservative persuasion (Exhibit 4).

On the other hand, the company seldom submits to community groups that oppose its plans to build new stores. The number of such challenges has increased steadily and is now running at about 100 a year. Wal-Mart's "biggest barrier to growth is . . . opposition at the local level," says Carl Steidtmann, Deloitte Research's retail economist. The Stop Wal-Mart movement has been bolstered of late by a series of academic studies that have debunked the notion that a new big-box store boosts employment and sales and property-tax receipts. "The net increases are minimal as the new big-box stores merely capture sales from existing business in the area," concludes a new study of Wal-Mart's impact in Mississippi. "I see it pretty much as a zero-sum game," says co-author Kenneth E. Stone, an economics professor at Iowa State University.

EXHIBIT 4 Wal-Mart by the Numbers The world's largest company generates some amazing statistics

30	44%	4	14%	82%	71%
Supermarkets closed since Wal-Mart **saturated** Oklahoma City	**Turnover rate** for Wal-Mart's hourly workers per year	Number of Wal-Marts in Vermont, the **fewest of any state**	How much **lower** average grocery prices are where Wal-Mart competes	Percentage of **U.S. households** that made a Wal-Mart purchase last year	**Price drop** for George jeans at Britain's Asda since Wal-Mart bought it in '99
Data: Retail Forward Inc.	Data: Wal-Mart Stores Inc.	Data: Wal-Mart Stores Inc.	Data: UBS Warburg	Data: Retail Forward Inc.	Data: Wal-Mart Stores Inc.

The most hotly contested battleground at the moment is Contra Costa County, near San Francisco. In June, county supervisors enacted an ordinance that prohibits any retail outlet larger than 90,000 square feet from devoting more than 5% of its floor space to food or other nontaxable goods. Wal-Mart promptly gathered enough signatures to force a referendum, scheduled for March. Complains County Supervisor John Gioia: "Local planning should be done by our locally elected board and not by a corporate office in Bentonville, Arkansas." Robert S. McAdam, Wal-Mart's vice-president for government relations, says corporate-sponsored referenda, which Wal-Mart has promoted elsewhere in California, are "a perfectly legitimate part of the process."

Supercenter Nation

Meanwhile, the United Food & Commercial Workers union is stepping up its long-standing attempts to organize Wal-Mart stores, with current campaigns in 45 locations. For UFCW locals that represent grocery workers, the issue is nothing less than survival. The Wal-Mart supercenter—the principal vehicle of the company's expansion—is a nonunion dagger aimed at the heart of the traditional American supermarket, nearly 13,000 of which have closed since 1992.

Patterned after the European hypermarket, the supercenter is a combination supermarket and general merchandise discounter built to colossal scale. Wal-Mart didn't introduce the supercenter to America, but it has amassed a 79% share of the category since it moved into food and drug retailing by opening its first such store in 1988. Today, Wal-Mart operates 1,386 supercenters and is the nation's largest grocer, with a 19% market share, and its third-largest pharmacy, with 16%.

Wal-Mart plans to open 1,000 more supercenters in the U.S. alone over the next five years. Retail Forward estimates that this supercenter blitzkrieg will boost Wal-Mart's grocery and related revenues to $162 billion from the current $82 billion, giving it control over 35% of U.S. food sales and 25% of drugstore sales. Market-share gains of such magnitude in a slow-growth business necessarily will come at the expense of established competitors—especially the unionized ones, which pay their workers 30% more on average than Wal-Mart does, according to the UFCW. Retail Forward predicts that for every new supercenter that Wal-Mart opens, two supermarkets will close, or 2,000 all told.

To the low-price, low-cost operator go the spoils. Isn't that how capitalism is supposed to work? Certainly, the supercentering of America can be expected to result in huge savings at the cash register. On average, a Wal-Mart supercenter offers prices 14% below its rivals', according to a 2002 study by UBS Warburg.

However, those everyday low prices come at a cost. As the number of supermarkets shrinks, more shoppers will have to travel farther from home and will find their buying increasingly restricted to merchandise that Wal-Mart chooses to sell—a growing percentage of which may be the retailer's private-label goods, which now account for nearly 20% of sales. Meanwhile, the failure of hundreds of stores will cost their owners dearly and put thousands out of work, only some of whom will find jobs at Wal-Mart, most likely at lower pay. "It will be a sad day in this country if we wake up one morning and all we find is a Wal-Mart on every corner," says Gary E. Hawkins, CEO of Green Hills, a family-owned supermarket in Syracuse, N.Y.

For suppliers, too, Wal-Mart's relentless pricing pressure is a mixed blessing. "If you are good with data, are sophisticated, and have scale, Wal-Mart should be one of your most profitable customers," says a retired consumer-products executive. Unlike many retailers, the company does not charge "slotting fees" for access to its shelves and is unusually generous in sharing sales data with manufacturers. In return, though, Wal-Mart not only dictates delivery schedules and inventory levels but also heavily influences product specifications. In the end, many suppliers have to choose between designing goods their way or the Wal-Mart way. "Wal-Mart really is about driving the cost of a product down," says James A. Wier, CEO of Simplicity Manufacturing, a lawn-mower maker that decided to stop selling to Wal-Mart last fall. "When you drive the cost of a product down, you really can't deliver the high-quality product like we have."

Critics also argue that Wal-Mart's intensifying global pursuit of low-cost goods is partly to blame for the accelerating loss of U.S. manufacturing jobs to China and other low-wage nations. "It's hard to tease out, but Wal-Mart is definitely part of the dynamic, and given its market share and power, probably a significant part," says Jared Bernstein, a labor economist at the liberal Economic Policy Institute. The $12 billion worth of Chinese goods Wal-Mart bought in 2002 represented 10% of all U.S. imports from China.

For obvious reasons, Wal-Mart has de-emphasized the "Made in America" campaign that founder Sam Walton started in the mid-1980s to great promotional effect. "Where we have the option to source domestically we do," says Ken Eaton, Wal-Mart's senior vice-president for global procurement. However, he adds, "there are certain businesses, particularly in the

U.S., where you just can't buy domestically anymore to the scale and value we need." In recent years, Wal-Mart increasingly has sought additional cost advantages by bypassing middlemen and buying finished goods and raw materials from foreign manufacturers. By contracting directly with a handful of denim manufacturers in Southeast Asia, the company has driven down the retail price of the George brand jeans it sells in Britain and Germany to $7.85 from $26.67. Says Eaton: "The mind-set around here is, we're agents for our customers."

"The Wal-Mart Phenomenon"

Wal-Mart's philosophy doesn't cut any ice with Wilbur L. Ross Jr., a financier and steel tycoon who soon will close on the purchase of beleaguered textile manufacturer Burlington Industries Inc. Ross contends that Wal-Mart is costing Americans jobs "not only as a business strategy, but as a lobbying strategy"—that is, by using its influence in Washington to oppose import tariffs and quotas and promote free-trade pacts with Third World countries, including the Southeast Asian countries that supply Wal-Mart with denim. "Everybody is now scurrying around trying to find the lowest price points," Ross complains. "It's the Wal-Mart phenomenon."

High on a wall inside Wal-Mart headquarters is a paper banner with a provocative question in big block letters: "Who's taking your customers?" Beneath it, "Wanted" poster style, hang photos of the CEOs of two dozen of America's largest retailers—Target, Kroger, Winn-Dixie Stores, Walgreen, and so on. None looks very happy, perhaps because they know that the only way to get off the wall is to fail utterly. Although Kmart is reorganizing under the federal bankruptcy code, a photo of its CEO continues to hang in Wal-Mart's rogues' gallery and no doubt will remain there for as long as Kmart operates even a single store.

Growth will only add to the clout that the Bentonville colossus now wields. There might well come a time, though, when Wal-Mart's size poses as much of a threat to the company itself as it does to outsiders. "Their biggest danger is just managing size," observes a long-time supplier. Adds Babson College's Hoopes: "The history of the last 150 years in retailing would say that if you don't like Wal-Mart, be patient. There will be new models eventually that will do Wal-Mart in, and Wal-Mart won't see it coming." Right now, though, Wal-Mart's day of reckoning seems a very long way off.

With Diane Brady, Mike France, Tom Lowry, Nanette Byrnes, and Susan Zegel in New York; Michael Arndt, Robert Berner, and Ann Therese Palmer in Chicago; and bureau reports

Source: Anthony Bianco and Wendy Zellner, "Is Wal-Mart Too Powerful?" BusinessWeek, October 6, 2003, 100–110.

Case 6-10

Blair Water Purifiers India

"A pity I couldn't have stayed for Diwali," thought Rahul Chatterjee. "But anyway, it was great to be back home in Calcutta." The Diwali holiday and its festivities would begin in early November 1996, some two weeks after Chatterjee had returned to the United States. Chatterjee worked as an international market liaison for Blair Company Inc. This was his eighth year with Blair Company and easily his favorite. "Your challenge will be in moving us from just dabbling in less developed countries [LDCs] to our thriving in them," his boss had said when Chatterjee was promoted to the job last January. Chatterjee had agreed and was thrilled when he was asked to visit Bombay and New Delhi in April. His purpose on that trip was to gather background data on the possibility of Blair Company entering the Indian market for home water purification devices. The initial results had been encouraging and had prompted the second trip.

Chatterjee had used his second trip primarily to study Indian consumers in Calcutta and Bangalore and to

This case was written by Professor James E. Nelson, University of Colorado at Boulder. He thanks students in the class of 1996 (batch 31), Indian Institute of Management, Calcutta, for their invaluable help in collecting all the data needed to write this case. He also thanks Professor Roger Kerin, Southern Methodist University, for his helpful comments. The case is intended for educational purposes rather than to illustrate either effective or ineffective decision making. Some data as well as the identity of the company are disguised.

gather information on possible competitors. The two cities represented quite different metropolitan areas in terms of location, size, language, and infrastructure, yet both cities faced similar problems in terms of the water supplied to their residents. Those problems could be found in many LDCs and were favorable to home water purification.

Information gathered on both visits would be used to make a recommendation on market entry and on the elements of an entry strategy. Executives at Blair Company would compare Chatterjee's recommendation to those from two other Blair Company liaisons who were focusing their efforts on Argentina, Brazil, and Indonesia.

Indian Market for Home Water Filtration and Purification

Like many things in India, the market for home water filtration and purification took a good deal of effort to understand. Yet despite expending this effort, Chatterjee realized that much remained either unknown or in conflict. For example, the market seemed clearly a mature one, with four or five established Indian competitors fighting for market share. Or was it? Another view portrayed the market as a fragmented one, with no large competitor having a national presence and perhaps 100 small regional manufacturers, each competing in just one or two of India's 25 states. Indeed, the market could be in its early growth stages, as reflected by the large number of product designs, materials, and performances. Perhaps with a next-generation product and a world-class marketing effort, Blair Company could consolidate the market and stimulate tremendous growth—much like the situation in the Indian market for automobiles.

Such uncertainty made it difficult to estimate market potential. However, Chatterjee had collected unit sales estimates for a 10-year period for three similar product categories: vacuum cleaners, sewing machines, and color televisions. In addition, a Delhi-based research firm had provided him with estimates of unit sales for Aquaguard, the best-selling water purifier in several Indian states. Chatterjee had used the data in two forecasting models available at Blair Company along with three subjective scenarios—realistic, optimistic, and pessimistic—to arrive at the estimates and forecasts for water purifiers shown in Exhibit 1. "If anything," Chatterjee had explained to his boss, "my forecasts are conservative because they describe only first-time sales, not any replacement sales over the 10-year forecast horizon." He also pointed out that his forecasts applied only to industry sales in larger urban areas, which was the present industry focus.

One thing that seemed certain was that many Indians felt the need for improved water quality. Folklore, newspapers, consumer activists, and government officials regularly reinforced this need by describing the poor

EXHIBIT 1
Industry Sales Estimates and Forecasts for Water Purifiers in India, 1990–2005 (thousands of units)

		Unit Sales Forecast Under		
Year	Unit Sales Estimates	Realistic Scenario	Optimistic Scenario	Pessimistic Scenario
1990	60			
1991	90			
1992	150			
1993	200			
1994	220			
1995	240			
1996		250	250	250
1997		320	370	300
1998		430	540	400
1999		570	800	550
2000		800	1,200	750
2001		1,000	1,500	850
2002		1,300	1,900	900
2003		1,500	2,100	750
2004		1,600	2,100	580
2005		1,500	1,900	420

quality of Indian water. Quality suffered particularly during monsoons because highly polluted water entered treatment plants and because of numerous leaks and unauthorized withdrawals from water systems. Such leaks and withdrawals often polluted clean water after it had left the plants. Politicians running for national, state, and local government offices also reinforced the need for improved water quality through election campaign promises. Governments at these levels set standards for water quality, took measurements at thousands of locations throughout the nation, and advised consumers when water became unsafe.

During periods of poor water quality many Indian consumers had little choice but to consume the water as they found it. However, better-educated, wealthier, and more health-conscious consumers took steps to safeguard their families' health and often continued these steps all year. A good estimate of the number of such households, Chatterjee thought, would be around 40 million. These consumers were similar in many respects to consumers in middle- and upper-middle-class households in the United States and the European Union. They valued comfort and product choice. They saw consumption of material goods as a means to a higher quality of life. They liked foreign brands and would pay a higher price for such brands as long as those products outperformed competing Indian products. Chatterjee had identified as his target market these 40 million households plus another 4 million households whose members had similar values and lifestyles but made little effort to improve water quality in their homes.

Traditional Method for Home Water Purification

The traditional method of water purification in the target market relied not on a commercially supplied product but on boiling. Each day or several times a day, a cook, maid, or family member would boil two to five liters of water for 10 minutes, allow it to cool, and then transfer it to containers for storage (often in a refrigerator). Chatterjee estimated that about 50 percent of the target market used this procedure. Boiling was seen by consumers as inexpensive, effective in terms of eliminating dangerous bacteria, and entrenched in a traditional sense. Many consumers who used this method considered it more effective than any product on the market. However, boiling affected the palatability of water, leaving the purified product somewhat "flat" tasting. Boiling also was cumbersome, time-consuming, and ineffective in removing physical impurities and unpleasant odors. Consequently, about 10 percent of the target market took a second step by filtering their boiled water through "candle filters" before storage. Many consumers took this action despite knowing that water could become recontaminated during handling and storage.

Mechanical Methods for Home Water Filtration and Purification

About 40 percent of the target market used a mechanical device to improve their water quality. Half of this group used candle filters, primarily because of their low price and ease of use. The typical candle filter contained two containers, one resting on top of the other. The upper container held one or more porous ceramic cylinders (candles) which strained the water as gravity drew it into the lower container. Containers were made of plastic, porcelain, or stainless steel and typically stored between 15 and 25 liters of filtered water. Purchase costs depended on materials and capacities, ranging from Rs. 350 for a small plastic model to Rs. 1,100 for a large stainless-steel model (35 Indian rupees was equivalent to US $1.00 in 1996). Candle filters were slow, producing 15 liters (one candle) to 45 liters (three candles) of filtered water in 24 hours. To maintain this productivity, candles regularly had to be removed, cleaned, and boiled for 20 minutes. Most manufacturers recommended that consumers replace candles (Rs. 40 each) either once a year or more frequently, depending on sediment levels.

The other half of this group used "water purifiers," devices that were considerably more sophisticated than candle filters. Water purifiers typically employed three water-processing stages. The first removed sediments, the second objectionable odors and colors, and the third harmful bacteria and viruses. Engineers at Blair Company were skeptical that most purifiers claiming the latter benefit could deliver on their promise. However, all purifiers did a better job here than candle filters. Candle filters were totally ineffective in eliminating bacteria and viruses (and might even increase this type of contamination) despite advertising claims to the contrary. Water purifiers generally used stainless-steel containers and sold at prices ranging from Rs. 2,000 to Rs. 7,000, depending on the manufacturer, features, and capacities. Common flow rates were one to two liters of purified water per minute. Simple service activities could be performed on water purifiers by consumers as needed. However, more complicated service required that units be taken to a nearby dealer or necessitated an in-home visit from a skilled technician.

The remaining 10 percent of the target market owned neither a filter nor a purifier and seldom boiled their water. Many consumers in this group were unaware of water problems and thought their water quality was acceptable. However, a few consumers in this group refused to pay for products that they believed were mostly ineffective. Overall, Chatterjee believed that only a few consumers in this group could be induced to change their habits and become customers. The most attractive segments consisted of the 90 percent of households in the target market that boiled, boiled and filtered, only filtered, or purified their water.

All the segments in the target market showed a good deal of similarity in terms of what they thought important in the purchase of a water purifier. According to Chatterjee's research, the most important factor was product performance in terms of sediment removal bacteria and virus removal, capacity (in the form of storage or flow rate), safety, and "footprint" space. Purchase price also was an important concern among consumers who boiled, boiled and filtered, or only filtered their water. The next most important factor was ease of installation and service, with style and appearance rated almost as important. The least important factor was warranty and the availability of financing for purchase. Finally, all segments expected a water purifier to be warranted against defective operation for 18 to 24 months and to perform trouble-free for 5 to 10 years.

Foreign investment in India

India appeared attractive to many foreign investors because of government actions begun in the 1980s during the administration of Prime Minister Rajiv Gandhi. The broad label applied to these actions was *liberalization.* Liberalization had opened the Indian economy to foreign investors, stemming from a recognition that protectionist policies had not worked very well and that Western economies and technologies—seen against the collapse of the Soviet Union—did. Liberalization had meant major changes in approval requirements for new commercial projects, investment policies, taxation procedures, and, most important, the attitudes of government officials. These changes had stayed in place through the two national governments that followed Gandhi's assassination in 1991.

If Blair Company entered the Indian market, it would do so in one of three ways: (1) joint working arrangement. (2) joint venture company, or (3) acquisition. In a joint working arrangement Blair Company would supply key purifier components to an Indian company, which would manufacture and market the assembled product. License fees would be remitted to Blair Company on a per-unit basis over the term of the agreement (typically five years, with an option to renew for three more). A joint venture agreement would have Blair Company partnering with an existing Indian company expressly for the purpose of manufacturing and marketing water purifiers. Profits from the joint venture operation would be split between the two parties per the agreement, which usually contained a clause describing buy/sell procedures available to the two parties after a minimum time period. An acquisition entry would have Blair Company purchasing an existing Indian company whose operations then would be expanded to include the water purifier. Profits from the acquisition would belong to Blair Company.

Beyond understanding these basic entry possibilities, Chatterjee acknowledged that he was no expert in the legal aspects of the project. However, two days spent with a Calcutta consulting firm had produced the following information. Blair Company had to apply for market entry to the Foreign Investment Promotion Board, Secretariat for Industrial Approvals, Ministry of Industries. The proposal would go before the board for an assessment of the relevant technology and India's need for the technology. If approved by the board, the proposal then would go to the Reserve Bank of India, Ministry of Finance, for approvals of any royalties and fees, remittances of dividends and interest (if any), repatriation of profits and invested capital, and repayment of foreign loans. While the process sounded cumbersome and time-consuming, the consultant assured Chatterjee that the government usually completed its deliberations in less than six months and that his consulting firm could "virtually guarantee'' final approval.

Trademarks and patents were protected by law in India. Trademarks were protected for seven years and could be renewed on the payment of a prescribed fee. Patents lasted for 14 years. On balance, Chatterjee had told his boss that Blair Company would have "no more problem protecting its intellectual property rights in India than in the United States—as long as we stay out of court." Chatterjee went on to explain that litigation in India was expensive and protracted. Litigation problems were compounded by an appeal process that could extend a case for a generation. Consequently, many foreign companies preferred arbitration, as India was a party to the Geneva Convention covering foreign arbitral awards.

Foreign companies were taxed on income arising from Indian operations. They also paid taxes on any interest, dividends, and royalties received and on any capital gains received from a sale of assets. The government offered a wide range of tax concessions to foreign investors, including liberal depreciation allowances and generous deductions. The government offered even more favorable tax treatment if foreign investors would locate in one of India's six Free Trade Zones. Overall, Chatterjee thought that corporate tax rates in India probably were somewhat higher than those in the United States. However, so were profits; the average return on assets for all Indian corporations in recent years was almost 18 percent, compared to about 11 percent for U.S. corporations.

Approval by the Reserve Bank of India was needed for the repatriation of ordinary profits. However, approval could be obtained easily if Blair Company could show that repatriated profits were being paid out of export earnings of hard currencies. Chatterjee thought that export earnings would not be difficult to realize because of India's extremely low wage rates and its central location in regard to wealthier South Asian countries. "Profit repatriation is really not much of an issue, anyway," he thought. Three years might pass before profits of any magnitude could be realized; at least five years would pass before substantial profits would be available for repatriation. Approval of repatriation by the Reserve Bank might not be required at that time, given liberalization trends. Finally, if repatriation remained difficult, Blair Company could undertake cross-trading or other actions to unblock profits.

Overall, investment and trade regulations in India in 1996 meant that business could be conducted much more easily than ever before. Hundreds of companies from the European Union, Japan, Korea, and the United States were entering India in all sectors of the country's economy. In the home appliance market, Chatterjee could identify 11 such firms: Carrier, Electrolux, General Electric, Goldstar, Matsushita, Singer, Samsung, Sanyo, Sharp, Toshiba, and Whirlpool. Many of those firms had yet to realize substantial profits, but all saw the promise of a huge market developing over the next few years.

Blair Company, Inc.

Blair Company was founded in 1975 by Eugene Blair after he left his position in research and development at Culligan International Company. Blair Company's first product was a desalinator used by mobile home parks in Florida to remove salt from the brackish well water supplied to residents. The product was a huge success, and markets quickly expanded to include nearby municipalities, smaller businesses, hospitals, and bottlers of water for sale to consumers. Geographic markets also expanded, first to other coastal regions near the company's headquarters in Tampa, Florida, and then to desert areas in the southwestern United States. New products were added rapidly as well, and by 1996 the product line included desalinators, particle filters, ozonators, ion exchange resins, and purifiers. Industry experts generally regarded the product line as superior in terms of performance and quality, with prices higher than those of many competitors.

Blair Company sales revenues for 1996 would be almost $400 million, with an expected profit close to $50 million. Annual growth in sales revenues had averaged 12 percent for the last five years. Blair Company employed over 4,000 people, with 380 having technical backgrounds and responsibilities.

Export sales of desalinators and related products began at Blair Company in 1980. Units were sold first to resorts in Mexico and Belize and later to water bottlers in Germany. Export sales grew rapidly, and Blair Company found it necessary to organize its international division in 1985. Sales in that division also grew rapidly and would reach almost $140 million in 1996. About $70 million would come from countries in Central America and South America, $30 million from Europe (including shipments to Africa), and $40 million from South Asia and Australia. The international division had sales offices, small assembly areas, and distribution facilities in Frankfurt, Germany; Tokyo, Japan; and Singapore.

The Frankfurt office had provided the impetus in 1990 for the development and marketing of Blair Company's first product targeted exclusively at consumer households—a home water filter. Sales engineers at the Frankfurt office began receiving consumer and distributor requests for a home water filter soon after the fall of the Berlin Wall in 1989. By late 1991 two models had been designed in the United States and introduced in Germany (particularly to the eastern regions), Poland, Hungary, Romania, the Czech Republic, and Slovakia.

Blair Company executives watched the success of the two water filters with great interest. The market for clean water in LDCs was huge, profitable, and attractive in a socially responsible sense. However, the quality of water in many LDCs was such that a water filter usually would not be satisfactory. Consequently, in late 1994 executives had called for the development of a water purifier that could be added to the product line. Engineers had given the final design in the project the brand name Delight. For the time being Chatterjee and the other market analysts had accepted the name, not knowing if it might infringe on an existing brand in India or in the other countries under study.

The Delight Purifier

The Delight purifier used a combination of technologies to remove four types of contaminants from potable water: sediments, organic and inorganic chemicals, microbials or cysts, and objectionable tastes and odors. The technologies were effective as long as the contaminants in the water were present at "reasonable" levels. Engineers at Blair Company had interpreted this to mean the levels described in several World Health Organization (WHO) reports on potable water and had combined the technologies to purify water to a level above WHO standards. Engineers had repeatedly assured Chatterjee that Delight's design in terms of technologies should not be a concern. Ten units operating in the company's testing laboratory showed no signs of failure or performance deterioration after some 5.000 hours of continuous use. "Still," Chatterjee thought, "we will undertake a good bit of field testing in India before entering. The risks of failure are too large to ignore. And besides, the results of our testing would be useful in persuading consumers and retailers to buy."

Chatterjee and the other market analysts still faced major design issues in configuring technologies into physical products. For example, a "point of entry" design would place the product immediately after water entry to the home, treating all water before it flowed to all water outlets. In contrast, a "point of use" design would place the product on a countertop, on a wall, or at the end of a faucet and treat only water arriving at that location. Based on cost estimates, designs of competing products, and his understanding of Indian consumers, Chatterjee would direct the engineers to proceed only with point of use designs for that market.

Other technical details had not yet been worked out. For example, Chatterjee had to provide engineers with suggestions for filter flow rates, storage capacities (if any), unit layout, and overall dimensions, plus a number of special features. One such feature was the possibility of a small battery to operate the filter for several hours in case of a power failure (a common occurrence in India and many other LDCs). Another might be one or two "bells or whistles" to tell cooks, maids, and family members that the unit indeed was working properly. Yet another might be an "additive" feature that would permit users to add fluoride, vitamins, or even flavorings to their water.

Chatterjee knew that the Indian market eventually would require a number of models. However, at the outset of market entry, he probably could get by with just two—one with a larger capacity for houses and bungalows and the other a smaller-capacity model for flats. He thought that model styling and specific appearances should reflect a Western, high-technology design to distinguish the Delight purifier from competitors' products. To that end, he had instructed a graphics artist to develop two ideas that he had used to gauge consumer

EXHIBIT 2
Wall-Mount and Countertop Designs

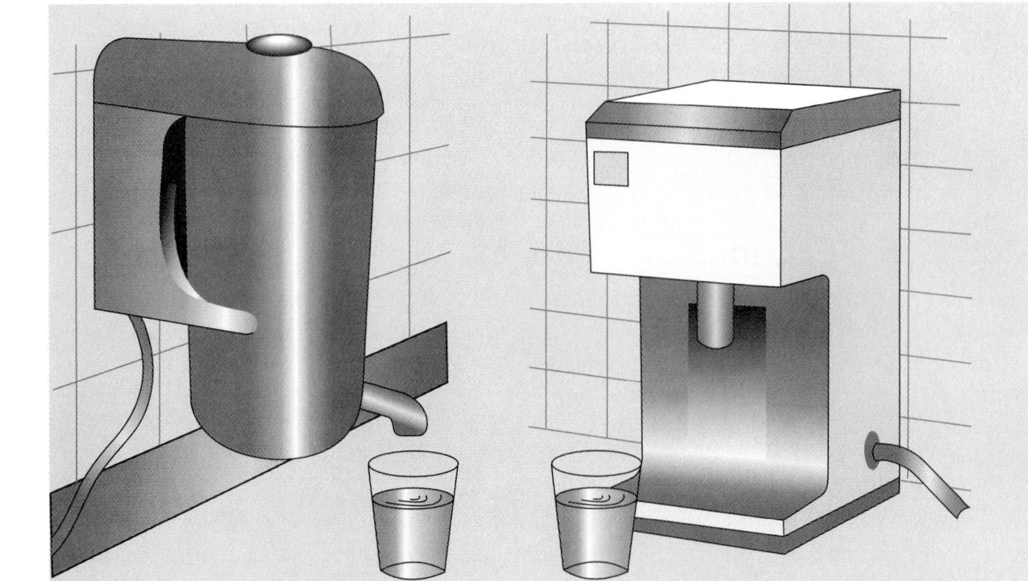

reactions on his last visit (see Exhibit 2). Consumers liked both models but preferred the countertop design to the wall-mount design.

Competitors

Upward of 100 companies competed in the Indian market for home water filters and purifiers. While information on most of those companies was difficult to obtain, Chatterjee and the Indian research agencies were able to develop descriptions of three major competitors and brief profiles of several others.

Eureka Forbes

The best established competitor in the water purifier market was Eureka Forbes, a joint venture company established in 1982 between Electrolux (Sweden) and Forbes Campbell (India). The company marketed a broad line of "modern, lifestyle products," including water purifiers, vacuum cleaners, and mixers/grinders. The brand name used for its water purifiers was Aquaguard, a name so well established that many consumers used it to refer to other water purifiers or to the entire product category. Aquaguard, with its 10-year market history, was clearly the market leader and came close to being India's only national brand. However, Eureka Forbes had recently introduced a second brand of water purifier called PureSip. The PureSip model was similar to Aquaguard except in its third-stage process, which used a polyiodide resin instead of ultraviolet rays to kill bacteria and viruses. This meant that water from a PureSip purifier could be stored safely for later use. Also in contrast to Aquaguard, the PureSip model needed no electricity for its operation.

However, the biggest difference between the two products was how they were sold. Aquaguard was sold exclusively by a 2,500-person sales force that called directly on households. In contrast, PureSip was sold by independent dealers of smaller home appliances. Unit prices to consumers for Aquaguard and PureSip in 1996 were approximately Rs.5,500 and Rs.2,000, respectively. Chatterjee believed that unit sales of PureSip were much lower than unit sales for Aquaguard but were growing at a much faster rate.

An Aquaguard unit typically was mounted on a kitchen wall, with plumbing required to bring water to the purifier's inlet. A two-meter-long power cord was connected to a 230-volt AC electrical outlet—the Indian standard. If the power supply dropped to 190 volts or lower, the unit would stop functioning. Other limits of the product included a smallish amount of activated carbon, which could eliminate only weak organic odors. It could not remove strong odors or inorganic solutes such as nitrates and iron compounds. The unit had no storage capacity, and its flow rate of one liter per minute seemed slow to some consumers. Removing water for storage or connecting the unit to a reservoir tank could affect water quality adversely.

Aquaguard's promotion strategy emphasized personal selling. Each salesperson was assigned to a specific neighborhood and was monitored by a group leader, who in turn was monitored by a supervisor. Each salesperson was expected to canvass his or her neighborhood, select prospective households (those with annual incomes exceeding Rs.70,000), demonstrate the product, and make an intensive effort to sell the product. Repeated sales calls helped educate consumers about their water quality and reassure them that Aquaguard service was readily available. Television commercials and advertisements in magazines and newspapers (see Exhibit 3) supported the personal selling efforts. Chatterjee estimated that Eureka Forbes would spend about Rs. 120 million on all sales activities in 1996, or roughly 11 percent of its sales revenues. He estimated that about Rs. 100 million of that Rs. I 20 million would be spent in the form of sales commissions. Chatterjee thought the company's total advertising expenditures for the year would be only about Rs. 1 million.

Eureka Forbes was a formidable competitor. The sales force was huge, highly motivated, and well managed. Moreover, Aquaguard was the first product to enter the water purifier market, and the name had tremendous brand equity. The product itself was probably the weakest strategic component, but it would take a lot to convince consumers of this. And while the sales force provided a huge competitive advantage, it represented an enormous fixed cost and essentially limited sales efforts to large urban areas. More than 80 percent of India's population lived in rural areas, where water quality was even lower.

Ion Exchange

Ion Exchange was the premier water treatment company in India, specializing in the treatment of water, processed liquids, and wastewater in industrial markets. The company began operations in 1964 as a wholly owned subsidiary of British Permutit. Permutit divested its holdings in 1985, and Ion Exchange became a wholly owned Indian company. The company currently served customers in a diverse group of industries, including nuclear and thermal power stations, fertilizers, petrochemical refineries, textiles, automobiles, and

EXHIBIT 3
Aquaguard Newspaper Advertisement

home water purifiers. Its home water purifiers carried the family brand name ZERO-B (Zero-Bacteria).

ZERO-B purifiers used a halogenated resin technology as part of a three-stage purification process. The first stage removed suspended impurities with filter pads, the second eliminated bad odors and taste with activated carbon, and the third killed bacteria by using trace quantities of polyiodide (iodine). The last feature was attractive because it helped prevent iodine deficiency diseases and permitted purified water to be stored up to eight hours without fear of recontamination.

The basic purifier product for the home carried the name Puristore. A Puristore unit typically sat on a kitchen counter near the tap, with no electricity or plumbing hookup needed for its operation. The unit stored 20 liters of purified water. It sold to consumers for Rs. 2,000. Each year the user had to replace the halogenated resin at a cost of Rs. 200.

Chatterjee estimated that ZERO-B captured about 7 percent of the Indian water purifier market. Probably the biggest reason for the small share was a lack of consumer awareness. ZERO-B purifiers had been on the market for less than three years. They were not advertised heavily and did not enjoy the sales effort intensity of Aquaguard. Distribution also was limited. During Chatterjee's visit, he could find only five dealers in Calcutta carrying ZERO-B products and none in Bangalore. The dealers he contacted were of the opinion that ZERO-B's marketing efforts soon would intensify; two had heard rumors that a door-to-door sales force was planned and that consumer advertising was about to begin.

Chatterjee confirmed the latter point with a visit to a Calcutta advertising agency. A modest number of 10-second television commercials soon would be aired on the Zee TV and DD metro channels. The advertisements would focus on educating consumers with the position "It is not a filter." Instead, ZERO-B was a water purifier and was much more effective than a candle filter in preventing health problems. Apart from this advertising effort, the only form of promotion used was a point of sale brochure that dealers could give to prospective customers (see Exhibit 4).

On balance, Chatterjee thought that Ion Exchange could be a major player in the market. The company had over 30 years' experience in the field of water purification and devoted upward of Rs. 10 million each year to corporate research and development. "In fact," he thought, "all Ion Exchange really needs to do is recognize the market's potential and make it a priority within the company." However, that might be difficult to do because of the company's emphasis on industrial markets. Chatterjee estimated that ZERO-B products would account for less than 2 percent of Ion Exchange's 1996 total sales, estimated at Rs. 1 billion. He thought the total marketing expenditures for ZERO-B would be around Rs. 3 million.

Singer

The newest competitor to enter the Indian water purifier market was Singer India Ltd. Originally, Singer India was a subsidiary of the Singer Company, located in the United States, but a minority share (49 percent) was sold to Indian investors in 1982. The change in ownership led to the construction of manufacturing facilities in India for sewing machines in 1983. The facilities were expanded in 1991 to produce a broad line of home appliances. Sales revenues in 1996 for the entire product

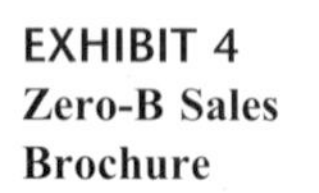

EXHIBIT 4
Zero-B Sales Brochure

line—sewing machines, food processors, irons, mixers, toasters, water heaters, ceiling fans, cooking ranges, and color televisions—would be about Rs. 900 million.

During Chatterjee's time in Calcutta he had visited a Singer Company showroom on Park Street. Initially he had hoped that Singer might be a suitable partner to manufacture and distribute the Delight purifier. However, much to his surprise, he was told that Singer now had its own brand on the market, Aquarius. The product was not yet available in Calcutta but was being sold in Bombay and Delhi.

A marketing research agency in Delhi was able to gather some information on the Singer purifier. The product contained nine stages (!) and sold to consumers for Rs.4,000. It removed sediments, heavy metals, bad tastes, odors, and colors. It also killed bacteria and viruses, fungi, and nematodes. The purifier required water pressure (8 psi minimum) to operate but needed no electricity. It came in a single countertop model that could be moved from one room to another. The life of the device at a flow rate of 3.8 liters per minute was listed as 40,000 liters—about four to six years of use in the typical Indian household. The product's life could be extended to 70,000 liters at a somewhat slower flow rate. However, at 70,000 liters, the product had to be discarded. The agency reported a heavy advertising blitz accompanying the introduction in Delhi, emphasizing television and newspaper advertising, plus outdoor and transit advertising as support. All 10 Singer showrooms in Delhi offered vivid demonstrations of the product's operation.

Chatterjee had to admit that the photos of the Aquarius purifier shown in the Calcutta showroom looked appealing. And a trade article he found had described the product as "state of the art" in comparison to the "primitive" products now on the market. Chatterjee and Blair Company engineers tended to agree—the disinfecting resin used in Aquarius had been developed by the U.S. government's National Aeronautics and Space Administration (NASA) and had been proved to be 100 percent effective against bacteria and viruses. "If only I could have brought a unit back with me," he thought. "We could have some test results and see just how good it is." The trade article also mentioned that Singer hoped to sell 40,000 units over the next two years.

Chatterjee knew that Singer was a well-known and respected brand name in India. Further, Singer's distribution channels were superior to those of any competitor in the market, including those of Eureka Forbes. The most prominent of Singer's three distribution channels were the 210 company-owned showrooms in major urban areas around the country. Each sold and serviced the entire line of Singer products. Each was very well kept and was staffed by knowledgeable personnel. Singer products also were sold throughout India by over 3,000 independent dealers, who received inventory from an estimated 70 Singer-appointed distributors. According to the marketing research agency in Delhi, distributors earned margins of 12 percent of the retail price for Aquarius, while dealers earned margins of 5 percent. Finally, Singer employed over 400 salespersons who sold sewing machines and food processors door to door. As with Eureka Forbes, the direct sales force sold products primarily in large urban markets.

Other Competitors

Chatterjee was aware of several other water purifiers on the Indian market. The Delta brand from S & S Industries in Madras seemed to be a carbon copy of Aquaguard except for a more eye-pleasing countertop design. According to the promotional literature, Delta offered a line of water-related products: purifiers, water softeners, iron removers, desalinators, and ozonators. Another competitor was Alfa Water Purifiers, Bombay. That company offered four purifier models at prices from Rs.4,300 to Rs.6,500, depending on capacity. Symphony's Spectrum brand sold well around Bombay at Rs.4,000 each but removed only suspended sediments, not heavy metals or bacteria. The Sam Group in Coimbatore recently had launched its Water Doctor purifier at Rs.5,200. The device used a third-stage ozonator to kill bacteria and viruses and came in two attractive countertop models with 6- and 12-liter storage, respectively. Batliboi was mentioned by the Delhi research agency as yet another competitor, although Chatterjee knew nothing else about the brand. Taken together, unit sales of all purifiers at these companies plus ZERO-B and Singer probably would account for around 60,000 units in 1996. The remaining 190,000 units would be Aquaguards and PureSips.

At least 100 Indian companies made and marketed candle filters. The largest probably was Bajaj Electrical Division, whose product line also included water heaters, irons, electric light bulbs, toasters, mixers, and grillers. Bajaj's candle filters were sold by a large number of dealers who carried the entire product line. Candle filters produced by other manufacturers were sold mostly through dealers who specialized in small household appliances and general hardware. Probably no single manufacturer of candle filters had more than 5 percent of any regional market in the country. No manufacturer attempted to satisfy a national market. Still, the candle filters market deserved serious consideration: perhaps Delight's entry strategy would attempt to "trade up" users of candle filters to a better, safer product.

Finally, Chatterjee knew that the sales of almost all purifiers in 1996 in India were in large urban areas. No manufacturer targeted rural or smaller urban areas, and at best, Chatterjee had calculated, existing manufacturers were reaching only 10 to 15 percent of the entire Indian population. An explosion in sales would come if the right product could be sold outside metropolitan areas.

Recommendations

Chatterjee decided that an Indian market entry for Blair Company was subject to three "givens," as he called them. First, he thought that a strategic focus on rural or smaller urban areas would not be wise, at least at the start. The lack of adequate distribution and communication infrastructure in rural India meant that any market entry would begin with larger cities, most likely on the west coast.

Second, market entry would require manufacturing the units in India. Because the cost of skilled labor in India was around Rs. 20 to Rs.25 per hour (compared to $20 to $25 per hour in the United States), importing complete units was out of the question. However, importing a few key components would be necessary at the start of the operation.

Third, Blair Company should find an Indian partner. Chatterjee's visits had produced a number of promising partners: Polar Industries, Calcutta; Milton Plastics, Bombay; Videocon Appliances, Aurangabad; BPL Sanyo Utilities and Appliances, Bangalore: Onida Savak, Delhi; Hawkins India, Bombay: and Voltas, Bombay. All those companies manufactured and marketed a line of high-quality household appliances, had one or more strong brand names, and had established dealer networks (a minimum of 10,000 dealers). All were involved to greater or lesser degrees with international partners. All were medium-size firms—not so large that a partnership with Blair Company would be one-sided and not so small that they would lack managerial talent and other resources. Finally, all were profitable (15 to 27 percent return on assets in 1995) and looking to grow. However, Chatterjee had no idea if any company would find the Delight purifier and Blair Company attractive or might be persuaded to sell part or all of their operations as an acquisition.

Field Testing and Product Recommendations

The most immediate decision Chatterjee faced was whether to recommend a field test. The test would cost about $25,000, placing 20 units in Indian homes in three cities and monitoring their performance for three to six months. The decision to test really was more than it seemed; Chatterjee's boss had explained that a decision to test was really a decision to enter. It made no sense to spend this kind of time and money if India was not an attractive opportunity. The testing period also would give Blair Company representatives time to identify a suitable Indian company as a licensee, joint venture partner, or acquisition.

Fundamental to market entry was product design. Engineers at Blair Company had taken the position that the purification technologies planned for Delight could be "packaged in almost any fashion as long as we have electricity." Electricity was needed to operate the product's ozonator as well as to indicate to users that the unit was functioning properly (or improperly, as the case might be). Beyond this requirement, anything was possible.

Chatterjee thought that a modular approach would be best. The basic module would be a countertop unit much like the one shown in Exhibit 2. The module would outperform anything on the market in terms of flow rate, palatability, durability, and reliability and would store two liters of purified water. Two additional modules would remove iron, calcium, or other metallic contaminants that were specific to particular regions. For example, Calcutta and much of the surrounding area suffered from iron contamination, which no filter or purifier on the Indian market could remove to a satisfactory level. Water supplies in other areas in the country were known to contain objectionable concentrations of calcium, salt, arsenic, lead, or sulfur. Most Indian consumers would need neither of the additional modules, some would need one or the other, but very few would need both.

Market Entry and Marketing Planning Recommendations

Assuming that Chatterjee recommended proceeding with the field test, he would need to make a recommendation concerning the mode of market entry. In addition, his recommendation should include an outline of a marketing plan.

Licensee Considerations. If market entry was in the form of a joint working arrangement with a licensee, Blair Company's financial investment would be minimal. Chatterjee thought that Blair Company might risk as little as $30,000 in capital for production facilities and equipment, plus another $5,000 for office facilities and equipment. Those investments would be completely offset by the licensee's payment to Blair Company for technology transfer and personnel training. Annual fixed costs to Blair Company should not exceed $40,000 at the outset and would decrease to $15,000 as soon as an Indian national could be hired, trained, and left in charge. The duties of this individual would be to work with Blair Company personnel in the United States and with management at the licensee to see that units were produced per Blair Company's specifications. Apart from this activity, Blair Company would have no control over the licensee's operations. Chatterjee expected that the licensee would pay royalties to Blair Company of about Rs. 280 for each unit sold in the domestic market and Rs. 450 for each unit that was exported. The average royalty probably would be around Rs. 300.

Joint Venture/Acquisition Considerations. If entry was in the form of either a joint venture or an acquisition, financial investment and annual fixed costs would be much higher and would depend largely on the scope of operations. Chatterjee had roughed out some estimates for a joint venture entry, based on three levels of scope (see Exhibit 5). His estimates reflected what he thought were reasonable assumptions for all needed investments plus annual fixed expenses for sales activities, general administrative overhead, research and development, insurance, and depreciation. His estimates allowed for the Delight purifier to be sold either through dealers or through a direct, door-to-door sales force. Chatterjee thought that estimates of annual fixed expenses for market entry through acquisition would be identical to those for a joint venture. However, estimates for the investment (purchase) might be considerably higher, the same, or lower. It depended on what was purchased.

Chatterjee's estimates of Delight's unit contribution margins reflected a number of assumptions: expected economies of scale, experience-curve effects, the costs of Indian labor and raw materials, and competitors' pricing strategies. However, the most important assumption was Delight's pricing strategy. If a skimming strategy was used and the product was sold through a dealer channel, the basic module would be priced to dealers at Rs. 5,500 and to consumers at Rs. 5,900. "This would give us about a Rs. 650 unit contribution once we got production flowing smoothly," he thought. In contrast, if a penetration strategy was used and the product was sold through a dealer channel, the basic module would be priced to dealers at Rs. 4,100 and to consumers at Rs. 4,400 and would yield a unit contribution of Rs. 300. For simplicity's sake, Chatterjee assumed that the two additional modules would be priced to dealers at Rs. 800 and to consumers at Rs. 1,000 and would yield a unit contribution of Rs. 100. Finally, he assumed that all products sold to dealers would go directly from Blair Company to the dealers (no distributors would be used).

If a direct sales force was employed instead of dealers, Chatterjee thought that the prices charged to consumers would not change from those listed above. However, sales commissions would have to be paid in addition to the fixed costs necessary to maintain and manage the sales force. Under a skimming price strategy, the sales commission would be Rs. 550 per unit and the unit contribution would be Rs. 500. Under a penetration price strategy, the sales commission would be Rs. 400 per unit and the unit contribution would be Rs. 200. These financial estimates, he would explain in his report, would apply to 1998 or 1999, the expected first year of operation.

Skimming versus penetration was more than just a pricing strategy. Product design for the skimming strategy would be noticeably superior, with higher performance and quality, a longer warranty period, more features, and a more attractive appearance compared with the design for the penetration strategy. Positioning also most likely would be different. Chatterjee recognized several positioning possibilities: performance and taste,

EXHIBIT 5
Investments and Fixed Costs for a Joint Venture Market Entry

	Operational Scope		
	Two Regions	Four Regions	National Market
1998 market potential (units)	55,000	110,000	430,000
Initial investment (Rs. thousands)	4,000	8,000	30,000
Annual fixed overhead expenses (Rs. thousands)			
Using dealer channels	4,000	7,000	40,000
Using direct sales force	7,200	14,000	88,000

value for the money/low price, safety, health, convenience, attractive styling, avoidance of diseases and health-related bills, and superior American technology. The only position he considered "taken" in the market was that occupied by Aquaguard—protect family health and service at your doorstep. While other competitors had claimed certain positions for their products, none had devoted financial resources to a degree that prevented Delight from dislodging them. Chatterjee believed that considerable advertising arid promotion expenditures would be necessary to communicate Delight's positi ing. He would need estimates of those expenditures his recommendation.

"If we go ahead with Delight, we'll have to mc quickly," Chatterjee thought. "The window of oppor nity is open, but if Singer's product is as good as tl claim, we'll be in for a fight. Still, Aquarius see vulnerable on the water pressure requirement and price. We'll need a product category 'killer' to win."

Case 6-11

Murphy Brewery Ireland, Limited

Patrick Conway, marketing director for Murphy's, picked up his issue of *The Financial Times* and read the following headline on May 13: "Grand Met, Guinness to Merge." He pondered the impact on his firm. Guinness was Murphy's most formidable competitor not only in Ireland but worldwide. Since a staff meeting was already scheduled for later Tuesday morning, he decided to examine the article closely and discuss it with his team. As he read on, the £22.3 billion merger between two of the four largest distillers (Seagram's headquartered in Canada and Allied Domecq, another British company, were the other two) appeared to have much synergy. The article pointed out that the geographic and brand fits were good between the two companies. The new firm, which will be called GMG, will be approximately equal in size to such major multinationals as Unilever, Procter & Gamble, and Philip Morris.[1]

During the 11 AM staff meeting, Patrick brought the merger to the attention of his colleagues. His company was in the middle of preparing its 1998 global marketing plan, and this news brought some urgency to the t ahead. Patrick stated that he felt a major assessment Murphy's status in the worldwide market was need He called on David Ford, his export manager, examine Murphy's position in the British and Europ markets. He said he would phone Michael Foley Heineken USA (distributor of Murphy's in the states) report on Murphy's progress there and asked Dan Lea to look into Murphy's status in Ireland. He asked e man to report back to him within a week.

As part of his personal preparation, Patrick deci to dig into the files and reacquaint himself with company history, since he had joined the firm only a f years previously. He also wanted to find out more ab the merger. He rang the communications department clip and route all articles from business publications this topic to him. Patrick considered the impact th developments would have on Murphy's brands.

In 1997 Murphy's had become a truly internatio brand that maintained a unique identity in Ireland. T name Murphy, the most common surname in the ent country, is recognized internationally for its Ir heritage. Exhibit 1 shows that about 85 percent Murphy's sales came from export business in 1996 a that the company now employs 385 people. He loca a report from several years earlier that provided historical perspective on the company.

This case was prepared by Patrick E. Murphy, professor of marketing, University of Notre Dame, Indiana, and former visiting professor of marketing, University College Cork in Ireland, and Don O'Sullivan, lecturer in marketing, Department of Management and Marketing, University College Cork. The case was distributed by the European Case Clearinghouse.

This case is intended to serve as a basis for a class discussion rather than to illustrate either effective or ineffective handling of a business situation. The authors would like to thank Patrick Conway, David Ford, and Dan Leahy of Murphy Brewery Ireland and Michael Foley of Heineken USA for their assistance in writing this case.

[1] John Willman and Ross Tieman, "Grand Met, Guinness to Merge," *Financial Times*, Tuesday, May 13, 1997, p. 1.

Historical Background

James J. Murphy and Company Limited was foun in 1856 in Cork City, Ireland, by the four Murp brothers—James, William, Jerome, and Francis. In 18 they were described as follows: "These gentlem applied themselves with energy and enterprise to

EXHIBIT 1 Export Sales versus Total Company Volumes

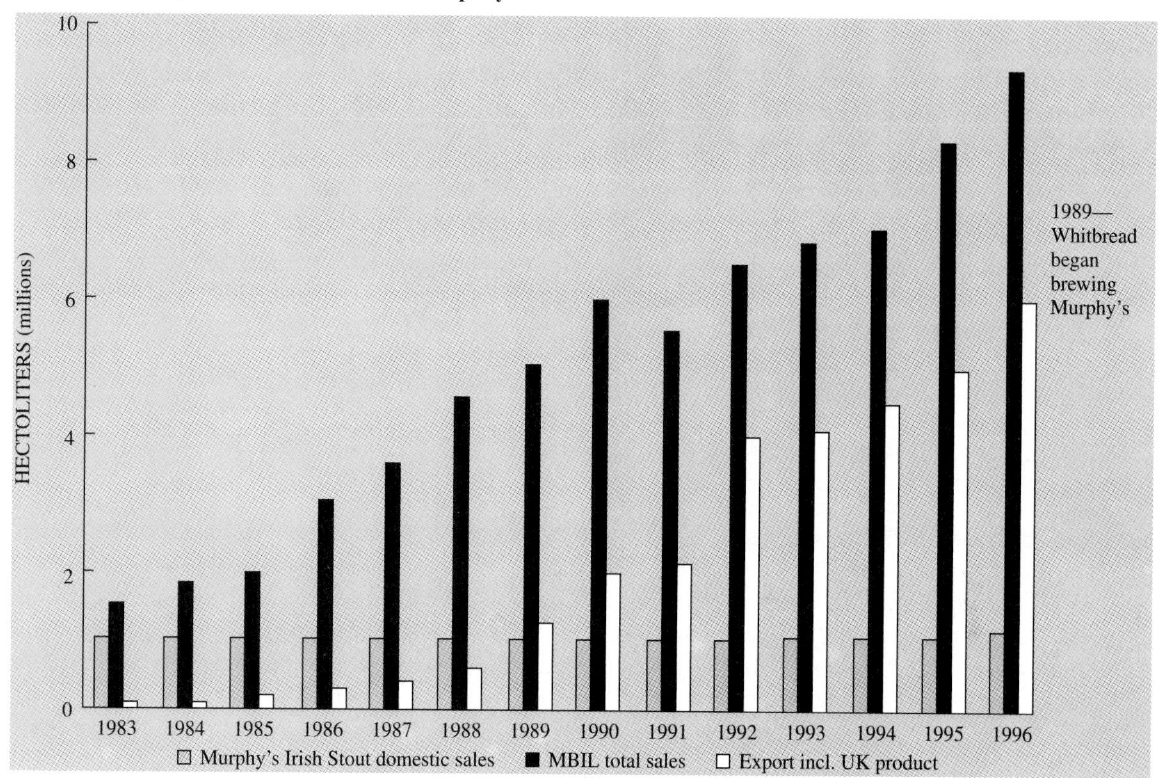

manufacture of an article, the reputation of which now extends far beyond the South of Ireland where the firm's stout and porter have been long and favorably known and where they command a very exclusive sale."[2]

James J. Murphy inherited the family business skills. His grandfather, also called James, had founded, with his brothers, the distillery James Murphy and Company in Midleton, County Cork (15 miles to the east of Cork City), in 1825. These Murphy brothers prospered as ship owners and tea importers and had been paid quite a large sum of money before founding their distillery. This company experienced significant growth and in 1867 amalgamated with four Cork distilleries to create Cork Distilleries Company Ltd. That firm enjoyed great success over the next century and in 1966 joined with the Dublin distillery John Jameson and Son and John Power and Son to create Irish Distillers Limited.

The Murphy Brewery is located at Lady's Well in Cork, whose name derives from a celebrated well on the hill opposite of the premises. It was dedicated to Our Lady and believed to possess miraculous properties. To the present day, pilgrimages take place to the shrine every year in the month of May. During the nineteenth century Lady's Well was one of Cork's largest breweries and was mentioned in the 1890 publication *Noted Breweries of Great Britain and Ireland,* which indicated that Murphy's Stout had become a formidable rival to Guinness in the south of Ireland.[3]

Initially, Murphy's brewed porter, but it switched exclusively to stout (the name *stout* denotes strong beers—see Exhibit 2 for a description of the product), and this remained its sole beer product until 1965. Over the years the brewery acquired a number of licensed products and developed a wholesale spirits and soft drinks bottling business.

Although Murphy's opened up trade in London, Manchester, South Wales, and other parts of England early in the twentieth century, the company began experiencing financial problems in the 1960s. There was considerable anxiety among the staff of 200 in Murphy's Brewery Cork concerning the continuity of their employment in the early 1970s. At that time they had an English partner (Watney and Mann), which wanted to dissolve the partnership. Colonel John J. Murphy,

[2] *Murphy Brewery Limited: A Profile*, undated.

[3] Company sources.

EXHIBIT 2
What Is Stout, and How Was It Promoted?

Source: Partially adapted from Brendan O'Brien, *The Stout Book* (Dublin; Anna Livia Press, 1990).

Stout is a black beer with a thick white head. The black color is due mainly to the fact that it contains malted barley which is roasted in a similar way to coffee beans. The creamy white head is created from the "initiation" and "surging" of bubbles of nitrogen and carbon dioxide gas as the beer is poured. The gas enters the keg and forces the beer out. It is actually the nitrogen which causes the tight, creamy head.

The word *stout* has long been used to describe strong beers; it also meant stout, as in stout ale. The strength may have been in terms of taste or alcohol or both. Standard stout ranges in alcohol content from 4 percent to 5 percent. The word *stout* gradually made the transition from adjective to noun. The basic constituent of stout is barley, which consists mainly of starch. The barley becomes a malt and during this process is converted to sugar, which is fermentable. When the malt is roasted beyond the normal limits, this gives the stout its unusual dark hue. The highly roasted dark malt is 500 times darker than a pale malt and adds its distinctive color as well as flavor.

The resulting sugary liquid, called wort, is eventually formed. At this stage hops are added and boiled with wort to produce the liquid. When boiled for an hour or two, the hops release oils and resins which produce the characteristic bitterness and aroma. A comparison of the bitterness level among the leading brands of stout conducted by the European Brewery Convention found that Guinness rates 45 to 48 European units of bitterness, Beamish 40, and Murphy's 36 to 38.

Stout is synonymous with Ireland, and nowhere else is stout as popular or as intrinsically part of everyday life. The criterion by which a pub often is judged is likely to be whether it sells a good pint of stout. In the pub, pouring pints is seen as having a major impact on product quality. Stout is poured in two stages. First the glass is filled to 75 percent capacity and allowed to "settle" so that the creamy head will separate from the dark body. To top off the pint, the tap is pushed forward slightly until the head rises just below the rim. This activity takes a minute or two and results in stout taking longer to pour. Interestingly, the product is poured in one go/pull outside Ireland.

Stout has its roots in colder climates in Ireland and Scandinavia, and traditionally it has been a winter brew. Comments such as "typically consumed in the dark winter months" and " a seasonal beer brewed only in the winter" are used regularly by stout breweries worldwide. Stout is thought to be a drink suited to quiet, reflective slipping. Both in Ireland and worldwide, it is now a year-round drink.

To return to the definition, stout is often considered a strong drink. Therefore, both Murphy's and Guinness have extensively used strength in their marketing and advertising. Murphy's utilized a circus strongman who was shown lifting a horse off the ground with the label "Murphy's Stout gives strength" for many years in the late 1800s and 1900s. Guinness has utilized posters throughout Ireland depicting superhuman strength achieved by drinking Guinness with the slogan "Guinness for strength."

chairman of Murphy's, stated that "we are confident that we can satisfy" certain financial conditions to meet the demands of the creditors. The company at this time was well over 100 years old and had overcome difficult periods in the past.

In February 1975 Murphy's approached Heineken N.B. (the Amsterdam-based brewery which had been founded by Garard Adriann Heineken the same year the Murphy brothers opened their brewery in Ireland) with a proposal to begin a licensing operation for Heineken in Ireland. Heineken examined the possibilities of the Irish market and found them favorable, and a license agreement was signed. A marketing company, Heineken Ireland Limited, was set up as a fully owned subsidiary of Heineken N.B. Heineken was well known for its lager beer, which complemented the Murphy's Irish Stout offering.

Murphy's new policy of expanding as a broad-based competitor to the leading brands (e.g., Guinness and Beamish and Crawford) worked well at first. However, the company was hit by recessionary problems, and J. J. Murphy and Company Limited went into receivership in 1982. At that time the company employed 235 people. On July 14, 1982, the *Cork Examiner* confirmed a commitment from the Dutch brewing company Heineken to invest 1.6 million pounds in the brewery.

In 1983 Heineken International purchased the assets of James J. Murphy and Company Limited, which was then in receivership. Murphy Brewery Ireland Limited became a wholly owned subsidiary of Heineken International, a move which gave a new lease on life to Murphy's Brewery. This development preserved the long and respected tradition of brewing in the Cork area and the well-known brand name. Since then Murphy Brewery Ireland Limited has continued its brewing and marketing of Murphy's Irish Stout and Heineken. The adoption of Murphy's Irish Stout by Heineken International as one of its corporate brands meant that the brand became available to drinkers worldwide.

The Heineken Era

Heineken International is the world's second largest brewer (Exhibit 3) and a private company. Its flagship Heineken lager, the world's most exported beer, and the Amstel brand are also brewed under license by third parties. They are produced in over 100 plants and sold in 170 countries on all continents. The Heineken brand is sold in the same green bottle and promoted with the same brand imagery in the same price tier in China, Spain, the United States, and elsewhere. Heineken was the first beer to be imported into the United States after Prohibition was lifted in 1933. The United States is now its largest market.

Murphy's management during the Heineken years has been led by four managing directors. Currently, Marien Kakabeeke, a native of Holland, serves in that position. He assumed the post in August 1993. Heineken has demonstrated its commitment to Murphy's by opening a new office complex in the old Malthouse at the brewery. Murphy's became accredited in 1992 with the ISO 9002 mark for all aspects of operations—the first brewery in Europe to achieve that distinction.

Murphy's Brands and Packaging

Internationally, Murphy's Irish Stout (MIS) is now available in 63 countries worldwide, up from only 20 in 1992. Export sales of the brand grew by almost 200 percent during 1996. Growth markets include the United States, where MIS sales increased 163 percent, and Germany, France, Spain, Italy, and the Netherlands, where sales volumes grew 82 percent. MIS's output has grown by 700 percent in the last decade. Most of this increase was fueled by international consumption, with sales in Ireland increasing only 10 percent over that time (Exhibit 1).

This growth is reflected in an increased turnover for MBI from Ir £125 million to Ir £140 million. The total company volume now stands at almost 950,000 hectoliters.

For most of its first 135 years Murphy's Irish Stout was available only in draft form in pubs throughout Ireland. A packaging innovation (draughtflow cans) was launched in October 1992. A plastic device (called a widget) is fitted into the bottom of the can which nitrates the liquid after the can is opened, creating the famous creamy head and giving the product a publike taste. Consumer acceptance of the can is reflected in the distribution growth of the product, which makes it available in off-licenses/liquor stores. Within Europe a 330-milliliter cream-colored can is sold, while in the United States a 14.9-ounce can is marketed. One distinguishing feature of the can in Europe is the message

EXHIBIT 3
World's Largest Brewers, 1994

Source: Havis Dawson, "Brand Brewing." *Beverage World*, October 1995, p. 52. 1994 is the latest year available.

Company	HQ	Prod./Vol.[1]	World share	% of Sales in Exports
Anheuser-Busch	United States	105.1	9%	6%
Heineken	Netherlands	59.6	4.8	89
Miller	United States	50.1	3.9	5
Kirin	Japan	35.1	2.7	5
Foster's	Australia	34.7	2.7	73
Carlsberg	Denmark	30.4	2.3	82
Danone Group	France	27.7	2.4	65
Guinness	United Kingdom	24.2	2.1	84

[1] Production/volume is measured in hectoliters: 1 hectoliter = 26.4 gallons or .85 barrel.

"Chill for at least two hours. Pour contents into glass in one smooth action. Best before end—see base," which is reprinted in four languages on the cans.

Another packaging innovation for MIS was developed in 1995. A draughtflow bottle is now available in both the U.S. and European markets. The 500-milliliter (16.9-oz.) bottle has a long neck and is dark brown in color. It is used as a powerful unique differentiating point for the brand. The back labels acclaim the benefits of the draughtflow technology. Warning labels concerning alcoholic beverages are shown on the U.S. labels.

Murphy's Irish Amber, a traditional Irish ale, was launched in 1995 as Murphy's Irish Red Beer in Germany and France. It is brewed in Cork but is not available domestically in Ireland. In the United States Murphy's Irish Amber was introduced in both draft and a 12-ounce bottle in September 1996. The bottles are amber in color. The label's dark blue and red colors accented by gold signal a high-quality product. Compelled by the need for a stronger Murphy's portfolio due to increased interest in genuine red beers, the company believed this product would be successful. Thus far, Murphy's Irish Amber's success has far exceeded expectations.

Murphy's also offers Heineken's low-alcohol beer called Buckler. It contains 1/2 of 1 percent alcohol and about half the calorie content of normal beer. It sells in 330-milliliter bottles in bars, off-licenses, and supermarkets in the served markets.

The Competition

After returning from a business trip to the Continent a week later, Patrick Conway found on his desk a stack of articles sent to him from the communications department discussing the Guinness–Grand Met merger. Before turning his attention to them, he reflected on what he knew regarding the Guinness brand both in Ireland and elsewhere. Guinness Stout was the pioneer in this category and an even older firm than Murphy's. It was founded in 1759 by Arthur Guinness in Dublin. It was now the eighth largest brewer in the world in terms of volume, with over a 2 percent market share. Murphy's parent, Heineken, is in second place worldwide (Exhibit 3).

Guinness is brewed in almost 50 countries and sold in over 130.[4] In the stout category, it is the proverbial "500-pound gorilla" in that it commands a 70 to 90 percent share in almost all markets. When it moves, Murphy's and other competitors invariably pay close attention. The Guinness name defines the stout market in most countries and is the "gold standard" against which all other competing brands are measured. The company's marketing prowess is well known in that Guinness Stout is positioned as "hip in the United Kingdom," "traditional in Ireland," and a source of "virility" in Africa; a special microbrew is aimed at "creating a new generation of beer snobs" in the United States. Guinness plans to continue targeting continental Europe, the United States, and Asia in a bid to expand its markets and grow its business.

Guinness has been very successful in building its stout brand around the world. The company is identified with its quirky advertising campaigns in Ireland and its high profile regarding other marketing and promotional endeavors. One significant effort involved the Irish national soccer team, which endorsed Guinness as its official beer for the 1994 World Cup. Sales of Guinness Stout rose dramatically in the United States during the World Cup finals. Another U.S.-based promotion program designed to appeal to the over 40 million Americans of Irish descent was the "Win Your Own Pub in Ireland" contest. This competition has been going on for several years and is featured in Guinness's Web page currently. Third, the huge development of the Irish pub concept around the world helped Guinness brands abroad and contributed to an increase in export sales of 10 percent in 1996. The company launched the Guinness pub concept in 1992, and there are now 1,250 "Guinness" Irish pubs in 36 countries. Four hundred more are expected to open in 1997.[5]

Patrick turned his attention to several articles about the Guinness and Grand Met merger. A rationale for the merger was that these firms could acquire new brands more easily than they may be able to find new consumers in the U.S. and European marketplace, where alcohol consumption is falling, the population is aging, and concerns about health are rising. The new firm will be a formidable force in the race to open up new markets in liquor and beer. The companies have complementary product lines and will be divided into four major divisions (Exhibit 4). The Guinness Brewery worldwide division will feature its signature stout, Harp (a lager), Kilkenny (a red ale), Cruzcampo (a Spanish beer), and Red Stripe.

[4] Company fact sheet.

[5] Barry O'Keeffe, "'Black Stuff' Underpins Profit Raise at Guinness," *The Irish Times*, March 21, 1997.

EXHIBIT 4
GMG Brands

Source: "GMG Brands: What the Two Sides Will Contribute," *Financial Times,* May 13, 1997, p. 27.

Division	Turnover (millions)	Pretax Profit (millions)
Guinness Brewing Worldwide:	£2,262	£283
Guinness Stout, Harp, Cruzcampo (Spanish), Red Stripe		
United Distillers & Vintners		
(Guinness Brands)	£2,468	£791
Dewar's, Gordon's Gin, Bell's, Moet Hennessey, Johnnie Walker, Black and White, Asbach		
(Grand Met Brands)	£3,558	£502
Smirnoff, Stolichnaya, J&B (whisky), Gilbey's Gin, Jose Cuervo, Grand Marnier, Bailey's, Malibu, Absolut		
Pillsbury	£3,770	£447
Pillsbury, Green Giant, Old El Paso, Häagen-Dazs		
Burger King	£ 859	£167

Note: Turnover and pretax profit numbers denote millions of pounds sterling.

The Economist noted that even though GMG will be the seventh largest company in the world, it faces major obstacles. One is that even though its brands are very well known, the combined company will lack focus. Grand Met has a long history of trying its hand at different businesses but has done so with mixed success. Guinness, however, has an even longer history of not doing much besides brewing beer, and its spirits business has been a struggle for the firm. *The Economist*'s conclusion gave Mr. Conway encouragement and reflected his own impression when the magazine stated: "Unless GMG manages to show very rapidly that they can mix these ingredients into something fairly tasty, then pressure will grow on it to simplify itself."[6]

Patrick recalled that Guinness is not the only competitor of Murphy's. Beamish & Crawford, also located in Cork, was founded in 1792 and currently employs about 200 people. In 1987 the company joined the Foster's Brewing Group. The primary brands offered by the company are Beamish (stout), Foster's (lager), and Carling Black Label (lager).

Beamish stout is available in most pubs throughout the southern part of Ireland. The brand is positioned on its Irishness, the heritage of Beamish Stout, and the fact that it is the only Irish stout exclusively brewed in Ireland. In the last three years Beamish has been marketed in Europe (Italy and Spain mostly) and North America (Canada and the United States). It is distributed through the Foster's Brewing Group in those markets.

[6] "Master of the Bar," *The Economist,* May 17, 1997, p. 73.

The Irish Market

Dan Leahy sent Patrick the following report on the market for Murphy's in Ireland. His memo discussed both the importance of pub life in the country and the competitive situation. Patrick read with interest Dan's assessment of the Irish market:

> With a population of less than 4 million people, the Irish market is small in international terms. However, it is the market in which stout holds the largest share at nearly 50 percent of all beer sales. With one of the youngest populations in the developed world and one of the fastest-growing economies, it is an important and dynamic market for all stout producers. This is added to by the fact that the three competitors—Murphy's, Guinness, and Beamish—all use their Irishness as a key attribute in product positioning. A presence in the Irish market is viewed as being central to the authenticity of the Irishness claim.
>
> Pubs have long been a central part of Irish life, particularly in rural areas, where pubs are semi-social centers. Irish pubs are regularly run by owner-operators who buy products from different breweries. This is quite different from most international markets, where pubs tend to be run by or for the breweries. For example, in the Dutch market Heineken has 52 percent of the outlets. Partly as a result of this, Irish consumers are highly brand-loyal. Also, in the Irish market, breweries engage in higher levels of promotion.
>
> Irish pubs are perceived very positively in many parts of the world. They are seen as places which are accessible to all the family. Irish pubs are intimately linked with musical sessions and viewed as being open, friendly places to visit. This positive perception

has resulted in a proliferation of Irish-themed pubs, particularly in the last decade. This development has been used extensively by Guinness and lately by Murphy's as a means of increasing distribution.

Guinness dominates the Irish stout market with an 89 percent market share. Murphy's and Beamish have roughly equal shares of the rest of the market. Guinness's dominance of the market is reflected in the fact that the term *Guinness* is synonymous with stout. In many parts of the country it is ordered without reference to its name simply by asking for "a pint." Similarly, in Britain 1 million pints of Guinness are sold every day, with 10 million glasses a day sold worldwide.

Guinness Ireland turned in a strong performance in 1996 with sales up 8 percent to 764 million pints.[7] The company began a 12-million-pound advertising campaign last year called "The Big Pint" and engaged in extensive billboard advertising emphasizing the size and strength of the brand.

In Ireland, Beamish Stout is positioned as a value for money, Irish stout selling at 20 pence (10 percent) lower than the competitors. It is slightly ahead of Murphy's currently in the race for second place in Ireland. As with Murphy's, Beamish's traditional base has been in the Cork-area market. Today, 1 in every 4 pints of stout consumed in Cork is Beamish and 1 in every 14 pints in Ireland is Beamish.

Within the lager market in Ireland, Heineken dominates with nearly 40 percent of the market, while Budweiser and Carlsberg (both distributed by Guinness) each have just over a 20 percent market share. Harp, which once held an overwhelming 80 percent share, now accounts for only 8 percent.

Murphy's is priced on a par with Guinness in all markets in the country. The average price of a pint of stout in the market is Ir £2.00.

In parts of the market where demand for the brand is low, Murphy's has begun selling the product in an innovative 3/5-keg (a keg is a barrel containing 50 liters) size. This ensures that the product reaches the customer at the desired level of quality.

Murphy's has pursued market growth through the development of export markets and development of the take-home market. The development of these markets is driven by the fact that the domestic draught market is mature with static sales over the last number of years. In 1995 pub sales fell by almost 2.5 percent, while off-license sales grew by 37 percent. The growth in the off-license business is due in part to the impact of the new stronger drunk-driving legislation and in-home summer consumption.[8]

Both of these markets rely heavily on canned and bottled packaging for the product. Traditionally this has posed a difficulty for stout products as there is a perceived deterioration in quality compared to the draught version. Murphy's is selling its product in bottles and dedicating some advertising to the superior bottled taste and using it as a differentiating feature for all of Murphy's products and using the draught bottle as a brand icon for the firm.

Conway thought about the report on the Irish market and how difficult it was to compete against Guinness and the extreme brand loyalty of the Irish consumer to it. He thought about the new three-year 5-million-pound advertising campaign launched in 1996 and hoped that the unique approach would win new customers. One memorable TV ad featured a group of Japanese samurai warriors who arrive in a line at a bar, knock back bottles of Murphy's, and leave while a Guinness drinker drums his fingers on the counter waiting for his pint to settle. Conway believed that brand awareness was growing. One successful promotional endeavor is the company's sponsorship of the Murphy's Irish Open, which was part of the PGA European Golf Tour.

He knew that strides were being made in the distribution network outside its traditional stronghold of Cork City and County. One of the inducements the company was using was a lower trade price to the pubs so that they made more on each pint sold. The company followed this philosophy internationally as well in the effort to compete with Guinness.

He also recalled two *Irish Times* articles that gave his and Kakabeeke's views on the importance of the Irish market to the company. He asked his secretary to retrieve them from the files and routed them to the marketing group. Conway was quoted as saying, "Murphy's believes it has to have an advertising spend comparable to Guinness if it is ever to achieve a critical mass in Ireland. We have to differentiate ourselves, and there's no use doing it with a whisper. A better market share in Ireland would also provide Murphy's Irish Stout with a backbone from which to grow exports."[9] Mr. Kakabeeke said that "the brewery is not happy with the 5 percent position in the Irish market and with the level of domestic growth being achieved by Murphy's Irish Stout. I feel that sales can be improved in Ireland."[10]

[7] O'Keeffe, "'Black Stuff' Underpins Profit Raise at Guinness."

[8] Paul O'Kane, "Murphy Boosts Exports," *The Irish Times*, March 7, 1996.

[9] Paul O'Kane, "Murphy's Aims to Double Its Sales in Three Years," *The Irish Times*, June 14, 1996.

[10] O'Kane, "Murphy Boosts Exports."

The UK and Continental European Markets

The United Kingdom (England, Scotland, Wales, and Northern Ireland), Ireland's closest neighbor, represents the world's largest stout market in terms of consumption at 60 million hectoliters. The total population of the UK is approximately 60 million consumers. Murphy's market share stands at 15 percent, while Guinness (78 percent) and Beamish (6 percent) are the other two major competitors. MIS was launched in the UK in 1985 and has enjoyed continued growth in that market since then. Murphy's success in the UK may be attributed to several factors.

First, Heineken and Murphy's are distributed in the UK through the Whitbread Beer Company in Luton. Whitbread has an association with over 27,000 pubs in the country, which translates to an automatic distribution network for Murphy's products. Recently Whitbread has opened a series of themed bars under the banner "J. J. Murphy and Company" throughout the country. These outlets reflect the desired image for Murphy's and help raise the profile of the brand in the UK. As a point of comparison, Beamish is distributed in 10,000 outlets in Britain.

Second, Murphy's has also been successful with its advertising in the UK. Its continuing advertising theme "Like the Murphy's, I'm not bitter" campaign is a tongue-in-cheek poke at Guinness's taste. The campaign has received several awards and has resulted in a unique identity developed for the brand (see Exhibit 2 on stout). The firm has also sponsored the Murphy's English Open Golf Championship for five years.

Third, the brand has gained momentum since it was voted product of the year by the UK Vintners in 1990. Murphy's has a strong position in the minds of the British who prefer darker ales. The brand represents a viable option to those who do not like the taste of Guinness and/or seek an alternative to their favorite UK-based brands such as Thomas Hardy, Newcastle, Samuel Smith, Watney's, and Young's.

MIS is available in all Western European markets. It has excellent distribution in the Netherlands, where Heineken is headquartered. Guinness's recent Irish pub expansion program has also helped raise awareness for all entries in the Irish stout category. Murphy's experienced dramatic growth in volume and market share across Europe in 1996.

In Germany, the establishment of Murphy's Trading GmbH, a wholly owned subsidiary of Murphy Brewery Ireland, allows for greater focus and control of the Murphy's brands within this critical market. The year 1996 also saw Murphy's gain the exclusive beer rights to Paddy Murphy's, the largest chain of Irish theme pubs throughout Germany. Also, in Denmark MIS is distributed in the Paddy Go Easy chain in several Danish cities.

In 1996 new markets were developed in Eastern Europe, including Hungary and the Czech Republic. The potential of the emerging Russian market is also anticipated. With the introduction of the brand in Finland, Murphy's is now available in all the Nordic countries.

The American Market

As he reached for the phone to ring Michael Foley, current CEO of Heineken USA (Van Munching & Co. is the importer's name) and former managing director of Murphy Brewery Ireland from 1989 to 1993, Patrick thought about the United States. He knew that the United States, with its 270 million consumers and general high standard of living, represents the most lucrative beer market in the world. The $40 billion beer market in the United States is dominated by the "giants" Anheuser-Busch (10 brands and 45 percent market share), Miller (9/23 percent), and Coors (7/11 percent).[11]

Michael gave Patrick a status report on the Murphy's brand in the United States as of June 1997. Michael reiterated that the U.S. strategy is to "build slowly" and gain acceptance of Murphy's products by endorsement by customers rather than attempting to buy market share with mass advertising. The plan is to "keep off TV because it is too expensive." Murphy's is seeking a premium brand positioning aimed at the specialty imported niche rather than the mass market.

Foley indicated that he was very optimistic about the Murphy growth possibilities in the United States. "Our 1996 sales were up 180 percent, and our target is 1 million cases by mid-1998," he said. Both Murphy's Irish Stout and Irish Amber are meeting the expectations set for them by Heineken USA.

Murphy's Irish Stout has been available in the United States since 1992 and has experienced steady growth since then. MIS has been on a gradual progression, from 100,000 gallons in 1992 to 400,000 gallons in 1994 and 600,000 gallons in 1995. It is now on tap at over

[11] "Domestic Beer Shipments Drop 2.1% in '95 While Volume Dips 1.7%," *Beverage Industry*, January 1996, pp. 24–32.

5,000 bars and pubs throughout the country. The distribution tends to be concentrated in the eastern corridor running from Boston through New York City (the largest market) to Washington, D.C. Another area of intense distribution is in south Florida. The "gold coast" area running from Miami to Fort Lauderdale is a stronghold for Murphy's, partially due to its attraction to British tourists who are already familiar with the brand. Other areas of focus for MIS are the major metropolitan areas of Chicago, Los Angeles, and San Francisco.

For the off-premises/carryout market, MIS has been available in cans since 1993. Their size is 14.9 ounces, and they are cream colored (like the "head" of the drink) and are priced relative to domestic U.S. beers at a premium level—$1.76 versus $1.99 for Guinness in the same size can. Foley stated that cans generally signify a "down market product" and the company would like to present more of a prestige image. Therefore, in September 1996 Murphy's introduced the draughtflow bottle in the United States. While Foley believes the glass package is "more premium," the company has experienced a problem with it in the United States. The serving size of 16.9 ounces is not correct for the market since most beer glasses hold only 12 ounces. The usual price is $1.99 per bottle. The size is not that important for in-home consumption, but in bars where MIS is sold by packages rather than on draft, this is a significant issue for the company. Another issue that has arisen is that the thick brown bottle takes substantially longer to cool than does a can.

Murphy's Irish Amber was introduced into the American market in late 1996. Its on-premise penetration has exceeded company expectations, and according to Foley, '"the product is doing very, very well. It is the 'real deal' and replacing nonauthentic Irish products such as Killian's in many areas." The product is available in six-packs for off-site consumption. The rich-looking green and red package makes it attractive. The company has positioned it against Bass Ale and other premium-quality ales. Its price is in the $7.50 range, which is substantially higher than many of the specialty imports, which cost $4.00 to $6.00 per six-pack. Killian's sometimes is sale priced as low as $3.99, but its regular price is in the $5.50 to $6.00 range, and Sam Adams Red and Pete's Wicked Ale are priced at $5.49 and S5.99, respectively. Bass Ale, however, carries an even higher price ($7.79) than Murphy's.

Conway thanked Foley for his update on the status of the Murphy's brands in the United States and asked if Michael could spend a few minutes discussing trends in the beer market within the country. "I know import sales are increasing about 7 percent a year in the United States and that Heineken is the leading import brand," said Conway, "But where does Guinness fall?" Foley responded that they were in tenth place, while Bass Ale held down the eighth spot and beer imports from Ireland held the sixth position among all countries (Exhibits 5 and 6). Foley said that he recalled reading that the top 20 brands (out of a total of 400 import brands) account for 90 percent of U.S. import sales.

Patrick asked about trends in the U.S. beer market. "It has been flat the last several years," said Foley. "The most significant recent trend domestically is the growth in microbreweries." Michael said he remembered seeing on a Web site that microbreweries, brewpubs, and regional specialty breweries totaled almost 1,300 in early 1997.[12] The microbrewery category has grown tenfold to 500 in 10 years. However, it still accounted for only a paltry 2 percent of the U.S. market in 1995.

Conway said good-bye and was just about to hang up when Foley said, "I almost forgot, but someone passed an article from *The Wall Street Journal* by me a few weeks ago that talked about Guinness and the microbrewery boom. I will send it to you with the other material" (Exhibit 7).

Murphy's World Market Positioning and Marketing

Dan Leahy stopped by Patrick Conway's office and handed him the information requested on Murphy's status in the world market. Patrick glanced at the statistics assembled by Dan and noticed that the specialty category (into which MIS and MIA both fell) had grown over the last few years (Exhibit 8). He was concerned that it was the second smallest of the five categories.

Dan left a revision of the Murphy's Positioning Statement on which Patrick and his colleagues had been working for several months. It read:

> Murphy's is a symbol of everything authentically "Irish." Its warm history takes time to discover but its taste is easy to appreciate.

Supporting this positioning was the image of Ireland that Murphy's planned to convey in its marketing strategy (Exhibit 9). While the words in the exhibit are a bit stereotypical, they describe the perception of both the country and its people. It is in this context that Irish products are viewed by consumers in other counties. The

[12] "Craft-Brewing Industry Fact Sheet—February 1997," http://www.Beertown.org/craftbrew.html.

EXHIBIT 5 Leading Imported Beer Brands in the United States (thousands of 2.25-gallon cases)

Brand	Importer	Origin	1992[1]	1993	1994[2]	% Change 1993–1994
Heineken	Van Munching & Co.	Netherlands	26,700	29,200	31,200	6.8%
Corona Extra	Barton/Gambrinus	Mexico	13,000	14,000	16,000	14.3
Molson Ice	Molson USA	Canada	–	3,000	10,000	–
Beck's	Dribeck Importers	Germany	9,650	9,700	9,720	0.2
Molson Golden	Molson USA	Canada	8,500	8,600	8,700	1.2
Amstel Light	Van Munching & Co.	Netherlands	5,500	6,000	7,500	25.0
Labatt's Blue	Labatt's USA	Canada	5,900	6,200	6,500	4.8
Bass Ale	Guinness Import Co.	United Kingdom	2,850	3,390	4,160	22.7
Tecate	Labatt's USA	Mexico	2,900	3,400	4,000	17.6
Guinness Stout	Guinness Import Co.	Ireland	3,100	3,650	3,970	8.8
Foster's Lager[3]	Molson USA	Canada	3,500	3,700	3,800	2.7
Moosehead	Guinness Import Co.	Canada	3,400	3,350	3,340	−0.3
Molson Light	Molson USA	Canada	1,900	2,000	2,200	10.0
Dos Equis	Guinness Import Co.	Mexico	1,900	2,060	2,120	2.9
St. Pauli Girl	Barton Brands	Germany	2,200	2,000	2,000	0.0
Labatt's Ice	Labatt's USA	Canada	–	845	1,910	–
Molson Canadian	Molson USA	Canada	1,640	1,690	1,710	1.2
Labatt's Light	Labatt's USA	Canada	1,100	1,020	1,100	7.8
Corona Light	Barton/Gambrinus	Mexico	1,100	1,000	1,000	0.0

[1] Revised.
[2] Estimated.
[3] The gradual production switch from Australia to Canada began in April 1992.

EXHIBIT 6
Imported Beer Market
Market Share by Supplier, 1994 (Estimated)

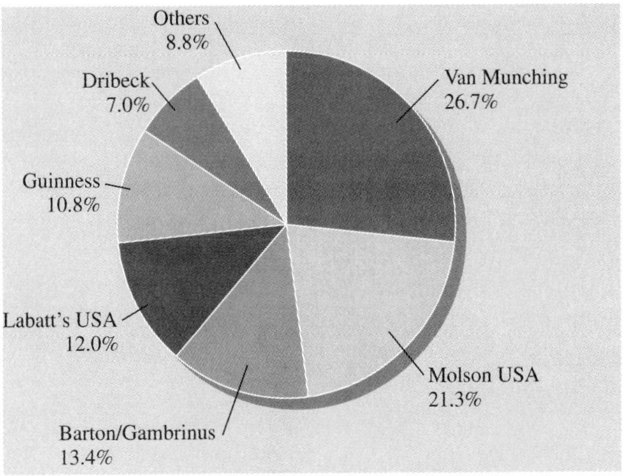

Van Munching 26.7%
Molson USA 21.3%
Barton/Gambrinus 13.4%
Labatt's USA 12.0%
Guinness 10.8%
Dribeck 7.0%
Others 8.8%

elements of the marketing mix were summarized by Dan in several accompanying pages.

The product consists of the two brands—Murphy's Irish Stout and Murphy's Irish Amber/Red Beer (MIA/RB). It is sourced in Ireland except for the UK and New Zealand markets. Ongoing new product development continues in line with positioning, umbrella branding, and premium packaging.

The distribution objective is one of controlled distribution growth. The focus is on quality Irish bars/pubs and specialty beer outlets. Package variants are available in low-volume outlets. Dual stocking of MIS and MIA/RB will occur wherever possible. Exclusivity is a goal but not a prerequisite for stocking. The existing Heineken distribution network will continue to be used wherever possible.

EXHIBIT 7
Buoyed by Boom in Microbrews, Guinness Pours Its Cash into TV

Source: Elizabeth Jensen, *The Wall Street Journal,* February 10, 1997, p. B2.

Guinness Import Co. poured about 33 percent more of its signature dark draft stout in the United States last year as the microbrew boom helped lift import sales by creating a new generation of beer snobs. Now Guinness hopes to keep the beer taps flowing with its first large-scale U.S. TV ad campaign for the Irish-brewed brand, breaking today.

At a time when sales of all beer in the United States rose just 1 percent last year, several of Guinness Import's major brands, including Harp lager and Bass ale, posted double-digit gains. Overall, sales of Guinness Import's brands (including Moosehead, whose distribution rights Guinness is shedding, effective at the end of March) grew 20 percent to about 17 million cases last year, according to Guinness.

The company's success is one of the factors that contributed to an estimated 10 percent rise in the sale of beers last year, according to Frank Walters, senior vice president of research at M. Shanken Communications, publisher of *Impact*, which tracks beer sales. Final numbers on sales of domestic beers are expected to be flat, although it's estimated that the tiny microbrewery and specialty segment jumped more than 20 percent, "It's a good economy, and people are indulging themselves more," says Mr. Walters of the sales of more-expensive imports.

Guinness stout's fast sales pace in bars and stores lifted it to the number 6 or 7 ranking among imports, up from ninth place in 1995, according to Mr. Walter's estimates. Guinness Import, a unit of Guinness PLC of London, attributes its success to changing consumer tastes in the wake of the microbrew explosion and a more intense distribution and marketing effort. "People are getting more into beers with taste," said Sheri Roder, marketing development director for Guinness Import, "and at the same time, we've gotten behind our brands more."

There have been eye-catching promotions, such as the annual "Win Your Own Pub in Ireland" contest, now in its fourth year. A "Great Guinness Toast," on February 28, hopes to get into the *Guinness Book of World Records* for the largest number of people making a toast. And the number of outlets selling the brand jumped by 20 percent in 1996.

Even more unusual, Guinness has been sending out a force of "draft specialists" armed with thermometers and training brochures to visit bars and make sure they're serving Guinness under the best possible conditions. Brewers can't own bars, so they can't control whether tavern owners serve the product in sparkling clean glasses or how often they flush out built-up yeast in the lines that carry the beer from the keg to the tap.

With distribution and the quality program in place, Guinness decided the time was right to launch the TV campaign. "There's no point in advertising a lot when people can't find you," says Ms. Roder. "There's a likelihood now that people will be able to find a pint of Guinness, poured well to our exacting standards. You don't want to get people too excited about something they can't find."

The TV ad campaign, with the tag line "Why Man Was Given Five Senses," will air through St. Patrick's Day, March 17, in 18 major markets, including New York, Los Angeles, and Atlanta. Guinness won't say what it is spending on the ad campaign, which will run in late prime-time and sports programs, but calls it a significant media buy. Chicago viewers of the Super Bowl saw the ad run twice; Guinness also has spots in NBC's high-rated Thursday prime-time lineup.

The quirky ad, which goes through the ritual of ordering a pint of Guinness, from the nod to the bartender to the long wait for the beer to settle, was created by Weiss, Stagliano of New York City. It got a five-week tryout in Chicago and Boston last fall with convincing results: Sales of Guinness in Boston were up 24 percent in December over a year earlier, compared with just an 11 percent gain for the rest of the Guinness portfolio, while in Chicago, sales are up 35 percent from a year ago, with distribution up 22 percent.

EXHIBIT 8
World Beer Market

Category	1994	1995	1996	Volume (Hectoliters)
Specialty	6.6%	7.4%	8.2%	103,000,000
Sophistication	11.9	12.4	12.9	162,000,000
Standard savings	63.5	62.7	61.0	763,000,000
Stay fit	15.9	15.5	15.8	189,000,000
Stay clear	2.1	2.0	2.1	24,000,000
Total	100	100	100	1,241,000,000

EXHIBIT 9
Image of Ireland

Perception of Country	Personality of People
Green	Relaxed
Environmentally friendly	Sociable
Natural	Friendly
Unspoiled	Different
Lost Arcadia	Humorous/witty
Underdeveloped	Pub atmosphere

The pricing strategy is one of price parity with major specialty competitors. A reasonable margin is being offered to the trade. In fact, the company prices its products slightly below the competition to the trade as an enticement to carry the products.

The promotion and communications strategy is multipronged. The brands' Irish heritage and origin continue to be reinforced. The company engages in tactical advertising and promotion rather than larger-scale strategic campaigns. For example, St. Patrick's Day and Irish music nights are exploited. The communication focus is on both brands in most markets. The company plans to use still rather than electronic media to convey the authentic Irish image of the brands.

Murphy's Future Direction

Patrick Conway assembled the reports on the Irish, UK, European, and American markets as well as the world positioning and strategy. He circulated them to the members of his group with a memo calling a meeting in early June 1997. Conway indicated that he wanted to develop a long-term strategy for the Murphy's brand to take to Heineken management rather than develop a knee-jerk reaction to the Guinness–Grand Met merger.

He believed that Murphy's reputation was improving both in Ireland and throughout the world. He did not want to jeopardize the gains made in the last several years. However, he was concerned with the stagnant nature of the beer industry in Europe and North America. He called a meeting for June 10, 1997, to discuss the marketing strategy for Murphy's.

Before he met with the marketing department members, he stopped by Marien Kakabeeke's office. The managing director reminded him of the corporate goal for Murphy's, which is 20 percent of the world's stout market by the year 2000. "I know that is ambitious, Patrick, but I am confident you and your staff can achieve it."

"Do you realize that the Cork Brewery is almost at capacity now?" asked Patrick. "Even if we stimulate demand, how will we be able to meet it with production limits? Also, recall that we expanded the brewery in 1995."[13]

When Patrick, D. Ford, and Dan Leahy sat down that morning to discuss the future of Murphy's, they considered several questions:

How important is a strong showing in the Irish domestic market to Murphy's? Must it make a strong showing there to be successful worldwide?

Should Murphy's employ a global rather than local marketing strategy worldwide? The "I'm not bitter" campaign has been successful in the United Kingdom, so should several possible strategies be used, especially in the large markets of the United States and continental Europe?

[13] Paul O'Kane, "Murphy's Plans Major Expansion," *The Irish Times*, August 16, 1995.

Is Murphy's destined to be a "niche" product forever? Will these brands ever reach a place where they command a substantial market share?

Should the company continue to make the two brands only at the Cork brewery for the lucrative U.S. market, or should it consider making the product in that country? It worked for automobiles; why not beer?

Will Murphy's ever be able to achieve the status of other products that are famous for their Irish heritage, such as Guinness, Bailey's Irish Cream, Jameson Irish Whiskey, Waterford Crystal, and Belleek China?

Case 6-12

Dairyland Seed Company

The morning sun was shining brightly as Tom Strachota, Chief Executive Officer for Dairyland Seed, drove up Highway 45 in southeast Wisconsin in late February 1999. Because of the snow cover on either side of the road, it was not immediately apparent that these fields were the sites of research plots that have generated some of the most cutting-edge biotechnologies in the seed industry. Tom couldn't help but smile as he reflected on the past few years' accomplishments. He was particularly pleased with the success of their line of soybean varieties tolerant to the DuPont Chemical Company's Sulfonylurea herbicides. Dairyland had pioneered the technology—a credit to Dairyland's long-standing commitment to research and development.

However, a lot had happened in the soybean market since the introduction of the Sulfonylurea Tolerant Soybean (STS) varieties five years ago. Competition in the STS seed market had intensified as competitors developed and promoted their own varieties. While Tom believed Dairyland still enjoyed some advantage in the expanding enhanced trait soybean seed business, other seed companies were making rapid progress in many of the same markets.

The market share growth of Round-Up® tolerant soybean varieties was one of the newest challenges. These new varieties enabled Monsanto, manufacturer of the well-known Round-Up® herbicide, to compete directly with DuPont's STS. Initially, limited amounts of Round-Up® tolerant seeds constrained growth, but Monsanto has taken major steps to ensure greater supplies in each of the past two years. As a result, Round-Up® tolerant seeds captured between 35–40 percent market share in 1998 and projections are that Round-Up® tolerant seeds will command as much as 50 percent of the market this year.

Dairyland had not been caught off guard by the Round-Up® tolerant technology, of course. In fact, Dairyland had acquired a license to develop its own Round-Up® tolerant soybean varieties. Dairyland researchers have been successful in developing several varieties that have fared extremely well in state yield trials and in the marketplace this year.

Combined, Dairyland's STS and Round-Up® tolerant varieties account for over 60 percent of Dairyland's soybean sales. This is remarkable given that STS traits entered the market in 1993, and Round-Up® in 1996. However, the growing importance of these varieties brings with it new challenges for Dairyland. By marketing both STS and Round-Up® tolerant varieties, Dairyland is in a position where Tom must manage business relationships with competitors in the chemical and biotechnology market, namely DuPont and Monsanto. With the market demands for Round-Up® tolerant technology, how closely should he establish his business relationship with Monsanto? He wondered what the impact of partnering with Monsanto might be on his carefully developed alliance with DuPont.

Adding to Tom's new challenges, agricultural chemical and biotechnology companies have chosen to become further committed to the seed industry by

"Partnering Strategies in the BioTech World: The Case of Dairyland Seed Company" by Mark P. Leach, Luiz Mesquita and W. David Downey in *Journal of Business and Industrial Marketing*, 2002. Republished with permission of the Publisher, Emerald.

Dr. Mark P. Leach is Assistant Professor of Marketing, Loyola Marymount University; Mr. Luiz Mesquita is a Doctoral Student of Management, Purdue University; and Dr. W. David Downey is Professor and Director, Center for Agricultural Business, Purdue University.

The authors would like to thank Dairyland Seed for permission to develop this case around issues facing their organization. The generous contributions of information and time by Tom Strachota (CEO), John Froelich (Director of Sales), and the many others at Dairyland Seed are gratefully acknowledged. In addition, they would like to recognize the contributions of Danny Kennedy (Co-Leader for North American Markets, Monsanto Global Seed Group as of February 1999), and Tom Matya (Director of Strategic Marketing, DEKALB Genetics Corporation). Note: This case was prepared as the basis for class discussion rather than to illustrate either effective or ineffective handling of an administrative situation.

acquiring or establishing joint ventures with larger seed firms. Of particular interest to Tom were DuPont's 20 percent ownership position in Pioneer, and Monsanto's recent acquisitions of Asgrow and DEKALB—two major seed companies. These mergers have caused these two major technology suppliers to become more tightly allied with Dairyland's direct competitors. What might this mean to Dairyland's access to future technologies? Success had certainly brought a new set of problems, and positioning was going to be especially important for Dairyland to ensure continuity of its role as a cutting-edge seed producer.

Company Background

Simon and Andrew Strachota founded the Dairyland Seed Company in 1907. In 1920, Andrew retired, leaving his brother Simon to head the company. When Simon died unexpectedly in 1940, his son Orville left college and returned home to run the company. At 79, Orville Strachota continues to be active in the business and serves as Chairman of Dairyland's Board. However, his three sons, Steve, Tom, and John Strachota, have managed day-to-day operations of the company for over 10 years.

Dairyland began as Strachota Seeds. The company operated out of the Strachota family's general store in eastern Wisconsin. White Dutch Clover Seed was their primary product. But when the market for White Dutch Clover suddenly dropped off in 1955, Orville shifted to the production of alfalfa seed—a product with rapidly growing demand driven by Wisconsin dairy farmers searching for better forages for their cows. Dairy continued to grow in importance in their region. In 1963 Orville decided to change the name of the company to Dairyland Seed Company to reflect its commitment to the market.

Dairyland continued to respond to challenges and opportunities in the seed industry as they arose. They began to produce and market seed corn on a large scale in 1961. As soybeans began to develop in the United States in the 1960s, Dairyland also added soybean seed to their product line.

Today, Orville Strachota's three sons, Steve (President), Tom (Chief Executive Officer), and John (Vice President), jointly manage Dairyland Seed. The company is privately held, with majority stock owned by the Strachota family. Of the over 800 companies listed by the American Seed Trade Association, Dairyland is the only American family-owned seed company with proprietary research in alfalfa, corn, and soybeans. Dairyland's board of directors, which includes family stockholders and outside directors, meets quarterly to review business strategy and plans.

The company is divided into seven functional operating areas: management, finance, research, production, distribution, marketing, and sales. Dairyland employs approximately 100 people plus seasonal help. Executive management is located at Dairyland's headquarters in West Bend, Wisconsin, while research, sales, and production employees are located throughout the company's market and production area. Dairyland's production/processing plants are in Mt. Hope and West Bend, Wisconsin. In addition, five research stations are located in Otterbein, Indiana; Sloughhouse, California; Gibson City, Illinois; Clinton, Wisconsin; and Gilbert, Iowa.

Dairyland has built its image around new product development and is well known in the upper-Midwest for innovation. Orville Strachota established a commitment to research early in the company's history. Today, over 40 percent of the company's employees work in research and development, making it the largest department in the company. Management believes Dairyland has a competitive advantage in certain markets with its continued commitment to research and development.

The Marketing Mix at Dairyland

Product

Dairyland his worked hard to build its image around quality products, its high standards of business ethics, and as a successful family-run business. This message is intentionally promoted in a myriad of ways including a highly visible commitment to research, maintaining a first-class physical plant, demonstrating employee pride in the organization, and the active involvement of Orville and three third-generation principals. Tom Strachota believes the positioning effort over the years has resulted in a positive and consistent image of Dairyland among customers and competitors alike. Tom believes that this image is very important and valuable.

The focus of Dairyland has been on high-yielding genetics rather than on specific traits. This commitment to high-performance genetics is captured in their statement of values:

1. Dairyland has a responsibility to its customers to deliver consistently high-performing products.
2. New traits are of value only if they add to the consistency of performance or bring more profit to the farmer.
3. No single genetic trait is of value by itself.

Tom Strachota puts it this way; "It is better to have high-yielding genetics with no specialty traits, than to have specialty traits with poor genetics." Guided by these values, researchers at Dairyland have developed a product mix that consists of varieties of alfalfa, corn, and soybean seed.

Alfalfa

Dairyland is especially proud of its success with alfalfa varieties. According to company executives, Dairyland has the world's largest alfalfa breeding program. Dairyland's alfalfa lineup includes several specialty alfalfa varieties from which the farmer can choose to match their particular needs (e.g., varieties suited for wet soil conditions, other varieties for high traffic fields, etc.). Strachota is quick to mention recent successful innovations Dairyland has made in the release of patented Sequential Maturity Alfalfa™ products that provide farmers with more high quality forage.

Corn

Dairyland's seed corn business has grown steadily since hybrid corn was first introduced into their product line in 1961. Seed corn now plays an important role in their overall strategy. Dairyland currently offers over 40 corn varieties that have been bred to meet the unique needs of the upper-Midwestern states. The company's "Stealth" hybrid corn breeding program (which emphasizes required growers to make increasingly more complex decisions about inputs—(seed, chemicals, and fertilizer), and the spectrum of knowledge required has grown prohibitively large. Many farmers favor retailers that can provide more technical advice to growers and maintain superior service standards. As such, a growing percentage of Dairyland's business flows through these intermediaries, and Dairyland is continuing to look for appropriate resale partners with which to license.

Promotion

Dairyland uses a wide variety of promotional programs to communicate the benefits of its soybean seed to farmers. The Dairyland Soybean Management Guide provides farmers with technical and practical advice on the best soybean production methods. Each year, the company produces a pocket-sized Dairyland seed reference guide and calendar. There is a quarterly newsletter called "The Leader" that communicates a variety of information to the customer. Other promotional efforts include tours of research and production facilities, crop management clinics, field days at Dairyland test plots, and maintenance of "show case" quality facilities.

Most of Dairyland's advertising is direct mail from an extensive database maintained on all dealers and customers. The internal database is supplemented by mailing lists from other sources. In addition, the company includes ads in state farm publications, magazines (especially Soybean Digest), agricultural newspapers, etc. Occasionally DSMs will prepare brief ads or radio announcements for local areas to promote a field day or educational program in that area.

Dealers are offered a wide range of individual and customer incentives intended to promote sales. Traditional caps, jackets, etc. are all available to dealers and their customers. In addition, dealers may work toward larger value gifts (e.g., television sets or trips to Florida are common, and even a car in the case of Dairyland's Stealth seed corn program). District sales managers are also offered sales incentives and bonus awards for achievement in increasing the sales of Dairyland's three product lines. Individual award programs depend on the specific activities that Dairyland is attempting to promote throughout the year.

Pricing

Dairyland's seed is priced slightly above the market average in all product lines (see Exhibit 1). "This is a strategy designed to encourage the premium quality image that is the core of our marketing strategy, and to generate margins necessary to support an aggressive research and development program," says Tom Strachota. "We believe farmers are willing to pay a little higher price when we deliver high quality seed, consistent performance, dependability, and cutting-edge technology." Although Dairyland seeds may not be the highest priced alternative in the market, this philosophy generally places Dairyland's average prices at 5–10 percent above the average in market. "The idea is to realize that we can't price like the market leader, but we can deliver the best overall value," Tom argues.

EXHIBIT 1
Estimated Industry Average Seed Prices for 1998

	Alfalfa	Corn	Soybeans
Average Retail Price—industry	$189	$99	$19.00
Average Retail Price—Dairyland	$193	$95	$18.65
Average Discounted Price—industry	$176	$78	$15.20

Based on the 1998 price list of Pioneer, Novartis, Mycogen, DEKALB, and Cargill companies.

Tom Strachota believes that this premium value strategy is highly successful. Dairyland has enjoyed an increase in its soybean sales for the last five years. This includes an increase in 1997 despite not having Round-Up® Ready soybeans; STS accounted for over one-third of Dairyland's soybean sales in 1997.

Channel Partners

Chemical companies like DuPont and Monsanto are using seed companies to bring their products to market. The developers of the biotechnology have sought to use a combination of seed production and distribution companies as well as licensing agreements with distributors and small seed companies in order to achieve access to growers with a high level of service. Dairyland has among its channel partners two main providers of biotechnology: DuPont and Monsanto. Among these partners, Dairyland has worked most closely in the past with DuPont. Through this relationship with DuPont, Dairyland has marketed its seed varieties of STS soybeans.

DuPont

DuPont began licensing with several larger seed companies over five years ago, giving them the right to sublicense to other smaller seed firms. While Dairyland was one of the first seed companies licensed to produce and sell STS seed, there are now nearly 100 seed companies who have been licensed to sell the STS technology. These companies have developed more than 170 varieties of STS seeds. The more aggressive companies include Dairyland Seeds, Asgrow (recently purchased by Monsanto), Pioneer, Stine Seed, Countrymark and GROWMARK, and Novartis Seed. Even though Asgrow is owned by Monsanto, it still maintains a licensing contract with DuPont.

Discussions between DuPont and Dairyland were opened in the mid-80s. Acquisition of the Sulfonylureas germplasm by Dairyland occurred in the late 80s. DuPont selected Dairyland for its strong reputation in soybean development and its independent research capability. The relationship is not exclusive, however. Other companies received the germplasm and have had the opportunity to develop their own tolerant varieties.

The agreement between Dairyland and DuPont stipulates formation of a "joint-commercialization" team to review the marketing strategies for STS. Dairyland and DuPont agreed that in marketing the product, DuPont would sell herbicides and help farmers understand the benefits of STS, while Dairyland would sell seed and talk about the benefits of STS as they relate to seed selection. The joint marketing strategy was a tremendous success as the salesforces of each company were able to establish mutually supportive professional relationships. As the STS technology represents important market potential for DuPont, Dairyland anticipates continued marketing support. DuPont's efforts have clearly helped position Dairyland as one of the leading developers of Sulfonylurea Tolerant Soybeans.

DuPont has basically maintained their aggressive marketing strategy to promote the use of STS seed varieties in the market through programs that include sizable advertising and incentive programs. They have executed major herbicide launches that include TV in major markets and heavy print media advertising. DuPont sales representatives will support local agricultural chemical dealers and seed companies with educational programs in local markets and support plot tours to demonstrate the new technology. DuPont has elected not to place any premium on the Sulfonylurea herbicides.

DuPont has relied heavily on media campaigns to successfully increase its brand name and product awareness among users. However, they have recently been forced to recognize the rapid growth of Round-Up® technology, and the potential cost savings and ease of the Round-Up® system to the farmer. While most industry experts have predicted the increase of Round-Up® soybeans, almost no one expected acceptance to be as rapid as it developed in the 1997 and 1998 markets (see Exhibit 2).[1]

DuPont has responded by increasing commitment with the seed industry substantially with the recent purchase of 20 percent of Pioneer Hybrid International stock and the holding of two seats on Pioneer's board of directors in 1997. Pioneer and DuPont also have announced the formation of a new joint venture called Optimum whose purpose is to bringing new value-added crops to market, such as high-oil corn, etc. It is clear that DuPont will be working more closely with Pioneer than with any other seed company. However, Dairyland feels that DuPont has not abandoned its STS technology or its initial seed industry partners. DuPont's relationship with other seed companies has remained the same. Time will tell whether DuPont's new relationship with Pioneer will have an impact on other seed industry firms.

In addition, DuPont made a substantial change in its pricing strategy—announcing a 75 percent price cut in August 1997 on its STS-related herbicides. This price reduction was a clear attempt to level the economics of

[1] Estimation by Dairyland executives, based on reports of the American Seed Trade Association. Assuming the development of high-yielding varieties of soybean. Seeds out of the bag (does not include bin seed).

EXHIBIT 2
Estimated Market Share for STS and Round-Up® Tolerant Soybean Seed Varieties

	1996	1997	1998	1999*	2000*
STS Varieties	7%	8–12%	10–15%	15–20%	20–25%
Round-Up Ready	3%	18–20%	35–40%	45–50%	50–60%

*The economic situation faced by producers varies widely by region. This table is based on 1998 University of Wisconsin yield trials on three varieties of Dairyland seed.

EXHIBIT 3
Alliances in the Supply Chain

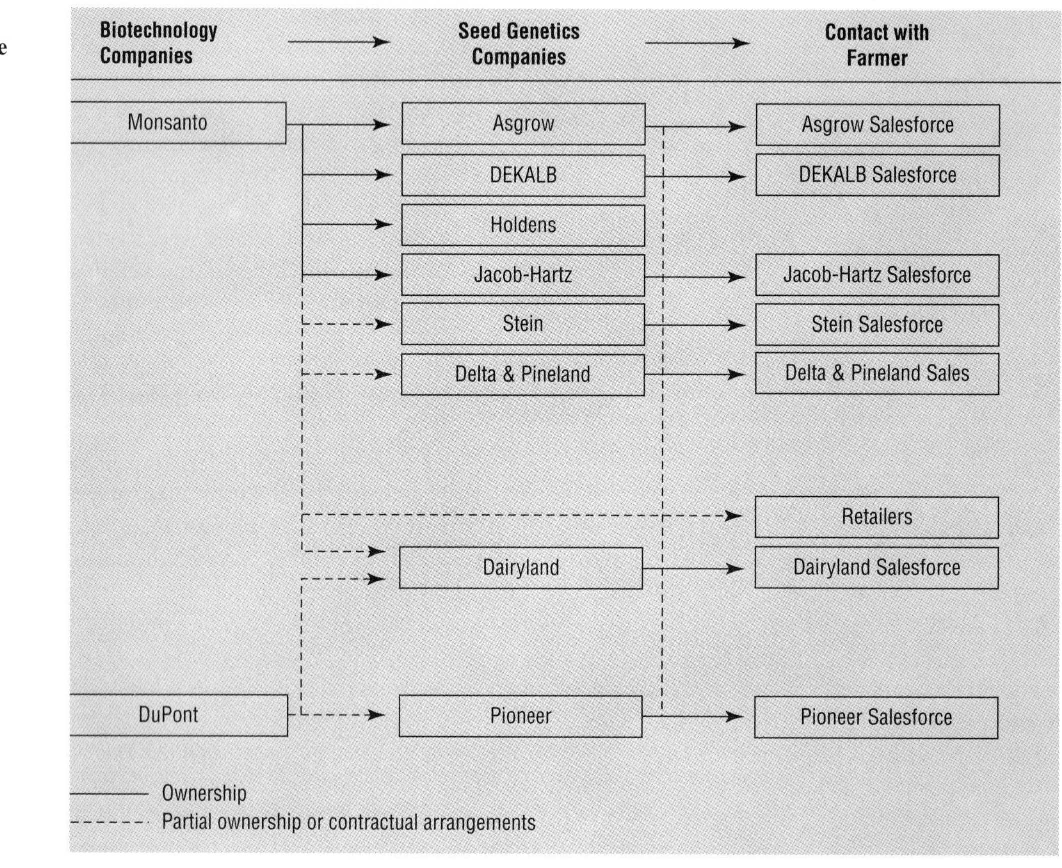

the farmer's decision process in choosing which herbicide resistant technology to embrace. On an average basis, the farmer would pay approximately $28 per acre for Round-Up® tolerant seeds (including a $6.50 technology fee). The herbicide would cost about $15 per acre per application. With the new lower price, DuPont claims it can offer the farmer superior protection (longer weed control) for basically the same price. Dairyland believes that its STS seeds outperform most competitors' Round-Up® varieties and so it continues to be committed to the STS technology.

Monsanto and Round-Up® Ready

Monsanto's Round-Up® Ready technology has been under development for some time. From its introduction, market growth has been limited only by supply. In 1994 and 1995, Round-Up® tolerant soybeans hit the market with limited quantity and sold out. In 1996 they sold out with a 3 percent market share. In 1997 supplies sold out, this time with approximately 20 percent market share. In 1998 Round-Up® soybeans did not sell out, but did capture nearly 40 percent of the market.

Dairyland did not have Round-Up® technology initially. In fact, Dairyland was not licensed to market Round-Up® soybeans in 1997, but it did enter into an arrangement with Monsanto in 1998. Tom attributes Dairyland's ability to license with Monsanto to Dairyland's commitment to quality, and the recognition that Dairyland receives for being the first to market with STS herbicide-resistant soybeans.

Recently Monsanto has escalated its activity in the seed industry. Through its acquisitions, partnerships, and incentive programs, Monsanto has effectively elevated its position in the seed supply chain (see Exhibit 3). These acquisitions and partnerships are part of a continuing effort of Monsanto to strengthen its position in the market for new biotechnological products. This is consistent with Monsanto's strategic vision, "to create cutting-edge environmental solutions in order to assure sustainable growth for our company," says Monsanto's CEO Robert Shapiro (Monsanto Press Release, 1998).[2]

In 1996, Monsanto Company acquired Asgrow Agronomics. Asgrow is a major U.S. soybean seed company with international operations. According to Monsanto's executive vice president, Hendrik A. Verfaillie: "Asgrow's strength in soybeans is particularly important to us as we accelerate the sales of our Round-Up® soybeans and other new soybean products to formers worldwide. The acquisition of Asgrow Agronomics strengthens our ability to quickly move our innovations into the marketplace" (Monsanto Press Release, 1998). Other examples of recent Monsanto acquisitions and alliances include:

- In December 1997, Monsanto Company, Asgrow Seed Company, and Stine Seed Company announced a collaboration agreement. This research agreement was reportedly designed to further improve and develop soybean genetics and related technologies.
- On December 4, 1998, DEKALB Genetics became a wholly-owned subsidiary of Monsanto.
- Monsanto also bought Holdens in early 1997. Holdens is a major supplier of corn genetics to both large and independent seed companies.
- In June 1998 Monsanto signed an agreement to purchase Cargill's international seed operations in Latin America, Asia, Africa, and parts of Europe. This acquisition includes seed research, production, and testing facilities in 21 countries and distribution systems in 51 countries.

Through these partnerships, Monsanto has acquired a solid distribution network that should facilitate rapid seed product introduction. Also, through gearing research to complement one another, these new alliances will achieve synergies in new product development. Thus, at the same time Dairyland's initial soybean technology partner (i.e., DuPont) has become more tightly allied with one of Dairyland's key competitors (i.e., Pioneer), Monsanto has been managing its relationships with several other Dairyland competitors.

Another way that Monsanto is managing the supply-chain of its Round-Up® Ready technology is through incentive programs. Monsanto has established an incentive structure for seed manufactures, for agricultural retailing, and for growers. For example, growers who use both Round-Up® Ready soybeans and Monsanto's YieldGard Bt corn on a high percentage of acres are given a rebate.

Given the demand for Round-Up® Ready soybeans, Monsanto has been able to charge a technology fee to growers. This fee was originally $5 per 50-pound bag, but was increased to $6 for spring 1999 (the price increase was coupled with a price reduction of Round-Up® Ready herbicide so that the overall cost to a customer was essentially the same).

One incentive that Monsanto provides to seed suppliers is a special handling fee. For suppliers, Monsanto provides 10 percent of this fee back to the supplier (i.e., $0.60). In addition, if a supplier meets certain share-of-business requirements, Monsanto will rebate another 10 percent (i.e., $0.60) to the supplier. These requirements include having 90 percent of herbicide-resistant soybeans sold be Round-Up® Ready soybeans, 85 percent of herbicide-resistant corn be Round-Up® Ready corn, and 90 percent of corn borer insect-protected corn be YieldGard Bt corn. In order to obtain the additional 10 percent, all three share-of-business requirements must be met. Together, these two rebates can more than double the retail profit on a bag of seed.

For any seed company, this program can generate a lot of money. For a firm selling 100,000 bags of soybeans, meeting these requirements would mean receiving $60,000. Likewise, for a firm selling 500,000 units, this means an additional $300,000 in revenue. Given the relatively low profit margin on a bag of soybeans, this provides substantial incentive for suppliers to sell products with Monsanto technologies.

However, for companies like Dairyland who are allied with other biotechnology channel partners, Monsanto's incentive structure raises several issues. First of all, with such an attractive inducement to sell Round-Up® tolerant soybeans, should Dairyland continue to develop its relationship with DuPont? Furthermore, because this offer will shape decisions made by other genetic companies, a result may be the decrease in the number of companies providing STS technologies. Will DuPont continue to aggressively market STS even when they foresee markets becoming less attainable? Is this an opportunity for Dairyland, or a threat to its position in the market?

[2] Monsanto press releases are available online at http://www.monsanto.com/monsanto/media.

Another concern for Dairyland is that not all of Monsanto's business partners operate under the same set of restrictions. Due to prior contractual arrangements, neither Novartis nor Pioneer is required to pay Monsanto the $6.50/bag technology fee. However, each of these firms charges this fee to customers. This raises concerns of the equity of Monsanto business relationships, as this money may provide a source of funds for research and development that is not available to most Round-Up® tolerant soybean suppliers, or allow a significant disparity in dealer or retail pricing.

Danny Kennedy, Co-President of Asgrow Seed, believes Monsanto's success stems from its ability to add value to the farmer by capitalizing on the synergies from its portfolio of companies and technologies representing several sectors in agriculture. He states that Monsanto considers its involvement in agricultural business to be a core part of the overall technology platform. This view is consistent with the strategic actions of Monsanto. Since heading up the company in 1995, Robert Shapiro has spun off the core chemical business to focus on being the "main provider of the agricultural biotechnology. . ." (Monsanto Press Release, 1998).

With regard to herbicide-resistance technology, Monsanto executives see both seed and biotechnology as key ingredients to their long-term strategy. Danny Kennedy realizes that seed is the distribution system by which Monsanto technologies reach the farmer. He believes that seed will drive farmers' decisions in the future, and states that, "farmers will buy seed that is specialized genetically to suit their own feed stock needs, grain market needs, consumer needs, etc." Asgrow and DEKALB have competitive advantages in some regions, however, because small firms can have a strong presence in certain regions and market niches, he believes that Monsanto cannot afford not to license other seed firms with its new technologies. As an example of the commitment of Monsanto to licensing its technology to the broad market (family and small firms), as of February 1999 Monsanto has already agreed to licensing its technology to more than 200 seed firms.

Other Providers of Herbicide-Tolerant Soybean Technology

Although Dairyland has business partnerships with DuPont and Monsanto, there are several other chemical and biotechnical firms that operate in this market. AgrEvo, is the third player in the herbicide-resistant seed market. AgrEvo's herbicide, Liberty, targets a broad spectrum of broad leaf weeds. The Liberty technology was late to enter the market. Early efforts of AgrEvo to bring its herbicide-resistance technology to the seed market were through Asgrow and Holdens. This strategy has proven to be problematic, especially since Monsanto now owns both. AgrEvo has been licensing its technology to other seed companies, though it has been less successful than Monsanto and DuPont to bring its technology to the market. While pricing of the AgrEvo product is not yet clear, it appears that AgrEvo may choose a premium price strategy rather than a licensing fee as Monsanto has chosen. Liberty is faster-acting than Round-Up® but has about the same kill spectrum for weeds and grasses as Round-Up®.

American Cyanamid has maintained a significant share of the soybean herbicide market with Pursuit®, which is used with nonherbicide-tolerant soybean varieties. Recently, they have cut prices approximately 40 percent so that its use is competitively priced with Round-Up® Ultra and DuPont's Symphony. Thus, American Cyanamid continues to represent a major market challenge for DuPont/STS and Monsanto Round-Up® products. If DuPont is to be successful, it will be necessary to demonstrate a significant advantage over this and other traditional herbicide alternatives. Another relatively new release is Flexstar® by Zeneca, a formulation intended for broadleaf weed control in soybeans.

Competitive Environment in the Soybean Seed Industry

Dairyland faces a wide range of competitors in their diverse market area (see Exhibit 4). Some competitors are large international companies such as Pioneer, DEKALB, and Novartis Seeds that have broad product lines that parallel Dairyland's. Furthermore, there are a large number of regional and local seed companies who offer all or part of the seed products sold by Dairyland. Some of Dairyland's competitors develop and sell proprietary products, while others sell public varieties that are genetically identical to each other, but carry the producer's own label. Many of these smaller companies are aggressive and have strong loyalties within their own local market areas.

Competition is intense in all three product lines. Pioneer is the clear industry leader in the seed corn market with an estimated market share of about 42 percent. There is no dominant supplier in alfalfa although alfalfa has always been one of Dairyland's strengths. Pioneer has become aggressive in the soybean market with an estimated 14 percent share. Asgrow recently announced that it was the leader in soybean share with 16 percent. Accurate market share information is difficult to obtain and to interpret since many seed companies are privately held and the market is so geographically fractured.

EXHIBIT 4 Estimated 1998 National Market Share

	Percent of Soybean Acres
Farmer Saved Seed	32.5%
Public Varieties	15.0%
Private Varieties:	
Asgrow (Monsanto)	16.0%
Pioneer	14.0%
DEKALB (Monsanto)	≅5.0%
Novartis	≅5.0%
Stine	≅5.0%
Jacob-Hartz (Monsanto)	<5.0%
Cokers (Sandoz)	<5.0%
FS (GROWMARK)	<5.0%
Mycogen	<5.0%
Others	≅8.0%
Total Private	(52.5%)
Total	100.0%

Aggregate market share information is also often misleading because it varies dramatically among local market areas. For example, while Dairyland Seed does not have a large market share on a national basis (i.e., less than 2 percent), in some core market areas, their market share may run as high as 30 percent.

Most soybean seed companies are marketing some STS varieties. However, these companies differ basically in their enthusiasm and commitment to the technology. Among the major players, a few of them are worth mentioning. Asgrow has had STS products developed since 1993. Asgrow has not priced their STS varieties at a premium relative to their non-STS varieties. Cenex, a major cooperative in the upper-Midwest, has introduced an STS product, and DEKALB has STS products in the market. Other seed companies, such as Stine, have introduced STS varieties but lack breadth in this product line.

A major new player in the STS market is Pioneer. Consistent with Pioneer's general pricing strategy, it is pricing its STS products at a premium relative to its non-STS products. Many in the industry expect the new relationship of DuPont and Pioneer will result in additional introductions of enhanced trait seeds.

John Froelich feels that one of Dairyland's competitive advantages continues to be their lead in the development of STS varieties. While some companies are still working to improve the performance of their STS varieties, Dairyland executives feel that their "commanding lead" allows them to concentrate on introducing enhanced traits into varieties that have already proven to be strong performers. Pursuing this strategy, Dairyland researchers have successfully bred additional traits into the STS product line. New Dairyland varieties have demonstrated resistance to a series of plant diseases, such as white mold, brown stem rot, and phytophtora. Dairyland believes these new traits will be particularly important in "niche" markets where these diseases are problematic.

Dairyland has responded to the growing market demand for Round-Up® Ready soybeans by introducing several new varieties for the '98 and '99 selling seasons. So far, over 30 percent of Dairyland's sales today come from Round-Up® Ready products. John Froelich expects this trend to continue to the end of the 1999 selling season. Research is currently underway to introduce still more Round-Up® Ready varieties in the future.

Asgrow is expected to continue the aggressive introduction of new soybean varieties. This Monsanto-affiliate is marketing a new "stacked traits" variety—one that has resistance to both STS and Round-Up® herbicides. Monsanto has not given other seed companies the legal right to offer "stacked trait" varieties. On the other hand, DuPont has announced that it will allow companies already licensed to sell (STSs) to develop and market stacked trait soybean varieties. It is unclear what Monsanto's intentions are for the future.

Dairyland's Customer Focus

Putting the customer first has always been the core of Dairyland's business philosophy. As Orville Strachota puts it, Dairyland's objective has always been to treat farmers fairly and understand their needs. If you have a good product at a fair price with good service and hold true to your word, you've got a customer and a friend for life.

However, customer buying behavior is changing. On today's large farms, more people influence decisions, and farmers are more business-oriented. Tom Matya, Director of Strategic Marketing for DEKALB Genetics Corporation, finds customers today to be more economically focused, more highly educated in germplasm and herbicides, and less brand loyal than 10 years ago. Although there is still a strong sense of loyalty, he attributes the increase in brand switching by customers today to the rapid acceleration of product innovation, and the leapfrogging of technologies.

Farmers today have been characterized as being value-driven. Farmers must justify the economics of the variety that is being purchased, and understand the mix of products that work together to provide optimal solutions. This may be one reason for the increase in sales through agricultural retailers. Through their ability to provide customers bundled packages and product expertise on everything from seeds to chemicals, agricultural retailers are providing farmers with added value through expertise, convenience, and often through creative discounting.

EXHIBIT 5
Percentage of Dairyland Soybean Sales

Year	STS Sales	Round-Up® Sales	Conventional Sales
1993	<1%	0%	99%
1994	6%	0%	94%
1995	31%	0%	69%
1996	41%	0%	59%
1997	40%	1%	59%
1998	41%	21%	38%
1999 est.	41%	32%	27%

Farmer customers have a high level of risk aversion. Both John Froelich from Dairyland Seed and Tom Matya from DEKALB agree that farmers will be more inclined to test new technologies themselves before converting large numbers of acres to a new product. However, if the product works, adoption moves quickly.

Similarly, Tom Strachota foresees that farmers will become more focused on high-quality genetics and less driven by new specialty traits until they have been proven in the field. However, the growth of herbicide-tolerant varieties of soybean in general and Round-Up® Ready soybeans in particular, provides evidence that specialty traits are highly desired by today's farmers. At Dairyland, herbicide-tolerant soybeans accounted for 62 percent of total soybean sales in 1998 and are expected to increase to 73 percent in 1999 (see Exhibit 5).[3]

Dairyland has been encouraged by experiences reported by many of their key accounts who have been aggressively testing the STS and Round-Up® Ready seed on their farms. The net result has been an increase in their purchases of Dairyland STS. John Froelich believes that the sales increases further demonstrate that performance continues to be the major factor for many business-minded farmers. Yet John is quick to recognize that the differences in performance may not be enough for many farmers who simply like the convenience of Round-Up®.

John relates a Monsanto study showing approximately 95 percent of the farmers using the Round-Up® Ready system experienced "satisfaction" with the product. "That is, they got what they thought they would get with their product," John says. "I believe this means these farmers did not expect to have higher yields, but were focusing on a wider span of weed control. On the other hand," John continues, "I believe the initial impact of Round-Up® Ready will be dimmed by performance of the Round-Up® Ready varieties as farmers have more data and experience to really evaluate the results."

Dairyland believes that in many regions the STS varieties will continue to show a performance advantage over the newer Round-Up® tolerant beans. However, they believe their current advantage is temporary and the Round-Up® tolerant beans will soon equal STS varieties in performance. Further, because of all the variables involved, this performance advantage is increasingly difficult to prove. John Froelich expects that most independent seed companies will continue to work with both Monsanto and DuPont in order to cover all the bases. Yet the appeal of Round-Up® Ready soybeans is unmistakable. Many farmers have had much experience with Round-Up® and are very comfortable with its use.

However, some of the economic appeal of the Round-Up® system has been reduced by recent competitive actions. Prices on both DuPont's Synchrony and American Cyanamid's Pursuit have been cut substantially, making purchase decisions less dependent on price. Dairyland believes that much of the customer demand for the Round-Up® system was the up-front cost savings that the system provided for farmer customers. If this was a major purchase motive, the virtual elimination of Round-Up® Ready's cost savings advantage may reduce the demand for Round-Up® tolerant varieties (see Exhibit 6).

A lot has changed in the soybean market in the few years since Dairyland introduced that first line of herbicide-tolerant soybean varieties. The excitement created by the advent of biotechnology has led to a rapidly changing environment where Dairyland's biotechnology suppliers are becoming more closely aligned with its competitors and where soybean seed customers are demanding the inclusion of biotechnological traits in addition to high-yielding genetics. As Tom puzzles over his current situation, and how to best manage his relationships with his technology suppliers and his customers, he is also keenly aware that herbicide tolerance is just the tip of the proverbial biotech iceberg. What will that next market-changing trait be, and when will it be developed? Will he have access to develop varieties with that trait? What types of relationships will he be managing in the future? Tom sits back from his desk and smiles. Yes, there hasn't been a more interesting time to be in the seed industry.

[3] Dairyland.

EXHIBIT 6
Economic Decisions Faced by Customers*

	Yield/ acre	Seed costs/acre	Herbicide costs/acre†
Dairyland Round-Up® 2341 variety			Round-Up® Ultra
One application of Herbicide	61	29.73**	35.00
Two applications of Herbicide			5.00††
Dairyland STS variety			Synchrony
One application of Herbicide	61	18.63	35.00
Two applications of Herbicide			25.00
Dairyland Conventional 256 variety			Pursuit
One application of Herbicide	64	18.63	35.00
Two applications of Herbicide			25.00

*The economic situation faced by producers varies widely by regions. This table is based on 1998 University of Wisconsin yield trials on three varieties of Dairyland seed.

**Seed costs include seed, and applicable technology fees (i.e., $19.98+(1.5*$6.50)=$29.73).

†Herbicide costs are based on manufactures suggested application rates and include a $5.00/acre application fee, and an estimated $10.00 for pre-plant and burn-down.

††The warranty for a second application of herbicide for Round-Up® customers depends on the producer following specific planting and application guidelines. Dairyland believes many farmers will not meet these requirements.

Dairyland Case Questions

Three alternative product strategies that Tom Strachota might take with Dairyland Seed are:

1. Attempt to associate more strongly with Monsanto and sell over 90 percent Round-Up® Ready herbicide-resistant seed.
2. Continue with the status quo and produce both Round-Up® Ready and STS beans letting the market dictate the level of each.
3. Attempt to associate more strongly with DuPont and focus on STS herbicide-resistant beans.

For EACH of these alternatives answer the following four questions:

1. What are the pros and cons of each strategy?
2. Are there other significantly different strategies that Dairyland should consider?
3. What would you recommend Dairyland do in the immediate future and why?
4. How can Dairyland remain family-owned and a successful seed business in the future?

Case 6-13

International Business Machines

The directors were just sitting down for the first IBM board meeting of the year on Jan. 28 when CEO Samuel J. Palmisano dropped a bombshell. For years, the board had lavished wealth upon Louis V. Gerstner Jr., keeping his pay in line with other pinstriped superstars across Corporate America. But in a surprise break from the past, Palmisano asked the board to cut his 2003 bonus and set it aside as a pool of money to be shared by about 20 top executives based on their performance as a team. Palmisano doesn't want to say how much he's pitching in, but insiders say it's $3 million to $5 million—nearly half his bonus.

A crowd-pleasing gesture? It was just his latest salvo. Five days earlier, he took aim at a bastion of power and privilege at Big Blue, the 92-year-old executive management committee. For generations, this 12-person body presiding over IBM's strategy and initiatives represented the inner sanctum for every aspiring Big Blue executive. Palmisano himself was anointed back in 1997, a promotion that signaled the shimmering possibilities ahead. But on Jan. 23, the CEO hit the send button on an e-mail to 300 senior managers announcing that this venerable committee was *finito*, kaput. Palmisano instead would work directly with three teams he had put in place the year before—they comprised people from all over the company who could bring the best ideas to the table. The old committee, with its monthly meetings, just slowed things down.

All the while, Palmisano was piecing together an audacious program to catapult IBM back to the zenith of

EXHIBIT 1
Blueprint for Big Blue
CEO Palmisano wants to bring back the days when IBM was revered as a great company. Here's how he plans to do it.

An Egalitarian Culture Palmisano has made a radical proposal to his board: Take several million dollars from his 2003 bonus and give it to his top execs based on teamwork.
Says Sam "If you say you're about a team, you have to be a team. You've got to walk the talk, right?"

Bureaucracy-Busting Big Decisions Decisions at IBM long ran through the 12-member Corporate Executive Committee. Palmisano replaced it with three teams—operating, strategy, and technology—to move more quickly.
Says Sam "Bureaucracy is an inhibiter to excellence.

A Unifying Goal IBM acted like fiefdoms: software, chips, computers. Palmisano created a unifying strategy: e-business on demand, to deliver tech like a utility. This requires all hands on deck.
Says Sam "It was about appealing to the pride of the 320,000 people to go to the next level."

Agenda Setter IBM was once the tech leader. Now, it's using R&D to leap ahead with grid computing and self-healing software.
Says Sam "IBM should be setting the industry agenda. We shouldn't let some small venture-based firm with 10 people do it. That's a joke.

Talent Magnet The company is spending $100 million to teach 30,000 employees to lead, not control their staff, so workers won't feel like cogs in a machine.
Says Sam "If you look at people's frustration, it's this inability to connect in a big place with a lot of smart people."

Squeaky-Clean Finances Palmisano is quieting criticism of IBM's accounting practices. He has allocated $4 billion to fully fund the U.S. pension plan. IBM also is paying more in taxes.
Says Sam "Write about somebody else. The pension plan is funded, the tax rate is up."

Good Works Palmisano wants IBM to give back. IBM is the leader in volunteer time. Now, he's considering more volunteers to mentor teachers and build computer systems for schools.
Says Sam "There's an attractiveness about being part of an enterprise that can make a difference."

technology (Exhibit 1). It started at an Aug. 5 strategy meeting, when he asked his team to draw up a project as epochal as the mainframe computer—IBM's big bet from 40 years ago. Through the day, the team cobbled together a vision of systems that would alter the very nature of how technology is delivered. IBM would supply computing power as if it were water or electricity. But how to tackle a project this vast? No one knew where to begin. A frustrated Palmisano abruptly cut short the meeting and gave the team 90 days to assemble and launch the megaproject. Three months later, the CEO unveiled "e-business on demand." Standing in New York's American Museum of Natural History, not far from the hulking dinosaurs whose fate IBM narrowly skirted, Palmisano vowed to lead a new world of computing. "We have an opportunity to set the agenda in our industry," he says.

After one year on the job, Palmisano is putting his imprint on the company—and with a vengeance. Sure, IBM roared back to strength in the late '90s. But Palmisano is out to remake the company and hoist it back to greatness. Through much of the 20th century, under the leadership of Thomas J. Watson and his son, Thomas Jr., IBM not only ruled computing and defined the American multinational, it was the gold standard for corporations. From the days of tabulating machines all the way to the Space Age, when its mainframes helped chart the path to the moon, IBM was a paragon of power, prestige, and farsightedness. It was tops in technology, but also a leader in bringing women and minorities into a well-paid workforce and in creating a corporate culture that inspired lifelong loyalty. "We stood for something back then," Palmisano says.

To return IBM to greatness, the 51-year-old Palmisano is turning the company inside out. He's the first true-blue IBMer to take the reins since the company's fall from grace more than a decade ago. And while the new CEO never criticizes his predecessor, who rescued IBM and pushed many key technologies, Palmisano is quietly emerging as the antithesis of Gerstner. Where Gerstner raked in money, Palmisano makes a point of splitting the booty with his team. While Gerstner ruled IBM regally, Palmisano is egalitarian. The revolution he is leading spells the end of the imperial CEO at IBM. "Creativity in any large organization does not come from one individual, the celebrity CEO," Palmisano says. "That stuff's B.S. Creativity in an organization starts where the action is—either in the laboratory, or in R&D sites, at a customer place, in manufacturing."

If that sounds like the IBM of old, that's exactly what Palmisano is hoping for. The flattening of the organization, the lowering of CEO pay, the emphasis on teams—it's all part of his broad campaign to return to IBM's roots. Palmisano believes that core values remain in what he calls the company's DNA, waiting to be awakened. And he thinks that this message, which might have elicited chortles during the tech boom, resonates in the wake of the market crash and corporate scandals. More important, he believes that only by returning to what made IBM great can the company rise again to assume its place of leadership in America and the world.

At the heart of Palmisano's plan is e-business on demand (Exhibit 2). The project, which is already gobbling up a third of IBM's $5 billion research and development budget, puts Big Blue in the vanguard of a massive computing shift. The company starts by helping customers standardize all of their computing needs. Then, in the course of the next 10 years, it will handle growing amounts of this work on its own massive computer grids. And this won't be just techie grunt work. The eventual goal is to imbue these systems with deep industrial expertise so that IBM is not only crunching numbers and dispatching e-mails but also delivering technology that helps companies solve thorny technical problems—from testing drugs to simulating car crashes. It's a soaring vision. But Palmisano has believers. "Sam is aiming to go where the market's going, not to where it's been," says Cisco Systems Inc. CEO John Chambers.

The obstacles he faces are immense. Start with the technology. The vision of on-demand computing is downright audacious. It proposes joining all of the thousands of computers and applications in enormous enterprises, and putting them to work seamlessly and in unison—not only in-house, but with partners and customers. Assembling the pieces will require every bit of IBM's vaunted smarts, and a scrap of luck as well. IBM officials say only 10% of the technology needed for this system is ready. And many of the necessary pieces, including futuristic software programs that will heal themselves, are at the basic test stage in IBM's labs. "There are huge, huge technical challenges," says A. Richard Newton, dean of the College of Engineering at the University of California at Berkeley.

Palmisano faces an equally imposing job at home. To make good on his vision, he must turn IBM itself into

EXHIBIT 2
The Evolution of E-Business on Demand

IBM is pushing a new strategy called e-business on demand that could cut tech users costs by 50%. But getting there could take a decade of rolling out new technologies and new ways of doing business.

STAGE 1	**Simplify** Typically, companies have different brands of gear, creating a Tower of Babel. The first step is to build a unified network. That means getting the hundreds of servers down to a dozen or so, and using open standards so all the pieces of gear speak to one another.
STAGE 2	**Efficiency** Too often, servers run idle and software sits on shelves. This phase ekes more out of the equipment through virtualization, a process by which many machines appear to be one. If one server is busy, software automatically farms out work to the others.
STAGE 3	**Grids** The technology has to be supersize. Corporations will be able to link all their networks and data centers to create a gigantic computing grid so that businesses can access information and computing power whenever they need to.
STAGE 4	**Utility** If a company runs out of capacity, it can buy computing power from a supplier on an as-needed basis instead of building a new data center. The company just flips a switch, and presto! it taps into a supplier's data center and gets billed for what it uses.
STAGE 5	**Expertise** This is the Big Kahuna: It's when customers get a new generation of Web services that speed up tasks. Take a drug company. Software that captures the myriad knowledge of researchers could be available to the entire research staff to hasten drug discovery.

a user of on-demand computing and become a prototype for its customers. This entails recharting the path of every bit of information flowing inside the company. It means not just shifting the computer systems, but redefining nearly everyone's job. And if IBM meets resistance to these changes, it could stumble in producing the new technology. This could undermine IBM's $800 million marketing campaign for e-business on demand—and scare away customers in droves. Such a failure could punish IBM financially, forcing a retreat toward fiercely competitive markets such as servers and chips. "The two most important parts of their business—services and software—are tied to the [on-demand] strategy," says Gartner analyst Tom Bittman. "They need to succeed."

Is history on Palmisano's side? Try to think of a great technology company that took a life-threatening fall and then scratched and clawed all the way back to the very top. Westinghouse? Digital Equipment? Xerox? Some have survived. But if Palmisano leads IBM back to the summit, Big Blue will be the first full-fledged round-tripper.

To get there, he must win a brutal battle raging among the titans of tech. From Hewlett-Packard Co. to Microsoft Corp., the industry's bruisers are all pushing research into next-generation computing systems that will rival IBM's. Big Blue appears to be better positioned than its foes, thanks to a wider range of offerings. But, warns Irving Wladawsky-Berger, IBM's general manager for e-business on demand: "In 1996, we had the benefit of being considered irrelevant. [Microsoft's William H.] Gates and [Steven A.] Ballmer felt pity on us. Now they are all watching us. If we don't move fast, they will pass us" (Exhibit 3).

The new initiative provides Palmisano with a prodigious tool to remake the company. Gerstner's reforms began the process, directing IBM toward software and services. But Palmisano's e-business on demand goes much further. It extends into nearly every nook of Big Blue, from its sales force and its army of systems consultants to the big brains cooking up the software code in the research and development labs. Management expert Jim Collins, author of *Good to Great*, says Palmisano's willingness to think and act boldly bodes well, and recalls earlier outsize bets in IBM's history, such as the development of the tabulating machine. "It reminds me of what Tom Watson Sr. did during the Depression," he says.

Palmisano already is banking on winning his share of the new business. Last year IBM saw revenue slip 2%, to $81.2 billion, with earnings tumbling 54% to $3.6 billion. But this year Palmisano is counting on e-business on demand to fuel the hottest sales growth at Big Blue since 1995. Analysts predict 9% revenue growth this year. And Palmisano expects 40%—nearly $3 billion—to come from new offerings in e-business on demand. These include servers running the free Linux operating system and grid software that pools the power of scores of networked computers into a virtual supercomputer.

By pursuing this plan, Palmisano is fleeing the brutish world of hardware and seeking refuge in profitable software and services businesses. He bulked up for this drive last year by spending $3.5 billion for PricewaterhouseCoopers Consulting and another $2.1 billion for Rational Software Corp., a maker of software tools to write programs. And why not? According to IBM's internal research, 60% of the profits in the $1 trillion high-tech industry will come from software and services by 2005. That's up from 45% in 2002. "We're just going where the profit is," Palmisano says.

And he's leading Big Blue in a way it has never been led before. One year before Palmisano disbanded the Executive Management Committee, he had put in place his management teams for the future. He created three of them: strategy, operations, and technology. Instead of picking only high-level executives for each team, Palmisano selected managers and engineers most familiar with the issues. "Heads are spinning," says J. Bruce Harreld, senior vice-president for strategy. "He's reaching six levels down and asking questions."

Talk to Palmisano for an hour and he'll mention teamwork 20 times. His entire on-demand strategy hinges upon it. Why? For IBM to come up with a broad array of on-demand technologies in a hurry, the whole company has to work smoothly from one far-flung cubicle to another. That means bringing researchers in touch not only with product developers, but with consultants and even customers. Only by reaching across these old boundaries will IBM find out what customers are clamoring for—and produce it fast.

To head up this process, Palmisano has chosen Wladawsky-Berger, the renowned Cuban-born computer scientist who was IBM's e-biz guru in the 1990s. Today, Wladawsky-Berger's mission is to drive the strategy across the company. In the last two months, he has assembled 28 people working in every division of IBM into what he calls a "virtual team." These are Wladawsky-Berger's on-demand agents. They nose around their areas of expertise, looking for on-demand possibilities. New servers coming out later this year, for example, will be equipped to dispatch excess work to other machines on the network.

Still, it's no easy job coaxing separate divisions to dance in unison. Clashes are common, for example, when IBM's 160,000 Global Service workers descend into the research labs. Last year, researchers were hard at work on a program for supply chains in the electronics industry. Consultants ordered up a quick version of the same program for a carmaker. The two sides battled briefly until the researchers adapted a program for cars, and then went back to work on electronics. The consultants' timeframe, says William Grey, manager of IBM's Finance Research, "is milliseconds. Ours is five years. There's a cultural gap that needs to be bridged."

The key is getting IBM itself to function as an e-business-on-demand enterprise. To drive this message through the company, Palmisano in January grabbed a star manager, Linda Sanford, and put her in charge of internal e-business on demand. Sanford, a senior vice-president, had revived IBM's storage business and was viewed as a bona fide up-and-comer at Big Blue. "I take a senior vice-president who has a great job, and say, 'O.K., you're going to make IBM on demand,'" Palmisano says. "Then, 320,000 people say, 'Holy . . . , this guy's serious."

Sanford faces an imposing job. First, she has to supervise the overhaul of IBM's massive supply chain. That means piling $44 billion of purchases into a single system. It's a slog. It means pushing IBM's engineers to switch to company-approved suppliers. Then a procurement rep is assigned to each development team, to make sure that they all use industry standard parts. It's intrusive. But like the rest of the on-demand program, it focuses the company onto a single effort. And it should pay dividends. Palmisano expects the entire initiative to yield 5% productivity gains, worth $2 billion to $3 billion a year, for the next five to 10 years.

Sanford also is working to create an online inventory of IBM's knowledge. She's turning the company's intranet into a giant collaboration portal. One feature is an "expertise locator" that helps an employee find, say, a software engineer with expertise in building databases in Linux. But at a meeting of the operations team at Armonk, N.Y. on a cold mid-February morning, a frustrated Sanford told key executives, including Palmisano, that the concept was a hard sell.

Palmisano, his face cupped in his hands, looked concerned. "There's a huge level of expectation on this portal," he said. "I just hope we can deliver." Sanford responded with a blunt message: If Palmisano wants the portal to succeed, he and his teams must lead by example, offering their own areas of expertise within a 30-day deadline. "We have to lead the way," she said.

For Palmisano, this means rallying the biggest brains and deepest thinkers in the company to the cause. In January he flew to Harvard University in Cambridge for a meeting with IBM's top computer scientists. His message was simple and straightforward: The dream of on-demand computing hinged upon their ability to produce technology breakthroughs.

While scientists are wrestling with future iterations of on-demand computing, IBM's sales team is rolling out the first products. New IBM servers include a feature called "hypervisors." These allow technicians to monitor as many as 100 servers at a time, shifting work from one machine to another. A new program from IBM's Tivoli group performs similar work, patrolling the network, constantly on the lookout for servers running short of memory. When it finds one, it automatically shifts the work to other computers. This is a key aspect of on-demand computing, and a potential money saver. Once systems can distribute work, companies will be able to run their servers at a high level, much closer to capacity. This reduces costs. And if work piles up, customers will ship excess tasks to IBM.

Many of them, IBM hopes, will eventually exit the computing business altogether and ship all their digital work to IBM. American Express likes the idea. A year ago, before Palmisano even came up with the new vision, AmEx signed a seven-year, $4 billion services contract with Big Blue. At first blush it looks like a standard outsourcing deal. The company has shifted its computers and 2,000 tech employees to IBM. But what makes it different is the economics. AmEx pays only for technology it uses every month. The advantages? AmEx is looking to save hundreds of millions of dollars over the course of the contract. And with IBM running the system, says Glen Salow, chief information officer at American Express, "they can upgrade technology five times faster."

Palmisano's vision for e-business on demand stretches beyond the technical challenges to the realm of human knowledge. In the services division, IBM has experts on industries ranging from banking to metals to autos. He wants to gather their knowhow—"deep process insights," he calls it—into the systems. Eventually, he sees IBM's on-demand offerings reinventing the company's corporate customers and shaking up entire industries.

IBM is developing 17 different industrial road maps for on demand. Pharmaceuticals is one. There, a computer grid will handle simulation and modeling to reduce the number of clinical trials needed. That, IBM says, could lead to improving the success rates of drugs, now from 5% to 10%, to 50% or better. IBM also believes it can help cut the time it takes to identify and launch a new drug to three to five years, down from 10 to 12, slicing the pre-launch cost of drug development to less than $200 million, from $800 million.

It's a splendid vision—and far too rich with opportunity for IBM alone. Microsoft has more cash than any tech company—$43 billion—and its .net Windows initiative is an effort to rule the next generation of computing every bit as ambitious as Palmisano's. But Microsoft trails Big Blue in the upper end of the corporate computing world. Sun Microsystems, an early advocate of on demand computing, is pushing its own effort to develop software, called N1, that will more efficiently manage Sun gear. Sun claims N1 will offer superior performance—at one-tenth the cost—because the software is designed only for Sun products. "Diversity is great in your workforce," says Sun Executive Vice President Jonathan Schwartz. "It sucks in your data center." IBM software head Steven A. Mills shoots back: "Nothing they have in N1 is unique."

EXHIBIT 3 'We Have Reinvented Ourselves Many Times'

Last year, when Sam Palmisano took the top job at IBM Corp., pundits figured he would settle in as the caretaker of former CEO Louis V. Gerstner Jr.'s strategy. Not Palmisano. He's blazing his own trail. The new CEO is streamlining management, emphasizing teamwork, and re-jiggering compensation—starting with his own. At IBM's snow-covered headquarters in Armonk, N.Y., and in an e-mail exchange, Palmisano talked with BusinessWeek *Computer Editor Spencer E. Ante about his mission to make IBM great again.*

What inspired you to try and make IBM a great company again?

IBM is one of the few companies in the world where people refer to themselves as IBMers. There's an attractiveness about being part of an institution that can do great things beyond generating financial results and paying a lot of money.

I kept thinking about an approach that would energize all the good of the past and throw out all the bad: hierarchy and bureaucracy. Get rid of all that trash. People stay at IBM for pride. It's about appealing to the pride of the people of IBM to go drive to the next level.

How are you going to measure IBM's greatness?

I think about it in four or five dimensions. If you're leading the industry agenda, you should be gaining share in your core segments.

In the financials, there should be real consistency in earnings. It's about cash flows and balance sheets. It's the flexibility to fund the IBM pension fund for $4 billion. Why? Because it's the right thing to do, and you can afford to do it. It's being an employer of choice. People want to be here and want to make a big difference. So it's attrition rates. And the last dimension is being viewed as a valuable citizen. Getting people involved and using their skills to help local communities, whether that's Austin, Texas or Stuttgart.

Are you remaking IBM's core values?

No. Think about the early days of IBM. Bold moves. Diversity. I think 28 years before it was legislated, we paid equal pay for women. There was a lot that was great in the old IBM. These Watsons did not play to lose. In 1933, Thomas J. Watson Sr. gave a speech at the World's Fair, "World Peace through World Trade." We stood for something, right?

The DNA of the IBM company is what it always stood for. But get rid of the bad in the DNA, which was rigid behavior, starched white shirts, straw hats, singing company songs. I lived it. I sang the songs. That caused us to become insular, focused on ourselves. Beating up your colleagues was more important than winning in the marketplace. Lou [Gerstner] did a lot to knock all that down.

Why did you ask the board to cut your 2003 bonus?

If you say you're about a team, you have to be a team. You have to walk the talk, right? I can't have a big gap between me and my team.

We're talking about a pool of money that the board historically allocated to the chief executive. I recommended the board take the money and give it to the top officers of IBM. [There are] more than 20. The board will determine the exact size of this pool [and will determine bonuses] based on teamwork.

How do you balance your new job and family time?

It's incredibly tough to find the right balance. The workload just never lets up. On weekends I get up early and work until the kids get up. Then I go do whatever the family wants to do. People at IBM are used to getting e-mails from me early in the morning and late at night. On weekends, Sunday afternoons have pretty much become work times for me. It comes down to my family and IBM. I pretty much say no to everything else. I know it makes some people mad when I can't attend their events, but at least I'm consistent on that point.

A stronger contender is Hewlett-Packard, thanks to its array of hardware, software, and services. Analysts say HP leads IBM in a few important niches. HP, for example, has software called Utility Data Center, that shifts work across all of a company's computers, networks, and storage devices.

For now, IBM's wide-angle vision and broader range of technology gives it the overall lead. But to keep ahead, Palmisano maintains a routine of near-constant work. Even while on a Vermont ski vacation in early March, Palmisano spent a snowy Sunday afternoon reading briefing papers while his family hit the slopes. Rest assured, Palmisano won't be getting his weekends back anytime soon. He is remaking IBM, and that's a job that could last a full decade. If he pulls it off, though, a giant of technology will be reborn.

By Spencer E. Ante in Armonk, N.Y.

Source: "The New Blue", BusinessWeek, March 17, 2003, 80–88.

Case 6-14

L'Oréal Nederland B.V.

Yolanda van der Zande, director of the Netherlands L'Oréal subsidiary, faced two tough decisions and was discussing them with Mike Rourke, her market manager for cosmetics and toiletries. "We have to decide whether to introduce the Synergie skin care line and Belle Couleur permanent hair colorants," she told him. Synergie had recently been introduced successfully in France, the home country for L'Oréal. Belle Couleur had been marketed successfully in France for two decades. Mr. Rourke responded:

> Yes, and if we decide to go ahead with an introduction, we'll also need to develop marketing programs for the product lines. Fortunately, we only need to think about marketing, since the products will still be manufactured in France.

Ms. van der Zande replied:

> Right, but remember that the marketing decisions on these lines are critical. Both of these lines are part of the Garnier family brand name. Currently Ambre Solaire (a sun screen) is the only product we distribute with the Garnier name in the Netherlands. But headquarters would like us to introduce more Garnier product lines into our market over the next few years, and it's critical that our first product launches in this line be successful.

This case was prepared by Frederick W. Langrehr, Valparaiso University; Lee Dahringer, Butler University; and Anne Stöcker. This case was written with the cooperation of management solely for the purpose of stimulating student discussion. All events and individuals are real, but names have been disguised. We appreciate the help of J. B. Wilkinson and V. B. Langrehr on earlier drafts of this case.

Mr. Rourke interjected, "But we already sell other brands of L'Oréal products in our market. If we introduce Garnier, what will happen to them?" After some more discussion, Ms. van der Zande suggested:

> Why don't you review what we know about the Dutch market. We've already done extensive marketing research on consumer reactions to Synergie and Belle Couleur. Why don't you look at it and get back to me with your recommendations in two weeks.

Background

In 1992 the L'Oréal Group was the largest cosmetics manufacturer in the world. Headquartered in Paris, it had subsidiaries in over 100 countries. In 1992, its sales were $6.8 billion (a 12 percent increase over 1991) and net profits were $417 million (a 14 percent increase). France contributed 24 percent of total worldwide sales, Europe (both western and eastern countries, excluding France) provided 42 percent, and the United States and Canada together accounted for 20 percent; the rest of the world accounted for the remaining 14 percent. L'Oréal's European subsidiaries were in one of two groups: (1) major countries (England, France, Germany, and Italy) or (2) minor countries (the Netherlands and nine others).

The company believed that innovation was its critical success factor. It thus invested heavily in research and development and recovered its investment through global introductions of its new products. All research was centered in France. As finished products were developed, they were offered to subsidiaries around the world. Because brand life cycles for cosmetics could be very short, L'Oréal tried to introduce one or two new products per year in each of its worldwide markets. International subsidiaries could make go/no go decisions on products, but they generally did not have direct input into the R&D process. In established markets such as the Netherlands, any new product line introduction had to be financed by the current operations in that country.

L'Oréal marketed products under its own name as well as under a number of other individual and family brand names. For example, it marketed Anaïs Anaïs perfume, the high-end Lancôme line of cosmetics, and L'Oréal brand hair care products. In the 1970s it acquired Laboratoires Garnier, and this group was one of L'Oréal's largest divisions. In France, with a population of about 60 million people, Garnier was a completely separate division, and its sales force competed against the L'Oréal division. In the Netherlands, however, the market was much smaller (about 15 million people), and Garnier and L'Oréal products would be marketed by the same sales force.

Dutch consumers had little, if any, awareness or knowledge of Garnier and had not formed a brand image. The Garnier sunscreen was a new product, and few Dutch women knew about the brand. It was therefore very important that any new Garnier products launched in the Netherlands have a strong concept and high market potential. To accomplish this, the products needed to offer unique, desired, and identifiable differential advantages to Dutch consumers. Products without such an edge were at a competitive disadvantage and would be likely not only to fail but to create a negative association with the Garnier name, causing potential problems for future Garnier product introductions.

The Dutch Market

In the late 1980s, 40 percent of the Dutch population (about the same percentage as in France) was under 25 years old. Consumers in this age group were the heaviest users of cosmetics and toiletries. But as in the rest of Europe, the Dutch population was aging and the fastest-growing population segments were the 25-or-older groups.

Other demographic trends included the increasing number of Dutch women working outside the home. The labor force participation rate of women in the Netherlands was 29 percent. That was much lower than the 50 percent or above in the United Kingdom or the United States, but the number of women working outside the home was increasing faster in the Netherlands than it was in those countries. Dutch women were also delaying childbirth. As a result of these trends, women in the Netherlands were exhibiting greater self-confidence and independence; women had more disposable income, and more of them were using it to buy cosmetics for use on a daily basis.

Despite their rising incomes, Dutch women still shopped for value, especially in cosmetics and toiletries. In the European Union (EU), the Netherlands ranked fourth in per capita income, but it was only sixth in per capita spending on cosmetics and toiletries. Thus, Dutch per capita spending on personal care products was only 60 percent of the amount spent per capita in France or Germany. As a result of both a small population (15 million Dutch to 350 million EU residents) and lower per capita consumption, the Dutch market accounted for only 4 percent of total EU sales of cosmetics and toiletries.

Synergie

Synergie was a line of facial skin care products that consisted of moisturizing cream, antiaging day cream, antiwrinkle cream, cleansing milk, mask, and cleansing gel. It was made with natural ingredients, and its advertising slogan in France was "The alliance of science and nature to prolong the youth of your skin."

Skin Care Market

The skin care market was the second largest sector of the Dutch cosmetics and toiletries market. For the past five quarters unit volume had been growing at an annual rate of 12 percent, and dollar sales at a rate of 16 percent. This category consisted of hand creams, body lotions, all-purpose creams, and facial products. Products in this category were classified by price and product type. Skin care products produced by institutes such as Shisedo and Estée Lauder were targeted at the high end of the market. These lines were expensive and were sold through personal service perfumeries that specialized in custom sales of cosmetics and toiletries. At the other end of the price scale were mass-market products such as Ponds, which were sold in drugstores and supermarkets. In the last couple of years a number of companies, including L'Oréal, had begun to offer products in the midprice range. For example its Plénitude line was promoted as a high-quality, higher-priced—but still mass-market—product.

Skin care products also could be divided into care and cleansing products. Care products consisted of day and night creams; cleansing products were milks and tonics. The current trend in the industry was to stretch the lines by adding specific products targeted at skin types, such as sensitive, greasy, or dry. An especially fast-growing

EXHIBIT 1 **Usage of Skin Care Products by Dutch Women**

Product	Percentage of Women Using
Day cream	46%
Cleansers	40
Mask	30
Tonic	26
Antiaging cream	3

EXHIBIT 2 **Sales Breakdown for Skin Care Products in Supermarkets and Drugstores**

Type of Store	Unit Sales (%)	Dollar Sales (%)
Supermarkets	18%	11%
Drugstores	82	89
	100	100

EXHIBIT 3 **Sales Breakdown for Skin Care Products by Type of Drugstore**

Type of Drugstore	Unit Sales (%)	Dollar Sales (%)
Chains	57%	37%
Large independent	31	39
Small independent	12	24
	100	100

category consisted of antiaging and antiwrinkling creams. Complementing this trend was the emphasis on scientific development and natural ingredients.

Almost 50 percent of the 5 million Dutch women between the ages of 15 and 65 used traditional skin care products. The newer specialized products had a much lower penetration, as shown in Exhibit 1.

The sales breakdown by type of retailer for the middle- and lower-priced brands is shown in Exhibits 2 and 3.

Competition

There were numerous competitors. Some product lines, such as Oil of Olaz (Oil of Olay in the United States) by Procter & Gamble and Plénitude by L'Oréal, were offered by large multinational companies; other brands, for example, Dr. vd Hoog and Rocher, were offered by regional companies. Some companies offered a complete line, while others, such as Oil of Olaz, offered one or two products. Exhibit 4 lists a few of the available lines along with the price ranges and positioning statements.

The Dutch market was especially competitive for new brands such as Oil of Olaz and Plénitude. The rule of thumb in the industry was that share of voice for a brand (the percentage of total industry advertising spent by the company) should be about the same as its market share. Thus, a company with a 10 percent market share should have had advertising expenditures around 10 percent of total industry advertising expenditures. But there were deviations from this rule. Ponds, an established and well-known company with loyal customers, had about 9 percent share of the market (units) but accounted for only about 2.5 percent of total industry ad expenditures. Alternatively, new brands such as Oil of Olaz (10 percent market share, 26 percent share of voice) and Plénitude (5 percent market share, 13 percent share of voice) spent much more. The higher ad spending for these brands was necessary to develop brand awareness and, ideally, brand preference.

Any innovative products or new product variations in a line could be quickly copied. Retailers could develop and introduce their own private labels in four months; manufacturers could develop a competing product and advertising campaign in six months. Manufacturers looked for new product ideas in other countries and then transferred the product concept or positioning strategy across national borders. They also monitored competitors' test markets. Since a test market typically lasted nine months, a competitor could introduce a product before a test market was completed.

Consumer Behavior

Consumers tended to be loyal to their current brands. This loyalty resulted from the possible allergic reaction to a new product. Also, facial care products were heavily advertised and sold on the basis of brand image. Thus, users linked self-concept with a brand image, and this increased the resistance to switching. While all consumers had some loyalty, the strength of this attachment to a brand increased with the age of the user. Finally, establishing a new brand was especially difficult since Dutch women typically purchased facial creams only once or twice a year. Dutch women were showing an increasing interest in products with "natural" ingredients, but they were not as familiar as the French were with technical product descriptions and terms.

Market Research Information

Earlier, Mike Rourke had directed his internal research department to conduct some concept and use tests for the Synergie products. The researchers had sampled 200 women between the ages of 18 and 55 who used skin

EXHIBIT 4 Competitive Product Lines of Cosmetics

	Price Range (Guilders)*	Positioning
Lower End		
Nivea Visage†	9.50–11.50	Mild, modest price, complete line
Ponds	5.95–12.95	Antiwrinkle
Middle		
Dr. vd Hoog	10–11.95	Sober, nonglamorous, no illusions, but real help, natural, efficient, relatively inexpensive
Oil of Olaz (Procter & Gamble)	12 (day cream only)	Moisturizing, antiaging
Plénitude (L'Oréal)	10.95–19.95	Delay the signs of aging
Synergie	11.95–21.95	The alliance of science and nature to prolong the youth of your skin
Upper End		
Yves Rocher	10–26.95	Different products for different skins, natural ingredients
Ellen Betrix (Estée Lauder)	12.95–43.50	Institute line with reasonable prices, luxury products at nonluxury prices

*One dollar = 1.8 guilders; one British pound = 2.8 guilders; 1 deutschmark = 1.1 guilders.
†Although Nivea Visage had a similar price range to Dr. vd Hoog, consumers perceived Nivea as a lower-end product.

EXHIBIT 5 Buying Intentions for Synergie Products

	All Participants	Plénitude Users	Dr. vd Hoog Users	Other Brand Users
Price Not Known				
Antiaging daycream				
After trial	5.37*	5.63	5.00	5.42
After use	5.26	5.55	5.08	5.17
Moisturizing cream				
After trial	5.34	5.60	5.38	5.11
After use	5.51	5.74	5.56	5.22
Price Known				
Antiaging daycream				
After trial	3.75	4.13	3.82	3.44
After use	3.60	3.76	3.54	3.54
Certainly buy†	24%	21%	23%	27%
Moisturizing cream				
After trial	4.08	4.36	4.17	3.77
After use	4.06	4.26	4.13	3.78
Certainly buy	39%	52%	38%	30%

*Seven-point scale with 7 being most likely to buy.
†Response to a separate question asking about certainty of buying with "certainly buy" as the highest choice.

care products three or more times per week. They sampled 55 Plénitude users, 65 Dr. vd Hoog users, and 80 users of other brands.

The participants reacted positively to Synergie concept boards containing the positioning statement and the terminology associated with the total product line. On a seven-point scale with 7 being the most positive, the mean score for the Synergie line for all the women in the sample was 4.94. The evaluations of the women who used the competing brands, Plénitude and Dr. vd Hoog, were similar at 4.97 and 4.88, respectively.

The researchers then conducted an in-depth analysis of two major products in the line: antiaging day cream and moisturizing cream. Participants reported their buying intentions after they tried the Synergie product once and again after they used it for a week. Some participants were told the price, and others did not know the price. The results of this analysis are shown in Exhibit 5.

Belle Couleur

Belle Couleur was a line of permanent hair coloring products. It had been sold in France for about two decades and was the market leader. In France the line had 22 shades that were mostly natural shades and a few strong red or very bright light shades. It was positioned as reliably providing natural colors with the advertising line "natural colors, covers all gray."

Hair Coloring Market

There were two types of hair coloring: semipermanent and permanent. Semipermanent colors washed out after five or six shampooings. Permanent colors disappeared only as the hair grew out from the roots. Nearly three-quarters (73 percent) of Dutch women who colored their hair used a permanent colorant. Over the past four years, however, the trend had been toward semipermanent colorants, with an increase from 12 percent to 27 percent of the market. Growth in unit volume during those years for both types of colorant had been about 15 percent per annum. The majority of unit sales in the category were in chain drugstores (57 percent), with 40 percent equally split between large and small independent drugstores. Food retailers accounted for the remaining 3 percent.

Competition

In the Netherlands 4 of 10 total brands accounted for 80 percent of the sales of permanent hair colorants, compared to 2 brands in France. Exhibit 6 gives the market share of the leading permanent color brands in the period 1987–1989. Interestingly, none of them had a clear advertising positioning statement describing customer benefits. By default, then, Belle Couleur could be positioned as "covering gray with natural colors."

Hair salons were indirect competitors in the hair coloring market. The percentage of women who had a hairstylist color their hair was not known, nor were the trends in the usage of this method known. It was projected that as more women worked outside the home, home coloring probably would increase because it was more convenient.

L'Oréal's current market entry (Recital) was the leading seller, although its share was declining. Guhl's and Andrelon's increases in shares between 1986 and 1989 reflected the general trend toward using warmer shades, and these two brands were perceived as giving quality red tones. In the late 1980s Guhl had changed its distribution strategy and started selling the brand through drug chains. In 1987 less than 1 percent of sales were through drug outlets; in the first quarter of 1990 drug-outlet sales had reached nearly 12 percent. Guhl also had become more aggressive in its marketing through large independents, with its share in those outlets climbing from 16 to 24 percent over the same period. Both the increasing shares of the smaller brands and the decreasing shares of the leaders sparked a 60 percent increase in advertising in 1989 for all brands of hair coloring.

Consumer Behavior

Consumers perceived permanent hair color as a technical product and believed its use was very risky. As a result, users had strong brand loyalty and avoided impulse purchasing. When considering a new brand, both first-time users and current users carefully read package information and asked store personnel for advice.

Traditionally, hair colorants had been used primarily to cover gray hair. Recently, however, coloring hair had become more of a fashion statement. This partially accounted for the increased popularity of semipermanent hair coloring. In one study the most frequently cited reason (33 percent) for coloring hair was to achieve warm/red tones; another 17 percent reported wanting to lighten their hair color, and covering gray was cited by 29 percent. It was likely that the trend toward using colorants more for fashion and less for covering gray reflected the increase in hair coloring by consumers less than 35 years old. In 1989, 46 percent of Dutch women

EXHIBIT 6 **Major Brands of Hair Colorant**

Market Shares of	1987	1988	1989
Upper end (14.95 guilders)			
Recital (L'Oréal brand)	35%	34%	33%
Guhl	9	12	14
Belle Couleur (12.95 guilders)	—	—	—
Lower-priced (9.95 guilders)			
Andrelon	12	14	17
Poly Couleur	24	23	21
Others	20	17	15
Total	100	100	100

EXHIBIT 7 **Hair Coloring by Age (%)**

	1986	1989
Less than 25 years	35%	50%
25–34	24	54
35–49	32	55
50–64	24	33
65 and over	15	19

EXHIBIT 8
Buying Intentions

	Price-Unaware	Price-Aware	After Use
Certainly buy (5)	18%	26%	29%
Probably buy (4)	60	57	30
Don't know (3)	12	5	9
Probably not (2)	7	7	11
Certainly not (1)	3	6	21
Total	100%	100%	100%
Mean score	3.85	3.92	3.35

(up from 27 percent in 1986) colored their hair with either semipermanent or permanent hair colorants. Exhibit 7 contains a breakdown of usage by age of user.

Hair coloring was purchased almost exclusively in drugstores; only 3 percent of sales were through supermarkets. The percentage of sales for drug outlets was chains, 58 percent; large independents, 22 percent; and small independents, 20 percent.

Market Research

As with Synergie, Mr. Rourke had the L'Oréal market researchers contact consumers about their reactions to Belle Couleur. Four hundred twelve Dutch women between the ages of 25 and 64 who had used hair colorant in the last four months were part of a concept test, and 265 of those women participated in a use test. A little over 25 percent of the participants colored their hair every six weeks or more often, while another 47 percent did it every two to three months. (The average French user colored her hair every three weeks.) Nearly 60 percent used hair color to cover gray, while the remainder did it for other reasons.

After being introduced to the concept and being shown some sample ads, participants were asked their buying intentions. The question was asked three times—before and after the price was given and after Belle Couleur was used. The results are shown in Exhibit 8.

In most product concept tests (as with the Synergie line) buying intentions declined once the price was revealed. For Belle Couleur, buying intentions increased after the price was given but decreased after actual use. As the exhibit shows, the percentage of participants who would probably or certainly not buy the product after using it increased from 13 to 32 percent. In Exhibit 9 only participants who gave negative after-use evaluations of Belle Couleur are included, and they are grouped according to the brands they were using at the time.

To try to determine why some users didn't like the product, the dissatisfied women were asked to state why they disliked Belle Couleur. The results are shown in Exhibit 10.

Many of the women thought that their hair was too dark after using Belle Couleur and said it "didn't cover gray." Those who thought Belle Couleur was different from expected were primarily using the blond and chestnut brown shades of colorant. This was expected, since in France Belle Couleur was formulated to give a classical, conservative dark blond color without extra reflections or lightening effects and the product had not been modified for the Dutch test. The competing Dutch-manufactured hair colorant competitors, by contrast, were formulated to give stronger lightening effects. Thus, some of the negative evaluations of Belle Couleur were due to the fact that Dutch women tended toward naturally lighter hair colors, and the French toward darker shades.

Role of Distributors

Distributors' acceptance of the two product lines was critical for L'Oréal's successful launch of both Synergie and Belle Couleur. At one time, manufacturers had more control in the channel of distribution than did retailers. Retailers, however, had been gaining power as a result of the increasing size of retailers, the development of chains with their central buying offices, and the proliferation of new brands with little differentiation from brands currently on the market. Retailers had also increasingly been offering their own private-label products, since they earned a higher-percentage profit margin on their own brands.

Following are the criteria, listed in order of importance (3 being "most important"), that retailers used to evaluate new products:

1. Evidence of consumer acceptance 2.5
2. Manufacturer advertising and promotion 2.2
3. Introductory monetary allowances 2.0
4. Rationale for product development 1.9
5. Merchandising recommendations 1.8

L'Oréal's goal for developing new products was to introduce only products that had a differential advantage

EXHIBIT 9 Purchase Intentions and Evaluation of Belle Couleur by Brand Currently Used

		Brand Currently Used			
	Total Sample	Andrelon	Poly Couleur	Guhl	Recital (L'Oréal)
After-Use Purchase Intentions of Belle Couleur					
Probably not (2)	11%	12%	12%	14%	5%
Certainly not (1)	21	24	29	20	5
	32%	36%	41%	34%	10%
Overall mean score	3.35	3.4	3.1	3.4	3.95
Evaluation of Final Color of Belle Couleur					
Very good (1)	25%	24%	31%	22%	35%
Good (2)	43	40	31	44	49
Neither good or bad (3)	10	10	14	6	8
Bad (4)	12	14	5	18	8
Very bad (5)	9	12	19	10	. . .
Mean	2.37	2.5	2.5	2.5	1.89
Comparison to Expectations					
Much better (1)	11%	12%	14%	14%	14%
Better (2)	26	12	21	24	38
The same (3)	29	38	26	28	32
Worse (4)	19	24	19	18	11
Much worse (5)	15	14	19	16	5
Mean	3.0	3.17	3.07	2.98	2.57
Compared with Own Brand					
Much better (1)		17%	17%	24%	14%
Better (2)		21	19	24	32
The same (3)		21	31	14	30
Worse (4)		21	12	16	16
Much worse (5)		19	21	22	8
Mean		3.05	3.02	2.88	2.73

Note: Data for total sample not available.

EXHIBIT 10 Reasons for Negative Evaluations of Belle Couleur by Brand Currently Used

		Brand Currently Used			
	Total Sample	Andrelon	Poly Couleur	Guhl	Recital (L'Oréal)
Hair got dark/darker instead of lighter	13%	14%	17%	14%	5%
Irritates skin	8	10	7	2	11
Ammonia smell	5	7	—	2	—
Didn't cover gray	5	12	2	4	3
Color not beautiful	5	7	5	6	3
Color different from expected	5	5	10	4	3

Note: Some of the cell sizes are very small, and caution should be used when comparing entries of less than 10 percent.

with evidence of consumer acceptance. It did not want to gain distribution with excessive reliance on trade deals or higher than normal retail gross margins. L'Oréal also wanted to have its Garnier product lines extensively distributed in as many different types of retailers and outlets as possible. This approach to new product introduction had been effective for L'Oréal, and it currently had a positive image with Dutch retailers. L'Oréal was perceived as offering high-quality, innovative products supported with good in-store merchandising.

For L'Oréal's current products, 35 percent of sales came from independent drugstores, 40 percent from drug chains, and 25 percent from food stores. For all manufacturers, drug chains and supermarkets were increasing in importance. These stores required a brand with high customer awareness and some brand preference. The brands needed to be presold since, unlike independent drugstores, there was no sales assistance.

Introducing a line of products rather than just a product or two resulted in a greater need for retail shelf space. Although the number of new products and brands competing for retail shelf space frequently appeared unlimited, the space itself was a limited resource. With Belle Couleur, L'Oréal had already addressed this issue by reducing the number of Belle Couleur colorants it planned to offer in the Netherlands. Although 22 shades were available in France, L'Oréal had reduced the line to 15 variations for the Netherlands. As a result, 1.5 meters (about five linear feet) of retail shelf space was needed to display the 15 shades of Belle Couleur. Synergie required about half this shelf space.

Decision Time

After reviewing the information on the market research on the two product lines, Ms. van der Zande summarized the situation. L'Oréal Netherlands could leverage its advertising of the Garnier name by promoting two lines at once. Consumers would hear and see the Garnier name twice, not just once. As a result, Dutch consumers might see Garnier as a major supplier of cosmetics and toiletries. But she was concerned about the selling effort that would be needed to sell the L'Oréal brands that were already in the Dutch market and at the same time introduce not just one but two new brand name product *lines*. The Dutch L'Oréal sales force would have to handle both family brands, since the much lower market potential of the Netherlands market could not support a separate Garnier sales force, as in France. She was also concerned about retailer reaction to a sales pitch for two product lines.

Ms. van der Zande reflected that she was facing three decision areas. First, she had to decide if she should introduce one or both product lines, and she had to make this decision knowing that L'Oréal would not reformulate the products just for the Dutch market. Second, if she decided to introduce either one or both of the product lines, she needed to develop a marketing program. This meant she had to make decisions on the promotion of the product line(s) to both retailers and consumers as well as the pricing and distribution of the line(s). Third, given that the Garnier product introductions might negatively affect the sales of her current product lines, she needed tactical marketing plans for those products.

Case 6-15

A.T. Kearney and the New "Defining Entity"

IVEY

Richard Ivey School of Business
The University of Western Ontario

Michael Carter prepared this case under the supervision of Professor Donald W. Barclay solely to provide material for class discussion. The authors do not intend to illustrate either effective or ineffective handling of a managerial situation. The authors may have disguised certain names and other identifying information to protect confidentiality.

It was early Monday morning, September 22, 1996, and Brian Harrison, president of A. T. Kearney (Canada), was in his Chicago office preparing for an upcoming meeting. A. T. Kearney, headquartered in Chicago, Illinois, was one of the world's largest and most respected global management consulting firms. On Friday, Brian was to meet with the rest of the Toronto management team to review the activities of the firm since its acquisition by Electronic Data Systems (EDS) just over a year ago and to discuss the strategic direction of the firm moving forward. Of particular interest to the management team were the challenges A.T. Kearney faced in trying to take advantage of the new relationship it shared with EDS, a leader in the global Information Services industry.

From a client perspective, many new opportunities were created by the acquisition. Clients could take advantage of a much broader range of services. In essence, the new EDS/A.T. Kearney organization was striving to become a "one-stop-shop," capable of servicing every client requirement. However, many consultants were concerned about the ability of these two very different organizations, with different skill sets and culture, to work together in blending their services into a broad, seamless continuum. Senior consultants wondered about the implications it would have for the overall market strategy of the firm, and the changes that would have to be made for these two companies to benefit fully from the acquisition. Brian prepared himself for what he expected would be a rather lively discussion around this very issue.

Sipping his coffee, Brian smiled as he reviewed the results of a recent A. T. Kearney survey of information technology practices and perceptions at some of the world's largest corporations. Senior executives at Global 1000 companies were interviewed to explore their evolving attitudes toward the role of information technology in their core businesses. Information technology (IT) issues had indeed emerged on "the CEO Agenda." One particular excerpt caught Brian's attention:

> The results suggest a fundamental shift away from the days when information technology was viewed as one tactical item among others used to improve business productivity. No longer is IT just another tool the CEO might use to accomplish cost savings and operational ends. Today, information technology can help solve product problems, set new levels of service and create new distribution and communication channels. It has become sufficiently important to be included in the process of setting a company's strategic objectives.

The study reached the following main conclusions:

- Technology has been integrated into business strategy
- Technology investments will increase
- Corporations are embracing the philosophy of restructuring and reengineering
- Senior management is becoming technology-literate as, across all industries, major corporations increasingly view themselves as "technology-oriented companies"
- Senior management expresses satisfaction with return on technology investment, even in the absence of precise measurements.

These results were no surprise to Brian Harrison, who had played a key role in EDS's acquisition of A.T. Kearney and the subsequent merger of the firm into its new parent. The largest buy-out of a management consulting firm in history had been a bold strategic move for both organizations. The results of the survey highlighted the growing importance of technology as an area of concern and interest among senior management at the world's largest corporations, many of which were clients of A. T. Kearney.

Fred Steingraber, A. T. Kearney's CEO since 1983, suggested:

> The days are past when senior management could remain aloof from the adoption of new technology and still expect to increase quality, productivity, market share, and profits. Today, every enterprise is a high-technology business to the extent that technology, strategy and operational decisions must be made simultaneously to ensure a competitive advantage in the marketplace.

Industry

In 1994, general management consulting firms billed an estimated $40 billion of services to corporations around the globe. The world's top fifteen consulting companies, with over 91,000 consultants, accounted for $18 billion of this total.[1] In particular, services related to information technology (i.e., IT planning, IT strategy, strategic procurement of hardware and software solutions) and process reengineering accounted for almost half of the total fees billed to clients. This segment was expected to grow faster than any other through the turn of the century at an annual rate of up to 15 per cent. Fred Steingraber suggested that total fees for the management consulting industry would double by the year 2000. So why all the growth in consulting?

Many suggested that it had to do with management's need for expert assistance as companies pushed further into the global marketplace and started to rethink strategy for the 21st century. Combined with increasing business uncertainty, senior executives would continue to look for guidance on the way their industries were headed, how to align business processes with strategy, how to empower employees, and how technology could be used to attain competitive advantage. For numerous reasons, it was often more effective for the agent of such changes to come from the outside. Heavy downsizing and cost cutting efforts by many companies in recent years also played a major role in the continued growth of the consulting industry, since corporations around the world had created their own shortage of capable staff.

[1] According to Consultants News—*Chicago Tribune*, "Consulting firms are no longer put on the shelf and forgotten," Wednesday, September 27, 1995.

Coupled with strong growth, the management consulting industry was also undergoing tremendous change. This transformation was being driven by significant trends in the marketplace, some of which included:

- The convergence of telecommunications, technology and information services, dramatically altering the structure of business and how companies competed in the global marketplace;
- The rapid pace of technology development and the movement of technology to the "front line" of operations and the desktop;
- The need to rapidly develop, customize and market new products and services world-wide.

Global clients, accompanied by global issues, were becoming the norm. There was a need to continuously demonstrate greater industry expertise, deep business knowledge and in-depth thought leadership to guide clients into the future and ensure flexibility in a rapidly changing environment. It was becoming a requirement that leading-edge information technology be incorporated into implementable solutions, as technology and convergence played an increasing role in driving strategy, and in restructuring industries.

Engagements were becoming longer with greater emphasis placed on achieving performance targets, and fees increasingly tied to tangible results. Consultants were evolving as "partners" in long-term business relationships. Fred Steingraber commented:

> For a long time, much of the industry's focus was on single-dimension projects. Now the leading consulting firms must possess multidisciplinary consulting capability to secure meaningful relationships with clients worldwide. The idea that consultants are just there for a single project has all but disappeared. Management consulting has new requirements and must develop enhanced capabilities to remain competitive and to be prepared to serve clients effectively in the 21st century.

Competition

The lines between strategy, operations and information systems consulting continued to blur. A broad range of service capabilities would be required for firms to achieve high impact, tangible results and the ability to position themselves in the high value-added end of management consulting. An integrated service continuum from strategy formulation to implementation was the direction in which many international players were heading.

(I) The "Big Six"—Classic IT Firms

The "Big Six" accounting firms (Price Waterhouse, Deloitte & Touche, KPMG, Coopers & Lybrand, Ernst and Young, and Andersen) were enjoying annual growth rates in excess of 15 percent. A large part of this growth was supported by their large share of the fast-growing IT/BPR (Business Process Reengineering) consulting market and a strong push into operations consulting as IT became increasingly strategic in nature and instrumental for reengineering.

(II) Operational and Strategic Firms

Traditional consulting firms like McKinsey, BCG, Bain, and Booz Allen & Hamilton, who were best known for their strategic expertise, were broadening their service offerings as they moved aggressively downstream into operations consulting. Both strategy and operational consultants were pushing information technology as clients demanded more implementation capabilities, and reengineering required information technology resources.

(III) Systems Integrators and System Vendors

Classical IT firms such as EDS, CSC (Computer Sciences Corporation), IBM, and Cap Gemini had moved into more traditional management consulting markets, recognizing that IT had become increasingly strategic in nature and critical for reengineering. With the exception of EDS, CSC, and Cap Gemini, these firms had built practices in the business and IT consulting area from the ground up.

(IV) New Information Technology Entrants

Some of the fastest-growing players were the new information technology entrants, such as AT&T and Oracle who, along with Andersen, had spotted the opportunity to consolidate client relationships by selling "upstream" consulting services on top of their core outsourcing and system integration skills. AT&T, for one, started AT&T Solutions in early 1995 to offer end-to-end solutions supplied through various units. They positioned themselves as the 'Technology Life Cycle Management' company who would increase their value to clients by tying computer and communications solutions to the customer's strategic business objectives. Many of these capital-strong, technology-oriented firms were establishing consulting practices through the acquisition of smaller generalists. Some industry analysts suggested that these IT giants would claim over 15 percent market share before the turn of the century.

Results to date suggested that full-service firms were performing better in terms of growth and profitability

(Exhibit 1). Many were expanding and integrating their service portfolio, supporting the belief that technology and high value-added consulting went hand-in-hand. Industry observers had noted several competitors merging practices in convergent industries like telecommunications, media, entertainment, and consumer electronics. Many of the operational, generalist, and IT players continued to evaluate potential merger/alliances to enhance their service portfolio (Exhibit 2).

A.T. Kearney

Founded in 1926, A.T. Kearney had evolved into one of the world's dominant management consulting practices. Its approach was to develop realistic solutions and help clients implement recommendations that generated tangible results and improved competitive advantage. The firm was well known for its ability to deliver value and results throughout the management process, from strategy development to business and market analysis to operations, process, and technology transformation. This mix of strategy and operations, combined with a focus on implementation, had differentiated A.T. Kearney from its competitors and driven the firm's outstanding results for over a decade. The leaders of the firm emphasized strong, lasting relationships (at the CEO level) with fewer, larger clients. To this end A. T. Kearney had been quite successful. Continuously challenging themselves to exceed their clients' expectations, more than 75 percent of their business volume was generated from clients who had used A. T. Kearney's services the previous year.

While striving to help global clients gain and sustain competitive advantage, A. T. Kearney pursued its own goals of globalization, growth and leadership. Before integrating with Management Consulting Services (MCS), EDS's management consulting arm, the firm had 40 offices in 22 countries. It was expected that over 65 percent of A. T. Kearney's revenues would be generated outside of the United States by 1997. This was quite remarkable considering that only 10 percent of revenues came from outside the United States as late as 1980. Accompanying its aggressive move towards globalization, A. T. Kearney had experienced tremendous growth over the last decade. From a staff of only 230 in 1984 to over 1,100 consultants in 1994, the firm had enjoyed double digit revenue growth for each of the last 13 years. A.T. Kearney had doubled its size every three years since 1983 and was recently listed in *Consultants News* as one of the five fastest-growing consulting firms in the world. Brent Snell, a Principal in the Toronto office, suggested that A. T. Kearney was, in fact, "growth-constrained only by having insufficient numbers of highly qualified new people at all levels of the organization."

EXHIBIT 1 Vertically Integrated Firms Perform Better

Source: *Consultants News*, A. T. Kearney.

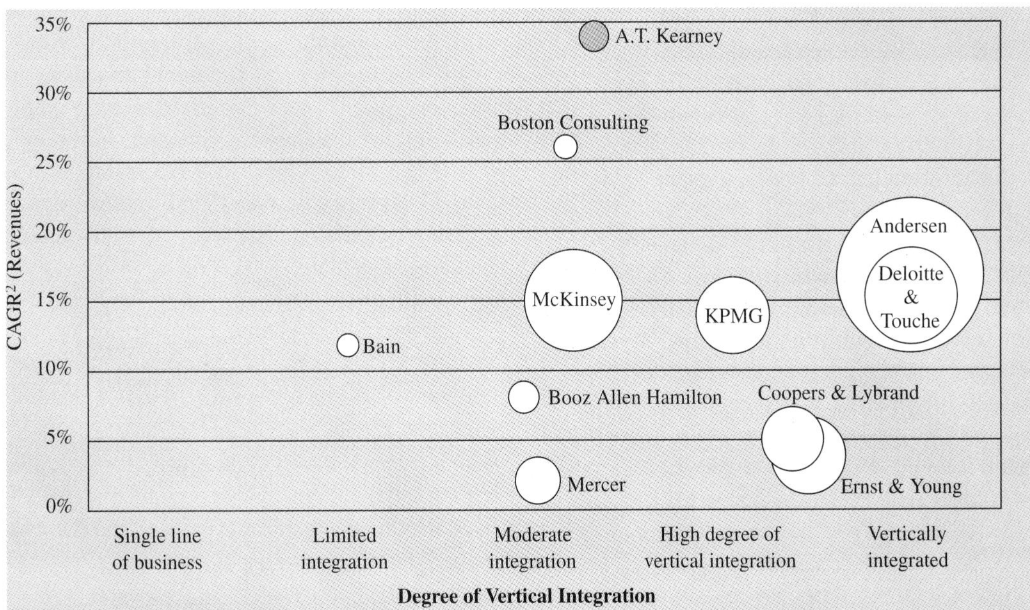

EXHIBIT 2 Major Service Offerings of Leading Consulting and Information Technology Services Firm

Sources: A. T. Kearney, Gartner Group.

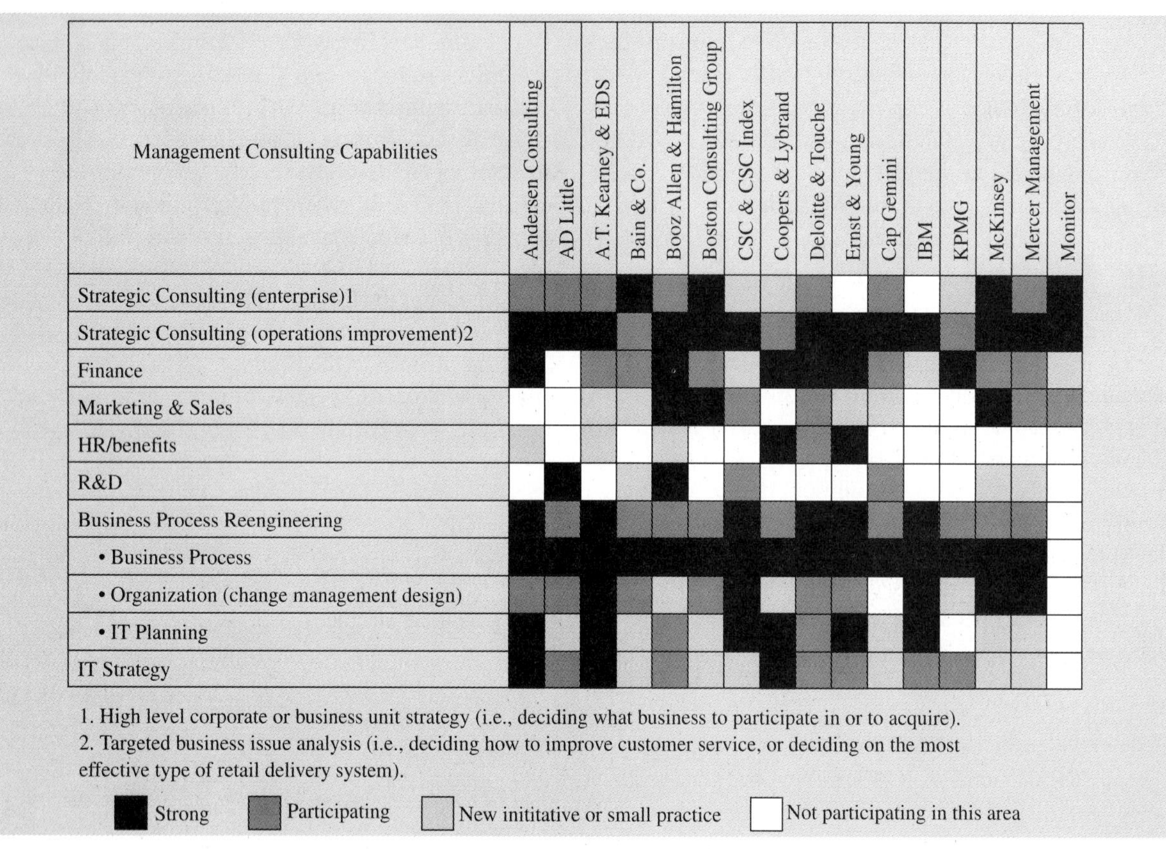

Electronic Data Systems (EDS)

EDS started in 1962 with Ross Perot and a $1,000 investment. The fledgling company began by offering routine data processing services for Dallas-area companies on computers they didn't even own. In 1985, a year after Perot sold the information technology giant to General Motors for an estimated $2.5 billion, EDS reported revenues of $3.4 billion, a 264 percent improvement from the previous year. By 1995, as a subsidiary of the auto manufacturer, EDS was making most of its money running the computer networks of its clients more efficiently than they could. It helped customers use information and technology to recast their economics and to identify and seize new opportunities. This translated into 90,000 employees in 41 countries and revenues that were expected to exceed $12 billion. Considered by many to be the inventor of 'outsourcing', EDS had established itself as a world leader in information technology services (Exhibit 3).

EDS was very much a part of everyone's world. For soccer's World Cup of 1994, EDS developed the largest and most complex information system of its kind for the world's largest single sporting event (seen more than 31 billion times around the world). Instant information on each match, player biographies, and historical information for every World Cup ever played were available to some 15,000 journalists covering the matches in nine cities across the United States. In 1995 in the United States alone, EDS processed over 2.2 million Automated Banking Machine (ABM) transactions, 1.2 billion credit card authorizations and 500,000 airline reservations.

EDS defined its business as "shaping how information is created, distributed, shared, enjoyed, and applied for the benefit of businesses, governments, and individuals around the world." Its service offering included four different types of products:

1. *Systems Development*—EDS designed, developed, and implemented systems that supported and improved its clients' business processes and the way they served their customers.
2. *Systems Integration*—EDS became the single point of contact for a client, responsible for directing multiple vendors and ensuring that combinations of

EXHIBIT 3 EDS and Its Major Competitors in the Computer Service Market

Sources: The companies, Disclosure Inc.—*The Wall Street Journal*, August 8, 1995.

Company	Location	Sales* (billions USD)	Net Income* (millions USD)	Major Customers
Electronic Data Services	Plano, Texas	$10.50	821.9	GM, Xerox, American Express Bank, Inland Revenue, Bethlehem Steel
Computer Sciences (CSC)	El Segundo, California	3.37	110.7	General Dynamics, Hughes Aircraft, Lucas Industries, Department of Defense
Andersen Consulting	Chicago, Illinois	3.45	N.A.	Bell Atlantic, LTV, British Petroleum, London Stock Exchange
Integrated Systems Solutions (a unit of IBM)	White Plains, New York	N.A.	N.A.	BankAmerica, McDonnell Douglas, Amtrak, Eastman Kodak

* Latest fiscal year for each company as of August 1995.
N.A. = Not available.

EXHIBIT 4 Estimated Market Size and Growth (in $ billions)

Source: EDS Marketing Strategic Service Unit Market. Analysis, February 1995, Gartner Group.

Service Continuum	1994	CAGR	1999
Management Consulting	$ 40.0	14.20%	$ 80.0
Systems Development	50.8	6.10	68.3
Systems Integration	56.2	11.90	98.7
Systems Management	120.2	9.10	185.8
Process Management	21.5	35.60	98.3
Estimated Total Market	$288.7		$531

hardware, software, communications, and human resources worked together.

3. *Systems Management*—EDS assumed strategic management responsibility for a client's information technology resources.
4. *Process Management*—EDS provided comprehensive management of business processes, such as customer service, insurance claims processing, telemarketing, accounts payable, accounts receivable, and leadership and employee training programs.

By adding these types of information technology services to management consulting, the size of the global market ballooned to an estimated $280 billion. Growth in both industries was expected to be tremendous (Exhibit 4).

Under the leadership of Chief Executive Officer Les Alberthal since 1986, EDS had maintained its reputation as a hard-driving, results-oriented business. It had also lessened the firm's dependence on General Motors from 73 percent of revenues in 1986 to 39 percent in 1993. In 1995, the majority of EDS's revenue (over 75 percent) was generated from systems integration and systems management. A professional sales force focused on long-term contracts, generated over 70 percent of EDS's revenues from clients within the United States and almost 50 percent from corporations whose core business was manufacturing.

But for almost a decade, while EDS was making its fortune running other companies' mainframe computer operations, competition intensified, and margins began to deteriorate on these traditional lines of business. EDS started to look towards "higher value-added" services rather than data processing. This translated into business-process reengineering and client server technology, two trends that were reshaping the corporate landscape. EDS entered the management consulting industry as part of a strategy to offer business solutions rather than simply IT solutions to its customers.

EDS-Management Consulting Services (MCS)

EDS had been involved in management consulting since 1985 and formalized its efforts by creating MCS in 1993. By leveraging its tradition and strengths, MCS brought a new dimension to EDS. Over a short two-year period, EDS had built MCS into an organization of 1300 people, with 30 offices in 20 countries, generating an estimated $200 million in revenues. During its first year, MCS services were sold through the EDS sales force to give the firm a chance to get organized internally. During its second year, the consultants were selling on their own. The goals and objectives of the new Strategic Services Unit were simple:

- Grow and be profitable while building a world-class management consulting organization;
- Help grow EDS through leveraged downstream-influenced revenue; and
- Act as a catalyst for EDS by bringing in new skills, particularly in relationship management and developing industry knowledge.

Despite the ability to combine expertise and intellectual capital with the delivery capability of EDS, MCS was having difficulties getting off the ground. In 1994 alone, the young organization lost an estimated $23 million. By approaching clients alongside EDS as an IT firm, MCS lacked a clear positioning in the marketplace as a formidable 'consulting' practice. One former MCS consultant suggested, "Any company would have had its difficulties turning a profit in such a short period of time, particularly considering the enormous growth rate of MCS." The majority of this growth came internally through a hiring frenzy while the growth in clients was not so quick. "It's hard to achieve profitability with half your staff not billing," commented the ex-MCS consultant. Rapid growth made it difficult for MCS to put in place some of the necessities for success in the global market. Lack of uniform business systems and processes, and inconsistent consulting methodologies, human resource practices, billing rates and quality measures all translated into an inconsistent positioning in the marketplace. Another struggle for MCS was in establishing its own culture. There were a tremendous number of highly talented people, but coming together so quickly from so many different places, made it impossible to establish a unified identity. The firm lacked a sense of cohesion among its broad base of consultants.

A. T. Kearney—Acquired by EDS and Merged with MCS (September 1995)

The acquisition of A. T. Kearney was the first significant move by an information technology firm into the upper echelon of the management consulting leagues. EDS had purchased seven management consulting firms over the last two years, but none of this magnitude. Gary Fernandez, EDS vice chairman and new chairman of A. T. Kearney, commented:

> The addition of the A. T. Kearney team builds on the progress EDS has made to date in creating a world-class management consulting organization. Our enhanced management consulting capability coupled with EDS's traditional information technology and process management expertise represents a powerful combination of business insight, industry experience, and global delivery capability to help our clients successfully undertake enterprise-wide transformation initiatives.

EDS agreed to buy A. T. Kearney for $300 million in cash and contingency payments, plus a stock incentive provision of seven million shares to be earned at a rate of 10 percent a year by A. T. Kearney partners and 100 other key individuals. The total bill was estimated at just over $600 million. It was determined that the MCS practice would be integrated into the new A. T. Kearney, maintaining the brand name, procedures, policies, and standards that had made the Chicago-based firm one of the world's leading management consulting practices. Fred Steingraber would continue to function as the company's CEO. For the first time in EDS's long history, a fully independent subsidiary was created in order to assure the integrity and objectivity of a world-class management consulting firm. This subsidiary provided EDS with a credible, ready-made consulting practice that would have taken far too long for EDS to develop on its own.

This was an excellent match for both A. T. Kearney and MCS as consulting organizations because of the synergistic and complementary industry, functional, and geographic strengths. The operational and technology consulting strengths of MCS complemented the strategy and high value-added operational strengths of A. T. Kearney. The integration provided A. T. Kearney with an influx of new, talented consultants that were necessary for the firm to ramp up its capabilities and reach critical mass in many of its markets. Together, they brought an unparalleled spectrum of capabilities to clients. The combination of locations ensured that a broad and well-positioned global organization was in place to service clients worldwide. Industry coverage was also well matched and balanced; for example, A. T. Kearney was exceptionally strong in manufacturing, while MCS had particular strengths in the communications and electronics industries.

When EDS's information services and technology capabilities were added to the mix, the ability to have a near seamless link of strategy through implementation was created. One competitor suggested:

> The market is demanding integrated business and technology services. I think it will be tough for them, but it's the right move. It's very difficult to do process improvement as A. T. Kearney does and not leverage that into implementing systems.

The combined capabilities brought a range of skills and leading-edge solutions to clients of both A. T. Kearney and EDS. For clients involved in reengineering and transformation, process and functional issues could be addressed concurrently with the enabling technology and implementation issues. In addition, implementation expertise could be tapped into earlier in the development process. The relationship with EDS also helped ensure the availability of major investment resources for A. T. Kearney. It provided the infrastructure to support its rapid growth both from a geographic and practice development perspective. The relationship with A. T. Kearney gave the information technology giant the key high-level perspectives on business issues which helped it to sell its outsourcing and systems integration services.

A. T. Kearney was a key part of the EDS vision to become the new "Defining Entity." For A. T. Kearney, the partnership with EDS had placed it in a stronger position to pursue its goals of growth, globalization, and leadership. According to Fred Steingraber, A. T. Kearney viewed itself as "one of a new breed of management consultancies, rich in resources, global in reach, and integrated in solution delivery." Both companies felt the merger had provided them with a tremendous opportunity to take the lead in bringing the "next generation" of professional services capabilities to clients worldwide.

Risks, Challenges, and Obstacles

Despite all of the optimism of A. T. Kearney and EDS, skeptics were lining up to criticize the strategy. Many wondered whether vertically integrating services, so that a single consulting firm offered end-to-end consulting solutions, was an inevitable trend, and even if it was, integrating the existing MCS into A. T. Kearney would be no easy task. One such critic was James Kennedy, publisher of Consultants News:

> First you have entirely different cultures. What you are going to get is the propeller heads meeting the button downs. Kearney has been selling top management for decades, while EDS, which has only been in the consulting business since 1993, has been dealing mostly with the systems people. We're talking about two different levels here.

He went on to say:

> Consulting firms are very fragile entities. They cannot be transplanted easily. You have something equivalent to organ rejection when you try to mix and match consultants from one company with another. There are huge egos here.

Referring to the acquisition by the General Motors subsidiary, one A. T. Kearney consultant was quoted as saying, "We would go from being an independent, uninhibited place to being a small piece of the country's largest company. Talk about culture shock." Independence was a major issue for many A. T. Kearney consultants. It was felt that IBM Solutions was essentially created to sell IBM hardware solutions. The relationship between MCS and EDS was not much different. Many consultants feared that A. T. Kearney would be viewed as the front end for EDS. If so, this could have significant implications for A. T. Kearney's ability to both attract and retain good people—the main assets of any professional services firm. Some wondered whether there would be a mass exodus from the Kearney ranks. Clients had parallel concerns. Would A. T. Kearney still be able to maintain its objectivity in helping clients choose the right suppliers? Would clients continue to use A. T. Kearney services, particularly if they competed against EDS or General Motors?

One Year Later (September 1996)

No one would say that the first year had been easy. However, most would argue that it was successful. The integration of MCS into A. T. Kearney had gone smoothly. With 60 offices in over 30 countries, the consulting practice had grown to over 3,500 employees, 2,400 of whom were consultants. In 1995, revenues soared to $650 million which placed A. T. Kearney as the 11th largest consulting firm in the world (Exhibits 5 and 6) and the number two firm in the high value-added segment of the market. The marketplace had received the marriage between A. T. Kearney and EDS with open arms. In fact through June 1996, the two companies partnered on more than 20 successful initiatives resulting in $1.4 billion in new business for EDS and $140 million for A. T. Kearney. Perhaps the most exciting collaboration between the two companies was a 10-year engagement with Rolls-Royce worth over $900 million. Even more remarkable, its independence from EDS and its business systems and culture had been maintained. With almost no turnover of staff throughout the integration and absolutely no turnover of clients, A. T. Kearney had further established itself as a strong and successful player in the management consulting industry.

What Next?

Despite the consulting firm's success to date, Brian Harrison knew that the greatest potential from the merger had yet to be realized. The integration of MCS into A. T. Kearney was the first step. Now EDS and A. T. Kearney sought to take advantage of the synergy created from the merger by leveraging the capabilities of both organizations. While significant revenue had been generated to date from joint clients, most collaborative initiatives had been in response to client demand, or to competitive pressures created by a bidding process. In almost all cases, A. T. Kearney had reacted to opportunities, rather than having taken the initiative and proactively sought them out. One example of this was the Rolls Royce project. Competing with CSC for the engagement, EDS decided to include its consulting arm in the service mix since the services of CSC Index, CSC's consulting division, had been offered. The selling process was not initiated with both service offerings in mind. Most managers felt that a more proactive approach to similar situations was the ultimate objective of the firm. The question was how to make this happen. Leveraging and combining each others' strengths in the marketplace was a must.

Several courses of action were available to the two organizations in light of the merger. Substantial cross-marketing opportunities were created because of the minimal client overlap. EDS had significant positions in health care, insurance, communications and electronics, aerospace and defense industries, while A. T. Kearney's strengths resided in manufacturing, consumer products, transportation, and chemical/pharmaceuticals. They shared mutual strengths in industries such as automotive,

EXHIBIT 5 Top Consulting Firms for 1995 (in $ millions)

Source: Worldlink, September/October 1996, p. 15–25.

Rank	Company	Revenues
1	Andersen	4,200
2	McKinsey & Company	1,800
3	Ernst & Young	1,500
4	KPMG	1,500
5	Deloitte & Touche	1,400
6	Coopers & Lybrand	1,200
7	Mercer Management	1,000
8	Price Waterhouse	1,000
9	Booz Allen & Hamilton	785
10	Towers Perrin[1]	767
11	A.T. Kearney	650
12	Boston Consulting Group	550
13	Cap Gemini	548
14	Arthur D. Little	514
15	Bain	375

[1] Estimate of 1994 revenues only.

EXHIBIT 6 A. T. Kearney Growth & Performance Unparalleled in the Industry[1]

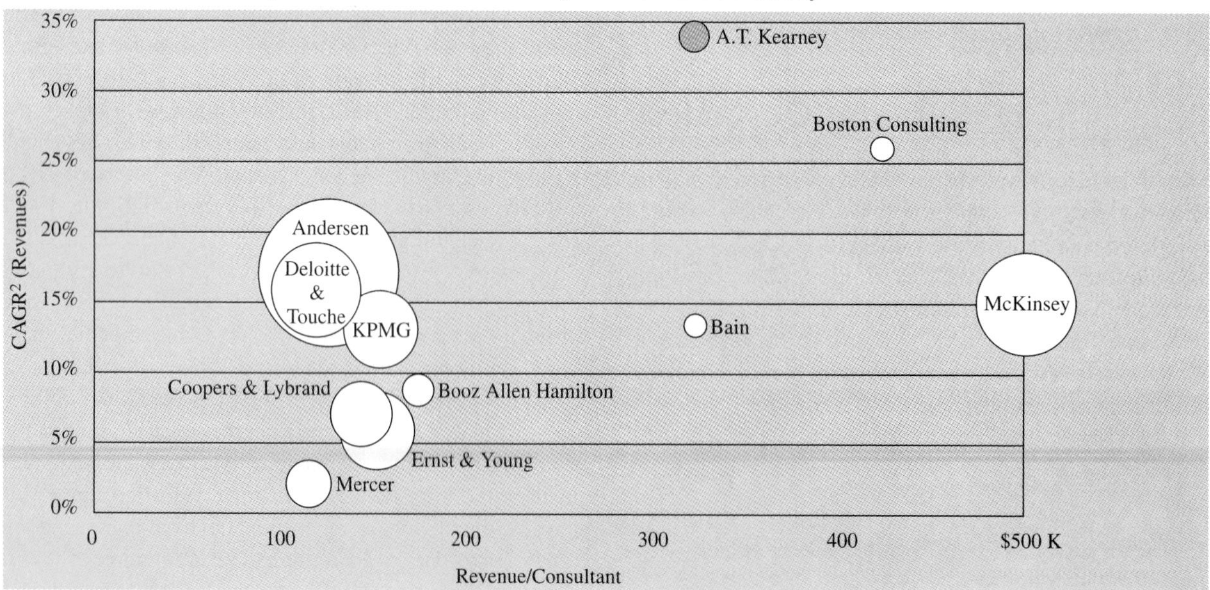

[1] Source: *Consultants News.*
[2] Growth measured between 1990–1995.

financial services, energy and retail. Products and services that had made each company successful in the past could be offered to each others' clients.

Another opportunity was to offer the combined menu of these very same products to a whole new set of clients looking for a "one-stop-shop," where A. T. Kearney and EDS were not in a position to service these accounts effectively in the past. Most of the reactive collaborative initiatives to date had taken the form of one of these two approaches.

Brian, however, suggested this was not the primary purpose of the merger. Instead, there was an opportunity to draw on the strengths of both organizations and develop entirely new products. For example, these would be in the category of enterprise-wide transformation initiatives or in the development of technology-enabled strategies. Offered to either existing or new clients, these new products would significantly differentiate the new enterprise from its competition, and generate revenue streams that neither A. T. Kearney nor EDS could have enjoyed without this partnership. This was what Brian considered to be the most attractive opportunity. For example, A. T. Kearney and EDS had recently embarked on the development of a new service called CoSourcing. Once completed, this would be a collaborative initiative that integrated business process reengineering, information technology, outsourcing, and organizational transformation to deliver significant performance enhancements to prospective clients. However, before this or any other new initiative could possibly work, significant changes to both organizations had to occur, particularly with respect to sales and account management. The objective of these changes would be to create an environment where the two companies could remain apart, but at the same time, work together.

Brian sat back in his chair and remembered a comment Fred had made almost a year ago, when the merger was finalized:

> The offer has provided us with a catalyst in terms of looking at the next generation of success criteria that will be critical in this industry in the future. It has caused a lot of people to ponder the future of the consulting industry.

With this in mind, Brian began to prepare for his upcoming meeting on Friday.

Case 6-16

Camar Automotive Hoist

In September 2000 Mark Camar, president of Camar Automotive Hoist (CAH), had just finished reading a feasibility report on entering the European market in 2001. CAH manufactured surface automotive hoists, a product used by garages, service stations, and repair shops to lift cars for servicing (Exhibit 1). The report, which had been prepared by CAH's marketing manager, Pierre Gagnon, outlined the opportunities in the European Union and the available entry options.

Mr. Camar was not sure if CAH was ready for this move. While the company had been successful in expanding sales into the U.S. market, he wondered if this success could be repeated in Europe. He thought that with more effort, sales could be increased in the United States. However, there were some positive aspects to the European idea. He began reviewing the information in preparation for the meeting the following day with Mr. Gagnon.

This case was prepared by Gordon McDougall, Wilfrid Laurier University, as the basis for class discussion rather that to illustrate either effective or ineffective handling of an administrative situation.

Camar Automotive Hoist

Mr. Camar, a design engineer, had worked for eight years for the Canadian subsidiary of a U.S. automotive hoist manufacturer. During those years he had spent considerable time designing an aboveground, or surface, automotive hoist. Although Mr. Camar was very enthusiastic about the unique aspects of the hoist, including a scissor lift and wheel alignment pads, senior management expressed no interest in the idea. In 1990, Mr. Camar left the company to start his own business with the express purpose of designing and manufacturing the hoist. He left with the good wishes of his previous employer, who had no objections to his plans to start a new business.

Over the next three years Mr. Camar obtained financing from a venture capital firm; opened a plant in Lachine, Quebec; and began manufacturing and marketing the hoist, which was called the Camar Lift (see Exhibit 1).

From the beginning Mr. Camar had taken considerable pride in the development and marketing of the Camar Lift. The original design included a scissor lift

EXHIBIT 1 Examples of Automotive Hoists

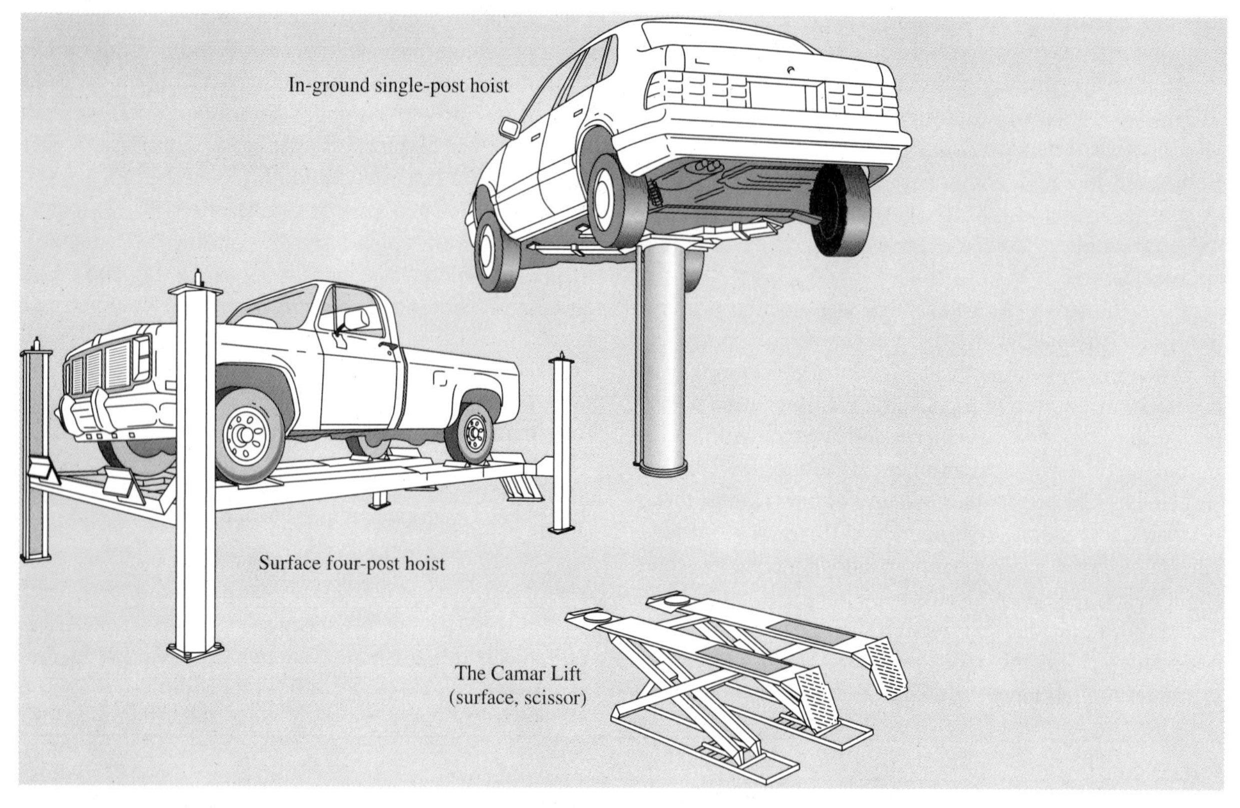

and a safety locking mechanism which allowed the hoist to be raised to any level and locked in place. Also, the scissor lift offered easy access for the mechanic to work on the raised vehicle. Because the hoist was fully hydraulic and had no chains or pulleys, it required little maintenance. Another key feature was the alignment turn plates that were an integral part of the lift. The turn plates would allow mechanics to perform wheel alignment jobs accurately and easily. Because it was a surface lift, it could be installed in a garage in less than a day.

Mr. Camar continually made improvements to the product, including adding more safety features. In fact, the Camar Lift was considered a leader in automotive lift safety. Safety was an important factor in the automotive hoist market. Although hoists seldom malfunctioned, when they did, it often resulted in a serious accident.

The Camar Lift developed a reputation in the industry as the "Cadillac" of hoists; the unit was judged by many as superior to competitive offerings because of its design, the quality of the workmanship, the safety features, the ease of installation, and the five-year warranty. Mr. Camar held four patents on the Camar Lift, including the lifting mechanism on the scissor design and a safety locking mechanism. A number of versions of the product were designed that made the lift suitable (depending on the model) for a variety of tasks, including rustproofing, muffler repairs, and general mechanical repairs.

In 1991 CAH sold 23 hoists and had sales of $172,500. During the early years the majority of sales were to independent service stations and garages specializing in wheel alignment in the Quebec and Ontario market. Most of the units were sold by Mr. Gagnon, who was hired in 1992 to handle the marketing side of the operation. In 1994 Mr. Gagnon began using distributors to sell the hoist to a wider geographic market in Canada. In 1996 he signed an agreement with a large automotive wholesaler to represent CAH in the U.S. market. By 1999 the company had sold 1,054 hoists and had sales of $9,708,000 (Exhibit 2). In 1999 about 60 percent of sales were to the United States, with the remaining 40 percent going to the Canadian market.

Industry

Approximately 49,000 hoists were sold each year in North America. Hoists typically were purchased by any automotive outlet that serviced or repaired cars, including new car dealers, used car dealers, specialty

EXHIBIT 2
Camar Automotive Hoist, Selected Financial Statistics (1997–1999)

Source: Company records.

	1997	1998	1999
Sales	$6,218,000	$7,454,000	$9,708,000
Cost of sales	4,540,000	5,541,000	6,990,000
Contribution	1,678,000	1,913,000	2,718,000
Marketing expenses*	507,000	510,000	530,000
Administrative expenses	810,000	820,000	840,000
Earnings before tax	361,000	583,000	1,348,000
Units sold	723	847	1,054

* Marketing expenses in 1999 included advertising ($70,000), four salespeople ($240,000), the marketing manager, and three sales support personnel ($220,000).

shops (for example, mufflers, transmission, wheel alignment), chains (for example, Firestone, Goodyear, Canadian Tire), and independent garages. It was estimated that new car dealers purchased 30 percent of all the units sold in a given year. In general, the specialty shops focused on one type of repair, such as mufflers or rustproofing, while "nonspecialty" outlets handled a variety of repairs. While there was some crossover, in general CAH competed in the specialty shop segment and, in particular, shops that dealt with wheel alignment. This included chains such as Firestone and Canadian Tire as well as new car dealers (for example, Ford) which devoted a certain percentage of their lifts to the wheel alignment business and independent garages that specialized in wheel alignment.

The purpose of a hoist was to lift an automobile into a position where a mechanic or serviceperson could easily work on the car. Because different repairs required different positions, a wide variety of hoists had been developed to meet specific needs. For example, a muffler repair shop required a hoist where the mechanic could gain easy access to the underside of the car. Similarly, a wheel alignment job required a hoist that offered a level platform where the wheels could be adjusted and there was easy access for the mechanic. Mr. Gagnon estimated that 85 percent of CAH's sales were to the wheel alignment market to service centers such as Firestone, Goodyear, and Canadian Tire and to independent garages that specialized in wheel alignment. About 15 percent of sales were made to customers who used the hoist for general mechanical repairs.

Firms that purchased hoists were part of an industry called the automobile aftermarket. This industry was involved in supplying parts and service for new and used cars and was worth over $54 billion at retail in 1999 while servicing the approximately 14 million cars on the road in Canada. The industry was large and diverse; there were over 4,000 new car dealers in Canada, over 400 Canadian Tire stores, over 100 stores in each of the Firestone and Goodyear chains, and over 220 stores in the Rust Check chain.

The purchase of an automotive hoist was often an important decision for a service station owner or dealer. Because the price of hoists ranged from $3,000 to $15,000, this was a capital expense for most businesses.

For the owner-operator of a new service center or car dealership the decision involved determining what type of hoist was required and what brand would best suit the company. Most new service centers and car dealerships had multiple bays for servicing cars. In these cases the decision would involve what types of hoists were required (for example, in-ground, surface). Often more than one type of hoist was purchased, depending on the service center/dealership needs.

Experienced garage owners seeking a replacement hoist (the typical hoist had a useful life of 10 to 13 years) usually would determine what products were available and then make a decision. If the garage owners were also mechanics, they probably would be aware of two or three types of hoists but would not be very knowledgeable about the brands or products currently available. Garage owners and dealers who were not mechanics probably knew very little about hoists. The owners of car or service dealerships often bought the product that was recommended and/or approved by the parent company.

Competition

Sixteen companies competed in the automotive lift market in North America: 4 Canadian and 12 U.S. firms. With the advent of the North American Free Trade Agreement in 1989, the duties on hoists between the two countries were phased out over a 10-year period, and in 1999 exports and imports of hoists were duty-free. For Mr. Camar, the import duties had never played a part in

EXHIBIT 3 North American Automotive Lift Unit Sales by Type, 1997–1999

Source: Company record.

	1997	1998	1999
In-ground			
Single-post	5,885	5,772	5,518
Multiple-post	4,812	6,625	5,075
Surface			
Two-post	27,019	28,757	28,923
Four-post	3,862	3,162	3,745
Scissor	2,170	2,258	2,316
Other	4,486	3,613	3,695
Total	48,234	50,187	49,272

any decisions; the fluctuating exchange rates between the two countries had a far greater impact on selling prices. In the last three years the Canadian dollar had fluctuated between $0.65 and $0.70 versus the U.S. dollar ($1.00 CDN bought $0.65 U.S.) and forecasted rates were expected to stay within that range.

A wide variety of hoists were manufactured in the industry. The two basic types of hoists were in-ground and surface. As the name implies, in-ground hoists required a pit to be dug "in-ground" where the piston that raised the hoist was installed. In-ground hoists were either single-post or multiple-post, were permanent, and obviously could not be moved. In-ground lifts constituted approximately 21 percent of total lift sales in 1999 (Exhibit 3). Surface lifts were installed on a flat surface, usually concrete. Surface lifts came in two basic types: post lift hoists and scissor hoists. Compared to in-ground lifts, surface lifts were easy to install and could be moved if necessary. Surface lifts constituted 79 percent of total lift sales in 1999. Within each type of hoist (for example, post lift surface hoists) there were numerous variations in terms of size, shape, and lifting capacity.

The industry was dominated by two large U.S. firms, AHV Lifts and Berne Manufacturing, that together held approximately 60 percent of the market. AHV Lifts, the largest firm, with approximately 40 percent of the market and annual sales of about $60 million, offered a complete line of hoists (in-ground and surface) but focused primarily on the in-ground market and the two-post surface market. AHV Lifts was the only company that had its own direct sales force; all the other companies used only wholesalers or a combination of wholesalers and a company sales force. AHV Lifts offered standard hoists with few extra features and competed primarily on price. Berne Manufacturing, with a market share of approximately 20 percent, also competed in the in-ground and two-post surface markets. It used a combination of wholesalers and company salespeople and, like AHV Lifts, competed primarily on price.

Most of the remaining firms in the industry were companies that operated in a regional market (for example, California, British Columbia) and/or offered a limited product line (for example, four-post surface hoist).

Camar had two competitors that manufactured scissor lifts. AHV Lift marketed a scissor hoist that had a different lifting mechanism and did not include the safety locking features of the Camar Lift. On average, the AHV scissor lift was sold for about 20 percent less than the Camar Lift. The second competitor, Mete Lift, was a small regional company with sales in California and Oregon. It had a design that was very similar to that of the Camar Lift but lacked some of its safety features. The Mete Lift, which was regarded as a well-manufactured product, sold for about 5 percent less than the Camar Lift.

Marketing Strategy

As of early 2000, CAH had developed a reputation for a quality product backed by good service in the hoist lift market, primarily in the wheel alignment segment.

The distribution system employed by CAH reflected the need to engage in extensive personal selling. Three types of distributors were used: a company sales force, Canadian distributors, and a U.S. automotive wholesaler. The company sales force consisted of four salespeople and Mr. Gagnon. Their main task was to service large "direct" accounts. The initial step was to get the Camar Lift approved by large chains and manufacturers and then, having received the approval, sell to individual dealers or operators. For example, if General Motors approved the hoist, CAH could sell it to individual General Motors dealers. CAH sold directly to the individual dealers of a number of large accounts, including General Motors, Ford, Chrysler, Petro-Canada, Firestone, and Goodyear. CAH had been successful in obtaining manufacturer approval from the big three automobile manufacturers in both Canada and the United States. Also, CAH had received approval from service companies such as Canadian Tire and Goodyear. To date, CAH had not been rejected by any major account, but in some cases the approval process had taken over four years.

In total, the company sales force generated about 25 percent of the unit sales each year. Sales to the large "direct" accounts in the United States went through CAH's U.S. wholesaler.

The Canadian distributors sold, installed, and serviced units across Canada. Those distributors handled the Camar Lift and carried a line of noncompetitive automotive equipment products (for example, engine diagnostic equipment, wheel-balancing equipment) and noncompetitive lifts. They focused on the smaller chains and the independent service stations and garages.

The U.S. wholesaler sold a complete product line to service stations as well as manufacturing some equipment. The Camar Lift was one of five different types of lifts that the wholesaler sold. Although the wholesaler provided CAH with extensive distribution in the United States, the Camar Lift was a minor product within the wholesaler's total line. While Mr. Gagnon did not have actual figures, he thought that the Camar Lift probably accounted for less than 20 percent of the total lift sales of the U.S. wholesaler.

Both Mr. Camar and Mr. Gagnon felt that the U.S. market had unrealized potential. With a population of 264 million people and over 146 million registered vehicles, that market was almost 10 times the size of the Canadian market (population of over 30 million and approximately 14 million vehicles). Mr. Gagnon noted that the six New England states (population of over 13 million), the three largest mid-Atlantic states (population of over 38 million), and the three largest Mideastern states (population of over 32 million) were all within a day's drive of the factory in Lachine. Mr. Camar and Mr. Gagnon had considered setting up a sales office in New York to service those states, but they were concerned that the U.S. wholesaler would not be willing to relinquish any of its territory. They also had considered working more closely with the wholesaler to encourage it to "push" the Camar Lift. It appeared that the wholesaler's major objective was to sell a hoist, not necessarily the Camar Lift.

CAH distributed a catalog-type package with products, uses, prices, and other required information for both distributors and users. In addition, CAH advertised in trade publications (for example, *AutoInc.*), and Mr. Gagnon traveled to trade shows in Canada and the United States to promote the Camar Lift.

In 1999, Camar Lifts sold for an average retail price of $10,990 and CAH received on average $9,210 for each unit sold. This average reflected the mix of sales through the three distribution channels: (1) direct (where CAH received 100 percent of the selling price), (2) Canadian distributors (where CAH received 80 percent of the selling price) and (3) the U.S. wholesaler (where CAH received 78 percent of the selling price).

Both Mr. Camar and Mr. Gagnon felt that the company's success to date had been based on a strategy of offering a superior product that was targeted primarily at the needs of specific customers. The strategy stressed continual product improvements, quality workmanship, and service. Personal selling was a key aspect of the strategy; salespeople could show customers the advantages of the Camar Lift over competing products.

The European Market

Against this background, Mr. Camar had been thinking of ways to maintain the rapid growth of the company. One possibility that kept coming up was the promise and potential of the European market. The fact that Europe had become a single market in 1993 suggested that it was an opportunity that should at least be explored. With this in mind, Mr. Camar asked Mr. Gagnon to prepare a report on the possibility of CAH entering the European market. The highlights of Mr. Gagnon's report follow.

History of the European Union

The European Union (EU) had its basis in the 1957 Treaty of Rome, in which five countries decided it would be in their best interest to form an internal market. Those countries were France, Spain, Italy, West Germany, and Luxembourg. By 1990 the EU consisted of 15 countries (the additional 10 were Austria, Belgium, Denmark, Finland, Greece, Ireland, the Netherlands, Portugal, Sweden, and the United Kingdom) with a population of over 376 million people. Virtually all barriers (physical, technical, and fiscal) in the EU were scheduled to be removed for companies within the EU. This allowed the free movement of goods, persons, services, and capital.

In the last 15 years many North American and Japanese firms had established themselves in the EU. The reasoning for this was twofold. First, those companies regarded the community as an opportunity to increase global market share and profits. The market was attractive because of its size and lack of internal barriers. Second, there was continuing concern that companies not established within the EU would have difficulty exporting to the EU due to changing standards and tariffs. To date, this concern had not materialized.

Market Potential

The key indicator of the potential market for the Camar Lift hoist was the number of passenger cars and commercial vehicles in use in a particular country. Four countries in Europe had more than 20 million vehicles in use, with Germany having the largest domestic fleet, 44 million vehicles, followed in order by Italy, France, and the United Kingdom (Exhibit 4). The number of vehicles

EXHIBIT 4
Number of Vehicles (1997) and Population (2000 estimate)

Country	Vehicles in Use (thousands) Passenger	Small Commercial	New Vehicle Registrations (thousands)	Population (thousands)
Germany	41,400	2,800	3,500	82,100
France	28,000	4,900	2,200	59,000
Italy	33,200	2,700	1,800	56,700
United Kingdom	23,500	4,000	2,200	59,100
Spain	15,300	2,800	1,000	39,200

was an important indicator since the more vehicles there were in use, the greater the number of service and repair facilities which needed vehicle hoists and potentially the Camar Lift.

An indicator of the future vehicle repair and service market was the number of new vehicle registrations. The registration of new vehicles was important, as it maintained the number of vehicles in use by replacing cars that had been retired. Again, Germany had the most new cars registered in 1997 and was followed in order by France, the United Kingdom, and Italy.

Based primarily on the fact that a large domestic market was important for initial growth, the selection of a European country should be limited to the "Big Four" industrialized nations: Germany, France, the United Kingdom, and Italy. In an international survey companies from North America and Europe ranked European countries on a scale of 1 to 100 on market potential and investment site potential. The results showed that Germany was favored for both market potential and investment site opportunities, while France, the United Kingdom, and Spain placed second, third, and fourth, respectively. Italy did not place in the top four in either market or investment site potential. However, Italy had a large number of vehicles in use, had the fourth largest population in Europe, and was an acknowledged leader in car technology and production.

Little information was available on the competition within Europe. There was no dominant manufacturer as there was in North America. At that time there was one firm in Germany that manufactured a scissor-type lift. That firm sold most of its units within the German market. The only other available information was that 22 firms in Italy manufactured vehicle lifts.

Investment Options

Mr. Gagnon felt that CAH had three options for expansion into the European market: licensing, a joint venture, or direct investment. The licensing option was a real possibility, as a French firm had expressed an interest in manufacturing the Camar Lift.

In June 2000, Mr. Gagnon had attended a trade show in Detroit to promote the Camar Lift. At the show he met Phillipe Beaupre, the marketing manager for Bar Maisse, a French manufacturer of wheel alignment equipment. The firm, located in Chelles, France, sold a range of wheel alignment equipment throughout Europe. The best-selling product was an electronic modular aligner which enabled a mechanic to utilize a sophisticated computer system to align the wheels of a car. Mr. Beaupre was seeking a North American distributor for the modular aligner and other products manufactured by Bar Maisse.

At the show Mr. Gagnon and Mr. Beaupre had a casual conversation in which both explained what their respective companies manufactured, exchanged company brochures and business cards, and went on to other exhibits. The next day Mr. Beaupre sought out Mr. Gagnon and asked if he might be interested in having Bar Maisse manufacture and market the Camar Lift in Europe. Mr. Beaupre felt that the lift would complement Bar Maisse's product line and the licensing would be beneficial to both parties. They agreed to pursue the idea. Upon his return to Lachine, Mr. Gagnon told Mr. Camar about those discussions, and they agreed to explore the possibility.

Mr. Gagnon called a number of colleagues in the industry and asked them what they knew about Bar Maisse. About half had not heard of the company, but those who had commented favorably on the quality of its products. One colleague with European experience knew the company well and said that Bar Maisse's management had integrity and the firm would make a good partner. In July Mr. Gagnon sent a letter to Mr. Beaupre stating that CAH was interested in further discussions and enclosing various company brochures, including price lists and technical information on the Camar Lift. In late August Mr. Beaupre responded, stating that Bar Maisse would like to enter a three-year licensing agreement with CAH to manufacture the Camar Lift in Europe. In exchange for the manufacturing rights, Bar Maisse was prepared to pay a royalty rate of 5 percent of gross sales. Mr. Gagnon had not yet responded to this proposal.

A second possibility was a joint venture. Mr. Gagnon had wondered if it might not be better for CAH to offer a counterproposal to Bar Maisse for a joint venture. He had not worked out any details, but he felt that CAH would learn more about the European market and probably make more money if it was an active partner in Europe. Mr. Gagnon's idea was a 50-50 proposal in which the two parties shared the investment and the profits. He envisaged a situation where Bar Maisse would manufacture the Camar Lift in its plant with technical assistance from CAH. Mr. Gagnon also thought that CAH could get involved in the marketing of the lift through the Bar Maisse distribution system. Further, he thought that the Camar Lift, with proper marketing, could gain a reasonable share of the European market. If that happened, Mr. Gagnon felt that CAH was likely to earn greater returns with a joint venture.

The third option was direct investment, in which CAH would establish a manufacturing facility and set up a management group to market the lift. Mr. Gagnon had contacted a business acquaintance who recently had been involved in manufacturing fabricated steel sheds in Germany. On the basis of discussions with his acquaintance, Mr. Gagnon estimated the costs involved in setting up a plant in Europe at (1) $250,000 for capital equipment (welding machines, cranes, other equipment), (2) $200,000 in incremental costs to set up the plant, and (3) carrying costs to cover $1 million in inventory and accounts receivable. While the actual costs of renting a building for the factory would depend on the site location, he estimated that annual building rent, including heat, light, and insurance, would be about $80,000. Mr. Gagnon recognized that these estimates were guidelines but felt that the estimates were probably within 20 percent of the actual costs.

The Decision

As Mr. Camar considered the contents of the report, a number of thoughts crossed his mind. He began making notes concerning the European possibility and the future of the company:

- If CAH decided to enter Europe, Mr. Gagnon would be the obvious choice to head up the direct investment option or the joint venture option. Mr. Camar felt that Mr. Gagnon had been instrumental in the success of the company to date.
- While CAH had the financial resources to go ahead with the direct investment option, the joint venture would spread the risk (and the returns) over the two companies.
- CAH had built its reputation on designing and manufacturing a quality product. Regardless of the option, Mr. Camar wanted the firm's reputation to be maintained.
- Either the licensing agreement or the joint venture appeared to build on the two companies' strengths: Bar Maisse had knowledge of the market, and CAH had the product. What troubled Mr. Camar was whether this apparent synergy would work or whether Bar Maisse would seek to control the operation.
- It was difficult to estimate sales under any of the options. With the first two (licensing and a joint venture), it would depend on the effort and expertise of Bar Maisse; with the third, it would depend on Mr. Gagnon.
- CAH's sales in the U.S. market could be increased if the U.S. wholesaler would "push" the Camar Lift. Alternatively, the establishment of a sales office in New York to cover the Eastern states also could increase sales.

As Mr. Camar reflected on the situation, he knew he probably should get additional information, but it wasn't obvious exactly what information would help him make a yes or no decision. He knew one thing for sure: He was going to keep this company on a "fast growth" track, and at tomorrow's meeting he and Mr. Gagnon would decide how to do it.

Case 6-17

Procter & Gamble Co.

It's Mother's Day, and Alan G. "A.G." Lafley, chief executive of Procter & Gamble Co., is meeting with the person he shares time with every Sunday evening—Richard L. Antoine, the company's head of human resources. Lafley doesn't invite the chief financial officer of the $43 billion business, nor does he ask the executive in charge of marketing at the world's largest consumer-products company. He doesn't invite friends over to watch *The Sopranos*, either. No, on most Sunday nights it's just Lafley, Antoine, and stacks of reports on the performance of the company's 200 most senior executives. This is the boss's signature gesture. It shows his determination to nurture talent and serves notice that little escapes his attention. If you worked for P&G, you would have to be both impressed and slightly intimidated by that kind of diligence.

On this May evening, the two executives sit at the dining-room table in Antoine's Cincinnati home hashing over the work of a manager who distinguished himself on one major assignment but hasn't quite lived up to that since. "We need to get him in a position where we can stretch him," Lafley says. Then he rises from his chair and stands next to Antoine to peer more closely at a spreadsheet detailing P&G's seven management layers. Lafley points to one group while tapping an empty water bottle against his leg. "It's not being felt strongly enough in the middle of the company," he says in his slightly high-pitched voice. "They don't feel the hot breath of the consumer."

If they don't feel it yet, they will. Lafley, who took over when Durk I. Jager was pressured to resign in June, 2000, is in the midst of engineering a remarkable turnaround. The first thing Lafley told his managers when he took the job was just what they wanted to hear: Focus on what you do well—selling the company's major brands such as Tide, Pampers, and Crest—instead of trying to develop the next big thing.

Now, those old reliable products have gained so much market share that they are again the envy of the industry. So is the company's stock price, which has climbed 58%, to $92 a share, since Lafley started, while the Standard & Poor's 500-stock index has declined 32%. Banc of America analyst William H. Steele forecasts that P&G's profits for its current fiscal year, which ended June 30, will rise by 13%, to $5.57 billion, on an 8% increase in sales, to $43.23 billion. That exceeds most rivals'. Volume growth has averaged 7% over the past six quarters, excluding acquisitions, well above Lafley's goal and the industry average.

The conventional thinking is that the soft-spoken Lafley was exactly the antidote P&G needed after Jager. After all, Jager had charged into office determined to rip apart P&G's insular culture and remake it from the bottom up. Instead of pushing P&G to excel, however, the torrent of proclamations and initiatives during Jager's 17-month reign nearly brought the venerable company to a grinding halt.

Enter Lafley. A 23-year P&G veteran, he wasn't supposed to bring fundamental change; he was asked simply to restore the company's equilibrium. In fact, he came in warning that Jager had tried to implement too many changes too quickly (which Jager readily admits now). Since then, the mild-mannered 56-year-old chief executive has worked to revive both urgency and hope: urgency because, in the previous 15 years, P&G had developed exactly one successful new brand, the Swiffer dust mop; and hope because, after Jager, employees needed reassurance that the old ways still had value. Clearly, Lafley has undone the damage at P&G.

What's less obvious is that, in his quiet way, Lafley has proved to be even more of a revolutionary than the flamboyant Jager. Lafley is leading the most sweeping transformation of the company since it was founded by William Procter and James Gamble in 1837 as a maker of soap and candles (Exhibit 1). Long before he became CEO, Lafley had been pondering how to make P&G relevant in the 21st century, when speed and agility would matter more than heft. As president of North American operations, he even spoke with Jager about the need to remake the company.

So how has Lafley succeeded where Jager so spectacularly failed? In a word, style. Where Jager was gruff, Lafley is soothing. Where Jager bullied, Lafley persuades. He listens more than he talks. He is living proof that the messenger is just as important as the message. As he says, "I'm not a screamer, not a yeller. But don't get confused by my style. I am very decisive." Or as Robert A. McDonald, president of P&G's global fabric and home-care division, says, "people want to follow him. I frankly love him like my brother."

Indeed, Lafley's charm offensive has so disarmed most P&Gers that he has been able to change the company profoundly (Exhibit 2). He is responsible for P&G's largest acquisitions ever, buying Clairol in 2001

EXHIBIT 1
Lafley's Vision

Outsourcing If it's not a core function the new P&G won't do it. Info tech and bar-soap manufacturing have already been contracted out. Other jobs will follow.

Acquisitions Not everything has to be invented in company labs. Lafley wants half of all new-product ideas to come from the outside.

Building Staff Managers are under much closer scrutiny, as Lafley scans the ranks for the best and the brightest and singles them out for development.

Brand Expansion The Crest line now includes an electric toothbrush and tooth-whitening products along with toothpaste. Lafley is making similar moves elsewhere.

Pricing P&G isn't just the premium-priced brand. It will go to the lower end if that's where opportunity lies.

EXHIBIT 2 P&G Turning the Tide

Data: Banc America securities.

Fabric and Home Care	Beauty Care	Baby and Family Care	Health Care	Snacks and Beverages
Lafley has aggressively cut costs in the company's largest division. But Tide in particular faces intense competition from lower-priced rivals. To compensate, Lafley is introducing high-margin products, such as the Swiffer Duster.	Lafley has quickly expanded this business by acquiring Clairol and Wella. But the company has less expertise here and still has to prove it can grow internally.	P&G now vies with Kimberly-Clark to dominate the disposable-diaper market. But competition has pushed prices down, which is why this division has the slowest profit-margin growth.	With its SpinBrush and tooth-whitening products, P&G has regained the lead in oral care from Colgate. The division will get a lift from distributing heart-burn drug Prilosec over the counter. But the pharmaceutical business depends on one big seller, Actonel for osteoporosis.	Because the division generates the company's lowest profit margins many expect Lafley to continue to extricate P&G from these businesses. He has already sold Crisco and Jiff to J.M. Smuckers.
Sales* 29%	Sales 28%	Sales 23%	Sales 13%	Sales 7%
Operating Profit Margin 25%	Operating Profit Margin 23%	Operating Profit Margin 17%	Operating Profit Margin 18%	Operating Profit Margin 15%
Outlook Very Good	Outlook Good	Outlook Good	Outlook Mixed	Outlook Weak

*Share of total sales. Estimates for fiscal year ending June 30, 2003

for $5 billion and agreeing to purchase Germany's Wella in March for a price that now reaches $7 billion. He has replaced more than half of the company's top 30 officers, more than any P&G boss in memory, and cut 9,600 jobs. And he has moved more women into senior positions. Lafley skipped over 78 general managers with more seniority to name 42-year-old Deborah A. Henretta to head P&G's then-troubled North American baby-care division. "The speed at which A.G. has gotten results is five years ahead of the time I expected," says Scott Cook, founder of software maker Intuit Inc., who joined P&G's board shortly after Lafley's appointment.

Still, the Lafley revolution is far from over. Precisely because of his achievements, Lafley is now under enormous pressure to return P&G to what it considers its rightful place in Corporate America: a company that is admired, imitated, and uncommonly profitable. Nowhere are those expectations more apparent than on the second floor of headquarters, where three former chief executives still keep offices. John Pepper, a popular former boss who returned briefly as chairman when

Jager left but gave up the post to Lafley last year, leans forward in his chair as he says: "It's now clear to me that A.G. is going to be one of the great CEOs in this company's history."

But here's the rub: What Lafley envisions may be far more radical than what Pepper has in mind. Consider a confidential memo that circulated among P&G's top brass in late 2001 and angered Pepper for its audacity. It argued that P&G could be cut to 25,000 employees, a quarter of its current size. Acknowledging the memo, Lafley admits: "It terrified our organization."

Lafley didn't write the infamous memo, but he may as well have. It reflects the central tenet of his vision—that P&G should do only what it does best, nothing more. Lafley wants a more outwardly focused, flexible company. That has implications for every facet of the business, from manufacturing to innovation. For example, in April he turned over all bar-soap manufacturing, including Ivory, P&G's oldest surviving brand, to a Canadian contractor. In May, he outsourced P&G's information-technology operation to Hewlett-Packard Co.

No bastion has been more challenged than P&G's research and development operations. Lafley has confronted head-on the stubbornly held notion that everything must be invented within P&G, asserting that half of its new products should come from the outside. (P&G now gets about 20% of its ideas externally—up from about 10% when he took over.) "He's absolutely breaking many well-set molds at P&G," says eBay Inc.'s CEO, Margaret C. "Meg" Whitman, whom Lafley appointed to the board.

Lafley's quest to remake P&G could still come to grief. As any scientist will attest, buying innovation is tricky. Picking the winners from other labs is notoriously difficult and often expensive. And P&G will remain uncomfortably reliant on Wal-Mart Stores Inc., which accounts for nearly a fifth of its sales. Lafley is looking to pharmaceuticals and beauty care for growth, where the margins are high but where P&G has considerably less experience than rivals.

The biggest risk, though, is that Lafley will lose the P&Gers themselves. Theirs is a culture famously resistant to new ideas. To call the company insular may not do it justice. Employees aren't kidding when they say they're a family. They often start out there and grow up together at P&G, which only promotes from within. Cincinnati itself is a small town: Employees live near one another, they go to the same health clubs and restaurants. They are today's company men and women—and proud of it.

Lafley is well aware of his predicament. On a June evening, as he sits on the patio behind his home, he muses about just that. The house, which resembles a Tuscan villa and overlooks the Ohio River and downtown Cincinnati, is infused with P&G history. Lafley bought it from former CEO John G. Smale three years before he was named chief executive. A black-and-gold stray cat the family feeds sits a few feet away and watches Lafley as he sips a Beck's beer. The clouds threaten rain. "I am worried that I will ask the organization to change ahead of its understanding, capability, and commitment," Lafley admits.

For most of its 166 years, P&G was one of America's preeminent companies. Its brands are icons: It launched Tide in 1946 and Pampers, the first disposable diaper, in 1961. Its marketing was innovative: In the 1880s, P&G was one of the first companies to advertise nationally. Fifty years later, P&G invented the soap opera by sponsoring the *Ma Perkins* radio show and, later, *Guiding Light.*

Its management techniques, meanwhile, became the gold standard: In the 1930s, P&G developed the idea of brand management—setting up marketing teams for each brand and urging them to compete against each other. P&G has long been the business world's finest training ground. General Electric Co.'s Jeffrey R. Immelt and 3M's W. James McNerney Jr. both started out on Ivory. Meg Whitman and Steven M. Case were in toilet goods, while Steven A. Ballmer was an assistant product manager for Duncan Hines cake mix, among other goods. They, of course, went on to lead eBay, AOL Time Warner and Microsoft (Exhibit 3).

But by the 1990s, P&G was in danger of becoming another Eastman Kodak Co. or Xerox Corp., a once-great company that had lost its way. Sales on most of its 18 top brands were slowing; the company was being outhustled by more focused rivals such as Kimberly-Clark Corp. and Colgate-Palmolive Co. The only way P&G kept profits growing was by cutting costs, hardly a strategy for the long term. At the same time, the dynamics of the industry were changing as power shifted from manufacturers to massive retailers. Through all of this, much of senior management was in denial. "Nobody wanted to talk about it," Lafley says. "Without a doubt, Durk and I and a few others were in the camp of 'We need a much bigger change.'"

When Jager took over in January, 1999, he was hell-bent on providing just that—with disastrous results. He introduced expensive new products that never caught on while letting existing brands drift. He wanted to buy two huge pharmaceutical companies, a plan that threatened

EXHIBIT 3 P&G's Family Tree

The CEOs who preceded Lafley launched ambitious projects but also oversaw a gradual erosion of P&G's core brands.

1981–90	1990–95	1995–99	1999–2000
John Smale moves P&G into the health-care and beauty business, which becomes central to the company. His decision to expand its food and beverage division doesn't amount to nearly as much.	Edwin Artzt helps bring P&G to the world, and cosmetics to P&G, through the purchase of Max Factor and Cover Girl. But sales of major brands slow—as international expansion and new-product launches take precedence.	John Pepper pushes into developing markets such as China and Russia and starts to revamp the company's international structure. But sales remain weak, and much of P&G's profit gains come from cost-cutting.	Durk Jagar tries to jump-start innovation by launching expensive new products, which flop, and by trying to shake up P&G's stodgy culture, which quickly demoralizes many employees.

P&G's identity but never was carried out. And he put in place a companywide reorganization that left many employees perplexed and preoccupied. Soaring commodity prices, unfavorable currency trends, and a tech-crazed stock market didn't help either. At a company prized for consistent earnings, Jager missed forecasts twice in six months. In his first and last full fiscal year, earnings per share rose by just 3.5% instead of an estimated 13%. And during that time, the share price slid 52%, cutting P&G's total market capitalization by $85 billion. Employees and retirees hold about 20% of the stock. The family began to turn against its leader.

But Jager's greatest failing was his scorn for the family. Jager, a Dutchman who had joined P&G overseas and worked his way to corporate headquarters, pitted himself against the P&G culture, contending that it was burdensome and insufferable, says Susan E. Arnold, president of P&G's beauty and feminine care division. Some go-ahead employees even wore buttons that read "Old World/New World" to express disdain for P&G's past. "I never wore one," Arnold sneers. "'The old Procter is bad, and the new world is good.' That didn't work."

On June 6, 2000, his 30th wedding anniversary, Lafley was in San Francisco when he received a call from Pepper, then a board member: Would he become CEO? Back in Cincinnati, a boardroom coup unprecedented in P&G's history had taken place.

As Lafley steps into the small study in his house three years later, a Japanese drawing on the wall reminds him of what it was like to become CEO. The room, with its painting of a samurai warrior and red elephant-motif wallpaper, alludes to his stint running P&G's Asian operations. Bookshelves hold leather-bound volumes of Joseph Conrad and Mark Twain. A simple wooden desk faces the window. Lafley focuses on the drawing, which depicts a man caught in a spider's web; it was given to him by the elder of his two sons, Patrick. "In the first few days, you are just trying to figure out what kind of web it is," he says.

In a sense, Lafley had been preparing for this job his entire adult life. He never hid the fact that he wanted to run P&G one day. Or if not the company, then a company. That itself is unusual since, like almost all P&Gers, Lafley has never worked anywhere else. After graduating from Hamilton College in 1969, Lafley decided to pursue a doctorate in medieval and Renaissance history at the University of Virginia. But he dropped out in his first year to join the Navy (and avoid being drafted into the Army). He served in Japan, where he got his first experience as a merchandiser, supplying Navy retail stores. When his tour of duty ended in 1975, he enrolled in the MBA program at Harvard Business School. And from there, he went directly to Cincinnati.

When he was hired as a brand assistant for Joy dish detergent in 1977 at age 29, he was older than most of his colleagues and he worried that his late start might hinder his rise at P&G. Twice within a year in the early 1980s, Lafley quit. "Each time, I talked him back in only after drinking vast amounts of Drambuie," says Thomas A. Moore, his boss at the time, who now runs biotech company Biopure Corp. On the second occasion, then-CEO John Smale met with Lafley, who had accepted a job as a consultant in Connecticut. Without making any promises, Smale says he told Lafley that "we thought there was no limit on where he was going to go."

Sure enough, Lafley climbed quickly to head P&G's soap and detergent business, where he introduced Liquid Tide in 1984. A decade later, he was promoted to head the Asian division. Lafley returned from Kobe, Japan, to Cincinnati in 1998 to run the company's entire North

American operations. To ease the transition home, he and his younger son, Alex, who was then 12, studied guitar together. Two years later, Lafley was named CEO.

Along the way, he developed a reputation as a boss who stepped back to give his staff plenty of responsibility and helped shape decisions by asking a series of keen questions—a process he calls "peeling the onion." And he retained a certain humility. He still collects baseball cards, comic books, and rock 'n' roll 45s. Whereas some executives might have a garage full of antique cars or Harley-Davidsons; Lafley keeps two Vespa motor scooters. "People wanted him to succeed," says Virginia Lee, a former P&Ger who worked for Lafley at headquarters and overseas.

As CEO, Lafley hasn't made grand pronouncements on the future of P&G. Instead, he has spent an inordinate amount of time patiently communicating how he wants P&G to change. In a company famed for requiring employees to describe every new course of action in a one-page memo, Lafley's preferred approach is the slogan. For example, he felt that P&G was letting technology rather than consumer needs dictate new products. Ergo: "The consumer is boss." P&G wasn't working closely enough with retailers, the place where consumers first see the product on the shelf: "The first moment of truth." P&G wasn't concerned enough with the consumer's experience at home: "The second moment of truth."

Lafley uses these phrases constantly, and they are echoed throughout the organization. At the end of a three-day leadership seminar, 30 young marketing managers from around the world present what they have learned to Lafley. First on the list: "We are the voice of the consumer within P&G, and they are the heart of all we do." Lafley, dressed in a suit, sits on a stool in front of the group and beams. "I love the first one," he laughs as the room erupts in applause.

When he talks about his choice of words later, Lafley is a tad self-conscious. "It's *Sesame Street* language—I admit that," he says. "A lot of what we have done is make things simple because the difficulty is making sure everybody knows what the goal is and how to get there."

Lafley has also mastered the art of the symbolic gesture. The 11th floor at corporate headquarters had been the redoubt of senior executives since the 1950s. Lafley did away with it, moving all five division presidents to the same floors as their staff. Then he turned some of the space into a leadership training center. On the rest of the floor, he knocked down the walls so that the remaining executives, including himself, share open offices. Lafley sits next to the two people he talks to the most, which, in true P&G style, was officially established by a flow study: HR head Antoine and Vice-Chairman Bruce Byrnes. As if the Sunday night meetings with Antoine weren't proof enough of Lafley's determination to make sure the best people rise to the top. And Byrnes, whom Lafley refers to as "Yoda"—the sage-like *Star Wars* character—gets a lot of face time because of his marketing expertise. As Lafley says, "the assets at P&G are what? Our people and our brands."

Just as emblematic of the Lafley era is the floor's new conference room, where he and P&G's 12 other top executives meet every Monday at 8 a.m. to review results, plan strategy, and set the drumbeat for the week. The table used to be rectangular; now it's round. The execs used to sit where they were told; now they sit where they like. At one of those meetings, an outsider might have trouble distinguishing the CEO: He occasionally joins in the discussion, but most of the time the executives talk as much to each other as to Lafley. "I am more like a coach," Lafley says afterward. "I am always looking for different combinations that will get better results." Jeff Immelt, who asked Lafley to join GE's board in 2002, describes him as "an excellent listener. He's a sponge."

And now, Lafley is carefully using this information to reshape the company's approach to just about everything it does. When Lafley describes the P&G of the future, he says: "We're in the business of creating and building brands." Notice, as P&Gers certainly have, that he makes no mention of manufacturing. While Lafley shies away from saying just how much of the company's factory and back-office operations he may hand over to someone else, he does admit that facing up to the realities of the marketplace "won't always be fun." Of P&G's 102,000 employees, nearly one-half work in its plants. So far, "Lafley has deftly handled the outsourcing deals, which has lessened fear within P&G," says Roger Martin, a close adviser of Lafley's who is dean of the University of Toronto's Joseph L. Rotman School of Management. All 2,000 of the information-technology workers were moved over to HP. At the bar-soap operations, based entirely in Cincinnati, 200 of the 250 employees went to work for the Canadian contractor.

Lafley's approach to selling P&G products is unprecedented at the company, too: He argues that P&G doesn't have to produce just premium-priced goods. So now there's a cheaper formulation for Crest in China. The Clairol deal gave P&G bargain shampoos such as Daily Defense. And with Lafley's encouragement, managers have looked at their most expensive products to make sure they aren't too costly. In many cases, they've actually lowered the prices.

And Lafley is pushing P&G to approach its brands more creatively. Crest, for example, isn't just about toothpaste anymore: There's also an electric toothbrush, SpinBrush, which P&G acquired in January, 2001 (see Appendix). P&G is also willing to license its own technologies to get them to the marketplace faster. It joined with Clorox Co., maker of Glad Bags, last October to share a food-wrap technology it had developed. It was unprecedented for P&G to work with a competitor, says licensing head Jeffrey Weedman. The overall effect is undeniable. "Lafley has made P&G far more flexible," says Banc of America's Steele.

But Lafley still faces daunting challenges. Keeping up the earnings growth, for example, will get tougher as competitors fight back and as P&G winds down a large restructuring program—started under Jager but accelerated under Lafley. Furthermore, some of the gains in profit have resulted from cuts in capital and R&D spending, which Lafley has pared back to the levels of the company's rivals. And already, P&G has missed a big opportunity: It passed up the chance to buy water-soluble strips that contain mouthwash. Now, Listerine is making a bundle on the product.

Nor are all investors comfortable with growth through acquisitions. The deals make it harder for investors to decipher earnings growth from existing operations. Then there's the risk of fumbling the integration, notes Arthur B. Cecil, an analyst at T. Rowe Price Group Inc., which holds 1.74 million P&G shares. "I would prefer they not make acquisitions," he says. Already, Clairol hair color, the most important product in P&G's recent purchase, has lost five points of market share to L'Oréal in the U.S., according to ACNeilsen Corp.

Making deals, however, could be the only way to balance P&G's growing reliance on Wal-Mart. Former and current P&G employees say the discounter could account for one-third of P&G's global sales by the end of the decade. Meanwhile, the pressure from consumers and competitors to keep prices low will only increase. "P&G has improved its ability to take on those challenges, but those challenges are still there," says Lehman analyst Ann Gillin.

Still, Lafley may be uniquely suited to creating a new and improved P&G. Even Jager agrees that Lafley was just what the company needed. "He has calmed down the confusion that happened while I was there," says the former CEO. Jager left a letter on Lafley's desk the day he resigned telling his successor not to feel responsible for his fall. "You earned it," he recalls writing. "Don't start out with guilt."

Lafley says he learned from Jager's biggest mistake. "I avoided saying P&G people were bad," he says. "I enrolled them in change." Lafley, a company man through and through, just can't resist trying out a new slogan.

Source: Robert Berner, "P&G", *BusinessWeek,* July 7, 2003, 52–63.

Appendix to Case 6-17

Darin S. Yates had watched many consumer focus groups at Procter & Gamble Co., but he had never witnessed a response like this. Out of a panel of 24 consumers evaluating a new electric toothbrush, 23 raved about the product, begging to take it home. "We were just blown away," the 36-year-old brand manager recalls.

But Yates, team leader on the new toothbrush, never imagined how successful the Crest SpinBrush would be. While most electric brushes cost more than $50, SpinBrush works on batteries and sells for just $5. Since that focus group in October 2000, it has become the nation's best-selling toothbrush, manual or electric. In P&G's last fiscal year, it posted more than $200 million in global sales, helping Crest become the consumer-product maker's 12th billion-dollar brand. It has also helped Crest reclaim the title as No. 1 oral-care brand in the U.S., a position it lost to Colgate-Palmolive's Colgate brand in 1998. "It's hard for P&G's business models to conceive of a business growing as quickly as SpinBrush," Yates says.

One reason is that P&G didn't conceive SpinBrush to begin with. Four Cleveland-area entrepreneurs developed the gizmo in 1998 with the idea of selling it to P&G. They parlayed a $1.5 million investment into a $475 million payout. Three of them even went on the P&G payroll for a year and a half to shepherd the product—something unheard of at the insular company. Says John Osher, the lead entrepreneur behind SpinBrush: "My job was to not allow P&G to screw it up."

SpinBrush marks a dramatic departure for the 165-year-old company. For once, P&G didn't insist on controlling every step, from product development to pricing. Instead, it harnessed its greatest strength—the ability to market and distribute products—to the innovation and risk-taking ability of a tiny startup that wasn't constrained by the culture inside P&G's Cincinnati headquarters. The strategy is not without risks or cultural challenges. P&G had to bend on how it packaged, manufactured, shipped, and worked its mighty marketing machine. And the story isn't over: The SpinBrush founders question if the product will reach its potential once it is fully enveloped in P&G's big-company culture. "I'm not sure you can teach an elephant to dance," Osher says.

Even so, the acquisition of SpinBrush says a lot about the leadership of Alan G. Lafley, who became chief executive in June 2000, when predecessor Durk I. Jager was ousted. Jager, a combative change agent, had pushed P&G to ramp up development of new products. He shook P&G's identity with proposals to buy two large pharmaceutical companies. In the end he overreached, missing earnings forecasts.

Lafley has been more deft. He has refocused the company on the big brands that drive earnings, including Pampers, Tide, and Crest. Like Jager, he has made acquisitions. But the $4.9 billion purchase of Clairol, P&G's largest ever, and SpinBrush have been closer to P&G's core strengths in hair and oral care than Jager's forays with Iams pet food and PUR water-filter systems.

Those moves have helped Lafley find a balance between sales and profit growth—something that eluded his predecessor. P&G has exceeded Wall Street's earnings estimates in the last three reported quarters, while at the same time increasing share in its markets through higher promotional and ad spending. For the fiscal year ended June 30, analysts expect P&G's operating earnings to climb 9% to $5 billion, reversing a prior-year decline. Such gains will get harder, though, as savings from a $6 billion restructuring started under Jager start to wind down.

Still, Lafley is proving to be a radical strategic thinker by P&G standards. When Kimberly-Clark Corp. launched a moist toilet paper last year, he went against P&G's make-it-here mentality by acquiring a manufacturer of a similar product. That let him parry Kimberly more quickly and tied up less money in the capital-intensive business. Recent negotiations to outsource P&G's 6,000-employee, back-office operations would also have been unlikely at the old P&G. The move reflects Lafley's efforts to focus the company on its core strengths and suggests further payroll cuts ahead.

The SpinBrush saga also shows a new recognition that not all great ideas originate at P&G. Lafley has made clear that as many as a third of P&G's new product ideas may come from outside, and he has stepped up efforts to identify and acquire other small companies. But perhaps the biggest change for P&G was in SpinBrush's pricing. P&G usually prices its goods at a premium, based on the cost of technology. But competitors now follow new products more quickly, eroding P&G's pricing power. With SpinBrush, P&G reversed its usual thinking. It started with an aggressive price, then found a way to make a profit. If P&G had conceived SpinBrush, admits Yates, "my gut tells me we would not have priced it where we did."

That's just the opportunity John Osher and his three colleagues saw when they had the SpinBrush brainstorm back in 1998. Osher, 55, had spent most of his career inventing things and selling them to big companies. His latest creation had been the Spin Pop, a lollipop attached to a battery-powered plastic handle, in which the candy spun at the press of a button. He had teamed up on the Spin Pop with John R. Nottingham and John W. Spirk, the principals of a Cleveland industrial design firm, and their in-house patent lawyer, Lawrence A. Blaustein. The Spin Pop had recently sold to Hasbro for millions and the men were looking for another way to utilize the technology.

They can't remember who came up with the concept, but they know it came from their group walks through the aisles of their local Wal-Mart, where they went for inspiration. They saw that electric toothbrushes, from Sonicare to Interplak, cost more than $50 and for that

EXHIBIT 4 Different Strokes for P&G

The marketing giant broke a lot of its own rules when it launched the SpinBrush. Here's what it did:

Looked Outside	Empowered the Inventors	Got Aggressive on Price
SpinBrush wasn't invented at P&G. Instead, the company bought it from a group of entrepreneurs.	To make sure the new toothbrush didn't get smothered by the P&G bureaucracy, the inventors were hired for the first year to help with everything from packaging to logistics.	Instead of starting at the high end and cutting prices as competitors moved in, P&G started low and made it harder for newcomers to steal market share.

reason held a fraction of the overall toothbrush market. They reasoned: Why not create a $5 electric brush using the Spin Pop technology? At just $1 more than the most expensive manual brushes, they figured many consumers would trade up. They spent 18 months designing and sourcing a high-quality brush that wouldn't cost more than $5, batteries included. "If it had cost $7.99, we wouldn't have gone forward," Osher says.

They also formulated an exit strategy: Sell it to P&G. In 1998, they saw that Colgate toothpaste was dethroning Crest, the market champ since the early 1960s. Colgate edged out Crest by launching Total and pitching it around the new theme of whitening. P&G, meanwhile, clung to its cavity-fighting message. Colgate gained 5.6 percentage points of market share in 1998, giving the company 29.6% of the market, vs. P&G's 25.6%. "We knew that P&G would be very hungry," says Nottingham.

But first they had to prove the product could sell. They couldn't afford to advertise and sell SpinBrush at that low price. So they resorted to the marketing ploy they used with Spin Pop: packaging that said, "Try Me" and that allowed the consumer to turn the brush on in the store. They also hired a former Clorox salesman, Joseph A. O'Connor, who had years of experience selling to Wal-Mart and other big chains.

When they tested SpinBrush in Meijer Inc., a Midwest discount chain, in October 1999, it outsold the leading manual brush nearly 3 to 1, convincing Meijer to carry it. Using that sales data, they cracked drugstore chain Walgreen Co. and caught the interest of Wal-Mart in early 2000. To help close that deal, O'Connor persuaded a health and beauty aid manager at a Phoenix Wal-Mart to buy 240 SpinBrushes. "They sold out over the weekend," he recalls.

In 2000, the entrepreneurs sold 10 million SpinBrush units, more than triple the existing 3 million U.S. electric toothbrush market. With that record, it wasn't hard for Osher to get an appointment at P&G in July. The company had another reason to take notice: Colgate's recently launched ActiBrush electric toothbrush, at $19.95, was off to a fast start, too.

Yates, a financial manager on the Crest brand, headed a team to evaluate SpinBrush. P&G code-named the project Julius, after basketball great Julius Erving. With approval to negotiate a purchase and focus group reactions off the charts, Yates moved fast. A deal to buy the startup closed in January, 2001, six months after the first meeting with Osher.

The deal's structure was unprecedented for P&G. Instead of paying a lump sum, P&G would pay $165 million up-front with an "earn-out" payment in three years based on a formula pegged to financial results. The up-front payment alone—nearly four times SpinBrush's prior year sales of $43 million—was rich by P&G's standards. The company paid three times sales for Clairol. But P&G was banking on faster sales growth from SpinBrush.

The deal had another unique feature: Osher, Blaustein, and O'Connor agreed to join the company for the three-year earn-out period with a mandate of keeping the business entrepreneurial. They would become part of a 27-person team headed by Yates that would have authority to bend any P&G rules that interfered with the business. The entrepreneurs would guide the team and had carte blanche to go higher within P&G to resolve conflicts.

And there were conflicts aplenty. Some P&Gers questioned the "Try Me" feature, fearing the batteries would wear out. Others wanted to stop store deliveries for three months so P&G could build inventories. Still others worried about having more automated factories in China. In the end, though, "they would listen to us and fight their own bureaucracy," says Osher.

Yates broke the the biggest rule of all for a company whose heritage is in marketing—he didn't advertise SpinBrush for the first seven months. The traditional P&G model for a launch calls for heavy TV advertising from the outset and a high enough price to help carry that cost. But Yates didn't want the ad expense, which could force him to raise prices, until sales could support it. "I didn't want to mess up the economic structure of the business," he says.

P&G now sells SpinBrush in about 35 countries, marking its quickest global rollout ever. And it's added a multitude of models, including ones with replaceable heads. Colgate earlier this year launched Motion, a SpinBrush look-alike, at the same price. In a recent earnings conference call, Colgate CEO Reuben Mark admitted that the company had cut the price of ActiBrush from $19 to $12 because of the competition.

P&G and the SpinBrush founders agreed to an early payout in March, 21 months ahead of schedule. Osher's employment contract ended that month, and O'Connor's and Blaustein's ended in June. P&G pushed for the deal because SpinBrush's sales so far exceeded plans that the company faced the prospect of a much bigger payout if it waited, Osher says. The founders settled on a final payment of $310 million. The total price of $475 million was about 2.3 times last fiscal year's sales, a price some analysts consider a steal.

But Osher and his partners had their own reason for getting out early—they wanted to hedge their bets. They're uncertain whether SpinBrush will live up to its potential as it is further folded into P&G. Osher had an exit interview with Lafley in May in which the CEO vowed to keep SpinBrush on course. Osher has no doubt about Lafley's sincerity. It's just that he is still not sure an elephant can learn to dance.

By Robert Berner in Chicago

Source: "Why P&G's Smile Is So Bright," *BusinessWeek*, August 12, 2002, 58–60.

Case 6-18

Hewlett-Packard Co.

Since taking over as chief executive of Hewlett-Packard Co. 18 months ago, Carleton S. "Carly" Fiorina has pushed the company to the limit to recapture the form that made it a management icon for six decades. Last November, it looked like she might have pushed too hard. After weeks of promising that HP would meet its quarterly numbers, Fiorina got grim news from the finance department. While sales growth beat expectations, profits had fallen $230 million short. The culprit, in large part, was Fiorina's aggressive management makeover. With HP's 88,000 staffers adjusting to the biggest reorganization in the company's history, expenses had risen out of control. And since new computer systems to track the changes weren't yet in place, HP's bean counters didn't detect the problem until 10 days after the quarter was over. "It was frantic. The financial folk were running all around looking for more dollars," says one HP manager.

One might expect a CEO in this spot to dial down on such a massive overhaul. Not Fiorina. After crunching numbers in an all-day session on Saturday and offering apologies for missing the forecast to HP's board at an emergency meeting Sunday, Fiorina told analysts she was raising HP's sales growth target for fiscal 2001 from 15% to as much as 17%. "We hit a speed bump—a big speed bump—this quarter," she said in a speech broadcast to employees a few days later. "But does it mean, 'Gee, this is too hard?' No way. In blackjack, you double down when you have an increasing probability of winning. And we're going to double down."

The stakes couldn't be higher—both for Fiorina and for the Silicon Valley pioneer started in a Palo Alto garage in 1938. Just as founders Bill Hewlett and David Packard broke the mold back then by eliminating hierarchies and introducing innovations such as profit-sharing and cubicles, Fiorina is betting on an approach so radical that experts say it has never been tried before at a company of HP's size and complexity. What's more, management gurus haven't a clue as to whether it will work—though the early signs suggest it may be too much, too fast. Not content to tackle one problem at a time, Fiorina is out to transform all aspects of HP at once, current economic slowdown be damned. That means strategy, structure, culture, compensation—everything from how to spark innovation to how to streamline internal processes. Such sweeping change is tough anywhere, and doubly so at tradition-bound HP. The reorganization will be "hard to do—and there's not much DNA for it at HP," says Jay R. Galbraith, professor at the Institute for Management Development in Lausanne, Switzerland.

Fiorina believes she has little choice. Her goal is to mix up a powerful cocktail of changes that will lift HP from its slow-growth funk of recent years before the company suffers a near-death experience similar to the one IBM endured 10 years ago and that Xerox and others are going through now. The conundrum for these behemoths: how to put the full force of the company behind winning in today's fiercely competitive technology business when they must also cook up brand-new megamarkets? It's a riddle, says Fiorina, that she can solve only by sweeping action that will ready HP for the next stage of the technology revolution, when companies latch on to the Internet to transform their operations. "We looked in the mirror and saw a great company that was becoming a failure," Fiorina told employees. "This is the vision Bill and Dave would have had if they were sitting here today."

At its core lies a conviction that HP must become "ambidextrous." Like a constantly mutating organism, the new HP is supposed to strike a balance: It should excel at short-term execution while pursuing long-term visions that create new markets. It should increase sales and profits in harmony rather than sacrifice one to gain the other. And HP will emphasize it all—technology, software, and consulting in every corner of computing, combining the product excellence of a Sun Microsystems Inc. with IBM's services strength.

To achieve this, Fiorina has dismantled the decentralized approach honed throughout HP's 64-year history.

Until last year, HP was a collection of independently run units, each focused on a product such as scanners or security software. Fiorina has collapsed those into four sprawling organizations (Exhibit 1). One so-called back-end unit develops and builds computers, and another focuses on printers and imaging equipment. The back-end divisions hand products off to two "front-end" sales and marketing groups that peddle the wares—one to consumers, the other to corporations. The theory: The new structure will boost collaboration, giving sales and marketing execs a direct pipeline to engineers so products are developed from the ground up to solve customer problems. This is the first time a company with thousands of product lines and scores of businesses has attempted a front-back approach, a strategy that requires laser focus and superb coordination.

Just as radical is Fiorina's plan for unleashing creativity. She calls it "inventing at the intersection." Until now, HP has made stand-alone products, from $20 ink cartridges to $3 million Internet servers. By tying them all together, HP hopes to sniff out new markets at the junctions where the products meet. The new HP, she says, will excel at dreaming up new e-services and then making the gear to deliver them. By yearend, for example, HP customers should be able to call up a photo stored on the Net using a handheld gizmo and then wirelessly zap it to a nearby printer. To create such opportunities, HP has launched three "cross-company initiatives"—wireless services, digital imaging, and commercial printing—that are the first formal effort to get all of HP's warring tribes working together.

EXHIBIT 1 HP the Fiorina Way

When Fiorina arrived at HP, the company was a confederation of 83 autonomous product units reporting through four groups. She radically revamped the structure into two "back-end" divisions–one developing printers, scanners, and the like, and the other computers. These report to "front-end" groups that market HP's wares. Here's how the overhaul stacks up:

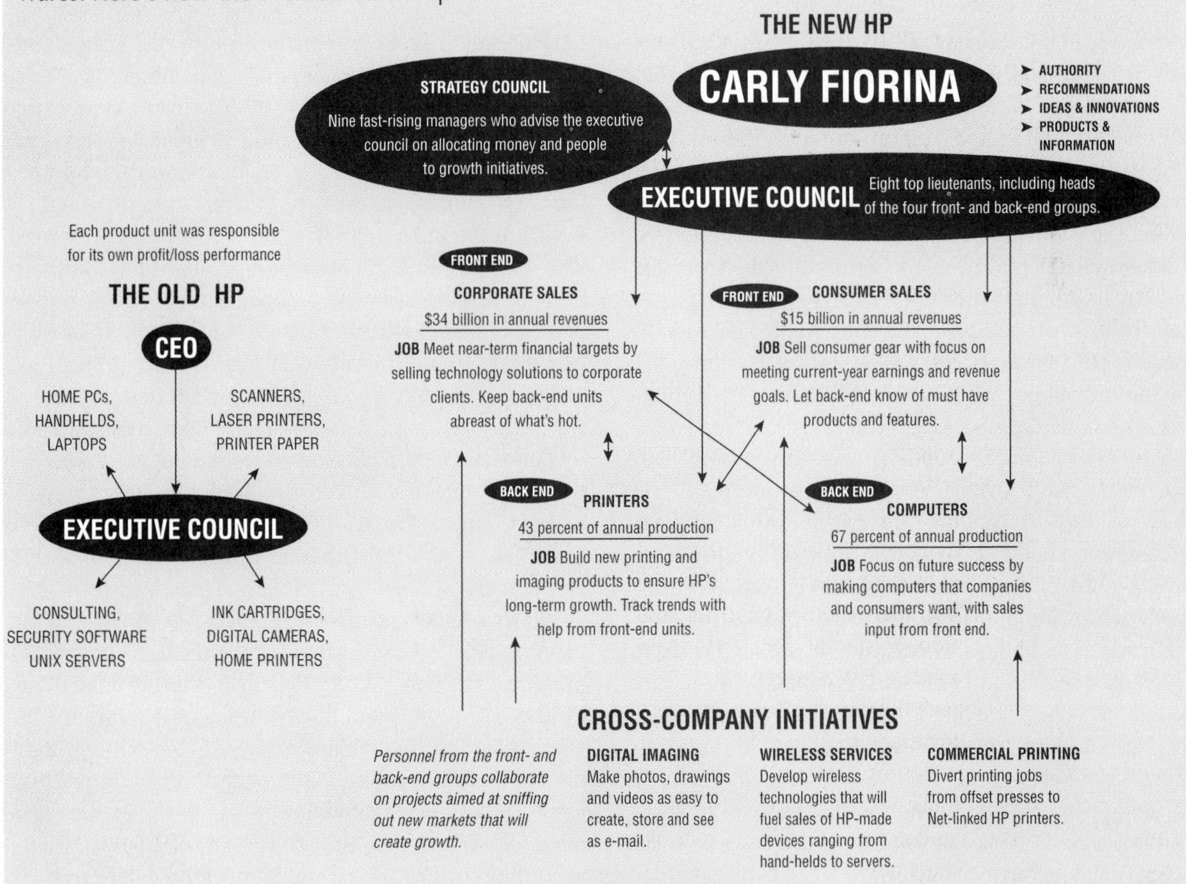

EXHIBIT 2 The Assessment

Benefits

HAPPIER CUSTOMERS Clients should find HP easier to deal with, since they'll work with just one account team.

SALES BOOST HP should maximize its selling opportunities because account reps will sell all HP products, not just those from one division.

REAL SOLUTIONS HP can sell its products in combination as "solution"—instead of just PCs or printers—to companies facing e-business problems.

FINANCIAL FLEXIBILITY With all corporate sales under one roof, HP can measure the total value of a customer, allowing reps to discount some products and still maximize profits on the overall contract.

Risks

OVERWHELMED WITH DUTIES With so many products being made and sold by just four units, HP execs have more on their plates and could miss the details that keep products competitive.

POORER EXECUTION When product managers oversaw everything from manufacturing to sales, they could respond quickly to changes. That will be harder with front-and back-end groups synching their plans only every few weeks.

LESS ACCOUNTABILITY Profit-and-loss responsibility is shared between the front-and back-end groups so no one person is on the hot seat. Finger-pointing and foot-dragging could replace HP's collegial cooperation.

FEWER SPENDING CONTROLS With powerful division chiefs keeping a tight rein on the purse strings, spending rarely got out of hand in the old HP. In the fourth quarter, expenses soared as those lines of command broke down.

Will her grand plan work? (Exhibit 2). It's still the petri-dish phase of the experiment, so it's too soon to say. But the initial results are troubling. While she had early success, the reorganization started to run aground nine months ago. Cushy commissions intended to light a fire under HP's sales force boosted sales, but mostly for low-margin products that did little for corporate profits. A more fundamental problem stems directly from the front-back structure: It doesn't clearly assign responsibility for profits and losses, meaning it's tough to diagnose and fix earnings screwups—especially since no individual manager will take the heat for missed numbers. And with staffers in 120 countries, redrawing the lines of communication and getting veterans of rival divisions to work together is proving nettlesome. "The people who deal with Carly directly feel very empowered, but everyone else is running around saying, 'What do we do now?'" says one HP manager. Another problem: Much of the burden of running HP lands squarely on Fiorina's shoulders. Some insiders and analysts say she needs a second-in-command to manage day-to-day operations. "She's playing CEO, visionary, and COO, and that's too hard to do," says Sanford C. Bernstein analyst Toni Sacconaghi.

Fiorina gets frosty at the notion that her restructuring is hitting snags. "This is a multiyear effort," she says. "I always would have characterized Year Two as harder than Year One because this is when the change really gets binding. I actually think our fourth-quarter miss and the current slowing economy are galvanizing us. When things are going well, you can convince yourself that change isn't as necessary as you thought." Fiorina also dismisses the need for a COO: "I'm running the business the way I think it ought to be run."

If Fiorina pulls this off, she'll be tech's newest hero. The 46-year-old CEO already has earned top marks for zeroing in on HP's core problems—and for having the courage to tackle them head-on. And she did raise HP's growth to 15% in fiscal 2000 from 7% in 1999. If she keeps it up, a reinvigorated HP could become a blueprint for others trying to transform technology dinosaurs into dynamos. "There isn't a major technology company in the world that has solved the problem she's trying to address, and we're all going to learn from her experience," says Stanford Business School professor Robert Burgelman.

Fiorina needs results—and fast. For all its internal changes, HP today is more dependent than ever on maturing markets. While PCs and printers contributed 69% of HP's sales and three-fourths of its earnings last year, those businesses are expected to slow to single-digit growth in coming years, with falling profitability. Last year, HP was tied with Compaq as the leading U.S. maker of home PCs and sold 60% of home printers, according to IDC. Those numbers make it hard to boost market share. In corporate computing—where the company is banking on huge growth—HP has made only minor strides toward capturing lucrative business such as consulting services, storage, and software. And the failure of Fiorina's $16 billion bid to buy the consulting arm of PricewaterhouseCoopers LLP leaves her without a strong services division to help transform HP from high tech's old reliable boxmaker into a Net powerhouse, offering e-business solutions.

Careening

With the tech sector slowing, this may be the wrong time to make a miracle. In January, HP said its revenue and earnings would fall short of targets for the first quarter, and Fiorina cut her sales-growth estimates to about 5%—a far cry from the mid-teens she had been promising. In late January, the company announced it was laying off 1,700 marketing workers. HP's stock, which has dropped from a split-adjusted $67 in July to less than $40, is 19% below its level when Fiorina took the helm.

It's not just Fiorina's lofty goals that are so radical, but the way she's trying to achieve them. She's careening along at Net speed, ordering changes she hopes are right—but which may need adjustment later. That goes even for the front-back management structure. "When you sail, you don't get there in a straight line," Fiorina argues. "You adjust your course to fit the times and the current conditions." Insiders say that before the current slowdown, she expected HP to clock sales growth of 20% in 2002 and thereafter—a record clip for a $50 billion company. Fiorina won't confirm specific growth goals but says the downturn doesn't change her long-term plan.

Her overambitious targets have cost her credibility with Wall Street, too. While she earned kudos for increasing sales growth and meeting expectations early on, she has damaged her reputation by trying to put a positive spin on more troubled recent quarters. HP insiders say that while former CEO Lewis E. Platt spent a few hours reviewing the results at the end of each quarter, Fiorina holds marathon, multiday sessions to figure out how to cast financials in the best light. Not everyone is impressed. "I grew up with HP calculators, but they don't work right anymore," jokes Edward J. Zander, president of rival Sun Microsystems. "Everything they mention seems to be growing 50%, but the company as a whole only grows 10%." Fiorina says HP has accurately reported all segments of its business and that she makes no special effort to spin the results. "The calculators still work fine," she says.

Fiorina was well aware of the challenges when she joined HP, but she also saw the huge untapped potential. She had grown to admire the company while working as an HP intern during her years studying medieval history at Stanford University. Later, as president of the largest division of telecommunications equipment maker Lucent Technologies Inc., she learned the frustrations of buying products from highly decentralized HP. When HP's board asked her to take over, she jumped at the chance to show off her management chops. While she had spearheaded the company's spin-off from AT&T in 1996, then CEO Richard A. McGinn got all the credit.

"Perfectly Positioned"

Soon after signing on, Fiorina decided the front-back structure was the salve for HP's ills. With the help of consultants, she tailored the framework to HP's needs and developed a multiyear plan for rejuvenating the company. Step One would be to shake up complacent troops. Next, Fiorina set out to refine a strategy and "reinvent" HP from the ground up, a task she expected would take most of 2000. Only then—meaning about now—would HP be ready to unleash its potential as a top supplier of technology for companies revamping their businesses around the Web.

That's where the cross-company initiatives come in. So far, HP has identified three. There's the digital-imaging effort to make photos, drawings, and videos as easy to create, store, and send as e-mail. A commercial-printing thrust aims to capture business that now goes to offset presses. And a wireless services effort might, say, turn a wristwatch into a full-function Net device that tracks the wearer's heart rate and transmits that info to a hospital. "All the great technology companies got great by seeing trends and getting there first—and they're always misunderstood initially," says Fiorina. "We think we see where the market is going and that we're perfectly positioned."

The first chapters of Fiorina's plan came off as scripted. When she replaced 33-year HP veteran Platt on a balmy July day in 1999, Fiorina swept in with a rush of fresh thinking and made headway—for a time. She ordered unit chiefs to justify why HP should continue in that line of business. And she gave her marketers just six weeks to revamp advertising and relaunch the brand. After a few days on the job, she met with researchers who feared that Fiorina—a career salesperson—would move HP away from its engineering roots. She wowed them. In sharp contrast to the phlegmatic Platt, Fiorina moved through the crowd, microphone in hand, exhorting them to change the world. "There was a lot of skepticism about her," says Stan Williams, director of HP's quantum science research program. "But she was fantastic."

If she was a hit with engineers, it took a bit longer to win over HP's executive council. For years, these top execs had measured HP's performance against its ability to meet internal goals, but rarely compared its growth rates to those of rivals. In August, Fiorina rocked their cozy world when she shared details of her reorganization—and of her sky-high growth targets. She went to a whiteboard and compared HP with better-performing competitors: Dell Computer in PCs, Sun in servers, and IBM in services. She issued a challenge: If the executives could show her another way to hit her 20% growth target by 2002, she would postpone the restructuring, insiders say. Five weeks later, the best alternative was a plan for just 16% growth. The restructuring would start by yearend.

She dove into the details. While Platt ran HP like a holding company, Fiorina demanded weekly updates on key units and peppered midlevel managers with 3 a.m. voice mails on product details. She injected much needed discipline into HP's computer sales force, which had long gotten away with lowering quotas at the end of each quarter. To raise the stakes, she tied more sales compensation to performance and changed the bonus period from once a year to every six months to prevent salespeople from coasting until the fourth quarter. While some commissions were tied to the number of orders rather than the sales amount and contributed to the earnings miss, Fiorina has fixed the problem and accomplished her larger goal of kick-starting sales. "You can feel the stress her changes are causing," says Kevin P. McManus, a vice-president of Premier Systems Integrators, which installs HP equipment. "These guys know they have to perform."

This play-to-win attitude has started to take root in other areas. Take HP Labs. In recent years, the once proud research and development center made too many incremental improvements to existing products, in part because engineers' bonuses were tied to the number, rather than the impact, of their inventions. Now, Fiorina is focusing HP's R&D dollars on "big bang" projects. Consider Bob Rau's PICO software, which helps automate the design of chips used in electronic gear. Rau had worked for years on the project, but the technology languished. Last spring, Rau told Fiorina that the market for such systems was projected to grow to $300 billion as appliance makers built all sorts of Net-enabled gadgets. Within days, Fiorina created a separate division that operates alongside the two back-end groups and has grown to 250 people. Besides Rau's software, it will sell other HP technologies such as new disk drives to manufacturers. "It was like we'd been smothered for four years and someone was finally kind enough to lift the pillow off our face," says Rau.

Rough Edges

With Phase One of her transformation behind her, Fiorina launched a formal reinvention process last spring (Exhibit 3). First up: cutting expenses. Over nine days, a 12-person team came up with ways to slash $1 billion by fiscal 2002. HP could save $100 million by outsourcing procurement. It could trim $10 million by letting employees log their hours online rather than on cardboard time cards. And the company could revamp its stodgy marketing by consolidating advertising from 43 agencies into two. That would save money and, better yet, focus HP's campaigns on Fiorina's big Web plans rather than on its various stand-alone products.

But when the big changes really started to kick in, Fiorina's plan started to bog down. In the past, HP's product chieftains ran their operations, from design to sales and support. Today, they're folded into the two back-end units, leaving product chiefs with a far more limited role. They're still responsible for keeping HP competitive with rivals, hitting cost goals, and getting products to market on time. But they hand those products to the front-end organizations responsible for marketing and selling them.

The arrangement solves a number of long-standing HP problems. For one, it makes HP far easier to do business with. Rather than getting mobbed by salespeople from various divisions, now customers deal with one person. It lets HP's expert product designers focus on what they do best and gives the front-end marketers authority to make the deals that are most profitable for HP as a whole—say, to sell a server at a lower margin to customers who commit to long-term consulting services. "You couldn't miss how silly it was the old way if you were part of the wide-awake club," says Scott Stallard, a vice-president in HP's computing group. "A parade of HP salesmen in Tauruses would pull up and meet for the first time outside of the customer's building." These advantages, though, aren't enough to convince management experts or many HP veterans that a front-back approach will work at such a complex company. How do back-end product designers stay close enough to customers to know when a new feature becomes a must-have? Will executives, now saddled with thousands of HP products under their supervision, give sufficient

EXHIBIT 3
Carly to HP: Snap to It

Even before she took charge at HP in mid-1999, Fiorina had formulated a three-phase plan for returning the company to its former glory. Some highlights:

Phase I, 1999

Prepare the ground

SPREAD THE GOSPEL Held "Coffee with Carly" sessions in 20 countries to boost morale. Convinced top lieutenants that HP needs to match the growth of rivals.

ONE IMAGE Merged HP's fragmented ad effort under one all-encompassing "Invent" campaign.

SPARK INNOVATION Reoriented HP's R&D lab away from incremental product improvements and toward big-bang projects such as nanotechnology for making superpowerful chips.

Phase II, 2000

Improve growth and profits in core businesses

CONSOLIDATE Folded HP's 83 product divisions into four units: two product development units that work with two sales and marketing groups—one aimed at consumers, the other corporations.

SET STRATEGY Created a nine-person Strategy Council to allocate resources to the best opportunities rather than leaving strategy to product chieftains.

WHACK COSTS Lower expenses by $1 billion by revamping internal processes to tap the power of the Web.

Phase III, 2001 and Beyond

Build new markets

TRIGGER NEW PRODUCT CATEGORIES Establish cross-company initiatives to develop altogether new Net-related businesses.

WOO CUSTOMERS Offer soup-to-nuts solutions for customers by creating teams from across HP that sell to major accounts.

GOOD CORPORATE CITIZEN Use HP's resources to create subsidized or low-cost computer centers and services to make the Net available to everyone.

attention to each of them to stay competitive? And with shared profit-and-loss responsibility between front and back ends, who has the final say when an engineer wants to take a flier on expensive research? "You just diffuse responsibility and authority," says Sara L. Beckman, a former HP manager who teaches at the Haas Business School at the University of California at Berkeley. "It makes it easier to say, 'Hey, that wasn't my problem.'"

Indeed, the front-back plan is showing some rough edges. While HP cited many reasons for its troubling fourth-quarter results, the reorganization is probably front and center. Freed from decades-old lines of command, employees spent as if they had already hit hypergrowth. In October alone, the company hired 1,200 people. Even dinner and postage expenses ran far over the norm. Such profligate spending was rare under the old structure where powerful division chiefs kept a tight rein on the purse strings. "They spent too much money on high-fives and setting themselves up to grow the following quarter," says Salomon Smith Barney analyst John B. Jones.

That situation could improve over time. Fiorina rushed the reorganization into place before the company's information systems were revamped to reflect the changes. Before Fiorina arrived, each product division had its own financial reporting system. It was only on Nov. 1 that HP rolled out a new *über*-system so staffers could work off the same books. Although it's too soon to say whether it's a winner, HP claims the system will let it watch earnings in powerful new ways. Rather than just see sales for a product line, managers will be able to track profits from a given customer companywide or by region. That way they can cut deals on some products to boost other sales and wind up with a more lucrative relationship.

Another restructuring red flag is the way Fiorina now sets strategy, a big departure from "The HP Way"—the principles laid out by the founders in 1957. Based on the belief that smart people will make the right choices if given the right tools and authority, "Bill and Dave" pushed strategy down to the managers most involved in each business. The approach worked. Not only did HP dominate most of its markets, but low-level employees unearthed new opportunities for the company. "HP was always the exact opposite of a command-and-control environment," says former CEO Platt. Although Platt wouldn't comment on Fiorina directly, he says, "Bill and Dave did not feel they had to make every decision." HP's $10 billion inkjet printer business, for example, got its start in a broom closet at HP's Corvallis (Ore.) campus, where its inventors had to set up because they had no budget.

Eyes on the Prizes

Fiorina isn't waiting for another broom-closet miracle. Since the halcyon mid-'90s, the old HP way hasn't worked quite as well. The last mega-breakthrough product HP introduced was the inkjet printer, in 1984. Growth had slowed to just 4% in the six months before Fiorina took over. To give HP better direction, Fiorina has created a nine-person Strategy Council that meets every month to allocate resources, set priorities, and advise her on acquisitions and partnerships. "This is a company that can do anything," Fiorina says. "But it can't do everything."

Again, the move makes sense on paper. By steering the entire company, the council can focus HP on a few big Internet prizes rather than myriad underfunded pet projects. But this top-down engine could backfire. Experts point out that except for visionaries like Apple Computer's Steve Jobs or IBM's Thomas J. Watson Jr., it's rare for the suits in the corner office to be able predict the future—especially in a market as fast-changing as the Net. "If we were to go too far toward top-down, it would not be right for this company," acknowledges Debra L. Dunn, HP's vice-president of strategy.

To be sure, Fiorina is quick to embrace ideas from below if she thinks they'll solve a problem. This spring, Sam Mancuso, HP's vice-president of corporate accounts, proposed a team-based plan that advances the front-back approach. Time was, PC salespeople weren't allowed to sell, say, printers. Mancuso has fixed that by pulling together 20-person teams to concentrate on the top 75 corporate customers. The teams create an "opportunity map" for each customer, tracking the total amount of business HP could possibly book. Then the team analyzes what deal would maximize earnings for HP. Mancuso says his operation has boosted sales to top customers by more than 30% since May. "We're taking the handcuffs off, so now we can be more aggressive," Mancuso says.

The shackles may be off, but HP still lags its competitors in many areas. For all HP's talk of becoming a Net power, in the fourth quarter, Sun held 39% of the market for Unix servers preferred by e-businesses, according to IDC. HP is in second place with 23% share, a slight improvement over the year before. But it faces growing competition from third-place IBM, which just introduced a product line that many analysts say handily outperforms HP's servers. "HP is just not making much headway," says Ellen M. Hancock, CEO of Exodus Communications Inc. Her company uses 62,000 servers in its Web hosting centers, virtually none of them from HP. And most of HP's Net schemes, such as Cartogra, a service that lets consumers post pictures on the Web, have failed to catch on.

Even fans of Fiorina acknowledge she has a ways to go. While wireless juggernaut Nokia Corp. just signed a deal to use HP software, Chairman Jorma Ollila questions how successful Fiorina's turnaround is likely to be. "Carly is very impressive," he says. "But the jury is still out on HP." Says Cisco Systems Inc. CEO John T. Chambers, who named Fiorina to his board on Jan. 10: "I'd bet that Carly will be one of the top 5 or 10 CEOs in the nation. But she has still got to get them running faster." Fiorina wouldn't disagree and says she plans to keep upping her bets. "The greatest risk is standing still," she says. She should hope she has picked the right cards, because she's gambling with Silicon Valley's proudest legacy.

Source: Peter Burrows, "The Radical," *BusinessWeek,* February 19, 2001, 70–74, 76, 78, 80.

Case 6-19

Nanophase Technologies Corporation

The 2001 business year was finished and **Nanophase Technologies Corporation**, the industry leader in commercializing nanotechnology, had just reported financial results to shareholders. It was a discouraging year for the Romeoville, Illinois company, with revenues declining to $4.04 million from $4.27 million in 2000. The year was disappointing in other respects as well. **Nanophase** reported a loss of $5.74 million for 2001, even though management had been optimistic about achieving operating profitability. Reflecting on the Statement of Operations shown in Appendix Table 1 and the Balance Sheet in Appendix Table 2, the company's President and CEO, stated:

> "2001 was disappointing in terms of revenue growth due to the economic recession, especially in the manufacturing sector that represents our primary customer and business development market, and the events in September, which lingered through the end of the year," stated Joseph Cross, President and CEO. "However we believe that the company had several outstanding accomplishments that provide a solid basis for future revenue growth." (Nanophase Technologies Corporation, Press Release, February 20, 2002)

Later, Cross expanded on the operating results and future prospects when Nanophase hosted a quarterly conference call for investors which was broadcast over the Internet and posted on the company Web site (www.nanophase.com). In the transcript of his prepared remarks, Cross said:

> "Entering 2002, we believe that the company is stronger and better positioned than at any time in its history. We have established the vital delivery capabilities to succeed with our enlarged platform of nanoengineering technologies and delivery capability investments, our market attack is broader and at the same time better focused, the infrastructure - people and equipment are ready to deliver, our processes have been proven demonstrably scalable and robust, and we have strengthened the company's supply chain." (Nanophase Technologies Corporation, Fourth Quarter Conference Call, February 21, 2002)

While Cross was encouraged about the future, there were reasons to be cautious. After all, the company had been in business since 1989 and had not yet earned a profit. Questions arose about 2002, because the U.S. economy was only beginning to emerge from a significant manufacturing recession. Nanophase management remembered that in 2001, after its largest customer had expanded and extended its supply agreement, a weak economy had caused the customer to delay receipt of shipments of zinc oxide powder during the year to adjust inventory. Given the short notice provided by the customer, Cross had indicated that the company would not be able to find additional business to fill the revenue shortfall. Later in 2001, a UK company, Celox, Ltd., failed to fulfill a purchase contract for a catalytic fuel additive which resulted in a substantial loss of revenues and a nonrecurring inventory adjustment. In late November, Nanophase announced a temporary hourly manufacturing furlough until January 7, 2002 to enable the company to reduce existing inventory and lower its cost of operations during the holiday period. (Nanophase Technologies Corporation, Press Releases: October 25 and November 14, 2001 and February 20, 2002).

Transition times from start-up to commercialization exceeding ten years were not unusual for companies developing emerging technologies. Typically new high technology firms struggled with product development, experienced set-backs in bringing products to market and were slow to earn profits. Nanophase experienced some of these problems, but the company had managed to achieve a solid record of revenue growth since introducing it's first commercial products in 1997. Exhibit 1 summarizes the revenues, profit (loss) and cost of revenues for the 1993-2001 time period.

Nanophase records revenue when products are shipped, when milestones are met regarding development arrangements or when the company licenses its technology and transfers proprietary information. Cost of revenue generally includes costs associated with commercial production, customer development arrangements, the transfer of technology and licensing fees. It does not include all of the costs incurred by the company. Gross margin, a useful indicator of a businesses move toward profitability, can be calculated as revenue minus cost of revenue divided by revenue.

Nanophase Technologies Corporation was prepared by Dr. Lawrence M. Lamont, Professor Emeritus of Management, Washington and Lee University. Case material is prepared as a basis for class discussion and not designed to present illustrations of either effective or ineffective handling of administrative problems.

The author gratefully acknowledges Nanophase Technologies Corporation for reviewing the accuracy of the case study and granting permission to reproduce certain materials used in the preparation.

EXHIBIT 1 Revenue, Costs and Profit (Loss), 1993–2001

Source: SEC form 10-K, 1997 and 2002.

Year	Revenues	Net Profit (Loss)	Cost of Revenues
2001	$4,039,469	$(5,740,243)	$4,890,697
2000	4,273,353	(4,518,327)	4,754,485
1999	1,424,847	(5,117,067)	2,610,667
1998	1,303,789	(5,633,880)	3,221,996
1997	3,723,492	(3,072,470)	3,935,766
1996	595,806	(5,557,688)	4,019,484
1995	121,586	(1,959,874)	532,124
1994	95,159	(1,287,772)	167,746
1993	$25,625	(729,669)	61,978

What is Nanotechnology?

Nanotechnology is the science and technology of materials at the nanometer scale—the world of atoms and molecules. It is a multi-disciplinary science drawing on chemistry, biology, engineering materials, mathematics and physics. Scientists use nanotechnology to create materials, devices and systems that have unusual properties and functions because of the small scale of their structures. Nanophase uses the technology in its patented manufacturing processes to produce nanocrystalline materials, like microfine zinc oxide powder, sold as a component material to producers of industrial and consumer products, such as cosmetics. See Appendix Table 3 for additional description.

Over the next 20–30 years, it is expected that nanotechnology will find applications in chemicals and engineering materials, optical networking, memory chips for electronic devices, thin film molecular structures and biotechnology. Experts predict that the technology could spawn a new industrial revolution. According to Mihail Roco, senior advisor for nanotechnology at the National Science Foundation's Directorate for Engineering: "This is a technology that promises to change the way we live, the way we combat disease, the way we manufacture products, and even the way we explore the universe. Simply put, nanoscale manufacturing allows us to work with the fundamental building blocks of matter, at the atomic and molecular levels. This enables the creation of systems that are so small that we could only dream about their application years ago." "Because of nanotechnology, we'll see more changes in the next 30 years than we saw in all of the last century." (Roco, 2001)

Because nanotechnology promises to impact so many different industries, the National Nanotechnology Initiative has received the financial support of the United States government. The annual letter sent by the Office of Science and Technology Policy and the Office of Management and Budget to all agencies put nanotechnology at the top of R&D priorities for fiscal year 2001. The expenditures have reflected the priority, and in fiscal 2001 actual federal expenditures for nanotechnology were $463.85 million. In 2002, Congress enacted a fiscal year nanotechnology appropriation of $604.4 million. The 2003 budget request was set at $710.2 million, another substantial increase reflecting the continuing interest and commitment to the commercial potential of the technology. (www.nano.gov)

History of Nanophase Technologies Corporation

Nanophase Technologies Corporation traces its beginnings to the mid-1980's and the research of Richard Siegel, who developed the "physical-vapor synthesis" (PVS) method for producing nanocrystalline materials at the Argonne National Laboratory, southwest of Chicago. Siegel, an internationally known scientist, co-founded the company in 1989 after receiving funding from the Argonne National Laboratory-University of Chicago Development Corporation. The mission of Nanophase was to produce nanostructured materials by developing and applying the PVS process. For several years, the company was located in Burr Ridge, Illinois. In 2000, Nanophase expanded its manufacturing capabilities and moved its headquarters to a facility in Romeoville, Illinois. The original Burr Ridge manufacturing facility was also retained and is currently the main source of PVS production. The Romeoville addition enables the company to increase its manufacturing operations and expand its customer application technology to meet future demand. (Stebbins, 2000; www.nanotechinvesting.com; Nanophase Technologies Corporation, 2000 Annual Report)

Developing the Technology

From its beginning as a 1989 start-up, Nanophase emphasized the development of technology, the pursuit of patents and the design of manufacturing processes to transition the company from R&D to a commercial enterprise. Through 1995, the majority of the company's revenues resulted from government research contracts. From this research, the company developed an operating capacity to produce significant quantities of nanocrystalline materials for commercial use. At the same time, Nanophase was involved with potential customers to facilitate the development of products that would utilize the capabilities of the PVS process. During 1996, Nanophase began emerging from product development and in 1997, the first complete year of commercial operations, the company significantly increased its revenues from sales to businesses.

Protecting Intellectual Property

Nanophase was also successful in protecting its technology, equipment and processes with patents. Early in 2002, the company had 38 U.S. and foreign patents, patent applications, or licenses covering core technologies and manufacturing processes. (Nanophase Technologies Corporation, Fourth Quarter Conference Call, February 21, 2002) Intellectual property such as patents and trade secrets are valuable because they protect many of the scientific and technological aspects of the company's business and result in a competitive advantage.

Reducing Manufacturing Costs

Nanophase placed importance on research and technology development to reduce manufacturing costs. Although the company de-emphasized the pursuit of revenue from government research contracts in 1995, research was funded by the company to improve manufacturing processes for commercial production. For example, in 2001, Nanophase made expenditures to improve PVS manufacturing technology in product quality and output quantity. Nanophase was successful in reducing variable manufacturing cost by 40 to 65% (including a 25% reduction in manufacturing staff) and increased reactor output by 100 to 200% depending on the material. The company was also successful in commercializing a new, lower-cost manufacturing process, trademarked NanoArc Synthesis (TM). The new process promises to further cut some production costs by an estimated 50 to 90%, increase production output rates by estimated factors of 2 to 10 times, and permit the use of less expensive raw materials. The process also will allow Nanophase to increase the variety of nanocrystalline products available for sale and address the needs of potential customers who need nanoparticles in liquid solutions and dispersions. (Nanophase Technologies Corporation, Press Release, February 20, 2002; Fourth Quarter Conference Call, February 21, 2002)

Financing Operations

To date, Nanophase has financed operations from a private offering of approximately $19,558,069 of equity securities and an initial public offering in 1997 of 4,000,000 common shares at $8.00 a share to raise $28,837,936 for continued development of the company. (SEC form 10-K405, 1997) In 2000, Nanophase entered into an agreement with BASF (its largest customer) to borrow $1.3 million to finance the purchase and installation of new equipment to meet the customer's requirements during 2001-2002. (Nanophase Technologies Corporation, Press Release, December 8, 2000)

Nanophase will need additional financing to complete another year of operations. At the end of 2001, the balance sheet indicated that about $7.4 million was available from cash and investments. Nanophase has reported cumulative losses of $34,754,188 from inception through December 31, 2001. (Nanophase Technologies Corporation, 2001 Annual Report)

Transition and Changes in Management

To speed the transition to a commercial venture, executives with experience in developing high-technology businesses were hired. According to critics, Nanophase had too many development projects under way and did not have enough products and customers to generate a dependable revenue stream. As a result, the company lost its focus and progress fell behind expectations.

Joseph E. Cross came to Nanophase in November 1998 as a Director and President and Chief Operating Officer. In December 1998, Cross was promoted to CEO and he continues to serve in that capacity. Cross brings a background of directing high-technology start-ups and managing rapid growth and turnaround operations. His biography is in Appendix Table 4.

According to Cross, Nanophase was focused more on pure research than on finding practical applications for nanoengineered materials and making money. Cross stated: "We had a bunch of scientists but didn't have any engineers or a sales distribution or manufacturing system." (Stebbins, 2001) Since his appointment, Cross and his management team have been concentrating on six major areas:

1. Emphasizing new business development to expand revenues.
2. Achieving a positive gross margin on products.
3. Increasing the technology and intellectual property base by developing new manufacturing processes and establishing patents and trademarks.
4. Reducing manufacturing costs by using less expensive raw materials, increasing output rates and yields and reducing supply chain costs.
5. Increasing manufacturing skills and the capability to produce products to address current and new market opportunities.
6. And, strategically positioning the company for economic recovery.

Following his appointment to CEO, Cross moved quickly to expand and strengthen the management team in the areas of marketing, manufacturing, technology and engineering. Exhibit 2 shows the executive officers of the company, including their title, year of appointment and previous business experience. At the end of 2001, Nanophase had approximately 51 full-time employees.

Nanophase also attracted an impressive outside Board of Directors to provide management and technical advice to the Company. In addition to Cross, the Board included Donald Perkins, retired Chairman of the Board of Jewel Companies, a Chicago retail supermarket and drug chain; James A. Henderson, former Chairman and CEO of Cummins Engine Company; Richard Siegel, co-founder and internationally known scientist; Jerry Pearlman, retired Chairman of Zenith Electronics Corporation and James McClung, a Senior Vice President and a corporate officer for FMC Corporation. Donald Perkins currently serves as Chairman of the Nanophase Board of Directors. (www.nanophase.com)

The Science of Nanotechnology at Nanophase

Nanotechnology is used to produce nanocrystalline particles in powder form using metallic materials such as aluminum, cerium, copper, iron and zinc. The extremely small size of the particles, combined with the properties of surface atoms gives nanoparticles unusual chemical, mechanical, electrical and optical properties that often exceed those of the original raw materials.

Different technologies are used to achieve these results, but two of the most important are Physical Vapor Synthesis (PVS) and Discrete Particle Encapsulation (DPE). Exhibit 3 illustrates the PVS process patented and used by Nanophase.

The PVS process uses a solid metallic wire or rod which is heated in a reactor to high temperatures (about 3000 F) using jets of thermal energy. The metal atoms boil off, creating a vapor. A reactive gas is introduced to cool the vapor, which condenses into liquid molecular clusters. As the cooling process continues, the molecular clusters are frozen into solid nanoparticles. The metal atoms in the molecular clusters mix with reactive gas (e.g., oxygen atoms), forming metal oxides such as zinc and aluminum oxide. The nanocrystalline particles are near-atomic size. For example, about nine hundred million zinc oxide crystals could be spread across the head of a pin in a single layer. (Nanophase Technologies Corporation, 2000 Annual Report)

Because of the PVS process, Nanophase is able to produce nanoparticles with properties that are highly desirable to customers. These product features include spherical, nonporous particles of uniform size and large surface area, particles virtually free of chemical residues and particles that flow freely without clustering together. The company is also able to use the PVS

EXHIBIT 2 Profile of Executive Officers

Company Officer	Title	Joined	Previous Experience
Joseph Cross	Pres. and CEO	1998	Senior Management
Daniel Billicki	VP Sales and Mkt.	1999	Senior Management
Dr. Richard Brotzman	VP R&D	1994	Research Director
Dr. Donald Freed	VP Bus. Development	1995	Senior Marketing
Jess Jankowski	VP and Controller	1995	Controller
Dr. Gina Kritchevsky	Chief Technology Officer	1999	Business Development
Robert Haines	VP Operations	2000	Manufacturing

EXHIBIT 3 Nanophase Patented PVS Process

Source: www.nanophase.com

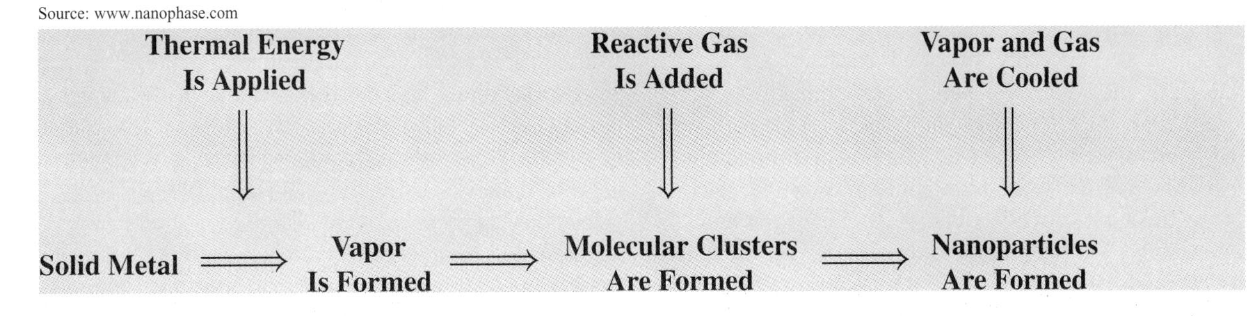

process and NanoArc Synthesis (TM) to custom-size the particles for a customer's application.

In some applications, the nanoparticles created by the PVS process require additional surface engineering to meet customer requirements. Nanophase has developed a variety of surface treatment technologies to stabilize, alter or enhance the performance of nanocrystalline particles. At the core of these surface treatment technologies is the patented Discrete Particle Encapsulation (DPE) process. DPE uses selected chemicals to form a thin durable coating around nanoparticles produced by the PVS process to provide a specific characteristic such as preventing the particles from sticking together or enabling them to be dispersed in a fluid or polymer to meet specific customer needs. (SEC form 10-K405, 1997)

Product Markets and Customer Applications

Substantial commercial interest has developed in nanotechnology because of its broad application. Although most companies refuse to disclose their work with the technology, it is likely that materials science, biotechnology and electronics will see much of the initial market development. Nanotechnology has already attracted the interest of large companies like IBM (using the technology to develop magnetic sensors for hard disk heads); Hewlett-Packard (using the technology to develop more powerful semiconductors); 3M (producing nanostructured thin film technologies); Mobil Oil (synthesizing nanostructured catalysts for chemical plants) and Merck (producing nanoparticle medicines). In other applications, Toyota has fabricated nanoparticle reinforced polymeric materials for cars in Japan and Samsung Electronics is working on a flat panel display with carbon nanotubes in Korea. (Roco, 2001)

Nanophase is not active in all of the areas. Instead, the company focuses selectively on products and market opportunities in materials science that can be developed within 12–18 months. Longer range product applications in the 18–36 month time frame were also of interest, but they were pursued mainly to give the company a pipeline of new, future opportunities. Nanophase evaluated markets by using criteria such as revenue potential, time-to-market and whether or not a product developed for one application could be successfully modified for sale in other markets.

Dr. Donald Freed, Vice President of business development, explained the company's strategy for commercializing nanotechnology: "Opportunities for nanomaterials will mature at different rates, and there are substantial opportunities in the near term—those with a not too demanding level of technical complexity. There are truly different problems in nanotechnology, such as those falling into the realm of human genetics or biotechnology. So we are successfully pursuing a staged approach to developing products for our customers." Freed further explained that this staged approach to developing customer applications enables the company to build product-related revenues while also expanding its foundations for developing more complicated applications. Nanophase was established in six product markets and was developing one potential market that met its time-to-market criteria of 12 to 18 months. (Nanophase Technologies Corporation, Press Release, October 31, 2000; Nanophase Technologies Corporation, 2000 Annual Report; Analyst Presentation, 2000)

Healthcare and Personal Products

The largest product market for Nanophase was zinc-oxide powder used as an inorganic ingredient in sunscreens, cosmetics and other health care products produced by the BASF cosmetic chemicals group. In early 2001, BASF signed an exclusive long-term purchase contract in which Nanophase agreed to supply a product that met technical and FDA regulatory requirements for active cosmetic ingredients. When added to a sunscreen the specially designed particles are small enough to allow harmless light to pass through the sunscreen while the ultraviolet light bounces off the particles and never makes it to the skin. Zinc-oxide formulations also eliminate the white-nose appearance on the user's skin without a loss of effectiveness. BASF Corporation is a diversified $30 billion global corporation and the third largest producer of chemicals and related products in the United States, Mexico and Canada. Sales to this company accounted for 75.5 percent of Nanophase revenues in 2001. (SEC form 10-Q, May 15, 2002)

In another healthcare application, Schering-Plough Corporation uses Nanophase zinc oxide as an ingredient in Dr. Scholl's foot spray to act as a fungicide and prevent the nozzle from clogging. (Stebbins, 2000) The unique properties of nanoparticles has also enabled their use in antifungal ointments and as odor and wetness absorbents. Both customers continue to explore opportunities for Nanophase products in other areas. The company estimated the market potential for its products in the healthcare and cosmetics market at approximately $45 million. (Nanophase Technologies Corporation, Press Release, October 31, 2000; Nanophase Technologies Corporation, 2000 Annual Report; SEC form 10-K, 2000; Stebbins, 2000)

Environmental and Chemical Catalysts

Nanophase was beginning to sell cerium dioxide to a manufacturing company that supplied one of the three largest automobile companies in the U.S. with catalytic converters for installation on a new car model. The product replaced expensive palladium, which was used in the converters to reduce exhaust emissions. Because a pound of nano-size particles has a surface area of 5.5 acres, less active material was needed to produce comparable emission results saving the customer money and space. Catalysts promised to be a rapidly growing market for Nanophase. Opportunities in industry for new types of nanoparticles to catalyze chemical and petroleum processes and for other environmental applications offered the potential to generate $30–$60 million in revenues. (Nanophase Technologies Corporation, Press Release, October 31, 2000; Nanophase Technologies Corporation, 2000 Annual Report)

Ceramics and Thermal Spray Applications

Nanoparticles were sold for the fabrication of structural ceramic parts and components used in corrosive and thermal environments. The properties of the company's materials enabled the rapid fabrication of ceramic parts with improved hardness, strength and inertness. Fabrication costs were lower because nanoparticles reduced the need for high temperatures and pressures and costly machining during the manufacturing process. Nanophase worked with parts fabricators to design and develop ceramic parts and components using its technologies and materials. (SEC form 10-K405, 1997)

Nanophase products were also used in thermal spray materials to repair worn or eroded metal parts on naval vessels and replace conventional ceramic coatings where properties such as abrasion and corrosion resistance and tensile strength were needed for longer service life. For example, the U.S. Navy uses thermal sprays incorporating aluminum and titanium oxides to recondition worn steering mechanisms in ships and submarines. With less wear and barnacle growth on the bow planes used to steer, the Navy expects to save $100 million a year when the program is fully implemented. Nanophase sells its products to U.S. Navy approved contractors who formulate the spray with nanoparticles and then apply it to critical parts. In addition to the Navy, Nanophase has several development programs with industrial companies involving similar applications. According to Dr. Donald Freed, Vice President of Business Development, "Our materials are being evaluated in such diverse applications as improving wear resistance in the plastics molding industry and in protective coatings for industrial equipment, gas turbine and aircraft engines." The company estimates the potential market for these and similar applications to be in the range of $25 million. (Nanophase Technologies Corporation, Press Release, October 31, 2000)

Transparent Functional Coatings

Nanophase has translated the technology used to make transparent sunscreens into ingredients for coatings designed to improve the scratch resistance of high gloss floor coatings, vinyl flooring and counter tops. Apparently, nanoparticles fit so tightly together that they make vinyl flooring up to five times more scratch resistant than existing products. Additionally, Nanophase is pursuing a number of opportunities for abrasion resistant coatings. Eventually the products may end up in automobile and appliance finishes, eyeglass lense coatings, fabrics and medical products. According to management, the opportunity in transparent functional coatings is estimated at $50–$60 million. (Nanophase Technologies Corporation, Press Release, October 31, 2000; Nanophase Technologies Corporation, 2000 Annual Report)

Conductive and Anti-static Coatings

Nanophase produces indium/tin oxide and antimony/tin oxide formulations for use as conductive and anti-static coatings for electronic products. The nanoparticle coatings are stored and used at room temperatures, which is an economic advantage to manufacturers. Indium/tin oxide is used primarily as a conductive coating to shield computer monitors and television screens from electromagnetic radiation. The world market for indium/tin oxide conductive coatings is estimated at $10–$20 million.

Antimony/tin oxide materials are used for transparent anti-static coatings in electronic component packaging. Nanophase replaced coatings based on carbon black and/or evaporated metals. The key advantage of nanoparticles in this market is that the transparent coatings maintained anti-static protection while enabling end-users to see the contents inside a package. (Nanophase Technologies Corporation, 2000 Annual Report)

Ultrafine Polishing

The newest application for Nanophase was the use of nanoparticles to create ultra smooth, high quality polished surfaces on optical components. The company provided NanoTek (R) metal oxides engineered specifically for polishing semiconductors, memory disks, glass photo masks and optical lenses. The application was made possible because of the 2001 technology advances in the core PVS process, commercialization of the new NanoArc Synthesis (TM) process, and the improved technology for preparation of stable dispersions of nanocrystalline metal oxides. Nanophase received orders of $100,000 and $200,000 for the materials in early 2002 and expected the application to quickly grow to annual revenues of approximately $500,000. (Nanophase Technologies Corporation, Press Release, February 21, 2002)

Nanofibers—A Developing Market

In a developing market called Nanofibers, engineered nanoparticles that could be incorporated directly into fibers for better wear properties and ultraviolet resistance were being developed. It was expected that the customer solution would result in a more stain and wear-resistant fiber with a high level of permanence. The products were being co-developed with leading companies producing nylon, polyester and polypropylene fibers for industrial carpets and textiles. Nanophase estimated that the applications could be commercialized in about 18 months with a potential market opportunity of several million dollars. (Nanophase Technologies Corporation, Fourth Quarter Conference Call, February 21, 2002)

Business Model and Marketing Strategy

Business Model

For most of its revenues, the Nanophase business model used direct marketing to customers. Teams worked collaboratively with prospective customers to identify an unsatisfied need and apply the company's proprietary technology and products to solve a problem. In most cases, the nanocrystalline materials were custom engineered to the customer's application. International and some domestic sales were made through trained agents and distributors that served selected markets. Nanophase was also engaged in on-going research, technology licensing and strategic alliances to expand revenues. The markets served were those where the technology and nanocrystalline materials promised to add the most value by improving the functional performance of a customer's product or the economic efficiency of a process.

Marketing Strategy

The marketing strategy used a business development team to work on nanotechnology applications with new customers. Business development activities included evaluation and qualification of potential markets, identification of the lead customers in each market and the development of a strategy to successfully penetrate the market. Nanophase then formed a technical/marketing team to provide an engineered solution to meet the customer's needs. Since one-third of the company staff had a masters or doctorate in materials-related fields, including chemistry, engineering, physics, ceramics and metallurgy, Nanophase had the expertise to understand the customer's problem, determine the functions needed and apply nanocrystalline technology. The team formed a partnership with the customer to create a solution that delivered exceptional value. After a satisfactory solution was achieved, application engineering and customer management staff were moved to a sales team organized along market lines. The sales team was expected to increase revenue by selling product and process solutions and broadening the customer base in the target market. Customers and applications were carefully selected so the science and materials would represent a technology breakthrough thus enabling the customer to add substantial value to its business, while at the same time making Nanophase a profitable long-term supplier. (Nanophase Technologies Corporation, 2001 Annual Report)

Although Nanophase focused its strategy in the markets previously mentioned, applications existed in related markets where the performance of products could be improved using similar technologies without extensive re-engineering. Based on market research, these included applications in fibers, footwear and apparel, plastics and polymers, paper, pigments and other specialty markets. The company strategy in these instances was to pursue only those applications which fit its primary business strategy and were strongly supported by a significant prospective customer.

Nanophase permitted prospective customers to experiment with small research samples of nanoparticles. About eight different products, branded NanoTek (R), were available for sale in quantities ranging from 25 grams to 1 kilogram. The samples included Aluminum Oxide, Antimony/ Tin Oxide, Cerium Oxide, Copper Oxide, Indium/ Tin Oxide, Iron Oxide, Yttrium Oxide and Zinc Oxide. They were sold by customer inquiry and on the Nanophase web site in different particle sizes and physical properties. Prices for research materials ranged from $0.80 to $10.00 per gram depending on the product and the quantity desired. (www.nanophase.com)

Customer inquiries were initiated by a variety of methods including the Nanophase web page, trade journal advertising, telephone inquiries, attendance and participation at trade shows, presentations and published papers, sponsorship of symposia and technical conferences and customer referrals. Management and staff followed-up on inquiries from prospective customers to determine their needs and qualify the customer and application as appropriate for a nanotechnology solution. Cross described the process as developing a collaborative relationship with the customer. "Our particular sort of chemistry enables people to do things they can't do any other way. To make that happen, you have to have a close relationship with a customer. You have to make it work in their process or their product. So it is indeed providing a solution; not just the powder that we make, which is nanocrystalline in nature. Its formulating the powder to work in a given application." (CNBC Dow Jones Business Video, 1999)

Using management and staff to build collaborative relationships with customers was time consuming and expensive. Exhibit 4 provides the annual selling, general and administrative expenses for the years 1993–2001. While not all of the expenses can be attributed to personal selling, the expenditures are indicative of the substantial growth of the expense category as Nanophase built the business development and marketing capability to commercialize its business. Management expected that these expenses would decrease or stabilize as the markets for the company's products developed.

EXHIBIT 4 Selling, General and Administrative Expense, 1993–2001

Source: www.nanophase.com; Nanophase 2001 Annual Report; SEC form 10-K405, 1997.

Year	Expenditures
2001	$3,798,543
2000	3,388,758
1999	3,641,736
1998	3,594,946
1997	2,074,728
1996	1,661,504
1995	1,150,853
1994	799,558
1993	556,616

In a few instances, Nanophase leveraged its resources through partnerships with organizations and individuals focused on market-specific or geographic-specific areas. For example, licensees and agents were used to increase manufacturing, engineering and sales representation. The agents were specialized by geographic region and the types of products they were permitted to sell. Ian Roberts, Director of U.S. and International Sales stated: "The use of experienced sales agents in selected markets is a fast and cost effective way to multiply the Nanophase sales strategy. The agents bring years of industry experience and contacts to the task of introducing nanoparticles to potential customers. We intend to form close partnerships with selected agents for specific products to speed product introduction and horizontal applications." (Nanophase Technologies Corporation, Press Release, November 27, 2000)

In November 2000, Nanophase appointed Wise Technical Marketing, specialists in the coatings industry, to represent the line of NanoEngineered Products (TM) in the Midwest and the Gillen Company LLC to promote the NanoTek (R) metal oxides in Pennsylvania and surrounding areas. Nanophase also announced the appointment of Macro Materials Inc., specialists in thermal spray materials and technology, as its global, nonexclusive agent for marketing and sales of the company's line of NanoClad (TM) metal oxides for thermal spray ceramic coatings.

Nanophase retained international representation in Asia through associations with C.I. Kasei Ltd. and Kemco International of Japan. C.I. Kasei was the second largest customer, accounting for 9.4 percent of Nanophase revenues in 2001. Kasei was licensed to manufacture and distribute the Company's NanoTek (R) nanocrystalline products, while Kemco represented conductive coatings. Nanophase was also working with customers in Europe and intended to expand its European presence as part of its future marketing strategy. (Nanophase Technologies Corporation, Press Release, November 27, 2000; Nanophase Technologies Corporation, 2000 Annual Report; SEC form 10-Q, May 15, 2002)

Competition

Competition in nanomaterials is not well-defined because the technology is new and several potential competitors are start-up businesses. However, the situation is temporary and eventually Nanophase could face competition from large chemical companies, new start-ups and other industry participants. Five types of industry participation seem to exist.

First, there were several large chemical companies located in the United States, Europe and Asia already involved in manufacturing and marketing of silica, carbon black and iron oxide nanoparticles sold as commodities to large volume users. The companies have a global presence and include prestigious names such as Bayer AG, Cabot Corporation, Dupont, DeGusa Corporation, Showa Denka and Sumitoma Corporation. All of these companies are larger and more diversified than Nanophase and pose a significant threat because they have substantially greater financial and technical resources, larger research and development staffs and greater manufacturing and marketing capabilities.

Second, there are OEMs making nanoparticles for use in their proprietary processes and products. For example, Eastman Kodak makes nanoparticles for use in photographic film. Similarly, the technology attracted the interest of other large OEM's like IBM, Intel, Lucent Technologies, Hitachi, Mitsubishi, Samsung, NEC, Thermo Electron, Micron Technology, Dow Chemical, Philips Electronics and Hewlett-Packard. They are pursuing applications that involve optical switching, biotechnology, petroleum and chemical processing, computing and microelectronics. These companies are potential competitors in the sense that they could sell nanoparticles not needed in their own operations to outside customers, putting them into competition with Nanophase.

Third, is the group of start-up companies shown in Exhibit 5 that will compete directly with Nanophase. These competitors, funded by venture capital or other private sources, are located in the United States, Canada, Europe and the Middle East. Most were founded in the 1990's after nanotechnology began to gain attention. For example, Oxonica Ltd., Nanopowder Enterprises Inc. and TAL Materials are spin-off firms out of university and government research laboratories. They were founded by scientists and engineers attempting to commercialize a nanotechnology developed while they were employed in a research organization. Richard Laine, a scientist at the University of Michigan, was a driving force behind the founding of TAL Materials. TAL was incorporated to commercialize the nanotechnologies developed in the Science and Engineering Department at the University. (Spurgeon, 2001) Most of the firms listed in Exhibit 5 have not yet reached commercial production. Nanophase is presently the only firm capable of producing substantial quantities of nanoparticles to rigid quality standards. The company is acknowledged by industry peers as the world leader in the commercialization of nanomaterials.

Fourth, there are firms that hold process patents or supply commercial equipment to nanotechnology firms, but also have the capability to produce nanomaterials in small quantities using an alternative manufacturing process. These companies, while not competitors at present, could enter the nanocrystalline materials market and compete with Nanophase in the future. Plasma Quench Technologies is an example. This company, which holds a process patent, recently spun out two small development companies, NanoBlok and Idaho

EXHIBIT 5
Summary of Potential Nanophase Competitors

Source: Company Internet Web sites.

Company	Location	Year Founded	Public/Private
Lightyear Technologies Inc.	Vancouver	1996	Private
Argonide Corporation	Florida	1994	Private
TAL Materials Inc.	Michigan	1996	Private
Altair Nanotechnologies Inc.	Wyoming	1999	Private
Nanomat	Ireland	1995	Private
Oxonica Ltd.	England	1999	Private
Nanopowders Industries	Israel	1997	Private
Nanopowder Enterprises, Inc.	New Jersey	1997	Private
Nanosource Technologies, Inc.	Oklahoma	Unknown	Private

TitaniumTechnologies, to produce titanium powders using the company's patented plasma quench manufacturing process.

Finally, Altair Nanotechnologies is an emerging competitor that has a natural resource position in titanium mineral deposits. Altair is developing the technology to produce nanoparticles such as titanium dioxide in commercial quantities. The company is completing a manufacturing plant and offering its products for sale on an Internet Web site. (www.altairtechnologies.com)

Recent Developments

As the U.S. economy dramatically slowed during 2001, companies around the world delayed the receipt of shipments and rescheduled purchase orders for future delivery. Nanophase was impacted by the slowdown, but the company continued to aggressively pursue applications of nanoparticles with selected customers in each of its product markets. Fortunately, the interest level in nanotechnology remained and some customers continued to move forward on the business development projects already initiated. Despite some setbacks, the results of Nanophase's R&D and intensified business development activities slowly began to show results.

April 24, 2002

On April 24, Joseph Cross, President and Chief Executive Officer, offered some observations about the position of the company:

> Cross said that the company entered 2002 with a wider array of improved technology applications tools than it entered 2001 with, and has significantly increased momentum in business development in several markets. "The improvement in our core PVS Technology, commercialization of our new NanoArc Synthesis (TM) process technology, and multiple application developments during the last half of 2001 and this far into 2002, provide an integrated platform of nanotechnologies that should allow the company to engineer solutions across more markets," explained Cross." (Nanophase Technologies Corporation, Press Release, April 24, 2002)

May 29, 2002

Nanophase completed a private placement of 1.37 million newly issued shares of common stock for a gross equity investment of $6.85 million. Nanophase plans to use the net proceeds to fund the continued development and capacity expansion of its NanoArc Synthesis (TM) process technology, expand marketing and business development activities, increase process capability and capacity in the PVS process and for general corporate purposes. (Nanophase Technologies Corporation, Press Release, May 29, 2002)

June 26, 2002

Nanophase announced a strategic alliance with Rodel, Inc., a part of the Rohm and Haas Electronic Materials Group. Rodel is a global leader in polishing technology for semiconductors, silicon wafers and electronic storage materials. The company will combine its patented technology with Nanophase's new nanoparticle technology to develop and market new polishing products for the semiconductor industry. The alliance is a five-year partnership and supply agreement with appreciable revenues targeted for 2003 and a planned ramp in volume through 2005 and beyond. Nanophase believes that the revenue opportunities approach the size of the Company's personal care and sunscreen markets. Rodel, headquartered in Phoenix, Arizona, has operations throughout the United States, Asia and Europe. (Nanophase Technologies Corporation, Press Releases, June 26 and June 28, 2002)

July 24, 2002

Nanophase announced financial results for the first two quarters of 2002. Revenues were $3.07 million compared with first half 2001 revenues of $2.12 million for a revenue growth of 45% year-over-year. Gross margin for the first half of 2002 averaged a positive 12% of revenues versus the annual 2001 average of a negative 21%. The company reported a net loss for the first half of 2002 of $2.72 million, or $0.20 per share, compared with a net loss for the first half of 2001 of $2.38 million, or $0.18 per share. Appendix Table 5 shows the comparative results for the first two quarters of operations.

Commenting on the balance of 2002, President Cross noted:

> While we are somewhat concerned with general market conditions and the normal market slowness that we expect during the summer, we remain cautiously positive about 2002. Based on information from current and prospective customers, we currently believe additional orders will be received during July through September toward our annual revenue target. Although orders are always subject to cancellation or change, and these estimates are based on various product mix, pricing, and other normal assumptions, we are maintaining our 2002 revenue target of $7.00 million or an anticipated revenue growth of approximately 75% compared to 2001. (Nanophase Technologies Corporation, Press Release, July 24, 2002)

Synopsis

The 2001 business year had proven to be difficult for Nanophase. The economic recession in the manufacturing sector of the economy had impacted the company's primary customer base; the manufacturing firms using nanomaterials in their processes and products. While interest continued to remain strong in the potential of nanotechnology, it was still difficult to stimulate interest among prospective customers who were also facing economic challenges and declining business activity, Finally, as the third quarter of 2002 rolled in, a slowly improving economic environment was on the horizon. Maybe 2002 and the years that followed would be the breakout years management was planning for.

APPENDIX TABLE 1 Statements of Operations (Years ended December 31)

Source: Nanophase Technologies Corporation, 2001 Annual Report.

	2000	2001
Revenue		
Product revenue	$3,824,159	$3,650,914
Other revenue	449,194	388,555
Total revenue	4,273,353	4,039,469
Operating Expense		
Cost of revenue	4,754,485	4,890,697
R&D expense	1,837,036	1,601,671
Selling, general and administrative expense	3,388,758	3,798,543
Total operating expense	9,980,279	10,290,911
Loss from operations	(5,706,926)	(6,251,442)
Interest Income	1,188,599	511,199
Loss before provision for income taxes	(4,518,327)	(5,740,243)
Provision for income taxes	—	—
Net loss	$(4,518,327)	$(5,740,243)
Net loss per share	$(0.34)	$(0.42)
Common shares outstanding	13,390,741	13,667,062

APPENDIX TABLE 2 Balance Sheets (Years ended December 31)

Source: Nanophase Technologies Corporation, 2001 Annual Report.

	2000	2001
Assets		
Current Assets:		
Cash and cash equivalents	$473,036	$582,579
Investments	16,831,721	6,842,956
Accounts receivable	1,238,334	1,112,952
Other receivables, net	144,818	67,449
Inventories, net	892,674	956,268
Prepaid expenses and other current assets	770,200	381,696
Total current assets	20,350,783	9,943,900
Equipment and leasehold improvements, net	3,266,245	8,914,745
Other assets, net	213,135	325,743
Total Assets	$23,830,163	$19,184,388
Liabilities and Stockholders Equity		
Current Liabilities		
Current portion of long-term debts	$285,316	$714,135
Current portion of capital lease obligations		48,352
Accounts Payable	824,338	1,233,466
Accrued Expenses	884,780	732,427
Total Current Liabilities	1,994,434	2,728,380
Long-term debt	827,984	758,490
Long-term portion of capital lease obligations		53,900
Stockholders' equity		
Preferred stock, $.01 par value; 24,088 authorized and none issued	—	—
Common stock, $.01 par value; 25,000,000 shares authorized and 13,593,914 shares issued and outstanding at December 31, 2000; 12,764,058 shares issued and outstanding at December 31, 1999	135,939	137,059
Additional paid-in capital	49,885,751	50,260,747
Accumulated deficit	(29,013,945)	(34,754,188)
Total stockholders' equity	21,007,745	15,643,618
Total liabilities and stockholders' equity	$23,830,163	$19,184,388

APPENDIX TABLE 3 Nanocrystalline Materials (Nanoparticles)

Source: SEC form 10-K, 2001.

Nanocrystalline materials generally are made of particles that are less than 100 nanometers (billionths of a meter) in diameter. They contain only 1,000s or 10,000s of atoms, rather than the millions or billions of atoms found in larger size particles. The properties of nanocrystalline materials depend upon the composition, size, shape, structure, and surface of the individual particles. Nanophase's methods for engineering and manufacturing nanocrystalline materials results in particles with a controlled size and shape, and surface characteristics that behave differently from conventionally produced larger-sized materials.

APPENDIX TABLE 4 Biographical Profile of Joseph E. Cross, Chief Executive Officer

Source: The Wall Street Transcript, January 22, 2001.

Joseph E. Cross is CEO of Nanophase Technologies Corporation. Mr. Cross has been a Director since November 1998 when he joined Nanophase as President and Chief Operating Officer. He was promoted to Chief Executive Officer in December 1998. From 1993–1998, Mr. Cross served as President and CEO of APTECH, Inc., an original equipment manufacturer of metering and control devices for the utility industry and as President of Aegis Technologies, an interactive telecommunications company. He holds a BS in Chemistry and attended the MBA program at Southwest Missouri University. He brings a background of successfully directing several high-technology start-ups, rapid growth and turnaround operations.

APPENDIX TABLE 5 Statements of Operations (Six months ended June 30)

Source: Nanophase Technologies Corporation, Press Release, July 24, 2002.

	June 30, 2001	June 30, 2002
Revenue		
Product revenue	$1,937,489	$2,829,773
Other revenue	183,815	239,755
Total revenue	2,121,304	3,069,528
Operating Expense		
Cost of revenue	1,857,122	2,696,720
R&D expense	800,189	1,003,726
Selling, general and administrative, expense	2,226,949	2,091,319
Total operating expense	4,884,260	5,791,765
Loss from operations	(2,762,956)	(2,722,237)
Interest Income	416,616	61,177
Interest Expense	(17,664)	(56,282)
Other, net	(12,000)	(50)
Loss before provision for income taxes	(2,376,004)	(2,717,392)
Provision for income taxes	(30,000)	(30,000)
Net loss	(2,406,004)	(2,747,392)
Net loss per share	$(0.18)	$(0.20)
Common shares outstanding	13,628,562	13,980,694

References

Nanophase Technologies Corporation-Press Releases

Nanophase Announces Second Quarter and First Half 2002 Results, July 24, 2002. PRNewswire.

Nanophase Technologies Provides Additional Information at Annual Shareholder Meeting, June 28, 2002. PRNewswire.

Rodel Partners with Nanophase Technologies to Develop and Market Nanoparticles in CMP Slurries for Semiconductor Applications, June 26, 2002. PRNewswire.

Nanophase Technologies Completes Private Equity Financing, May 29, 2002. PRNewswire.

Nanophase Technologies Announces First Quarter 2002 Results, April 24, 2002. PRNewswire.

Nanophase Receives Order for Ultrafine Optical Polishing Application, February 21, 2002. PRNewswire.

Nanophase Technologies Announces Fourth Quarter and 2001 Results, February 20, 2002. PRNewswire.

Nanophase Announces Temporary Hourly Manufacturing Furlough, November 14, 2001. PRNewswire.

Nanophase Technologies Announces Third Quarter 2001 Results, October 25, 2001. PRNewswire.

Nanophase Technologies Announces Capital Investment, December 8, 2000. PRNewswire.

Nanophase Technologies Increases Sales Representation, November 27, 2000. PRNewswire.

Experts From Nanophase Elaborate on New Technology Opportunities, October 31, 2000. PRNewswire.

Online Magazine and Newspaper Articles

Spurgeon, Brad, "Nanotechnology Firms Start Small in Building Big Future," January 29, 2001. *International Herald Tribune*. www.iht.com.

CEO Interview with Joseph E. Cross, January 22, 2001. Reprinted from The Wall Street Transcript. Roco, Mihail C. "A Frontier for Engineering," January, 2001. www.memagazine.org. Stebbins, John, "Nanophase Expects to Turn Tiniest Particles into Bigger Profits," November 5, 2000. www.bloomberg.com

Transcripts of On-line Conference Calls, Analyst Presentations and Personal Interviews

An Interview with Joseph Cross, President and CEO of Nanophase Technologies Corporation, January 2002. www.nanophase.com.

Fourth Quarter Conference Call, February 21, 2002. www.nanophase.com Analyst Presentation, 2000. www.nanophase.com.

CNBC/Dow Jones Business Video, February 9, 1999.

SEC Documents

SEC form 10-K, 2002.

SEC form 10-Q, May 15, 2002.

SEC form 10-K, 2001.

SEC form 10-K, 2000.

SEC form 10-K405, 1997.

Annual Reports

Nanophase Technologies Corporation, 2001 Annual Report.

Nanophase Technologies Corporation, 2000 Annual Report.

Web Sites

www.altairtechnologies.com

www.argonide.com

www.ltyr.com

www.nano.gov

www.nanomat.com

www.nanophase.com

www.nanopowders.com

www.nanopowderenterprises.com

www.nanosourcetech.com

www.nanotechinvesting.com

www.oxonica.com

www.plasmachem.de

www.talmaterials.com

Case 6-20

CUTCO International

It was CUTCO Cutlery's 1997 midyear companywide meeting in Olean, New York. Record sales and profits had been achieved for the first six months. CUTCO had seen record weekly shipments in June. Over 27,000 packages had gone out just the week before. Unlike some recent years, needed inventory was in place to meet seasonal demand. Further, record sales and profits were projected for the entire year. CUTCO employees could look forward to significant year-end profit-sharing bonuses.

The management team was proud of these achievements. However, Erick Laine (CEO/president, ALCAS Corporation), Fran Weinaug (president/CEO, CUTCO International), Bob Haig (president/COO, Vector Marketing Corporation), Mike Lancellot (president, Vector East), Don Muelrath (president, Vector West), and Jim Stitt (president/CEO, CUTCO Cutlery Corporation) were not satisfied. Growth was at record levels but not at plan.

According to Erick Laine, "Sales are up 11 percent over 1996, not the 20 to 25 percent we looked for. International sales in particular have been way off

This case was prepared by William F. Crittenden at Northeastern University and Victoria L. Crittenden at Boston College as the basis for class discussion rather than to illustrate effective or ineffective handling of a managerial situation. The Direct Selling Education Foundation provided partial funding for the development of this case. Revised 2001.

projections (15 percent growth versus the expected 75 percent). Although we've made some important adjustments, the second half of the year is unlikely to compensate."

He continued: "Other direct sales firms have had enormous success in the international arena. International markets are attractive to direct sellers. Direct selling allows market entry without fighting the battles of brand identity and entrenched distribution systems. With limited brick and mortar requirements, direct selling allows one to grow rapidly. We know it's [the market] there to be gotten."

CUTCO's corporate vision statement (Exhibit 1) to be the world's "largest, most respected and widely recognized" cutlery firm required substantial growth. Although product development and company acquisitions might be part of the strategic mix, management clearly viewed the international market as a critical element to growth. Yet decisions regarding which markets to enter, which approach to use, and the sequencing and timing of entry still needed to be made.

EXHIBIT 1

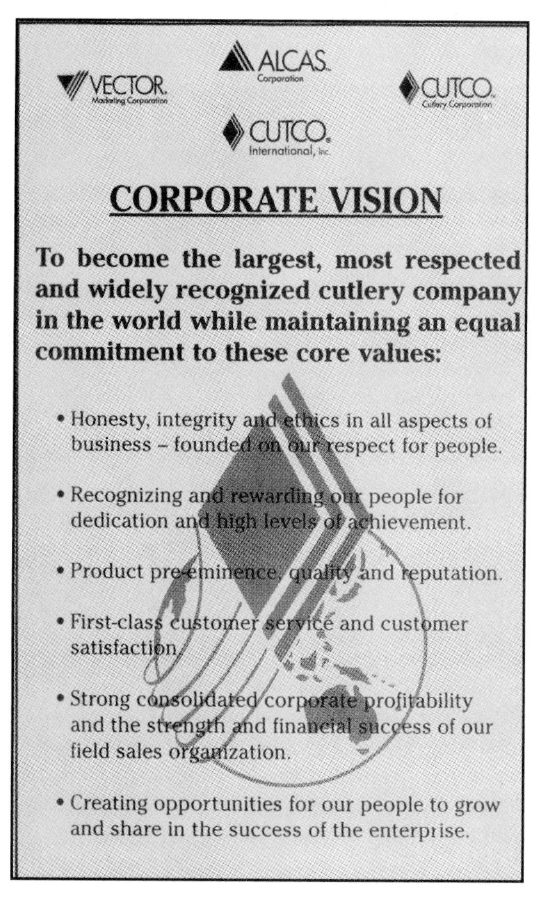

The ALCAS Corporation (the Parent)

In 1949 Alcoa and CASE Cutlery formed a joint venture, ALCAS Cutlery Corporation, to produce kitchen cutlery known as CUTCO. The product was exclusively marketed via in-home demonstrations by WearEver, Inc. (However, CUTCO and WearEver products were treated as separate entities and were not sold together.) In 1972, Alcoa bought out CASE and ALCAS became wholly owned by Alcoa. In 1982, the local management of ALCAS, headed by Erick Laine, a longtime Alcoa employee, purchased the company from Alcoa. Management converted ALCAS into a privately held corporation with headquarters in Olean, New York. Ownership remains closely held by five of the top managers. In 1996, the company acquired KA-BAR Knives, an established sporting knife company. Exhibit 2 outlines the corporate structure. Worldwide revenues from direct marketing and direct sales operations exceeded $100 million in 1996. (Sales just exceeded $20 million in 1987.) All corporations within ALCAS operate as profit centers.

CUTCO Cutlery covers a broad range of food preparation knives as well as scissors and hunting, fishing, and utility knives. (Exhibits 3 through 10 show examples of CUTCO products.) The product line is identified as "CUTCO—*The World's Finest Cutlery*." Product pricing is consistent with this positioning at the high end of the spectrum. The product is sold as individual open stock, in wood block sets, or in a variety of gift boxed sets. According to Mark George (now international sales director and a former CUTCO sales representative), numerous features make CUTCO the world's finest cutlery: "the ergonomically designed handle, the thermo-resin handle material, the full tang triple rivet construction, the high-carbon, stain-resistant steel, and the exclusive Double-D® edge. All products are backed by the CUTCO 'Forever Guarantee.'"

Recognizing the importance of satisfied customers, CUTCO devoted considerable space in its Olean headquarters to its service department. The company has a goal of two to three days' turnaround on knives returned for free sharpening or guarantee issues.

CUTCO cutlery is marketed in North America by Vector Marketing Corporation. During peak selling periods, Vector Marketing operates around 400 offices in Canada and the United States. CUTCO is sold primarily by college students who are recruited to work during vacations as sales representatives. (Exhibit 11 shows the

EXHIBIT 2

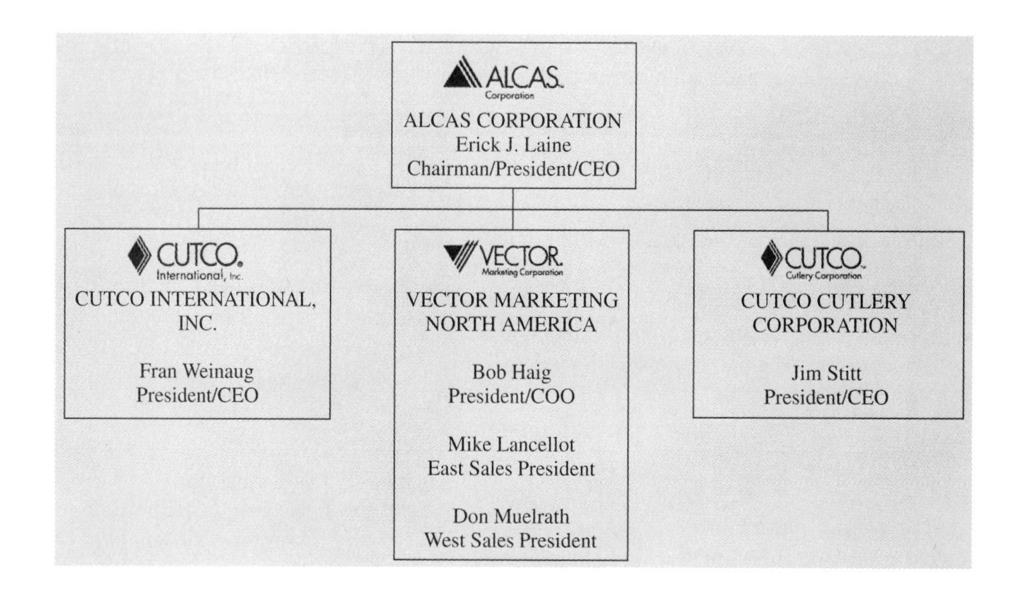

EXHIBIT 3

EXHIBIT 4

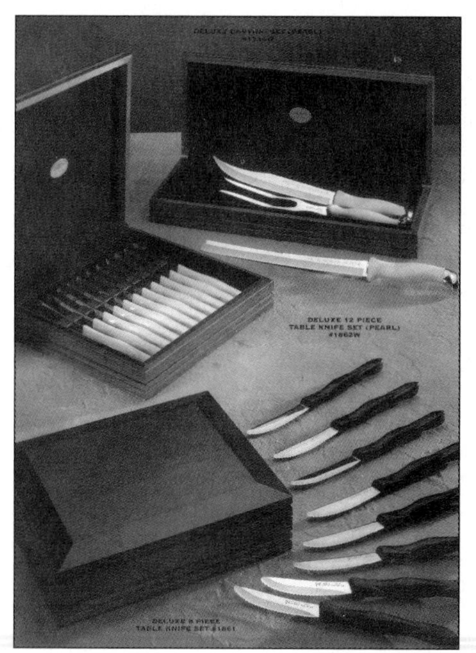

EXHIBIT 5

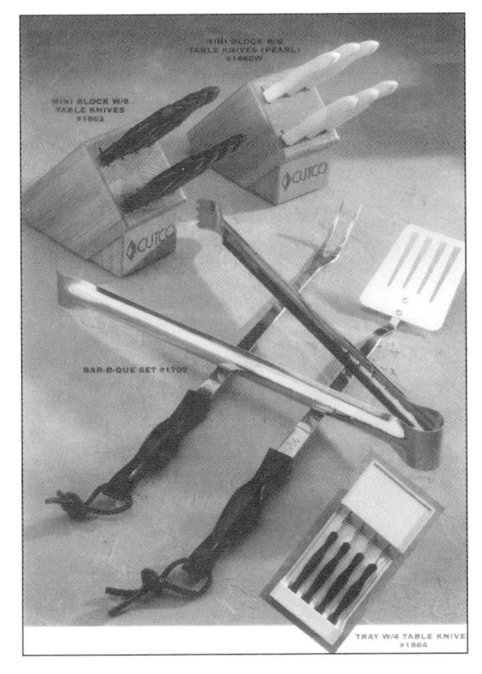

EXHIBIT 6

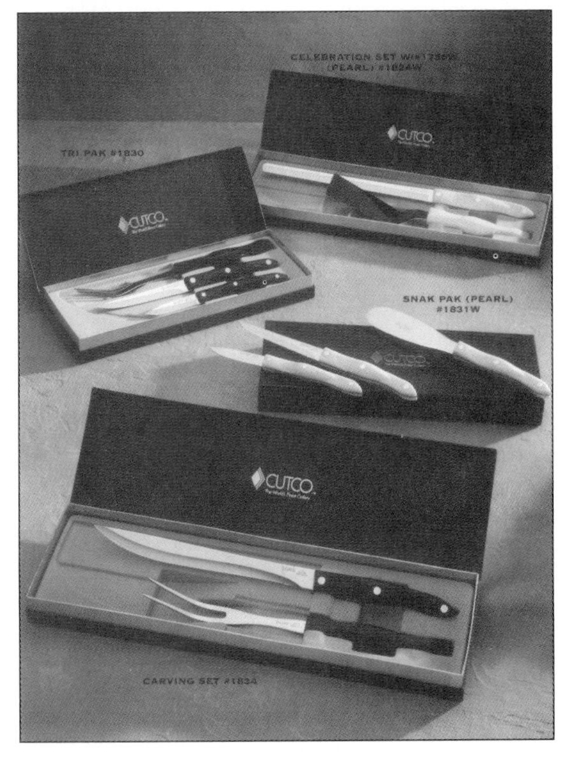

EXHIBIT 7

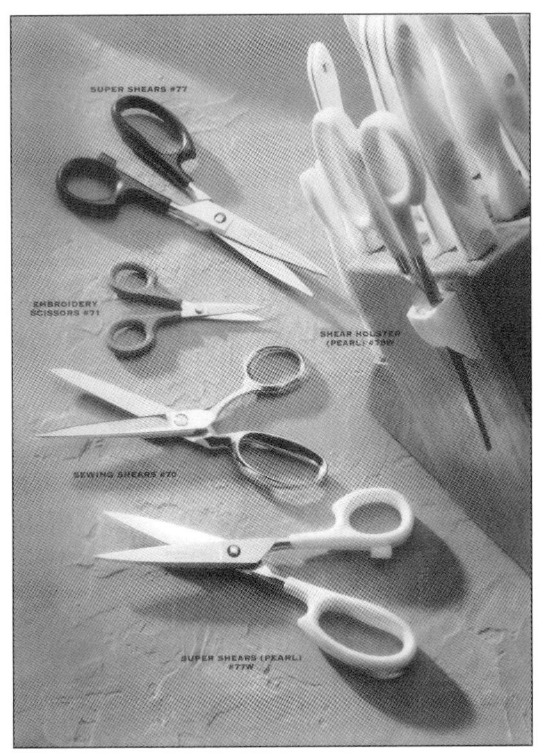

EXHIBIT 8

EXHIBIT 9

typical seasonal percentage of sales for CUTCO products.) Some students continue to sell during the school year. Recruiting, training, and ongoing management of the sales force are done utilizing over 200 district offices. Over 200 temporary branch offices are opened during the summer months and are staffed by college students with prior selling and management experience. All sales representatives are independent contractors. Sales training is completed over a three-day period. Vector has experimented with some catalog sales and has special policies in place that demonstrate sensitivity to its sales representatives. The typical CUTCO customer has household income of approximately $60,000, is well educated (with most holding a bachelor's degree and some with postgraduate degrees), is married with older children, holds a professional or managerial position, is approximately 40 to 54 years old, is a homeowner, and enjoys cooking, gardening, reading, and traveling.

CUTCO Cutlery Corporation manufactures CUTCO products in Olean, New York, and sells at wholesale to Vector and CUTCO International. Unlike many manufacturers, CUTCO has reduced outsourcing in recent years and has backward integrated into plastic molding (e.g., knife handles and cutting boards) and wood blocks. Jim Stitt, CUTCO Cutlery Corporation president and CEO, attributed the company's ability to stay competitive to its skilled work force and considerable investment in high-technology equipment. Additionally, the company processes its product very differently from competitors to provide a high level of product distinction (e.g., its unique recessed edge grind, freezing the blades, applying a mirror polish finish to the blades).

EXHIBIT 10 Fisherman's Solution

A total fillet knife system. Designed for lake, coastal or stream fishing. The high-carbon, stain-resistant steel blade adjusts and locks from 6" to 9" to fillet any size fish. A patented Cam-Lock secures the blade tightly at any length. The Zytel® inner track system assures the blade's smooth adjustment. The sheath pivots open to become a gripper to help clean, skin and fillet or remove a hook. Notched line cutter and a built-in sharpening stone with a groove for fish hooks complete the sheath.

FISHERMAN'S SOLUTION
A total fillet knife system. Designed for lake, coastal or stream fishing.
The high-carbon, stain-resistant steel blade adjusts and locks from 6" to 9" to fillet any size fish. A patented Cam-Lock secures the blade tightly at any length. The Zytel® inner track system assures the blade's smooth adjustment. The sheath pivots open to become a gripper to help clean, skin and fillet or remove a hook. Notched line cutter and a built-in sharpening stone with a groove for fish hooks complete the sheath.

EXHIBIT 11 Seasonal Sales

January–April	17%
May–August	67
September–December	16

EXHIBIT 12 Cutlery Sales by Retail Outlet, 1996

Mass merchants	33%
Department stores	20
Specialty stores	15
Warehouse clubs	13
Catalog showrooms	5
Other[1]	14

Note: Mass merchants, specialty stores, and warehouse clubs have gained in the past 10 years, with the "Other" category seeing the greatest decline as a percentage of the total.

[1] Includes hardware stores, home centers, supermarkets, drug stores, and direct mail.

Cutlery

Cutlery is a term applied collectively to all types of cutting instruments. More specifically, in the United States it refers to knives employed in the preparation of food and for sporting and utility use. The first U.S. cutlery factory was established in Worchester, Massachusetts, in 1829. As American steel improved in quality and decreased in price, the industry developed steadily, particularly in the Northeastern states. (Exhibit 12 provides industry cutlery sales by retail outlet for 1996.)

Cutting instruments are clearly of worldwide importance—numerous international manufacturing sites have gained some renown. Sheffield in the United Kingdom and Soligen in Germany are especially well known for cutlery. However, substantial innovation at the high end and inexpensive imports at the other have hurt some of the sectors that are long known for expertise and quality. For example, the cutlery industry in Sheffield has been reduced from over 300 firms to around 12 in the past 35 years. Several cutlery manufacturers recently have expanded into other product lines, including kitchen tools, pantryware, and garden implements.

While the number of successful cutlery firms was declining, cutlery sales increased throughout the 1990s. Sales were especially strong in specialty product segments (e.g., multitool, pizza cutters, potato peelers, nonstick cheese slicers, under-the-counter knife blocks), with new product innovations initially targeting upscale channels. In 1995 and 1996, U.S. consumers demonstrated renewed interest in known brands of cutlery rather than private-label goods and were buying more expensive brands.

In addition to specialty product segments, many cutlery vendors had begun focusing on niche markets such as bridal registries and Internet shopping. Regarding registries, Howard Ammerman, vice president of sales for J.A. Henckels (USA), stated, "Catching consumers early helps to avoid the looming issue of affordability. [Bridal] Registries are our opportunity to gain the next generation of Henckels' cutlery customers. They need to know why they're spending the money for high-end cutlery, and that it's a lifetime investment."[1]

By 1996, some knife manufacturers and retailers also were testing the Internet as a medium for promoting and selling cutlery products. According to Brice Hereford, national sales manager at Lamson & Goodnow, "We were most intrigued by the demographics. The demographics of an Internet browser—typically a college-educated person with above-average income—fits well with the profile of most consumers of high-end cutlery. This type of person is much more likely to buy an $80 chef's knife."[2]

Direct Selling

Direct selling is a method of marketing and retailing consumer goods directly to the consumer without reliance on direct mail, product advertising, or fixed retail outlets. Most direct selling employs independent salespeople to call on consumers, mainly in their homes, to show and demonstrate products and obtain orders. The goods are then supplied by the company either directly to the consumer or through the salesperson who obtained the order. The direct sales industry exceeds US$80 billion in annual worldwide sales. The United States represents less than 25 percent of total sales. Leading international direct sales firms include Avon, Tupperware, Shaklee, Stanhome, Amway, and Mary Kay Cosmetics. The Direct Selling Association, a worldwide trade association, represents most leading direct sales firms.

Generically, direct selling is a push marketing strategy. Direct selling is an especially effective strategy for products and services with a high personal selling elasticity, where procrastination in purchasing is easy, and when the product is a household item that benefits from demonstration in that environment. Push marketing strategies have been effectively realized by direct selling firms entering newly emerging economies where distribution systems, supporting infrastructure, and capital access are limited. Further, direct selling jobs are often attractive to citizens in such economies. Direct selling often is seen as the ultimate in equal-income-earning

[1] The *Weekly Newspaper for the Home Furnishing Network*, April 14, 1997.

[2] *The Weekly Newspaper for the Home Furnishing Network*, February 26, 1996.

opportunity, with no artificial barriers based on age, race, sex, or education. Independent contractors have flexible hours and can pursue earnings full-time or while pursuing an education, raising a family, or holding down another job.

Two general forms of direct selling exist: party plan and one-on-one. With the party plan method, a salesperson presents and sells products to a group of customers attending a party in one of the customer's homes. The intention is to demonstrate the quality and value of a product to a group of people, many of whom then will purchase the product. The party, however, is more than just a sales presentation and often is viewed as a socializing opportunity for busy people. The party host/hostess is principally responsible for identifying, qualifying, and inviting attendees. Tupperware and Mary Kay Cosmetics principally utilize the party plan approach. The one-on-one approach is more personalized and requires the salesperson to focus on the needs and economic demand of each potential customer. This approach is especially useful when customers may require detailed instruction regarding product quality differences or appropriate use of the product.

CUTCO's Major Competitors

Henckels

J.A. Henckels Zwillingswerk Inc., a 266-year-old German manufacturer, is a dominant player in the upscale cutlery market and has a global presence in over 100 countries, with long-established subsidiaries in Canada, China, Denmark, Japan, the Netherlands, Spain, Switzerland, and the United States. Significant growth in sales over recent years has been attributable to increased accounts, the expansion of existing accounts, and a broadening of the company's customer base through the development of non-German sources for the production of moderately priced products for multiple channels under the Henckels International logo. Through non-German sources, Henckels has been able to offer additional price points: EverEdge, a never-needs-sharpening, Japanese-made brand has a suggested retail price of $29.99 for a seven-piece set; the Brazilian-made Classic and Traditional forged lines are considered a cost-efficient alternative at $149.99 to the German-made brands. The company offers over 10 brands in fine-edge and never-needs-sharpening cutlery, and its products are available in virtually every high-profile retail account worldwide.

Further stimulating demand for Henckels Cutlery has been the development of specialty gift sets, providing a prestigious presentation of commonly grouped individual items. Henckels also has taken a strong stance on advertising to build brand awareness, substantially increasing its television, co-op, and bridal advertising budget in recent years. Henckels also has attempted to be innovative through new packaging (e.g., clam sets) and in working with retailers to develop appropriate displays. (A clam set is one or more products in thermoformed packaging that allows a full view of product, shelf appeal, potential customer opportunity to grasp the handle, and blade protection. Clam sets can be pegged or self-supported on a shelf.) Numerous retailers and catalog firms have begun to advertise and sell their Henckels offerings through Internet Web sites. Henckels recently added new handles with an ergonomic "open-flow" design to comfortably accommodate each individual hand while maintaining safety.

In 1995, Henckels acquired German-based Wilkens tableware, moving the firm into the silverplate and stainless-steel flatware business. In 1996, the U.S. subsidiary doubled its available warehouse space to improve delivery performance. Recent estimates suggest that Henckels USA will have $70 million in 1997 trade sales. Karl Pfitzenreiter, president of J.A. Henckels, USA, explained, "We want to double our growth every five years, which we have so far been able to do by maintaining a 15 percent average annual growth rate in the U.S."[3]

Fiskars

Fiskars, founded in 1649, is the oldest industrial company in Finland and one of the oldest in the Western world. Over the years the company has solidified a reputation as a premier steel and ironworks company manufacturing a widening range of architectural, industrial, agricultural, and houseware-related products. Main market areas include North America and Europe, with 1997 estimated sales of US$550 million (of which over 90 percent was generated outside Finland). Headquartered in Helsinki, Fiskars has subsidiaries and/or manufacturing in Canada, the Czech Republic, Denmark, France, Germany, Hungary, India, Italy, Mexico, Norway, Poland, Russia, Sweden, the United Kingdom, and the United States. Markets targeted for further development or new expansion include Eastern Europe, Southeast Asia, Australia, and Latin America. The company is considered to be very strong financially and a major innovator in its many diverse product lines.

[3] The *Weekly Newspaper for the Home Furnishing Network*, October 7, 1996.

The Montana adjustable bread knife and the Raadvad cutter for bread, cabbage, and lettuce were examples of recent innovations. Fiskars cutlery features a full tang with synthetic handles, ergonomically designed and weighted and balanced to correspond to the blade length. Gift sets are housed in handcrafted solid walnut boxes lined with velveteen fabric and intended as heirlooms. Individual units may be purchased in clam shell packaging. Fiskars's worldwide sales of cutlery products are estimated to be US$70 million. Products in its homeware lines include scissors, knives, kitchen gadgets, and sharpeners. Trademarks include Alexander, Fiskars, Gerber, Montana, Raadvad, Knivman, Kitchen Devils, DuraSharp, and CutRite. The upscale Alexander line features such gift sets as a four-piece steak knife set retailing for US$197 and a two-piece carving set at US$260. Fiskars products are carried primarily in upscale channels, but the company continues to target mass merchants with select lines within its wide array of products. The Consumer Products Group generated 59 percent of its 1997 net sales in the United States. A 35 percent jump in U.S. sales was at least partly attributable to a strengthening U.S. dollar.

In late 1994, as part of its overall expansion strategy, Fiskars acquired Rolcut & Raadvad, a supplier of kitchen cutlery and garden tools. In July 1997 a greenfield startup, A/O Baltic Tool, began production of garden tools. In August 1997 Fiskars agreed to acquire the Italian knife manufacturer Kaimano S.p.A.

According to Stig Stendahl, the company president, "Our goal is to generate one-fourth of sales from new products which have been in the market for less than three years. Fiskars has gained a lot of positive publicity thanks to innovative product development and design."[4]

CUTCO International

In 1990, Vector Canada was established as the company's first international marketing entity. Patterned after the U.S. sales model of utilizing college students as salespeople, the international entry is considered to be quite successful. (Sales should approximate US$7.5 million in 1997.) Fueled by the rather immediate success in Canada, the company entered into the Korean marketplace in 1992 as Vector Korea.

[4] President's Message on Fiskars Web page, 1997.

CUTCO Korea

CUTCO entered into the Korean marketplace with the student salesperson model that had been successful in the United States and Canada. CUTCO's strategy for entering Korea was to utilize U.S.-trained, Korean-born managers to oversee administrative operations. CUTCO Korea operated in the student salesperson mode from May 1992 until early 1995. Sales were nowhere near company expectations during this 2½-year period. With the student program faltering, CUTCO Korea began entertaining, in early 1995, the group selling (party plan) approach to selling.

Tae S. Kim, former Korean manager in charge of administration and finance and current national administration manager for CUTCO Australia, identified two major reasons for the lack of success of CUTCO's original college program approach in Korea:

1. *Cultural.* Korean college students do not value earning income during their college days in the same manner as college students in the Western part of the world do. Money is not a motivating factor for Korean students since their parents continue to provide total financial support. Mr. Kim described Korean students as less aggressive and uncertain about going into sales.
2. *Distribution.* Korean students generally do not own automobiles. The vast majority utilize public transportation (subway or bus), which does not make it easy to make sales calls.

Once CUTCO Korea understood and accepted the fact that the student model could not work in Korea, a group selling approach, with a revised commission structure, was quickly implemented. This model started in March 1995 with five female-managed offices. At that point, Korean sales exploded. The typical Korean sales representative is now a married, middle-class female age 20 to 50. The student program was abolished completely by the end of 1995. There were 21 female-managed offices by February 1996, and 1996 sales hit US$8.2 million. Unfortunately, due to the loss of sales offices, the temporary relocation of a key employee to head up a Philippine pilot office, and a very weak Korean economy, 1997 sales were likely to fall significantly below 1996 levels.

CUTCO United Kingdom

In 1992, the company conducted a "college program" trial in the United Kingdom. An English-speaking country with a well-educated population exceeding 60 million, the United Kingdom seemed a promising market, with approximately US$1.4 billion in direct sales. Although sales were reasonably successful, high expenses (e.g., office and warehousing rent, recruiting ads) led the company to delay entry. Instead, in 1995, the company made a trial entry using a group sales (party plan) approach. This approach was not successful, and CUTCO's intention remains to re-enter with the college program in 1999.

Distributorships

The company has utilized one independent distributor in Mauritius. Sales there are small but growing. CUTCO has tried out two other distributorships, but neither succeeded. In the distributor agreement, CUTCO sells to the distributor on wholesale terms and the distributor organizes, develops, and manages its own sales force. Chris Panus (CUTCO international finance manager) indicated that the company spent a lot of time selecting, training, and developing these distributors and wondered if the effort—versus opening up its own operation—was worth it.

CUTCO Australia

In 1996, CUTCO entered Australia. The entry was modeled after Vector Marketing in the United States and Canada. Unlike the Korean entry, CUTCO Australia began with experienced CUTCO sales and administration people. Stephen McCarthy, national sales manager for CUTCO Australia, has been with CUTCO since 1986. Steve had a reputation as a top CUTCO sales manager. Tae Kim was transferred from Korea and appointed national administration manager for CUTCO Australia. In addition to Steve and Tae, CUTCO moved five American managers to Australia. Each of these five had been with CUTCO between 7 and 13 years, and each manages his own sales office in Australia. (Three offices are in Sydney, and two are in Melbourne.) Plans were to have a total of 21 sales offices by the end of 1998.

Australia appeared to offer a significant opportunity. According to Mark George, "Australia is a territory with 19 million English-speaking, qualified-income people and a university school break starting in November and ending in February. The culture is similar to that in the U.S."

With annual sales expected to be A$3.0 million by the end of 1997, CUTCO Australia had definitely beat the odds of the typical international startup. CUTCO products were virtually unheard of in Australia in 1996. McCarthy reported, "The Australians thought our method of marketing knives was crazy. Our solicitors, our accountants, our consultants . . . all said, 'Students? You have got to be crazy!' They could not have been more wrong! Australian students like being entrepreneurial and goal-oriented. The student model is working wonderfully in Australia."

McCarthy's goal is to make Australia the CUTCO hub for the Asia–Pacific region. He envisions an all-Asian office to manage Singapore, Thailand, and Hong Kong as well as a proposed entry into New Zealand by 1999. As with Canada and other countries entered, he says that the long-term plan is to turn management of CUTCO Australia over to the Australians.

CUTCO Germany

In 1996 CUTCO began sales in Germany. Direct sales are extremely popular in Germany (almost US$5 billion), and other U.S. direct sales firms had experienced great success there. However, Germany appeared to be another country where recruiting college students would be difficult. Therefore, based on its Korean experience, CUTCO pursued a party plan format in Germany. The profile of sales representatives was similar to that in Korea. Unfortunately, a sales director heading up the German expansion left the company and sales had not achieved the hoped-for level of success, with 1997 sales around US$400,000 (approximately two-thirds of goal).

CUTCO Costa Rica

A launch in Costa Rica was made in June 1997. Two managers, from inside CUTCO, were available for transfer. One manager, a Spanish speaker with a Hispanic background, was from New York; the other was from Puerto Rico.

According to Mark George, "We picked Costa Rica because it was a small market with a nice middle- and upper-class structure. It is a safe place to do business, and although it's a small country, we believe we can develop Spanish-speaking managers who can help establish markets for CUTCO in the rest of Latin America. People are well educated, and the literacy rate is around 97 percent. We utilize the university student model, which helps us qualify the recruit to be able to get into the market that can afford our product."

International Market Expansion

CUTCO International was established in 1994 as a wholly owned subsidiary of ALCAS Corporation to manage the marketing and distribution of CUTCO products on an international basis. According to Fran

Weinaug: "International operations are currently in the developmental stage." The management team had initially set a goal of wanting to open two countries each year for the foreseeable future.

Weinaug, George, and Panus all understood that a multitude of diverse issues could spring up in international markets. They had already experienced currency fluctuations, nontariff barriers, import duties, and language and gender considerations in recruiting sales representatives, plus variability in country laws for direct selling. Further, opening a market required a major outlay of capital. There are considerable cost-of-living considerations for expats (e.g., housing, cars, start-up funds). To facilitate market entry in places where language is a barrier, management has used an in-country sales manager and in-country financial officer. Selling a high-end set of cutlery isn't the same as selling plasticware or cosmetics, and using in-country managers requires a lengthy training process.

To ensure timely international delivery, CUTCO ships and warehouses product at each international site. Freight, warehousing, and insurance add approximately 10 percent to total costs. On a country-by-country basis, the company goal was to be at breakeven, covering annual costs, by its third year.

By mid-1997 international operations had yet to be profitable. Noting this lack of international profitability, Erick Laine commented, "Developing international markets is a very costly process, but we're convinced it's worth it for the long term—and we're grateful we have the financial resources to wait it out."

For the near term (in addition to a 1997 pilot test in the Philippines), Laine, Weinaug, and their management team are deciding among such diverse countries as Argentina, Austria, Brazil, Ireland, Italy, Japan, Mexico, Poland, Taiwan, and the United Kingdom. Longer-term markets under consideration include China, Hong Kong, India, and South Africa. (Exhibit 13 provides worldwide direct sales data.)

Weinaug, George, and Panus know that CUTCO management expects to move quickly into several of these new markets. During strategy meetings they have been fielding a laundry list of questions from the rest of the CUTCO management team. In developing a recommended sequence of countries for market entry (along with an overall entry timetable), the management team needs immediate answers to the following questions:

1. What criteria should CUTCO use to select countries for market entry?
2. Which countries offer the best market opportunities for CUTCO products?
3. What should be the composition of the new country's management team?
4. Should CUTCO continue to develop countries using both the party plan/hostess program approach and the college program approach?

EXHIBIT 13
Worldwide Direct Sales Data

Source: World Federation of Direct Selling Associations.

	Year	Retail Sales (U.S.$)	Number of Salespeople
Argentina	1996	1.004 billion	410,000
Australia	1996	2.02 billion	615,000
Austria	1996	340 million	40,000
Belgium	1996	111 million	13,500
Brazil	1996	3.5 billion	887,000
Canada	1996	1.825 billion	875,000
Chile	1996	180 million	160,000
Colombia	1996	400 million	200,000
Czech Republic	1996	75 million	70,000
Denmark	1996	50 million	5,000
Finland	1995	120 million	20,000
France	1995	2.1 billion	300,000
Germany	1995	4.67 billion	191,000
Greece	1996	41 million	25,000
Hong Kong	1995	78 million	98,000
Hungary	1996	53 million	110,000
India	1995	70 million	12,000
Indonesia	1995	192 million	750,000
Ireland	1995	19 million	5,000
Israel	1996	80 million	14,000
Italy	1996	2.12 billion	375,000
Japan	1996	30.2 billion	2,500,000
Korea	1995	1.68 billion	475,988
Malaysia	1995	640 million	1,000,000
Mexico	1996	1.3 billion	1,060,000
Netherlands	1993	130 million	33,750
New Zealand	1996	126.5 million	76,000
Norway	1996	90 million	9,000
Peru	1996	295 million	177,000
Philippines	1996	320 million	630,000
Poland	1996	155 million	220,000
Portugal	1995	60 million	23,000
Russia	1995	300 million	250,000
Singapore	1996	96 million	34,500
Slovenia	1994	58 million	15,500
South Africa	1994	330 million	100,000
Spain	1995	652 million	123,656
Sweden	1996	90 million	50,000
Switzerland	1996	245 million	5,700
Taiwan	1995	1.92 billion	2,000,000
Thailand	1996	800 million	500,000
Turkey	1996	98 million	212,000
United Kingdom	1996	1.396 billion	400,000
United States	1995	19.50 billion	7,200,000
Uruguay	1995	42 million	19,500
Total		79.5715 billion	22,291,094

Case 6-21

Smith & Nephew—Innovex

At the beginning of March 2000, James Brown, CEO of Smith & Nephew, S.A. (S&N), was in a meeting with Josep Serra, Director of the Medical Division.

Almost six months earlier, on September 29,1999, they had signed an agency contract with Innovex whereby Innovex employees would promote S&N's moist wound healing (MWH) products Allevyn®, Intrasite® Gel and Opsite®[1] to primary care centres[2] in Galicia and Asturias. It was the first time S&N had used the services of a contract or outsourced sales force in Spain.

Among other things, the contract specified that the agreement would expire on March 29, 2000.

Brown and Serra had to assess the results of their collaboration with Innovex and decide not only what to do in Galicia and Asturias but also, more generally, what their policy should be with respect to the sales personnel who promoted the company's MWH products in the rest of Spain.

Smith & Nephew, S.A. (S&N)

Smith & Nephew, S.A. (S&N) was the Spanish subsidiary of the Smith & Nephew group (for information on the group, see Exhibit 1).

Founded in Spain in 1963, S&N sold in Spain the healthcare products manufactured by the Smith & Nephew group in various countries, mainly the United Kingdom and the United States, though it also imported products from France, Germany and South Africa, among others.

With annual sales of more than 4,000 million pesetas, the Spanish subsidiary had two commercial divisions: a medical division, and a surgical division. Between them these two sold all of the group's product ranges and families except consumer healthcare products, which were sold almost exclusively in the United Kingdom and some former Commonwealth countries. The company also had an administrative and finance division.

At the beginning of the year 2000, James Brown had been with the Smith & Nephew group for 18 years. He had been appointed CEO of the Spanish subsidiary in 1993. He reported to the Managing Director for Continental Europe, who was responsible for various countries in the north and south of continental Europe. The Managing Director for Continental Europe, in turn, reported to the Group Commercial Director, who was a member of the Group Executive Committee, along with the chief executive, the three presidents of the group's Global Business Units, and other senior executives.

The Spanish subsidiary had been the official supplier of certain healthcare products during the 1992 Barcelona Olympics. It had had ISO 9002 certification for several years and had almost finished computerising its entire sales network.

Since November 1998 S&N had been using the services of a specialized shipping and logistics company, which, under contract, took care of the reception of imported goods, storage, stock control, order preparation, and transport and delivery to the customer's address. Given its small workforce of fewer than 100 people, S&N also outsourced certain other services, such as payroll administration and social security paperwork, legal and tax advice, design and execution of advertising materials, organization of sales conventions, etc.

And yet the company had an uneven profit record, and its management faced certain challenges. For example, throughout 1998 and 1999 the pound sterling had steadily appreciated against the peseta, giving rise to a steady increase in the peseta cost of the products sold in Spain, most of which were imported from the United States and the United Kingdom.

Selling prices in the Spanish market for healthcare products were significantly lower than in other European countries. Also, in Spain it was more difficult to raise prices because the Social Security Administration often did its purchasing by a system of open

Case of the Research Department at IESE. Prepared by Professor Lluis G. Renart. May 2000. It is intended to be used as a basis for class discussion rather than to illustrate either effective or ineffective handling of an administrative situation.
Last edited: 1/16/01

[1] Allevyn®, Opsite® and Intrasite® Gel are registered trademarks of T. S. Smith & Nephew Ltd. Innovex™ and Quintiles™ are registered trademarks of Quintiles Transnational Corporation.

[2] Also known as health centres, basic health areas, or, previously, outpatient clinics. They delivered primary care services to the population covered by Spanish Social Security. There were some 3,000 primary care centres in the country as a whole, each tied to a referral hospital. A hospital and the group of primary care centres tied to it made up what was known as a health management area.

EXHIBIT 1 The Smith & Nephew Group

This global medical device company, headquartered in London, traced its origins back to 1856, when Thomas James Smith founded a pharmacy in Hull in the United Kingdom.[1]

In 1896, the founder brought his nephew Horatio Nelson Smith into the business as a partner, giving rise to the name Smith & Nephew. The company grew rapidly with the addition of products such as elastic adhesive bandages (Elastoplast), plaster casts (Gypsona), and sanitary towels (Lilia), often through acquisitions.

In 1999, the group reported worldwide sales of 1,120 million pounds sterling[2], with earnings of 171 million pounds[3] before tax and extraordinary income. In that year the group had activities in 90 countries. Geographically, the sales revenues were distributed as follows: 19 percent in the UK, 20 percent in continental Europe, 43 percent in America, and the remaining 18 percent in Africa, Asia and Oceania.

The main product ranges or families sold worldwide were: orthopaedics and trauma (mainly hip and knee prostheses, and trauma implants, 26 percent of worldwide sales); endoscopy (particularly knee and shoulder arthroscopy, 18 percent); wound management (e.g., Allevyn®, Opsite®, and Intrasite® Gel, 21 percent); orthosis and rehabilitation, casting and bandaging (bandages and plaster casts), and otology (prostheses and instrumentation for microsurgery of the inner ear) (together, 18 percent); and consumer healthcare (17 percent).

In the 1999 Annual Report, Chris O'Donnell, Chief executive, declared:

> We are concentrating our strategic investment on the three markets of orthopaedics [implants and trauma procedures], endoscopy, and wound management.

Each of these three Global Business Units was headed by a president.

In these three specialties, or in some of their subspecialties, the Smith & Nephew group held first or second place in the global ranking. In its three priority business units it expected to grow both organically and through acquisitions, whereas growth in its other businesses would be basically organic.

The group invested 4 percent of its sales revenue in research and development. One of its latest developments, precisely in the Wound Management GBU, was Dermagraft, a dressing of human tissue developed through bioengineering processes, which made it possible to heal certain types of chronic ulcers, such as diabetic foot ulcers, in just a few weeks. Although at the beginning of the year 2000 it was already being sold in some countries, Dermagraft was not yet available in Spain.

To summarize, starting from the British parent company, the group had evolved to the point where it had a broad range of ever more high-tech healthcare products that were sold around the globe.

[1] In fact, Thomas Southall had founded a pharmacy in Birmingham as early as 1820, and Southalls (Birmingham) Ltd. had been acquired by Smith & Nephew in 1958. So the roots of the company could be said to stretch back even further, to 1820.

[2] Equivalent to approximately 1,800 million dollars or euros, or almost 300,000 million pesetas, at the exchange rates prevailing at the beginning of March 2000. On January 1, 1999, the exchange rate of the peseta had been irrevocably fixed at a rate of 166.386 pesetas per euro. At the beginning of 1999, the euro had traded at 1.18 dollars, but over the year had steadily slipped against the dollar until by the end of February 2000 one euro was practically equal to one dollar. Thus, the peseta was quoted at 166 pesetas per dollar, and 267 pesetas per pound sterling. At the beginning of the year 2000 the pound sterling, the Greek drachma, the Swedish krona and the Danish krone had not joined the euro.

[3] Data about the group are taken from the Smith & Nephew plc "1999 Annual Report and Accounts." For more information, go to <http://www.smith-nephew.com>.

bidding, and because other competitors were less affected by the strength of the dollar and sterling.

Commercialization of Healthcare Products in Spain

According to EC directives, before a healthcare product could be commercialized, it first had to obtain the "CE marking" from an authorized body in any EU member country. In addition to this, in Spain the company commercializing the product had to submit, generally to the Ministry of Health or the regional government, a "market introduction report". Once these requirements had been met, the product could be marketed and sold.

However, given the way Social Security operated in Spain, the second key requirement for a product to achieve widespread use was for the product to gain approval from the Social Security Administration as a reimbursable product. Reimbursable products were identified by what was known as the *cupón precinto* or "Social Security coupon"[3]. As is explained in greater detail later on, obtaining reimbursable status as certified

[3] Only products classed as "medical accessories" (under Royal Decree Legislative 9/1996 of January 15, which regulates the selection of medical accessories, their financing from Social Security funds or government funds earmarked for healthcare, and the basis on which they may be supplied and dispensed to outpatients) could apply for reimbursement.

by the Social Security coupon was critical for sales of a particular product through pharmacies, though not strictly necessary for its use in hospitals.

The Social Security coupon was a rectangle printed on the packaging of each unit of product, with perforated edges to allow it to be detached. On it were printed the initials A.S.S.S. ("Social Security healthcare"), the commercial name of the product, certain data about the product and manufacturer, and the price.

Healthcare Products Sold in Pharmacies

In the case of drugs and healthcare products sold in pharmacies, patients covered by Social Security had to obtain a prescription from their Social Security physician, who would usually have her office in a primary care centre. They could then take the prescription to any pharmacy to obtain the medicine. At the time of purchase, the patient would have to pay 40 percent of the retail price (except for pensioners and the chronically ill, for whom prescriptions were completely free). Before handing over the product, the pharmacist would cut out the Social Security coupon and staple it to the prescription, so as later to be able to obtain reimbursement of the remaining 60 percent (or 100 percent if sold to a pensioner or chronic patient) from the Social Security Administration.

If a drug or healthcare product was authorized for sale but did not have the Social Security coupon, a patient could still apply to the Social Security Administration's own medical inspection service for reimbursement as an exceptional case, but this was a very laborious procedure with no guarantee of success. The alternative was to pay the full 100 percent of the retail price. In either case use of the product was seriously inhibited, above all if there were alternative healthcare products on the market that had similar therapeutic qualities and were reimbursable.

Given the pressure to contain health spending in the Spanish state budget, it was quite possible for a more modern and more efficient yet more expensive drug or healthcare product not to obtain Social Security approval because an alternative product was available which, while not so advanced from a therapeutic point of view and possibly less efficient, could cover the same need.

Healthcare Products Used in Hospitals and Primary Care Centres

In hospitals, whether a healthcare product was reimbursable or not had no direct impact on sales (though it did affect them indirectly, as we shall see later). Private hospitals and clinics purchased healthcare products in the normal way, paying the price freely agreed with the manufacturer or distributor.

Hospitals and primary care centres belonging to the Social Security Administration, in contrast, used a system of procurement by public bidding. Usually, an individual hospital or primary care centre, or all of the hospitals and primary care centres in a particular geographical area, would issue an invitation to tender once a year, specifying the quantity and characteristics of the products they wanted to purchase. All of this would be set out in a bidding document, which would also specify the information and other things required of prospective bidders, the bid closing date, the selection criteria, etc.

Healthcare Products for Ulcer and Wound Care

Traditionally, the main wound care products were elastic adhesive bandages, gauzes, and the classic dressings. These constituted what was known as the wet-to-dry method. In the year 2000, wet-to-dry dressings were still commonly used in the management of acute wounds, where it was possible to predict the duration of the healing process. They were products with a low unit value, and so whether they were reimbursable or not was practically irrelevant, as hardly anybody went to the doctor to get a prescription for a roll of plaster.

From the early 80s onward, however, a new method, known as moist wound healing, began to be adopted in the treatment of chronic ulcers[4]. It was found that wounds healed more quickly if they were kept moist and protected from infection, allowing the passage of moisture vapour and maintaining the physiological temperature.

Over the years a variety of products for moist wound healing (MWH) came onto the market, such as polyurethane dressings, hydrocolloids, alginates, hydrocellular dressings, and carbon moist wound dressings.

In Spain, in 1999, the total market for MWH products was worth around 3,200 million pesetas at manufacturer's prices. Of this total, around 1,870 million was sold through pharmacies and around 1,300, to hospitals and clinics. A large proportion of the total MWH market consisted of hydrocolloids.

[4] Chronic ulcers are ulcers of unpredictable duration. The healing process can easily go on for several months. The most common causes of chronic ulcers are continuous pressure on a particular part of the body (e.g., bedsores) or vascular or circulatory problems. A chronic ulcer can be shallow or deep, and in serious cases can lead to necrosis, gangrene, and may even require amputation of the affected part.

The main competitors in the MWH product category were C.S. (with a market share of around 35 percent), Danplast (22 percent), and Smith & Nephew (9 percent).[5]

The Medical Division of Smith & Nephew, S.A. (S&N)

Under the overall management of Josep Serra, the medical division's sales and marketing activities were carried out by a sales team and a marketing team. In 1999 the division had total sales in the region of 3,000 million pesetas, shared between three product families: wound care (1,000 million); casting and bandaging; and orthosis, rehabilitation and aids for everyday living (2,000 million between these last two families).

Of the 1,000 million pesetas in wound care, around 600 million were wet-to-dry and around 400 million, moist wound healing (MWH) products.

At the beginning of the year 2000, S&N competed in only three categories of MWH products (in various sizes and varieties):

- Intrasite® Gel, a cleansing hydrogel that regenerated the ulcer, debriding and absorptive, sold in packs of five 15g units (see Exhibit 5). It had the Social Security coupon. In 1999, S&N had sold 130 million pesetas of the product and had a market share in this subcategory in the order of 40 percent of sales through pharmacies.
- The Allevyn® range, a controlled absorption hydrocellular dressing (see Exhibit 6). Three sizes of the range had the Social Security coupon. In 1999, S&N had sold 170 million pesetas of the product and had a market share in this subcategory in the order of 50 percent of sales through pharmacies.
- The Opsite® range, a transparent polyurethane dressing. Six sizes of the range had the Social Security coupon. In 1999, S&N had sold 100 million pesetas of the product and had a market share in this subcategory in the order of 90 percent of sales through pharmacies.

These products had various technical advantages that made the healing of an ulcer or wound faster, safer and less painful.

However, the correct prescription, use and application of MWH products required certain knowledge that only doctors and nurses were likely to have. This meant that patients and their relatives very rarely influenced the type of product used.

Nevertheless, a significant volume of MWH products was sold through pharmacies. It was true that it was always a doctor who prescribed the use of a particular product. But, often, a relative of a housebound chronically ill patient would go to the pharmacy, obtain the product free of charge, and then give it to the nurse who, in the course of a home visit, would apply the dressing.

The management of S&N's medical division estimated that slightly over 50 percent of their MWH products were sold through pharmacies.

Almost all the remainder, just under 50 percent, was used in hospitals and primary care centres belonging to the Social Security administration.

S&N Medical Division's Sales and Promotional Activities

The division's *sales* efforts, strictly speaking (i.e. activities undertaken to generate orders and invoices), were conducted in three channels:

1. Sales to Social Security hospitals and primary care centres were made by bidding in yearly auctions[6]. Products that won a contract would be supplied and billed over the course of the year, and were used either in the hospital or primary care centre itself, or during home visits.
2. Sales to pharmacies were accomplished through pharmaceutical wholesalers or cooperatives, which replenished their stocks at regular intervals without S&N having to make hardly any effort to sell to them.
3. Lastly, the medical division's own sales representatives sold directly to private hospitals and large private clinics, or indirectly, through healthcare product wholesalers/ distributors, to other private hospitals and clinics, geriatric homes and the private practices of doctors and vets.

The division's *promotional* efforts were targeted at doctors and, above all, nurses. The aim was to bring the products to their attention, explain their advantages and how to use them, give the doctors and nurses an opportunity to try them out, and explain to them the differential therapeutic advantages of the company's products compared with older or competing alternatives.

When dealing with healthcare professionals working in the public health system, the sales representatives'

[5] Throughout the case, unless stated otherwise, the market shares of specific products refer to the pharmacies channel, which was monitored by IMS, a market research services company. Market share data for hospitals were difficult to estimate, as they depended on the outcome of the bidding process.

[6] In 1999, S&N had bid in almost 500 auctions.

mission was also to persuade doctors and nurses to issue favourable reports on S&N's products.

Lastly, an important goal of the promotional effort was to ensure, once a contract had been won and the S&N product was in use in a given healthcare facility, that the product was always at hand for any doctor or nurse who needed it.

As Josep Serra remarked:

> It's a major training and "merchandising" challenge seeing to it that the products we sell are available on every floor, in every consulting room, on every trolley, and that they are used correctly.

Promotional Tasks Carried Out in the Field by the Medical Division's Own Sales Representatives

The national sales manager supervised two regional sales managers. Between them the two regional sales managers had 18 sales representatives and three commission agents, who did all the sales and promotional work for all the division's products. (Exhibit 7).

This sales team's coverage of the Spanish market as a whole was considered poor, particularly compared with the division's main competitors. It was estimated that it covered almost 100 percent of the hospitals but only 20 percent of the primary care centres. In contrast, Danplast, S.A. was thought to have around 50 sales representatives, and another major competitor, C.S., S.A., more than 40.

S&N's marketing manager estimated that to be able to provide a satisfactory level of promotional and sales service for the medical division's products throughout Spain, they would need about 40 sales representatives. Without that number it would be impossible to visit all the primary care centres.

One of the division's sales representatives nominally covered the area of Galicia. But given the size of the region,[7] in practice he only ever had time to visit hospitals and clinics and healthcare product wholesalers.

In 1999 the medical division's full-time sales representatives had sold an average of 150 million pesetas each, at an average cost per representative of 8.5 million pesetas, including salary, incentives, Social Security, vacations, travelling expenses, etc.

The division's three remaining commission agents (previously it had had five or six of them) had between them sold 150 million pesetas. The agent for the region of Extremadura was a company that had been working with S&N for about eight years. The other two agents were individuals. One covered the islands of Majorca and Ibiza, selling only S&N products. The other covered the island of Menorca, offering a very wide range of products by different companies, exclusively to hospitals. Both had been working with S&N for around 20 years, and in both cases the relationship was considered stable.

The commission agents had agency contracts. They visited only hospitals, that is to say, they did not promote the products to primary care centres. According to Serra, "They go for the guaranteed sales, what I mean is, they try to sell the products for which there's already a demand. They don't make much effort to introduce new products. They're undoubtedly more profitable than having full-time representatives of our own in those territories. That would be too expensive, in the case of Extremadura because its so extensive, and in the other cases because they're islands."

When they made a sale without going through a bidding process, the commission agents would close the deal and pass the order on to S&N, which would serve the goods, invoice the customers and collect payment. The commission agents were only responsible for collecting debts from private (nonpublic) customers, and earned a commission of between 7 percent and 10 percent. When there was an auction, the commission agents would gather the necessary information, so that S&N executives could prepare the documentation and put in a bid.

Other Promotional Activities Carried Out by the Marketing Department: Advertising, Seminars, "Study Days"

In addition to the sales and promotional activities carried out by the medical division's sales team, the marketing department, consisting of a marketing manager and two product managers, carried out a number of complementary activities.

These consisted mainly of:

- Advertising the division's products through inserts in medical journals and through special brochures.
- Attending nursing conferences organized by the professional associations of nurses for particular medical specialities. For example, in 1999 S&N had attended four conferences, including one in Bilbao on gerontological nursing. Attending a medium-sized conference could cost S&N around 3 million pesetas. A conference could be attended and sponsored by some 15–20 companies.

[7] Galicia has an area of 29,575 km^2 and is almost square in shape. In 1998 its population was approximately 2,716,000. Asturias is elongated and narrow in shape, with an area of 10,604 km^2 (approx. 200 x 50 km), and in 1998 had 1,060,000 inhabitants.

- Study days: These were meetings, organized entirely by S&N and generally held in a hotel, with a specific scientific interest provided by a guest speaker. Following the guest speaker's lecture, an S&N product manager would present the company's products for the application in question. The meeting would end with a colloquium and aperitifs.

In 1999 23 study days had been held, each of which had been attended by around 65 specially invited nurses. The average cost per study day had been around 300,000 pesetas. To make the most of these occasions, it was vital to carry out close personal follow-up.

Social Security Approval for the Allevyn® Range and First Contacts with Innovex

Up until April 1998, only two of Smith & Nephew, SA.'s MWH products had the Social Security coupon and were therefore reimbursable: Intrasite® Gel and Opsite®. In fact, hardly any other medical division product had the coupon.

In April 1998, after a long wait, S&N's Allevyn® product was finally granted the right to carry the prized coupon. This was an important development, as Allevyn® was potentially a similarly priced but functionally superior substitute for hydrocolloids, which accounted for a large proportion of the total market for MWH products.

Allevyn® was already sold by bidding to hospitals and primary care centres. Now, with the Social Security coupon, it seemed set to achieve a significant volume of sales through the pharmacy channel. With sales potential to hospitals and primary care centres currently in the order of 1,100 million pesetas, its potential market could therefore be considered to be augmented by a further 1,600 million or so, in the pharmacy channel, despite the fact that only some of the sizes in which the product was sold were reimbursable by Social Security.

As we said earlier, in order to bid in Social Security procurement auctions, a product did not have to be reimbursable. However, doctors and nurses preferred, when starting treatment of a wound or ulcer in hospital, to use products that *were* reimbursable because that made it much easier for the patient to continue the treatment at home, using the same products as in hospital.

Conversely, if a particular product was *not* reimbursable, doctors and nurses were sometimes reluctant to use it, even in hospital, so as not to have to change the patient's prescription on discharge and prescribe a different product that *was* reimbursable and would therefore be free of charge for the patient.

First Fruitless Contact with Innovex

In March 1998, with approval of Allevyn® now imminent, the medical division's top executives contacted Innovex, an international company already established in Spain that specialized in providing contract sales teams for the pharmaceutical and medical devices industry (see Exhibit 2 for information on Quintiles Transnational Corporation and its Innovex division.)

They were keen to explore the possibility of contracting a team of Innovex sales representatives to reinforce the efforts being made by the medical division's own sales team to promote its MWH products to primary care centres.

Smith & Nephew's Spanish subsidiary had never worked with Innovex previously, nor with any other company that offered this kind of contract sales services. But they knew that it was a fairly common practice among their competitors in the healthcare industry, particularly when launching new products onto the market.

Also, colleagues in the group's United Kingdom offices confirmed that they had worked with Innovex and thought highly of the company. One or two other companies that provided services similar to those of Innovex were contacted for the purpose of comparison.

In the end, however, the idea of working with Innovex was dropped for fear that the necessary level of sales and profitability might not be attained.

Developments in the Period April 1998 to February 1999

Between April and June 1998, sales of Allevyn® rose sharply, only to flatten out again in the following months.

By February 1999, the management of the medical division were concerned that if they did not take decisive action, Allevyn® was in danger of being sidelined, with a share of only 2 percent or 3 percent of the total MWH market in Spain.

In this situation, they decided that the only course of action was, on the one hand, to intensify and extend the promotional activities aimed at customers already covered by the company's sales team; and on the other, to achieve fuller coverage of primary care centres in the underserved regions of Valencia, Andalusia, Galicia and Asturias.

The medical division's managers were in a tight spot: there seemed to be a potentially profitable opportunity to promote Allevyn® to primary care centres, but CEO James Brown and his superiors would be reluctant to add to the company's workforce.

EXHIBIT 2 The Quintiles Transnational Group and Its Innovex Division

Innovex Spain, S.L. was the Spanish subsidiary of Innovex Inc., which in turn was a division of Quintiles Transnational Corp. Both had their headquarters in North Carolina, United States[1].

At the end of 1998 the Quintiles group had more than 18,000 employees in 31 countries and that year reported net revenue of 1,188 million dollars. Of this total, 583 million had been generated in the United States and 340 million in the United Kingdom.

The Quintiles group provided full, outsourced research, sales, marketing, healthcare policy consulting and information management services to pharmaceutical, biotechnology, medical devices and healthcare companies throughout the world.

For example, a pharmaceutical laboratory could turn to the Quintiles group to take care of anything from the basic research needed to synthesize a new molecule or active substance (Phase 1), plus any of the intermediate phases of research and development, clinical trials by physicians and hospitals, data compilation, etc., to the management of the new drug approval and registration process (Phase 4). Then, if it wanted, the laboratory could also hire the Quintiles group to do all the marketing and actually bring the product to market.

Innovex Inc. was a division of the Quintiles group that specialized in sales and marketing services for third parties.

In 1998, Innovex Inc. was present in 19 countries and had more than 7,000 sales representatives, sales managers and marketing directors. In that year its sales teams had made an average of almost two million product presentations per month.

Innovex had been present in Spain since 1996, when it had acquired an existing Spanish company that was already active in the business of providing contract sales teams. Subsequently it had extended, or intended to extend, its services to other areas connected with the commercialization of drugs or medical devices, such as marketing and sales strategy consulting, training, communication, resource optimization, etc.

As Jesus Polanco, CEO of Innovex's Spanish subsidiary, pointed out:

> "It's not just a matter of 'getting people out knocking on doors'. In line with the group's general approach, we aim to create value by carefully managing each sales territory, monitoring the costs and results of our actions, collecting and compiling the valuable commercial information generated in each territory, and so on."

See Exhibit 3 for various examples of Innovex's more recent projects in Spain.

At the end of 1999, Innovex's Spanish subsidiary had a team of 152 people. Of these, 17 belonged to the management team, while the remaining 135 made up the sales force that went out 'knocking on doors'. Seventy-seven of the sales representatives were full-time Innovex employees, with open-ended contracts, while the remaining 58 had temporary contracts linked to a particular job for a client.

[1] Data are taken from Quintiles Transnational Corp.'s "Annual Report 1998." For further details, go to <http://www.corporate.quintiles.com> and <http://www.innovexglobal.com>.

Steps towards an Agreement with Innovex

In March 1999 the management of S&N's medical division got back in touch with Innovex to explore the feasibility of contracting a team of medical sales representatives to promote the products of the Opsite®, Intrasite® Gel and Allevyn® ranges in the regions of Spain hitherto least well covered by the company's own sales staff and commission agents.

In all, they considered the possibility of contracting from Innovex a team of 10 sales representatives and an area manager to serve Galicia [3], Asturias [1], Andalusia [3] and Valencia [3].

Ideally, S&N's management would have preferred to contract a sales team that would devote only 50 percent of its time to promoting S&N's products.

Unfortunately, at that time they were unable to find any other company in the healthcare sector that needed Innovex sales representatives working half-time for precisely the hours that would fit in with S&N's requirements, in the same geographical areas and for the six-month period S&N envisaged.

It was therefore agreed that the sales team contracted from Innovex should devote 100 percent of its time to promoting S&N's MWH products to primary care centres.

In view of the cost this would represent, S&N's management asked Innovex to submit a formal offer for the provision of just two sales representatives to promote S&N's MWH products to primary care centres in Galicia and Asturias. At that time, Arturo, the

EXHIBIT 3 Examples of Recent Projects Carried Out by Innovex in Spain in the Field of Contract Sales Teams

Zeneca

Before Zeneca merged with Astra to form Astra-Zeneca, it planned to launch two new products in the same year. To do this, Zeneca's sales force required reinforcement in the form of 65 people hired from Innovex for a period of two years to carry out visits to cardiologists, neurologists, psychiatrists and general practitioners.

The main goal was rapid market share gain to block the entry of competitors.

However, it would have been too expensive to keep the 65 people on for a second phase focused on maintaining the products' market presence.

Géminis

Géminis was the new generic Pharmaceuticals division of Novartis, which marketed out-of-patent products.

As it was a new division, the company did not want to hire extra sales representatives until they had seen what results the new division was capable of achieving. Note that promoting generics requires a different sales approach, both when selling to doctors and when selling to pharmacies.

The task Innovex undertook between 1998 and 2000 initially required a team of 12 promotors, later expanded to 17.

Pierre Fabre

Pierre Fabre contracted a team of seven "beautician" promotors from Innovex to persuade and educate pharmacists to recommend, for each individual customer, the most appropriate Klorane® product from among a wide range of shampoos and hair creams.

Cardionetics

At the beginning of the year 2000, Innovex was preparing to set up a "virtual" company, i.e. using only temporary employees, to commercialize in Spain an innovative portable ECG device for monitoring and diagnosing abnormal heart rhythms as a person went about his normal daily activities.

It would be responsible for all the functional areas involved in commercialization, including, among other activities, the deployment of a contract sales team.

[1] Data are taken from Quintiles Transnational Corp.'s "Annual Report 1998." For further details, go to <http://www.corporate.quintiles.com> and <http://www.innovexglobal.com>.

company's only sales representative in Galicia, only had time to visit the region's hospitals, so the primary care centres were more or less neglected.

If Innovex's offer was accepted, it would be very much an experiment. After six months, they would decide whether the system should be extended to other areas of Spain where the primary care centres were also relatively poorly served, such as Valencia and Andalusia.

S&N's management chose to conduct the trial in Galicia and Asturias because, of all the poorly covered areas, Galicia was the most suitable.

On July 2, 1999, Jesus Polanco, for Innovex, presented the project to the top managers of S&N's medical division (see Exhibit 4 for a summary of his presentation).

On September 29, 1999, after clarifying and discussing certain details without making any substantial changes, James Brown and Jesus Polanco signed the contract for a term of 6 months, i.e. to March 29, 2000. Besides the operational details, the contract included clauses regulating confidentiality, contract termination in the event of non-compliance by either of the parties, etc.

Lastly, S&N undertook not to hire any of the Innovex employees involved in the project, and agreed to pay Innovex compensation equal to a percentage of the employees' base salary if it did. In the case of the sales representatives, the compensation would be equal to 20 percent of 2.8 million pesetas per sales representative per year.

Execution of the Contract

As soon as the contract was signed, Innovex proceeded to select the two sales representatives. S&N gave its approval to the candidates chosen:

- Isabel, the person selected for Galicia, to be based in Vigo, already had some experience of medical sales visits. The S&N products she would have to promote were already known and used in the region, thanks to the hospital work done by Arturo, the local representative, who lived in Corunna. This meant that the new sales representative would have some local support.
- The person chosen for Asturias, Federico, had little experience but the right profile and plenty of enthusiasm. Asturias had the added disadvantage of having

EXHIBIT 4 Summary of the Presentation Given on July 2, 1999 by Innovex's Jesus Polanco to the Top Management of Smith & Nephew, A.A.'s Medical Division

- The plan was to conduct a trial campaign to promote the products Opsite®, Intrasite® Gel and Allevyn® in the four provinces of Galicia and in Asturias using a team hired from Innovex, whose target contacts would be nurses. If the trial objectives were achieved, the scheme would be extended to other geographical areas.
- The contract would have a term of six months.
- The team contracted from Innovex would consist of two sales representatives, a project manager, and a clerical assistant. The latter two would devote two days a month to the project. The sales representatives would receive five days' training.
- The sales representatives would devote their efforts exclusively to promoting the above mentioned S&N products.
- The fee per sales representative would be 35,102 pesetas per day actually worked, i.e. neither sick leave nor vacations would be billed.

The daily cost given above would include:

- Salary and social security.
- Health insurance and accident and third party cover.
- Monthly food + travel expenses, including the sales representatives' travelling, parking and telephone expenses up to a maximum of 80,000 pesetas per person per month.
- Vacations.
- All expenses deriving from the vehicles used by Innovex personnel in providing the contracted services.
- Costs of personnel selection by Innovex (in particular the cost of press adverts, costs associated with the selection interview, and the costs of hiring). Innovex would only select people who matched the profile and culture required by S&N.
- All aspects of payroll and associated costs, company cars, and the telephone expenses of the project manager.
- The costs of the administration department.

The following items were not included in the price per day previously given:

- Incentives for the sales representatives[1].
- Promotions aimed at doctors and customers.
- Promotional materials, samples, etc., which would have to be provided by S&N.
- Trips and field visits by S&N executives.
- Training costs. S&N would be responsible for all training in products, therapeutic areas and customers.
- Innovex would be responsible for managing the sales team. The two companies would agree on the kind of reporting and information S&N thought necessary in order to monitor the team's activities.

In an appendix, Jesus Polanco's presentation also described:

- The recommended profile for the sales representatives.
- The selection process.
- The functions of the Innovex project manager, who would liaise between the two companies.
- The responsibilities of Innovex's human resources department.
- The responsibilities of Innovex's finance department.

Finally, the presentation included a page stressing the advantages of using a sales team contracted from Innovex as opposed to a company-employed sales team.

[1] In the end no incentives were established.

been neglected during the previous two years following the death of S&N's previous sales representative, who had not been replaced. Because of this, in Asturias there had not even been the momentary surge in sales registered in other parts of Spain after Allevyn® got the Social Security coupon; and the products Federico would have to promote were practically unknown in the region.

Both the Innovex sales representatives were given two weeks' training. In the first week they had three days' instruction on the products they would be promoting (given by S&N), and one day on sales techniques

EXHIBIT 5 Intrasite® Gel Range

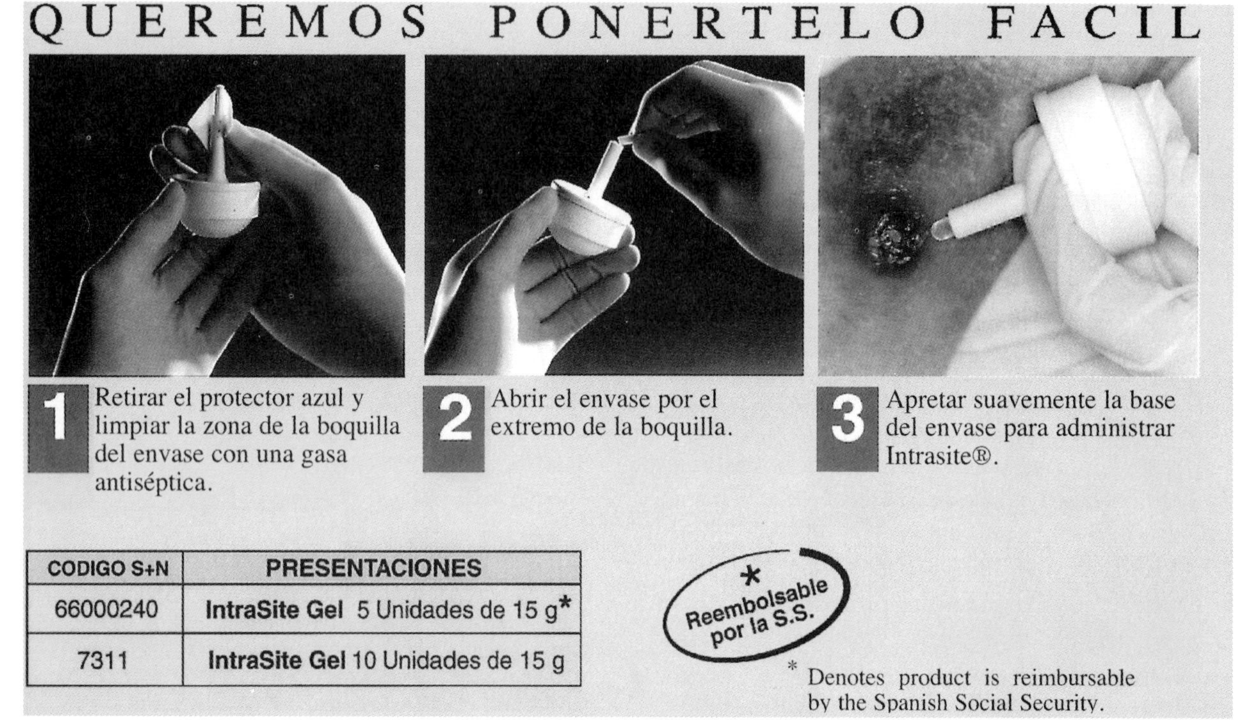

CODIGO S+N	PRESENTACIONES
66000240	**IntraSite Gel** 5 Unidades de 15 g*
7311	**IntraSite Gel** 10 Unidades de 15 g

(given by Innovex). The second week was given over to on-the-job training, accompanied by one of S&N's regional sales managers.

Following this, towards the middle of October 1999, they took up their posts in their respective sales territories and started to visit customers, using a list of primary care centres provided by Innovex and approved by S&N. The centres were ranked on an ABC basis according to their purchasing potential.

The regional sales manager for the central-northern area of S&N's medical division approved the sales routes proposed by Innovex, and after the first week started to accompany the two new representatives on their rounds.

According to the medical division sales manager, "We treated them as if they were our own employees."

It should be said, however, that about two weeks after Isabel, the representative for Galicia, had taken up her post, the marketing department held two study days in Vigo and Corunna, which had already been scheduled from earlier. This gave Isabel a chance to make contacts much more quickly than she could have done without the study days.

In Galicia, Isabel's promotional activities were concentrated in the provinces of Orense (342,000 inhabitants) and Pontevedra (904,000 inhabitants).

Both sales representatives took about three months to adapt to the normal pace of work.

Evaluation of the Results

At the end of February 2000, the director of S&N's medical division, together with his sales manager and marketing manager, analysed the results on the basis of the data available at the time.

With regard to costs, the average amount billed by Innovex to S&N had been 810,000 pesetas per sales representative per month.

With regard to sales, they had data from the territorial sales analysis (ATV)[8] for the last quarter of 1999, and internal billing data up to January 2000.

Everybody agreed that the results had been very different in the two areas:

In Galicia:

According to the October-December ATV report, the market share of Allevyn®, Intrasite® Gel and Opsite®, in pesetas, for the whole of Galicia had increased from 3.3 percent to 6.4 percent of the total value of MWH products sold. In Orense and in Pontevedra, the increase had been from 5.4 percent to 12 percent.

[8] The company IMS conducted a panel study of pharmaceutical retailers. Usually, it only provided aggregate data for the whole of Spain. The territorial sales analysis *(análisis territorial de ventas, ATV)* was a special service that IMS provided, offering the same data broken down by geographical areas similar in size to postal districts.

EXHIBIT 6 Allevyn® Range

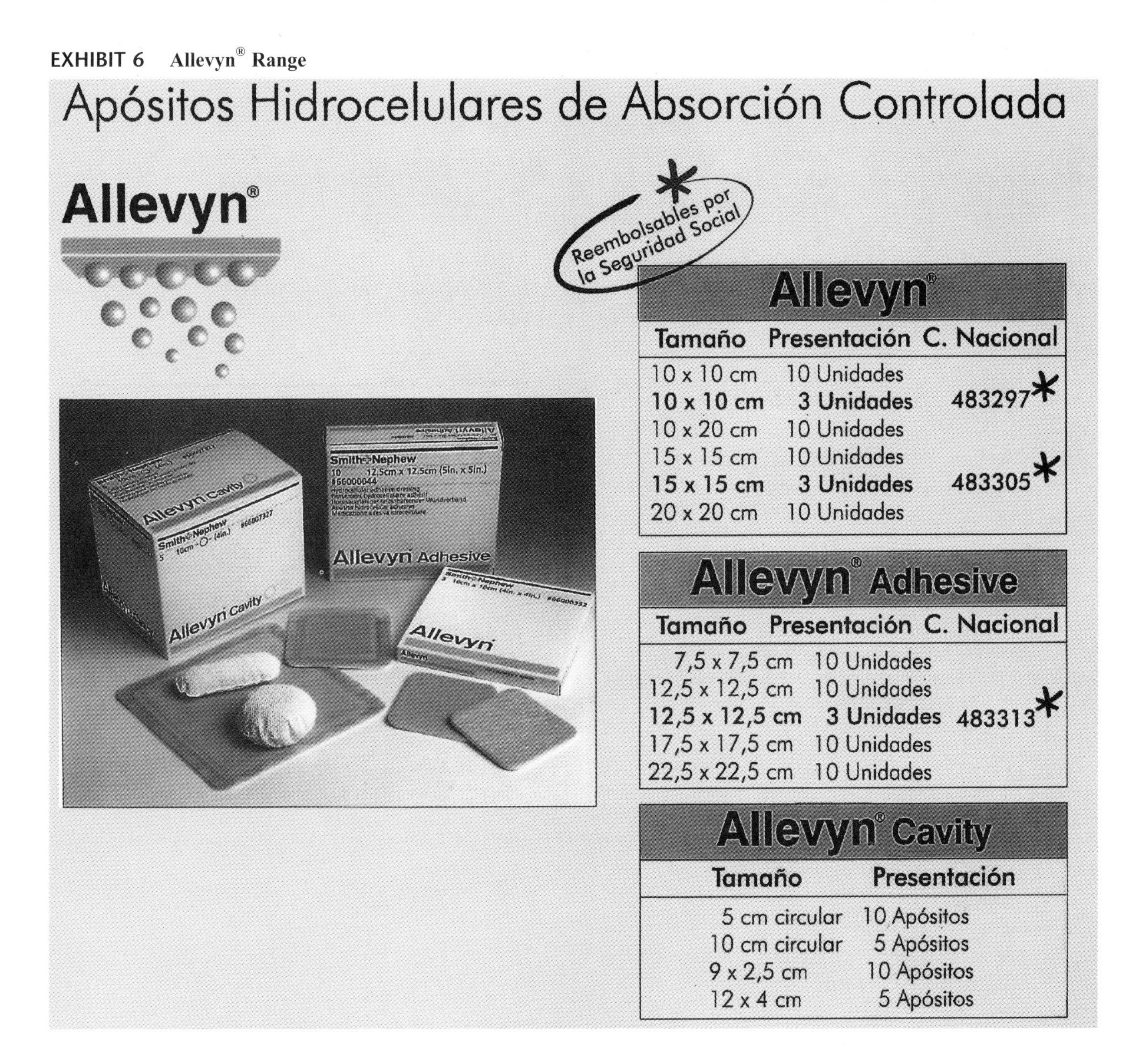

The additional sales revenue (on top of the minimal revenue obtained previously in the region) amounted to around 5,133,000 pesetas in four months (October 1999–January 2000 inclusive)[9] The gross margin had been 1,540,000 pesetas, i.e. 30 percent on average.

In Asturias:

The market share of the three products, in the last quarter of 1999, had increased from 0.9 percent to 2.36 percent of total sales, in pesetas, of all MWH products sold by all companies in Asturias.

The additional sales revenue amounted to only 1,484,000 ptas. in four months (October 1999–January 2000 inclusive),[10] with a gross margin of 371,000 pesetas (25 percent).

The difference in gross margin was due to the fact that the sales representative in Asturias had sold more products that had a lower gross margin. S&N's sales representatives did not know the gross margin of the products they sold. Only indirectly, through marketing actions, were they encouraged to sell higher gross margin products. Essentially, the difference in gross margin between Galicia and Asturias could be said to be due to chance factors.

[9] 606,000 pesetas. in October; 1,042,000 in November; 1,779,000 in December 1999; and 1,706,000 in January 2000.

[10] 134,000 pesetas in October: 252,000 in November; 528,000 in December 1999; and 570,000 in January 2000.

EXHIBIT 7 Sales Representatives' Legal Status

1. Salaried sales representatives

According to labour legislation in force in Spain in the year 2000, sales representatives who were integrated in a company's workforce had a "labour" contract of employment with that company. In the light of certain court rulings, a worker could be understood to be integrated in a company's workforce when he was unable to organize his professional activity at his own discretion, when his place of work was on the company's premises, and when he was subject to working hours stipulated by the company.

In the event of dismissal, such a sales representative could challenge the company's decision before the labour courts and require them to decide on the "fairness" or "unfairness" of the dismissal. If the dismissal was declared unfair, the company had to pay the worker severance payment or compensation equal to 45 days' salary per year of service up to a maximum of 42 months' salary.

If the company chose to terminate the employment relationship on any of the objective grounds for dismissal specified by the Workers' Statute (Article 52), it had to pay the worker, at the time of notification of termination, compensation equal to 20 days' salary per year of service up to a limit of 12 months' salary. Again in this case, the worker could challenge the dismissal and ask the court to declare it unfair. If in the end the company was unable to demonstrate the existence of objective grounds and the dismissal was declared unfair, the company would have to pay the worker compensation equal to 45 days' salary per year of service up to a maximum of 42 months' salary. Exceptionally, however, if the dismissed worker was hired under the terms of Law 63/1997, which provided for urgent measures to improve the labour market and promote stable employment, the above did not apply. Instead, in such cases, if the dismissal was found to be unfair, the company was obliged to pay compensation equal to 33 days' salary per year of service up to a maximum of 24 months' salary.

2. Sales representatives with an agency contract

According to the Agency Contract Law (Law 12/92 of May 27), a company could decide to establish a commercial relationship with a sales agent.

The features that defined a sales agent's commercial relationship with the company were:

- His place of work was not on the company's premises.
- He was not subject to working hours that were set by the company.
- In his professional activities he acted independently and organized his work as he saw fit.
- He could assume the business risk of the activities he performed, but this circumstance was not considered a defining feature of a commercial agency relationship and therefore was not sufficient by itself to prevent the relationship from being declared one of employment.

Any disputes that might arise between the parties in the execution of the commercial agency contract were resolved by the civil courts.

Unless otherwise expressly agreed by the parties, the company was not obliged to pay any compensation upon termination of the contract. Nevertheless, the commercial agent could claim compensation if by his work he had added new customers to the company's customer base. In any case, whether or not this right arose, and in what circumstances, would depend on the specific content of the agreement between by the parties.

Given that the relationship was not one of employment, the company was not obliged to pay Social Security contributions for the sales agent.

In response to the low sales in Asturias, the regional sales manager felt that Federico would have to improve his sales technique, in particular his closing abilities.

Sales Projection

In view of the actual results achieved, the medical division's marketing manager estimated that, if new Innovex sales representatives were introduced in other geographical areas, each one of them could be expected to generate roughly the following sales:

Month 1	**450,000 pesetas.**
Month 2	**900,000** "
Month 3	**1,650,000** "
Month 4	**2,225,000** "
Month 5	**2,700,000** "
Month 6	**3,000,000** "
Month 7 onward	**3,000,000 pesetas each month.**

Assuming a gross margin of 30 percent and average Innovex billing steady at 810,000 pesetas per representative per month, breakeven for a representative would be reached in the fifth month (2,700,000 × 30% = 810,000 pesetas of gross margin).

If these sales and margin forecasts were accurate, from month 6 onward the company would generate new gross income of 90,000 pesetas per month (gross margin less the amount billed by Innovex).

Other Considerations

The following are comments made by the director of the medical division and his sales and marketing managers, during their meeting, as they analyzed the facts and figures:

- "Innovex gives us a chance to try things out, to start working with new people and new regions, with a controlled level of risk. Then we can decide whether or not we want to actually hire the people once they've proved they can work profitably."
- "You have to remember that Innovex takes over a whole range of management tasks. During the trial period in Galicia and Asturias all we had to do was approve a bill of 1.6 million pesetas each month. And monitor sales as we wanted. Everything else (payroll, checking the expense sheets, mileage, and so on) was taken care of by Innovex."
- "If the Asturias salesman doesn't perform as well as expected, we can ask Innovex to replace him. And it'll be up to them to carry out the selection, hiring, sales training, etc."
- "Before we replace the salesman, though, we need to be sure it's him who's letting us down, rather than the sales potential of the territory itself, or lack of support on our part."
- "I suspect that Innovex doesn't pay its salespeople very highly. Take our sales representative in Galicia, for example. I'm already starting to worry that one of our competitors will notice our sudden gain of market share, realise that this person is worth her salt, or at least has potential, and offer her a permanent job with better pay."
- "Is it feasible to use Innovex sales representatives in the medium and long term? Or do companies just use them for tactical sales drives that never last more than 6 or 9 months?"

The Decision

Given the results of the trial, Brown and Serra now faced a set of alternatives deriving from the possible combinations of three variables:

1. To use salaried sales representatives or to use contract sales representatives employed by Innovex
2. Level of geographical coverage
3. Timing: when would be best to do one thing or another?

For example, without trying to be exhaustive, the above three variables could be combined in different ways to generate at least the following possible courses of action:

1. Terminate the contract with Innovex and leave the areas of Galicia and Asturias as they were before, i.e., with a single representative, Arturo, visiting hospitals.
2. Renew the contract with Innovex for another six months, only for Galicia and Asturias, in order to prolong the trial and so obtain more reliable data on sales trends and to verify whether the sales and financial performance could be consolidated.
3. Terminate the contract with Innovex and proceed immediately to hire:
   a. One salaried sales representative for Galicia.
   b. Two salaried sales representatives, one for Galicia and one for Asturias.
   c. Two or three salaried sales representatives for Galicia and one for Asturias, as in the original plan.

And in the rest of Spain:

4. Sign a new agreement with Innovex to establish contract sales representatives in all or some of the regions currently lacking coverage: Valencia (2 or 3 representatives) and Andalusia (2 or 3 representatives). The contract could be for six months or one year. Following that, introduce own salaried sales representatives in all or some of those regions, depending on the level of sales and profitability attained in each one.
5. Directly hire a certain number of salaried sales representatives for those same underserved regions.

Finally, if they decided to hire new salaried sales representatives, they would have to decide whether it was better for the representatives to work in tandem, as Isabel and Arturo had done in Galicia, i.e., with Arturo visiting mainly hospitals and Isabel visiting primary care centres; or whether it would be better to divide up the territory and for each representative to visit both hospitals and primary care centres in the part of the territory assigned to him or her.

Obviously, for each of these options they would have to weigh up the costs and the benefits, both in strictly financial terms and in terms of sales and marketing strategy.

In this latter respect, CEO James Brown was starting to get excited at the thought of the strategic possibilities that would be opened up if he ever reached the position of having a sales team fully deployed throughout Spain.

At the same time, however, he needed to make sure that the Smith & Nephew group's Spanish subsidiary reported a profit, as he personally desired and as the company's year 2000 budget demanded.

Case 6-22

Sun Microsystems (B)

Scott G. McNealy looks mighty calm for a man running a company whose stock has cratered. In the past two years, shares in Sun Microsystems Inc. have plunged from $64 to a lowly $3.28. A cool $195.1 billion in market cap has evaporated. Subtract Sun's cash from the equation, and investors value the company at barely $1.63 per share, less than they'd pay for a slice of pizza. Now, from the coffee bars to the research and development labs of Silicon Valley, the buzz is that Sun, long a symbol of ingenuity and dynamism, is looking more and more like a relic of a free-spending era that's long gone.

McNealy, Sun's chairman and chief executive, says he's not fazed. Throughout Sun's 20-year history, he has grappled with crises before, struggling to convince skeptical investors, customers, and employees that Sun could transform itself. Each time, he pulled it off. In the early 1990s, tech pundits said Sun should ditch its workstation business and jump on the cheap Intel-Microsoft Windows bandwagon. McNealy wouldn't listen. He went the other direction and built bigger and more powerful machines, setting up Sun to take advantage of the Internet boom. These days, the 48-year-old CEO, dressed in his trademark jeans and sneakers, says matter-of-factly that he understands why investors are treating his stock so poorly. "We're not making money."

Worse, sales have taken a nosedive, down 32%, to $12.5 billion, from a high of $18.3 billion two years ago, as net losses over the past five quarters, excluding special charges, have mounted to $307 million (Exhibit 1). In the past two years, gross profit margins have skidded by 20%. Top managers, including highly regarded President Edward J. Zander, have jumped ship. And yet McNealy clings tightly to the formula that has worked for him before. It calls for stubbornness, hard work, and faith that the research and innovation that have kept Sun at the head of the industry through the years will come to the rescue.

There's no time to waste. A fearsome posse of competitors, from Dell Computer to Microsoft and Intel, is battering its way into Sun's core market for computer servers, selling low-cost machines at a fraction of Sun's price. A few years ago, servers powered by Microsoft Windows software and Intel chips couldn't perform in the same league with Sun. Now they can. Worse, Linux' open-source software is making inroads into McNealy's market. It's created by legions of volunteers, and it's free—a price that's hard to beat. McNealy finds himself selling the tech equivalent of a Mercedes in a market of Honda buyers. "Sun will need to reinvent its business model," says Henry W. Chesbrough, a management professor at Harvard Business School.

Try saying that to McNealy. He maintains there's a home for Sun at the very top of the industry, safely above the Linux- and Microsoft-powered hoi polloi. He fiercely resists the notion that Sun's sophisticated servers could ever follow the brutal course of a commodity market. At the mention of the word "commodity," McNealy's eyes flash, and the Harvard alum growls that "a hammer is a commodity, a nail is a commodity. A computer is not a commodity."

But if those $4,000 boxes rolling off the assembly lines at Dell Computer Corp. aren't technically commodities, they behave very much like them, pummeling prices in Sun's core business. Consider Sun customer E*Trade Group Inc. In August, the $1.3 billion online financial-services company finished yanking out 60 Sun servers that cost $250,000 apiece and replaced them with 80 Intel-powered Dell servers running Linux that cost just $4,000 each. That took a huge bite out of expenses, including a one-time depreciation of the Sun gear and big maintenance fees. The savings so far: Nearly $13 million—and the company expects to shave another $11 million annually from its $220 million tech budget. "It wasn't a hard decision," says Joshua S. Levine, chief technology officer at E*Trade. And here's the really painful part: When the Intel-powered machines break, E*Trade doesn't bother calling a repairman. It just junks the server and plugs in a new one.

McNealy is battling disposable computers. And even when he looks away from the cheap Dells, he finds little relief. In the pricey side of the business, IBM, with its horde of consultants, is swooping into Corporate America offering the ultimate in no-headache computing: It will take over the entire burden of running corporate computer systems for clients. Says Microsoft Corp. Chairman William H. Gates III: "In terms of products that meet the market's needs, [McNealy's] in tough shape."

Yet McNealy has a plan, one that he says will lift Sun not only back to profits but to the apex of the Information Economy (Exhibit 2). At the heart of the plan is Sun's classic franchise: heavy research and top-of-the-line computer systems. In a world of specialty players, Sun is a rare bird that designs its own

EXHIBIT 1 The Problem: Rivals and Technologies Are Undermining Prices . . .

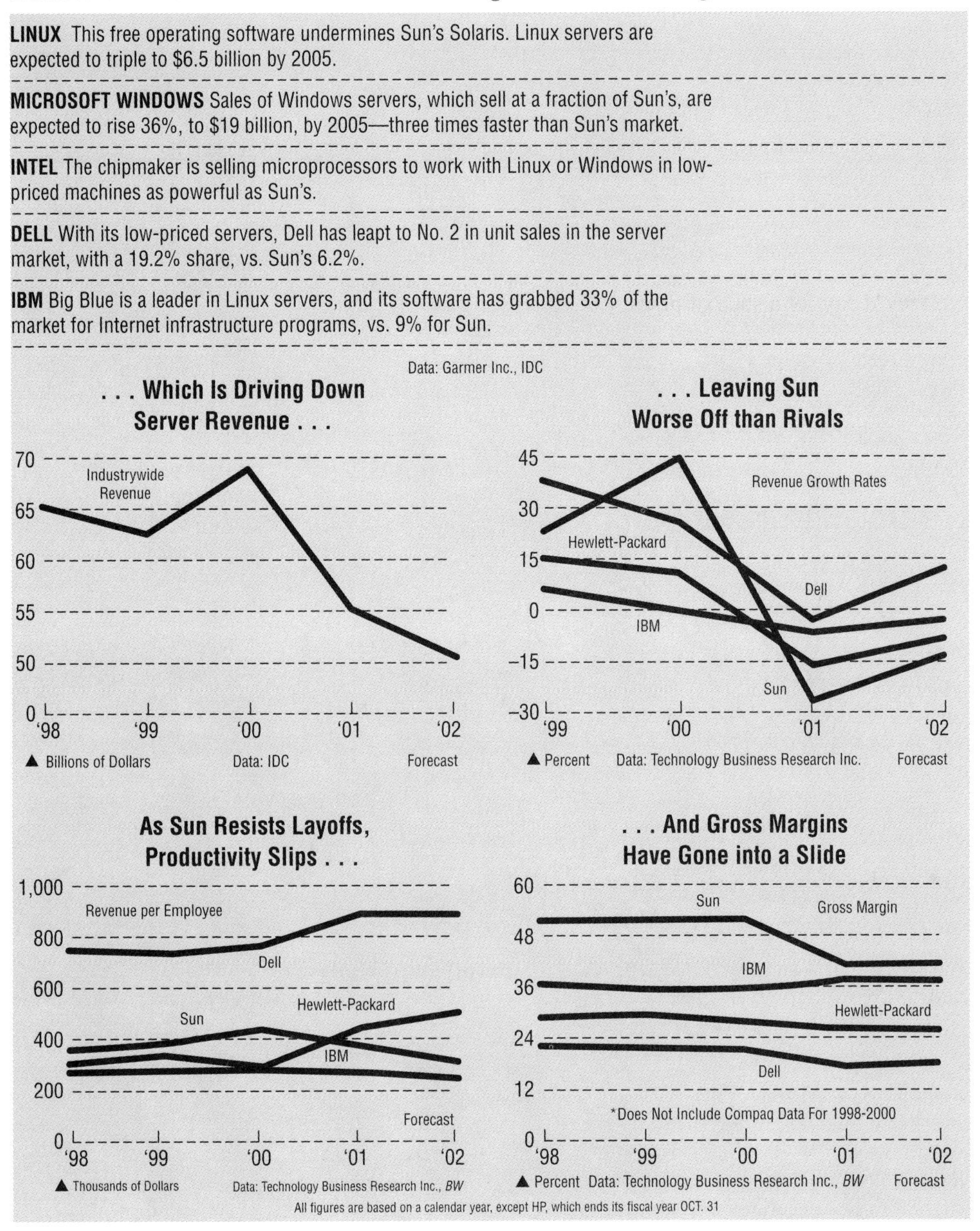

chips and writes its own server software and computer chips. And McNealy's sticking to his integrated model. He's pouring research dollars into network software. His goal, stunningly ambitious, is to have Sun servers and Sun software running superefficient networks of the future—marvels that run virtually free of human attention. In other words, while investors worry about Sun's very survival, McNealy, ever the contrarian, is plotting a path to supremacy.

And he has certain strengths to build on. By hacking costs, McNealy has stanched much of the bleeding and says Sun will break even by next year's second quarter. Net income has taken a beating, but Sun has generated cash in every quarter of the downturn. In the fiscal quarter that ended in September, Sun's cash total was $2.6 billion, up $140 million from the kitty in the fall of 2000. Tack on $2.6 billion in marketable securities, and McNealy has $5.2 billion to play with. He's using that

EXHIBIT 2 The Solution: McNealy's Plan for Reigniting Sun

FOLLOW THE MONEY Software products generate gross margins around 80%, twice that of servers. McNealy had dedicated 1,000 salespeople to software. He's also spending $900 million on it, half Sun's R&D budget.

LEARN TO LOVE LINUX Customers are clamoring for Linux, the free operating software. In the fall, Sun rolled out Linux on its low-end servers. With time, Linux will run on the powerful boxes too.

TAKE ON CUTTHROAT RIVALS In a bid to grab 30% of the market for supercheap Linux servers in a couple of years, McNealy has unveiled new servers priced as low as $2,700. He's using Intel chips and outsourcing production in an effort to still make money at that price

BEEF UP SERVICES Sun has doubled its force of consultants, to 13,000, over the past three years, getting 32% of revenues from services. Longer term, he hopes to offer more lucrative consulting.

PUSH INNOVATION McNealy is betting the farm that his outsize R&D budget will help Sun become the first company to provide software for smart networks that look after themselves—without calling on costly human help.

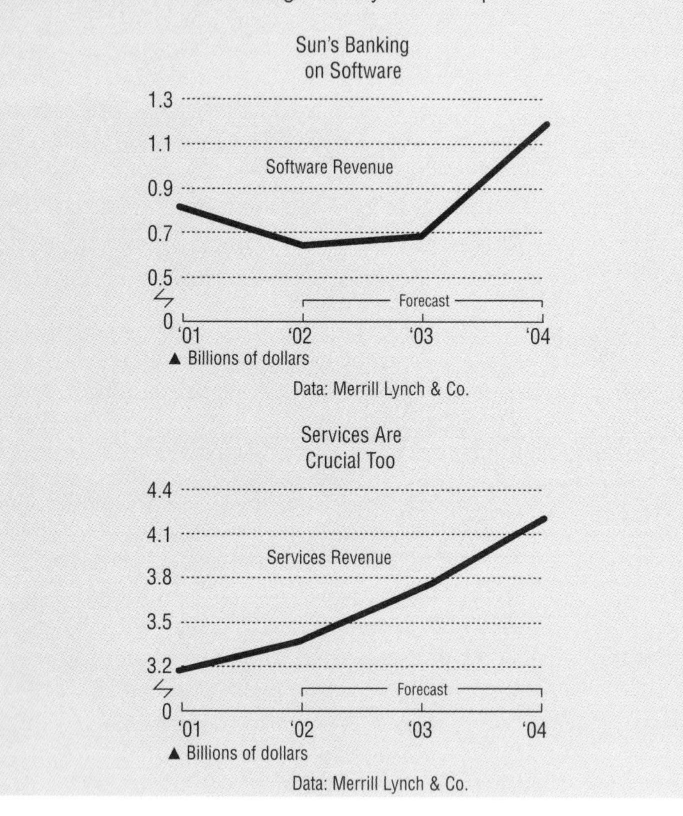

money to tidy up the books and spice up Sun's image. In the most recent quarter, Sun also bought back $500 million worth of stock and paid off $200 million in debt, bringing debt levels down to $1.5 billion. And he's spending $70 million on a worldwide ad blitz.

But the clock's ticking. Analysts say McNealy has only two years before low-end technologies in operating systems and chips catch up to his own. That's precious little time to defend the company from the onslaught—and to broaden his high-margin beachhead in software. It's fears about Sun's business model that are giving investors the willies. And financial worries are on the rise. On Oct. 16, Standard & Poor's lowered Sun's credit rating from a BBB+ to BBB, saying that Sun's profits would be too unpredictable in the coming year.

McNealy recognizes that hardware is unlikely to produce fat boom-level profits again. He's hoping that higher-margin software, which now makes up only 5%

of Sun's revenue and an estimated 9% of profits, will pick up the slack. He won't predict when, but a bullish report from Merrill Lynch & Co. says that within two years Sun could generate up to 9% of revenues from software. That would tack on an estimated $417 million in gross profits.

To reach that target, McNealy needs faultless execution and more than a little luck. He must come up with new network software that matches the best in the business, from IBM's to Microsoft's. It's a tough challenge for a box maker. Indeed, McNealy can only hope the company learned from its failure in the late '90s when it treated software as an ugly stepchild to its booming server business—and blew a golden chance to run away with the market for e-business software.

McNealy must also plow into services, but without disrupting relationships with consulting partners, such as Electronic Data Systems Corp., that install Sun systems. Perhaps most difficult, he must convince workers, many of whom hold stock options that are deep under water, to bust their gut for a company many in the tech world are writing off. And they must hurry: If the cheap servers climbing up the food chain catch up to Sun's top line before McNealy's plan has traction, he's in trouble.

As McNealy leads his company up this steep slope, he'll doubtless face some tough choices. Like the pioneers who tossed their beloved pianos and rocking chairs before crossing the raging Missouri, he'll likely be forced to let loose a few of his precious technologies. High on the list are Sun's proprietary Sparc chips and Solaris server software, which together eat up more than $200 million of R&D investment annually, according to analysts. But even here McNealy faces a dilemma. First, he has lots of customers who rely on maintenance and upgrades for these proprietary components. Cutting back R&D could cripple an important source of revenue. What's more, if he ditches the very pieces that make Sun special, he runs the risk of tumbling into the cutthroat commodity world below.

Will McNealy hoist Sun back to the top? More likely is a Sun that settles into a specialty niche, providing high-margin servers with all the bells and whistles built in, a path similar to the one trod by Apple Computer Inc. in the consumer market. A drearier possibility: Sun could follow the footsteps of Digital Equipment Co., which failed to keep up with cost-saving changes in the computer industry and was eventually bought by Compaq Computer Corp. in 1998 for $9.6 billion. "In a couple of years, if Sun can't turn it around, it could be acquired for its installed base and technology," says Steven Milunovich, a managing director at Merrill Lynch.

If McNealy comes up short, the effects will be felt far and wide. The ideas pouring out of Sun's labs have made the midsize computer maker into an outsize thought leader. Indeed, Sun has been strong enough to take on mighty Microsoft. Its Java programming language, which works on any operating system, remains an alternative to a Windows-dominated world. And many in the computer industry maintain that integrated manufacturers, like Sun and Apple, which focus on entire systems, generate far more creativity than the component-based champions such as Microsoft, Intel, and Dell.

Yet creativity doesn't always win the day. And as Sun struggles, Microsoft grows stronger. On Nov. 1, when U.S. District Judge Colleen Kollar-Kotelly upheld a settlement among Microsoft, the Bush Administration, and nine states, the software giant emerged virtually unscathed from a four-year antitrust case, which Sun actively supported. McNealy refuses to talk about the settlement. "I don't get paid to get aggravated," he says.

Still, McNealy has long enjoyed a parallel career as the industry's anti-Microsoft ringleader. But now he barely has time for Bill-baiting. He has a company to rescue. Friends say it's times like these that get McNealy fired up. Tony Scott, chief information officer at General Motors Co., who worked at Sun in the late 1980s and played club ice hockey with McNealy, says McNealy is doing his job with the intensity he always brought to the ice. "He'll put his body on the line to get the job done," says Scott, now a Sun customer.

McNealy is gripping the reins tighter than ever. He's working to put in place the management controls and succession planning learned at the side of the man he considers his mentor, former General Electric Co. Chairman and CEO Jack Welch. McNealy has cut a layer of management that kept him from execs on the front lines. He's acting like a battlefield sergeant, making sure his managers are following his strategy for facing the low-cost onslaught. In October, McNealy even moved his office from Sun's headquarters in Santa Clara, Calif.—a landmark building constructed in 1888—to Menlo Park so he could be closer to a customer center where he's spending most of his time these days.

When he's not meeting with customers, McNealy is making needed repairs to his company. In July, he created an executive vice-president position for software for the first time, organized all of Sun's consulting under one person, and assigned 1,000 salespeople to hawk Sun software.

But McNealy's first big management changes didn't come off as hoped. About 18 months ago, he started

EXHIBIT 3 Tough Decisions for Sun

Data: *BusinessWeek*

McNealy faces challenges. Here's what experts say he should do:

The Dilemma	The Fix
CHIPS Sun must decide if it can afford to spend $200 million a year designing its own microprocessor, the Sparc, when it and Fujitsu are the only two major companies using the chip.	• McNealy can phase Intel chips into most of Sun's servers over time. Power-hungry users will still pay a premium for high-end Sparc machines—at least until Intel crashes the party.
LINUX Customers want choices, and that's what they get with the open-standard Linux operating system.	• Phase in Linux on Sun servers, starting with the low end. As Linux improves, cut back Solaris.
EXPENSES If sales continue to slide, McNealy may have to tighten expenses even more than the 20% payroll cuts he has made so far.	• At 14% of sales, Sun's R&D budget needs reduction surgery. And McNealy may have to proceed with further job cuts.
MICROSOFT-BAITING Does Sun really stand a chance taking on Microsoft with StarOffice, a low-cost knockoff of the software giant's popular Office program?	• McNealy has to pick his fights with Microsoft. Give this one up. It's a distraction.

work on a succession plan patterned after what he had learned while sitting on the board at GE. McNealy believed the timing was perfect. Several longtime execs, including Zander, wanted to leave the company. By last spring, McNealy had his plan in place.

When Zander left, McNealy would eliminate the president's position. When John Shoemaker, head of Sun's computer unit, retired, McNealy would ax that position, too. This would cut out two layers of management, and more execs would report directly to the CEO. Just like Welch at GE, McNealy planned to evaluate and train a new generation of leaders. At an April, 2002, powwow for Sun's 200 vice-presidents, he unveiled his plan.

Then it blew up in his face. Instead of presenting a cohesive management plan, McNealy, over the course of a month, dribbled out separate announcements for each of the five executives leaving the company, culminating with Zander. Coupled with the downturn in Sun's business, it looked as though the top people were jumping ship—or McNealy was forcing them out. "When they said Ed was leaving, that's when I said to myself, 'Maybe I should think about looking for another job,'" says one former Sun employee. Sun's stock dropped 10% the week after Zander announced he was leaving. McNealy was so flabbergasted by the debacle he called Welch to ask what he did wrong. "Jack said, 'Don't worry about it. They'll forget about it soon enough,'" says McNealy.

Other concerns promptly leaped to the fore, led by Sun's plunging stock. For months, as Sun shares descended into single figures, McNealy turned a deaf ear to Wall Street and resisted further layoffs. He wanted to keep positioning the company, he said, to cash in on the tech recovery. But to a skeptical market he looked less like a determined visionary than a CEO in dangerous denial. On Oct. 17, with Sun's stock wallowing around $3, McNealy finally bowed to the market and announced a second round of layoffs. Combined with last year's cuts, he will have slashed 20% of the company's 43,700 workers.

Now he's hurrying to save money in operations. This year, Sun has shaved $600 million in costs from its supply chain. That has saved five points on its gross margins. "If we hadn't done that, we'd be dead," says Marissa Peterson, executive vice-president of worldwide operations at Sun.

To kick-start business in the low end, McNealy is making a tactical retreat in servers (Exhibit 3). He has opened up a place for the commodity components, Linux and Intel chips, in his economy offerings. To proclaim his newfound love of Linux, McNealy showed up at a Feb. 7 conference in San Francisco in the costume of a penguin, the Linux mascot. The challenge for McNealy is to crack open a door to low-cost business without encouraging high-end customers to swarm through and switch to the cheaper fare.

McNealy has aggressive goals for the Linux servers. He's not airing them publicly, but several Sun

EXHIBIT 4

Data: Sun Microsystems Inc.

SUN'S ELDORADO

Sun is staking its software future on a vast project to automate the work in complex data networks. In September, Sun unveiled its nascent effort, called N1. Here's what it aims to do by mid-decade:

ONE SYSTEM Think of N1, as one huge operating system for the network. The software will automatically manage all of the computers, storage, and switches, making them work together as one giant machine.

VIRTUAL RESOURCES The software views all the tech gear in a corporate data center as one virtual pool of resources. If a big project taps out the supercomputer, N1 will automatically route the work to other computers.

LOW-COST COMPUTING By running computers close to capacity, the system will reduce the need for new machines. The software also will manage and update software installations. That will eliminate many of the tasks now handled by squadrons of systems administrators.

executives say McNealy has told them that within the next two years he wants to grab 30% of what will then be a $6.5 billion market, according to researcher IDC. To take on cutthroat rivals, McNealy is keeping costs low and outsourcing production of Sun's Linux machines, which start at $2,700. That's a highly ambitious goal, given that Sun has no market share today. But if McNealy can hit his target, the low-end gear could add $400 million in gross profits in 2004.

That may be just enough to cover the slide in sales of Sun's midrange Solaris machines. The trouble with such calculations is that Dell and its low-cost collaborators represent a fast-moving target—one that slashes prices to woo new business. Merrill Lynch estimates that from 2001 to 2004, revenue in Sun's midrange will fall 60%, to $1.7 billion. That translates into an estimated $500 million hit on profits.

McNealy's bid hinges on his ability to focus the company on a handful of key initiatives. One is services. As Sun extends its business from the boxes to the broader network, it will be up to the service staff to help customers install the full gamut of Sun offerings. IBM has mastered this approach. And McNealy, who long denigrated the industry's march toward services, is now following suit. Sun has 13,000 service consultants, double three years ago. And while they're dwarfed by IBM's 180,000 consultants and HP's 65,000-member force, they appear to be gaining traction. In the most recent quarter ended Sept. 30, service revenues were up 9%, to $879 million. Patricia C. Sueltz, Sun's executive vice-president in charge of consulting, targets $1 billion in quarterly services revenue by next year.

Equally vital for McNealy is software. While Sun has been a bold software innovator, coming up with such advances as Java, software has remained a niche business marked by Sun's failure to turn leading-edge technology into sales and profits. Now McNealy needs it more than ever. Software is at the center of his vision of a Sun-driven networked world—and it delivers gross profit margins of 80%. It's little surprise that McNealy is plowing more than half of his R&D budget into software, much of it for Web applications.

Again, Sun risks new battles with old friends as the company plunges into different businesses. For years, Net software maker BEA Systems Inc. was an enthusiastic Sun partner. It created software to run on Sun's Solaris servers that let customers deliver applications effortlessly via the Web. Now, Sun's assault on the Web-software business has pushed BEA into the arms of chip giant Intel. Why? Unlike Sun, Intel isn't likely to compete in software. Now BEA is shipping a Linux version of its software to run on Intel chips, and sales are taking off. In the last year, Sun's share of the BEA installed base has tumbled from 75% to 55%.

At the heart of McNealy's vision is an ambitious software project called N1 (Exhibit 4). Sun's software developers have been working on the technology for two years, tucked away in a space-age data center at Sun's Sunnyvale (Calif.) facility. The idea is to create vast networks in which the software administers itself. If one computer runs out of memory, the software seeks spare capacity elsewhere on the network. If the software develops a glitch, the program itself will work to fix it, without calling on costly human administrators. Sun will be releasing the first components of the program by the end of the year.

The trouble is, McNealy must invest heavily in N1 just to stay in step with competitors. IBM and HP are hard at work on very similar systems. On Oct. 30, IBM CEO Samuel J. Palmisano told customers that he was betting the future of his company on a vast, N1-type project called "on-demand computing." He's investing billions to develop new products and will spend $800 million on the marketing. And although HP CEO Carleton S. Fiorina keeps it quiet, HP's version of N1, called Utility Data Center, already has 450 engineers behind it and 10 customers in pilot projects.

With all these challenges, it might make sense for McNealy to shelve his ongoing war with Microsoft. But he has trouble letting it rest. Since May, he's been offering a low-cost office-applications package to battle Microsoft's ubiquitous Office desktop suite. This is David taking on Goliath without the slingshot. McNealy's colleagues urge him to focus on more pressing threats. Before a Sept. 18 speech to Sun customers at San Francisco's Moscone Center, his vice-president for software, Jonathan Schwartz, bet his boss $2 that he couldn't avoid mentioning Microsoft during his speech. McNealy took the bet—and collected his money after his talk.

At the event, Sun's first big customer conference in seven years, dreadlocked drummers on stage were pounding a beat when McNealy jumped up, beating on a drum of his own. He promptly launched into a 45-minute stump speech defending Sun, one of the last of the integrated computer makers. "There is no automobile-integration industry," he says. "You get a car fully assembled. They even wash it for you." Jokes and debating points aside, McNealy has to get Sun making money again. Only then will he convince the world that Sun can shine anew.

By Jim Kerstetter in Menlo Park, Calif., with Jay Greene in Seattle and bureau reports

Source: "Will Sun Rise Again?" *BusinessWeek*, November 25, 2002, 120–130.

Case 6-23

Telus Mobility—What to do with Mike

IVEY

Richard Ivey School of Business
The University of Western Ontario

In early 2001, Wade Oosterman reflected on TELUS Corporation's recent acquisition of Clearnet Communications Inc. As executive vice-president of sales and marketing at the new TELUS Mobility, Oosterman was eager to realize the synergies from merging the two compatible personal communications services (PCS) networks of TELUS and Clearnet to achieve a stronger competitive position in the Canadian consumer wireless market. However, his attention soon turned to Mike, a completely separate digital wireless network that was extremely important to TELUS.

What implications did the recent changes have for Mike? From a broader perspective, given the continued advancement in wireless technology and the increasingly competitive industry climate, what changes, if any, would need to be made to TELUS's short-medium term strategy for Mike? New risks and potential opportunities that needed to be considered. For example, Mike was tied to one handset manufacturer, competition was making aggressive moves, and new technology platforms and migration paths to these needed to be considered. Mike had been incredibly successful within the high revenue commercial market, but Oosterman knew that it would be a challenge to defend that position and continue to grow the business. He started by reviewing the broad landscape of the industry.

Jack Wong prepared this case under the supervision of Professor Don Barclay solely to provide material for class discussion. The authors do not intend to illustrate either effective or ineffective handling of a managerial situation. The authors may have disguised certain names and other identifying information to protect confidentiality.

The Canadian Wireless Communications Industry

Cellular phone service was first introduced in Canada in 1985. Since then, the industry has experienced unprecedented growth. In 2000 alone, a record 5.9 percent of Canadians adopted wireless, representing a net addition of 1.8 million users. This brought the penetration of wireless services across the Canadian population to 28.4 percent. To put this in perspective, it took over 10 years for the Canadian wireless industry to add its first 1.8 million customers.

Canadian Wireless Penetration Rates

	Net Additions (#) (million)	Net Additions (%)	Total Penetration (%)
2000	1.8	5.9	28.4
1999	1.5	5.0	22.5
1998	1.1		17.5

Industry analysts expected robust growth in the wireless sector to continue over the next five years. Current estimates for wireless penetration in 2005 range from 57 percent to 70 percent. These forecasts translate into gains of between 8.8 million and 12.8 million new wireless subscriptions over this period. Experience overseas illustrates that these forecasts are reasonable. Already in Finland and Italy, over 70 percent of the population was using wireless phones.

It is widely believed that wireless subscriptions will eventually reach, or possibly even exceed, 100 percent of the population. In spite of the fact that the addressable market is in the range of 80 percent to 85 percent of the population (excluding the very young and elderly), it is believed that many customers will utilize two or even more wireless devices. While a majority of wireless users communicate through digital PCS phones, new devices such as personal digital assistants (PDAs) manufactured by companies like Palm and Handspring have been gaining popularity.

Consumer demand for freedom, mobility and "anywhere, anytime" access to information has fuelled the development of wireless telemetry applications and user-relevant mobile Internet services. Also, advanced second and third generations of wireless technology (2.5G, 3G) bring the promise of broadband, which will allow for high-speed data transmissions and the introduction of more robust features and services. The convergence of wireless technology and the Internet makes such high penetration increasingly possible.

Economics

In an immensely capital-intensive industry, network operators invest billions in building wireless infrastructure. Wireless phones use radio waves to transmit and receive sound through a wideband radio frequency or channel. A network requires numerous cell sites to be deployed throughout its coverage area. Cell sites are radio antenna towers that transmit signals to and from wireless handsets. Also, switches are required to co-ordinate call traffic, interconnect calls with local and long distance landline telephone companies, and compile billing information. The final significant capital expenditure for operators consists of fees paid to the federal government for spectrum licences that are awarded through an auction process. As the spectrum of radio frequencies is a valuable finite resource, spectrum assignment is regulated and controlled by federal government agencies, such as Industry Canada.

Given the high level of fixed costs in the industry, considerable attention is paid to particular metrics once a network is established and operational. In particular, there are four key elements in the profit dynamic in the wireless industry (see Exhibit 1 for historical performance of major industry players):

Subscribers

Currently, industry success is primarily measured by subscriber growth. Network operators generate revenue from subscribers who use their service. Naturally, this means that the acquisition of new users is a foremost objective in order to recover the heavy fixed investment. In Canada, the major industry players have been aggressively targeting new entrants to the market as opposed to focusing on converting subscribers from competitors.

Cost of Acquisition (COA)

COA refers to the cost of acquiring a network subscriber. While wireless handsets typically cost consumers from $50 to $250, in most cases the handset costs have been subsidized by network operators to encourage greater adoption by users. Industry research has shown that, in the consumer market, up-front handset costs are the largest inhibitor for potential new subscribers. This has led many network operators to subsidize the cost of handsets in an effort to boost subscriber additions. A common tactic in the industry involves offering customers free handsets while tying them to long-term contracts, ensuring that the initial handset costs would be recovered over time.

Handset manufacturers such as Ericsson, Nokia, Motorola and Samsung decrease the wholesale price of their handsets as they realize economies of scale, learning curve effects in production, and advances in component technology (semiconductor, screen, battery). However, because wireless networks operate on different technology platforms, some more established than others, certain operators benefit from a substantial handset cost advantage.

EXHIBIT 1
Historical Performance of Major Wireless Industry Players

	2000*	1999	1998	1997
Subscribers				
Mike	–	210,121	114,095	44,549
Clearnet PCS	–	349,210	194,374	50,676
TELUS PCS	2,156,000	1,099,000	963,000	823,000
Bell Mobility	2,340,000	1,797,000	1,475,000	
Rogers AT&T	2,514,000	2,153,100	1,737,600	1,552,100
Microcell	922,500	484,487	282,174	n/a
ARPU				
Mike	–	68.91	73.32	72.28
Clearnet PCS	–	46.97	49.60	44.24
TELUS PCS	59.00	60.00	70.00	76.00
Bell Mobility	46.00	51.00	60.00	
Rogers AT&T	46.00	49.00	54.00	59.00
Microcell	43.55	47.08	58.40	n/a
Churn				
Mike	–	1.64%	1.28%	1.50%
Clearnet PCS	–	1.87%	1.54%	0.47%
TELUS PCS	n/a	1.40%	1.30%	1.20%
Bell Mobility	1.50%	1.80%	n/a	n/a
Rogers AT&T	2.36%	1.86%	1.90%	1.63%
Microcell	2.20%	2.10%	2.10%	n/a
COA				
Mike	–	$578	$619	$603
Clearnet PCS	–	$544	$662	$1,107
TELUS PCS	537	360	412	338
Bell Mobility	n/a	n/a	n/a	n/a
Rogers AT&T	$441	$391	$525	$623
Microcell	$388	$421	$687	n/a
MOU				
Mike	–	378	358	315
Clearnet PCS	–	249	202	182
TELUS PCS	271	218	219	200
Bell Mobility	n/a	n/a	n/a	n/a
Rogers AT&T	263	216	202	213
Microcell	185	190	257	n/a

* 2000 numbers for TELUS PCS are adjusted figures to reflect acquisitions.

Additional costs that are considered in the calculation of COA are sales, marketing and advertising costs that include commissions, gifts with purchase, and rebates.

Average Revenue per Subscriber Unit (ARPU)

Not surprisingly, the average revenue per subscriber unit per month is an important target, one that operators would logically seek to maximize. However, over the past few years, ARPU has been decreasing within the industry. Despite Canada's relatively low wireless penetration rate among developed nations, Canadian airtime prices are among the least expensive in the world. The aggressive pricing strategies of some players, eager to gain new users, have led to a highly competitive market. A multitude of airtime packages now exists to meet the needs of a variety of users. Business customers continue to represent the most lucrative segment of the wireless market. Many believe that the introduction of new services, such as wireless Internet, will have a positive impact on ARPU in the future.

Churn

Churn refers to the rate at which clients leave an operator's network. Given the substantial costs incurred in acquiring a subscriber, customer retention is critical. Every network operator wants to realize a payback on COA before losing a customer, especially wireless service providers with a high handset subsidy structure and no-contract policies. Unfortunately, this is not always achievable and churn is unavoidable. Customers leave for a number of reasons including relocation, insufficient network coverage and poor customer service. Industry churn in 2000 was approximately two percent, indicating that an average network operator lost two percent of its subscriber base each month of the year.

Year 2000 Key Metrics of Industry Players

	TELUS Mobility	Bell Mobility	Rogers AT&T	Micro-cell
Subscribers	2,156,000	2,340,000	2,514,000	922,500
COA	$537	n/a	$441	$388
ARPU/month	$59	$46	$46	$44
Churn/month	1.95%	1.5%	2.36%	2.20%

Company Background

In setting the strategic direction for Mike, Oosterman had to consider that two companies with distinct histories had just come together—Clearnet and TELUS.

Clearnet

Clearnet was founded in 1984 as a subsidiary of Lenbrook Inc., a private Canadian company specializing in electronics marketing and distribution. Clearnet was created to give Lenbrook a foothold in the specialized mobile radio (SMR) service industry. SMR systems allow for radio conversations between users through simple walkie-talkie devices that operate in a push-to-talk mode in which a user cannot hear the other(s) while transmitting. Clearnet's SMR business targeted dispatch companies like taxi fleets, fire departments, paramedic squads, police departments, construction services and parcel delivery companies.

Headquartered in Pickering, Ontario (and later Scarborough), Clearnet became the first and largest licensed SMR operator in Canada. The company attained its Canadian leadership position in SMR by increasing its 800 megahertz (MHz) spectrum position, securing smaller regional operators, and acquiring Motorola's Canadian SMR business. Clearnet also operated a wholly owned dealership division, Clearnet Business Communication Centres, that sold and serviced the company's range of wireless technologies.

In 1996, Clearnet introduced the digital Mike network, becoming the first and only Canadian wireless communications company to provide fully integrated two-way radio, mobile telephone, and alphanumeric paging services in a single handset on a single network. Mike was targeted primarily at business workgroup users.

In 1997, Clearnet launched digital PCS in Canada's largest urban centres, becoming the first Canadian company to operate two digital wireless networks. Compared to existing wireless analog phone technology, PCS offered consumers superior call clarity, lighter handsets, longer battery life and enhanced security. As PCS was intended for the growing individual consumer market, Clearnet expanded its distribution network to include flagship stores in major Canadian cities, a wide variety of retailers, and eventually corporate-owned in-mall stores.

The company's success was attributable to its industry foresight, strategic partnerships and unique supplier relationships. Clearnet saw the advantage of accumulating radio spectrum in the expectation of emerging digital technologies that would utilize radio frequencies more efficiently and creatively. Initially, the spectrum was used for two-way dispatch radio services. However, Clearnet understood that owning spectrum was like owning precious real estate. As cellular technology developed, Clearnet was well positioned because it owned the right to offer high revenue cellular/PCS services on those radio frequencies that other companies, at the time, did not see value in. The company was successful at raising the capital necessary to construct its digital networks. Clearnet's initial public offering in 1994 resulted in $121 million. Also, strategic alliances with wireless giants Motorola and Nextel Communications gave Clearnet cutting-edge technology and research and development (R&D) capability, while exclusive alliances with leading industry suppliers, such as Lucent Technologies Canada, provided vendor financing arrangements and industrywide recognition.

Telus

TELUS Corporation is one of Canada's leading telecommunications companies, providing a full range of communications products and services. Originally Alberta's provincial telephone service provider, TELUS merged with BC Tel, its counterpart in British Columbia, in 1999, retaining the TELUS name. Since then, TELUS has aggressively pursued Eastern Canadian markets in an effort to become a national telecommunications service provider. Through expansion and acquisitions (e.g., Quebec Tel purchase), TELUS soon began to provide voice, data, Internet, advertising and wireless services to Central and Eastern Canada, in addition to servicing its home markets in Western Canada.

In 2000, TELUS acquired Clearnet in what was the largest transaction in Canadian telecommunications history. This move allowed TELUS to create a national wireless company with an industry leadership position in overall revenue, revenue growth, revenue per subscriber and wireless spectrum position. Technological synergies were apparent, as Clearnet's digital PCS network operated on the same CDMA technology platform as that of TELUS. To otherwise realize its national ambition, TELUS would have had to brave the risks and time-to-market delays associated with building its own greenfield digital network in Central-Eastern Canada. Additionally, Clearnet offered an extensive national retail and dealer distribution system.

The newly combined company, under the name TELUS Mobility, ended 2000 with more than 2.1 million subscribers across Canada, pro forma annual revenue of more than $1.7 billion, more than 4,000 employees, and digital coverage of 22.6 million of the 31 million total Canadian population that TELUS had licences to cover. TELUS had inherited Mike from Clearnet as one of its key offerings.

The Mike Network

The Mike network is an enhanced specialized mobile radio (ESMR) system based on iDEN (integrated digital enhanced network), a proprietary technology of Motorola. To date, it is the only technology in the world with the ability to integrate four distinct services in a single portable phone: digital telephone, dispatch radio (Mike's Direct Connect), alphanumeric paging and data transmission. iDEN networks have been deployed worldwide in countries such as Canada, the United States, Argentina, Brazil, China, Colombia, Israel, Japan, Korea, Mexico, the Philippines and Singapore.

In Canada, TELUS is the sole operator of iDEN and offers service in British Columbia, Alberta, Ontario and Quebec. These four provinces represent 85 percent of the Canadian population. In the United States, iDEN is operated by Nextel, with whom TELUS enjoys a strong partnership. This has allowed for the introduction of value-added features for Mike clients. For example, Mike users are able to use their handsets in the United States, at local Canadian rates, without paying any roaming fees.

Target Customers

Clearnet's initial marketing strategy for Mike was directed at existing dispatch and two-way radio users. The appeal to these users was obvious. Mike's digital technology gives users higher quality transmission and greater geographic coverage than SMR systems. Since a considerable number of dispatch subscribers also use cellular phones and paging services, Mike would eliminate the need for businesses to subscribe to multiple services. Clearnet began converting its existing SMR client base to its ESMR system, Mike. The other primary target market consisted of commercial users with a mobile work force, such as real estate firms and other sales-driven companies.

As Mike possessed all the capabilities of PCS, along with additional functionality, its target market broadened to include traditional "white collar" businesses. Over time, Mike users would include airlines, film and television companies, government agencies and utilities. Mike's positioning evolved to that of "a universal communication tool designed to save businesses time and money." It became clear that Mike had incredible market potential, much of which still remains untapped.

Products and Services

All Mike handsets are manufactured by Motorola. See Exhibit 2 for descriptions of TELUS Mobility's Mike product line. Since its launch, Motorola has regularly introduced new handsets, continually incorporating improvements in features and design. For example, the palm-sized iDEN i1000 handset offered sophisticated buyers the first phone with a built-in speaker phone, while still satisfying their demand for handsets featuring sleek "form factor." The latest Mike handsets are "dot-com ready," built with microbrowsers to allow users to connect with wireless Internet services. Internet services are the same on Mike as on TELUS PCS, enabling users to access news, directories, restaurant and movie listings, and other entertainment-related information. Also, Mike handsets support mobile computing by acting as a modem that can connect to laptop computers.

Mike's Direct Connect

Mike's competitive advantage lies in its Direct Connect feature. While cellular phones can now offer features such as digital clarity, secure calling, text messaging and longer battery life, they have not been able to duplicate the digital two-way radio feature of iDEN. Mike's Direct Connect allows users to contact each other instantly at the touch of a button. Unlike telephones, Direct Connect does not require any dialing or ringing, eliminating the delay and frustration from waiting for connections and playing "telephone tag." Direct Connect allows users to talk to one person at a time (private mode) or to many (group mode).

EXHIBIT 2 Mike Handsets—Product Descriptions

Features					
Weight - Phone plus std Battery (g)	170	204	243.5	170	170
Size	11.5cm × 5.6cm × 3cm	13.2cm × 5.4cm × 3.6cm	13.4cm × 5.4cm × 3.6cm	11.5cm × 5.6cm × 3cm	11.5cm × 5.6cm × 3cm
Talktime (minutes)	180	330	330	180	180
Standby Time (hours)	28hrs	85	85	50	50
Display	Large 4-line backlit display	Large 4-line backlit display	Large 4-line backlit display	Large 8-line backlit display	Large 8-line backlit display
Multi-language support	English, French, Portuguese, and Spanish	English, French, Portuguese, and Spanish	English, French, Portuguese, and Spanish	English, French, Portuguese, and Spanish	English, French, Portuguese, and Spanish
Phone					
Speed Dial	100 entries	100 entries	100 entries	250 consolidated phone book entries	250 consolidated phone book entries
Speakerphone	Yes	No	No	Yes	Yes
Phone Only Mode	Yes	Yes	Yes	Yes	Yes
Name and Number Scrolling Display	Yes	Yes	Yes	Yes	Yes
Consolidated Directory Programming	Yes	Yes	Yes	Yes	Yes
Call Waiting/Call Hold	Yes	Yes	Yes	Yes	Yes
Call Forwarding	Yes	Yes	Yes	Yes	Yes
Vibra Call	Yes	No	Yes	Yes	Yes
Any Key Answer	Yes	Yes	Yes	Yes	Yes
Keypad Lockout	Yes	Yes	Yes	Yes	Yes
Selectable Ring Styles	Yes	Yes	Yes	Yes	Yes
One-touch Emergency Dial	Yes	Yes	Yes	Yes	Yes
Last 10 Calls sent/ received	Yes	Yes	Yes	Yes	Yes
Missed Call Indicator	Yes	Yes	Yes	Yes	Yes
Quickstore of Phone Numbers	Yes	Yes	Yes	Yes	Yes
Quickstore of Private IDs	Yes	Yes	Yes	Yes	Yes
Wireless Modem	Yes	Yes	Yes	Yes	Yes
Dot Com Ready	Yes	Yes	Yes	Yes	Yes
Mike Smart Card Enabled	No	No	No	Yes	Yes
Certified to Military Standard 810 C/D/E for mechanical shock and vibration	No	No	Yes	No	Yes
Java 2 Micro Edition™ (J2ME) Ready	No	No	No	Yes	Yes
Direct Connect (Private Call)					
Directory	100	100	100	250 consolidated phone book entries	250 consolidated phone book entries

EXHIBIT 2 (continued)

Call Alert Stacking	Yes	Yes	Yes	Yes	Yes
Caller ID / Name Display	Yes	Yes	Yes	Yes	Yes
Vibra Alert	Yes	No	Yes	Yes	Yes
Direct Connect (Group Call)					
Programming Talkgroups	30	30	30	30	30
Message Mail Slots	16	16	16	16	16

Mike Networks

Clearnet recognized the growing value that Mike created in certain industries and capitalized on this opportunity to foster loyalty among Mike customers. In 1998, Clearnet introduced Mike Networks, expanding the functionality of Direct Connect to allow instant contact, not only within one's own organization of Mike users, but also with other groups of Mike users. Without Mike Networks, only an organization's own Mike users can communicate with one another using Direct Connect.

Construction Net, the first Mike Network, was embraced by the construction sector, which realized the value of instant contact with industry partners. In Eastern Canada, Construction Net grew to include more than 650 construction businesses, 4,000 subscribers, and associations such as the Ontario Road Builders Association and the Greater Toronto Home Builders Association. It became evident that construction companies looking to operate at peak efficiency would have to be a part of Construction Net.

Each of the Mike Networks was designed around specific communities to give users efficient and cost-effective access to business partners. Mike Networks now exists in Professional Services, Construction, Media and Entertainment, Health and Social Services, Transportation and Automotive, Friends and Family, and Hospitality and Travel services.

Pricing

Unlike the consumer segment of the market, commercial users demonstrate less sensitivity to the price of handsets. Their purchase decisions are more influenced by the cost effectiveness of a service's rate plans. TELUS currently prices Mike handsets between $49.99 and $249.99. To respond to varying business communication needs, TELUS offers 11 monthly rate plans designed for individual users, small teams or larger businesses that start at $30 per user. Available plans offer flexible features and add-ons, such as unlimited local evening calling and long distance, designed for travellers and heavy business users. See Exhibit 3 for Mike Service Plans. Mike also offers a cost saving Account Pooling feature that allows a user's unused dollars to be applied to the excess minutes of another user in the organization (see Exhibit 4).

Distribution

Initially, Mike was sold through two competing channels of distribution: Clearnet Business Communication Centres and an independent dealer network. As the sales process for Mike simplified, distribution grew to include Clearnet stores and national retailers with a wireless category focus. Because Mike sales typically involve multiple users and handsets, its sales cycle still remains longer than that of PCS. Also, it remains a challenge for sales representatives to clearly articulate the benefits of Mike's Direct Connect without a live demonstration of the feature. Even then, it is often not until a customer is personally using Direct Connect that they understand and appreciate the utility it provides.

Communication

Clearnet launched iDEN services under the brand name Mike to create a brand that is simple to say, easy to remember and bilingual. Mike also allowed Clearnet to differentiate itself from the brands of competitors, which at the time of Mike's introduction were geared primarily towards consumers (e.g., Liberti, Amigo, Fido). In addition, Mike was clearly positioned for business users while Clearnet's other digital network, PCS, was focused on the mass consumer market. Mike existed in a very formidable and dynamic competitive context.

Competition

Bell Mobility

Bell Mobility, a division of Bell Canada, offers analog cellular and digital PCS, paging, two-way messaging and data services to customers in Ontario and Quebec. In a competitive market, Bell Mobility has chosen to focus its efforts on value as opposed to aggressive pricing. The company was the first in Canada to offer a mobile

EXHIBIT 3 Mike Service Plans

Rate Plan	Phone 40	Dispatch 40	Work 40	Work 65	Work 100	Work 150	Travel 75	Travel 150	Travel 250
Monthly Fee	$40	$40	$40	$65	$100	$150	$75	$150	$250
Target Audience	Phone Users	Heavy Dispatch Users	Multi-function Users	Multi-function Users	Multi-function Users	Heavy multi-function Users	Travelers	Travelers	Travelers
Total combined minutes or messages									
	Up to 400	Unlimited + Unlimited Direct Connect	267	650	1000 + Unlimited Message Mail	1500 + Unlimited Message Mail and Direct Connect	250 + Unlimited Message Mail	600 + Unlimited Message Mail and Direct Connect	1250 + Unlimited Message Mail and Direct Connect
Anytime rate									
Phone	10c/min (up to 400 mins)	n/a	15c/min	10c/min	10c/min	10c/min	30c/min	25c/min	20c/min
Direct Connect (private and group)	20c/min (up to 200 mins)	Unlimited (private), 20c/min (group)	15c/min	10c/min	10c/min	Unlimited (private), 10c/min (group)	30c/min	Unlimited (private)	Unlimited (private)
Message Mail	20c/message (up to 200 messages)	n/a	15c/message	10c/message	Unlimited	Unlimited	Unlimited	Unlimited	Unlimited
Additional Airtime									
Phone	20c/min	20c/min	20c/min	20c/min	20c/min	10c/min	30c/min	25c/min	20c/min
Direct Connect	20c/min	20c/min (group)	20c/min	20c/min	20c/min	10c/min (group)	30c/min	Unlimited	Unlimited
Message Mail	20c/message	20c/message	15c/message	10c/message	Unlimited	Unlimited	Unlimited	Unlimited	Unlimited
Unlimited Add-ons									
Unlimited evenings and weekends (phone)	$15	$25	$15	$15	$10	Included	n/a	n/a	n/a
Unlimited Direct Connect	n/a	Included	$20	$15	$10	Included	$10	Included	Included
Unlimited Message Mail	$5	$5	$5	$5	Included	Included	Included	Included	Included
Unlimited Surf	$10	$10	$10	$10	$10	$10	$10	$10	$10
Unlimited Surf-A-Lot	$15	$15	$15	$15	$15	$15	$15	$15	$15

EXHIBIT 3 (continued)

Optional Add-on									
Mike Online (mobile computing)	$5 (+ airtime)	$5 (+ airtime)	$5 (+ airtime)	$5 (+ airtime)	$5 (+ airtime)	$5 (+ airtime)	$5 (+ airtime)	$5 (+ airtime)	$5 (+ airtime)
Included Features									
	Basic voice, mail, caller ID, call waiting, call forwarding		Basic voice mail, caller ID, call waiting, call forwarding		Advanced voice mail, caller ID call waiting, call forwarding		Direct Connect wide area, voice mail, caller ID, call waiting, call forwarding		Wide area, advanced voice mail, caller ID, call waiting, call forwarding

browser service on PCS, allowing users to access the Internet from their phones. Similar to Mike's data capabilities, its Digital Data to Go service allows digital PCS phones to send and receive e-mail, surf the Internet, and send and receive faxes. Bell Mobility offers a solid product mix backed by an extensive network of dealers, established customer service and financial stability. The company also continues to leverage its connection to other Bell Canada Enterprises (BCE) companies through service bundling.

In 2000, Bell Mobility launched wireless e-mail services through handheld devices manufactured by Research In Motion (RIM). Driving the appeal of RIM wireless handhelds are features such as alphanumeric keyboards, thumb-operated trackwheels, and integrated e-mail/organizer software. The devices can also be synchronized with laptops and desktops. Users can send and receive e-mail; forward attachments; update schedules, contacts and task lists; and access traditional paging services.

While PCS phones and Mike handsets allow for basic access to e-mail, their current design and size limit effectiveness, as the screens are small and data must be entered using numeric keypads (e.g., the letter "L" is entered by pressing the "5" key three times). Additionally, wireless phones currently require users to retrieve e-mail. RIM handhelds are designed to remain on and continuously connected to the wireless network, automatically notifying users when e-mail is received. Users save time because they do not have to initiate routine connections to check for messages.

RIM has been an industry success story and its Blackberry handhelds have been extremely popular among professional business users. However, its current lack of voice calling capability limits its ability to act as a complete communications solution. RIM handsets are sold by Bell Mobility's corporate sales force and its retail and dealer networks. Also, RIM has its own corporate sales force tasked with selling wireless e-mail solutions to corporate customers.

Rogers AT&T Wireless

Rogers AT&T Wireless is one of Canada's largest national wireless communications service providers, offering subscribers a wide selection of products and services. With extensive network coverage and over 6,000 points of distribution, it provides analog cellular, digital PCS, paging, and wireless data services nationwide. Rogers also offers RIM handsets, which complement its line of communication products. The company intends to compete vigorously for all customer

EXHIBIT 4 Mike Account Pooling

Account pooling allows individuals belonging to a particular account to make use of the unspent dollars from the monthly plan(s) of other individuals within the same account. Those unused dollars are automatically applied to other users' excess minutes at their per-minute rate. At the time of this case, no other provider provided such service. Below is an example of account pooling:

Example	Bill	Sue	John	Account Total
Monthly Rate	$40 +	$100 +	$100	= $240
Actual Usage	$40 +	$55 +	$150	= $245
Additional Usage	$0 +	($45) +	$50	= $ 5
Amount Due (greater of total monthly rates and total actual usage)				$245
Charges from other companies	$40 +	$100 +	$150	= $290

Savings under account pooling: $45

segments and in all markets based on the strengths of its broad digital service coverage and extensive distribution network.

Like Bell Mobility, Rogers's wireless business unit leverages the capabilities of other Rogers companies. Consumers benefit from the bundling of core cable TV, digital TV, high-speed Internet access, and wireless communication services. Research has shown that over 60 per cent of U.S. customers are interested in receiving all their communication services from one provider on one bill. This can be an effective retention tool provided that services delivered meet the expectations of consumers.

In 2001, Rogers launched a wireless product specifically targeted at the youth market under a completely separate brand called iD. Analysts predict that the wireless penetration rate among 14-year-olds to 19-year-olds will grow from 1.2 million to 3.8 million in two years. Fuelling the growth and high adoption rates is the availability of Internet services. In Europe, short message services (SMS) is an incredibly popular form of communicating, where users send short text messages to and from wireless phones. Instant messaging is a low-latency, short form of Internet messaging that is used by large communities of users, allowing participants to identify "buddies" and see when members of their "buddy list" are online to chat. Rogers intends to build a similar community among users aged 14 to 24.

Microcell

Microcell Telecom first launched PCS in November 1996, under the brand Fido. Fido was positioned as an everyday communications tool, and its consumer proposition was based primarily on price, with a focus on fairness and simplicity. Service was marketed in communities where 56 percent of the Canadian population resides. Distribution was initially achieved through corporate flagship stores in major city centres and has since expanded to include major electronics retailers. In 1999, the company introduced two data products, Fido E-Mail and FidoData. Together, these products delivered mobile e-mail and wireless connectivity to the customer's data environment, including the Internet and corporate intranets. At the end of 2000, Microcell reported 922,527 customers on Fido postpaid and Fidomatic prepaid services.

Microcell's PCS network is based on the global system for mobile communications (GSM). GSM is an older technology platform for PCS and is the prevalent standard in Europe. In North America, a majority of PCS providers selected the more technologically advanced CDMA standard for PCS. While CDMA offers superior call clarity, soft call handoffs, and more efficient use of wireless spectrum, these differences are not easily discernible by consumers. GSM allows Microcell to enjoy a significant cost advantage in the procurement of handsets, as there are many manufacturers and models to choose from.

Fido has experienced considerable success in the youth market. Approximately 70 percent of its sales are to youth. However, unlike Rogers's iD, Microcell has positioned its pre-paid service, Fidomatic, to this segment. Traditionally, pre-paid churn is higher than that of post-paid, while ARPU is typically lower.

As Oosterman worked through the above scenario, a number of risks and opportunities surfaced.

The Current Situation—Risks

Highly Competitive and Uncertain Wireless Communications Industry

The ability of a service provider to compete successfully is based on factors such as pricing, distribution, services and features, ease of use, quality of geographic and in-building coverage, image and brand recognition, customer service, reliability of service, and customer satisfaction. With five major digital networks, including Mike, in the Canadian wireless market, new pricing, aggressive advertising and innovative marketing approaches are anticipated. The increase in demand for wireless Internet communication device options could bring new competitors to the market (e.g., mobile satellite). Also, the Canadian government has actively encouraged more competition in the industry.

Dependency on Motorola

To date, Mike has relied on one handset manufacturer, Motorola. The presence of multiple manufacturers in the PCS market has allowed competitors to choose from a wider selection of economically priced handsets. The cost of iDEN handsets is higher than the cost of those used on networks of certain competing technologies and is subsidized by TELUS. In the absence of competitive supply, there is no assurance that the cost of iDEN handsets will remain competitive visà-vis the cost of others or that they will be available in sufficient quantities, on a timely basis, to satisfy demand.

iDEN's Future

The wireless industry is in the process of adopting advanced second (2.5G) and third generation (3G) technologies that are expected to deliver high-speed wireless IP and data services. Various operators are announcing plans to permit existing wireless protocols to migrate to 2.5G in 2001 and subsequently 3G over the next two to three years. TELUS Mobility's CDMA protocol has a reasonable and cost-effective migration path to 2.5G and 3G (W-CDMA), as does Microcell's GSM protocol (UMTS). TELUS's Mike service uses an iDEN technology protocol that already has packet data capability, a primary feature of 2.5G. However, iDEN is not compatible with any other digital protocol. It has not yet been determined how it will migrate to 3G. iDEN may become obsolete or provide no cost-effective migration path to allow for the competitive provision of 3G service.

In addition, there can be no assurance that the Direct Connect technology that is now unique to iDEN will not become available on other technology platforms, especially with the emergence of 3G technologies. Oosterman knew that while his immediate concern was Mike's short- to medium-term strategy, any actions would have to be consistent with TELUS's overall long-term vision.

The Current Situation—Opportunities

Virtual Private Networks

Virtual private networks (VPN) are a growing aspect of the Mike business. Mike VPNs deliver dedicated coverage, customized handset services and high-volume airtime packages, allowing clients to incorporate Mike on a very broad scale. Mike's greatest VPN success to date is a 10-year contract with General Motors of Canada Ltd. for its 14-million-square-foot Autoplex in Oshawa, Ontario, the largest auto plant in North America. The VPN concept has also been employed in other sectors. In the area of public safety, the Durham Regional Police Service has employed Mike as a digital communications solution. There are many potential areas where the customized services of VPNs could be deployed (e.g., university campuses). However, the institutional sales process requires a significant investment of time. In order for VPNs to be economically viable, customers must be organizations with user bases large enough to warrant the development of customized solutions.

New Products

In spring of 2001, Motorola announced the introduction of the first Java technology-enabled handsets in North America, which will be available for iDEN. Positioned by Motorola as a digital personal companion, the handsets enable users to download and run applications that meet individual user needs. For example, a handset could be customized to allow a particular user to schedule meetings in a datebook, submit expense reports remotely and play the latest Sega games. This is in addition to the existing features available through iDEN. To allow for personal handheld computing, the handsets are equipped with flash memory, which permits the storage of several applications. Motorola plans to pre-install applications such as productivity tools and a Sega game. The handsets can retrieve information using the phone's "always on" Internet access, without the need to establish a dial-up connection, and its offline capabilities allow applications to be run even when disconnected from the network. The handsets will also feature interchangeable faceplates in a variety of colors.

New Segments

The powerful functionality offered by iDEN, coupled with demand trends in the wireless industry, makes it clear that businesses are not the only ones who could benefit from the services of Mike. For example, basic two-way radios have been gaining popularity among everyday users. The radios are limited to communication over short distances (four to 10 kilometres) and, as they do not require a cellular network, users are not required to pay any service fees. The devices are used by families to keep in touch in shopping malls, amusement parks and while hiking.

Mike's strategy could be altered to focus more heavily on additional market segments. For example, Mike handsets could be bundled in two to target consumers who would benefit from PCS handsets integrated with Direct Connect capability. However, expanding Mike's target market to explicitly include consumer segments is not without risk. To date, Mike has been clearly positioned to business users, who have very different needs from everyday consumers. PCS handsets have been marketed and designed with consumers in mind. For example TELUS offers PCS handsets with features such as color screens and integrated MP3 player capability. While iDEN may offer some distinct feature advantages over PCS, a considerable investment has been made to build TELUS's consumer PCS brand. A key objective for TELUS Mobility is to minimize market confusion, while optimizing performance on key wireless industry metrics (subscribers, ARPU, COA and churn). Any decision to enter new segments would therefore require additional consideration.

Conclusion

Oosterman knew that with TELUS's acquisition of Clearnet now complete, he must reevaluate the strategy for Mike. However, he was concerned about what criteria to use to make this decision. He also realized that he didn't have a lot of time to gather more information before he made this strategic choice. Things were moving too quickly to do more extensive analysis. What was the best course to take for Mike in the competitive wireless market that would result in future success for TELUS Mobility?

GLOSSARY

AMPS Advanced Mobile Phone Service. The North American analog cellular phone standard

Analog An older method of wireless transmission that uses a continuous electrical signal (sound waves), which is easily intercepted or scanned, leading to the possibility of eavesdropping and fraud. Used in traditional cellular (AMPS) service.

ARPU Average Revenue Per User. Total monthly revenue generated, divided by the average subscriber base in the period examined.

Broadband Broadband refers to telecommunication in which a wideband of frequencies is available to transmit information, allowing more information to be transmitted in a given amount of time (much as more lanes on a highway allow more cars to travel on it at the same time).

CDMA Code Division Multiple Access. A digital technology used by PCS providers. The newest PCS standard prevalent in North America.

Cellular Network Any mobile communications network with overlapping radio cells. Common term describing older, analog networks.

Churn Typically expressed as a rate per month for a given measurement period, equal to the number of subscribers disconnected divided by the average number of the entire installed base of subscribers.

Digital The newer method of wireless transmission (versus analog) in which speech is converted into binary digits (various combinations of 0 and 1). These digits are transmitted to a receiver and converted back into speech within a fraction of a second. Comparing analog to digital is like comparing a vinyl record to a CD. Because computer data is already in digital form, digital transmission also facilitates data-based services on a PCS network.

Dual-mode Handset A wireless phone capable of supporting both digital and analog communications.

ESMR Enhanced Specialized Mobile Radio.

GSM Global System for Mobile Communications. A digital technology used by PCS providers. The prevalent standard in Europe.

Handset The device (phone) with which a subscriber accesses a wireless network.

iDEN Integrated Digital Enhanced Network. A digital technology that integrates the services of PCS with digital two-way radio communications.

Licence The right to exclusive use of a particular block or blocks of spectrum. Industry Canada awards radio communication licenses in Canada. In 1995, Industry Canada awarded four national PCS licences in the 1.9 GHz spectrum band to encourage competition in the mobile wireless marketplace. Microcell and Clearnet were both awarded national licences of 30 MHz of spectrum.

MOU Minutes of Usage. The amount of time a user spends connected to the network. An average of this, measured monthly, is often used to compare usage on different wireless networks.

PCS Personal Communications Services. Digital mobile wireless service that offers voice communication plus a number of other capabilities, such as e-mail, fax and text messaging. PCS also offers subscribers improved voice quality and security. The term PCS distinguishes this type of wireless service from older analog technology.

PDA Personal Digital Assistant. Term for any small mobile hand-held device that provides computing and information storage and retrieval capabilities for personal or business use, often for keeping schedule calendars and address book information at hand.

Postpaid PCS A form of PCS in which the customer opens a wireless account and receives a monthly invoice. The alternative is prepaid PCS.

Prepaid PCS A form of PCS in which customers do not receive a monthly invoice from their wireless service provider. Rather, they buy increments of airtime as required. Prepaid PCS services have airtime rates that are higher than traditional postpaid services. They are more appropriate for occasional users or for customers who want to closely control their wireless costs. Also, because there is no credit risk for the network operator, prepaid customers do not have to submit to a credit check.

Roaming The ability to travel freely between compatible wireless networks.

SMR Specialized Mobile Radio. Two-way radio system typically used by dispatch companies (e.g., taxi fleets, construction services).

SMS Short Message Service. A feature available on handsets that allows customers to send and receive short alphanumeric messages.

Single-mode Handset A wireless phone capable of supporting only one type of communication (e.g., digital only).

TDMA Time Division Multiple Access. A digital technology used by PCS providers.

3G Third Generation. A generic name for mobile systems that will offer high-speed data and voice services. First Generation = analog cellular, Second Generation = digital PCS.

2.5G 2.5G describes the state of wireless technology and capability between the second and third generations of wireless technology. The term describes services of a higher data rate than PCS, though not as advanced as those promised by 3G.

* From www.microcell.ca and whatisit.techtarget.com.

Resource List

1. 3gnewsroom.com
2. anywhereyougo.com
3. Bruno, L. 2000. Broadband Unwired. Red Herring, 83: 280–282.
4. Diamond, R. What's Up at Palm. Wireless Business and Technology, 1(1): 68–71.
5. Drummond, M. 2001. Wireless at Work. Business 2.0, 3.6.2001: 68–83.
6. Girard, K. 2001. The Palm Phenom. Business 2.0, 4.3.2001: 74–80.

7. Neil, K., & Hibbard, J. 2000. Spectrum Shortage. Red Herring, 83: 284–290.
8. Phan, S. 2000. Who Needs a PC? Business 2.0, 11.14.2000: 52–57.
9. Smith, W. 2001. Surviving the Wireless Disruption. Wireless Business and Technology, 1(1): 64–66.
10. Splevin, G. 2001. Product Roundup—Wireless Devices. Wireless Business and Technology, 1(1): 86–87.
11. whatisit.techtarget.com
12. Williamson, A. 2001. What Does It All Mean? Wireless Business and Technology, 1(1): 72.
13. www.3g-generation.com
14. www.bce.ca
15. www.bellmobility.ca
16. www.clearnet.com
17. www.fido.ca
18. www.mformobile.com
19. www.microcell.ca
20. www.motorola.com
21. www.nextel.com
22. www.rim.net
23. www.rogers.com
24. www.TELUS.com
25. www.wbt2.com
26. Young, L. 2001. Tapping into Youth Wireless Market. Marketing Magazine, 4.9.2001: 2.
27. Zeichick, A. 2000. 3G Wireless Explained. Red Herring, 83: 314–317.

Case 6-24

Tri-Cities Community Bank*

Case A: Balanced Scorecard Development

Tri-Cities Community Bank (TCCB) is located in the Midwest U.S. and has a total of 10 branches grouped into two divisions, the southern division (SD) and the northern division (ND). Each division consists of five branches; each branch employs a branch president, branch vice-president/chief loan officer, customer service representatives, loan representatives, mortgage loan originators, head tellers, tellers, and administrative assistants. All branches are located within a 60-mile radius.

TCCB has enjoyed strong financial success over the past few years but continues to look for ways to improve its performance. The strategic direction of the bank is reviewed annually at a meeting of top bank officials and outside consultants. The purpose of the meeting is to outline the vision and mission of the bank and to ensure all top managers understand and agree on the direction of the organization. In 1997, TCCB management adopted the master strategy of balancing profits with growth to ensure the bank remains an independent entity existing to provide quality service and products to an increasingly diverse customer base.

Chris Billings recently was promoted from marketing director to SD president. The promotion came just as Chris finished her evening Master of Business Administration (MBA) degree in December 1999. As part of her graduate studies, she was introduced to the balanced scorecard (BSC), a performance measurement system that directs decision makers toward long-term value-creating activities. Chris thought the BSC could be used to improve the financial performance of TCCB. In late December 1999, she approached the chief executive officer (CEO) and requested permission to implement the new program.

TCCB's CEO was apprehensive about the new program. His reluctance stemmed from his own unfamiliarity with the BSC and Chris's short tenure as SD president. The CEO also was concerned about whether Chris's ideas would be accepted by the ND president and ND branch employees. Finally, he was uncertain about the BSC's benefits. At the same time, however, the CEO didn't want to respond negatively to Chris's first efforts as SD president. To appease Chris without totally committing the bank to implement the BSC, the CEO agreed to allow Chris to begin the process of developing the BSC in the five branches of her division. In turn, Chris agreed to make a presentation to the CEO and the bank's Board of Directors in three

* BY Tom Albright, Stan Davis, and Aleecia Hibbets.

months. In this meeting, Chris would present BSC concepts and how she planned to use the program to improve the financial performance of her branches. Given the short period of time to design a pilot study, Chris wondered how she could convince the Board of Directors to give her permission to implement the BSC. She knew she must convince the SD branch presidents of its value.

On January 7th, 2000, Chris met with her branch presidents to discuss the BSC program and enlist their help in developing balanced scorecards for their branches. She began the meeting by distributing a handout (Exhibit A1) highlighting the key objectives of the BSC. She used the handout to inform the branch presidents of the four business "perspectives" (categories of measures to be included on the BSC). The example measures she included on the handout were from a hospital that had implemented the BSC. Because she didn't have example measures from a bank using the BSC, she wanted to show measures from another service industry for the branch presidents to consider. As the handout shows, the hospital uses operating margin and cost per case as their primary financial measures, recommendation ratings from outgoing patients and discharge timeliness information as customer measures, length of stay and readmission rate (patients being admitted again for the same injury or illness) for the internal business measures, and employee training and retention measures in the learning and growth perspective. She then instructed the branch presidents to work together to develop meaningful measures to be included on branch BSCs. While each branch would eventually develop a branch-specific scorecard, she believed the branches were similar enough to allow branch presidents to work together initially. The group was to meet again in six weeks to discuss their progress in developing branch BSCs.

The group meeting on February 25th did not go as well as Chris had hoped. While the branch presidents had done a good job of identifying areas that needed attention within each branch, the information presented could, at best, only be considered as raw materials necessary to build a BSC program. Much work was needed prior to implementing the program.

With time running out, Chris grew concerned about the scheduled meeting with the Board of Directors on March 31st. She had nothing concrete to present at the meeting and worried she might not receive permission to pursue the program if she did not make a solid presentation to the Board. Chris's goal is to present a group of quantifiable measures that are linked through causal relationships and that lead to improvement of key financial measures.

One of the primary benefits of the BSC comes through mapping causal relationships from nonfinancial performance measures to financial measures. Nonfinancial measures are categorized into three perspectives: Learning and Growth, Internal Business Processes, and Customer Focus. The cause and effect linkages in the BSC will occur in the following manner: If *learning* improves, then *internal processes* will improve. If *internal processes* improve, then *customer value* will increase. If *customer value* increases, *financial performance* will improve. Financial performance is the ultimate evaluation of a firm's strategy. If financial performance improves significantly, the firm's strategy is successful. Thus, if the strategy is good, the measures of the nonfinancial perspectives will be lead indicators of increasing value that will ultimately be proven by improved financial measures.

Exhibit A2 provides a list of performance measures developed by the branch presidents and notes Chris took during meetings with them. Exhibit A3 illustrates a sample cause-and-effect chain. For example, as shown in Exhibit A3, if employees receive training in sales effectiveness, customer service, product profitability, and local bank knowledge, they will be better equipped to provide customers with higher-quality service. TCCB measures the effectiveness of the training programs by having employees take in-house tests on various training topics. By increasing employee knowledge and skills, higher-quality referrals and cross-sell proposals will take place, leading to higher customer satisfaction and greater customer retention. Maintaining the current customer base provides the basis for growth in deposit and loan balances, while a greater number of successful referrals and cross-sells increase noninterest income.

Chris wants to prepare a series of cause-and-effect chains to illustrate to the Board of Directors how the BSC can be used to improve performance on three key financial measures: loan balances, deposit balances, and noninterest income. She knows that any program emphasizing improvement in these three measures has a strong chance of receiving approval. An example of a cause-and-effect chain appears in Exhibit A3.

Assignment

Prepare a presentation for the Board of Directors that explains how the BSC may be used to help TCCB achieve its strategic goals. Include in your presentation the following:

1. A table that categorizes each of the measures in Exhibit A2 into one of the four BSC perspectives. State why you placed a measure in a particular perspective.

EXHIBIT A1 Key Business Perspectives and Lead/Lag Indicators

Source: Adapted from Kaplan and Norton's 1996 *Translating Strategy into Action: The Balanced Scorecard* (1996) and The Strategy-Focused Organization (2001).

Key Business Perspectives

- **Financial Perspective** – *How do we look to our shareholders?*
  - The financial objectives of the organization serve as the focus of all activities. Every measure selected for a balanced scorecard should be part of a causal chain that results in improved performance on financial objectives.
  - Some examples of financial perspective objectives in the hospital industry include operating margins, cost per case, and capital fund-raising.

- **Customer Perspective** – *How do customers view us?*
  - In the customer perspective, Organizations must identify key customers and market segments. Organizations must also determine how they add value for customers and seek to deliver better products and services that are tailored to specific customer needs.
  - Some examples of customer perspective objectives in the hospital industry include improved recommendation ratings and discharge timeliness.

- **Internal Business Perspective** – *At what must we excel?*
  - For the internal business perspective, Organizations identify those processes that must be improved or created in order to reach the objectives of the customer and financial perspectives.
  - Some examples of internal business perspective objectives in the hospital industry include reducing the readmission rate (for the same medical condition) and increasing the doctor-to-patient contact time.

- **Learning and Growth Perspective** – *How do we continue to improve and create value?*
  - To achieve the lofty standards set in the previous three objectives, organizations must invest in their people and infrastructure. For this perspective, organizations identify where resources are needed and craft a plan to enable its employees to achieve the objectives of the other perspectives.
  - Some examples of learning and growth perspective objectives in the hospital industry include increased employee training and retention, improved information technology systems, and adequate staffing for all shifts.

Lead and Lag Indicators

Nonfinancial measures (NFMs) selected in the customer, internal business process, and learning and growth perspectives serve as *lead indicators* of improvement in financial objectives because improvement in these NFMs often "lead" or precede the improvement observed in financial measures. Likewise, the financial measures selected in the financial perspective are often called *lag indicators* because improvement in these financial measures often "lags" or comes after the improvement in the NFMs.

EXHIBIT A2 Performance Measures for TCCB Balanced Scorecards

- Outstanding Loan Balances
- Deposit Balances
- Number of Products per Customer
- Number of New Customers
- Non-Interest Income-income earned from fees on services and products provided by the bank. NII includes fees associated with CDs, ATM cards, insurance policies, lock boxes, annuities, brokerage accounts, checking accounts, and travelers' checks.
- New Loans Created
- New Accounts
- New Products Introduced
- Employee Training Hours
- Customer Satisfaction
- Customer Retention
- Employee Satisfaction
- Sales Calls to Potential Customers
- Thank-You Calls/Cards to New & Existing Customers
- Employee Turnover
- Referrals-referrals occur when an employee suggests a customer see another branch employee for more information about a product
- Cross-Sells-selling multiple products to a customer when the customer comes in for only one product

Notes from Branch Presidents' Meetings

The most important financial measures are loan balances, deposit balances, and noninterest income. Everything we do should be aimed toward improving these three financial measures.

Customer satisfaction must be improved. Because we are a small community bank, we rely on delivering quality services with a "hometown" feel. We rely on word-of-mouth advertising as much as we do radio and newspaper ads.

Our employees must have training in several different areas, including sales techniques, customer service, and product knowledge/profitability. This type of training would improve the interactions between our employees and customers, allowing tellers and Customer Sales Representatives to recognize customer needs and make more effective referrals and new product offerings.

EXHIBIT A3 Cause-and-Effect Chain Illustration for TCCB

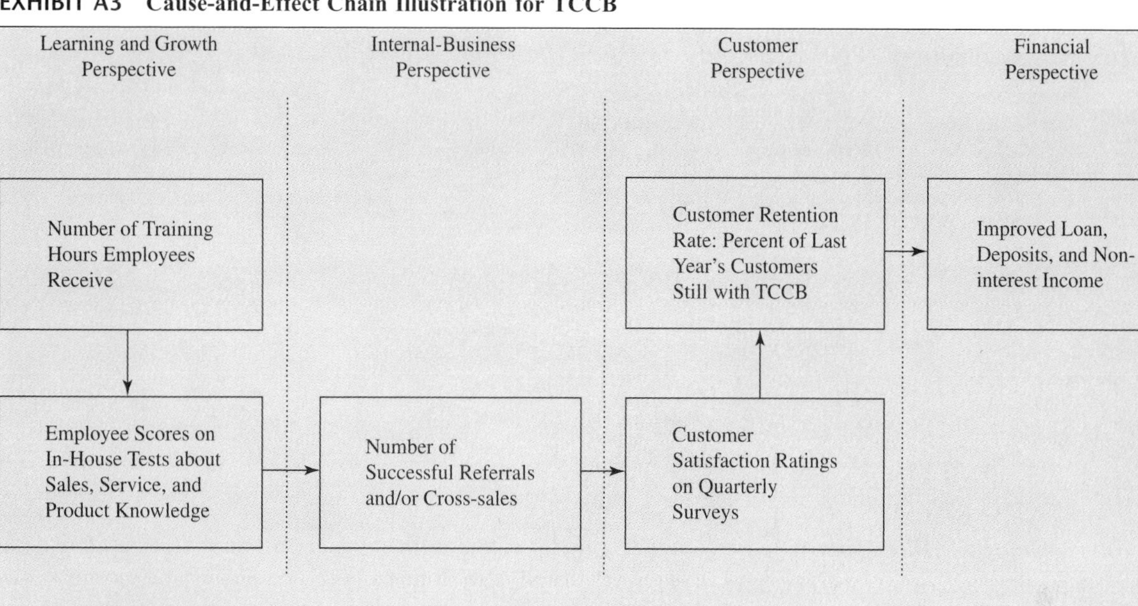

Causal Chain Explanation

If employees receive training in sales effectiveness, customer service, product profitability and local bank knowledge, then better customer service and higher quality interactions with existing clients can take place. TCCB employees will be better able to ascertain the needs of customers, thereby making higher quality referrals and cross-sell proposals to customers, and customers will be more satisfied and choose to continue banking with TCCB. Increased referrals or cross-sales increases non-interest income and provides the basis for growth in deposit and loan balances.

2. Two cause-and-effect chains similar to the one shown in Exhibit A3. Use the measures listed in Exhibit A2, or suggest other measures you feel are appropriate. *Be sure to include a Causal Chain Explanation* with your answer.

Case B: Assessing Financial Improvement

The presentation to the Board of Directors was well received and Chris secured permission for a pilot study of the BSC in the five SD branches. She had one year to convince the CEO and Board of Directors of the BSC's ability to improve branch performance. During the year, all five SD branches implemented the BSC. However, each manager brought his or her individual style to the implementation process.

Now, the one-year trial period is over, and Chris has collected data to determine whether the program was successful. Because no unusual business situations occurred during the year, Chris believes any changes in performance among the adopting branches can be attributed to the BSC. Exhibit B1 reports financial data on loan balances, deposit balances, and noninterest income for the years ended June 30, 2001, and June 30, 2000, respectively. The SD branches, Branches A–E in Exhibit B1, began their BSC programs on July 1, 2000.

As part of her program assessment, Chris interviewed several employees at each branch.[1] Turnover of tellers has always been a significant issue for the branches. In the past, the tellers would leave the bank if they could find a job that paid as little as $.25 more per hour. The interviews are summarized below.

Branch A

Customer Service Representative–Mary Richards

One reason for implementing the BSC is to help us reach our branch goals. Everyone understands that our strategy is to balance loans, deposits, and Certificates of Deposit, with growth. For example, to create greater loan volume, we are willing to accept a lower profit margin on each loan. The BSC helps clarify our strategy.

[1] Most excerpts are actual comments gathered from interviews assessing a balanced scorecard implementation.

EXHIBIT B1 Branch Performance on Key Financial Indicators

	As of June 30, 2001			As of June 30, 2000		
Branch	Loan Balance (Million $)	Deposit Balance (Million $)	Noninterest Income (NII) (Thousand $)	Loan Balance (Million $)	Deposit Balance (Million $)	Noninterest Income (NII) (Thousand $)
A	39.3	85.1	476.0	35.9	77.0	411.0
B	58.1	104.5	428.0	49.7	101.4	399.0
C	63.7	136.3	529.0	56.1	124.0	474.0
D	46.7	93.1	291.0	45.1	86.7	276.0
E	54.4	109.3	343.0	53.9	108.2	344.0
F	42.9	87.5	345.0	41.9	88.5	335.0
G	64.5	115.2	498.0	64.5	114.8	477.0
H	33.2	78.2	230.0	32.7	77.8	233.0
I	51.1	93.7	293.0	50.8	91.6	280.0
J	71.2	150.8	589.0	68.0	145.0	571.0

Loan Representative–Mike Moore

We have to work at our scorecard measures. They're not easy, but they are realistic. The process seems fair because my measures are just as hard as the other scorecards I've seen. Of course, the measures on my co-workers' scorecards may be different from mine, but everyone has to work hard.

Head Teller–Paul Franks

If we meet or exceed our targets, we are eligible to earn cash bonuses. Each month the top performers are recognized and rewarded. There's also a $1,000 reward per quarter to the individual who performs the best on his or her scorecard.

Branch B

Loan Representative–Pamela Wise

As I understand it, the BSC is a tool to measure our progress in achieving the goals established by management. In our case, we want to meet the financial needs of a growing community, yet keep a small-town feeling to our services.

Teller–Glenda Smalley

Some of my scorecard measures are challenging, but no more so than the other scorecards I have seen. The measures are difficult but not unattainable. I think the BSC is being used to encourage us to do better. We are rewarded when we improve. For example, our performance on the BSC helps to determine our year-end bonuses, as well as promotions and raises.

Branch C

Customer Service Representative–Bill Sorensen

Sure, I understand why we implemented the balanced scorecard. Its purpose is to promote teamwork among tellers, loan officers, and customer service representatives. Also, it helps everyone understand our goals and how to reach them.

Mortgage Loan Originator–Debbie Hansen

The scorecard taught us how everyone has a part in achieving branch goals by selling, cross-selling, serving as a communication port, and making customers feel welcome. Management wanted a lot of employee feedback when we were deciding to start the BSC. They wanted to be sure we knew about the program.

Administrative Assistant–Lou Martin

When we reach our BSC goals as a branch on a quarterly basis, we throw a big party. Individually, we can earn time off, up to a day every two months, if we do well on the BSC. Unfortunately, some of my scorecard measures are next to impossible to achieve.

Branch D

Loan Representative–Gary Smith

As I understand it, the BSC is for charting growth. We had to determine which measures were important to the company. Thus, our branch manager asked a few questions when we were deciding which measures to include on the scorecards. I think she helped focus our ideas.

Customer Service Representative–Al Taylor

My scorecard measures are not impossible; they are fair. All of our measures are probably about the same difficulty. There are some incentives to achieve our goals. For example, we can earn $50 each month if we meet our individual BSC goals. Our branch president is always looking for better ways to reward us for good BSC performance.

Branch E

Loan Representative–Ann Stone

In our branch, the BSC is to keep track of what we're doing and to compare our performance with others. I don't see it as a big deal. I reached all of my goals within two months of starting the program.

Teller–Pete Jones

I think the scorecard is used just to keep up with people's activities. I'm not sure any tangible rewards are associated with my performance on the BSC. If I do poorly, I'll probably be fired, however. On the other hand, keeping my job may be considered a tangible reward.

Administrative Assistant–Daniel Hughes

We didn't get to participate very much in developing our scorecards. Management just came in one day and told us about the new performance measurement system.

Loan Representative–Tim Vines

I've read that the scorecard is supposed to help companies with their strategy. It's difficult to get an idea of our strategy from management. Maybe what I do helps us achieve our strategic goals—who knows?

Chris believed the BSC had been a success. She expressed her confidence to the CEO about winning Board approval for her plan to expand the BSC to all branches. However, she understood the board would require hard evidence before approving a plan. Chris also understood she must be prepared to answer questions about what went right and what went wrong during the pilot study in the SD branches.

Assignment

1. Prepare an analysis to determine whether the BSC appears to have had an effect.
2. Summarize your results in a presentation appropriate for the Board of Directors.
3. Identify differences in implementation quality that may explain variation in performance among branches A–E. What implementation recommendations would you make to ND managers who are considering adopting the balanced scorecard?

Source: Tom Albright is the J. Reese Phifer Faculty Fellow at the Culverhouse School of Accountancy, University of Alabama, Tuscaloosa, AL. He can be reached at (205) 348-2908 or Talbrigh@cba.ua.edu.

Stan Davis is an assistant professor at the Babcock Graduate School of Management, Wake Forest University, Winston-Salem, NC. He can be reached at (336) 758-4492 or stan.davis@mba.wfu.edu.

Aleecia Hibbets is a doctoral student at the Culverhouse School of Accountancy, University of Alabama. Tuscaloosa, AL. She can be reached at (205) 348-0149 or ahibbets@cba.ua.edu.

Case 6-25

Cima Mountaineering, Inc.

"What a great hike," exclaimed Anthony Simon as he tossed his Summit HX 350 hiking boots into his car. He had just finished hiking the challenging Cascade Canyon Trail in the Tetons north of Jackson, Wyoming. Anthony hiked often because it was a great way to test the hiking boots made by Cima Mountaineering, Inc., the business he inherited from his parents and owned with his sister, Margaret. As he drove back to Jackson, he began thinking about next week's meeting with Margaret, the president of Cima. During the past month they had been discussing marketing strategies for increasing the sales and profits of the company. No decisions had been made, but the preferences of each owner were becoming clear.

Lawrence M. Lamont is professor of management at Washington and Lee University, and Eva Cid and Wade Drew Hammond are seniors in the class of 1995 at Washington and Lee, majoring in management and accounting, respectively. Case material was prepared as a basis for class discussion and not designed to present illustrations of either effective or ineffective handling of administrative problems. Some names, locations, and financial information have been disguised.

As illustrated in Exhibit 1, sales and profits had grown steadily for Cima, and by most measures the company was successful. However, growth was beginning to slow as a result of foreign competition and a changing market. Margaret observed that the market had shifted to a more casual, stylish hiking boot that appealed to hikers interested in a boot for a variety of uses. She favored a strategy of diversifying the company by marketing a new line of boots for the less experienced weekend hiker. Anthony also recognized that the market had changed, but he supported expanding the existing lines of boots for mountaineers and hikers. The company had been successful with those boots, and Anthony had some ideas about how to extend the lines and expand distribution.

EXHIBIT 1
Cima Mountaineering, Inc., Revenues and Net Income, 1990–95

Year	Revenues	Net Income	Profit Margin (%)
1995	$20,091,450	$857,134	4.27%
1994	18,738,529	809,505	4.32
1993	17,281,683	838,162	4.85
1992	15,614,803	776,056	4.97
1991	14,221,132	602,976	4.24
1990	13,034,562	522,606	4.01

EXHIBIT 2
Cima Mountaineering, Inc., Income Statement, Years Ended December 31, 1995, and December 31, 1994

	1995	1994
Net sales	$20,091,450	$18,738,529
Cost of goods sold	14,381,460	13,426,156
Gross margin	5,709,990	5,312,373
Selling and admin. expenses	4,285,730	3,973,419
Operating income	1,424,260	1,338,954
Other income (expenses)		
Interest expense	(160,733)	(131,170)
Interest income	35,161	18,739
Total other income (net)	(125,572)	(112,431)
Earnings before income taxes	1,298,688	1,226,523
Income taxes	441,554	417,018
Net income	$ 857,134	$ 809,505

"This is a better way to grow," he thought. "I'm concerned about the risk in Margaret's recommendation. If we move to a more casual boot, then we have to resolve a new set of marketing and competitive issues and finance a new line. I'm not sure we can do it."

When he returned to Jackson that evening, Anthony stopped by his office to check his messages. The financial statements shown in Exhibits 2 and 3 were on his desk, along with a marketing study from a Denver consulting firm. Harris Fleming, vice president of marketing, had commissioned a study of the hiking boot market several months earlier to help the company plan for the future. As Anthony paged through the report, two figures caught his eye. One was a segmentation of the hiking boot market (Exhibit 4), and the other was a summary of market competition (Exhibit 5). "This is interesting," he mused. "I hope Margaret reads it before our meeting."

History of Cima Mountaineering

As children, Anthony and Margaret Simon had watched their parents make western boots at the Hoback Boot Company, a small business they owned in Jackson, Wyoming. They learned the craft as they grew up and joined the company after college.

In the late 1960s the demand for western boots began to decline, and the Hoback Boot Company struggled to survive. By 1975 the parents were close to retirement and seemed content to close the business, but Margaret and Anthony decided to try to salvage the company. Margaret, the older sibling, became the president, and Anthony became the executive vice president. By the end of 1976, sales had declined to $1.5 million and the company earned profits of only $45,000. It became clear that to survive, the business would have to refocus on products with a more promising future.

Refocusing the Business

As a college student, Anthony attended a mountaineering school north of Jackson in Teton National Park. As he learned to climb and hike, he became aware of the growing popularity of the sport and the boots being used. Because of his experience with western boots, he also noticed their limitations. Although the boots had good traction, they were heavy and uncomfortable and had little resistance to the snow and water always present in the mountains. He convinced Margaret that Hoback should explore the possibility of developing boots for mountaineering and hiking.

In 1977 Anthony and Margaret began 12 months of marketing research. They investigated the market, the

EXHIBIT 3 Cima Mountaineering, Inc., Balance Sheet, Years Ending December 31, 1995, and December 31, 1994

	1995	1994
Assets		
Current assets		
Cash and equivalents	$ 1,571,441	$ 1,228,296
Accounts receivable	4,696,260	3,976,608
Inventory	6,195,450	5,327,733
Other	270,938	276,367
Total	12,734,089	10,809,004
Fixed assets		
Property, plant, and equipment	3,899,568	2,961,667
Less: accumulated depreciation	(1,117,937)	(858,210)
Total fixed assets (net)	2,781,631	2,103,457
Other assets		
Intangibles	379,313	568,087
Other long-term assets	2,167,504	1,873,151
Total fixed assets (net)	$18,062,537	$15,353,699
Liabilities and shareholder equity		
Current liabilities		
Accounts payable	$ 4,280,821	$ 4,097,595
Notes payable	1,083,752	951,929
Current maturities of long-term debt	496,720	303,236
Accrued liabilities		
Expenses	2,754,537	2,360,631
Salaries and wages	1,408,878	1,259,003
Other	1,137,940	991,235
Total current liabilities	11,162,648	9,963,629
Long-term liabilities		
Long-term debt	3,070,631	2,303,055
Lease obligations	90,313	31,629
Total long-term liabilities	3,702,820	2,334,684
Other liabilities		
Deferred taxes	36,125	92,122
Other noncurrent liabilities	312,326	429,904
Total liabilities	14,672,043	12,820,339
Owner's equity		
Retained earnings	3,390,494	2,533,360
Total liabilities and owner's equity	$18,062,537	$15,353,699

competition, and the extent to which Hoback's existing equipment could be used to produce the new boots. By the summer of 1978 Hoback had developed a mountaineering boot and a hiking boot that were ready for testing. Several instructors from the mountaineering school tested the boots and gave them excellent reviews.

The Transition

By 1981 Hoback was ready to enter the market with two styles of boots: one for the mountaineer who wanted a boot for all-weather climbing and the other for men and women who were advanced hikers. Both styles had water-repellent leather uppers and cleated soles for superior traction. Distribution was secured through mountaineering shops in Wyoming and Colorado.

Hoback continued to manufacture western boots for its loyal customers, but Margaret planned to phase them out as the hiking boot business developed. However, because they did not completely understand the needs of the market, they hired Harris Fleming, a mountaineering instructor, to help them with product design and marketing.

EXHIBIT 4 Segmentation of the Hiking Boot Market

	Mountaineers	Serious Hikers	Weekenders	Practical Users	Children	Fashion Seekers
Benefits	Durability/ruggedness Stability/support Dryness/warmth Grip/traction	Stability Durability Traction Comfort/protection	Lightweight Comfort Durability Versatility	Lightweight Durability Good value Versatility	Durability Protection Lightweight Traction	Fashion/style Appearance Lightweight Inexpensive
Demographics	Young Primarily male Shops in specialty stores and specialized catalogs	Young, middle-aged Male and female Shops in specialty stores and outdoor catalogs	Young, middle-aged Male and female Shops in shoe retailers, sporting goods stores, and mail order catalogs	Young, middle-aged Primarily male Shops in shoe retailers and department stores	Young Marrieds Male and female Shops in department stores and outdoor catalogs	Young Male and female Shops in shoe retailers, department stores, and catalogs
Lifestyle	Adventuresome Independent Risk taker Enjoys challenges	Nature lover Outdoorsman Sportsman Backpacker	Recreational hiker Social, spends time with family and friends Enjoys the outdoors	Practical Sociable Outdoors for work and recreation	Enjoys family activities Enjoys outdoors and hiking Children are active and play outdoors Parents are value-conscious	Materialistic Trendy Socially conscious Nonhikers Brand name shoppers Price-conscious
Examples of brands	Asolo Cliff Raichle Mt. Blanc Salomon Adventure 9	Raichle Explorer Vasque Clarion Tecnica Pegasus Dry Hi-Tec Piramide	Reebok R-Evolution Timberland Topozoic Merrell Acadia Nike Air Mada, Zion Vasque Alpha	Merrell Eagle Nike Air Khyber Tecnica Volcano	Vasque Kids Klimber Nike Merrell Caribou	Nike Espirit Reebok Telos Hi-Tec Magnum
Estimated market share	5% Slow growth	17% Moderate growth	25% High growth	20% Stable growth	5% Slow growth	28% At peak of rapid growth cycle
Price range	$210–$450	$120–$215	$70–$125	$40–$80	Up to $40	$65–$100

EXHIBIT 5 Summary of Competitors

Source: Published literature and company product brochures, 1995.

Company	Location	Mountaineering (Styles)	Hiking (Styles)	Men's	Women's	Children's	Price Range
Raichle	Switzerland	Yes (7)	Yes (16)	Yes	Yes	Yes	High
Salomon	France	Yes (1)	Yes (9)	Yes	Yes	No	Mid
Asolo	Italy	Yes (4)	Yes (26)	Yes	Yes	No	High
Tecnica	Italy	Yes (3)	Yes (9)	Yes	Yes	No	Mid/high
Hi-Tec	United Kingdom	Yes (2)	Yes (29)	Yes	Yes	Yes	Mid/low
Vasque	Minnesota	Yes (4)	Yes (18)	Yes	Yes	Yes	Mid/high
Merrell	Vermont	Yes (5)	Yes (31)	Yes	Yes	Yes	Mid
Timberland	New Hampshire	No	Yes (4)	Yes	No	No	Mid
Nike	Oregon	No	Yes (5)	Yes	Yes	Yes	Low
Reebok	Massachusetts	No	Yes (3)	Yes	Yes	Yes	Low
Cima	Wyoming	Yes (3)	Yes (5)	Yes	Yes	No	High

A New Company

During the 1980s Hoback prospered as the market expanded along with the popularity of outdoor recreation. The company slowly increased its product line and achieved success by focusing on classic boots that were relatively insensitive to fashion trends. By 1986 sales of Hoback Boots had reached $3.5 million.

Over the next several years distribution was steadily expanded. In 1987 Hoback employed independent sales representatives to handle the sales and service. Before long, Hoback boots were sold throughout Wyoming, Colorado, and Montana by retailers specializing in mountaineering and hiking equipment. Margaret decided to discontinue western boots to make room for the growing hiking boot business. To reflect the new direction of the company, the name was changed to Cima Mountaineering, Inc.

Cima Boots Take Off

The late 1980s was a period of exceptional growth. Demand for Cima boots grew quickly as consumers caught the trend toward healthy, active lifestyles. The company expanded its line for advanced hikers and improved the performance of its boots. By 1990, sales had reached $13 million and the company earned profits of $522,606. Margaret was satisfied with the growth but was concerned about low profitability as a result of foreign competition. She challenged the company to find new ways to design and manufacture boots at a lower cost.

Growth and Innovation

The next five years were marked by growth, innovation, and increasing foreign and domestic competition. Market growth continued as hiking boots became popular for casual wear in addition to hiking in mountains and on trails. Cima and its competitors began to make boots with molded footbeds and utilize materials that reduced weight.[1] Fashion also became a factor, and companies such as Nike and Reebok marketed lightweight boots in a variety of materials and colors to meet the demand for styling in addition to performance. Cima implemented a computer-aided design (CAD) system in 1993 to shorten product development and devote more attention to design. Late in 1994, Cima restructured its facilities and implemented a modular approach to manufacturing. The company switched from a production line to a system in which a work team applied multiple processes to each pair of boots. Significant cost savings were achieved as the new approach improved the profit and quality of the company's boots.

The Situation in 1995

As the company ended 1995, sales had grown to $20.0 million, up 7.2 percent from the previous year. Employment was at 425, and the facility was operating at 85 percent of capacity, producing several styles of mountaineering and hiking boots. Time-saving innovations and cost reduction also had worked, and profits reached

[1] Two processes are used to attach the uppers to the soles of boots. In classic welt construction, the uppers and soles are stitched. In the more contemporary method, a molded polyurethane footbed (including a one-piece heel and sole) is cemented to the upper with a waterproof adhesive. Many mountaineering boots use classic welt construction because it provides outstanding stability, while the contemporary method often is used with hiking boots to achieve lightweight construction. Cima used the classic method of construction for mountaineering boots and the contemporary method for hiking boots.

EXHIBIT 6
The Glacier MX 350 Mountaineering Boot

an all-time high. Margaret, now 57, was still president, and Anthony remained executive vice president.

Cima Marketing Strategy

According to estimates, 1994 was a record year for sales of hiking and mountaineering boots in the United States. Retail sales exceeded $600 million, and about 15 million pairs of boots were sold. Consumers wore the boots for activities ranging from mountaineering to casual social events. In recent years, changes were beginning to occur in the market. Inexpensive, lightweight hiking boots were becoming increasingly popular for day hikes and trail walking, and a new category of comfortable, light "trekking" shoes was being marketed by manufacturers of athletic shoes.

Only a part of the market was targeted by Cima. Most of its customers were serious outdoor enthusiasts. They included mountaineers who climbed in rugged terrain and advanced hikers who used the boots on challenging trails and extended backpacking trips. The demand for Cima boots was seasonal, and most of the purchases were made during the summer months, when the mountains and trails were most accessible.

Positioning

Cima boots were positioned as the best available for their intended purpose. Consumers saw them as durable and comfortable with exceptional performance. Retailers viewed the company as quick to adopt innovative construction techniques but conservative in styling. Cima intentionally used traditional styling to avoid fashion obsolescence and the need for frequent design changes. Some of the most popular styles had been in the market for several years without any significant modifications. The Glacier MX 350 shown in Exhibit 6 and the Summit HX 350 boot shown in Exhibit 7 are good examples. The MX 350, priced at $219.00, was positioned as a classic boot for men and had a unique tread design for beginning mountaineers. The Summit HX 350 was priced at $159.00 and was a boot for men and women hiking rough trails. Exhibit 8 describes the items in the mountaineering and hiking boot lines, and Exhibit 9 provides a sales history for Cima boots.

Product Lines

Corporate branding was used, and "Cima" was embossed on the leather on the side of the boot to enhance consumer recognition. Product lines were also branded, and alphabetic letters and numbers were used to differentiate items in the line. Each line had different styles and features to cover many of the important uses in the market. However, all the boots had features that the company believed were essential to positioning. Standard features included water-repellent leather uppers and high-traction soles and heels. The hardware for the boots was plated steel, and the laces were made of tough, durable nylon. Quality was emphasized throughout the product lines.

Glacier Boots for Mountaineering

The Glacier line featured three boots for men. The MX 550 was designed for expert all-weather climbers

EXHIBIT 7
The Summit HX 350 Hiking Boot

EXHIBIT 8
Cima Mountaineering, Inc., Mountaineering and Hiking Boot Lines

Product Line	Description
Glacier	
MX 550	For expert mountaineers climbing challenging mountains. Made for use on rocks, ice, and snow. Features welt construction, superior stability and support, reinforced heel and toe, padded ankle and tongue, step-in crampon insert, thermal insulation, and waterproof inner liner. Retails for $299.
MX 450	For proficient mountaineers engaging in rigorous, high-altitude hiking. Offers long-term comfort and stability on rough terrain. Features welt construction, deep cleated soles and heels, reinforced heel and toe, padded ankle and tongue, step-in crampon insert, and waterproof inner liner. Retails for $249.
MX 350	For beginning mountaineers climbing in moderate terrain and temperate climates. Features welt construction, unique tread design for traction, padded ankle and tongue, good stability and support, and a quick-dry lining. Retails for $219.
Summit	
HX 550	For experienced hikers who require uncompromising performance. Features nylon shank for stability and rigidity, waterproof inner liner, cushioned midsole, high-traction outsole, and padded ankle and tongue. Retails for $197.
HX 450	For backpackers who carry heavy loads on extended trips. Features thermal insulation, cushioned midsole, waterproof inner liner, excellent foot protection, and high-traction outsole. Retails for $179.
HX 350	For hikers who travel rough trails and a variety of backcountry terrain. Features extra cushioning, good stability and support, waterproof inner liner, and high-traction outsole for good grip in muddy and sloping surfaces. Retails for $159.
HX 250	For hikers who hike developed trails. Made with only the necessary technical features, including cushioning, foot and ankle support, waterproof inner liner, and high-traction outsole. Retails for $139.
HX 150	For individuals taking more than day and weekend hikes. Versatile boot for all kinds of excursions. Features cushioning, good support, waterproof inner liner, and high-traction outsoles for use on a variety of surfaces. Retails for $129.

EXHIBIT 9
Cima Mountaineering, Inc., Product Line Sales

	Unit Sales (%)		Sales Revenue	
Year	Mountaineering	Hiking	Mountaineering	Hiking
1995	15.00%	85.00%	21.74%	78.26%
1994	15.90	84.10	22.93	77.07
1993	17.20	82.80	24.64	75.36
1992	18.00	82.00	25.68	74.32
1991	18.80	81.20	26.71	73.29
1990	19.70	80.30	27.86	72.14

looking for the ultimate in traction, protection, and warmth. The MX 450 was for experienced climbers taking extended excursions, while the MX 350 met the needs of less-skilled individuals beginning climbing in moderate terrain and climates.

Summit Boots for Hiking

The Summit line featured five styles for men and women. The HX 550 was preferred by experienced hikers who demanded the best possible performance. The boot featured water-repellent leather uppers, a waterproof inner liner, a cushioned midsole, a nylon shank for rigidity, and a sole designed for high traction. It was available in gray and brown with different types of leather.[2] The Summit HX 150 was the least expensive boot in the line, designed for individuals who were beginning to take more than the occasional "weekend hike." It was a versatile boot for all kinds of excursions and featured a water-repellent leather upper, a cushioned midsole, and excellent traction. The HX 150 was popular as an entry-level boot for outdoor enthusiasts.

Distribution

Cima boots were distributed in Arizona, California, Colorado, Idaho, Montana, Nevada, New Mexico, Oregon, Washington, Wyoming, and western Canada through specialty retailers selling mountaineering, backpacking, and hiking equipment. Occasionally, Cima was approached by mail order catalog companies and chain sporting goods stores offering to sell its boots. The company considered the proposals but had not used those channels.

Promotion

The Cima sales and marketing office was located in Jackson. It was managed by Harris Fleming and staffed with several marketing personnel. Promotion was an important aspect of the marketing strategy, and advertising, personal selling, and sales promotion were used to gain exposure for Cima branded boots. Promotion was directed toward consumers and to retailers that stocked Cima mountaineering and hiking boots.

Personal Selling

Cima used 10 independent sales representatives to sell its boots in the Western states and Canada. Representatives did not sell competing boots, but they sold complementary products such as outdoor apparel and equipment for mountaineering, hiking, and backpacking. They were paid a commission and handled customer service in addition to sales. Management also was involved in personal selling. Harris Fleming trained the independent sales representatives and often accompanied them on sales calls.

Advertising and Sales Promotion

Advertising and sales promotion also were important promotional methods. Print advertising was used to increase brand awareness and assist retailers with promotion. Advertising was placed in leading magazines such as *Summit, Outside,* and *Backpacker* to reach mountaineers and hikers with the message that Cima boots were functional and durable and had classic styling. In addition, cooperative advertising was offered

[2] Different types of leather are used to make hiking boots. *Full grain:* High-quality, durable, upper layer of the hide. It has a natural finish and is strong and breathable. *Split grain:* Underside of the hide after the full-grain leather has been removed from the top. Light weight and comfort are the primary characteristics. *Suede:* A very fine split-grain leather. *Nubuk:* Brushed full-grain leather. *Waxed:* A process in which leather is coated with wax to help shed water. Most Cima boots were available in two or more types of leather.

Mountaineering and hiking boots are made water-repellent by treating the uppers with wax or chemical coatings. To make the boots waterproof, a fabric inner liner is built into the boot to provide waterproof protection and breathability. All Cima boots were water-repellent, but only styles with an inner liner were waterproof.

to encourage retailers to advertise Cima boots and identify their locations.

Sales promotion was an important part of the promotion program. Along with the focus on brand name recognition, Cima provided product literature and point of sale display materials to assist retailers in promoting the boots. In addition, the company regularly exhibited at industry trade shows. The exhibits, staffed by marketing personnel and the company's independent sales representatives, were effective for maintaining relationships with retailers and presenting the company's products.

Pricing

Cima selling prices to retailers ranged from $64.50 to $149.50 a pair, depending on the style. Mountaineering boots were more expensive because of their construction and features, while hiking boots were priced lower. Retailers were encouraged to take a 50 percent margin on the retail selling price, and so the retail prices shown in Exhibit 8 should be divided by two to get the Cima selling price. Cima priced its boots higher than competitors did, supporting the positioning of the boots as the top-quality product at each price point. Payment terms were net 30 days (similar to competitors), and boots were shipped to retailers from a warehouse in Jackson, Wyoming.

Segmentation of the Hiking Boot Market

As Anthony reviewed the marketing study commissioned by Harris Fleming, his attention focused on the market segmentation shown in Exhibit 4. It was interesting, because management had never seriously thought about the segmentation in the market. Of course, Anthony was aware that not everyone was a potential customer for Cima boots, but he was surprised to see how well the product lines met the needs of mountaineers and serious hikers. As he reviewed the market segmentation, he read the descriptions for mountaineers, serious hikers, and weekenders carefully because Cima was trying to decide which of these segments to target for expansion.

Mountaineers

Mountain climbers and high-altitude hikers are in this segment. They are serious about climbing and enjoy risk and adventure. Because mountaineers' safety may depend on their boots, they need maximum stability and support, traction for a variety of climbing conditions, and protection from wet and cold weather.

Serious Hikers

Outdoorsmen, who love nature and have a strong interest in health and fitness, are the serious hikers. They hike rough trails and take extended backpacking or hiking excursions. Serious hikers are brand-conscious and look for durable, high-performance boots with good support, a comfortable fit, and good traction.

Weekenders

Consumers in this segment are recreational hikers who enjoy casual weekend and day hikes with family and friends. They are interested in light, comfortable boots that provide a good fit, protection, and traction on a variety of surfaces. Weekenders prefer versatile boots that can be worn for a variety of activities.

Foreign and Domestic Competition

The second part of the marketing study that caught Anthony's attention was the analysis of competition. Although Anthony and Margaret were aware that competition had increased, they had overlooked the extent to which foreign bootmakers had entered the market. Apparently, foreign competitors had noticed the market growth and were exporting their boots aggressively into the United States. They had established sales offices and independent sales agents to compete for the customers served by Cima. The leading foreign brands, such as Asolo, Hi-Tec, Salomon, and Raichle, were marketed on performance and reputation, usually to the mountaineering, serious hiker, and weekender segments of the market.

The study also summarized the most important domestic competitors. Vasque and Merrell marketed boots that competed with Cima, but others were offering products for segments of the market where the prospects for growth were better. As Anthony examined Exhibit 5, he realized that the entry of Reebok and Nike into the hiking boot market was quite logical. They had entered the market as consumer preference shifted from wearing athletic shoes for casual outdoor activities to wearing a more rugged shoe. Each was marketing footwear that combined the appearance and durability of hiking boots with the lightness and fit of athletic shoes. The result was a line of fashionable hiking boots that appealed to brand and style-conscious teens and young adults. Both firms were expanding their product lines and moving into segments of the market that demanded lower levels of performance.

Margaret and Anthony Discuss Marketing Strategy

A few days after hiking in Cascade Canyon, Anthony met with Margaret and Harris Fleming to discuss marketing strategy. Each had read the consultant's report and studied the market segmentation and competitive summary. As the meeting opened, the conversation went as follows:

Margaret: It looks like we will have another record year. The economy is growing, and consumers seem confident and eager to buy. Yet I'm concerned about the future. The foreign bootmakers are providing some stiff competition. Their boots have outstanding performance and attractive prices. The improvements we made in manufacturing helped control costs and maintain margins, but it looks like the competition and slow growth in our markets will make it difficult to improve profits. We need to be thinking about new opportunities.

Harris: I agree, Margaret. Just this past week we lost Rocky Mountain Sports in Boulder, Colorado. John Kline, the sales manager, decided to drop us and pick up Asolo. We were doing $70,000 a year with them, and they carried our entire line. We also lost Great Western Outfitters in Colorado Springs. They replaced us with Merrell. The sales manager said that the college students there had been asking for the lower-priced Merrell boots. They bought $60,000 last year.

Anthony: Rocky Mountain and Great Western were good customers. I guess I'm not surprised, though. Our Glacier line needs another boot, and the Summit line is just not deep enough to cover the price points. We need to have some styles at lower prices to compete with Merrell and Asolo. I'm in favor of extending our existing lines to broaden their market appeal. It seems to me that the best way to compete is to stick with what we do best, making boots for mountaineers and serious hikers.

Margaret: Not so fast, Anthony. The problem is that our markets are small and not growing fast enough to support the foreign competitors that have entered with excellent products. We can probably hold our own, but I doubt if we can do much better. I think the future of this company is to move with the market. Consumers are demanding more style, lower prices, and a lightweight hiking boot that can be worn for a variety of uses. Look at the segmentation again. The "Weekender" segment is large and growing. That's where we need to go with some stylish new boots that depart from our classic leather lines.

Anthony: Maybe so, but we don't have much experience working with the leather and nylon combinations that are being used in these lighter boots. Besides, I'm not sure we can finance the product development and marketing for a new market that already has plenty of competition. And I'm concerned about the brand image that we have worked so hard to establish over the past 20 years. A line of inexpensive, casual boots just doesn't seem to fit with the perception consumers have of our products.

Harris: I can see advantages to each strategy. I do know that we don't have the time and resources to do both, so we had better make a thoughtful choice. Also, I think we should reconsider selling to the mail order catalog companies that specialize in mountaineering and hiking equipment. Last week I received another call from REI requesting us to sell them some of the boots in our Summit line for the 1997 season. This might be a good source of revenue and a way to expand our geographic market.

Margaret: You're right, Harris. We need to rethink our position on the mail order companies. Most of them have good market penetration in the East, where we don't have distribution. I noticed that Gander Mountain is carrying some of the Timberland line and that L.L. Bean is carrying some Vasque styles along with its own line of branded boots.

Anthony: I agree. Why don't we each put together a proposal that summarizes our recommendations, and then we can get back together to continue the discussion.

Harris: Good idea. Eventually we will need a sales forecast and some cost data. Send me your proposals, and I'll call the consulting firm and have them prepare some forecasts.

I think we already have some cost information. Give me a few days, and then we can get together again.

The Meeting to Review the Proposals

The following week, the discussion continued. Margaret presented her proposal, which is summarized in Exhibit 10. She proposed moving Cima into the "Weekender" segment by marketing two new hiking boots. Anthony countered with the proposal summarized in Exhibit 11. He favored extending the existing lines by adding a new mountaineering boot and two new Summit hiking boots at lower price points. Harris presented sales forecasts for each proposal, and after some discussion and modification, they were finalized as shown in Exhibit 12. Cost information was gathered by Harris from the vice president of manufacturing and is presented in Exhibit 13. After a lengthy discussion in which Margaret and Anthony were unable to agree on a course of action, Harris Fleming suggested that each proposal be explored further by conducting marketing research. He proposed the formation of teams from the Cima marketing staff to research each proposal and present it to Margaret and Anthony at a later date. Harris presented his directions to the teams in the memorandum shown in Exhibit 14. The discussion between Margaret and Anthony continued as follows:

Margaret: Once the marketing research is completed and we can read the reports and listen to the presentations, we should have a better idea of which strategy makes the best sense. Hopefully, a clear direction will emerge and we can move ahead with one of the proposals. In either case, I'm still intrigued with the possibility of moving into the mail order catalogs, since we really haven't developed these companies as customers. I just wish we knew how much business we could expect from them.

Anthony: We should seriously consider them, Margaret. Companies like L.L. Bean, Gander Mountain, and REI have been carrying a selection of hiking boots for several years. However, there may be a problem for us. Eventually the catalog companies expect their boot suppliers to make them a private brand. I'm not sure this is something we want to do, since we built the company on a strategy of marketing our own brands that are made in the U.S.A. Also, I'm concerned about the reaction of our retailers when they discover we are selling to the catalog companies. It could create some problems.

Harris: That is a strategy issue we will have to address. However, I'm not even sure what percentage of sales the typical footwear company makes through the mail order catalogs. If we were to solicit the catalog business, we would need an answer to this question to avoid exceeding our capacity. In the proposals I asked each of the teams to provide an estimate for us. I have to catch an early flight to Denver in the morning. It's 6:30; why don't we call it a day.

The meeting was adjourned at 6:35 P.M. Soon thereafter, the marketing teams were formed, with a leader assigned to each team.

EXHIBIT 10 Margaret's Marketing Proposal

MEMORANDUM

TO: Anthony Simon, Executive Vice President
Harris Fleming, Vice President of Marketing
FROM: Margaret Simon, President
RE: Marketing Proposal

I believe we have an excellent opportunity to expand the sales and profits of Cima by entering the "Weekender" segment of the hiking boot market. The segment's estimated share of the market is 25 percent, and according to the consultant's report, it is growing quite rapidly. I propose that we begin immediately to develop two new products and prepare a marketing strategy as discussed below.

Target Market and Positioning

Male and female recreational hikers looking for a comfortable, lightweight boot that is attractively priced and acceptable for short hikes and casual wear. Weekenders enjoy the outdoors and a day or weekend hike with family and friends.

The new boots would be positioned with magazine advertising as hiking boots that deliver performance and style for the demands of light hiking and casual outdoor wear.

Product

Two boots in men's and women's sizes. The boots would be constructed of leather and nylon uppers with a molded rubber outsole. A new branded line would be created to meet the needs of the market segment. The boots (designated WX 550 and WX 450) would have the following features:

	WX 550	WX 450
Leather and nylon uppers	X	X
Molded rubber outsole	X	X
Cushioned midsole	X	X
Padded collar and tongue	X	X
Durable hardware and laces	X	X
Waterproof inner liner	X	

Uppers: To be designed. Options include brown full-grain, split-grain, or suede leather combined with durable nylon in two of the following colors: beige, black, blue, gray, green, and slate.
Boot design and brand name: To be decided.

Retail Outlets

Specialty shoe retailers carrying hiking boots and casual shoes and sporting goods stores. Eventually mail order catalogs carrying outdoor apparel and hiking, backpacking, and camping equipment.

Promotion

Independent sales representatives
Magazine advertising
Co-op advertising
Point of sale display materials
Product brochures
Trade shows

Suggested Retail Pricing

WX 550: $89.00
WX 450: $69.00

Competitors

Timberland, Hi-Tec, Vasque, Merrell, Asolo, Nike, and Reebok.

Product Development and Required Investment

We should allow about one year for the necessary product development and testing. I estimate these costs to be $350,000. Additionally, we will need to make a capital expenditure of $150,000 for new equipment.

EXHIBIT 11 Anthony's Marketing Proposal

MEMORANDUM

TO: Margaret Simon, President
Harris Fleming, Vice President of Marketing
FROM: Anthony Simon, Executive Vice President
RE: Marketing Proposal

We have been successful with boots for mountaineers and serious hikers for years, and this is where our strengths seem to be. I recommend extending our Glacier and Summit lines instead of venturing into a new, unfamiliar market. My recommendations are summarized below:

Product Development
Introduce two new boots in the Summit line (designated HX 100 and HX 50) and market the Glacier MX 350 in a style for women with the same features as the boot for men. The new women's Glacier boot would have a suggested retail price of $219.00, while the suggested retail prices for the HX 100 and the HX 50 would be $119.00 and $89.00, respectively, to provide price points at the low end of the line. The new Summit boots for men and women would be the first in the line to have leather and nylon uppers as well as the following features:

	HX 100	HX 50
Leather and nylon uppers	X	X
Molded rubber outsole	X	X
Cushioned midsole	X	X
Padded collar and tongue	X	X
Quick-dry lining	X	X
Waterproof inner liner	X	

The leather used in the uppers will have to be determined. We should consider full-grain, suede, and nubuck since they are all popular with users in this segment. We need to select one for the initial introduction. The nylon fabric for the uppers should be available in two colors, selected from among the following: beige, brown, green, slate, maroon, and navy blue. Additional colors can be offered as sales develop and we gain a better understanding of consumer preferences.

Product Development and Required Investment
Product design and development costs of $400,000 for the MX 350, HX 100, and HX 50 styles and a capital investment of $150,000 to acquire equipment to cut and stitch the nylon/leather uppers. One year will be needed for product development and testing.

Positioning
The additions to the Summit line will be positioned as boots for serious hikers who want a quality hiking boot at a reasonable price. The boots will also be attractive to casual hikers who are looking to move up to a better boot as they gain experience in hiking and outdoor activity.

Retail Outlets
We can use our existing retail outlets. Additionally, the lower price points on the new styles will make these boots attractive to catalog shoppers. I recommend that we consider making the Summit boots available to consumers through mail order catalog companies.

Promotion
We will need to revise our product brochures and develop new advertising for the additions to the Summit line. The balance of the promotion program should remain as it is since it is working quite well. I believe the sales representatives and retailers selling our lines will welcome the new boots since they broaden the consumer appeal of our lines.

Suggested Retail Pricing

MX 350 for women:	$219.99
HX 100:	$119.00
HX 50:	$ 89.00

Competitors
Asolo, Hi-Tec, Merrell, Raichle, Salomon, Tecnica, and Vasque.

EXHIBIT 12 Cima Mountaineering, Inc., Sales Forecasts for Proposed New Products (Pairs of Boots)

	Project 1		Project 2		
Year	WX 550	WX 450	MX 350	HX 100	HX 50
2001–02	16,420	24,590	2,249	15,420	12,897
2000–01	14,104	21,115	1,778	13,285	11,733
1999–2000	8,420	12,605	897	10,078	9,169
1998–99	5,590	8,430	538	5,470	5,049
1997–98	4,050	6,160	414	4,049	3,813

Note: Sales forecasts are expected values derived from minimum and maximum estimates.
Some cannibalization of existing boots will occur when the new styles are introduced. The sales forecasts provided above have taken into account the impact of sales losses on existing boots. No additional adjustments need to be made.
Forecasts for WX 550, WX 450, HX 100, and HX 50 include sales of both men's and women's boots.

EXHIBIT 13 Cima Mountaineering, Inc., Cost Information for Mountaineering and Hiking Boots

	Inner Liner	No Inner Liner
Retail margin	50%	50%
Marketing and Manufacturing Costs		
Sales commissions	10	10
Advertising and sales promotion	5	5
Materials	42	35
Labor, overhead, and transportation	28	35

Cost information for 1997–98 only. Sales commissions, advertising and sales promotion, materials, labor, overhead, and transportation costs are based on Cima selling prices. After 1997–98, annual increases of 3.0 percent apply to marketing and manufacturing costs and increases of 4.0 percent apply to Cima selling prices.

EXHIBIT 14 Harris Fleming's Memorandum to the Marketing Staff

MEMORANDUM

TO: Marketing Staff
CC: Margaret Simon, President
Anthony Simon, Executive Vice President
FROM: Harris Fleming, Vice President of Marketing
SUBJECT: Marketing Research Projects

Attached to this memorandum are two marketing proposals (see case Exhibits 10 and 11) under consideration by our company. Each proposal is a guide for additional marketing research. You have been selected to serve on a project team to investigate one of the proposals and report your conclusions and recommendations to management. At your earliest convenience, please complete the following.

Project Team 1: Proposal to enter the "Weekender" segment of the hiking boot market.
Review the market segmentation and summary of competition in Exhibits 4 and 5. Identify consumers who would match the profile described in the market segment and conduct field research using a focus group, a survey, or both. You may also visit retailers carrying hiking boots to examine displays and product brochures. Using the information in the proposal, supplemented with your research, prepare the following:

1. A design for the hiking boots (WX 550 and WX 450). Please prepare a sketch that shows the styling for the uppers. We propose to use the same design for each boot, the only difference being the waterproof inner liner on the WX 550 boot. On your design, list the features that your proposed boot would have, considering additions or deletions to those listed in the proposal.
2. Recommend a type of leather (from among those proposed) and two colors for the nylon to be used in the panels of the uppers. We plan to make two styles, one in each color for each boot.
3. Recommend a brand name for the product line. Include a rationale for your choice.

EXHIBIT 14 (concluded)

4. Verify the acceptability of the suggested retail pricing.
5. Prepare a magazine advertisement for the hiking boot. Provide a rationale for the advertisement in the report.
6. Convert the suggested retail prices *in the proposal* to the Cima selling price and use the sales forecasts and costs (shown in Exhibits 12 and 13) to prepare an estimate of before-tax profits for the new product line, covering a five-year period starting in 1997–98. Assume annual cost increases of 3.0 percent and price increases of 4.0 percent beginning in 1998–99. Discount the future profits to present value, using a cost of capital of 15.0 percent. Use 1996–97 as the base year for all discounting.
7. Determine the payback period for the proposal. Assume product development and investment occur in 1996–97.
8. Provide your conclusions on the attractiveness of these styles to mail order catalog companies and their customers. You may wish to review current mail order catalogs to observe the hiking boots featured. Assuming that Cima is successful selling to mail order catalog companies, estimate the percentage of our sales that could be expected from these customers.
9. Prepare a report that summarizes the recommendations of your project team, including the advantages and disadvantages of the proposal. Be prepared to present your product design, branding, pro forma projections, payback period, and recommendations to management shortly after completion of this assignment.
10. Summarize your research and list the sources of information used to prepare the report.

Project Team 2: Proposal to extend the existing lines of boots for mountaineers and hikers.

Review the market segmentation and summary of competition in Exhibits 4 and 5. Identify consumers who match the profile described in the market segment and conduct field research using a focus group, a survey, or both. You also may visit retailers carrying hiking boots to examine displays and product brochures. Using the information in the proposal, supplemented with your research, prepare the following.

1. Designs for the hiking boots (HX 100 and HX 50). Please prepare sketches showing the styling for the uppers. We propose to use a different design for each boot, so you should provide a sketch for each. On each sketch, list the features that your proposed boots would have, considering additions or deletions to those listed in the proposal. No sketch is necessary for the mountaineering boot, MX 350, since we will use the same design as the men's boot and build it on a women's last.
2. Recommend one type of leather (from among those proposed) and two colors for the nylon to be used in the panels of the uppers. We plan to make two styles, one in each color for each boot.
3. Verify the market acceptability of the suggested retail pricing.
4. Prepare a magazine advertisement for your hiking boots. Include a rationale for the advertisement in the report.
5. Using the suggested retail prices *in the proposal*, convert them to the Cima selling prices and use the sales forecasts and costs (shown in Exhibits 12 and 13) to prepare an estimate of before-tax profits for the new products covering a five-year period starting in 1997–98. Assume annual cost increases of 3.0 percent and price increases of 4.0 percent beginning in 1998–99. Discount the profits to present value using a cost of capital of 15.0 percent. Use 1996–97 as the base year for all discounting.
6. Determine the payback period for the proposal. Assume product development and investment occur in 1996–97.
7. Provide your conclusions on the attractiveness of these styles to mail order catalog companies and their customers. You may wish to review current mail order catalogs to observe the hiking boots featured. Assuming that Cima is successful selling to mail order catalog companies, estimate the percentage of our sales that could be expected from these customers.
8. Prepare a report that summarizes the recommendations of your project team, including the advantages and disadvantages of the proposal. Be prepared to present your product design, pro forma projections, payback period, and recommendations to management shortly after completion of this assignment.
9. Summarize your research and list the sources of information used to prepare the report.

Name Index

Subject Index

C

J

Q

R

T